THE ENCYCLOPEDIA OF OPERA

THE ENCYCLOPEDIA OF OPERA

EDITED BY LESLIE ORREY

Advisory Editor Gilbert Chase

Pitman Publishing Limited

First published 1976

PITMAN PUBLISHING LTD
Pitman House, 39 Parker Street, London WC2B 5PB

PITMAN MEDICAL PUBLISHING CO. LTD
42 Camden Road, Tunbridge Wells, Kent TN1 2QD

FOCAL PRESS LTD
31 Fitzroy Square, London W1P 6BH

PITMAN PUBLISHING PTY LTD
Pitman House, 158 Bouverie Street, Carlton, Victoria 3053, Australia

PITMAN PUBLISHING
COPP CLARK PUBLISHING
517 Wellington Street West, Toronto, M5V 1G1, Canada

SIR ISAAC PITMAN AND SONS LTD
Banda Street, P.O. Box 46038, Nairobi, Kenya, East Africa

PITMAN PUBLISHING CO. S.A. (PTY) LTD
Craighall Mews, Jan Smuts Avenue, Craighall Park, Johannesburg 2001, South Africa

ISBN: 0 273 00237 6
G3555:15

This book was designed and produced by
RAINBIRD REFERENCE BOOKS LTD
Marble Arch House, 44 Edgware Road,
London W2, England

House Editor: Perry Morley
Assistant Editor: Raymond Kaye
Designer: Trevor Vincent
Picture Research: Krystyna Baran

Text filmset by Jolly & Barber Ltd, Rugby, Warwickshire, England
Printed and bound by
Dai Nippon Printing Co. Ltd, Tokyo, Japan

Introduction

The first operatic reference book was compiled by Leone Allacci, the Vatican Librarian, and published in Venice in 1666, when opera was in its infancy. A much enlarged version, *Drammaturgia di Leone Allacci accresciuta e continuata fino all'anno MDCCLV,* was published in Venice in 1755. It remained the work of a librarian, relying on printed sources. It included drama as well as opera, and its Italian bias was so pronounced that it did scant justice to the theatre of other nations, with even the works of Lully absent from its pages. Even from Italy there were some startling omissions, as for instance Monteverdi's *Orfeo* and Pergolesi's *Serva Padrona.*

A more ambitious work, and the first of any comprehensiveness to restrict itself to opera, was the *Dictionnaire lyrique, ou Histoire des opéras* of Félix Clément and Pierre Larousse, published in Paris. No date was given, but it must have been about 1868. Four supplements were subsequently issued, bringing the work up to 1880, and it was finally revised and augmented by Arthur Pougin in 1905. The treatment is somewhat idiosyncratic, with a disproportionate attention devoted to French works; the dating of especially Italian 18th-century works erratic.

A contemporary Italian publication, the *Opera e operisti: Dizionario lirico, 1541–1902* of Carlo Dassori (Genoa 1903), lists 3,628 composers and 15,406 operas, but limits its information to dates of the operas and births and deaths of the composers. A more determined effort at a complete list of operas was that compiled by John Towers of Pennsylvania, *Dictionary-Catalogue of Operas and Operettas which have been performed on the public stage* (Morgantown, W. Va., 1910). Like Dassori, it includes no critical or biographical information. In three parts, it lists: (1) operas in alphabetical order, with no dates, but with names, nationalities and birth and death dates of composers (more than 28,000 entries); (2) composers and their operas in alphabetical order; (3) librettos in alphabetical order, with no composers or authors mentioned, but giving the number of times each has been set to music.

Since then opera has continued to proliferate, and today a complete list might contain up to 60,000 entries. The most thoroughgoing catalogue, which is certainly not exhaustive, is to be found in the index volume of the *Enciclopedia dello spettacolo* (Rome, 1954–66, 10 volumes), with over 100,000 entries of 'spectacles' of every kind – plays, ballets and films as well as operas. An indispensable and unique work is Alfred Loewenberg's *Annals of Opera* (Cambridge 1943; revised edition, by Frank Walker, Geneva 1955). This gives details of some 4,000 operas, arranged chronologically from 1597. In its breadth of scholarship combined with impeccable accuracy it constitutes one of the most remarkable reference tools available to the opera student.

To these general reference works and chronologies we must add those dealing with single cities and opera houses such as Jacques Gabriel Prod'homme's *L'Opéra, 1669–1925* (Paris 1925), which includes a chronological list of first performances at the Paris Opéra from 1671 to 1925. Several Italian scholars were active in this field during the 19th century, e.g. Paolo Emilio Ferrari with his

Spettacoli drammatico-musicali e coreografici in Parma dall'anno 1628 all anno 1883 (Parma 1884); or Luigi Bignami, with *Cronologia di tutti gli spettacoli rappresentati nel Gran Teatro Comunale di Bologna dalla solenne sua apertura 14 maggio 1763 a tutto l'autunno del 1880* (Bologna 1880). The activities of most important centres have been chronicled in this way.

Without the librettist, the singer, or the stage designer there would be no opera; but information on them in reference-book form is not handily available. The art of the librettist has been studied by Ulderico Rolandi, *Il Libretto per musica attraverso i tempi* (Rome 1951) and, more recently, by Patrick J. Smith, *The Tenth Muse* (New York 1970, London 1971), but there is no dictionary of librettists, the nearest approach being the US Library of Congress *Catalogue of Opera Librettos Printed Before 1800*, edited by Oscar Sonneck (Washington, D.C., 1914, 2 volumes). This gives alphabetical lists of librettos (over 12,000) and librettists. Similarly, stage design, in importance equal or superior to the music in the early days of opera, has been the subject of much research, but information in compact reference-book form is not available. As to singers, there is the *Unvergängliche Stimmen: Kleines Sängerlexikon* by K. J. Kutsch and Leo Riemens (Bern and Munich 1962), translated by Harry Earl Jones as *A Concise Biographical Dictionary of Singers* (Philadelphia, New York and London 1969). A revised German edition has appeared (1975), doubling the number of entries from about 1,500 to about 3,000. But this concentrates on those singers whose voices have been recorded, and thus perforce ignores the singers of the past, besides limiting the range of present-day performers. Regrettably, too, it is far from reliable.

Since the invention of the gramophone (phonograph), record companies have made a feature of singers, with uncountable discs of operatic artists. Some idea of the vast quantity involved can be obtained by considering a recent publication, *Smetana on 300 Records* by John R. Bennett (Blandford, Dorset, 1975). Catalogues such as Schwann's or *The Classical Catalogue* issued quarterly by the *Gramophone*, give particulars of operas and artists currently available on disc, tape and cassette. Of the singers in the present encyclopedia most of those who have worked in the 20th century have recorded their voices; operas that have been recorded complete, or have been filmed, have been indicated (see below under Abbreviations).

It is clear that in order to be reasonably complete an operatic reference book covering operas, the places where they have been and are performed, and even the briefest biographical notes of all who contribute to opera (composers, librettists, singers, conductors, designers, and producers), would have to exceed by far the modest 3,000 entries of the present work. The first attempt at such a survey seems to be that by David Ewen, in his *Encyclopedia of the Opera* (New York 1955, revised 1963, and again as *The New Encyclopedia of the Opera*, New York 1971), followed by the *Concise Oxford Dictionary of Opera* by Harold Rosenthal and John Warrack (London 1964, 1972). The present encyclopedia is the first to be illustrated.

The main criterion in choosing items for inclusion in this book has been their relevance to the contemporary scene. Operas from the past have been included if they are historically important, or if they have had important revivals. Performers of the past have been limited to a selection of those who made significant contributions to the operatic art. To many, including the editor, the omissions here are regrettable; their absence made space for the inclusion of some (still all too few) of the exciting young artists of today. 'Opera' has been given the widest and broadest definition, as a 'theatrical presentation illumined by music'. The musical content must be substantial, so that the 'play with incidental music' is ruled out; but the definition is wide enough to embrace opera, operetta, and 'musical', all of which are viable music theatre today. The treatment has had to be condensed, and this has entailed some sacrifice in dealing with the familiar repertory of western Europe so that space could be found for a somewhat fuller treatment of operatic activities in the United States, Canada, Latin America, Czechoslovakia, and the USSR. The same need for compression has decreed the curtailment or complete suppression of the plots of standard operas to make way for more extended discussion of new or out-of-the-way operas. Further information can be found in Gustave Kobbé, *The Complete Opera Book* (London and New York 1919, 8th ed. rev. Harewood, London and New York 1969); Mark Lubbock, *The Complete Book of Light Opera* (London and New York 1962); Peter Gammond and Peter Clayton, *A Guide to Popular Music* (London 1960; New York 1961 as *Dictionary of Popular Music*); Cecil Michener Smith, *Musical Comedy in America* (New York 1950) and others listed in the article Opera Handbooks.

It is appropriate at this point that I should pay a warm tribute to my collaborators, with whom it has been a pleasure to work. The specialized knowledge they have brought to the task has been of inestimable value, and they have given unstintedly of their time. Only those who have embarked on such an undertaking can fully appreciate the frustrations inherent in the search for accuracy. This is most apparent perhaps as it concerns living performers, many of whom seem either to have been able to dispense with the formality of birth, or to have seen the light of day at different times in different places; but even when dealing with the not-so-remote past one is all too frequently faced with the problem of reconciling two or more impeccable but contradictory authorities – as it may be Hugo Riemann's *Musiklexikon* (Leipzig 1882 and later editions), Theodore Baker's *Biographical Dictionary of Musicians* (New York 1900; 5th edition New York 1958; with supplement by Nikolas Slonimsky, New York 1971) and Loewenberg's *Annals of Opera*. I must also offer a special word of thanks to Mr Tai Kanō, chief librarian of the Tokyo Broadcasting System 1951–66, for information about opera in Japan. Finally, I am indebted to the editorial staff of Rainbird Reference Books Ltd, who have been responsible for the conception and production of the encyclopedia. Guided by the alert and indefatigable Miss Perry Morley, they have watched over all stages of the work with the utmost care, their one concern for the excellence of the finished article. They have scrutinized each entry with microscopic thoroughness, thus at one and the same time both lightening and increasing my burden: for to confess that such errors as remain are my sole responsibility becomes in consequence less of a convention and more of a reality than usual.

LESLIE ORREY, *Editor* Richmond, Surrey, 4 November 1975

Contributors

AB *Alan Blyth*
After several journalistic posts began to contribute music criticism to the BBC publication, the *Listener*, and *The Times* (London), for which he continues to write. Associate editor of *Opera* magazine and a regular contributor to the *Gramophone*; broadcasts frequently on operatic subjects; author of *The Enjoyment of Opera* (1969) and short biographies of Janet Baker and Colin Davis. A contributor to *Grove's Dictionary of Music and Musicians*, 6th edition (in preparation).

FGB *Frank Granville Barker*
Between 1953 and 1973 edited, successively, the journals *Plays and Players, Music and Musicians,* and *Books and Bookmen* (London); contributed regular reviews of opera in performance and on records to journals in various parts of the world; author of *Stars of the Opera* (1949), *Voices of the Opera* (1951), and, with Geoffrey Handley-Taylor, *John Gay and the Ballad Opera* (1956). Now a freelance writer, a music critic of the *Daily Express*, the London correspondent of *Opera News* (New York), and a contributor to many journals and books on opera.

JB *Julian Budden*
Chief producer, Opera (radio) for the BBC. Author of *The Operas of Verdi* (Volume 1, 1973; Volumes 2 and 3 in preparation). A contributor to many journals and magazines, and to *Grove's Dictionary of Music and Musicians*, 6th edition; broadcasts frequently.

GC *Gilbert Chase*
Professor in Comparative Studies at the University of Texas in Austin, teaching the history of American music. Founder director of the Inter-American Institute for Musical Research; has lectured extensively in the United States, Latin America and Europe. Former Director of the School of Music at the University of Oklahoma, Professor of American Musical History and Latin American Studies at Tulane University, Senior Research Fellow at the Institute for Studies in American Music, Brooklyn College, CUNY, and Ziegele Visiting Professor of Music at the State University of New York at Buffalo. His many publications include *The Music of Spain* (1941, 2nd revised edition 1959); *A Guide to Latin American Music* (1945, 2nd revised edition 1962); *America's Music: From the Pilgrims to the Present* (1955, 2nd revised edition 1966); *The American Composer Speaks: A Historical Anthology* (1966); and *Contemporary Art in Latin America* (1971).

EF *Elizabeth Forbes*
Freelance music critic and journalist; member of editorial board of *Opera* magazine (London); contributor to *Financial Times, Musical Times, Music and Musicians*, and other specialist publications; also to *Grove's Dictionary of Music and Musicians*, 6th edition.

NG *Noël Goodwin*
Music and dance critic for the *Daily Express* (London) since 1956; Executive Editor, *Music and Musicians*, 1965–71; now Associate Editor, *Dance and Dancers*; broadcasts frequently on musical matters; contributor to *Encyclopaedia Britannica*, 15th edition, and to *Grove's Dictionary of Music and Musicians*, 6th edition.

EJ *H. Earle Johnson*
Assistant Professor of Music at Clark University (Worcester, Mass.); Visiting Professor at College of William and Mary (Williamsburg, Va.); author of four books including *Operas on American Subjects* (1964); contributor to many journals and books including *Dictionary of American Biography; Die Musik in Geschichte und Gegenwart; Notes* (published by the American Music Library Association) and *The Musical Quarterly*.

MK *Malena Kuss*
Argentine-born musicologist and pianist living in the United States. A recipient of several awards, she has made a special study of Argentine opera and has contributed articles on Latin American music to *Die Musik in Geschichte und Gegenwart*, the *Composers of the Americas* series, the *Yearbook for Inter-American Musical Research*, and *Heterofonía* (Mexico City). Her Ph.D. dissertation, *Nativistic Strains in Argentine Operas Premiered at the Teatro Colón (1908–1972)* is in progress.

CM *Carl Morey*
Associate Professor of Music History, University of Toronto, since 1970; Academic Secretary, Graduate Department of Music there 1973–6; founder and first head of the Department of Music, University of Windsor (Ontario), 1964; Visiting Professor of Musicology at Colorado College (1966, 1969), and Indiana University (1970). Has con-

tributed many reviews and articles to *Acta Musicologica* (Basel), *Canadian Forum*, *Music and Letters* (London), *Opera Canada*, etc.; contributor to *The Encyclopedia of Music in Canada* (in preparation); *The Concise Oxford Dictionary of Opera* (revised edition, in preparation), and *Grove's Dictionary of Music and Musicians*, 6th edition.

GN *Geoffrey Norris*
Studied music in England and the Soviet Union, has written a number of articles on Russian music, and has edited the Russian section of *Grove's Dictionary of Music and Musicians*, 6th edition. He is the author of *Rakhmaninov* (1976), is preparing a book on Shostakovich, and lectures in music history at the Royal Northern College of Music.

LO *Leslie Orrey*
Lately head of Music Department, Goldsmiths' College, University of London; has also taught in the United States, as Visiting Professor of Music at Ohio State University and San Jose State College, California. Author of *Bellini* (1969), *A Concise History of Opera* (1972), *Programme Music* (1975) and *Gluck* (1976). Contributor to many periodicals including *Music and Letters* and *Musical Times* (London).

PS *Patric Schmid*
Founder and director of Opera Rara (London); has been responsible for the first modern revivals of Meyerbeer's *Il Crociato in Egitto*, Mercadante's *Orazi e Curiazi*, Donizetti's *Torquato Tasso*, the original version of Mayr's *Medea in Corinto*, etc. Musical director of the Hintlesham Festival, 1972–3; artistic adviser to the Northern Ireland Opera Trust. Has special knowledge of 19th-century opera and performers.

JT *John Tyrrell*
Studied Cape Town, Oxford, and Brno Universities. D.Phil. from Oxford with a dissertation on Janáček's operas. Associate Editor, *Musical Times* (London), since 1972; editor responsible for articles on musicologists and writers on music, *Grove's Dictionary of Music and Musicians*, 6th edition. Has special knowledge of Czech music.

Editorial note

Some points of treatment require explanation:

We have given the titles of all operas in their original languages, where they were written in English, French, German, Italian, or Spanish. For those written in Czech, Polish, Russian, or some other language less commonly known in English-speaking countries, we have used an English title, choosing in most cases a literal translation of the original. In a few instances we have kept to well-known English titles that are not translations of the original (e.g. *The Bartered Bride*). For consistency, we have capitalized titles in all languages as they would be in English.

Dates of works, unless otherwise noted, are those of first stage production. We have retained old-style English dates before 1752 when the Gregorian calendar was adopted. Russian dates are given in new style.

Place names are generally given as currently spelled in the country concerned, except for a few cities (Munich, Prague, etc.) where readers will be more familiar with the English rendering; when a city has changed its own name (St Petersburg, Petrograd, Leningrad) we give the form under which it was known at the time. In certain entries, current or historical alternative forms are printed in parentheses.

All personal names are printed as the owner would spell them, complete with accents. For names transliterated from the Cyrillic script, we have based our system upon that used in *Grove's Dictionary of Music and Musicians*, 6th edition. We have, however, retained the inconsistent but familiar form in a few instances (e.g. Tchaikovsky, not Chaykovsky).

Cross-references within entries are indicated by the use of SMALL CAPITALS.

ABBREVIATIONS

ABC	American Broadcasting Company
acad.	academy
Amer.	American
art. dir.	artistic director
b.	born
BBC	British Broadcasting Corporation
BNOC	British National Opera Company
BT	Burgtheater, Vienna
c.	century
c.	*circa*
CC	City Center, New York
CG	Covent Garden (Royal Opera House), London
char.	character
CI	Comédie-Italienne, Paris
co.	company
COC	Canadian Opera Company
Col	Coliseum, London
comp.	composed, composer, composition
cons.	conservatory (or equivalent in any language)
d.	died
des.	designed (by), designer
DL	Drury Lane, London
Eng.	English
ENO	English National Opera
EOG	English Opera Group
fest.	festival
Fr.	French
Ger.	German
Gr.	Greek
HM	Her (His) Majesty's Theatre, London
HNT	Hof- und Nationaltheater, Munich
It.	Italian
KO	Komische Oper, Berlin
KT	Kärntnerthor-Theater, Vienna
Lat.	Latin
LC	Lincoln Center, New York
lib.	librettist, libretto (by)
m.	married
MdC	Maestro di Cappella, Maître de Chapelle (also Kapellmeister, i.e. the job, not strictly the title)
Met	Metropolitan Opera, New York
mus.	music (by)
mus. dir.	musical director
NT	National Theatre
O.	Opera (or equivalent in any language, e.g. Paris O. = Paris Opéra)
OC	Opera Company
OH	Opera House
orch.	orchestra
perf.	performance, performed (by), performer
prod.	produced (by), producer, production
PRT	Prinzregententheater, Munich
PT	Provisional Theatre, Prague
pub.	publication, published (by)
RAH	Royal Albert Hall, London
RAM	Royal Academy of Music, London
RCM	Royal College of Music, London
RFH	Royal Festival Hall, London
Sc.	La Scala (T. alla Scala)
SO	Scottish Opera
Sp.	Spanish
SW	Sadler's Wells, London
T.	Theatre (or equivalent in any language, e.g. T. de la Monnaie = Théâtre de la Monnaie; T. S. Carlo = Teatro San Carlo; T. a. d. Wieden = Theater auf der Wieden)
TI	Théâtre-Italien, Paris
TL	Théâtre-Lyrique, Paris
tr.	translated (by), translation
univ.	university
WNO	Welsh National Opera
O	recorded (complete)
★	filmed (complete)

Colour Plates

Page 49 Stage set by Alessandro Sanquirico for *Anna Bolena*
50 Teatro Amazones, Manaus
67 Grace Bumbry as Amneris in *Aida*
68 Jean-Baptiste Faure in *L'Africaine*
109 Nadězda Kniplová as Jenůfa
110–11 *The Fair* by Mstislav Dobuzhinsky
112 Gwyneth Jones and David Ward in *Don Carlos*
153 *Nabucco*
154 Stage model for *Tristan und Isolde*
171 Costume design by Erté for *Madama Butterfly*
172 Curtain design by Yuri Pimenov for *Pagliacci*
172 Design by Amable for *Tannhäuser*
213 Costume design by Isak Rabinovich for *Love for Three Oranges*
214–5 Set by David Hockney for *The Rake's Progress*
216 Teatro alla Scala, Milan, painted by Inganni Angelo
257 Alexandra Hunt and William Neill in *Of Mice and Men*
258 Ascot scene, designed by Cecil Beaton, for the film of *My Fair Lady*
275 Sena Jurinac in *Der Rosenkavalier*
276 *Salomé*, painted by Gustave Moreau
317 Henriette Sontag as Rosina in *Il Barbiere di Siviglia*
318–19 Set by Karl Friedrich Schinkel for *Die Zauberflöte*
320 Amy Shuard in *Turandot*

A

Aachen [Fr. Aix-la-Chapelle], W. Germany, has a small but significant provincial opera house. SCHINKEL built a theatre there, 1825. Musicians associated with Aachen have incl. BUSCH, 1912–19, and KARAJAN, 1935–42. LO

Abbado, Claudio, b. Milan, 26 Jun 1933. Italian conductor. Won major international prizes before taking up career equally divided between opera house and concert hall. In 1971 appointed mus. dir. of Sc., Milan, and principal cond. of the Vienna Philharmonic. Guest appearances with all major orchs and in principal opera houses. FGB

Abbott, Emma *see* EMMA ABBOTT ENGLISH OPERA CO.

Abencérages, Les, ou L'Étendard de Grenade (*The Abencerrages, or The Standard of Granada*), opera, 3 acts, CHERUBINI, lib. JOUY, based on Jean-Pierre Florian's novel, *Gonzalve de Cordoue*. Paris O., 6 Apr 1813; revived Florentine Maggio Musicale, 1957. Wr. in adulation of Napoleon, who was present, it tells of the final overthrow of the Moors under their chieftain Almansor at Granada in 1492. LO

Aborn Opera Company, US touring co. organized by Milton and Sargent Aborn in 1902 for standard works of light opera and musical comedy at popular prices with seasons mainly in Brooklyn and Baltimore. The co. toured for 20 years. The Aborns managed the Century Co. in NY, 1913–15, without success. EJ

Abraham, Paul [Pál], b. Apatin, now in Yugoslavia, 2 Nov 1892; d. Hamburg, 6 May 1960. Hungarian composer. Studied mus. acad. Budapest, soon devoted himself to operetta. After collaborating with LEHÁR in *Friederike* (1928) and *Land des Lächelns* (1929) wrote several on his own of which *Viktoria und ihr Husar* (Vienna 1930★) has been the most successful. Emigrated to USA, 1938; *The White Swan* prod. NY, 1939. Returned to Europe 1950. LO

Abstrakt Oper No. 1, opera, 7 scenes, BLACHER, lib. EGK. Radio Frankfurt, 28 June 1953; staged Mannheim, 17 Oct 1953; Boston, 19 Apr 1956. LO ○

Académie de Musique *see* PARIS

Academy of Music *see* NEW YORK

Acis and Galatea, described variously as masque, serenata, or opera, 2 acts, HANDEL, lib. GAY and others. Cannons, Edgware, Middlesex, 1719?; public perf. London, Lincoln's Inn T., 13 Mar 1731; NY, Park T., 21 Nov 1842; revived, EOG, Aldeburgh Fest., 1966. Very popular in London in 18th c. and later. Acis (ten.) in love with Galatea (sop.), is destroyed by the giant Polyphemus (bass), but his soul lives on in the shape of a purling stream. LO ○

Acis et Galatée, *pastorale héroique*, 3 acts and prologue, LULLY, lib. Jean-Galbert de Campistron (1656–1723). First perf., privately, 6 Sept 1686 at a reception for the Dauphin at the Château d'Anet, later in Sept at the Palais Royal. HANDEL later used the story in ACIS AND GALATEA. LO

Ackté, Aino, b. Helsinki, 23 Apr 1876; d. Nummela, 8 Aug 1944. Finnish soprano. Debut 1897, Paris O., as MARGUERITE and sang there for six years, incl. premiere of Samuel Rousseau's *Cloche du Rhin* (1898). She sang at the NY Met, 1904–6; London debut at CG, 1907, as ELSA. Repertory incl. GLUCK'S ALCESTE, JULIETTE, THAÏS, MICAËLA, NEDDA, SENTA, ELISABETH and EVA. In 1910 she sang in the first London perf. of SALOME, where the power of her singing and the seductiveness of her acting caused a sensation. EF

Adalgisa, sop., young priestess, in love with Pollione in NORMA

Adam, Adolphe Charles, b. Paris, 24 July 1803; d. Paris, 3 May 1856. French composer. Actively discouraged from music by his parents, was largely self-taught until in 1817 he was allowed to enter the Paris Cons., where he was influenced by BOÏELDIEU. Set up in 1847 an operatic venture, the T. National, disastrously cut short by the 1848 revolution. *Opéras comiques* incl. POSTILLON DE LONGJUMEAU, *Le Brasseur de Preston* (1838), ROI D'YVETÔT, and *Si J'étais Roi* (1852). Best known as comp. of the ballet *Giselle* (1841). Wrote musical criticism and *Derniers Souvenirs d'un Musicien* (Paris 1859), a most engaging volume of memoirs. LO

Adam, Theo, b. Dresden, 1 Aug 1926. German bass-baritone. Member Dresdener Kreuzchor as a boy. Debut Dresden Staats O., 1949. Member Berlin Staats O., 1952. First appeared at Bayreuth in MEISTERSINGER and as King Henry (LOHENGRIN), 1954; also WOTAN, 1963, AMFORTAS, 1968, and HANS SACHS, 1968. Salzburg Fest. OCHS, 1969, and WOZZECK,

Acis and Galatea. EOG, London, CG, 12 Sept 1966; produced COPLEY; sets Henry Bardon; costumes David Walker. Victor Godfrey as Polyphemus

1972. CG debut as Wotan, 1967. PIZARRO in 1970 bicentenary of FIDELIO, T. a. d. Wien, cond. BERNSTEIN. Other roles incl. KING MARK and PHILIPPE. One of the leading Wagnerian heroic bass-bars. AB

Theo Adam in the title role of DESSAU's *Einstein*, Berlin Staats O., 16 Feb 1974; sets and costumes Andreas Reinhardt; produced Ruth Berghaus

Adamberger, Valentin, b. Munich, 6 July 1743; d. Vienna, 24 Aug 1804. Austrian tenor. After successes in London and Italy was recalled to Vienna, 1880, by the Emperor to sing in the new NT there. Friend of MOZART; created BELMONTE. LO

Adami, Giuseppe, b. Verona, 4 Feb 1878; d. Milan, 12 Oct 1946. Italian librettist. A music critic for *La Sera*, his first libretto, in association with WILLNER and Heinrich Richert, was RONDINE in 1917, then came TABARRO, 1918, *La Via della Finestra* for ZANDONAI, 1919, and, with Renato Simoni, TURANDOT. PS

Adam und Eva, oder Der erschaffene, gefallene, und wieder aufgerichtete Mensch (*Adam and Eve, or The Creation, Fall and Redemption of Man*), Johann Theile (1646–1724), lib. Richter. The first opera in the newly built T. at Hamburg, 1678. A church opera; music lost. LO

Adelaide. During the 19th c. opera made sporadic appearances, e.g. CENERENTOLA at the Victoria T. in 1844, and valuable work was done by the Elizabethan Trust in the 1950s (*see* AUSTRALIA). Opera is now given in the Festival Centre, which embraces a theatre/concert hall seating 2,000; the Playhouse, *c.* 630 seats; and an open-air amphitheatre. LO

Adele, sop., the maid in FLEDERMAUS

Adelson e Salvini, *opera semi-seria*, 3 acts, BELLINI, lib. Andrea Leone Tottola. Naples, Real Collegio di Musica, S. Sebastiano, Feb 1825. Later revised form (2 acts, with recitative replacing orig. spoken dialogue) pub. but never perf. Main chars: Nelly (sop.) Fanny (contr.) Salvini (ten.) Adelson (bar.) Struley (bass) Bonifacio (basso buffo). Salvini, a painter, is hopelessly in love with Nelly, fiancée of the Irish peer, Lord Adelson, his friend and patron. He foils an attempt by Nelly's uncle, Struley, to abduct her, but hearing a pistol shot, is convinced that Nelly has been killed. He is dissuaded from suicide by the discovery that she is alive. Cured of his passion he becomes engaged to his pupil, Fanny; Adelson weds Nelly. Bellini's first opera, written in florid ROSSINI style. Never revived since first perf. JB

Adina, sop., the heroine of ELISIR D'AMORE

Adler, Kurt Herbert, b. Vienna, 2 Apr 1905. Austrian, later American, conductor and manager. TOSCANINI's assistant at Salzburg Fest., 1936; settled in USA, 1938. After cond. Chicago O., 1938–43, went to San Francisco, where later, in 1953, he followed Gaetano Merola (1881–1953) as dir. LO

Adler, Peter Herman, b. Jablonec, Czechoslovakia, 2 Dec 1899. Czech, later American, conductor. After cond. opera at Brno, 1923, was first cond. at the Bremen T., 1928–31. Cond. orch. in Kiev, 1932–7; to USA in 1939. Dir. NBC TV Opera, 1949–60, and dir., National Education TV since 1969. LO

Admeto, Re di Tessaglia (*Admetus, King of Thessaly*), opera, 3 acts, HANDEL, lib. 'altered' from Aurelio Aureli's *L'Antigona Delusa da Alceste* prob. by Nicola Haym. London, HM, 31 Jan 1727; revived Abingdon, 7 May 1964. Story basically that of ALCESTE. LO

Adriana Lecouvreur, opera, 4 acts, CILEA, lib. Arturo Colautti after play by SCRIBE and Ernest Legouvé. Milan, T. Lirico, 6 Nov 1902; London, CG, 8 Nov 1904; New Orleans, 5 Jan 1907. Main chars: Adriana (sop.) Maurizio (ten.) Princesse de Bouillon (mezzo-sop.) Michonnet (bar.) Adriana, famous star at the Comédie-Française, loves Maurizio, Count of Saxony, who for political reasons has a liaison with the Princesse de Bouillon. Adriana saves her rival from a compromising situation. Later she insults the Princess under cover of a recitation from Racine. Adriana is herself poisoned by a bunch of violets sent by the Princess, and dies in the arms of Maurizio, watched by her faithful Michonnet, the stage manager who also loves her. Cilea's best-known opera, frequently performed in Italy. Last heard at CG 1906. JB O
See Kobbé

Aegyptische Helena, Die *see* ÄGYPTISCHE HELENA

Aeschylus, b. Eleusis, nr Athens, 525 BC; d. Gela, Sicily, 456 BC. Greek dramatist. Titles of about 80 plays are known, but only seven are extant. Operas based on his plays incl.: *Prometheus* (ORFF; FAURÉ, *Prométhée*; Maurice Emmanuel, *Prométhée Enchaîné*, 1915); the *Oresteia* trilogy (Sergei Taneyev, 1895; WEINGARTNER; MILHAUD); *The Suppliants* (Emmanuel, *Salamine*, 1929). LO

Africaine, L' (*The African Girl*), opera, 5 acts, MEYERBEER, lib. SCRIBE. Paris, O., 28 Apr 1865; London, CG, 22 July 1865 (in It.); NY, 1 Dec 1865 (in It.). Main chars: Vasco da Gama (ten.) Selika (mezzo-sop.) Nelusko (bar.) Inez (sop.) Don Diego (bass) Don Pedro (bass) Don Alvar (ten.). Vasco returns to Portugal from an expedition bringing two captives, Selika and Nelusko. The royal councillors refuse his request for another ship, he denounces them and is imprisoned. Inez arranges Vasco's freedom by marrying Don Pedro, who undertakes an expedition to the new land beyond Africa. Nelusko wrecks the ship on Madagascar. Selika saves Vasco's life by marrying him, but the ceremony is interrupted by Inez's song of farewell. Selika, moved by Inez's love for Vasco, reunites the lovers, and kills herself by inhaling the poisonous scent of the manchineel tree. Convinced it would be his masterpiece, Meyerbeer worked on *L'Africaine* for a quarter of a century, finishing only days before his death, a year before the opera's first prod. PS

Agathe, sop., the heroine in FREISCHÜTZ

Agrippina, opera, 3 acts, HANDEL, lib. Vincenzo Grimani. Venice, T. S. Giovanni Crisostomo, 28 Dec 1709. Main chars: Agrippina (sop. or mezzo-sop.) Poppea (sop.) Ottone (contr.) Nerone (sop.) Pallante (bar.) Narciso (mezzo-sop.) Claudio (bass). During the absence of her husband, the emperor Claudio, in Britain, Agrippina intrigues to ensure the succession of her son Nerone, using the freedmen Pallante and Narciso. Surprised by Claudio's unexpected return, she poisons his mind against Ottone, to whom he has decreed the succession for having saved his life. Poppea, Ottone's betrothed, sets herself to thwart Agrippina's plans, making use of the fact that Nerone and Claudio are both in love with her. She places the two men in a compromising position, and so extracts from the emperor permission to marry Ottone, who is willing to renounce the succession for her sake. Agrippina exculpates herself, and Nerone is declared the future emperor. Probably the only opera produced by Handel during his Italian tour, it is a typical Venetian drama of intrigue. Occasionally staged in Germany in a modern arrangement (pub. Bärenreiter, 1956). JB

Aguiari, Lucrezia, b. Ferrara, 1743; d. Parma, 18 May 1783. Italian soprano. The natural child of a nobleman, known as *La Bastardella*, her phenomenal range and agility were praised by MOZART, who heard her sing at Parma in 1770 and transcribed some of the passages she executed. In an era of great singers her technique surpassed that of all her rivals. LO

Ägyptische Helena, Die (*The Egyptian Helen*), opera, 2 acts, R. STRAUSS, lib. HOFMANNSTHAL. Dresden, 6 June 1928; NY Met, 6 Nov 1928; Salzburg Fest. (revised version) 1933. Main chars: Helena (sop.) Menelaus (ten.) Aithra (sop.) Altair (bar.). The magic potion of

the Egyptian sorceress Aithra makes Menelaus, returned from Troy, forgive his faithless Helen. FGB
See Mann, *Richard Strauss* (London 1964; New York 1966); Kobbé

Ahronovitch, Yuri, b. Leningrad, 13 May 1932. Russian conductor. Studied at Leningrad Cons., and with Kurt Sanderling and Nathan Rachlin. Career began as orchestral cond. at Saratov, where he eventually appeared with the opera co. After leaving Russia, Western operatic debut at Cologne in VERDI's OTELLO, 1974; London, CG, debut, BORIS GODUNOV, 1975; US debut at Chicago with FIDELIO, 1975. AB

Aida, opera, 4 acts, VERDI, lib. GHISLANZONI based on a plot by Auguste Mariette. Cairo, Opera House, 24 Dec 1871; Milan, Sc., 8 Feb 1872; Paris, O., 22 Mar 1880 (with extended ballet music); NY, Acad of Mus., 26 Nov 1873; London, CG, 22 June 1876. Main chars: Aida (sop.) Amneris (mezzo-sop.) Radames (ten.) Amonasro (bar.). Radames, captain of the Egyptian guard, is in love with Aida, an Ethiopian slave, but is loved by Amneris, princess of Egypt. Aida's father, Amonasro, King of Ethiopia, is discovered among the newly captured Ethiopian prisoners. Aida, instigated by Amonasro, forces Radames to betray his country's secrets. Radames is condemned to be immured alive; Aida voluntarily shares his fate. Among the most popular of Verdi's mature operas, its grandeur of spectacle makes it especially suitable for open-air perf. JB O
See Kobbé

air (Fr. *air*, Ger. *Arie*, It. *aria*) 1. Song or extended melody. Fr. and Eng. term (in British usage until *c.* 1900) equivalent to the It. ARIA. 2. Term used in ballad and pastiche operas in indicating the source of a melody. E.g. in BEGGAR'S OPERA, ''Tis woman that seduces all mankind' (Air: 'The bonny gray-eyed morn'). JB

Aix-en-Provence, France. The still-extant Salle d'Opéra was built in 1775; operas were given there in 18th c. with stars from Paris O. Summer fests have been held since 1948, usually in the open-air theatre in the Archbishop's Palace. LO

Albanese, Licia, b. Bari, 22 July 1913. Italian soprano (US citizen 1945). Studied with Giuseppina Baldassare-Tedeschi. After singing in MADAMA BUTTERFLY, where she was understudying, 1934, won national song contest 1935. Debut 1935, Parma; NY Met debut 1940. Took part in first broadcast from the stage of the Met, where she was an admired singer for 25 years with over 40 roles and more than 1,000 perfs. Broadcast and recorded, under TOSCANINI, BOHÈME and TRAVIATA. LO

Albani, Emma [Marie Louise Cécile Emma Lajeunesse], b. Chambly, Que., 1 Nov 1852; d. London, 3 Apr 1930. Canadian soprano. Moved to Albany, NY, as a girl; her singing in the cathedral choir resulted in a fund to send her to Europe, 1868. Assumed the name Albani in her benefactors' honour. Studied with DUPREZ in Paris and Francesco Lamperti in Milan. Debut Messina, 1869, in SONNAMBULA. Began 24-year association with CG, 1872; m. Ernest Gye, CG dir., 1878. A famous interpreter of Wagnerian roles. Farewell appearance RAH, 14 Oct 1911. Made a DBE, 1925. PS
See autobiography, *Forty Years of Song* (London 1911)

Albéniz, Isaac, b. Camprodón, 29 May 1860; d. Camboles-Bains, France, 16 June 1909. Spanish composer. Of his several operas and *zarzuelas*, the most important are *Henry Clifford*, Barcelona, 1895, and esp. *Pepita Jiménez*, Barcelona, 1896, and elsewhere. LO

Alberich, bass-bar., a Nibelung in RHEINGOLD, SIEGFRIED and GÖTTERDÄMMERUNG

Albert, Eugen (Eugène Francis Charles) d', b. Glasgow, 10 Apr 1864; d. Riga, Latvia, 3 Mar 1932. French pianist and composer. Studied

Albert Herring, EOG production 1962, Act II sc. 1. Kenneth Macdonald as Albert; FISHER as Lady Billows; produced GRAHAM; designed PIPER

initially with his father, then at National Training School, London (which later became the RCM), and with LISZT in Vienna. One of the most brilliant pianists of his time. Became Ger. by adoption; all his 20 operas except TIEFLAND and *Flauto Solo* (1905) orig. prod. there. Operas that found favour outside Germany were *Die Abreise* (Frankfurt 1898; London, King's T., Hammersmith, 1925) and *Die Toten Augen* (Dresden 1916; Chicago 1923; NY, Met, 1924). LO

Albert Herring, opera, 3 acts, BRITTEN, lib. CROZIER after Maupassant's story, *Le Rosier de Madame Husson*. Glyndebourne, 20 June 1947; Tanglewood, 8 Aug 1949. Main chars: Albert Herring (ten.) Lady Billows (sop.) Sid (bar.) Nancy (mezzo-sop.) Mrs Herring (contr.) Miss Wordsworth (sop.). Britten's second chamber opera and first comedy. In describing the election of a May King, rather than a May Queen, as the only virtuous villager in the fictitious Loxford, Suffolk, the comp. deploys formal arias, duets and ensembles, and parodies some operatic conventions, yet genuine feeling tempers the humour. Albert appears a real person, not just a figure of fun. Prod. in Canada, the USA, and Germany. AB O
See Kobbé

Alboni, Marietta [Maria Anna Marzia], b. Cesena, 6 Mar 1823; d. Ville d'Avray, nr Paris, 23 June 1894. Italian contralto. Studied Bologna, where ROSSINI met her and taught her the contr. parts of his operas. After debut Bologna, 1842, appeared in many It. opera houses, also in Germany, Austria, and Russia. Engaged CG, 1847, as rival to LIND; appeared in London several times in the 1850s; visited USA 1853. Retired 1863 on her m. to Count Pepilo. One of the outstanding singers of her time. LO

Alcina, produced and designed ZEFFIRELLI, Venice Fest., 19 Feb 1960, the first performance of this work in Italy, with SUTHERLAND and Monica Sinclair

Alceste 1. Opera, 3 acts, GLUCK, lib. CALZABIGI, derived from EURIPIDES. Vienna, BT, 26 Dec 1767. 2. Opera, 3 acts, mus. recast and added to by Gluck, Calzabigi's text tr. and much altered by François Louis Gaudi Duroullet. Paris O., 23 Apr 1776; London (in It. for BANTI's benefit), King's T., 30 Apr 1795, and (in Eng., tr. TROUTBECK) HM, 2 Dec 1904; Wellesley College, Mass., 11 Mar 1938. At least 12 other operas on this theme are known, incl. ADMETO. LO
See Cooper, *Gluck* (London 1935)

Alceste, ou le Triomphe d'Alcide (*Alceste, or The Triumph of Hercules*), *tragédie lyrique*, prologue and 5 acts, LULLY, lib. QUINAULT. Paris O., 10 Jan 1674. The king, Admète, will die unless someone can be found to take his place. Alceste, his queen, volunteers, and dies. She is brought back from Hades by Alcide (Hercules). Revived London, O. Centre, 17 Dec 1975. LO

Alcina, *opera seria*, 3 acts, HANDEL, lib. Antonio Marchi based on ARIOSTO's *Orlando Furioso*. London, CG, 27 Apr 1727. Main chars: Alcina (sop.) Ruggiero (mezzo-sop.) Bradamante (contr.) Morgana (sop.) Oronte (ten.). Bradamante, disguised as a soldier, searches for her lover Ruggiero, held captive by the sorceress Alcina. Morgana, mistress of Alcina's captain Oronte, falls in love with Bradamante, believing her to be a man. Alcina genuinely loves Ruggiero; after various misunderstandings Bradamante and Ruggiero escape; Alcina's magic kingdom is destroyed. Important modern revivals: London, St Pancras Fest., 1957, Venice 1960, London, CG, 1962. JB O

Alda [Davis], Frances, b. Christchurch, 31 May 1883; d. Venice, 18 Sept 1952. New Zealand soprano. Studied Paris, with MARCHESI DE CASTRONE. Paris OC, 1904 in MANON. 1906–8 sang in London, Brussels, Parma, Buenos Aires and Milan, where she sang in first It. LOUISE (1908) and met GATTI-CASAZZA, whom she m. in 1910. Engaged by him for NY Met (debut in RIGOLETTO, 1908) where she remained, except for the 1910–11 season, until 1929. Created roles in CYRANO DE BERGERAC, HADLEY's *Cleopatra's Night* (1920) and HERBERT's *Madeleine* (1914). LO
See autobiography (under Gatti-Casazza), *Men, Women, and Tenors* (Boston 1937)

Aldeburgh Festival. Founded 1948 by BRITTEN, CROZIER, and PEARS; held at Britten's

home town, Aldeburgh, on the Suffolk coast. Programme has usually reflected the tastes of Britten and Pears. Imogen Holst, GRAHAM, Philip Ledger, and Steuart Bedford have as dirs contributed actively to its programmes, Graham being responsible for many prods, and Bedford conducting them. First perfs at the fest. have incl. many Britten operas and his Church Parables (in nearby Orford church), and works by WILLIAMSON, WALTON, BERKELEY and Harrison Birtwistle. Opera prods have been larger in scale since the conversion of the Maltings at Snape into a concert hall/opera house, 1968 (burned down 1969, rebuilt 1970), notably the premieres there of DEATH IN VENICE, 1973, and of the revised *Paul Bunyan* (BRITTEN), 4 June 1976. AB
See Ronald Blythe (ed.), *Aldeburgh Anthology* (London 1973)

Alessandro, *opera seria*, 3 acts, HANDEL, lib. Paolo Antonio Rolli. London, Haymarket T., 5 May 1726. Hamburg (in Ger., airs and final chorus in It.), 7 Nov 1726, and Brunswick, 6 Aug 1728. One of several of Handel's operas perf. at Hamburg. LO

Alessandro Stradella, opera, 3 acts, FLOTOW, lib. Wilhelm Friedrich. Hamburg, 30 Dec 1844; London, DL, 6 Jun 1846; NY, 29 Nov 1853. Story based on incidents in life of the It. comp. A. Stradella, *c.* 1642–82. LO

Alfano, Franco, b. Posillipo, nr Naples, 8 Mar 1876; d. San Remo 27 Oct 1954. Italian composer. He studied at the Naples and Leipzig Cons. Debut, as a concert pianist, in Berlin, 1896. His first operatic success was with RISURREZIONE (Turin 1904), still occasionally heard in Italy. In 1926 TOSCANINI commissioned him to complete from PUCCINI's sketches the third act of TURANDOT; Alfano's ending is regularly heard today. Of his 11 operas (incl. the unfinished *I Cavalieri e la Bella*) the first five follow the tradition of Puccini, MASCAGNI and GIORDANO. From 1920 onward a more individual, symphonic approach is discernable. *La Leggenda di Sakuntala* (Bologna 1921) is his most stylistically advanced; *L'Ultimo Lord* (Naples 1930) is partly indebted to the language of INTERMEZZO. JB

Alfonso, Don, bar., the cynical bachelor of COSÌ FAN TUTTE

Alfonso und Estrella, opera, 3 acts, SCHUBERT, lib. Franz von Schober. Comp. 1822. Schubert sent it to MILDER-HAUPTMANN, who hoped to mount it in Berlin, but nothing came of this. First perf., in a mutilated version, by LISZT, Weimar, 24 Jun 1854. Other mangled attempts, with lib. rewritten and music revised, at Karlsruhe, 1881, and Vienna, 1882. LO

Alfredo, ten., Violetta's lover in TRAVIATA

Alkestis, opera, 1 act, Egon Wellesz, lib. HOFMANNSTHAL, based on drama by EURIPIDES. Mannheim, 20 Mar 1924. EF

Alkmene, opera, 3 acts, KLEBE, lib. composer after KLEIST. Berlin, Deutsche O., 25 Sept 1961. Main chars: Alkmene (sop.) Jupiter (bass) Amphitryon (ten.) Cleanthis (sop.) Sosias (bar.) Mercury (bar.). Jupiter assumes the form of Amphitryon, the Theban general, in order to press his attentions on Alkmene. EF

Allegra, Salvatore, b. Palermo, 13 July 1898. Italian composer. His operas are: *Ave Maria*, Perugia 1934; *I Viadanti*, 1936; *Il Medico sul Malgrado*, based on MOLIÈRE, Kassel 1938; *Romulus*, Naples 1952. Has also wr. operettas and musical comedies. LO

Allen, Thomas, b. Seaham, Co. Durham, 10 Sept 1944. English baritone. A season in the Glyndebourne chorus, then debut, 1969, with the WNO as FIGARO (BARBIERE DI SIVIGLIA). First heard at CG in 1971 as Donald in BILLY BUDD, he sang the title role of this opera with the WNO in 1972. Now a member of CG company, he sings Figaro and ALMAVIVA (NOZZE DI FIGARO), GUGLIELMO, PAPAGENO, Paolo (SIMONE BOCCANEGRA), VALENTIN, SCHAUNARD, Dominik (one of the suitors in ARABELLA) and Sid (ALBERT HERRING). His fine voice, innate musicality and acting

Right: Thomas Allen (right) as Figaro and ALVA as Almaviva in ROSSINI's BARBIERE DI SIVIGLIA, London, CG, 20 Oct 1975; produced Michael Rennison; designed Moshe Mussman

ability were demonstrated at the premiere of VOICE OF ARIADNE (Aldeburgh 1974), when he sang Count Marco Valerio. EF

Allin, Norman, b. Ashton-under-Lyne, Lancashire, 19 Nov 1884; d. London, 26 Oct 1973. English bass. Studied Manchester. Debut, 1926, with Beecham Opera Company as the Old Hebrew in SAMSON ET DALILA. Sang with that co. until 1922, then became a dir. of newly formed BNOC. At CG in international seasons, 1926–33, roles incl. BARTOLO (NOZZE DI FIGARO), which he also sang at Glyndebourne's first season, 1934. With the Carl Rosa Company, 1942–9: MÉPHISTOPHÉLÈS, SARASTRO, FASOLT, HAGEN, HUNDING, OCHS, Don BASILIO, (BARBIERE DI SIVIGLIA), and Falstaff (LUSTIGEN WEIBER VON WINDSOR) were among his roles. He had a true, voluminous bass. An early stalwart of opera in Eng. AB

Almaviva 1. Ten., the Count in BARBIERE DI SIVIGLIA. 2. Bar., the Count in NOZZE DI FIGARO

Almaviva, Countess, sop., wife of Count Almaviva in NOZZE DI FIGARO

Almira, opera, 3 acts, HANDEL, lib. Friedrich Feustking based on an It. lib. by Giulio Pancieri. Hamburg, 8 Jan 1705. Handel's first opera, and a polyglot affair. The scene is set in Spain, the arias are in both Ger. and It., the dance music is Fr. in style. It ran for 20 nights. LO

Alonso, Francisco, b. Granada, 9 May 1887; d. Madrid, 18 May 1948. Spanish composer. His more than 100 *zarzuelas* incl. *La Calesera*, *Las Corsarias*, *La Perfecta Casada* and *La Picarona*. FGB

Althouse, Paul, b. Reading, Pa., 2 Dec 1889; d. New York, 6 Feb 1954. American tenor. Studied Philadelphia and NY; debut Philadelphia. NY Met debut in first US perf. of BORIS GODUNOV – the first US singer without European experience engaged there. Stayed at Met until 1922, then studied Europe, returning as a WAGNER singer (the first US TRISTAN), 1934–40. After retirement from stage became a successful singing teacher. LO

alto *see* CONTRALTO

Alva, Luigi, b. Lima, 10 Apr 1927. Peruvian tenor. European debut as ALFREDO at T. Nuovo, Milan, 1954. Sang in MATRIMONIO SEGRETO at 1955 opening of Piccola Sc., Milan, repeating the opera at Edinburgh, 1957. Has sung at Aix-en-Provence (1957), London CG (1960), Glyndebourne (1961), NY Met (1964), and other major opera houses. A stylish singer with a flexible voice, he specializes in MOZART (DON GIOVANNI, COSÌ FAN TUTTE, ZAUBERFLÖTE) and ROSSINI (BARBIERE DI SIVIGLIA, CENERENTOLA, TURCO IN ITALIA, ITALIANA IN ALGERI). Other roles include FENTON (FALSTAFF) and NEMORINO. EF

Alvarez, Marguerite d', b. Liverpool, 1886; d. Alassio, Italy, 18 Oct 1953. English contralto, of Peruvian parentage. Studied at Brussels Cons. Debut as DALILA in Rouen; as Fidès (PROPHÈTE) at Manhattan OH, 1909; and in HÉRODIADE and LOUISE in HAMMERSTEIN's inaugural London season, 1911. She sang AMNERIS at CG, 1914. Appeared at a number of European opera houses; also with the Boston and Chicago opera cos. In 1944 she appeared in the film *Till We Meet Again*. Her autobiography, *Forsaken Altars*, was published in London 1954. PS

Alvaro, ten., the hero in FORZA DEL DESTINO

Alzira, opera, prologue and 2 acts, VERDI, lib. CAMMARANO after VOLTAIRE. Naples, T. S. Carlo, 12 Aug 1845. Main chars: Alzira (sop.) Zamoro (ten.) Gusman (bar.). Alzira, an Inca princess, betrothed to Zamoro, is forced into a political marriage with the Spanish governor, Gusman. Zamoro, believed dead, reappears, leads an unsuccessful revolt against the Spaniards and stabs Gusman at the wedding ceremony. But Gusman forgives him before dying. Verdi's least successful opera. Revived at Rome O., 1967, with Virginia Zeani, Gianfranco Cecchele, and Cornell MacNeil, cond. BARTOLETTI. JB

Amadis, *tragédie en musique*, prologue and 5 acts, LULLY, lib. QUINAULT based on 14th-c. romance *Amadis de Gaule*. Paris O., 18 Jan 1684. Several other comps. have treated the same subject including HANDEL, 1715, and J. C. BACH, 1779. LO

Amahl and the Night Visitors, chamber opera, 1 act, MENOTTI, lib. composer. Inspired by Hieronymus Bosch's painting *Adoration of the Magi*, and the first opera designed for TV. NY NBC, 24 Dec 1951; first staged perf. Indiana Univ., 21 Feb 1952. Main chars: Amahl (boy sop.) Mother (mezzo-sop.) Kaspar (ten.) Melchior (bar.) Balthazar (bar.) The Page (bar.). A crippled boy has only his crutches to offer the Holy Child. These he gives to the Magi and is healed. The work receives regular Christmas perfs on TV in the USA. EJ O

Amara [Armaganian], Lucine, b. Hartford, Conn., 1 Mar 1927. American soprano of Armenian origin. Studied San Francisco, singing in chorus of O. there. In 1948 won $2,000 prize and scholarship to univ. of S. California. Debut NY Met, 1950, in DON CARLOS. Besides singing regularly there, has appeared in Europe in ARIADNE AUF NAXOS, Glyndebourne and Edinburgh, 1954; Stockholm, 1955; and in AIDA, Vienna Staats O., 1960. LO

Amato, Pasquale, b. Naples, 21 Mar 1878; d. Jackson Heights, NY, 12 Aug 1942. Italian baritone. Studied Naples Cons. Debut Naples, T. Bellini, as GERMONT; NY debut in same role at Met, 1908; London CG, with Naples San Carlo Company, 1904, but did not return. At Met, created Jack Rance (FANCIULLA DEL WEST); the title role in CYRANO DE BERGERAC; and Napoleon in GIORDANO's *Madame Sans-Gêne*. His many records show the full, vibrant tone, clarity of diction, and sincerity of interpretation that made him one of the great VERDI and *verismo* baritones of his day. AB

Amelia, sop., the heroine in BALLO IN MASCHERA

Amelia Goes to the Ball, *opera buffa*, 1 act, MENOTTI, lib. composer. Philadelphia, Curtis Inst., where the comp. was a student, 1 Apr 1937 (in Eng.); NY, Amsterdam T., 11 Apr 1937; San Remo, 4 Apr 1938 (in It. as *Amelia al Ballo*); NY Met, 3 Mar 1938; Liverpool, 19 Nov 1956. The first American comic opera at the Met. EJ

Ameling, Elly, b. Rotterdam, 8 Feb 1938. Dutch soprano. Studied Rotterdam with Jo Bollenkamp; Paris with Pierre Bernac. Won competitions in 's-Hertogenbosch, 1956, and Geneva, 1958. Most of career to date spent in concert and recital work. Debut as Ilia in IDOMENEO with Nederlandse O., 1973. AB

American Opera Company. Founded by Mrs Jeannette Thurber in 1885 to prod. opera in Eng. With Theodore Thomas as dir. and a youthful co., largely of Americans, the first season opened at the Acad. of Music, NY, 4 Jan 1886. Twelve operas were tastefully staged, incl. works by MOZART, FLOTOW, NICOLAI, WAGNER, and DELIBES. Two national tours followed the 66 NY perfs, but the public did not respond. The National Opera Company continued its work for one season (1888) with many members from the earlier group. EJ

American Opera Society. Founded 1951 for presenting little-known or neglected operas in concert form. Perfs are usually given in Carnegie Hall, NY with soloists of the calibre of CABALLÉ, GEDDA and SUTHERLAND. The many operas thus sung have incl. PARIDE ED ELENA, STRANIERA, ROSSINI's OTELLO and SEMIRAMIDE. The founder, moving spirit, and dir. is Allen Sven Oxenburg. LO

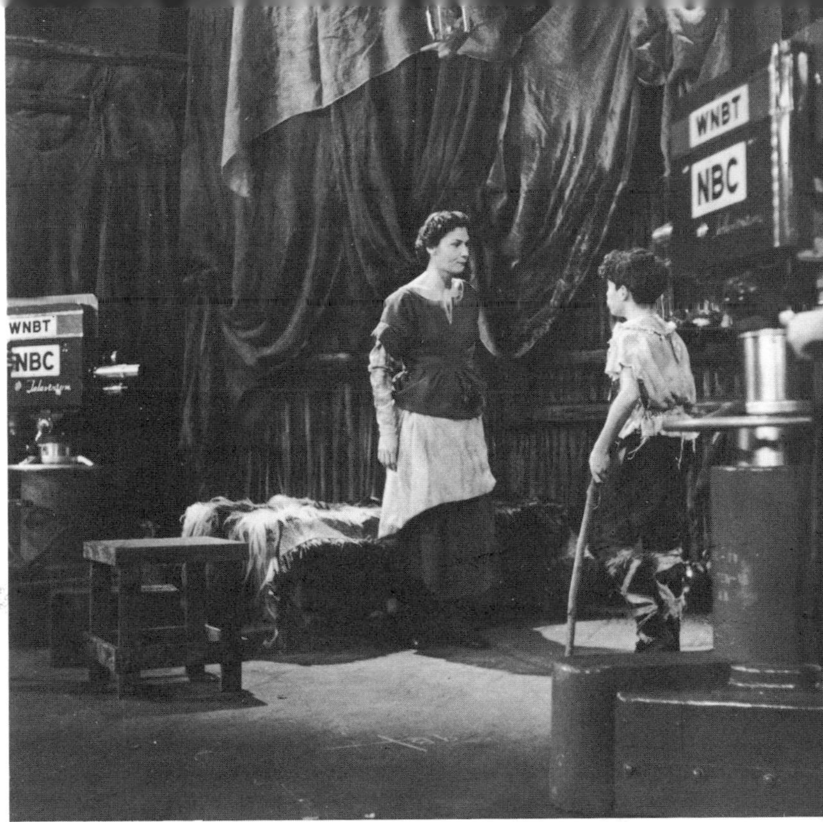

Amahl and the Night Visitors, NBC, 24 Dec 1951. Rosemary Kuhlmann as the Mother; Chet Allen as Amahl

Amfortas, bar., the guardian of the Grail in PARSIFAL

Amico Fritz, L' (*Friend Fritz*), opera, 3 acts, MASCAGNI, lib. P. Suardon (N. Daspuro) after novel by Erckmann-Chatrian. Rome, T. Costanzi, 31 Oct 1891; London, CG, 23 May 1892; Philadelphia, 8 June 1892. Main chars: Fritz (ten.) Suzel (sop.) David (bar.) Beppo (mezzo-sop.). Fritz, a rich farmer, falls in love with Suzel, a girl on his estate, but refuses to relinquish his bachelor status. Through the machinations of Rabbi David their wedding is eventually brought about. Mascagni's second greatest success after CAVALLERIA RUSTICANA; still occasionally revived in Italy. The Intermezzo and the 'Cherry Duet' are well known as excerpts. JB O
See Kobbé

Amneris, mezzo-sop. or contr., the King of Egypt's daughter in AIDA

Amonasro, bar., the King of Ethiopia in AIDA

Amore dei Tre Re, L' (*The Love of Three Kings*), opera, 3 acts, MONTEMEZZI, lib. BENELLI, adapted from his verse drama. Milan, Sc., 10 Apr 1913; NY Met, 2 Jan 1914; London, CG, 27 May 1914. Main chars: Fiora (sop.) Avito (ten.) Manfredo (bar.) Archibaldo (bass). King Archibaldo kills his daughter-in-law, Fiora, poisoning her lips so that her lover, Avito, and her husband, Manfredo, both die after kissing her. EF O

Amsterdam, Netherlands. Opera, at first predominantly It., has been perf. in Amsterdam since 1680. A Fr. company was active from 1788 to 1855, and the Hollandse O. (1886–94) perf. works by Dutch as well as foreign comps. A Netherlands Wagner society was founded in 1893, and broadened its repertory in 1912 to incl. other comps. The present Nederlandse O., based in Amsterdam, opened in 1946 with BOHÈME. *See also* NETHERLANDS. EF

Anacréon ou l'Amour Fugitif, *opéra-ballet*, 2 acts, CHERUBINI, lib. R. Mendouze. Paris, OC, 4 Oct 1803; Vienna, Redoutensaal (concert version in Ger.), 14 Apr 1805. The splendid overture is still sometimes played. LO

Anders, Peter, b. Essen, 1 July 1908; d. Hamburg, 10 Sept 1954. German tenor. Studied Berlin with Lula Mysz-Gmeiner. Debut in BELLE HÉLÈNE, Berlin 1931. Worked at various Ger. houses before joining Berlin Staats O., 1936; most of the rest of his career there. British debut at 1950 Edinburgh Fest., as Bacchus in ARIADNE AUF NAXOS under BEECHAM, who took him to CG in 1951 as an outstanding WALTHER VON STOLZING. One of the most deservedly popular Ger. lyric tenors before and just after World War II. Sang heavier roles from 1950 onward. AB

Andersen, Hans Christian, b. Odense, 2 Apr 1805; d. Copenhagen, 4 Aug 1875. Danish writer of children's and fairy stories. STANFORD, ENNA, STRAVINSKY, Ernst Toch, and WAGNER-RÉGENY are among more than 20 composers who have drawn on his tales for opera plots. LO

Anderson, Marian, b. Philadelphia, Pa., 17 Feb 1902. American contralto. Gifted with a fine, warm, and rich voice, she was the first Negro singer to perf. in a major role at the NY Met, in 1955 (ULRICA). Her career was mainly as a concert artist. LO

Andrea Chénier, opera, 4 acts, GIORDANO, lib. ILLICA. Milan, Sc., 28 Mar 1896; NY, Acad. of Mus., 13 Nov 1896; London, Camden Town T. (in Eng.), 16 Apr 1903. Set in Paris at time of the Revolution. Main chars: Chénier (ten.) Charles Gérard (bar.) Countess de Coigny (sop.) Madeleine (sop.). Gérard, a servant and revolutionary, is secretly in love with the Countess's daughter, Madeleine, who is in love with the poet Chénier. At a ball Madeleine invites Chénier to improvise a poem on love, but instead he sings of the sufferings of the poor. Chénier, now in disfavour with the revolutionaries, meets Madeleine in secret; they are discovered by Gérard, now in favour with the authorities. He and Chénier fight, and Gérard is wounded. The lovers escape, but later Chénier is captured, and condemned to death by Gérard's evidence. Madeleine pleads with Gérard, who yields, but the mob is implacable. Madeleine and Chénier die together. LO O
See Kobbé

Andrésen, Ivar, b. Christiania (now Oslo), 27 July 1896; d. Stockholm, 26 Nov 1940. Norwegian bass. Debut at Stockholm, 1919, as AMONASRO, then engaged at Dresden. Bayreuth debut 1927 as Gurnemanz (PARSIFAL); CG, 1930, as FAFNER; NY Met the same year as DALAND; and at Glyndebourne, 1935, as SARASTRO. Repertory incl. all WAGNER's bass roles – Hermann (TANNHÄUSER), King Henry (LOHENGRIN), KING MARK, POGNER, HUNDING, and HAGEN. EF

Andriessen, Hendrik Franciscus, b. Haarlem, 17 Sept 1892. Dutch composer. Studied Amsterdam Cons. His works incl. two operas: *Philomela*, 23 June 1950, by Nederlandse O. at Amsterdam during Holland Fest.; and *De Spiegel uit Venetië (The Mirror from Venice)*, pub. 1964. EF

Angeles, Victoria de los, b. Barcelona, 1 Nov 1923. Spanish soprano. First sang Countess ALMAVIVA, Barcelona, 1945; MANON and MIMI with GIGLI, Madrid, 1947. First heard in Britain in BBC broadcast of VIDA BREVE, 1948. Debuts in 1950 at London, CG, as Mimi; Milan, Sc., in title role of ARIADNE AUF NAXOS, and NY Met as MARGUERITE. Acclaimed in Europe and N. and S. America for singing of unusual richness of tone, flexibility of technique, and warmth of feeling in roles emphasizing femininity of character; and for song programmes that often include fruits of research into the heritage of Spanish song. NG
See Rosenthal, *Sopranos of Today: Studies of Twenty-five Opera Singers* (London 1956)

Angélique, opera, 1 act, IBERT, lib. Nino. Paris, T. Bériza, 28 Jan 1927; NY, 8 Nov 1937; London, Fortune T., 20 Feb 1950. Angélique is a constantly nagging wife, whose husband Boniface is persuaded by his friend Charlot that the only way of getting rid of her is to put her up for sale. The song 'Pauvre Madame Boniface' owes much to the old Paris vaudeville tradition. FGB

Aniara, opera, 2 acts, BLOMDAHL, lib. Erik Lindegren, based on the epic poem by the Swedish writer Harry Martinson. Stockholm, Royal O., 31 May 1959; Edinburgh, King's T., 3 Sept 1959; London, CG, 1 Sept 1960; Montreal, 31 May 1967. Main chars: Daisy Doodle (sop.) Blind Poetess (sop.) Mimarobe (bar.). A spaceship, carrying refugees from an Earth devastated by atomic warfare to a settlement on Mars, collides with an asteroid and is knocked off course, doomed to fly forever through infinite space. EF

Anna, Donna, sop., daughter of the Commendatore in DON GIOVANNI

Anna Bolena, opera, 2 acts, DONIZETTI, lib. ROMANI. Milan, T. Carcano, 26 Dec 1830; London, HM, 8 July 1831; New Orleans, Nov 1839. Main chars: Anna (sop.) Giovanna (sop.) Smeton (mezzo-sop.) Percy (ten.) Enrico (bass). Enrico (Henry VIII of England) loves Giovanna (Jane Seymour) and wants to be rid of Anna Bolena (Ann Boleyn), his queen. On the appearance of Percy, Anna's former lover, a charge of adultery is fabricated against Anna. She is condemned and executed. Donizetti's 30th opera and first masterpiece. Revival at Sc., Milan, in 1957 with CALLAS in the title role was important to the revaluation of Donizetti. JB O

Anna Bolena. CALLAS in the title role, Milan, Scala, 1957; produced VISCONTI; designed N. BENOIS

Annie Get Your Gun, musical, music and lyrics BERLIN, book Herbert and Dorothy Fields. NY, Imperial T., 16 May 1946; London, Coliseum, 7 June 1947. EJ O★
See Lubbock

Ansseau, Fernand, b. Boussu-Bois, nr Mons, 6 Nov 1890. Belgian tenor. Debut Dijon, 1913, in HÉRODIADE, but his career really began after World War I, singing in Fr. and Belg. opera houses, CG and Chicago, 1923–8. At his best in Fr. operas such as MANON and GOUNOD's FAUST; noteworthy for the beauty of his vocal line and the care and artistry he brought to each role. LO

Antheil, George, b. Trenton, NJ, 8 July 1900; d. New York, 12 Feb 1959. American composer. Studied with BLOCH and in Europe. Wrote music that was considered advanced at the time. Of his three operas *Transatlantic*, to his own lib. (Frankfurt, May 1930, in Ger.) was the most successful. Other operas are *Helen Retires* (1934) and *Volpone* (1953). LO
See autobiography, *Bad Boy of Music* (New York 1945; London 1947)

Antigone, opera, 3 acts, HONEGGER, lib. COCTEAU, based on SOPHOCLES. Brussels, T. de la Monnaie, 28 Dec 1927; Paris O., 26 Jan 1943; NY, 16 April 1969. Main chars: Antigone (mezzo-sop.) Ismène (sop.) Hémon (bar.) Créon (bar.) Tirésias (bass). Antigone defies Créon's ban on the burial of her brother, and dies with her lover Hémon, Créon's son. This has been the subject of some 30 operas incl. ones by ZINGARELLI and ORFF. EF

Antigono, *dramma per musica,* 3 acts, GLUCK, lib. METASTASIO (first set by HASSE, 1744). Rome, T. Argentino, 9 Feb 1756. Typical Metastasio plot, *not* derived from SOPHOCLES. Main chars: Berenice, Queen of Egypt; King Antigono of Asia; his son Demetrius. The music already foreshadows something of the mature Gluck. LO

Antonia, sop., Hoffmann's third lover in CONTES D'HOFFMANN

Antony and Cleopatra, opera, 3 acts, BARBER, lib. adapted from SHAKESPEARE by ZEFFIRELLI. NY Met, 16 Sept 1966, commissioned for the opening of the new opera house at Lincoln Center. LO

Antwerp [Antwerpen, Anvers], Belgium. Est. 1893, the Koninklijke Vlaamse (Royal Flemish) O. is based in Antwerp. *Herbergprinses (Tavern Princess)* and *De Bruid der Zee (The Bride from the Sea)*, operas by a native of the city, BLOCKX, had their first perfs there in 1896 and 1901 respectively. About 12 operas are given each season. Mus. dir. Frits Celis. In 1971 two companies merged to form the Vlaamse Kameropera (Flemish Chamber O.). EF

Apollo et Hyacinthus, *lateinische Komödie*, 9 intermezzos, MOZART, lib. Rufinus Widl. Salzburg, 13 May 1767. Mozart's second stage work, wr. at the age of 11. JB

Apotheker, Der *see* SPEZIALE

Appia, Adolphe, b. Geneva, 1 Sept 1862; d. Nyon, 29 Feb 1928. Swiss scenographer whose theories profoundly influenced designers in the early years of the 20th c. A fanatical admirer of WAGNER's music, he was opposed to the prevailing realism of the theatre, and sought an 'ideal' solution in which simple spatial structures and subtle (electric) lighting reinforced the inner essence of the drama rather than distracted with unnecessary externals. His severe designs, drab in colour, contrasted sharply with the over-luxuriant Wagner decor of BRÜCKNER and met with little approval at the time, but provided the starting point of Wagner's post-World War II Bayreuth productions. His theories were embodied in two treatises, *La Mise-en-Scène du drame Wagnérien* (Paris 1895) and *Die Musik und die Inscenierung* (Munich 1899). LO

appoggiatura (It. 'leaning'). An 18th- and early 19th-c. ornament consisting of an unharmonized auxiliary note occurring on a strong beat and resolving onto an adjacent harmony note. Very frequent in It. music, especially at recitative cadences. Sometimes written in small notation, sometimes unwritten, but expected of the performer according to convention. In Italy this ornament persisted until *c.* 1850, though since *c.* 1835 its use had been widely regarded as optional. JB

Arabella, opera, 3 acts, R. STRAUSS, lib. HOFMANNSTHAL. Dresden, 1 July 1933; London, CG, 17 May 1934; NY Met, 10 Feb 1955. Main chars: Arabella (sop.) Mandryka (bar.) Zdenka (sop.) Matteo (ten.) Graf Waldner (bass) Adelaide (mezzo-sop.) the Fiakermilli (sop.). The story, set in romantic Vienna, concerns the impoverished Graf Waldner's attempt to find a wealthy husband for his daughter Arabella. FGB ○

Arabella, London, CG, Apr 1973. HARPER in the title role; Raymond Wolansky as Mandryka; produced R. HARTMANN; designed Peter Rice

See Mann, *Richard Strauss* (London 1964; New York 1966); Kobbé

Arabian Nights' Entertainments, The, stories, wr. in Arabic, popularized in the W. in the early 18th c. by Fr. tr. by Antoine Galland (1644–1715). Operas drawing on this collection are: CADI DUPÉ; BARBIER VON BAGDAD; WEBER's *Abu Hassan*, 1811; REYER's *La Statue*, 1861; MÂROUF. *Aladdin*, not in the 1,001 Nights, is the subject of operas by several composers including ISOUARD, Adalbert Gyrowetz (1819), BISHOP (1826), Lodovico Ricci (1826), and ATTERBERG. LO

Aragall, Giacomo [Jaime], b. Barcelona, 6 June 1940. Spanish tenor. Debut as Gaston in *Gerusalemme* at T. La Fenice, Venice, 1963, the first 20th-c. revival of VERDI's revised version of LOMBARDI ALLA PRIMA CROCIATA. First appeared at Sc., Milan, as RODOLFO; then London, CG, as DUCA DI MANTUA, 1967; and NY Met in same role, 1968. Has since sung leading lyric ten. roles in Verdi, MASSENET and PUCCINI all over the world. The *travesti* role of

Romeo in CAPULETI ED I MONTECCHI was rewritten for him for the 1966 Sc. prod. He has a voice of remarkably beautiful quality and sings with great refinement. FGB

Araia [Araja], Francesco, b. Naples, 25 Jun 1709; d. Italy, *c.* 1770. Italian composer. After writing several operas in Italy, he went to Russia in 1735, composing there the first opera to a Russian text, Aleksandr Sumarokov's *Cephalus and Prokris* (1755). He composed several other operas for the Russian court before retiring to Bologna some time after Peter III's death in 1762. GN

Arakishvili, Dimitri Ignatyevich, b. Vladikavkaz (now Ordzhonikidze), 23 Feb 1873; d. Tbilisi, 13 Aug 1953. Georgian composer. Studied Moscow, 1894–1901, but was always drawn toward the folk music of his native Georgia. He composed the earliest Georgian national opera, *The Legend of Shota Rustaveli* (1919), and also the comic opera, *Life-Joy* (1927). GN

Archers, The, *or The Mountaineers of Switzerland*, opera, 3 acts, CARR, lib. William Dunlap, founded on an anonymous lib., *Helvetic Liberty, or The Lass of the Lake*, pub. London, 1792. NY, John Street T., July 1796. The second opera based on William Tell (cf. GRÉTRY), and the first American opera of which some of the music is extant. LO

Arden Muss Sterben, opera, 2 acts, GOEHR, lib. Erich Fried, freely based on the anonymous Eng. 16th-c. play, *Arden of Faversham*. Hamburg Staats O. (which commissioned the work), 5 Mar 1967; London, SW, 17 Apr 1974 (as *Arden Must Die*, tr. Geoffrey Skelton). Main chars: Arden (bass) Alice (mezzo-sop.) Mosbie (ten.). Goehr's first major opera deals with the attempts, instigated by his wife, to assassinate Arden. A black comedy of dramatic force, it points a number of morals. The vocal and instrumental style is tough but accessible. The Hamburg premiere audience objected to what it supposed was the political attitude expressed in the spoken epilogue; this was omitted from the first London perf. AB

Arditi, Luigi, b. Crescentino, Piedmont, 16 July 1822; d. Hove, Sussex, 1 May 1903. Italian composer and conductor. Studied Milan Cons. Began as a violinist; debut as cond. 1843, Vercelli. Left Italy for the New World, 1846; in 1854 cond. the first opera at NY Acad. of Music. Cond. at HM, London, in 1858, subsequently touring continental Europe. Cond. first London perfs of MEFISTOFELE (1880), CAVALLERIA RUSTICANA (1891), and HÄNSEL UND GRETEL, which had a run at Daly's T. in 1894. LO

See autobiography, *My Reminiscences* (London and New York 1896)

Argentina. Argentina has the strongest tradition of native opera in Latin America. Transplanted from Europe to satisfy a small but influential urban social class, opera in Argentina incorporated ethnic elements early in its development and thus became a vehicle for asserting the country's cultural identity. Twentieth-c. attention has been focused on GINASTERA's three operas, the product of a strong dramatic tradition going back to 1897, when BERUTI's *Pampa*, lib. Guido Borra based on Eduardo Gutiérrez's novel *Juan Moreira*, and considered as the first national opera, was first performed.

Opera was introduced to Buenos Aires by It. cos touring the area as early as 1823. Regular opera seasons began when a co. recruited by Mariano Pablo Rosquellas prod. BARBIERE DI SIVIGLIA at the Coliseo Provisional, 27 Sept 1825. The earliest operas written in Buenos Aires were by resident foreign comps such as Prósper Fleuriet's *Le 14 Juillet* (1854); the first opera comp. by a native Argentinian was Francisco Hargreaves' *La Gatta Bianca* (Buenos Aires, T. de la Victoria, 11 Jan 1877). Beruti's first three operas stirred interest in Europe; he also started both the Creole and indigenist trends in Argentine lyric theatre with *Pampa* and *Yupanki* (1899). Commissioned for the first season of the new T. Colón, *Aurora* (1908) by PANIZZA, was inspired by an episode from Argentine history. Literary nationalism was also adopted by Eduardo García-Mansilla (1871–1930) in his second opera *La Angelical Manuelita* (1917).

The influence of Italy and France was strong, not only through the repertory of travelling cos but also because most promising young comps studied in Paris or Milan. This European training enabled local comps to acquire the necessary dramatic tools to establish sophisticated levels of craftsmanship. While the exoticism of their libs enabled the comps to display lavish settings and their newly acquired orchestral techniques, the Argentine operas of the formative period (1908–24) used It. or Fr. as the standard languages for perf. BOERO's *Tucumán* (1918) was the first opera which, based on a national subject, was sung in Spanish at the T. Colón. Although all his operas with premieres in the 1920s were perf. in Spanish, it was the successful *El Matrero* (1929) that firmly established the language in national theatre. While *El Matrero* and GAITO's *La Sangre de las Guitarras* (1932) remain the most successful works inspired by the national tradition, it was also adopted by Gaito in *Lázaro* (1929), the first Argentine opera to incorporate a *tango*; Enrique Mario Casella (1891–1948), whose *Chasca* (1939) is the first of a trilogy of native legends; Raúl H. Espoile (1888–1958); and Alfredo Pinto (1891–1968).

Distant pre-Columbian traditions provided the basis for the first fully 'ethnic' opera, *Huemac* (1916) by Pascual de Rogatis (b. 1880), based on a Toltec legend as interpreted by Spanish chroniclers. Other such operas are *Tabaré* (1925) and *Las Vírgenes del Sol* (1939), both by Alfredo L. Schiuma (1885–1963); *Ollantay* (1926) by Gaito; *La Leyenda del Urutaú* (1934) by Gilardo Gilardi (1889–1963); *La Novia del Hereje* (1935) by de Rogatis; *Siripo* (1937) by Boero; *Lin-Calel* (1941) by Arnaldo D'Espósito (1907–1945), the most successful Argentine opera after *El Matrero*; and *El Oro del Inca* (1953) by Héctor Iglesias Villoud (b. 1913). Of the eight operas prod. at the T. Colón that follow established modern European trends, only three show ethnic elements: CASTRO's *Proserpina y el Extranjero* (1951), SCIAMMARELLA's *Marianita Limeña* (1957), and DON RODRIGO.

Argentine dramatic prod. of the last 20 years has sharply declined. Some younger opera comps incl. Mario Perusso (b. 1936), whose *La Voz del Silencio* was first perf. at the T. Colón, 23 Nov 1969; Claudio Guidi Drei (b. 1927), *Medea* (lib. comp., T. Colón, 3 July 1973); Juan Carlos Zorzi (b. 1936), *El Timbre* (T. Argentino, La Plata, 19 June 1975); and Antonio Tauriello (b. 1931), *Les Guerres Picrocholines* (unperf.), which imaginatively combines puppetry, mimicry, and electronic music with more conventional means.

An almost complete collection of microfilmed opera scores is available at the Library of Congress, Washington D.C. *See also* LATIN AMERICA. MK

See Gesualdo, *La Historia de la Música en la Argentina*, 3 vols (Buenos Aires 1961)

Argentina, T. *see* ROME

aria (It. 'air'). Song or air. Generic term for self-contained vocal solo such as constitutes the main formal unit of Italian opera in the 18th c. and to a decreasing extent in the 19th. From *c.* 1690 to *c.* 1770, arias were built on a large-scale ternary design usually qualified as *da capo*. Later this gave way to the aria in two contrasted movements, which flourished especially during the 1830s and 1840s. As Italian opera becomes more continuous in form the term *scena ed aria* tends to replace the plain 'aria'. *See also* CABALETTA, CAVATINA.

arietta. dim. of aria. Smaller in scale, occasionally found in *opera buffa*.

arioso. Having the lyrical character of an aria without its formal properties. JB

Ariadne auf Naxos, opera, 1 act with prologue, R. STRAUSS, lib. HOFMANNSTHAL. In the original 1-act version, without prologue, given after BOURGEOIS GENTILHOMME, Stuttgart, 25 Oct 1912; London, HM, 27 May 1913. In the fuller version, Vienna, 4 Oct 1916; London, CG, 27 May 1924; NY, Juilliard, 5 Dec 1934. Main chars: Ariadne (and the Prima Donna in the Prologue) (sop.) Bacchus (and the Tenor in the prologue) (ten.) Zerbinetta (sop.) the Composer (prologue only) (sop.). The *bourgeois gentilhomme* has engaged both an opera company and a *commedia dell'arte* troupe who must entertain his guests simultaneously, which gives rise to tantrums in the prologue and hilarity in *Ariadne auf Naxos* itself. FGB ○

See Mann, *Richard Strauss* (London 1964; New York 1966); Kobbé

Ariane et Barbe-Bleue, opera, 3 acts, DUKAS, lib. MAETERLINCK, wr. (1901) expressly for the composer. Paris, OC, 10 May 1907; NY Met, 29 Mar 1911; London, CG, 20 Apr 1937, by artists from Paris. Not perf. since, though till then had been seen in Vienna, Brussels, and Italy. Strongly influenced by PELLÉAS ET MÉLISANDE. In this version Barbe-Bleue (Bluebeard) has not killed his wives but imprisoned them. Ariane, his latest, tries to free them, but they prefer captivity: moral – the only person you can free is yourself. LO

Arianna, L', opera, prologue and 8 scenes, MONTEVERDI, lib. RINUCCINI. Mantua, 28 May 1608. Monteverdi's second opera, wr. for wedding of Francesco Gonzaga to Margareta di Savoia; also chosen to open the T. S. Moisè, Venice, 1639. Music lost, all but a famous 'lament', which became the pattern for similar pieces by CAVALLI and PURCELL. LO

Arié, Raphael, b. Sofia, 22 Aug 1920. Bulgarian bass. Studied Sofia, where he joined the local opera company after World War II. First prize at Geneva competition, 1946, led to engagement at Sc.; debut there in LOVE FOR THREE ORANGES, 1947. Created Trulove in RAKE'S PROGRESS at Venice, 1951. Grand Inquisitor in DON CARLOS, Salzburg, 1960. AB

arietta *see* ARIA

Ariodant, *drame lyrique*, 3 acts, MÉHUL, lib. HOFFMAN. Paris, T. Favart (OC), 11 Oct 1799. Subject derived from ARIOSTO's *Orlando Furi-*

Ariadne auf Naxos, Berlin Staats O., 21 June 1964; designed Wilfried Werz; produced Erhardt Fischer

oso; Méhul's own favourite opera, and admired by BERLIOZ. In Apr 1799 BERTON had prod. an opera at the OC on the same subject, *Montano et Stéphanie*. LO

Ariodante, opera, 3 acts, HANDEL, lib. Antonio Salvi from ARIOSTO's *Orlando Furioso*. London, CG, 19 Jan 1735. Main chars: Ariodante (mezzo-sop.) Ginevra (sop.) Dalinda (sop.) Polinesso (contr.) the King (bass). Ariodante, betrothed to Ginevra, daughter of the King of Scotland, has a rival in Polinesso, Duke of Albania. Polinesso makes use of the maid, Dalinda, to produce false evidence of Ginevra's unchastity. Ginevra is saved from execution by Polinesso's dying confession and the return of Ariodante, believed dead. The opera is occasionally revived. JB O

arioso *see* ARIA

Ariosto, Lodovico, b. Reggio, 4 Sept 1474; d. Ferrara, 6 June 1533. Italian poet whose *Orlando Furioso* (1510), a sequel to Matteo Boiardo's *Orlando Innamorato* (1487), has been the source of more than 20 operas, incl.: *Angelica (e Medoro)* (PORPORA, 1722, GRAUN, 1749, Ambroise THOMAS, *Angélique et Médor*, 1843); *Alcine* (CAMPRA, 1705, ALCINA, 1735); *Ariodant(e)* (ARIODANTE, 1735, ARIODANT, 1799); *Roland* (LULLY, 1685, PICCINNI, 1778). LO

Arkel, bass, the blind king in PELLÉAS ET MÉLISANDE

Arkhipova, Irina Konstantinovna, b. Moscow, 2 Dec 1925. Soviet mezzo-soprano. She sang with the Sverdlovsk O. 1954–6; joined the Bolshoy, 1956, making her debut as CARMEN. She is one of the most prominent Soviet singers of the day: her wide-ranging, versatile voice is always at the service of an intelligent and powerfully dramatic acting ability. Her AZUCENA at Orange (1972), with CABALLÉ as LEONORA, led to her CG debut in the same role on 22 Apr 1975. Her large repertory incl. Marina (BORIS GODUNOV), Marfa (KHOVANSHCHINA), Lyubasha (TSAR'S BRIDE), AMNERIS, EBOLI, CHARLOTTE, Polina (QUEEN OF SPADES), and many Soviet roles. She has toured extensively in W. Europe and the USA. GN

Arlecchino, *'ein theatralisches Capriccio'*, opera, 1 act, BUSONI, lib. composer on themes from the Commedia dell'Arte. Zürich, 11 May 1917; radio perf. (in Eng., tr. DENT), BBC, 27 Jan 1939; Glyndebourne, 25 June 1954; concert perf., NY, 11 Oct 1951. LO

Arlesiana, L' *(The Girl from Arles)*, opera, 4 acts, CILEA, lib. Leopoldo Marenco after DAUDET. Milan, T. Lirico, 27 Nov 1897; revised there in definitive version, 22 Oct 1898. Philadelphia, 11 Jan 1962. Main chars: Federico (ten.) Rosa Mamai (mezzo-sop.) Vivetta (sop.) Metifio (bar.) Baldassare (bar.) L'Innocente (mezzo-sop.). Federico, a young farmer, about to marry a girl from Arles, receives proof that she is the mistress of Metifio, a drover. At first in despair, Federico eventually agrees to marry his foster sister, Vivette. But a visit from Metifio reawakens his jealousy and he kills himself. JB

Arlésienne, L' *(The Girl from Arles)*, incidental music, BIZET, to DAUDET's play. Paris, Vaudeville T., 1 Oct 1872. Though not an opera this *mélodrame* contains more significant vocal and instrumental music than many an *opéra comique*: 27 numbers, wr. for a small orch. of 26 players. Daudet's play was 'a story of various levels of disastrous love', and as such a forerunner of CARMEN, already simmering in Bizet's mind. LO O

Arme Heinrich, Der (*Poor Henry*), opera, 3 acts, PFITZNER, lib. James Grun based on a medieval legend. Mainz, 2 Apr 1895. LO

Armide, opera, 5 acts, GLUCK, lib. QUINAULT (previously set by LULLY). Paris O., 23 Sept 1777; London, CG (in Fr.), 6 July 1906; Falmouth (in Eng., tr. M. and E. Radford), 24 Nov 1936; NY Met, 14 Nov 1910. Gluck's last important work, it has never had the appeal of ORFEO ED EURIDICE or the two IPHIGÉNIE operas. Its lack of robustness and (except in the last act) drama is compensated for by the tenderness of the love music and the musical delineation of the two principal characters, Renaud and Armide. LO
See Cooper, *Gluck* (London and New York 1935)

Armide et Renaud, *tragédie lyrique*, 5 acts, LULLY, lib. QUINAULT, based on GERUSALEMME LIBERATA. Paris O., 15 Feb 1686. Renaud, crusader and invincible warrior, falls into the toils of the enchantress, Armide, who in turn falls in love with him. After dalliance in her magic garden and palace Renaud is eventually recalled to a sense of duty. Armide, distracted, causes the destruction of her palace by fire and earthquake, perishing in the flames. The more than 40 operas on this subject incl. those by HANDEL (1711), TRAETTA (1761), GLUCK (1777), HAYDN (1784), ROSSINI (1817), and DVOŘÁK (1904). LO

Armstrong, Sheila, b. Ushington, Northumberland, 13 Aug 1942. English soprano. Studied RAM, London, and made her debut in 1966 as Belinda in DIDO AND AENEAS at Glyndebourne, where she has also sung ZERLINA, PAMINA, and Fiorilla (TURCO IN ITALIA). She first sang at CG in 1973, as MARCELLINA, returning in 1974 as Nannetta (FALSTAFF). Her voice is not large, but pure-toned and well projected. EF

Arne, Thomas Augustine, b. London, 12 Mar 1710; d. London, 5 Mar 1778. English composer. Worked in a solicitor's office for three years before becoming a full-time musician. His large output for the theatre embraces incidental music, especially for SHAKESPEARE's plays; masques (*Comus*, 1738, *The Judgment of Paris*, 1740, both at London, DL, and *Alfred*, at Cliveden, Buckinghamshire, 1740, which included the song 'Rule, Britannia'); and several attractive light operas at CG (THOMAS AND SALLY, LOVE IN A VILLAGE, *The Cooper*, 1772) that have proved more durable than his more ambitious, through-composed Italian-style operas ARTAXERXES and *L'Olimpiade* (1764). His stage connections extended to his sister, Susanna Maria (Mrs Cibber, 1714–66), who sang in Johann Friedrich Lampe's *Amelia* (1732) and in Arne's setting of Addison's *Rosamond* (1733), later becoming a famous tragic actress; and to his wife, Cecilia Young (*c.* 1711–89), who sang in It. opera and could compete on almost equal terms with the imported foreign vocalists. LO
See Langley, *Doctor Arne* (Cambridge 1938)

Arnold, ten., Swiss patriot, hero of GUILLAUME TELL

Arnold, Samuel, b. London, 10 Aug 1740; d. London, 22 Oct 1802. English composer, engaged by BEARD at CG, 1765, where his pasticcio work, *The Maid of the Mill* (lib. BICKERSTAFFE, founded on Samuel Richardson's *Pamela*), was prod., 31 Feb 1765. Between then and 1802 he was responsible for nearly 50 stage works of all kinds, many of them true comic operas. LO

Arnould, Madeleine Sophie, b. Paris, 13 Feb 1740; d. Paris, 22 Oct 1802. French actress, singer, and wit. The leading sop. at Paris O., 1757–78, then superseded by R. LEVASSEUR. Created title role in IPHIGÉNIE EN AULIDE and was the first Fr. Euridice (GLUCK). Subject of opera by PIERNÉ, 1927. Her portrait by Jean Baptiste Greuze is in the Wallace Collection, London. LO

Aroldo *see* STIFFELIO

Arrangements and revivals 1. Composers themselves have frequently retouched their operas, sometimes producing what is virtually a new work, as GLUCK did with ORFEO ED EURIDICE and ALCESTE. The most famous, and most drastic, instance is FIDELIO. HANDEL, MOZART, WAGNER (the Paris TANNHÄUSER), VERDI (DON CARLOS), MEYERBEER (L'ÉTOILE DU NORD), HINDEMITH (CARDILLAC), R. STRAUSS (ARIADNE AUF NAXOS) are only a few of the composers who have in greater or lesser degree modified their own works on later revivals. 2. Conductors and composers have frequently interfered with others' operas; a notorious example was RIMSKY-KORSAKOV's treatment of BORIS GODUNOV. The 19th c. was particularly unscrupulous: FREISCHÜTZ appeared as *Robin des Bois*, ZAUBERFLÖTE masqueraded as *Les Mystères d'Isis*, and BISHOP 'adapted' everything in sight. Even Wagner had no compunction over rescoring Gluck. Today controversies centre on the 'realizations' of the scores of 17th-c. composers such as CAVALLI and MONTEVERDI. LO

Arrieta y Corera, (Pascual) Emilio, b. Puente la Reina, 21 Oct 1823; d. Madrid, 11 Nov 1894. Spanish composer. Studied in Milan; operas incl. *Ildegonda*, 1849, and *La Conquista di Granada*, 1850; but his lasting fame rests on his 50 *zarzuelas*, notably *Marina*, 1855, which he extended into a 3-act opera with additional arias for TAMBERLIK (Madrid 1871). Also popular still is *El Dominó Azul*, 1853. FGB

Arroyo, Martina, b. New York, 2 Feb 1940. American soprano. First sang in US premiere of ASSASSINIO NELLA CATTEDRALE, Carnegie Hall, NY, 1958; won Met 'Auditions of the Air' the same year. Engaged for small parts there; debut perfs with Vienna Staats O. and Deutsche O., Berlin. Member of Zürich O., 1963–8. Gained international acclaim on replacing NILSSON as AIDA at NY Met, 1965. Debut at CG, London, as Aida, 1968, followed concert perf. as Valentine (HUGUENOTS) at RAH. Has brought a voice of lustrous timbre and agile flexibility, rich in lower range, to major dramatic roles in most VERDI, and some ROSSINI, operas. NG

Artaxerxes, *opera seria*, 3 acts, ARNE, lib. composer, tr. from METASTASIO. London, CG, 2 Feb 1762; NY, 31 Jan 1828. Arne's most ambitious and successful attempt at writing a big opera in the It. style. Revived Camden Fest., Handel Opera Society, 14 Mar 1962. There are nearly 50 other operas with this title, mostly to Metastasio's text, first set by VINCI, 1730. LO

Artôt, [Marguerite Joséphine] Désirée [Montagney], b. Paris, 21 July 1835; d. Berlin, 3 Apr 1907. Belgian mezzo-soprano, later soprano. Studied with VIARDOT; concert debut, Brussels, 1857. Paris O. debut, 1858, as Fidès (PROPHÈTE), at MEYERBEER's suggestion. Sang in Italy and Berlin with success. As a sop., London debut 1863, HM, singing VIOLETTA and ADALGISA; CG 1864 and 1866. In Russia in 1868 TCHAIKOVSKY is said to have proposed to her, but on 18 Sept she married the Spanish bar. Mariano Padilla y Ramos. Retired 1887 to teach. PS

Arundell, Dennis Drew, b. London, 22 July 1898. English producer, author, and translator. Prod. first stage perf. of SEMELE, Cambridge, 1925; other prods there were HISTOIRE DU SOLDAT and ROI DAVID (in his own tr., 1931). At SW prod. first perfs in England of QUATTRO RUSTEGHI, 1946, and of a JANÁČEK opera, KÁT'A KABANOVÁ, 1951. His prods. abroad include PETER GRIMES in Helsinki and MOZART operas in Adelaide for the Elizabethan Trust (1956). His scholarly writings include his books *The Critic at the Opera* (London 1957) and *The Story of Sadler's Wells, 1683–1964* (London 1965). LO

Ascanio in Alba, *festa teatrale*, 2 acts, MOZART, lib. Giuseppe Parini. Milan, T. Regio Ducale, 17 Oct 1771. Main chars: Ascanio (sop.) Silvia (sop.) Venere (sop.) Aceste (ten.). At the bidding of his mother, Venere (Venus), Ascanio (Ascanius) woos his destined bride, Silvia, in disguise. Revived at Salzburg Fest., 1967. JB ○

Asmus, Rudolf, b. Zlín (now Gottwaldov), 30 Oct 1921. Czech bass. Studied in Ostrava; joined the opera chorus in 1941. He was a member of the Brno O. (1944–53) and Prague NT (1953–9), achieving his greatest success as BORIS GODUNOV. He won special fame for his portrayal of the Forester in CUNNING LITTLE VIXEN, a role which he repeated in the celebrated FELSENSTEIN prod. in Berlin (1956). Since 1956 he has been a member of the Berlin KO, where his repertory has incl. several MOZART roles and ROCCO. JT

Assassinio nella Cattedrale, L', opera, 2 acts and interlude, PIZZETTI, lib. composer based on Thomas Stearns Eliot's *Murder in the Cathedral*, 1935. Milan, Sc., 1 Mar 1958; NY, 17 Sept 1958; Coventry T., 12 June 1962, by SW Co.; London, SW, 3 July 1962. LO

Athens *see* GREECE

Atlantide, L', opera, 4 acts, TOMASI, lib. Francis Didelot, based on the novel by Pierre Benoit. Mulhouse, 26 Feb 1954. (Not to be confused with *La Atlántida*, cantata by FALLA based on the epic poem in Catalan by Jacinto Verdaguer, completed after the comp.'s death by Ernesto Halffter and prod. Milan, Sc., 14 June 1962.) FGB

Atlantov, Vladimir Andreyevich, b. Leningrad, 19 Feb 1939. Russian tenor. From 1963 he was a member of the Kirov (also undergoing training at Sc., Milan, 1963–5), and since 1967 has been a member of the Bolshoy co. His full-toned voice has been particularly effective in such roles as ALFREDO, Don JOSÉ, Hermann (QUEEN OF SPADES), and Vladimir Igorevich (PRINCE IGOR). GN

Attaque du Moulin, L' *(The Attack on the Mill)*, opera, 4 acts, BRUNEAU, lib. GALLET. Paris, OC, 23 Nov 1893; London, CG, 4 July 1894; NY, New T., 8 Feb 1910. Based on story by ZOLA pub. in *Les Soirées de Médan* (1880), founded on an episode in the Franco-Prussian war. The betrothal of Françoise, daughter of the miller Merlier, to Dominique, a Flemish peasant, is interrupted by warlike sounds. The mill is attacked by Germans, Dominique is seized and condemned to be shot at daybreak. He escapes by stabbing a sentry; Merlier, condemned to die in his stead, is taken out and shot, but almost immediately Dominique, who has joined the Fr. forces, arrives with a Fr. squadron shouting 'Victory!' The opera was intended as an anti-war tract, stressing its horrors and its uselessness. LO

Atterberg, Kurt, b. Göteborg, 12 Dec 1887. Swedish composer. His five operas include *Fanal*, 1934, based on HEINE's *Der Schelm von Bergen* and *Stormen*, 1948, based on SHAKESPEARE's *The Tempest*. LO

Attila, opera, prologue and 3 acts, VERDI, lib. Temistocle Solera with additions by PIAVE after Zacharias Werner's *Attila, König der Hunnen*. Venice, T. La Fenice, 17 Mar 1846; London, HM, 14 Mar 1848; NY, Niblo's Garden, 15 Apr 1850. Main chars: Odabella (sop.) Foresto (ten.) Ezio (bar.) Attila (bass). Attila has sacked the city of Aquileia whose fugitives under Foresto proceed to found Venice; he refuses a pact with the Roman general, Ezio (Aetius); among his captives is Odabella, Foresto's betrothed. Attila is turned back from the gates of Rome by Pope Leo. An attempt on his life during a feast is thwarted by Odabella. Odabella, now Attila's bride, stabs him to death in the presence of Ezio and Foresto. The opera was popular in Italy during the 1840s; revived by SW, London, in 1963 as part of the 150th anniversary celebrations of Verdi's birth. JB O

Auber, Daniel François Esprit, b. Caen, 29 Jan 1782; d. Paris, 12 May 1871. French composer. After overcoming family opposition, studied with CHERUBINI. Initial failures were followed in 1820 by the successful *La Bergère Châtelaine* at the Paris OC. MUETTE DE PORTICI was the most celebrated of all his operas; FRA DIAVOLO, GUSTAVE III, and DIAMANTS DE LA COURONNE were among those that remained in the international repertoire throughout the 19th c. His more than 40 comic and serious works, few of which are heard today, also incl. *Fiorella*, 1826, *Le Philtre*, 1831, *Manon Lescaut*, 1856, and *Le Premier Jour de Bonheur*, 1868. Auber became member of Fr. Acad. in 1829, dir. of the Paris Cons. in 1842, and MdC to Napoleon III in 1859. PS

Aubert, Louis François Marie, b. Paramé, Ille-et-Vilaine, 19 Feb 1877; d. Paris, 10 Jan 1968. French composer. His one opera, *La Forêt Bleue*, lib. Jacques Chenevière based on PERRAULT's fairy tales, comp. 1904–10, was perf. Geneva, 7 Jan 1913, and Boston, 8 Mar 1913. LO

Auden, Wystan Hugh, b. York, 21 Feb 1907; d. Vienna, 28 Sept 1973. English poet and librettist. Wrote, with KALLMAN, libs for RAKE'S PROGRESS, ELEGY FOR YOUNG LOVERS, BASSARIDS, and NABOKOV's *Love's Labour's Lost*. Also wrote lib. for BRITTEN's early *Paul Bunyan*, 1941. LO

Audran, Edmond, b. Lyon, 12 Apr 1840; d. Tierceville, 17 Aug 1901. French composer. Educated École Niedermeyer; had musical posts in Marseille before returning to Paris. Wrote some 20 operettas between 1862 and 1901, very popular in France and Britain. Best known are MASCOTTE, 1880, and *La Poupée*, 1896. LO

Aufstieg und Fall der Stadt Mahagonny (*Rise and Fall of the city of Mahagonny*), opera, 3 acts, WEILL, lib. BRECHT. Leipzig, 9 Mar 1930; London, SW, 16 Jan 1963; NY, 4 Mar 1970. A satire on the corruption and false values of modern society, set to music that flouted operatic conventions and exploited the dissonant techniques and jazz of its time. LO O

Augsburg, W. Germany. Opera is given in the Stadts. O., where KERTESZ was mus. dir., 1958–63; present dir., Gabor Otväs. The *Intendant* is P. EBERT. LO

Austin, Frederic, b. London, 30 Mar 1872; d. London, 10 Apr 1952. English baritone and administrator. Sang under RICHTER at CG, 1908, in RING DES NIBELUNGEN in Eng. Was with BEECHAM's co. 1915–20. Sang Peachum in his own arrangement of BEGGAR'S OPERA at the Lyric T., Hammersmith, 1922, then joined BNOC, becoming its artistic director. LO

Austin, Sumner Francis, b. London, 24 Sept 1888. English baritone, producer, and administrator. Studied Dresden; debut Potsdam, 1914, in BRÜLL's *Das Goldener Kreuz*. Interned in Germany during World War I; joined Old Vic Co. on return to England, making this and its successor, SW, his life's work, as singer, producer (over 20 operas including Nicholas Gatty's *The Tempest*, 1920, SMYTH's *Fête Galante*, 1923, and many from the standard repertoire), and administrator. LO

Austral [Wilson], Florence, b. Richmond, nr Melbourne, 26 Apr 1896; d. Sydney, 15 May 1968. Australian soprano. Studied Melbourne Cons., 1914, and later in NY. Debut, BRÜNNHILDE, with BNOC, 1922. Appeared frequently at CG and elsewhere in the interwar years, chiefly in WAGNER roles which her rich, warm voice well suited. From 1940 lived in

Australia, teaching singing at Cons. of Newcastle, nr Sydney. LO

Australia. Throughout the 19th c. opera in Australia was a matter of visiting cos, a state of affairs not finally remedied until the 1950s. The chief of these visiting cos were the Anna Bishop Co., touring 1850–60; the Martin Simonson It. Grand Opera Co., 1886–7; and the Quinlan Co., dirs BEECHAM and Thomas Quinlan, 1912 and 1913, giving e.g. DEBUSSY'S *L'Enfant Prodigue* and FANCIULLA DEL WEST. Another appreciable event was MELBA's farewell tour in 1924; it was followed by others which also included famous European singers. The pattern continued for a time after World War II until 'national' (really regional) cos were formed in Melbourne and Sydney. A merger of these two was mooted in 1954 under the title Elizabethan Theatre Trust, but in the event the Trust set up its own co., and several seasons of increasing artistic merit were given under the aegis of the Trust, with well-known Australian singers who had made their main careers in Europe returning for shorter or longer periods to add lustre to the performances. In 1965 there was a tour by SUTHERLAND with a co. dir. by her husband BONYNGE. The Trust became the Australian Opera Co. in 1969 with the prospect of its own opera house in Sydney, finally opened 28 Sept 1973 with WAR AND PEACE under the co.'s mus. dir. DOWNES, during whose tenure of office the standard of perfs was raised considerably. Downes was succeeded by Bonynge in 1975. *See* ADELAIDE, MELBOURNE, SYDNEY. AB

Austria. Apart from VIENNA most of the *Land* capitals, such as Graz, Klagenfurt, Innsbruck, Linz, have operatic seasons of varying length and significance. Important annual international festivals are held at SALZBURG and BREGENZ. JB

Azora, Daughter of Montezuma, opera, 3 acts, HADLEY, lib. David Stevens. Chicago O., 26 Dec 1917. For other Montezuma operas *see* GRAUN and MONTEZUMA. LO

Azucena, contr., the gypsy in TROVATORE

B

Baccaloni, Salvatore, b. Rome, 14 Apr 1900; d. 31 Dec 1969. Italian bass. Studied with KASCHMANN. Debut 1922, Rome, as BARTOLO (BARBIERE DI SIVIGLIA). Engaged by TOSCANINI for Sc., 1926, where the cond. advised him to specialize in *buffo* parts. CG debut 1928 as Varlaam (BORIS GODUNOV). Glyndebourne as LEPORELLO (1936) and returned as BARTOLO (NOZZE DI FIGARO), OSMIN, DON ALFONSO, and DON PASQUALE (his most famous role). NY Met debut 1940 as Bartolo (*Nozze di Figaro*). *Don Pasquale* was revived for him the same season, and he remained at the house in *buffo* roles for 22 years. Rotund, sometimes outrageous, comic bass performer. AB

Bach, Johann Christian, b. Leipzig, 5 Sept 1735; d. London, 1 Jan 1782. German composer, youngest son of Johann Sebastian Bach. Wr. 13 operas for Naples, Mannheim, and Paris, but mostly for London, where from 1762 he was comp. to the King's T. When ORFEO ED EURIDICE was first sung in England (1770) Bach provided some additional arias. His music has a graceful limpidity – a style which the young MOZART, who came to know and love the 'English Bach', was to build upon with greater dramatic force. LO

Bacquier, Gabriel, b. Béziers, 17 May 1924. French baritone. Debut Nice, then sang in Brussels (1953), Paris OC (1956), Paris O. (1958), Aix-en-Provence (1960), Glyndebourne (1962), and CG (1964). He has also appeared at Sc., the Colón, Buenos Aires, San Francisco, and NY Met. Equally at home in Fr. and It. opera, he sings VALENTIN, ESCAMILLO, and GOLAUD, as well as DON GIOVANNI, ALMAVIVA (NOZZE DI FIGARO), Riccardo (PURITANI), and RIGOLETTO. A forceful actor with a strong voice, his most successful role is probably SCARPIA. EF

Gabriel Bacquier (right) as Malatesta and R. DAVIES as Ernesto in DON PASQUALE, London, CG, 28 Feb 1973; designed and produced PONNELLE

Janet Baker as Penelope in RITORNO D'ULISSE IN PATRIA, Glyndebourne, 1972

Badings, Henk, b. Bandoeng [Bandung], Java, 17 Jan 1907. Dutch composer. He has wr. three radio operas, *Liefde's Listen* (*Love's Stratagems*, 1948), *Orestes* (1954), which won the Italia prize, and *Asterion* (1957), as well as a chamber opera for TV, *Salto Mortale* (1959). *De Nachtwacht* (*The Nightwatch*) was prod, by the Kon. Vlaamse (Royal Flemish) O. at Antwerp, 1950; his *Martin Korda, DP* was first perf. by the Nederlandse O. at the 1960 Holland Fest. EF

Bahr-Mildenburg [Mildenburg von Bellschau], Anna, b. Vienna, 29 Nov 1872; d. Vienna, 27 Jan 1947. Austrian dramatic soprano. Stage debut 1895 Hamburg; sang leading Wagnerian roles at Bayreuth from 1897. Engaged by MAHLER 1898, as permanent member of Vienna Staats O.; became *Kammersängerin* 1901. Appeared at CG, London, as ISOLDE, 1906, and as KLYTEMNESTRA in Eng. premiere of ELEKTRA, 1910. Retired 1917; subsequently active as teacher and Wagnerian prod. Famous roles: Donna ANNA, FIDELIO, Rezia (OBERON), AIDA, SENTA, VENUS, and SALOME. With husband, Hermann Bahr, wr. *Bayreuth und das Wagner-Theater* (1910). JB

Bailey, Norman, b. Birmingham, 23 Mar 1933. English bass-baritone. Trained in Vienna; debut there 1959 (CAMBIALE DI MATRIMONIO). Engaged at various Ger. opera houses, he sang bar. roles in NABUCCO, RIGOLETTO, TROVATORE, BALLO IN MASCHERA, SIMONE BOCCANEGRA, and TOSCA, at the same time taking on the German bass-bar. repertory: Pizarro (FIDELIO), KLINGSOR, FLIEGENDE HOLLÄNDER, Doctor Schön (LULU), Orest (ELEKTRA), and WOTAN. London debut 1968, SW, as HANS SACHS, a part he repeated at CG, Hamburg, Brussels, Munich, and Bayreuth (1969). He sang Wotan in the RING DES NIBELUNGEN in Eng. at the London Col., 1973; also Kutuzov (WAR AND PEACE). EF

Baker, Janet, b. Hatfield, Yorkshire, 21 Aug 1933. English mezzo-soprano. Studied near her home, then in London with Helene Isepp and Meriel St Clair. Debut 1956 Oxford Univ. O. Club (SECRET), followed by GLUCK's ORPHÉE ET EURYDICE (Morley College, 1958), the Sorceress (DIDO AND AENEAS, 1959 Bath Fest.), and Pippo (GAZZA LADRA, 1959, Wexford Fest.). Sang Dido in PURCELL's opera at the Barber Institute, Birmingham, 1961, followed at the same venue, all cond. by Sir Anthony Lewis, by several HANDEL roles, notably ARIODANTE (1964) and the title part in *Orlando* (1966). EOG debut 1962, Aldeburgh, as Dido; Polly (BEGGAR'S OPERA, 1963); Lucretia (RAPE OF LUCRETIA, 1964), and again in a new prod. (1970). SO debut 1967 as DORABELLA, then Dido (TROYENS, 1969), OCTAVIAN (1971), and The Composer (ARIADNE AUF NAXOS, 1975). Glyndebourne roles after her debut as Dido (1965) incl. Diana (CALISTO, 1970) and, memorably, Penelope (RITORNO D'ULISSE IN PATRIA, 1972). CG debut 1966 as Hermia (MIDSUMMER NIGHT'S DREAM), then Dido (TROYENS, 1970, 1972) and Vitellia (CLEMENZA DI TITO, 1974). For SW, later the ENO, she first appeared as POPPEA (1972), then MARGUERITE (DAMNATION DE FAUST) and MARIA STUARDA (1973), and CHARLOTTE (1976). Her vivid stage personality, her utter conviction and her intense projection of words inform all her perfs. Awarded DBE 1976. AB

Baku, Azerbaijan SSR. The first Azerbaijan opera was LEYLI AND MEDZHNUN. More recent works have incl. Fikret Amirov's *Seville* (1953), Ahmed Hajiyev's and Kara Karayev's *Fatherland* (1945), and Muslim Mahomayev's *Shakh Ismail* (1919) and *Nergiz* (1935). GN

Balfe, Michael (William), b. Dublin, 15 May 1808; d. Rowney Abbey, Hertfordshire, 20 Oct 1870. Irish composer and baritone. A proficient violinist, he moved to London aged 16, playing in the DL orch. Vocal debut 1825, Norwich, as Kaspar (FREISCHÜTZ); travelled to Italy where he studied with GALLI. Became principal bar. of TI, Paris, 1827, on ROSSINI's recommendation. In Palermo, 1830, he comp. the first of his 29 operas, *I Rivali di se Stesso*. *The Siege of Rochelle* (1835) was the first of many London successes incl. *The Maid of Artois* (1836), *Falstaff* (1838), and his most famous work, BOHEMIAN GIRL. He m. the Hungarian sop. Lina Roser. Retired 1864. His last work, *The Knight of the Leopard*, was perf. four years after his death (as *Il Talismano*). His statue stands in the T. Royal, DL, scene of many of his greatest successes. PS
See Kenney, *A Memoir of M. W. Balfe* (London 1875)

Ballad of Baby Doe, The, opera, 2 acts, D. MOORE, lib. John Latouche. Central City, Col., 7 July 1956; NY CC 3 Apr 1958; Berlin and Belgrade 1961. Commissioned by Serge Koussevitsky Fund in the Library of Congress. Main chars: Tabor (bar.) Augusta (mezzo-sop.) Baby Doe (sop.) Mama McCourt (mezzo-sop.) Wm J. Bryan (bass). In Leadville, Col., during the late 19th-c. goldrush, Horace Tabor divorces his wife to marry Baby Doe, a notorious beauty from Wisconsin. Tabor loses his money and influence, but after his death she remains faithful to his memory, spending 36 years in a lonely shack at a worthless silver mine where, in 1935, she is frozen to death. EJ

Un Ballo in Maschera, London, CG, 20 Feb 1975; produced SCHENK; designed Jürgen Rose

ballad opera, Eng. term for an opera, usually comic, the music adapted from previously comp. or more usually traditional sources. BEGGAR'S OPERA is typical; about 50 were comp. during the next 30 years. Though the term is confined to Britain it has parallels in some *opéras comiques* and *Singspiele.* LO

Ballet Comique de la Royne, a dramatic ballet, devised by Balthasar de Beaujoyeulx, music by Lambert de Beaulieu and Jacques Salmon, for wedding of Mlle de Vaudemont (the French queen's sister) to the Duc de Joyeuse. Paris, Petit-Bourbon Palais, 15 Oct 1581. A fusion of drama and ballet anticipating by some 100 years the *comédies-ballets* of LULLY and MOLIÈRE. LO

ballet in opera. In Italy the 18th- and 19th-c. tradition was for an independent ballet to be danced between the acts of an opera; the Fr. tradition, stemming from LULLY and Louis XIV, was for ballet to be an integral part of the opera. When GLUCK adapted his It. operas for Paris he had to add ballets. That ballet need not be incongruous is demonstrated by e.g. AIDA, PRINCE IGOR, and BARTERED BRIDE, where the dancing evolves naturally, convincing both musically and dramatically. LO

Ballo in Maschera, Un (*A Masked Ball*), opera, 3 acts, VERDI, lib. Antonio Somma after SCRIBE's lib. for GUSTAVE III (Paris 1833). Rome, T. Apollo, 17 Feb 1859 (original action transferred from Sweden to Boston, Mass., for reasons of censorship); NY, Acad. of Mus., 11 Feb 1861; London, Lyceum, 15 June 1861. Main chars: Riccardo (ten.) Amelia (sop.) Renato (bar.) Oscar (sop.) Ulrica (mezzo-sop.). Riccardo, colonial governor, loves Amelia, the wife of his faithful secretary, Renato. Ulrica, a fortune teller, prophesies Riccardo's murder by a friend. Later Riccardo is apparently compromised with Amelia, and Renato joins a conspiracy against him and murders him at a masked ball. Among the most successful of Verdi's 'middle-period' operas. JB ○
See Kobbé

Baltimore Civic Opera. Began in 1932 as an opera workshop; by 1950 was giving professional perfs under Eugène Martinet. Gen. dir. Robert J. Collinge, with PONSELLE as artistic dir. LO

Bampton, Rose, b. Cleveland, Ohio, 28 Nov 1908. American soprano. Studied Curtis Institute, Philadelphia. Debut 1929, Chautauqua, as contr. Sang as contr. with Philadelphia O. and at the Met until 1936, then changed to sop., beginning at Met 1937 with LEONORA (TROVATORE), followed (1942) by WAGNER sop. roles in TANNHÄUSER, LOHENGRIN, and PARSIFAL. Though she has sung at CG (AMNERIS, 1937) her career has mainly been in NY (Met and CC) and in Buenos Aires. LO

banda (It. 'band'), term for stage band in It. opera. A miscellaneous group of instruments mainly of the clarinet, trumpet, and tuba families; common in 19th-c. works. First well-known example: ROSSINI, *Ricciardo e Zoraide* (Naples 1818).

banda turca (It. 'Turkish band'), triangle, cymbals, and bass drum used as a single unit of percussion. JB

Bánk Bán, opera, 3 acts, ERKEL, lib. Béni Egressy based on play by József Katona. Budapest 9 Mar 1844. Along with *Hunyadi László* (1844), Erkel's most popular work, still perf. in Hungary. LO ○★

Banti [Giorgi], Brigitta, b. Monticelli d'Ongina, ?1756; d. Bologna, 18 Feb 1806. Italian soprano. A street singer, she sang her way to Paris where Pierre Jacques de Vismes heard her in a café and hired her for the O. 1776. She sang at the Pantheon, London, 1778. 'More perfect, more impassioned, more divine singing, perhaps, was never heard,' one critic wr., but da PONTE called her 'ignorant, stupid, indolent, addicted to carousals, dissolute amusement and the bottle'. She triumphed in all the musical centres of Italy and Germany. It was for Banti that HAYDN wrote his *Scena di Berenice*. She m. the dancer Zaccaria Banti. Considered unteachable, she remained unable to read music until her death. She bequeathed her larynx – said to be of an extraordinary size – to the city of Bologna. PS

Barbaia, Domenico, b. Milan, *c.* 1775; d. Posilippo, 16 Oct 1841. Italian impresario. A man of extraordinary energy and flair who, beginning as a coffee-shop proprietor, became manager of the T. S. Carlo, Naples, 1809–24 and, from 1821, simultaneously managed the KT and T. a. d. Wien, Vienna. Also took over Sc. 1826, before returning to Naples. Commissioned works by ROSSINI, DONIZETTI, BELLINI, and C. WEBER, and engaged many of the star singers of his time such as LABLACHE, Giuditta GRISI, and PASTA. LO

Barber, Samuel, b. West Chester, Pa., 9 Mar 1910. American composer. Studied Curtis Institute of Music (aged 13 when he entered); won *Prix de Rome* aged 25, the Pulitzer Prize twice and has benefited from the encouragement of TOSCANINI, MOLINARI-PRADELLI, and other major conds. His first full-length opera was VANESSA, commissioned by the NY Met, the first US opera prod. there in 11 years and the first in BING's regime. A second opera, ANTONY AND CLEOPATRA, was commissioned for the opening of the new opera house in Lincoln Center, beginning the season of 1966–7. Its resounding failure is partly attributed to a bad lib., scenic over-prod., and circumstances of the moment. The work was rewr. to a new lib. by MENOTTI for a more modest prod. by the Juilliard School, in the 1974–5 season. EJ

Barber of Bagdad, The *see* BARBIER VON BAGDAD

Barber of Seville, The *see* BARBIERE DI SIVIGLIA

Barbier, Jules, b. Paris, 8 Mar 1822; d. Paris, 16 Jan 1901. French librettist, collaborating with CARRÉ in writing libs for DINORAH, PHILÉMON ET BAUCIS, ROMÉO ET JULIETTE, GOUNOD's *Polyeucte*, MÉDECIN MALGRÉ LUI, CONTES D'HOFFMANN, MASSÉ's *Pygmalion* and *Les Noces de Jeanette*, and others. LO

Barbiere di Siviglia, Il (*The Barber of Seville*) 1. *opera buffa*, 4 acts, PAISIELLO, lib. Giuseppe Petrosellini after BEAUMARCHAIS. St Petersburg, 26 Sept 1782; London, HM, 11 June 1789; New Orleans, 12 July 1810. Main chars: Rosina (sop.) Almaviva (ten.) Figaro (bar.) Bartolo (bass) Basilio (bass). Count Almaviva loves Rosina, ward and destined bride of Dr Bartolo. With the help of Figaro, a barber, he enters Bartolo's house disguised as a drunken soldier, and later as a music teacher; he bribes the Notary into marrying him to Rosina in Bartolo's absence. Very popular in Europe around the turn of the 18th–19th c. until eclipsed by ROSSINI's work. ○
2. *Opera buffa* (orig. title: *Almaviva o sia l'Inutile Precauzione*), 2 acts, Rossini, lib. Cesare Sterbini. Rome, T. Argentina, 20 Feb 1816; London, HM, 10 Mar 1818; NY, Park T., 3 May 1819. Main chars: Rosina (mezzo-sop.). Almaviva (ten.) Figaro (bar.) Bartolo (bass) Basilio (bass) Berta (mezzo-sop.). The plot is the same as in (1). A classic of It. comic opera. JB ○
See Kobbé

Barbieri, Francisco Asenjo, b. Madrid, 3 Aug 1823; d. Madrid, 17 Feb 1894. Spanish composer and musicologist who began his career playing in military and strolling street bands. His 77 *zarzuelas* brought authentic Sp. songs and dances into the lyric theatre then domi-

Il Barbiere di Siviglia (ROSSINI), CG, 1967. G. EVANS (left) as Dr Bartolo and ROULEAU as Don Basilio; produced Maurice Sarrazin; designed Jean-Denis Malclès

nated by foreign influences. His classic successes are *Pan y Toros* (*Bread and Bulls*, 1864) and *El Barberillo de Lavapiés* (*The Little Barber of Lavapiés*, 1874). *Pan y Toros* presents a musical picture of Madrid in the time of Goya. Also popular is *Jugar con Fuego* (*Playing with Fire*, 1851). FGB

Barbieri-Nini, Marianna, b. Florence, *c.* 1820; d. Florence, 27 Nov 1887. Italian soprano. A pupil of PASTA and VACCAI, her first success was in a revival of LUCREZIA BORGIA (Florence 1840); created sop. leads in VERDI's *I Due Foscari* (Rome 1844), MACBETH, CORSARO, and in works by PACINI and MERCADANTE; retired 1856. An outstanding '*donna di forza*' whose rare artistry more than made up for an unprepossessing appearance. JB

Barbier von Bagdad, Der (*The Barber of Bagdad*), opera, 2 acts, CORNELIUS, lib. comp., based on ARABIAN NIGHTS ENTERTAINMENTS. Weimar 15 Dec 1858; NY Met 3 Jan 1890; London, Savoy T., 9 Dec 1891. LO

barcarolle (It. *barcaruola*, 'boating song'). In romantic opera often used to describe a piece evocative of sailing, rowing, or the sea in general. Traditionally tranquil and in 6/8 rhythm (but see ELISIR D'AMORE for a barcarolle in 2/4). Famous examples in MUETTE DE PORTICI, CONTES D'HOFFMANN, and MASCAGNI's *Silvano*. JB

Barcelona, Spain. Its famous opera house, the Gran T. del Liceo, originally built 1847 with a capacity of 4,000, was destroyed by fire 1861. The present house (capacity *c.* 3,500) opened 20 Apr 1862. Its annual season extends Nov–Mar, with international casts and visiting cos. FGB

Bardi, Count *see* FLORENTINE CAMERATA

Bari, Italy. The earliest theatre still in use is the T. Piccini, opened 1854 with POLIUTO. Main opera house is the T. Petruzzelli, one of the largest in Italy, capacity 4,000, opened 14 Feb 1903 with HUGUENOTS. LO

baritone, male voice midway in pitch between TENOR and BASS, partaking in quality of the latter rather than the former. LO

Barnett, John, b. Bedford, 15 July 1802; d. nr Cheltenham, 16/17 Apr 1890. English composer, with Prussian father (real name Beer) and Hungarian mother. His numerous stage works incl. an opera, *Farinelli* (1838), and *The Mountain Sylph* (1834), his best work, the first important English romantic opera. LO

Barraud, Henry, b. Bordeaux, 23 Apr 1900. French composer. Dir. mus., French Radio, 1937–44. His operas are: *La Farce de Maître Pathelin*, 1-act comic opera (Paris, OC, 1948); *Numance*, lib. Salvador de Madariaga (Paris, O., 1955); and *Lavinia*, lib. Félicien Marceau (Aix-en-Provence 1961). EF

Barrault, Jean-Louis, b. Vésinet, 8 Sept 1910. French actor, producer, and manager. Dir. VIE PARISIENNE at the Palais-Royal, Paris, 1958, himself playing the Brazilian. At the Paris O. he has prod. WOZZECK (1963); at the NY Met GOUNOD's FAUST (1965) and CARMEN (1967); at Sc. *Faust* (1966). Re-dir. *La Vie Parisienne* at Cologne 1969, in honour of OFFENBACH's 150th anniversary. Dir., Odéon, Paris, 1959–68. EF

Barrientos, Maria, b. Barcelona, 10 Mar 1883; d. Ciboure, France, 8 Aug 1946. Spanish coloratura soprano. First sang aged 15 in Barcelona, then, after further study in Milan, Sc. debut as LAKMÉ. Sang in London at CG only as ROSINA, 1903, but appeared regularly in Italy, Spain, and South America. Retired for a time 1913, emerging for NY Met debut 1916 (LUCIA DI LAMMERMOOR). Remained at Met until 1920, during which time *Lakmé*, PURITANI, and SONNAMBULA were revived for her. Retired 1939. FGB

Barsova, Valeriya Vladimirovna, b. Astrakhan, 13 June 1892; d. Sochi, 13 Dec 1967. Soviet soprano. Studied with her sister, Mariya Vladimirovna, then with Umberto Mazetti at the Moscow Cons. Debut 1919 with ZIMIN's Private O., then sang with the Bolshoy 1920–48. Was successful in a wide range of roles, incl. Lyudmila (RUSLAN AND LYUDMILA) and VIOLETTA. She also sang the roles of GILDA and MANON. GN

Barstow, Josephine, b. Sheffield, 27 Sept 1940. English soprano. Debut 1964 (MIMI) with Opera for All. After a year in the Glyndebourne chorus, she sang at SW (1967), with WNO (1968), at CG (1969), Aix-en-Provence (1971), and Geneva (1972). An outstanding interpreter of modern works, she created Denise (KNOT GARDEN) and Marguerite in Gordon Crosse's *Story of Vasco* (London, Col., 1974), and took part in the first London perfs of WAR AND PEACE (1972), DEVILS OF LOUDUN (1973), and BASSARIDS (1974). She scored a particular success as Emilia Marty (MAKROPULOS CASE) and her repertory incl. FIORDILIGI, Idamantes and Electra (IDOMENEO), VIOLETTA, Elisabeth (DON CARLOS), and LADY MACBETH. EF

Left: Josephine Barstow and Minoo Golvala in Bohème, produced 1964–5 by Opera for All, a small co. presenting opera in English, touring the smaller towns of Britain with *c.* 8 singers and a pianist, based on the London Opera Centre, itself a subsidiary of CG

Bartered Bride, The (*Prodaná nevěsta*), opera, 3 acts, Smetana, lib. Sabina. Prague, PT, 30 May 1866 (2 acts, spoken dialogue); Prague, PT, 25 Sept 1870 (3 acts, through-comp.); London, DL, 26 June 1895; Chicago, Haymarket, 20 Aug 1893. Main chars: Mařenka (sop.) Jeník (ten.) Kecal (bass) Vašek (ten.) Circus master (ten.) Esmeralda (sop.). Mařenka loves Jeník, but her parents wish her to marry Vašek, the son of Mícha and Háta. Kecal, the marriage-broker, seems to be successful in persuading Jeník not to marry Mařenka and instead to receive 300 gulden and the promise that Mařenka will marry 'none but Mícha's son'; Mařenka has been 'bartered'. What Mařenka and the rest of the outraged village do not know is that Jeník is Mícha's long-lost eldest son by his first wife. Jeník wins not only Mařenka but the 300 gulden, while Mícha grudgingly admits that the simple-minded Vašek (who appears dramatically dressed up as a bear to help out a visiting circus) would make an unsuitable husband. Smetana's most popular opera and, with its appealing tunes and colourful folk atmosphere, the only one to find a permanent place in world repertory. JT O★
See Kobbé; Large, *Smetana* (London 1970)

Bartók, Belá, b. Nagyszentmiklós, 25 Mar 1881; d. New York, 26 Sept 1945. Hungarian composer. Although his operatic output was confined to a single work, Duke Bluebeard's Castle, its extraordinary dramatic power gives it an importance beyond that normally accorded to a one-act piece. In it, the comp. showed an exceptional feeling for Bluebeard's tormented soul, and expressed it in a melodic line of great flexibility and a free tonality that was peculiarly apt to the exotic nature of the story. AB

Bartoletti, Bruno, b. Sesto Fiorentino, 10 June 1926. Italian conductor. Studied Florence Cons. before joining the city's T. Comunale as a *répétiteur*; debut there 1953 as a cond. (Rigoletto). From then on established himself as one of the leading conds of It. opera of his generation. In charge of It. opera at Copenhagen 1957–60. Chicago Lyric T. debut 1957, principal cond. there since 1964. Regular cond. at Rome O. since 1965. Has also championed modern repertory in Italy. AB

Bartolo, Don 1. Bass, Rosina's guardian in Barbiere di Siviglia. 2. Bass, the doctor in Nozze di Figaro.

Basel [Bâle; also Basle], Switzerland. In 1834 the T. auf dem Blömlein opened, where operas by Auber, Boïeldieu, Mozart, J. F. Halévy, and Meyerbeer were given. This became a school 1872. A new theatre, opened 1875 with Don Giovanni; burned down 1904 and the present Stadttheater opened 20 Sept 1909 with Tannhäuser. Operas by Swiss comps incl. Huber were given there, also first Swiss perf. of Rosenkavalier (1911) and, 1924, first two parts of Ring des Nibelungen with Appia's decor. Present mus. dir. Armin Jordan. LO

Basilio, Don 1. Ten., music master in Nozze di Figaro. 2. Bass, music master in Barbiere di Siviglia.

Basoche, La, *opéra comique*, 3 acts, Messager, lib. Albert Carré. Paris, OC, 30 May 1890; London (Eng. tr. Harris and Eugène Oudin), Royal English O. House, 3 Nov 1891, following Ivanhoe; Chicago, Jan 1893. Set in Louis XII's Paris. 'La Basoche' is a guild of Parisian students; plot hinges on a student, Clément Marot, elected King of the Basoche, being mistaken for Louis XII. LO
See Lubbock

bass (It. *basso*) is the lowest male voice; **bass-baritone** combines attributes of deep bass with baritone quality; **basso cantante** (It. 'singing bass'), a voice with an esp. lyric quality; **basso**

profundo (It. 'deep bass'), a voice with extremely low TESSITURA. LO

Bassarids, The, opera, 1 act with intermezzo, HENZE, lib. AUDEN and KALLMAN, based on EURIPIDES' *The Bacchae*. Salzburg (in Ger. tr. as *Die Bassariden*) 8 Aug 1966; Santa Fe 7 Aug 1968; London, Col., 10 Oct 1974, cond. and prod. by comp. Main chars: Dionysus (ten.) Pentheus (bar.) Agave (Venus) (mezzo-sop.) Autonoe (Proserpine) (sop.) Captain of the Guard (Adonis) (bar.) Tiresias (Calliope) (ten.). King Pentheus, endeavouring to suppress the Dionysian side of his nature, is torn to pieces by the Bacchantes, who incl. his mother Agave. During the intermezzo, four of the characters act out the Judgment of Calliope. EF

bass-baritone *see* BASS

Bassi, Carolina, b. Naples, 10 Jan 1781; d. Cremona, 12 Dec 1862. Italian contralto. Daughter of the actors Giovanni Bassi and Gaetanina Grassi, Carolina became prima donna of the Giovinetti Napoletani co. at the age of eight. Later she secretly m. Pietro Manna, a nobleman of Cremona, who encouraged her career. She graduated from comic roles in Trieste, to *opera seria* in Livorno and Florence after which she retired for five years, reappearing at Sc. 1812. Operas wr. expressly for her incl. MEYERBEER's *Semiramide Riconosciuta*, G. S. MAYR's *Tamerlano*, PACINI's *Vallace*, MERCADANTE's *Ezio*, MARIA STUARDA, and ROSSINI's *Bianca e Faliero*. Last appearance 1828, T. La Fenice, although she was persuaded, during a visit to Vienna with her son, the comp. Ruggero Manna, to appear in concert. She was considered in her time to be the greatest rival of COLBRAN. PS

Bassi, Luigi, b. Pesaro, 5 Sept 1766; d. Dresden, 13 Sept 1825. Italian baritone. Debut 1779, Pesaro, in Pasquale Anfossi's *Il Curioso Indiscreto*. Engaged at Prague O. 1784; created title role in DON GIOVANNI; entered employment of BEETHOVEN's patron, Prince Lobkowitz, 1806; re-engaged at Prague under C. WEBER 1814; moved to Dresden 1815 where he later assumed direction of the O. A great singing actor of his day. JB

basso cantante *see* BASS

basso continuo *see* CONTINUO

basso profundo *see* BASS

Bastianini, Ettore, b. Siena, 24 Sept 1922; d. Sirmione, 25 Jan 1967. Italian baritone. Debut 1945, as bass, Ravenna (COLLINE). Debut 1951, as bar. (GERMONT). Sang Andrey in first staged perf. of WAR AND PEACE (Sc., 1953). NY Met debut 1953 (Germont). Salzburg Fest. 1960–1 (DI LUNA). CG debut 1962 (RENATO). He was one of the leading VERDI baritones of his day. AB

Bastien und Bastienne, opera, 1 act, MOZART, lib. Friedrich Wilhelm Weiskern and Andreas Schachtner from FAVART's parody of DEVIN DU VILLAGE. Vienna *c.* Sept 1768, privately (house of Anton Mesmer, the hypnotist); London, Daly's T., 26 Dec 1894; NY 26 Oct 1916. Chars: Bastien (ten.) Bastienne (sop.) Colas (bass). A village soothsayer reconciles two young lovers. A work of the infant Mozart that is sometimes revived as a curtain raiser. JB O

Battaglia di Legnano, La (*The Battle of Legnano*), opera, 4 acts, VERDI, lib. CAMMARANO after François Joseph Méry's *La Bataille de Toulouse*. Rome, T. Argentina, 27 Jan 1849. Main chars: Arrigo (ten.) Rolando (bar.) Lida (sop.) Federico (bass). Arrigo returns after long absence to Milan to fight in the wars of the Lombard League, and finds his fiancée Lida married to his friend Rolando. The two comrades defy Federico (Frederick Barbarossa). Arrigo joins the Knights of Death. Rolando, having circumstantial evidence of intrigue between Lida and Arrigo, locks the latter in a high tower from which he escapes to take part in the battle and kill Federico. Verdi's contribution to the It. national cause of 1848-9, it is seldom revived today. JB

Battistini, Mattia, b. Contigliano, Rieti, 8 Feb 1857; d. Colle Baccaro, Rieti, 8 Nov 1928. Italian baritone. Studied with Alessandro Orsini and Pietro Persechini; debut 1878, Rome. One of the outstanding singers of his day, with a remarkable technique and a fine voice which maintained its quality until he was nearly 70. His wide repertory incl. MOZART, It. and Fr. operas, and WAGNER. Acclaimed widely through Europe and Russia, he sang infrequently at CG, and never at the Met. LO

Bavaria, W. Germany. Formerly an independent kingdom. *See* BAYREUTH; MUNICH; NUREMBERG; LUDWIG II OF BAVARIA. LO

Baylis, Lilian, b. London, 9 May 1874; d. London, 25 Nov 1937. English theatre manager. She took over the management of the Old Vic from her aunt, Emma Cons, 1898, and reopened SW 1931, running both theatres till her death. Her policy of opera in Eng., and her

Bayreuth. 1962 production of TRISTAN UND ISOLDE by Wieland WAGNER with WINDGASSEN and Birgit NILSSON in the title roles

encouragement of British singers, were directly responsible for the development of the SW co., later the ENO. EF

Bayreuth, W. Germany. Wagner Fest. inaugurated here, 1876, with RHEINGOLD. Ran into financial difficulties; no more perfs until PARSIFAL (1882). From 1883 has been the scene of an annual pilgrimage, with WAGNER's music dramas given in the Festspielhaus, and under the control of Wagner's descendants; Cosima Wagner 1883–1908; S. WAGNER 1909–1930; Winifred Wagner 1931–44, and, after a gap due to World War II, since 1951 WIELAND and Wolfgang WAGNER. Conds, singers, designers, and producers taking part have incl. some of the most distinguished Ger. and foreign artists in the operatic world. The Munich Fest., inaugurated 1901 and the Salzburg Fest., 1925, were modelled on Bayreuth. LO

Festspielhaus (Festival Playhouse). When WAGNER's plans for a festival theatre in Munich, to designs by SEMPER, came to nought, he turned to nearby Bayreuth. The foundation stone was laid 1872, but the theatre was not opened until 1876, with the first complete RING DES NIBELUNGEN perf. Intended as a temporary building, of wood and brick, the auditorium seats 1,800, on one tier only. With a covered orch. and ample stage facilities it forms a well-nigh perfect setting for Wagner's grand conceptions. LO

Markgräfliches Opernhaus. This opera house is the sole complete survivor of the theatres designed by the BIBIENA family, built for Friedrich Margrave of Bavaria and his wife Sophia (sister of Frederick the Great) by G. BIBIENA 1748. LO

Beard, John, b. London (?), *c.* 1717; d. Hampton, 5 Feb 1791. English tenor. A Chapel Royal chorister, sang ten. in HANDEL oratorios (incl. first London perf. of *Messiah*, 1743) and operas (PASTOR FIDO, *Arminio*, 1737, BERENICE), all at CG, and in 1737 in DEVIL TO PAY at DL. During next 20 years he was constantly singing at these two theatres, and when John Rich died (1761) he took over the management of CG. Described as possessing 'an extremely fine English voice', he maintained national prestige in an era dominated by foreign singers. Macheath (BEGGAR'S OPERA) was one of his best parts. Increasing deafness made him retire 1767. LO

Beatrice di Tenda, opera, 2 acts, BELLINI, lib. ROMANI. Venice, T. La Fenice, 16 Mar 1833; New Orleans, 5 Mar 1842. Main chars: Beatrice (sop.) Agnese (mezzo-sop.) Orombello (ten.) Filippo (bar.). Filippo Visconti, Duke of Milan, is tired of his wife, Beatrice, and in love with Agnese, who in turn loves Orombello. Discovering that Orombello loves Beatrice, Agnese denounces them both to Filippo, who, finding them together, has them arrested. Later Agnese, filled with remorse, begs Filippo to spare her rival's life; but Filippo, hearing that Beatrice's followers have rebelled against him, signs her death warrant. A fiasco at its premiere but subsequently popular for a while. Recent revivals date from 1959. JB ○

Béatrice et Bénédict, *opéra comique*, 2 acts, BERLIOZ, lib. comp. after SHAKESPEARE's *Much Ado About Nothing*. Baden-Baden 9 Aug 1862; Weimar 8 Apr 1863 (in Ger.), Karlsruhe 6 Apr 1888 (with recitatives by MOTTL replacing spoken dialogue); Glasgow 24 Mar 1936, NY, Carnegie Hall (concert perf.), 21 Mar 1960. Main chars: Béatrice (mezzo-sop.) Bénédict (ten.) Hero (sop.) Ursula (contr.) Don Pedro (bass) Claudio (bar.) Somarone (bar.). The lib. follows Shakespeare, omitting the near-tragedy of Don Juan's plot against Claudio and Hero and replacing the comic Dogberry and Verges by a cond., Somarone. Berlioz's last opera. JB ○
See Kobbé

Beatrix Cenci, opera, 2 acts, GINASTERA, lib. (in Sp.) William Shand and Alberto Girri after Percy Bysshe Shelley's *The Cenci* (1819) and Stendhal's tr. of contemporary chronicles as *Chroniques Italiennes* (1837). NY CC 14 Mar 1973. Main chars: Count Francesco Cenci (bass-bar.) Beatrix Cenci (sop.) Lucrecia (contr.) Orsino (ten.) Bernardo (boy sop.). Set in 16th-c. Rome and Petrella, a re-creation of the gory events surrounding the life of Beatrix Cenci, executed in Rome in 1599 at the age of 22 for complicity in her father's murder. MK

Beaumarchais, Pierre-Augustin Caron de, b. Paris, 24 Jan 1732; d. Paris, 18 May 1799. French adventurer, wit, and dramatist. He played the harp, and was for a time music master to Louis XV's daughters. Chiefly known for his two comedies, *Le Barbier de Seville* (1775) (*see* PAISIELLO and ROSSINI) and *La Folle Journée, ou Le Mariage de Figaro* (1784), the basis of MOZART's opera. Also lib., esp. of TARARE, with a preface in which the musico-dramatic problems of opera are discussed. LO

Beckmann [Reed], Judith, b. Jamestown, N. Dak. American soprano. A pupil of Lotte LEHMANN, she won the San Francisco Opera Auditions 1961. European debut, Brunswick (FIORDILIGI); then sang at Düsseldorf, Berlin, Munich, Frankfurt, Hamburg, and

Vienna. Sang MARGUERITE, San Francisco 1970; London debut at CG 1974 (TATYANA). A lyric sop. with a well-prod. voice and a fine stage presence, she also sings AGATHE, EVA, ARABELLA, VIOLETTA, and Mistress Ford (FALSTAFF). At Hamburg since 1971. EF

Beckmesser, bar., the town clerk in MEISTERSINGER

Beecham, (Sir) Thomas, b. St Helens, 29 Apr 1879; d. London, 8 Mar 1961. English conductor; operatic debut in WRECKERS (London 1909). From 1910 dir. operatic seasons with own co. at CG, introducing to Britain VILLAGE ROMEO AND JULIET, ELEKTRA, SALOME, ROSENKAVALIER, ARIADNE AUF NAXOS, BORIS GODUNOV with SHALYAPIN, and NIGHTINGALE. During World War I dir. opera in Eng. at DL, Shaftesbury and Aldwych Ts, London; first cond. MOZART at Salzburg Fest. 1932 and was apptd principal cond. CG, becoming art. dir. 1933; dir. three seasons at NY Met during World War II. Last CG appearance 1951 (MEISTERSINGER); revived BOHEMIAN GIRL for Fest. of Britain 1951. Last operatic season at T. Colón, Buenos Aires, 1958. One of the few British conds of his day with international standing. His repertoire was vast, with special leaning toward Mozart. JB

Beethoven, Ludwig van, b. Bonn, 15 or 16 Dec 1770; d. Vienna, 26 Mar 1827. Like every comp. of his time he had operatic ambitions, contemplating subjects such as Faust, Ulysses, Undine, Grillparzer's *Melusin*, Collin's *Bradamante*, and GOETHE's *Claudine von Villa Bella*. He even wr. to the Imperial T., Vienna, 1807, proposing himself as court comp., guaranteeing one grand opera and one operetta a year. But though he wrote incidental music and the substantial *Prometheus* ballet (1800), his only completed opera was FIDELIO. LO

The Beggar's Opera, drawn by William Hogarth (1697–1764)

Beggar's Opera, The, ballad opera, 3 acts, PEPUSCH, lib. GAY. London, Lincoln's Inn Fields T., 3 Feb 1728; NY 3 Dec 1750. Chars: Macheath (bass) Polly Peachum (sop.) Lucy Lockit (sop.) Mrs Peachum (mezzo-sop.). The highwayman Macheath's love for and betrayal of Polly, his imprisonment and reprieve on the day of execution, provides the excuse to poke fun at politicians (Macheath is based on Horace Walpole), It. opera (the Polly–Lucy rivalry paralleling that between BORDONI and CUZZONI), and the manners and pretensions of Eng. high society. Revived many times, esp. by F. AUSTIN, BRITTEN, and BLISS, 1953, for a film with Laurence Olivier as Macheath. PS ○★

Béjart, Maurice [Maurice-Jean Berger], b. Marseille, 1 Jan 1927. French choreographer and producer, mainly occupied with ballet. Bayreuth invited him to comp. choreography for bacchanale in TANNHÄUSER (1961). Art. dir. of T. de la Monnaie, where he prod. CONTES D'HOFFMANN (1961) and LUSTIGE WITWE (1963). LO

Bekker, Paul, b. Berlin, 11 Sept 1882; d. NY, 7 Mar 1937. German administrator and writer. *Intendant,* Prussian State T., Kassel, 1925; dir. Wiesbaden State T., 1927–32. Music critic, writing for papers in Berlin and Frankfurt. Wr. biographies of OFFENBACH (1909), SCHREKER (1919), WAGNER (1931, and a history of opera, *Wandlungen der Oper* (Zürich and Leipzig 1934), tr. Mendel (NY 1935; London 1936). LO

bel canto (It. 'beautiful singing'). A question-begging term that came into general use about the beginning of the 20th c. to describe whatever method was currently being claimed as teaching the art of It., classical singing. Today it more usually categorizes It. opera *c.* 1810–50. JB

Belcore, bar., the sergeant in ELISIR D'AMORE

Belgium. Opera is perf. in ANTWERP, BRUSSELS, Ghent, LIÈGE. Among Belgian opera comps are Jean Absil (b. 1893; *Fanson,* 1947), BENOÎT, BLOCKX, Auguste de Boeck (1865–1937), FRANCK, GILSON, GOSSEC, GRÉTRY, POUSSEUR, Léon Jongen (b. 1884), Sylvain Dupuis (1856–1931), and Victor Vreuls (1876–1944). *See* FLEMISH OPERA. LO

Belgrade. The first opera perf. in the city was IN THE WELL (1894); the first Serbian opera was Binički's *At Dawn* (1903). The Belgrade O. (housed in the NT building of 1869) was founded 1920, after establishment of Yugoslav state. It maintains a large repertory, with a bias toward Slavonic music. GN

Belle Hélène, La (*Fair Helen*), operetta, 3 acts, OFFENBACH, lib. MEILHAC and L. HALÉVY. Paris, T. des Variétés, 17 Dec 1864; London (in Eng.), Adelphi, 30 June 1866; Chicago 31 May 1867. Revived London, SW, 31 May 1963. An amusing and topical skit on the theme of Helen of Troy and Paris. LO
See Lubbock

Bellezza, Vincenzo, b. Bitonto, 17 Feb 1888; d. Rome, 8 Feb 1964. Italian conductor. Studied Naples Cons. under Alessandro Longo (piano) and Giuseppe Martucci (cond.). Debut 1908, T. S. Carlo, Naples; on staff of the NY Met 1926–35; returned to Italy 1938; latterly associated with the Rome O. He cond. in all the major European and US theatres. JB

Bellincioni, Gemma [Cesira Matilde], b. Como, 18 Aug 1864; d. Naples, 23 Apr 1950. Italian soprano. Taught by her father; debut 1881, Naples, in Carlo Pedrotti's *Tutti in Maschera*; at HM, London, 1889. Created Santuzza (CAVALLERIA RUSTICANA), the role in which she made her CG debut 1895. She was the first FEDORA and a noted VIOLETTA, MANON, and CARMEN. She m. the ten. Roberto Stagno (1836–97). Their daughter, Bianca Bellincioni, sang at CG 1914. Gemma Bellincioni retired 1911 and taught in Berlin, Vienna and, from 1932, at the Naples Cons. Her autobiography, *Io e il Palcoscenico*, was published in Italy in 1920. PS

Bellini, Vincenzo, b. Catania, 2 Nov 1801; d. Puteaux, nr Paris, 23 Sept 1835. Italian composer. Studied Naples Cons. with ZINGARELLI; his first opera, *Adelson e Salvini*, was perf. 1825 by fellow students. He achieved national fame with PIRATA, in which the prevailing Rossinian style receives a new, romantic inflexion; the tendency away from display toward simple and expressive declamation reaches its limit in STRANIERA. In SONNAMBULA and NORMA a new balance is struck between virtuosity and musical expression. PURITANI shows Bellini grappling with new problems of scale and musical design. Bellini's is the most influential voice in It. romantic opera after ROSSINI's. The melodic style of which he remained the supreme master permeated the works of his contemporaries and successors. Of his 10 operas, seven have libs by ROMANI, to whose verses the comp. by his own account owed much of his inspiration; and in fact his musical style is deeply rooted in the It. language. His operas have always been vehicles for star singers. JB
See Weinstock, *Bellini, His Life and Operas* (New York 1971; London 1972)

Belmonte, ten., the hero of ENTFÜHRUNG AUS DEM SERAIL

Benda, Jiří Antonín, b. Staré Benátky, 30 June 1722; d. Köstritz, 6 Nov 1795. Czech composer. One of a large family of Czech musicians, he became violinist in the Berlin court of Frederick II 1742, and MdC to the Duke of Gotha 1750. His compositions incl. several *Singspiele* (e.g. *Der Dorfjahrmarkt*, 1775) and It. operas, but it is chiefly for his four 'duodramas' (or melodramas) that he is remembered. *Ariadne auf Naxos* (1775) and *Medea* (1775) influenced not only contemporaries such as MOZART (in ZAIDE) but also later Czechs like FIBICH. JT

Bendl, Karel, b. Prague, 16 Apr 1838; d. Prague, 20 Sept 1897. Czech composer and conductor. A successful and influential cond. at the Prague Hlahol choral society (1865–77), he also held several cond. posts abroad before settling permanently in Prague 1881. Though he is largely forgotten today he was a very popular comp. in his time: his *Lejla* (1868, lib. KRÁSNOHORSKÁ) was the second Czech opera to be pub. (BARTERED BRIDE was the first). His music is eclectic, borrowing from Ger. and Fr. romanticism and, in *Matka Míla* (1895) from It. *verismo*; he set one of his 12 operas to an It. lib., another to a Ger. one, though his early and more successful works like *Břetislav* (1870) and *The Old Bridegroom* (*Starý ženich*, 1882) have texts by Krásnohorská and SABINA respectively. His *Indian Princess* (*Indická princezna*, 1877) was the first Czech operetta. JT

Benedict, [Sir] Julius, b. Stuttgart, 27 Nov 1804; d. London, 5 June 1885. German, naturalized British, conductor and composer. Studied with Johan Nepomuka [Johann Nepomuk] Hummel and C. WEBER, on whose recommendation he became cond. Vienna KT 1823. Cond, T. S. Carlo, Naples, 1825, where he wrote the first of his eight operas, *Giacinta ed Ernesto* (1827). Settled in London 1835; cond. DL. Toured USA 1850 as LIND's accompanist. His most successful opera was *The Lily of Killarney* (CG, 8 Feb 1862). Benedict was knighted in 1871. PS

Benelli, Sem, b. Prato, *c.* 1875; d. Genoa, 18 Dec 1949. Italian dramatist. Two of his plays have been turned into operas: *La Cena delle Beffe*, 1909 (GIORDANO, 1924), and AMORE DEI TRE RE. LO

Benelli, Ugo, b. Genoa. Italian tenor. Has sung light lyrical roles in most It. houses, specializing in ROSSINI and DONIZETTI. CG debut 1974 as Ernesto (DON PASQUALE); Glyndebourne debut 1967 (NEMORINO); returned 1970 to sing Narciso (TURCO IN ITALIA). A refined, fluent singer. AB

Benjamin, Arthur, b. Sydney, 18 Sept 1893; d. London, 10 Apr 1960. Australian composer. Lived in England after 1921. Operas are: *The Devil Take Her* (London, RCM, 1931); PRIMA DONNA; *A Tale of Two Cities*, lib. Cedric Cliffe after DICKENS (London, SW, 23 July 1957); *Tartuffe*, vocal score only complete at his death (SW, 30 Nov 1964). FGB

Bennett, Richard Rodney, b. Broadstairs, 29 Mar 1936. English composer. Studied with BERKELEY and Pierre Boulez. After several instrumental compositions, wrote one-act opera *The Ledge* (1951). The full-length MINES OF SULPHUR was successfully prod. by SW, who then commissioned another work, PENNY FOR A SONG, a comedy based on a play by John Whiting that proved dramatically less gripping. For CG he wr. VICTORY. His style is readily accessible, vocally and instrumentally, and closely related to dramatic incident for which his experience in writing film scores has been helpful. AB

Benois, Alexandre [Aleksandr Nikolayevich], b. St Petersburg, 4 May 1870; d. Paris, 9 Feb 1960. Russian painter and designer. Came of a family connected with the theatre and the arts: great-grandfather had been dir. T. La Fenice, Venice; grandfather designed the Bolshoy T., Moscow. Primarily associated with DYAGILEV's Russian Ballet, Benois did a number of opera decors: for GÖTTERDÄMMERUNG 1903, and (for Sc.) for LUCIA DI LAMMERMOOR, WERTHER, and MANON LESCAUT. LO

Benois, Nicola [Nikolay Aleksandrovich], b. St Petersburg, 2 May 1901. Russian stage designer, son of A. BENOIS, with whom he worked in Paris. Invited 1925 by TOSCANINI to design for Sc. prods of BORIS GODUNOV and KHOVANSHCHINA he moved to Italy, becoming Sc. chief designer. Apart from notable prods there (FEDORA, 1956; BALLO IN MASCHERA, 1957; RIENZI, 1963) his work has been seen in Hamburg, Buenos Aires, Montreal (TROVATORE and NABUCCO, Expo' 67), and San Francisco. LO

Benoît, Pierre [also Peter] Léonard Léopold, b. Harlebeke, 17 Aug 1834; d. Antwerp, 8 Mar 1901. Belgian composer, active in promoting Flemish national music. Studied Brussels Cons. 1851–5; after a period in Paris, settled in Antwerp 1863, founding (1867) Flemish School of Music there. His Flemish operas are: *Het Dorp in 't Gebergte (The Village in the Mountains)*, 1856; *Isa*, 1864; *Willem de Zwijger (William the Silent)*, 1876; *Pompeja*, 1896. LO

Benvenuto Cellini, opera, 2 acts, BERLIOZ, lib. Léon de Wailly and Auguste Barbier. Paris, O., 20 Sept 1838; Weimar 20 Mar 1852 in 4 acts and 18 Feb 1856 tr. CORNELIUS, with recitative in place of dialogue; London, CG, 25 June 1853 (cond. BERLIOZ); NY, Philharmonic Hall (concert perf.), 22 Mar 1965. Main chars: Cellini (ten.) Teresa (sop.) Balducci (bass) Fieramosca (bar.) Ascanio (mezzo-sop.) Pope Clement (bass). The plot concerns the adventures of the famous Florentine goldsmith in his rivalry with Fieramosca for the hand of Balducci's daughter Teresa, and the casting of his masterpiece, the statue of Perseus. Berlioz's first opera; its failure persuaded him to salvage some of its music in the overture, *Carnival Romain*. JB O
See Kobbé

Bérain, Jean, b. St Mihiel, Lorraine, 28 Oct 1637; d. Paris, 25 Jan 1711. One of the most important designers in history of Fr. theatre. With LULLY, RACINE, and MOLIÈRE, devised fetes for perf. in park of Versailles, and, 1680, was apptd by Louis XIV to design all the opera and ballet for the O. His work, full of fantasy, elegant, light of touch, created the typically Fr. decor, traces of which can be seen to this day; the *chinoiserie* he cultivated made its mark beyond his lifetime, in e.g. the early ballets of Jean Georges Noverre and entertainments at the Viennese court such as GLUCK's *Le Cinesi* (1754); while the exuberant headdresses of the Parisian Folies-Bergère and other revues can trace their ancestry to him. LO

Berenice, opera, 3 acts, HANDEL, lib. Antonio Salvi. London, CG, 29 May 1737. Main chars: Berenice (sop.) Selene (mezzo-sop.) Alessandro (sop.) Demetrio (mezzo-sop.) Arsace (mezzo-sop.). Berenice, Queen of Egypt, is under political pressure from Rome to marry Alessandro, but she herself loves Demetrio, himself in love with Selene, her sister. Berenice orders Selene to marry Arsace; Demetrio believing Selene faithless conspires with an enemy ruler, for which Berenice has him condemned to death; then, impressed with Alessandro's nobility (he once saved Demetrio's life) she agrees to marry him, par-

Ugo Benelli as Nemorino in ELISIR D'AMORE, at his Glyndebourne debut in 1967; decor ZEFFIRELLI

dons Demetrio, and allows him to marry Selene. Unsuccessful; nowadays known by the minuet which forms part of the overture. JB

Berg, Alban, b. Vienna, 9 Feb 1885; d. Vienna, 24 Dec 1935. Austrian composer. Began studying music aged 18. His meeting with Schönberg proved the turning point in his musical life, and he followed in his contemporary's revolutionary path when he wrote his major works, as can be heard in his WOZZECK and the unfinished LULU, which are among the most arresting musical dramas of the 20th c. AB

Berg, (Carl) Natanael, b. Stockholm, 9 Feb 1879; d. Stockholm, 15 Oct 1957. Swedish composer. Studied Stockholm, Paris, and Vienna, then for some years practised as a veterinary surgeon. His five operas, comp. to his own texts, were all prod. in Stockholm: *Leila* (1912), based on BYRON's *Giaour*, *Engelbrekt* (1929), *Judith* (1936), based on the play by HEBBEL, *Birgitta* (1942), and *Genoveva* (1947), also adapted from a play by Hebbel. EF

Bergamo. It. city at the foot of the Lombardian Alps. Birthplace of DONIZETTI and RUBINI, and home of G. S. MAYR, who founded its music school 1806; this now houses the Centro di Studi Donizettiani, which has promoted a number of rare Donizetti revivals at the T. Donizetti since World War II. JB

Berganza, Teresa, b. Madrid, 16 Mar 1935. Spanish mezzo-soprano. Early experience in Sp. operetta (*zarzuela*) from 1955. International debut 1957, Aix-en-Provence Fest. (DORABELLA); US debut 1958, Dallas, Texas, as Neris (MÉDÉE; with CALLAS); British debut 1958, Glyndebourne (CHERUBINO), repeated 1959 together with title role in CENERENTOLA; CG debut 1960 (ROSINA). A voice of uncommon range and agility in coloratura-mezzo roles such as ROSSINI originally comp., and in 18th-c. opera (HANDEL etc.), with warmth of personality that makes vocal display integral to character. A popular concert singer. NG

Berger, Erna, b. Dresden, 19 Oct 1900. German soprano of perennially youthful timbre and sparkling agility. Debut 1926, Dresden, as First Boy in ZAUBERFLÖTE. Berlin Städtische O. 1930–2; Berlin Staats O. from 1934. Active during this time at Bayreuth and Salzburg, and CG debut 1934 (MARCELLINA); returned CG 1948–9. NY Met debut 1949 (SOPHIE). Outstanding in MOZART, incl. a dazzling QUEEN OF THE NIGHT and a beautiful GILDA. Retired 1955 but continued to teach: pupils incl. STREICH. NG

Berglund, Joel (Ingemar), b. Torsåker, 4 June 1903. Swedish bass-baritone. Studied Stockholm; debut there 1929 as Monterone (RIGOLETTO). Sang FLIEGENDE HOLLÄNDER (Bayreuth 1942). Appeared at NY Met 1945–9; dir. Stockholm Royal O., 1949–52. Best known as a WAGNER singer, he was a particularly fine HANS SACHS and a notable WOTAN, but his repertory incl. many other roles, such as MÉPHISTOPHÉLÈS, SCARPIA, and Jokanaan (SALOME). EF

Bergonzi, Carlo, b. Parma, 13 July 1924. Italian tenor. Studied Parma Cons. Debut 1948, Lecce, as FIGARO (BARBIERE DI SIVIGLIA). After three years as bar. and more study, emerged as ten. 1951, Bari (ANDREA CHÉNIER). Has since become one of the leading It. tens of his era. London debut 1953, Stoll T., as ALVARO, a role he sang at his CG debut (1962) and again in 1975. US debut 1955, Chicago; NY Met debut 1956 (RADAMES). His pure, even line and expansive style were invaluable in an age not flush with VERDI tenors of his quality. AB

Berio, Luciano, b. Oneglia, 24 Oct 1925. Italian composer. His opera, *Amores*, was perf. at Holland Fest., 1972. LO

Berkeley, (Sir) Lennox, b. Oxford, 12 May 1903. English composer. Studied Paris with Nadia Boulanger 1926–33. His work is chiefly orch. and chamber music; always thoughtful and fastidious, operas are *Nelson* (London, SW, 1953); DINNER ENGAGEMENT; and the 1-act *Ruth* (London, Scala T., 1956). FGB

Berkshire Music Center Opera School (Tanglewood), Stockbridge, Mass. Summer home of the Boston Symphony Orch. A workshop programme occasionally staging new or unusual works, as PETER GRIMES (6 Aug 1946), ALBERT HERRING (1949), TENDER LAND (parts revised; 1954). Guest dirs and faculty are in residence each season; students are young professionals. EJ

Berlin. Like most court centres, the city had some opera in the 17th c., but its operatic history really begins with Frederick the Great of Prussia (reigned 1740–86). GRAUN was his MdC; operas were given either in nearby Potsdam (Sans Souci), or in the new Hofoper (also called the Lindenoper from its site in the Unter den Linden), opened in 1742 and later to be the home of the Staats O. In 1786 the Komödienhaus in the Gendarmenmarkt became the Königliches National-Theater; here *Singspiele* were played, incl. ENTFÜHRUNG AUS DEM

Berlin. The new Komische Oper, completed 1966 and designed by K. Nierade and F. Kühin

SERAIL (1788). The two theatres shared an *Intendant* in the early 19th c. Yet another theatre was the Königstadt-Theater, built 1824, where ROSSINI's, VERDI's, and other It. operas were performed.

The **Deutsche Oper**, Bismarckstrasse, W. Berlin, opened in 1912 as the Deutsches Opernhaus, a private foundation. Taken over by the city in 1924, it bore the name **Städtische Oper** (Municipal O.) 1925–34, and again for a time after World War II, during which the building was destroyed (1942). In 1961 the Deutsche O. returned to its rebuilt home on the original Charlottenburg site, after a period in the former T. des Westens. Chief conds have incl. WALTER and STIEDRY. The repertory has been very wide since World War II; several important premieres have been given. Present dir. is MAAZEL.

The Soviet military authorities set up the **Komische Oper**, Behrenstrasse, E. Berlin, in 1947. Under dir. of FELSENSTEIN, a reformer and innovator, often controversial in operatic prods, it acquired its international reputation and a repertoire ranging from MONTEVERDI to BRITTEN and GERSHWIN.

The **Kroll-Oper** had its origins in the impresario Kroll's summer theatre, where from 1850 opera was incl. on the programme. This establishment was taken over in 1896 in connection with Kaiser Wilhelm II's much-delayed plans for a new Berlin opera house. The Kroll theatre itself, after a number of extensions and modifications, had to be wholly rebuilt, reopening in 1924. It was then linked administratively with the Staats O. (it often served as its alternative theatre), but retained its artistic independence. Under KLEMPERER, 1927–31, it entered its greatest, most adventurous – and final – period, with prods of CARDILLAC, ERWARTUNG, GLÜCKLICHE HAND, OEDIPUS REX, and the premiere of NEUES VOM TAGE. The building housed the Reichstag after the fire of 1933 and was destroyed toward the end of World War II.

The **Staatsoper,** more fully the Deutsche Staatsoper, of E. Berlin is the descendant of the original Hof- or Königliche Oper. In 1821, under the dir. of SPONTINI, the premiere of FREISCHÜTZ was staged. The repertoire, under Spontini and MEYERBEER, was cosmopolitan rather than national. Later associated with the co. were WEINGARTNER, MUCK, and R. STRAUSS. The sequence of distinguished names continued with BLECH, E. KLEIBER, FURTWÄNGLER, and C. KRAUSS. Twice the victim of hostilities in World War II, the Staats O. reopened on its old Unter den Linden site in 1955, after spending the intervening postwar years in the Admiralspalast, Friedrichstrasse. It is now E. Germany's chief operatic showcase in Berlin, with a traditional repertoire. JB/LO

Berlin, Irving [Israel Baline], b. Temun, Eastern Russia, 11 May 1888; moved to USA 1892. Russian, later American, composer. His first popular success was *Say It With Music*. While on leave during World War I he prod. an all-soldier show called *Yip, Yip, Yaphank*. A successful series of *Music Box Revues* (1921–4 incl.) was staged lavishly in a theatre built for them, constituting a chapter in the history of the Broadway theatre. After an infertile period during the Depression, in which he lost his fortune, Berlin came back with *As Thousands Cheer* (1933). Following World War II came *This Is the Army*, his second all-soldier show, ANNIE GET YOUR GUN, the first Broadway show for which he comp. the entire score (as distinguished from a sheaf of songs), and CALL ME MADAM. EJ

See Freedland, *Irving Berlin* (New York and London 1974)

Berlioz, (Louis) Hector, b. La Côte-Saint-André, Isère, 11 Dec 1803; d. Paris, 8 Mar 1869. French composer and critic. Son of a doctor, he renounced the study of medicine for music. His teachers at Paris Cons. were LESUEUR and Antonín Reicha; but his musical ideals were derived from BEETHOVEN's symphonies and the operas of GLUCK and SPONTINI. In 1827 he began an opera, *Les Francs Juges*, of which only the overture survives. First theatrical commission, BENVENUTO CELLINI, had hostile reception. An accomplished writer and the music critic of the *Journal des Debats* from 1835, he wr. his own text for TROYENS. It was composed 1858–60 and intended for the Paris O.; but only the second part of it, *Les Troyens à Carthage* was ever perf. in his lifetime. He enjoyed better fortune in England and Germany, where under LISZT *Benvenuto Cellini* was resurrected at Weimar, and his final opera BÉATRICE ET BÉNÉDICT was given in several cities. Berlioz's operas are stamped by the same boldness and originality that informs everything he wrote. In *Troyens* he achieves Wagnerian proportions without WAGNER's methods, which were to him abhorrent. His edition of ORFEO ED EURIDICE, made for VIARDOT in 1859, is still in general use. A dedicated romantic in the spirit of HUGO, he infused a theatrical verve into many of his religious and concert-hall works. DAMNATION DE FAUST, a dramatic cantata, was first given as an opera in Monte Carlo in 1893 and is sometimes so perf. today. In general, despite the championship of Liszt and Charles Hallé, Berlioz's full stature was not recognized until the 20th c. JB

Bern [Berne], Switzerland. There were occasional perfs of opera in the 18th c., in a converted ballroom, by visiting troupes. In the Hôtel de Musique, built in 1767–9, opera was given during the 18th c. (e.g. ZAUBERFLÖTE, 1796), with more activity in the 19th c. esp. under Julius Edele, dir. 1838–43.

A new Stadt T. was opened 1903, the first opera being TANNHÄUSER. Here 6–8 operas are mounted each season. Present mus. dir. Klaus Weise. LO

Bernacchi, Antonio, b. Bologna, 23 June 1685 (?); d. Bologna, Mar 1756. Italian sopranist, 'the best singer in Italy' (*London Daily Journal*, 2 July 1729). Sang in several HANDEL operas in London beginning with revival of RINALDO 1717, in which he sang Goffredo which Handel had originally wr. for female contr., and AMADIS. Also created title role in *Lotario* (1729) and Arsace in *Partenope* (1730). Gifted with a small voice, his singing appealed more to connoisseurs than to the general public. LO

Bernardi, Mario, b. Kirkland Lake, Ontario, 20 Aug 1930. Canadian conductor. Studied Venice, Salzburg, and Toronto. Cond. frequently at SW 1964–8 (QUEEN OF SPADES, MADAMA BUTTERFLY, BALLO IN MASCHERA) and at Aldeburgh (GLORIANA). US debut 1967, San Francisco. Cond. of Vancouver O. Assn 1962–8, O. Guild, Montreal, 1965–7, and mus. dir. of Toronto O. Fest., later COC, with which he is mainly associated. LO

Hector Berlioz's TROYENS, London, CG, 17 Sept 1969; VEASEY as Dido; produced Minos Volanakis; designed Nicholas Georgiadis

Bernauerin, Die: Ein Bayrisches Stück *(The Bernauer Girl: A Bavarian Tale)*, opera, 2 acts, ORFF, lib. comp. in old Bavarian dialect based on 17th-c. ballad. Stuttgart, Staats O., 15 June 1947. A play with music rather than a true opera. LO

Bernstein, Leonard, b. Lawrence, Mass., 25 Aug 1918. American conductor and composer. Cond. first US perf. of PETER GRIMES and MAMELLES DE TIRÉSIAS; has made numerous guest appearances at CG, Sc., and Vienna as well as NY Met (FALSTAFF, 1964). Comp. two operas: TROUBLE IN TAHITI and CANDIDE and the musical WEST SIDE STORY. LO

Berry, Walter, b. Vienna, 8 Apr 1929. Austrian baritone. First studied engineering; entered Vienna Acad. of Music 1947. Engaged Vienna Staats O. 1950: first major role 1953 as Masetto (DON GIOVANNI). UK debut 1954 with Vienna co. at RFH as Antonio (NOZZE DI FIGARO). Became much admired in major MOZART roles (FIGARO, PAPAGENO, Don ALFONSO), and US debut 1958, Chicago, as Figaro. Has sung over 50 roles, from WOZ-

ZECK to Frank (FLEDERMAUS). A voice of firm technique and expressive colour. NG

Bertini, Gary, b. Bessarabia, 1 May 1927. Israeli conductor. Founded the Israel Chamber Ensemble 1966, with which he has cond. DOCTEUR MIRACLE, MEDIUM, CONSUL, CLEMENZA DI TITO, and ORFEO ED EURIDICE. Debut with SO 1971, cond. BARBIERE DI SIVIGLIA; has since returned for NOZZE DI FIGARO, BORIS GODUNOV, and COSÌ FAN TUTTE. At Hamburg he cond. the first perf. of TAL's *Ashmedai* (1971), and BILLY BUDD; at Jerusalem the premiere of Tal's *Masada 967* (1973) and MOSÈ IN EGITTO. While at Caesarea he cond. the Hamburg prod. of MOSES UND ARON (1974). EF

Berton, Henri Montan, b. Paris, 17 Sept 1767; d. Paris, 22 Apr 1844. French violinist, composer, conductor. Dir. first perf. in France of NOZZE DI FIGARO. Of his *c.* 50 operas the most successful was *Montano et Stéphanie* (1799), which long retained its place in the repertory. Others of interest are *Aline, Reine de Golconde* (1803; also treated by BOÏELDIEU and DONIZETTI) and the thriller, *Les Rigueurs du Cloître* (1790). LO

Beruti, Arturo, b. San Juan, 27 Mar 1862; d. Buenos Aires, 3 Jan 1938. Argentine composer. Trained in Europe (1884–*c.*1890), where his first operas were prod.: (*Vendetta*, 1892; *Evangelina*, 1893; *Taras Bulba*, 1895). Comp. the first Argentine national opera, *Pampa* (1897), based on Eduardo Gutiérrez's novel *Juan Moreira*, and followed it with *Yupanki* (1899), lib. Enrique Larreta, tr. into It. by José Tarnassi for its Buenos Aires premiere with CARUSO. After *Khrysé* (1903) and *Horrida Nox* (1908) came *Los Héroes* (1919), his only opera prod. at the T. Colón. MK

Besch, Anthony, b. London, 5 Feb 1924. English producer. Gained his earliest operatic experience with the Oxford Univ. O. Club; prod. SCHAUSPIELDIREKTOR (Glyndebourne 1957). At SW, 1959–66, dir. TANNHÄUSER, ANDREA CHÉNIER, ARIADNE AUF NAXOS, COMTE ORY, GAZZA LADRA, and QUEEN OF SPADES. For SO his prods incl. VERDI's OTELLO, GOUNOD's FAUST, ALBERT HERRING, COSÌ FAN TUTTE, ALCESTE (GLUCK), and CATILINE CONSPIRACY. He prod. BERKELEY's *Castaway* (1967) and Harrison Birtwistle's *Punch and Judy* (1968) for the EOG, Elisabeth Lutyens's *Time off. . . Not a Ghost of a Chance* and NOSE for the New O. Co. Directed CLEMENZA DI TITO (CG, 1974) and ZAUBERFLÖTE for ENO at the Col 1975. Has also prod. in the USA. EF

Besuch der Alten Dame, Der (*The Visit of the Old Lady*), opera, 3 acts, EINEM, lib. Friedrich Dürrenmatt based on his play, *The Visit*. Vienna Fest. 23 May 1971; Glyndebourne 31 May 1973 LO

Betrothal in a Monastery *see* DUENNA

Bettelstudent, Der, (*The Beggar Student*), operetta, MILLÖCKER, lib. F. Zell (pseud. of Camillo Walzell) and GENÉE. Vienna, T. a. d. Wien, 6 Dec 1882; London, Alhambra T., 12 Apr 1884. Revived Bregenz 1956. One of the most popular of all the Viennese operettas, with nearly 5,000 perfs in Ger. 1896–1921. LO *See* Lubbock

Bettinelli, Bruno, b. Milan, 4 June 1913. Italian composer. His first opera, *Il Pozzo e il Pendolo*, based on POE's story, *The Pit and the Pendulum*, comp. 1957–8, was prod. at Bergamo 1967; *La Smorfia* was perf. at Como 1959. EF

Betz, Franz, b. Mainz, 19 Mar 1835; d. Berlin, 11 Aug 1900. German baritone. Debut 1856, Hanover; member of Staats O., Berlin, 1859–97; created HANS SACHS; sang WOTAN in Bayreuth, 1876; also FALSTAFF in first Berlin prod. JB

Bevignani, Enrico, b. Naples, 29 Sept 1841; d. Naples, 29 Aug 1903. Italian conductor and composer. His one opera *Caterina Blum* (Naples 1863) was very successful and much admired by TCHAIKOVSKY. Resident cond., HM 1864–70 and CG 1870–7; also cond. Moscow, St Petersburg, and NY. JB

Bianca e Fernando, *opera semi-seria*, 2 acts, BELLINI, lib. Domenico Gilardoni after play by Carlo Roti; Naples, T. S. Carlo, 30 May 1826 (as *Bianca e Gernando*); Genoa, T. Carlo Felice, 7 Apr 1828 with altered music, and text revised by ROMANI. Main chars: Bianca (sop.) Fernando (ten.) Filippo (bass bar.) Carlo (bar.). Fernando, son of Carlo, Duke of Agrigento, imprisoned by the usurper, Filippo, visits his enemy's court in disguise and together with his sister Bianca, whom Filippo hopes to marry, penetrates to their father's dungeon cell just as the people of Agrigento rise in rebellion against the tyrant. Bellini's second opera, successful in both versions. JB

Bibiena family. A dynasty of scenographers and architects. Real name Galli; came from Bibbiena in Tuscany, settled in Bologna. 1. **Ferdinando Galli** Bibiena, b. Bologna, 18 Aug 1657; d. Bologna, 1743; 2. **Giuseppe,** b.

Bibiena family. A scene by Giuseppe Bibiena illustrating the favourite central and diagonal perspective developed from Andrea Palladio's (1508–80) Teatro Olimpico at Verona, in turn based on the ancient Greek theatres

Parma, 5 Jan 1696; d. Berlin, 1757, son of (1); 3. **Antonio,** b. Parma, 1700; d. Milan, 1774, son of (1); 4. **Carlo,** b. Vienna, 1725; d. Florence, 1787, son of (2); 5. **Francesco,** b. Bologna, 12 Dec 1659; d. Bologna, 20 Jan 1739, brother of (1). They worked largely as a team and identification of individual contributions is difficult. Designed theatres for Rome, Verona, Nancy, Dresden, Bayreuth (Giuseppe's work, still extant), Vienna, and elsewhere. Inside the theatre their lavish decorations repeated the florid fantasy of their architecture. They introduced innovations such as the *scena al angola* or diagonal perspective replacing the traditional central perspective (attributed to Ferdinando *c.* 1700) and transparent scenery lighted from behind (1723, Giuseppe). Their endless inventiveness can be seen in the drawings preserved in Vienna and elsewhere, and esp. in the Bayreuth opera house. LO

See Oenslager, *Stage Design* (London and New York 1975)

Bible, Frances, b. Sackets Harbor, NY. American mezzo-soprano. Studied Juilliard School, NY; debut Chautauqua (GONDOLIERS). NY CC since 1948. Has also appeared at San Francisco, Vancouver, Central City, Col. (creating Augusta Tabor in BALLAD OF BABY DOE), and at Glyndebourne. A versatile artist, very much at home in the modern repertory. LO

Biblical operas. The Bible, esp. the Old Testament and the Apocrypha, has been a quarry for a quantity of operas. At least 16 comps have used the story of Judith, incl. N. BERG, GOOSSENS III, HONEGGER, NAUMANN, REZNIČEK, and SEROV. The *fin de siècle* Salome vogue yielded two important operas, SALOME and HÉRODIADE. JOSEPH and SAMSON ET DALILA continue the Fr. interest in sacred drama which began with Michel Montéclair's *Jephté*, 1732. The first Ger. opera, ADAM UND EVA, was Biblical. Among other operas are BERKELEY'S *Ruth* (1956), PRODIGAL SON, CASTELNUOVO-TEDESCO'S *Saul* (1960), MALIPIERO'S *Il Figliuolo Prodigo* (1953) and *L'Iscariota* (1971), and DEBORA E JAELE. LO

Bickerstaffe, Isaac, b. *c.* 1735; d. St Malo, 1812. Irish playwright. Wrote libs for ARNE (THOMAS AND SALLY), ARNOLD (*The Maid of the Mill*, based on Samuel Richardson's *Pamela*, 1765), Charles Dibdin (*The Padlock*, after CERVANTES, 1768; *A School for Fathers*, based on Richardson's *Lionel and Clarissa*, 1770), SHIELD, and others. His work was superior to most prod. in England at that time. LO

Bilibin, Ivan Yakovlevich, b. Tarkhovka, nr St Petersburg, 14 Aug 1876; d. Leningrad, 7 Feb 1942. Russian artist. Known esp. for his richly colourful book illustrations, an art which he occasionally transferred to the theatre, notably in his costumes and sets for the premiere of GOLDEN COCKEREL. GN

Billington [Weichsel], Elizabeth, b. London, prob. 1765; d. Venice, 25 Aug 1818. English soprano of German parentage. She m. the double-bass virtuoso, James Billington, 1783. Debut 1786, CG (LOVE IN A VILLAGE). Appeared in Naples 1794 in Francesco Bianchi's *Iñes de Castro*. The eruption of Vesuvius coincided with her debut and was blamed on the appearance of a Protestant heretic on the stage of the T. S. Carlo. It was after the first perf. also that her husband died of apoplexy. Her 'sweet and captivating voice' ranged three octaves. She retired 1809; settled in Venice 1817. PS

Below: Ivan Bilibin's design for Act IV of TALE OF TSAR SALTAN; produced Kirov T., Leningrad, 1937

Below: Billy Budd. The main deck and quarter-deck. Produced London, CG, 1964, by Basil Coleman; designed PIPER

Billy Budd, opera, 2 acts (orig. 4), BRITTEN, lib. E. M. Forster and CROZIER, derived from Herman Melville's unfinished novel. London, CG, 1 Dec 1951; Bloomington, Ind., 5 Dec 1952 (staged). Main chars: Billy Budd (bar.) Captain Vere (ten.) Claggart (bass). Set on board ship, it deals with the false charge brought by Claggart against Budd, who kills the tyrannical master-of-arms, when his stutter will not let him defend himself verbally. One of several operas by Britten in which an innocent char. exhibits a fatal flaw in his make-up. Musically, the work is taut and dramatic, showing Britten's usual aptitude in characterization and timing. The scoring is rich and evocative, the thematic interrelationship close. Successful on TV, with PEARS, who created the role, as Captain Vere. AB O
See Kobbé

Bing, (Sir) Rudolf, b. Vienna, 9 Jan 1902. Austrian, later British, opera manager and impresario. Studied Vienna. Manager of concert agency 1923. Held managerial appointments at Darmstadt and Berlin, where he worked for C. EBERT, who brought him to Glyndebourne 1934; became gen. mgr 1936. Helped to start the Edinburgh Fest., becoming its first gen. mgr 1947–9. Gen. mgr, NY Met, 1950–72. AB
See autobiography, *5,000 Nights at the Opera* (London and New York 1972)

Bishop, (Sir) Henry (Rowley), b. London, 18 Nov 1786; d. London, 30 Apr 1855. English conductor and composer. Studied under Francesco Bianchi. Mus. dir., CG, 1810 and King's T. 1816. Wr. 57 operas 1804–34, many in partnership, besides much other music for the theatre. Adapted many operas for the English stage incl. DON GIOVANNI, BARBIERE DI SIVIGLIA, and GUILLAUME TELL. He is remembered today for 'Lo, Here the Gentle Lark', and 'Home, Sweet Home' (from *Clari, Maid of Milan*, 1823), which was used in ANNA BOLENA. PS

Bispham, David Scull, b. Philadelphia, 5 Jan 1857; d. NY, 2 Oct 1921. Baritone, the first American singer to achieve international standing. Studied Florence and Milan; debut 1891, London (BASOCHE). At DL 1892 (TRISTAN UND ISOLDE), engaged by CG 1893. Met debut 1896 (MEISTERSINGER). Had a repertory of over 50 roles ranging from light opera to VERDI and WAGNER – particularly praised in the latter. LO
See autobiography, *A Quaker Singer's Recollections* (New York 1920)

Bittner, Julius, b. Vienna, 9 Apr 1874; d. Vienna, 19 Jan 1939. Austrian composer. His *c.* 10 operas, to his own libs, were highly regarded in the Germany of his time, but made no mark outside his own country and have not proved lasting. LO

Bizet, Georges, b. Paris, 25 Oct 1838; d. Bougival, nr Paris, 3 June 1875. French composer. At Paris Cons. 1849–57, studying composition with J. F. HALÉVY, but the strongest early influence on him was that of GOUNOD. From the first he was drawn toward the theatre, and in 1857 he and LECOCQ shared the prize offered by OFFENBACH for a one-act *opéra comique*, DOCTEUR MIRACLE. Won the *Prix de Rom* 1857 with a cantata. While in Rome he wrote his third opera (his first, a very early comp., was *La Maison du Docteur*, never perf., never pub.); this was *Don Procopio* (1858–9), posthumously perf. in 1906. Returning to Paris he began a long struggle for recognition as a comp. Of three operas attempted in the 1860s only PÊCHEURS DE PERLES and JOLIE FILLE DE PERTH reached completion and perf., with only moderate success; of the five-act *Ivan le Terrible* (lib. Arthur Leroy and Henri Trianon) four acts were completed (1865), but this was not perf. until 1946. One or two other projects were begun, or contemplated; there are MS fragments of *La Coupe du Roi de Thule* (1868) and *Clarissa Harlowe* (1870–1). DJAMILEH was a failure, but the incidental music to ARLÉSIENNE at last gave him a taste of success. Even his last and incomparably greatest opera, CARMEN, was slow to make an impression, but the power and originality of this work needs no advocacy today, acknowledged as it is among the handful of operatic masterpieces of the very highest quality. LO

See Curtiss, *Bizet and his World* (London 1959, 1964)

Bjoner, Ingrid, b. Krakstad, nr Oslo, 8 Nov 1927. Norwegian soprano. Studied Oslo Cons. and at Frankfurt Hochschule für Musik. At Wuppertal 1957–9 (debut as Donna ANNA) graduating to Deutsche O. am Rhein, 1959–61. Bayreuth debut 1960 as Freia (RHEINGOLD) and GUTRUNE. Member of the Bavarian Staats O., Munich, since 1961. NY Met debut 1961 (ELSA); CG debut 1967 (SENTA). Her roles incl. most of the leading WAGNER and R. STRAUSS *hochdramatische* roles and FIDELIO. Her voice is powerful and true and her acting is sound. AB

Björling, Jussi (Johan), b. Stora Tuna, 5 Feb 1911; d. Stockholm, 9 Sept 1960. Swedish tenor. Sang in public from the age of six; stage debut 1930, Stockholm as the Lamplighter (MANON LESCAUT). Other debuts: Chicago 1937 (DUCA DI MANTUA), NY Met 1938 (RODOLFO), CG 1939 (MANRICO). The possessor of one of the most beautiful ten. voices of the century, and a most elegant singer, his repertory ranged from Ottavio (DON GIOVANNI) to CAVARADOSSI, and he was much admired as DON CARLOS, Riccardo (BALLO IN MASCHERA), DES GRIEUX (MANON), and GOUNOD'S FAUST and ROMÉO. EF

Björling, Sigurd, b. Stockholm, 2 Nov 1907. Swedish baritone. Debut 1935, Royal O., Stockholm, as Alfio (CAVALLERIA RUSTICANA). Sang WOTAN at the first postwar Bayreuth Fest. (1951) and has appeared at San Francisco (1950), CG and Sc. (1951), the NY Met (1952–3), and all over Europe. Best known for his WAGNER roles – the Dutchman (FLIEGENDE HOLLÄNDER), WOLFRAM, TELRAMUND, KURWENAL, and AMFORTAS – he has sung DON GIOVANNI, ALMAVIVA (NOZZE DI FIGARO), many VERDI characters, SCARPIA, Balstrode (PETER GRIMES), MATHIS DER MALER, and Wilhelm Peterson-Berger's *Arnljot*, in a career lasting 40 years. EF

Blacher, Boris, b. China, 6 Jan 1903; d. Berlin, 30 Jan 1975. German composer. His operas are *Fürstin Tarakanova* (Wuppertal 1941); FLUT; ROMEO UND JULIA (Radio Berlin 1947; staged Salzburg Fest. 1950); *Der Grossinquisitor* (1947); *Die Nachtschwalbe* (1948); PREUSSISCHES MÄRCHEN; ABSTRAKT OPER NO. 1; ALKMENE; *Rosamunde Floris* (1960); ZWISCHENFÄLLE BEI EINER NOTLANDUNG; ZWEIHUNDERTTAUSEND TALER; *Yvonne, Prinzessin von Burgund* (Wuppertal 1973). LO

Blachut, Beno, b. Ostrava, 14 June 1913. Czech tenor. Studied Prague Cons. 1935–9; sang in Olomouc opera 1939–41, and joined Prague NT 1941. Has sung both lyric ten. roles (José, the Prince in RUSALKA, Ctirad in ŠÁRKA) and dramatic and heroic roles (DALIBOR, RADAMES, and FLORESTAN); more recently he excelled in buffo parts, such as Beneš (DEVIL'S WALL) and Mr Brouček (MR BROUČEK'S EXCURSIONS). The isolation of Czechoslovakia during World War II and after prevented his fine, resonant ten. voice, one of the noblest of his generation, from winning the international recognition it merited. JT

Blackham, Joyce, b. Rotherham, 1 Jan 1935. English soprano. Joined SW from Guildhall School of Music 1955; debut as Olga (EUGENE ONEGIN). After three seasons as mezzo-sop. she changed to sop. and won popular successes in roles dependent on voluptuous sex appeal of both voice and appearance, incl. CARMEN and several classic operettas, notably BELLE HÉLÈNE, OFFENBACH'S *Barbe-Bleue*, and LUSTIGE WITWE. CG debut 1958 as Esmeralda (BARTERED BRIDE). She married the bar. GLOSSOP. NG

Blech, Leo, b. Aachen, 21 Apr 1871; d. Berlin, 24 Aug 1958. German composer and conductor; studied at Berlin Hochschule für Musik and with HUMPERDINCK at Frankfurt. Resident cond., Aachen, 1893–9, and German T., Prague, 1899–1906. Later associated with Berlin, as cond. of Staats O. 1906–23 and its mus. dir.-gen. from 1913; art. dir., Deutsche (Städtische) O.; cond. Staats O. 1926–37 (retaining his post despite his Jewish origins), also Volks O., 1924. During World War II he cond. at Stockholm, returning to the Deutsche O., Berlin, 1949. Comp. several operas of which the one-act comedy *Versiegelt* (Hamburg 1908) was the most popular. JB

Blegen, Judith, b. Lexington, Ky, 27 Apr 1941. American soprano. She sang MANON at Santa Barbara while still a student at the Curtis Institute, Philadelphia. Engaged at Nuremberg 1966; she sang in PELLÉAS ET MÉLISANDE (Spoleto 1966) and as PAPAGENA (Salzburg 1967), also appearing in Vienna. US debuts: NY Met 1970, San Francisco 1972, Chicago 1973. Gifted with a beautiful lyric sop. voice and a charming stage presence, she has a repertory that incl. BLONDE, SUSANNA, ZERLINA, ROSINA, ADINA, JULIETTE, and SOPHIE. She sang Emily in HELP, HELP, THE GLOBOLINKS! (Santa Fe 1969). CG debut 1975 (DESPINA). EF

Bliss, (Sir) Arthur, b. London, 2 Aug 1891; d. London, 27 Mar 1975. English composer, Master of the Queen's Musick 1953 until his death. Wr. OLYMPIANS and *Tobias and the Angel* (1960), lib. Christopher Hassall, which was conceived as a TV opera, but later adapted for the theatre. EF

Blitzstein, Marc, b. Philadelphia, Pa., 2 Mar 1905; d. Martinique, 22 Jan 1964. American composer. Studied composition at Curtis Institute, Philadelphia, in Paris with Nadia Boulanger, and with SCHÖNBERG in Berlin. Becoming an ardent propagandist of left-wing causes, his first important work was CRADLE WILL ROCK. *No For An Answer* was wr. 1941. REGINA (1949), however, carried no overt political message. Blitzstein's tr. and adaptation of DREIGROSCHENOPER (Brandeis Univ. 1952, NY 1953) had a run of several years in an Off-Broadway theatre. He was working on an opera on Sacco and Vanzetti at the time of his death. EJ

Bloch, Ernest, b. Geneva, 24 July 1880; d. Portland, Oreg., 15 July 1959. Swiss, later American, composer. His one opera, *Macbeth,* 3 acts, lib. Edmond Fleg after SHAKESPEARE, comp. *c.* 1903, was prod. Paris, OC, 30 Nov 1910. Revived Geneva 1968–9; concert perf. London, RFH, 9 July 1975. LO

Blockx, Jan, b. Antwerp, 25 Jan 1851; d. Antwerp, 26 May 1912. Flemish composer, pupil of BENOÎT at Antwerp School of Music, of which he became dir. 1901. Of his seven operas, mostly to libs by the poet Nestor de Tière, *Herbergprinses* (Antwerp 1896 and, in Fr., as *Princesse d'Auberge*, Brussels 1898), *Thyl Uilenspiegel* (Brussels 1900), and *De Bruid der Zee* (Antwerp 1901; Fr. version, *La Fiancée de la Mer*, Brussels 1902) were the most successful. *De Bruid der Zee* was revived in Brussels in 1958. LO

Blodek, Vilém, b. Prague, 3 Oct 1834; d. Prague, 1 May 1874. Czech composer. Known chiefly for his comic opera IN THE WELL. *Zítek*, a historical-romantic opera, was left incomplete at his death. JT

Blomdahl, Karl-Birger, b. Växjö, 19 Oct 1916; d. Växjö, 17 June 1968. Swedish composer. Studied at Stockholm with Hilding Rosenberg and in Paris and Rome. ANIARA was a great success. A later opera, *Herr von Hauchen*, was also perf. in Stockholm (1965), where the comp. taught at the Royal Acad. of Music. EF

Blonde [Blondchen], sop., the maid in ENTFÜHRUNG AUS DEM SERAIL.

Bloomington, Ind., Indiana University Opera Theater. The world's largest school opera-producing organization, estab. 1948 and giving *c.* 32 perfs over 10 months of *c.* 8 works. Standard light and grand opera with many novelties; professional singers, supplemented by students. Premieres incl.: WEILL, *Down in the Valley* (1948); JUMPING FROG OF CALAVERAS COUNTY; Bernard Rogers, *The Veil* (1950); Norman Dello Joio, *The Ruby* (1955); Walter Kaufmann, *The Scarlet Letter* (1961) and *A Hoosier Tale* (1965); John C. Eaton, *Heracles* (1972). The Opera T. has also presented MOTHER OF US ALL (1973), WOZZECK (1974) and DOKTOR FAUST (28 Nov 1974). Art. dir. Wilfred C. Bain. EJ

Bluebeard's Castle *see* DUKE BLUEBEARD'S CASTLE

Bluthochzeit (*Blood Wedding*), opera, 2 acts, FORTNER, lib. Enrique Beck based on LORCA's *Bodas de Sangre*. Cologne 8 June 1957 for the opening of the new opera house. Another opera has been composed on the same theme by SZOKOLAY. LO

La Bohème, London, CG, 20 Oct 1974; produced COPLEY; designed Julia Trevelyan Oman. Veriano Luchetti as Rodolfo; Helena Döse as Mimi

Colour plate: Stage set by SANQUIRICO for ANNA BOLENA showing 'the Park of Windsor Castle'; produced T. Carcano, Milan, 26 Dec 1830

Boatswain's Mate, The, opera, 1 act, SMYTH, lib. comp. based on story by W(illiam) W(ymark) Jacobs. Perf. in Germany, 1914, prevented by outbreak of war. London, Shaftesbury T., 28 Jan 1916. Chars: Harry Benn (ten.) Mrs Waters (sop.) Ned Travers (bar.). Mrs Waters, landlady of The Beehive, rejects proposals of marriage from Harry, ex-boatswain. His friend, Ned, pretends to be a burglar so that he can play the hero and win Mrs Waters' favour. She captures Ned, and to teach Harry a lesson tells him she has shot the burglar. After the repentant Harry gives himself up, the matter is straightened out and Mrs Waters takes a fancy to Ned. PS

Boccaccio, Giovanni, b. Florence (?), 1313; d. Certaldo, 21 Dec 1375. Italian novelist and poet. His *Decameron* (*c.* 1350) has provided the source for a few operas: Rodolphe Kreutzer, *Imogène* (Paris 1796); HÉROLD, *Le Muletier* (Paris 1823), AUDRAN, *Gillette de Narbonne* (Paris 1882), and Carlo Chavez, *Panfilo and Lauretta* (NY 1957). LO

Boccaccio, operetta, 3 acts, SUPPÉ, lib. F. Zell (pseud. of Camillo Walzell) and GENÉE. Vienna, Carl T., 1 Feb 1879; revived Bregenz 1953 and Munich, Gärtnerplatz T., 1964. Based on life of BOCCACCIO. One of Suppé's most successful works. LO
See Lubbock

Bockelmann, Rudolf, b. Bodenteich, 2 Apr 1890; d. Dresden, 9 Oct 1958. German baritone. Successively engaged at Leipzig (debut in LOHENGRIN, 1921), Hamburg Staats O. (1926–32), Berlin Staats O. (1932–45). From 1928 regularly sang at Bayreuth; appeared also in London, Vienna, and Chicago. A Wagnerian singer *par excellence*, whose known Nazi sympathies put an end to his career after Germany's defeat in World War II. JB

Bodanzky, Artur, b. Vienna, 16 Dec 1877; d. NY, 23 Nov 1939. Austrian conductor; joined Vienna Imperial O. 1896 as violinist; became MAHLER's assistant 1902 and later chief cond.; cond. first perfs at CG, 1914, of PARSIFAL; chief Ger. cond., NY Met, 1915. JB

Boero, Felipe, b. Buenos Aires, 1 May 1884; d. Buenos Aires, 9 Aug 1958. Argentine composer. Studied Buenos Aires and Paris. Of his nine stage works (wr. 1913–38) six were premiered at the T. Colón. *Tucumán* (1918) was the first opera on a national subject sung in Sp. at the T. Colón; *Raquela* (1923) the first work to incorporate dances from the gaucho's regional folklore into an operatic score. His most popular and established masterpiece is *El Matrero* (*The Rogue*, 1929), based on Yamandú Rodríguez's symbolistic play. MK

Bohème, La (*The Bohemian Girl*), opera, 4 acts, PUCCINI, lib. ILLICA and GIACOSA after Henri Murger's novel, *Scènes de la Vie de Bohème*. Turin, T. Regio, 1 Feb 1896; Manchester (in Eng.) 22 Apr 1897; London, CG (in Eng.), 2 Oct 1897; (in It.) 1 July 1899; Los Angeles (in It.) 14 Oct 1897. Main chars: Mimi (sop.) Rodolfo (ten.) Musetta (sop.) Marcello (bar.) Schaunard (bar.) Colline (bass). Tragedy and comedy in the lives and loves of impoverished artists in Paris. Rodolfo falls in love with Mimi but abandons her for her own good on realizing that she is a consumptive. She returns to die in his arms. Puccini's fourth and best-loved opera. JB O★
See Kobbé

Bohemian Girl, The, opera, 3 acts, BALFE, lib. BUNN based on a ballet-pantomime by SAINT-GEORGES, 1839. London, DL, 27 Nov 1843; NY, 25 Nov 1844. The most successful Eng. opera of the early 19th c.; revived by BEECHAM (CG 1951). LO

PARCO NEL CASTELLO DI WINDSOR

nell'Opera Anna Bolena

Böhm, Karl, b. Graz, 28 Aug 1894. Austrian conductor. Studied law, then music at Graz and Vienna. Posts at Graz 1917, and Munich Staats O. 1921; became gen. mus. dir., Darmstadt, 1927–31. Hamburg 1931–4; Dresden 1934–43; Vienna 1943–5. After World War II held a similar post in Vienna but resigned, 1954, after a year. Has cond. at many of the world's great opera houses incl. CG, NY Met and for many years at Bayreuth and Salzburg Fests, where his WAGNER and MOZART interpretations have been notable. LO

Böhme, Kurt, b. Dresden, 5 May 1908. German bass, distinguished in WAGNER and R. STRAUSS. Debut 1930, Dresden, as Kaspar (FREISCHÜTZ). Resident Dresden O. to 1950, then Bavarian Staats O., Munich. CG debut 1936 with Dresden O. as Commendatore (DON GIOVANNI); returned 1956 as FASOLT and HAGEN. NY Met debut 1954. A singer of dark-hued force of char. and rock-firm vocal line. NG

Bohnen, Michael, b. Cologne, 2 May 1887; d. Berlin, 26 Apr 1965. German bass-baritone. Studied Cologne; debut 1910, Düsseldorf (FREISCHÜTZ). Principal engagements: Berlin Staats O. 1913–21; NY Met 1922–32 (debut 1923 in SCHILLING's *Mona Lisa*). Sang in first US perf. of JONNY SPIELT AUF. Also sang under BEECHAM at DL and at Bayreuth. Returned to Berlin 1932; *Intendant* at Berlin Städtische O. 1945–7. Also made films: ROSENKAVALIER (1920); ABRAHAM's *Victoria und ihr Husar* (1932). Had a big voice of extensive compass and was a convincing actor. LO

Boïeldieu, François Adrien, b. Rouen, 16 Dec 1775; d. Jarcy, 8 Oct 1834. French composer. Wrote *c.* 40 operas, sometimes in collaboration with AUBER, CHERUBINI, HÉROLD, and others. After some instruction from the organist of Rouen cathedral moved to Paris *c.* 1795; had his first real success with CALIFE DE BAGDAD. Went to St Petersburg 1803; wr. several operas there incl. *Aline Reine de Golconde* (1804) and *Télémaque* (1806). Returned to Paris 1811. His later operas incl. *Jean de Paris* (1812), *Le Petit Chaperon Rouge* (1818), and his masterpiece, DAME BLANCHE. LO

Boito, Arrigo [Enrico], b. Padua, 24 Feb 1842; d. Milan, 10 June 1918. Italian composer and man of letters. Son of an It. artist and a Polish countess. Studied Milan Cons. under Alberto Mazzucato. During the 1860s active as a critic and propagandist for the reform of It. opera and the regeneration of the country's instrumental tradition. For his fellow pupil FACCIO he wrote the lib. of *Amleto* (Genoa 1865) and comp. to his own text MEFISTOFELE which failed disastrously. Subsequent work as tr. and lib. appeared under the anagrammatic pseudonym, Tobia Gorrio, incl. the lib. of GIOCONDA, until the vindication of *Mefistofele*, 1875, brought its comp. international fame. As lib. he worked with VERDI on the revision of SIMONE BOCCANEGRA, and later wr. for him the libs of OTELLO and FALSTAFF. His own NERONE, the work of a lifetime, he brought to an end after four acts in 1916. Although *Mefistofele* is sometimes revived Boito's reputation today rests more on his literary than on his musical achievements, on the influence that he exerted on the artistic ideals of his time, and above all on the part he played in the final flowering of Verdi's genius. JB

Bolivar, opera, 3 acts and 10 scenes, MILHAUD, lib. Madeleine Milhaud and Jules Supervielle. Paris, O., 12 May 1950. Main chars: Manuela (sop.) Maria-Teresa (sop.) Precipitation (mezzo-sop.) Bolivar (bar.) Bovès (bass) Nicador (ten.). Wr. 1943, this historical drama is based on the life of Simon Bolivar, the early 19th-c. S. American patriot. EF

Bologna, Italy. A centre of opera since the early 17th c. T. Comunale inaugurated by GLUCK's *Il Trionfo di Clelia* (1763). Here MARIANI dir. the It. premiere of DON CARLOS (1867) and those of LOHENGRIN (1871) and TANNHÄUSER (1872), the first WAGNER operas to be given in Italy. Bologna has in the past prided itself on its receptiveness to new operatic ideas. It now has frequent visits from E. European cos such as those from Belgrade and Sofia. JB

Bolshoy Theatre *see* MOSCOW

Bomarzo, opera, 2 acts, GINASTERA, lib. (in Sp.) Manuel Mujica Láinez, based on his novel *Bomarzo*, set in 16th-c. Italy. Washington DC, Opera Society of Washington, 19 May 1967; NY CC 14 May 1968; Kiel 29 Nov 1970. Main chars: Pier Francesco Orsini (ten.) Silvio de Narni (bar.) Girolamo and Maerbale Orsini (bars) Gian Corrado Orsini (bass) Julia Farnese (sop.) Pantasilea (mezzo-sop.) Diana Orsini (contr.) Shepherd (child). Silvio de Narni, the Astrologer, gives Pier Francesco Orsini, Duke of Bomarzo, a potion which should secure him immortality. Instead, it is fatal poison. Except for the interludes separating each scene, *Bomarzo* stands closer to the style of BEATRIX CENCI than to that of the earlier DON RODRIGO. As in *Beatrix Cenci*'s ballet music, Ginastera revives Renaissance instrumental dance

Colour plate: The Teatro Amazones, Manaus, Brazil, designed by Bernardo Antonio Oliveira Braga and opened 31 Dec 1896. Built at the height of the rubber boom, no expense was spared to make it one of the most lavish opera houses in the world. Lured by huge fees, opera companies and famous singers and dancers made the 26-day journey up the Amazon to perform there. PATTI came from Paris to give a single performance.

forms for the erotic ballet, embodying the Duke's hallucinatory sexual fantasies, which caused the work to be called 'shocking' and 'topless opera'; the regime of Juan Carlos Onganía banned it from the T. Colón in 1967. Dramatically effective in this scene is the chorus, intoning 'love' in over 40 languages. The 'circular libretto' is an attempt to apply to opera the 'flashback' technique familiar in film and novel. *Bomarzo* is the first opera by Ginastera to display aleatory means; the fifth soliloquy is a particularly effective example of aleatory instrumental writing to match the dramatic intensity of recited verse. MK O

Bonci, Alessandro, b. Cesena, nr Bologna, 10 Feb 1870; d. Viserba, 10 Aug 1940. Italian tenor. Studied Rossini Cons., Pesaro; debut 1896 Parma, as FENTON (FALSTAFF). CG debut 1900. Sang frequently in USA, with Manhattan O. Co. at NY Met, 1908, and in Chicago, 1914. Had a lyric rather than a dramatic voice, excelling in the Italian repertory of the early 19th century. LO

Bonhomme, Jean, b. Ottawa, 14 Feb 1936. Canadian tenor. Originally studied law but in 1961 turned to singing; studied in Montreal with JOBIN and at the Royal Cons. O. School, Toronto. Debut 1964, Stratford Fest., Ontario, as Don BASILIO (NOZZE DI FIGARO). Sang RODOLFO with the COC in Toronto 1965; SW 1964, CG 1965. US debut 1971, Sante Fe; appearances in Paris, Budapest, many cities in N. America. A lyric ten. capable of great power and intensity. CM

Jean Bonhomme as Cavaradossi in TOSCA, London, CG, 21 Oct 1972; produced ZEFFIRELLI; scenery Renzo Mongiardino; costumes Marcel Escoffier

Bononcini, Giovanni, b. Modena, 18 July 1670; d. Vienna (?), 9 Aug 1747. Italian composer. Wr. *c.* 20 operas, several prod. in London as part of HANDEL's Royal Acad. of Music. He was in London 1720–32. LO

Bonynge, Richard, b. Epping, NSW, 29 Sept 1930. Australian conductor. Trained as a pianist; debut as cond. 1963, Vancouver (FAUST). CG debut 1964 (PURITANI), with his wife, SUTHERLAND, as Donna Elvira. Has cond. at Vienna, Hamburg, Florence; NY Met debut 1970 (NORMA). Other operas he cond. for Sutherland incl. GIULIO CESARE, SONNAMBULA, LUCIA DI LAMMERMOOR, FILLE DU RÉGIMENT, SEMIRAMIDE, TRAVIATA, and MASSENET's *Esclarmonde*, revived at San Francisco, 1974. Apptd mus. dir. Australian O., 1975. EF

Boquet, Louis René, b. Paris, 1717; d. Paris, 7 Dec 1814. Costume designer. Worked with BOUCHER at Paris O. Designed costumes and scenery for RAMEAU's *Fêtes de l'Hymen* (1762), DARDANUS, and CASTOR ET POLLUX. LO

Bordeaux, France. Opera was heard there in the 18th c.; SERVANDONY was designing decor for RAMEAU's operas there 1745. The fine Grand Théâtre, still standing, was built 1780 (architect, Victor Louis). Since World War II its importance has increased, under directors MARCOUX, 1948–51 and Roger Lalande, from 1952. The present dir. is Gerhard Boireau. First perf. of PETER GRIMES in Fr. was given there 1954. During recent years it has joined with Toulouse in sharing productions. LO

Bordoni, Faustina, b. Venice, 1700; d. Venice, 4 Nov 1781. Italian soprano. Member of Venetian nobility, she studied with Michelangelo Gasparini, and was a protégée of Benedetto Marcello. Sensational debut in Carlo Francesco Pollarolo's *Ariodante* (Venice 1716). HANDEL heard her at the Vienna Court T. 1724 and engaged her for London; debut 5 May 1726 in ALESSANDRO. Her bitter rivalry with CUZZONI culminated in a famous perf. of BONONCINI's *Astianatte* which ended with the divas pulling each other's hair. In 1730 she m. HASSE; moved to Dresden 1731, where she appeared until 1763, then moved to Vienna, finally retiring to Venice in 1775. Her voice ranged from B flat to G below high C, and she was noted for her beauty, her singing, and her acting. PS

Kim Borg as DON GIOVANNI at Glyndebourne, 1956

Borg, Kim, b. Helsinki, 7 Aug 1919. Finnish bass. Studied at the Sibelius Acad., Helsinki; debut 1951, Århus, Denmark. Has sung at Stockholm, Glyndebourne (1956), NY Met (1959), Budapest, Moscow, Salzburg, and Hamburg. A versatile singer, his roles incl. DON GIOVANNI, ALMAVIVA (NOZZE DI FIGARO), Don ALFONSO, PIZARRO, MÉPHISTOPHÉLÈS, KING MARK, BORIS GODUNOV, PIMEN, Rangoni (*Boris Godunov*), PHILIPPE and Schigolch (LULU). He took part in the first perf. of VISITATION. EF

Borgatti, Giuseppe, b. Cento, 17 Mar 1871; d. Reno, Lago Maggiore, 18 Oct 1950. Italian tenor. Studied Bologna; debut 1892 Castelfranco Venuto (GOUNOD's FAUST). After being invited by TOSCANINI to sing SIEGFRIED at Sc. went on to become one of the leading It. Wagnerian singers of his time, perf. widely in Europe and S. America. LO

Borgioli, Dino, b. Florence, 15 Feb 1891; d. Florence, 12 Sept 1960. Italian tenor. Studied Florence. Debut 1917, Milan, as Fernando (FAVORITE). CG debut 1925 (EDGARDO and DUCA DI MANTUA); returned there regularly until 1939. US debut Chicago 1928. Sang CAVARADOSSI to MUZIO's TOSCA at San Francisco debut 1932; NY Met 1934–5. Glyndebourne as OTTAVIO (1937–9) and Ernesto in DON PASQUALE (1938). Producer for New London O. Co. at Cambridge T. after World War II. One of the most elegant, refined tens of the interwar years, particularly renowned in the music of DONIZETTI, BELLINI, and for his ALFREDO. AB

Bori, Lucrezia [Lucrecia Borja y Gonsalez de Riancho], b. Valencia, 24 Dec 1887; d. NY, 14 May 1960. Spanish soprano. Studied Milan; debut 1908, T. Costanzi, Rome (MICAËLA). Engaged by Sc., was OCTAVIAN in It. premiere of ROSENKAVALIER under SERAFIN. NY Met debut 1912 (MANON). In 1915 a throat operation interrupted her career, which was resumed at Monte Carlo 1919. Returned to the Met 1921, remaining there until retirement 1936. A distinguished artist esp. in Fr. and It. roles, her beauty and acting matching her singing. LO

Boris Godunov, opera, prologue and 4 acts, MUSORGSKY, lib. comp. after PUSHKIN and Nikolay Mikhaylovich Karamzin. Musorgsky's 1st version 1868–9: Leningrad 16 Feb 1928; London, SW, 30 Sept 1935; Musorgsky's 2nd version 1871–2: St Petersburg, Mariinsky T., 17 Feb 1873 (excerpts), Mariinsky T., 8 Feb 1874 (complete); London, CG, 19 May 1948; RIMSKY-KORSAKOV's 1st revised version 1896: St Petersburg Cons., 10 Dec 1896; Rimsky-Korsakov's 2nd revised version 1906–8: Paris, O., 19 May 1908; Moscow, Bolshoy, 17 Oct 1908; NY Met 19 Mar 1913; London, DL, 24 June 1913. Main chars: Boris Godunov (bass) Fyodor (mezzo-sop.) Prince Vasily Shuysky (ten.) Pimen (bass.) the Pretender (at first Grigory, then Dmitry) (ten.) Marina Mnishek (mezzo-sop.) Varlaam (bass) the Hostess (mezzo-sop.) Simpleton (ten.). An apathetic crowd is made to plead with Boris to accept the crown; he is crowned. Pimen, writing in his chronicle, tells Grigory that the Tsarevich Dmitry would have been his age, had he not been murdered by Boris. Grigory resolves to pose as Dmitry; he meets Varlaam and Misail at an inn on the Lithuanian border, where guards come to arrest him; but he escapes. Boris is haunted by feelings of guilt; Shuysky tells him that the Pretender is gaining support in Poland. The Pretender, in Poland, falls in love with Marina Mnishek; she makes it clear that she wishes to be Empress of Russia. Shuysky describes Boris's mental torment to the council of Boyars; Boris enters, collapses, and dies. The Pretender invades Russia and attracts popular support at the forest at Kromy; the Simpleton reflects on the disaster which is to befall Russia. Musorgsky's first version of the opera had only seven scenes; in the second version the original scene 6 (outside St Basil's) was omitted, but the two scenes comprising the Polish Act (Act 3) and the Kromy scene (Act 4 scene 2) were added. Rimsky-Korsakov, in his first revision, tampered not only with Musorgsky's harmony and orchestration but also with the dramatic content: he made drastic cuts, and reversed the order of the last two

scenes, so that the opera ended with Boris's death. His second revision, restoring the cuts but retaining the reversal of the Act 4 scenes, forms the basis of most perfs today. GN O★
See Kobbé

Borkh, Inge, b. Mannheim, 26 May 1917. German soprano. Began career as actress. Studied singing Vienna and Milan. Operatic debut 1940, Lucerne, as Czipra (Zigeunerbaron). Magda (Consul) at Basel (1952) caused a sensation. Other debuts: San Francisco 1953 (Elektra); RFH, London, 1955 (Elektra); NY Met 1958 (Salome); CG 1959 (Salome). In first perf. at CG (1967) of Frau ohne Schatten, as Dyer's Wife. Other leading roles incl. Turandot and Lady Macbeth. Her voice was bright and incisive, her acting sustained and highly dramatic. AB

Borodin, Aleksandr Porfiryevich, b. St Petersburg, 12 Nov 1833; d. St Petersburg, 27 Feb 1887. Russian composer. Like all the members of the so-called *moguchaya kuchka*, or Mighty Handful, Borodin acquired his musical education more through experience than formal tuition, and very much under the influence of Mily Alekseyevich Balakirev (1837–1910). His first stage work was the opera farce in 5 scenes, *The Bogatyrs* (1867), to a lib. by Viktor Krylov and largely based on themes from Hérold, Meyerbeer, Offenbach, Rossini, Serov, Verdi, and others. His next opera, *Tsar's Bride*, did not progress beyond sketches wr. 1867–8, and the collective Mlada, for which he wrote the fourth act in 1872, was never perf. He worked on his masterpiece, Prince Igor, 1869–70 and 1874–87, but it was unfinished at his death and was completed and partly orchestrated by Rimsky-Korsakov and Aleksandr Glazunov (1865–1936). GN

Boston, Mass. An important centre for opera in the United States. The first opera staged there (concert perfs had hitherto been the rule) was *The Farmer*, a ballad opera, 1794. Operatic visitors from the 1850s onward incl. Giulia Grisi, and Mario, Patti, Sontag, Alboni, the Mapleson Co. (from 1878), and Grau's French Co. (from 1879).

Boston Opera Company. Organized 1908 with a new opera house which opened Nov 1909. Leading singers were engaged, often by arrangement with the NY Met, and new works by Debussy, Raoul Laparra, Rakhmaninov, Bizet, Aubert, Février, and Converse were staged. About 90 perfs were given each season. A tour to Paris (Apr–June 1913) proved frustrating and in May 1915 the co. filed for bankruptcy. Max Rabinoff acquired the assets and toured for two years as the Boston National O. Co. before capitulating in 1917. After World War I the Met visited Boston, followed by brilliant seasons of the Chicago O. Co. during the 1920s. The opera house was demolished in 1958. For many years the Met has given 10–15 perfs annually, usually of standard works, at present in the John B. Hines Memorial Auditorium. These augment resident efforts.

Boris Godunov. Sketch of stage setting by Konstantin Yuon for Dyagilev's Russian Opera tour in Paris, 1913

In the early 1930s Boris Goldowsky formed the **New England Opera Theater** which, making Boston its headquarters, toured extensively with a repertory incl. works by Mozart and Vaughan Williams. This co. was succeeded by the Opera Society of Boston in 1958.

Opera Society of Boston. Established 1958. About 15 perfs each year, often of works done for the first time in the USA, e.g. Mathis der Maler; Intolleranza 1960; Moses und Aron; Troyens; Benvenuto Cellini; and Roger Sessions's Montezuma. Founder and dir., Sarah Caldwell (the first woman to conduct at NY Met., in Jan 1976). EJ
See Eaton, *The Boston Opera Company 1909–1915* (New York 1965)

Boucher, François, b. Paris, 23 Sept 1703; d. Paris, 30 May 1770. French painter and designer. Worked for Pompadour's private theatre, also designed scenery and costumes for Indes Galantes. When Jean Monnet took over the OC in the Foire St Laurent (1743) Boucher contributed to the decor of this, and from 1752 designed for Monnet. Also designed for the O. after Servandony left (1764). LO

Bouffes Parisiens *see* PARIS

Bouffons, Guerre des *see* PARIS

Boughton, Rutland, b. Aylesbury, 23 Jan 1878; d. London, 24 Jan 1960. English composer. In 1914 went to live at Glastonbury, where he sought to found a kind of Eng. Bayreuth, with perfs of DIDO AND AENEAS, scenes from WAGNER, IPHIGÉNIE EN TAURIDE, and his own operas IMMORTAL HOUR, *Alkestis* (1922), and his 'Arthurian' trilogy, *The Birth of Arthur* and *The Round Table* (1920, though both wr. earlier), and *The Queen of Cornwall* (1924). LO

Bouilly, Jean Nicolas, b. La Coudraye, Indre-et-Loire, 23 Jan 1763; d. Paris, 14 Apr 1842. French librettist. His text for GAVEAUX's *Léonore* was the basis of operas by PAER (LÉONORE, OU L'AMORE CONJUGAL, Dresden 1804), G. S. MAYR (*L'Amore Conjugale*, Padua 1805), and FIDELIO. Also wr. libs for AUBER, BOÏELDIEU, CHERUBINI (DEUX JOURNÉES), MÉHUL, and others. LO

Boulevard Solitude, opera, 1 act (7 scenes), HENZE, lib. comp. and Grete Weil. Hanover 17 Feb 1952; London, SW (New O. Co.), 25 June 1962; Santa Fe 2 Aug 1967. Main chars: Manon (sop.); Armand des Grieux (ten.) Lescaut (bar.) Lilaque *père* (ten.) Lilaque *fils* (bar.). The plot is a version in modern dress, of MANON LESCAUT, set in Paris during the latter part of the 1940s. EF

Bourgeois Gentilhomme, Le (*The Bourgeois as Gentleman*), *comédie-ballet*, MOLIÈRE, music LULLY. Château de Chambord 14 Oct 1670. It satirized the *nouveau riche* M. Jourdain, aping the manners of the aristocracy, whose foolishness in turn was exposed, and ridiculed the current Orientalist craze. Though more a play with music than an opera there were songs as well as dances. Molière's text was later embodied in ARIADNE AUF NAXOS. LO ○

Bowman, James, b. Oxford, 6 Nov 1941. English counter-tenor of exceptional richness of timbre and vigour of projection. Boy chorister, Ely Cathedral; trained with Michael Howard. Debut 1967 with EOG, Aldeburgh Fest., as Oberon (MIDSUMMER NIGHT'S DREAM); toured this to San Francisco (US debut), Montreal, Paris, Brussels. Since appeared with major success in HANDEL operas, incl. SEMELE (SW debut 1970), FAIRY QUEEN, CALISTO (as Endymion; Glyndebourne 1970), INCORONAZIONE DI POPPEA (Nederlandse O. 1971). CG debut 1972, creating Priest-Confessor/God the Father (Maxwell DAVIES's *Taverner*). Much-admired concert soloist and member of Early Music Consort. NG

Braham [Abraham] John, b. London, 20 Mar 1777; d. London, 17 Feb 1856. English tenor, later baritone, and composer. Studied with his uncle Myer Lyons, known as Leoni; concert debut CG aged 10. After teaching piano for several years reappeared as a singer at Bath 1794. At DL 1796, with the Italian O. 1796–7,

James Bowman as Endymion in CALISTO, Glyndebourne, 23 May 1974; produced Patrick Lobby; designed John Berry

and sang at Sc. 1798–9. London's first MAX and created Huon (OBERON). Later became a bar.; was a famous GUILLAUME TELL and DON GIOVANNI; toured the USA 1840–2. His last appearance was in London in concert 1852. In his last years he became a canon at Canterbury and changed his name to Meadows. PS

Braithwaite, Warwick, b. Dunedin, 9 Jan 1898; d. London, 18 Jan 1971. New Zealand conductor. Studied London, RAM. Cond. of O'Mara O. Co. 1919; joined BNOC 1922. His main work was with SW 1933–9 and after 1960. He was musical director of the WNO, 1956–60. LO

Brambilla, Marietta, b. Cassano d'Adda, 6 June 1807; d. Milan, 6 Nov 1875. Italian contralto. One of the most important of the 19th c., she created the roles of Maffeo Orsini (LUCREZIA BORGIA) and Pierrotto (LINDA DI CHAMOUNIX). Studied Milan Cons.; stage debut 1827, King's T., London, as Arsace (SEMIRAMIDE). Her four sisters were also singers: Annetta, Laura, and more importantly, Giuseppina (1819–1903), a contr. at Sc. 1841–57, and Teresa (1813–95), who created GILDA. Their niece, also Teresa (1845–1921) m. PONCHIELLI, and created the role of Lucia in his *I Promessi Sposi* (1872). There were also five Milan Brambilla sisters, daughters of the comic-opera comp., Paolo Brambilla (1786–1838), the most celebrated of them Erminia and the mezzo-sop., Amalia (d. 1880). The latter was the wife of the ten. Giovanni Battista Verger, and mother of the bar. Napoleone Verger. PS

Brangäne, mezzo-sop., Isolde's attendant in TRISTAN UND ISOLDE

Brannigan, Owen, b. Annitsford, nr Newcastle, 10 Mar 1908; d. Annitsford, 10 May 1973. English bass. Studied at Guildhall School of Music, London. Debut 1943 with SW on tour at Newcastle (SARASTRO); sang regularly with that co. 1944–9, 1952–8. Also appeared with the EOG and at Glyndebourne. Created Swallow (PETER GRIMES), Collatinus (RAPE OF LUCRETIA), Noye (BRITTEN's *Noyes Fludde*), 1958, Bottom (MIDSUMMER NIGHT'S DREAM), Dr Hasselbacher (OUR MAN IN HAVANA). Also sang a wide range of *buffo* parts. AB

Branzell, Karin, b. Stockholm, 24 Sept 1891; d. California, 15 Dec 1974. Swedish mezzo-soprano. Debut 1912, Stockholm (d'ALBERT's *Izeyl*), where she appeared for the next decade. Sang the Nurse at the first Berlin perf. of FRAU OHNE SCHATTEN (1920). She was then engaged at the NY Met (1924–44), Bayreuth (1930–1), and CG (1935–8). Though her powerful voice and wide range were particularly effective in Wagnerian roles – FRICKA and Waltraute (RING DES NIBELUNGEN), BRANGÄNE, ORTRUD, and MAGDALENA – she also sang AZUCENA, AMNERIS, Konchakovna (PRINCE IGOR), DALILA, and Herodias (SALOME). EF

Bratislava [Pressburg], Czechoslovakia. It. opera was given from 1791 and a theatre completed 1886 (renovated 1970–2), in which opera was presented in Ger. and Hungarian. The first perf. of an opera in Slovak (BARTERED BRIDE, translated) was given by the newly founded Slovak NT, 1919. NEDBAL (1923–30) and his nephew Karel Nedbal (1930–8) helped to estab. the co. The partition of Czechoslovakia and the departure of the Czech members in 1939 had a serious effect on standards, but the break was helpful in bringing about a fully Slovak co., a movement to which the perfs of native Slovak operas by SUCHOŇ and CIKKER gave further impetus. The Nová scéna (New Scene) provides a second stage for operetta and musicals. JT

Braun, Victor, b. Windsor, Ontario, 4 Aug 1935. Canadian baritone. After singing with the COC, engaged at Frankfurt 1963. Sang at San Francisco 1968; CG debut 1969 in SEARLE's HAMLET, which he had previously sung at Toronto. Has appeared at Sc., Vienna, Salzburg, and Munich. His repertory incl. DON GIOVANNI, ALMAVIVA (NOZZE DI FIGARO), GUGLIELMO, DI LUNA, GERMONT, Posa (DON CARLOS), EUGENE ONEGIN, ESCAMILLO, and MARCELLO. EF

Braunfels, Walter, b. Frankfurt, 19 Dec 1882; d. Cologne, 19 Mar 1954. German composer. Of his eight operas the most successful was *Don Gil von der Grünen Hosen*, based on Tirso da Molina (Vienna 1924). Among the others are *Prinzessin Brambilla*, based on HOFFMANN (his first, 1909); *Till Eulenspiegel* (Stuttgart 1913), and *Die Vögel*, based on Aristophanes (Munich 1920). LO

Brazil. Indigenous Brazilian opera in its early days was greatly boosted when Spanish-born José Zapata y Amat est. in Rio de Janeiro the Imperial Academia de Música e Ópera Nacional (1857–65) which trained Brazilian singers to perf. European repertory works in Portuguese and encouraged the comp. of native operas. Financially supported by Dom Pedro II, emperor of Brazil 1841–89, the Academia realized its goals in the premiere, 14 Dec 1860, of the 2-act comic opera, *A Noite de São João* by Elías Álvares Lôbo (1834–1901), lib. novelist José M. de Alençar (1829–77). This was the first Brazilian opera on a native subject sung in Portuguese by Brazilian singers, prod. T. Lírico Fluminense, the 1860 name for the reconstructed Real T. de São João (1813–24), and cond. GOMES. This prod. preceded by one year the premiere of Gomes's first stage work and his only opera with a Portuguese lib., 3-act *A Noite no Castelo*.

The aims of the Academia were revived in the late 19th c. by Leopoldo Miguez (1850–1902), founder of O. Centro Artístico (1893) and the comp. of two Wagnerian-style dramatic poems based on libs by Henrique M. Coelho Neto (1864–1934), the 3-act *Os Saldunes* (1896), and 2-act *Pelo Amor!* (1897). Other Brazilian comps of Miguez's generation who wrote operas in European styles were Manuel Joaquim de Macedo (1847–1925), comp. of the unperf. but pub. 4-act *Tiradentes*; and Henrique Oswald (1854–1931), protégé of Dom Pedro II and comp. of three unperf. It.-style operas, the 3-act *Croce d'Oro*, 1-act comic *Il Neo* (1900), and 2-act *Le Fate* (1902).

At the same time, other comps continued the trend toward literary nationalism started by Gomes in GUARANY by setting Brazilian literary subjects to music. A staunch defender of perfs in native Portuguese, Alberto Nepomuceno (1864–1920) used Afro-Brazilian rhythms in the overture of his unfinished lyric comedy *O Garatuja* (1904). Also based on a native subject is the 1-act *Moema* (1894) by Delgado de Carvalho (1872–1921), lib. comp. and Assís Pacheco (1865–1937), himself the comp.-lib. of four operas, 1-act *Jací*, 1-act *Dor!* (1900), 1-act *Moema*, and *Cléopatra*.

Because of the terms of theatre managers' contracts, many Brazilian operas were perf. in Rio up to about 1930. However, the 20th-c. comps who developed a distinctly Brazilian symphonic and chamber music were never able to match the great advance of native opera that culminated in Gomes's European success. The eight operas by VILLA-LOBOS are probably the least known among his comps. He was the least successful of three nationalist comps to set libs based on José Pereira de Graça Aranha's (1868–1931) legendary folk hero Pedro de Urdemales or Malazarte, with his 3-act, unperf. *Malazarte* (comp. 1921). The others were Oscar Lorenzo Fernândez (1897–1948) with his 4-act *Malazarte* (Rio de Janeiro 1941), from which the popular symphonic *Betugue* was excerpted and M. Camargo Guarnieri (b. 1907) with the 1-act *Pedro Malazarte* (Rio de Janeiro 1952, 1959), lib. Mario de Andrade (1893–1945). Other 20th-c. Brazilian opera comps incl. the prolific Francisco Mignone (b. 1897), a master of chamber song; the best known of his three operas is the 3-act *O Contratador de Diamantes* (comp. 1921), lib. Gerolamo Bottoni based on a play by Alfonso Arinos (Rio de Janeiro 1924), from which the *Congada* from Act II is a popular symphonic excerpt; Eleazar de Carvalho (b. 1912), comp. of the 2-act *A Discoberta do Brasil* (comp. *c.* 1938); José de Lima Siqueira (b. 1907), comp. of two recent scores: *A Compadecida*, lib. Ariano Suassuna (Rio de Janeiro 1961), and the 2-act *Gimba* (1960), lib. Gianfrancesco Guarnieri; Claudio Santoro (b. 1919), comp. of the puppet opera *Zé Brasil* (1949); and Edino Krieger (b. 1928), whose stage oratorio *Natividade do Rio* (1965), lib. Luiz Paiva de Castro, was commissioned for the city's quadricentennial celebrations.

Experimental works incl. the published 1-act chamber opera *Contato* (comp. 1966–8) by Jorge Antunes (b. 1942), which combines conventional means with radio receptor, theremin and generator; and several integrated-art works by the same comp., such as *Ambiente I* (1965) and *Cromoplastofonia II* (1966) and *III* (1968), that exploit the five senses (hearing, sight, touch, smell, and taste). MK

See Corrêa de Azevedo, *Relação das Óperas de Autores Brasileiros* (Rio de Janeiro 1938); Béhague, *The Beginnings of Musical Nationalism in Brazil* (Detroit 1971); Chase, *Introducción a la Música Americana Contemporánea* (Buenos Aires 1958); de Andrade, *Francisco Manuel da Silva e seu Tempo*, 2 vols (Rio de Janeiro 1967); *Composers of the Americas*, vols 3, 4, 7, 9, 13 and 16 (Washington, D.C. 1955–)

Brecht, Bertolt, b. Augsburg, 10 Feb 1898; d. Berlin 15 Aug 1956. German playwright and satirist, preaching against the false values of capitalism and the doctrines of Nazi Germany. Found a sympathetic collaborator in WEILL (DREIGROSCHENOPER, *Der Jasager* (1930), and AUFSTIEG UND FALL DER STADT MAHAGONNY. More recently DESSAU has set VERURTEILUNG DES LUKULLUS, and *Puntila* (Berlin 1966). LO

Brecknock, John, b. Long Eaton, Derbyshire, 29 Nov 1937. English tenor. Studied Birmingham School of Music; engaged at SW 1966. Sang for Glyndebourne Touring O. 1971 and in Canada 1973; CG debut 1974 FENTON (FALSTAFF). A leading ten. with the ENO, he has a lyric, flexible voice whose brilliant upper register enables him to sing ALMAVIVA (BARBIERE DI SIVIGLIA) and COMTE ORY with particular success. A stylish interpreter of MOZART, he also sings ALFREDO, Paris (BELLE HÉLÈNE),

Camille (LUSTIGE WITWE), and Anatol (WAR AND PEACE). He created the title role of Gordon Crosse's *Story of Vasco* (London, Col., 1974). EF

Bregenz, Austria. For *c.* 20 years a summer Fest. has been held there in the open air on Lake Bregenz, members of Vienna Staats O. perf. operettas, MOZART, and lightweight 18th- and early 19th-c. operas. LO

Bremen, W. Germany, one of the many Ger. cities that serve as a proving ground for young artists. Past mus. dirs have incl. A. NEUMANN (1882–5) and GURLITT (1914–27). SEIDL was there as cond. 1883–5. Present opera house dates from 1950, replacing one bombed during World War II. LO

Brescia, Italy. T. degli Erranti built 1664; an opera perf. there 1688 (Marc Antonio Ziani's *Tullo Ostilio*). Alterations were made during 18th c.; it became the T. Nuovo. Renamed T. Nazionale 1797 and, after further modifications, the present T. Grande 1810, opening with G. S. MAYR's *Ifigenia in Aulide*. Its dirs have incl. FACCIO, TOSCANINI, CAMPANINI, and (dir. his own operas) MASCAGNI. The revised 3-act version of MADAMA BUTTERFLY was played here, 28 May 1904. LO

Bretón, Tomás, b. Salamanca, 29 Dec 1850; d. Madrid, 2 Dec 1923. Spanish composer. Throughout his life championed the cause of true Sp. music which he believed had been stifled by It. influence ever since the time of FARINELLI. Of his half-dozen operas *Los Amantes de Teruel* (1889), *Garín* (1892), and *La Dolores* (1895) won him glory in Spain during his lifetime and some recognition abroad as far as Milan, Prague, Vienna, and S. America. Of his *zarzuelas* VERBENA DE LA PALOMA achieved legendary success. He became Professor of Composition at the Madrid Cons.; taught Pablo Casals. FGB

Bréval, Lucienne [Berthe Agnes Lisette Schilling], b. Berlin, 4 Nov 1869; d. Neuilly, 15 Aug 1935. Swiss, naturalized French, soprano, educated Geneva. Debut 1892, Paris, as Selika (AFRICAINE). Created many roles, e.g. GRISÉLIDIS, SALAMMBÔ, and PÉNÉLOPE; was a noted WAGNER singer and an outstanding CARMEN. A vigorous singer and powerful personality, she dominated the Paris O. for 30 years. LO

Brilioth, Helge, b. Lund, 7 May 1951. Swedish tenor associated with WAGNER roles. Studied Salzburg Mozarteum and Santa Cecilia Acad., Rome. Joined Stockholm Royal O. 1959 as bar., changed to ten. from 1965. Ten. debut Stockholm (Don JOSÉ); progressed via the title role in VERDI's OTELLO to WAGNER. Debuts: Bayreuth Fest. 1969 (SIEGMUND); Salzburg Easter Fest. 1970 (SIEGFRIED); CG 1970 (Siegmund); NY Met 1972 as Tristan (TRISTAN UND ISOLDE). A singer of firm vocal line and forthright dramatic character. NG

brindisi (It., from *fare un brindisi*, 'to drink a toast'). Drinking song in It. opera. Famous examples are in LUCREZIA BORGIA, CAVALLERIA RUSTICANA, MACBETH, TRAVIATA, VERDI's OTELLO. JB

Bristow, George Frederick, b. Brooklyn, NY, 19 Dec 1825; d. NY, 13 Dec 1898. American composer. His 'Grand Romantic Opera', RIP VAN WINKLE, was the first by an American comp. on an American subject. A second opera, *Columbus*, was not completed. EJ

British National Opera Company. Formed from members of BEECHAM's opera co. 1922. Dir. successively by PITT and F. AUSTIN (from 1924), it perf. an international repertoire in CG and in the provinces. Important services to Eng. opera incl. the premieres of PERFECT FOOL and Alexander Mackenzie's *The Eve of St John* (1924), and perfs 1924 of HUGH THE DROVER and BOUGHTON's *Alkestis*. The co. was dissolved 1929. JB

Britten, (Edward) Benjamin, b. Lowestoft, 22 Nov 1913. Studied with Frank Bridge, John Ireland, and Arthur Benjamin. Wr. instrumental works and film scores before embarking seriously on opera. First stage work was *Paul Bunyan* (1941, revised 1974), wr. while

Benjamin Britten's *The Golden Vanity*, produced and designed GRAHAM; Vienna Boys' Choir, Aldeburgh Fest., 3 June 1967

he was in the USA. PETER GRIMES brought him to immediate prominence as a major comp. Grimes was the first of Britten's 'outsider' heroes, for whom his succeeding operas also show such sympathy. His next large-scale opera was BILLY BUDD. In between came two chamber operas, RAPE OF LUCRETIA and ALBERT HERRING, both wr. for the newly formed EOG. GLORIANA, wr. for Queen Elizabeth II's Coronation, was again a large-scale work, poorly received at first but since vindicated for its picturesque invention and acute characterization. TURN OF THE SCREW treats of innocence corrupted in a score that is thematically integrated to catch the eerieness of the original. Likewise, MIDSUMMER NIGHT'S DREAM catches the mystery and fascination of the play. Britten then turned to the original form of Church Parable in three works inspired by medieval chant and Japanese Noh plays, CURLEW RIVER, BURNING FIERY FURNACE, and PRODIGAL SON, each seeking freedom from the conventions of the stage, and employing highly stylized movement. OWEN WINGRAVE tackled the problems of writing for TV and was later transferred successfully to the stage. DEATH IN VENICE, a score of great ingenuity and economy, converted Thomas Mann's novella into a convincing dramatic form, and showed the comp. developing still further his style of thematic cross-reference. All these works demonstrate the rare gift for theatrical timing combined with music both apt and approachable while entirely avoiding the merely facile. Three works for children, LET'S MAKE AN OPERA (1949), *Noyes Fludde* (1958), and *The Golden Vanity* (1967) have shown his sympathy in writing for children to act. His rewriting of BEGGAR'S OPERA and his realization of DIDO AND AENEAS (1951) are further evidence of the range of his genius. Founded the Aldeburgh Fest. 1948 with PEARS, for whom he has wr. many major roles in his operas. AB

Brno [Brünn], Czechoslovakia. Opera was first perf. in the Reduta T. (built 1600–5), used now for operetta. Regular operatic perfs took place in Ger. from 1882 in the newly built T. on the Ramparts, and in Czech from 1884 in a less opulent renovated building in Veveří Street (where the premiere of JENŮFA took place). With Czech independence in 1918 the German T. became the seat of the Brno NT and a fine tradition, particularly in JANÁČEK, was built by V. NEUMANN, CHALABALA, and SACHS. After World War II, the Veveří T., which had been bombed, was demolished. The Janáček T., opened 1965, became the chief opera theatre; the old German T. was renamed the Mahen T. and is used for plays. Chief cond. JÍLEK. JT

Brod, Max, b. Prague, 27 May 1884; d. Tel Aviv, 20 Dec 1968. German writer. His favourable review of the Prague JENŮFA (1916) encouraged JANÁČEK to ask him to tr. the work into Ger. This initiated a fruitful friendship during which Brod tr. all Janáček's mature operas except MR BROUČEK'S EXCURSIONS. He was more than a tr.: his German versions often incorporate revisions of the text (e.g. in CUNNING LITTLE VIXEN, 1924) which did not always win Janáček's approval. He contributed to and tr. SCHWANDA THE BAGPIPER and tr. Czech operas by NOVÁK, FOERSTER, and KŘIČKA into Ger. His writings on Czech music incl. the first book on Janáček. JT

Bronze Horse, The *see* CHEVAL DE BRONZE

Brook, Peter, b. London, 21 Mar 1925. English producer. Dir. of prods, CG, 1947–50; prod. BORIS GODUNOV, BOHÈME, NOZZE DI FIGARO, the first perf. of OLYMPIANS and a controversial prod. (1947), with decor by Salvador Dali, of SALOME. At the NY Met, he has dir. GOUNOD'S FAUST (1953) and EUGENE ONEGIN (1958). EF

Broschi, Carlo *see* FARINELLI

Brouček's Excursions *see* MR BROUČEK'S EXCURSIONS

Brouwenstijn, Gré, b. Den Helder, 25 Aug 1915. Dutch soprano. Studied Amsterdam; debut there 1947 (TOSCA), then sang with Nederlandse O. for five seasons. London debut 1951, CG (AIDA) and sang there regularly until 1962, incl. fine perfs as VERDI'S DESDEMONA (1955) and Elisabeth (DON CARLOS, 1958). Bayreuth debut 1954 (ELISABETH) and sang there in two subsequent years. Also appeared at Glyndebourne (LEONORE, 1955), Chicago, San Francisco, Buenos Aires, and Vienna. An intelligent and warm soprano. AB

Browne, Sandra, b. Point Fortin, Trinidad, 27 July 1947. Trinidadian mezzo-soprano. Studied NY. British operatic debut 1972 with the WNO as Ismene (NABUCCO). Sang Man Friday in OFFENBACH'S *Robinson Crusoe* at the Camden Fest. 1973 and POPPEA with Kent O. 1974. Has appeared with the ENO as ROSINA, OCTAVIAN, and CARMEN. Sang DORABELLA with the WNO 1975. EF

Brownlee, John, b. Geelong, 7 Jan 1900: d. NY, 10 Jan 1969. Australian baritone. A protégé of MELBA, he sang at her CG farewell perf. (1926). Engaged at the Paris O. 1927–36, he sang in MASSENET's *Esclarmonde*, HÉRODIADE, THAÏS, GUILLAUME TELL, ROMÉO ET JULIETTE, and PELLÉAS ET MÉLISANDE. Sang at CG 1930–6 and at Glyndebourne 1935–9, where he was much admired as DON GIOVANNI, ALMAVIVA (NOZZE DI FIGARO), and Don ALFONSO. A member of the co. at the NY Met 1937–57, his vast repertory ranged from WAGNER and VERDI to R. STRAUSS and PUCCINI. Became head of the Manhattan School of Music 1957. EF

Bruch, Max, b. Cologne, 6 Jan 1838; d. Friedenau, nr Berlin, 2 Oct 1920. German composer. Wr. three operas: *Scherz, List und Rache*, lib. GOETHE (Cologne 1858); *Loreley*, lib. Emmanuel Geibel (Mannheim 1863); *Hermione*, lib. E. Hopffer based on SHAKESPEARE's *The Winter's Tale* (Berlin 1872). LO

Brückner, Max, b. 1855; d. 1912. German scenographer. Worked with his brother and father, who was scenographer at Coburg-Gotha. Designed scenery for Berlin, Dresden, Weimar, and for Duke of Meiningen. Designed decor for first perf. of RING DES NIBELUNGEN and PARSIFAL, and for a Bayreuth revival of TANNHÄUSER (1891). Brückner's principles have been out of favour since the work of APPIA, Gordon Craig, and their successor, W. WAGNER; but his work was fully approved by R. WAGNER himself, who indeed liked it so much that he chose him to design for Bayreuth. LO
See Oenslager, *Stage Design* (London and New York 1975)

Brüll, Ignaz, b. Prostějov [Prossnitz], Moravia, 7 Nov 1846; d. Vienna, 17 Dec 1907. Moravian composer. Of his 10 operas the most successful was *Das Goldene Kreuz*, lib. Salomon Mosenthal, based on play by MÉLESVILLE and Nicholas Brazier: Berlin, 22 Dec 1875; London, Adelphi T. (in Eng. as *The Golden Cross*, by Carl Rosa Co.), 2 Mar 1878; NY 19 July 1879. LO

Bruneau, Alfred, b. Paris, 3 Mar 1857; d. Paris, 15 June 1934. French writer and composer. He had aspirations toward a 'reformed' Fr. opera – libs dealing with social problems of the time, music incorporating the Wagnerian LEITMOTIV technique and permeated with symbolism – high ideals not quite matched by perf. Of his 12 operas, usually indebted to his friend ZOLA for their plots, the most successful were RÊVE, ATTAQUE DU MOULIN, MESSIDOR, and OURAGAN. LO
See Hervey, *Alfred Bruneau* (London and New York 1907)

Brünnhilde, sop., Wotan's favourite Valkyrie in WALKÜRE, SIEGFRIED and GÖTTERDÄMMERUNG. *See* these three operas *under* RING DES NIBELUNGEN

Brunswick [Braunschweig], W. Germany. Having close associations with Hanover, it was one of the few places in continental Europe where HANDEL operas were perf. during his lifetime. Present theatre dates from 1948, replacing one destroyed during World War II. LO

Bruscantini, Sesto, b. Civitanova, 10 Dec 1919. Italian baritone. Debut 1946, Civitanova (COLLINE); then appeared at Sc. 1949, Rome O. 1950, Glyndebourne 1951, Salzburg 1952, Chicago 1961, and San Francisco 1967, specializing in the comic operas of MOZART, CIMAROSA, ROSSINI, and DONIZETTI, singing both bass and bar. roles. Also sings in *bel canto* operas (LUCIA DI LAMMERMOOR, FAVORITE, and PURITANI), in Fr. works (PÊCHEURS DE PERLES, WERTHER, and THAÏS), and the VERDI bar. repertory (RIGOLETTO, DI LUNA, GERMONT, RENATO, IAGO, and FORD). A stylish singer with impeccable diction, and a fine actor, especially in comedy, he sings the FIGARO of Mozart, PAISIELLO, and Rossini, and it was in the last-mentioned composer's BARBIERE DI SIVIGLIA that he made his CG debut (1971). EF

Brussels [Brussel; Bruxelles]. Opera in the Belgian capital has a long history. A theatre, more or less on present site of Théâtre Royale de la Monnaie, was built 1700. A second theatre, built 1819, was burned down 1855; the present theatre dates from 1856 (architect Joseph Poelaert). T. de la Monnaie frequently gave versions of many operas by BELLINI, DONIZETTI, and VERDI before Paris did. A particularly splendid era began in 1872 with Joseph Dupont (1838–99) as cond., joined later (1886–9) by Lapissida as dir. Another brilliant period opened in 1900 under Maurice Kufferath (1852–1919) and Guillaume Guide (1859–1937). The long list of premieres at T. de la Monnaie incl. HÉRODIADE, SIGURD, GWENDOLINE, SALAMMBÔ, FERVAAL, as well as the first Fr. versions of TANNHÄUSER (1873), MEISTERSINGER VON NÜRNBERG (1885), and AIDA (1871). After 1918 the direction was in the hands of Corneil de Thoran and Jean Van Glabbeke; the Belgian author Paul Spaak joined them 1920 until his death (1936). After 1943 Thoran was sole dir. The permanent co. was disbanded 1959, opera now being provided by visiting companies. *See also* FLEMISH OPERA. LO

Buenos Aires. Interior of Salón Dorado, Teatro Colón. The theatre, opened 1908, was the second of that name in the city, the first functioning 1857–88. The second was designed by Tamburini, assisted by his pupil Victor Meano, and completed after the latter's death by the Belgian Julio Dormal. It was the last of the great, ornate and sumptuous international opera houses in the flamboyant 19th-c. manner.

Bucchi, Valentino, b. Florence, 29 Nov 1916. Italian composer. Studied with DALLAPICCOLA and FRAZZI. His opera *Il Giuoco* was prod. 1944, Florence; a revised version, *Il Giuoco del Barone*, was heard on It. Radio 1956 and perf. Spoleto 1958. Other operas incl.: *Les Jeux de Robin et de Marion* (1952), *Il Contrabasso*, based on CHEKHOV (1954), *Una Notte in Paradiso* (1960), and *Il Cocodrillo* (1969), all staged at Florence. He has ed. a version of MONTEVERDI's ORFEO (1966). EF

Bucharest [Bucureşti], Capital of Romania. A theatre was built there 1784; visiting It. and Ger. cos provided opera until mid-19th c. The Teatru cel Mare was built 1852 (opened 31 Dec), becoming the NT only in 1877. A Romanian co. was estab. in the 1850s, with a largely It. repertory. Under Gheorge Stefanescu, Romanian opera and opera in Romanian became more estab., with a complete season 1885–6. The Asociaţa Liricŭ Romîna was founded 1919, transformed into the State O. 1921, and becoming the Teatru de Opera si Balet 1944. The theatre was severely damaged by earthquake in 1940, and by bombs in 1944; it was eventually rebuilt in 1953. LO

Büchner, Georg, b. Godelau, 17 Oct 1813; d. Zürich, 18 Feb 1837. German playwright whose work has come to be appreciated only in the present century. Operas based on his work are: DANTONS TOD; WOZZECK (A. BERG, 1925, GURLITT, 1926, and PFITZNER, 1950); *Leonce und Lena* (Julius Weismann, 1925, and Kurt Schwaen, 1961); *Der Günstling* (WAGNER-RÉGENY, 1935). LO

Budapest. Capital of Hungary. The Pestí Magyar Színház (NT) was opened 1837, and under ERKEL gave operas, first of all mainly It., and in It., but increasingly in the Hungarian language, and with Hungarian operas becoming more frequent. Erkel's *Báthory Mária* (1840) was followed by operas by Károly Thern, Ferenc Doppler (1825–83), György Császár, Ignaz Bognár, and Károly Hüber. Another, more important, comp. was Mihály Mosonyi (1815–70) (*Szép Ilona*, 1861). A new theatre, the Operház, one of the most beautiful in Europe, was opened on 27 Sept 1884 with one act of LOHENGRIN, one of BÁNK BÁN, and one of Erkel's *Hunyadi László*. A second opera house, the Városi Szinház (City T.) was opened 1911; several Hungarian premieres have been given there. Conds, either resident or visiting, associated with Budapest opera have incl. MAHLER, NIKISCH, KLEMPERER, R. STRAUSS, WALTER, E. KLEIBER, SCHALK, FURTWÄNGLER, and KNAPPERTSBUSCH. Its present reputation stands high. LO

Buenos Aires. The main centre for opera in ARGENTINA from the early 19th c.

Teatro Colón. The focus of much of the city's musical activity, the lavish 2,478-seat opera house in French Renaissance style was built to satisfy the growing demands of the It. immigrant population which settled in large numbers between 1890 and 1914. Giving over 200 perfs a year, it has been officially subsidized by the city since 1931. It has stimulated indigenous opera by holding yearly contests and has prod. 47 operas by 28 Argentine comps from PANIZZA's *Aurora* (1908), commissioned for the inaugural season, to Claudio Guidi-Drei's *Medea* (1973). The theatre's permanent orchestra, chorus, and ballet were est. 1925. Performers there of international stature have incl. SHALYAPIN, CARUSO, B. NILSSON. World premieres incl. FALLA's *Atlántida*, cond. CASTRO (1963). Other 20th-c. prods incl. NIGHTINGALE; OEDIPUS REX; RAKE'S PROGRESS; JENŮFA; RAPE OF LUCRETIA; LULU; FIERY ANGEL; HINDEMITH's *Hin und Zurück;* PADMÂVATÎ; JEANNE D'ARC AU BÛCHER, and Mario Perusso's *La Voz del Silencio* (1969), designed by Ariel Bianco. The theatre opened 25 May 1908 with AIDA, cond. MANCINELLI. MK

See Caamaño (ed.), *La Historia del Teatro Colón (1908–1968)*, 3 vols (Buenos Aires 1969)

Buesst, Aylmer, b. Melbourne, 28 Jan 1883. Australian conductor. Was with Moody-Manners Co. 1914–16, with BEECHAM's company between 1916 and 1920, and with BNOC 1922–9. LO

Bulgaria. The chief musical centre is Sofia, the capital, but there are also important opera cos at Stara Zagora (founded 1946), Varna (1947), Ruse (1949), and Plovdiv (1953). The earliest Bulgarian opera was *Siromakhkinya* (1900) by Emanuil Manolov (1860–1902), though Georgi Atanasov (1881–1931), a pupil of MASCAGNI, is considered to be the founder of the Bulgarian opera tradition. He comp. six operas, employing a nationalist idiom that has largely been taken up by most later Bulgarian comps: Pancho Vladigerov (b. 1899: *Tsar Kaloyan*, 1936), Veselin Stoyanov (b. 1902: *The Women's Kingdom*, 1935; *Salammbô*, 1940; *Cunning Peter*, 1958), PIPKOV, Marin Goleminov (b. 1908: *Ivaylo*, 1959), Parashkev Hadjiyev (b. 1912: *Once Upon a Time*, 1957; *The Madcap*, 1959; *Albena*, 1962; *July Night*, 1964; *Master Carvers*, 1966), and Konstantin Iliyev (b. 1924: *The Master of Boyana*, 1962). Asen Karastoyanov (b. 1893), Georgi Zlatev-Cherkin (b. 1905), Yosif Tsankov (b. 1911), Iliya Iliyev (b. 1912) and Viktor Raychev (b. 1920) are particularly known for operetta.

There are several Bulgarian singers who have become well known internationally, notably CHRISTOFF, GHIAUROV, and WELITSCH. GN

Bülow, Hans (Guido) von, b. Dresden, 8 Jan 1830; d. Cairo, 12 Feb 1894. German conductor and pianist. It was the premiere of LOHENGRIN that decided him to become a professional musician and a champion of WAGNER. He m. LISZT's daughter Cosima (later Cosima Wagner) 1857. Became chief cond., Royal O., Munich, 1864, where he cond. the premieres of MEISTERSINGER and TRISTAN UND ISOLDE. When Cosima deserted him for Wagner he left Munich to tour Europe. The first of the modern virtuoso conds. FGB

Bumbry, Grace, b. St Louis, 4 Jan 1937. American mezzo-soprano, later soprano. Studied at Music Acad. of the West, Santa Barbara, with Lotte LEHMANN. Joint winner (with ARROYO) of NY Met auditions 1958. Debut 1960, Paris O. (CARMEN). Bayreuth 1961 (VENUS), first black singer to appear at that house. CG debut 1963 (EBOLI); NY Met debut 1965 in same role. Salzburg Fest. as LADY MACBETH 1964–5, CARMEN 1966–7. First sop. role, Santuzza (CAVALLERIA RUSTICANA) (Vienna Staats O., 1966), followed by SALOME (CG, 1970), and TOSCA (Met, 1971). Has a vibrant, imposing voice, dark at the bottom, gleaming but not always of steady quality at top. Her dramatic interpretations are always effectively projected by her commanding stage personality. AB

Grace Bumbry as LADY MACBETH, her debut at Salzburg Fest. 1964; produced SCHUH, with FISCHER-DIESKAU as Macbeth

Bunn, Alfred, b. ?, 8 Apr 1798; d. Boulogne, 20 Dec 1860. English manager and librettist. From 1835 in charge of both DL and CG; *c.* 1835 attempted to estab. an Eng. opera at DL with operas by BALFE (*Maid of Artois*, 1836; BOHEMIAN GIRL; *The Daughter of St Mark*, 1844), BENEDICT's *Brides of Venice* (1843), and MARITANA. Libs incl. *Maid of Artois* and *Maritana*. LO

Buona Figliuola, La (*The Good Girl*), opera, 3 acts, PICCINNI, lib. GOLDONI after Samuel Richardson's *Pamela* (1740). Rome, T. delle Dame, 6 Feb 1760; London, HM, 25 Nov 1766; Madison, Wis., 6 Jan 1967. Main chars: La Cecchina (sop.) Armidoro (ten.) Il Marchese (ten.) Lucinda (sop.) Sandrina (sop.) Paoluccia (sop.) Tagliaferro (bar.) Mengotto (bar.). La Cecchina, an orphan girl, loves and is loved by her master, the Marchese, to the envy of her fellow servants Sandrina and Paoluccia, the jealousy of Mengotto, who also loves her, and the annoyance of Lucinda, the Marchese's sister, whose own matrimonial prospects would be compromised if her brother were to marry beneath him. Tagliaferro, a Ger. soldier, reveals that La Cecchina is a Baroness; so all ends happily. Piccinni's most famous opera, widely perf. in Italy and abroad during the 18th c. JB

Burghauser, Jarmil, b. Písek, 21 Oct 1921. Czech composer. A freelance comp. (pupil of KŘIČKA and JEREMIÁŠ) as well as a cond. pupil of TALICH and a musicologist (author of a thematic catalogue of DVOŘÁK's works and an editor of the complete Dvořák edition), he has comp. four operas. These incl. *The Miser* (*Lakomec*, 1950, after MOLIÈRE), *Caroline and the Liar* (*Karolinka a lhář*, 1955, after GOLDONI) and *The Bridge* (*Most*, 1967). JT

Burgtheater *see* VIENNA

Burian, Emil František, b. Plzeň, 11 June 1904; d. Prague, 9 Aug 1959. Czech composer and producer, nephew of Karel BURIAN. A composition pupil of FOERSTER at the Prague Cons., he was active in the interwar period in experimental theatre, where he made good use of his versatile gifts as poet, dramatist, publicist, film dir., administrator, singer, and comp., notably in the Prague-based, 'Theatre D' (1933–41), which he founded. Of his six operas it is *Maryša* (1940), a sombre folk tragedy in the tradition of JENŮFA, that remains in the Czech repertory. JT

Burian, Karel, b. Rousínov, 12 Jan 1870; d. Senomaty, 25 Sept 1924. Czech tenor, uncle of E. F. BURIAN. Debut 1891, Brno; in the next decade sang in Cologne, Hanover, Hamburg, and Budapest. From Dresden (1902–10) he made many guest appearances: in London, Paris (under R. STRAUSS, with DESTINN) and from 1906 regularly at the NY Met. He also sang frequently at Prague NT but was never a regular member of the co. His Brno debut (Jeník in BARTERED BRIDE followed the next evening by DALIBOR) showed his versatility: not only did he excel in the lyrical Czech repertory but was equally suited to dramatic and heroic parts, particularly Wagnerian. He was blessed with a faultless technique and a robust constitution that survived 117 Wagnerian perfs in a single year (1905). Some considered his beautiful and powerful voice superior to CARUSO's; he was also an excellent linguist (at home in Czech, Ger., Fr., It., and Hungarian) and a singer of exceptional intelligence and musicianship. JT

Burkhard, Paul, b. Zürich, 21 Dec 1911. Swiss composer and conductor. Was MdC at Bern, Stadt T., 1932–4, and mus. dir. Zürich, Schauspielhaus, 1939–44, and 1945–57 in charge of Radio Beromünster orch. Has wr. several operettas of which *Der Schwarze Hecht* (1939; revised as *Feuerwerk*, 1950) has had most success; also a comic opera, *Casanova in der Schweiz* (1942). LO

Burkhard, Willy, b. Leubringen, 17 Apr 1900; d. Zürich, 18 June 1955. Swiss composer. Active in many fields, he wrote only one opera, *Die Schwarze Spinne* (1948). LO

Burnacini, Lodovico Ottavio, b. probably Mantua, 1636; d. Vienna, 12 Dec 1707. Italian architect and designer. Worked for over 40 years at court of Leopold I, Vienna, designing settings and sometimes costumes for more than 400 stage works. He built a theatre in the Hofburg (destroyed 1683) seating 2,000, in which his and CESTI's POMO D'ORO was perf. 1667 and 1668. LO

Burney, Charles, b. Shrewsbury, 12 Apr 1726; d. Chelsea, London, 12 Apr 1814. English music historian and composer. His *History of Music* (4 vols, London 1776–89; reprinted, London 1935, 2 vols) and the accounts of the journeys he undertook in preparing the work are invaluable sources as to comps and perfs of his time, though characteristically prejudiced against earlier comps such as MONTEVERDI. His *Life of Metastasio* (3 vols, 1796) still remains the only substantial account in Eng. of the great It. librettist. LO

Burning Fiery Furnace, The, church parable, 1 act, BRITTEN, lib. William Plomer, derived from the Old Testament story (Book of Daniel) of Shedrach, Meschach and Abednego. Orford Church 9 June 1966. Second of the comp.'s three Church Parables. Main chars: Nebuchadnezzar (ten.) Astrologer (bar.) Misael (ten.) Ananias (bar.) Azarias (bass). Musical material is derived from plainsong heard during the Processional. Requires small chamber orch., with considerable emphasis on exotic percussion sounds. An arresting re-creation of the famous story for perf. in church. AB ○

Burrowes, Norma, b. Bangor, 24 Apr 1944. British soprano. Studied RAM with Flora Nielsen and later with Rupert Bruce-Lockhart. Debut 1970 with Glyndebourne Touring co. (ZERLINA), Fiorilla for same co. in TURCO IN ITALIA (1971). CG debut 1970 as Fiakermilli (ARABELLA), returned 1975 for Woodbird (SIEGFRIED). Salzburg Fest. (BLONDE) 1971–3. Debut with ENO at Col. 1971 (Blonde), has returned for Oscar (BALLO IN MASCHERA) and SOPHIE. ZERBINETTA with SO 1975. Blonde at Paris O. 1976. She m. cond. Steuart Bedford. One of the most attractive of British light sops with a pure, natural voice, used intelligently and brilliantly. AB

Burrows, Stuart, b. Cilfynydd, 1933. Welsh tenor. Formerly a schoolmaster, he turned to professional singing after winning first prize at the 1959 National Eisteddfod. Debut 1963 with WNO at Cardiff as Ismaele (NABUCCO); CG 1967 as Beppe (PAGLIACCI); in USA with San Francisco O. 1967 (TAMINO). Has since been a

Stuart Burrows as Lensky and KNIGHT as Olga in EUGENE ONEGIN, London, CG, July 1974; produced Charles Hamilton, designed Julia Trevelyan Oman

frequent guest in USA, incl. NY Met., and with Vienna Staats O., winning much renown for elegance of line and vibrant warmth of tone as a MOZART stylist in particular, and with comparable qualities in lyric ten. roles of VERDI and PUCCINI. NG

Busch, Fritz, b. Siegen, 13 Mar 1890; d. London, 14 Sept 1951. German conductor. Studied Cologne; after appointments in Riga (1909), Aachen (1912), and Stuttgart (1918) went to Dresden, where he gave premieres of DOKTOR FAUST, CARDILLAC, and ÄGYPTISCHE HELENA. Left Germany 1933, moved to Glyndebourne 1934 where he was mus. dir. until his death. LO

Busenello, Giovanni Francesco, b. Venice, 24 Sept 1598; d. Legnago, Venice, 27 Oct 1659. Italian poet, 'historically the first great librettist' (Patrick Smith, *The Tenth Muse*). Wrote four libs for CAVALLI (*Gli Amori d'Apollo e di Dafne*, 1640; *Didone*, 1641; *La Prosperità Infelice di Giulio Cesare, Dittatore*, 1646; *Statira*, 1655), and that for INCORONAZIONE DI POPPEA. LO

Bush, Alan, b. London, 22 Dec 1900. English composer. Educated at RAM and Univ. of Berlin. Subjects of operas influenced by his Communist belief. They incl. *Wat Tyler* (1950), given its first British perf. at SW 1974, *The Sugar Reapers*, and *Men of Blackamoor* (1955), all prod. in E. Europe and all with libs by his wife Nancy. His style is predominantly traditional, often with strong characterization. AB

Busoni, Ferruccio, b. Empoli, Tuscany, 1 Apr 1866; d. Berlin, 27 July 1924. Italian composer and pianist. Was a child prodigy as a pianist. Became a teacher and virtuoso pianist while carrying on career as a comp. His four operas are much admired by specialists but seldom reach the stage. *Die Brautwahl* (1912), based on a story by HOFFMANN, was followed by the delightful one-act *capriccio*, ARLECCHINO (1917). *Turandot* (1917), another short opera, is in many ways more faithful to GOZZI's fable than PUCCINI's work. However, DOKTOR FAUST (1925) is probably his greatest work in this genre, dealing with the familiar subject in a noble, discerning manner, although its somewhat severe intellectual approach probably precludes it from ever entering the regular repertory. AB

Busser, Henri, b. Toulouse, 16 Jan 1872; d. Paris, 30 Dec 1973. French composer and conductor. Cond. Paris O., also mus. dir, OC, 1939–41. Operas incl. *Colomba* (1920) and *Le Carrosse du Saint-Sacrement* (1948), both based on MÉRIMÉE, and *Les Noces Corinthiennes* (1922), based on a poem by Anatole France. LO

Bussotti, Sylvano, b. Florence, 1 Oct 1931. Italian composer. His theatre pieces incl. *Géographie Française* (Darmstadt 1959), *Memoria* (Palermo 1962), and *La Passion selon Sade* (NY and Palermo 1965). Has wr. operas for marionettes, *Nottetempolunapark* (Florence 1954), *Arlechinbatocieria* (Florence 1955), and *Tre Mascare in Gloria* (Aix-en-Provence 1956). EF

Byron, George Gordon, Lord, b. London, 22 Jan 1788; d. Missolonghi, 19 Apr 1824. English poet and dramatist. Works on which some 16 operas are based incl.: *The Giaour*, 1813 (N. BERG, *Leila*, 1912); *Parisina*, 1815 (DONIZETTI, 1833); *Manfred*, 1817 (Enrico Petrella, 1872); *Don Juan*, 1819 (FIBICH, *Hedy*, 1896); *Marino Faliero*, 1821 (Donizetti, 1835); *Cain*, 1821 (LATTUADA, 1957); *The Two Foscari*, 1821 (DUE FOSCARI). LO

C

cabaletta (It. 'short melodic air'), the concluding usually fast, movement of a large-scale aria or ensemble in It. opera (see also STRETTA). In general use *c.* 1820–1880, the word also connotes a musical form involving the repetition of a melodic period mostly with intervening ritornello and a coda designed to stimulate applause. JB

Caballé, Montserrat, b. Barcelona, 12 Apr 1933. Spanish soprano. Studied Liceo Cons., Barcelona; won gold medal there 1954. Debut 1957, Basel O. At Bremen from 1960 where she sang her first VIOLETTA and TATYANA. Sc. 1960 as Flower Maiden (PARSIFAL). Mexico City 1964 (MANON). Caused a sensation in a concert perf. at Carnegie Hall, NY, in title role of LUCREZIA BORGIA (1965). Debuts: Glyndebourne 1965 (MARSCHALLIN and Countess ALMAVIVA); NY Met 1965 (MARGUERITE); CG 1972 (Violetta). During 1970s became leading exponent of *bel canto* roles in which she is a perfectionist in spinning a pure line and taking care over vocalization. Also a considerable singer of MOZART, R. STRAUSS, VERDI, and PUCCINI. AB

Caccini, Giulio, b. Rome, *c.* 1545; d. Florence, 10 Dec 1618. Italian singer, composer, member of Florentine Camerata. Contributed much esp. in his publication *Le Nuove Musiche* (1602) to the development of recitative. His *Dafne* (1597?, lib. RINUCCINI) was comp. about the same time as PERI's setting, but was possibly never performed and the music is lost. With Peri comp. EURIDICE (lib. Rinuccini, 1600); also (1600) made a separate setting of *Euridice*, pub. 1601, the first pub. opera. Daughter, Francesco (b. Florence, 1581) was also a singer (*Euridice*, Florence, 1600) and was the first woman to wr. an opera, *La Liberazione di Ruggiero* (1625). LO

cadenza (It. 'cadence'), a term transferred to the improvisatory passage in free time interpolated before the final cadence of a movement during the 18th c. During the 19th c. cadenzas were increasingly wr. out by the comps themselves. JB

Cadi Dupé, Le (*The Cadi Duped*), *opéra comique*, 1 act, MONSIGNY, lib. Pierre René Lemonnier after the ARABIAN NIGHTS. Paris, Foire St Laurent, 4 Feb 1761. Rewr. by GLUCK, new version produced Vienna, Schönbrunn T., Dec 1761. LO

Cadman, Charles Wakefield, b. Johnstown, Pa., 24 Dec 1881; d. Los Angeles, 30 Dec 1946. American composer. Studied Pittsburgh; moved to Los Angeles where he became teacher, lecturer, and critic. With other musicians, painters, and writers Cadman shared the view that the true American voice was that of the Indian (a view not widely shared by the public). SHANEWIS was readily acclaimed on first hearing at the Met, but few prods of the Indianist movement have stood the test of time. Cadman's other operas incl. an 'operatic cantata', *The Sunset Trail* (Denver 1922 and later perf. by Chicago Civic O.); the one-act *Garden of Mystery* (1925), based on Nathaniel Hawthorne's *Rappacini's Daughter*; and *A Witch of Salem* (Chicago 1926). EJ

Caffarelli [Gaetano Majorano], b. Bitonto, 12 Apr 1710; d. Naples, 31 Jan 1783. Italian male soprano, one of the greatest of 18th-c. castrati. Pupil of PORPORA; debut 1724, Rome; thereafter sang in all the principal opera houses in Europe. Sang in HANDEL's *Faramondo* (1738) and SERSE, and created Sextus in GLUCK's *La Clemenza di Tito* (Naples 1752). Retired with a fortune, as did so many castrati. LO

Cahill, Teresa, b. Rotherhithe, 25 Sept 1946. English soprano. Debut 1967 while still a student. Winner of the John Christie Award (1970), she sings at Glyndebourne, CG, Santa Fe, with the Handel O. Society, the EOG and SO. Her most successful appearances have been in MOZART roles, ZERLINA and Donna ELVIRA (DON GIOVANNI), FIORDILIGI, PAMINA, and Servilia (CLEMENZA DI TITO), but she also sings IOLANTA, SOPHIE, and Miss Wordsworth (ALBERT HERRING). EF

Calaf, ten., the hero of TURANDOT

Caldara, Antonio, b. Venice 1670; d. Vienna, 28 Dec 1736. Italian composer. Imperial comp. to Charles VI in Vienna from 1714; from 1716 assistant MdC to FUX. His more than 60 operas, often to ZENO's libs, incl. *Achille in Sciro* (lib. METASTASIO, 1736) and *Ifigenia in Aulide* (lib. Zeno, 1718), the first opera based on this classical theme. LO

Calderón de la Barca, Pedro, b. Madrid, 17 Jan 1600; d. Madrid, 25 May 1681. Spanish dramatist and poet, regarded as second only to Félix de Lope de Vega in his time. In addition to a huge output of plays in many forms, he wrote the text of the first known *zarzuela*, *El Jardín de Falerina*, perf. Buen Retiro Palace, Madrid, 1648. His first to be given at the actual Palace of La Zarzuela was *El Golfo de las Sirenas*, on 17 Jan

1657. The comps of the music for these and his other *zarzuelas* are not known. Calderón also wrote libs for two operas, *La Púrpura de la Rosa* and *Celos Aun del Aire Matan* (*Jealousy is Always Fatal*) with music by Juan Hidalgo, perf. 1660. Operas adapted from his plays incl. FRIEDENSTAG, EGK's *Circe*, and MALIPIERO's *La Vita è Sogno*. FGB

Calife de Bagdad, Le, *opéra comique*, 1 act, BOÏELDIEU, lib. Claude Godard d'Aucour de St-Just, based on the ARABIAN NIGHTS. Paris, OC, 16 Sept 1800; New Orleans, 2 Mar 1806; London, HM, 11 May 1809. Other operas by GARCÍA I (1813) and PACINI (1825). LO

Calisto, La, opera, 3 acts, CAVALLI, lib. Giovanni Battista Faustini. Venice, T. S. Apollinare, autumn 1651. Revived Glyndebourne 1969, and Schwetzingen 1975. LO ○

Callas, Maria [Cecilia Sophia Anna Maria Kalogeropoulos], b. NY, 3 Dec 1923. Greek soprano. Her vocal and dramatic versatility made her the *prima donna assoluta* of her generation. Taken to Greece aged 14; studied Athens Cons. mainly with Elvira de Hidalgo. Sang Santuzza in student prod. of CAVALLERIA RUSTICANA a few days before 15th birthday. Joined Athens Royal O. Professional debut aged 16 in BOCCACCIO; in 1942 took over title role in TOSCA at short notice with much success. Italian debut (Verona 1947) as GIOCONDA launched main career as protégée of SERAFIN. At Venice, 1947–9, she sang TURANDOT, ISOLDE, BRÜNNHILDE, but career took new direction after major success (Dec 1948) as Elvira (PURITANI), having replaced CAROSIO and learned role in six days, in same season as she sang Brünnhilde. First sop. since Lilli LEHMANN to

Colour plate: BUMBRY as Amneris in AIDA, London, CG, 24 Jan 1968; produced Peter Potter; designed Nicholas Georgiadis

Left: Teresa Cahill as Zerlina and SIEPI in the title role of DON GIOVANNI, London, CG, Nov–Dec 1973; produced COPLEY; scenery and costumes Stefanos Lazaridis

Below: Maria Callas as TOSCA and GOBBI as Scarpia, two of their greatest roles, London, CG, 5 July 1965; produced ZEFFIRELLI; designed Renzo Mongiardino. This was Callas's last performance at CG.

Lith. Ch. Fernique, 15, r. de Clichy, Paris.

927

FAURE

Rôle de Nélusko dans l'Africaine

range freely from dramatic to lyric roles. Her successes at Sc. from 1951, CG from 1952, Chicago Lyric T. from 1954, NY Met from 1956, are chronicled in bibliography noted below, with distinctive triumphs as NORMA, TRAVIATA, and TOSCA. In spite of flawed vocal technique, her exceptional artistry revitalized many forgotten operas, at the same time as her glamour of personality and temperament for controversy (which ranged from a libel action against a pasta factory to disputes with opera managements) attracted a wider public interest in opera generally. 1952–64 she recorded principal roles in 22 different operas, incl. four she never sang on stage (BOHÈME, CARMEN, MANON LESCAUT, PAGLIACCI), plus second versions of *La Gioconda*, *Norma*, and LUCIA DI LAMMERMOOR. On stage she sang 43 different roles in over 500 perfs (documented total: 535). She withdrew from stage perfs in late 1960s (her last was Tosca, CG, 5 July 1965); turned actress for the title role in Pier Paolo Pasolini's film of *Medea*, 1970, and gave operatic master classes in NY. A brief return to concert platform occurred on extensive US and European tour, 1972–3, singing operatic excerpts with DI STEFANO. They relied much on public personality at the expense of vocal resource, and maintained her own earlier precept: 'When my enemies stop hissing, I'll know I've failed.' NG

See Ardoin and Fitzgerald, *Callas* (London 1974); Galatopoulos, *Callas: la Divina* (London 1963; rev. 1966); Jellinek, *Callas: Portrait of a Prima Donna* (New York 1960; London 1961, 1965). Full critical discography by Galatopoulos in *Records and Recording* (London, Mar 1972), documentation of stage roles in Ardoin and Fitzgerald, *op. cit.* and further discography.

Call Me Madam, musical, BERLIN, book Russell Crouse and Howard Lindsay; lyrics Berlin. NY, Imperial T., 12 Oct 1950; London, Col., 15 Mar 1952. A lady with no other qualification than wealth is appointed ambassador to a tiny European principality. EJ ★

See Lubbock

Calvé, Emma [Rose Calvert], b. Décazeville, Aveyron, 15 Aug 1858; d. Millau, 6 Jan 1942. French soprano. Pupil of MARCHESI DE CASTRONE, debut 1882, T. de la Monnaie (MARGUERITE). From 1884 principal sop. at Paris OC, where (1892) she sang Santuzza in first Fr. perf. of CAVALLERIA RUSTICANA, a part she also sang in her CG debut the same year. First sang at NY Met (1893) Santuzza and CARMEN, in which role she was at her greatest. She created Suzel (AMICO FRITZ), MASSENET's *Sapho* (OC 1897) and Anita (NAVARRAISE). LO

See autobiography, tr. Gilder, *My Life* (New York and London 1922)

Calzabigi, Raniero, b. Livorno, 23 Dec 1714; d. Naples, July 1795. Italian adventurer and librettist, friend of Casanova. Began as an admirer of METASTASIO, whose works he ed. and pub. (Paris 1755). After a period in Paris, *c.* 1750–8, arrived Vienna 1761, when he collaborated with GLUCK in the ballet *Don Juan*. His *c.* 10 libs incl. *Le Danaïde* (DANAÏDES), *Semiramide*, sent to Gluck 1778, but never set by him, and, most important, the three set by Gluck, ORFEO ED EURIDICE, ALCESTE, and PARIDE ED ELENA. LO

Cambert, Robert, b. Paris, *c.* 1628; d. London, 1677. French composer, wrote the first Fr. opera, POMONE, a *pastoral* in five acts and a prologue, lib. Pierre Perrin, perf. 19 Mar 1671 at the newly established Académie Royale de Musique. A second, *Les Peines et les Plaisirs d'Amour*, followed, autumn 1671. When Perrin's privilege was overturned by LULLY Cambert left Paris and settled in London. LO

Colour plate: FAURE as he appeared in the premiere of AFRICAINE, Paris O., 1865

Emma Calvé as CARMEN, which she sang at Paris OC, London CG, NY Met, and elsewhere. She was considered one of the best Carmens of her day.

Cambiale di Matrimonio, La (*The Marriage Contract*), *farsa*, 1 act, ROSSINI, lib. G. ROSSI after comedy by Camillo Federici. Venice, T. S. Moisè, 3 Nov 1810; NY, 14 Oct 1829. Main chars: Fanny (sop.) Clarina (mezzo-sop.) Edoardo (ten.) Tobia (bass) Slook (bar.). Sir Tobias Mill, an English businessman, has signed a contract making over his daughter Fanny to a Canadian merchant, Slook: but Fanny loves Edoardo, and with Slook's help the young couple outwit the avaricious parent. Rossini's first perf. opera. JB O

Cambridge, England. DENT's prod. of ZAUBERFLÖTE (1911) in his own tr. led to a reappraisal in Britain of MOZART's stature as an opera comp. During his professorship there, 1926–41, Dent encouraged opera, and works such as PURCELL's *King Arthur*, FAIRY QUEEN, and POISONED KISS were staged. Since World War II prods have incl. SIR JOHN IN LOVE, RAKE'S PROGRESS (both 1958), LIEBERMANN's *L'École des Femmes* (1958), and BIZET's *Don Procopio* (1959); also a prod. of the original version of ARIADNE AUF NAXOS which helped to launch the career of the young cond. David Atherton. LO

Camden Festival *see* LONDON

Camerata *see* FLORENTINE CAMERATA

Cammarano, Salvatore, b. Naples, 19 Mar 1801; d. Naples, 17 July 1852. Italian librettist. From a family associated with the stage, he worked as a scene painter and stage manager at the T. S. Carlo, Naples. He wr. a number of prose dramas before turning to opera libs 1834; provided DONIZETTI with LUCIA DI LAMMERMOOR 1835. Donizetti set a further seven Cammarano libs incl. ROBERTO DEVEREUX, POLIUTO, MARIA DI ROHAN, and *Maria de Rudenz*. Cammarano also provided VERDI with the texts for his operas ALZIRA, BATTAGLIA DI LEGNANO, LUISA MILLER, and TROVATORE. PS

Campanini, Cleofonte, b. Parma, 1 Sept 1860; d. Chicago, 19 Dec 1919. Italian conductor. Assistant, NY Met, 1883; dir. It. opera, CG, 1900–12; cond. and art. dir. Manhattan OH, 1906–9; first chief cond. of Chicago Civic O. 1910 till his death. Also appeared at leading opera houses in Europe and S. America, incl. Sc. (1903–6). JB

Campiello, Il, *opera buffa*, 3 acts, WOLF-FERRARI, lib. Mario Ghisalberti, based on GOLDONI. Milan, Sc., 12 Feb 1936. Il Campiello is a small square in Venice, the scene in the opera of a climactic street fight between two women – tenors in *travesti*. LO

Campo, Conrado del, b. Madrid, 28 Oct 1879; d. Madrid, 16 Mar 1953. Spanish composer. Attended Madrid Cons. but largely self-taught, influenced at first by the music of R. STRAUSS and FRANCK. His 13 operas incl. *Los Amantes de Verona* (*Romeo and Juliet*; 1909), *El Final de Don Alvaro* (1874), and *El Avapiés* (1874). He succeeded BRETÓN as Professor of Comp., Madrid Cons. FGB

Campra, André, b. Aix-en-Provence, 4 Dec 1660; d. Versailles, 29 June 1744. French composer whose *c.* 20 *tragédies lyriques* and *opéras-ballets* formed an important link between LULLY and RAMEAU. They incl. *Tancrède* (TL 1702), in which a woman appeared for the first time on the Fr. lyric stage; *Alcine* (TL 1705); *Idoménée* (TL 1712); *Achille et Deidamie* (TL 1735). His *L'Europe Galante* (opera-ballet; 1697) was the pattern for INDES GALANTES. LO

Canada. The principal centre for operatic prod. is TORONTO, followed by MONTREAL and VANCOUVER. Organizations also regularly present 2–3 operas each year in Edmonton, Calgary, and Winnipeg, which three cities together with Vancouver formed Opera West (1972), a co-operative venture to give a prod. in more than one city.

The Stratford Shakespearean Fest. began operatic prod. 1956 with RAPE OF LUCRETIA (with RESNIK, TOUREL, and VICKERS) and has usually presented at least one opera each summer, incl. several Canadian works. Opera is also an important part of summer activities of the National Arts Centre Orch. under BERNARDI in Ottawa, and at the Guelph Spring Fest. under Nicholas Goldschmidt.

The difficulty of presenting opera in a vast country of small population has to some extent been overcome by the Canadian Broadcasting Corporation (CBC). The transmission of studio perfs led to the formation of the CBC O. Co. 1948, which presented a wide variety of both standard and novel works. TV transmission of opera began 1953. Altogether, the CBC has given over a 100 different operas; it also transmits perfs provided by foreign broadcasting systems.

Among Canadians who have comp. operas in recent years are Raymond Pannell, Murray Schafer, SOMERS, Healey Willan, and WILSON. CM

Candide, operetta, BERNSTEIN, book Lillian Hellman, lyrics Richard Wilbur, John Latouche, and Dorothy Parker, based on

VOLTAIRE. NY, Martin Beck T., 1 Dec 1956; revised, Broadway T., 11 Mar 1974. EJ O

Caniglia, Maria, b. Naples, 5 May 1906. Italian soprano. Studied Naples. Debut 1930, Turin (CHRYSOTHEMIS). Sang at Sc. 1930–42 and again after World War II. CG debut 1937 (TOSCA); NY Met debut 1938 as Amelia (SIMONE BOCCANEGRA). Returned to CG 1939 and again with the Sc. co. 1950. She was for many years a favourite at the Verona Arena. Her voice was full and vibrant, apt to be squally. Much admired as Tosca, AIDA, and ADRIANA LECOUVREUR. AB

Canio, ten., the leader of the strolling players in PAGLIACCI

cantabile (It. 'songlike', 'singable'). The standard term in 19th-c. It. opera for a short, lyrical movement, incl. the first, slow movement of a double ARIA or CAVATINA. JB

Cantelli, Guido, b. Novara, 27 Apr 1920; d. Paris, 24 Nov 1956. Italian conductor. One of the most brilliant of his generation. Had only just turned his attention to opera and was apptd mus. dir., Sc., 1956, when killed in air crash. LO

Canterbury Pilgrims, The, opera, 3 acts, STANFORD, lib. Gilbert Arthur A'Beckett after Geoffrey Chaucer. London, DL, 28 Apr 1884 (Carl Rosa Co.). Reginald de Koven (1859–1920) wr. an opera on same subject, commissioned by NY Met, 1917. LO

Capecchi, Renato, b. Cairo, 6 Nov 1923. Italian bass-baritone. Debut 1949, Reggio Emilia (AMONASRO); sang in the premiere of MALIPIERO's *Allegra Brigata* (Sc. 1950). Has appeared at the NY Met (1951), San Francisco (1960), Salzburg (1961), CG (1962), and at all the major It. opera houses. His repertory, of over 280 roles, ranges from the comic operas of MOZART and ROSSINI to *verismo* works such as FEDORA, ADRIANA LECOUVREUR, and IRIS; it also incl. LEONORE 40/45 and GLÜCKLICHE HAND. EF

Čapek, Karel, b. Malé Svatoňovice, Bohemia, 9 Jan 1890; d. Prague, 25 Dec 1938. Czech novelist and dramatist. The best-known Czech writer between the two world wars. His play *Krakatit* has been made into an opera by both Jiří Berkovec (1961) and KAŠLÍK (1961) and his MAKROPULOS CASE provided JANÁČEK with one of his finest libs. Tibor Andrašan's opera *The White Disease* (1968) is based on Čapek's play *Bíla Nemoc*. JT

Cappuccilli, Piero, b. Trieste, 9 Nov 1929. Italian baritone. Debut 1957, T. Nuovo, Milan (TONIO); Sc. debut 1964 as Enrico (LUCIA DI LAMMERMOOR). CG debut 1967 (GERMONT); since sung there as IAGO (1974) and RENATO (1975). NY Met debut 1960 (Germont). Salzburg 1975 as Posa (DON CARLOS). One of the leading It. bars of his day with a dark, incisive tone; particularly notable in the roles of Iago, Renato, and SIMONE BOCCANEGRA. AB

Capriccio, opera, 1 act, R. STRAUSS, lib. C. KRAUSS. Munich, 28 Oct 1942; London, CG, 22 Sept 1953; New York, Juilliard, 2 Apr 1954. Main chars: the Countess (sop.) Flamand (ten.) Olivier (bar.) the Count (bar.) Clairon (contr.) La Roche (bass). This delicate conversation-piece, in which the musician Flamand and the poet Olivier are rival suitors of the Countess, dramatizes the question whether words or music are of greater importance in opera. The comp.'s final work for the stage, it reveals many of the artistic problems he had wrestled with all his life. FGB O

See Mann, *Richard Strauss* (London 1964; New York 1966); Kobbé

Capuana, Franco, b. Fano, 29 Sept 1894. Italian conductor. Studied Naples. After cond. Palermo, Genoa, Brescia, and Turin went to T.S. Carlo, Naples, 1930–7; Sc. 1937–40 and 1946–52 (mus. dir. from 1949). Cond. premieres of GHEDINI's *Pulce d'Oro* (Genoa 1940), MALIPIERO's *Sette Canzoni* (Rome 1949) and the first Italian performance of JENŮFA (Venice 1941). LO

Capuleti ed i Montecchi, I (*The Capulets and the Montagues*), opera, 2 acts, BELLINI, lib. ROMANI after Matteo Bandello (?). Venice, T. La Fenice, 11 Mar 1830; London, 20 July 1833; New Orleans, 4 Apr 1847. Main chars: Romeo (mezzo-sop.) Giulietta (sop.) Tebaldo (ten.) Capellio (bar.) Lorenzo (bar.). The story of Romeo and Juliet simplified. Bellini's sixth opera, partly constructed from the music of the unsuccessful *Zaire* (Parma 1829). Often revived during the 19th c. with Romeo's death substituted by the corresponding scene in VACCAI's setting, also to the same lib by Romani. JB

Carafa [di Colobrano], Michele Enrico, b. Naples, 17 Nov 1787; d. Paris, 26 July 1872. Italian composer. After an army career he settled in Paris where most of his 35 operas were prod. They incl. *La Fiancée de Lammermoor* (1828) and *Masaniello* (OC 27 Dec 1827), prod. two months before MUETTE DE PORTICI on the same subject. LO

Carmen, *opéra comique*, 4 acts, BIZET, lib. MEILHAC and L. HALÉVY based on MÉRIMÉE's story, 1845. Paris, OC, 3 Mar 1875; London, HM (in It.), 22 June 1878; NY, Acad. of Music (in It.), 23 Oct 1878; first perf. in Eng. HM 27 Jan 1879; first perf. in Fr. in England, HM 1886, with GALLI-MARIÉ as Carmen. The original spoken dialogue replaced by recitative by GUIRAUD (Vienna, in Ger., 23 Oct 1875). Main chars: Carmen (mezzo-sop.) Don José (ten.) Micaëla (sop.) Escamillo (bar.). Don José, a corporal of dragoons, is infatuated by the gypsy girl Carmen and follows her to the mountains. She soon tires of him, however, attracted by the dashing toreador Escamillo. A fight between Escamillo and José nearly ends in Escamillo's death. José leaves with his country sweetheart Micaëla, who has brought word that his mother is dying. On the day of the bullfight, José, enraged by Carmen's love for Escamillo, kills her and then gives himself up. The lib. of the opera differs in some essentials from Mérimée's novel, which contains no

Left: I Capuletti ed i Montecchi. ARAGALL as Romeo, Scala, 1965–6; produced Renato Castellani; designed Ezio Frigerio

Carmen. TROYANOS as Carmen, London, CG, 6 June 1974; produced GELIOT; scenery Jenny Beavan and Donald Fielding; costumes Jenny Beavan

Cardillac, opera, 3 acts, HINDEMITH, lib. Ferdinand Lion, based on HOFFMANN's *Das Fräulein von Scuderi*. Dresden 9 Nov 1926; London, Queen's Hall (concert), 18 Dec 1936; revised version lib. comp., Zürich 20 June 1952; Sante Fe 26 July 1967; London, New O. Co. at SW, 11 Mar 1970. Main chars: Cardillac (bar.) his daughter (sop.) a Lady (sop.) an Officer (ten.) a Cavalier (ten.) The goldsmith Cardillac cannot bear to part with the jewelry he makes, and murders each customer after a sale. EF O★

Carlos, Don, bar., Leonora's brother in FORZA DEL DESTINO

Carl Rosa Opera Company. Founded 1875 by Karl Rose, a Ger. violinist living in England, for presentation of opera in Eng. The most successful and longlived Eng. touring co. it gave many British premieres incl. MANON, BOHÈME, and ANDREA CHÉNIER and first perfs in Eng. of WAGNER; it also commissioned works by British comps. Ceased 1958. LO

Carlyle, Joan, b. Wirral, 6 Apr 1931. English soprano. Debut 1955, CG, as Frasquita (CARMEN). Remained a principal sop. with the co. for 15 years singing wide variety of lyric roles. Sang Zdenka (later title role) in first UK prod. of ARABELLA (1964). Sang Jenifer (MIDSUMMER MARRIAGE); MIMI, VERDI's DESDEMONA, and Countess ALMAVIVA were among her most sympathetic roles. AB

Carmelites, The *see* DIALOGUES DES CARMÉLITES

Micaëla and does not glamorize Carmen and her smuggler associates. LO O★
See Kobbé

Carmen Jones, musical, marrying BIZET's CARMEN music to new lib. and lyrics by HAMMERSTEIN II. NY, Broadway T., 2 Dec 1943, beginning a run of over 500 perfs. It is the Carmen story in essence, but the setting is the American South and Chicago; the time, World War II. Carmen Jones works in a parachute factory; Escamillo has become Husky Miller, a prizefighter, and Don José is Corporal Joe. The final scene is outside the stadium where Miller is about to fight. In 1954 Otto Preminger prod. and dir. a film of this with an all-Negro cast, starring Harry Belafonte and Dorothy Dandridge. LO O★

Carmina Burana (*Songs of Benediktbeuren*, a monastery in the foothills of the Bavarian Alps), opera, 3 parts, ORFF, lib. adapted by comp. from a 13th-c. Latin codex. Frankfurt, Staats O., 8 June 1937; San Francisco, 3 Oct 1958; London, RFH (concert perf.), 26 Jan 1960. Orff's most widely played stage work. LO O

Carnival (Fr. *carnaval*; It. *carnevale*; Ger. *Karneval*). The main operatic season in continental European, esp. It. opera houses, lasting from 26 Dec to the following Shrove Tuesday. A commission to write an opera for the opening of the Carnival Season was a high honour. LO

Caron [Meuniez], Rose-Lucile, b. Monerville, Seine-et-Oise, 17 Nov 1857; d. Paris, 9 Apr 1930. French soprano, studied Paris Cons.; debut, 1884, T. de la Monnaie (ROBERT LE DIABLE). Created Brunehilde in SIGURD and title role in SALAMMBÔ. Sang for several years in Paris O., where she was the first Fr. SIEGLINDE (1893) and DESDEMONA in VERDI's OTELLO (1894). She also excelled as ELISABETH, as FIDELIO, and as Donna ANNA. Her singing was largely confined to the cities of Paris and Brussels. LO

Carosio, Margherita, b. Genoa, 7 June 1908. Italian soprano. Debut 1924, Novi Ligure (LUCIA DI LAMMERMOOR). CG 1928 as Musetta (BOHÈME). Returned with T. S. Carlo, Naples, co. as VIOLETTA and NEDDA (1946) and with Sc. as ADINA (1950). Sc. debut 1929. She had a light, lyric sop. of considerable character, and acted with charm and pathos. AB

Carousel, musical, RODGERS, book and lyrics HAMMERSTEIN II, based on Ferenc Molnar's *Liliom*. NY, Majestic T., 19 Apr 1945; London, DL, 7 June 1950; revived NY CC 1954. EJ O★
See Lubbock

Carr, Benjamin, b. London, 12 Sept 1768; d. Philadelphia, Pa., 24 May 1831. American publisher, composer, and singer (sang in LOVE IN A VILLAGE, NY 15 Dec 1794). His opera, ARCHERS, was one of the first by an American citizen, and the second on William Tell. LO

Carré, Michel, b. Paris, 1819; d. Argenteuil, 27 June 1872. French librettist and translator. Very prolific; either on his own or in collaboration with others, chiefly BARBIER, supplied libs for most of the Fr. comps of his time, esp. BIZET (PÊCHEURS DE PERLES), GOUNOD (FAUST, MIREILLE), MEYERBEER (DINORAH), Ambroise THOMAS (MIGNON), and REYER (*La Statue*, 1861). Trs incl. NOZZE DI FIGARO, COSÌ FAN TUTTE, and LUSTIGEN WEIBER VON WINDSOR. LO

Carreras, José Maria, b. Barcelona, 1946. Spanish tenor. Debut 1969, Barcelona, as Ismaele (NABUCCO). London debut 1971, RFH; CG debut 1974 (ALFREDO). Has sung in Italy, Vancouver, Vienna, and NY (City O. and Met). Has a lyrical, keenly focused voice, and his repertory incl. the ten. roles in LUCREZIA BORGIA, MARIA STUARDA, *Caterina Cornaro* (DONIZETTI), LUCIA DI LAMMERMOOR, BEATRICE DI TENDA, LOMBARDI, LUISA MILLER, RIGOLETTO, and BALLO IN MASCHERA. He also sings ROMÉO and PINKERTON. EF

Carron [Cox], Arthur, b. Swindon, 12 Dec 1900. English tenor. Debut 1929, Old Vic, London; a prominent member of the Old Vic and later SW until 1935. NY Met 1935–46; CG 1947–51. At his best a fine, resonant heroic ten., excellent in dramatic parts. LO

Carson, Clarice, b. Montreal, 23 Dec 1936. Canadian soprano. Debut 1962, Montreal, as the Mother (AMAHL AND THE NIGHT VISITORS). NY CC 1965–6; debut as Countess ALMAVIVA. Joined the Met O. National Touring Co. 1966–7, then joined the regular co. Sang Chicago and Barcelona 1969, and with SO 1970. Her voice is of such variety and agility that she sang CONSTANZE at the 1969 Stratford Fest., but she also has power and dramatic presence; an outstanding TOSCA. CM

Caruso, Enrico, b. Naples, 25 Feb 1873; d. Naples, 2 Aug 1921. Italian tenor. Debut 1894, Naples, in GOUNOD's FAUST. Created leading ten. roles in FEDORA, ADRIANA LECOUVREUR,

and FRANCHETTI's *Germania*, 1902. Sang regularly at CG 1903–7, where his RODOLFO esp. popular; from 1908 to the end of his career principally associated with NY Met. The most popular ten. of his age, he excelled equally in the *verismo* and the *bel canto* repertoires. JB
See Robinson, *Caruso: His Life in Pictures* (London and New York 1957)

Carvalho [Carvaille], Léon, b. Mauritius, 18 Jan 1825; d. Paris, 29 Dec 1897. French manager and producer. Sang for a time, Paris OC; dir., TL, 1856–8, then stage manager at the O. Dir., OC, 1876–87, but when this was burned down with loss of 130 lives Carvalho was imprisoned for alleged negligence; reinstated 1891. An enterprising dir., operas mounted by him incl. TROYENS À CARTHAGE (TL 1863), CONTES D'HOFFMANN (OC 1881), LAKMÉ (OC 1883), MANON (OC 1884), and BRUNEAU's operas. He m. MIOLAN-CARVALHO (1853). LO

Casa, Lisa della, b. Burgdorf, nr Bern, 2 Feb 1919. Swiss soprano, famous for leading roles in R. STRAUSS operas. Wartime debut 1941, Solothurn-Biel (CIO-CIO-SAN); member of Zürich O. 1943–7. Following personal success at Salzburg Fest. 1947, as Zdenka (ARABELLA), became regular member of Vienna Staats O. and Bavarian Staats O., Munich. Later outstanding as Arabella, Countess (CAPRICCIO), and first singer since Lotte LEHMANN to appear successively in all three principal roles in ROSENKAVALIER. British debut 1951, Glyndebourne (Countess ALMAVIVA); Bayreuth 1952 (EVA); CG 1953, with Bavarian O., as Arabella; NY Met in 1953–4 season. Sang in premieres of W. BURKHARD's *Die Schwarze Spinne* and PROZESS in which she took three roles. Her voice is often likened to 'peaches and cream' in its beauty of legato line, subtlety of colour, and radiance of feeling, and much admired in MOZART, HANDEL, oratorio, and song programmes. She m. music critic Dragan Debelievic. NG
See Rosenthal, *Sopranos of Today* (London 1956)

Lisa della Casa as ARABELLA, London, CG, 29 Jan 1965; produced R. HARTMANN; designed Peter Rice

Cassel *see* KASSEL

Cassilly, Richard, b. Washington, DC, 14 Dec 1927. American tenor. Studied Peabody Cons., Baltimore. Debut 1954 in SAINT OF BLEECKER STREET on Broadway. Joined NY City O. and first appeared as Vakula in TCHAIKOVSKY's *Vakula the Smith*. Chicago Lyric O. debut 1959 as Laca (JENŮFA). First European appearance as Raskolnikoff in SUTERMEISTER's *Crime and Punishment* (Geneva 1965), the year he joined Hamburg Staats O. (debut as CANIO). CG debut 1968 (Laca); other roles there: FLORESTAN, SIEGMUND and VERDI's OTELLO. Vienna Staats O. debut 1970 (TANNHÄUSER); at Sc. as SAMSON 1970, at NY Met as RADAMES 1973. His big, vibrant ten. and committed acting have adorned many heroic roles. AB

Casson, (Sir) Hugh, b. Hampstead, London, 23 May 1910. British architect and designer. The chief architectural designer of the 1951 Fest. of Britain, he designed the massive sets for GLUCK's ALCESTE (1953) and INCORONAZIONE DI POPPEA (1962) at Glyndebourne, and for TROILUS AND CRESSIDA (CG 1954). EF

Castagna, Bruna, b. Bari, 15 Oct 1908. Italian contralto. Debut 1925 Mantua in BORIS GODUNOV; engaged by T. Colón 1925–8, then Sc. 1928–33. NY debut 1934, Hippodrome T., in CARMEN. Engaged by NY Met 1936–45 (debut as AMNERIS, 2 Mar 1936). LO

Castelnuovo-Tedesco, Mario, b. Florence, 3 Apr 1895; d. Hollywood, Cal., 16 Mar 1968. Italian composer. His eight operas incl. a marionette opera, *Aucassin et Nicolette* (Florence Maggio Musicale 1952); *Il Mercanto di Venezia* (Florence 1961), and *The Importance of Being Earnest* (1962). LO

Casti, Giovanni Battista, b. Acquapendente, Viterbo, 29 Aug 1724; d. Paris, 5 Feb 1803. Italian poet and librettist, court poet to Francis II in Vienna. His lib. for SALIERI's *Prima la Musica e poi le Parole* (1786) deals with the relationship between words and music – a theme taken up again in CAPRICCIO. LO

Castil-Blaze [François Henri Joseph Blaze], b. Cavaillon, 1 Dec 1784; d. Paris, 11 Dec 1857. Writer and critic. Wrote *De l'Opéra en France*, 2 vols (Paris 1820) and *Les Théâtres Lyriques de Paris*, 3 vols (Paris 1847–56). Also tr. into Fr. several operas incl. FIDELIO (Brussels 1847), NOZZE DI FIGARO, DON GIOVANNI, ZAUBERFLÖTE, and GAZZA LADRA. His maltreatment of OBERON as *Robin des Bois* (1824, trenchantly attacked by BERLIOZ) is a classic example of the misuse of the adapter's function. LO

Castor et Pollux, opera, 5 acts, RAMEAU, lib. Pierre Joseph Bernard. Paris, O., 24 Oct 1737; Glasgow (amateur prod.), 24 Oct 1937. Revived Paris 1754 with many changes from 1737 version; chosen for reopening of Paris O. after World War I, 17 Jan 1919. Perf. Florence Maggio Musicale 1935. Other operas by WINTER (Paris, O., 1806); Francesco Bianchi (Florence

1780); Georg Joseph Vogler (Munich 1787); Vincenzo Federici (1803). LO ○
See Girdlestone, *Jean-Philippe Rameau: His Life and Work* (London 1957)

castrato (It. from *castrare*, 'to emasculate'), a eunuch. An alternative term is *evirato* (from *evirare*, 'to emasculate'). A feature of It. *opera seria*, 17th–early 19th c., the vogue being at its height during the late Baroque era when castrati embodied the ideals of artificiality popular at the time. Famous castrati incl. Farinelli, Guadagni, and Senesino, who created leading roles for Handel. JB
See Heriot, *The Castrati in Opera* (London 1956)

Castro, Juan José, b. Avellaneda, Provincia de Buenos Aires, 7 Mar 1895; d. Buenos Aires, 3 Sept 1968. Argentine composer and conductor. Studied Buenos Aires with Manuel Posadas, Gaito, and Eduardo Fornarini, and Paris with d'Indy. Cond. T. Colón 1928–68 where he dir. the local premiere of Retablo de Maese Pedro (1942) and the posthumous world premiere of Falla's *La Atlántida* in its original Catalan version, 1963. His four operas are *La Zapatera Prodigiosa* (1943) and *Bodas de Sangre* (1952), both to libs by Lorca; *Proserpina y el Extranjero* (Sc. 1952), a version of the Persephone myth, which won the Verdi prize; and *Cosecha Negra*, unfinished and unperf.; orch. entrusted to Eduardo Ogando (comp. 1961). MK

Catalani, Alfredo, b. Lucca, 19 June 1854; d. Milan, 7 Aug 1893. Italian composer. Studied Paris and Milan. His first opera, *Elda* (Turin 1880) was refashioned as Loreley. His other operas, all given at Sc., are *Dejanice* (1883), *Edmea* (1886), and Wally, generally considered his masterpiece. Often taxed by his countrymen for his cosmopolitan style, Catalani was a thoughtful, sensitive artist with real imagination and a highly developed sense of the orch. He was much admired by Mahler and Toscanini, who rated him above Puccini; but the lack of a confident musical personality has militated against the survival of his works. JB

Angelica Catalani in Portugal's *Semiramide*, in which she made her London debut at the King's T., 13 Dec 1806

Catalani, Angelica, b. Sinigaglia, 10 May 1780; d. Paris, 12 June 1849. Italian soprano. Debut 1797, T. La Fenice, Venice. Appeared in other It. cities and then a sensational London debut 1806, where she sang till 1813 and again 1824 and 1828, her powers undiminished. She was notorious for over-embellishing her arias. She and her husband Valabrègue, a soldier-diplomat, ran the Paris TI on and off, 1813–18, disastrously. PS

Catania. A town on the east coast of Sicily; birthplace of Bellini. The Museo Belliniano contains documents and relics relating to the comp. Opera season at the T. Massimo Bellini usually runs from Jan to May. JB
See Hughes, *Great Opera Houses* (London 1956; New York 1959)

Catiline Conspiracy, The, opera, 2 acts, Hamilton, lib. comp., commissioned SO. Stirling, MacRobert T., 16 Mar 1974. Main chars: Fulvia (sop.) Sempronia (mezzo-sop.) Aurelia (mezzo-sop) Cicero (ten.) Quintus (ten.) Catiline (bar.) Caesar (bar.) Crassus (bass). Rome, 64–63 BC. The ambitious and unscrupulous Catiline obtains wealthy patrician support for his election as consul, against the democratic Cicero, as a first step toward overthrowing the republic and replacing it with his own dictatorship. He raises a secret conspiracy, but in the election he is defeated by Cicero, on whom he vows revenge. His plot is betrayed by Quintus via Fulvia and, after Cicero has disclosed it in the Senate, Catiline is hounded out. He flees Rome to lead a rebel army, but is mortally wounded in battle; the republic is preserved. Hamilton's music achieves a modern equivalent to Verdi's in expressive eloquence and theatrical impact within a serial idiom, often using traditional operatic devices, and portrays a wealth of individual char. in word setting of exceptional clarity. NG

Cavalieri, Caterina or Katharina [Franziska Kavalier], b. Währing, nr Vienna, 19 Feb 1760; d. Vienna, 30 June 1801. Austrian soprano. A pupil of Salieri, she sang only in Vienna; debut 1775, It. O., and from 1777 till its demise in 1787, at the Ger. Court O. Impressed by her 'flexible throat', MOZART comp. CONSTANZE for her, Mme Silberklang (SCHAUSPIELDIREKTOR) and Donna ELVIRA's aria, 'Mi tradì' for the Viennese revival of DON GIOVANNI, 1788. She retired 1793. JB

Cavalieri, Emilio di, b. Rome, *c.* 1550; d. Rome, 10 Mar 1602. Italian composer and member of Florentine Camerata. Wr. several stage works of which most important is the sacred opera *La Rappresentazione di Anima e di Corpo*, perf. in Oratory of S. Filippo Neri, Rome, Feb 1600. The first church opera, a continuation of the Liturgical Drama. Adapted by Bernhard Paumgartner for Salzburg Fest., 1968; recorded by Archive, cond. MACKERRAS, 1969. LO ○

Cavalieri, Lina, b. Viterbo, 25 Dec 1874; d. Florence, 8 Feb 1944. Italian soprano. Debut Lisbon (NEDDA); later sang leading roles in Italy, France, England, and USA; from 1906 onward increasingly associated with NY and Chicago.

Reputed the most beautiful singer of her time, Cavalieri was most successful in the lighter lyrical roles. JB

Cavalleria Rusticana (*Rustic Chivalry*), opera, 1 act, MASCAGNI, lib. Guido Menasci and Giovanni Targioni-Tozzetti after play by Giovanni Verga. Rome, T. Costanzi, 17 May 1890; Philadelphia, Grand O. House, 9 Sept 1891; London, Shaftesbury T., 19 Oct 1891. Main chars: Santuzza (sop. or mezzo-sop.) Lola (sop. or mezzo-sop.) Turiddu (ten.) Alfio (bar.). Turiddu, a returned soldier, has been neglecting his mistress Santuzza for the sake of his former love, Lola, now married to Alfio. Santuzza betrays them to Alfio, who provokes Turiddu to a duel and kills him. Mascagni's first perf. and most popular opera, it inaugurated the tradition of *verismo* and was hailed throughout Europe as heralding the rebirth of It. opera after VERDI. JB ○★
See Kobbé

Cavalli [Caletti-Bruni], Pietro Francesco, b. Crema, 14 Feb 1602; d. Venice, 14 Jan 1676. Italian composer. He took the name of Cavalli from his patron. Wrote *c.* 40 operas, chiefly for Venice, beginning with *Le Nozze di Teti e di Peleo* (1639); 28 are extant, and several have been revived recently incl. *Egisto* (Sante Fe 1974), ERISMENA, ORMINDO, *Rosinda* (Oxford 1973), and *Scipio Africano* (Drottningholm 1973). LO

Cavaradossi, ten., the hero of TOSCA

cavatina (It. from *cavare*, 'to extract'; application uncertain). Term in general use in 19th-c. Italy up to *c.* 1880 denoting a principal singer's first aria, usually in two movements (although '*Largo al factotum*' in BARBIERE DI SIVIGLIA has one). In Ger. and Fr. opera (*cavatine* or *Kavatine*') describes any short, slow aria (e.g. '*Und ob die Wolken*' in FREISCHÜTZ or '*Comme autrefois*' in PÊCHEURS DE PERLES). Used in modern times, rather misleadingly, to denote the slow movement of a double aria (see CANTABILE). In late 18th c. the form *cavata* is sometimes found. JB

Caverne, La, *drame lyrique*, 3 acts, LESUEUR, lib. P. Dercy. Paris, T. Feydeau, 15 Feb 1793. The subject, which gave some ideas to MÉLESVILLE for ZAMPA, is drawn from Alain-René Le Sage's *Gil Blas*: the rescue of Séraphine, daughter of Count Alvar de Guzman, abducted by bandits whose headquarters is a cave. Lesueur's best work. MÉHUL wrote an opera on same subject (1795). LO

Cebotari, Maria, b. Kishinev, Bessarabia, 10 Feb 1910; d. Vienna, 9 June 1949. Russian soprano. Debut 1931, Dresden (MIMI) where she sang Aminta in the first perf. of SCHWEIGSAME FRAU. Engaged at Berlin 1936–44, Vienna 1946–9. CG debut 1936, returning in 1947 during the visit of the Vienna Staats O. A superb interpreter of MOZART and R. STRAUSS, she sang SUSANNA, Countess ALMAVIVA, ZERLINA, Donna ANNA, SOPHIE, and SALOME. She created roles in ROMEO UND JULIA and DANTONS TOD. EF

Cavalleria Rusticana, London, CG, 16 Dec 1959; produced and designed ZEFFIRELLI

Cecchina, La *see* BUONA FIGLIUOLA

Cellier, Alfred, b. Hackney, 1 Dec 1844; d. London, 28 Dec 1891. English conductor and composer. Mus. dir., Prince's T., Manchester, 1873–5; later cond. GILBERT and SULLIVAN operas at the O. Comique (in the Strand, London) and also in the USA and Australia. Of his numerous operettas the greatest success was scored by *Dorothy* (London, Lyric T., 1888), a rewriting of his *Nell Gwynne* (Manchester 1876). LO

Cenerentola, La, ossia La Bontà in Trionfo (*Cinderella, or The Triumph of Goodness*), *opera buffa*, 2 acts, ROSSINI, lib. Jacopo Ferretti after Charles Guillaume Étienne, and based on PERRAULT. Rome, T. Valle, 25 Jan 1817; London, HM, 8 Jan 1820; NY, Park T., 27 June 1826; revived, new edition, Alberto Zedda, Florence 1971. Main chars: Cenerentola (mezzo-sop.) Ramira (ten.) Dandini (bar.) Don Magnifico (bass). The Cinderella story shorn of its supernatural elements. Rossini's most popular opera after BARBIERE DI SIVIGLIA. JB O
See Kobbé

Central City, Colorado, a summer school for young professionals offering 13 opera prods, 1957–63; dir. Nathaniel Merrill. BALLAD OF BABY DOE and R. WARD's *The Lady from Colorado* (1964) were first given there. Recent policy is for works of lighter character, or for dramas staged for the entire season. EJ

Cervantes, Miguel de, b. Alcalá de Henares, 1547; d. Madrid, 23 Apr 1616. Spanish novelist, dramatist, and poet. His *Don Quixote* (1605, 1615) has been the basis of many operas incl. MASSENET's *Don Quichotte*, the most famous, CALDARA's *Don Chisciotte* and *Sancio Panza*, DONIZETTI's *Il Furioso*, IBERT's *Le Chevalier Errant*, MENDELSSOHN's *Die Hochzeit des Camacho*; RETABLO DE MAESE PEDRO. His *El Teatro Magico* was drawn on for HENZE's *Das Wundertheater* and ORFF's *Astutuli*. Operas based on other of his works incl. BARRAUD's *Numance*, and GRÉTRY's *Le Trompeur*. FGB

Cesti, Marc'Antonio [Pietro Antonio], b. Arezzo, 5 Mar 1623; d. Florence, 14 Oct 1669. Italian composer. He worked chiefly in Venice, for which he wrote *c.* eight operas, but his most famous work, POMO D'ORO, a spectacle opera, of prodigious scenic display, was written for Vienna, 1667. LO

Chabrier, Emmanuel, b. Ambert, Puy-de-Dôme, 18 Jan 1841; d. Paris, 13 Dec 1894. French composer. His operas are *L'Étoile*, *opéra bouffe*, 3 acts, lib. Eugène Leterrier and Albert Vanloo, 1877; *Une Éducation Manquée*, 1-act operetta by same libs, 1879; GWENDOLINE; ROI MALGRÉ LUI. The first two have been revived in the USA (NY, 1968, and Aspen Col. 1959). Of *Briséïs*, lib. MENDÈS and Georges Ephraim Michel [E. Mikhaël], one act only was completed (perf. Paris O., 8 May 1899). His gay, unorthodox and sometimes brash music had an important influence on later Fr. music, although in *Gwendoline* and *Briséïs* his emulation of WAGNER blurred his characteristically Fr. outlook on art. Chabrier was a close friend of the Impressionist painters, and possessed a remarkable collection of their works. LO.
See Myers, *Emmanuel Chabrier and His Circle* (London 1969; Rutherford, N.J. 1970)

Miguel de Cervantes' *Don Quixote* was the basis for many operas including FRAZZI's *Don Chisciotte*, produced at the Florence Maggio in 1952; decor by the distinguished painter Giorgio de' Chirico (b. 1888).

chaconne (Fr. of Sp. derivation). A moderately slow dance in triple pulse time with an accent on the second beat. From LULLY's time it was usually the concluding dance in Fr. *tragédie lyrique* and in operas imitated from the Fr. (e.g. TRAETTA's *Antigona* and even ORFEO ED EURIDICE). JB

Chailly, Luciano, b. Ferrara, 19 Jan 1920. Italian composer. Two of his operas, *Una Domanda di Matrimonio* (1957) and *Era Proibito* (1963), had their premieres at the Piccola Sc., Milan. Others are: *Ferrovia Sopraelevata* (Bergamo 1955), *Il Canto del Cigno* (Bologna 1957), *La Riva delle Sirti* (Monte Carlo 1959), *Procedura Penale* (Como 1959), *Il Mantello* (Florence 1960), *Vassiliev* (Genoa 1967), and *Markheim* (Spoleto 1967). He has also wr. an operatic adaptation of DOSTOYEVSKY's novel, *The Idiot*. Mus. dir., Sc., 1969–71. EF

Chalabala, Zdeněk, b. Uherské Hradiště, 18 Apr 1899; d. Prague, 4 Mar 1962. Czech conductor. A pupil of F. NEUMANN and JANÁČEK in Brno. Cond. Brno 1925–36, then moved to Prague as Dramaturg and cond. After World War II cond. Ostrava, Brno, and Bratislava before becoming head of opera at the Prague NT (1953). One of the finest and most intelligent postwar Czech conds, excelling in large-scale works, notably the Russ. repertory. JT

Chaliapin, Feodor *see* SHALYAPIN

Chamber opera, opera wr. for reduced numbers of performers, both singers and esp. orch. Developed in the 20th c. partly by force of circumstances (expense of GRAND OPERA and accommodation problems), partly as reaction against the colossal theatrical apparatus demanded by WAGNER and R. STRAUSS. The 18th-c. INTERMEZZO had two or three soloists on stage, with a small, mainly string, orch.; the modern SĀVITRI has three characters only, TELEPHONE two, VOIX HUMAINE only one. BRITTEN in RAPE OF LUCRETIA reduced his orch. to a handful of soloists; in 1919 STRAVINSKY in HISTOIRE DU SOLDAT dispensed with the pit, putting his small selection of instrumentalists side by side with the players on stage. The practice is likely to increase rather than diminish. LO

Chapí y Lorente, Ruperto, b. Villena, nr Alicante, 27 Mar 1851; d. Madrid, 25 Mar 1909. Spanish composer. Studied Rome and Paris; of his eight operas, *Roger de Flor*, *La Bruja*, and *Circe* won him the name of 'the Spanish Massenet' among his devotees, but it was his 155 *zarzuelas* that brought him his wide popularity. His masterpiece in this form, *La Revoltosa* (1897), was keenly admired by SAINT-SAËNS; *La Patria Chica* (1907), *La Chavala* (1898), and *El Milagro de la Virgen* (1884) have kept their place in the repertoire. FGB

Charlotte, sop., Werther's lover in WERTHER

Charpentier, Gustave, b. Dieuze, Meurthe, 25 June 1860; d. Paris, 18 Feb 1956. French composer. Pupil of MASSENET and *Prix de Rome* winner, now remembered solely for his *verismo* working-class opera LOUISE. Its sequel, JULIEN, was a failure. LO

Chausson, Ernest, b. Paris, 21 Jan 1855; d. Limay, 10 June 1899. French composer. Studied with MASSENET and later with FRANCK. His only opera, *Le Roi Arthus* (others mentioned in some reference books are incidental music to plays), wr. 1886–95 in emulation of TRISTAN UND ISOLDE, was perf. Brussels, T. de la Monnaie, 30 Nov 1903. The lib., by the comp., bears a similarity to *Tristan*, dealing with Lancelot's guilty love for Guinevere, and Mordred's betrayal to King Arthur. LO

Chautauqua Opera Association, Chautauqua, NY. Founded 1874 as a centre of Sunday School activity by the Methodist Episcopal Church with programmes of Bible courses, literary lectures, and 'lyceum' entertainment during the summer, and by selected groups on tour during the winter. It now has a non-sectarian summer programme of master classes and operas given by advanced students of the Juilliard School of Music. Six or seven operas are perf. during July and August, and one musical comedy with guests from the NY Met and a professional orch. Dir. Leonard Treash. EJ

Chekhov, Anton Pavlovich, b. Taganrog, 29 Jan 1860; d. Badenweiler, 14/15 July 1904. Russian writer. In the West known particularly for his plays, yet it was in his many short stories that he contributed most to the development of Russ. literature. Several have inspired operas, incl.: *I've Forgotten!* 1882 (Iosif Pribik, 20th c.); *Surgery*, 1884 (Pierre Octave Ferroud, 1928; Ostroglazov); *Romance with a Double Bass*, 1886 (Dubensky, 1916; SAUGUET, *La Contrebasse*, 1932; Bucchi, *Il Contrabasso*, 1954); *The Witch*, 1886 (Boris Yanovsky, 1916; Vladimir Vlasov and Vladimir Fere, radio 1961; staged 1965); Pietro Argentino, *The Boor*, comp. 1957).

Dramatic works on which operas are based incl.: *On the High Road*, 1885 (Nottara, 20th c.); *Swan Song*, 1887–8 (CHAILLY, *Il Canto del Cigno*, 1957); *The Bear*, 1888 (Dobronić, *Vječnaja Pamjat*, also based on GOGOL's *Taras Bulba*, 1947; WALTON, 1967); *The Proposal*, 1888–9 (Chailly, *Una Domanda di Matrimonio*, 1957); *The Wedding*, 1889–90 (Vladimir Erenberg, 1916). GN

Cherepnin, Nikolay Nikolayevich, b. St Petersburg, 15 May 1873; d. Issy-les-Moulineaux, nr Paris, 27 June 1945. Russian composer and conductor. It was in his edition that SOROCHINTSY FAIR became known in the West. He lived in France from 1921. GN

Cherubini, Maria Luigi, b. Florence, 14 Sept 1760; d. Paris, 15 Mar 1842. Italian theorist and composer. Lived most of his life in Paris, where he was Dir. of the Cons. 1821–42. Wrote 25 operas, from *Il Quinto Fabio* (Alessandria 1780) to *Ali Baba* (Paris 1833, lib. SCRIBE and MÉLESVILLE, based on the ARABIAN NIGHTS). The most important are: LODOÏSKA; MÉDÉE;

DEUX JOURNÉES; *Anacréon* (1803); *Faniska* (wr. for Vienna, perf. there, KT, 25 Feb 1806). His best operas, wr. in the *opéra-comique* tradition, well constructed, with good and often exciting orchestration, pointed the way to the romantic opera of C. WEBER and the Grand Opera of MEYERBEER. BEETHOVEN admired him more than any other living comp., and imitated him in FIDELIO. *Médée,* his masterpiece, has been revived this century, notably by CALLAS. LO
See Deane, *Cherubini* (London 1965)

Cherubino, sop., the Countess's page in NOZZE DI FIGARO

Cheval de Bronze, Le (*The Bronze Horse*), *opéra féerique*, 3 acts, AUBER, lib. SCRIBE. Paris, OC, 23 Mar 1835; London, CG (in Eng.), 14 Dec 1835; NY (in Eng.), 23 Oct 1837. Revised, 4 acts, Paris, O., 21 Sept 1857. Chars: Yang, prince of China (ten.) Tsing Sing (bass) Peki (sop.) Stella (sop.). The mandarin, Tsing Sing, is turned to stone by one of his wives. Peki, another of his wives, flies on the magic bronze horse to seek the aid of Stella, a fairy princess, and with her magic bracelet breaks the spell, on the understanding that the mandarin will divorce her and allow her to marry her true love, a farmer. Seldom perf. today, Auber's score was notable for its imaginative quasi-Chinese scoring. PS

Maria Chiara as Micaëla in a Milan Scala production of CARMEN, 1973–4; produced Mauro Bolognini; decor Pier Luigi Samaritani; costumes Cloë Obolenski

Chiara, Maria, b. Oderzo, 24 Nov 1939. Italian soprano. Studied Venice Acad. Debut 1965, Venice (DESDEMONA in VERDI's OTELLO). Debut at Verona Arena as LIÙ (1969). Sc. debut 1972 (MICAËLA); CG debut 1973 (Liù). Her other roles incl. VIOLETTA, MIMI, AMELIA, and CIO-CIO-SAN. One of the most promising and expressive of younger It. sops, always using her beautiful voice sensitively. AB

Chicago. The Chicago-Philadelphia organization (1910–21) was formed from the carry-over of the defunct Manhattan O. in NY. Notable for artists of highest rank and for unusual works, often by Fr. comps, this co. served both cities and toured extensively (excepting 1914–15), incl. Boston in its seasons. CAMPANINI was Gen. Dir. 1913–19. After HAMMERSTEIN I's death (1919) the Chicago O. Assn was estab., then the Chicago Civic O. Co. with Samuel Insull as Chairman and principal guarantor, GARDEN as Dir., and POLACCO as principal cond. Soon after the new Opera House was built (1928) the entire Chicago operatic scene came to a halt with the Depression and the collapse of the Insull fortunes.

Ravinia Park, from 1911 to 1931, had a 10-week season during the summer of standard works, slightly abbreviated, with eminent singers and occasional novelties. Louis Eckstein was guarantor. Revived later as Ravinia Fest., it included presentations by the Chicago Orchestra.

The Chicago Lyric O. (founded 1954) now presents standard fare and a few novelties, with the best singers obtainable from Europe and the USA. EJ
See Davis, *Opera in Chicago 1850–1965* (New York 1966)

Children's operas. Though there were cos of child performers in the 18th c. the vogue for operas specially for children is modern. Two were comp. in Germany in 1931 – FORTNER's *Cress Ertrinkt* and HINDEMITH's *Wir Bauen eine Stadt*; in 1932 MILHAUD wrote *À Propos de Bottes* and *Un Petit Peu de Musique*, followed by *Un Petit Peu d'Exercise* (1934). COPLAND's first opera was a 'play opera' for high schools, *The Second Hurricane* (1937). LET'S MAKE AN OPERA combines children and adults, as does BRITTEN's *Noyes Fludde*. Other examples are by Aleksandr Grechaninov (1864–1956) (*The Dream of a Little Christmas Tree* and *The Castle House*, both 1911, and *The Cat, the Fox and the Rooster*, 1919); MENOTTI (HELP, HELP, THE GLOBOLINKS!); BUSH; BENNETT (*All the King's Men*, 1969); WILLIAMSON (*Julius Caesar Jones*, 1966), and WILSON (*The Selfish Giant*, Toronto 1973). In Moscow there is a Music T. for Children, dir. Natalia Saz, a pupil of STANISLAVSKY. LO

Chile *see* LATIN AMERICA

Chisholm, Erik, b. Glasgow, 4 Jan 1904; d. Rondebosch, Cape Town, 7 June 1965. Scottish conductor and composer. He cond. first British stage perfs of TROYENS, BÉATRICE ET BÉNÉDICT, and DUKE BLUEBEARD'S CASTLE. His own operas incl. *Feast of Samhain*, *Simoon*, *Dark Sonnet*, *Murder in 3 Keys* (NY 1954), *Black Roses*, and *Inland Woman* (Capetown 1954; London 1957). He was Professor of Music at Cape Town Univ. from 1945 until his death. EF

Chlubna, Osvald, b. Brno [Brünn], 22 July 1895; d. Brno, 30 Oct 1971. Czech composer. A pupil of JANÁČEK, he scored the final act of Janáček's first opera ŠÁRKA for its perf. in 1925 and, with another pupil Břetislav Bakala, was responsible for the reorchestration and changed ending (1930) of FROM THE HOUSE OF THE DEAD. His seven operas incl. *Catullus's Vengeance* (*Pomsta Catullova*, 1921), *The Love Affairs of the Lord of Heslov* (*Freje pána z Heslova*, 1949), and *The Cradle* (*Kolébka*, 1963). JT

chorus 1. A body of singers who sing and act as a group, either in unison or harmony. 2. Any musical number wr. for such a body. The chorus played little part in It. opera until *c.* 1750; in Fr. *tragédie lyrique* it was important from the start. JB

Christie, John, b. Glyndebourne, 14 Dec 1882; d. Glyndebourne, 4 July 1962. English theatre owner. With his wife, MILDMAY, he built and founded GLYNDEBOURNE O., whose repertory at first reflected his own taste for MOZART and the It. 19th-c. repertory. In 1954 the theatre, house, grounds, and gardens were conveyed to the Glyndebourne Arts Trust, to ensure the future of the opera house. EF

Christoff, Boris, b. Sofia, 18 May 1918. Bulgarian bass. Debut 1946, Rome (COLLINE), Sc. debut 1947 (BORIS GODUNOV), CG debut 1949, also as Boris. Other Russ. operas in which he sings are IVAN SUSANIN, PRINCE IGOR, KHOVANSHCHINA, and MAID OF PSKOV. His repertory incl. GOUNOD's FAUST, MEFISTOFELE, MOSÈ IN EGITTO, ROBERT LE DIABLE, and many roles in VERDI operas: ATTILA, Zaccaria (NABUCCO), PHILIPPE, Procida (VÊPRES SICILIENNES), and Fiesco (SIMONE BOCCANEGRA). His black-toned, resonant voice and strong stage personality make him the ideal exponent of Boris, which he has sung all over the world. EF

Christophe Colomb, opera, 2 parts and 27 scenes, MILHAUD, lib. CLAUDEL. Berlin, Staats O., 5 May 1930; London, BBC, 16 Jan 1937; NY, Carnegie Hall (concert), 1952. Main chars: Colomb (bar.) Isabella (sop.) King of Spain (bass). The narrator (speaking role) announces the work as 'The Book of the Life and Voyages of Christopher Columbus, who discovered America'. EF

Chrysothemis, sop., Elektra's sister in ELEKTRA

Chueca, Federico, b. Madrid, 5 May 1848; d. Madrid, 20 June 1908. Spanish composer. Of his numerous *zarzuelas*, the most famous is *La Gran Vía* (1886), jointly comp. with J. VALVERDE, and presented in a modified form as *Castles in Spain* (London 1906). FGB

Church operas. Opera as a branch of theatre has some roots in liturgical drama, and E. di CAVALIERI's *La Rappresentazione di Anima e di Corpo* is the first church opera. BRITTEN has revived the practice in his church operas CURLEW RIVER, BURNING FIERY FURNACE, and PRODIGAL SON, and in his children's opera *Noyes Fludde*. MACONCHY's church opera, *The Jesse Tree* was performed at Dorchester Abbey, 7 Oct 1970. LO

Boris Christoff as BORIS GODUNOV and PASHLEY as Fyodor, London, CG, 23 Nov 1974; produced Ande Anderson; designed WAKHEVITCH

Ciboulette, operetta, 3 acts, HAHN, lib. Robert de Flers and Francis de Croisset. Paris, T. des Variétés, 7 Apr 1923. Hahn's most successful operetta, revived Marseille, 1974–5 season. LO
See Lubbock

Ciceri, Pierre-Luc-Charles, b. St Cloud, 17 or 18 Aug 1782; d. St Cléron, 22 Aug 1868. French designer. At Paris O. from 1809, succeeding Jean-Baptiste Isabey (1767–1855) as scenic dir. 1810. Specialized in exteriors. Designed for fairytale operas and ballets; also did decor for LISZT's *Don Sancho* (1825), MUETTE DE PORTICI (1828), COMTE ORY (1828), GUILLAUME TELL (1829), ROBERT LE DIABLE (1831). His scenery was romantic, full of lush vegetation and fanciful architecture, but attempted realistic portrayal. LO

Cid, Le, opera, 4 acts, MASSENET, lib. Adolphe d'Ennery, GALLET, and Édouard Blau, based on CORNEILLE's drama, 1637. Paris, O., 30 Nov 1885; New Orleans, 23 Feb 1890. Other operas based either on Corneille or his Sp.

source *Las Mocedas del Cid* by Guilhem de Castro (1621), incl. HANDEL's *Rodrigo* (1707 or 1708) and *Flavio* (1723); SACCHINI's *Chimene* (1784), and CORNELIUS's *Le Cid* (1865). LO
See Harding, *Massenet* (London 1970; New York 1971)

Cikker, Ján, b. Banská Bystrica, 29 July 1911. Slovak composer. Studied under KŘIČKA and NOVÁK, Prague Cons. 1930–6 and with WEINGARTNER, Vienna 1936–7. Became professor of composition at Bratislava Acad. 1951. His first two operas, *Juro Jánošík* (1954) and *Beg Bajazid* (1957) deal with Slovak subjects, the first a folk legend, the second historical fiction; later operas – *Mister Scrooge* (1963, after DICKENS), *Resurrection* (*Vzkříšení*, 1962, after TOLSTOY), *A Play of Love and Death* (*Hra o lasce a smrti*, 1971, after Romain Rolland) and *Coriolanus* (1974, after SHAKESPEARE) – employ not only international subjects but a musical technique that owes much to Ger. expressionism and serialism. He is the best-known Slovak opera comp. and his works, *Resurrection* in particular, have had several productions abroad. JT

Cilea, Francesco, b. Palmi, 26 July 1866; d. Varazze, 20 Nov 1950. Italian composer. Studied Naples Cons.; later dir. there (1916–35). His operas are *Gina* (Naples 1889), *Tilda* (Florence 1892) ARLESIANA, ADRIANA LECOUVREUR, *Gloria* (Milan 1907; revived 1932), *Il Matrimonio Selvaggio* (wr. 1909, unperf.). A competent practitioner of *verismo* opera who combined composition with a distinguished acad. career and whose masterpiece, *Adriana Lecouvreur*, survives in the repertoire. JB

Cimarosa, Domenico, b. Aversa, 17 Dec 1749; d. Venice, 11 June 1801. Italian composer. Studied Naples Cons. S. Maria di S. Loreto; from 1772 active as leading It. opera comp. with PAISIELLO: chamber comp. to Catherine the Great, St Petersburg, 1787–90, and MdC to Emperor Leopold II, Vienna, 1790–2; returned to Naples, and died on his way to Russia, a victim of the anti-Napoleonic reaction in his native city. Of his more than 60 operas MATRIMONIO SEGRETO was his masterpiece and is still revived today. In the serious genre, the neo-classical *Gli Orazi ed I Curiazi* (Venice 1796) looks forward to future trends in It. opera. JB

Cinq-Mars, *opéra dialogué*, 4 acts, GOUNOD, lib. Paul Poirson and GALLET, based on Alfred de Vigny's novel, 1826. Paris, OC, 5 Apr 1877; Leeds (in Eng. by Carl Rosa Co.), 26 Oct 1900. LO

Church operas. The EOG's production of CURLEW RIVER; Orford Church, 1964 Aldeburgh Fest., the cast included TEAR as the Madwoman; SHIRLEY-QUIRK as the Ferryman; Bryan Drake as Taverner; GARRARD as the Abbot.

Cinti-Damoreau, Laure [Cinthie Montalant], b. Paris, 6 Feb 1801; d. Paris, 25 Feb 1863. French soprano. Studied Paris Cons.; debut aged 18 TI, Paris, as CHERUBINO, graduating to principal roles 1821. Paris O. debut 1826 (FERNAND CORTEZ). Sang in Brussels 1827 where she m. the ten., L. C. Damoreau. Remained at the O. till 1835, then at the OC until 1842, retiring 1846. From 1834 she taught singing at the Paris Cons., and pub. an album of romances and a book on singing. She sang in the first perfs of five ROSSINI operas, *Il Viaggio a Reims*, *Le Siège de Corinthe*, MOSÈ IN EGITTO, COMTE ORY, and GUILLAUME TELL. PS

Cio-Cio-San (sop.), the heroine of MADAMA BUTTERFLY

City Center *see* NEW YORK

claque (Fr. 'slap, smack'). A group, a section of the audience, whose function is to lead the applause. Organized under a leader, paid by one or more performers; the others may be paid, or may be provided with free tickets. Not unknown at CG and the NY Met, it is more a feature of continental European opera houses, as in Vienna, Sc., and other It. theatres. LO

Claudel, Paul, b. Villeneuve, 6 Aug 1868; d. Paris, 23 Feb 1955. French writer, poet and librettist, with close links with the Symbolist writers. Wrote libs for CHRISTOPHE COLOMB, JEANNE D'ARC AU BÛCHER, and MILHAUD's trilogy *Orestie* (Berlin 1963). Renzo ROSSELLINI's *L'Annonce Faite à Marie* (1972) is based on Claudel's poetic drama of that name (1912). LO

Clemenza di Tito, La (*The Clemency of Titus*), *opera seria*, 2 acts, MOZART, lib. METASTASIO adapted Caterino Mazzolà. Prague, 6 Sept 1791; London, HM, 27 Mar 1806; Tanglewood, 4 Aug 1952. Main chars: Vitellia (sop.) Servilia (sop.) Annio (mezzo-sop.) Sesto (mezzo-sop.) Tito (ten.). Vitellia, humiliated by Tito's neglect of her claim to be his Empress, incites her admirer Sesto (Sextus) to murder him; but the plot is unsuccessful and Tito, having earlier renounced Servilia to her lover Annio (Annius) pardons the conspirators. Mozart's last It. opera, widely perf. as long as the neoclassical vogue persisted. Recently it has begun to re-enter the repertoire. Metastasio's lib. was first set by CALDARA (1734), and by *c.* 20 other comps incl. GLUCK (1752). JB O

Cleva, Fausto, b. Trieste, 17 May 1902; d. 6 Aug 1971. Italian-born conductor, migrated to USA 1920. Attached to NY Met, where he was chief cond. of It. operas 1938–42. Cond., San Francisco O., 1942–4 and 1949–55, after which returned to the Met. Art. dir., Chicago O., 1944–6. LO

cloud machines. The invention of these devices for suspending performers above the stage was attributed to Filippo Brunelleschi (1377–1446), whose Paradiso in S. Felice in Florence was improved by Francesco d'Angelo (*fl.* 15th c.) by adding cottonwool clouds to the machinery. Their heyday was in SPECTACLE OPERA by designers such as TORELLI, BURNACINI, and SERVANDONY, not only for the DEUS EX MACHINA but for other flying and celestial effects. Their construction was described in Niccola Sabbatini's famous *Pratica di Fabricar Scene, e Machine ne' Teatri* (Ravenna 1638). LO

Cluj. Town in Romania; the cultural centre of Transylvania. It has the Romanian O. House (founded 1919) and the Magyar O. (1948). GN

Cluytens, André, b. Antwerp, 26 Mar 1905; d. Neuilly, Paris, 3 June 1967. Belgian conductor. Dir. opera at Antwerp 1927–32, Toulouse 1932–5, and Lyon 1935. After World War II cond. Paris O. and OC. From 1956 he appeared successfully in USA. JB

Coates, Albert, b. St Petersburg, 23 Apr 1882; d. Milnerton, nr Cape Town, 11 Dec 1953. Anglo-Russian composer and conductor. Studied Leipzig Cons. under NIKISCH, who appointed him coach at the Leipzig O. Engaged as chief cond., Elberfeld, 1906–8; after periods at Dresden and Mannheim he became for five years principal cond. St Petersburg. Escaping from Russia during the Revolution he made England his home. Cond. frequently at CG and made guest appearances at leading opera houses in Europe and America, settling in S. Africa 1940. His operas incl. *Samuel Pepys* (Munich 1929) and *The Pickwick Papers* (CG 1936). JB

Cocteau, Jean, b. Maisons-Laffitte, Seine-et-Oise, 5 July 1889; d. Paris, 12 Oct 1963. French writer. An important figure in the Parisian Theatre of the 1920s, active in plays, revues, films. Operas based on his works are: ANTIGONE; PAUVRE MATELOT; OEDIPUS REX, and VOIX HUMAINE. LO

Coelho, Ruy, b. Alcácer do Sal, 3 Mar 1891. Portuguese composer. Studied with HUMPERDINCK and SCHÖNBERG. His 11 operas incl. *Inês de Castro*, *Crisfal*, and *Belkiss*. Music critic of the daily *O Diário de Notícias*. FGB

Coertse, Mimi, b. Durban, 12 June 1932. South African soprano. Studied S. Africa and Vienna, where she began her long association with the QUEEN OF THE NIGHT; also sang CG 1956–8. A coloratura sop.; other roles are OLYMPIA, GILDA, and ZERBINETTA. LO

Cola Rienzi, der Letzte der Tribunen (*Cola Rienzi, the Last of the Tribunes*), grand opera, 5 acts, WAGNER, lib. composer after E. Bulwer Lytton. Dresden, 20 Oct 1842; NY, 4 Mar 1878; London, HM (in Eng.), 27 Jan 1879. Main chars: Cola Rienzi (ten.) Irene (sop.) Colonna (bass) Adriano (mezzo-sop.) Orsini (bass) Raimondo (bass). Orsini and Colonna and their respective followers clash in an attempt to carry off Irene, Rienzi's sister. Adriano, Colonna's son, defends her; Raimondo the Papal Legate invests Rienzi with power to restore order in Rome. Adriano forestalls his father's attempt to murder Rienzi. At Adriano's request Rienzi pardons the conspirators. Orsini and Colonna lead an attack on Rome and are defeated and killed. His father's death turns Adriano into an enemy of Rienzi, and the people, led by Raimondo and Adriano, turn against Rienzi: only Irene stands by him. The Capitol is fired: Irene and Rienzi die in the flames. JB
See Kóbbe

Colas Breugnon: The Master of Clamecy, opera, 3 acts, KABALEVSKY, lib. V. G. Bragin and composer after Romain Rolland. Leningrad, Maly T., 22 Feb 1938; revised version, Moscow, Stanislavsky-Nemirovich-Danchenko Music T., 20 Mar 1971. Main chars: Colas Breugnon (bar.) Selina (mezzo-sop.) Jacqueline (sop.) Gifflard (bass) Curé (bass) Duke (ten.) Mademoiselle de Termes (sop.). Colas and Selina are in love. Gifflard (who also covets Selina) spreads a rumour that Colas is enamoured of Mademoiselle de Termes, a guest whom the tyrannical Duke has brought from Paris. In a jealous rage, Selina tells the tipsy Curé to marry her to Gifflard. Thirty years pass (during which time Colas has been living with his former love, Jacqueline), and the Duke takes away to his castle the sculpture of Selina which Colas has carved. The Duke's soldiers bring the plague to the town. Jacqueline dies; Colas meets Selina, and the couple are reconciled. At the castle, Gifflard tells the Duke that Colas is a rebel; the Duke destroys Colas's sculpture of Selina. Seeing his finest work mutilated, Colas feigns repentence for his activities, and promises to carve a statue of the Duke. At its unveiling, this is revealed to be a sculpture of the Duke sitting back-to-front on a donkey. Ridiculed, the Duke retreats to his castle. Though Kabalevsky's first stage success, criticism of (primarily) the lib caused him to make substantial revisions of his early version, where, for example, the opera ends with Colas throwing open the gates of the castle to the Clamecy rioters. In the second version, it is the forces of art rather than arms that win the day. GN

Colbran, Isabella (Angela), b. Madrid, 2 Feb 1785; d. Bologna, 7 Oct 1845. Spanish soprano. Studied with Francesco Pareja and Girolamo Crescentini; debut 1801, Paris. Sang successfully Sc., 1807, and in 1811 engaged by BARBAIA for Naples; debut as PAISIELLO's Nina. She became Barbaia's mistress. ROSSINI wr. ELISABETTA REGINA D'INGHILTERRA for her. She deserted Barbaia to live with Rossini, and created roles in ten of his operas, incl. *Armida*, *Zelmira*, and SEMIRAMIDE. They m. 15 Mar 1822. She appeared in London without success 1823. Rossini left her for Olympe Pélissier and Colbran retired to Bologna. PS

Coliseum *see* LONDON

colla voce (It. 'with the voice'), an instruction to an accompanist to abandon strict time and follow whatever rhythmic licence the singer chooses to employ. Mostly used with reference to individual phrases only. JB

Collier, Marie, b. Ballarat, 16 Apr 1926; d. London, 8 Dec 1971. Australian soprano. Debut 1952, with Victoria National O., Melbourne, as Santuzza (CAVALLERIA RUSTICANA); subsequently toured Australia as Magda (CONSUL). Joined CG 1956, with major success as Musetta (BOHÈME). Created Hecuba in KING PRIAM; title role in Western Europe premiere of KATERINA IZMAYLOVA (CG 1963); Emilia Marty in British premiere of MAKROPULOS CASE; Christine Mannon in MOURNING BECOMES ELECTRA (1968). US debut 1964 with San Francisco O. (Katerina Izmaylova). Also gained widespread success as TOSCA and as MARIE. On stage a flamboyant, dramatic personality with vibrant voice of brilliant timbre and emotional commitment to the highly charged roles she favoured. She died in fall from window. NG

Colline, bass, one of the four Bohemians in BOHÈME

Collingwood, Lawrance Arthur, b. London, 14 Mar 1887. English conductor. Studied St Petersburg Cons. Taken on the music staff at the Old Vic, London, 1919; principal cond., SW, 1931. His own opera *Macbeth* prod. there 1934, and he cond. the first London perfs of SNOW MAIDEN and TALE OF TSAR SALTAN, and of the original version of BORIS GODUNOV. Mus. dir. SW, 1940–6, and during the Lillian Baylis Centenary Fest. there (1974) cond. NOZZE DI FIGARO. EF

Cologne [Köln], W. Germany. The city has one of the leading opera houses in the German Federal Republic. Otto Lohse, KLEMPERER, Eugen Szenkar were among its mus. dirs during and after World War I, Klemperer introducing (1917–24) several new works to the country, incl. KÁT'A KABANOVÁ (1922). The opera house was destroyed during World War II and a new house, with an attractive modern design and good acoustics, was opened 1957. Mus. dirs have incl. SAWALLISCH (1959–63) and KERTESZ (1963–73). By 1975 a complete cycle of MOZART's major operas from IDOMENEO to CLEMENZA DI TITO had been brought into the repertory, all prod. PONNELLE. AB

Colombia *see* LATIN AMERICA

Colón, Teatro *see* BUENOS AIRES

coloratura (It. 'colouring'), a bastard term meaning brilliant vocal passage work, for which the It. equivalent is FIORITURA; but today the word is beginning to be used even in Italy in its Eng. sense. JB

coloratura soprano, a sop. who specializes in showy, high-lying parts such as QUEEN OF THE NIGHT, LAKMÉ, and ZERBINETTA. JB

Coltelacci, Giulio, b. Rome, 12 Apr 1916. Italian scenographer. Has both des. and prod. for many It. theatres incl. Sc., Verona (GIOCONDA, 1973), and Florence Maggio Musicale. LO

Coltellini, Marco, b. Livorno, ?13 Oct 1719; d. St Petersburg, 1777. Important 18th-c. Italian librettist, friend of GLUCK, TRAETTA, and others of the 'operatic reform' movement. After working at Parma was appointed 'Theatre Poet' at Viennese court 1764; similar post at St Petersburg from 1772. Wrote about 18 libs, some set more than once, for Traetta (*Ifigenia in Tauride*, 1763) MOZART (FINTA GIARDINIERA, FINTA SEMPLICE), GASSMANN, HASSE, SALIERI (*Armida*, 1771), and HAYDN (*L'Infedeltà Delusa*, 1773). LO

Columbia University, Brander Matthews Theater *see* NEW YORK

comédie-ballet, a term used esp. by LULLY and MOLIÈRE to describe prods at Louis XIV's court, e.g. MONSIEUR DE POURCEAUGNAC, *Le Bourgeois Gentilhomme*. An important link between the *ballet du cour* and Fr. opera, which has always preserved a dance element. Term first used in *Les Fâcheux* (Charles Louis Beauchamp), perf. Vaux 1660. LO

comédie mêlée d'ariettes, term used in mid-18th-c. France to describe *opéra comique*. Plays, in prose or in verse, interspersed with songs, by FAVART, SEDAINE, MARMONTEL, and others. LO

Comedy on the Bridge (*Veselohra na Mostě*), radio opera, 1 act, MARTINŮ, lib. Václav Kliment Klicpera. Czechoslovak Radio, 18 Mar 1937; London, Lamda T., 10 Oct 1965; NY, Hunter Playhouse, 28 May 1951. Main chars: Popelka (sop.) Jan (bar.) the Brewer (bass) Eva (contr.) the Schoolmaster (ten.). The two pairs and the schoolmaster assemble on a bridge linking enemy and friendly territory; they are not allowed to pass by the sentries on either side. This situation allows the unfolding of their stories: their loves, their jealousies, and reconciliations. Martinů's simple and effective radio opera is ideally served by Klicpera's text, a witty satire on war and bureaucracy. JT

comic opera, a somewhat nebulous term applied to an opera that is light and amusing, similar in some respects to OPÉRA COMIQUE or SINGSPIEL, but not to be confused with them since these terms indicate certain restrictions to which comic opera may not necessarily conform. LO

commedia dell'arte, popular It. improvised comedy, 16th–18th c., with stock characters (Pantaloon, Arlequino, Pulcinello) and situations (scheming lovers, cunning servants, duped masters). It underlies much of OPERA BUFFA, and several works from early 20th c. show a revived interest, e.g. ARLECCHINO, ARIADNE AUF NAXOS, and even, esp. in the last act, ROSENKAVALIER. LO

comprimario (It. 'junior lead', 'second part'). Duennas or chaperons, servants, confidants, come into this class, which often provides good opportunities for young singers to show their paces. LO

Comte Ory, Le (*Count Ory*), opera, 2 acts, ROSSINI, lib. SCRIBE and Charles Gaspard Delestre-Poirson. Paris, O., 20 Aug 1828; London, HM, 28 Feb 1829; NY, 22 Aug 1831. Main chars: Adèle (sop.) Isolier (mezzo-sop.) Ory (ten.) Raimbaud (bar.). Ory, a notorious rake, attempts the virtue of the Lady Adèle, disguising himself first as a hermit, then as the mother superior of a company of nuns – his own followers *en travesti*; admitted to Adèle's castle they all become drunk; Ory's designs are thwarted, partly by Isolier, his page, also in love with Adèle, and finally by the return of her brother from the Crusades. Rossini's only comic opera in Fr.: very popular at the Paris O. where after 1846 it was frequently coupled with A. ADAM's *Giselle*. JB

Constanze, sop., Belmonte's lover in ENTFÜHRUNG AUS DEM SERAIL

Le Comte Ory, Paris OC, 29 Dec 1968; designed François Gaveau; produced Michel Grochot. Left to right: Eliane Manchet as Lady Adèle, Marie Luce Bellary as Ragonde (a servant), Jean-Christophe Benoît as Raimbaud

Consul, The, opera, 3 acts, MENOTTI, lib. comp. Philadelphia, 1 Mar 1950; NY, Barrymore T., 15 Mar 1950; London, Cambridge T., 7 Feb 1951. Main chars: Magda Sorel (sop.) John Sorel (bass-bar.) Mother (contr.) Secretary (sop.). In a consulate 'somewhere in Europe', Magda, wife of a revolutionary patriot, 'lover of freedom', tries to procure an emigration visa and is thwarted by a high government official. Played widely in continental Europe; the work was revived NY CC, 1973. EJ

Contes d'Hoffmann, Les (*The Tales of Hoffmann*), opera, 3 acts, OFFENBACH, left unfinished and completed by GUIRAUD, lib. BARBIER based on play, *Les Contes Fantastiques d'Hoffmann* (1851) by Barbier and CARRÉ. Paris, OC, 10 Feb 1881; NY, Fifth Avenue T. (in Fr.), 10 Oct 1882; London, Adelphi T. (in Ger.), 17 Apr 1907; HM (in Eng. under BEECHAM) 12 May 1910. A new edition has recently been prepared by BONYNGE (prod. Seattle, NY Met, Sydney). Based on three stories by HOFFMANN, from *Nachstücke*, 1817 (act I), *Fantasiestücke in Callots Manier*, 1814–15 (act II), and *Die Serapionsbrüder*, 1819–21 (act III). Offenbach's most ambitious work relates Hoffmann's unfulfilled loves with Olympia, a mechanical doll (act I); with the Venetian courtesan Giulietta (act II); with the consumptive Antonia (act III) – thwarted by the evil influences of, in turn, Dr Coppelius, the magician Dapertutto, and Dr Miracle. LO ○★
See Newman, *More Opera Nights* (London 1954)

continuo, short for It. *basso continuo* (Eng. 'thorough-bass'). A bass line, called 'continuo' because it is the one wholly continuous element in a composition; the basis of Baroque music from the *stile rappresentativo* of the earliest operas to that of HANDEL. Normally played on a keyboard instrument with or without a string bass, the player filling out the harmony *ad lib*, sometimes guided by figures or accidentals below the stave. Keyboard continuo remained in force for *recitativo secco* until *c.* 1820 in *opera seria* and *c.* 1840 in *opera buffa*. JB

contralto, the lowest range in the female voice, distinguished from SOPRANO and MEZZO-SOPRANO not only by pitch but by darker colouring. LO

Converse, Frederick Shepherd, b. Newton, Mass., 5 Jan 1871; d. Westwood, nr Boston, 8 June 1940. American composer. His *The Pipe of Desire* (Boston 1906) was the first US opera perf. at NY Met, 1910. LO

Convitato di Pietra, Il (*The Stone Guest*), opera, Giuseppe Gazzaniga (1743–1819), lib. Giovanni Bertati. Venice, 5 Feb 1787. The forerunner of DON GIOVANNI. Very popular in its time; revived Siena 30 Aug 1973. LO

Cooper, Emil, b. Kherson, Ukraine, 20 Dec 1877; d. NY, 16 Nov 1960. Russian conductor. Studied Odessa, Vienna, Moscow. Cond. premiere of GOLDEN COCKEREL. Went with DYAGILEV to Paris 1909. Left Russia 1922; cond., Chicago O., 1929–31; NY Met, 1944–50, then with Montreal O. Guild, where he cond. local premiere of CONSUL. Has also cond. Russ. opera at CG and Sc. LO

Copenhagen [København]. Ger., It., and Fr. opera cos visited Copenhagen in the early 18th c. The first grand opera to a Danish text, NAUMANN's *Orfeus og Eurydice*, was given at the Royal T. 1786, when Naumann became dir. The present theatre, which houses the Danish Royal O., dates from 1874. *See* DENMARK. EF

Copland, Aaron, b. Brooklyn, NY, 14 Nov 1900. American composer. His two operas are a children's opera, *The Second Hurricane* (1937), and TENDER LAND. LO

Copley, John, b. Birmingham, 12 June 1933. English producer. First worked at CG as the Apprentice in GUTHRIE's prod. of PETER GRIMES (1950). SW as stage manager, later prod. (TABARRO, 1957). After a period as deputy stage manager, CG, became resident prod. Began by reviving other prods' work, but since the late 1960s has been responsible for many of the house's most inventive stagings, incl. COSÌ FAN TUTTE, NOZZE DI FIGARO, DON GIOVANNI, ORFEO ED EURIDICE, BOHÈME, and ELISIR D'AMORE. At the same time, he has worked regularly with the ENO at the Col, notably on prods of CARMEN, TROVATORE, TRAVIATA, MARIA STUARDA, and ROSENKAVALIER. US debut 1972, Dallas (LUCIA DI LAMMERMOOR). One of the most lively and imaginative prods, with a particular flair in clarifying char. relationships. AB

Coq d'Or, Le *see* GOLDEN COCKEREL

Corbeil, Claude, b. Rimouski, Quebec, 17 Apr 1940. Canadian bass-baritone. First appeared in opera on TV from Montreal, 1965. Sang in PÉRICHOLE in Quebec City 1967; since then at CG, NY CC, Philadelphia Lyric, and regularly with most cos in Canada. He has a fine lyric bass voice, effective in such roles as COLLINE and Bluebeard (DUKE BLUEBEARD'S CASTLE), and an engaging stage presence. CM

Franco Corelli as Licinio (VESTALE), in which he made his Milan Scala debut, 14 Nov 1954, in a performance celebrating the 180th anniversary of SPONTINI's birth. The cast included CALLAS, ROSSI-LEMENI, STIGNANI; decor Pietro Zuffi; produced VISCONTI; conducted Antonio Votto

Corder, Frederick, b. London, 26 Jan 1852; d. London, 21 Aug 1932. English composer, conductor, and translator. From RAM, London, won Mendelssohn Scholarship, studied Cologne under Ferdinand Hiller. Opera, *Nordisa*, perf. Liverpool 1887 (Carl Rosa Co.). A WAGNER champion, tr. RING DES NIBELUNGEN and TRISTAN UND ISOLDE; his tr. of WALKÜRE was the first to be sung in Eng. (1895). LO

Corelli [Dario] Franco, b. Ancona, 8 Apr 1921. Italian tenor. Debut 1951, Spoleto (Don JOSÉ). Sc. debut 1954 as Licinio (VESTALE); CG debut 1957 (CAVARADOSSI). Since 1961 he has sung at the NY Met. The strength of his heroic ten. voice is shown to best advantage in roles such as POLLIONE, Gualtiero (PIRATA), POLIUTO, ERNANI, and MANRICO; he is also admired as ANDREA CHÉNIER, DICK JOHNSON, CALAF, and WERTHER. EF

Corena, Fernando, b. Geneva, 22 Dec 1916. Swiss-Italian bass. Studied Geneva and Milan. Debut 1947 Trieste, as Varlaam (BORIS GODUNOV). NY Met debut 1954 (LEPORELLO) and has since sung there more than 350 times, mostly in all the It. *buffo* parts. CG debut 1960 as Don BARTOLO (ROSSINI'S BARBIERE DI SIVIGLIA). Famous roles incl. FALSTAFF, DON PASQUALE, Sacristan (TOSCA), and DULCAMARA. AB

Corneille, Pierre, b. Rouen, 6 June 1606; d. Paris, 1 Oct 1684. French dramatist. His tragedies, with those of RACINE and perhaps Alexandre Hardy (c. 1570–1632), exploiting the conflict between duty and honour, and passion, were the models for ZENO and METASTASIO. Dramas that have furnished subjects for operas are: *Horace*, 1640 (SALIERI, 1786); *Le Cid*, 1636/7 (MASSENET; HANDEL, *Flavio*, 1723; SACCHINI, 1764; PAISIELLO, 1775; Johan Wagenaar, 1916); *Polyeucte*, 1641/2 DONIZETTI; GOUNOD); *Sophonisba*, 1663 (TRAETTA, 1761; CALDARA, 1708). His brother, Thomas (1625–1709), also a dramatist, wrote *Médée*, on which Marc-Antoine Charpentier and CHERUBINI both based operas, and also made a verse tr. of MOLIÈRE's *Dom Juan, Le Festin de Pierre* (1677). LO

Cornelius, Peter, b. Mainz, 24 Dec 1824; d. Mainz, 26 Oct 1874. German composer. For a time worked with LISZT at Weimar, where his masterpiece BARBIER VON BAGDAD was perf. Other operas are *Der Cid* (1965) and *Gunlöd*, unfinished, completed by Carl Hoffbauer, perf. posthumously 1891. Cornelius wrote his own libs. LO

Corregidor, Der (*The Magistrate*), comic opera, 4 acts, WOLF, lib. Rosa Mayreder-Obermeyer after Pedro Antonio de Alarcón's novel *El Sombrero de Tres Picos (The Three-cornered Hat)*. Mannheim, 7 June 1896; London, RAM, 13 July 1934; NY, Carnegie Hall, 5 Jan 1959 (concert perf.). Comedy about a Magistrate (ten.) whose attempts to seduce Frasquita (mezzo-sop.), the wife of the Miller (bar.), all bring humiliations on his own head. The comp. worked two of his earlier songs into the story. FGB
See Kobbé

Corsaro, Il (*The Corsair*), opera, 3 acts, VERDI, lib. PIAVE after BYRON. Trieste, T. Grande, 25 Oct 1848; London, Camden Fest., 15 Mar 1966. Main chars: Corrado (ten.) Gulnara (sop.) Medora (sop.) Seid (bar.). Corrado leaves his beloved Medora to lead an expedition against Pasha Seid. He is captured, then rescued from prison by the Pasha's favourite slave, Gulnara, who kills her master. Together they return to Corrado's island to find Medora dying. Verdi's 13th opera, unsuccessful and rarely revived. JB

Corsi, Jacopo *see* FLORENTINE CAMERATA

Cortez, Viorica, b. Jassy. Romanian contralto. Began career as concert singer; operatic debut 1965, Toulouse (DALILA). Member of Bucharest O. since 1966. CG debut 1968 (CARMEN), returned as AMNERIS (1971), Carmen (1974). US debut 1970, Philadelphia (Carmen). Roles incl. EBOLI, CHARLOTTE, ADALGISA, LAURA, and KUNDRY. AB

Cosa Rara, Una, o sia Bellezza ed Onestà (*A Rare Thing, or Beauty and Honesty*), *dramma giocoso*, 2 acts, MARTÍN-Y-SOLER, lib. da PONTE, after Luis Vélez de Guevera. Vienna, BT, 17 Nov 1786; London, 10 Jan 1789. Main chars: Isabella (sop.) Lilla (sop.) Ghita (sop.) Giovanni (ten.) Lubino (bar.) Tita (bar. or bass) Corrado (ten.) Lisargo (buffo bass). Lilla, a peasant girl, intended by her brother Tita as a bride for the magistrate Don Lisargo, is pursued by Prince Giovanni and his chamberlain Corrado; but despite all their threats and blandishments she remains true to her lover Lubino. Martín-y-Soler's most famous opera, popular throughout Europe for nearly 50 years. MOZART quotes a passage from it in the music for the banquet scene in his opera DON GIOVANNI. JB

Così fan Tutte, o sia La Scuola degli Amanti (*All Women So Do, or The School for Lovers*), *dramma giocoso*, 2 acts, MOZART, lib. da

Così fan Tutte. Act I sc 2 of CG production, London, 4 July 1968. Sets designed by Henry Bardon; costumes David Walker; produced COPLEY. Left to right: LORENGAR as Fiordiligi; Waldimiro Ganzarolli as Guglielmo; Keith Engen as Alfonso; ALVA as Ferrando; VEASEY as Dorabella

PONTE. Vienna, BT, 26 Jan 1790; London, HM, 9 May 1811; NY Met, 24 Mar 1922. Chars: Fiordiligi (sop.) Dorabella (mezzo-sop.) Ferrando (ten.) Guglielmo (bar.) Despina (sop.) Don Alfonso (bass). For the sake of a bet Ferrando and Guglielmo woo and win each other's sweethearts in disguise. Mozart's third and last complete collaboration with da Ponte; rated low during the 19th c. due to its supposed immorality. JB O★
See Kobbé; Dent, *Mozart's Operas* (London 1913; reissued 1960)

Carlo Cossutta in the title role and KANAWA as Desdemona in VERDI's OTELLO, London, CG, 24 May 1974; produced Peter Potter; designed WAKHEVITCH

Cossotto, Fiorenza, b. Vercelli, 22 Apr 1935. Italian mezzo-soprano. Studied Turin and Sc., Milan, where she first sang small roles. Debut 1959, Verona, as Preziosilla (FORZA DEL DESTINO); CG debut 1959 as Neris (MÉDÉE); Sc. major debut 1962 as Leonora (FAVORITE); NY Met debut 1968 (AMNERIS). Has also appeared regularly at Vienna and Paris. A leading mezzo in It. opera, with a rich voice. AB

Cossutta, Carlo, b. Trieste, 8 May 1932. Italian tenor. Brought up in Argentina; debut there 1956 in a small theatre as ALFREDO. First appearance at T. Colón 1958 as Cassio (VERDI's OTELLO). CG debut 1964 (DUCA DI MANTUA); his more than 100 perfs there have incl. TURIDDU, Otello (his first 1974), and MANRICO. Has also sung many of these parts at Vienna, Chicago, and Paris. NY Met debut 1973 (POLLIONE). Sang RADAMES with Sc. in Moscow (1974). One of today's leading robust tens, with a full, vibrant tone that he uses with discrimination. His Otello is one of the best sung since World War II. AB

Costanzi, Teatro *see* ROME

Costume. Early operatic costume tended to be ornate and flamboyant; designers such as BÉRAIN and BOQUET allowed their fancies free play with little thought of dramatic appropriateness. The move toward authenticity in costume came with GLUCK and MOREAU, continued in the 19th c. by SPONTINI and esp. WAGNER. For modern designers costume is an important aspect of the whole stage decor, with carefully thought-out colour schemes that reflect both the period and the mood of the work in hand. LO

See Laver, *Costume in the Theatre* (London 1964; New York 1965)

Cotogni, Antonio, b. Rome, 1 Aug 1831; d. Rome, 15 Oct 1918. Italian baritone, prominent among It. singers in second half of 19th c. Debut 1852, Rome. After some years at Sc., came to London, CG, where he sang regularly for 20 years. Much admired by VERDI; very successful as singing teacher of J. DE RESZKE, BATTISTINI, LAURI-VOLPI, GIGLI, and STABILE. LO

Cotrubas, Ileana, b. Galatà, Romania, 9 June 1939. Romanian soprano. Studied Bucharest Cons.; debut at the Bucharest State O. in small roles. Joined Frankfurt O. 1968, where roles incl. SOPHIE, PAMINA, ANTONIA, GILDA, and MÉLISANDE. British debut 1969, Glyndebourne (Mélisande), returning there (1970) for title role in CALISTO. CG debut 1971 (TATYANA) and has since sung there a variety of roles incl. NORINA and VIOLETTA, a role which she sang at the Vienna Staats O. with great success (1971). Sc. debut 1975 (MIMI), as eleventh-hour replacement for FRENI. Her interpretations are sincere and appealing, and expressed through her vibrant tone that is also capable of extraordinarily accurate coloratura. AB

Count, Countess. For characters beginning with this title, *see under* first name

countertenor, high male voice with a range approximately between tenor and alto; today generally means 'male alto' using exclusively head tone or 'falsetto'. BRITTEN was the first modern comp. to write a countertenor part in an opera in MIDSUMMER NIGHT'S DREAM; but in revivals of 18th-c. *opera seria* countertenors often substitute for the original *alti castrati*. JB

Court Opera *see* HOFOPER

Covent Garden, Royal Opera House *see* LONDON

Cowen, (Sir) Frederic Hymen, b. Kingston, Jamaica, 29 Jan 1852; d. London, 6 Oct 1935. English composer and conductor. Among his 4 operas, *Pauline* (London, Lyceum T, 1876) was the first Eng. opera commissioned by Carl Rosa. LO

Cox, Jean, b. Gadsden, Alabama, 16 Jan 1932. American tenor. Studied Boston and Rome. Began career in various small Ger. houses during the 1950s. Bayreuth debut 1956 as Steersman (FLIEGENDE HOLLÄNDER); first major appearance 1967 (LOHENGRIN); has returned regularly since as Erik (*Fliegende Holländer*), PARSIFAL, and SIEGFRIED, roles he has sung in most major continental European houses; CG debut as Siegfried, 1975. Possesses a strong *Heldentenor* and has a handsome stage presence. AB

Cracow [Kraków], Poland. Dirs of the O. in the 19th c. incl. Józef Damse (1788–1852), who wrote over 50 operas, operettas, and pastiches, Hilarius Meciszewski, comp. of 17 operas, and Stanisław Duniecki (1839–70), whose works prod. at Cracow incl. *Dożynki czyli Pierwsze Wrazenia* (*Harvest Festival*, or *First Impressions*, 1865), *Pokusu* (*Temptation*), and *Odaliski* (1866). Władysław Zeleński's *Goplana* (1896) received its premiere there, becoming one of the most popular Polish operas. *See also* POLAND. EF

Cradle will Rock, The, musical play, 2 acts, BLITZSTEIN, lib. comp. NY, 15 June 1937. Scheduled for perf. through a Federal theatre project, it was cancelled at the last minute, and took place at the 48th St T. without costumes or scenery. First fully staged NY CC, 11 Feb 1960, when its protest (a conflict between steel unions and capitalist society) seemed rather tame. EJ O

Crespin, Régine, b. Marseille, 23 Mar 1927. French soprano. Debut 1950, Mulhouse (ELSA), singing the same role at the Paris O. the following year. She has sung at Bayreuth (1958), Glyndebourne (1959), CG (1960), NY Met (1962), Aix-en-Provence and San Francisco (1966). Her repertory incl. FEDRA (Sc. 1959), VESTALE, Mme Lidoine (DIALOGUES DES CARMÉLITES), PÉNÉLOPE, both Didon and Cassandre in TROYENS, SIEGLINDE, KUNDRY, and Rezia (OBERON). Her warm, vibrant voice and exemplary diction make her an especially fine MARSCHALLIN. EF

Cricket on the Hearth, The *see* HEIMCHEN AM HERD

Crivelli, Filippo, b. Milan, 27 Mar 1928. Italian producer. Worked with ZEFFIRELLI 1954–9 and with VISCONTI. Prod. BOHÈME (Genoa 1958) and since then has been active in

Italy, France, Belgium, Germany, Israel, the Netherlands, and the USA. Has prod. new operas by CHAILLY, MORTARI, VIOZZI, and others. Has also prod. for It. TV, e.g. RITA (1961). LO

Crociato in Egitto, Il (*The Crusader in Egypt*), opera, 2 acts, MEYERBEER, lib. G. ROSSI. Venice, T. La Fenice, 7 Mar 1824; London, King's T., 3 June 1825. The last and most successful of Meyerbeer's six It. operas. Chars: Armando (mezzo-sop., orig. castrato) Palmide (sop.) Felicia (contr.) Adriano (ten.) Aladino (bass). Armando d'Orville, a knight of Rhodes, has been left for dead in Egypt, during the sixth crusade. He assumes the name Elmireno and becomes a confidant of the Sultan, Aladino, whose daughter, Palmide, he secretly converts to Christianity and marries. Armando's uncle, Adriano, arrives to sue for peace. Elmireno's true identity is discovered and leads to battle, and the Christians are sentenced to death. Armando saves the Sultan's life when the Grand Vizier attempts to overthrow Aladino. Armando and Palmide are reunited, and a treaty of peace is signed. The opera remained in the repertoire until the second half of the 19th c. Meyerbeer supervised the prod. in Paris in 1825, which led to his remaining in the Fr. capital to comp. his Fr. grand operas. Revived in London by Opera Rara, 30 Jan 1972. PS

Crooks, Richard Alexander, b. Trenton, NJ, 26 June 1900. American tenor. Operatic debut 1927, Hamburg (CAVARADOSSI); same role, Philadelphia 1930. With NY Met 1933–43, with appearances in San Francisco, Chicago, and elsewhere. Specialized in the It. and Fr. repertory. Retired 1946. LO

Cross, Joan, b. London, 7 Sept 1900. English soprano, producer, teacher; leading figure in SW and EOG. Studied Trinity College of Music, London; joined Old Vic chorus under BAYLIS 1924; first solo roles there as First Lady (ZAUBERFLÖTE), and CHERUBINO. Before SW re-opened (1931) had sung leading roles in MOZART, WAGNER, VERDI, PUCCINI. Principal sop., SW, 1931–46, and dir. of co. 1943–5. Specially distinguished at this time as MARSCHALLIN, SIEGLINDE, Donna ANNA. CG debut 1934 (DESDEMONA in VERDI'S OTELLO with MELCHIOR); also sang MICAËLA there with SUPERVIA as CARMEN. Created Ellen Orford (PETER GRIMES); founder member with BRITTEN of EOG and created principal roles in his later operas, incl. RAPE OF LUCRETIA, ALBERT HERRING, GLORIANA, TURN OF THE SCREW. Prod. ROSENKAVALIER, CG 1947, and others for SW, Nederlands O., Phoenix O. Retired from singing 1955; continued teaching interpretation and stage char. at National School of Opera she first formed with Anne Wood 1948, until it was absorbed in London O. Centre, 1963. Her perfs are remembered for their depth of feeling and warmth of female char. in addition to superior vocal style. Awarded CBE 1951. NG

See Rosenthal, *Sopranos of Today* (London 1956)

Il Crociato in Egitto. Production at Milan, Scala, 1826

Crown Diamonds, The *see* DIAMANTS DE LA COURONNE.

Crozier, Eric, b. London, 14 Nov 1914. English producer and librettist. Co-founder with BRITTEN and PIPER of EOG. Prod. PETER GRIMES (SW 1945 and Tanglewood 1946); RAPE OF LUCRETIA (Glyndebourne 1946). Wrote libs of ALBERT HERRING, LET'S MAKE AN OPERA, BILLY BUDD (with E. M. Forster), and BERKELEY'S *Ruth.* LO

Crucible, The, opera, 4 acts, R. WARD, lib. Bernard Stambler from the play by Arthur Miller. NY CC, 26 Oct 1961; Wiesbaden 1963. Main chars: Rev. Samuel Parris (ten.) Rev. John Hale (bar.) Thomas Putnam (bass) Betty (sop.) Tituba (contr.). Witchcraft accusations and Salem trials of 1692 with terror, violence, charges, and counter-charges. EJ O

Cruz, Ramón de la, b. Madrid, 1731; d. Madrid 1794. Spanish dramatist. A minor government official and successful writer of satirical sketches about the life and people of Madrid in his day. His most valuable contribution to his native culture was to change the subject matter of the *zarzuela* from heroic mythology to the activities of everyday life. His brief collaboration with RODRÍGUEZ DE HITA prod. *Las Segadores de Vallecas* (1768) and LABRADORAS DE MURCIA; subsequent works incl. *Los Jardineros de Aranjuez* (1768) with Pablo Esteve, *Las Foncarraleras* (1769) with Ventura Galván, and *El Licenciado Farfulla* (1776) with music by Antonio Rosales. FGB

Cuba *see* LATIN AMERICA

Cuénod, Hugues, b. Coiseaux-sur-Vevey, 26 June 1902. Swiss tenor. Studied Basel Cons. and privately in Vienna. After teaching at Geneva Cons., stage debut 1928, T. des Champs Elysées, Paris. Created role of Sellem (RAKE'S PROGRESS). CG debut 1954 as Astrologer (GOLDEN COCKEREL); has appeared regularly at Glyndebourne in char. roles since. Has specialized in parts such as Don BASILIO (NOZZE DI FIGARO), the Astrologer, and grotesque roles in Baroque opera, for which his light, high, agile ten. is well suited. AB

Cui, César Antonovich, b. Vilna [Vilnius], Lithuania, 18 Jan 1835; d. Petrograd, 24 Mar 1918. Of Fr. descent, he was one of the leading figures of the Russ. *moguchaya kuchka* (Mighty Handful). His operas are: *A Prisoner in the Caucasus* (1883), *The Mandarin's Son* (1878), *William Ratcliff* (1869), Act I of the collective MLADA, *Angelo* (1876), *Le Flibustier* (1894), *The Saracen* (1899), *A Feast in Time of Plague* (1901), *Mam'selle Fifi* (1903), *Matteo Falcone* (1907), *The Captain's Daughter* (1911), and three children's operas. He completed SOROCHINTSY FAIR. Not even his finest opera, *William Ratcliff,* has remained in the repertory. GN

The Cunning Little Vixen, Komische Oper, Berlin, 30 May 1956; produced FELSENSTEIN; designed Rudolf Heinrich; ASMUS as the Forester

Cunning Little Vixen, The (*Příhody lišky Bystroušky*), opera, 3 acts, JANÁČEK, lib. comp. after Rudolf Těsnohlídek's novel *Liška Bystrouška* (1920). Brno, NT, 6 Nov 1924; London, SW, 22 Mar 1961; NY, Hunter College Playhouse, 7 May 1964. Main chars: the Vixen (sop.) the Fox (sop.) the Forester (bar.) the Schoolmaster (ten.) the Parson (bass) Harašta (bass). The Forester catches the little Vixen and brings her up in the farmyard but she escapes and, after a short courtship, marries the Fox. The Forester's drinking companions commiserate with him over his loss, which is somehow linked in their minds with the disappearance of the gypsy girl, Terynka (not seen on stage), whom Harašta the poacher marries. It is also Harašta who shoots the Vixen, but the Forester finds one of her cubs and the cycle begins again. Despite its unusual subject matter and staging problems this is one of Janáček's most appealing operas, wr. at the height of his maturity. JT O

Curlew River, 1 act, BRITTEN, lib. William Plomer derived from the Noh play, *The Sumida River*. Orford Church, 13 June 1964 as part of the Aldeburgh Fest.; Katonah, NY, 26 June 1966. First of the comp.'s three Church Parables. Main chars: Madwoman (ten.) Ferryman (bar.) Traveller (bar.). A highly stylized setting of a miracle story, based musically on a plainsong heard during the Processional. The setting has been transposed from Japan to the English Fenlands. Roles are performed by the 'monks' who change from their habit into the characters they are to play and back again at the close before the Recessional. The seven instrumentalists are also dressed as monks. A work, lasting about 70 minutes like the other church parables, of great economy and concentration, breaking new ground in the operatic field when first perf. AB O

Curtin, Phyllis, b. Clarksburg, W. Va., 3 Dec 1930. American soprano. Engaged at the NY City O. since 1953; debut 1946, Tanglewood, as Second Niece (PETER GRIMES). A fine MOZART singer, her repertory incl. Countess ALMAVIVA and FIORDILIGI (her NY Met debut role in 1961). She created SUSANNAH and Cathy in FLOYD's *Wuthering Heights*. She appeared in the first NY perf. of TROILUS AND CRESSIDA (1955) and sang Ellen Orford (PETER GRIMES) with SO at Edinburgh (1968). EF

Cuzzoni, Francesca, b. Parma, *c.* 1700; d. Bologna, 1770. Italian soprano. Debut 1719,

Venice; moved to London 1722 and sang with great success in many of HANDEL's operas. The rivalry between her and BORDONI, which came to physical violence on stage during a perf. of BONONCINI's *Astianatte* (1727), has unfortunately overshadowed the memory of her vocal abilities, for she was one of the most accomplished singers of her age. LO

Cyrano de Bergerac, opera, 4 acts, ALFANO, lib. Henry Cain based on ROSTAND's play, 1891. Rome, T. Reale, 22 Jan 1936. W. DAMROSCH's *Cyrano*, NY Met, 27 Feb 1913, lib. William James Henderson, is based on the same play. LO

Czar and Carpenter *see* ZAR UND ZIMMERMANN

czardas, Hungarian folk dance with strong national characteristics not known to have existed before the 19th c. Consists of a slow section followed by a fast; figures frequently in Hung. romantic opera and in Viennese operetta (e.g. FLEDERMAUS).The term is spelled *csárdás* in Hung. JB

Czechoslovakia. The rise of opera coincided with the decline of the Czech nation. With the removal of the Hapsburg Emperor to Vienna and the effects of the Thirty Years' War, Prague's status sank to that of a provincial capital. Czech almost died out as a cultural language and 18th-c. Czech opera comps such as BENDA and MÜLLER wrote in Ger. Czech opera began only with the Czech National Revival early in the 19th c.: ŠKROUP's *The Tinker* (1823) was the first opera written to a Czech text. It was not, however, until SMETANA that a national school of opera grew up, for which the Prague PT (1862) and NT (1881) provided a home. Smetana's example was followed by BENDL, BLODEK, and others but he stood alone in the sheer quality of his work. While their nationalist content has ensured that 100 years later works such as DALIBOR, BARTERED BRIDE, and LIBUŠE still occupy a special position in Czech consciousness, Smetana's operas, like the less dramatic operas of DVOŘÁK and FIBICH, have proved poor exports.

Czech opera has traditionally focused on PRAGUE, where its course has been shaped by comp.-conds like KOVAŘOVIC and OSTRČIL, but with the establishment of the Czechoslovak Republic (1918) theatres built by the wealthy Ger. populations in PLZEŇ (1832), BRNO (1882), BRATISLAVA (1886), and OSTRAVA (1908) passed eventually into Czechoslovak hands. From the provincial capitals only one truly great figure emerged: JANÁČEK, whose works have proved the most internationally viable of any Czech operas. But neither in Moravia nor Bohemia did any significant operatic school develop after Smetana. Some of the most successful Czech operatic comps, e.g. MARTINŮ and WEINBERGER, spent most of their lives abroad, while the most influential Czech teachers, NOVÁK, FOERSTER, HÁBA, were more at home outside opera. Though the large number of Czechoslovak opera houses (also in Ústí nad Labem, Liberec, České Budějovice, Olomouc, Opava, Košice, Banská Bystrica) and a generous state subsidy have allowed many operas to be wr. and prod. since 1950s, few have been accepted into the general Czech repertory. Operas by PAUER, KREJČÍ, and J. FISCHER have proved some of the most durable. Slovakia's later development has prod. two outstanding and internationally accepted opera comps in CIKKER and SUCHOŇ.

The Czechs have always perf. opera in the vernacular and, particularly after the expulsion of the large Ger. population after World War II, opera has become less international than in western Europe. Few foreign singers appear on the Czechoslovak stage, and, since they have few opportunities for singing Ger., It., and Fr. opera in anything but Czech, few Czech singers have made successful careers outside Czechoslovakia (recent exceptions are DVOŘÁKOVÁ, KNIPLOVÁ, PŘIBYL, and JANKŮ). One beneficial result of this has been the fine teamwork that one expects from any Czechoslovak co. Though cultural directions were affected under Communism (from 1948), particularly in the early period with its emphasis on Soviet and socialist realist repertory, Czechoslovak opera has in many respects gained from state monopoly not least in the sheer quantity of opera that is comp. and perf. JT

D

da capo aria, an ARIA in the mus. form A B A, the second 'A' often not wr. out, the singer being given the instruction, at the end of 'B', '*da capo*' (back to the beginning). In the days of *opera seria*, in the 18th century, singers would improvise ORNAMENTATION on the second 'A'. LO

Dafne, opera, prologue and 6 scenes, PERI, lib. RINUCCINI. Florence, Palazzo Corsi, 1597 (?). The first opera, music lost. The same lib. in a Ger. version by Martin Opitz, set by Heinrich Schütz (1585–1672) was perf. Torgau, nr Dresden, 1627. This work was the first Ger. opera; music lost. LO

Daguerre, Louis-Jacques-Mande, b. Corneilles, Seine-et-Oise, 18 Nov 1787; d. Bry-sur-Marne, 10 July 1851. French photographer and designer. Important in history of lighting in the theatre. Made his name at T. Ambigu, Paris, with spectacular presentations of melodramas, producing scenic illusions by magic lantern and diorama. Assisted CICERI and Charles Cambon in installing new lighting (gas) and panorama in new Paris O., Salle de la rue le Peletier. LO

Daisi *see* TWILIGHT

Daland, bass, Norwegian sea captain in FLIEGENDE HOLLÄNDER

Dalayrac, Nicolas, b. Muret, Languedoc, 8 June 1753; d. Paris, 27 Nov 1809. French composer. Began as a barrister, and in 1774 had commission in the guards of Comte d'Artois at Versailles. First stage work a *comédie mêlée d'ariettes*, *l'Éclipse totale* (1782). Some 55 other comedies followed, of which NINA OU LA FOLLE PAR AMOUR was the most famous. He bridged the gap between the *ancien régime* and the post-revolutionary period. LO

d'Albert *see* ALBERT, Eugen d'

Dalibor, opera, 3 acts, SMETANA, lib. Josef Wenzig, tr. into Czech by Ervín Špindler. Prague, New Town T., 16 May 1868; Chicago, Sokol Hall, 13 Apr 1924; Edinburgh, King's T., 17 Aug 1964. Main chars: Dalibor (ten.) Milada (sop.) Beneš (bass) King Vladislav (bar.) Jitka (sop.). The knight Dalibor is imprisoned for avenging his friend's death. Milada, the sister of the man he has killed, is captivated by his noble bearing and falls in love with him. Dressed as a boy, she gains access to him by helping his gaoler Beneš. Her plan to free Dalibor is betrayed and though she storms the castle with her followers and rescues him, she receives a mortal wound and dies in his arms. Smetana's heroic opera is also one of his most tightly constructed, and makes use of Lisztian thematic transformation. JT O
See Large, *Smetana* (London 1970)

Dalila, mezzo-sop., Samson's seductress in SAMSON ET DALILA

Dalis, Irene, b. San Jose, Calif., 8 Oct 1929. American mezzo-soprano. Heard while studying in Milan by MÖDL and recommended to Oldenburg Staats T. Debut there 1953 (EBOLI); NY Met 1957 same role. CG 1958 (BRANGÄNE); Bayreuth 1961 (ORTRUD), and 1962 became the first American to sing KUNDRY at Bayreuth under KNAPPERTSBUSCH, a role also heard on records made from live perfs at the fest. A voice of deep and eloquent timbre, more sensuous than brilliant in character. NG

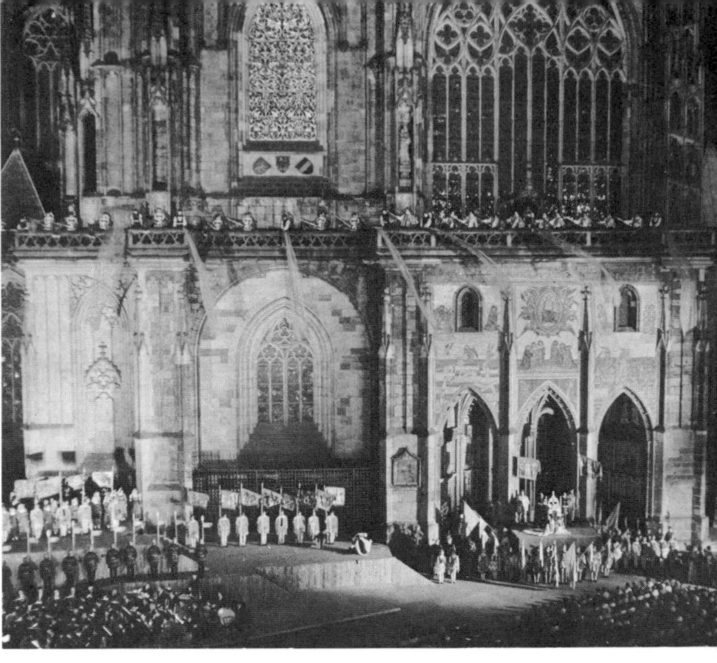

Dalibor, Prague Castle, June 1960; produced KAŠLÍK; designed SVOBODA

Dallapiccola, Luigi, b. Pisino, Istria, 3 Feb 1904; d. Florence, 19 Feb 1975. Italian composer. Studied Graz, Trieste, and Florence; debut 1926 as a concert pianist. His opera VOLO DI NOTTE (*Night Flight*, based on Antoine de Saint-Exupéry's book *Vol de Nuit*) was prod. 1940 Florence. His best-known dramatic work was PRIGIONIERO. Others incl. *Job* (Rome 1950), a dramatic oratorio, and *Ulisse*, adapted by the comp. from Homer's *Odyssey* (German O., West Berlin, 1968). EF

Dalla Rizza, Gilda, b. Verona, 12 Oct 1892. Italian soprano. Debut 1912, Bologna (CHARLOTTE). PUCCINI admired her, and wrote Magda (RONDINE) for her; she also created LAURETTA and was the first It. SUOR ANGELICA (Rome 1919). Engaged by TOSCANINI at Sc., 1923, where she created roles (she sang over 50) in ZANDONAI'S *Giulietta e Romeo* (1922) and PICCOLO MARAT. Retired 1939, to teach; has recently done some producing. LO

Dallas, Texas, USA. Dallas Civic O. founded 1957 by Lawrence Kelly (d. 1974); succeeded by Nicola Rescigno, art. dir. since 1957. Presents seasons of a few operas with first-rate international singers; prods mostly of standard works. LO

Dal Monte, Toti [Antonietta Meneghel], b. Mogliano Veneto, nr Treviso, 27 June 1893; d. Treviso, 25 Jan 1975. Italian soprano. Studied with B. MARCHISIO; debut Sc. 1916 (FRANCESCA DA RIMINI). Sang there for several seasons under TOSCANINI. US debut 1924, Chicago; NY Met same year (LUCIA DI LAMMERMOOR). With a small but pure voice of great agility, she concentrated on the lighter roles in which she was unsurpassed. LO

Damase, Jean Michel, b. Bordeaux, 27 Jan 1928. French composer. His operas are: *Madame de . . .* lib. Jean Anouilh, based on a story by Louise de Vimorin (Monte Carlo 1970); *Colombe* (Bordeaux 1961); *Eurydice* (Bordeaux Fest. 1972); *L'Héritière*, lib. Louis Dacreux, based ultimately on JAMES's *Washington Square* (Nancy 1974). LO

Dame Blanche, La (*The White Lady*), *opéra comique*, 3 acts, BOÏELDIEU, lib. SCRIBE, based on SCOTT's *Guy Mannering*, 1815, and *The Monastery*, 1820. Paris, OC, 10 Dec 1825; London, DL, 9 Oct 1826; NY, 24 Aug 1827. Boïeldieu's masterpiece, maintaining its popularity well into the middle of the 19th c.; 1,000 perfs at OC by 1864. LO O
See Kobbé

Damiani, Luciano, b. Bologna, 14 July 1923. Italian designer. Designed MATRIMONIO SEGRETO (1955), the opening prod. at the Piccola Sc., Milan; also MACBETH, and FIERY ANGEL at T. La Fenice, Venice. At Sc. he has des. LOUISE (1957), BATTAGLIA DI LEGNANO (1961), Turchi's *Buon Soldato Svejk* (premiere), and CAVALLERIA RUSTICANA (1962); Florence, WOZZECK (1963); Salzburg, ENTFÜHRUNG AUS DEM SERAIL (1965); Vienna, DON GIOVANNI (1967); Rome, TROVATORE (1967); Buenos Aires, LUISA MILLER (1968); Verona Arena, DON CARLOS (1969); Deutsche O., Berlin, BARBIERE DI SIVIGLIA (1970). EF

Damnation de Faust, La, *légende dramatique*, 4 parts, BERLIOZ, lib. comp. and Almire Gandonnière, based on Gérard de Nerval's Fr. version of GOETHE's *Faust*. Never intended for the stage, it has nevertheless been mounted as an opera, Monte Carlo, 18 May 1893; Liverpool (Carl Rosa Co.), 3 Feb 1894; New Orleans, 1894. LO O

Damoreau, Laure Cinti *see* CINTI-DAMOREAU

Damrosch, Leopold, b. Posen [Poznań], 22 Oct 1832; d. NY, 15 Feb 1885. German conductor. Went to NY 1871, founding NY Symphony Society 1878. Principal cond., NY Met, 1884, giving perfs of MOZART, WAGNER, BEETHOVEN, and Fr. and It. operas in Ger. After he died of pneumonia his place was taken by his son, Walter (*see below*). LO

Damrosch, Walter, b. Breslau [Wrocław], 30 Jan 1862; d. NY, 22 Dec 1950. American conductor and composer. At NY Met 1885–91, dir. US premieres of TRISTAN UND ISOLDE, MEISTERSINGER VON NÜRNBERG, and the RING DES NIBELUNGEN. After forming the Damrosch Opera Co., 1894–9, returned to Met 1900–3. Also a comp.; wr. five operas incl. *The Dove of Peace* (1912). LO

Damrosch Opera Company. Founded by W. DAMROSCH, 1894, to present Ger. operas, esp. WAGNER. Opened NY Met 1895 with TRISTAN UND ISOLDE; toured USA with a co. of international singers. MELBA joined the Co. 1897, when its name became Damrosch-Ellis Co. (Ellis was Melba's manager). It was dissolved 1900. LO

Danaïdes, Les, *tragédie-opéra*, 3 acts, lib. (in It.) CALZABIGI, tr. into Fr. and altered by Du Roullet and Baron Tschudi, Paris, O., 26 Apr 1784; advertised as by GLUCK, only later revealed as entirely the work of SALIERI. Calzabigi sent the lib. to Gluck from Naples; Gluck sent it, without Calzabigi's knowledge or consent, to Du Roullet in Paris. A notable work, revealing Salieri as a comp. of some power. LO

Danco, Suzanne, b. Brussels, 22 Jan 1911. Belgian soprano. Debut 1941, Genoa (FIOR-

Luciano Damiani's set for CAVALLERIA RUSTICANA, produced STREHLER at Milan Scala, 1965–6

DILIGI). British debut 1948 at Edinburgh with Glyndebourne O. (Fiordiligi). CG 1951 (MIMI). Also sang at Sc. and throughout Italy, specializing in Mozartian and in modern roles. AB

D'Annunzio, Gabriele, b. Pescara, 12 Mar 1863; d. Vittoriale, 1 Mar 1938. Italian dramatist. His plays which have formed the bases of operas are: *Francesca da Rimini*, 1902 (ZANDONAI); *La Figlia di Jorio*, 1904 (FRANCHETTI, PIZZETTI); *La Nave*, 1908 (MONTEMEZZI); *Fedra*, 1909 (Pizzetti); *Parisina*, 1912 (MASCAGNI). LO

Dante Alighieri, b. Florence, May 1265; d. Ravenna, 14 Sept 1321. Italian poet. His *Divina Commedia* (*c.* 1300), and particularly the *Inferno* section, has been a potent source of inspiration to comps, esp. in the 19th c. Of the *c.* 20 operas on the *Francesca da Rimini* episode only the one by ZANDONAI (FRANCESCA DA RIMINI, based on D'ANNUNZIO) has met with a large degree of acceptance. LO

Dantons Tod (*Danton's Death*), opera, 2 parts, EINEM, lib. BLACHER, after the drama by BÜCHNER. Salzburg 6 Aug 1947; NY, City O., 9 Mar 1966. Main chars: Danton (bar) Robespierre (ten.) Camille Desmoulins (ten.) Lucille Desmoulins (sop.). The denunciation, trial, and execution of the revolutionary hero and martyr. EF

Dapertutto, bar., the magician in the second episode of CONTES D'HOFFMANN

Daphne, opera, 1 act, R. STRAUSS, lib. J. GREGOR. Dresden, 15 Oct 1938; Milan, Sc., 1942; NY, Town Hall (concert), 10 Oct 1960. Main chars: Daphne (sop.) Gaia (mezzo-sop.) Apollo (ten.) Leukippos (ten.) Peneios (bass). This 'bucolic tragedy' treats the myth of Daphne, daughter of Peneios and Gaia, who is turned into a tree after Apollo, disguised as a herdsman, has killed her lover Leukippos and tried to seduce her. FGB O
See Mann, *Richard Strauss* (London 1964; New York 1966); Kobbé

Dardanus, *tragédie lyrique*, prologue and 5 acts, RAMEAU, lib. Clerc de la Bruère. Paris, O., 19 Nov 1739; revived with second half rewr., 23 Apr 1744, Paris O., and again in 1760, with scenery inspired by Giambattista Piranesi. Modern perf., 1934, Algiers. The classical story is enlivened by the librettist with magic, a monster (cf. IDOMENEO) and with opportunities for scenic splendour. Another *Dardanus* by SACCHINI (1771). LO

Dargomyzhsky, Aleksandr Sergeyevich, b. Tula government, 14 Feb 1813; d. St Petersburg, 17 Jan 1869. Russian composer. The opera *Esmeralda* (comp. 1839, perf. 1847), and the one-act opera-ballet *The Triumph of Bacchus* (comp. 1848, perf. 1867), based on an earlier cantata setting of PUSHKIN's poem, met with little success. A project for another opera, *Rogdana*, was abandoned. *Rusalka* (comp. 1855, perf. 1856) was received more enthusiastically and is still perf., displaying as it does a fine sense of drama and humour. His most significant achievement was STONE GUEST, which uses the innovatory 'melodic recitative' closely following the inflections of the text, a technique influencing much later 19th-c. Russ. opera. GN

Daudet, Alphonse, b. Nîmes, 13 May 1840; d. Paris, 16 Dec 1897. French novelist, whose tales, highly esteemed during his lifetime, are now almost totally forgotten. Of these *Sapho* (1884) was used by MASSENET (1897) and *Tartarin sur les Alpes* (1885) by Émile Pessard (1888). ARLESIANA was based on his play, *L'Arlésienne*, but for musicians this lives rather in the incidental music BIZET wr. for it (*see* ARLÉSIENNE). LO

Daughter of the Regiment, The *see* FILLE DU RÉGIMENT

David, ten., the apprentice in MEISTERSINGER

David, opera, 5 acts, MILHAUD, lib. Armand Lunel. Jerusalem 1 June 1954 (concert perf.); Milan, Sc., 2 Jan 1955; Hollywood Bowl, 22 Sept 1956. Main chars: David (bar.) Saul (bass) Bathsheba (sop.) Jesse (bass) Goliath (bass) Samuel (bass). This version of the biblical story from the Old Testament Books of Samuel I and II, was wr. to commemorate the 3,000th anniversary of Israel. EF

David, Félicien César, b. Cadenet, Vaucluse, 13 May 1810; d. St Germain-en-Laye, 29 Aug 1876. French composer. His symphonic ode *Le Désert* (1844), extravagantly praised by BERLIOZ, ushered in an era of exoticism in Fr. opera, as in his own *Lalla-Rookh* (1862) based on T. MOORE. The Orientalism – the evocation of the 'mysterious East' – was continued by GOUNOD, BIZET, DELIBES, and RABAUD. LO

Davide, Giacomo, b. Presezzo, nr Bergamo, 1750; d. Presezzo, 31 Dec 1830. Italian tenor. Studied with Nicola Sala; debut Paris in PERGOLESI's *Stabat Mater*. Sang Naples 1790; London 1791, when MOUNT-EDGCUMBE described him as 'the first tenor of his time,

Maxwell Davies's *Taverner*. The Wheel of Fortune, Act II, sc. 2, London, CG, 12 July 1972; produced GELIOT; decor KOLTAI

possessing a powerful and well-toned voice'. Retired to Bergamo 1812, although he is known to have sung at Lodi 1820. His pupils incl. his son, Giovanni (*see below*), and Andrea Nozzari. PS

Davide, Giovanni, b. Naples, 15 Sept 1790; d. St Petersburg, 1864. Italian tenor. Studied with his father (*see above*). He created roles in ROSSINI'S TURCO IN ITALIA, OTELLO, *Ricciardo e Zoraide* (1818), *Ermione* (1819), *La Donna del Lago* (1819), and *Zelmira* (1822). BELLINI revised BIANCA E FERNANDO for him, Genoa, 1828. London debut 1829. He possessed an extraordinary range of three octaves, from B flat to B flat above high C, and a superlative technique. He lost his voice 1841 and retired to open a school of singing in Naples; subsequently became opera manager, St Petersburg. PS

Davies, Peter Maxwell, b. Manchester, 27 June 1934. English composer. Studied Manchester Univ. and Royal Manchester College of Music. Wrote *Taverner* for CG (1972), after comp. several quasi-dramatic scores for his own group, originally Pierrot Players, later Fires of London. His style of writing is highly original and full of acute characterization. AB

Davies, Ryland, b. Cwm, Ebbw Vale, 9 Feb 1943. Welsh tenor. Studied Royal Manchester College of Music; joined Glyndebourne Chorus and awarded first John Christie prize for further study. First major role NEMORINO for Glyndebourne Touring Co. (1967). Glyndebourne 1968 (BELMONTE), and has returned for FERRANDO and LENSKY. CG debut 1969 as Hylas (TROYENS); has since sung there as FERRANDO, ALMAVIVA (BARBIERE DI SIVIGLIA), FENTON (FALSTAFF), Ernesto (DON PASQUALE) and in other roles. Salzburg 1970 as Cassio (VERDI'S OTELLO). US debut 1970, San Francisco (Ferrando); NY Met debut 1975 (Ferrando). He m. Anne HOWELLS. Possesses an attractive light lyric ten. and is a good actor. AB

Davis, Colin, b. Weybridge, 25 Sept 1927. English conductor. Gained his earliest operatic experience with the Chelsea O. Group 1950; first cond. at SW 1958 (ENTFÜHRUNG AUS DEM SERAIL) and at Glyndebourne 1960 (ZAUBERFLÖTE). Mus. dir. SW, 1961–5, cond. the first London perfs of CUNNING LITTLE VIXEN, ASSASSINIO NELLA CATTEDRALE, and AUFSTIEG UND FALL DER STADT MAHAGONNY, as well as the premiere of MINES OF SULPHUR. CG debut 1965 (NOZZE DI FIGARO), NY Met debut 1967 (PETER GRIMES). Cond. the first perf. of KNOT GARDEN; became mus. dir. of the Royal O. 1971. His interpretations of MOZART (DON GIOVANNI, CLEMENZA DI TITO) and BERLIOZ (TROYENS) are particularly admired, and, 1974, he began a cycle of the RING. EF

De Angelis, Nazareno, b. Rome, 17 Nov 1881; d. Rome, 14 Dec 1962. Italian bass. Sang as a boy in Sistine Choir. Debut 1903 as Acquila (LINDA DI CHAMOUNIX). Regular bass at Sc. and other It. houses until 1939. US debut 1910, Chicago. One of the most impressive basses of his era. AB

Death in Venice, 2 acts, BRITTEN, lib. Myfanwy Piper, derived from the novella of Thomas Mann. The Maltings, Snape, 16 June 1973; London, CG, 18 Oct 1973: NY Met, 18 Oct 1974. Main chars: Aschenbach (ten.) nine bar. roles; Tadzio (dancing role). A faithful rethinking in musical terms of the Mann book staying close to the original. Long central role, with several interior monologues, wr. for PEARS. Many thematic cross-references. In spite of some uncertainty in the Grecian fantasy at the end of the first half, the work has been considered a worthy summation of Britten's impressive contribution to the genre, while at the same time extending still further the range and daring of his dramatic ideas. AB O

De Begnis, Giuseppe, b. Lugo, 1793; d. NY, Aug 1849. Italian bass. Most celebrated *buffo* of the first half of the 19th c. Debut 1813, Modena, in Stefano Pavesi's *Ser Marcantonio*. Created Dandini (CENERENTOLA). In Bologna he appeared in PAER'S *Agnese* with the sop. Giuseppina Ronzi (*see below*), whom he m. shortly

Left: Giuseppina Ronzi de Begnis in MOSÈ IN EGITTO, first performed in London in Italian as *Pietro l'Eremita* at Haymarket T., 22 Apr 1822. Albert Edward Chalon (1780–1860), whose drawing is shown here, illustrated a number of singers of the period.

afterwards. They made their debut Paris, 1819, and 1821–7 sang in London. 1823–4 they dir. opera in Bath, and 1834–7 in Dublin. PS

De Begnis, Giuseppina Ronzi, b. Milan, 11 Jan 1800; d. Florence, 7 June 1853. Italian soprano. Renowned for her acting ability, she possessed a voice of great sweetness and flexibility, managed with considerable skill and taste. In Bologna she appeared with the *buffo*, Giuseppe DE BEGNIS, whom she m. For DONIZETTI, she created the sop. roles in *Fausta* (1832), *Sancia di Castiglia* (1832), MARIA STUARDA, *Gemma di Vergy* (1834), and ROBERTO DEVEREUX. She retired after her husband's death in 1849. Her daughter m. the ten. Gaetano Fraschini. PS

Debora e Jaele, opera, 3 acts, PIZZETTI, lib. comp. based on the Old Testament story of Deborah and Jael. Milan, Sc., 16 Dec 1922. LO

Debrecen, Hungary. The opera co. (formed 1952) perf. at the Csokonai T., built 1865. GN

Debussy, (Achille) Claude, b. St Germain-en-Laye, 22 Aug 1862; d. Paris, 25 Mar 1918. French composer. Entered Paris Cons. 1873 as piano student; transferred to GUIRAUD's composition class 1880. Won *Prix de Rome* 1884, but left before completing the statutory three years' residence. During career as one of the most original and influential comps of his time, he considered various subjects for opera, incl. the Tristram legend and works by SHAKESPEARE, HEINE, and POE, but he comp. only PELLÉAS ET MÉLISANDE. Its Symbolist drama of dream-like fantasy, expressed in music of subtle colours and shifting allusions, represents a furthermost limit of Romanticism, and was a turning point in operatic evolution. NG
See Lockspeiser, *Debussy, His Life and Mind*, 2 vols (London and New York 1962–5)

Decembrists, The (*Dekabristy*), opera, 4 acts, SHAPORIN, lib. Vsevolod Rozhdestvensky, after ideas by A. K. Tolstoy and P. E. Shchogolev. Leningrad, 1925, two scenes only (as *Paulina Goebbel*); Moscow, Bolshoy T. (complete), 23 June 1953. Main chars: Ryleyev (bar.) Bestuzhev (bass) Prince Dmitry Shchepin-Rostovsky (ten.) Elena (sop.). The action is set against the Decembrist uprising, 1825. Dmitry is prevented by his mother from marrying Elena; he leaves the estate, which is well known for tyranny over the peasants, and goes to St Petersburg to join Ryleyev, one of the leaders of the revolutionary movement. The uprising takes place, and, to celebrate the suppression of the rebels, a courtier organizes a masked ball. Elena attends, and is pursued by a knight; recognizing him as the Tsar, Elena pleads with him to let her share Dmitry's fate. She joins the Decembrists on their way to exile in Siberia. The revolution has failed, but Bestuzhev tells the people, 'From a spark rises a flame.' Shaporin's lyric opera has retained a key place in the Soviet repertory. GN

decor *see* DESIGNING FOR OPERA

De Fabritiis, Oliviero, b. Rome, 13 June 1902. Italian conductor. Rome O. 1933–43; also cond. Vienna, Paris, South America, and Edinburgh Fest. (1963). One of the leading conds of It. opera of the day. AB

Deidamia, opera, 3 acts, HANDEL, lib. Paolo Antonio Rolli. London, Lincoln's Inn Fields, 21 Jan 1741; Hartford, Conn., 25 Feb 1959. Main chars: Deidamia (sop.) Ulisse (mezzo-sop.) Achille (sop.) Licomede (bass) Fenice (bar.) Nerea (sop.). The young Achille (Achilles), living disguised as a girl in the palace of Licomede (Lycomedes, King of Scyros), is unmasked by Ulisse (Ulysses) and Fenice (Phoenix) and summoned to the Trojan War. Before setting out he m. the king's daughter, Deidamia, who has fallen in love with him. Handel's last opera. Revived SW, 3 July 1968. Other operas on same subject by CAMPRA (*Achille et Déidamie*, 1735) and CAVALLI (*La Deidamia*, 1644). JB

Delibes, (Clément Philibert) Léo, b. St Germain-du-Val, 21 Feb 1836; d. Paris, 16 Jan 1891. French composer. Born into a musical family, he studied with his mother, then with A. C. ADAM at the Paris Cons. At 19 wr. the first of many successful operettas, followed by the ballets *La Source*, *Coppélia*, and *Sylvia*. Wrote three operas for the OC, *Le Roi l'a Dit* (1873), *Jean de Nivelle* (1880), and his best work LAKMÉ. His last opera, *Kassya*, was completed after his death by MASSENET. Professor of comp. at the Cons. from 1881 and a member of the Institut de France from 1884. A man of unfailing good humour and a comp. of charming melody enhanced by piquant orchestration. FGB

Delius, Frederick, b. Bradford, 29 Jan 1862; d. Grez-sur-Loing, France, 10 June 1934. English composer, of German-Dutch descent. Wrote several operas, some of them never prod. It was largely thanks to BEECHAM that his operas were first staged in England after their Ger. premieres. They are, in order of completion, *Irmelin* (wr. 1892), *The Magic Fountain* (1893), KOANGA, VILLAGE ROMEO AND JULIET, *Margot la Rouge* (1902), *Fennimore and Gerda* (wr. 1910). Delius's music is generally late romantic in style, influenced by Impressionism, rich-textured, and chromatic. FGB

Della Casa, Lisa *see* CASA

Del Monaco, Mario, b. Florence, 27 July 1915. Italian tenor. First sang aged 13 in MASSENET's *Narcisse* at Mondaldo. Gave up institutional study at Rome 1935 after six months in favour of self-instruction from gramophone records. Debuts: Pesaro 1939 (TURIDDU); Sc. 1941 (PINKERTON); CG 1946 (CAVARADOSSI) with San Carlo O., Naples; San Francisco 1950 (RADAMES); NY Met 1950 as DES GRIEUX (MANON LESCAUT). During 1950s one of the most popular and highly-paid singers at NY Met in various It. roles that displayed a voice of exceptional volume and intensity. NG

De Luca, Giuseppe, b. Rome, 25 Dec 1876; d. NY, 26 Aug 1950. Italian baritone. Debut 1897, Piacenza (VALENTIN); Sc. debut 1903 as ALBERICH (RHEINGOLD). Created Gleby in GIORDANO's *Siberia* (1903), and SHARPLESS. CG debut 1907 (Sharpless); NY Met debut, 1915 as FIGARO (BARBIERE DI SIVIGLIA); sang title role at the premiere of GIANNI SCHICCHI, Ping in the first US perf. of TURANDOT, and appeared in NY until 1941. His large repertory incl. MOZART's FIGARO, LEPORELLO, and DON GIOVANNI, many VERDI roles, and Zurga (PÊCHEURS DE PERLES). EF

Demon, The, opera, 3 acts, RUBINSTEIN, lib. Pavel Aleksandrovich Viskovatov after Mikhail Lermontov. St Petersburg, Mariinsky T., 25 Jan 1875; London, CG, 21 June 1881; Los Angeles, Mason O. House, 18 Feb 1922. Main chars: Prince Gudal (bass) Tamara (sop.) Prince Sinodal (ten.) Demon (bar.) Angel (contr.). In the midst of a storm the Demon appears. He sees Tamara and is struck by her beauty. Prince Sinodal, on his way to marry Tamara, is held up by the storm and camps in a wild gorge. The Demon appears; robbers attack the camp and Sinodal is killed. When Tamara hears of his death, she begs her father (Prince Gudal) to let her enter a nunnery. Here the Demon appears; at first he is thwarted by the Angel, but then manages to kiss Tamara. She dies, and the Angel carries her soul to Paradise, leaving the Demon alone once more. An impressive, if melodramatic opera, *The Demon* is still perf. often by Russ. opera cos. GN

De Murska, Ilma, b. Zagreb, 1836; d. Munich, 14 Jan 1889. Croatian soprano. Studied with MARCHESI DE CASTRONE. Debut 1862, Florence, then appeared in Pest, Hamburg, Berlin, Barcelona, and Vienna. At HM, London, 1865, as LUCIA DI LAMMERMOOR, LINDA DI CHAMOUNIX, Amina (SONNAMBULA), and the QUEEN OF THE NIGHT, and appeared regularly in Britain until 1873. Toured America and Australasia 1873–6. Her voice, which spanned three octaves, began to deteriorate 1880 and she became a singing teacher in NY. She later retired to Munich, where she committed suicide. PS

Denhof Opera Company. Founded 1910 by Ernst Denhof to give perfs of the RING DES NIBELUNGEN in Eng. in the provinces, the first perf. being in Edinburgh, Feb-Mar 1910. The repertory was enlarged to incl. other WAGNER, some R. STRAUSS (the Co., gave the first perf. of ELEKTRA in Eng. 1911), PELLÉAS ET MÉLISANDE, and ZAUBERFLÖTE. After the inevitable financial difficulties BEECHAM (who had been one of the conds) took over in 1913, the singers being eventually absorbed into his own co. LO

Denmark. Foreign composers who visited Copenhagen during the 18th c. incl. KEISER, GLUCK, SARTI, whose operas to Danish texts, *Gram og Signe* and *Tronfølgen i Sidon* (*The Succession in Sidon*), were popular, and Paolo Scalabrini, whose *Kjærlighed uden Strømper* (*Love without Stockings*) was a brilliant satire on Sarti's style. NAUMANN, whose *Orfeus og Eurydice* (1786) was the first grand opera written to a Danish text, was mus. dir. of the Court O. Meanwhile a national school was developing, with operas on subjects from Danish history and legend: Johann Ernst Hartmann's *Balders Død* (Balder's Death), 1779, and *Fiskerne* (*The Fishermen*), 1780; Friedrich Ludwig Aemilius Kunzen's *Holger Danske* (1789) and *Erik Ejegod* (1795); Frederik Kuhlau's *Elverhøj* (1828). Johann Peter Emilius Hartmann (1805–1900), the grandson of J. E. Hartmann, comp. numerous operas, incl. two with texts by ANDERSEN, *Ravnen* (*The Raven*), 1832, and *Liden Kirsten* (*Little Kirsten*), 1846. Peter Arnold Heise (1830–79) wr. *Paschaens Datter* (*The Pasha's Daughter*), prod. 1869 and *Drot og Mark* (*King and Marshall*), perf. 1878. Christian Hornemann (1840–1906), whose style influenced NIELSEN, comp. an ambitious opera, *Aladdin*; Nielsen's own *Saul og David* (1920) and MASKARADE still retain their popularity, especially the latter. Another popular 19th-c. comp. was ENNA. In the 20th c. Hakon Børresen's *Den Kongelige Gæst* (*The Royal Guest*), 1919, and *Kadara* (1921), Jørgen Bentzon's *Saturnalia* (1944), and the chamber operas of Svend S. Schultz are particularly notable. EF

Dent, Edward Joseph, b. Ribston, Yorkshire, 16 July 1876; d. London, 22 Aug 1957. English scholar, writer, translator, and champion of opera in Eng. At Cambridge from 1902 (Prof. of Music, 1926–41). His MOZART prods there drew renewed attention to the operas and prompted his study, *Mozart's Operas* (London 1913). His *c.* 30 translations, beginning with ZAUBERFLÖTE (1911), aimed always at intelligibility and creditability, and incl. EUGENE ONEGIN, ARLECCHINO, BALLO IN MASCHERA, LIEBESVERBOT, QUATTRO RUSTEGHI, and other VERDI and Mozart operas; many were for years standard at the Old Vic and later at SW. Other important books were *Alessandro Scarlatti: His Life and Works* (London 1905; 2nd edn with preface and notes by Frank Walker, London 1960) and *Foundations of English Opera* (Cambridge 1928). LO

De Reszke, Édouard, b. Warsaw, 22 Dec 1853; d. Garnek, 25 May 1917. Polish bass, brother of Jean DE RESKE. Studied Warsaw; debut Paris premiere of AIDA (1876). CG 1880–4; debut Paris O. 1885 as MÉPHISTOPHÉLÈS, a role he made peculiarly his own. At DL 1887–90 embarked on some of the great WAGNER roles, esp. HANS SACHS, KING MARK, KURWENAL, and HAGEN. Sang several seasons NY Met, from 1890. Retired from the stage 1903; died in poverty in Poland. One of the great operatic basses, a fine actor with an imposing stage presence. LO

De Reszke, Jean [Jan Mieczysław], b. Warsaw, 14 Jan 1850; d. Nice, 3 Apr 1925. Polish tenor.

Studied with his mother, a singer, then in Milan with Antonio Cotogni, as a bar.; debut Jan 1874, Venice, in FAVORITE (singing as Giovanni di Reschi). Appeared in London 1874 in same role; Paris debut 1876 as Fra Melitone (FORZA DEL DESTINO), singing as Jean de Reszke. He restudied as a ten. with Giovanni Sbriglia; ten. debut 9 Nov 1879, Madrid (ROBERT LE DIABLE). MASSENET heard him sing in Brussels and wrote CID for him. Appeared at DL, London, 1887 as RADAMES, Raoul (HUGUENOTS),

LOHENGRIN, and FAUST, and sang CG 1888 in AFRICAINE. US debut 1891, Chicago (Lohengrin); NY 1891 (ROMÉO). Last appeared at the Met 19 Mar 1901, then sang PAGLIACCI in Paris, and retired to teach there and, after 1919, in Nice. He frequently appeared with his brother Édouard DE RESZKE, and also with their sister, the sop. Joséphine De Reszke (1855–91). PS

Dermota, Anton, b. Kropa, 4 June 1910. Yugoslav tenor, who made his career in Austria. Debut 1936, Vienna Staats O. (ALFREDO); remained there throughout his long career. Salzburg Fest. debut 1938 (Don OTTAVIO). One of the leading Mozartian tens of his day; but also a fine DAVID, FLORESTAN, and latterly PALESTRINA. Stylish, mellifluous singer. He is much sought after as a teacher. AB

Dernesch, Helge, b. Vienna, 3 Feb 1939. Austrian soprano. Studied Vienna Acad. Debut 1961, Bern, moving to Wiesbaden 1963 and Cologne. Bayreuth debut 1965 as Wellgunde (RHEINGOLD) and a Flower Maiden (PARSIFAL); progressed in following seasons to ELISABETH, EVA, Freia (*Rheingold*), and GUTRUNE. Sang BRÜNNHILDE (SIEGFRIED, 1969; GÖTTERDÄMMERUNG, 1971), FIDELIO (1971), ISOLDE (1972) at Salzburg Easter Fest. cond. KARAJAN. UK debut 1968 with SO (Gutrune), returning as LEONORE, the MARSCHALLIN, and Isolde. CG debut 1970 (SIEGLINDE) and has returned for CHRYSOTHEMIS, Leonore, and the Marschallin. One of the leading lighter dramatic voices of the day. AB

Left: Édouard De Reszke as MÉPHISTOPHÉLÈS

De Sabata, Victor *see* SABATA

Left: Jean De Reszke as ROMÉO

Desdemona, sop., Otello's wife in OTELLO (ROSSINI and VERDI)

Déserteur, Le (*The Deserter*), *drame en prose, mêlée de musique*, 3 acts, MONSIGNY, lib. SEDAINE. Paris, TI, 6 Mar 1769; NY, 8 June 1787. Very popular in France and Germany, revived as late as 1843. An English adaptation, music Charles Dibdin, appeared London 1773. Founded on a real-life incident; one of Monsigny's best works. LO

Des Grieux, ten., the hero of MANON and MANON LESCAUT

Designing for opera. Early operatic design was in the hands of architects such as BURNACINI, the BIBIENA, MAURO, and GALLIARI families; the legacy of their lavish SPECTACLE OPERAS is still with us. 19th-c. It. designers such as SANQUIRICO, FERRARIO, and ROVESCALLI, and SCHINKEL in Germany followed this architectural tradition. In France design in the 19th c. was a corporate effort, some designers specializing in exteriors, others in interiors, while everywhere lighting improvements were influencing decor. In Germany the realistic settings that were usual and approved of by WAGNER gave place to the sparer sets favoured by Wieland and Wolfgang WAGNER based on the theories of APPIA and Gordon Craig. Russ. designers such as Viktor Bakst, BENOIS, and others brought vivid primary colours and a new sense of excitement to the stage, and the cinema opened up other avenues. Economic stringencies have forced present-day designers to experiment with new materials and have encouraged them to venture into bald presentations, sometimes beyond what is visually acceptable, while the search for 'originality' is in danger of going against the intentions, implicit or explicit, of the comp. LO

Désormière, Roger, b. Vichy, 13 Sept 1898; d. Paris, 25 Oct 1963; French conductor. After working with the Dyagilev Ballet, he was engaged at the Paris OC, where he cond. the premieres of ROUSSEL's operetta *Testament de Tante Caroline* (1937), MILHAUD's *Esther de Carpentras* (1938), Marcel Delannoy's *Ginevra* (1942), and SAUGUET's *Gageure Imprévue* (1944). Also cond. ARIADNE AUF NAXOS, CHABRIER's *Éducation Manquée* and ÉTOILE, MASSENET's *Don Quichotte*, and PELLÉAS ET MÉLISANDE, which he brought to CG 1949. Dir. OC 1944–5; retired 1950. EF

Despina, sop., the maid in COSÌ FAN TUTTE

Dessau, Paul, b. Hamburg, 19 Dec 1894. German conductor and composer. Began career 1913 as coach at Hamburg, then cond. at Bremen 1914, Cologne 1919, Mainz 1924, and Berlin, Städtische O. 1925–33. Moved to USA 1939; back to Germany 1948. His operas incl. *Das Verhör des Lukullus* (*see* VERURTEILUNG DES LUKULLUS); *Puntila*, lib. BRECHT (1966); *Lanzelot* (Berlin 1969); and several children's operas. EF

Destinn [Kittl], Emmy, b. Prague, 26 Feb 1878; d. České Budějovice, 28 Jan 1930. Czech soprano. One of the leading dramatic singers during the early part of the c., noted particularly for her WAGNER and PUCCINI singing but also an outstanding exponent of the Slavonic repertory. Studied Prague with Marie Loewe-Destinn, whose name she assumed for professional purposes. Debut 1898, Berlin, as Santuzza (CAVALLERIA RUSTICANA). CG debut 1904 (Donna ANNA) and returned every year until 1914. NY Met debut 1908 (AIDA). Sang SENTA at the first Bayreuth prod. of FLIEGENDE HOLLÄNDER (1901). Created role of Minnie (FANCIULLA DEL WEST). Under the name Ema Destinnová returned to CG as Aida, 1919. Retired 1921. Her highly individual voice can still be heard on her many records, but they cannot convey all the histrionic effect of her fine acting. AB

Destouches, André, b. Paris, *c.* 1672; d. Paris, 8 Feb 1749. French composer, dir. of Paris O. 1728–31. Best known for a *pastorale héroïque*, *Issé*, a spectacle opera (1697). His 8 other operas incl. *Télemaque et Calypso* (1714) and *Sémiramis* (1718). LO

Detroit Grand Opera Association. Founded 1962. Two operas Jan–Apr, *c.* 20 perfs. Resident singers with occasional guests. Novelties incl. CHERUBINI's *Portuguese Inn*, the rock opera *Joseph and His Technicolor Dreamcoat*, and WEILL's *Der Jasager*. David Di Chiera, Administrative Head. EJ

deus ex machina (Lat. 'the god from the machine'). The device goes back to EURIPIDES, who used a sort of crane to lower the deity to the arena. By end of 16th c. the descent from above the stage was made in a CLOUD MACHINE. Used 17th c. and later as an arbitrary means of resolving the dramatic complexities of the plot. LO

Deutekom, Christina, b. Amsterdam, 28 Aug 1932. Dutch soprano. Having sung small parts with Nederlandse O. (1965) and at Barcelona (1966), she scored a success as the QUEEN OF THE NIGHT, Munich, Vienna, and NY Met (1967), CG (1968), and San Francisco (1969). Her secure coloratura technique is heard to best advantage in roles such as CONSTANZE, FIORDILIGI, and ROSSINI's *Armida*, but she also sings LUCIA DI LAMMERMOOR, NORMA, PURITANI, ATTILA, BALLO IN MASCHERA, LOMBARDI, and VÊPRES SICILIENNES. EF

Deutsche Oper am Rhein. Düsseldorf and Duisburg form the Deutsche O. am Rhein, one of the leading N. Ger. cos. Both built new houses after the war, Düsseldorf 1956, Duisburg 1950. In an age when co. work was becoming more and more a thing of the past, the Deutsche O. am Rhein managed to continue the repertory and ensemble system with considerable success. AB

Deux Journées, Les (*The Water Carrier*; in Ger., *Der Wasserträger*), *comédie-lyrique*, 3 acts, CHERUBINI, lib. BOUILLY. Paris, T. Feydeau, 16 Jan 1800; London, CG, 14 Oct 1801; New Orleans, 12 Mar 1811. First perf. in Eng., by Carl Rosa, Princess's T., London, 27 Oct 1875; revived Glasgow 2 May 1950. A famous rescue opera, very popular in its day; perf. Vienna 1802, and had an influence on FIDELIO. The plot concerns the escape from Paris of Count Armand, who, befriended by the Water Carrier, escapes concealed in a barrel. LO

The Devils of Loudun, Berlin Staats O. 4 Oct 1975; produced Erhard Fischer; designed Wilfried Werz. Peter Olesch as Father Rangier; Fritz Hübner as Father Barré; Krystyna Szostek-Radkowa as Jeanne des Anges

Devil and Daniel Webster, The, folk opera, 1 act, Douglas MOORE, lib. comp. after a story by Stephen Vincent Benét. NY, Amsterdam T. (American Lyric O.), 17 May 1939. In the course of Jabez Stone's wedding festivities, in mid-19th-c. New Hampshire, with Daniel Webster as honoured guest, Scratch, a lawyer, enters as fiddler and, by his conduct, brings a realization that Jabez has sold his soul to the Devil. Jabez and his bride decide to ask Webster's aid. Webster demands a trial; a jury of damned souls from America's past is summoned. His powers of oratory at length turn the tide of condemnation and Jabez is saved. EJ O

Devil and Kate, The (*Čert a Káča*), opera, 3 acts, DVOŘÁK, lib. Adolf Wenig. Prague, NT, 23 Nov 1899; Oxford, 22 Nov 1932. Main chars: Jirka (ten.) Káča (mezzo-sop.) Marbuel (bass) Lucifer (bass) the Lady of the Manor (sop.). No one wants to dance with the garrulous and unattractive Káča, so she offers to dance 'with the Devil'. Marbuel promptly appears and takes her to Hell with him. The shepherd Jirka volunteers to rescue her – an easy operation since Hell is delighted to be rid of her. The Lady of the Manor, hearing that the Devil is coming for her, also enlists Jirka's services. In return for her abolishing serfdom he

frightens Marbuel away by bringing Káča to the manor. After RUSALKA, Dvořák's most popular opera, especially in Czechoslovakia, where its folk char. still has a wide appeal. JT
See Clapham, *Antonín Dvořák: Musician and Craftsman* (London and New York 1966)

Devils of Loudun, The (*Diably z Loudun*), opera, 3 acts, PENDERECKI, lib. comp. based on John Whiting's dramatization of the book by Aldous Huxley. Hamburg, 20 June 1969; Santa Fe, 14 Aug 1969; London, Col, 1 Nov 1973. Main chars: Jeanne des Anges (sop.) Grandier (bar.) Baron de Laubardemont (ten.) Father Barré (bass). A worldly priest, Urbain Grandier, is accused of devilish practices, his chief traducer being the hysterical prioress Jeanne des Anges. He refuses to confess, and after torture is burned at the stake. EF ○

Devil's Wall, The (*Čertova Stěna*), opera, 3 acts, SMETANA, lib. KRÁSNOHORSKÁ. Prague, New Czech T., 29 Oct 1882. Main chars: Vok (bar.) Jarek (ten.) Hedvika (sop.) Michálek (ten.) Záviš (contr.) Beneš (bass) the Devil (bass) Katuška (sop.). Jarek's vow not to marry Katuška until Vok, his master, marries is overheard by the Devil, who, disguised as the disreputable hermit Beneš, confuses everyone and nearly succeeds in preventing Vok's marriage with Hedvika. The climax of the opera is the Devil's damming of the Vltava, which threatens to engulf Vok in the abbey to which he has retired. Smetana's last opera, intended as a comic romance, has a rich and often complex score with fine ensembles. JT ○
See Large, *Smetana* (London 1970)

Devil to Pay, The, or, The Wives Metamorphos'd, ballad opera, anon., lib. Charles Coffey and John Mottley. London, DL, 22 Apr 1731. A knockabout farce of no distinction, connected with the *Singspiel* as follows: 1. Ger. version as *Der Teufel ist Los: oder, Die Verwandelten Weiber* (Berlin 1743), perhaps with the original tunes; 2. new version, Johann Christoph Standfuss, lib. WEISSE (Leipzig 1752); 3. Fr. version, *Le Diable à Quatre*, PHILIDOR, lib. SEDAINE (Paris 1756); GLUCK added music when this was perf. Vienna 1759; 4. new Ger. version, HILLER, lib. Weisse (Leipzig 1766). LO

Devin du Village, Le (*The Village Soothsayer*), *opéra comique*, 1 act, ROUSSEAU, lib. comp. Fontainebleau, 18 Oct 1752; Paris, O., 1 Mar 1753; London, DL, arr. BURNEY, 21 Nov 1766; NY 21 Oct 1790. Wr. in emulation of SERVA PADRONA, whose 1752 Paris perf. began *La Guerre des Bouffons*. LO ○

Dexter, John, b. Derby, 2 Aug 1925. English producer. Prod. BENVENUTO CELLINI (CG 1966), then worked at the Hamburg Staats O.: dir. VÊPRES SICILIENNES (1969), FROM THE HOUSE OF THE DEAD, BILLY BUDD, BORIS GODUNOV, and BALLO IN MASCHERA (1973). He prod. DEVILS OF LOUDUN for ENO (1973), and re-dir. *Vêpres Siciliennes* for NY Met and Paris O. 1974, the year he was appointed Dir. of Prods at the Met. EF

Diable Boiteux, Le (*The Limping Devil*), *opéra comique*, FRANÇAIX, lib. comp. based on a story by Alain René Le Sage, 1707. Paris, at house of Princess Polignac, 1937, and Palermo, International Soc. for Contemporary Music conference, 1949. The story was used by HAYDN for his first stage work, *Der Krumme Teufel* (Vienna 1752). LO

Diaghilev *see* DYAGILEV

Dialogues des Carmélites, Les (*The Carmelites*), opera, 3 acts, POULENC, lib. Georges Bernanos after a novel by Gertrude von le Fort and a film scenario by the Rev. Fr Raymond Bruckberger and Philippe Agostini. Milan, Sc., 26 Jan 1957; San Francisco, 20 Sept 1957; London, CG, 16 Jan 1958. Main chars: Blanche (sop.) First Prioress (sop.) New Prioress (sop.) Mère Marie (mezzo-sop.) Chevalier (ten.) Marquis (bar.). The opera tells the moving story of the martyrdom of a group of Carmelite nuns during the Fr. Revolution. The serious tone and tender expressiveness of the music for this work come as a surprise after the comp.'s earlier stage works. FGB

Les Dialogues des Carmélites, Elsie Morison as Blanche and Jeannette Sinclair as Soeur Constance, in the UK premiere, CG, 16 Jan 1958; produced WALLMANN; designed WAKHEVITCH; conducted KUBELIK

Justino Diaz in the 1968–9 Milan Scala production of *L'Assedio di Corinto*, the Italian translation of ROSSINI's *Le Siège de Corinthe*, first performed at Barcelona, 24 July 1827, tr. Calisto Bassi

Diamants de la Couronne, Les (*The Crown Diamonds*), *opéra comique*, 3 acts, AUBER, lib. SCRIBE and SAINT-GEORGES. Paris, OC, 6 Mar 1841; Brussels, 25 Nov 1841; NY, 14 July 1843. London, Princess T., 2 May 1844 (in Eng.). Main chars: Catarina (sop.) Don Henrique (ten.) Diana (sop.) Rebolledo (bass). The young and beautiful queen of Portugal plans to fill her country's depleted treasury by selling the crown jewels, and replacing them with imitations, and to do so masquerades as La Catarina, queen of the brigands. Don Henrique, a young nobleman, falls in love with Catarina, and with the help of Diana, his former fiancée, saves Catarina from capture. PS

Diaz, Justino, b. Puerto Rico, 29 Jan 1940. American bass. Debut 1957, Puerto Rico, as Ben (TELEPHONE). NY Met debut 1963 as Monterone (RIGOLETTO); 1966 created Antony (ANTONY AND CLEOPATRA) at the opening of the new Met. Sang Mahomet II in ROSSINI's *Assedio di Corinto*, Sc. 1969; has appeared at Spoleto, Salzburg, and Barcelona. His repertory incl. ATTILA, da Procida (VÊPRES SICILIENNES), DON GIOVANNI, MEFISTOFELE, Friar Lawrence (ROMÉO ET JULIETTE), and ESCAMILLO. EF

Dickens, Charles, b. Landsport, 7 Feb 1812; d. Gadshill, 9 June 1870. English novelist. Works on which operas are based: *The Pickwick Papers*, 1836–7 (COATES); *A Christmas Carol*, 1843 (CIKKER, *Mr Scrooge*); *The Cricket on the Hearth*, 1846 (GOLDMARK, HEIMCHEN AM HERD; ZANDONAI, *Il Grillo del Focolare*, 1908, Alexander Mackenzie, 1914); *A Tale of Two Cities* (BENJAMIN). Also wrote lib. for John Hullah's *The Village Coquette* (1836). LO

Dickie, Murray, b. Bishopstown, 2 Apr 1924. Scottish tenor. Began professional career after World War II service; debut New London O. Co., Cambridge T., 1947, as ALMAVIVA (BARBIERE DI SIVIGLIA). CG 1948–52 in various roles incl. DAVID, TAMINO, BASILIO (NOZZE DI FIGARO), and created Curé in OLYMPIANS. From 1952 under permanent contract at Vienna Staats O., singing full repertory of lyric ten. roles incl. Pedrillo (ENTFÜHRUNG AUS DEM SERAIL), Jacquino (FIDELIO), and appearing at Salzburg and other fests. NY Met debut 1961. First British singer to receive Austrian courtesy title of *Kammersänger*. His light, flexible voice and cheerful personality expresses a particular talent for matching humour of char. to musical style. NG

Dick Johnson, ten., the hero of FANCIULLA DEL WEST

Dido and Aeneas, opera, PURCELL, lib. Nahum Tate based on VIRGIL's *Aeneid*. Josias Priest's Boarding School for Young Gentlewomen, Chelsea, prob. Christmas 1689; in public 1700; not staged again until 1895, Lyceum, by students of the RCM; NY, Juilliard School of Music, 18 Feb 1932 (staged). Main chars: Dido (sop.) Belinda (sop.) Aeneas (bar.) Sorceress (mezzo-sop.). Set in Carthage, the opera retells the story of Dido's love for Aeneas and her death after he is tricked by the Sorceress and witches into leaving her. Purcell's only true opera; a landmark in early operatic history. The integration of music, text, song, and dance into one simple artistic entity makes it one of the few 17th-c. works valid within today's concept of mus. drama. A prologue exists in the lib. but if set, music is lost. PS O

Di Luna, Count, bar., a young noble in love with Leonora in TROVATORE

Dimitri [Dmitri], ten., the Pretender in BORIS GODUNOV

Dimitrij, opera, 4 acts, DVOŘÁK, lib. Marie Červinková-Riegrová after SCHILLER and Ferdinand Mikovec. Prague, New Czech T., 8 Oct 1882. Main chars: Dimitrij (ten.) Marfa (sop.) Marina (sop.) Xenie (mezzo-sop.) Šujský (bar.). After the death of Boris Godunov, Dimitrij and his wife Marina arrive with Polish troops in Moscow, where Dimitrij wins the people's affection and even the acknowledgment of his supposed mother, Marfa, the widow of Ivan the Terrible. He foils a plot by Šujský but pardons him after the intercession of Godunov's daughter, Xenie. Marina's jealousy, exacerbated by the growing Polish-Russian animosity, is inflamed when she overhears Dimitrij offering marriage to Xenie and she denounces him as a pretender. Marfa is asked to swear that he is not; when Dimitrij stops her he is shot dead by Šujský. Despite the fine choral writing and strong Russian flavour Dvořák did not know BORIS GODUNOV. Hoping to make the work more dramatic he revised it in 1894; KOVAŘOVIC restored much of the original in 1906. JT
See Clapham, *Antonín Dvořák: Musician and Craftsman* (London and New York 1966)

Di Murska, Ilma *see* DE MURSKA

d'Indy, Vincent *see* INDY

Dinner Engagement, A, opera, 1 act, BERKELEY, lib. Paul Dehn. Aldeburgh 17 June 1954. The witty plot deals with the attempt of the impoverished Lord and Lady Dunmow to marry off their daughter Susan to a Prince, successfully in the end but for reasons they did not imagine. FGB

Dinorah (*Le Pardon de Ploërmel*), *opéra comique*, 3 acts, MEYERBEER, lib. BARBIER and CARRÉ. Paris, OC, 4 Apr 1859; London (in It.), 26 July 1859; New Orleans, 4 Mar 1861. Main chars: Hoël (bar.) Dinorah (sop.) Corentin (ten.). A magician reveals the location of a buried treasure to Hoël, a goatherd, but warns him that the first one to touch it will die. Dinorah, believing Hoël has deserted her, goes mad. She is saved from drowning by her lover, and on seeing Hoël regains her sanity. Hoël promises to abandon his quest. A favourite role of PATTI, and a mainstay of the repertoire until the beginning of this c., but rarely perf. today. Dinorah's Shadow Song (*Ombre Légère*) is a favourite coloratura showpiece. PS

Dippel, Andreas, b. Kassel, 30 Nov 1866; d. Hollywood, 12 May 1932. German tenor and impresario. Debut 1887, Bremen; at Breslau 1892–3 and Vienna O. 1893–8. NY Met debut 1890 in US premiere of FRANCHETTI's *Asrael*, 1888. A leading ten. there, with a vast repertory, 1898–1908. Joint manager there with GATTI-CASAZZA 1908–10; 1910–13 manager of Chicago O. LO

Di Stefano, Giuseppe, b. Molta, nr Catania, 24 July 1921. Italian tenor. Studied with Luigi Montesanto at Milan. Debut 1946, Reggio Emilia, as DES GRIEUX (MANON LESCAUT). NY Met debut 1948 (DUCA DI MANTUA). Swiftly became most sought-after It. ten. in VERDI and PUCCINI after earlier period in lighter parts to which his tone was perhaps more naturally suited. CG debut 1961 (CAVARADOSSI). His voice was warm and appealing, his manner ardent even when his style became coarser. AB

Dittersdorf, Karl Ditters von [Karl Ditters], b. Vienna, 2 Nov 1739; d. Neuhof, 24 Oct 1799. Austrian composer. His 15 It. *opere serie* were less important historically than his 29 Ger. *Singspiele* of which *Doktor und Apotheker* (1786) is the best known. LO

Djamileh, *opéra comique*, 1 act, BIZET, lib. GALLET, based on Alfred de Musset's poem *Namouna* (1833). Paris, OC, 22 May 1872; Manchester, 22 Sept 1892; London, CG, 13 June 1893; Boston, Boston O., 24 Feb 1913. Also revived Paris OC 1933 and Hintlesham Fest. (Essex), July 1971. Speldiano buys a new slave girl for his master, Haroun, every month; Djamileh, at the end of her month, having fallen in love with Haroun, plots with Splendiano to disguise her and re-admit her. The ruse succeeds, and Haroun falls in love with her. LO

Dobbs, Mattiwilda, b. Atlanta, Ga., 11 July 1925. American soprano. Debut 1952, Holland Fest. in NIGHTINGALE; has sung at Sc. and Glyndebourne (1953), CG (1954), San Francisco (1955), NY Met (1957), and Wexford (1965), where she appeared in FINTA GIARDINIERA. A secure technique allied to a naturally attractive voice has enabled her to sing coloratura roles such as ZERBINETTA, the Queen of Shemakhan (GOLDEN COCKEREL), OLYMPIA, and the QUEEN OF THE NIGHT, also more lyrical parts such as GILDA. EF

Dobroven, Issay Aleksandrovich, b. Nizhny-Novgorod (now Gorki), 27 Feb 1894; d. Oslo, 9 Dec 1953. Russian conductor. Debut 1919, Bolshoy T., Moscow, and then cond. at Dresden 1923, Vienna 1924, Sofia 1927, and Budapest 1936. Settled in Stockholm 1941, and both cond. and prod. many operas there, incl. EUGENE ONEGIN and ROMEO UND JULIA. First cond. Sc. 1949 (KHOVANSHCHINA) and CG 1952 (BORIS GODUNOV). Though best known for his interpretations of 19th-c. Russ. comps, in particular MUSORGSKY and RIMSKY-KORSAKOV, he was also an idiomatic cond. of 20th-c. works, such as ARIADNE AUF NAXOS and HONEGGER's JUDITH. EF

Docteur Miracle, Le, operetta, 1 act, BIZET, lib. Léon Battu and L. HALÉVY. Paris, Bouffes-Parisiens, 9 Apr 1857; London, Park Lane Group, 8 Dec 1957; Newhaven, Conn., 14 July 1962. In 1856 OFFENBACH offered a prize for an opera, ¾ hour long, 4 characters, orch. not more than 30. Winners (the judges were J. F. HALÉVY, SCRIBE, AUBER, Ambroise THOMAS, GOUNOD) were LECOCQ and Bizet, who shared the prize. LO

Doctor Miracle, bass, the doctor in the third episode of CONTES D'HOFFMANN

Dodon, bass, the king in GOLDEN COCKEREL

Dohnanyi, Christoph von, b. Berlin, 8 Sept 1929. German conductor. Studied Munich and in USA; cond. Frankfurt, Lübeck, Kassel, Berlin, Munich, Cologne, and other German cities. Mus. dir. Frankfurt O. from 1968, which he brought to the Edinburgh Fest. 1970. Cond. the world premiere of BASSARIDS and has been responsible for notable perfs of other modern operas, incl. MINES OF SULPHUR, FIERY ANGEL, and LULU, which he cond. in San Francisco (1971). CG debut 1974 (SALOME). Apptd mus. dir. Hamburg O. from 1977. EF

Doktor Faust, opera, two prologues, an interlude, 3 scenes, BUSONI, lib. comp. based on the Faust legend and Christopher Marlowe's *Dr Faustus*, 1589. Dresden, 21 May 1925; NY, 1 Dec 1964. Busoni's most ambitious work, left unfinished by him, completed by his pupil Philipp Jarnach (b. 1892). Has had revivals (Florence Maggio Musicale 1955, Berlin 1955, Hanover 1968) but has not established itself in the repertory. LO O

Domanínská, Libuše, b. Brno [Brünn], 4 July 1924. Czech soprano. Studied Brno Cons. debut 1945, Brno, as Blaženka (SECRET). A member of the Brno NT 1945–55 and in 1955 joined the Prague NT. Though she sings a variety of roles, she is known particularly for her SMETANA and JANÁČEK: her portrayals of JENŮFA and KÁT'A KABANOVÁ emphasize their gentleness, nobility and moral authority. JT

Domgraf-Fassbänder, Willi, b. Aachen, 19 Feb 1897. German baritone. Studied Aachen; debut there 1922. Engagements followed in various Ger. houses before he became a principal bar. with the Berlin Staats O. (1930–46). First British appearance on opening night of Glyndebourne (1934) as FIGARO (NOZZE DI FIGARO); returned there 1935 and 1937, when his GUGLIELMO and PAPAGENO were much admired. After World War II he appeared at Vienna, Munich, and Hanover. Had one of the most mellifluous, well-schooled voices of the years between the two world wars; also a strong actor. AB

Domingo, Placido, b. Madrid, 21 Jan 1941. Spanish tenor. Internationally renowned in VERDI, PUCCINI, and other It. and Fr. *verismo* operas. Son of *zarzuela* singers, who emigrated to Mexico 1950. Debut there aged 16 in *Gigantes y Cabezudos* (*Giants and Bigheads*), *zarzuela* by FERNÁNDEZ CABALLERO. Joined Mexican National O. first as bar.; ten. debut 1961 (ALFREDO). US debut 1961, Dallas Civic O., as Arturo (LUCIA DI LAMMERMOOR) with SUTHERLAND. Member of Israel National O. 1962–5. NY City O. 1966; created title role in DON RODRIGO. European debuts 1967–8 at Vienna (DON CARLOS); Hamburg (TOSCA and LOHENGRIN); Berlin (BALLO IN MASCHERA). NY Met 1968 as Maurizio (ADRIANA LECOUVREUR); Sc. 1969 (ERNANI); CG 1971 (CAVARADOSSI). His singing combines heroic ardour with expressive musicality and intensity of character. Proficient pianist and cond. (student of Igor Markevitch). NG

Domino Noir, Le, *opéra comique*, 3 acts, AUBER, lib. SCRIBE. Paris, OC, 2 Dec 1837; London, CG (in Eng.), 16 Feb 1838; NY (in Fr.), 7 June 1843. Opened the first regular Fr. opera season in London, St James's T., 15 Jan 1849. LO

Placido Domingo as Radames, AIDA, London, CG, Jan 1974

Don, Donna. For characters beginning with this title, see under first name

Don Carlos, grand opera, 5 (or 4) acts, VERDI, lib. (in Fr.) François Joseph Méry and du LOCLE after SCHILLER. Paris, O., 11 Mar 1867; Naples, T. S. Carlo, 2 Dec 1872 (partially revised); Milan, Sc., 10 Jan 1884 (revised into 4 acts); London, CG, 4 June 1867; NY, Acad. of Music, 12 Apr 1877. Main chars: Carlos (ten.) Elisabeth (sop.) Eboli (mezzo-sop.) Posa (bar.) Grand Inquisitor (bass) Philippe (bass). Don Carlos, Infante of Spain, is torn between a hopeless love for his stepmother Elisabeth, to whom he was once engaged, and a passionate desire to bring freedom to the Netherlands. He quarrels with his father, Philippe, who surprises him in a last tryst with Elisabeth; but he is saved from the Inquisition by the apparition of his grandfather Carlos (Emperor Charles V). Verdi's 25th and most 'epic' opera. In 1886 he authorized a conflation of the four- and five-act versions which is sometimes heard today (e.g. in the 1958 VISCONTI/GIULINI prod. at CG). Most opera houses keep to the 1884 four-act revision. Recent prods have occasionally added material from the original version which had been cut before the 1867 premiere. JB O
See Kobbé

Don Giovanni, o sia Il Dissoluto Punito (*Don Juan*, or *The Rake Punished*), *dramma giocoso*, 2 acts, MOZART, lib. da PONTE after Giovanni Bertati's *Il Convitato di Pietra*. Prague 29

Oct 1787; Vienna, BT, 7 May 1788 (with three extra numbers); London, HM, 12 Apr 1817; NY, Park T., 23 May 1826. Main chars: Don Giovanni (bar.) Donna Anna (sop.) Donna Elvira (sop.) Zerlina (sop.) Don Ottavio (ten.) Masetto (bass) Leporello (bar./bass) Commendatore (bass). Don Juan, in his insatiable quest for amorous adventure, is finally dragged down to Hell by the statue of the Commendatore whom he has killed in a duel after attempting to seduce his daughter, Donna Anna. The second of Mozart's It. comic operas wr. with da Ponte; throughout the 19th c. generally acknowledged as his dramatic masterpiece. ○ ★

Several other operas on the same theme incl. those by Giuseppe Gazzaniga, *Il Convitato di Pietra* (1787); Vincenzo Righini, *Il Convitato di Pietra* (1877), and STONE GUEST. JB

Donizetti, Gaetano, b. Bergamo, 29 Nov 1797; d. Bergamo, 8 Apr 1848. Italian composer. Studied with G. S. MAYR in Bergamo and Stanislao Mattei in Bologna. His opera *Enrico di Borgogna* (Venice 1818) led to commissions from the principal cities of Italy, esp. Rome and Naples, where (1826) he received a three-year contract to provide four operas a year. Early successes incl. *L'Ajo nell'Imbarazzo* (1824), *Le Convenienze ed Inconvenienze Teatrali* (1827), *L'Esule di Roma* (1828). His international fame began with ANNA BOLENA, in which for the first time his musical personality is fully realized. The death of BELLINI in 1835 left him for a while in undisputed command of the It. operatic field. Among his romantic masterpieces of the 1830s are LUCREZIA BORGIA, LUCIA DI LAMMERMOOR, and the sentimental comedy ELISIR D'AMORE. The refusal of the Neapolitan censors to allow his POLIUTO caused him to break his associations with that city, and his last active years were divided mainly between Paris and Vienna, where in 1842 he was apptd MdC and Court Comp. to the Emperor. The best works of that period are FILLE DU RÉGIMENT, FAVORITE, LINDA DI CHAMOUNIX, DON PASQUALE, MARIA DI ROHAN, and *Don Sébastien* (1843). Although several of his 66 operas have always remained in the popular repertory, Donizetti has been the principal victim of the Wagnerian reaction against It. *bel canto* opera. A recent revaluation of that tradition within which he was a master craftsman has led to a better appreciation of his merits. But because he wr. too fast and too much, many of his operas fail to sustain their opening promise despite an innate melodic freshness and moments of real dramatic power. JB

See Ashbrook, *Donizetti* (London 1965)

Donna del Lago, La (*The Lady of the Lake*), opera, 2 acts, ROSSINI, lib. Andrea Leone Tottola after SCOTT's *The Lady of the Lake*. Naples, T. S. Carlo, 24 Sept 1819; London, HM, 18 Feb 1823; NY, 26 Aug 1829. Main chars: Elena (sop.) Malcolm (mezzo-sop.) Roderigo (ten.) Giacomo (ten.) Douglas (bass). Giacomo (King

Don Giovanni, London, CG, 18 Apr 1973; sets and production Stefanos Lazaridis and COPLEY, much acclaimed by critics. GLOSSOP in the title role; G. EVANS as Leporello; Gwynne Howell as Commendatore

James V of Scotland), losing his way during a hunt incognito, is received into the house of his enemy, the Black Douglas, whose daughter Elena (Helen) is to be married against her will to the rebel chief Roderigo (Roderick Dhu). In the subsequent uprising Roderigo is killed; Elena pleads successfully for her father's life and is permitted to marry her lover Malcolm. Rossini's 29th opera, popular in Italy and other countries until the mid-19th c.; modern taste has generally found it too florid. JB

Donna Diana, opera, 3 acts, REZNIČEK, lib. comp. based on Moreto y Cavaña's *El Lindo Don Diego* (1654). Prague, 16 Dec 1894. Rezniček's most successful opera. LO

Donne Curiose, Le (*The Inquisitive Ladies*), opera, 3 acts, WOLF-FERRARI, lib. Luigi Sugana based on GOLDONI's play of same name. Munich, in Ger. as *Die Neugierigen Frauen*, 27 Nov 1903; NY Met (in It. for the first time), 3 Jan 1912. LO

Don Pasquale, *opera buffa*, 3 acts, DONIZETTI, lib. Giacomo Ruffini after Angelo Anelli's *Ser Marc'Antonio*. Paris, TI, 3 Jan 1843; London, HM, 29 June 1843; New Orleans 7 Jan 1845. Main chars: Norina (sop.) Ernesto (ten.) Malatesta (bar.) Pasquale (bass). Don Pasquale, an elderly bachelor, has decided to marry in order to spite his nephew, Ernesto. The wife found for him is his nephew's betrothed, who conducts herself after the ceremony in such a way that Pasquale is only too anxious to be rid of her. Wr. for the star quartet of Giulia GRISI, RUBINI, TAMBURINI, and LABLACHE, this is the ripest of Donizetti's comic operas. JB O
See Kobbé

Don Rodrigo, Buenos Aires, T. Colón, 24 July 1964; produced Jorge Petraglia; designed L. Rey

Don Quixote *see* CERVANTES

Don Rodrigo, opera, 3 acts, GINASTERA, Sp. lib. Alejandro Casona based on historical legend of the last Visigothic King of Spain (d. 711). Buenos Aires, T. Colón, 24 July 1964; NY CC, 22 Feb 1966. Main chars: Don Rodrigo (ten.) Florinda (sop.) Don Julián (bar.) Teudiselo (bass) Fortuna (mezzo-sop.). Rodrigo, having defeated his rivals to become king of the Visigoths in N. Africa, meets Florinda, daughter of Don Julián and one of his supporters. During Rodrigo's coronation the crown slips from Florinda's hands, a symbol of foreboding reinforced when Rodrigo opens the Cave of Toledo's iron chest, revealing an Islamic prophecy of doom for its violator. Rodrigo lusts after Florinda and rapes her; she appeals to her father to avenge her, and Julián orders the invasion that secured Arab domination of Spain for over seven centuries. Full of remorse, Rodrigo, a wandering beggar, dies in Florinda's arms. With WOZZECK as his formal prototype Ginastera sets a masterful lib. that fuses the Mozarabic, Arab, and Christian literary traditions in a musical language combining free atonality with serial techniques. MK

Donzelli, Domenico, b. Bergamo, 2 Feb 1790; d. Bologna, 31 Mar 1873. Italian tenor. Studied Bergamo; debut there 1808. ROSSINI wrote *Torvaldo e Dorliska* for him, and in 1831 he created POLLIONE. Sang throughout Italy, in Vienna, and at the TI, Paris, 1824–31; appeared in London 1829–33. At the age of 51 he created Ruiz in Donizetti's *Maria Padilla* at Sc., after which he retired to Bologna. Regarded as the first dramatic ten.; the critic Henry Chorley noted his astonishing high A from the chest 'without resorting to falsetto', adding 'when he gave out high notes there was no peril of his blood vessels' (referring to a perf. of DONIZETTI's *Zoraide di Granata*, in which the ten. Amerigo Sbigoli burst a blood vessel and died in trying to copy Donzelli's full-voiced high notes). PS

Don Pasquale, London, CG, 9 Feb 1973; produced and designed PONNELLE

Dorabella, sop., one of the two sisters in COSÌ FAN TUTTE

Dorn, Heinrich [Ludwig Egmont], b. Königsberg (now Kaliningrad), 14 Nov 1804; d. Berlin, 10 Jan 1892. German conductor and composer. Conducted opera at Hamburg, Riga (following WAGNER), and Berlin (succeeding NICOLAI) 1849–68. His 10 operas incl. *Die Nibelungen*, to a text rejected by MENDELSSOHN, prod. 1854 when Wagner was at work on his own RING DES NIBELUNGEN. LO

Dorus-Gras [Steenkiste], Julie [Aimée Josèphe], b. Valenciennes, 7 Sept 1805; d. Paris, 6 Feb 1896. Belgian soprano. Studied with her father, leader of the orch. in Valenciennes; debut at concert 1814. Studied Paris Cons.; debut 1825 Brussels; Paris O. debut 1830 (COMTE ORY); in 1833 m. Gras, first violinist at the O. Retired 1851. Her most notable creations were Marguerite de Valois (HUGUENOTS), Pauline (DONIZETTI's *Les Martyrs*); she was also Lucie de Lammermoor in Donizetti's revision of LUCIA DI LAMMERMOOR for Paris. PS

Dostoyevsky, Fyodor Mikhaylovich, b. Moscow, 11 Nov 1821; d. St Petersburg, 9 Feb 1881. Russian writer. Not until the 20th c. have his advanced ideas appealed to opera comps, and then mainly in the West: in the USSR his reputation has been insecure largely because of his conservatism, morbidity, and religious conviction. His works on which operas are based incl.: *White Nights*, 1848 (operas by Tsvetayev, 1933; Luigi Cortese, 1973); *Christ, the Boy, and the Christmas Tree*, 1848 (Vladimir Rebikov's *The Christmas Tree*, 1903); *The Gambler*, 1866 (PROKOFIEV, 1929); *Memoirs from the House of the Dead*, 1862 (FROM THE HOUSE OF THE DEAD); *Crime and Punishment*, 1866 (Arrigo Pedrollo's *Delitto e Castigo*, 1926; RASKOLNIKOFF, 1948); *The Idiot*, 1868–9 (Valerian Bogdanov-Berezovsky's *Nastasya Filippovna*, 1968); *The Brothers Karamazov*, 1879–80 (JEREMIÁŠ's *Bratři Karamazovi*, 1928; BLACHER's dramatic oratorio *Der Grossinquisitor*, 1948). GN

Downes, Edward Thomas, b. Aston, nr Birmingham, 17 June 1924. English conductor. Studied Birmingham Univ. and the RCM with VAUGHAN WILLIAMS and Reginald Owen Morris. Began career as horn player in several orchs. Decided to become a cond. and studied with SCHERCHEN at Zürich. Carl Rosa 1951 as *répétiteur*. Joined CG staff 1952 as *répétiteur*. First cond. for co. on tour of Rhodesia 1953 (BOHÈME). From then on cond. wide range of repertory at CG, incl. new prods of FREISCHÜTZ, TURANDOT, KATERINA IZMAYLOVA, and AIDA. Mus. dir., Australian O., 1971–5, cond. first perf. (WAR AND PEACE) in new opera house 1973. Tr. several Russ. operas into Eng. AB

D'Oyly Carte Opera Company. Founded 1876 by the Eng. impresario Richard D'Oyly Carte (1844–1901) for presentation of the comic operas of GILBERT and SULLIVAN. Its London base after 1881 was the Savoy T. built by D'Oyly Carte; it tours extensively in the British Isles, the United States and elsewhere in the world. LO

Dramaturg. Ger., with no exact equivalent in Eng., for the person in Ger. theatres with the responsibility for adapting plays and esp. libs (*see* LIBRETTO) to the conditions prevailing in the particular theatre. LO

drame lyrique. Fr. term for opera

dramma giocoso (It. 'humorous drama'), a comic opera with possibly more serious overtones. MOZART gave this name to DON GIOVANNI. LO

dramma per musica (It. 'drama through or by means of music'), 17th-c. name for what we should now call a 'serious' opera. LO

Dreaming about Thérèse *see* DRÖMMEN OM THÉRÈSE

Dreigroschenoper, Die (*The Threepenny Opera*), opera, prologue and 8 scenes, WEILL, lib. BRECHT. Berlin, T. am Schiffbauerdamm, 31 Aug 1928; NY, Empire T., 13 Apr 1933; London, Royal Court T., 9 Feb 1956. A modern reworking of BEGGAR'S OPERA, set by Weill in a popular style. Extraordinarily successful in Germany and, in an adaptation by BLITZSTEIN, in the USA in the 1950s (first perf. Brandeis Univ. Fest., Waltham, Mass., 14 June 1952). LO O★

Dresden, E. Germany. One of Germany's main operatic centres from earliest times. Dirs of Dresden opera incl. Heinrich Schütz in the 17th c., HASSE in the 18th. C. M. WEBER, apptd dir. 1816, brought a Ger. element to the repertoire which had been till then exclusively It. His successors incl. WAGNER (1841–8) and in the present c. REINER, BUSCH, and BÖHM. Until World War II Dresden prided itself on its pioneering record. Wagner's first 'repertory' operas were originally prod. here; all of R. STRAUSS's operas but three had their premieres here. The opera house, completed 1841, burned down and rebuilt from the original plans (1869–78), was bombed 1944. Present-day perfs are given in the modern Schauspielhaus. JB

Drömmen om Thérèse (*Dreaming about Thérèse*), chamber opera-in-the-round, WERLE, lib. Lars Runsten, based on ZOLA's short story, *Pour une Nuit d'Amour*. Stockholm, 26 May 1964; Edinburgh, King's T., 2 Sept 1974. Main chars: Thérèse (sop.) Julien (bar.) Colombel (ten.). Thérèse's price to Julien for a night of love is the disposal of the corpse of Colombel, whom she has accidentally killed, but Julien throws himself into the river after the dead body. The audience sits surrounding a circular stage, with the 26-piece orch. behind the spectators. Speech and melodrama are extensively used, while the action unfolds out of strict time sequence. EF

Drottningholm, Sweden. The Court T. in the palace of Drottningholm, nr Stockholm, was originally built 1754; burned down 1762, it was rebuilt 1764–6, restored, after a long period of neglect, 1912, and reopened 1948 for summer seasons of operas by MONTEVERDI, HANDEL, GLUCK, GRÉTRY, CIMAROSA, and MOZART. The stage machinery and much of the original scenery are still in use. EF

Drury Lane Theatre *see* LONDON

Dublin. There was a fair amount of operatic activity in Dublin in the 18th c. RINALDO was heard 1711; ARNE visited the city several times, with his operas *Alfred* (really a masque) and *Eliza* (1755). GLUCK'S ORFEO ED EURIDICE was first heard in Eng. there, 1784. Touring cos visited from 1871 when the Gaiety T. was opened until *c.* 1928. Since 1941 the Dublin Grand O. Society has been enterprising in bringing visiting cos from continental Europe and in prod. operas in conjunction with Radio Eireann orch. LO
See Walsh, *Opera in Dublin, 1705–1797* (Dublin 1973)

Duca di Mantua, Il, ten., the Duke of Mantua in RIGOLETTO

Due Foscari, I (*The Two Foscari*), opera, 3 acts, VERDI, lib. PIAVE after BYRON's drama. Rome, T. Argentina, 3 Nov 1844; London, HM, 10 Apr 1847; Boston, 10 May 1847. Main chars: Lucrezia (sop.) Jacopo (ten.) The Doge (bar.). Jacopo Foscari, son of the Doge of Venice, has been unjustly condemned to imprisonment and exile by the Council of Ten. The Doge, knowing him to be innocent, is obliged none the less to ratify the decree, despite the protests of Jacopo's wife Lucrezia. As he boards the ship that will take him to Crete Jacopo dies of heartbreak; his father is forced to resign his position. Verdi's sixth opera, nowadays more popular with specialists than with the general public; rarely revived. JB

Duenna, The, or The Betrothal in a Monastery (*Obrucheniye v Monastyre*), opera, 4 acts, PROKOFIEV, lib. comp. after Richard Brinsley Sheridan. Leningrad, Kirov T., 3 Nov 1946; NY, Greenwich Mews Playhouse, 1 June 1948. Main chars: Don Jerome (ten.) Louisa (sop.) Antonio (ten.) Don Mendoza (bass) the

Colour plates. Facing page: Antonie Denygrová in the title role of RUSALKA and HAKEN as the Water Goblin, Prague, Smetana T., 29 Jan 1960; produced KAŠLÍK; designed SVOBODA

Overleaf: Design (1940) by Mstislav Dobuzhinsky (1875–1957) for MUSORGSKY's opera SOROCHINTSY FAIR, produced Michael Chekhov, with choreography by George Balanchine, was performed by the New Opera Company, New York, 1942. Dobuzhinsky left Russia in 1917 after an active career there and worked for many European theatres before moving to New York in 1939.

Colour plate: DON CARLOS, London, CG, 1968, produced and designed VISCONTI. G. JONES as Elisabeth and D. WARD as Philippe

Duenna (contr.). Don Jerome, a Seville nobleman, wants Louisa, his daughter, to m. the elderly Don Mendoza, but she is in love with Antonio. By deceiving her father, Louisa m. Antonio; and Don Mendoza is tricked into m. the Duenna. The work differs from Prokofiev's other comic opera LOVE FOR THREE ORANGES in that the grotesquerie and satire (the tipsy monks in Act 4, for example) are contrasted with the more lyrical music associated with the lovers. GN

Dugazon [Lefèvre], Louise Rosalie, b. Berlin, 18 June 1755; d. Paris, 22 Sept 1821. French actress and mezzo-soprano. Began as dancer, first appearance as singer at CI, Paris, 1774; m. actor Dugazon 1776. Excelled as *comédienne*, the best *opéra-comique* singer of her day, much admired by GRÉTRY. Absent from stage during Revolution, reappeared 1795, continuing until her retirement 1804. LO

Duisburg *see* DEUTSCHE OPER AM RHEIN

Dukas, Paul, b. Paris, 1 Jan 1865; d. Paris, 17 May 1935. French composer. Wr. only one opera, ARIANE ET BARBE-BLEUE, but also orchestrated first 3 acts of his master GUIRAUD's *Frédégonde* (1895), and ed. several of RAMEAU's operas for the publisher Durand. LO

Duke Bluebeard's Castle, sometimes *Bluebeard's Castle* (*A Kékszakállú Herceg Vára*), 1 act, BARTÓK, lib. Béla Balázs. Budapest, 24 May 1918; NY CC, 2 Oct 1952. London, Rudolf Steiner Hall, 16 Jan 1957. Main chars: Judith (sop.) Bluebeard (bass). Bluebeard, portrayed more sympathetically than in other versions of his story, is made by his latest bride Judith to open his secret doors one by one, as if stripping away layers of his char. so as in the end to lay bare his soul. Eventually she, too, departs behind the last door leaving him once again alone and despairing. The fine text caught the comp.'s imagination, and he wr. one of his most passionate and highly coloured scores, marvellously attuned to the tortured hearts of the two principals. AB ○
See Kobbé

Dulcamara, bass, the quack doctor in ELISIR D'AMORE

Dumas, Alexandre I, b. Villers-Cotterêts, 24 June 1802; d. Dieppe, 5 Dec 1870. French novelist and dramatist. Works on which operas are based incl.: *Henry III et sa Cour*, 1829, a historical drama with a very 'operatic' plot (FLOTOW's *Duchesse de Guise*, 1846); *Charles VII chez des Grands Vassaux*, 1831 (DONIZETTI's *Gemma di Vergy*, 1831; CUI's *The Saracen*, 1899); *Les Demoiselles de St Cyr*, 1843 (SAINT-SAËNS's *Ascanio*); *Les Trois Mousquetaires*, 1844 (Isadore de Lara's opera of same name, 1921). LO

Dumas, Alexandre II, b. Paris, 28 July 1824; d. Paris, 27 Nov 1895. French novelist and dramatist, natural son of the above. His novel *La Dame aux Camélias*, 1848, dramatized by himself, 1852, very successful in 19th c., was the basis for TRAVIATA. LO

Duni, Egidio Romoaldo, b. Matera, nr Naples, 9 Feb 1709; d. Paris, 11 June 1775. Italian composer. Settled in Paris, important in history of *opéra comique*. His *c.* 30 examples incl. NINETTE À LA COUR, *La Buona Figliuola* (Parma, 1757, based on Samuel Richardson's *Pamela*), and *La Fée Urgèle* (1765) – an early version of the RUSALKA story. LO

Dunn, Geoffrey, b. London, 13 Dec 1903. English tenor, producer, and translator. Studied London RAM. With Margaret Ritchie and Frederick Woodhouse founded, 1930, INTIMATE OPERA CO. His numerous trs incl. ASSASSINIO NELLA CATTEDRALE, CORREGIDOR, INCORONAZIONE DI POPPEA, IVROGNE CORRIGÉ, *Das Verhör des Lukullus* (*see* VERURTEILUNG DES LUKULLUS); VIE PARISIENNE. LO

Duprez, Gilbert Louis, b. Paris, 6 Dec 1806; d. Passy, 23 Sept 1896. French tenor. Studied Paris Cons., with Alexandre Choron; after unsuccessful debut 1825 (Odéon) went to Italy for further study. Created role of EDGARDO; returned to Paris, sang at O. 1837–45, creating roles in BENVENUTO CELLINI, FAVORITE, and *Les Martyrs* (POLIUTO). Later became a successful teacher. LO
See his *Souvenirs d'un chanteur* (Paris 1880)

Düsseldorf *see* DEUTSCHE OPER AM RHEIN

Dustmann-Mayer, Luise, b. Aachen, 22 Aug 1831; d. Charlottenburg, Berlin, 2 Mar 1899. German dramatic soprano. Debut 1849, Breslau; later engaged at Kassel under SPOHR. Member, Vienna Staats O. 1857; taught singing at the Cons. She made guest appearances abroad and was a friend of Johannes Brahms and WAGNER. JB

Duval, Denise, b. Paris, 23 Oct 1921. French soprano. First sang at the Paris O. 1947 as Salome (HÉRODIADE), and at OC the same year in MADAMA BUTTERFLY. At Glyndebourne 1962 (PELLÉAS ET MÉLISANDE). Though a fine TOSCA, Musetta (BOHÈME),

Left: Denise Duval as Elle in VOIX HUMAINE, a role which she created at the Paris OC, 6 Feb 1959

THAÏS, and Giulietta (CONTES D'HOFFMANN), she is best known as an interpreter of POULENC's operas. She created the roles of Thérèse (MAMELLES DE TIRÉSIAS) and Elle (VOIX HUMAINE), and sang Blanche at the first Paris perf. of DIALOGUES DES CARMÉLITES (1957). Her Concepción in HEURE ESPAGNOLE was also much admired. Retired 1965 because of ill health. EF

Dvořák, Antonín, b. Nelahozevez, Bohemia, 8 Sept 1841; d. Prague, 1 May 1904. Czech composer. Studied at the Prague Organ School 1857–9 and played viola in Komzák's orch. (later the Prague PT Orch.) 1859–71. Johannes Brahms was a dominant influence, especially in his large symphonic and chamber output. From 1884 onwards Dvořák made many visits to England, for which he wr. several choral works. Dir., National Cons. NY, 1892–5 where in addition to his well-known instrumental works from this period he contemplated setting an opera based on *Hiawatha*. On his return to Prague he resumed his teaching at the Cons., begun 1891. His 10 operas began with *Alfred* (1870, prod. 1938) and ended with *Armida* (1904); the first to be perf. was *King and Charcoalburner* (*Král a uhlíř*), (second version, 1874), followed by *Vanda* (1876), *The Cunning Peasant* (*Šelmá sedlák*, 1878), and *The Stubborn Lovers* (*Trvdé palice*, 1874, prod. 1881). His best operas were those that made use of a typical Czech milieu, such as JACOBIN and DEVIL AND KATE and it is his good humour, almost sentimental lyricism, and sheer musicianship that keep his works alive in Czechoslovakia rather than any powerful feeling for the stage or dramatic qualities – lacking even in his historical opera DIMITRIJ. His most popular work is the fairy-tale opera RUSALKA. JT
See Clapham, *Antonín Dvořák, Musician and Craftsman* (London 1966)

Dvořáková, Ludmila, b. nr Prague, 11 July 1923. Czech soprano. Studied Prague Cons. Began career at Ostrava and Bratislava in 1950s as lyric sop., graduating to heavier roles when she reached Prague. Debut 1960 Berlin Staats O. (OCTAVIAN). Sang her first WALKÜRE BRÜNNHILDE there 1962, her first ISOLDE 1964 at Karlsruhe. NY Met debut 1966 (LEONORE). CG debut 1966 as Brünnhilde in complete RING cycle. Bayreuth debut 1965 (GUTRUNE and VENUS); has sung Brünnhilde in *Walküre* and SIEGFRIED there 1966, KUNDRY 1969, and ORTRUD 1971. Rich, affecting dramatic sop. and good actress, helped by pleasing appearance. AB

Dyagilev, Sergey Pavlovich, b. Novgorod Government, 31 Mar 1872; d. Venice, 19 Aug 1929. Russian impresario. For some years a close associate of STRAVINSKY, several of whose works he prod. for the first time: NIGHTINGALE, MAVRA, RENARD, *The Wedding* (1923), and OEDIPUS REX, a work comp. specially for the 20th anniversary of Dyagilev's life in the theatre but which was so little to his liking that it only had a concert perf. (1927). Dyagilev is particularly known for the Ballet Russe which he formed 1909. And it was also in his Paris prods that a number of Russ. operas were first heard in the West, notably BORIS GODUNOV (1908), MAID OF PSKOV (1909), and KHOVANSHCHINA (1913). GN

Dzerzhinsky, Ivan Ivanovich, b. Tambov, 9 Apr 1909. Russian composer. A graduate of Leningrad Cons., he rose to fame in 1936 when Stalin attended a perf. of his first opera QUIET FLOWS THE DON and saw it as a model of the 'socialist realism' he was advocating in art. Of his 11 other operas *Virgin Soil Upturned* (1937)

Antonín Dvořák's DEVIL AND KATE, Prague, National T., 9 Sept 1966; produced Přemysl Kočí; designed Zdeněk Seydl. Dalibor Jedlička as Marbuel and Slávka Procházková as Káča.

and *The Fate of a Man* (1961), both based on novels by Mikhail Sholokhov, are still perf. in the USSR. His recent operas incl. *Grigory Melekhov* (1967), a sequel to *Quiet Flows the Don*, and *Hostile Whirlwinds* (1969). His style is characterized by simple harmony and lyrical melody, often imitative of Russ. folk music. GN

E

Eames, Emma, b. Shanghai, 13 Aug 1865; d. NY, 13 June 1952. American soprano. Her American parents took her to the USA in 1870. Studied with Clara Munger, Boston; with MARCHESI DE CASTRONE, Paris, 1886. Debut 13 Mar 1889, Paris, as JULIETTE. Created role of Colombe (SAINT-SAËNS's *Ascanio*). Appeared as MARGUERITE at London, CG, 1891; NY Met debut, 14 Dec 1891, as Juliette. A favourite with Brit. and US audiences for the next 18 years. Retired 1909, after disagreement with GATTI-CASAZZA, reappearing in Boston for two perfs of TOSCA (1911) and DESDEMONA in VERDI's OTELLO (1912). After 1912 she gave recitals with her second husband, the bar. Emilio di Gogorza. Autobiography, *Some Memories and Reflections* (New York and London 1927). PS

East Germany *see* GERMANY

Easton, Florence, b. Middlesbrough, 25 Oct 1884; d. NY, 13 Aug 1955. English soprano. Studied London, RCM, and Paris; debut with Moody-Manners Co. After engagements at Berlin, 1907–13, and Hamburg, 1914–16, went to NY Met, 1917–29, singing in US premieres of GIANNI SCHICCHI and KING'S HENCHMAN. Her amazing repertory of 150 roles included BRÜNNHILDE, ISOLDE, TOSCA, and TURANDOT, besides such widely different parts as CIO-CIO-SAN and CARMEN. LO

Ebert, Carl, b. Berlin, 20 Feb 1887. German producer. Studied with REINHARDT. Gen. dir. Darmstadt 1927–31, then at Berlin Städtische O. until 1933. With BUSCH and CHRISTIE founded Glyndebourne Fest. 1934. After World War II was dir. of Opera Dept, Univ. of S. California, 1948–56, and prod. at Glyndebourne 1947–59. Rejoined Berlin Städtische O. 1956–61, and at NY Met 1959–62. His insight into the stage and his understanding of the problems of producing opera have made him one of today's most influential prods. LO

Ebert, Peter, b. Frankfurt, 6 Apr 1918. Son of the above. German producer. Has worked in places as far apart as Glyndebourne, Toronto Univ. Opera Dept, Augsburg, and Glasgow, where he has been with SO since its inception in 1962. His prods there have incl. VERDI's OTELLO, 1962, TROYENS, 1969, and WALKÜRE, 1971. LO

Eboli, mezzo-sop., in love with Don Carlos and lady-in-waiting to Elisabeth, in DON CARLOS

Écho et Narcisse, opera, 5 acts, GLUCK, lib. Baron Tschudi. Paris, O., 24 Sept 1779. Gluck's last opera; a failure. Revived in revised form 8 Aug 1780, with little better success. Based on the fable in Ovid's *Metamorphoses*. The action is slender, but work contains some of Gluck's most delicate music. LO

Ecuador *see* LATIN AMERICA

Edgar, opera, 4 acts, PUCCINI, lib. Ferdinand Fontana after Alfred de Musset's *La Coupe et les Lèvres* (1832). Milan, Sc., 21 Apr 1889; Ferrara, 28 Feb 1892 (revised into 3 acts); NY, Waldorf-Astoria, 12 Apr 1956. Main chars: Fidelia (sop.) Tigrana (mezzo-sop.) Edgar (ten.) Frank (bar.). Edgar, a young Belgian, is torn between his love for Fidelia and a former mistress, the gypsy girl Tigrana, now loved by Fidelia's brother Frank. Edgar defends Tigrana against enraged villagers and elopes with her. Tiring of her, he joins a military expedition under Frank. He is brought home apparently dead in a coffin, having been killed in action, but the coffin is found to be empty, and the Monk who was preaching over it reveals himself as Edgar. He is about to leave with Fidelia, when Tigrana stabs her to death. Puccini's second and least successful opera. JB

Edgardo, ten., Lucia's lover in LUCIA DI LAMMERMOOR

Edinburgh. The annual July Fest. was begun in 1947 under the inspiration of BING. Opera is provided by visiting companies (there is no permanent Edinburgh co.). The Glyndebourne Co. was the first, 1947–51. Since 1952 there have been visits from the Hamburg, Piccola Scala, Stuttgart, Stockholm, and Belgrade operas.

The Edinburgh Fest. maintains high standards but is handicapped by the lack of a proper opera house. LO

Egk, Werner, b. Auchsesheim, Augsburg, 17 May 1901. German composer. Studied with ORFF in Munich, and from 1935 to 1941 was a cond. at the Berlin Staats O. First opera *Col-*

umbus, given on Munich radio in 1933, staged at Frankfurt, 1942. He has also comp. *Peer Gynt* (Berlin 1938); *Circe* (Berlin 1948); IRISCHE LEGENDE; REVISOR; VERLOBUNG IN SAN DOMINGO; and *17 Tage und 4 Minuten* (Stuttgart 1966). His operas are frequently perf. in Germany and Austria. EF

Ehrling, (Evert) Sixten, b. Malmö, 3 Apr 1918. Swedish conductor. From 1939 to 1960 he worked at the Stockholm Royal O., first as coach, from 1944 as cond., and from 1953 as mus. dir. Cond. ANIARA (1959) at the premiere in Stockholm, at Edinburgh the same year, and in London during the Stockholm Opera's visit to CG (1960), when he also cond. BALLO IN MASCHERA and FLIEGENDE HOLLÄNDER. San Francisco debut 1969 (FIDELIO); NY Met 1973 (PETER GRIMES). Cond. RING cycle at Met, 1975. EF

Einem, Gottfried von, b. Bern, 24 Jan 1918. Austrian composer. His operas incl. DANTONS TOD; PROZESS; *Der Zerrissene (The Confused)*, Hamburg 1964; and BESUCH DER ALTEN DAME. EF

Eine Nacht in Venedig *see* NACHT IN VENEDIG, EINE

Eisinger, Irene, b. Kosel, 8 Dec 1903. German soprano. Studied in Berlin. Debut 1926, Basel. Berlin, Kroll T., 1928–31; Salzburg Fest. 1930–3; Glyndebourne 1934–9. Appeared at CG as GRETEL and ADELE (1936–7 season). Lived in England from 1938. A delightful soubrette singer whose DESPINA and BLONDE adorned Glyndebourne's earliest seasons. Repeated the former role with the co. at 1949 Edinburgh Fest. AB

Eléazar, ten., father of Rachel in JUIVE

Elegie für Junge Liebende, Die *see* ELEGY FOR YOUNG LOVERS

Elegy for Young Lovers, opera, 3 acts, HENZE, lib. AUDEN and KALLMAN. Schwetzingen (in Ger. tr. as *Die Elegie für Junge Liebende*), 20 May 1961; Glyndebourne, 19 July 1961; NY, 29 Apr 1965. Main chars: Gregor Mittenhofer (bar.) Elisabeth Zimmer (sop.) Hilda Mack (sop.) Carolina (mezzo-sop.) Toni Reischmann (ten.) Dr Reischmann (bass). The poet Mittenhofer, a monster of selfishness, battens on his entourage for inspiration, allowing his young mistress and her lover to die in order to provide material for his muse. EF

Elektra. MASTILOVIĆ (left) as Elektra and MEYER as Klytemnestra, London, CG, 2 Nov 1973

Elektra, opera, 1 act, R. STRAUSS, lib. HOFMANNSTHAL after SOPHOCLES. Dresden, 25 Jan 1909; NY, Manhattan OH, 1 Feb 1910 (in Fr.!); London, CG, 19 Feb 1910. Main chars: Elektra (sop.) Klytemnestra (mezzo-sop.) Orest (bar.) Chrysothemis (sop.) Aegisth (ten.). Elektra waits for the return of her brother Orest to avenge the murder of their father Agamemnon by his wife Klytemnestra and her lover Aegisth. Strauss and Hofmannsthal, working together for the first time, transformed the classical Greek tragedy into a music drama of compelling depravity and frenzy. FGB O
See Mann, *Richard Strauss* (London 1964; New York 1966); Kobbé

Élisa, ou Le Voyage au Mont Bernard (*Élisa, or the Journey to Mount Bernard*), opera, 2 acts, CHERUBINI, lib. Reveroni Saint-Cyr. Paris, T. Feydeau, 13 Dec 1794. Remarkable not so much for the music as for the exploitation of Alpine scenery, with a glacier, a storm, and an avalanche (cf. Loutherberg's *An Avalanche in the Alps* in the Tate Gallery, London). LO

Elisabeth, sop., daughter of the Landgrave in TANNHÄUSER

Elisabetta, Regina d'Inghilterra (*Elizabeth, Queen of England*), opera, 2 acts, ROSSINI, lib. Giovanni Schmidt after Sophia Lee's *The Recess*. Naples, T. S. Carlo, 4 Oct 1815; London, 30 Apr 1818. Main chars: Elisabetta (sop.) Matilda (sop.) Enrico (mezzo-sop.) Leicester (ten.) Norfolk (ten.). Elisabetta (Elizabeth I) in love with the Earl of Leicester, is furious to learn from the Duke of Norfolk that her favourite is secretly married to Matilda. Thwarted in her attempt to make Leicester give up his wife, she has him thrown into prison under sentence of death. Finally Norfolk's villainy is unmasked and the Queen pardons Leicester and his wife. Rossini's first opera to dispense with *recitativo secco*, following the new Neapolitan practice. The overture is the same as that for BARBIERE DI SIVIGLIA. JB

Elisir d'Amore, L' (*The Love Potion*), opera, 2 acts, DONIZETTI, lib. ROMANI after SCRIBE's

L'Elisir d'Amore. Gala performance, London, CG, 18 Dec 1975; produced COPLEY; designed Beni Montresor; G. EVANS as Dulcamara

Le Philtre. Milan, T. Canobbiana, 12 May 1832; London, Lyceum, 10 Dec 1836; NY, Park T., 22 May 1844. Main chars: Adina (sop.) Nemorino (ten.) Belcore (bar.) Dulcamara (bass). Nemorino, a young farmer, hopelessly in love with the rich young landowner Adina, buys from the travelling quack doctor Dulcamara what he believes is a potion that will make her fall in love with him: it is in fact a bottle of Bordeaux. Donizetti's masterpiece in the sentimental-comic vein. JB O★
See Kobbé

Elmendorff, Karl, b. Düsseldorf, 25 Jan 1891; d. Taunus, 21 Oct 1962. German conductor. Studied Cologne. Held posts in Wiesbaden, Mannheim, and Munich; a frequent cond. at Bayreuth 1927–42. Mus. dir., Dresden, 1942–5; Kassel, from 1949. Has also cond. at Berlin Staats O. and Florence Maggio Musicale. A WAGNER specialist, he did much to revive VERDI in Germany, besides championing Czech operas (JENŮFA and JACOBIN, Dresden 1943) and presenting 20th-c. works. LO

Elsa, sop., the heroine of LOHENGRIN

Elvira, Donna 1. Sop., one of the ladies seduced by DON GIOVANNI. 2. Sop., the heroine of ERNANI

Emma Abbott English Opera Co., founded 1878 by the US singer and managed by her husband, Eugene Wetherell. As the sole star of a youthful co. of 60, Miss Abbott supervised every aspect of prod. Abridged versions of works incl. *Les Cloches de Corneville (The Chimes of Normandy)*, MARTHA, NORMA, *Ruy Blas*, ERNANI, and TRAVIATA were edited and perf. in Eng. for appeal to communities where higher standards would fail. Her tours through the Middle and far West bolstered civic and social pride while doing no great violence to the music. Thirty-five new opera houses were dedicated by the co. 1878–80. EJ

Emperor Jones, The, opera, 2 acts, GRUENBERG, lib. Kathleen de Jaffe based on the play by Eugene O'Neill. NY Met, 7 Jan 1933; San Francisco 1933; Amsterdam, Rome 1952. Main chars: Brutus Jones (bar.) Henry Smithers (ten.) Old Nature Witch (sop.) Congo Witch Doctor (dancer). On an island in the West Indies, Jones, an ex-Pullman porter, crap shooter, murderer, fugitive from justice, rules his Caribbean tribesmen with all the trappings of royalty. Smithers warns him of his deposition; Jones flees through the jungle, has hallucinations of seeing his victims, sheds his 'royal' garments, then ends his life with his last bullet. EJ

Enfant et les Sortilèges, L' (*The Child and the Magic Spells*), opera, 2 acts, RAVEL, lib. Colette. Monte Carlo, 21 Mar 1925; San Francisco, 19 Sept 1930; Oxford, 3 Dec 1958. Main char.: the Child (mezzo-sop.). Skilful elements of parody in this exquisite score keep the fantasy free from sentimentality. FGB O
See Kobbé

English Music Theatre Co. *see* ENGLISH OPERA GROUP

English National Opera (ENO), previously Sadler's Wells Opera Co. (SW). Opened officially under its new name at London Coliseum 3 Aug 1974 with TRAVIATA. LO

English Opera Group (EOG). An opera co. formed 1947 by BRITTEN, PIPER and CROZIER for the perf. of new operas. Besides mounting several by Britten, it has prod. operas by BERKELEY, Brian Easdale, and WALTON. Closely identified with Aldeburgh; it has also toured in continental Europe and Canada. Re-formed 1975 as English Music Theatre Co. LO

Enna, August, b. Nakskov, 13 May 1860; d. Copenhagen, 3 Aug 1939. Danish composer. His first opera, *Agleia*, was prod. at Copenhagen (1884); he wrote more than a dozen others, most of them also first perf. in Copenhagen and some of them based on ANDERSEN. They incl. *Heksen (The Witch)*, 1892; *Kleopatra*, 1894; *Aucassin og Nicolette*, 1896; *Pigen med Svovlstikkerne (The Little Match-Girl)*, 1897; *Prinsessen paa Ærten (The Princess and the Pea)*, 1900; *Nattergalen (The Nightingale)*, 1912; *Gloria Arsena*, 1917; and *Komedianter (The Comedians)*, 1920. EF

Enriquez, Franco, b. Florence, 20 Nov 1907. Italian theatre and TV producer. Was assistant to C. EBERT and GRAF; since World War II his work has been seen frequently in Milan, Naples, Rome, and Venice, in both standard and modern works, and he has also prod. at CG (NORMA, 1953). More recent prods have included KHOVANSHCHINA (Florence Fest. 1973) and SIMONE BOCCANEGRA (Verona 1973). LO

Entführung aus dem Serail, Die (*The Elopement from the Harem*), opera, 3 acts, MOZART, lib. Gottlieb Stephanie after Christoph Friedrich Bretzner. Vienna, BT, 16 July 1782; London, CG, 24 Nov 1827; NY, German OH, 16 Feb 1860. Main chars: Constanze (sop.) Blondchen (or Blonde) (sop.) Belmonte (ten.) Pedrillo (ten.) Osmin (bass). Belmonte and his servant, Pedrillo, try to rescue their respective sweethearts, Constanze and Blondchen, from the harem of Pasha Selim. Discovered in the act of escaping by Osmin, keeper of the harem, they are apprehended but eventually pardoned and set free by the magnanimous Pasha. Mozart's first great success, with which German opera came of age. JB O
See Kobbé

entr'acte (*Fr.*) 1. Interval between the acts of an opera. 2. An instrumental movement between two acts, usually following an interval, very occasionally replacing it. *See* INTERMEZZO. JB

Equivoci, Gli (*The Doubles*), opera, 2 acts, S. STORACE, lib. da PONTE after SHAKESPEARE's *Comedy of Errors*. Vienna, BT, 27 Dec 1786; London, Camden Fest., 20 Feb 1974. Some of the music was incl. in other Storace operas, as *No Song, No Supper* (1790) and *The Pirates* (1792). LO

Erda, contr., the Earth Goddess in RING DES NIBELUNGEN

Erede, Alberto, b. Genoa, 8 Nov 1909. Italian conductor. Studied Genoa, Milan, and Basel, also with WEINGARTNER and BUSCH, whose assistant at Glyndebourne he became (1935–9). After World War II in charge of New London Opera Co. In 1937–8 made tour of USA, giving opera in some 70 towns with Salzburg Opera Guild. Cond. radio premiere of OLD MAID AND THE THIEF and was a principal cond. at NY Met for several seasons. Mus. dir. of Deutsche Oper am Rhein 1958–62. LO

Erhardt, Otto, b. Breslau (now Wrocław), 18 Nov 1888; d. San Carlos de Bariloche, Argentina, Feb 1971. German producer. Studied Munich, Berlin, and Oxford. Prod. first Ger. stage perf. of FAVOLO D'ORFEO, Breslau, 1913. Held posts at Stuttgart, 1920–7; chief prod. Dresden 1927–33, till forced to leave Germany by the Nazis. At CG, 1933–5, at T. Colón, 1938–60. Prod. first perfs of HINDEMITH's *Mörder, Hoffnung der Frauen,* and ÄGYPTISCHE HELENA. LO

Erismena, L', opera, prologue and 3 acts, CAVALLI, lib. Aurelio Aureli. Venice, T. S. Apollinare, Jan 1655. Several modern revivals, e.g. London BBC, ed. Lionel Salter, 1967, and at 1974 Holland Fest., ed. Alan Curtis, prod. and dir. SANJUST. LO

Erkel, Ferenc, b. Gyula, 7 Nov 1810; d. Budapest, 15 June 1893. Hungarian composer. A key figure in the Hung. nationalist movement, in his eight operas on Hung. subjects he created a distinctively Hung. operatic language, seen at its most characteristic in *Hunyadi László* and BÁNK BÁN. His other operas are: *Báthori Mária* (1840), *Sarolta* (1862), *Dózsa György* (1874), *Brnakovics György* (1867), *Névtelen Hosök* (1880) and *István Király* (1885). LO

Ernani, opera, 4 acts, VERDI, lib. PIAVE after HUGO's *Hernani*, 1830. Venice, T. La Fenice, 9 Mar 1844; London, HM, 8 Mar 1845; NY, Park T., 15 Apr 1847. Main chars: Elvira (sop.) Ernani (ten.) Carlo (bar.) Silva (bass). Donna Elvira, loved by her guardian Don Ruy Gomez de Silva, and courted by Carlo (Charles, King of Spain), is in love with Ernani, an outlawed nobleman turned bandit. When Carlo removes her from Silva's palace, Silva and Ernani join in a plot against his life. The conspirators are discovered and pardoned by Carlo, newly elected Holy Roman Emperor as Charles V. Ernani is restored to his estates and allowed to marry Elvira; but having forfeited his life to Silva, kills himself when the old man comes to claim the fulfilment of his vow. Verdi's fifth opera and the first to bring him world fame. (BELLINI began an opera on the same subject.) Its vitality and freshness of invention has kept it intermittently in the repertory. JB O

Erwartung (*Expectation*), monodrama, 1 act, SCHÖNBERG, lib. Marie Pappenheim. Prague, 6 June 1924; NY, 15 Nov 1951; London, SW, 4 April 1960. A woman (sop.) is searching for her lover in a dark wood, and eventually discovers his dead body. EF O

Escamillo, bar., the Toreador in CARMEN

Esser, Hermin, b. Rheydt, 1 Apr 1948. German tenor. Studied Düsseldorf. First appeared

Krefeld. Bayreuth debut 1966 as Froh (RHEINGOLD); has since sung LOHENGRIN, TANNHÄUSER, DAVID, LOGE among other roles there. British debut as TRISTAN with SO 1973. AB

Étoile, L' (*The Star*), *opéra bouffe*, 3 acts, CHABRIER, lib. Eugène Leterrier and Albert Vanloo. Paris, Bouffes-Parisiens, 28 Nov 1877; NY (as *The Merry Monarch*), 18 Aug 1890. A frothy *jeu d'esprit* described by both Charles Koechlin and STRAVINSKY as 'a little masterpiece'. LO
See Myers, *Emmanuel Chabrier and His Circle* (London 1969; Rutherford, N.J. 1970)

Étoile du Nord, L' (*The North Star*), *opéra comique*, 3 acts, MEYERBEER, lib. SCRIBE. Paris, OC, 16 Feb 1854; London, CG, 19 July 1855 (in It., with recitatives and additional mus. by Meyerbeer); New Orleans, 5 Mar 1855. A second revision of *Ein Feldlager in Schlesien* (lib. L. Rellstab), Berlin 7 Dec 1844. Written for Jenny Lind, who did not in fact sing the first perf. It was revised for Vienna as *Vielka*, 18 Feb 1847, with Jenny Lind in the title role. Main chars: Catherine (sop.) Peters (bass) Danilowitz (ten.) Georges (ten.) Prascovia (sop.). Peter the Great, disguised as the carpenter, Peters, woos Catherine. She takes her brother Georges's place in the Russian army. Mistaken for a conspirator, she is ordered to be shot, and is wounded escaping. Deranged, she is brought to the Tsar's palace. Seeing Peters she regains her sanity, and is made his Tsarina. One of the most successful operas of the 19th c., it remained in the repertoire until 1901; famous Catherines included PATTI, MIOLAN-CARVALHO and SEMBRICH. The opera was revived at the Camden Fest., London, 25 Feb 1975, by Opera Rara. PS

Eugene Onegin (*Evgeny Onegin*), lyric scenes, 3 acts, TCHAIKOVSKY, lib. composer and Konstantin Shilovsky, after PUSHKIN's poem. Moscow, Maly T., 29 Mar 1879; London, Olympic T., 17 Oct 1892; NY (concert perf.), 1 Feb 1908. Main chars: Tatyana (sop.) Olga (contr.) Onegin (bar.) Lensky (ten.). Tchaikovsky's lyrical masterpiece, this remains his most popular opera. GN ○
See Kobbé

Euridice, L', opera, prologue and 6 scenes, PERI, lib. RINUCCINI. Florence, Palazzo Pitti, 6 Oct 1600, for wedding of Henri IV of France with Maria de' Medici. The first opera the mus. of which is preserved. Rinuccini's lib., dealing with the story of Orpheus and Eurydice, was also set by CACCINI in 1602. LO ○

Euripides, b. Salamis, 480 BC; d. Pella, *c.* 406 BC. Greek dramatist. About 20 operas have been based on his tragedies, the more important being: *Alkestis* (GLUCK, BOUGHTON, 1922, Egon Wellesz, 1924); *The Bacchae* (Wellesz, 1931, GHEDINI, 1948, BASSARIDS); *Hippolytus* (RAMEAU, 1733); *Iphigenia in Aulis* (Gluck); *Iphigenia in Tauris* (Gluck); *Medea* (CHERUBINI, 1797); *Orestes* (KŘENEK, *Leben des Orest*, 1930). LO

Euryanthe, opera, 3 acts, C. WEBER, lib. Helmine von Chezy based on 13th-c. Fr. romance. Vienna, KT, 25 Oct 1823; London, CG, 29 June 1833; NY Met, 23 Dec 1887. Main chars: Euryanthe de Davoie (sop.) Eglantine de Poiset (mezzo-sop.) Lysiart de Forêt (bar.) Adolar de Nevers (ten.) Louis VI (bass). LO ○
See Kobbé

Eva, sop., the heroine of MEISTERSINGER

Evangelimann, Der (*The Evangelist*), opera, 2 acts, KIENZL, lib. composer based on story by Leopold Florian Meissner. Berlin Staats O., 4 May 1895; London, CG, 2 July 1897; Liverpool (in Eng., Moody-Manners Co.) Apr 1914; Chicago 3 Nov 1923. Revived, Vienna Volks O., 3 Oct 1973. Combining Wagnerian sophistication with It. *verismo* in the working out of a homely but melodramatic story of crime and repentance, it was extremely popular, with more than 5,000 perfs in 40 years. LO

Evans, Geraint, b. Pontypridd, 16 Feb 1922. Welsh baritone. Internationally acclaimed in MOZART, BRITTEN, and title roles in FALSTAFF and WOZZECK. Studied Guildhall School of Music, London, Hamburg and Geneva. Joined CG 1948; debut as Nightwatchman (MEISTERSINGER VON NÜRNBERG). Continued regular CG appearances to 1970s, steadily building reputation there and at Glyndebourne Fest.

Eugene Onegin. Curtain by GOLOVIN for production by the Kirov T., Leningrad, 1926

Geraint Evans as PAPAGENO, London, CG, 25 July 1966; produced Peter Hall; designed John Bury

1950–61, as MOZART's FIGARO, LEPORELLO, and PAPAGENO. Created Flint in BILLY BUDD (1952), Mountjoy in GLORIANA (1953), Antenor in TROILUS AND CRESSIDA (1954), all at CG. First sang Falstaff at Glyndebourne 1957; BECKMESSER at CG 1957; Wozzeck at CG 1960. Debuts abroad quickly followed, incl. San Francisco 1959; Milan, Sc., 1960; Vienna, Staats O., 1961; Salzburg Fest. 1962; NY Met, 1964. His singing unites warmth of tone and expression with instinctive sense of theatrical char. and endearing personality, creating memorable stage portraits.

His own success helped to gain prestige for British singers abroad from the 1960s. He has given master classes in interpretation (incl. TV), and prod. operas for WNO, Edinburgh Fest., San Francisco and Chicago. Made CBE 1959; knighted 1969. NG

Evans, Nancy, b. Liverpool, 19 Mar 1915. English mezzo-soprano. Studied with John Tobin and TEYTE. Sang small roles at CG before World War II. Debut with EOG alternating in first perfs of RAPE OF LUCRETIA as Lucretia (1946). Created Nancy (ALBERT HERRING, 1947). Also sang DIDO with EOG. Glyndebourne, in small roles, 1957–60. AB

Everding, August, b. Bottrop, Westphalia, 31 Oct 1928. German producer. Studied philosophy and drama at Bonn and Munich. Began career producing plays in Munich, where he also prod. his first operas from 1965, followed by TRISTAN UND ISOLDE at Vienna Staats O. (1967), the premiere of SEARLE's HAMLET at Hamburg (1968), FLIEGENDE HOLLÄNDER at Bayreuth (1969), SALOME at CG (1970), *Tristan und Isolde* at the NY Met (1971), and DON GIOVANNI at Paris O. (1975). One of the most thought-provoking producers of the day. AB

evirato *see* CASTRATO

Ezio, *opera seria*, 3 acts, HANDEL, lib. METASTASIO, London, King's T., 15 Jan 1732. Metastasio's text, one of his best, was set by over 25 comps incl. GLUCK, TRAETTA, 1754, GRAUN, 1755, and MERCADANTE, 1827. LO

F

Faccio, Franco [Francesco], b. Verona, 8 Mar 1840; d. Monza, 21 July 1891. Italian conductor and composer. A fellow pupil of BOITO at the Milan Cons., he was initially active as a comp. His two operas *I Profughi Fiamminghi* (Milan 1863) and *Amleto* (Genoa 1865), lib. Boito, were considered adventurous for their time. From 1867 he turned to conducting; dir. premiere of the revised FORZA DEL DESTINO in 1869 at Sc., and became chief cond. in 1871. Also cond. European premiere of AIDA (1872), and world premieres of the revised SIMONE BOCCANEGRA (1881), DON CARLOS (1884), and VERDI's OTELLO (1887). Introduced the late works of WAGNER to Italy. Professor of harmony at the Milan Cons. from 1868; taught SMAREGLIA. As a comp., Faccio is musicianly but little more; but he was the greatest It. cond. between MARIANI and TOSCANINI. JB

Fafner, bass, one of the two giants in RHEINGOLD

Fair Maid of Perth, The *see* JOLIE FILLE DE PERTH

Fairy Queen, The, masque, 5 acts with prologue, PURCELL, lib. Elkanah Settle, based on SHAKESPEARE's *A Midsummer Night's Dream*. London, Dorset Gardens, Apr 1692. The score was lost for two centuries (20 guineas were offered for its recovery in 1700) and was found in 1901 by John South Shedlock while cataloguing the RAM library. It was given in concert perf. London 15 June 1901. First modern stage perf. Cambridge 10 Feb 1920; also San Francisco 30 Apr 1932. Constant Lambert's adaptation re-opened CG after World War II in 1946. PS ○

Fairy-tale operas. The fairy tale has appealed to a number of composers. *See* ANDERSEN, the GRIMM brothers, PERRAULT, WILDE; also ARABIAN NIGHTS ENTERTAINMENTS. Operas from other sources incl. FAIRY QUEEN and MIDSUMMER NIGHT'S DREAM, UNDINE, RUSALKA, and SNOW MAIDEN. LO

Falcon, Marie Cornélie, b. Paris, 28 Jan 1812; d. Paris, 27 Feb 1897. French dramatic soprano. Her short career (her voice gave out *c.* 1840) coincided with a brilliant era in Fr. opera. Debut 1832, Paris O., as Alice (ROBERT LE DIABLE); created Mme Anckarström (GUSTAVE III, 1833), Morgiani (CHERUBINI's *Ali Baba*, 1833), Rachel (JUIVE, 1835), and Valentine (HUGUENOTS, 1836). LO

Fall, Leo, b. Olmütz (now Olomouc), Moravia, 2 Feb 1873; d. Vienna, 16 Sept 1925. Czech composer of operettas. Studied Vienna Cons.; after posts as cond. in Germany returned to Vienna 1904 when his career as comp. began. Of his operettas, *Die Dollarprinzessin* (Vienna, Carl T., 2 Nov 1907) was the most successful, with over 600 perfs. Others of note, heard like *Die Dollarprinzessin* outside Vienna, are: *Der Fidele Bauer*, lib. Viktor Léon (Mannheim 1908; London 1910); *Die Geschiedene Frau*, lib. Léon (Vienna 1908; London 1910); *Der Liebe Augustin* (Berlin 1912; London 1913); *Madame Pompadour* (Vienna 1922; London 1933). Like J. STRAUSS and LEHÁR of the Second Viennese Operetta School, Fall exploited the Viennese waltz, with its nostalgic fusion of champagne gaiety and wistfulness; his operettas, charming, slight, inhabit a make-believe world. LO
See Lubbock

Falstaff, London CG, 10 May 1961; produced and designed ZEFFIRELLI. G. EVANS as Falstaff; RESNIK as Alice Ford; FRENI as Nannetta

Falla, Manuel de, b. Cádiz, 23 Nov 1876; d. Alta Gracia, Argentina, 14 Nov 1946. Spanish composer. In his youth he comp. five *zarzuelas*, of which only *Los Amores de la Inés* (1902) was perf., but without success. After composition studies with PEDRELL (1902–4), his first opera VIDA BREVE won first prize in a Madrid competition (1905), but remained unprod. until 1913, at Nice. It has since been widely but infrequently perf., like the second of his two pub. operas, RETABLO DE MAESE PEDRO. Falla, who lived in Paris, 1907–14, also made Frédéric Chopin's mus. the basis of an unpub. comic opera, *Fuego Fátuo* (*Will o' the Wisp*, 1918). Falla settled in Argentina from 1939, and left at his death the unfinished *La Atlántida*, a 'scenic cantata' for chorus and orch. on a Catalan epic poem by Mosén Jacinto Verdaguer. Following its completion by Ernesto Halffter and concert premiere at Barcelona (1961), it was prod. as a stage work at Sc. in 1962. NG
See Pahissa, *Falla, His Life and Works* (London 1954)

Falstaff, *commedia lirica,* 3 acts, VERDI, lib. BOITO after SHAKESPEARE. Milan, Sc., 9 Feb 1893; London, CG, 19 May 1894; NY Met, 4 Feb 1895. Main chars: Falstaff (bar.) Fenton (ten.) Nannetta (sop.) Alice (sop.) Meg (mezzo-sop.) Quickly (contr.) Ford (bar.). An operatic version of *The Merry Wives of Windsor* with elements borrowed from the chronicle plays: the misadventures of the 'fat knight in love'. Verdi's last and most musicianly opera. JB ○
See Kobbé

Fanciulla del West, La (*The Girl of The Golden West*), opera, 3 acts, PUCCINI, lib. Guelfo Civinini and Carlo Zangarini after David Belasco's *The Girl of the Golden West.* NY Met, 10 Dec 1910; London, CG, 29 May 1911; Rome, T. Costanzi, 12 June 1911. Main chars: Minnie (sop.) Dick Johnson (ten.) Jack Rance (bar.). Minnie, owner of an inn in the Californian mountains and self-appointed 'schoolmarm' to the miners of 1849, falls in love with Dick Johnson, a bandit in disguise. She saves his life from the Sheriff, Jack Rance,

by cheating at cards, and later prevents him from being lynched by the miners. Puccini's seventh opera; the work is more popular with connoisseurs of the comp. than with the public at large. JB ○
See Kobbé

Faninal, von, bar., Sophie's father in ROSENKAVALIER

Fanny, mus. play by Harold Rome, based on a book by Samuel Nathaniel Berman and Joshua Logan from stories by Marcel Pagnol. NY, Majestic T., 4 Nov 1954; Munich 16 Dec 1955; London, DL, 15 Nov 1956. EJ ★
See Kobbé

Farinelli [Carlo Broschi], b. Andria, nr Bari, 24 Jan 1705; d. Bologna, 15 July 1782. Italian castrato. The most celebrated castrato of the 18th c., he studied with his father and brother, the comps Salvatore and Riccardo Broschi, and later with PORPORA. Debut, 1720, Naples, in a serenata by his teacher (to METASTASIO's first text); operatic debut in Porpora's *Eumene* (Rome 1721). He had a 'penetrating, well-rounded, luscious, clear and even soprano voice' reaching D above high C, combined with amazing agility and flexibility. His appearance in London in *Artaserse* (1734) by HASSE and his brother, created a sensation, causing women to swoon. In 1737 he was hired to assuage the melancholy of Philip v of Spain by singing him, it is said, the same four songs every night for 10 years. Dir. of the Spanish Court O. 1747–59. PS

Farrar, Geraldine, b. Melrose, Mass., 28 Feb 1882; d. Ridgefield, Conn., 11 Mar 1967. American soprano. Studied Boston, NY, Paris, and Berlin; debut 1901, Berlin (GOUNOD's FAUST). After further study with Lilli LEHMANN and appearances in Berlin, Paris, and Monte Carlo, made her debut at NY Met (ROMÉO ET JULIETTE, 1906); remained there until her retirement in 1922. One of the outstanding performers there, at her best in lyric roles and operas such as MADAMA BUTTERFLY and MANON, which were imbued with a rare radiance by her personal beauty and artistic integrity. LO
See autobiography, *Such Sweet Compulsion* (New York 1938, 1970)

Farrell, Eileen, b. Willimantic, Conn., 13 Feb 1920. American soprano. Studied NY; sang Marie in concert version of WOZZECK, Carnegie Hall, 1950. Sang at San Francisco and Chicago before joining NY Met, 1960 (debut in GLUCK's ALCESTE). Gifted with a fine, big voice, she excels in WAGNER roles, which she has sung not only at the Met but elsewhere. LO

Fasolt, bass, one of the two giants in RHEINGOLD

Fassbänder, Brigitte, b. Berlin, 3 July 1939. German mezzo-soprano. Studied Nuremberg and with her father W. DOMGRAF-FASSBÄNDER. Joined Bavarian Staats O. in 1961 and has remained with co. ever since. Also appeared regularly at the Munich Fests in MOZART and R. STRAUSS roles. Salzburg Fest. since 1972 as DORABELLA. CG debut as OCTAVIAN, 1971. AB

Fatinitza, operetta, 3 acts, SUPPÉ, lib. F. Zell (Camillo Walzell) and GENÉE based on SCRIBE's *Circassienne*. Vienna, Carl T., 5 Jan 1876; London, Alhambra T. (in Eng.), 20 June 1878; NY, 14 Apr 1879; revived Munich 1950 in new version by E. Rogati and Bruno Uher. Suppé's first full-length operetta. LO

Fauré, Gabriel Urbain, b. Pamiers, 12 May 1845; d. Paris, 4 Nov 1924. French composer. Apart from some incidental mus., esp. that to PELLÉAS ET MÉLISANDE written for Prince of Wales's T., London (1898), his only stage works were PROMÉTHÉE and PÉNÉLOPE. LO

Faure, Jean-Baptiste, b. Moulins, 15 Jan 1830; d. Paris, 9 Nov 1914. French baritone. Studied at the Paris Cons. and the Madeleine, played in the orch. of the Odéon and sang in the chorus of TI before his solo debut in MASSÉ's *Galathée* (OC 20 Oct 1852). After eight years there he became principal bar. Among the many roles he created were MÉPHISTOPHÉLÈS (1859), Nelusko (AFRICAINE, 1865), Posa (DON CARLOS, 1867), and HAMLET (Ambroise THOMAS), 1868. He was also a celebrated DON GIOVANNI, GUILLAUME TELL and Nevers (HUGUENOTS). CG debut DINORAH (1860); appeared there regularly for 16 years. Last Paris appearance at O., 13 May 1876, as Hamlet; final stage appearance was in Vienna in 1878. In 1859 m. Caroline Lefebvre (1828–1905), a singer at OC. PS

Faust, opera, 5 acts, GOUNOD, lib. BARBIER and CARRÉ based on GOETHE's *Faust*. Paris, TL, 19 Mar 1859; London, HM, 11 June 1863; Philadelphia, 18 Nov 1863. Gounod's most successful opera and one of the most widely perf. ever written. Main chars: Faust (ten.) Méphistophélès (bass) Marguerite (sop.). Faust barters his soul with Méphistophélès in exchange for, not power or wealth, but youth. He ravishes Marguerite, who after being con-

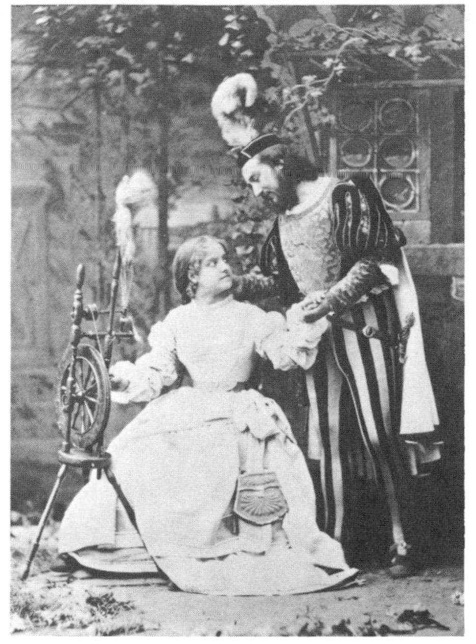

Left: Faust (GOUNOD), London, CG, 1864; MARIO in the title role; PATTI as Marguerite, her first at CG; she was criticized for being 'too flippant', refused to modify her interpretation and left the company in a tantrum. She returned in 1865 in the same role.

Right: La Favola d'Orfeo, ENO production at the London Coliseum, 25 May 1970; designed Yolanda Sonnabend; produced Patrick Libby. Shirley Chapman (seated, centre) as the Messenger who has brought news of Eurydice's death.

demned to death for the killing of her child, is finally forgiven and transported to heaven, while Faust must keep his bargain with Méphistophélès. LO ○
See Kobbé

Faust, opera, 2 acts, SPOHR, lib. Joseph Karl Bernard derived from Maximilian von Klinger's *Fausts Leben, Thaten und Höllenfahrt*. Dresden, 1 Sept 1816 (cond. C. WEBER); London, Prince's T., 1840 (in Eng., tr. John Wray Mould). *Not* based on GOETHE. Main chars: Faust (bar.) Mephistopheles (bass) Count Hugo (ten.) Cunigund (sop.). There is no Valentin, Siebel, or Marguerite. LO

Favart, Charles Simon, b. Paris, 13 Nov 1710; d. Belleville, 12 Mar 1792. French librettist. His over 150 libs were witty and eminently suited to musical settings; the 18th-c. *opéra comique* of DUNI, GRÉTRY, GLUCK, MONSIGNY, and PHILIDOR depends on the type of lib. he originated. His wife, Marie, 1727–72, was an accomplished actress and singer. LO

Favola d'Orfeo, La (*The Tale of Orpheus*), opera, prologue and 5 acts, MONTEVERDI, lib. Alessandro Striggio. Mantua, probably in Palazzo Ducale, 22 (?) Feb 1607. Monteverdi's score, pub. 1609, lay forgotten for so long after the initial perfs and presented so many problems (realization of *continuo*, instrumentation, the whole question of 17th-c. It. operatic style) that it would be hazardous to suggest a modern revival before that of the Oxford Univ. O. Club, 7 Dec 1925 (in Eng.), cond. by Jack Westrup; first fully professional prod. in England, SW (in It.), 5 Oct 1965. In Feb 1975 the Oxford Univ O. Club celebrated its jubilee by presenting *Orfeo* again in a more authentic form prepared by Jane Glover and cond. by her. It has with justice been described as 'the first opera', containing as it does the ingredients – arias, ensembles, dramatic recitatives, instrumental interludes, confrontation, tension, release, etc. – of all later operas. It recounts the nuptials of Orpheus and Eurydice; her death and Orpheus's grief; his journey to the underworld; the joyous return of the happy pair, followed by tragedy with (as it is a fable) a contrived happy end. LO ○

favola per musica (It. 'fable [composed] with music'). Applied in 17th c. to musical settings of legends or myths, e.g. the Orpheus myth. LO

Favorite, La, grand opera, 4 acts, DONIZETTI, lib. Alphonse Royer and Gustave Vaëz after F. T. de Baculard d'Arnaud's *Le Comte de Comminges*. Paris, O., 2 Dec 1840; New Orleans, 9 Feb 1843; London, DL, 18 Oct 1943. Main chars: Leonore (mezzo-sop.) Ferdinand (ten.) Alphonse (bar.) Balthazar (bass). Ferdinand, a young novice, falls in love with Leonore, mistress of Alphonse (Alfonso XI of Castile) without knowing who she is. Alphonse, threatened with excommunication by the Father Superior, Balthazar, unless he returns to his lawful wife, bestows Leonore on Ferdinand, now a captain in the army. On discovering his bride's iden-

La Favorite. Milan Scala production of the Italian *La Favorita*, 1961–2; produced WALLMANN; designed N. BENOIS

tity, Ferdinand returns to the monastery, where Leonore follows him in male disguise, and dies in his arms. More familiar in its Italian form *La Favorita*, without ballet, it still holds the stage in Italy today. The air 'Spirto gentil' from Act IV is one of the most famous in the ten. repertory. JB ○
See Kobbé; Ashbrook, *Donizetti* (London 1965)

Fedora, opera, 3 acts, GIORDANO, lib. Arturo Colautti after SARDOU. Milan, T. Lirico, 17 Nov 1898; London, CG, 5 Nov 1906; NY Met, 5 Dec 1906. Main chars: Fedora (sop.) Loris (ten.) Olga (mezzo-sop.) De Siriex (bar.). Princess Fedora Romanov, determined to avenge her fiancé's murder, discovers the assassin to be one Count Loris Ipanov, with whose wife the dead man had carried on an intrigue. Fedora falls in love with him but is too late to save him from the consequences of her earlier plotting. She takes poison and dies in his arms. Giordano's most popular opera after ANDREA CHÉNIER. JB ○
See Kobbé

Fedorovich, Sophie, b. Minsk, 15 Dec 1893; d. London, 31 Jan 1953. Russian, naturalized British, designer. Better known as a designer for ballet, in particular for the Rambert and SW companies, she also designed sets and costumes for TRAVIATA (SW 1946; CG 1948), MADAMA BUTTERFLY, TOSCA (CG 1950), DIDO AND AENEAS (Aldeburgh Fest. 1951), and ORFEO ED EURIDICE (CG 1953). EF

Fedra (*Phaedra*), opera, 3 acts, PIZZETTI, lib. D'ANNUNZIO based on EURIPIDES' *Hippolytus*. Milan, Sc., 20 Mar 1915 (comp. 1909–12). LO
See Gatti (tr. Moore), *Ildebrando Pizzetti* (London 1951)

Feen, Die (*The Fairies*), opera, 3 acts, WAGNER, lib. composer after GOZZI's *La Donna Serpente*. Munich, 29 June 1888 (posthumous). Main chars: Ada (sop.) Arindel (ten.) Gernot (buffo-bass) Gunther (buffo-ten.). King Arindel of Tramond has married the fairy Ada, whom he is fated to lose if he should curse her under the stress of some calamity apparently caused by her. He fails the test, and Ada is turned into a stone. But his grief finally undoes the spell and he is allowed to enter fairyland as her husband. Wagner's first opera, written at Würzburg in 1833 and influenced by C. WEBER and LORTZING. JB

Felsenstein, Walter, b. Vienna, 30 May 1901; d. Berlin, 8 Oct 1975. Austrian producer. After working in various Ger. theatres, he was apptd *Intendant* of the Berlin KO (1947). He then dir. many prods noteworthy for their dramatic consistency, incl. NOZZE DI FIGARO, ZAUBERFLÖTE, FREISCHÜTZ, BARTERED BRIDE, TANNHÄUSER, CARMEN, CONTES D'HOFFMANN, VERDI's OTELLO and TRAVIATA. He also prod. operettas such as FLEDERMAUS, ZIGEUNERBARON and NACHT IN VENEDIG, and 20th-c. works such as SCHWEIGSAME FRAU, KLUGE, ALBERT HERRING and, esp.,

CUNNING LITTLE VIXEN, which was given at Sc. and other European opera houses. EF

Fenice, La *see* VENICE

Fenton, ten., Anne's lover in LUSTIGEN WEIBER VON WINDSOR and FALSTAFF

Fernand Cortez, ou La Conquête du Mexique, grand opera, 3 acts, SPONTINI, lib. JOUY and Joseph Alphonse Esménard. Paris, O., 16 Dec 1808; 28 May 1817 in revised form. Main chars: Cortez (ten.) Amazily (sop.) Montezuma (bass) Telasco (bar.) Alvaro (ten.). Cortez, engaged in the conquest of Mexico, loves Amazily, daughter of King Montezuma, and hopes by their marriage to bring about peace. He quells a mutiny among his own troops, burns his boats, and with the help of Amazily, now a Christian, rescues his brother from being sacrificed to the Aztec gods. Montezuma finally agrees to the marriage. Spontini's second grand opera, intended to celebrate Napoleon's conquest of Spain. In the second, definitive version the action is re-ordered and a stage cavalry charge eliminated. For other operas on this theme *see* AZORA, DAUGHTER OF MONTEZUMA and MONTEZUMA. JB

Fernández Caballero, Manuel, b. Murcia, 14 Mar 1835; d. Madrid, 26 Feb 1906. Spanish composer (and youngest of 18 brothers). Remembered for his more than 100 *zarzuelas*, many of which he dictated to his son Mario after his sight had failed. They incl. *Château Margaux* (1887), *Gigantes y Cabezudos* (1898), *El Dúo de la Africana* (1893), and *La Viejecita.* FGB

Ferne Klang, Der (*The Distant Sound*), opera, 3 acts, SCHREKER, lib. composer. Frankfurt, 18 Aug 1912 (comp. 1906–9). LO

Ferrando, ten., Dorabella's lover in COSÌ FAN TUTTE

Ferrario, Carlo, b. Milan, 8 Sept 1833; d. Milan, 12 May 1907. Italian scenographer, assoc. for many years with Sc., where he designed sets for MEFISTOFELE, GIOCONDA and many other operas. After a short break when he worked for T. Argentina, Rome, and T. Carcano, Milan, returned to Sc. for the premieres of VERDI's OTELLO and FALSTAFF. One of most important It. designers of second half of 19th c., and much admired by Verdi. LO

Ferrari-Trecate, Luigi, b. Alessandria, Piedmont, 25 Aug 1884; d. Rome, 17 Apr 1964. Italian composer. His 12 operas include *Regina Ester* (Faenza 1900); *La Bella e il Mostro* (Milan 1926), and *La Capanna dello Zio Tom* (after Harriet Beecher Stowe's *Uncle Tom's Cabin*, Parma 1953). LO

Ferrier, Kathleen Mary, b. Higher Walton, Lancashire, 22 Apr 1912; d. London, 8 Oct 1953. English contralto. Her beauty of voice and personality won her worldwide acclaim mainly as a concert singer (esp. in Johann Sebastian Bach, HANDEL, MAHLER). Turned to singing after winning competitive fest. prize, Carlisle 1937. Died from cancer at the height of her fame, having sung only two operatic roles: created title role in RAPE OF LUCRETIA (Glyndebourne Fest. 1946); sang Orfeo in ORFEO ED EURIDICE there 1947, Holland Fest. 1949, CG 1953 (two perfs only, the second being her last public appearance). Instinctive dignity and serenity of spirit in perf. were combined with vitality of char. and a quality of compassion unparalleled in modern vocal experience. Awarded CBE 1953. NG
See Kathleen Ferrier (London 1971), comprising Ferrier, *The Life of Kathleen Ferrier* (1955) and Cardus, *Kathleen Ferrier – A Memoir* (1954)

Fervaal, *action musicale*, prologue and 3 acts, d'INDY, lib. composer. Brussels, T. de la Monnaie, 12 Mar 1897; Paris, OC, 10 May 1898. Written under the influence of WAGNER and esp. PARSIFAL, it employed the *Leitmotif* technique and exploited the symbolism fashionable at the time. LO
See Cooper, *French Music, From the Death of Berlioz to the Death of Fauré* (London 1951)

festa teatrale (It. 'theatrical festival'). Name given to the sumptuous spectacle opera written in the 17th and 18th c. to commemorate special occasions such as royal births or weddings. LO

Festival of Two Worlds *see* SPOLETO

Festivals. Seasons of opera, usually during summer months, either in addition to regular opera seasons (e.g. Vienna Fest.) or in locations that have no regular opera (e.g. EDINBURGH). Sometimes dedicated to one composer (e.g. Bayreuth, the oldest of them). Among the more important are AIX-EN-PROVENCE, ALDEBURGH, GLYNDEBOURNE, HOLLAND, MAGGIO MUSICALE FIORENTINO, MUNICH, SALZBURG, SCHWETZINGEN, SPOLETO, VENICE, WEXFORD. For USA *see* article on UNITED STATES OF AMERICA. LO

Feuersnot (*Fire Famine*), opera, 1 act, R. STRAUSS, lib. Ernst von Wolzogen on an idea suggested by Strauss derived from a Flem. legend, *The Quenched Fires of Oudenaarde*. Dres-

den, 21 Nov 1901; London, HM, 9 July 1910; Philadelphia, 1 Dec 1927. Strauss's second opera and the first prod. at Dresden. LO
See Mann, *Richard Strauss* (London 1964; New York 1966); Del Mar, *Richard Strauss*, Vol. 1 (London and New York 1962)

Février, Henry, b. Paris, 2 Oct 1875; d. Paris, 8 July 1957. French composer. His operas are: *Le Roi Aveugle* (1906), based on a Norweg. legend; MONNA VANNA (1909); *Gismonda* (Chicago 1919); *La Damnation de Blanche-Fleur* (Monte Carlo 1920); *La Femme Nue* (Monte Carlo 1929); *Carmosine* (1913). Also wrote three operettas. LO

Fiamma, La (*The Flame*), opera, 3 acts, RESPIGHI, lib. Claudio Guastalla after Hans Wiers-Jenssen's *The Witch*. Rome, T. Reale, 23 Jan 1934; Chicago O., 2 Dec 1935. Main chars: Silvana (sop.) Donello (ten.) Basilio (bar.) Eudossia (mezzo-sop.). Silvana, daughter of the witch Agnese di Cervia and second wife of Basilio, Exarch of Ravenna, is unable to prevent her mother from being lynched. Agnes curses the Exarch's family, her own daughter included, for whom she predicts a similar fate. Silvana falls in love with her stepson Donello and confesses her adultery to the ailing Exarch, who falls dead at the news; his mother accuses Silvana of killing him by witchcraft. Arraigned before the bishop, Silvana fails to defend herself and is condemned. The eighth of Respighi's nine operas. JB

Fibich, Zdeněk, b. Všebořice, 21 Dec 1850; d. Prague, 15 Oct 1900. Czech composer. Studied at Leipzig Cons., 1865–7, and in Paris and Mannheim before returning to Prague in 1871. Apart from brief appointments at the Prague NT he lived from composition – his vast output incl. 600 works. Besides two lost early operas, he wrote seven operas and a melodrama trilogy, *Hippodamia*, 1890–1, the culmination of his very successful concert melodramas (e.g. *Christmas Eve*). Both SCHUMANN and WAGNER influenced his development. Perhaps to the detriment of his popularity he was the most internationally orientated of late 19th-c. Czech comps: evident from his choice of libs like *The Bride of Messina* (*Nevěsta Messinská*, 1884, after SCHILLER), *The Tempest* (1895, after SHAKESPEARE) and *Hedy* (1897, after BYRON). His earlier and uneven *Bukovín* (*Bouře*, 1874, lib. SABINA) and *Blaník* (1881, lib. KRÁSNOHORSKÁ) have Czech subjects, as does his masterpiece ŠÁRKA (1897), wr. like *Hedy* and *The Fall of Arkun* (*Pád Arkuna*, 1900) to a lib. by Anežka Schulzová, who inspired Fibich to the erotic fervour of his late works. JT

Fidelio, CG, 9 Nov 1967; PŘIBYL as Florestan and G. JONES as Leonore; produced COPLEY; designed Hainer Hill

Fidelio, oder Die Eheliche Liebe (*Fidelio, or Wedded Love*) 1. Opera (technically a *Singspiel*), 3 acts, BEETHOVEN, lib. Josef Sonnleithner based on LÉONORE, OU L'AMOUR CONJUGAL; Vienna, T. a. d. Wien, 20 Nov 1805. 2. Revised, 2 acts, by Stefan von Breuning, Vienna, T. a. d. Wien, 29 Mar 1806. 3. Revised again, 2 acts, by Georg Friedrich Treitschke, Vienna, KT, 23 May 1814; London, HM (in Ger.), 18 May 1832 (a selection had been heard in 1822, CG); NY, Park T., 9 Sept 1839. 3. is the one normally sung today, but 1 was perf. by R. STRAUSS, Berlin, 20 Nov 1905, and has since been occasionally heard. This is the grandest of all rescue operas. Florestan (ten.), imprisoned, is saved through the steadfastness of his wife, Leonore (sop.). The work never fails to make its emotional impact, the Chorus of Prisoners and the rescue scene in the final act being particularly impressive. LO
O★
See Kobbé and, particularly, Winton Dean in Arnold and Fortune (eds), *The Beethoven Companion* (London 1971)

Fiery Angel, The (*Ognenny angel*), opera, 5 acts, PROKOFIEV, lib. composer after Valery Bryusov. Paris 25 Nov 1954 (concert perf.); Venice, T. La Fenice, 29 Sept 1955; London, SW, 27 July 1965; NY, CC, 22 Sept 1965. Main chars: Renata (sop.) Ruprecht (bass) Heinrich (bar.). Renata mistakes Ruprecht for her former love, Heinrich. Ruprecht (himself in love with Renata) takes her to Cologne to look for Heinrich. But she is repulsed by the sight of Heinrich; Ruprecht fights him, loses, but wins

Renata. Renata, repulsed now by Ruprecht's strong physical passion for her, throws a knife at him and accuses him of being possessed by the Devil. The Inquisitor, investigating reports of demonic possession at a nunnery, sentences Renata to be burned alive for dealing with evil. In this work (comp. 1919–27), Prokofiev vividly portrays his characters' emotions, which are here whipped up to horrific intensity by the intrusion of elements of mysticism, sorcery, and the supernatural. The opera was never prod. in the composer's lifetime; material taken from it was used for the Third Symphony (1928). GN

Figaro 1. Bar., the barber in ROSSINI'S BARBIERE DI SIVIGLIA. 2. Bar., Count Almaviva's valet in NOZZE DI FIGARO.

Figlia di Jorio, La (*Jorio's Daughter*), opera, 3 acts, FRANCHETTI, lib. from D'ANNUNZIO'S tragedy. Milan, Sc., 29 Mar 1906. Main chars: Mila (sop.) Aligi (ten.) Lazzaro (bar.). Mila, pursued as a witch by Abruzzi peasants, is saved by Aligi, who falls in love with her though he is engaged to be married. Their love scene, in a mountain cave, is interrupted by Aligi's father Lazzaro, who has his son beaten and tied up. But Aligi escapes and kills his father as he is about to rape Mila. Mila accuses herself of the murder and is burned by the mob. A typical *verismo* opera. This drama was also set by PIZZETTI, 1954. JB

Fille de Madame Angot, La (*Madame Angot's Daughter*), *opérette*, 3 acts, LECOCQ, lib. Paul Siraudin, Louis François Clairville, and Victor Koning. Brussels, T. Alcazar, 4 Dec 1872 (a run of 500 nights); London, St James's T. (in Fr.), 17 May 1873; NY (in Fr.), 25 Aug 1873. Lecocq's most successful work, founded on a vaudeville by A. F. E. Maillot, *Madame Angot, ou La Poissarde Parvenue*. LO
See Lubbock

Fille du Régiment, La (*The Daughter of the Regiment*), *opéra comique*, 2 acts, DONIZETTI, lib. SAINT-GEORGES and Jean François Alfred Bayard. Paris, OC, 11 Feb 1840: Milan, Sc., 30 Oct 1840 (in It. with recitatives); New Orleans, 2 Mar 1843; London, HM, 27 May 1847. Main chars: Marie (sop.) Tonio (ten.) Marquise (mezzo-sop.) Sulpice (bar.). Marie, *vivandière* and mascot of Sulpice's regiment, is loved by Tonio, a mountaineer, who enlists for her sake. Identified as niece to a marquise, she must leave the regiment and undergo a lady's education. But the attractions of army life are too strong, and she marries Tonio, now an officer. Donizetti's first Fr. opera, much admired by MENDELSSOHN. Famous excerpts from the work include Marie's farewell and a Rat-a-plan chorus. JB ○
See Kobbé

Filmed opera. PAGLIACCI, filmed by Mario Costa in 1949 with GOBBI and Gina Lollobrigida

Filmed opera. The melodramatic plots of 19th-c. opera made an appeal even before the sound film: CARMEN was prod. several times in the silent days. The sound film and esp. colour photography revolutionized the filming of opera. The success of filmed musicals encouraged dirs to tackle the difficulties attendant on filming 'opera'. So far few have been comp. specially for the medium; the first was *The Robber Symphony* (1935) and perhaps the best known is *Les Parapluies de Cherbourg* (1963). Filmed operas are marked ★ in this book. LO

Filosofo di Campagna, Il (*The Country Philosopher*), *opera buffa*, 3 acts, GALUPPI, lib. GOLDONI. Venice, 26 Oct 1754; London, 6 Jan 1761; Boston, 26 Feb 1960. Galuppi's most famous work, and one of the best examples of 18th-c. *opera buffa*. LO

finale (It.). The final number of an act, when sung by an ensemble. In early 18th-c. *opera seria*, usually an ensemble of soloists. In *opera buffa* and 19th-c. opera a central act-finale usually forms the main architectural feature of the work. JB

Fine, Wendy, b. Durban. South African soprano. Studied Vienna Music Acad. After engagements at Bern and Wiesbaden, joined Cologne co. Bayreuth debut as Flower Maiden

Finland. A performance of TROVATORE at the Savonlinna Castle 19 July 1968. ACKTÉ started some summer seasons from 1912 which continued until 1930. The festival was revived by the town, a popular resort, 1967; TALVELA became chairman of the artistic committee 1972.

in PARSIFAL (1969). Bavarian Staats O. as MARIE (1971). CG debut as GUTRUNE (1972), and has since appeared there as FIORDILIGI, ELVIRA (DON GIOVANNI), Musetta (BOHÈME), and JENŮFA. AB

Finland. Opera was mostly sung in German at Helsinki until 1852, when Fredrik Pacius (1809–91) comp. *Kung Karls Jakt* (*King Charles's Hunt*) to a Swedish text. Pacius also wrote *Prinsessan af Cypros* (*The Princess of Cyprus*, 1860) and *Loreley* (1887). The only opera by Jean Sibelius (1865–1957), *Jungfruburen* (*The Maiden's Bower*), also had a Swed. text; it was first perf. at the Helsinki City Hall, 7 Nov 1896. The first opera comp. to a Finnish lib. was *Pohjan Neiti* (*Maid of the North*) by Oskar Merikanto (1868–1924), wr. 1898 and prod. at Viipuri (now Vyborg, in USSR), 1908. Merikanto's other operas were *Elinan Surma*, prod. Helsinki, 1910, and *Regina von Emmeritz*, also given at Helsinki, 1920. Erkki Melartin (1875–1937) based his opera *Aino* (1909) on a story from the Kalevala epic, Selim Palmgren's (1878–1951) *Daniel Hjort* was given at Åbo (Turku) in Swed. (1910) and at Helsinki in Fin. (1929). Leevi Madetoja (1887–1947) wrote two successful operas, *Pohjalaisia* (*The Bothnians*), prod. 1924, and *Juha* (1935). Aarre Merikanto (1893–1958), son of Oskar Merikanto, comp. another version of *Juha*, perf. on Radio Helsinki in 1958. Tauno Pylkkänen (b. 1918) has written several operas, one of which, with the Swed. title *Vargbruden* (*The Wolf's Bride*), won an international competition organized by It. radio in 1950. Summer fests are held at HELSINKI and at Savonlinna (from 1967). EF

Finta Giardiniera, La (*The Pretended Garden Girl*), *opera buffa*, 3 acts, MOZART, lib. COLTELLINI after CALZABIGI. Munich, 13 Jan 1775; NY, Mayfair T., 18 Jan 1927; London, Scala T., 7 Jan 1930. Main chars: Sandrina (sop.) Arminda (sop.) Ramiro (mezzo-sop.) Count Belfiore (ten.) the Podestà (ten.) Serpetta (sop.) Nardo (bar.). Violante, deserted by her lover, Belfiore, who believes her dead, goes in pursuit of him disguised as a woman gardener, Sandrina, and is employed by the Podestà (Mayor), whose daughter, Arminda, Belfiore is now courting. A merry-go-round of amorous relationships results; but all turns out well, with only the Podestà left unmarried. Still perf. in Germany and Austria, in an early Ger. tr. with spoken dialogue replacing recitatives. (The It. recitatives from Act 1 have been lost.) JB O

Finta Pazza, La (*Feigned Madness*), opera, prologue and 3 acts, Francesco Sacrati, lib. Giulio Strozzi. Venice, T. Novissimo, 14 Jan 1641. Given in Paris, Salle du Petit-Bourbon, 14 Dec 1645 – the second, possibly the first, It. opera to be heard and seen in France. LO

Finta Semplice, La (*The Pretended Simpleton*), *opera buffa*, 3 acts, MOZART, lib. COLTELLINI after GOLDONI. Salzburg, 1 May 1769; London, Palace T., 12 Mar 1956; Boston, 27 Jan 1971. Main chars: Rosina (sop.) Giacinta (sop.) Ninetta (sop.) Fracasso (ten.) Polidoro (ten.) Cassandro (bass) Simone (bass). Rosina, a Hungarian baroness, practises her wiles on the infatuated brothers, Cassandro and Polidoro, so that they will allow her own brother to marry their sister Giacinta. Mozart's first opera to be publicly perf. Rarely revived except as a curiosity. JB

Finto Stanislao, Il *see* GIORNO DI REGNO

Fiordiligi, sop., one of the two sisters in COSÌ FAN TUTTE

fioritura (It. 'blossoming', 'efflorescence'). In music, a florid decoration. The pl. is *fioriture*. *See also* COLORATURA. LO

Fischer, Jan F[rank], b. Louny, 15 Sept 1921. Czech composer. After studies at Prague Acad. he made a successful career in incidental and film mus. His operas, most of which have had several productions in Czechoslovakia and abroad, incl. a comedy, *The Bridegrooms* (*Ženichové*, 1957), a tragic opera about the Nazi

La Finta Pazza, design by TORELLI for Paris, 1645, engraved by Nicolas Cochin (1610–86)

era, *Romeo, Juliet and Darkness* (*Romeo, Julie a tma*, 1962), and a chamber opera, *Oh Mr Fogg!* (1971, after Jules Verne), making use of mus. theatre devices. JT

Fischer, Ludwig, b. Mainz, 13 Aug 1745; d. Berlin, 10 July 1825. German bass singer. First achieved fame in Munich (1778); at N. Singspiel, Vienna, 1780–3, where he created OSMIN, 1782. After successful engagements in Paris, Germany, and Italy, he was apptd a permanent member of the court opera at Berlin, 1789. Much admired by MOZART, who intended to rewrite for him the title role in IDOMENEO, he himself comp. a *Singspiel*, *Der Kritikanter und der Trinker*, containing the well-known 'Im kühlen Keller sitz' ich hier'. JB

Dietrich Fischer-Dieskau as FALSTAFF, in which he excelled in every way

Fischer-Dieskau, Dietrich, b. Berlin, 28 May 1925. German baritone. Debut 1948, Berlin, as Posa (DON CARLOS). He has sung in Vienna, Munich (1949), Bayreuth (1954), Salzburg (1957), London (CG 1965), and many other cities. His large repertory incl. DON GIOVANNI, ALMAVIVA (NOZZE DI FIGARO), MACBETH, RENATO, FALSTAFF, WOLFRAM, AMFORTAS, Jochanaan (SALOME), Barak (FRAU OHNE SCHATTEN), and Mandryka (ARABELLA). He sang Mittenhofer at the first perf. of ELEGY FOR YOUNG LOVERS, and also sings WOZZECK, MATHIS DER MALER, and DANTONS TOD. An excellent *Lieder* singer and a musicianly cond. EF

Fisher, Sylvia, b. Melbourne, 1910. Australian soprano. Studied Melbourne Cons.; became known as concert singer before travelling to Britain, 1947. Joined CG; debut 1949 as LEONORE. Principal sop. CG to 1958 singing variety of roles incl. Countess ALMAVIVA, ELSA, ISOLDE, and BRÜNNHILDE. Specially admired as the MARSCHALLIN, SIEGLINDE, Kostelnička (JENŮFA), for perfs of spirited char. and womanly feeling. Foreign debuts: Rome O. 1952; Chicago Lyric O. 1959. Became assoc. with several roles in BRITTEN's operas, and toured USSR with EOG 1964. Further successes as Queen Elizabeth I in GLORIANA (SW 1966), and created Miss Wingrave in OWEN WINGRAVE (BBC TV 1971; CG 1973). NG
See Rosenthal, *Sopranos of Today. Studies of Twenty-five Opera Singers* (London 1956)

Fitelberg, Gregor [Grzegorz], b. Daugavpils [Dünaburg; Dvinsk], Latvia, 18 Oct 1879; d. Katowice, Poland, 10 June 1953. Polish conductor. Studied at Warsaw, and in 1905 at Berlin founded the Young Poland Group with SZYMANOWSKI and other comps. Cond. at Warsaw from 1907, at the Vienna Staats O., 1911–14, at St Petersburg, 1914–18, and Moscow, 1919–20. Cond. of the Dyagilev ballet in Paris, London, Monte Carlo, and Spain, 1921–4. EF

Flagstad, Kirsten, b. Hamar, 12 July 1895; d. Oslo, 7 Dec 1962. Norwegian soprano, the greatest WAGNER sop. of her time. Studied with her mother and Ellen Schytte-Jacobsen. Debut, 1913, Oslo, in TIEFLAND. Continued to perf. in Scandinavia until 1933 when she sang small roles at Bayreuth. Pre-eminence as a Wagner singer began in 1935 with SIEGLINDE at NY Met. Thereafter her position was as-

Left: Kirsten Flagstad as ISOLDE, in a very characteristic pose

sured. Sang at CG, 1936–7; made many appearances there after World War II. Outside Wagner she made notable appearances in NY in GLUCK's ALCESTE and in London as DIDO in PURCELL's opera. Though limited as an actress her imposing stage presence and above all her magnificent voice always commanded attention. In 1959–60, after she had retired from the stage, she was dir. of Den Norske (Norwegian) O. at Oslo. LO
See autobiography (narrated to Louis Biancolli), *The Flagstad Manuscript* (New York 1952)

Flaubert, Gustave, b. Rouen, 12 Dec 1821; d. Croisset, 8 May 1880. French novelist. Works on which opera are based: *Madame Bovary*, 1857 (Emanuel Bondeville, 1950; SUTERMEISTER); *Salammbô*, 1862 (REYER); *Hérodias*, pub. as one of *Trois Contes*, 1877 (HÉRODIADE). LO

Fledermaus, Die (*The Bat*), operetta, 3 acts, J. STRAUSS, lib. Carl Haffner and GENÉE, derived from a *vaudeville*, *Le Réveillon*, by MEILHAC and L. HALÉVY, in turn based on a Ger. comedy, *Das Gefängnis*, by Roderich Bendix. Vienna, T. a. d. Wien, 5 Apr 1874; NY, Stadt T. (in Ger.), 21 Nov 1874; London, Alhambra T. (in Eng.), 18 Dec 1876. The classic operetta of all time, now accepted (since MAHLER's perf., Vienna O., 1894) everywhere alongside operatic comedies. For synopsis and esp. the details of the transformations from a fairly simple comedy of mistaken identity to the final elaborate plot, *see* Newman, *Opera Nights* (London 1943). LO ○★

Flemish opera. Opera in Flemish (i.e. Dutch as spoken in Belgium) is centred on Antwerp. Its est. at the time of the Flem. national revival was due in the first place to BENOÎT. He wrote the Flem. opera, *Het Dorp in 't Gebergte* (*The Village in the Mountains*), 1856. Other Flem. opera comps incl. Joseph Mertens (1834–1901), who wrote six operas, the best being *De Zwarte Kapitein* (*The Black Captain*), 1877; BLOCKX; Auguste de Boeck (1865–1937); GILSON; Albert Dupuis (b. 1877); Arthur Meulemans (b. 1884); and Marcel Poot (b. 1901). LO

Fliegende Holländer, Der (*The Flying Dutchman*), opera, 3 acts, WAGNER, lib. composer after HEINE. Dresden, 2 Jan 1843; Munich, 4 Dec 1864 with revisions; London, DL, 23 July 1870; Philadelphia, Acad. of Mus. (in It.), 8 Nov 1876. Main chars: Senta (sop.) Erik (ten.) Dutchman (bar.) Daland (bass). The well-known story of the captain Vanderdecken compelled to sail the seven seas until redeemed by the love of a pure-hearted woman. Sometimes given in the continuous one-act version as the comp. originally intended. JB ○★
See Kobbé

Florence, Italy. Here opera was born as *dramma per musica* (*see* FLORENTINE CAMERATA), and never ceased to thrive. The T. della Pergola opened in 1656 with one of the earliest comic operas, *La Tancia*; it alone survives from the many theatres promoted in rivalry by the learned Accademia of the city. The T. Politana Fiorentino Vittorio Emmanuele, built without a roof in 1864, roofed in 1883, and renamed T. Comunale in 1932, has been since 1933 the centre of the Maggio Musicale Fiorentino and an associated International Mus. Congress. At-

Der Fliegende Holländer, Berlin Staats O., 3 Oct 1968; designed Wilfried Werz; produced Erhard Fischer

tached to the T. Comunale there is an operatic training school. JB

Florentine Camerata, The. An 'academy' of comps, theorists, and men of letters, founded in the late 16th c., whose aim was to revive Greek tragedy according to the description given by Aristotle with words 'sweetened by music'. To this end they evolved a declamatory style of solo singing called *recitar cantando*, from which opera developed. Early examples incl. DAFNE and EURIDICE, CACCINI's *Rapimento di Cefalo* (pub. 1602): all settings of libs by RINUCCINI. Members incl. Count Bardi (at whose house the Camerata met), Jacopo Corsi, and E. DI CAVALIERI. The Camerata's importance is mostly historical. JB

Florestan, ten., Leonore's husband in FIDELIO

Flotow, Friedrich von, b. Teutendorf, 26 Apr 1812; d. Darmstadt, 24 Jan 1883. German composer. Of his 18 operas only MARTHA has held the stage, though *Le Naufrage de la Méduse* (Paris 1939) and ALESSANDRO STRADELLA had some success in their day. *Intendant* at Schwerin, 1856–63. LO

Floyd, Carlisle, b. Latta, S.C., 11 June 1926. American composer. Studied at Florida State Univ. and Univ. of Syracuse. Phyllis Curtin and Mack Harrell were so impressed with SUSANNAH that they offered to sing in it; hence the first perf. at Florida State, 24 Feb 1955. Floyd's operas incl. *Wuthering Heights*, commissioned by Santa Fe O. Assoc., perf. 16 July 1958 and, revised, NY CC, 9 Apr 1959; *The Passion of Jonathan Wade*, NY CC 12 Nov 1962; and OF MICE AND MEN. EJ

Flut, Die (*The Tide*), chamber opera, 1 act, BLACHER, lib. comp. Radio Berlin, 20 Dec 1946; Dresden Staats O., 7 Mar 1947; Boston, 19 Apr 1956; London, St Pancras, 8 Mar 1960. Chars: the Girl (sop.) the Young Man (ten.) the Sailor (bar.) the Banker (bass). A party of four are trapped on a wrecked ship by the tide. The girl announces her love for the sailor, but when the tide recedes she leaves with the young man, who has murdered the banker for his money. EF

Flying Dutchman, The *see* FLIEGENDE HOLLÄNDER

Fodor-Mainvielle, Joséphine, b. Paris, 13 Oct 1789; d. St Genis, nr Lyon, 14 Aug 1870. French soprano. Daughter of the violinist and comp. Joseph Fodor, she moved with her family to St Petersburg in 1794 where, in 1810, she made her debut in Valentino Fioravanti's *Le Cantatrici Villane*. M. the actor Mainvielle, 1812, and appeared in Stockholm and Copenhagen. Paris debut (OC 1814) unsuccessful. However, she appeared successfully at the TI, and in London (1816), and Italy before her first great triumph as Paris's first ROSINA (1819). Sang in Naples and Vienna (1822–5) for BARBAIA, and in 1825 reappeared as SEMIRAMIDE in Paris. Her voice failed and she was unable to finish the perf. She last sang in Bordeaux in 1831. PS

Foerster, Josef Bohuslav, b. Prague, 30 Dec 1859; d. Nový Vestec, 29 May 1951. Czech composer. The best known of a long line of Czech musicians, he studied at the Prague Organ School (1879–82) and held several organ posts in Prague before working as a mus. teacher and critic in Hamburg (1893–1903) and Vienna (1903–18), where MAHLER befriended him. Though an impressive symphonist he is remembered chiefly for his fine choral works. He wrote six operas, of which the second, *Eva* (1899) to a text by Gabriela Preissová and like JENŮFA set in Moravia, is the best known. His lyrical gifts are also evident in *Debora* (1893) and *Jessika* (1905, later called *The Merchant of Venice*). His later operas, all to his own libs, were less successful. JT

Force of Destiny, The *see* FORZA DEL DESTINO

Ford, bar., a citizen of Windsor in FALSTAFF

Forrester, Maureen, b. Montreal, 25 July 1930. Canadian contralto. Sang in CONSUL, LOUISE, and BORIS GODUNOV in Montreal (1955–6), then concentrated on a career as one

La Forza del Destino, London, CG, Dec 1973. CAPECCHI as Melitone; D. WARD as Padre Guardiano

of the finest *Lieder* and oratorio singers of the day. At height of concert career she returned to opera as Orfeo in ORFEO ED EURIDICE (Toronto 1962). In 1969 she sang in NY CC prod. of GIULIO CESARE and then appeared increasingly in opera. COC debut as FRICKA (1971); NY Met debut as ERDA (1975); also sang Dame Quickly in FALSTAFF (1974) and BRANGÄNE (1975) in Montreal. She has a voice of great tonal variety and wide range combined with fine and subtle musicality. CM

Forsell, John [Johan], b. Stockholm, 6 Nov 1868; d. Stockholm, 30 May 1941. Swedish baritone. Had a distinguished career as a singer, mainly at Stockholm, 1896–1909; also appeared on other stages incl. in London (as DON GIOVANNI, a role for which he was especially famous) and NY Met. *Intendant*, Stockholm, 1923–39; also known as a singing teacher. LO

Fortner, Wolfgang, b. Leipzig, 12 Oct 1907. German composer. His operas include a school opera, *Cress Ertrinkt* (1931); *Der Wald*, an early TV opera (1953, staged Essen, 1954); BLUTHOCHZEIT, based on LORCA's *Bodas de Sangre*; *In seinem Garten liebt Don Perlimplin Belisa* (also based on Lorca, Schwetzingen 1962); and *Elisabeth Tudor* (Berlin 1972). LO

Forza del Destino, La (*The Force of Destiny*), opera, 4 acts, VERDI, lib. PIAVE after Angelo Pérez de Saavedra's *Don Alvaro*. St Petersburg, 10 Nov 1862; Milan, Sc., 27 Feb 1869 in new definitive version; NY, Acad. of Mus., 24 Feb 1865; London, HM, 22 June 1867. Main chars: Leonora (sop.) Alvaro (ten.) Carlo (bar.) Padre Guardiano (bass) Preziosilla (mezzo-sop.) Melitone (bar.). Don Alvaro, son of a Spanish governor and an Inca princess, accidentally kills the father of his beloved, Donna Leonora. His fate is to be responsible for the deaths of her and her brother, through no fault of his own. JB ○
See Kobbé

Forzano, Giovacchino, b. Florence, 19 Nov 1883; d. Rome, 18 Oct 1970. Italian producer and librettist. Prods incl. premieres of NERONE, TURANDOT, TRITTICO, GIORDANO's *La Cena delle Beffe* (1920), and ZANDONAI's *I Cavalieri di Ekebù* (1925). Has been active in many European theatres incl. CG (1926, 1931). Has written over 20 libs incl. LODELETTA, GIANNI SCHICCHI, PICCOLO MARAT, WOLF-FERRARI's *Sly* (1927), and SUOR ANGELICA. LO

Foss [Fuchs], Lukas, b. Berlin, 15 Aug 1922. German, later American, composer; in USA from 1937. Operas incl.: JUMPING FROG OF CALAVERAS COUNTY; a TV opera, *Griffelkin*, lib. Alastair Reid, 6 Nov 1955, and prod. Karlsruhe 1973; and a nine-minute mini-opera, *Introductions and Goodbyes*, lib. MENOTTI (Spoleto 1960). LO

Four Saints in Three Acts, opera, 4 acts, V. THOMSON, lib. G. STEIN, scenario Maurice Grosser. Wadsworth Athenaeum, Hartford, Conn., 8 Feb 1934. Sponsored by the Friends and Enemies of Modern Music as opening event for their new auditorium. The all-Negro cast (Thomson's suggestion), was a decisive factor in the work's charm, in the clarity of its diction, and in heightening the sense of novelty. A work of superior imagination. Has had several subsequent perfs in USA, incl. a run on Broadway, and was heard in Paris, 1952, with the 1952 NY cast. EJ ○

Fra Diavolo, ou L'Hôtellerie de Terracine (*Brother Devil, or The Inn at Terracine*), *opéra comique*, 3 acts, AUBER, lib. SCRIBE. Paris, OC, 28 Jan 1830; London, DL, 1 Feb 1831; Philadelphia, Pa., 16 Sept 1831; NY, 17 Oct 1831 (in Fr.). Main chars: Zerlina (sop.) Lady Pamela (mezzo-sop.) Fra Diavolo (ten.) Lorenzo (ten.) Lord Cockburn, or Rocburg (bar.). The adventures, intrigues, and final capture of the Marchese di San Marco, whose chief occupation is highway robbery. JB ★
See Kobbé

Françaix, Jean René, b. Le Mans, 23 May 1912. French composer. His operas are: DIABLE BOITEUX; a 1-act comedy, *L'Apostrophe*, 1942; *La Main de Gloire*, Bordeaux 1950, based on the story by Gérard de Nerval (1832); *Paris à Nous Deux*, 1954; and *La Princesse de Clèves*, 1965. LO

France. Apart from Paris, the main centre, opera can be heard at Aix-en-Provence, Avignon, Bordeaux, Colmar, Mulhouse and Strasbourg (Opéra du Rhin), Lille, Lyon, Marseille, Nancy, Nice, Orange, Rouen, and Toulouse. In the early 1970s efforts were made to bring other towns such as Angers, Tours, and Grenoble into a scheme aimed at promoting artistic activities in the provinces. For Fr. comps see A. C. ADAM, AUBER, AUBERT, AUDRAN, BERTON, BIZET, BOÏELDIEU, BRUNEAU, BUSSER, CAMBERT, CAMPRA, CHABRIER, CHARPENTIER, CHAUSSON, CHERUBINI, DAVID, DEBUSSY, DELIBES, DESTOUCHES, DUKAS, FAURÉ, FRANÇAIX, FRANCK, GAVEAUX, GOUNOD, GUIRAUD, HÉROLD, HERVÉ, IBERT, ISOUARD, LALO, LECOCQ, LESUEUR, LULLY, MAILLART, MEYERBEER,

MONSIGNY, OFFENBACH, PHILIDOR, POULENC, RAMEAU, RAVEL, REYER, ROUSSEL, SAINT-SAËNS, SAUGUET, TOMASI, LO

Francesca da Rimini, opera, 4 acts, ZANDONAI, lib. arr. Tito RICORDI II from D'ANNUNZIO's play. Turin, T. Regio, 19 Feb 1914; London, CG, 16 July 1914; NY Met, 22 Dec 1916. Main chars: Francesca (sop.) Paolo (ten.) Gianciotto (bar.) Malatestino (ten.). Francesca, about to marry Gianciotto Malatesta, is taken from her home by his handsome younger brother Paolo, whom she mistakes for her future husband. She joins Paolo on the battlements during the fight against the Ghibellines and sees Malatestino the youngest brother wounded in the eye. She is visited by Paolo after a long absence and together they read the romance *Lancelot of the Lake*, and fall into each other's arms. Malatestino, whose advances Francesca has repulsed, betrays the guilty couple to Gianciotto who, catching them *in flagrante delicto*, kills Paolo. Zandonai's most famous opera; an unusually refined instance of the so-called veristic style. JB

Franchetti, Alberto, b. Turin, 18 Sept 1860; d. Viareggio, 4 Aug 1942. Italian composer. Studied with Felix Draeseke at Dresden and at Munich. A wealthy man, he had the means to mount his nine operas under good conditions. The best of them were *Asrael*, his first (Brescia 1888); *Germania* (Milan 1902, CG 1907); and FIGLIA DI JORIO. LO

Franci, Carlo, b. Buenos Aires, 18 July 1927. Italian conductor and composer. Studied Rome. Cond., Radio Orch., Dublin, 1955–7 and Italian radio, Rome, 1961–3. Debut as opera cond. Spoleto, 1959, HÄNSEL UND GRETEL. Besides important revivals of ROSSINI has cond. premieres of operas by Niccolò Castiglione, HENZE, LUALDI, PERAGALLO, ROTA, and TOSATTI. LO

Frankfurt. The new Städtischen Bühnen complex, designed by Otto Apel and opened in 1963

Franck, César, b. Liège, Belgium, 10 Dec 1822; d. Paris, 8 Nov 1890. French composer (naturalized 1873). Completed two operas: *Le Valet de Ferme*, *opéra comique*, 2 acts, lib. Alphonse Royer and Gustave Vaëz, comp. 1851–2, never perf.; and *Hulda*, 4 acts and epilogue, lib. Charles Grandmougin, based on Bjørnstjerne Bjørnson's play, comp. 1882–5, perf. Monte Carlo, 8 Mar 1894. *Ghisèle*, lib. Gilbert Augustin, was completely sketched 1888–9, orchestration completed by five of Franck's pupils: perf. Monte Carlo, 5 Apr 1896. LO

Frankfurt, W. Germany. The opening of the opera house in 1880 signalled the birth of one of Germany's most eminent companies, under conds of such distinction as WEINGARTNER, C. KRAUSS, and, until the Nazis came to power, STEINBERG. Perfs ceased during World War II, when the opera house was destroyed. It was rebuilt in 1951. SOLTI became mus. dir., 1951, remaining there until appointed to CG, London, in 1961. MATAČIĆ and DOHNÁNYI were among his successors. Premieres at the house have incl. FERNE KLANG (1912), VON HEUTE AUF MORGEN (1930), and CARMINA BURANA (1937). AB

Franklin, David, b. London, 17 May 1908; d. Worcester, 26 Oct 1973. English bass. After being a schoolmaster, heard by BUSCH, who engaged him to sing at Glyndebourne (1936) as the Commendatore (DON GIOVANNI). Also sang SARASTRO and Banquo (MACBETH) there. Became leading bass at CG after World War II, remaining with the resident co. until forced to give up singing through ill health in 1950. Roles incl. Sarastro, POGNER, OCHS, ROCCO, COLLINE, KING MARK, and HUNDING. Created Mars in OLYMPIANS. Later lib. of Phyllis Tate's opera *The Lodger* (1958). AB

Frau ohne Schatten, Die (*The Woman without a Shadow*), opera, 3 acts, R. STRAUSS, lib. HOFMANNSTHAL. Vienna, Staats O., 10 Oct 1919; San Francisco, 18 Sept 1959; London, SW, 1966 (Hamburg Co.); London, CG, 14 June 1967. Main chars: Emperor (ten.) Empress (sop.) Barak (bass) Barak's Wife (sop.) Nurse (mezzo-sop.). This symbolic fairy tale is the most ambitious, even pretentious, work undertaken by Strauss and Hofmannsthal. No thumbnail synopsis can do justice to its depth as an allegory on the supreme importance of

Left: Die Frau ohne Schatten, designed SVOBODA; produced R. HARTMANN; London, CG, 12 June 1967; KING as the Emperor

Right: Olive Fremstad as ISOLDE at the NY Met

unselfishness. It has been described as 'the last Wagnerian opera of inner psychology and also the last pantomime opera'. FGB O
See Mann, *Richard Strauss* (London 1964; New York 1966); Kobbé

Frazzi, Vito, b. San Secondo Parmense, 1 Aug 1888; d. Florence, 8 July 1975. Italian composer. His operas incl.: *Re Lear* (Bologna 1939); *L'Ottava Moglie di Barbablu* (Florence 1940); *Don Chisciotte* (Florence 1952); also *Il Giardino Chiuso* (not perf.). EF

Freischütz, Der (*The Free Shooter*), opera, 3 acts, C. WEBER, lib. Friedrich Kind based on a tale in the *Gespensterbuch* (1811) of Johann August Apel and Friedrich Laun [Friedrich August Schulze]. Berlin, Schauspielhaus, 18 June 1821; London, Lyceum (in Eng. tr. W. MacGregor Logan as *The Seventh Bullet*), 22 July 1824; NY, Park T., 2 Mar 1825; London, CG (in Ger., the first major opera in London in that language), 9 May 1832. Main chars: Max (ten.) Agathe (sop.) Kaspar (bass) Kuno (bass). Max bargains with the Black Huntsman (Samiel, speaking part) for seven magic bullets, cast by Kaspar in the Wolf's Glen at midnight. With six he wins the contest to decide who shall succeed Kuno as head ranger. The seventh he fires at a dove, really his bride, Agathe, transformed by the Black Huntsman. The bullet is deflected and Kaspar dies in Agathe's place. Max reveals his pact and is given a year to atone. A work of major significance, it brought romanticism and new tradition to German opera. PS O★
See Kobbé; Warrack, *Carl Maria von Weber* (London and New York 1968)

Fremstad, Olive [Anna Augusta Olivia Petersen], b. Stockholm, 14 Mar 1871; d. Irvington, NY, 21 Apr 1951. Swedish, later American, soprano. After debut in PATIENCE (Boston 1890), went for further study to Lilli LEHMANN in Berlin; debut, 1895, Cologne (AZUCENA). Engagements in London, Vienna, Bayreuth, and Munich followed; in 1903 went to NY Met (debut in WALKÜRE), remaining there until 1914 as one of its leading WAGNER singers, ranking among the finest Wagner interpreters of her day. Sang title role in first Met perf. of SALOME (1907). Willa Cather's novel, *The Song of the Lark*, was inspired by her. LO
See biography: Mary Watkins Cushing, *The Rainbow Bridge* (New York 1954)

Freni, Mirella, b. Modena, 27 Feb 1935. Italian soprano. Debut, 1956, Modena (MICAËLA). Has sung at Glyndebourne (1960), CG (1961), Sc., Wexford (1962), Chicago (1963), NY Met (1965), Salzburg (1966), and San Francisco (1967). Her beautiful, lyric sop. voice and charming stage presence make her an ideal ZERLINA, SUSANNA, Elvira (PURITANI), ADINA, Marie (FILLE DU RÉGIMENT), MARGUERITE, MANON, MIMI, LIÙ and Nannetta (FALSTAFF). Also sings VIOLETTA and DESDEMONA (OTELLO). EF

Mirella Freni as Nannetta, with ALVA as Fenton, in FALSTAFF, produced ZEFFIRELLI, London, CG, 10 May 1961

Fretwell, Elizabeth, b. Melbourne, 13 Aug 1923. Australian soprano. Debut, 1947, Australian Nat. O. (SENTA). Moved to Britain 1954. Sang AIDA (title role) and Musetta (BOHÈME) for Dublin Grand O., then joined SW from 1955 as principal sop. Debut there as First Lady (ZAUBERFLÖTE). Much admired as VIOLETTA, LEONORE and as first Brit. singer in title role of ARIADNE AUF NAXOS (from 1961). Created Blanche in GARDNER's *The Moon and Sixpence* (1957). A singer of consistent tonal freshness and dramatic feeling. She returned to Australia in 1970. NG

Frezzolini, Erminia, b. Orvieto, 27 Mar 1818; d. Paris, 5 Nov 1884. Italian soprano. Daughter of the *buffo* Giuseppe Frezzolini (1789–1861), DONIZETTI's first DULCAMARA. Debut Florence 1838 (BEATRICE DI TENDA). After appearing in minor Italian houses, she triumphed in Milan 1840 as LUCREZIA BORGIA. M. ten. Antonio Poggi with whom she appeared in London in 1842. Returning to Italy, she created the roles of Giselda (LOMBARDI ALLA PRIMA CROCIATA, 1843) and GIOVANNI D'ARCO (1845) at Sc., and Camilla in MERCADANTE's *Orazi e Curiazi* at T. S. Carlo (1846). By the time of her Paris debut (PURITANI, 1853) her voice had lost its freshness and did not please. She was moderately successful in America (the first NY GILDA), but did not sing in Europe again. PS

Frick, Gottlob, b. Ölbronn, Württemberg, 28 July 1906. German bass. Studied at Stuttgart. After engagement in chorus there and in several smaller opera houses was at Dresden 1940–50, Berlin Städtische O. 1950–3, and since then at Munich and Vienna. Has also sung at CG and NY Met. A versatile artist, at his best in WAGNER and other Ger. operas. LO

Fricka, sop., Wotan's wife in RING DES NIBELUNGEN

Fricsay, Ferenc, b. Budapest, 9 Aug 1914; d. Basel, 20 Feb 1963. Hungarian conductor. Studied with BARTÓK and KODÁLY. Cond. debut Szeged, 1933. Principal cond., Budapest O., 1939–45. Salzburg Fest. 1947 (premiere DANTONS TOD); returned there for premieres of MARTIN's *Le Vin Herbé* (1948) and ORFF's *Antigonae* (1949). Mus. dir., Berlin Städtische O., 1951–2; Bavarian State O., Munich, 1956–8; Deutsches Opernhaus, Berlin, 1961–3. AB

Friedenstag (*Peace Day*), opera, 1 act, R. STRAUSS, lib. J. GREGOR with assistance from ZWEIG, who provided the intial scenario, based on CALDERÓN's *La Redención de la Breda*, 1625. Munich, 24 July 1928; Los Angeles, 2 Apr 1967. A plea for tolerance and a criticism of militarism. LO
See Mann, *Richard Strauss* (London 1964; New York 1966)

Friedrich, Götz, b. Naumburg, 4 Aug 1930. German producer. Studied stagecraft before being engaged by FELSENSTEIN for the Berlin KO, remaining there for 20 years, first as assistant to Felsenstein, then as a prod. in his own right from 1959 onward. Also worked at Vienna, Stuttgart, Copenhagen, and Stockholm, where he was responsible for a notable JENŮFA, seen at the Edinburgh Fest. (1974). Holland Fest., since 1972, where he prod. controversial versions of FALSTAFF (1972), AIDA (1973), and NOZZE DI FIGARO (1974). First Bayreuth prod., TANNHÄUSER (1972), caused a furore. Prod. dir., Hamburg since 1973. Began producing the RING DES NIBELUNGEN at CG in 1974. Also prod. opera for TV. AB

Friml, Rudolf, b. Prague, 7 Dec 1879; d. NY, 12 Nov 1972. Czech, later American, composer. Student of DVOŘÁK; moved to USA in 1906 as accompanist. Wrote *c.* 24 operettas, incl. *The Firefly* (1912); *High Jinks* (1913); ROSE MARIE; and VAGABOND KING. Orchestrated in the traditional way and well sung, their elegance made no concessions to ragtime or jazz. He also wrote for films. LO

From the House of the Dead (*Z Mrtvého Domu*), opera, 3 acts, JANÁČEK, lib. composer after DOSTOYEVSKY's novel *Memoirs from the House of the Dead* (1861). Brno, NT, 12 Apr 1930 (Bakala-Chlubna adaptation); Prague, NT, 24 Apr 1964 (Janáček's ending); Edinburgh, King's T., 5 Sept 1964; London, SW, 28 Oct 1965 (Janáček's ending and orchestration); NET O. (TV), 3 Dec 1969. Main chars: Petrovič (bar.) Aljeja (mezzo-sop.) Camp Commandant (bass) Luka (ten.) Skuratov (ten.) Šiškov (bass-bar.). Petrovič's arrival and departure frame these scenes from a Siberian prison camp, where inmates relate their past histories against a background of prison activity. Act 2 provides light-hearted contrast with a feast and two plays acted by the prisoners. Though lacking a conventionally coherent 'plot', this is perhaps Janáček's finest and certainly his most concentrated opera. JT O
See Ewans, *Janáček's Tragic Operas* (London 1976)

Fry, William Henry, b. Philadelphia, Pa., 10 Aug 1815; d. Santa Cruz, West Indies, 1864. First American composer of grand opera: *Leonora*, lib. adapted from Edward Bulwer-Lytton's play *The Lady of Lyons* (1838), prod. Philadelphia, 4 June 1845 and NY Acad. of Mus. (in It.), 1858. LO

Fuchs, Marta, b. Stuttgart, 1 Jan 1898; d. Stuttgart, 22 Sept 1974. German soprano. Studied in Stuttgart, Munich, and Milan. Debut, 1928, Aachen, as mezzo-sop., turning to the dramatic sop. roles when she moved to Dresden in 1930. Berlin Staats O. 1936–44; Stuttgart 1945 onward. Bayreuth debut 1933 (KUNDRY) and sang there until 1942, her ISOLDE and BRÜNNHILDE being much admired. Only CG appearances with the Dresden State O. (1936) as MARSCHALLIN, ARIADNE (under R. STRAUSS), and Donna ANNA. One of the leading dramatic sops of her day; sang with great feeling and clarity. AB

Fuga, Sandro, b. Mogliano Veneto, Treviso, 26 Nov 1906. Italian composer. His opera *La Croce Deserta* was prod. at Bergamo, 1950. *Otto Schnaffs*, based on a story by Guy de Maupassant, was staged at Turin, 1950. *Confessione* was heard on It. radio in 1960. He is dir., Turin Cons. EF

From the House of the Dead, Prague, NT, 10 May 1958; designed SVOBODA; produced Hanuš Thein

Fugère, Lucien, b. Paris, 22 July 1848; d. Paris, 15 Jan 1935. One of the outstanding French baritones of his day. After studying sculpture, he next became a commercial traveller; his first singing engagement was at the Bouffes-Parisiens in OFFENBACH's *Mme l'Archiduc* (1874), and his long career at the OC began in 1877 (MASSÉ's *Les Noces de Jeanette*). Created roles in many operas incl.: ROI MALGRÉ LUI, BASOCHE, TROYENS, LOUISE, GRISÉLIDIS, and JONGLEUR DE NOTRE-DAME, and was the first Fr. SCHAUNARD (1904). His large repertory was confined almost exclusively to Fr. opera and MOZART, of which his sure vocal technique and brilliant acting skill made him an ideal interpreter. LO

Furtwängler, Wilhelm, b. Berlin, 25 Jan 1886; d. Baden-Baden, 30 Nov 1954. German conductor, his allegiance divided between concert hall and opera house. Chief cond. Mannheim 1915–20. After a period of orchestral cond. resumed contact with opera 1924, at Berlin Staats O. Thereafter he made frequent appearances at CG, Paris O., Vienna, Salzburg, and Bayreuth, also at Sc. and for It. radio. Under a cloud in his native Germany at outbreak of World War II, he soon regained favour with the Nazis, and as a consequence was refused permission to cond. in USA. LO

Fux, Johann Josef, b. Hirtenfeld, nr Graz, 1660; d. Vienna, 13 Feb 1741. Austrian theorist and composer. Became Court Composer, Vienna, 1698; Imperial Conductor 1715. Of his 19 operas the last three were *feste teatrali* on the grandest scale: *Angelica Vincitrice di Alcina* (lib. Pietro Pariati, from ARIOSTO's *Orlando Furioso*), perf., on huge fishpond in park of Imperial Palace, La Favorita, 1716; *Elisa*, another open-air perf. in park of La Favorita 1719; *Costanza e Fortezza*, 1723 – also open-air. LO
See Wellesz, *Fux* (London 1965)

G

Gabrielli, Caterina, b. Rome, 12 Nov 1730; d. Rome, 16 Feb 1796. Italian soprano, a brilliant singer and colourful personality, dominating 18th-c. operatic stage from Naples to Russia. Daughter of Prince Gabrielli's cook, hence nickname 'La Cochetta'. BURNEY praised her highly as singer and actress, admiring her elegance of phrasing, her 'accent and precision in her divisions, superior to every singer of her time'. Sang in several of GLUCK's early operas. LO

Gadzhibekov *see* HAJIBEYOV

Gaito, Constantino, b. Buenos Aires, 3 Aug 1878; d. Buenos Aires, 14 Dec 1945. Argentine composer. Studied Naples. His operas were all first perf. at T. Colón except *Shafras* (perf. T. Politeama 1907 before T. Colón was opened). They progressed from the Italian *I Doria* (unperf., comp. 1911–14), *Caio Petronio* (1919), and *Fior di Neve* (1922) to operas on ethnic subjects, such as *Ollantay* (1926), the 1-act *Lázaro* (1929), in which the urban *tango* was first used in an opera by an Argentine composer, and on to his most popular score, *La Sangre de las Guitarras* (1932), which successfully incorporated dances from the *gaucho* regional folklore. Gaito and BOERO are two of the most accomplished Argentine nationalist opera composers. MK

Gallet, Louis, b. Valence, 1835; d. 1895. French librettist. Libs incl. those for BIZET's *La Coupe du Roi de Thule* (1868), *Don Rodrigue* (with Édouard Blau, 1873), and DJAMILEH; ATTAQUE DU MOULIN and RÊVE; MASSENET's ROI DE LAHORE, CID (with Adolphe Philippe d'Ennery and Édouard Blau), and *Marie Magdeleine* (1873); SAINT-SAËNS's *La Princesse Jaune* (1872), *Étienne Marcel* (1879), *Proserpine* (1887), *Ascanio* (1890), *Dejanire* (1898), and *Frédégonde* (1895). LO

Galli, Filippo, b. Rome, 1783; d. Paris, 3 June 1853. Italian bass. Debut, 1801, as ten., Naples. After an illness in 1810, he became a bass, and made his debut in the premiere of ROSSINI's *L'Inganno Felice* (Venice 1812). He sang in Milan and Barcelona, and also created for Rossini the roles of Fernando in GAZZA LADRA, and *Maometto Secondo*. Paris debut 1821. Sang at the King's T., London, 1827; in Spain 1828; in Mexico 1832–6. Destitute in 1842, he was given the post of professor of singing and declamation at the Paris Cons. His brother, Vincenzo (1798–1858), was also a bass and enjoyed an international career. PS

Galliari family. An 18th-c. Piedmontese dynasty of designers: **Giovanni** (1672–1722), his three sons **Giovanni Antonio** (1714–83), **Bernardino** (1707–94), **Fabrizio** (1709–90), also **Giovanni** (1746–1818), son of Fabrizio. They worked communally, like the BIBIENA family; active Turin, Milan, Innsbruck, Berlin. Designed for the opera that opened the new Sc. in 1778. LO

Galli-Curci, Amelita, b. Milan, 18 Nov 1882; d. La Jolla, California, 26 Nov 1963. Italian soprano. Self-taught. Debut, 1909, Trani. After singing successfully throughout Italy, she moved to America in 1916, joining the NY Met in 1921. She retired from the stage in 1930. A lyric sop. with a firm line and impeccable *fioritura*, she was at her best in the lighter roles of *bel canto* opera. JB

Above: The Gambler, Bolshoy T., Moscow, Apr 1974. VISHNEVSKAYA as Polina and Aleksey Maslenikov as Aleksey

Galli-Marié [Marié de l'Isle], Célestine, b. Paris, Nov 1840; d. Vence, 22 Sept 1905. French mezzo-soprano, taught by her father, Claude Marié de l'Isle. After debut (Strasbourg 1862), joined Paris OC where she remained until 1885. Man Friday in OFFENBACH'S *Robinson Crusoé* (1867) was written for her; she also created MIGNON (1866) and CARMEN (1875). In 1864 MASSÉ had suggested MÉRIMÉE'S *Carmen* to SARDOU as a possible lib., with Galli-Marié in mind. Her playing of Carmen emphasized the realism and earthiness of Mérimée's gypsy, thereby shocking Parisian audiences: of her Mignon it was said: 'Mignon *is* Galli-Marié; no other artist should sing it.' She also sang WAGNER roles. One of the most intelligent and dedicated singers of her day. LO

Left: Célestine Galli-Marié in the role of MIGNON, which she created in 1866

Galuppi, Baldassare, b. Burano, 18 Oct 1706; d. Venice, 3 Jan 1785. Italian composer, assoc. mostly with Venice, apart from a three-year period spent at the Russian Imperial Court, 1766–8. Of his 95 operas, 20 have GOLDONI libs, among which the light-hearted comedy FILOSOFO DI CAMPAGNA (1754) is occasionally heard today. JB

Gambler, The (*Igrok*), opera, 4 acts, PROKOFIEV, lib. composer after DOSTOYEVSKY. Brussels, T. de la Monnaie, 29 April 1929; NY, 85th Street Playhouse, 4 April 1957; Edinburgh, 28 Aug 1962; Moscow, 14 Mar 1963 (concert performance). Main chars: General (bass) Polina (sop.) Marquis (ten.) Grandmama (mezzo-sop.) Aleksey (ten.). At the spa of Roulettenburg, the General is in debt to the Marquis, and is hoping for an inheritance from Grandmama; but she loses her fortune at the gambling tables, and the General's stepdaughter, Polina, has to face the prospect of marrying the Marquis. Aleksey, the General's servant who is in love with Polina, tries to win the 50,000 francs the General needs to repay the Marquis, and instead wins 200,000 francs. Polina, in a state of hysteria, throws the money in his face. In this work Prokofiev, like Dostoyevsky, reveals a deep understanding of human nature, combined with a powerful ability to re-create it in musical terms. Throughout the piece, the extreme emotions ignited by the effects of avarice gradually increase in intensity toward the explosive dénouement. GN

García, Manuel (1) del Popolo Vicente, b. Seville, 22 Jan 1775; d. Paris, 2 June 1832. Spanish tenor, composer, and teacher. At six he became a chorister in Seville Cathedral, where he studied with Antonio Ripa. He adopted García as his professional name and in his teens was active as singer, actor, and comp. of some short comic operas. Opera debut in PAER'S *Griselda* (Paris, 11 Feb 1808). Went to Naples 1811. He created the role of Egeo in MEDEA IN CORINTO with his wife, Joacquina Sitches, as Ismene and his daughter, the five-year-old MALIBRAN, as one of Medea's children.

ROSSINI wrote one of the principal parts in ELISABETTA, REGINA D'INGHILTERRA for him and Count ALMAVIVA (BARBIERE DI SIVIGLIA). He sang in Angelica CATALANI's co. in Paris, and in London from 1816 to 1825, when he took his own opera co. to NY and Mexico, losing all his money to bandits. He returned to Paris and the opera stage, then devoted himself to teaching. His pupils incl. his daughters, Maria Malibran and VIARDOT, his son Manuel Patricio Rodríguez GARCÍA, and NOURRIT. Rossini considered him a fine comp., but his operas are forgotten. PS

García, Manuel (II) Patricio Rodríguez, b. Zafra, Catalonia, 17 Mar 1805; d. London, 1 July 1906. Spanish baritone and teacher. Studied with his father, GARCÍA I, ZINGARELLI, Auguste Panseron, and F. J. Fétis. Operatic debut, 1825, with his father's co. in NY as FIGARO (BARBIERE DI SIVIGLIA). His father sang Count ALMAVIVA, his mother, Joacquina Sitches sang Berta, and his sister, MALIBRAN, ROSINA. He considered his voice tremulous, 'one of the deadly sins in singing', and after a year in the Fr. Army in 1830, devoted himself to teaching at the Paris Cons. and the RAM, London. His pupils incl. LIND, MARCHESI DE CASTRONE, SANTLEY, and his own son, Gustavo, also an opera singer. In 1854 he invented the laryngoscope. His *Traité Complet de l'Art du Chant* (Paris 1847) is considered the greatest treatise on singing techniques. He lived to be 101. PS

Gardelli, Lamberto, b. Venice, 8 Nov 1915. Italian, later Swedish, conductor. Studied Liceo Musicale Rossini, Pesaro, and later at Rome. Assistant to SERAFIN in early stages of career. Resident cond., Royal Swedish O., Stockholm, 1946–55. Worked at Budapest O. 1955–61. US debut, Carnegie Hall, 1964 concert perf. of CAPULETI ED I MONTECCHI; Met, 1966 (ANDREA CHÉNIER). British debut at Glyndebourne 1964 (MACBETH), CG 1969 (VERDI's OTELLO). One of the most telling exponents of Verdi's opera today. AB

Garden, Mary, b. Aberdeen, 20 Feb 1877; d. Aberdeen, 3 Jan 1967. Scottish soprano. Taken as a child to USA, studied singing there, then went to Paris, under MARCHESI DE CASTRONE, FUGÈRE and others. Debut, 1900, Paris, taking title role in LOUISE when Marthe Rioton fell ill. Chosen by DEBUSSY to create MÉLISANDE (1902). US debut, Manhattan OH, 1907, as THAÏS (US premiere), and in 1909 sang (and danced) SALOME. Joined Chicago O. 1910, which she managed for one lavish, artistically successful but financially disastrous

Mary Garden as SALOME, Manhattan Opera House, NY, 1909

season, 1919–20. With her striking presence, keen intelligence, fine voice, and outstanding acting ability, she was one of the operatic personalities of her time. LO
See Garden and Biancolli, *Mary Garden's Story* (New York 1951; London 1952)

Gardner, John, b. Manchester, 2 Mar 1917. English composer. Mus. master at Repton School 1939, then mus. staff CG 1946–53. Works, chiefly in orch. and chamber music, incl. the opera *The Moon and Sixpence*, based on the Somerset Maugham novel, prod. SW 24 May 1957, and *The Visitors*, Aldeburgh, 1972. FGB

Garnier, Jean-Louis-Charles, b. Paris, 6 Nov 1825; d. Paris, 1898. Architect, designer of Paris O. Won *Prix de Rome* 1848, and competition for design of the new Paris opera house, 1860, but the building was not completed until 1875. Also designed Monte Carlo Casino and Opera House 1879, and the tombs of BIZET, MASSÉ, and OFFENBACH in Paris. LO

Garrard, Don, b. Vancouver, 31 July 1929. Canadian bass. Studied Toronto and Santa Barbara, with Lotte LEHMANN and John Charles Thomas. Debut in title role of DON GIOVANNI on Canadian TV. English debut with SW (1961). Has sung title role in ATTILA, SILVA, SARASTRO, ROCCO, Fernando (GAZZA LADRA), Raleigh (GLORIANA), and Trulove (RAKE'S PROGESS), a role he also sang at Glyndebourne in 1975, when he was also heard

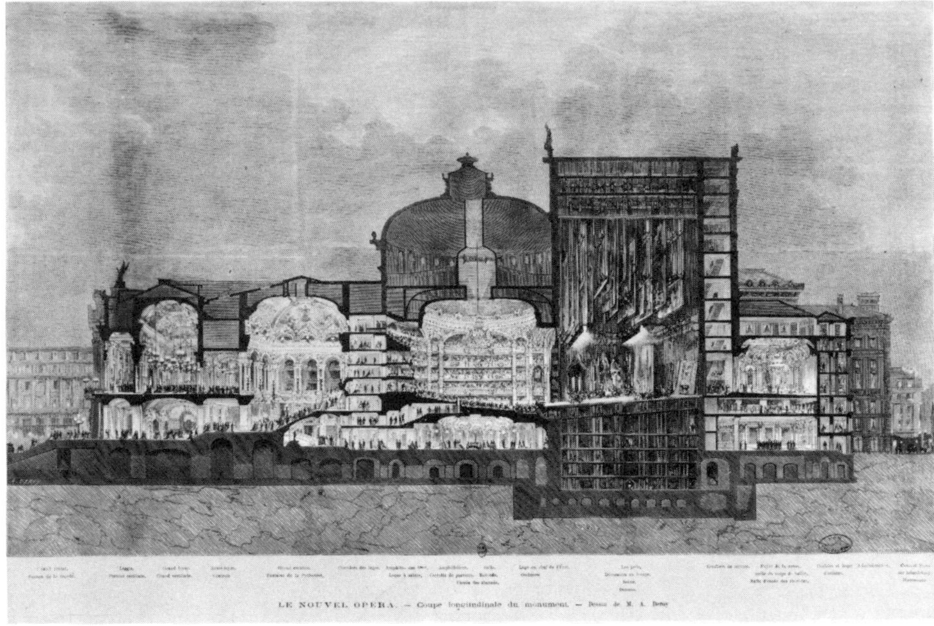

Jean-Louis-Charles Garnier's design for the Paris O., completed 1875

as Gremin (EUGENE ONEGIN), which he sang at CG in 1971, having made his debut in that house as Ferrando in TROVATORE (1970). Hamburg debut 1968. Has also sung Wanderer (SIEGFRIED) with the ENO at the London Coliseum. He has a warm, sympathetic voice and is a good actor. JB

Garrick, David, b. Hereford, 19 Feb 1717; d. London, 20 Jan 1779. English actor, whose new, more naturalistic style of playing influenced opera both indirectly, through his contact with Jean-Georges Noverre (1727–1810), whose *Lettres sur la Danse* (1760) greatly influenced GLUCK, and directly, through singers such as GUADAGNI whom he coached. His play (with George Colman), *The Clandestine Marriage* (1766), was the source of MATRIMONIO SEGRETO. LO

Gassmann, Florian Leopold, b. Brüx (now Most), Czechoslovakia, 3 May 1729; d. Vienna, 20 Jan 1774. Bohemian composer. After studying in Italy, with Padre Martini at Bologna, and working in Venice, went to Vienna 1762, succeeding Johann Georg Reutter as MdC in 1772. Began by writing *opere serie*, but his place in the history of opera rests on his *opere buffe*, often to GOLDONI's libs, such as *La Contessina* (1770) and *La Notta Critica* (1768). LO

Gatti-Casazza, Giulio, b. Udine, 3 Feb 1869; d. Ferrara, 2 Sept 1940. Italian impresario. Followed his father as manager of T. Municipale, Ferrara, 1893. This led to similar position at Sc. 1898, where he worked with TOSCANINI and brought non-It. operas such as PELLÉAS ET MÉLISANDE and works of WAGNER to Milan. Went to NY Met as general manager in 1908, remaining there until retirement, 1935. His regime, among the most illustrious in the Met's history, consolidated its reputation as a great international opera house. LO
See autobiography, *Memories of the Opera* (New York 1941)

Gavazzeni, Gianandrea, b. Bergamo, 25 July 1909. Italian conductor, composer, and writer. Studied Rome; debut as cond. Bergamo, 1940. Has cond. at Sc., debut 1944, and regularly since 1948, at Rome (BLOCH's *Macbeth*, 1953) and Florence. Cond. premieres of PIZZETTI's *Vanna Lupa*, Florence Maggio Musicale, 1948, and his ASSASSINIO NELLA CATTEDRALE and the first It. perf. of EMPEROR JONES, Rome 1952. LO

Gaveaux, Pierre, b. Béziers, 1761; d. Passy, 5 Feb 1825. French tenor and composer. Of his some 30 operas only one deserves mention – LÉONORE, OU L'AMOUR CONJUGAL (1798) – as being the first to treat the theme of FIDELIO. LO

Gay, John, b. Barnstaple, Sept 1685; d. London, 4 Dec 1732. English poet and playwright. Wrote the libs for ACIS AND GALATEA and BEGGAR'S OPERA. Produced by John Rich in 1728 with enormous success, wits said that it 'made Rich gay, and Gay rich'. Gay's sequel, POLLY, was prohibited from perf. by the government. The score was pub., however, and brought Gay £1,000. The opera failed when it was prod. 45 years after Gay's death. PS

Gaztambide y Garbayo, Joaquín, b. Tudela, 7 Feb 1822; d. Madrid, 18 Mar 1870. Spanish composer. Of his 44 *zarzuelas*, *La Mensajera* (1849) helped to establish the popularity of the genre after a considerable period of neglect. FGB

Gazza Ladra, La (*The Thieving Magpie*), *opera semiseria*, 2 acts, ROSSINI, lib. Giovanni Gherardini after Jean Marie Théodore Baudouin d'Aubigny's and Louis Charles Caigniez's *La Pie Voleuse*. Milan, Sc., 31 May 1817; London, HM, 10 Mar 1821; Philadelphia, Pa., Oct 1827. Main chars: Ninetta (sop.) Giannetto (ten.) Isacco (ten.) the Podestà (buffo-bass) Pippo (mezzo-sop.) Fernando (bass). Ninetta, engaged to Giannetto, son of the farmer in whose house she works as a maid, is suspected of having sold some of her employer's silverware. The Podestà presses the charge because she has repulsed his advances. Condemned to death, Ninetta is on her way to execution when the real thief is discovered – a magpie. The overture is especially well known. JB

La Gazza Ladra, London, SW Opera, 15 May 1969. Produced BESCH, designed Peter Rice. *Left to right:* Harold Blackburn as the Podestà (Mayor); Louis Browne as Giannetto, and Margaret Curphey as Ninetta

Gedda [Ustinov], Nicolai, b. Stockholm, 11 July 1925. Swedish tenor of Russian parentage. Debut, 1952, Stockholm (POSTILLON DE LONGJUMEAU). In 1953 he sang at Sc. in the premiere of Orff's *Trionfo d'Afrodite*. First appeared at Paris O. and CG, 1954, at Salzburg and NY Met, 1957. Fluent in six languages, he is equally at home in Russ., Ger., It., and Fr. opera. His vast repertory ranges from GLUCK, HAYDN, and MOZART to WAGNER (LOHENGRIN), VERDI, and PUCCINI; among his most successful roles are FAUST, Vincent (MIREILLE), DES GRIEUX (MANON), Huon (OBERON), and BENVENUTO CELLINI. He sang Anatol in the first perf. of VANESSA. EF

Geiger-Torel, Herman, b. Frankfurt am Main, 13 July 1907. German, later Canadian, stage director and producer. Studied Frankfurt. After work at Frankfurt, Salzburg, and in France and Czechoslovakia, went as stage dir. to T. Colón, Buenos Aires, 1938–40, and other places in S. America. Stage dir. of Toronto Cons. of Music Opera School, 1948, and in 1950 founded COC, retiring in 1975. Prod. over 50 perfs of 36 operas including premieres of SOMERS's *Louis Riel*, 1967 and WILSON's *Heloise and Abelard*, 1973; also Canadian premieres of ELEKTRA, SALOME, GÖTTERDÄMMERUNG, and BORIS GODUNOV. LO

Geliot, Michael, b. London, 29 Sept 1933. English producer. Began work as dir. of theatre and opera while still at Cambridge. Then was staff prod. at both SW and Glyndebourne. One of his earliest successes was AUFSTIEG UND FALL DER STADT MAHAGONNY at SW (1963). Debut at CG with Maxwell DAVIES's *Taverner* (1972); also new CARMEN (1973). Art. dir., WNO, since 1970, for whom he has done several major prods. WOZZECK at Holland Fest. (1974); FIDELIO at Munich Fest. (1974). His prods are approached from an original, often controversial point of view. AB

Gencer, Leyla, b. Istanbul, 10 Oct 1928. Turkish soprano. Studied at Istanbul. Debut, as Santuzza (CAVALLERIA RUSTICANA), Ankara 1950. Then studied in Italy with Giannina Arangi-Lombardi and Apollo Granforte. First It. appearance at Arena Flegrea, Naples, also as Santuzza, 1953. Other debuts: 1957, Sc. (Mme Lidoine in premiere of DIALOGUES DES CARMÉLITES) and Vienna Staats O. (VIOLETTA); 1962, CG (Elisabeth in DON CARLOS and Donna ANNA) and Glyndebourne (Countess ALMAVIVA). She returned to CG for ANNA BOLENA, 1965; most famous in this and other DONIZETTI roles, such as LUCREZIA BORGIA, Elisabetta (ROBERTO DEVEREUX), MARIA STUARDA, and Antonina (*Belisario*), to which her dramatic and pathetic accents are best suited. AB

Genée, (Franz Friedrich) Richard, b. Danzig (now Gdańsk), 7 Feb 1823; d. Baden, nr Vienna, 15 June 1895. German conductor, composer, but principally librettist. With F. Zell (pseudonym of Camillo Walzel) supplied books for MILLÖCKER – BETTELSTUDENT and

Gasparone, 1884; J. STRAUSS – *Cagliostro in Wien (C. in Vienna),* 1875, and NACHT IN VENEDIG; SUPPÉ – BOCCACCIO and FATINITZA; also, with Carl Haffner, FLEDERMAUS. Tr. works by OFFENBACH, HERVÉ, LECOCQ, AUDRAN, and SULLIVAN. His own operettas incl. *Der Seekadett* (*The Naval Cadet*), 1876; *Der Geiger aus Tirol (The Fiddler from Tyrol*), 1857; and *Nanon* (lib. Genée and Zell), 1877. LO

Generali [Mercandetti], Pietro, b. Masserano, 23 Oct 1783; d. Novara, 3 Nov 1832. Italian composer. He wrote his earliest works for the church. His first opera *Gli Amanti Ridicoli* was prod. in Rome, 1800, when he was only 17. In the next 29 years he wrote 44 operas. The most important are *Adelina* (Venice 1810), which ROSSINI has been accused of plagiarizing for BARBIERE DI SIVIGLIA; *I Baccanali di Roma* (Venice 1815); and *Il Voto di Jefte* (Florence 1827), a dramatic oratorio. In 1817 he became dir. of the Barcelona opera, a position he held for four years, after which he became MdC of Novara Cathedral, retiring from the operatic stage for five years. In his early works, he originated a number of forms of harmony and modulation that Rossini used to great effect. Ironically, Generali's later operas were criticized for being Rossinian. *Francesca da Rimini*, written for the 1829 reopening of La Fenice, was jeered off the stage with cries of 'Semiramide! Mosè!' PS

Generalintendant *see* INTENDANT

Geneva [Genève; Genf], Switzerland. Opera was first heard there in 18th c., and esp. after 1783 when a new theatre was built. In 1879 another theatre, an opera house similar to Paris O., was built; burned down 1951, it was replaced only in 1962. From then, and esp. since 1965 when GRAF took over the Grand T., Geneva opera has bloomed, staging estab. works with verve, reviving unfamiliar ones (e.g. BLOCH's *Macbeth*, 1968–9). From 1962 until his death in 1969 Ernest Ansermet was mus. dir. Present *Intendant* Jean-Claude Riber, apptd 1973; resident stage dir. Lotfi Mansouri. About ten operas are presented during each season. LO

Genoa [Genova], Italy. Its operatic life was dominated mainly by Venetian comps in the 17th and 18th c. In 1828 the T. Carlo Felice opened with BIANCA E FERNANDO (2nd version). Under MARIANI (1852–72) the standard of perf. was high and the repertory adventurous. Bombed in 1943, the theatre still awaits complete reconstruction. Annual operatic season Dec–Feb. JB

Genoveva, opera, 4 acts, SCHUMANN, lib. Robert Reinick, after TIECK's *Leben und Tod der Heiligen Genoveva* and HEBBEL's *Genoveva,* with some modifications by comp. Leipzig, 25 June 1850; London, DL, by students of RCM, 6 Dec 1893. Schumann's only opera. Has never entered the repertory; revived Florence Maggio Musicale, 1951. LO

Gentele, Göran, b. Stockholm, 20 Sept 1917; d. Sardinia, 18 July 1972. Swedish producer and manager. While prod. at the Stockholm Royal Opera (1950–63) he dir. BALLO IN MASCHERA in its historical Swedish setting, and the space opera ANIARA, – later seen at Edinburgh (1959) and CG (1960). In 1961 he prod. IPHIGÉNIE EN TAURIDE for CG, and in 1963 became dir. of the Stockholm Opera. Nominated to succeed BING as General Manager of the NY Met, he was killed in a car accident shortly after taking up the appointment. EF

Gerhard, Roberto, b. Valls, 25 Sept 1896; d. Cambridge, 5 Jan 1970. Spanish composer, later naturalized British. He studied with GRANADOS and SCHÖNBERG. Left Spain after the Civil War to take up residence in England at King's College, Cambridge. Comp. in all mus. forms. His single opera DUENNA was broadcast by the BBC (1949) and staged at Wiesbaden (1951). CBE in 1967. FGB

Gerl, Franz Xaver, b. Audorf, 30 Nov 1764; d. Mannheim, 9 Mar 1827. German bass and composer. Joined SCHIKANEDER's theatre co. as actor and singer *c.* 1788, supplied music for several prods and created SARASTRO. In 1765 he left Vienna for Brünn, where two of his *Singspiele* were prod. JB

Germany. In the 17th c. It. opera predominated. The few exceptions incl. the first opera in Ger., Heinrich Schütz's *Dafne*, a tr. of PERI's *Dafne* (1627); Sigmund Theophilus Staden's *Seelewig* (Nuremberg 1644), the first Ger. opera of which the music is preserved, and ADAM UND EVA. It. *opera seria* continued to dominate the 18th c., esp. in S. Germany and Austria; Ger. serious opera dates from Anton Schweitzer's *Alceste* (1773), followed by HOLZBAUER's *Günther von Schwartzburg* (1777), the first Ger. serious opera on a national subject. The characteristic 18th-c. contribution was the SINGSPIEL.

Of the scores of 19th-c. operas by Ger. comps, few remain in the repertory apart from those by BEETHOVEN, HUMPERDINCK, LORTZING, R. STRAUSS, WAGNER, and C. M. WEBER. Twentieth-c. comps incl. BLACHER, FORTNER, EGK, HINDEMITH, KLEBE, ORFF, and WEILL, but since World War II the only comp. of more than national significance to come to the fore is HENZE, though his influence has been limited since his conscious decision to leave his native land and work in Italy. His earlier operas exhibit a strongly lyrical and fantastic vein at odds with most of the developments in the country over the same period, from about 1952 to 1966. Most other comps have either carried on the serial style of SCHÖNBERG and his disciples or broken away into more experimental forms employing electronic methods and, more recently, multimedia forms, as in SOLDATEN. The more conventional of these comps have been von EINEM (most of whose works have had their premieres in Austria), Fortner, Klebe, and Egk. Blacher was rather more experimental, and Orff pursued his own, somewhat sterile style. ZIMMERMANN, before his untimely death, seemed to be the most adventurous of a younger generation. Other advanced comps, such as Karlheinz Stockhausen and his disciples, did not seem interested in opera as such, although they often used dramatic elements in their unorthodox works.

Opera is perf. in over 40 centres of **West Germany**, incl. AACHEN, BAYREUTH, BERLIN, Bremen, BRUNSWICK, COLOGNE, Dortmund, Duisburg and Düsseldorf (which jointly run the DEUTSCH OPER AM RHEIN), FRANKFURT, HAMBURG, HANOVER, KARLSRUHE, KASSEL, Kiel, Koblenz, Mainz, MANNHEIM, MUNICH, Nuremberg, SCHWETZINGEN, STUTTGART, WIESBADEN, and Wuppertal.

East Germany contains the important centres DRESDEN and LEIPZIG, also E. Berlin, where the Deutsche O. and Komische O. are situated, and HALLE and WEIMAR. Among comps are DESSAU, Gunter Kochan, Rainer Künod, Ernst Hermann Meyer, and Udo Zimmermann. LO/AB

Germont, bar., Alfredo's father in TRAVIATA

Gershwin, George, b. Brooklyn, NY, 26 Sept 1898; d. Hollywood, Cal., 11 July 1937. American composer. Studied piano with Ernest Hutcheson, harmony with Edward Kilenyi and Rubin Goldmark; also studied briefly with Nadia Boulanger in Paris. With Broadway as his goal, he wrote music for George White's *Scandals* (1919–24) and for 16 musical comeddies, incl. LADY, BE GOOD, *Oh, Kay* (1926), *Strike Up the Band* (1927), *Funny Face* (1927), *Girl Crazy* (1930), OF THEE I SING, and his masterpiece PORGY AND BESS. He continued writing for Broadway and Hollywood. EJ
See Schwartz, *Gershwin, His Life and Music* (Indianapolis 1973)

Gerusalemme Liberata (*Jerusalem Liberated*). It. epic poem by TASSO. Of the more than 30 operas based on this the most important are: MONTEVERDI's *Il Combattimento di Tancredi e Clorinda* (1624); ARMIDE (LULLY, GLUCK, ROSSINI, 1817, DVOŘÁK, 1904); RINALDO (HANDEL, TRAETTA, 1761, JOMMELLI, 1770). LO

Ghedini, Giorgio Federico, b. Cuneo, 11 July 1892; d. Nervi, 25 Mar 1965. Italian composer. His eight operas incl. *Re Hassan* (Venice 1939, revised version, Naples 1961); *La Pulce d'Oro* (Genoa 1940); *Le Baccanti* (Sc. 1948); *Billy Budd* (Venice 1949), and *Lord Inferno*, a radio play based on Max Beerbohm's *Happy Hypocrite*, which won the Italia Prize (1952) and was staged at the Piccola Sc. as *L'Ipocrita Felice* (1956). He also edited INCORONAZIONE DI POPPEA (1953). EF

Ghiaurov, Nicolai, b. Velingrad, 13 Sept 1929. Bulgarian bass. Distinguished in wide range of operas from MOZART to MUSORGSKY. Studied at Sofia and Moscow. Debuts: 1956, Sofia, as Don BASILIO (BARBIERE DI SIVIGLIA); 1958, Moscow, as MÉPHISTOPHÉLÈS; 1959, Sc., as Varlaam (BORIS GODUNOV); 1962, CG, as Padre Guardiano (FORZA DEL DESTINO); 1962, Vienna Staats O.; 1963, Chicago Lyric O.; 1965, NY Met. Widely admired for eloquence of Italianate style as *basso cantante*, esp. in VERDI, and for breadth of character and authority in title role of *Boris Godunov*. NG

Ghislanzoni, Antonio, b. Lecco, 25 Nov 1824; d. Caprino-Bergamasco, 16 July 1893. Italian writer. Among his *c.* 80 libs are those for AIDA; Alfredo CATALANI's *Edmea* (1886); Enrico Petrella's *I Promessi Sposi* (1869), based on Alessandro Manzoni's novel; and PONCHIELLI's *I Lituani* (1874). LO

Giacosa, Giuseppe, b. Turin, 21 Oct 1847; d. Turin, 2 Sept 1906. Italian dramatist and librettist. In collaboration with ILLICA wrote libs for BOHÈME, MADAMA BUTTERFLY, and TOSCA (he was the versifier of the partnership); with Luigi Illica, Tito Ricordi, Marco Praga, and Domenico Oliva wrote lib. for MANON LESCAUT. LO

Giannini, Vittorio, b. Philadelphia, Pa., 19 Oct 1903; d. NY, 28 Nov 1966. American composer. His six operas are: *Lucidia* (Munich 1934); *The Scarlet Letter* (Hamburg 1938), based on Nathaniel Hawthorne; *The Taming of the Shrew* (TV and NY CC 1956); *The Harvest* (Chicago 1961); *Rehearsal Call* (NY 1962); *The*

Servant of Two Masters, based on GOLDONI, NY CC 1967 (prod. posthumously). LO

Gianni Schicchi, *opera buffa*, 1 act, PUCCINI, lib. FORZANO. NY Met, 14 Dec 1918; London, CG, 18 June 1920. Main chars: Lauretta (sop.) Rinuccio (ten.) Schicchi (bar.). Gianni Schicchi, called in by Rinuccio Donati to falsify the will of a rich relative who has left everything to the Church, impersonates the dead man before witnesses and dictates a new will leaving the most valuable part of the legacy to himself – but as a dowry for his daughter, Rinuccio's betrothed. Puccini's only comic opera: the third of the TRITTICO. JB O
See Kobbé

Gibson, Alexander, b. Motherwell, 11 Feb 1926. Scottish conductor. Began career in London with SW and became its youngest ever mus. dir. in 1957. CG debut 1957, cond. TOSCA. Founded SO 1962, since cond. 40 of its prods incl. RING DES NIBELUNGEN. Regular guest with opera companies and symphony orchs in Britain and abroad. Since US debut in 1967 has returned to Britain every year for opera and concerts. FGB

Gielen, Michael Andreas, b. Dresden, 20 July 1927. Argentinian conductor of German extraction. Studied at Buenos Aires, where he became a *répétiteur* at the Colón. European debut, 1951, Vienna. Mus. dir. of the Royal Opera, Stockholm, 1960–5. Has cond. at Cologne, Aix-en-Provence, Munich and many other cities. Apptd mus. dir. of the Netherlands O. 1972. Particularly assoc. with modern works, he cond. the premiere of SOLDATEN; other 20th-c. operas Gielen has cond. incl. Josef Hauer's *Die Schwarze Spinne* (*The Black Spider*), OEDIPUS REX, DUKE BLUEBEARD'S CASTLE, and WOZZECK. EF

Gigli, Beniamino, b. Recanati, 20 Mar 1890; d. Rome, 30 Nov 1957. Italian tenor. Studied at S. Cecilia acad., Rome. Debut 1914, Rovigo, as Enzo (GIOCONDA); 1918 Sc., Milan, as Faust (MEFISTOFELE), under TOSCANINI. First appearance at NY Met in same role, 1920; sang there regularly until 1932. CG debut as ANDREA CHÉNIER, 1930 – which was among his most famous parts, others being NEMORINO, DES GRIEUX (MANON), RODOLFO, PINKERTON, CAVARADOSSI, and DUCA DI MANTUA. Audiences were consoled for his poor acting by his honeyed, impassioned singing: his voice was among the most natural and beautiful heard this c. Although his vocal taste was far from impeccable, he always drew a public – in concerts, after retirement, as much as in opera – by virtue of his direct, popular appeal. His earlier records in particular give a good idea of his singing. AB

Gilbert, (Sir) William Schwenk, b. London, 18 Nov 1836; d. Harrow, 29 May 1911. Playwright and librettist. His success in the straight theatre with e.g. *Pygmalion and Galatea* (1871) was entirely eclipsed by the fame of the operas written in collaboration with SULLIVAN, a partnership which began with *Trial by Jury* (1875) and ended with *The Grand Duke* (1896). Of libs written for other comps that to *The Mountebanks* (CELLIER, 1892) was the most successful. LO

Gilda, sop., Rigoletto's daughter in RIGOLETTO

Gilson, Paul, b. Brussels, 15 June 1865; d. Brussels, 3 Apr 1942. Flemish composer. Studied with François Gevaert, winning *Prix de Rome*, 1889. His operas are: *Prinses Zonneschijn* (Antwerp 1903; in Fr. as *Princesse Rayon de Soleil*, Brussels 1905); *Zeevolk* (Antwerp 1905; in Fr. as *Gens de Mer*, 1929); *Rooversliefde* (Antwerp 1906). LO

Giménez, Gerónimo *see* JIMÉNEZ, Jerónimo

Ginastera, Alberto E., b. Buenos Aires, 11 Apr 1916. Argentine composer of Italian and Spanish descent. Studied at Cons. Williams, Buenos Aires, 1925–35 and Cons. Nacional, with José Andre, José Gil and Athos Palma. A Guggenheim Fellowship took him to the USA 1945–7. His three operas DON RODRIGO, BOMARZO, and BEATRIX CENCI (commissioned by the Opera Society of Washington for the opening of the John F. Kennedy Center for the Performing Arts), reveal a growing preoccupation with the theatricality of madness, consistent with his statement that 'sex, violence and hallucination are three of the basic elements from which grand opera can be constructed'. From 1963 to 1971 he was dir. of the Latin American Center for Advanced Studies in composition at the Instituto Torcuato di Tella, later moving to live in Geneva, Switzerland. MK

Gioconda, La, opera, 4 acts, PONCHIELLI, lib. 'Tobia Gorrio', i.e. BOITO after HUGO's *Angelo, Tyran de Padoue* (1835). Milan, Sc., 8 Apr 1876; London, CG, 31 May 1883; NY Met, 30 Dec 1883. Main chars: Gioconda (sop.) Cieca (contr.) Alvise (bass) Laura (mezzo-sop.) Enzo (ten.) Barnaba (bar.). La Gioconda, a ballad singer of Venice, loves Enzo, a proscribed nobleman, but is herself pursued by Barnaba, a

Alberto Ginastera's DON RODRIGO, NY City Opera, Spring 1966; sets designed LEE; costumes Theoni V. Aldredge; produced Tito Capobianco

government spy. Enzo is in love with Laura, a Venetian senator's wife. As Laura has saved her mother from the mob, La Gioconda helps her to elude her husband's vengeance and to escape with Enzo to safety. She then kills herself. Ponchielli's only successful opera, famous for three arias and the ballet 'The Dance of the Hours'. It remains part of the NY Met repertory. JB O
See Kobbé

Gioielli della Madonna, I (*The Jewels of the Madonna*), opera, 3 acts, WOLF-FERRARI, lib. Enrico Golisciani and C. Zangarini. Berlin, Kurfürsten O., 23 Dec 1911 (in Ger. version of Hans Liebstöckl); Chicago, 16 Jan 1912 (in It.); London, CG, 30 May 1812. Main chars: Gennaro (ten.) Maliella (sop.) Rafaele (bar.). Gennaro, a poor young Neapolitan smith, steals the jewels from a statue of the Madonna to give to his beloved Maliella, herself involved with Rafaele, head of the Camorra. Wolf-Ferrari's only essay in *verismo*. JB
See Kobbé

Giordano, Umberto, b. Foggia, 27 Aug 1867; d. Milan, 12 Nov 1948. Italian composer. Studied Naples Cons., where he wrote his first opera, *Marina*. His next stage work, *Mala Vita* (Rome 1892, revived as *Il Vito*, 1897), satisfied the current taste for violent melodrama. His greatest success was ANDREA CHÉNIER, later rivalled by FEDORA. Other operas incl.: *Siberia* (Milan 1903); *Marcella* (Milan 1907); *Mese Mariano* (Palermo 1910); *Madame Sans-Gêne* (New York 1915 with FARRAR in the title role); *Giove a Pompei* (Rome 1921 in collaboration with FRANCHETTI); *La Cena delle Beffe* (Milan 1924); *Il Re* (Milan 1929). Like many of his generation, Giordano was sustained by the post-MASCAGNI tradition of *verismo*, of which he was a competent and occasionally inspired practitioner. JB

Giorgi Righetti, Geltrude, b. Bologna, 1793; d. *c.* 1850. Italian contralto. Debut, 1814, Bologna; moved to Rome where in 1816 she created the role of ROSINA. After an attack on the opera by an English journalist in 1822, she pub. her reply, 'Cenni di una donna gia cantante sopra il maestro Rossini . . .' In 1817, she was ROSSINI's first CENERENTOLA. She retired in 1836. PS

Giorno di Regno, Un (*King for a Day*), *opera buffa*, 2 acts, VERDI, lib. ROMANI after Pineu-Duval. Milan, Sc., 5 Sept 1840; London, Camden Fest., 21 Mar 1961. Main chars: Belfiore (bar.) Marchesa (sop. or mezzo-sop.) Giulietta (sop. or mezzo-sop.) Edoardo (ten.) Barone (buffo-bass) Tesoriere (buffo-bass). Belfiore, called upon to impersonate the Polish King Stanislaus in France, makes use of his false authority to unite a young couple in the teeth of parental opposition, and finally effects a reconciliation with his own fiancée, the Marchesa, who has tried in vain to make him drop his disguise. Verdi's second and only comic opera before FALSTAFF. A failure, rarely revived. JB

Giovanna d'Arco (*Joan of Arc*), opera, prologue and 3 acts, VERDI, lib. Temistocle Solera after SCHILLER. Milan, Sc., 15 Feb 1845. Main chars: Giovanna (sop.) Carlo (ten.) Giacomo (bar.). Giovanna (Joan of Arc) senses her divine mission, and receives from the despairing Carlo (the Dauphin) his sword and armour. After the relief of Orléans, Carlo declares his love for her; but angel voices have warned her never to yield to mortal passion. Her father, Giacomo, who has already promised to deliver her to the English, denounces her publicly at the coronation in Reims. However, convinced of her innocence, he then frees her from her prison and she leads the French troops once more, returning mortally wounded. Verdi's seventh opera, rarely revived. JB O

Girl of the Golden West, The *see* FANCIULLA DEL WEST

Giuditta (*Judith*), *musikalische Komödie*, 3 acts, LEHÁR, lib. Paul Knepler and Fritz Löhner. Vienna, O., 20 Jan 1934. Lehár's only opera and his last stage work – *not* based on the Bible story. LO O
See Lubbock

Giulini, Carlo Maria, b. Barletta, 9 May 1914. Italian conductor. Studied Rome. Mus. dir. of

It. radio 1946–51; cond. at Sc. 1951–6, and has since been much in demand at European centres including CG, Edinburgh, Florence, and Aix-en-Provence fests and also at Sc. One of the best of present-day conds. LO

Giulio Cesare in Egitto (*Julius Caesar in Egypt*), opera, 3 acts, HANDEL, lib. Nicola Francesco Haym. London, Haymarket T., 2 Mar 1724; Northampton, Mass., 14 May 1927. Main chars: Cesare (mezzo-sop.) Cleopatra (sop.) Sesto (sop.) Tolomeo (bass). Cesare (Julius Caesar) has pursued Pompey to Egypt, where Tolomeo (Ptolemy) has had him murdered. Hearing of Cesare's anger, Tolomeo decides to murder him also; he imprisons Pompey's widow and son. Cleopatra tries to charm Cesare to enlist his support against her brother Tolomeo, who meanwhile is frustrated in his attempt on Cornelia's virtue by the escaped Sesto (Sextus Pompeius, Pompey's son). A love scene between Cesare and Cleopatra is interrupted by the sound of a mob crying for Cesare's blood. Cesare swims to safety after a defeat by Tolomeo, finds a secret way to the royal palace and crowns Cleopatra sole queen of Egypt. With RODELINDA, Handel's most successful opera. JB ○

Gizziello [Gioacchino Conti], b. Arpino, Naples, 28 Feb 1714; d. Rome, 25 Oct 1761. Italian sopranist, pupil of D. Gizzi, whence is derived his name. Debut Rome, aged 15; sang Naples 1732–3, then taken by HANDEL to London, singing in his ARIODANTE, *Atalanta*, *Poro*, *Arminio*, *Giustino*, and *Partenope*. A rival to the great CAFFARELLI and FARINELLI, and a member of the latter's co., Madrid 1749–52. Described in 1736 as the best singer in Italy. One of his pupils was GUADAGNI. LO

Glasgow, Scotland. Opera given by touring cos. In addition the Glasgow Grand O. Soc. gave some notable perfs in the 1930s under CHISHOLM, esp. TROYENS (1935) and BÉATRICE ET BÉNÉDICT (1936). Its enterprise continued after World War II. Glasgow has been the centre of SO since its inception in 1962; since autumn 1975 the King's T. has been its permanent home. LO

Glinka, Mikhail Ivanovich, b. Novospasskoye [now Glinka], 1 June 1804; d. Berlin, 15 Feb 1857. Russian composer. Apart from lessons in Italy and Berlin (with Siegfried Dehn), he was self-taught in composition. But he occupies a seminal position in the history of music in Russia, and the striking innovations in his two completed operas, IVAN SUSANIN and RUSLAN AND LYUDMILA, had a lasting effect on the development of Russian music drama. GN
See Brown, *Mikhail Glinka* (London 1974)

Gloriana, 3 acts, BRITTEN, lib. William Plomer, from Lytton Strachey's *Elizabeth and Essex*. Commissioned by CG for the Coronation of Queen Elizabeth II and first prod. at a gala perf. in her presence, 8 June 1953, with CROSS as Elizabeth I. Main chars: Elizabeth I (sop.) Essex (ten.) Cecil (bar.). Although superficially a work of Tudor pageantry, *Gloriana* delves deeply into the char. of the queen and into the conflicting demands of royal duty and love. The score is fashioned with the comp.'s usual understanding of projecting private and public char. After disdain by critics and public alike, the work was favourably reassessed when revived by SW in the 1960s. AB
See Kobbé

Glossop, Peter, b. Sheffield, 6 July 1928. English baritone of worldwide acclaim in VERDI and other It. roles. Studied singing while working as bank clerk. Joined SW chorus 1952; promoted principal from 1953 and sang variety of leading roles there to 1963, winning international competition at Sofia, 1961, as Conti DI LUNA. Other debuts: 1961, CG, as Demetrius (MIDSUMMER NIGHT'S DREAM); 1965, Sc., as RIGOLETTO; 1966, Boston, as FALSTAFF; 1967, NY Met O. Co. at Newport Fest., as Rigoletto; 1968, Vienna Staats O.; 1973, NY Met as SCARPIA. His perfs are distinguished by burly vigour of expression, lyrical firmness of vocal line, and intensity of char., esp. as IAGO, Rigoletto, Scarpia, SIMONE BOCCANEGRA. Has appeared in filmed operas as Iago and TONIO under KARAJAN. He m. the sop. BLACKHAM. NG

Gluck, Christoph Willibald, b. Erasbach, 2 July 1714; d. Vienna, 15 Nov 1787. Composer, German, possibly Bohemian. Spent eight years, 1737–45, in N. Italy, writing It. operas. Visited London, 1746; worked with Mingotti's Opera Co., then settled in Vienna, 1750. There his contact with Count Giacomo Durazzo, director of Imperial Theatres in Vienna, 1754–64, CALZABIGI and the dancer Gasparo Angiolini turned his thoughts to a new concept of opera based on simplicity. The first 'reform' opera, ORFEO ED EURIDICE, 1762, was followed by ALCESTE (with a famous preface), 1767, and PARIDE ED ELENA, 1770 – all three with It. libs by Calzabigi. This reform style was continued in the operas written, in Fr., for Paris: IPHIGÉNIE EN AULIDE, 1774, ARMIDE, 1777, and IPHIGÉNIE EN TAURIDE, 1779. The reworkings of *Orfeo* as ORPHÉE and of *Alceste*, both in Fr.,

Right: Glyndebourne. A general view of the house and theatre from the gardens. The opera house is small, seating 800; the emphasis has been on perfection of ensemble in a range of operas that lend themselves to an intimate approach.

entailed considerable changes, in fact the Fr. *Alceste* is almost a new work; he also rewrote some of his earlier Viennese *opéras comiques*, inserting, esp. in *La Cythère assiégée*, elaborate *fioriture*. In his last opera, ÉCHO ET NARCISSE, he discarded the human tragedies of his 'reform' style in favour of a pastoral. His fame rests almost entirely on his 'reform' operas; in reverting to the principles of the FLORENTINE CAMERATA and the emphasis on dramatic truth he paved the way for WAGNER and 19th-c. music drama. LO

Glückliche Hand, Die (*The Favoured Hand*), music drama, 1 act, SCHÖNBERG, lib. composer. Vienna, 14 Oct 1924; Philadelphia, Pa., 11 Apr 1930. Main chars: the Man (bar.) a man and a woman (mimed roles). A man searches for his own identity and for artistic fulfilment. EF O

Glyndebourne. CHRISTIE's country house near Glynde, Sussex, where he, his wife MILDMAY, BUSCH, and C. EBERT founded the Glyndebourne Fest., in a small theatre built in the grounds, in 1934. The repertory at first was mainly MOZART. MACBETH was given its British premiere there, 1938. After World War II the repertory was widened. Premieres of RAPE OF LUCRETIA, ALBERT HERRING, and ELEGY FOR YOUNG LOVERS were given side by side with interesting prods of ROSSINI, R. STRAUSS (ARIADNE AUF NAXOS and others), and the co. took part in the first Edinburgh Fests. Busch was followed as chief cond. by V. GUI in 1951; PRITCHARD is now mus. dir. LO
See Hughes, *Glyndebourne, A History of the Festival Opera* (London 1965)

Gobbi, Tito, b. Bassano del Grappa, nr Venice, 24 Oct 1915. Italian baritone. Studied in Rome with Giulio Crimi. Debut (as student) 1935, T. Comunale, Gubbio, as Count Rodolfo (SONNAMBULA). Took small roles at Sc. while a 'cadet' there. First major role: GERMONT (Rome, T. Adriano, 1937). On the strength of that perf. engaged for T. Reale, Rome, where he remained a regular member of the co. until after World War II. First sang SCARPIA (one of his most famous roles) at Rieti 1940; Posa (DON CARLOS) and SIMONE BOCCANEGRA at Rome 1941; IAGO at T. S. Carlo, Naples, 1946; and FALSTAFF at T. Comunale, Florence, 1951. First CG appearance with Sc. co. 1950 as BELCORE and FORD; with the resident co. as RENATO 1953. Debut 1955, NY Met, as Scarpia. Has also appeared regularly at San Francisco and Chicago, where he made his debut as a prod. in 1965 with *Simone Boccanegra*, which he prod. at CG the same year. One of the most significant VERDI and PUCCINI baritones of the post-World War II era, with a gift for dramatic characterization and great tonal variety. AB

Godard, Benjamin, b. Paris, 18 Aug 1849; d. Cannes, 10 Jan 1895. French composer. Wrote eight operas, the most successful being *La Vivandière*, lib. Henri Cain; Paris, OC, 1 Apr 1895. Carl Rosa perf. it, in Eng., Liverpool 1896. LO

Goehr, Alexander, b. Berlin, 10 Aug 1932. British composer of German parentage. Studied in Paris with Olivier Messiaen. Goehr has wr. one major opera, ARDEN MUSS STERBEN; it shows his concise dramatic skill. AB

Goethe, Johann Wolfgang von, b. Frankfurt am Main, 28 Aug 1749; d. Weimar, 22 Mar 1832. German poet and playwright. Music's debt to him is considerable; the more than 50 operas based on his works include GOUNOD's FAUST, MIGNON, WERTHER, MEFISTOFELE, DOKTOR FAUST, as well as GOLDMARK's *Götz von Berlichingen* (1902), Max Ettinger's *Clavigo*

Tito Gobbi as FALSTAFF, one of his most memorable roles, and Ilva Ligabue as Alice Ford, London, CG, June 1974

(1926), Egon Wellesz's *Scherz, List und Rache* (1928), Arthur Meulemans's *Egmont* (1960), and numerous settings of his *Singspiele*, *Claudine von Villa Bella*, *Erwin und Elmire*, and *Jery und Bately*. Another *Singspiel*, *Die Fischerin*, set by Corona Schröter, contains the song, 'Erlkönig', also set by SCHUBERT. LO

Gogol, Nikolay Vasilyevich, b. Sorochintsy, 31 Mar 1809; d. Moscow, 4 Mar 1852. Russian writer. The nationalist idiom and sharp humour of his works have appealed to a large number of comps. Dramatic writings on which operas are based incl.: *The Inspector General*, 1835 (Tigran Chukhadjian, *Arifin Khilesi*, 1872; Karel Weis's operetta, *Der Revisor*, 1907; Dmitry Shvedov, comp. 1934; Eugen Zádor, 1935; Amilcare Zanella, *Il Revisore*, 1940; EGK, *Der Revisor*, 1957); *The Marriage*, 1833–41 (MUSORGSKY, incomplete opera comp. 1868, perf. 1909; Aleksandr Grechaninov, 1948; MARTINŮ, TV 1953, staged 1954; Alois Jiránek's musical comedy); *The Gamblers*, 1836–42 (SHOSTAKOVICH, projected opera). Many more operas have been based on stories contained in the collection *Evenings on a Farm Near Dikanka*, 1831–2: *Sorochintsy Fair* (three operas, incl. Musorgsky's unfinished one, comp. 1874–80; Boris Yanovsky, comp. 1899; and two operettas, incl. Aleksey Ryabov, 1936); *St John's Eve* (Tikots, comp. *c.* 1910–20); *May Night* (five, incl. Pyotr Petrovich Sokalsky, comp. 1876; RIMSKY-KORSAKOV, 1880; Nikolay Lysenko, *The Drowned Woman*, 1885; and an operetta by Ryabov, 1937); *The Lost Charter* (Yaroslavenko, *The Witch*, 1922); *Christmas Eve* (eight operas, incl. Lysenko's operetta, 1874, revised as opera 1883; Nikolay Afanasyev, *Vakula the Smith*, comp. 1875; TCHAIKOVSKY, *Vakula the Smith*, 1876; revised as *Cherevichki*, 1887; Nikolay Solovyov, *Vakula the Smith*, 1880; Rimsky-Korsakov, 1895; Abram Peysin, operetta, 1929); *Terrible Revenge* (Nikolay Kochetov, 1903). Other stories upon which operas have been based incl.: *The Portrait*, 1833–42 (Hilding Rosenberg, 1956); *The Nose*, 1833–5 (Shostakovich, 1930; Walter Kaufmann, 1953); *The Diary of a Madman*, 1834 (SEARLE, 1958); *The Overcoat*, 1839–41 (two operas, incl. Marttinen, 1965); *Taras Bulba*, 1833–42 (nine operas, incl. Pyotr Sokalsky, comp. 1878, revised as *The Siege of Dubno*, comp., 1905; Basil Kühner, 1880; Vladimir Kashperov, 1887; Lysenko, comp. 1890, perf. 1924; BERUTI, 1895; Marcel Rousseau, 1919; Trailin, 1914); *Viy*, 1833–42 (Gorelov, 1897; Karel Moor, 1903; Anton Dobronić, *Vječnaja Pamjat*, 1947, also based on CHEKHOV's *The Bear*; three operettas incl. Mikhail Verikivsky, comp. 1946). GN

Nikolay Gogol's *Taras Bulba* inspired several operas, including Nikolay Lysenko's (1842–1912) *Taras Bulba*, first produced at the Shevchenko T., Kiev, 1890. A recent production in the USSR is shown here with B. Gmyrya as Taras Bulba

Golaud, bass-bar., Mélisande's husband in PELLÉAS ET MÉLISANDE

Golden Cockerel, The (*Zolotoy Petushok*), opera, 3 acts, prologue and epilogue, RIMSKY-KORSAKOV, lib. Vladimir Ivanovich Belsky after PUSHKIN. Moscow, Solodovnikov T., 7 Oct 1909; London, DL, 15 June 1914; NY Met, 6 Mar 1918. Main chars: King Dodon (bass) Prince Gvidon (ten.) Prince Afron (bar.) Astrologer (high ten.) Queen of Shemakhan (sop.) Golden Cockerel (sop.). King Dodon's enemies threaten to attack his country. A golden cockerel, presented to him by the Astrologer, twice warns him of danger; he sends his two sons (Gvidon and Afron) to attack in a pincer movement, then goes to war himself, dressed in rusty armour. The king finds his soldiers dead (his sons' armies have killed one another in the pincer movement), then sees a silken tent; from it emerges the Queen of Shemakhan (of whom he has dreamed while asleep). She accepts his offer to become his queen. When the king returns home with his bride, the Astrologer claims her as payment for the cockerel; the king strikes him dead with his sceptre. The cockerel pecks Dodon's head; he dies, and the queen disappears. The Astrologer reappears and tells the audience not to take the story too seriously. Arguably Rimsky-Korsakov's finest opera, *The Golden Cockerel* met with severe censorship problems, because of its satire of Nicholas II's handling of the Russo-Japanese War. GN

Goldmark, Karl, b. Keszthely, 18 May 1830; d. Vienna, 2 Jan 1915. Austro-Hungarian composer. Of his seven operas the first, KÖNIGIN VON SABA, was widely played in Europe and the USA. Others are HEIMCHEN AM HERD and WINTERMÄRCHEN. LO

Goldoni, Carlo, b. Venice, 25 Feb 1707; d. Paris, 6 Feb 1793. Italian dramatist and librettist. The long list of comps for whom he wrote libs or who drew on his plays incl., in the 18th c., GALUPPI, HAYDN, PAISIELLO, PICCINNI, and SARTI, and in the 20th c. GIANNINI (*Servant of Two Masters*, 1967), MALIPIERO, MARTINŮ, and WOLF-FERRARI. LO
See Smith, *The Tenth Muse: A Historical Study of the Opera Libretto* (New York 1970; London 1971)

Goldovsky, Boris, b. Moscow, 7 June 1908. Russian, later American, conductor and manager. Studied in Moscow and Budapest; moved to USA 1930. Has been active in popularizing opera, through his work at Cleveland Inst. of Mus., the New England Cons. of Mus., Boston, and at the Berkshire Music Center; also as commentator for radio broadcasts from NY Met. Founder of New England O. Co. 1946. Has also worked as tr. of libs. LO

Golovin, Aleksandr Yakovlevich, b. Moscow, 1 Mar 1863; d. Detskoye Selo (now Pushkin), 17 Apr 1930. Russian stage designer. In the 1890s he was associated with ZIMIN, and later (in Paris) with DYAGILEV, for whom he designed a prod. of BORIS GODUNOV (1908) and the premiere of STRAVINSKY's ballet *The Firebird* (1910). GN

Goltz, Christel, b. Dortmund, 8 July 1912. German soprano. In the chorus at Furth; debut there, 1935, as AGATHE. At Dresden 1936–50. First sang at CG 1951 and at NY Met 1954, and has appeared in Berlin, Munich, Vienna, and Salzburg. Her strong, bright voice and the intensity of her acting make her an outstanding R. STRAUSS singer; SALOME, ELEKTRA, ARIADNE, ARABELLA and the Dyer's Wife (FRAU OHNE SCHATTEN) are among her finest roles. Her repertory also incl. FIDELIO, JENŮFA, Lisa (QUEEN OF SPADES), and MARIE. She created the title roles of ORFF's *Antigonae* (1949) and LIEBERMANN's *Penelope* (1954). EF

Gomes, António Carlos, b. Villa de São Carlos, Campinas, 11 July 1836; d. Belém, Pará, 16 Nov 1896. Brazilian composer. Studied with his father, Manuel José Gomes, and at the Rio de Janeiro Cons., 1860–3. The first opera, *A Noite no Castelo*, 1861, was his only Brazilian opera sung in Portuguese. After his second, *Joanna de Flandres*, 1863, he moved to Milan, where his most popular opera, GUARANY, was perf. Other operas written in Italy were *Fosca* (Sc. 1873) and *Salvator Rosa* (Genoa 1874), both to libs by GHISLANZONI; *Maria Tudor* (Sc. 1879), lib. Emilio Praga based on HUGO's drama, and *Côndor* (Sc. 1891). During a visit to his native Brazil, 1880–9, *Lo Schiavo* (*The Slave*) was prod. at T. Lírico Fluminense, Rio de Janeiro, 1889; it was restaged at T. Municipal, Rio, 1921, with choreography by Léonide Massine. Gomes was the only South American opera comp. to gain international recognition before GINASTERA; his music is generally Italianate in style, even in *Il Guarany* where the subject matter is Brazilian; but in *Lo Schiavo* native instruments such as chocalhos, maracas, and inubias enrich the orchestra to give an indigenous flavour to the Indian dance. MK

Gomez, Jill, b. New Amsterdam, British Guiana (now Guyana), 21 Sept 1942. British soprano; lived in Trinidad from age of 3 months until 1955. Studied RAM and Guildhall School of Mus. Debut 1968, Glyndebourne Touring co. as ADINA, at Glyndebourne itself as MÉLISANDE (1969). CG debut 1970, creating Flora (KNOT GARDEN). Created role of the Countess (VOICE OF ARIADNE) at Aldeburgh (1974). Has sung MOZART roles successfully with SO. Natural stage presence and pure, silvery voice. AB

Gondoliers, The, *or The King of Barataria*, operetta, 2 acts, SULLIVAN, lib. GILBERT. London, Savoy T., 7 Dec 1889. NY, 7 Jan 1890. Main chars: Giannetta (sop.) Tessa (mezzo-sop.) Marco (ten.) Giuseppe (bar.) Duke of Plaza-Toro (buffo) Duchess (contr.) Casilda (sop.) Luiz (ten.) Grand Inquisitor (bass-bar.). Through a baby-farmer's error, the two gondoliers Marco and Giuseppe are under consideration as rightful King of Barataria, and must reign jointly until the matter is resolved. Eventually the heir to the throne is identified as Luiz, servant to the Duke of Plaza-Toro and in love with his daughter Casilda. JB O
See Lubbock

Goodall, Reginald, b. Lincoln, 13 July 1905. English conductor. After study at RCM, London, and in Munich and Vienna, he joined the mus. staff at CG, 1936. Cond. with SW, 1944, where he cond. premiere of PETER GRIMES (1945). Cond. RAPE OF LUCRETIA at Glyndebourne (1946) and was apptd to the mus. staff of the newly formed Royal Opera, CG. Since MANON (1947), he has cond. many repertory operas there, but has also given notable perfs of WOZZECK, MEISTERSINGER, TRISTAN UND ISOLDE, and PARSIFAL. In 1970 at the Coliseum, he began to build up RING DES NIBELUNGEN with the SW co., and in 1973 cond. two complete cycles, sung in Eng., for which he received great critical acclaim. EF

Good Soldier Schweik, The, opera, 2 acts, KURKA, lib. Lewis Allen (pseud.) from the novel by Jaroslav Hasek. NY CC 23 Apr 1958; Dresden 10 Nov 1959; East Berlin, KO, 1960. Main chars: Schweik (ten.) Baroness (sop.) Lt Lukash (bar.) Fox (a dog). The scene is set in Bohemia before and after World War I. Joseph Schweik, personifying shrewd wisdom beneath a foolish exterior, becomes involved in absurd situations related through a series of tableaux. EJ

Goossens. Three generations of musicians, of Belgian origin. **Eugene I,** b. Bruges, 25 Feb 1845; d. Liverpool, 30 Dec 1906. Conductor. Joined Carl Rosa 1882; cond. first perf. in Eng. of TANNHÄUSER 1882. **Eugene II,** b. Bordeaux, France, 28 Jan 1867; d. London, 31 July 1958. Conductor. Worked with several companies, incl. Moody-Manners, before becoming principal cond. Carl Rosa, 1899–1915; then joined Beecham's co. **Eugene III,** b. London, 28 May 1893; d. London, 13 June 1962. Conductor and composer. As cond. worked mainly in the concert hall. Wrote two operas, JUDITH (comp. 1925) and *Don Juan de Mañara* (comp. 1934, perf. CG 1937), lib. Arnold Bennett based on MÉRIMÉE. LO

Goring Thomas, Arthur *see* THOMAS

Gorr, Rita [Marguerite Geimaert], b. Ghent, 18 Feb 1926. Belgian mezzo-soprano. Studied at Ghent and Brussels. Competition prize-winner Verviers 1946; Ostend 1949; Lausanne 1952. Debut, 1949, Antwerp, as FRICKA. Member Strasbourg O. 1949–52; Paris O. 1952–5 – resigned from boredom with minor roles. Other debuts: 1957 Bayreuth Fest. (Fricka); 1959 CG (AMNERIS); 1961 Edinburgh Fest. (IPHIGÉNIE EN TAURIDE, title role); 1962 NY Met. Much admired for richness of tone and intensity of vocal and dramatic character in these roles; also sings KUNDRY, ORTRUD, EBOLI, DALILA. NG

Gossec, François Joseph, b. Vergnies, Hainaut, 17 Jan 1734; d. Passy, nr Paris, 16 Feb 1829. Belgian-French composer. Between 1765 and 1803 wrote *c.* 20 operas mostly for Paris, popular in their day, now largely forgotten. When GLUCK left Paris in 1776 Gossec was entrusted with modifications to ALCESTE (Paris version). Cond. at Paris O. 1780–5. LO

Götterdämmerung *see* RING DES NIBELUNGEN

Götz, Hermann, b. Königsberg (now Kaliningrad), 7 Dec 1840; d. Hottingen, Switzerland, 3 Dec 1876. German composer. Remembered now by one opera, WIDERSPENSTIGEN ZÄHMUNG. LO

Gounod, Charles François, b. Paris, 17 June 1818; d. Saint-Cloud, Paris, 17 Oct 1893. French composer. Studied at Paris Cons. with PAER and LESUEUR; *Prix de Rome* 1839. His first opera, *Sapho*, was comp. in 1851, followed in 1854 by *La Nonne Sanglante*, based on M. G. Lewis's melodramatic novel *The Monk*. First success came in 1858 with MÉDECIN MALGRÉ LUI, followed in 1859 by the work for which he is universally known, FAUST. PHILÉMON ET BAUCIS (1860) and REINE DE SABA (1862), were not well received, but MIREILLE (1864) retrieved his fortune and reputation. Five more followed, of which only ROMÉO ET JULIETTE (1867) made a significant mark. The others are *La Colombe* (1866); CINQ-MARS (1877), *Polyeucte* (1878), and *Le Tribut de Zamora* (1881). LO

Goyescas, opera, 3 scenes, by GRANADOS, lib. Fernando Periquet. NY Met, 28 Jan 1916; Paris, O., 1919; London, RCM, 11 July 1951. Main chars: Rosario (sop.) Fernando (ten.) Paquiro (bar.) Pepa (mezzo-sop.). Characters and setting are suggested by paintings and drawings by Goya, whose work permeated the comp.'s creative and imaginative activity. The music of the opera was expanded from that of a suite of piano pieces bearing the same title. The aristocratic Rosario arouses the jealousy of her lover, Fernando, by paying attention to Paquiro, a torero. Pepa, Paquiro's sweetheart, is also enraged. Fernando escorts Rosario to a ball, where Paquiro challenges him to a duel. Rosario, who sings the famous 'The Lover and the Nightingale', meets Fernando briefly before the duel in which he is killed. Despite its hauntingly expressive music the opera has never been successful enough to find a place in the international repertoire. FGB
See Kobbé

Gozzi, Carlo, b. Venice, 13 Dec 1720; d. Venice, 14 Apr 1806. Italian playwright. Works on which operas are based incl.: *L'Amore delle Tre Melarance* (*The Love for Three Oranges*), 1761 (PROKOFIEV, 1921); *La Donna Serpente* (*Woman as Serpent*), 1762 (FEEN, 1888; Alfredo Casella, 1931); *Il Re Cervo* (*King Stag*), 1761 (KÖNIG HIRSCH, 1956); *Turandot*, 1762 (BUSONI, 1917; PUCCINI, 1926). LO

Graener, Paul, b. Berlin, 11 Jan 1872; d. Salzburg, 13 Nov 1944. German composer and conductor. His eight operas incl. *Don Juans Letztes Abenteuer* (*Don Juan's Last Adventure*),

1914; *Friedemann Bach*, 1931; and PRINZ VON HOMBURG (based on KLEIST), 1935. LO

Graf, Herbert, b. Vienna, 10 Apr 1904; d. Geneva, 5 Apr 1973. Austrian, later American, producer. Studied at Vienna; worked at Münster, Breslau (Wrocław), and Frankfurt before moving to USA, 1934. Stage dir. NY Met, 1936–60. While in USA also prod. several operas at Montreal, incl. Canada's first TRISTAN UND ISOLDE. Returned to Europe in 1960; 1960–3, art. dir. at Zürich and, from 1965 until his death, at Geneva, where he did much to enhance the importance of the Grand T. Also prod. at Salzburg, CG, Sc., and elsewhere. LO

Graham, Colin, b. Hove, Sussex, 22 Sept 1931. English producer. Assoc. with the EOG since 1953, he prod, the first perfs of BRITTEN's three Church Parables, *Noye's Fludde*, DEATH IN VENICE, WALTON's *Bear*, VOICE OF ARIADNE, as well as DIDO AND AENEAS, IDOMENEO, MIDSUMMER NIGHT'S DREAM, ALBERT HERRING, and RAPE OF LUCRETIA. For SO he has dir. PETER GRIMES, CENERENTOLA, PELLÉAS ET MÉLISANDE, and at Glyndebourne, MAW's *Rising of the Moon*. At SW he staged MINES OF SULPHUR and GLORIANA; at the Coliseum, where he is resident prod. for ENO, his prods incl. FORZA DEL DESTINO, CONTES D'HOFFMANN, WAR AND PEACE, MANON, MADAMA BUTTERFLY, and DON CARLOS. He dir. OWEN WINGRAVE for BBC TV and at CG, and staged *Death in Venice* at the Met. EF

Granados (y Campiña), Enrique, b. Lérida, 27 July 1867; d. at sea 24 Mar 1916 (the ship in which he was returning to Spain from NY was torpedoed by a U-boat). Spanish composer. Studied in Barcelona, which he later made his home. His operas incl. *María del Carmen* (1898), *Petrarca* (1901), *Follet* (1903), *Gaziel* (1906), *Liliana* (1911), and GOYESCAS (1916). FGB

La Grande Duchesse de Gérolstein, premiere, T. des Variétés, Paris, 1867; SCHNEIDER as the Duchess

Grande Duchesse de Gérolstein, La, *opéra bouffe*, 3 acts, OFFENBACH, lib. MEILHAC and L. HALÉVY. Paris, T. des Variétés, 12 Apr 1867; London, CG, 18 Nov 1867 – (last opera in Eng. there until 1919); NY 1867. Revived San Francisco 1973; WNO 1975. SCHNEIDER as the Duchess scored one of her greatest successes in this satire ridiculing the self-importance and incompetence of Europe's military ruling class. LO
See Lubbock

Grandi, Margherita, b. Hobart, Tasmania, 10 Oct 1899. Italian soprano. Studied with Giannina Russ. Debut, 1932, Milan, as AIDA and sang throughout Italy in subsequent years. British debut 1939, Glyndebourne, as LADY MACBETH. Cambridge T., with New London O. as TOSCA. CG debut, creating Diana in OLYMPIANS, 1949. Forceful, large-scale singer and actress. AB

Grand Opera 1. The popular name for serious opera which is sung throughout (i.e., no spoken dialogue). 2. The typical 19th-c. *grand opéra* of the Paris O., conceived on a large scale, lavishly produced, and including a substantial ballet, estab. by SPONTINI and above all by MEYERBEER. Its influence can be seen in VERDI and WAGNER. LO

Grant, Clifford, b. Sydney, 11 Sept 1933. Australian bass. After singing with New South Wales O., in 1965 he accompanied the SUTHERLAND tour of Australia. Joined SW 1966; US debut, 1966, San Francisco. The dark colour and resonance of his voice are specially suitable to the bass roles of VERDI and WAGNER, and his repertory incl. Zaccaria (NABUCCO), SPARAFUCILE, Padre Guardiano (FORZA DEL DESTINO), and PHILIPPE, as well as Henry the Fowler (LOHENGRIN), POGNER, FAFNER, HUNDING, and HAGEN. He also sings the Commendatore (DON GIOVANNI) and Trulove (RAKE'S PROGRESS). CG debut, 1974, as BARTOLO (NOZZE DI FIGARO). EF

Grassini, Josephina [Giuseppina], b. Varese, 8 Apr 1773; d. Milan, 3 Jan 1850. Italian contralto. Studied at Milan Cons.; debut, 1789, Parma, in comic opera. She turned successfully to *opera seria* three years later. Napoleon heard her in Milan after the battle of Marengo and engaged her for the O. where she created a sensation at her debut, 22 July 1800, and was known as 'the Tenth Muse'. She became very popular in London where she first appeared in 1804. She made her last appearance in Paris in 1829, then became a successful teacher. Her pupils incl. PASTA and her nieces Giulia and Giuditta GRISI. She m. César Ragani. PS

Grau, Maurice, b. Brno [Brünn], 1849; d. Paris, 14 Mar 1907. Czech impresario. Moved to USA as a boy. With Henry Abbey (1846–96), managed NY Met 1890–6, then until 1903 on his own. On the death of HARRIS took over CG, 1896–1900, thus for a time managing the two main opera houses of Britain and the USA. At the Met he gave operas in their original languages, championed the WAGNER music dramas, and introduced many star singers and conds to NY; it was one of the Met's brightest periods. LO

Graun, Karl Heinrich, b. Wahrenbrück, 7 May 1704 (?); d. Berlin, 8 Aug 1759. German composer and singer, MdC to Prince Frederick, later Frederick the Great. His *Cleopatra e Cesare* was the opening opera of Berlin's Unter den Linden Opernhaus, 7 Dec 1742. Wrote *c.* 30 operas, of which MONTEZUMA is interesting as an early example of a modern subject in 18th-c. opera. LO

Graz, Steiermark, Austria. Active operatically in 18th c.; Mingotti's Co. there, and a theatre built 1776. SCHALK was mus. dir. there one season, 1889–90. Opera is given in the Opernhaus, built 1899, damaged in 1944. *Intendant*, Carl Nemath; mus. dir. Berislav Klobucar. LO

Great Britain. Opera has largely centred on London, with minor but sometimes important subsidiary centres in Dublin, Glasgow, Edinburgh. There has been a wealth of comps since PURCELL, who with more luck and in different circumstances might, with John Dryden, have established an English Opera.

In the 18th c. HANDEL's *opere serie* were offset by BEGGAR'S OPERA and the lightweight vernacular opera of ARNE, ARNOLD, Charles Dibdin, and SHIELD. In the 19th c. BALFE, BARNETT, BISHOP, V. WALLACE were followed by COWEN and STANFORD, with SULLIVAN's comic operas in a class by themselves. Touring cos provided opera in the provinces, and sometimes in the capital. The 20th c. has seen important regional developments such as WNO and SO as well as Glyndebourne. The outstanding comps are BRITTEN and TIPPETT; others whose works have been heard abroad include DELIUS, BENNETT, BERKELEY, BUSH, GOEHR, and SEARLE. Singers have made the international grade since A. STORACE, KELLY, and BILLINGTON; the present-day list is too long to attempt. The first Englishman to cond. at an international season at CG was Alfred Mellon (1821–67), sharing it in 1855 with Michael Costa, who had settled in London. Early this century BEECHAM blazed a brilliant trail, followed by COATES, Sir Malcolm Sargent, Sir John Barbirolli and more recently DOWNES, GOODALL, MACKERRAS, and LOCKHART. LO

Greece. The National Hellenic Opera was organized in 1898 by Dinisios Lavangra, Greek comp. (1864–1941), beginning with BOHÈME, 1900. The National Lyric T. was opened 1940, becoming the National Opera, 1944. The National Opera Co. mounts summer open-air fests in Athens at the Herod Atticus T. adjoining the Acropolis, with their own or visiting cos. LO

Greek drama and legend have influenced opera since the time of the Florentine Camerata. MONTEVERDI and LULLY in the 17th c., RAMEAU and GLUCK in the 18th c. were the chief composers. The 19th c. with its emotional romanticism reacted against this (BERLIOZ was an exception), but a marked revival came with the 20th c. The Ger. August Bungert, 1845–1915, wrote a Homeric tetralogy on Wagnerian lines, perf. Dresden 1896–1903; other works incl. PROMÉTHÉE, ELEKTRA, Egon Wellesz's *Alkestis*, 1924, OEDIPUS REX, ANTIGONE, ORFF's *Antigonae*, 1949, OEDIPUS DER TYRANN, ALKMENE and KING PRIAM. (*See* AESCHYLUS, EURIPIDES, HOMER, SOPHOCLES.) LO

Greek Passion, The, opera, 4 acts, MARTINŮ, lib. composer after the novel by Nikos Kazantzakis. Zürich, Municipal T., 9 June 1961. Main chars: Grigoris (bass-bar.) Michelis (ten.) Kostandis (bar.) Yannakos (ten.) Manolios (ten.) Panait (ten.) Catherine (sop.) Lenio (sop.) Fotis (bass-bar.). A passion play is to be put on in a Greek village. The actors begin in their lives to take on characteristics of their parts so that the Christ, Manolios, son of a rich farmer, pleads compassion for a group of refugees. He is supported by his three 'apostles' (Michelis, Kostandis, Yannakos) and by the village prostitute, Catherine, who is to play Magdalene. The priest, Grigoris, an unwitting Pharisee, denies the refugees shelter and, feeling his authority usurped, excommunicates Manolios, who is then killed by Panait, the Judas. Wr. in Eng. at the end of his life, this is one of Martinů's most powerful and dramatic works

Colour plate: NABUCCO, London, CG, 21 Mar 1972, produced KAŠLÍK, scenery SVOBODA, costumes Jan Skalicky. D. WARD as Zaccaria.

with impressive choral scenes based on a close study of Orthodox church music. JT
See Šafránek, *Bohuslav Martinů* (London 1962); Large, *Martinů* (London 1975)

Gregor, Bohumil, b. Prague, 14 July 1926. Czech conductor. Studied at Prague Cons. and worked as *répétiteur* and cond. in Prague (1947–9), and under CHALABALA in Brno (1949–51). Head of opera at Ostrava 1958–62, then returned to Prague. Has cond. opera in most major cities, holding appointments in Stockholm (1965–9) and Hamburg (from 1969). Specialized in JANÁČEK. JT

Gregor, Joseph, b. Cernăuţi [Chernovtsy], Romania, 26 Oct 1888; d. Vienna, 12 Oct 1961. Austrian theatre historian and librettist. Wrote libs for FRIEDENSTAG, DAPHNE, and LIEBE DER DANAE. Among his writings *Das Russische Theater* (Zürich 1928) (*The Russian Theatre*, London 1930) is important. LO

Greindl, Josef, b. Munich, 23 Dec 1912. German bass. Studied Munich; debut there 1935. Berlin Staats. O. 1942–8; Städtische O. from 1948. Bayreuth 1943, and leading bass there since 1951. Has appeared frequently at Salzburg Fest. since 1956, and has been guest star in Europe and S. America. LO

Gretel, sop., Hänsel's sister in HÄNSEL UND GRETEL

Grétry, André Ernest, b. Liège, 11 Feb 1741; d. Montmorency, nr Paris, 24 Apr 1813. Belgian composer. Taste for opera developed in boyhood from hearing a touring co. in Liège. Travelled to Rome 1759, where his first opera was prod. 1765. Arrived Paris 1767, where his 50 operas, mostly *opéras comiques*, were prod. They incl.: HURON (1768), his first success, ZÉMIRE ET AZOR (1771), *Fausse Magie* (1775), RICHARD CŒUR-DE-LION (1784), *Le Caravane du Caire* (1783). His *Guillaume Tell* (1791), with lib. SEDAINE, antedates both ROSSINI's opera and SCHILLER's play. LO

Grimm, Friedrich Melchior von (Baron), b. Ratisbon, 26 Dec 1723; d. Gotha, 18 Dec 1807. German writer. Lived in Paris from 1750 until the Revolution. Edited the *Correspondance littéraire, philosophique et critique* 1753–90, circulating in Germany in ms and later pub. – an important source for the history of opera in France. LO

Grimm brothers: Jakob Ludwig, b. Hanau, 4 Jan 1785; d. Berlin, 20 Sept 1863; and **Wilhelm Carl,** b. Hanau, 24 Feb 1786; d. Berlin, 16 Dec 1859. German scholars whose collections of fairy tales, *Kinder- und Hausmärchen* (1812–15), have provided material for operas. The best known are HÄNSEL UND GRETEL and MOND. LO

Grisélidis, *conte lyrique*, prologue and 3 acts, MASSENET, lib. Armand Sylvestre and Eugène Morand. Paris, OC, 20 Nov 1901; NY, Manhattan OH, 19 Jan 1910. The story comes from G. BOCCACCIO, and appears as 'The pleasant comedy of patient Griselidis' in Geoffrey Chaucer's *Canterbury Tales*. Griselda, the wife who remains constant in the face of repeated hurts inflicted on her by her husband, was the subject of at least 12 18th-c. operas. BIZET began one, on a lib. by SARDOU. LO

Grisi, Giuditta, b. Milan, 28 July 1805; d. Robecco sul Naviglio, 1 May 1840. Italian mezzo-soprano. Eclipsed by the greater fame of her sister Giulia GRISI, and her cousin, the ballerina, Carlotta Grisi, she was nevertheless considered one of the most important mezzo-sops of the 19th c., despite a tragically short career. After studying at the Milan Cons., 1822–5, she appeared at the principal opera houses of Italy and at the TI. In Venice, 11 Mar 1830, she created the role of Romeo in CAPULETI ED I MONTECCHI for BELLINI, and was also the first to sing the title role in Luigi Ricci's opera *Chiara di Rosembergh*. She retired after m. Count Barni. PS

Grisi, Giulia, b. Milan, 28 July 1811; d. Berlin, 29 Nov 1869. Italian soprano. One of the most celebrated prima donnas of the 19th c. Her sister Giuditta GRISI and her aunt GRASSINI were famous mezzo-sops, her cousin, Carlotta Grisi, a celebrated ballerina. Studied with Marco Aureliano Marliani; debut, 1828, Bologna, as Emma in ROSSINI's *Zelmira*. Successes in Florence and Pisa led to a contract at Sc. where she created the role of ADALGISA. Dissatisfied with minor roles, she broke her contract to go to Paris, and never sang in Italy again. Debut 16 Oct 1832, TI, under Rossini's direction as SEMIRAMIDE, and during her 17-year reign at the TI created the role of Elvira (PURITANI, 1835). London debut 1834 in GAZZA LADRA, and appeared there regularly for 27 years. DONIZETTI wrote the role of NORINA for her in 1843. In 1844 she m. the ten. MARIO. They toured the USA together, 1854. She retired in 1861, making one final disastrous appearance as LUCREZIA BORGIA (London 1866). PS

Grist, Reri, b. NY, 1932. American soprano of captivating charm and vocal agility, widely

Colour plate: Stage model for first performance of TRISTAN UND ISOLDE, designed by Angelo QUAGLIO. This realistic stage setting was of a type approved of by WAGNER.

popular in Europe. Began singing at age of 16 while recovering from injury as dancer. Played Consuelo in original Broadway production of WEST SIDE STORY (1957). Opera debut, 1959, Santa Fe O., as ADELE. European debut, 1960, Cologne O., as QUEEN OF THE NIGHT; joined Zürich O. 1961. UK debuts: 1962, Glyndebourne Fest. as ZERBINETTA; CG as Queen of Shemakhan (GOLDEN COCKEREL). Frequent appearances Salzburg Fest. from 1964; NY Met from 1965; Vienna Staats O. from 1966. A distinctive sparkling timbre of voice and flexibility of technique ideal for MOZART soubrettes (SUSANNA, DESPINA, BLONDE), and lead roles in some DONIZETTI operas (LUCIA DI LAMMERMOOR, ELISIR D'AMORE, DON PASQUALE). Has also successfully appeared as ROSINA, GILDA, and in the title role in LAKMÉ. NG

Gruenberg, Louis Theodore, b. Brest Litovsk, Poland, 3 Aug 1884; d. Los Angeles, 9 June 1964. American composer. In USA from the age of two; attended schools in NY. Studied in Berlin (1903) with BUSONI, also at the Vienna Cons. Returned to USA 1919 and became enthusiastic over the possibilities of jazz, using it in *Daniel Jazz* (1923), a year before GERSHWIN'S *Rhapsody*. After discussions with Eugene O'Neill, Gruenberg secured permission to set EMPEROR JONES. Other operas are *Jack and the Beanstalk* (Juilliard School, 31 Nov 1930) and, for radio, *Green Mansions* (1937). EJ

Grümmer, Elisabeth, b. Diedenhofen, Alsace, 31 Mar 1911. German soprano. Actress at Aachen before becoming singer at the opera co. there, 1941, at KARAJAN'S behest. At Duisburg before being engaged at the Städtische O., Berlin, 1946. CG debut (as EVA) 1951 under BEECHAM. Bayreuth debut (as Eva) 1957. Excelled in that role and in MOZART and R. STRAUSS roles through her lovely voice, pure style, and natural stage personality. AB

Guadagni, Gaetano, b. Lodi, *c.* 1725; d. Padua, Nov 1792. Italian male contralto, later soprano. Pupil of GIZZIELLO. Sang in HANDEL'S oratorios in London where he met GARRICK who taught him acting. Became friend of GLUCK; created title roles in his ORFEO and *Telemacco*, 1765. Retired to Padua where he perf. operas in his house on a puppet stage. LO

Guarany, Il, opera, 4 acts, GOMES, lib. (in It.) Tomaso Scalvini, revised Carlo d'Ormeville, based on novel by José Martiniano de Alençar which he also adapted for the stage. Milan, Sc., 19 Mar 1870; Rio de Janeiro, T. Municipal, 2 Dec 1870; London, CG, 13 July 1872; NY, 3 Nov 1884. Main chars: Don Antonio de Mariz (bass) Cecilia (sop.) Pery, Il Guarany (ten.) Don Alvaro (ten.) Gonzales (bar.) Ruy-Bento (ten.) Alonso (bass) Pedro (bass) Chief of the Aimorè tribe (bass). Pery, of Guarani royal blood, rescues Cecilia, whom he loves, from the Spanish Gonzales, Ruy-Bento and Alonso, who have planned to deliver her into the hands of the enemy Aimorè tribe. Don Antonio (Cecilia's father) and his Portuguese retinue arrive in time to free the lovers, after the Indians have performed ritual dances to honour Il Guarany's impending death. Although Cecilia and Pery reach safety and freedom, Don Antonio dies when a dynamite charge that kills the Spanish villains explodes in his castle. *Il Guarany* was perf. an unprecedented 48 times at Rio's T. Municipal. Two years after its premiere the opera's *Preludio* was replaced by the popular *Symphonia do 'Guarany'* which contains the opera's chief motifs and became identified with Brazilian nationalism; it is often perf. on official occasions. MK

Güden, Hilde, b. Vienna, 15 Sept 1917. Austrian soprano. Debut, 1939, Zürich as CHERUBINO. At Munich 1941; Vienna 1946; CG 1947; NY Met 1950. Has also sung at Salzburg, Sc., and other major European opera houses. Able to encompass both lyric and coloratura roles, she excels in MOZART and R. STRAUSS. Her repertory incl. Ilia (IDOMENEO), SUSANNA, SOPHIE, ZERBINETTA, Aminta (SCHWEIGSAME FRAU), Marzelline (FIDELIO), GILDA, and also the part of Anne Trulove (RAKE'S PROGRESS). EF

Guerrero, Jacinto, b. Ajofrín, 16 Aug 1895; d. Madrid, 15 Aug 1951. Spanish composer. He comp. about 50 *zarzuelas*, of which the most famous are *Los Gavilanes* and *La Alsaciana*. FGB

Guglielmo, bar., Fiordiligi's lover in COSÌ FAN TUTTE

Gui, Henri, b. Bordeaux, 23 Oct 1923. French baritone. Originally a ten. operetta singer, he specializes in high Fr. bar. roles such as Pelléas (PELLÉAS ET MÉLISANDE) which he has sung at Vienna, Sc., Glyndebourne, and Strasbourg (1962, the DEBUSSY centenary year), Naples, San Francisco (1969), and Aix-en-Provence (1972). He also sings MALHEURS D'ORPHÉE (Piccola Scala, 1963, and Paris OC, 1972), Mercutio in ROMÉO ET JULIETTE (Wexford, 1967), the Duc de Rothesay in JOLIE FILLE DE PERTH (Wexford, 1968), and Henri de Valois in ROI MALGRÉ LUI. Modern operas in his repertory are JUNGE LORD, MINES OF SULPHUR, and Daniel Lesur's *Andrea del Sarto*, in whose first performance he took part (Marseille 1969). EF

Gui, Vittorio, b. Rome, 14 Sept 1885; d. Florence, 17 Oct 1975. Italian conductor. Studied Rome; debut there, 1907, GIOCONDA. Succeeded CAMPANINI at T. S. Carlo, Naples, 1910; 1925–8 mus. dir., new T. Torino, Turin. One of the founders and chief conds of Florence Maggio Musicale. Followed BUSCH as chief cond. at Glyndebourne, 1951; also cond. at CG and at other Continental European houses. LO

Guillard, Nicolas François, b. Chartres, 16 Jan 1752; d. Paris, 26 Dec 1814. French librettist. Of his 12 or so libs written for GRÉTRY, PAISIELLO, SALIERI, and others the best was IPHIGÉNIE EN TAURIDE, written for GLUCK – 'the best opera book that ever came into Gluck's hands' (Alfred Einstein). LO

Guillaume Tell (*William Tell*), grand opera, 4 acts, ROSSINI, lib. JOUY and H. E. F. Bis after SCHILLER. Paris, O., 3 Aug 1829; London, DL, 1 May 1830 (in Eng.); CG, 6 June 1845 (in Fr.); NY, Park T., 19 Sept 1831 (in Eng.); NY, 16 June 1845 (in Fr.). Main chars: Tell (bar.) Mathilde (sop.) Arnold (ten.) Jemmy (sop.) Gessler (bass). The story of William Tell, the shooting of the apple, the uprising of the Swiss against the Austrians, and the love of the Swiss patriot Arnold for the Austrian Mathilde. Rossini's last opera and his greatest in scope. JB O
See Kobbé

Guiraud, Ernest, b. New Orleans, 23 June 1837; d. Paris, 6 May 1892. French composer. His eight operas made little stir (one, *Piccolino*, 1876, was perf. by Carl Rosa, London 1879); today remembered solely for the recitatives he added to CARMEN for its first perf. in Vienna and for his completion of the orchestration of CONTES D'HOFFMANN. LO

Gunther, bar., Hagen's half-brother in GÖTTERDÄMMERUNG

Guntram, opera, 3 acts, R. STRAUSS, lib. composer. Weimar, 10 May 1894. The work was a failure, and even after a revision, with extensive cuts, it has not entered the repertory. LO

Guridi, Jesús, b. Vitoria, 25 Sept 1886; d. Madrid, 7 Apr 1961. Spanish (Basque) composer. Studied with d'INDY in Paris, then in Brussels and Cologne. His works include the operas *Mirentxu* (1910) and *Amaya* (1920), and the popular *zarzuela El Caserio* (1926). FGB

Gurlitt, Manfred, b. Berlin, 6 Sept 1890; d. Tokyo, 29 Apr 1972. German composer and conductor. After the rise to power of the Nazis he left Germany for Japan, where he cond. opera. His own comps incl. a setting of BÜCHNER's *Wozzeck*, prod. 1926. LO

Gustave III, *ou Le Bal Masqué* (*Gustavus III, or the Masked Ball*), opera, 5 acts, AUBER, lib. SCRIBE, on which Antonio Somma based his lib. for BALLO IN MASCHERA. Paris, O., 27 Feb 1833; London, CG (in Eng., tr. PLANCHÉ), 13 Nov 1833. LO

Gutheil-Schoder, Marie, b. Weimar, 10 Feb 1874; d. Bad Ilmenau, 8 Oct 1935. German soprano. Studied Weimar; debut there as First Lady in ZAUBERFLÖTE (1891). After guest engagements in Leipzig, Berlin, and Vienna, joined the Vienna Hofoper under MAHLER's regime. Her CARMEN, ELEKTRA, and OCTAVIAN were much admired. CG as Octavian (1913). Retired 1926. AB

Guthrie, Tyrone, b. Tunbridge Wells, 2 July 1900; d. Newbliss, 15 May 1971. English producer. Worked at the London Old Vic from 1933 before becoming dir. of SW. (1941). His outstanding prods during that period included TRAVIATA and an evocative, controversial CARMEN. Debut at CG with PETER GRIMES (1947); *La Traviata* there (1948). Debut at the Met, with *Carmen* (1952), returning for *La Traviata* (1957). Approached opera from a theatrical rather than musical standpoint; prods were notable for vivid handling of both principals and chorus. AB

Gutrune, sop., Gunther's sister in GÖTTERDÄMMERUNG

Guttman, Irving, b. Chatham, Ontario, 27 Oct 1928. Canadian producer. Studied in Toronto with GEIGER-TOREL, then began opera in Montreal in 1953. From 1956, many prods with Montreal Symphony Orch. and Montreal Opera Guild. US debut, 1958, Santa Fe, then work in many US cities incl. Houston, Philadelphia, Pittsburgh, European debut, 1969, Barcelona. With estab. of Vancouver O. Assoc., he became its first art. dir., 1960–74; since 1966 art. dir., Edmonton O. Assoc. CM

Guys and Dolls, musical, LOESSER, book Jo Swerling and Abe Burrows. NY, 46th Street T., 24 Nov 1950; London Coliseum, 28 May 1953. EJ ★

Gwendoline, opera, 2 acts, CHABRIER, lib. MENDÈS. Brussels, T. de la Monnaie, 10 Apr

1886; Paris, O., 17 Dec 1893. Chabrier's only completed tragic opera. Harald the Dane invades Britain; Gwendoline, daughter of the Saxon leader Armel, pleads with Harald to save Armel's life. He agrees, provided Armel will consent to his marriage to Gwendoline. But the Danes are treacherously murdered, at Armel's instigation. Harald, refusing to escape, is killed by Armel; Gwendoline stabs herself. LO
See Myers, *Emmanuel Chabrier and His Circle* (London 1969; Rutherford, N. J. 1970)

Gypsy Baron, The *see* ZIGEUNERBARON

H

Hába, Alois, b. Vizovice, 21 June 1893; d. Prague, 18 Nov 1973. Czech composer. Studied with NOVÁK in Prague (1914–15), in Vienna (1917–20) and with SCHREKER in Berlin (1920–2), and was influenced both by BUSONI and SCHÖNBERG. An enthusiastic advocate of microtonal music, he was professor of quarter-tone and sixth-tone composition at Prague Cons. (later Acad.) from 1923 and continued to teach there even after this department was closed in 1948. His second opera *The Mother* (*Matka*, 1931, under SCHERCHEN in Munich) employed quarter-tones much in the same way that Moravian folk singers use microtonal inflection to brighten or darken the mood of the music they are singing. A third opera (employing sixth-tones), *Thy Kingdom Come* (*Přijď království Tvé*, 1939–42), has not been perf. JT

habanera. Spanish dance, 2/4 time, of Cuban origin. The only notable example is 'L'amour est un oiseau rebelle' in CARMEN (Act I), the origin of which is a song in habanera rhythm, *El Arregilito*, by Sebastián Yradier. LO

Hadley, Henry Kimball, b. Somerville, Mass., 20 Dec 1871; d. NY, 6 Sept 1937. American composer. Most successful operas: AZORA, DAUGHTER OF MONTEZUMA, and *Cleopatra's Night*, lib. Alice Leal Pollock based on Théophile Gautier's story, *Une Nuit de Cléopatre*, NY Met 1920. LO

Hagen, bass, Alberich's son in GÖTTERDÄMMERUNG

Hahn, Reynaldo, b. Caracas, Venezuela, 9 Aug 1875; d. Paris, 28 Jan 1947. French composer and conductor. Of his eight stage works the most successful was the operetta CIBOULETTE, still played frequently in Fr. Also wrote a SHAKESPEARE opera, *Le Marchand de Venise* (1935). Dir. of Paris O, 1945–6. LO

Hajibeyov [Gadzhibekov], Uzeir Abdul Husein, b. Agjabedi, nr Shusha, 17 Sept 1885; d. Baku, 23 Nov 1948. Azerbaijani composer. Known particularly for the first Azerbaijani opera LEYLI AND MEDZHNUN, which makes use of folksong and the improvisatory *mugam*. He continued in this vein for his next operas: *Sheikh Sanan* (1909), *Rustam and Zokhrab* (1910), *Asli and Kerem* (1912), and *Shah Abbas and Khurshid Banu* (1912); his masterpiece is the epic *Kyor-ogly* (1937). *Garun and Leyda* (comp. 1915) was not staged; *Firuza* was unfinished. GN

Haken, Eduard, b. Shklin, Volyn, USSR, 28 Mar 1910. Czech bass. Studied singing privately and after singing in the Olomouc co. (1938–41), joined the Prague NT in 1941. His powerful, wide-ranging and distinctive voice has served both serious and comic roles in Czech opera, from the Water Goblin in RUSALKA (which he played in the 1964 Edinburgh tour) to KECAL. JT

Halévy [Lévy], Jacques François Fromental Élie, b. Paris, 27 May 1799; d. Nice, 17 Mar 1862. French composer. Studied Cons. with CHERUBINI; won *Prix de Rome* 1819. His masterpiece, JUIVE, appeared in 1835; of his other 36 operas those which had some success were *L'Éclair* (OC 1835); *La Reine de Chypre* (O. 1841); *La Dame de Pique*, lib. SCRIBE based on MÉRIMÉE's tr. of PUSHKIN (OC 1850). LO

Halévy, Ludovic, b. Paris, 1 Jan 1834; d. Paris, 3 May 1908. French librettist, nephew of J. F. HALÉVY. In collaboration with MEILHAC wrote libs for OFFENBACH's *Barbe-Bleue* (1866), BELLE HÉLÈNE, *Les Brigands* (1870), GRANDE DUCHESSE DE GÉROLSTEIN, PÉRICHOLE, and VIE PARISIENNE; for LECOCQ's *Le Petit Duc* (1878); for CARMEN. Collaborated with Léon Battu in DOCTEUR MIRACLE and with Hector Crémieux in ORPHÉE AUX ENFERS. LO

Halka (*Helen*), opera, 2 acts, MONIUSZKO, lib. Włodzimierz Wolski based on a story of Kazimierz Władysław Wojcicki. Wilno, 20 Dec 1847; first professional prod. (in 4 acts) Warsaw, 1 Jan 1903; London, University Coll., 8 Feb 1961. Moniuszko's most successful opera and the most popular Polish one. LO

Hall, Peter Reginald Frederick, b. Bury St Edmunds, 22 Nov 1930. English producer. He directed the first perfs of GARDNER's *Moon and*

Sixpence (SW 1957) and KNOT GARDEN (CG 1970). Responsible for notable prods at CG of MOSES UND ARON (1965), ZAUBERFLÖTE (1966), TRISTAN UND ISOLDE, and EUGENE ONEGIN (1971). At Glyndebourne he has dir. CALISTO (1970), RITORNO D'ULISSE IN PATRIA (1972), and NOZZE DI FIGARO (1973). Lord Olivier's successor as dir. (British) National Theatre, 1973. EF

Halle, E. Germany. One of the first Ger. towns to present opera, in 1654, A WAGNER Fest. on BAYREUTH lines was held here in 1910. HANDEL Fests have been a feature since 1922, in the Stadt T., built 1951, replacing the older T. des Friedens, destroyed 1945. LO

Hallström, Ivar Christian, b. Stockholm, 5 June 1826; d. Stockholm, 11 Apr 1901. Swedish composer. A prolific writer of opera and operetta, he frequently chose Scandinavian legend and folktale as the subject of his dramatic work. Operas incl.: *Hvita Frun på Drottningholm* (*The White Lady of Drottningholm*, 1847); *Mjölnarvargen* (*The Miller-Wolf*, 1871); *Den Bergtagna* (*The Bewitched*, 1874); *Vikingarne* (*The Vikings*, 1877); *Silverringen* (*The Silver Ring*, 1880); and *Den Ondes Snaror* (*The Devil's Snares*, 1900). His operetta *Neaga* (1885) had lib. by Carmen Sylva, Queen of Romania. EF

Hamburg, W. Germany. There was a theatre here in 1678, in the Gänsemarkt (Goosemarket), where ADAM UND EVA, the first Ger. opera, was staged, and where, in the early 18th c., operas by HANDEL, KEISER, TELEMANN, and by Fr. comps were given. After a period of quiescence Hamburg came back into prominence in 1874 with the building of the Stadt T., under the directorship of Bernhard Pollini. The long line of distinguished musicians assoc. since then with Hamburg includes MAHLER (1891–7), KLEMPERER (1910–14), BÖHM (1930–3), and JOCHUM (1933–44). In 1955 a new opera house replacing that bombed during World War II was opened. Since then the *Intendanten* have incl. RENNERT, TIETJEN, and LIEBERMANN. It is one of the most important and adventurous houses in Germany with a leaning toward the opera of our day. LO

Hamilton, Iain (Ellis), b. Glasgow, 6 June 1922. Scottish composer. He spent seven years in engineering training before winning a scholarship to the RAM in 1947, when he devoted his attention wholly to mus. and won four major composition prizes in his graduation year. Since 1961 he has lived and taught in USA, first at Duke Univ., N. Carolina, and from 1971 at City Univ., NY. He wrote and destroyed several youthful operatic works, but 1967–9 comp. two major operas still unperf.: *Agamemnon*, to his own lib., and *The Royal Hunt of the Sun*, after the play by Peter Schaffer. A breakthrough for him in opera occurred with CATILINE CONSPIRACY. NG

Hamlet, opera, 3 acts, SEARLE, lib. comp. taken from SHAKESPEARE. Hamburg Staats O. (in Ger.), 6 Mar 1968; Toronto, 12 Feb 1969; London, CG, 18 Apr 1969. Main chars: Hamlet (bar.) Claudius (ten.) Gertrude (mezzo-sop.) Ophelia (mezzo-sop.) Polonius (bass) Laertes (ten.) Player King (bass) Player Queen (sop.). A shortened version of Shakespeare's play. EF

Hamlet, opera, 5 acts, Ambroise THOMAS, lib. BARBIER and CARRÉ after SHAKESPEARE. Paris, O., 9 Mar 1868; London, CG (in It. as *Amleto*), 19 June 1869; NY, Acad. of Mus. (in It.), 22 Mar 1872. There are at least 19 operas with this title incl. those by FACCIO, MERCADANTE, ZAFRED, and SEARLE. LO

Hammerstein, Oscar I, b. Stettin (now Szczecin), 8 May 1846; d. NY, 1 Aug 1919. German, later American, impresario. Built Manhattan OH, NY, 1906, successfully competing with the Met until 1910 when it bought him out and restrained him from prod. opera in NY for 10 years. In 1911 built Kingsway OH, London (the Stoll T., now pulled down). Was also active in Philadelphia and Baltimore.

His nephew, **Oscar Hammerstein II,** b. 12 July 1895, is best known for the books and lyrics he wrote for musicals, incl. OKLAHOMA!; CAROUSEL; SOUTH PACIFIC; CARMEN JONES; and KING AND I. LO

Hammond, Joan, b. Christchurch, 24 May 1912. New Zealand soprano. Studied Sydney Cons., Vienna, and London with BORGIOLI. Debut Vienna, Volks O. as NEDDA (1939). Dublin O. Soc. as PAMINA (1940). English stage debut with Carl Rosa, as CIO-CIO-SAN (1942). CG debut (1948) as LEONORA (TROVATORE) and sang there as guest until 1951. SW 1951 and 1959 when she sang RUSALKA. Retired 1965. Rich, expressive lyric voice that was unfortunately not heard often enough in the opera house. Popular and prolific recording artist. AB

Hammond-Stroud, Derek, b. London, 10 Jan 1929. English baritone. Sang Taddeo (ITALIANA IN ALGERI) at St Pancras 1961, then joined SW, scoring a great success as BECKMESSER (1968). CG debut 1971 as FANINAL, has sung at Glyndebourne in BESUCH DER ALTEN DAME (1973); US debut (Houston 1975) as

Faninal. Repertory incl. PAPAGENO, Melitone (FORZA DEL DESTINO), TONIO, Cecil (GLORIANA), Napoleon (WAR AND PEACE), and ALBERICH (ENO, RING cycle, 1973). EF

Handel, George Frideric [Georg Friedrich Händel], b. Halle, 23 Feb 1685; d. London, 14 Apr 1759. German, naturalized English, composer. After a training in law at Halle Univ. he served his operatic apprenticeship at Hamburg under KEISER and prod. there his first opera ALMIRA (1705). Travelled in Italy 1706–10 where he comp. *Rodrigo* (Florence 1707), *Aci, Galatea e Polifemo* (Naples 1708), and AGRIPPINA, all in the prevalent It. idiom, which was to remain basic to his mature style. His entry into the service of the Elector of Hanover was preceded by a visit to England in 1710, where RINALDO was prod., 1711, with great success in a season that introduced It. opera to London. Handel returned there in 1712, overstaying his leave of absence from Hanover, whose Elector became George I of England in 1714. In 1715 *Amadigi* followed up the success of *Rinaldo*, and Handel was reconciled with the king. Mus. dir. 1716–20 to the Duke of Chandos at whose palace, Cannons, Edgware, ACIS AND GALATEA was first given. Dir. 1720–8 with BONONCINI and Attilio Ariosto of the 'Royal Acad. of Mus.', with the duty of engaging singers and comp. operas for regular yearly seasons. Successful at first, the Acad. foundered partly on rivalry and faction, partly as a result of the success of BEGGAR'S OPERA which satirized the more serious genre. Outstanding works of that period of the composer's work incl. *Radamisto* (1720), GIULIO CESARE (1724), *Tamerlano* (1724), and RODELINDA (1725).

After 1728 Handel continued to produce operas in association with the impresario John Heidegger, the most notable being *Orlando* (1733); but in 1734 the 'Opera of the Nobility', headed by the Prince of Wales, took over the King's T.; Handel moved to CG with a rival co., giving operas over the next three years which incl. such masterpieces as ARIODANTE and ALCINA, though they met with decreasing favour. His last opera DEIDAMIA failed outright. Meantime Handel had begun to shift his attention from opera to dramatic oratorio, secular and sacred. His great works in this genre incl. *Samson* (1743), SEMELE (1744), *Hercules* (1745), *Theodora* (1750), and finally *Jephtha* (1752). Perf. in concert form in Eng. and using large choruses, the so-called oratorios conform more nearly to modern notions of drama than do the operas, though they are less stageable but have none the less been staged. In his traditional It. works Handel carries the *opera seria* of the early 18th c. to its highest achievement. JB

Handel Opera Society. Founded in London 1955 under inspiration of DENT; dir. Charles Farncombe. By 1974 had staged 18 HANDEL works, first at Camden Fest., but since 1959 has given short seasons at SW. Perf. RINALDO (Halle 1961 and Berlin 1962); they have also perf. at Drottningholm, Sweden. LO

Hanover [Hannover], W. Germany. The first opera house was opened in 1689 with Agostino Steffani's *Enrico Leone*. During MARSCHNER'S period as MdC, 1831–59, he prod. his own operas there, with those of VERDI and LORTZING. A. NEUMANN gave the RING DES NIBELUNGEN there, 1882. A new Hof T., built 1853, and a private Stadt T., built 1877, were both destroyed in World War II; now replaced by the present theatre, built 1950. LO

Hänsel und Gretel, opera, 3 acts, HUMPERDINCK, lib. Adelheid Wette (the comp.'s sister) derived from the fairy tale by the Brothers GRIMM. Weimar, Hof T., 23 Dec 1893; London, Daly's T., 26 Dec 1894; NY, Daly's, 8 Oct 1895. Main chars: Hänsel (mezzo-sop.) Gretel (sop.) The Witch (mezzo-sop.) Peter (bar.) Gertrude (sop.). Hänsel and Gretel, sent by their mother to pick strawberries in the woods, are captured by the witch who intends to turn them into gingerbread, but they successfully trick her. Originally comp. as mus. for his sister's play for children, the score was extended by Humperdinck to develop its nursery tunes in a Wagnerian style. It was accepted by R. STRAUSS for prod. in Weimar and has become a worldwide Christmas entertainment. FGB O
See Kobbé

Hans Heiling, opera, prologue and 3 acts, MARSCHNER, lib. Eduard Devrient based on story by Karl Theodor Körner (originally intended for MENDELSSOHN). Berlin, Hof O., 24 May 1833; Oxford, 2 Dec 1953. The theme is the love of Hans, son of the Queen of the Earth Spirits, for a mortal. Marschner's best opera and an important link between WEBER and WAGNER. LO

Hanslick, Eduard, b. Prague, 11 Sept 1825; d. Baden, nr Vienna, 6 Aug 1904. Austrian critic and writer on aesthetics. His early approval of WAGNER (in 1846 he described TANNHÄUSER as 'the finest thing achieved in grand opera in at least 12 years') was later modified; his opposition to the theories of 'the New Music' incurred Wagner's enmity (Wagner's original name for the pedantic caricature BECKMESSER was Hans Lick). Cultured and intelligent, he was a more sympathetic critic than his Wag-

Hänsel und Gretel. PASHLEY as Gretel, Ann Howard as the Witch, and KERN as Hänsel, London, SW, 12 Dec 1967; produced SHAW; designed Jane Kingshill

nerian opponents have suggested. LO
See Pleasants (tr. and ed.), *Vienna's Golden Years of Music* (London 1951)

Hanson, Howard, b. Wahoo, Neb., 28 Oct 1896. American composer. Studied at Institute of Musical Art, NY, and American Acad., Rome. Dir., Eastman School of Music, Rochester, NY, 1924–64. He has comp. other musical works but his only opera is MERRY MOUNT. EJ

Hans Sachs, bass-bar., the cobbler in MEISTERSINGER

Hans Sachs, opera, 3 acts, LORTZING, lib. comp. and Philipp Reger based on play by Johann Ludwig Deinhardstein, 1827, which also gave some hints to WAGNER for MEISTERSINGER. Leipzig, 23 June 1840. LO

Hanuš, Jan, b. Prague, 2 May 1915. Czech composer. Studied with JEREMIÁŠ and has made a career in publishing. He has written four operas: *The Flames* (*Plameny*, 1956), *The Servant of Two Masters* (*Sluha dvou pánů*, 1959), *The Torch of Prometheus* (*Podhodeň Prometheova*), and *The Tale of One Night* (*Pohádka jedne noci*), the last two not perf. JT

Harewood, George, Earl of (George Henry Hubert Lascelles), b. London, 7 Feb 1923. English critic and administrator. Founded *Opera* magazine in 1950, editing it until 1953. Controller of Opera Planning at CG 1953–60. Art. Dir. of the Edinburgh Fest. 1961–6. Since 1972 Man. Dir. of the ENO. He revised and edited *Kobbé's Complete Opera Book* (1969). EF

Harmonie der Welt, Die (*The Harmony of the World*), opera, 5 scenes, HINDEMITH, lib. composer. Munich, Prinzregenten T., 11 Aug 1957. The plot is drawn from the life of the astronomer Johannes Kepler. LO

Harper, Heather, b. Belfast, 8 May 1930. British soprano. First studied piano at Trinity College, London; switched to singing while there. Debut Oxford Univ. O. Club 1954 (LADY MACBETH). This brought BBC TV appearances creating Luisita in *Mañana* by BENJAMIN and as VIOLETTA, both 1956, and MIMI 1957. Debuts: 1957, Glyndebourne Fest., as First Lady (ZAUBERFLÖTE); 1959, SW with New O. Co., as Ann Trulove (RAKE'S PROGRESS); 1962, CG, as Helena (MIDSUMMER NIGHT'S DREAM); 1967, Bayreuth Fest., as ELSA; 1971, Buenos Aires, as MARGUERITE. Much admired for consistent musicality and sympathetic womanliness of char. in such varied roles as Ellen Orford (PETER GRIMES) and GUTRUNE. Created Mrs Coyle in OWEN WINGRAVE (BBC TV 1971; CG 1973). Awarded CBE 1965. NG

Harris, Augustus (Sir), b. Paris, 1852; d. Folkestone, 22 June 1896. English impresario, son of Augustus Harris, stage manager at CG for 27 years. Began prod. opera at DL 1879, moving to CG 1888; man. there until his death. Worked hard to raise standards of perf.; from *c.* 1892 he insisted on operas being sung in their original language instead of in It. as previously. Prod. first CG RING DES NIBELUNGEN (under MAHLER 1892), and followed this by other WAGNER in Ger. CARMEN was sung in Fr. for the first time 1890. He also brought LEONCAVALLO, MASCAGNI, and PUCCINI to London when their works were given first perfs at CG, extending the repertory to incl. contemporary works by BRUNEAU, MASSENET, as well as those by native comps such as COWEN. LO

Hart, Lorenz, b. New York, 2 May 1895; d. New York, 22 Nov 1943. American librettist. Attended Columbia Univ. but left without a degree after considering a career in languages, literature, and journalism. His meeting with RODGERS established him as a librettist. A first success was *The Poor Little Ritz Girl* (1920), but *Garrick Gaieties* (1925), a revue by many young talents, set the Rodgers and Hart collaboration on course for 20 years. EJ

Hartmann, Karl Amadeus, b. Munich, 2 Aug 1905; d. Munich, 5 Dec 1963. German composer. His opera, *Des Simplicius Simplicissimus Jugend*, was first produced in Cologne in 1948; a revised version, *Simplicius Simplicissimus*, was published in 1955. EF

Hartmann, Rudolf, b. Ingolstadt, 11 Oct 1900. German producer and administrator. Studied art and stage design in Munich and Bamberg. After various posts in Germany, was engaged at the Berlin Staats O. 1934–8, where he began his collaboration with C. KRAUSS. General administrator at Munich 1938–44, staging the premieres of FRIEDENSTAG and of CAPRICCIO, which he has prod. with success several times since. After a period at Nuremberg he returned to Munich in his old post in 1953; remained there until he retired in 1967. Prod. the premiere of LIEBE DER DANAE (Salzburg 1952). At CG he was responsible for ELEKTRA (1953, still current in 1975), and a RING DES NIBELUNGEN prod. in 1954. His work was conservative and realistic, always responsive to and faithful to the opera in hand. AB

Hartt College of Music (affiliate of Univ. of Hartford, Conn.); John J. Zei, Chairman of O. Dept. Largely student perfs since 1942 of contemporary works (often in one act) by HINDEMITH, FRANCHETTI, MENOTTI, novelties by HANDEL, SUPPÉ, FALLA, and first perfs of *The Young God* by Edward Miller, and *The Unicorn in the Garden* by Russell Smith. Perfs given in Millard Auditorium of Fuller Music Center. Inactive since 1969. EJ

Harwood, Elizabeth, b. Kettering, 27 May 1938. English soprano. Engaged at SW in 1961; joint winner of the International Verdi Competition at Busseto (1963). She accompanied the SUTHERLAND tour of Australia (1965); CG debut 1967 as Fiakermilli (ARABELLA). Sings with SO, at Glyndebourne and Salzburg. Roles incl.: SEMELE, CONSTANZE, Countess ALMAVIVA, Donna ELVIRA (DON GIOVANNI), and FIORDILIGI, as well as LUCIA DI LAMMERMOOR, NORINA, GILDA, Oscar (BALLO IN MASCHERA), and MANON. She has also sung Bella (MIDSUMMER MARRIAGE). EF

Háry János, 5 parts and prologue, KODÁLY, lib. Béla Paulini and Zsolt Harsányi derived from a poem by János Garay. Budapest, 16 Oct 1926; NY CC, 19 Mar 1960. Main chars: Háry János (bass) Örzse (mezzo-sop.). Kodály's only opera, if this series of musical numbers interspersed with long stretches of dialogue can be so described. It is a fantasy about the prodigious liar popular in Hungarian folklore and his love for Marie Louise, Napoleon's wife and for a peasant girl Örzse, whom he eventually marries. The attractive score is more familiar in the orchestral suite, consisting of six numbers from the opera. AB O★
See Kobbé

Hasse, Johann Adolph, b. Bergedorf, nr Hamburg, baptized 25 Mar 1699; d. Venice, 16 Dec 1783. German composer. Though a German he so completely assimilated the It. *opera seria* style that he might be regarded as its chief exponent. In 1729 m. BORDONI; was MdC Dresden 1731–59, moving to Vienna after the Siege of Dresden. His *c.* 100 operas, often settings of METASTASIO, lacked the dramatic impact of his contemporaries JOMMELLI, TRAETTA and above all GLUCK. *Attilio Regolo* was revived at Göttingen 1971. LO

Haug, Hans, b. Basel, 27 July 1900; d. Lausanne, 15 Sept 1967. Swiss composer and conductor. Has wr. operas incl. two based on MOLIÈRE: *Tartuffe* (Basel 1937) and *Der Unsterbliche Kranke* (Zürich 1946). LO

Hauk, Minnie [Mignon Hauck], b. NY, 16 Nov 1851; d. Triebschen, Switzerland, 6 Feb 1929. American soprano. Studied NY with Achille Errani; debut, Brooklyn, as Amina (SONNAMBULA) when only 14, and was not 16 when she sang the lead in USA premiere of ROMÉO ET JULIETTE (NY 1867). London debut CG 1868. The first London and NY CARMEN (1878) – a role in which she was extraordinarily successful, singing it over 600 times. NY Met debut 1891 in AFRICAINE. Toured USA with her own opera co., then suddenly gave up her stage career and retired with her husband,

Minnie Hauk as CARMEN, her most famous role

Baron Ernst von Hesse-Wartegg, to WAGNER's villa on Lake Lucerne, where she died. LO
See autobiography (by Minnie de Wartegg), *Memories of a Singer* (London 1925)

Haydn, Franz Joseph, b. Rohrau, 31 Mar 1732; d. Vienna, 31 May 1809. Austrian composer. Wrote at least 25 operas beginning with *Der Krumme Teufel* (DIABLE BOITEUX, 1752) and ending with *L'Anima del Filosofo* (London 1791). Mostly written for Prince Esterházy, they incl. SPEZIALE (1768); *L'Incontro Improviso* (1775), a subject used previously by GLUCK and later MOZART, *L'Isola Disabitata* (1779), and *Armida* (1784). Those revived 20th c. incl.: MONDO DELLA LUNA; *L'Infedeltà Delusa* (Bregenz 1970); *Orfeo (L'Anima del Filosofo)* (Camden Fest. 1955); *La Vera Costanza* (Brunswick 1973–4), and *La Canterina* (London, Guildhall School of Music, 1974). LO

Hebbel, Christian Friedrich, b. Wesselburen, Schleswig-Holstein, 18 Mar 1813; d. Vienna, 13 Dec 1863. German poet and dramatist. Works on which operas are based incl.: *Judith*, 1840 (Max Ettinger, 1921; REZNIČEK's *Holofernes*, 1923; N. BERG's *Judith*, 1936); *Genoveva*, 1843 (SCHUMANN); *Der Rubin*, 1851 (d'ALBERT, 1893); *Agnes Bernauer*, 1852 (MOTTL, 1880); *Meloch*, 1850 (SCHILLINGS, 1906). He also wrote *Die Nibelungen*, a trilogy, 1855–62, not highly regarded by WAGNER. LO

Heger, Robert, b. Strasbourg, 19 Aug 1886. German conductor and composer. Studied Strasbourg, Zürich, and Munich. Debut Ulm, 1909. Chief appointments, Vienna Staats O., 1925–33, Berlin 1933–50, and Munich, 1950. Cond. at CG, 1925–35, and also in 1953 cond. London premiere of CAPRICCIO with the Munich co. Has written four operas. LO

Heimchen am Herd, Das (*The Cricket on the Hearth*), opera, 3 acts, GOLDMARK, lib. WILLNER based on the story by DICKENS. Vienna, O., 21 Mar 1896; London, Brixton T. (in Eng.), 23 Nov 1900; Philadelphia (in Eng.), 7 Nov 1912. Another *Cricket on the Hearth* by Alexander C. Mackenzie, 1914. LO

Heine, Heinrich [Harry], b. Düsseldorf, 13 Dec 1797; d. Paris, 17 Feb 1856. German poet and journalist. His *William Ratcliff* (1823) was the basis for operas by CUI (1869), MASCAGNI (1895), Xavier Leroux (1906), Cornelius Dopper (1909), Volkmar Andreae (1914). *Der Schelm von Bergen* (1846) was treated by ATTERBERG (*Fanal*, 1934), and Theodor Gerlach. For WAGNER's indebtedness to Heine see FLIEGENDE HOLLÄNDER. Heine lived in Paris from 1831; his reports from there on music to Ger. papers, esp. the *Augsburg Allgemeine Zeitung*, are important: 'he was the first to write about music and musicians not as an expert but as a journalist'. LO
See Graf, *Composer and Critic* (New York 1946; London 1947)

Heldentenor (Ger. 'heroic tenor'); the It. term is *tenor robusto*. A powerful voice capable of sustaining the big WAGNER and VERDI roles. LO

Helletsgruber, Luise, b. Vienna, ?1898; d. nr Vienna, 1 Jan 1967. Austrian soprano. Vienna O., 1922–42; Salzburg Fest., 1928–37; also sang frequently at Glyndebourne from 1934. A particularly stylish Mozart singer, her CHERUBINO and Donna ANNA were much admired. She died in a car accident. LO

Hello, Dolly! musical, music and lyrics Jerry Hermann, book Michael Stewart, adapted from Thornton Wilder's plays *The Matchmaker* and *The Merchant of Yonkers*. NY, St James T., 16 Jan 1964. Redirected with all-Negro cast, St James T., 11 Oct 1967. Revised with Negro cast, Minskoff T., Nov 1975. EJ O★

Help, Help, The Globolinks!, opera, 1 act, MENOTTI, lib. composer. Hamburg Staats O., 18 Dec 1968; Sante Fe, 1 Aug 1969. A science-fiction fantasy (earth is invaded by the Globolinks) 'for children and those who like children' (Menotti). LO

Helsinki [Helsingfors]. During the first half of the 19th c., opera was perf. in Ger. From 1852, when Fredrik Pacius's *Kung Karls Jakt* (*King Charles's Hunt*) was comp. to a Swedish text, opera was sung in that language; then in 1873 a permanent Finnish co. was founded. The first comp. of operas to Finnish texts was Oskar Merikanto (*see* FINLAND). Dir. Helsinki O., 1973–74 Leif Segerstam; succeeded Juhani Raiskinen. About eight operas given in a season Sept–May. Since 1973 TALVELA has been chairman of the Artistic Committee of the Summer Fest. EF

Heming, Percy, b. Bristol, 6 Sept 1883; d. London, 11 Jan 1956. English baritone. Studied London and Dresden (with George Henschel). Debut 1915, Beecham O. Co. as Mercutio in ROMÉO ET JULIETTE. Sang MARCELLO at CG on BNOC's opening night there (1922), and became one of its leading bars. SW 1933–5. Later an administrator. A notable AMFORTAS and SCARPIA. AB

Hempel, Frieda, b. Leipzig, 26 June 1885; d. Berlin, 7 Oct 1955. German soprano. Studied Berlin; debut there 1905. CG 1907, in MEISTERSINGER and LUSTIGEN WEIBER VON WINDSOR; Berlin Staats O. 1907–12. NY Met debut 1912 in HUGUENOTS, also sang at Bayreuth and Salzburg Fests; the first Berlin MARSCHALLIN. Retired from stage 1919. Early made a reputation as a MOZART singer and won high praise for her WAGNER. One of the great 20th-c. prima donnas, impeccable vocally, with a fine stage presence and acting abilities. LO

Henry VIII, opera, 4 acts, SAINT-SAËNS, lib. Léonce Détroyat and Armand Silvestre. Paris, O., 5 Mar 1883; London, CG, 14 July 1898. Despite the title the plot has no connection with SHAKESPEARE. LO
See Harding, *Saint-Saëns and His Circle* (London 1965)

Henze, Hans Werner, b. Gütersloh, 1 July 1926. German composer. Studied with FORTNER and René Leibowitz. His first full-length opera, BOULEVARD SOLITUDE, was followed by KÖNIG HIRSCH, PRINZ VON HOMBURG, ELEGY FOR YOUNG LOVERS, JUNGE LORD, and BASSARIDS. He has also comp. two radio operas, *Ein Landartz* (1951) and *Das Ende Einer Welt* (1953), an Italia prizewinner, which, together with *Das Wundertheater* (1948), an 'opera for actors', made up a triple bill staged at Frankfurt (1965) and in Eng. at the Camden Fest. (1966). More recent operas are *Der Floss der Medusa* (Nuremberg 1972) and *La Cubana* (Munich, May 1975). EF

Herbert, Victor, b. Dublin, 1 Feb 1859; d. NY, 26 May 1924. Irish-American composer. Educated in Germany, became competent cellist. In 1886 m. a singer, Therese Förster; went with her to NY Met where she sang and he played in the orch. Wrote two operas, *Natoma* (1911) and the 1-act *Madeleine* (1914), both perf. at the Met, and *c.* 35 operettas on which his fame largely rests. The most successful was *Naughty Marietta* (1910). LO
See Lubbock

Herincx, Raimund, b. London. English bass-baritone of Belgian parentage. Debut 1950; first heard in London (SW 1956) with WNO in MEFISTOFELE; then joined SW co. CG debut 1968 as King Fisher (MIDSUMMER MARRIAGE) and has sung all over Europe and America. Highly regarded as an interpreter of modern works, he created Segura (OUR MAN IN HAVANA, 1963), Faber (KNOT GARDEN, 1970), the White Abbot (Maxwell DAVIES's *Taverner*, 1972), and is a notable Shadow (RAKE'S PROGRESS). He has an immense repertory that incl. MÉPHISTOPHÉLÈS, ESCAMILLO, MACBETH, RIGOLETTO, and WOTAN. EF

Her (His) Majesty's Theatre *see* LONDON

Hérodiade, opera, 4 acts, MASSENET, lib. Paul Milliet and Henri Gremont (Georges Hartmann) based on FLAUBERT's *Hérodias*, 1877. Brussels, T. de la Monnaie, 19 Dec 1881; New Orleans, 13 Feb 1892; London, CG (as *Salome*), 6 July 1904. A simultaneous premiere at the Paris O. and in Milan had been planned by Massenet and RICORDI, but fell through owing to differences between Massenet and the new dir. of the O., Auguste Emmanuel Vaucorbeil. LO
See Harding, *Massenet* (London 1970; New York 1971)

Hérold, Louis Joseph Ferdinand, b. Paris, 28 Jan 1791; d. Paris, 19 Jan 1833. French composer. Entered Paris Cons. 1806, winning *Prix de Rome* 1812. First opera, *La Gioventù di Enrico V*, perf. Naples 1815; all his other operas and ballets given in Paris. Death came too soon; his last operas, ZAMPA and PRÉ AUX CLERCS, showed real potential, and deserved their popularity for the vigour of their style. His ballet *La Sonnambule* (1827) provided the plot for SONNAMBULA. LO

Herold, Vilhelm Kristoffer, b. Hasle, Bornholm, 19 Mar 1865; d. Copenhagen, 15 Dec 1937. Danish tenor. Sang at Copenhagen O. 1893–1915; debut in GOUNOD's FAUST; also appeared at Chicago, Stockholm, Oslo, Prague, and in Germany. CG debut 1904 (LOH-

Hans Werner Henze's BASSARIDS, performed by the ENO in its UK premiere at the London Coliseum, 10 Oct 1974; produced and conducted by the composer; designed by Timothy O'Brien and Tazeena Firth

ENGRIN), and returned there intermittently until 1907. Considered a stylish and elegant singer, he was also a fine Roméo (ROMÉO ET JULIETTE) and WALTHER VON STOLZING. Dir. of Copenhagen O. 1922–4. EF

Hertz, Alfred, b. Frankfurt, 15 July 1872; d. San Francisco, 17 Apr 1942. German, later American conductor. Debut Halle 1891. To USA 1902 as cond. of Ger. repertory at NY Met, remaining there till 1915. Cond. first PARSIFAL outside Bayreuth 1903, and several other US firsts (SALOME, ROSENKAVALIER), also world premiere of KÖNIGSKINDER. Left Met for San Francisco where he cond. guest perfs at San Francisco O. LO

Hervé [Florimond Ronger], b. Houdain, Pas de Calais, 30 June 1825; d. Paris, 4 Nov 1892. French conductor and composer, important in history of French operetta and English musical comedy. Wrote over 100 operettas, often to his own words. Among his more successful pieces were *Chilpéric* (1868); *Le Petit Faust* (a parody of *Faust*, 1868); MAM'ZELLE NITOUCHE. LO
See Hughes, *Composers of Operetta* (London and New York 1962)

Herz, Joachim, b. Dresden, 15 June 1924. German producer. At Dresden, Landes O., 1951–3; Berlin KO as assistant to FELSENSTEIN 1953–7; since then opera dir. at Leipzig. LO

Heš, Vilém, b. Týnec nad Labem, 3 July 1860; d. Vienna, 4 Jan 1908. Czech bass. Though with little formal training, he sang KECAL in Brno in 1880 and two years later joined the Prague NT. He went to Hamburg 1894 and permanently to Vienna 1896. He was one of the outstanding singers of his time, with a rich voice of wide compass and a versatility that embraced SARASTRO, Don BARTOLO (BARBIERE DI SIVIGLIA), and PAPAGENO. JT

Heuberger, Richard, b. Graz, 18 June 1850; d. Vienna, 28 Oct 1914. Austrian composer, critic, and writer. Wrote four operas incl. *Manuel Venegas* (1889) (*cf.* WOLF), and six operettas incl. *Don Quixote* (1910) and his first and most successful, *Der Opernball* (Vienna 1898; NY 1909). LO
See Lubbock

Heure Espagnole, L' (*The Spanish Hour*), opera, 1 act, RAVEL, lib. Franc-Nohain (Maurice Legrand) after his own farce. Paris, OC, 19 May 1911; London, CG, 24 July 1919; Chicago, 5 Jan 1920. Main chars: Concepción (sop.) Ramiro (bar.) Torquemada (ten.) Gonzalve (ten.) Don Inigo (bass). On the day that her husband Torquemada attends the public clocks in Toledo, Concepción is free for her love affairs. She is embarrassed by the presence of Ramiro, a muleteer, in the shop, but hides her lovers in clocks which she then persuades him to carry up to the bedroom. Finding the muscular muleteer a more attractive proposition than her effete lovers, she sends him to the bedroom also – without a clock. All ends happily when the returning husband sells each of the unsuccessful lovers a clock and thanks the muleteer for his help. If the story is very Sp., the mus. is no less Fr., full of wit in its combination of elegant lyricism, lively rhythms and ingenious orchestral sound effects. FGB O
See Kobbé

L'Heure Espagnol, London, SW, Apr 1965. Left to right: John Chorley as Torquemada, Robert Savoie as Don Inigo, Emile Belcourt as Gonzalve, BLACKHAM as Concepción, and David Bowman as Ramiro; produced BESCH; designed Peter Rice

Hiller [Hüller], Johann Adam, b. Wendisch-Ossig, 25 Dec 1728; d. Leipzig, 16 June 1804. German composer, important in history of *Singspiel*, writing *c.* 12 for Leipzig between 1766 and 1777. The most important are: *Der Teufel ist Los*, 1766 (based on DEVIL TO PAY); *Lottchen am Hofe*, 1767 (based on NINETTE À LA COUR); JAGD, 1770 (based on ROI ET LE FERMIER); *Der Dorfbarbier*, 1770. Hiller's simple, 'folksong' musical style befits the artless, rustic themes he dealt with. LO

Hindemith, Paul, b. Hanau, 16 Nov 1895; d. Frankfurt, 28 Dec 1963. German, naturalized American, composer. His first operas, CARDILLAC (1926), *Hin und Zurück* (1927) and NEUES VOM TAGE (1929), were prod. in Germany, as well as a children's opera, *Wir Bauen eine Stadt* (1931), but his best-known dramatic work, MATHIS DER MALER (comp. 1933–4), was banned by the Nazis, and received its first perf. in Switzerland 1938, a year after

Hindemith had moved to the USA. *Mathis*, not heard in Germany until 1946, was followed by HARMONIE DER WELT (Munich 1957), a study of the astronomer Kepler, and *The Long Christmas Dinner* (Mannheim 1961 and NY 1963), based on Thornton Wilder's play. EF

Hines, Jerome, b. Hollywood, 8 Nov 1921. American bass. Debut, 1941, San Francisco, as Monterone (RIGOLETTO); and at the NY Met in 1947 (minor role in BORIS GODUNOV). Sang Shadow (RAKE'S PROGRESS) with the Glyndebourne co. at Edinburgh (1953) and appeared at Bayreuth (1958–63) as Gurnemanz (PARSIFAL), KING MARK, and WOTAN. His repertory incl. MÉPHISTOPHÉLÈS, Swallow (PETER GRIMES), Grand Inquisitor (DON CARLOS), Dosifey (KHOVANSHCHINA), and Boris Godunov. EF

Hippolyte et Aricie, *tragédie lyrique*, prologue and 5 acts, RAMEAU, lib. Abbé Pellegrin. Paris, O., 1 Oct 1733; Boston, 11 Apr 1966; revived Marseille, O., 1973. Rameau's first opera. Pellegrin based his lib. on RACINE's *Phedre*, but elevated the love between Phaedra's stepson Hippolyte and Aricia, which had been a by-plot in Racine, to the main theme. LO

See Girdlestone, *Jean-Philippe Rameau: his Life and Work* (London 1957)

Hislop, Joseph, b. Edinburgh, 5 Apr 1884. Scottish tenor. Studied Stockholm where he began his career (1916) in what was to become one of his most noted roles – FAUST (GOUNOD). Sang regularly at CG 1920–8. US debut, 1920, Chicago. An admirable singer of PUCCINI and the Fr. repertory with a strong, expressive voice, which he used with taste. AB

Histoire du Soldat (*The Soldier's Tale*), STRAVINSKY, lib. Charles Ferdinand Ramuz. Lausanne, 28 Sept 1918; London (in Eng.), 10 July 1927, staged by Arts T. Club; NY (concert version), 23 Mar 1924. Described simply 'to be read, played and danced, in two parts', this moral tale, fitting into no convenient category and certainly not an 'opera', is yet important in the history of 20th-c. opera as it was in the van of that rejection of the complex apparatus of traditional opera to be seen in the work of BRECHT and WEILL and taken further in some of the post-World War II theatrical experiments. There is no singing, but the three speaking parts, the Soldier, the Devil and the Speaker, are sometimes notated with the rhythm of the music, provided by a chamber group of violin, double bass, clarinet, bassoon, cornet, trombone and percussion. The fourth character, the Princess, is mute, but she and the Devil are required to dance. Demanding no elaborate staging, and not even requiring an orchestral pit (the players are on stage), it was in deliberate contrast to the massive array demanded by Stravinsky's three great ballets, *Oiseau de Feu*, *Petrushka*, and *Le Sacre du Printemps*. LO

Histories of opera. The first in Eng. was by Henry Sutherland Edwards, *History of the Opera from Monteverdi to Donizetti* (London 1862) – an able and, for its time, reliable work. Richard Streatfeild's *The Opera* (London and Philadelphia 1897) brought the history up to date by incl. VERDI and WAGNER. BEKKER's *The Changing Opera*, tr. Arthur Mendel (New York 1935; London 1936) incl. opera post-World War I, with a strong bias toward Germany. DENT's *Opera* (Harmondsworth and New York 1940) is a useful survey. The most complete account in Eng. is Donald J. Grout's *A Short History of Opera* (New York and London, 2 vols, 1947; 2nd, one-vol. edn, New York and London 1966); it concentrates mainly on European opera, and treatment of moderns is rather sketchy. Leslie Orrey's *A Concise History of Opera* (London 1972) is very compressed, but with over 250 illustrations. An important Fr. publication is René Dumesnil's *Histoire Illustrée du Théâtre Lyrique* (Paris 1953). *See also* OPERA HANDBOOKS. LO

H.M.S. Pinafore or The Lass that Loved a Sailor, operetta, 2 acts, SULLIVAN, lib. GILBERT. London, Opéra Comique, 25 May 1878; Boston, 23 Sept 1878. Main chars: Ralph Rackstraw (ten.) Josephine (sop.) Captain Corcoran (bass-bar.) Sir Joseph Porter (buffalo) Little Buttercup (contr.) Dick Deadeye (bass). Sullivan's first world success. A satire on the traditions of the Royal Navy. JB

See Lubbock

Hoffman, François Benoît, b. Nancy, 11 July 1760; d. Paris, 25 Apr 1828. French librettist. Wrote libs for CHERUBINI (MÉDÉE), MÉHUL (incl. ARIODANT, *Le Trésor Supposé*), Jean-Baptiste Lemoyne's *Phèdre*, and others. LO

Hoffmann, Ernst Theodor Amadeus, b. Königsberg (now Kaliningrad), 24 Jan 1776; d. Berlin, 25 June 1822. German writer, music critic, conductor, and composer. Operas based on his writings incl. CARDILLAC, BUSONI's *Die Brautwahl* (1910), MALIPIERO's *I Capriccio di Callot* (1942), and most particularly CONTES D'HOFFMANN. Of Hoffmann's own operas UNDINE (1816) was a significant pointer toward the Ger. romanticism of MARSCHNER and C. WEBER. LO

H.M.S. Pinafore. D'Oyly Carte, 1966–7 tour; produced Herbert Newby. The backcloth was designed and made originally by Harkers in 1926; the scenery is also theirs although adapted in 1957 by Peter Goffin. Main characters, left to right: Clifford Parkes as the Bosun's Mate; George Cook as the Bosun; Christene Palmer as Little Buttercup; Donald Adams as Dick Deadeye

Hofmannsthal, Hugo von, b. Vienna, 1 Feb 1874; d. Rodaun, 15 July 1929. Austrian poet and playwright. He had acquired a reputation as a sensitive dramatist before his collaboration with R. STRAUSS, which lasted until his death, yielded six of the most important 20th-c. operas, ELEKTRA, ROSENKAVALIER, ARIADNE AUF NAXOS, FRAU OHNE SCHATTEN, ÄGYPTISCHE HELENA, and ARABELLA. LO

Hofoper (Ger. 'court opera'), opera, in 18th- and 19th-c. Germany and Austria, directly under the control of the imperial or princely court. LO

Holland *see* NETHERLANDS

Hollweg, Ilse, b. Solingen, 23 Feb 1922. German soprano. Studied with Gertrude Förstel in Cologne. Debut 1943 Saarbrücken. Became leading coloratura sop. at Düsseldorf (1946) where among other MOZART roles she graduated from BLONDCHEN to CONSTANZE. Has since been admired at Salzburg, Edinburgh, and Glyndebourne Fests, notably as ZERBINETTA, and in all major European opera houses. FGB

Holoubek, Ladislav, b. Prague, 13 Aug 1913. Slovak composer and conductor. After studies with NOVÁK he worked as an opera cond. in Slovakia, since 1958 as head of opera at Bratislava NT. His own works incl. *Stella* (1939), *Dawn* (*Svitanie*, 1941), *Longing* (*Túžba*, 1944), and *The Family* (*Rodina*, 1960). JT

Holst, Gustav, b. Cheltenham, 21 Sept 1874; d. London, 25 May 1934. English composer of Swedish descent. Studied with STANFORD. Wrote early operas in derivative styles; they were later suppressed by the comp. His first surviving work in the genre is SĀVITRI (1916), a one-act piece influenced by the comp.'s interest in Indian philosophy; it is strong on atmosphere, achieved by severe economy of means. PERFECT FOOL (1923), *At the Boar's Head* (1925), and *The Wandering Scholar* (1934) all show his feeling for the setting of short episodes involving wit and character, even if none is sufficiently vital to hold the stage regularly. AB

Holzbauer, Ignaz, b. Vienna, 17 Sept 1711; d. Mannheim, 7 Apr 1783. Austrian composer. Dir., Hof O., Vienna, 1745; MdC Stuttgart 1751, afterwards moving to Mannheim where he worked to further cause of Ger. opera (as opposed to It. opera and *Singspiel*). His *Günther von Schwarzburg* (Jan 1777), a subject from Ger. history, was a landmark, admired by MOZART who said: 'It is full of fire'; and some echoes of that fire can be heard in the coloratura of ZAUBERFLÖTE. LO

Homer. Ancient Greek poet or, in some views, a succession of traditional poets. The epics *Iliad* and *Odyssey* ascribed to him have inspired operas by August Bungert (*Homerische Welt*, a tetralogy); FAURÉ; Vittorio Gnecchi (*Cassandra*, 1905); Inglis Gundry (*The Return of Odysseus*, 1941); DALLAPICCOLA; HEGER (*Bettler Namenlos*, 1932); R. STRAUSS; STRAVINSKY; TIPPETT; Egon Wellesz (*Alkestis*, 1924); and others. See GREEK DRAMA AND LEGEND. LO

Homer, Louise [Louise Dilworth Beatty], b. Pittsburgh, Pen., 28 Apr 1871; d. Winter Park, Fla, 6 May 1947. American contralto. Studied Philadelphia and New England Cons., Boston, where she met and m. comp. Sidney Homer. After further study in Paris, debut 1898, Vichy in FAVORITE. After appearances at Brussels, CG, San Francisco (with the Met on tour), became leading contr. NY Met 1900–19. Was with Chicago O. 1920–5; San Francisco and Los Angeles 1926, back at Met 1927. Beginning in It. and Fr. operas she eventually moved over to Wagnerian music drama with great success. One of the finest artists in a splendid period at the Met. LO
See S. Homer, *My Wife and I* (New York 1939)

Honegger, Arthur, b. Le Havre, 10 Mar 1892; d. Paris, 27 Nov 1955. French-born composer of Swiss parentage. He studied in Zürich and Paris, becoming a member of the group 'Les

Six'. His operas incl. ROI DAVID (1921), JUDITH (1926), ANTIGONE (1927), a setting of COCTEAU's version of SOPHOCLES, *Aiglon* (Monte Carlo 1937), based on the play by ROSTAND and written in collaboration with IBERT, and several lighter works such as the operetta *Les Aventures du Roi Pausole* (Bouffes-Parisiens 1930). JEANNE D'ARC AU BÛCHER (1938), a lyric mystery play, is his most successful stage work. EF

Höngen, Elizabeth, b. Gevelsberg, Westphalia, 7 Dec 1906. German mezzo-soprano. Studied Berlin; debut 1933, Wuppertal. Düsseldorf 1935–40; Dresden 1940–3. Joined Vienna Staats O. 1943 (where her LADY MACBETH was acclaimed) and remained there for rest of career. CG debut with Vienna co. as DORABELLA (1947), returned to CG co. 1959 as Herodias (SALOME). NY debut 1951 as Herodias and KLYTEMNESTRA. Bayreuth as FRICKA (1951). Voluminous, highly dramatic voice, used with great intelligence. AB

Horaces, Les, *tragédie lyrique,* 3 acts, SALIERI, lib. GUILLARD based on CORNEILLE's *Horace.* Paris, O., 7 Dec 1786. The story, from Livy, of the Horatii and the Curiatii, the subject of Jacques-Louis David's painting *The Oath of the Horatii* (1784), has been used by other comps, notably CIMAROSA (1794) and MERCADANTE (1830). LO

Horký, Karel, b. Štěměchy, Moravia, 4 Sept 1909. Czech composer. A bassoonist and music teacher, he turned later to composition and was a pupil of KŘIČKA in Prague (1941–4). In addition to a very successful ballet *King Barleycorn* he has written several operas incl. *Jan Hus* (1950), *Poison from Elsinore* (*Jed z Elsinoru,* 1970) and *Daybreak* (*Svítání,* 1975). JT

Horne, Marilyn, b. Bradford, Penn., 16 Jan 1934. American mezzo-soprano. Debut, 1957, Gelsenkirchen. Has sung in Vienna, San Francisco (1960), Chicago (1961), Vancouver (1963), CG (1964), Sc. (1969), and NY Met (1970). With a voice of phenomenal range as well as great flexibility, she sings the ROSSINI mezzo-sop. coloratura roles: ROSINA, CENERENTOLA, Isabella (ITALIANA IN ALGERI), Arsace (SEMIRAMIDE), and Neocle (*Assedio di Corinto*) – and her repertory incl. MARIE, ADALGISA, EBOLI, Fidès (PROPHÈTE), and Jocasta (OEDIPUS REX). A fine CARMEN, she sang the leading role on the sound track for the film CARMEN JONES. EF

Hotter, Hans, b. Offenbach-am-Main, 19 Jan 1909. German bass-baritone, outstanding in WAGNER and the greatest WOTAN at post-1945 Bayreuth and elsewhere. Turned to singing from being organist and choirmaster and studied with Matthew Roemer, pupil of J. DE RESZKE. Opera debut, 1929, Opava, as Speaker (ZAUBERFLÖTE). Joined Hamburg Staats O. 1934–8. Following first Wotan at Munich 1937, became member of Munich co. from 1938 for remainder of career and made his home there. Close associate of R. STRAUSS: created roles of Kommandant (FRIEDENSTAG, 1938) and Olivier (CAPRICCIO, 1942), as well as gaining notable success as OCHS and Mandryka (ARABELLA). Also famous as FLIEGENDE HOLLÄNDER (title role); Grand Inquisitor (DON CARLOS); Cardinal Borromeo (PALESTRINA). CG debut 1947 with Vienna Staats O. as ALMAVIVA (NOZZE DI FIGARO); sang HANS SACHS and Wotan in Eng. there, 1948; returned for successive RING DES NIBELUNGEN perfs and was responsible for its CG prod. 1961–3. Regular appearances NY Met from 1950. Retired from major roles in late 1960s. Distinguished by breadth of musical sensibility and intensity of musical char. in addition to commanding stage presence. NG

Houston, Texas, USA. Houston Grand O. was founded 1955. First gen. dir., Walter Herbert; present administrator, David Gockley. Beginning cautiously with standard works, has gradually become more adventurous, adding new US operas such as SUSANNAH (1973), and, in 1975–6 season, FLOYD's new opera *Billy's Doll,* also first US perf. of RINALDO. About six operas a season are presented. LO

Howells, Anne, b. Southport, 12 Jan 1941. English mezzo-soprano. Studied Royal Manchester College, later with Vera Rosza. Debut, 1966, WNO, as Flora (TRAVIATA). CG debut 1967, same role. Glyndebourne debut 1967 as Erisbe (ORMINDO). Has since sung regularly in both houses. CG roles incl. DORABELLA, CHERUBINO, and ROSINA. Created Ophelia (SEARLE's HAMLET) and Lena (VICTORY), both at CG, and Cathleen (MAW's *The Rising of the Moon*) at Glyndebourne, where parts incl. Dorabella, the Composer (ARIADNE AUF NAXOS), and Minerva (RITORNO D'ULISSE IN PATRIA). AB

Hubay, Jenő, b. Budapest, 15 Sept 1858; d. Budapest, 12 Mar 1937. Hungarian violinist and composer. Has written six operas, of which *A Cremonai Hegedus,* based on François Coppée's play *Le Luthier de Crémone* (Budapest 1894; played elsewhere incl. NY), was the most successful. Another was *Anna Karenina* (Budapest 1915), based on TOLSTOY. LO

Huber, Hans, b. Eppenberg, nr Olten, 28 June 1852; d. Locarno, 25 Dec 1921. Swiss composer. His five operas, all but one prod. at Basel, were at one time popular in Switzerland, but have not reached a wider public. LO

Hugh the Drover, 2 acts, VAUGHAN WILLIAMS, lib. Harold Child. London, RCM, 4 July 1924. Main chars: Hugh (ten.) Mary (sop.) John the Butcher (bar.) The comp.'s best-known opera. Based on folk themes, it successfully incorporates them into a traditional romantic opera fabric in depicting the trials and tribulations of the hero and his love for Mary. Set in the Cotswolds during the Napoleonic wars. Prod. successfully by the BNOC and by SW. AB O
See Kobbé

Hugo, Victor, b. Besançon, 26 Feb 1802; d. Paris, 22 May 1885. French writer. His novels and plays on which *c.* 40 operas are based incl.: *Hernani*, 1830 (ERNANI); *Marion Delorme*, 1831 (PONCHIELLI, 1885); *Notre-Dame de Paris*, 1831 (Alberto Mazzucato, 1840) A. G. THOMAS, *Esmeralda*, 1883); *Le Roi s'amuse*, 1832 (RIGOLETTO); *Marie Tudor*, 1833 (PACINI, 1843; WAGNER-RÉGENY, *Der Günstling*, 1934); *Lucrèce Borgia*, 1833 (DONIZETTI); *Angelo*, 1835 (MERCADANTE, *Il Giuramento*, 1837; GIOCONDA); *Torquemada*, 1882 (ROTA, 1943). LO

Huguenots, Les, opera, 5 acts, MEYERBEER, lib. SCRIBE and Emile Deschamps. Paris, O., 29 Feb 1836; London, CG, 20 June 1842 (in Ger.); New Orleans, 29 Apr 1839. Main chars: Raoul de Nangis (ten.) Marguerite de Valois (sop.) Valentine (sop.) St Bris (bass) Nevers (bar.) Urbain (sop. or contr.). Raoul spurns Valentine believing her to be the mistress of the Count de Nevers, and challenges Nevers to a duel. From Marguerite he learns that Valentine is innocent, and risks his life to see her. He overhears the Catholic plot to slaughter the Huguenots, and in the course of the ensuing St Bartholomew's Day massacre, the lovers die at the hands of a mob led by St Bris, Valentine's father. WAGNER considered the fourth act among the finest moments in opera. It remained popular until the 1930s, and received a major revival at Sc. 1962 (in It.). PS O

Humperdinck, Engelbert, b. Siegburg, 1 Sept 1854; d. Neustrelitz, 27 Sept 1921. German composer. A student award allowed him to visit Italy, where he met WAGNER in 1879 and was invited to assist in the preparation of PARSIFAL for its first perf. at Bayreuth 1882. His own style was henceforward influenced by Wagner. He was obliged to teach for a living, first in Barcelona then in Frankfurt, until 1896, when the success of his HÄNSEL UND GRETEL enabled him to concentrate on composition. His later operas, which never achieved the success of the first, are *Dornröschen* (1902), *Die Heirat wider Willen* (1905), KÖNIGSKINDER, *Die Marketenderin* (1914), and *Gaudeamus* (1919). With *Hänsel und Gretel*, a curious mixture of German folk melody and Wagnerian polyphony, he estab. a style of fairy-tale opera imitated without success by several of his pupils. FGB

Hunding, bass, Sieglinde's husband in WALKÜRE

Hungary. Under three centuries of domiation first of the Turks and later that of the Austrian Habsburgs, Hungarian national feeling was stifled, and Hungarian opera began to blossom only in the 19th c.; the theatres at Eszterháza and Kismarton, associated with HAYDN, perf. only It. operas or occasionally operas in Ger. The first works in Hungarian were of the *Singspiel* type, e.g. *Pikkó Hertzeg és Jutka Perzsi* (*Prince Pikkó and Jutka Perzsi*), 1793, Budapest, by József Chudy, 1751–1813. His contemporaries were János Lavotta, 1761–1820, Antal Csermák, 1774–1882, and János Bihari, 1764–1827, all exploiting the Hungarian march and dance music known as

Hungary. Budapest Operaház, built 1875–84 and designed by Miklós Ybl (1814–91)

verbunkos. The first true Hungarian opera was *Béla Király Futása* (*The Flight of King Béla*), by Ignác Ruzitska, 1758–1823, at Klausenburg (now Cluj), 1822. Among 19th-c. comps were ERKEL, Mihály Mosonyi [Michael Brand], 1814–70 (*Szép Ilonka*, comic opera, 1861), GOLDMARK, HUBAY, Ferenc Sárosi, 1855–1913, Jenő Sztojanovics, 1846–1919, Mór Vavrinecz, 1858–1913, and the better-known Emil Ábrányi, b. 1882, BARTÓK, and KODÁLY. 20th-c. comps incl. Ferenc Farkas, b. 1905, Jenő Kenessey, b. 1906, Pál Kadosa, b. 1903, György Ránki, b. 1907, PETROVICS, and SZOKOLAY. Opera is perf. in BUDAPEST, DEBRECEN, PÉCS and Szeged. LO

Hunter, Rita, b. Wallasey, 15 Aug 1933. English soprano. After a season with the Carl Rosa, she was engaged at SW (1958) and at first sang small roles such as Berta (BARBIERE DI SIVIGLIA) and Marcellina (NOZZE DI FIGARO). First sang at CG 1963 as Third Norn (GÖTTERDÄMMERUNG). Emerged as a dramatic sop. 1964, singing SENTA and Odabella (ATTILA), but it was not until SW moved to the Coliseum (1968) that her full vocal potential was realized. NY Met debut 1972 as BRÜNNHILDE. She also sang Brünnhilde in the complete RING DES NIBELUNGEN cycle performed in English (1973) and is a fine LEONORA (TROVATORE), AMELIA, and Elisabeth (DON CARLOS). EF

Hurník, Ilja, b. Poruba, Moravia, 25 Nov 1925. Czech pianist and composer. Though he made his reputation initially as a pianist, he has comp. works in all genres, incl. two operas: *The Lady and the Robbers* (*Dama a lupiči*, 1966) and *Wise Men and Fools* (*Mudrci a bloudi*, 1972). JT

Huron, Le, *opera comique*, 2 acts, GRÉTRY, lib. MARMONTEL. Paris, TI, 20 Aug 1768. Grétry's first Paris success. A young Frenchman, b. Canada, brought up by tribe of Indians, goes to France, where his innocence contrasts with the artificiality of Fr. manners. An early instance of exploitation of theme of ROUSSEAU's exotic 'noble savage', as expounded in his *Discours* (1750). LO

Hurry, Leslie, b. London, 10 Feb 1909. English designer. Designed sets and costumes for CG prod. of TURANDOT (1947), RING DES NIBELUNGEN (1954), TRISTAN UND ISOLDE (1958), and SEARLE's HAMLET (1969). At SW he designed the first perf. of GARDNER's *Moon and Sixpence* (1957); also prods of ANDREA CHÉNIER (1959), VILLAGE ROMEO AND JULIET (1962), FIDELIO (1965), and QUEEN OF SPADES (1966). He also designed a production of ALBERT HERRING for the Stratford, Ontario, Fest. (1967). EF

Hüsch, Gerhard, b. Hanover, 2 Feb 1901. German baritone. Debut, 1923, Osnabrück; joined Bremen Staats T. and Cologne O. 1927, moving on to Berlin 1930–42. Guest appearances at Sc., CG, Hamburg, Dresden, Munich, Bayreuth. Though a persuasive singer on stage he has been more widely appreciated for his *Lieder* singing. LO

I

Iago, bar., Otello's 'ancient' in VERDI's OTELLO

Ibert, Jacques, b. Paris, 15 Aug 1890; d. Paris, 5 Feb 1962. French composer. Studied Paris Cons., won *Prix de Rome* 1919. Apptd Dir. of the Acad. de France in Rome 1937 and Asst Dir. of the Paris O. 1955. Operas incl.: *Andromède et Persée* (1920), ANGÉLIQUE, ROI D'YVETOT, *Gonzague* (1935) and *Aiglon* (1937), both with HONEGGER, *La Famille Cardinal* (1938), *Barbe-Bleu* (1943), and *Le Chevalier Errant* (1949). His comic operas are comp. in an unpretentious style, draw liberally on dance rhythms, and are often designed frankly as entertainment. FGB

Idomeneo, Re di Creta (*Idomeneus, King of Crete*), opera, 3 acts, MOZART, lib. Giambattista Varesco after Fr. lib. Antoine Danchet. Munich, 29 Jan 1781, revived Vienna, Mar 1786 in private perf. with two substitute numbers; Glasgow, 12 Mar 1934; Tanglewood, 4 Aug 1947. Main chars: Ilia (sop.) Elettra (sop.) Idomeneo (ten.) Idamante (sop. or ten.) Arbace (ten.). During a storm, Idomeneo, returning home from the Trojan Wars, has rashly vowed to sacrifice to Neptune in return for his own safety the first living creature he meets ashore. This turns out to be his own son Idamante. Already promised to Elettra, the prince has fallen in love with the captive Trojan princess, Ilia. After attempting to escape from fulfilling his vow, Idomeneo is released from it by the appearance of Neptune just as the sacrificial blow is about to be struck: Elettra returns to Greece, raging with jealousy: Idamante is able to marry Ilia. Mozart's first operatic masterpiece. JB O
See Kobbé

Illica, Luigi, b. Castell 'Arquato, 9 May 1857; d. Colombarone (Piacenza), 16 Dec 1919. Italian librettist. A well-known Milanese journalist, in 1892 began writing libs, incl. ANDREA

Colour Plate: Costume design for Cio-Cio-San in a Barcelona production of MADAMA BUTTERFLY, 1945, by Erté (Romain de Tirtoff; b. St Petersburg, 1892). Erté left Russia for Paris in 1912 where he designed for Folies-Bergère; he worked for the Ziegfeld Follies, New York, 1920–9. He designed for the Paris OC (MAMELLES DE TIRÉSIAS), Monte Carlo, and elsewhere.

CHÉNIER, *Cristoforo Colombo* and *Germania* for FRANCHETTI; IRIS, ISABEAU and *Le Maschere* for MASCAGNI; and works set by ALFANO, Vittorio Gnecchi and MONTEMEZZI. With GIACOSA he provided the texts for BOHÈME, MADAMA BUTTERFLY, MANON LESCAUT, and TOSCA. PS

Immortal Hour, The, opera, 2 acts, BOUGHTON, lib. play of same name by 'Fiona Macleod' (William Sharp), 1900. Glastonbury, 26 Aug 1914; London, Regent T., 13 Oct 1922 (a run of over 200 perfs); NY, 6 Apr 1926. Etain, of the fairy folk, marries Eochaidh, King of Ireland (a mortal), but is lured back to the Land of Heart's Desire from which she has come by Midir, a fairy prince. LO

Impresario, The *see* SCHAUSPIELDIREKTOR

Inbal, Eliahu, b. Jerusalem, 16 Feb 1936. Israeli conductor. Educated at Paris and Jerusalem, and at the Chigi Acad., Siena. Has cond. opera all over Italy since the mid-1960s. German debut Stuttgart with COSÌ FAN TUTTE (1973), and first Munich appearance with FORZA DEL DESTINO (1974). AB

Incoronazione di Poppea, L' (*The Coronation of Poppaea*), opera, prologue and 3 acts, MONTEVERDI, lib. BUSENELLO. Venice, T. SS Giovanni e Paolo, autumn 1642. The first opera based on an historical incident, and Monteverdi's masterpiece. Modern realizations are due to d'INDY, MALIPIERO, Giacomo Benvenuti (Florence Maggio Musicale, 1937), KŘENEK, Walter Goehr, LEPPARD (Glyndebourne, 29 June 1962), Alan Curtis, Stuart Bedford, and others. LO ○
See Arnold, *Monteverdi* (London and New York 1963)

Indes Galantes, Les (*The Gallant Indians*), *opéra-ballet*, prologue and 3 *entrées*, RAMEAU, lib. Louis Fuzelier. Paris, O., 23 Aug 1735; revived Paris, O., 1952, prod. M. LEHMANN. Its theme is the universal appeal of love, expounded by the three *entrées* which are: *Le Turc généreux*; *Les Incas de Peru* (the most dramatic and spectacular); *Les Fleurs*. A fourth, *Les Sauvages*, was added in 1736 (the first perf. had only the prologue and the first two *entrées*). Rameau was reproached for the noisiness and violence of his mus. – a frequent complaint through the centuries. LO ○
See Girdlestone, *Jean-Philippe Rameau: his Life and Work* (London 1957)

Indiana University Opera Theater *see* BLOOMINGTON

Indy, (Paul Marie Théodore) Vincent d', b. Paris, 27 Mar 1851; d. Paris, 2 Dec 1931. French composer. His six operas are an *opéra comique*, *Attendez-moi sous l'Orme*, Paris, OC, 11 Feb 1882; *Le Chant de la Cloche*, a *légende dramatique* based on SCHILLER, Brussels, T. de la Monnaie, 1909; FERVAAL; *L'Étranger*, T. de la Monnaie, 7 Jan 1903; a *drame sacré*, *La Légende de Saint-Cristophe*, Paris O., 9 June 1920; a *comédie musicale*, *Le Rêve de Cinyas*, comp. 1922–3, perf. Paris 1927. LO
See Demuth, *Vincent d'Indy, 1851–1931* (London 1951)

Innsbruck, Austria. A playhouse built here in 1652–4 was the first detached opera house in German-speaking lands; CESTI's *L'Argia* perf. there 1655, for Queen Christina of Sweden. A new theatre built 1846, was taken over by the town in 1886, and in 1945 became the Tiroler Landes T. Present administrator Helmut Wlasak. LO

Intendant, Generalintendant. Ger. equivalent of manager, general manager – the person responsible for the total administration of the theatre. LO

intermezzo (It. 'interlude'). 1. Short 2-act comic opera played between the acts of an 18th-c. *opera seria*: e.g. SERVA PADRONA. 2. An instrumental interlude played between scenes or acts when the stage is empty. JB

Intermezzo, opera, 2 acts, R. STRAUSS, lib. comp. Dresden, 4 Nov 1924; NY, LC, 11 Feb

Colour plates. Above: Curtain design by Yuri Pimenov (b. 1903) for PAGLIACCI, produced Bolshoy T., Moscow, 1957

Below: Design by Amable (-Petit; 1846–after 1911) for Act I of TANNHÄUSER, Paris, O., 13 May 1895, the first production of this opera at the new Palais de Garnier. Amable supplied a large number of designs to the Paris O. and to other theatres. His impressionistic designs, in the spirit of the time, were moving away from the ultra-realism favoured by WAGNER.

Intermezzo, in Andrew Porter's translation, Glyndebourne, 1974. Decor Martin Battersby, produced John Cox. Tom Lawlor as the Notary; SÖDERSTRÖM as Christine Storch

1963; Glyndebourne, 15 June 1974. Main chars: Christine Storch (sop.) Robert Storch (bar.) Baron Lummer (ten.) Anna (sop.). This slight yet charming comedy is unique in that it is autobiographical: a domestic storm in a teacup blew up when Strauss received, by mistake, a passionate love letter which fell into the hands of his shrewish wife. Other whimsical features are a tobogganing scene and a game of skat (the comp.'s favourite card game). It is musically most distinguished for the symphonic interludes between the 14 brief scenes, scored for unusually small orch. FGB
See Mann, *Richard Strauss* (London 1964; New York 1966); Kobbé

In the Well (*V Studni*), opera, 1 act, BLODEK, lib. SABINA. Prague, PT, 17 Nov 1867. Main chars: Veruna (contr.) Lidunka (sop.) Vojtěch (ten.) Janek (bass). Lidunka, a village beauty, loves Vojtěch, but her mother wants her to marry Janek, a rich old farmer. Undecided, she consults Veruna, the village witch, who advises her that on St John's Eve she will see the face of her future husband in a nearby well. Overhearing this, Janek climbs a tree above the well, and falls in. As he tries to get out, he startles Lidunka, who has come to see her future husband. Janek is disgraced and Lidunka's problem solved. This tuneful little work was after BARTERED BRIDE one of the most popular of local Czech operas and was much favoured by amateur companies. JT ○

Intimate Opera. Founded 1930 by DUNN, Margaret Ritchie, and Frederick Woodhouse for perfs of 18th-c. intermezzi and operas with two or three characters, and of modern operas with similar casting. Others associated with the co. have been Winifred Radford, ARUNDELL, and Joseph Horovitz; in 1952 Antony Hopkins became mus. dir., followed in 1963 by Stephen Manton. Working to high standards of singing and prod., the co. tours in the smaller centres of Britain. LO

Intolleranza 1960 (*Intolerance 1960*), opera, 2 acts, NONO, lib. composer. Venice, 13 Apr 1961; Boston, 22 Feb 1965. Main chars: the Emigrant (ten.) his Companion (sop.) a Tortured Man (bass). A condemnation of intolerance and indifference in the modern world, the opera has exerted a strong influence upon the younger generation of Italian composers. EF

Iolanta, opera, 1 act, TCHAIKOVSKY, lib. Modest Tchaikovsky after the Dane Henrik Hertz's *Kong Renés Datter*, tr. Konstantin Ivanovich Zvantsyev. St Petersburg, Mariinsky, 18 Dec 1892; Scarborough-on-Hudson, NY, Garden T. (Sleepy Hollow Country Club, in Russian), 10 Sept 1933; London, St Pancras Town Hall, 20 Mar 1968. Main chars: King René (bass) Iolanta (sop.) Ebn-Hakia (bar.) Vaudémont (ten.). Iolanta, protected in her father's castle, does not realize she is blind. King René arrives with a doctor, Ebn-Hakia, who says that Iolanta can only be cured if she knows she is blind and wants to see; but the king refuses. Vaudémont, betrothed to Iolanta since childhood, arrives at the castle and is captivated by her beauty. He tells her she is blind, and finally she is cured. The opera enjoyed enormous success in Russia, where it is still performed. GN ○★

Iolanthe or The Peer and the Peri, operetta, 2 acts, SULLIVAN, lib. GILBERT. London, Savoy T. and NY, Standard T., 25 Nov 1882. Main chars: Iolanthe (mezzo-sop.) Strephon (bar.) Phyllis (sop.) Queen of the Fairies (contr.) Lord Chancellor (buffo) Lord Tolloller (ten.) Lord Mountararat (bass) Private Willis (bar.). A satire on the British political system involving the rivalry of two peers of the realm, a Lord Chancellor and a half-mortal, half-fairy shepherd for the love of the shepherdess, Phyllis. JB ○

Iphigénie en Aulide (*Iphigenia in Aulis*), opera, 3 acts, GLUCK, lib. Bailly du Roullet based on RACINE's play *Iphigénie*, in turn based on EURIPIDES. Paris, O., 19 Apr 1774; Oxford, 20 Nov 1933; Philadelphia, 22 Feb 1935. Main chars: Agamemnon (bass) Calchas (bass) Iphigénie (sop.). The Greek fleet, *en route* for Troy, is becalmed in Aulis. Its commander, Agamemnon, is informed by the seer Calchas, that the gods require the sacrifice of his daughter, Iphigénie. She is reprieved at the last moment and spirited away to Tauris. Gluck's first opera wr. for Paris and his first unqualified success. LO

Iphigénie en Tauride (*Iphigenia in Tauris*), opera, 4 acts, GLUCK, lib. GUILLARD based on EURIPIDES. Paris, O., 18 May 1779; London, King's T., 7 Apr 1796; NY Met, 25 Nov 1916. Main chars: Iphigénie (sop.) Oreste (bass) Pylade (ten.). This follows on from IPHIGÉNIE EN AULIDE: Iphigénie, now a priestess of Diana in the Scythian capital of Tauris, finds herself impelled to consent to a sacrifice to appease the gods. The victim, one of two shipwrecked Greeks, turns out to be her brother, Oreste. At the last moment Diana calls off the sacrifice as a reward for the valour of Oreste's friend, Pylade. LO
See Kobbé

Iolanthe, London Coliseum, Aug 1973; produced Frank Hauser; designed Desmond Heeley; Anne Collins as the Queen of the Fairies

Ireland. Irish opera composers incl. BALFE, Augusta Holmès (*La Montagne Noire*, Paris O., 1895), KELLY, STANFORD and V. WALLACE; SULLIVAN was of Irish descent. T. MOORE's works have provided material for several operas, and Celtic legend has been the inspiration for operas by Robert O'Dwyer, *Eithne*, 1910, and Geoffrey Palmer, *Sruth na Maoile*, 1923 (both in Irish). *See* DUBLIN, WEXFORD. LO

Iris, opera, 3 acts, MASCAGNI, lib. ILLICA. Rome, T. Costanzi, 22 Nov 1898, revived in definitive form Milan, Sc., 19 Jan 1899; Philadelphia, 14 Oct 1902; London, CG, 8 July 1919. Main chars: Iris (sop.) Osaka (ten.) Kyoto (bar.) il Cieco (bass). Based on a brutal and decadent Japanese subject, *Iris* restored Mascagni's fortunes for a while. It is rarely revived now, though the 'Hymn to the Sun' survives as a concert piece. JB
See Kobbé

Irische Legende (*Irish Legend*), opera, 5 scenes, EGK, lib. comp. based on play *The Countess Cathleen* by William Butler Yeats. Salzburg, 17 Aug 1955. Main chars: Cathleen (sop.) Tiger (bass). The Devil causes a famine in Ireland, and barters food for souls. Cathleen offers her soul in exchange for the others, and is saved by angels from damnation. EF

Isabeau, *leggenda drammatica*, 3 parts, MASCAGNI, lib. ILLICA. Buenos Aires, T. Colón, 2 June 1911; Chicago, 12 Sept 1917. Main chars: Isabeau (sop.) Folco (ten.) il Re Raimondo (bar.) Giglietta (mezzo-sop.). For her reluctance to choose a husband, Isabeau is made to ride naked through the city streets at noon. The people pass an edict that all who dare look on her shall be put to death; it is disobeyed by the young woodman, Folco, a pure-hearted Peeping Tom. Isabeau, now in love with him, tries in vain to save him from the mob, then kills herself over his dying body. JB

Isolde, sop., the heroine of TRISTAN UND ISOLDE

Isouard, Nicolò, b. Malta, 6 Dec 1775; d. Paris, 23 Mar 1818. Maltese composer. Most of his 36 operas were written for Paris, where he went *c.* 1800, and were very popular there. The best of them is *Cendrillon* (1810), based on PERRAULT's Cinderella story. LO

Israel. Opera Israel was founded in 1947; the first opera perf. was THAÏS, starring Edis de Philippe, who with her husband Eben Zohar formed a permanent co., Israel National Opera, in 1958. Based on Tel Aviv, they also perf. in Haifa and Jerusalem. LO

Italiana in Algeri, L' (*The Italian Girl in Algiers*), *opera buffa*, 2 acts, ROSSINI, lib. Angelo Anelli. Venice, T. S. Benedetto, 22 May 1813; London, Haymarket, 26 Jan 1819; NY, 5 Nov 1832. Main chars: Isabella (contr.) Elvira (sop.) Lindoro (ten.) Taddeo (bar.) Mustafà (buffo-bass). Mustafà, tired of his wife Elvira, tries to get rid of her to his favourite slave, Lindoro, hoping to find a new wife from Europe. Isabella, Lindoro's beloved, arrives with her elderly admirer, Taddeo. Mustafà is immediately smitten. Isabella makes use of her hold over all three men to procure her own escape with Taddeo and Lindoro. JB O

Italy. The chief centres for opera are FLORENCE, MILAN, NAPLES, ROME and VENICE: others incl. BARI, BERGAMO, BOLOGNA, BRESCIA, CATANIA (Sicily), GENOA, PALERMO (Sicily), REGGIO EMILIA, SPOLETO, TRIESTE, TURIN, VERONA. Since MONTEVERDI there has never been a time when Italy lacked an important opera composer. The most important incl.: GALUPPI, JOMMELLI, PICCINNI, and TRAETTA in the 18th c.; BELLINI, DONIZETTI, ROSSINI, then VERDI, MASCAGNI, PUCCINI in the 19th c.; and in the 20th c. DALLAPICCOLA, MALIPIERO, NONO, PIZZETTI. LO

Ivanhoe, grand opera, 4 acts, SULLIVAN, lib. Julian Russell Sturgis after SCOTT. London,

Royal English O. House, 31 Jan 1891. Main chars: Ivanhoe (ten.) Bois-Guilbert (bar.) Rowena (sop.) Rebecca (sop.) King Richard (bass) Friar Tuck (bar.) Cedric the Saxon (bar.) Ulrica (contr.). Ivanhoe returns with King Richard I from the Third Crusade, both in disguise, to rescue the country from misrule by Prince John and his friends. Ivanhoe defeats the Templar, Brian de Bois-Guilbert, at the tournament at Ashby-de-la-Zouch. Bois-Guilbert abducts Rowena, ward of Cedric the Saxon and attempts the virtue of Rebecca, daughter of Isaac of York. Rebecca escapes from the Templar and nurses the wounded Ivanhoe back to health, while Richard I leads the men of Sherwood against Bois-Guilbert's castle, setting it on fire. He persuades Cedric to consent to Ivanhoe's marriage to Rowena. Ivanhoe fights Bois-Guilbert for Rebecca, accused of witchcraft, and kills him. Sullivan's only attempt at serious opera; a *succès d'estime* only but had a run of 160 perfs. JB

Ivan Susanin, opera, 4 acts and epilogue, GLINKA, lib. Georgy Fyodorovich Rozen. St Petersburg, Bolshoy T., 9 Dec 1836; London, CG, 12 July 1887; NY, Steinway Hall, 14 Nov 1871 (incomplete concert perf.); San Francisco, Veterans' Auditorium, 12 Dec 1936 (staged). Main chars: Ivan Susanin (bass) Antonida (sop.) Vanya (contr.) Sobinin (ten.). The distinctively Russian melodic traits which Glinka grafted on to an otherwise fairly Western-style opera structure were recognized by comps and critics alike as the starting point of a true nationalist musical culture in Russia; and the translucent orchestration made an impact that affected Russian music not only in the 19th c. but also in the 20th (right up to STRAVINSKY and PROKOFIEV). At the request of Nicholas I the title was changed to *A Life for the Tsar* (*Zhizn za Tsarya*); in Soviet times the original title has been restored. GN O
See Kobbé

Left: Ivan Susanin. O. PETROV in the title role at the Bolshoy T. (now the Mariinsky T.), St Petersburg, 27 Nov 1836

Ivan the Terrible *see* MAID OF PSKOV

Ivogün, Maria [Ilse von Günther], b. Budapest, 18 Nov 1891. Hungarian soprano. Studied Vienna. Debut, 1913, Munich (MIMI), remained there for 12 years. Ighino in first perf. of PALESTRINA (Munich 1917). Created ZERBINETTA in revised version of ARIADNE AUF NAXOS (Berlin 1916); CG debut in same role (1924). Sang GILDA the same season, returning in that role and as CONSTANZE in 1927. Appeared regularly in Chicago during the 1920s, and in NY, Lexington T., as Frau Fluth (LUSTIGEN WEIBER VON WINDSOR, 1923). Retired prematurely, in the 1930s, because of failing eyesight, and became a famous teacher; her many pupils included SCHWARZKOPF and STREICH. AB

Ivrogne Corrigé, L' (*The Reformed Drunkard*), *opéra comique*, 2 acts, GLUCK, lib. Louis Anseaume (1759) based on La Fontaine's tale *The Drunkard in Hell.* Vienna, BT, Apr 1760; London, Birkbeck College (in Eng. tr. DUNN) as *The Devil's Wedding*, 12 Mar 1931; Hartford, Conn., 26 Feb 1945. LO

J

Jacobin, The (*Jakobín*), opera, 3 acts, DVOŘÁK, lib. Marie Červinková-Riegrová. Prague, NT, 12 Feb 1889, (2nd version) 19 June 1898; Birmingham, Aston Univ., 30 Oct 1968. Main chars: the Count (bass) Bohuš (bar.) Julie (sop.) Filip (bass) Benda (ten.). Bohuš, the count's son, returns from France with his wife Julie and learns that his cousin Adolf is about to replace him as heir. Though Bohuš is arrested as a 'Jacobin', his wife, with the help of Benda the village schoolmaster, is able to change the count's mind. The opera contains one of Dvořák's most lovable characterizations, Benda, whose choir-practice scene (Act 2) is one of the opera's highlights. JT
See Clapham, *Antonín Dvořák, Musician and Craftsman* (London 1966)

Jadlowker, Hermann, b. Riga, 5 July 1877; d. Tel-Aviv, 13 May 1953. Latvian tenor. Studied at Vienna; debut, 1899, Cologne. After engagements in Berlin, Vienna, and Karlsruhe went to NY Met, 1910–13, debut in GOUNOD's FAUST, before returning to Berlin where he stayed for some years. Created Bacchus in ARIADNE AUX NAXOS (Stuttgart 1912). Though not a good actor his suave voice was well suited to MOZART and the older *bel canto* style. LO

Jagd, Die (*The Hunt*), *Singspiel*, 3 acts, HILLER, lib. WEISSE adapted from ROI ET LE FERMIER. Leipzig, 29 Jan 1770. 'The most popular opera in Germany before *Der Freischütz*' (Grout). LO

James, Henry, b. NY, 14 Apr 1843; d. Rye, England, 28 Feb 1916. American novelist, of Irish and Scottish ancestry. Settled in Europe 1875; lived *c.* 20 years in London, moved to Rye, Sussex, 1898; naturalized British subject 1915. His intricate and meticulous prose, reflecting his own searching attempt at grappling with the complexities of his characters, has stimulated several thoughtful comps of the present generation, as e.g. D. MOORE (*The Wings of the Dove*, 1961); BRITTEN (TURN OF THE SCREW and OWEN WINGRAVE); DAMASE (*L'Héritière*, based on *Washington Square*, Nancy 1974), and MUSGRAVE (VOICE OF ARIADNE). LO

Janáček, Leoš, b. Hukvaldy, Moravia, 3 July 1854; d. Ostrava, 12 Aug 1928. Czech composer. After studies in Brno, Prague, Leipzig, and Vienna, he settled in Brno in 1880 as a schoolteacher and was active as a choral cond. and mus. critic. Founded the Brno Organ School 1881; dir. until 1919. His first opera, ŠÁRKA (1887–8, revised 1918–24, prod. 1925) was influenced by Czech Romanticism and the second, *The Beginning of a Romance* (*Pocatek románu*, 1894), by Moravian folksong. It was not until JENŮFA (1904) that he found a personal style, characteristic in its directness and high emotional charge, its shortwindedness, frequent *ostinati*, intensely expressive harmony and voice parts modelled on the curves of Moravian speech against a dominant, idiosyncratically scored orch. part.

In two further works, *Fate* (*Osud*, 1903–7, prod. 1958) and MR BROUČEK'S EXCURSIONS (1920), Janáček experimented with operatically unconventional subject matter (thereafter a distinctive feature of his libs). After the success of *Jenůfa* in Prague (1916) and abroad four more operas followed: KÁT'A KABANOVÁ (1921), CUNNING LITTLE VIXEN (1924), MAKROPULOS CASE (1926), and FROM THE HOUSE OF THE DEAD (1930). Like *Jenůfa* these show a deep compassion and a belief in life and its renewal. The only Czech comp. with a number of works in the international operatic repertory, Janáček is one of the most original and powerful figures in 20th-c. opera. JT
See Vogel, *Leoš Janáček* (London 1962)

Janků, Hana (Svobodová-), b. Brno, 25 Oct 1940. Czech soprano. After winning a national singing competition in 1959 she was engaged at the Brno NT, where her repertory soon gravitated toward the heavier dramatic roles. Her greatest success has been as TURANDOT, a role in which she triumphantly replaced NILSSON at Sc. in 1967 and which she has repeated in Vienna, Verona, Stuttgart, Buenos Aires, Rome, and Mexico City. She has sung from 1970 in West Berlin (LEONORA, TOSCA, GIOCONDA), Düsseldorf (Tosca, ARIADNE, ELISABETH), and at CG (Tosca, 1973–4). She has a powerful, vibrant voice with a rich lower register and limpid, beautifully placed *mezza voce*. JT

Janowitz, Gundula, b. Berlin, 2 Aug 1937. Austrian soprano. Debut, 1959, Vienna Staats O., as Barbarina (NOZZE DI FIGARO); first sang at Bayreuth as a Flower Maiden (PARSIFAL, 1960). Has sung at Aix-en-Provence, Glyndebourne, Edinburgh, Salzburg, NY Met, and the Colón, Buenos Aires. Her MOZART roles incl. Ilia (IDOMENEO), Countess ALMAVIVA, Donna ANNA, FIORDILIGI, and PAMINA, while she also sings Odabella (ATTILA), Amelia (SIMONE BOCCANEGRA), AGATHE, the Empress (FRAU OHNE SCHATTEN), and ARABELLA. EF

Japan. Though lacking an opera house, Japan's interest in Western opera is lively. It was fostered by GURLITT, who lived in Japan from 1939 and organized the Gurlitt Opera Society in Tokyo, 1952. Numerous companies have visited Japan including the NY Met, 1975. At present the principal performing groups are: the Nikikai O. Co., founded 1952 by Mutsumu Shibata, a large group with a wide repertory of classical and modern; the Tokyo Chamber O. T., founded 1969 by Ryosuke Hatanaka, with a repertory of chamber opera from PERGOLESI to MENOTTI; the Kansai O. Co., founded 1949 by the cond. Takashi Asahima. Japanese comps incl. Osamu Shimizu (*Yokobue* and *Shuzenji Monogatari*) and Ikuma Dan (*Yuzuru*). About 100 Japanese operas have been written. LO

Jeanne d'Arc au Bûcher (*Joan of Arc at the Stake*), lyric mystery play, prologue and 10

Jeanne d'Arc au Bûcher, Buenos Aires, T. Colón, 17 May 1974; produced Cecilio Madanes; designed Guillermo de la Torre; decor Oscar Lagomarsino

scenes, HONEGGER, lib. CLAUDEL. Basel, 12 May 1938; Paris, 13 June 1939; London, RAH (concert), 4 Feb 1948; San Francisco, 15 Oct 1954; London, Stoll T. (staged), 20 Oct 1954. Main chars: Jeanne (actress) Frère Dominique (actor) the Virgin Mary (sop.) Archbishop Cauchon (ten.). Jeanne d'Arc, tied to the stake, relives her life and trial at the moment of her death. EF ★O

Jeník, ten., the hero of BARTERED BRIDE

Jenůfa (*Její Pastorkyňa – her Foster-daughter*), opera, 3 acts, JANÁČEK, lib. comp. based on a play by Gabriela Preissová (1890). Brno, NT, 21 Jan 1904; Prague, NT, 26 May 1916 (KOVAŘOVIC version); NY Met, 6 Dec 1924; London, CG, 10 Dec 1956. Main chars: Jenůfa (sop.) the Kostelnička (sop.) Laca (ten.) Števa (ten.). Laca, jealous that Jenůfa loves his half-brother Števa, disfigures her face with a knife. She gives birth in secret to Števa's child and when Števa refuses to marry her, her foster-mother, the Kostelnička, secretly kills the child fearing that it would be a hindrance to Jenůfa's union with the now penitent Laca. Laca and Jenůfa's wedding celebrations are interrupted by the discovery of the child's body; the Kostelnička confesses her crime and Jenůfa, understanding her motives, forgives her and seeks a new future with Laca. The Prague premiere under Kovařovic estab. both the opera's and Janáček's reputation; it is still his most popular opera and it was the first to pursue his favourite themes of compassion and renewal. JT O
See Ewans, *Janáček's Tragic Operas* (London 1976)

Jeremiáš, Otakar, b. Písek, 17 Oct 1892; d. Prague, 5 Mar 1962. Czech composer and conductor. After studying composition with NOVÁK, he became cond. of the Prague Radio Orch. 1929 and concentrated on a career in conducting and administration which culminated in his appointment as head of opera at the Prague NT (1948–9). His first opera, *The Brothers Karamazov* (*Bratři Karamazovi*, 1928), is a dramatic and well-constructed work whose orchestral fabric owes something to R. STRAUSS. A second opera, *Owlglass* or *Till Eulenspiegel* (*Enšpígl*, 1949), wr. during World War II, exploits the subversive aspects of its subject. JT

Jerger, Alfred, b. Brno [Brünn], 9 June 1889. Austrian baritone. Studied at Vienna. Began as a cond., then emerged as a singer, Munich 1919–21. Leading bar. Vienna 1921–53. Created Mandryka in ARABELLA (Dresden 1933); has also sung at Salzburg and CG. A most sympathetic interpreter of MOZART. More recently prod. opera, Volks O., Vienna. LO

Jeritza, Maria [Mimi Jedlitzka], b. Brno [Brünn], 6 Oct 1887. Czech soprano. Debut, 1910, Olomouc as ELSA. Two years later created the title role in ARIADNE AUF NAXOS at Stuttgart. Star of the Vienna Staats O. in a wide repertoire 1912–32. PUCCINI regarded her as the ideal TOSCA and she was R. STRAUSS's favourite interpreter for his leading roles. Sang at NY Met 1921–32, where she created for USA JENŮFA, TURANDOT, and other roles. Also famous for her THAÏS, CARMEN, and Minnie (FANCIULLA DEL WEST). First London appearance as Tosca (CG 1925). As beautiful in

appearance as in voice, an actress of imaginative conviction, she was one of the idols of the opera public until her abrupt early retirement on her marriage in 1935. Several years later made a few appearances, including a single perf. in FLEDERMAUS at the Met. FGB
See autobiography, *Sunlight and Song: A Singer's Life*, tr. Martens (London and New York 1924)

Jessonda, opera, 3 acts, SPOHR, lib. Eduard Heinrich Gehe based on A. M. Lemierre's *La Veuve de Malabar*. Kassel, 28 July 1823; London, Prince's T. (in Ger.), 18 June 1840; CG (in It.), 6 Aug 1853; Philadelphia, 15 Feb 1864. LO

Jewels of the Madonna, The *see* GIOIELLI DELLA MADONNA

Jílek, František, b. Brno [Brünn], 22 May 1913. Czech conductor. Studied composition, piano, and conducting (under CHALABALA) in Brno and then composition with NOVÁK in Prague (1935–7). He was a *répétiteur* under SACHS in Brno (1937–9) and after serving as opera cond. in Ostrava (1939–48), returned to Brno as cond. and *Dramaturg*, becoming head of opera in 1952. A discreet and self-effacing cond., he has continued the JANÁČEK tradition in Brno and built up a repertory of MARTINŮ operas with several world premieres. JT

Jiménez, Jerónimo, b. Seville, 10 Oct 1854; d. Madrid, 19 Feb 1923. Spanish composer. His numerous *zarzuelas* exploiting the gypsy tradition include *La Boda de Luis Alonso*, 1897, and *El Baile de Luis Alonso*, 1900, both based on the life of a famous popular dancer, 'La Tempranica', and one bearing the all-too-familiar title *El Barbero de Sevilla*. He was also first violinist, then Mus. Dir. of the T. Apolo in Madrid. FGB

Jirásek, Ivo, b. Prague, 16 July 1920. Czech composer and conductor. He has worked as an opera cond. in various Czech theatres and has written three operas: *Mr Johannes* (*Pan Johanes*, 1956), *Dawn over the Waters* (*Svítání nad vodami*, 1963), and *The Bear* (*Medvěd*, 1964, after CHEKHOV). JT

Jirko, Ivan, b. Prague, 7 Oct 1926. Czech composer and critic. A practising psychiatrist, he has written several operas. These incl. *Twelfth Night* (*Večer tříkrálový*, 1964), *The Strange Adventure of Arthur Rowe* (*Podivné dobrodružstvi Arthura Rowa*, 1969), *The Millionairess* (1972), and *The Strumpet* (1974). JT

Joan of Arc *see* GIOVANNA D'ARCO, JEANNE D'ARC AU BÛCHER

Jobin, Raoul, b. Quebec, 8 Apr 1906; d. Quebec, 13 Jan 1974. Canadian tenor. Debut, 1930, Paris O., as Tybalt (ROMÉO ET JULIETTE). Created Fabrice in SAUGUET's *Chartreuse de Parme* (Paris O., 1939). CG debut 1937 as DON JOSÉ; NY Met debut 1940 as DES GRIEUX (MANON). His repertory was mainly Fr. – WERTHER, Roméo (*Roméo et Juliette*), FAUST, Hoffmann (CONTES D'HOFFMANN), Nicias (THAÏS), Gérald (LAKMÉ), Julien (LOUISE), and Pelléas (PELLÉAS ET MÉLISANDE) – but he also sang CAVARADOSSI, CANIO, RADAMES, WALTHER VON STOLZING, and LOHENGRIN. EF

Jochum, Eugen, b. Babenhausen, 1 Nov 1902. German conductor. Studied Augsburg and Munich. Worked at Kiel, Mannheim, Duisburg, and Berlin before becoming mus. dir. of Hamburg Staats O. (1934–49). Since then has appeared regularly at all major Ger. houses. Bayreuth debut 1953 (TRISTAN UND ISOLDE). Returned there 1972 (PARSIFAL). One of the leading Wagnerian conductors of his generation. AB

Johnson, Edward, b. Guelph, Ontario, 22 Aug 1878; d. Toronto, 20 Apr 1959. Canadian tenor, later manager. Studied NY; debut Padua in ANDREA CHÉNIER. Sang in first It. PARSIFAL (Sc. 1914). Remained in Italy until 1919, creating ten. roles in NAVE, FEDRA, and ALFANO's *L'Ombra di Don Giovanni*. After two seasons at Chicago went to NY Met 1922, debut in AMORE DEI TRE RE. Remained there creating roles in KING'S HENCHMAN, MERRY MOUNT, and PETER IBBETSON, and singing a wide repertory that incl. Pelléas (PELLÉAS ET MÉLISANDE), SADKO, and VESTALE. In 1935 succeeded WITHERSPOON as gen. man. of the Met, remaining there in that capacity until 1950 when he went to Toronto University, Canada, to take up a position on the Mus. Faculty. LO
See Mercer, *The Tenor of his Time* (Toronto 1974)

Johnston, James, b. Belfast, *c.* 1900. Irish tenor. Debut, 1940, Dublin as DUCA DI MANTUA. Principal ten. SW 1945–50, CG 1950–8, where he created Hector (OLYMPIANS). His strong lyric-dramatic voice served him well in VERDI roles such as Gabriele Adorno, which he sang at the first British perf. of SIMONE BOCCANEGRA (SW 1948), and MANRICO. Also a notable Don José and CALAF. AB

Jolie Fille de Perth, La (*The Fair Maid of Perth*), opera, 4 acts, BIZET, lib. SAINT-GEORGES and Jules Adenis, based loosely on SCOTT's *Fair Maid of Perth* (1832). Paris, TL, 26 Dec 1867;

Manchester, 4 May 1917. Only been performed occasionally since that production. LO
See Curtiss, *Bizet and his World* (London 1959)

Jommelli, Niccolò, b. Aversa, 10 Sept 1714; d. Naples, 25 Aug 1774. Italian composer. Trained at the Naples Cons., his first opera was *L'Errore Amoroso* (Naples 1737). Soon recognized as one of the foremost among the so-called second Neapolitan school, he was in demand in all the leading cities of Italy and, thanks to his close friendship with METASTASIO, in Vienna. In the service of the Duke of Württemberg 1753–68 in Stuttgart, where he composed his most important opera, *Fetonte* (1768). His 70 operas incl. three intermezzos and a theatrical satire, *La Critica*. In his Stuttgart works he gives unusual prominence to the orch. and treats the formal conventions with a freedom worthy of GLUCK. In Germany he was regarded as one of the greatest comps of the mid-18th c. JB

Jones, Gwyneth, b. Pontnewynydd, nr Pontypool, 7 Nov 1936. Welsh soprano. Won scholarship to RCM while working as secretary; gained every available prize there and sang title role in ORPHÉE ET EURYDICE. Zürich International O. Studio and O. Co. 1961–3, changing from mezzo-sop. to sop. Debut 1963, CG, as Wellgunde (GÖTTERDÄMMERUNG) and WNO as LADY MACBETH. Major successes CG, 1964, taking over at short notice as LEONORE and LEONORA (TROVATORE). Foreign debuts, all 1966: Bayreuth Fest., SIEGLINDE; Vienna Staats O., Leonore; Dallas, Texas, Lady Macbeth; NY O. Soc., MÉDÉE. Then Sc. 1967, Leonora; NY Met from 1968. Later appeared more frequently in WAGNER in addition to It. repertory, and was engaged to sing BRÜNNHILDE throughout RING DES NIBELUNGEN cycle at Bayreuth Fest. 1975. A singer of eloquent emotional char. in chosen roles, with a voice of great beauty and radiance at its best, but sometimes lacking the consistency to sustain expressive intentions. NG

Jones, Parry, b. Blaina, 14 Feb 1891; d. London, 26 Dec 1963. Welsh tenor. Studied London, Italy and Germany. US debut 1914. D'Oyly Carte 1915. CG debut 1921 as TURIDDU. Sang heroic roles with BNOC 1922–8. Also appeared at Old Vic and SW in 1920s and 1930s. Reappeared at CG (1949–53) in a number of char. roles, notably as the Captain in WOZZECK, as MONOSTATOS, and as Shuisky (BORIS GODUNOV). AB

Jones, Sidney, b. London, 17 June 1861; d. Kew, 29 Jan 1946. English composer of musical comedies. His most popular, *The Geisha* (London, Daly's T., 25 Apr 1896), starring Marie Tempest, ran for two years; also prod. Munich, Gärtnerplatz T., 1898. His work was for long a standby of English amateur operatic societies. LO

Jongleur de Notre-Dame, Le (*The Juggler of Notre Dame*), *miracle*, 3 acts, MASSENET, lib. Maurice Léna. Monte Carlo, 18 Feb 1902; London, CG, 15 June 1906; NY, 27 Nov 1908. Based on story by Anatole France pub. in *L'Étui de Nacre*, 1892, in turn based on a medieval miracle play: Boniface offers to the Virgin his only accomplishment, dancing and juggling before the altar. The monks are horrified, but the Virgin accepts his homage. GARDEN persuaded Massenet to rewrite the part of Boniface *a travesti* for her. LO

Jonny Spielt Auf (*Jonny Strikes Up*), opera, 2 parts and 11 scenes, KŘENEK, lib. comp. Leipzig, 10 Feb 1927; NY Met, 19 Jan 1929. Main chars: Jonny (bar.) Daniello (bar.) Anita (sop.) Max (ten.). Jonny, a jazz-band leader, steals a priceless violin from Daniello, and becomes the most famous and successful violinist in the world. EF

Jonson, Ben, b. London, *c.* 11 June 1572; d. London, 6 Aug 1637. English dramatist. Dramas on which operas are based incl.: *Volpone*, 1606 (GRUENBERG, 1945; ANTHEIL, 1953; Francis Burt, 1960; ZIMMERMANN, 1957); *Epicoene*, 1609 (SALIERI, *Angiolina*, 1800; LOTHAR, *Lord Spleen*, 1930; SCHWEIGSAME FRAU, 1935). LO

José, Don, ten., the hero of CARMEN

Joseph, *opéra comique*, 3 acts, MÉHUL, lib. Alexandre Duval. Paris, T. Feydeau, 17 Feb 1807; Philadelphia, 15 Oct 1828; London, CG (in WEINGARTNER's version), 3 Feb 1914. Méhul's masterpiece, a biblical opera, very popular during 19th c. Mounted, 26 May 1899, at Paris O., spoken parts versified into recitative by Armand Silvestre to music by Louis-Albert Bourgault-Ducoudrey. The main characters are all male; the opera tells the story of Joseph's reconciliation with his brothers and his father in Egypt. Méhul's music is sober and restrained rather than exciting. LO

Journet, Marcel, b. Grasse, 25 July 1867; d. Vittel, 7 Sept 1933. French bass. Studied Paris Cons.; debut T. de la Monnaie, 1891. Sang frequently at CG, 1897–1907; NY Met 1900–08; Monte Carlo 1912–20. After World War I sang at Sc. under TOSCANINI. Possessed of a powerful and beautiful voice and admired as an actor, he perf. a wide range of the Fr., It., and Ger. repertory in a singing career that lasted *c.* 35 years. LO

Jouy, Victor Joseph Étienne de, b. Jouy, nr Versailles, 1764; d. St Germain-en-Laye, 4 Sept 1846. French librettist. Refashioned Andrea Tottola's *Mosè in Egitto* as *Moïse* (ROSSINI) and, with Hippolyte Bis, wrote GUILLAUME TELL. Other libs incl. ABENCÉRAGES, FERNAND CORTEZ, and VESTALE. LO

Juch, Emma, b. Vienna, 4 July 1863; d. NY, 6 Mar 1939. American soprano: her Austrian parents were naturalized US citizens, and Emma was born while they were visiting Austria. Debut, 1881, London, HM, as Philine (MIGNON); sang same role, NY Acad. of Music, same year. Joined the American O. Co. 1885 and in 1889 managed her own, the Emma Juch Grand Opera Co., touring for two years in USA, Canada, and Mexico. Retired from stage 1891. LO

Judith, 1. Opera, 3 acts, HONEGGER, lib. René Morax's play (1925) based on Judith and Holofernes story in the Apocrypha. Monte Carlo, 13 Feb 1926; Chicago (in Fr.), 27 Jan 1927. 2. Opera, 1 act, GOOSSENS III, lib. Arnold Bennett, also based on the Apocryphal story. London, CG, 25 June 1929; Philadelphia, 26 Dec 1929. Other Judith operas include those by SEROV, 1864; Albert Doppler, 1870; Charles Lefebvre, 1879; N. BERG, 1936 (Stockholm); Max Ettinger, 1921; REZNIČEK, *Holofernes*, 1923. LO

Juilliard School of Music *see* NEW YORK

Juive, La (*The Jewess*), opera, 5 acts, J. F. HALÉVY, lib. SCRIBE. Paris, O., 23 Feb 1835; New Orleans, T. d'Orléans, 13 Feb 1844; London, DL, 29 July 1846. Revived New Orleans 18 Oct 1973. Lib. had been offered to ROSSINI, who rejected it. In 15th c. Constance Cardinal Brogni is heading a Jewish persecution. Prince Léopold, under the assumed name Samuel, woos the Jewess Rachel. The lovers are denounced and, with Eléazar (Rachel's presumed father), are imprisoned. Rachel is persuaded by Léopold's intended bride to exonerate Léopold. She and Eléazar are condemned to death; Brogni offers to spare her if Eléazar will abjure his faith. He refuses, as does Rachel. Only when she is led to death does Eléazar reveal that Rachel is not his daughter but Brogni's long lost child. Both Rachel and Eléazar offered opportunities to dramatic singers such as NOURRIT, who created Eléazar, and VIARDOT. Eléazar was one of CARUSO's finest roles. LO

La Juive. CARUSO as Eléazar

Julien, *drame lyrique*, prologue and 4 acts, CHARPENTIER, lib. comp. Paris, OC, 4 June 1913; NY Met, 26 Feb 1914. A sequel to LOUISE. It made use of the mus. of an earlier *symphonie drame*, *La Vie du Poète*. It made little impression and has never been revived. LO

Julietta, or The Dream Book (*Snář*), opera, 3 acts, MARTINŮ, lib. Georges Neveux, tr. and

Julietta, Prague, National T., 5 Apr 1963; produced KAŠLÍK; designed SVOBODA; ŽÍDEK as Michel

arr. composer. Prague, NT, 16 Mar 1938. Main chars: Michel (ten.) Julietta (sop.). Michel, a travelling bookseller from Paris, has returned to a small coastal town, haunted by the memory of a girl (Julietta) singing from a window. But the inhabitants have now lost their memories. Michel, knowing nothing of this, finds their behaviour bewildering so that even his 'reality' seems empty and illusory and his encounters with Julietta unsatisfying. The railway station has disappeared and, unable to return, Michel finds himself in a 'Dream Office', where he thinks he hears Julietta calling him again, but, as is shown to him, there is no one there. *Julietta* is Martinů's most accomplished opera; exploring nostalgia and reality, it is well suited to his style. JT O
See Šafránek, *Bohuslav Martinů. His Life and Works* (London 1964); Large, *Martinů* (London 1975)

Juliette, sop., Roméo's lover in ROMÉO ET JULIETTE

Jumping Frog of Calaveras County, The, opera, 2 scenes, FOSS, lib. Jean Karsavina based on Mark Twain's story. Bloomington, Ind., 18 May 1950. LO

Junge Lord, Der (*The Young Lord*), opera, 3 acts, HENZE, lib. Ingeborg Bachmann based on a tale by Wilhelm Hauff. Berlin, Deutsche O., 7 Apr 1965; San Diego, Cal., 13 Feb 1967; London, SW (Cologne O.), 14 Oct 1969. Main chars: Lord Barrat (ten.) Sir Edgar (silent role) his Secretary (bar.) Luise (sop.) Wilhelm (ten.) Baroness Grünwiesel (mezzo-sop.). Sir Edgar introduces his nephew, Lord Barrat, to the polite society of a small Ger. town. The young man's atrocious behaviour is condoned until he is revealed as an ape. EF O

Jürgens, Helmut, b. Höxter a. d. Weser, 19 June 1902; d. Munich, 28 Aug 1963. German designer. Technical dir. at Düsseldorf 1930–8, then worked at Frankfurt, and from 1948 until his death was chief designer at the Bavarian Staats O., Munich. There he designed prods of operas by MOZART, WAGNER, VERDI and, in particular, R. STRAUSS, incl. SALOME, ROSENKAVALIER, DAPHNE, ELEKTRA, ARABELLA, LIEBE DER DANAE, ÄGYPTISCHE HELENA, ARIADNE AUF NAXOS, FRIEDENSTAG, and FRAU OHNE SCHATTEN. He also designed other 20th-c. works such as MATHIS DER MALER, PALESTRINA, JENŮFA, DUKE BLUEBEARD'S CASTLE; ORFF's KLUGE, *Antigonae*, BERNAUERIN, and CARMINA BURANA; EGK's *Peer Gynt* (1938), *Zaubergeige*, and *Columbus*; RASKOLNIKOFF and DANTONS TOD. At Hamburg he designed WOZZECK and MIDSUMMER NIGHT'S DREAM, and at Schwetzingen the premiere of ELEGY FOR YOUNG LOVERS. EF

Jurinac, Sena [Srebrenka], b. Travnik, 24 Oct 1921. Yugoslav soprano. Studied at Zagreb; debut there as MIMI (1942). Went to the Vienna Staats O. 1942 but debut not until after World War II, as CHERUBINO (1945). CG debut 1947 with Vienna co. as DORABELLA. Returned to sing CIO-CIO-SAN and OCTAVIAN with resident co. 1959; sang LEONORE in the 1961 KLEMPERER staging, and later MARSCHALLIN in VISCONTI's ROSENKAVALIER (1966). At Glyndebourne 1949–56, singing her noted Countess ALMAVIVA, FIORDILIGI, ELVIRA, and Composer (ARIADNE AUF NAXOS). In later part of career took on heavier roles such as Leonora (FORZA DEL DESTINO), Elisabeth (DON CARLOS), and TOSCA. One of the most attractive sops since World War II. AB

Juyol, Suzanne, b. Paris, 1 Jan 1920. French soprano. Debut, 1942, Paris O. as Margared (ROI D'YS); first sang at the OC as CHARLOTTE (1946). A dramatic sop. with a strong, keenly-projected voice, she has sung TOSCA, Santuzza (CAVALLERIA RUSTICANA), Marguerite (FAUST and DAMNATION DE FAUST), ARIANE ET BARBE-BLEUE, and FAURÉ's PÉNÉLOPE, as well as ORTRUD, BRÜNNHILDE (WALKÜRE and SIEGFRIED), and ISOLDE. EF

K

Kabalevsky, Dmitry Borisovich, b. St Petersburg, 30 Dec 1904. Russian composer. Studied Moscow Cons. His gifts for lyrical melody, sparkling orchestration, and highly effective choral writing are all evident in his first opera COLAS BREUGNON. His *Under Fire* (1943) was unsuccessful (largely because of a poor lib.), but much of the mus. was incorporated into *The Family of Taras* (1947, 2nd version 1950). Other operas are *Nikita Vershinin* (1955), *The Sisters* (1969), and the operetta *Spring Sings* (1957). GN

Kafka, Franz, b. Prague, 2 July 1883; d. Kierling, nr Vienna, 3 June 1924. Czech writer. Works on which operas have been based are: *Der Prozess*, 1925 (PROZESS; VISITATION); *America*, 1927 (Roman Haubenstock-Ramati, *Amerika*, Berlin 1966). LO

Kaiser, Georg, b. Magdeburg, 25 Nov 1878; d. Ascona, 5 June 1945. German dramatist. Leader of the Expressionist school of modern drama, and a potent force in the Ger. theatre between the two world wars. Operas to his libs or based on his plays are: *Der Protagonist*, 1926; *Der Zar lässt sich photographieren*, 1928; *Der Silbersee*, 1933 (all by WEILL); *Rosamunde Floris*, 1960 (BLACHER); *Juana*, 1926 (Max Ettinger); *Die Bürger von Calais*, play, 1914 (WAGNER-RÉGENY, 1939). LO

Kalisch, Alfred, b. London, 13 Mar 1863; d. London, 17 May 1933. English critic and translator. A champion of R. STRAUSS, tr. in Eng. SALOME, ELEKTRA, ARIADNE AUF NAXOS, ROSENKAVALIER (the latter used by ENO, 1975). Also tr. IRIS. LO

Kallman, Chester, b. Brooklyn, NY, 7 Jan 1921; d. Athens, 17 Jan 1975. American writer. Wrote lib. for Carlos Chávez's *Panfilo and Lauretta* (1957) and tr. DUKE BLUEBEARD'S CASTLE. Collaborated with AUDEN in libs for RAKE'S PROGRESS, ELEGY FOR YOUNG LOVERS, and NABOKOV's *Love's Labour's Lost*, and in tr. DON GIOVANNI, ZAUBERFLÖTE, and ANNA BOLENA. LO

Kálmán, Emmerich, b. Siófok, 24 Oct 1882; d. Paris, 30 Oct 1953. Hungarian composer of operettas. Studied at RAM, Budapest; BARTÓK and KODÁLY were fellow students. His first operetta was *Tártájárás*, Budapest 1908; perf. Vienna 1909, as *Herbstmanöver*, London 1912, as *Autumn Manoeuvres*. Other successful ones were *Die Csárdásfürstin* (Vienna 1915; London 1921), *Gräfin Mariza* (Vienna 1924; London 1938), and *Die Zirkusprinzessin* (Vienna 1926). The Magyar element is a prominent feature in them all. LO
See Lubbock

Kanawa, Kiri Te, b. Gisborne, 6 Mar 1944. New Zealand soprano. Studied in England at the London Opera Centre (1966). After minor appearances joined CG (1970) and made her debut in a major role with Countess ALMAVIVA (1971); has since sung MICAËLA, MARGUERITE, ELVIRA, DESDEMONA, and AMELIA (SIMONE BOCCANEGRA) among others. NY Met debut as Desdemona (1974); Glyndebourne as Countess (1973); Paris O. as Elvira (1975). One of the most promising lyrico-dramatic sops of recent years. AB

Kapellmeister *see* MAESTRO DI CAPPELLA

Kappel, Gertrude, b. Halle, 1 Sept 1884. German soprano. Studied Leipzig; debut, 1903, Hanover (TROVATORE). Sang in many of the principal opera houses including Munich 1927–31, CG, NY Met, 1928–36, and San Francisco 1933–7. One of the leading WAGNER and R. STRAUSS singers of her day. LO

Karajan, Herbert von, b. Salzburg, 5 Apr 1908. Austrian conductor and producer. Studied at Salzburg Mozarteum and Vienna Acad. Cond. at Ulm 1929, Aachen 1935; mus. dir. Aachen 1936. First appearance at Berlin Staats O. 1937; cond. there 1938–45. Art. dir., Vienna Staats O., 1956–64, Salzburg Fest. 1958–60 and again from 1964, often prod. as well as cond. Also in charge of Salzburg Easter Fest., at which he cond. and prod. RING DES NIBELUNGEN 1967–70, besides other WAGNER operas, and FIDELIO and BOHÈME. Appeared at Bayreuth 1951–2, at Sc. since 1948. NY Met debut 1968 with WALKÜRE. One of the most strikingly talented, idiosyncratic, sought-after conds of the day with a repertory ranging from MOZART to the Second Viennese School. Filmed Salzburg prods of CARMEN and VERDI's OTELLO, among others. AB

Karel, Rudolf, b. Plzeň [Pilsen], 9 Nov 1890; d. Terezín, 6 Mar 1945. Czech composer. One of DVOŘÁK's last pupils at the Prague Cons. His fairy-tale opera *Godmother Death* (*Smrt kmotřička*, 1933) has retained its popularity perhaps because of its strong folk roots and simple emotional appeal. Composition of *The Taming of the Shrew* (*Zkrocení zlé ženy*) was stopped by his imprisonment by the Nazis; a final opera *Three Hairs of an Old Wise Man* (*Tři vlasy děda Vševěda*, 1948) was sketched in concentration camp and completed by a pupil. JT

Karlsruhe, W. Germany. Home of Baden Staats. O., in the rebuilt Grosses Haus. A theatre was built there 1806–8; here first Ger. perf. of EURYANTHE was given, 1824. The first theatre burned down, 1847; Hof T. built 1851–3. Prod. of TANNHÄUSER there, 1855, began a long WAGNER tradition. It was destroyed 1944. Present mus. dir., Artur Grüber; dirs have incl. KEILBERTH, 1935–40. LO

Kaschmann [Kašman], Giuseppe, b. Lussimpiccolo, Istria, 14 July 1850; d. Rome, 7 Feb 1925. Italian baritone. Studied at Udine and Milan; debut 1876 Turin. Sang in NY Met's first season 1883. Was much admired as a WAGNER singer, but also had a wide repertory of Ger., It., and Fr. operas, and one of his favourite roles was HAMLET in Ambroise THOMAS's opera. LO

Kašlík, Václav, b. Poličná, 28 Sept 1917. Czech producer, composer, and conductor. Studied musicology and conducting and during World War II became cond. and prod. at the Prague NT. After the war he became increasingly interested in the application of experimental visual techniques to opera, and in televised and filmed opera. His own opera *Krakatit* (1961, after ČAPEK), an effective work which makes use of popular and jazz elements, was originally written for TV. Outside Czechoslovakia he is known chiefly as a prod., notably in collaboration with the designer SVOBODA, with whom he made his CG debut (PELLÉAS ET MÉLISANDE, 1969). Has since prod. NABUCCO and TANNHÄUSER in London and has worked in Berlin, Frankfurt, Munich (SOLDATEN), and Milan. JT

Kassel, W. Germany. Opera is given in the Staats T., opened 1959 replacing the Staats T. destroyed 1943. Has been important operatic centre at least since time of SPOHR, 1822–57; since World War II mus. dirs have included ELMENDORFF, Gerd Albrecht and, since 1972, LOCKHART, with Peter Löffler as the *Intendant* there. LO

Kát'a Kabanová, opera, 3 acts, JANÁČEK, lib. composer based on Vincenc Červinka's Czech translation (1918) of Aleksandr Ostrovsky's *The Storm* (1859). Brno, NT, 23 Nov 1921; London, SW, 10 Apr 1951; Cleveland, Karamu House, 26 Nov 1957. Main chars: Katěrina (Kát'a) (sop.) Boris (ten.) Kabanicha (contr.) Dikoj (bass) Tichon (ten.) Váňa (ten.) Varvara (mezzo-sop.). Kát'a, unhappily married to Tichon, takes advantage of his absence on a business trip to meet with Boris. When Tichon returns she is tormented by guilt, and, unnerved by a storm, she confesses to a company including Tichon and her evil mother-in-law, Kabanicha. Boris is sent to Siberia by his uncle Dikoj and Kát'a, after a final meeting with him, throws herself into the Volga. This is Janáček's most lyrical and passionate opera. JT O

See Ewans, *Janáček's Tragic Operas* (London 1976)

Katerina Izmaylova, with KNIPLOVÁ as Katerina and ŽÍDEK as Sergey; Prague, Smetana T., 14 May 1965; produced Karel Jernek; designed Oldřich Šimáček

Katerina Izmaylova, opera, 4 acts, SHOSTAKOVICH, lib. composer and A. Preys after

Kát'a Kabanová, Prague, National T., 3 June 1964; produced Hanuš Thein; designed SVOBODA. Marta Cihelniková as Kát'a and Libuše Márová as Varvara

Nikolay Leskov's story. Leningrad, Maly, as *Lady Macbeth of the Mtsensk District*, 22 Jan 1934; Moscow, Nemirovich-Danchenko Music T., 24 Jan 1934; Cleveland, Ohio, Severance Hall, 31 Jan 1935; London, Queen's Hall (concert perf.), 18 Mar 1936; revised version, Moscow, Stanislavsky-Nemirovich-Danchenko Music T., 26 Dec 1962. Main chars: Boris Izmaylov (bass) Zinovy Izmaylov (ten.) Katerina Izmaylova (sop.) Sergey (ten.) Sonetka (contr.). Katerina, bored with life, succumbs to the charms of Sergey, a worker on the estate, during the absence of her husband Zinovy. Boris (himself planning to seduce Katerina, his daughter-in-law) discovers the affair and has Sergey beaten. Katerina poisons some mushrooms; Boris eats them and dies. Later, while Sergey and Katerina are in the bedroom, Zinovy returns; Sergey kills him, and they hide the body in the cellar. During preparations for the marriage of Sergey and Katerina a drunken peasant discovers Zinovy's body and calls the police, who arrest the couple, and they are sent to Siberia. Sergey turns his attentions to Sonetka, a fellow convict, and Katerina, realizing that he had been using her simply to gain power, drowns herself, dragging Sonetka with her. The opera was intended to be part of a trilogy depicting Soviet womanhood, a project which Shostakovich never realized. In both versions, Katerina is portrayed more sympathetically than in the Leskov story (where, for example, she also murders her young coheir); and in the second version Shostakovich further avoided the implications of ruthlessness in Leskov's heroine by abandoning the opera's original title. Throughout the score, Katerina's intensely lyrical mus. is sharply contrasted with the often savage, grotesque satire in the mus. of the other characters. GN

Kecal, bass, the marriage broker in BARTERED BRIDE

Keilberth, Joseph, b. Karlsruhe, 19 Apr 1908; d. Munich, 21 July 1968. German conductor. Studied at Karlsruhe, where he became *répétiteur* 1925, and mus. dir. 1935–40. After Dresden (1945–50), moved to Munich where he remained until his death, first as cond. then mus. dir. (1959). He also cond. at Bayreuth, Edinburgh, and other fests. LO

Keiser, Reinhard, b. Teuchorn, 9 Jan 1674; d. Hamburg, 12 Sept 1739. German composer. The son of the organist at Weissenfels, he studied at the Thomasschule, Leipzig; after a spell as court MdC to the Duke of Brunswick he moved to Hamburg whose opera he dir. 1703–28, with a period of travel in Denmark and Germany 1717–22. He was the leading figure in the first short-lived phase of Ger. opera on the It. model that ended in 1733; his operas show both musical invention and dramatic power. Out of more than 40 works *Die Edelmuthige Octavia* (1705), *Massagnello* (1706), and *Der Lächerliche Prinz Jodelet* (1726) have attracted modern attention. JB

Kellogg, Clara Louise, b. Sumterville, S. Car., 12 July 1842; d. New Haven, Conn., 13 May 1916. American soprano. Educated NY. Debut, 1861, NY Acad. of Music as GILDA. London debut, HM 1867, singing in GOUNOD'S FAUST, TRAVIATA and DON GIOVANNI. In 1872 formed, with LUCCA, the Kellogg-Lucca Opera Co., which toured the USA 1872–4, and followed this with a co. of which she was in sole charge, supervising every aspect of the perfs from the tr. into Eng. to the chorus rehearsals and the details of the staging. A dedicated artist who did much to further the cause of opera in the USA. LO
See autobiography, *Memoirs of an American Prima Donna* (New York and London 1913)

Kelly, Michael, b. Dublin, 25 Dec 1762; d. Margate, 9 Oct 1826. Irish tenor. Studied singing in Naples, and appeared successfully on the It. stage under the name Occhelli. As a member of the Vienna Hof O. he came to know MOZART well, and created the roles of Don BASILIO and Don Curzio in NOZZE DI FIGARO (1786). In 1787 he went to London where he sang until he retired in 1811. He also comp. a number of operas. His *Reminiscences of M.K. of the King's Theatre* (London 1826) contains important information on Mozart. PS
See Kelly, *Solo Recital* (London 1972)

Kempe, Rudolf, b. Niederpoyritz, nr Dresden, 14 June 1910. German conductor. Studied with BUSCH at Dresden. Engaged Leipzig 1925 as *répétiteur*; debut as cond. there 1935. Mus. dir. Dresden O. 1949–52; similar post Munich 1952–4. Has since cond. frequently at important houses including NY Met (debut 1955, TANNHÄUSER), CG, Salzburg Fest. and Bayreuth (since 1960). A sensitive and versatile artist, equally illustrious in the It. as in the Ger. WAGNER/R. STRAUSS repertory, and a distinguished orchestral cond. LO

Kent Opera. Founded 1969 by Norman Platt, with Roger Norrington as mus. dir., Kent O. appears at Tunbridge Wells and Canterbury, also touring its prods in southern England. Operas perf. (in Eng.) incl. INCORONAZIONE DI POPPEA, NOZZE DI FIGARO, DON GIOVANNI, COSÌ FAN TUTTE, John Blow's *Venus*

and Adonis, TELEMANN's *Der Geduldige Sokrates*, Alan Ridout's *Pardoner's Tale* (specially commissioned) and, in lighter vein, H.M.S. PINAFORE and RUDDIGORE. The co. visited Lisbon, Jan 1974, giving perfs of *L'Incoronazione di Poppea*. EF

Kern, Jerome David, b. NY, 27 Jan 1885; d. NY, 11 Nov 1945. American composer. Trained in NY and in Europe, Kern began as comp. of mus. comedy; in the 1920s and 1930s moved into more substantial areas with more than 60 stage works incl. SHOW BOAT (1927), *The Cat and the Fiddle* (1931), *Music in the Air* (1932), and *Roberta* (1933), each illustrating his superior melodic talent and his firm grasp of musical materials. EJ

Kern, Patricia, b. Swansea, 14 July 1927. Welsh mezzo-soprano. Debut, 1952, with Opera for All as CENERENTOLA, a role for which she is renowned. Has sung with WNO, at Glyndebourne, SW (where she was first heard 1959 as the Witch in RUSALKA), and CG (debut, 1967, as ZERLINA). She has also appeared at Spoleto, Washington, NY City O., and in Canada. Excelling in ROSSINI's mezzo-sop. coloratura roles, she sings ROSINA, Isabella (ITALIANA IN ALGERI), Isolier (COMTE ORY), and Pippo (GAZZA LADRA), as well as CHERUBINO, Orlofsky (FLEDERMAUS), and Hänsel (HÄNSEL UND GRETEL). She created the part of Josephine in VIOLINS OF ST JACQUES (SW 1966). EF

Kertesz, Istvan, b. Budapest, 28 Aug 1929; d. Herzlia, Israel, 17 Apr 1973. Hungarian conductor. Assistant cond. Budapest 1954–6; mus. dir. Augsburg 1958–63, and of the Cologne O. from 1964 until his death. First cond. at Salzburg 1961 (ENTFÜHRUNG AUS DEM SERAIL), at CG 1966 (BALLO IN MASCHERA), and also worked at Sc., Berlin Staats O., the Colón, Buenos Aires, and at Edinburgh, Vienna, and Spoleto, where he cond. FIERY ANGEL (1959). In 1970 he brought the Cologne co. to London, SW, when his conducting of CLEMENZA DI TITO was particularly admired. Other operas in his repertory incl. FALSTAFF, SALOME, BILLY BUDD, and the original version of BORIS GODUNOV. EF

Khaikin [Khaykin], Boris Emmanuilovich, b. Minsk, 26 Oct 1904. Soviet conductor. Graduated from the Moscow Cons. in 1928, then cond. at the Stanislavsky Opera T. (1928–35). Principal cond. and art. dir. of the Maly T., Leningrad (1936–43) and of the Kirov T. (1943–54); and in 1954 he became a cond. at the Bolshoy T. He has been esp. active in promoting Soviet music, cond. the premieres of COLAS BREUGNON, DUENNA, and STORY OF A REAL MAN (PROKOFIEV), but also commands a wide repertory of Russian classical opera. Among his foreign perfs have been KHOVANSHCHINA (Florence 1963) and QUEEN OF SPADES (Leipzig 1964). GN

Kharkov *see* UKRAINE

Khovanshchina, opera, 5 acts, MUSORGSKY, lib. composer and Vladimir Stasov; completed, revised, and orchestrated by RIMSKY-KORSAKOV. St Petersburg, Kononov T., 21 Feb 1886; Mariinsky, 20 Nov 1911; London, DL, 1 July 1913; Philadelphia, Met. OH, 18 Apr 1928. Main chars: Prince Ivan Khovansky (bass) Prince Andrey Khovansky (ten.) Prince Vasily Golitsyn (ten.) Dosifey (bass) Shakhlovity (bar.) Marfa (mezzo-sop.) Emma (sop.). The action is set against the political insecurity of late 17th-c. Russia. Shakhlovity (the Regent Sofiya's agent) dictates a letter outlining the acts of treason planned by the Khovanskys; but Ivan Khovansky appears and declares his dedication to the royal family. Andrey enters in pursuit of Emma, but Marfa, his former love, intervenes; Dosifey, the leader of the Old Believers and a friend of the Khovanskys, restores order. The Khovanskys are denounced as traitors and, after Tsar Peter has gained control of Russia, Ivan Khovansky is assassinated and Golitsyn exiled. Finally the Old Believers (condemned by Peter) are joined by Andrey Khovansky and Marfa in a mass suicide by fire. A version of the opera based on Musorgsky's original manuscripts was made by Pavel Lamm and Boris Asafyev in 1931; a new orchestration by SHOSTAKOVICH (1959) forms the basis of most present-day perfs. GN O

Khrennikov, Tikhon Nikolayevich, b. Elets, 10 June 1913. Russian composer. Graduated from SHEBALIN's class at Moscow Cons. 1936; elected first secretary of the Soviet Comps' Union 1948. He comp. three operas: *Into the Storm* (1939, 2nd version, 1952), *Frol Skobeyev* (1950, 2nd version under the title *The Son-in-Law without Kith and Kin*, 1966), and *Mother* (1957). His 'song opera' *Into the Storm*, derivative in style and musically undistinguished, was the first Soviet opera in which Lenin appeared as a character. GN

Kienzl, Wilhelm, b. Waizenkirchen, 17 Jan 1857; d. Vienna, 3 Oct 1941. Austrian composer, one of the many in the WAGNER camp. His 10 operas, usually to his own words, had considerable success in Germany, with EVANGELIMANN reaching a wider public. It and *Der Kuhreigen*

Khovanshchina. Stage design by V. Y. Lowenthal (b. 1938) for Act I; produced People's T., Sofia, 1966

(1911) were played in Liverpool, in Eng., by Moody-Manners Opera Co. Kienzl also dir. opera at Amsterdam, Krefeld, Hamburg (1889–92), and Munich (1892–3). LO

Kiepura, Jan, b. Sosnowiec, 16 May 1902; d. NY, 15 Aug 1966. Polish tenor. Studied at Warsaw. Debut, 1924, Lvov as FAUST (GOUNOD). Vienna Staats O. debut 1926 and from then until 1938, singing such roles as TURIDDU, CALAF, and DES GRIEUX (MANON) with enormous success. Also appeared elsewhere in continental Europe and Buenos Aires. NY Met debut, 1938, as RODOLFO. Also a famous Danilo (LUSTIGE WITWE) with his wife Martha Eggerth as Hanna. Many films. His exciting voice was not always used with great taste; handsome stage presence. AB

Kiev *see* UKRAINE

King, James, b. Dodge City, Kansas, 22 May 1925. American tenor with major European reputation. Sang first as bar. while Professor of Mus., Univ. of Kansas City, 1952–61; changed to tenor in 1957 and studied with Martial Singher. Moved to Europe 1961 and joined Deutsche O., Berlin, 1962–5. Debuts: Berlin 1962 as Riccardo (BALLO IN MASCHERA); Salzburg Fest. 1962 as Achilles (IPHIGÉNIE EN AULIDE); Vienna Fest. 1964 at T. a. d. Wien as Apollo (DAFNE); Bayreuth Fest. 1965 as SIEGMUND; Vienna Staats O. 1965 as LOHENGRIN (title role); NY Met 1966 as FLORESTAN; CG 1967 as the Emperor (FRAU OHNE SCHATTEN). Distinguished by firm technique and forthright char. in wide range of Ger. repertory roles. NG

King and I, The, musical, RODGERS, book and lyrics HAMMERSTEIN II based on a novel *Anna and the King of Siam* by Margaret Landon. NY, St James's T., 29 Mar 1951; London, DL, 8 Oct 1953; revived NY, LC 6 July 1964. EJ ★○
See Lubbock

King David *see* ROI DAVID

King Mark, bass, King of Cornwall in TRISTAN UND ISOLDE

King Priam, opera, 3 acts, TIPPETT, lib. comp. derived from HOMER's *Iliad*. Commissioned by Koussevitsky Music Foundation. Coventry, Coventry T., 29 May 1962; London, CG, 5 June 1962; Karlsruhe, 26 Jan 1963. Main chars: Hecuba (sop.) Helen (mezzo-sop.) Achilles (ten.) Paris (ten.) Hector (bar.) Patroclus (bar.) Priam (bass-bar.). 'The mysterious nature of human choice' (Tippett). The choice of Priam in supposedly having the infant Paris killed, and in later restoring his patrimony; of Paris in taking Helen; of the Greeks in besieging Troy; of Hector in killing Patroclus; of Achilles in killing Hector; finally, Priam's acceptance of death as the price of dishonour when there is no choice left. Tippett's second opera replaces the luxurious textures of MIDSUMMER MARRIAGE with appropriately sparse instrumentation and athletic rhythms; the vocal writing is mainly declamatory. NG

King Roger, opera, 3 acts, SZYMANOWSKI, lib. comp. and Jaroslav Iwaszkiewicz. Warsaw, 19 June 1926; London, New O. Co. at SW, 14 May 1975. Main chars: King Roger (bar.) Queen Roxana (sop.) Shepherd/Dionysus (ten.). The opera deals with the struggle between Christianity and paganism when Roxana, wife of the medieval King Roger of Sicily, falls in love with a shepherd who is revealed as Dionysus. EF

King's Henchman, The, opera, 3 acts, TAYLOR, lib. Edna St Vincent Millay. NY Met, 17 Feb 1927. Main chars: Eadgar (bar.) Aethelwold (ten.) Aelfrida (sop.) Ase (contr.). King Eadgar of 10th-c. England has heard of the beauty of Aelfrida, a Devon princess. He sends his best friend Aethelwold to Devon where he and Aelfrida fall in love. Aethelwold returns news to King Eadgar that Aelfrida is too unattractive for his attention. When the King arrives he uncovers the deception and kills Aethelwold. EJ

King's Theatre, (Haymarket) *see* LONDON

Kipnis, Alexander, b. Zhitomir, Ukraine, 1 Feb 1891. Russian bass. Studied Warsaw and Berlin. In Germany when World War I broke out, but allowed to stay and work there. Debut Hamburg 1915. Sang at Wiesbaden, 1916–18 and Berlin, Städtische O., 1918–25. Moved to USA 1939; NY Met 1939–46, debut there 1940 (PARSIFAL). Sang at CG and Glyndebourne 1923–35, Staats O., Vienna, 1934–8, and a frequent visitor to Bayreuth and Salzburg Fests. His rich and resonant bass was one of the finest voices of the day, heard to great advantage in WAGNER and in roles such as ARKEL, BORIS GODUNOV, OCHS, and SARASTRO. LO

Kirov Theatre *see* LENINGRAD

Kirsten, Dorothy, b. Montclair, NJ, 6 July 1917. American soprano. Debut, 1940, Chicago, as Pousette (MANON), first sang at NY CC, 1944, as VIOLETTA and at the Met, 1945, as MIMI. Her repertory incl. MICAËLA, MARGUERITE, JULIETTE, LOUISE, Fiora (AMORE DEI TRE RE), MANON, MANON LESCAUT, CIO-CIO-SAN, TOSCA, and Minnie (FANCIULLA DEL WEST). She sang in the first US perf. of TROILUS AND CRESSIDA (1955) and DIALOGUES DES CARMÉLITES (1957), both at San Francisco. EF

Kiss, The (*Hubička*), opera, 2 acts, SMETANA, lib. KRÁSNOHORSKÁ after the tale by Karolina Světlá (1871). Prague, PT, 7 Nov 1876; Chicago, Blackston T., 17 Apr 1921; Liverpool, 8 Dec 1938. Main chars: Vendulka (sop.) Lukáš (ten.) Martinka (contr.) Paloucký (bass) Matouš (bass). Lukáš, recently widowed with a baby, wants to marry his former love Vendulka. Though delighted she refuses to let him kiss her before they are married; this leads to a quarrel and Vendulka flees to the mountains with her aunt Martinka, who takes part in border smuggling. Lukáš follows and asks for forgiveness and the couple are at last united. This was the first opera that Smetana comp. after going deaf, though there is little hint of this from its gentle and joyful music. During Smetana's lifetime this was his most popular opera after BARTERED BRIDE. JT ○
See Large, *Smetana* (London 1970)

Kiss Me Kate, musical, PORTER, book Samuel and Bella Spewak from SHAKESPEARE's *The Taming of the Shrew*. NY, New Century (formerly Jolson) T., 30 Dec 1948; London, Coliseum, 8 Mar 1951; Munich, 2 Dec 1955. EJ ★

Klafsky, Katharina, b. Mosonszentjános, 19 Sept 1855; d. Hamburg, 22 Sept 1896. Hungarian soprano. Studied at Vienna with MARCHESI DE CASTRONE; a leading sop. in Leipzig 1876–86, and Hamburg 1886–95. Sang with A. NEUMANN's travelling Wagner co. 1882, and with the Damrosch Opera Co. in USA 1895–6. Was m. three times; her third husband was the cond. Otto Lohse (1858–1925), whom she accompanied to the USA. She sang LEONORE and AGATHE in London, and her repertory was wide, but it was as a WAGNER singer that she was at her best. LO

Klebe, Giselher Wolfgang, b. Mannheim, 28 June 1925. German composer. His operas are: *Die Räuber*, after SCHILLER, Düsseldorf, 1957; *Die Ermörderung Cäsars*, 1 act, after SHAKESPEARE's *Julius Caesar*, Essen, 1959; *Die Tödlichen Wünsche*, after Honoré de Balzac, Düsseldorf, 1959; ALKMENE; *Figaro Lässt Sich Scheinen*, after Ödön von Horváth, Hamburg, 1963; *Jakobowsky und der Oberst*, after Franz Werfel, 1969; *Das Märchen von der Schönen Lilie*, Schwetzingen, 1969; *Ein Wahrer Held*, based on John Millington Synge's *Playboy of the Western World*, Zürich, 1975; *Das Mädchen von Domrémy*, Stuttgart, 1976. LO

Kleiber, Carlos, b. Berlin, 3 July 1930. German, later Argentinian, conductor. Son of E. KLEIBER. Engaged at the Deutsche O. am Rhein, Düsseldorf, 1956–64. Cond. at Zürich, Stuttgart, Munich, Vienna, Prague, and Hamburg. CG debut 1974 with ROSENKAVALIER, and the same year cond. TRISTAN UND ISOLDE

The Kiss, Prague, National T., 24 Feb 1960; produced PUJMAN; designed Karel Svolínsky. BLACHUT as Lukáš and Drahomíra Tikalová as Vendulka (right)

at Bayreuth. Other operas he has cond. incl. FREISCHÜTZ, CARMEN, VERDI'S OTELLO, ELEKTRA, and WOZZECK. EF

Kleiber, Erich, b. Vienna, 5 Aug 1890; d. Zürich, 27 Jan 1956. Austrian, naturalized Argentinian, conductor. Engaged at Darmstadt 1912, Wuppertal 1919, and Mannheim 1922. Mus. dir. of the Berlin Staats O. 1923–33, during which period he cond. the world premieres of WOZZECK (1925) and CHRISTOPHE COLOMB (1930). Resigning from the Staats O. over the banning of MATHIS DER MALER, he began an association with the Colón, Buenos Aires (1937) and cond. FLIEGENDE HOLLÄNDER (CG 1938). Returning to CG 1950, in three seasons he noticeably raised the orchestral standard of the co., cond. NOZZE DI FIGARO, ZAUBERFLÖTE, TRISTAN UND ISOLDE, RIGOLETTO, CARMEN, ROSENKAVALIER, and the first London perf. of *Wozzeck* (1952). EF

Kleist, Heinrich Wilhelm von, b. Frankfurt a. d. Oder, 18 Oct 1777; d. (by his own hand) Wannsee, nr Potsdam, 21 Nov 1811. German writer whose complex and contradictory mind in the emotional instability of the Germany of his time has found a sympathetic response today. Works on which operas are based: *Penthesilea*, 1808 (SCHOECK, Dresden 1927); *Michael Kohlhaas*, 1810 (KLENAU, Stuttgart 1933); *Der Prinz von Homburg*, 1810 (GRAENER, 1935, and HENZE); *Die Verlobung in San Domingo*, 1810 (EGK, 1963). LO

Klemperer, Otto, b. Breslau (now Wrocław), 14 May 1885; d. Zürich, 6 July 1973. German conductor. His operatic work was mainly before World War II, his first important post being at Prague NT, 1907–10, followed by Hamburg 1910–14, Strasbourg 1914–17, Cologne 1917–24, Wiesbaden 1924–7, and finally Berlin 1927 until the Nazi regime, when he left Germany. His Berlin period was his finest, giving memorable perfs of the standard repertory and operas by the modern comps HINDEMITH, SCHÖNBERG, and STRAVINSKY. After World War II he was at Budapest 1947–50, and also visited CG 1961, 1962 and 1963, cond. FIDELIO, ZAUBERFLÖTE, and LOHENGRIN. A devoted musician, at his best in works that matched his own seriousness of outlook. LO

Klenau, Paul von, b. Copenhagen, 11 Feb 1883; d. Copenhagen, 31 Aug 1946. Danish conductor and composer. His seven operas incl. *Kjartan und Gudrun* (1918, revised as *Gudrun auf Island*, 1924), *Michael Kohlhaas* (1933), based on KLEIST, and *Rembrandt van Rijn* (1937). LO

Klingsor, bass, the magician in PARSIFAL

Klose, Margarete, b. Berlin, 6 Aug 1902; d. Berlin, 14 Dec 1965. German mezzo-soprano. Studied Berlin. Debut 1927 at Ulm in KÁLMÁN'S *Gräfin Mariza*. Mannheim 1928–31, Berlin Staats O. 1932–49, Städtische O. 1949–58, Staats O. 1958–61. CG debut 1935 as ORTRUD; Bayreuth debut 1936 as Ortrud and sang leading roles there until 1942. One of the ranking German mezzo-sops of 1930–50, accomplished both in Wagnerian and more lyrical roles, among them Orphée (ORPHÉE ET EURYDICE) and CARMEN. AB

Kluge, Die (*The Clever Girl*), opera, 6 scenes, ORFF, lib. composer based partly on GRIMM'S *Die Kluge Bauerntochter* (*The Peasant's Clever Daughter*). Frankfurt, Staats O., 18 Feb 1943; Cleveland, Ohio, Karamu House, 7 Dec 1949; London, SW, 27 July 1959. LO

Klytemnestra, mezzo-sop., wife and murderess of Agamemnon in ELEKTRA

Knappertsbusch, Hans, b. Elberfeld, 12 Mar 1888; d. Munich, 25 Oct 1965. German conductor. Studied at Bonn Univ., then Cologne Cons. After appointments at Elberfeld 1913–18, Leipzig, and Dessau, succeeded WALTER as general mus. dir. Munich 1922–36, and had similar post Vienna 1938–9. A period as guest cond. followed (incl. Bayreuth from 1951), returning as cond. to Munich 1954. A renowned interpreter of WAGNER and R. STRAUSS. LO

Knight, Gillian, b. Redditch, Worcestershire. English mezzo-soprano. Engaged by the D'Oyly Carte company (1959–65) she sang Katisha (MIKADO), Ruth (PIRATES OF PENZANCE), Little Buttercup (H.M.S. PINAFORE), and Lady Jane (PATIENCE). She then joined SW, singing SUZUKI, Ragonde (COMTE ORY), Isabella (ITALIANA IN ALGERI), Juno (SEMELE), and CARMEN. CG debut 1970 as the Page in SALOME; created Rose Parrowe in Maxwell DAVIES's *Taverner* (1972). Her roles incl. Annina (ROSENKAVALIER), Helen (KING PRIAM), Olga (EUGENE ONEGIN), Fenena (NABUCCO), and Margret (WOZZECK). EF

Kniplová, Naděžda, b. Ostrava, 18 Apr 1932. Czech dramatic soprano. Studied at Prague Cons. 1947–53 and Acad. 1954–8; joined the Ústí nad Labem co. 1957; moved to Brno 1959, and Prague 1966. She has a powerful dramatic sop. voice and dominant stage presence which has been used with great effect as the Kostelnička in JENŮFA, Marty in the MAKROPULOS CASE or as LIBUŠE. She has also had an active career outside Czechoslovakia and Czech opera, particularly in WAGNER, singing BRÜNNHILDE under KARAJAN in Salzburg, in Turin (GÖTTERDÄMMERUNG), San Francisco (WALKÜRE), Vienna (RING DES NIBELUNGEN), and Barcelona (TRISTAN UND ISOLDE). Has sung in Tokyo with the Berlin O. and in Montreal with the Hamburg O. JT

Knipper, Lev Konstantinovich, b. Tiflis (now Tbilisi), 3 Dec 1898; d. Moscow, 30 July 1974. His first opera *The North Wind* (1930) was criticized for its modernist tendencies, but in subsequent works his style was tempered by an interest in the folk music of the various Soviet republics. This is evident in another opera *On Lake Baykal* (1948), based on Mongol themes. GN

Knot Garden, The, opera, 3 acts, TIPPETT, lib. comp. London, CG, 2 Dec 1970; Evanston, Ill., Northwestern Univ. Cahn Auditorium, 22 Feb 1974. Chars: Flora (sop.) Denise (sop.) Thea (mezzo-sop.) Dov (ten.) Mel (bar.) Faber (bar.) Mangus (bar.). Seven contemporaries whose personalities impinge on one another in the knot garden of their characters. Thea and Faber have a marriage grown stale and retreat from intimate communication; Faber lusts after the adolescent Flora, whom Thea protects. Dov, a white musician, and Mel, a black poet, are locked in a homosexual tangle. Their catalysts are Denise, a physically scarred revolutionary, and Mangus, a middle-aged analyst with allusions to SHAKESPEARE's Prospero as the 'man of power'. Tippett's third opera is distinguished by music that combines soaring cantilena, clarity of line and harmonic directness, exposing the nerve ends of varied human relationships with vivid yet subtle vocal writing and instrumental colour. NG O

Koanga, opera, prologue and 3 acts, DELIUS, lib. Charles Francis Keary after George Washington Cable's novel *The Grandissimes*. Elberfeld, 30 Mar 1904 (in Ger.); London, CG, 23 Sept 1935. Main chars: Koanga (bar.) Palmyra (sop.) Don José (bass). Palmyra, a mulatto, falls in love with Koanga, an African chieftain who has been captured and brought to work on a plantation. After a quarrel with the planter, Don José, Koanga escapes into the forest, where he causes a plague by means of voodoo. Palmyra and Koanga die together. It is interesting that Delius himself spent some of his early years as an orange planter in Florida. FGB O

Kobbé, Gustave, b. New York City, 3 Mar 1857; d. Babylon, L.I., 27 July 1918. American critic and writer, remembered now almost exclusively for his *Complete Opera Book* (1919; rev. 1954, 1969, by Earl of HAREWOOD). Other books incl. *Opera Singers* (1901) and *Wagner's Music-Dramas analysed* (New York 1904; London 1927). LO

Kodály, Zoltán, b. Kecskemét, 16 Dec 1882; d. Budapest, 6 Mar 1967. Hungarian composer. Studied in Budapest. Friend of and co-worker on Magyar folk music with BARTÓK. Of his three operas (made up of numbers with extensive dialogue), HÁRY JÁNOS (1926) is the most important and most often perf. It is largely based on Magyar music. Other semi-operas are: *The Spinning Room of the Székelys* (1932), in a single act, and *Czinka Panna* (1948), which deals with the 1848 national uprising and was wr. for its centenary. AB

Kokoschka, Oskar, b. Pöchlarn, 1 Mar 1886. German painter, of Austrian and Czech descent. Assoc. with Gustav Klimt and the Viennese Secession. Settled in England 1938 (Polperro, Cornwall), but removed to Switzerland 1947. Wrote lib. for HINDEMITH's *Mörder, Hoffnung der Frauen* (1921). Did some notable designs for ZAUBERFLÖTE (Geneva 1965) for GRAF. LO

Koltai, Ralph, b. Berlin, 31 July 1924. German-born British designer. Studied London. Debut as stage designer with ANGÉLIQUE at Fortune T. (1950). CG with controversial TANNHÄUSER (1955). Designed the following productions for SO: DON GIOVANNI (1964), BORIS GODUNOV (1965), RAKE'S PROGRESS (1967), ELEGY FOR YOUNG LOVERS (1970). Settings for Sadler's Wells (now ENO): AUFSTIEG UND FALL DER STADT MAHAGONNY (1963), RING DES NIBELUNGEN (1970–2). His work is distinguished by an imaginative, often original look. AB

Komissarzhevsky, Fyodor Petrovich, b. 1838; d. San Remo, 1 Mar 1905. Russian tenor. He sang at the Mariinsky Theatre (1863–80), where he created many Russian roles, including Vakula in TCHAIKOVSKY's *Vakula the Smith*, Don Juan in STONE GUEST, the Pretender in BORIS GODUNOV, and Levko in MAY NIGHT. His wife was the actress Vera Komissarzhevskaya. GN

Konetzni, Anni, b. 12 Feb 1902; d. Vienna, 6 Sept 1968. Austrian soprano. Studied at Vienna with SCHMEDES. Debut, 1927, Chemnitz, as a contr. but soon became a dramatic sop. Berlin Staats O. 1931–5, Vienna Staats O. 1935–54, singing all the heavier Wagnerian roles. CG debut 1935 as BRÜNNHILDE (RING), returned every season until World War II and again in 1951. NY Met debut 1934 as Brünnhilde. AB

Konetzni, Hilde, b. Vienna, 21 Mar 1905. Austrian soprano, sister of A. KONETZNI. Studied at Vienna and Prague. Debut, 1929, Chemnitz, as SIEGLINDE (to become one of her most famous roles). Prague 1932–6, Vienna Staats O. since 1936. CG debut, 1938, as MARSCHALLIN, replacing Lotte LEHMANN during a perf. when Lehmann fell ill; sang other roles 1938–9 and returned as LEONORE with the Vienna Staats O. 1947; as SIEGLINDE and GUTRUNE 1955. AB

König Hirsch (*King Stag*), opera, 3 acts, HENZE, lib. Heinz von Cramer based on the fairy tale by GOZZI. Berlin, Städtische O., 25 Sept 1956; revised version, as *Il Re Cervo*, Kassel 1963; Santa Fe, 4 Aug 1965. Main chars: King Leandro (ten.) Costanza (sop.) Tartaglia (bass-bar.) Checco (ten.) Coltellino (ten.) Scollatella (sop.). The King, brought up with wild animals in the forest, takes refuge there, in the form of a stag, from the wicked Tartaglia, who is eventually killed by his own hired assassin. EF

Königin von Saba, Die (*The Queen of Sheba*), opera, 4 acts, GOLDMARK, lib. Salomon Hermann Mosenthal. Vienna, O., 10 Mar 1875; Manchester (Carl Rosa, in Eng.), T. Royal, 12 Apr 1910; NY Met (in Ger.), 2 Dec 1885. Main chars: Assad (ten.) King Solomon (bar.) Sulamith (sop.) High Priest (bass) Queen of Sheba (mezzo-sop.). The opera tells of the downfall and final death in the desert of Assad, favourite of King Solomon. Betrothed to Sulamith, daughter of the High Priest, Assad has been ensnared by the beauty of the Queen of Sheba. Too late he is torn by remorse. LO
See Kobbé

Königskinder, Die (*The Royal Children*), opera, 3 acts, HUMPERDINCK, lib. Ernst Rosmer (Elsa Bernstein). NY Met, 28 Dec 1910; London, CG, 27 Nov 1911. Main chars: the Prince (ten.) the Goose-girl (sop.) the Witch (contr.) the Fiddler (bar.). The Goose-girl, who lives in the house of a witch, falls in love with a Prince disguised as a beggar. The Prince makes her his queen, but they are chased from the city. Lost and in despair, they die after eating the Witch's poisoned bread. In spite of some charming music the opera has fallen into neglect outside Germany. Originally written 1897 as a play with music, it made use of *Sprechstimme* later associated with SCHÖNBERG, which was deleted when the work was turned into an opera. FGB

Konjović, Petar, b. Čurug, 5 May 1883; d. Belgrade, 1 Oct 1970. Yugoslav composer. His first opera was *Miloš's Wedding* (1971), though he is better represented by the powerfully dramatic *Koštana* (1931). GN

Kónya, Sándor, b. Sarkad, 23 Sept 1923. Hungarian tenor. Studied Budapest and Hanover. Debut, 1951, Bielefeld, as TURIDDU. After several engagements in Germany joined Berlin Städtische O. 1955. Became internationally known after Wieland WAGNER chose him for title role in new prod. of LOHENGRIN at Bayreuth Fest. 1958. Further debuts at Sc. and San Francisco 1960; NY Met 1961 and CG 1963, both as Lohengrin. Admired for firmness of line and vigour of char. in wide range of It. repertory roles in addition to WAGNER. NG

Korngold, Erich Wolfgang, b. Brno [Brünn], 29 May 1897; d. Hollywood, 29 Nov 1957. Viennese composer. Son of music critic Julius

Korngold (1860–1945). His chief operas are the two one-act works *Der Ring des Polykrates* (1916) and *Violanta* (Munich 1916), and TOTE STADT. *Das Wunder der Heliane* (1927) was revived Ghent, Feb 1970. Began a new career in USA 1935, writing mus. for films; mus. dir. for Warner Brothers 1936. The film *Give Us this Night* (1936) had a miniature opera, *Romeo and Juliet*, inserted. LO

Košler, Zdeněk, b. Prague, 25 Mar 1928. Czech conductor. Studied composition with JEREMIÁŠ and conducting with Karel Ančerl at the Prague Acad. (1948–52). After serving as *répétiteur* at the Prague NT, he became head of opera at Olomouc (1958–62). He won first prize at the young conds' competition in Besançon (1956) and the Mitropoulos prize in New York (1963), where he was BERNSTEIN's assistant for a year. Head of opera in Ostrava (1962–6) and *Generalmusikdirektor* at the Berlin KO (1966–8) and became head of opera at Bratislava in 1971. He has had special success in conducting contemporary works and introduced several PROKOFIEV operas to Czechoslovakia. JT

Koussevitsky, Serge, b. Vizhny Volochek, 26 July 1874; d. Boston, 4 June 1951. Russian, later American, conductor. Primarily an orchestral cond., though he cond. some memorable perfs of Russian opera in Paris in 1921. Founded Berkshire Fest. 1937, and the Koussevitsky Music Foundation 1942, which commissioned, among other operas, PETER GRIMES, BALLAD OF BABY DOE, WALTON's *The Bear*, and KING PRIAM. Since 1950 the Foundation has been permanently endowed as 'The Serge Koussevitsky Music Foundation in the Library of Congress', the Library receiving the autograph scores of the works commissioned. LO

Kovařovic, Karel, b. Prague, 9 Dec 1862; d. Prague, 6 Dec 1920. Czech composer and conductor. Studied harp at Prague Cons. 1873–9 and composition with FIBICH. Worked as an orchestral harpist at the Prague NT 1879–85 before becoming a *répétiteur* and cond. Chief cond. of Prague NT 1900–20, where he did much to improve standards and diversify the repertory. He gave the premiere of RUSALKA (1901) and the crucial Prague premiere of JENŮFA (1916). Of his five operas *The Dogheads* (*Psohlavci*, 1898) is still occasionally played in Czechoslovakia, chiefly for its strong dramatic and patriotic elements. JT

Kozlovsky, Ivan Semyonovich, b. Maryanovka, Kiev Government, 24 Mar 1900. Ukrainian tenor. Studied in Kiev, sang at the Kharkov O. (1924) and Sverdlovsk O. (1925), then joined the Bolshoy in 1926. Possessing a highly individual and versatile voice, he is particularly noted for his interpretations of LENSKY, the Simpleton (BORIS GODUNOV), ALMAVIVA, Don JOSÉ, and LOHENGRIN. GN

Krásnohorská [Pechová], Eliška, b. Prague, 18 Nov 1847; d. Prague, 26 Nov 1926. Czech poet and librettist. She was an amateur musician and sang for many years in the Žofín Acad., where she met SMETANA. Though DVOŘÁK and JANÁČEK set some of her poems, she is better known for her opera libs for Smetana's *Lumír* (1870, not set), *Viola* (1871, incomplete), KISS (1876), SECRET (1878), and DEVIL'S WALL (1882); FIBICH's *Blaník* (1881), and BENDL's *Lejla* (1868), *Břetislav* (1870), *Karel Škréta* (1883), and *The Child of Tábor* (*Dítě Tábora*, 1892). Most of her work for Smetana was after he became deaf; her sympathetic correspondence was a source of encouragement. JT

Krásová, Marta, b. Protivín, 16 Mar 1901; d. Vráž u Berouna, 20 Feb 1970. Czech mezzo-soprano. She was a member of the Bratislava NT 1922–8, where she changed from sop. to mezzo-sop. and perf. AMNERIS and CARMEN. Joined Prague NT 1928; the leading mezzo-sop. until 1966. Her voice was of impressive power and extended to dramatic and coloratura roles. Sang most of the Czech repertory (incl. a famous portrayal of the Kostelnička in JENŮFA) as well as several contemporary works. JT

Kraus, Alfredo, b. Las Palmas, Canary I., 1928. Spanish tenor. Studied at Barcelona and Milan; prizewinner in Geneva international competition. Debut, 1956, Cairo O., as DUCA DI MANTUA. London debut, Stoll T., 1957 with visiting It. co. as ALFREDO; CG 1959 as EDGARDO. Then Sc. 1960 as Elvino (SONNAMBULA); US debut Chicago Lyric O. 1962 as NEMORINO; NY Met 1965 in RIGOLETTO; Salzburg Fest. as Don OTTAVIO under KARAJAN. A singer of enjoyable elegance of style and expressive line in lyric roles, incl. the Fr. repertory of MANON and WERTHER, GOUNOD's FAUST, and PÊCHEURS DE PERLES, in addition to It. roles. NG

Kraus, Otakar, b. Prague, 10 Dec 1909. Czech, later British, baritone. Studied Prague and Milan (with Fernando Carpi). Debut, 1935, Brno, as AMONASRO. At Bratislava 1936–9. Left Czechoslovakia for England after Hitler came to power. First London appearance in SOROCHINTSY FAIR at Savoy T. 1940. Carl Rosa 1943–6, when his SCARPIA and villains in CONTES D' HOFFMANN were much admired.

Otakar Kraus as the Doctor in WOZZECK, London, CG, 6 Apr 1970; produced S. F. AUSTIN; designed NEHER

Joined EOG 1946 and created Tarquinius (RAPE OF LUCRETIA). With Netherlands O. 1950–1 season. Created Nick Shadow (RAKE'S PROGRESS) at Venice 1951. Joined CG co. 1951 and remained with it until retirement in 1973, singing more than 40 roles, creating Diomede (TROILUS AND CRESSIDA) and King Fisher (MIDSUMMER MARRIAGE). Other important roles were IAGO, Scarpia, Caspar (FREISCHÜTZ), the Doctor (WOZZECK), KLINGSOR, and ALBERICH, which he sang at Bayreuth (1960–2). A powerful singing actor. AB

Krause, Tom, b. Helsinki, 5 July 1934. Finnish baritone. Studied at Vienna Acad. Debut, 1958, Städtische O., Berlin. Has sung at Bayreuth, Glyndebourne, Salzburg, Chicago and NY Met. A member of the co. at Hamburg, he created the title role of SEARLE's HAMLET there (1968). His repertory incl. DON GIOVANNI, Count ALMAVIVA (NOZZE DI FIGARO), GUGLIELMO, PIZARRO, Don Fernando (FIDELIO), WOLFRAM, ESCAMILLO, Orestes (ELEKTRA), the Count (CAPRICCIO), and Nick Shadow (RAKE'S PROGRESS). EF

Krauss, Clemens, b. Vienna, 31 Mar 1893; d. Mexico City, 16 May 1954. Austrian conductor. Studied Vienna. Posts included Frankfurt O., 1924–9; Vienna, 1929–35; Berlin, 1935–7; gen. mus. dir. Munich, 1937–42. A friend of R. STRAUSS and closely associated with his music, he cond. premieres of ARABELLA, FRIEDENSTAG, CAPRICCIO (for which he wrote the lib.), and LIEBE DER DANAE. He m. URSULEAC. LO

Krauss, Marie Gabrielle, b. Vienna, 24 Mar 1842; d. Paris, 6 Jan 1906. Austrian soprano. Studied Vienna Cons. and with MARCHESI DE CASTRONE. Debut, 1859, Vienna (GUILLAUME TELL). Remained there until 1867, then was with Paris TI until 1870. After a period touring, at Paris O. 1875–88, creating Pauline in GOUNOD's *Polyeucte*, Katherine of Aragon (HENRY VIII, 1883). Other roles incl. Rachel (JUIVE, at opening of GARNIER's O., 1875), GILDA, AIDA, FIDELIO, NORMA. Excelled almost equally as an actress, hence her nickname 'la Rachel chantante'. LO

Krejčí, Iša, b. Prague, 10 July 1904; d. Prague, 6 Mar 1968. Czech composer and conductor. Studied composition with NOVÁK 1927–9 and after working in Bratislava returned to Prague as chief cond. of radio orch. 1934–45. Head of opera at Olomouc 1945–58 and *Dramaturg* at Prague NT 1958–68. An early opera, *Antigona*, was revised for TV and then stage perfs (1965), but it is chiefly for his second opera, *Uproar in Ephesus* (*Pozdvižení v Efesu*, 1946, after SHAKESPEARE's *Comedy of Errors*) that he is known. This is a sparkling and deftly written neoclassical work, extensively perf. in Czechoslovakia. JT

Křenek, Ernst, b. Vienna, 28 Aug 1900. Austrian, naturalized American, composer. Studied at Vienna and Berlin. Moved to USA 1937; became an American citizen 1954. His operas incl. *Zwingburg* (Berlin 1924), *Leben des Orest* (Leipzig 1930), *Karl V* (Prague 1937), *Dark Waters* (Los Angeles 1950), *Pallas Athene Weint* (Hamburg 1955), *The Belltower* (Urbana, Ill. 1957), and *Der Goldene Bock* (Hamburg 1964), as well as a TV opera, *Der Zauberspiegel* (1966). His fame rests largely on JONNY SPIELT AUF (1927), the first jazz opera, which was enormously successful in its day, and exerted a powerful influence over many contemporary comps. EF

Kreutzer, Conradin, b. Messkirch, Baden, 22 Nov 1780; d. Riga, 14 Dec 1849. German composer and conductor, working principally in Vienna, at KT and Josephstadt T. He also had engagements at Stuttgart 1812–17, Donauschingen and Cologne 1840–6. Of *c.* 30 operas the best known was NACHTLAGER VON GRANADA (1834). LO

Křička, Jaroslav, b. Kelč, Moravia, 27 Aug 1882; d. Prague, 23 Jan 1969. Czech composer. As cond. of the Hlahol Choral Society in Prague (1911–20) and professor of comp. at Prague Cons. (1919–45), he played an active part in Czech musical life. He was a prolific comp.: he wrote 10 operas (incl. some for children) and several operettas. His best-known stage work is the Christmas opera *The Czech Crib* (*České jesličky*, 1949). JT

Krilovici, Marina, b. Bucharest. Romanian soprano. Debut Bucharest as VIOLETTA. Joined Hamburg Staats O. (1968). US debut as AIDA (1971); CG debut in same role (1971). Chicago as MIMI (1972). One of the leading lyric-dramatic singers of the day. AB

Krips, Josef, b. Vienna, 8 Apr 1902; d. Geneva, 13 Oct 1974. Austrian conductor. Studied with WEINGARTNER. Mus. dir. Karlsruhe, 1926–33, then left Germany for Vienna Staats O.; dismissed from there by the Nazis in 1938. Returned to Vienna after World War II, where he worked tirelessly to restore the Staats O. to its former glory. Has also cond. at CG, regularly at Salzburg Fest., and Florence Maggio Musicale. A well-loved personality, much admired for his MOZART. LO

Kroll Opera House *see* BERLIN

Krombholc, Jaroslav, b. Prague, 30 Jan 1918. Czech conductor. While studying composition at the Prague Cons. under NOVÁK and HÁBA (1938–42), he studied conducting with TALICH. He was engaged as a *répétiteur* at Prague NT in 1940 and after serving briefly as head of opera in Ostrava (1944) he returned to Prague NT, where he has held a number of positions, becoming chief cond. in 1963. Though he has concentrated on the Czech repertory, making recordings of operas by SMETANA, JANÁČEK, DVOŘÁK, FIBICH, CIKKER, and MARTINŮ, he also introduced WAR AND PEACE to the Prague NT and has cond. such works as ZAUBERFLÖTE, GOUNOD'S FAUST, and WOZZECK. He has also cond. abroad – in South America, Copenhagen, Vienna, Poland, France, London (1957–60), where he conducted BORIS GODUNOV, and at the Holland Fest. National Artist 1966. JT

Kubelík, Rafael (Jeronýmm), b. Býchory, 29 June 1914. Czech, naturalized Swiss, conductor and composer. The son of the violinist Jan Kubelík, he studied violin, cond. and comp. at Prague Cons. and became chief cond. of the Czech Philharmonic 1936. Cond. at the Brno NT from 1939 to 1941, when it closed. Left Czechoslovakia 1948; mus. dir. of the Chicago Symphony 1950–3, of CG 1955–8, where he gave the first London perfs of JENŮFA (1956) and TROYENS (1957), both in Eng. He has maintained his international reputation as a symphonic cond. (chiefly as principal cond. of the Bavarian Radio Symphony Orch. from 1961) but has also made several important opera recordings (including OBERON, LOHENGRIN, and PALESTRINA) and in 1971 became first permanent mus. dir. of the NY Met. Kubelík's five operas incl. *Cornelia Faroli* (on the life of Titian) prod. Augsburg 1972. JT

Kubiak, Teresa, b. Poland. Polish soprano. Debut, 1965, Lodz. British debut, 1971, Glyndebourne as Lisa (QUEEN OF SPADES). CG debut 1972 as CIO-CIO-SAN, returning for TOSCA and AIDA. NY Met debut, 1972, as Lisa. One of the most successful of younger lyric-dramatic sops with a robust voice of considerable allure; also a generous actress. AB

Kundry, sop., the enchantress in PARSIFAL

Kunz, Erich, b. Vienna, 20 May 1909. Austrian baritone. Studied at Vienna. Debut 1933, Opava as OSMIN. Glyndebourne, as member of chorus 1936. Debut 1940, Vienna Staats O. as BECKMESSER; came with that co. to CG 1947 and sang MOZART'S FIGARO, LEPORELLO, and GUGLIELMO, which he sang with Glyndebourne at Edinburgh 1948 and at Glyndebourne itself 1950. Bayreuth as Beckmesser 1943–4, 1951. NY Met debut 1952, as Leporello. One of the most amusing and characterful MOZART singers of his day, outstanding as PAPAGENO. Also noted in operetta. AB

Kurka, Robert, b. Cicero, Ill., 22 Dec 1921; d. NY, 12 Dec 1957. American composer. Studied at Columbia Univ. and with MILHAUD; served in World War II in Tokyo. Taught at City College (NY) and at Dartmouth. His opera GOOD SOLDIER SCHWEIK has been successful in the USA and Europe. EJ

Kurwenal, bar., Tristan's retainer in TRISTAN UND ISOLDE

Kurz, Selma, b. Bielitz (now Bielsko), 15 Nov 1874; d. Vienna, 10 May 1933. Austrian soprano. Studied at Vienna. Debut 1895, Hamburg, as mezzo-sop.; 1896 Frankfurt, as sop. (ELISABETH). Engaged by MAHLER for Vienna Hof. O. (1897); debut there 1899 (MIGNON). Sang there (992 perfs) between 1899 and 1927. Among her famous roles were MIMI, EVA, ZERBINETTA, Oscar (BALLO IN MASCHERA), VIOLETTA, LUCIA DI LAMMERMOOR, ROSINA, SOPHIE, first Urbain, later the Queen in HUGUENOTS. CG debut 1904 as GILDA, opposite CARUSO. Her renowned trill can be heard on her record of Oscar's 'Saper vorreste'. An affecting actress as well as singer. AB

Kussevitsky, Sergey *see* KOUSSEVITSKY

L

Lablache, Luigi, b. Naples, 6 Dec 1794; d. Naples, 23 Jan 1858. Italian bass of French and Irish parentage. Studied at the Cons. della Pietà de' Turchini, Naples; debut 1812, T. S. Carlino, in Silvestro Palma's *Erede senza Eredità*. Principal bass at Palermo for five years, then appeared at Sc. In Vienna, 1827, he sang MOZART'S Requiem and was a torchbearer at BEETHOVEN'S funeral. London debut 1830 (MATRIMONIO SEGRETO); Paris debut 1831. Created eight roles for DONIZETTI including DON PASQUALE (1843); appeared in the first perfs of BELLINI'S BIANCA E FERNANDO (1826), *Zaira* (1829) and PURITANI (1835). In London, where for a time he was Queen Victoria's singing master, he sang in premiere of MASNADIERI. Poor health forced him to retire in 1852. PS

Labradoras de Murcia, Las (*The Working Women of Murcia*), *zarzuela*, RODRÍGUEZ DE HITA, lib. CRUZ. Madrid, T. del Príncipe, 16 Sept 1769. The work is of the utmost importance in the development of the *zarzuela*, for it transformed folk elements into a work of art with *verismo* qualities before its time. Set in the silk-growing district of Murcia it involves characters accurately drawn from working life. A revealing complete perf. was given in 1896 to commemorate the centenary of the librettist's death. FGB

Labroca, Mario, b. Rome, 22 Nov 1896; d. Rome, 1 July 1973. Italian operatic manager, composer, and critic. Pupil of RESPIGHI and MALIPIERO. Administrator and art. dir. of T. Comunale, Florence and influential in founding the Florence Maggio Musicale, bringing first perfs in It. of works by BARTÓK, STRAVINSKY, BUSONI, and others. At Sc. 1947–9; at T. La Fenice from 1959, directing the Biennale Fest. there. Dir. of programmes for Radio Italiana 1949–58. LO

Lady, Be Good, musical, GERSHWIN, book Guy Bolton and Fred Thompson, lyrics Ira Gershwin. NY, Liberty T., 1 Dec 1924; London, 14 Apr 1926; revived, London, 25 July 1968. EJ ★

Lady Macbeth, sop., the heroine of MACBETH

Lady Macbeth of the Mtsensk District *see* KATERINA IZMAYLOVA

Lake George Opera Company, founded 1962, David Lloyd, General Dir. Five operas during summer, about 34 perfs, sung by resident talent with professional orch. Standard fare with few novelties, incl. David Amram's *Twelfth Night* (1968), in Queensbury School Auditorium, Glenns Falls. EJ

Lakmé, opera, 3 acts, DELIBES, lib. Edmond Gondinet and Philippe Gille, derived from Pierre Loti's *Le Mariage de Loti*. Paris, OC, 14 Apr 1883; London, Gaiety T., 6 Jun 1885; NY, Acad. of Mus., 1 Mar 1886. Main chars: Lakmé (sop.) Gérald (ten.) Nilakantha (bass) Mallika (mezzo-sop.) Frédéric (bar.). The setting is 19th-c. India under British rule. Lakmé, daughter of the Brahmin priest Nilakantha, falls in love with Gérald, a British officer, who has trespassed into a sacred garden. Nilakantha stabs Gérald, but Lakmé carries her lover away to safety. Realizing that the wounded Gérald will try to rejoin his regiment, she prepares a fatal poison which they drink together. The dazzling 'Bell Song' has made Lakmé a favoured role of TETRAZZINI, GALLI-CURCI, PONS, and SUTHERLAND. FGB ○
See Kobbé

Lalo, Édouard, b. Lille, 27 Jan 1823; d. Paris, 22 Apr 1892. French composer of Spanish descent. His first opera *Fiesque* won 3rd place in a competition at TL, Paris, 1866, but only a portion was ever perf. (at a *Concert national*, 1873). ROI D'YS was successfully given at the OC 1888; a third opera, of which he wrote only the first of four acts (rest by Arthur Coquard), *La Jacquerie*, was heard at Monte Carlo, 8 Mar 1895. His ballet *Namouna*, based on T. MOORE's *Lalla Rookh*, was performed at the Paris O. in 1882. LO

Lammers, Gerda, b. Berlin, 25 Sept 1915. German soprano. Began as a concert singer; opera debut as Ortlinde (WALKÜRE) at Bayreuth Fest. 1955, and MARIE on joining Kassel O. that year. An unheralded London appearance at CG, 1957, replacing GOLTZ in title role of ELEKTRA, brought her an overnight triumph in the literal sense, and an international reputation for heroic splendour of tone and breadth of expression. Sang Dido (DIDO AND AENEAS) at Ingestre Hall, Shropshire, 1958; KUNDRY at CG 1959. From 1960s concentrated again on concert singing from personal preference. NG

Lancaster, Osbert, b. London, 4 Aug 1908. English designer. Began work in opera with LOVE IN A VILLAGE for EOG (1952). First Glyndebourne sets for RAKE'S PROGRESS (1953), a British premiere, followed by FALSTAFF (1955), ITALIANA IN ALGERI (1957), PIETRA DEL PARAGONE (1964), HEURE ESPAGNOLE (1966), MAW's *Rising of the Moon* (1970). DON PASQUALE (SW 1954), PETER GRIMES (Sofia 1964), SORCERER, D'Oyly Carte. His stage designs have always been full of fantasy and, where appropriate, humour. AB

Langdon, Michael, b. Wolverhampton, 12 Nov 1920. English bass. He joined the CG chorus 1948, becoming a principal 1951. Creator of the He-Ancient in MIDSUMMER MARRIAGE (1955), he has sung a vast number of roles incl. OSMIN, the Commendatore (DON GIOVANNI), Don BASILIO (BARBIERE DI SIVIGLIA), MOSÈ IN EGITTO, the Grand Inquisitor (DON CARLOS), FAFNER, HUNDING, and HAGEN, Titurel (PARSIFAL) Varlaam (BORIS GODUNOV), and Waldner (ARABELLA). At CG, 1960, he first sang OCHS, and has since repeated the role over 100 times, at the Met, San Francisco, Paris, Vienna, in Germany, and with SO. He sings both Quince and Bottom in MIDSUMMER NIGHT'S DREAM. EF

Lanigan, John, b. Seddon, Victoria, 1921. Australian tenor. Won Sun Aria Competition 1945. Studied in London with BORGIOLI. Sang FENTON (FALSTAFF) and RODOLFO with London O. Co. at Stoll T. 1949. CG debut 1951 (BOHEMIAN GIRL) with BEECHAM, and later 1951 debut with resident co. as DUCA DI MANTUA. Sang many leading tenor roles before turning to char. parts in 1960s. A notable Laca (JENŮFA), JENÍK, Cassio (VERDI'S OTELLO), Shuysky (BORIS GODUNOV), and MIME. AB

Larsén-Todsen, Nanny, b. Hagby, 2 Aug 1884. Swedish soprano. Debut 1906 (AGATHE) at the Stockholm Royal O., where she sang until 1922 in the lyric sop. repertory. Turning to heavier, more dramatic (and especially Wagnerian) roles, she appeared at Sc. 1923, NY Met 1924–7, CG 1927 and 1930, and Bayreuth 1927–30, where her BRÜNNHILDE, KUNDRY, and ISOLDE were greatly admired. She also sang Donna ANNA, LEONORE, Rachel (JUIVE), TOSCA, and the MARSCHALLIN. EF

Lassalle, Jean-Louis, b. Lyon, 14 Dec 1847; d. Paris, 7 Sept 1909. French baritone. Studied at Lyon and Paris (Cons. and privately). Debut 1868 Liège (HUGUENOTS). Paris O. debut 1872 (GUILLAUME TELL), where he became principal bar. when FAURE left in 1876, creating roles in GOUNOD'S *Polyeucte* (1878), SIGURD, SAINT-SAËNS'S *Ascanio* (1890), HENRY VIII, and SAMSON ET DALILA. Sang at CG 1879–81 and 1888–93, and from 1891 was engaged for several seasons at NY Met. He possessed a beautiful voice which he managed with artistry; at his best in the Fr. repertory, he was also distinguished as a WAGNER singer. LO

Last Savage, The, opera, 3 acts, MENOTTI, lib. composer, originally in It. Paris, OC (in Fr. as *Le Dernier Sauvage*), 21 Oct 1963; NY Met, 23 Jan 1964. LO

Lászlo, Magda, b. Marosvásárhely, ?1919. Hungarian soprano. Debut with Budapest O. 1943–6, then moved to Italy. Created Mother in PRIGIONIERO (It. Radio 1949; Florence 1950). Eng. debut Glyndebourne Fest. 1953 in GLUCK'S ALCESTE (title role); returned 1962 as Poppea (INCORONAZIONE DI POPPEA), the first of several 17th-c. operas newly ed. and cond. by LEPPARD. CG debut 1954 creating Cressida (TROILUS AND CRESSIDA). Sings a wide range of modern operas, and combines bright, expressive vocal char. with uncommon grace of stage movement. NG

Osbert Lancaster's design for SORCERER, D'Oyly Carte, Manchester Opera House, 29 Mar 1971. Lancaster also designed the costumes; produced Michael Heyland

Latin America. The Peruvian and Mexican vice-regal courts were the settings for the perfs of the earliest operas wr. in the Sp. colonies. In the cultural centres Lima, Cuzco, and Mexico City, theatrical life followed closely that of Madrid, with operas wr. mostly by European comps serving in the vice-regal retinues. The Spaniard Tomás de Torrejón y Velasco arrived in Lima, Peru, 1667, in the entourage of Pedro Fernández de Castro y Andrade, Conde de Lemos (1632–72), 19th Viceroy of Peru, and was MdC, Lima Cathedral, 1676–1728. His 'all-sung' *La Púrpura de la Rosa* (Lima, Palace of 20th Viceroy Melchor Portocarrero Lasso de la Vega in honour of King Philip V's birthday, 19 Oct 1701), based on CALDERÓN'S mythological extravaganza of the same name, set in Madrid, 1660, by Juan Hidalgo, is considered to be the earliest surviving New World opera. The score (discovered and transcribed by Robert Stevenson) is now in the Nat. Library, Lima, but there is no music extant of a successful sacred play, *El Arca de Noé*, by Antonio Martínez de Meneses, Pedro Rosete Niño and Cáncer, prod. 11 Feb–2 Mar 1672. No comp. of its *música recitativa* was named, but Stevenson suggests it could have been the priest Lucas Ruiz de Ribayaz, also a member of the retinue of the Conde de Lemos.

The Milan-born Roque Ceruti (*c.* 1686–1760), who followed Torrejón as MdC of Lima Cathedral, comp. the mus. for the next vice-regal *festa*, the (lost) *comedia harmónica, El Major Escudo de Perseo* (Lima, Vice-Regal Palace, 17 Sept 1708), lib. Viceroy Manuel de Oms y Santa Pau, Marqués de Castelldosríus, who had brought Ceruti to Lima in 1708. Stevenson remarks on his use of the DA CAPO ARIA, and his preference for the It. *recitativo secco* over the more idiomatic way of setting Sp. narrative favoured by Torrejón. While northern Italians

(Ceruti and later Andrés Bolognesi) dominated the mus. comp. in Lima during the 18th c., southern Italians played the same role in the northern capital of Mexico City. To celebrate the name day of Philip V, Viceroy Fernando de Alencastre Noroña y Silva commissioned Manuel de Zumaya (c. 1678–1756) to write *La Parténope*, lib. Silvio Stampiglia (1664–1725), the first North Amer. opera wr. by a native Mexican (Mexico City, Vice-Regal Palace, 1 May 1711). The music is lost, but the lib., printed 1711, is in the Nat. Library, Mexico City. Zumaya is also credited with the earliest setting of the Rodrigo legend, *El Rodrigo* (1711), used later by the Colombian José María Ponce de León (1845–82) in *Florinda* (1880), the Chilean Gustavo Becerra-Schmidt (b. 1925), in *La Muerte de Don Rodrigo* (1958), and GINASTERA. Other comps active in Mexico incl. the Spaniard Matheo Tollis de la Roca, whose *La Casandra* was announced for perf. at Coliseo de la Cruz, Spain, 1737; and Bartolomé Massa (*c.* 1725–99), who, besides writing incidental mus. for plays, comp. the opera *Primero es la Honra* (Lima, Coliseo, 25 Dec 1762).

In Cuzco, Peru, the cathedral MdC Fray Esteban Ponce de León (*c.* 1692–1750) was probably the comp. of the comedy *Antíoco y Seleuco* (30 Nov 1743) and of the *Opera Serenata*, perf. Cuzco 1749 to celebrate Fernando Pérez de Oblitas' appointment as Bishop of Paraguay.

The arrival of It. touring cos in the first quarter of the 19th c. set off an It. opera craze that stifled the budding development of more regional and idiomatic types of music theatre. In Mexico City GARCÍA I reversed the growing practice of singing It. opera in Sp. (a practice estab. by royal ordinance in 1799, reinforced by the Reglamento Español de Teatros 1806, when PAISIELLO's BARBIERE DI SIVIGLIA was perf. in Sp.), with the Mexican premiere in It. of ROSSINI's BARBIERE DI SIVIGLIA, T. Provisional, 29 June 1827. García also led a co. that perf. Sp. opera at T. Principal, Havana, Cuba, 1810–32, where many of his own 44 operas were perf., e.g. *El Tío y la Tía* (1812) and *La Gitana por Amor* (1812). An early operatic market for Fr. and It. cos and mainstay of the ZARZUELA, Santiago de Cuba's and Havana's populations were enriched by the Fr. settlers fleeing Haiti after the 1791 revolution. Although the first Fr. opera co. from New Orleans visited Havana in 1800, a perf. of PICCINNI's *Didone Abbandonata* is reported as early as 12 Oct 1776, six years after its Rome premiere. A similar situation arose in Buenos Aires, where the premiere in It. of Rossini's *Barbiere di Siviglia* (27 Sept 1825) by the co. of the Sp. singer and comp. Mariano Pablo Rosquellas (1790–1859) had the effect of restricting the growing local taste for the Sp. *género mixto*, the practice of incorporating regional tunes and dances into plays on native subjects. Examples of this hybrid 19th-c. type of music theatre are the Mexican play *Los Plagiarios de la Malinche*, which called for the dancing of the *jarabe* and the *palomo*, and the 1-act Peruvian *zarzuela*, *Pobre Indio!* (Lima, 3 Mar 1868), lib. Juan Vicente Camacho (1829–72) and Juan Cossio (1833–81), mus. by Carlos Enrico Pasta (1817–98). The score incl. a *yaraví*, a *zamacueca*, and an overture that ended with the chorus from Peru's national anthem.

Opera in Latin Amer. countries developed along somewhat parallel lines during the 19th c., summarized as follows:

1. The comp., up to the late 19th c., of It.-style operas by native comps using It. or It.-translated libs. The earliest such work is *Le Due Gemelle* (1809), the only opera by the Brazilian church comp. Father José Mauricio Nuñes García (1767–1830). The Mexican Cenobio Paniagua (1821–82) gained national fame with the first of his three operas, *Catalina di Guisa* (comp. 1845, Mexico City 1859), a success matched by *Ildegonda* (Mexico City 1866, Florence 1869) by Paniagua's pupil Melesio Morales (1838–1908). *Macías*, 3 acts, by Puerto Rican Felipe Gutiérrez y Espinosa (1825–99), lib. Martín Travieso based on play of same name by Mariano José Larra, won a gold medal at San Juan's 1871 Exposition, and the first Venezuelan opera, *Virginia* (T. Caracas, 26 Apr 1873) was by José Angel Montero (1832–81), also comp. of 15 *zarzuelas*. The first Colombian opera was *Ester* (Bogotá, 12 July 1874) by José María Ponce de Léon; the first Cuban, the 1-act *La Hija de Jefté*, by Laureano Fuentes y Matons (1825–98), who also wrote 5 *zarzuelas*, lib. Antonio Arnao (Santiago de Cuba, T. Reina, 16 May 1875; later expanded into the 3-act *Seila*, Havana, T. Nacional, 5 Feb 1917). Also during one year in the 1870s were the premieres of the first It. operas by two River Plate comps: Francisco Hargreaves, *La Gatta Bianca* (Buenos Aires 1877; *see* ARGENTINA), and the Uruguayan, Tomás Giribaldi (1847–1930), with his *La Parisina* (Montevideo, T. Solís, 14 Sept 1878). *Zilia* or *Odio ed Amore*, by Gaspar Villate y Montes (1851–91) of Havana, lib. Temistocle Solera, was perf. at TI, Paris, 1 Dec 1877.

2. The setting of It., Fr. or, more rarely, Spanish or Portuguese, libs based on native subjects in eclectic European styles, a literary nationalism in vogue during the last third of 19th c. and best exemplified by GUARANY (1870), and BERUTI's *Pampa* (1897), both to It. libs. The earliest such work is Brazilian, *A Noite*

de São João (1860) by Elías Alvarez Lôbo (1834–1901) and José M. de Alençar (1829–77), but *Atahualpa*, 4 acts, by Pasta, lib. GHISLANZONI, is the first opera on an Inca subject (Lima, T. Principal, 11 Jan 1877, previously perf. Genoa 1875). Peruvian subjects had been used in 17th- and 18th-c. Europe, e.g. in the first known opera on such a theme, the anonymous setting of William Davenant's *The Cruelty of the Spaniards in Peru* (London 1658), and in INDES GALANTES. *Patria* by Hubert de Blanck (b. Utrecht 1856, residing in Havana 1883 until his death in 1932), lib. Ramón Espinosa de los Monteros (Havana, T. Tacón, 1 Dec 1899) was the first opera to dramatize a revolutionary episode from Cuban history. The 1-act *Yumurí*, by Eduardo Sánchez de Fuentes (1874–1944), lib. Rafael Fernández de Castro, based on a subject from colonial period (T. Albisu, 26 Oct 1898) is the comp.'s earliest nationalistic opera; his works incl. *zarzuelas*, operettas, and five other operas of which the most mature is *Kabelia*, 2 acts, lib. comp. (Havana, T. Nacional, 22 June 1942). The most genuine Cuban opera is held to be *La Esclava*, by José Mauri Esteve (1856–1937), lib. Tomás Juliá (T. Nacional, 6 June 1921).

3. An early type of mus. nationalism using native elements juxtaposed with eclectic dramatic techniques as in GOMES's *Lo Schiavo* (1889) and the Argentine Pascual de Rogatis's (b. 1880) *Huemac* (1916). The *episodio musical, Guatimotzín* (Mexico City, 13 Sept 1871) by the Mexican Aniceto Ortega (1823–75), incorporates Mexican themes in the *Marcha* and *Danza Tlaxcalteca*, as does *Atzimba*, 3 acts (1900) by the Mexican Ricardo Castro (1864–1907). The story of Atahualpa, the last Inca king of Peru (reigned 1525–33) has been the source of at least five operas, and the apocryphal Quechuan poem *Ollantai* is the subject of *Ollanta*, 3 acts (Lima, T. Principal, 26 Dec 1900) by the Peruvian José María del Valle Riestra (1859–1925); *Ollanta* (unperf., wr. *c.* 1900) by the Amer. Silas Gamaliel Pratt (1846–1916); *Ollantay* (Lima, T. Mazzi, 14 Feb 1919) by the Peruvian Reynaldo La Rosa (1852?–1954), and GAITO's *Ollantay* (Buenos Aires, T. Colón, 23 June 1926).

4. The establishment of distinct and mature national styles in the first half of the 20th c. through the assimilation of folk and urban popular elements into the learned academic craft of European-trained native comps, as in BOERO's *El Matrero* (1929), Gaito's *La Sangre de las Guitarras* (1932), and the Brazilian Oscar Lorenzo Fernândez's *Malazarte* (comp. 1931–3). Argentina and Brazil, with more modest operatic beginnings, have proved richer in the prod. of native opera than the seats of colonial culture, Peru and Mexico. From Peru comes Carlos Valderrama's (1887–1950) national trilogy *Época Primitiva, Época Colonial, y Época Actual* (Ica, 27 Feb 1930) and *Inty-Raymi* (Lima, T. Municipal, 2 Feb 1935); Teodoro Valcárcel's (1900–42) opera-ballet *Suray-Surita*; Andrés Sas's (b. 1900) *El Enfermo Imaginario* (1943), after MOLIÈRE's *Le Malade Imaginaire, El Hijo Pródigo* (1948), and the unfinished mus. comedy *Melgar*. From Mexico comes probably the best-known Mexican contemporary opera, *Tata Vasco* (Morelia, 12 Sept 1941) by Miguel Bernal Jiménez (1910–56); José Pablo Moncayo's (b. 1912) 1-act *La Mulata de Córdoba* (1948), and Luis Sandi's (b. 1905) 1-act *Carlota* (1949). The Cuban Amadeo Roldán's (b. Paris 1900, d. Havana 1939) 1-act mystery play *El Milagro de Anaquillé* (comp. 1928–9, perf. Havana 1960 as a ballet) incorporates Afro-Cuban rhythms, and the Cuban Alejandro García-Caturla's (1906–40) *Manita en el Suelo* (comp. 1934–7) is based on *buffo* Afro-Cuban mythology. From Colombia comes the 3-act *Furatena* by Colombia's most prolific comp. Guillermo Uribe-Holguín (b. 1880) and two operas by Luis Antonio Escobar (b. 1925), *La Princesa y la Arveja* (1957), a children's opera, and *Los Hampones* (1961). Among Uruguayan comps are Vicente Ascone (b. 1897), with *Paraná-Guazú* (Montevideo, T. Urquiza, 14 Aug 1930), and Ramón Rodríguez Socas (1886–1957) with *Urunday* (Montevideo, 25 Aug 1940). The most original Uruguayan opera is *Marti Gruni* (Montevideo, T. Solís, 26 Feb 1967) by Jaurés Lamarque Pons (b. 1917), lib. based on Florencio Sánchez's play of the same name, one of the few River Plate works to incorporate dances and instruments from the 19th-c. African slave population. Luis Delgadillo (b. 1887) from Nicaragua and Luis H. Salgado (b. 1903) from Ecuador have each wr. five operas; each has wr. an 'Indianist' work: Delgadillo's 1-act *Mabaltayán* (1942), lib. Rodolfo Arana Sándigo and Salgado's 3-act *Cumundá* (wr. 1940–54), lib. comp. based on J. L. Mera's 19th-c. novel of the Ecuadorian Amazonas.

5. The use of atonalism, 12-note and serial techniques as in DON RODRIGO, BOMARZO, and BEATRIX CENCI; and the partial adoption of electronic music and other experimental means as in the Brazilian Jorge Antunes's (b. 1942) multi-media works. Similar works from Chile are the 12-note chamber opera *La Sugestión* (1959) by Pablo Garrido Vargas (b. 1905), lib. Cipriano Rivas Cherif, and Becerra-Schmidt's *La Muerte de Don Rodrigo* (1958). From Mexico comes the 1-act *Misa de Seis* (Mexico City, Palacio Nacional de Bellas Artes, 21 June 1962), for five chars, masquerades and

small orch. by Carlos Jiménez-Mabarak (b. 1916). The premieres of the Peruvian César Bolaños's (b. 1931) *Lutero* and *Las Paredes* were both at Buenos Aires, Instituto Di Tella, 1965, and T. Agon, 1966, respectively; also from Peru is Pozzi Escot (b. 1931), whose *Intera* (1968) for piano and tape and *Aimu* (1969) for four groups of unspecified voices are both parts of an 'opera in progress', lib. comp. Scored in graphic notation is *Cocktail Party* (1970) for amplified instruments with piano obbligato and a variable number of guests, the second of two dramatic works by the Uruguayan Sergio Cervetti (b. 1940). MK
See Stevenson, *Foundations of New World Opera* (Lima 1973); *Composers of the Americas*, Vols 1–18 (Washington, D.C., 1955–72)

Lattuada, Felice, b. Caselle di Morimondo, nr Milan, 5 Feb 1882; d. Milan, 2 Nov 1962. Italian composer. His six operas incl. *La Tempesta*, lib. Arturo Rossato after SHAKESPEARE, 1922; *Le Preziose Ridicole*, lib. Rossato after MOLIÈRE, 1929; *Caino* (lib. based on BYRON's *Cain*), 1957. LO

Latvia. Since 1940 a republic of the USSR. An important national school of composition began to emerge during the years of Latvian independence (1919–40), and the first significant opera was *Banuta* (1920) by Alfreds Kalniņš (1879–1951); his historical opera *The Islanders* or *The Country's Awakening* was given in 1926. Subsequent operas have included *Fire and Night* (1921) and *Gods and Men* (1922) by Jānis Mediņš (b. 1890), *The Priestess* (1927) by Jāzeps Mediņš (1877–1947), and *Towards a New Shore* (1955), *The Green Mill* (1958), and *The Beggar's Opera* (1965) by Margeris Zariņš (b. 1910). Musical life is centred on Riga, the capital. Opera was given at the German theatre founded there in 1782; the National O. (now the Latvian State O. and Ballet T.) was established in 1919. GN

Laufer, Murray, b. Toronto, 26 Oct 1929. Canadian set designer, active in theatre and TV, and resident designer for St Lawrence Centre, Toronto. Beginning with LOVE FOR THREE ORANGES (1959), Laufer has designed more than 20 sets for the Canadian O. Co., incl. those for RING DES NIBELUNGEN. His style is essentially realistic, but often with an imaginative abstract quality. He is m. to the costume designer Marie Day. CM

Laura, sop., Enzo's lover in GIOCONDA

Lauretta, sop., Schicchi's daughter in GIANNI SCHICCHI

Lauri-Volpi, Giacomo, b. Rome, 11 Dec 1892. Italian tenor. Debut 1919, Viterbo, as Arturo (PURITANI); first sang at Sc. 1922 as DUCA DI MANTUA; at NY Met 1923 as ARNOLD; at CG 1925 as ANDREA CHÉNIER. His repertory encompassed both lyric and dramatic roles, incl. POLLIONE, EDGARDO, MANRICO, RADAMES, Hagenbach (WALLY), Enzo (GIOCONDA), PINKERTON, CAVARADOSSI, RODOLFO, DICK JOHNSON, and CALAF, which he sang at the first US perf. of TURANDOT (1926). EF

Lawrence, Marjorie, b. Deans Marsh, Victoria, 17 Feb 1900. Australian soprano. Debut 1932 Monte Carlo, as ELISABETH and first sang at Paris O. 1933 as ORTRUD. In Paris she sang Salome (HÉRODIADE), Rachel (JUIVE), AIDA, Donna ANNA, Valentine (HUGUENOTS), and REYER's Brünnhilde (SIGURD) as well as WAGNER's. NY Met debut 1935 in WALKÜRE and also sang THAÏS, ALCESTE, and SALOME. In 1941 she contracted polio and had to give up her stage career, though she sang VENUS at the Met (1943–4) and AMNERIS at the Paris O. (1946) after her illness. EF

Lawrence, Martin, b. London, 26 Sept 1909. English bass. Debut 1945 with the Carl Rosa co. as MÉPHISTOPHÉLÈS. 1946–8 he sang with the New London O. Co. at the Cambridge T., as DON PASQUALE, COLLINE, LEPORELLO, Don BARTOLO (NOZZE DI FIGARO), SPARAFUCILE, Pistol (FALSTAFF), and Don BASILIO (BARBIERE DI SIVIGLIA). He sang Devil's Hoof in BOHEMIAN GIRL at CG and Archbishop Sudbury in the first London stage perf. of BUSH's *Wat Tyler* at SW 1974. EF

Lear, Evelyn, b. NY, 18 Jan 1930. American soprano. Married to bar. STEWART. Debut 1959, Berlin Staats O., as the Composer (ARIADNE AUF NAXOS). Sang in the premieres of ALKMENE (Berlin 1961) and VERLOBUNG IN SAN DOMINGO (Munich 1963) and became a renowned exponent of LULU and MARIE. CG debut 1965 as Donna ELVIRA (DON GIOVANNI) and after singing at San Francisco and Chicago, she created Lavinia in MOURNING BECOMES ELECTRA (NY Met 1967), and Arkadina in PASATIERI's *The Seagull* (Houston 1974). A fine CHERUBINO and Countess ALMAVIVA, OCTAVIAN, and MARSCHALLIN, she also sings FIORDILIGI, TATYANA and Dido (TROYENS). EF

Lecocq, Alexandre Charles, b. Paris, 3 June 1832; d. Paris, 24 Oct 1918. French composer. Studied at the Cons. with J. F. HALÉVY; a fellow student was BIZET, with whom he shared the prize offered by OFFENBACH for an operetta, DOCTEUR MIRACLE (1857). Wrote over 50 operettas, incl. *Fleur-de-Thé* (1868, his first real success), FILLE DE MADAME ANGOT, *Giroflé-Girofla* (1874, frequently revived), *Ali Baba* (1888), and *La Belle au Bois Dormant* (1898). LO

Lee, Ming Cho, b. Shanghai, 3 Oct 1930. American designer. Student at Univ. of California at Los Angeles, then worked in NY with Joe Mielziner. Designed operas for Baltimore, and PETER IBBETSON and KÁT'A KABANOVÁ for Empire State Mus. Fest. In 1961 apptd resident designer, San Francisco, then returned to East Coast, becoming principal designer for Juilliard School O. T. Has also designed for NY CC, incl. premiere there of BOMARZO. LO

Leeuw, Ton de, b. Rotterdam, 16 Nov 1926. Dutch composer. Studied in the Netherlands and Paris. His radio oratorio, *Job*, won the Italia prize (1956) and his opera *Alceste* was shown on Dutch TV (1963). *De Droom* (*The Dream*), lib. comp., was first perf. in Amsterdam as part of the 1965 Holland Fest. EF

Legend of the Invisible City of Kitezh, The (*Skazaniye o Nevidimom Grade Kitezhe*), opera, 4 acts, RIMSKY-KORSAKOV, lib. Vladimir Ivanovich Belsky. St Petersburg, Mariinsky, 20 Feb 1907; London, CG, 30 Mar 1926; Ann Arbor, Mich., Hill Auditorium, 21 May 1932 (concert perf.); Philadelphia, Acad. of Mus., 4 Feb 1936 (staged). Main chars: Prince Vsevolod (ten.) Fevroniya (sop.) Grishka (ten.). Fevroniya, wife of Prince Vsevolod, is captured by Tartars, but Grishka helps her to escape. She is guided through a haunted forest and back to Kitezh by the spirit of the Prince. *Kitezh* contains two of the finest musical characterizations in any of Rimsky's operas: the maiden Fevroniya, and the drunken Grishka. GN

Legros, Joseph, b. Monampteuil, nr Laon, 7 Sept 1730; d. La Rochelle, 20 Dec 1793. French tenor. One of principal singers at Paris O., 1764–83. Created Achille (IPHIGÉNIE EN AULIDE), Admète (GLUCK'S ALCESTE), Pylade (IPHIGÉNIE EN TAURIDE), and Orphée (ORPHÉE ET EURYDICE). Two other Gluck roles he was associated with were Renaud (ARMIDE) and Cynire (ÉCHO ET NARCISSE). LO

Lehár, Franz [Ferencz], b. Komárom, 30 Apr 1870; d. Bad Ischl, 24 Oct 1948. Hungarian composer. Studied Prague Cons. and spent some years as a military bandmaster. An opera, *Kukuška* (*Kukuschka*), was perf. Leipzig 1896, without much success, but his real talent lay in operetta. *Wiener Frauen* (Vienna 1902) was the first of 30, ending with *Schön ist die Welt* (1931). LUSTIGE WITWE (1905) made his name overnight, and still retains its freshness, overshadowing the best of the others such as *Der Graf von Luxemburg* (1909); *Zigeunerliebe* (1910); *Frasquita* (1922); *Friederike* (1928); *Das Land des Lächelns* (*The Land of Smiles*, 1929). His farewell to the stage was GIUDITTA (1934) – an opera in a more serious vein. LO
See Grun, *Gold and Silver: The Life and Times of Franz Lehár* (London 1970).

Lehmann, Lilli, b. Würzburg, 24 Nov 1848; d. Berlin, 17 May 1929. German soprano. Taught singing by her mother, who had been leading sop. at Kassel under SPOHR. Debut Prague, as First Genie in ZAUBERFLÖTE. Berlin 1870–5, as lyric and coloratura sop. Sang in first RING DES NIBELUNGEN, 1876. NY Met debut 1885 as CARMEN; first ISOLDE and BRÜNNHILDE there, and became acknowledged as among the finest of WAGNER singers. Many appearances at Bayreuth and Salzburg Fests, becoming art. dir. of the latter. Excelling in MOZART and Wagner, she had a remarkable versatility, singing 170 roles in over 100 operas; one of the truly great singers. Her pupils included FARRAR and FREMSTAD. LO

Lehmann, Lotte, b. Perleberg, 27 Feb 1888. German, later American, soprano. Studied Berlin; debut Hamburg, 1909, in ZAUBERFLÖTE. Vienna Staats O. 1914–38; NY Met 1934–45; also frequent visitor to CG 1924–35. Her numerous roles incl. the Composer in ARIADNE AUF NAXOS, the Dyer's Wife in FRAU OHNE SCHATTEN, and Christine in INTERMEZZO, all three of which she created, ARABELLA, SUOR ANGELICA, LEONORE, SIEGLINDE, EVA, ELSA, and above all the MARSCHALLIN, which she sang at her last stage appearance NY Met 1945. One of the most beloved of opera singers of her time. LO

Lehmann, Maurice, b. Paris, 14 May 1895; d. Paris, 17 May 1974. French producer and manager. While administrator of the Paris O. 1945–6 and 1951–5, he dir. elaborate prods of INDES GALANTES, OBERON, and ZAUBERFLÖTE (all 1952). During his administration there was a revival of the HONEGGER and IBERT *L'Aiglon* (1952), as well as the first perf. of BARRAUD'S *Numance* (1950). He also prod. PIERNÉ'S *Fragonard* at the OC (1946) and PÉRICHOLE at the T. de Paris (1969). EF

Leider, Frida, b. Berlin, 18 Apr 1888; d. Berlin, 4 June 1975. German soprano. Studied

Berlin and Milan; debut 1915, Halle, in TANNHÄUSER. Engagements followed rapidly, at Hamburg 1919–23, Berlin Staats O. 1923–40. US debut 1928 with Chicago O. (WALKÜRE). Made frequent appearances at Bayreuth, CG (debut 1924 as ISOLDE), NY Met, and elsewhere. The beauty of her voice and the passionate intensity of her singing made her one of the most admired WAGNER exponents of her time. LO

Leigh, Adèle, b. London, 15 June 1928. English soprano who became operetta prima donna at Vienna Volks O. Studied RADA and with TEYTE; Juilliard School, NY. Resident sop. CG 1948–56: debut as Xenia (BORIS GODUNOV); notable successes as CHERUBINO, PAMINA, SOPHIE, MANON. Created Bella in MIDSUMMER MARRIAGE (CG 1955). Returned CG 1961 as OCTAVIAN. Joined Vienna Volks O. 1963, and sang numerous leading operetta roles with musical distinction in addition to personal charm and glamorous stage presence. US debut 1966, Boston O. Soc., as Musetta (BOHÈME). At Brighton Fest. 1974 she sang the role of Gabriella (VIE PARISIENNE) for Phoenix O. NG
See Rosenthal, *Sopranos of Today* (London 1956)

Leinsdorf, Erich, b. Vienna, 4 Feb 1912. Austrian conductor. Studied Vienna; assistant there to WALTER (1934) and TOSCANINI at Salzburg Fest. (1935–7). NY Met debut 21 Jan 1938 (WALKÜRE); succeeded BODANZKY as chief WAGNER cond. there until 1943. After period of orch. conducting became mus. dir. of NY City O. 1956–7, before returning to Met as consultant and cond. Dir. US premiere of DIALOGUES DES CARMÉLITES; also cond. at Tanglewood the 1805 version of FIDELIO and, for first time in Western hemisphere, the 1-act version of LOHENGRIN. Also cond. at T. Colón, the 1969 season. LO

Leipzig, E. Germany. Has had a long but uneven operatic history, beginning late in 17th c. During the 18th c. its importance lay in the *Singspiel*, under HILLER. From *c.* 1876 under A. NEUMANN the town became of more significance, with mus. dirs and conds such as SEIDL (1879–82), NIKISCH (1878–9), and MAHLER (1886–8). The 20th c. saw premieres of JONNY SPIELT AUF and AUFSTIEG UND FALL DER STADT MAHAGONNY.

Since World War II Leipzig has steadily increased in importance under *Intendanten* Max Kruger and HERZ, working in a new opera house replacing the one that was destroyed in 1943. LO

Leitmotiv (Ger. 'leading motive'), a musical fragment, melodic, rhythmic or harmonic, associated with a character, idea or thing, used as an identifying 'tag' and/or as an aid to structural cohesion. Developed most systematically by WAGNER; appearing in embryo before him, continued by post-Wagner comps, e.g. R. STRAUSS. LO

Leitner, Ferdinand, b. Berlin, 4 Mar 1912. German conductor. After studying in Berlin became BUSCH's assistant at Glyndebourne 1935. Engagements in Berlin 1943, Hamburg 1945–6 and Munich 1946–7. Mus. dir. Stuttgart 1947. Has appeared as guest cond. in opera houses in Europe and S. America. Cond. premiere of KLEBE's *Ein Wahrer Held* (Zürich 18 Jan 1975). LO

Leningrad. Founded in 1703 as St Petersburg, renamed Petrograd on 31 Aug 1914, and Leningrad on 26 Jan 1924. Opera has been given there since 1736, when ARAIA's *La Forza dell'Amore e dell'Odio* was perf. Toward the end of the 18th c. opera perfs became increasingly common at court and private theatres, including the Hermitage T. established by Catherine II, herself a competent librettist. The city's principal music theatres are now the Kirov and the Maly, the latter founded 1918 at the old Mikhaylovsky T. It was named the State Academic Comic Opera T. in 1920, the Petrograd State Maly Academic T. in 1921, and the State Academic Maly Opera T. in 1926; it received its present title,

Leningrad, The Kirov T., built as the Mariinsky T. in 1859–60; architect Alberto Cavos (1801–63), son of the Italian composer Caterino Cavos (1776–1840), who migrated to Russia *c.* 1800. It was rebuilt 1883–96.

Maly Opera and Ballet T., in 1964. It has been of particular importance in giving premieres of Soviet operas: *Lady Macbeth of the Mtsensk District* (1934, see KATERINA IZMAYLOVA), QUIET FLOWS THE DON (1935), COLAS BREUGNON (1938), and WAR AND PEACE (1946). Leningrad also has the Cons. Opera Studio (founded 1923) and the Musical Comedy T. (1927).

Kirov Theatre. Leningrad's principal opera theatre. From 1783 an opera company performed at the Stone (or Bolshoy) T., which in 1836 was reconstructed and given over entirely to opera (the Leningrad Cons. now stands on the site). In 1843 an Italian troupe ousted the Russian, which in 1845 moved to Moscow. Only in the mid-1850s did the Russian co. return to St Petersburg, performing at the T. Circus. This was burned down in 1859, rebuilt by Alberto Cavos (son of the comp. Caterino Cavos, the co.'s mus. dir. in the early 19th c.), and reopened in 1860 as the Mariinsky T. It was later rebuilt (1883–96). In 1917 the theatre was nationalized, and in 1920 named the State Academic Opera and Ballet Theatre. In 1935 it was dedicated to Kirov. Particularly during the 19th c. the co. gave many important premieres, among them PRINCE IGOR, CUI's *William Ratcliff* (1869), DARGOMYZHSKY's *Rusalka*, STONE GUEST, IVAN SUSANIN, RUSLAN AND LYUDMILA, the second version of BORIS GODUNOV (1874), NÁPRAVNÍK's *Dubrovsky* (1895 – Nápravník was mus. dir. from 1863 to 1916), RIMSKY-KORSAKOV's MAID OF PSKOV, MAY NIGHT, SNOW MAIDEN, *Christmas Eve* (1895) and *Serviliya* (1902), LEGEND OF THE INVISIBLE CITY OF KITEZH, DEMON, SEROV's *Judith* (1863) and *Rogneda* (1865), TCHAIKOVSKY's *The Oprichnik* (1874), *Vakula the Smith* (1876), MAID OF ORLEANS, *The Sorceress* (1887), QUEEN OF SPADES and IOLANTA, and FORZA DEL DESTINO. During the Soviet period it has staged operas by DZERZHINSKY (*Grigory Melekhov*, 1967), KABALEVSKY (*The Family of Taras*, 1950), PROKOFIEV (DUENNA, 1946), and Oles Chishko (*The Battleship Potyomkin*, 1937). GN

Lensky, ten., Onegin's friend in EUGENE ONEGIN

Leo, Leonardo [Lionardo Oronzo Salvatore de], b. San Vito degli Schiavi, 5 Aug 1694; d. Naples, 31 Oct 1744. Italian composer. Wrote both *opere serie* and *opere buffe*; his historical importance lies with the latter, as he was one of the developers of the concerted *finale*, to be used so effectively later by MOZART. LO

Leoncavallo, Ruggiero, b. Naples, 8 Mar 1858; d. Montecatini, 9 Aug 1919. Italian composer. Studied at Naples Cons., then led a nomadic life as singing teacher and accompanist in various countries in Europe, returning to Italy 1890 with the first part of a trilogy on the subject of Renaissance Italy; it was not perf. until after the remarkable success of PAGLIACCI (Milan 1892). However both *I Medici* (Milan 1893) and the youthful, newly revised *Chatterton* (Rome 1896) were both failures; only *La Bohème* (Venice 1897) enjoyed some success despite competition from PUCCINI's BOHÈME. ZAZA (Milan 1900) with its chorus-girl heroine was and remains Leoncavallo's second most popular opera. His remaining works are: *Der Roland* (Berlin 1904), *Maia and Melbruck* (Rome 1910), *Zingari* (London 1912), *La Reginetta della Rosa* (Rome 1912), *Are You There?* (London 1913), *La Candidata* (Rome 1915), *Goffredo Mameli* (Genoa 1916), *Prestammi tua Moglie* (Montecatini 1916), and the posthumously prod. *Edipo Re* (Chicago 1920); and the operettas *A Chi la Giarettiera?* (Rome 1919) and *Il Primo Bacio* (Montecatini 1923). Though often coupled with MASCAGNI, Leoncavallo is a more sophisticated if less original artist. Like WAGNER and BOITO he wrote his own libs. JB

Leonora 1. Sop., heroine of TROVATORE. 2. Sop., heroine of FORZA DEL DESTINO

Leonore, sop., wife of Florestan in FIDELIO

Léonore, ou L'Amour Conjugal (*Léonore, or Conjugal Love*), *opéra comique*, 2 acts, GAVEAUX, lib. BOUILLY. Paris, T. Feydeau, 19 Feb 1798. The first of the 'Leonora' operas – *see* FIDELIO. Based on a historical incident, which Bouilly relates in his *Mes Récapitulations* (1836); but Bouilly transferred the action to Spain. There is much spoken dialogue and 13 numbers of 'not negligible' music. LO
See Dean, in Arnold and Fortune (eds), *The Beethoven Companion* (London 1971)

Leonore 40/45, *opera semiseria*, 2 acts (7 scenes and a prologue), LIEBERMANN, lib. Heinrich Strobel. Basel, 26 Mar 1952. Main chars: Huguette (sop.) Alfred (ten.) Monsieur Émile (bar.). A young Frenchwoman and a German soldier meet at a concert in occupied Paris. They are separated when he is taken prisoner-of-war, but re-united by her guardian angel, M. Émile. EF

Leporello, bass, the Don's servant in DON GIOVANNI

Leppard, Raymond, b. London, 11 Aug 1927. English cond. Cond. HANDEL's *Samson* at Leeds and CG 1958, returning to CG in 1972 to cond. COSÌ FAN TUTTE. He has ed. and realized for perf. several 17th-c. operas. His version of INCORONAZIONE DI POPPEA was first given at Glyndebourne in 1962, and he cond. it there in 1964. He prepared and cond. FAVOLA D'ORFEO (1965) for SW, ORMINDO (1967) and CALISTO (1969) for Glyndebourne, RITORNO D'ULISSE IN PATRIA (1972) for Glyndebourne, and CAVALLI's *Egisto* (1974) for Santa Fe. He has also cond. with EOG at Aldeburgh. EF

Lescaut, bar., Manon's brother in MANON and MANON LESCAUT

Lesueur, Jean-François, b. Drucatplessiel, nr Abbeville, 15 Feb 1760; d. Paris, 6 Oct 1837. French composer. After a period in the provinces went to Paris (1884) and met SACCHINI, who urged him to write for the stage. CAVERNE (1793) was followed by *Paul et Virginie* (13 Jan 1794) and *Télémaque* (11 May 1796) – all at T. Feydeau. His OSSIAN (1804), the first to be played at the O. under its new title, *Académie Impériale*, won him the *Légion d'honneur* and a gold snuffbox from Napoleon inscribed 'L'Empereur des Français à l'Auteur des Bardes'. He was an inspector of instruction at the newly-formed (1795) Cons. de Musique, and one of BERLIOZ's teachers. His operas are important forerunners of Fr. grand opera. LO

Let's Make an Opera, opera, 2 parts, BRITTEN, lib. CROZIER. Aldeburgh, 14 June 1949; St Louis, Mo., 22 Mar 1950. Opera for children, with parts for children, and with songs for the audience. The child performers are most prominent in the second part, *The Little Sweep*, where the sweep's boy Sammy is rescued. LO

Levasseur, Nicolas Prosper, b. Bresles, 9 Mar 1791; d. Paris, 7 Dec 1871. French bass. Studied Paris Cons. Debut 1813, O. Sang for the first time in London in 1815 in G. S. MAYR's *Adelasia ed Aleramo*. Sang at the TI, Paris, 1819–27 and was principal bass at the O. 1828–53. Appeared at Sc. 1820 in MEYERBEER's *Margherita d'Anjou*, and returned to London in 1829 and 1832. He created many important bass roles, incl. those in ROSSINI's *Moïse* (1827), COMTE ORY (1828), and GUILLAUME TELL (1829), ROBERT LE DIABLE (1832), JUIVE (1835), HUGUENOTS (1836), and PROPHÈTE (1849). In 1841 he was apptd professor of lyric declamation at the Paris Cons. He retired to teach until in 1870 he went blind. PS

Levasseur, Rosalie [Marie Claude Josèphe], b. Valenciennes, 8 Oct 1749; d. Neuwied, 6 May 1826. French soprano. Followed ARNOULD as chief sop. at Paris O. As Mlle Rosalie sang L'Amour in premiere of ORPHÉE ET EURYDICE and later (as Levasseur), created title roles in ARMIDE and IPHIGÉNIE EN TAURIDE. LO

Levi, Hermann, b. Giessen, 7 Nov 1839; d. Munich, 13 May 1900. German conductor. Studied Mannheim. Principal cond., Munich, 1872, becoming mus. dir. 1894–6. Much admired for his WAGNER interpretations; cond premiere of PARSIFAL. LO

Levine, James, b. Cincinnati, Ohio, 23 June 1943. American conductor. Assistant cond., Cleveland Orch. 1964–70. Principal cond. NY Met from 1970; mus. dir. from 1975. LO

Lewis, Richard, b. Manchester, 10 May 1914. English tenor of Welsh parentage. Debut 1947, Glyndebourne, as Male Chorus (RAPE OF LUCRETIA) and in 1948 sang PETER GRIMES at CG. Has since sung all over the world, his repertory ranging from HANDEL, GLUCK, MOZART, and CHERUBINI to BEETHOVEN, VERDI, BIZET, MASSENET, and R. STRAUSS. He has a special aptitude for modern works, and created Troilus in TROILUS AND CRESSIDA (CG 1954), Mark in MIDSUMMER MARRIAGE (CG 1955), and Achilles in KING PRIAM (Coventry 1962). He also sings Alwa (LULU), the Captain (WOZZECK), Aron (MOSES UND ARON), and Captain Vere (BILLY BUDD). EF

Right: Richard Lewis as Achilles in KING PRIAM, London, CG, 19 May 1975; produced Sam Wanamaker; designed Sean Kenny

Leyli and Medzhnun (*Leyli i Medzhnun*), opera, 4 acts, HAJIBEYOV, lib. composer after Mohammed Fizuli's poem. Baku, 25 Jan 1908. Main chars: Heys (ten.) Leyli (sop.) Ibn Salam (ten.). Leyli and Heys are lovers, but Leyli's parents insist that she marry the wealthy Ibn Salam; Leyli faints, Heys (known as Medzhnun, or 'the madman') goes off to the desert. Here he is found by his father and a friend, but his love for Leyli has affected his mind and he cannot recognize them. Some Arabs take pity on him, and a soldier unsuccessfully pleads Heys's case with Leyli's father. Heys arrives at the wedding of Leyli and Ibn Salam, and later Leyli reveals to Ibn Salam that she and Heys are in love. Heys reappears and accuses her of betraying him; she dies in Ibn Salam's arms. In the final scene Heys dies at Leyli's tomb. Although *Leyli and Medzhnun* holds a key place in the history of Central Asian music, its highly specialized form of improvisation precluded any lasting influence on the development of viable opera in Azerbaijan. GN

Libretto and librettists. The libretto (It. 'booklet'), the text the comp. sets to music, has its roots in the theatre and literature; there are comparatively few successful operas that cannot be traced to plays or novels. The early It. pastoral plays led to It. and Fr. pastoral operas; ZENO and METASTASIO modelled their operas on RACINE and CORNEILLE; CALZABIGI in the 18th c. and HOFMANNSTHAL in the 20th c. turned to Greek drama. ROMANI turned constantly to the Fr. contemporary theatre, as did VERDI and PUCCINI; the WAGNER music dramas can be paralleled by 19th-c. poetic drama. Many libs in the prolific 18th and early 19th c. were the merest hackwork; dissatisfaction with poor standards led comps to write their own words (Wagner is the best known instance), but the result was not always a guarantee of a successful opera. LO
See Smith, *The Tenth Muse: A Historical Study of the Opera Libretto* (NY 1970; London 1971)

Libuše, opera, 3 acts, SMETANA, lib. Josef Wenzig, tr. into Czech by Ervín Špindler. Prague, NT, 11 June 1881. Main chars: Libuše (sop.) Přemysl (bar.) Chrudoš (bass) Šťáhlav (ten.) Krasava (sop.). Libuše, the mythical ruler of the Czechs, unable to assert her authority, marries Přemysl, the founder of the Přemyslide dynasty. Smetana wrote the work (1869–72) as a festival opera for the opening of the Prague NT and it is still played only on special national occasions. Its patriotic purpose is stressed by its ending with Libuše's prophecy of the history of the Czech nation. JT O
See Large, *Smetana* (London 1970)

Liebe der Danae, Die, (*The Love of The Danae*), opera, 3 acts, R. STRAUSS, lib. J. GREGOR. Salzburg, 14 Aug 1952; London, CG, 16 Sept 1953; Los Angeles, 1964 (in Eng.). Completed in 1940, but Nazi edicts prevented its official premiere even after the dress rehearsal Salzburg 16 Aug 1944. Main chars: Danae (sop.) Midas (ten.) Jupiter (bar.). The opera offers a cheerful combination of the mythical stories of Danae and Midas: Jupiter desires Danae for himself, but is finally touched by her devotion to Midas even when the latter is impoverished, and gives the couple his blessing. FGB
See Mann, *Richard Strauss* (London 1964; New York 1966); Kobbé

Liebermann, Rolf, b. Zürich, 14 Sept 1910. Swiss composer and administrator. Studied in Zürich and Vienna. His first opera, LEONORE 40/45 (1952), won him fame throughout Europe, and was followed by *Penelope* (Salzburg 1954) and *Die Schule der Frauen*, based on MOLIÈRE's *L'École des Femmes* (Louisville, Ky, 1955; 2nd version, Salzburg 1957). As *Intendant* of the Hamburg Staats O. (1959–72), he was responsible for the prod. there of a great number of modern and contemporary works. Since 1973 he has been Dir. of the Paris O. EF

Liebesverbot, Das (*Love's Interdict*), opera, 2 acts, WAGNER, lib. comp. after SHAKESPEARE's *Measure for Measure*. Magdeburg, 29 Mar 1836. Main chars: Friedrich (bass) Luzio (ten.) Isabella (sop.) Brighella (buffo-bass) Mariana (sop.) Dorella (sop.) Claudio (ten.). Friedrich, governor of Sicily, has issued a decree banning love-making under pain of death. Claudio, a victim, is interceded for by his sister, the novice Isabella; Friedrich agrees to a reprieve in return for Isabella's favours. She sends Mariana, Friedrich's estranged wife, to take her place at the rendezvous, suitably disguised. Friedrich is humiliated, and revokes the decree. Isabella marries Claudio's friend Luzio. Wagner's first opera to be perf. JB

Liège, Belgium. The town has had a theatre since 1702 and opera perfs since *c.* 1740. Perfs of operas by GRÉTRY and others were given at the T. La Douane, built 1767; today operas are perf. in the Grand T., a big auditorium inspired by the Paris Odéon, opened 1820 with ZÉMIRE ET AZOR. LO

Life for the Tsar *see* IVAN SUSANIN

Ligendza, Catarina, b. Stockholm, 18 Oct 1937. Swedish soprano. Studied Vienna Acad.,

Würzburg, and with GREINDL. Debut Linz; Saarbrücken 1966–70; at Deutsche O., West Berlin, since 1969; debut Sc. 1970. Bayreuth debut as BRÜNNHILDE 1971; sang ISOLDE there 1974; NY Met debut as LEONORE 1971; CG debut as SENTA 1972. One of the most sensitive dramatic sops of the day, with a notably lyrical timbre and an attractive presence. AB

Lighting in opera. The first opera houses were lit by candles. The Argand smokeless oil lamp, invented 1782, gave more control; it was superseded by gas in the early 1800s. Paris O. was fitted with gas lighting, 1822. Electricity, now universal, came into general use in the 1890s. Its flexibility made possible the lighting effects now basic to the whole concept of opera prod.; the lighting engineer is now an important member of the prod. team. LO

Light opera *see* OPERETTA

Lille, France. O. de Lille gives six or seven operas, Oct to Mar. T. Sébastopol offers musical comedy, Sept to Mar. Dir. Alexandre Vanderdonkct. LO

Lincoln Center *see* NEW YORK

Lind, Jenny [Johanna], b. Stockholm, 6 Oct 1820; d. Malvern, England, 2 Nov 1887. Swedish soprano. 'The Swedish Nightingale', Studied Stockholm Court T. School. Debut 1838 as AGATHE. Overwork damaged her voice and in 1841 she restudied with GARCÍA II in Paris. MEYERBEER heard her and engaged her for his *Ein Feldlager in Schlesien* in Berlin, although she did not sing the first perfs, and revised it for her for Vienna as *Vielka* in 1846. London debut 1847, and the same year she created MASNADIERI for VERDI. Idolized by the public, she considered opera 'immoral' and refused to sing 'evil' roles. In 1849 she retired from the opera stage to concentrate on concerts and oratorio. From 1850 she toured the USA and in 1852 m. the cond. Otto Goldschmidt in Boston. From 1856 they made their home in England. One of her last appearances was in her husband's *Ruth* (Düsseldorf 1870). From 1883 she taught singing at RCM. PS
See Bulman, *Jenny Lind, a Biography* (London 1956)

Linda di Chamounix (*Linda of Chamonix*), *opera semiseria*, 3 acts, DONIZETTI, lib. G. ROSSI, after a vaudeville *La Grâce de Dieu*. Vienna, KT, 19 May 1842; London, HM, 1 June 1843; NY, 4 Jan 1847. Main chars: Linda (sop.) Pierotto (contr.) Carlo (ten.) il Prefetto (bass) il Marchese (buffo-bass) Antonio (bar.).

Jenny Lind as Amina in the sleepwalking scene in SONNAMBULA, a contemporary print

Linda, daughter of poor parents, is loved by Carlo (Charles, Vicomte de Sirval), and pursued by his uncle, il Marchese. To escape his attentions she goes to Paris and is installed in an apartment by Carlo. Her father refuses to believe in her innocence and denounces her; Linda loses her reason, to regain it in the final act when her innocence is vindicated. JB
See Kobbé

Lindholm, Berit, b. Stockholm, 18 Oct 1934. Swedish soprano. Studied Stockholm at the opera school. Debut, Stockholm O. (1963). CG debut as CHRYSOTHEMIS (1966), returned for ISOLDE (1973), BRÜNNHILDE (1974), and Chrysothemis again (1975). Bayreuth debut, as Brünnhilde (1968). NY Met debut, also as Brünnhilde (1975). One of the leading dramatic sops of the day, particularly noted for her Isolde and Brünnhilde to which she brings comely looks and a vibrant, incisive voice. AB

Linz, Austria. The first opera given there was Antonio Draghi's *Ercole Acquistatore dell'Immortalità* in 1677. A Stadt T. has been discussed since 1940; opera is now given in the small Landes T., built 1958; present mus. dir. Theodor Gaschbauer. LO

Lisbon. Opera was first given regularly at the T. da Ribeira, opened Apr 1755 but destroyed seven months later by earthquake. The T. de S. Carlos, built as a replica of its namesake in Naples, was opened in 1793 and restored in 1940. It has continued to present international seasons up to the present day. FGB

List, Emanuel, b. Vienna, 22 Mar 1890. Austrian bass. After operatic debut Vienna 1922 as MÉPHISTOPHÉLÈS, engaged Berlin, 1923–33 and NY Met, 1933–50. Also sang at Salzburg and Bayreuth and has appeared at CG. He was especially admired in the WAGNER bass roles. LO

Liszt, Franz [Ferencz], b. Raiding, 22 Oct 1811; d. Bayreuth, 31 July 1886. Hungarian pianist, composer and conductor. Important for his championship of WAGNER and for his work as MdC at Weimar 1848–59. Works premiered there incl. LOHENGRIN (1850, while Wagner was in exile); GENOVEVA (1850); ALFONSO UND ESTRELLA (1854, drastically cut and altered); BARBIER VON BAGDAD (1858). Liszt's one-act opera *Don Sanche ou Le Château*, lib. Théaulon and Rancé, was perf. Paris O., 17 Oct 1825. LO
See Walker (ed.), *Franz Liszt, The Man and his Music* (London 1970)

Lithuania. Since 1940 a republic of the USSR. The first important Lithuanian opera was *Birute* (1921) by Mikas Petrauskas (1873–1937). This has been followed by such operas as *The Village on the Estate* (1942) by Stasys Šimkus (1887–1943), *Dalya* (1959) by Balys Dvarionas (b. 1904), *The Three Talismen* (1936), *Marite* (1953), and *City of the Sun* (1965) by Antanas Račiūnas (b. 1905), *The Rebels* (1957) by Julius Juzeliūnas (b. 1916), *Pilenay* (1956), *Vayva* (1958), and *The Daughter* (1960) by Vytautas Klova (b. 1926), *The Lost Birds* (1967) by Vytautas Laurušas (b. 1930) and *At the Crossroads* (1967) by Vytautas Paltanavičius (b. 1924). During Lithuanian independence (1919–40) an opera theatre was founded (1920) in the capital, Kaunas. In 1940 the capital was moved to Vilnius [Vilna], where opera has been given since 1842. The Opera and Ballet T. was established there in 1948; a new opera house was opened in 1971. GN

Little, Gwenlynn, b. Brampton, Ontario, 14 Apr 1937. Canadian lyric coloratura soprano. Studied at the Royal Cons. O. School, Toronto. Professional debut 1962 with COC as GILDA, then toured in USA with GOLDOVSKY's New England O. Co. Regular appearances throughout Canada; NY CC debut 1973 as SUSANNA and ZERLINA, two of her most successful roles. CM

Litvinne, Félia [Françoise-Jeanne Schütz], b. St Petersburg, 11 Oct 1860; d. Paris, 12 Oct 1936. Franco-Russian soprano. Studied in Paris with VIARDOT and MAUREL; debut, 1883, TI (SIMONE BOCCANEGRA). During next three years sang at Aix-les-Bains, Bordeaux, Genoa, Barcelona and elsewhere. In 1885 she appeared in NY at the Acad. T.; 1886–8 was engaged at T. de la Monnaie, Brussels. NY Met debut 1896 (HUGUENOTS). Though continuing to sing a wide variety of roles she began to concentrate on WAGNER, for which her dramatic, fine voice of wide range and magnificent resonance and her imposing stage presence made her well suited. CG debut, 1899, as ISOLDE. Left the stage in 1917 and devoted herself to teaching. LO

Liù, sop., the slave girl in TURANDOT

Ljubljana *see* YUGOSLAVIA

Lockhart, James, b. Edinburgh, 16 Oct 1930. Scottish conductor. Engaged in 1955 on the music staff at Münster. Cond. debut 1957 at Austin, Texas. He first cond. at SW 1960, at CG 1964–5, and has worked with SO 1962. Mus. dir. of the WNO 1968–73, he cond. notable perfs of ZAUBERFLÖTE, BORIS GODUNOV,

FALSTAFF, LULU and BILLY BUDD. In 1972 he became mus. dir. of the Kassel O., the first British cond. to hold such a post in Germany, and cond. a very wide repertory there, incl. the first Ger. perf. of YEOMAN OF THE GUARD. EF

Locle, Camille du, b. Orange, 16 July 1832; d. Capri, 9 Oct 1903. French administrator and librettist. Dir., Paris OC with Adolphe Leuven, 1870–4, then alone, 1874–6. Librettist, in association with others, of AIDA, DON CARLOS, and SIGURD and, by himself, of SALAMMBÔ. Collaborated with BOITO on Fr. tr. of VERDI's OTELLO. LO

Right: Lohengrin, London, CG, 8 Apr 1963, produced Josef Gielen; designed Hainer Hill. Lohengrin (Kolbjørn Hoiseth) is about to kill Telramund but has a change of heart and spares his life.

Lodoïska, *comédie héroïque* (opera), 3 acts, CHERUBINI, lib. Claude François Fillette-Loraux. Paris, T. Feydeau, 18 July 1791; NY, 4 Dec 1826. A melodramatic rescue opera: Lodoïska is incarcerated by Doulinsky in a castle on the Polish border; the castle is attacked and destroyed; Lodoïska is rescued by her lover, Florestan. Perf. Vienna 1802, much admired by BEETHOVEN, whose FIDELIO was influenced by it. Revived Sc., 1949. Other operas on same subject by Rodolphe Kreutzer (Paris, 1 Aug 1791); S. STORACE (London 1794); G. S. MAYR (1796); Luigi Caruso (1798). LO

Lodoletta, opera, 3 acts, MASCAGNI, lib FORZANO after Ouida's *Two Little Wooden Shoes*, 1874. Rome, T. Costanzi, 30 Apr 1917; NY Met, 12 Jan 1918. Main chars: Lodoletta (sop.) Flammen (ten.) Giannotto (bar.). The tragedy of a wholly innocent love affair between a Belgian village girl and a Bohemian painter from Paris. JB

Loesser, Frank, b. NY, 29 June 1910; d. NY, 28 July 1969. American composer. Graduated City College. Composed songs and lyrics, including 'Praise the Lord, and Pass the Ammunition' (1942), several achieving popular success. First entire score GUYS AND DOLLS (1950), followed by *The Most Happy Fella* (1956), and *How To Succeed in Business Without Really Trying* (1961). Loesser maintained other business interests, incl. mus. publishing and retailing. EJ

Left: Félia Litvinne as ISOLDE, the role which she sang in the first Paris performance of TRISTAN UND ISOLDE (1899) and in her London CG debut the same year

Loewe, Frederick, b. Vienna, 1901. Austrian, later American, pianist and composer. Studied in Vienna, moved to NY in 1924. Wrote several moderately successful works before achieving worldwide fame with *Brigadoon* (1947), *Paint Your Wagon* (1951), MY FAIR LADY (1956), and *Camelot* (1960), in copartnership with LERNER. EJ

Loge, ten., the god of fire in RHEINGOLD

Logroscino, Nicola, b. Bitonto, 22 Oct 1698; d. Palermo, *c.* 1765. Italian composer. Member of the Neapolitan School of *opera buffa* writers, one of the first to work on the problem of the 'concerted finale' in comic operas. LO

Lohengrin, opera, 3 acts, WAGNER, lib. comp. Weimar, 28 Aug 1850 (cond. LISZT); NY, 3 Apr 1871; London, CG, 8 May 1875. Main chars: Lohengrin (ten.) Elsa (sop.) Ortrud (sop. or mezzo-sop.) Telramund (bar.) König Heinrich (bass). Elsa, accused by Telramund of her brother's murder, is saved by the championship of Lohengrin, a knight of the Grail, who offers to wed her provided she promises never to ask his name. Ortrud and Telramund, however, work on her fears to make her break the promise on her wedding night. Wagner's last opera in traditional style. JB ○
See Kobbé

Lombard, Alain, b. Paris, 4 Oct 1940. French conductor. Studied with Suzanne Demarquez and Gaston Poulet. Debut, at age of 11, at Salle Gaveau, Paris. US debut with American Opera Society, NY. After winning Dmitri Mitropoulos Competition in 1966, became musical dir. of Miami Orchestra. Debut with NY City O. 1966 (DIALOGUES DES CARMÉLITES). NY Met debut with WERTHER (1971). Joined Strasbourg O. (1972) and became mus. dir., Opéra du Rhin (1974). AB

Lombardi alla Prima Crociata, I (*The Lombards on the First Crusade*), opera, 4 acts, VERDI, lib. Temistocle Solera after Tommaso Grossi's poem. Milan, Sc., 11 Feb 1843;

London, HM, 12 May 1846; NY, 3 May 1847. Main chars: Giselda (sop.) Oronte (ten.) Pagano (bass) Arvino (ten.). Two feuding brothers are reconciled through adherence to a holy cause, Pagano becoming a hermit in Syria, Arvino leading a contingent to the first crusade. Arvino's daughter Giselda is released by them from captivity in Antioch, but has meanwhile fallen in love with her captor, Oronte. Together they escape, but Oronte dies after receiving baptism at the hands of Pagano, who himself is killed during the final assault on Jerusalem. Verdi's fourth opera, remade as *Jérusalem* (Paris O., 26 Nov 1847) with several numbers rearranged, some new mus. added, and the plot altered. Main chars: Gaston (ten.) Roger (bass) Hélène (sop.) Comte de Toulouse (ten.). Less popular than the original version. JB O

London. Main centre of opera in the British Isles, and an important international centre. An opera house was projected, by Sir William Davenant, as early as 1639; but the Civil War intervened, and it was not until 1671 that the Dorset Garden T. was opened. There has been a continuous history of opera perfs since the early years of the 18th c., chiefly in the theatres listed below. *See also* GREAT BRITAIN.

Camden (formerly St Pancras) **Festival.** Inaugurated 1954 with RE PASTORE, restaged 1975. British premieres have incl. BLACHER's *The Tide* (1960), MALHEURS D'ORPHÉE (1960), HAYDN's MONDO DELLA LUNA (1960), *L'Infedeltà Delusa* (1964), and *L'Incontro Improviso* (1966); GIORNO DI REGNO, *Aroldo* (*see* STIFFELIO), and CORSARO; MARIA STUARDA; MASSENET's *Sapho* (1967), LEONCAVALLO's *La Bohème* (1970), and EQUIVOCI. There have been notable prods of DEIDAMIA (1955) and ALCINA (1957); CLEMENZA DI TITO (1957); FINTA GIARDINIERA (1956) and LUCIO SILLA (1967); ITALIANA IN ALGERI (1961), PIETRA DEL PARAGONE (1963), TURCO IN ITALIA (1965) and ELISABETTA, REGINA D'INGHILTERRA (1968); DONIZETTI's *Marin Faliero* (1967) and *Torquato Tasso* (1974); MASNADIERI (1962) and ÉTOILE DU NORD (1975). EF

Coliseum. Built by Sir Oswald Stoll, 1902, capacity 2,200. Used for revues and spectacular shows e.g., *White Horse Inn* (1931); VAGABOND KING (1937). After World War II some musicals were prod. there. Since 21 Aug 1968 the home of SW, now ENO. LO

Covent Garden, Royal Opera House. London's principal opera house. Built by John Rich in 1732, it housed a variety of musical and theatrical entertainments, ranging from HANDEL's later operas and oratorios to ballet, pantomime and pasticcio-opera. Burned down 1808: rebuilt 1809. OBERON was commissioned for perf. here in 1826. In 1847 the theatre set itself up as a rival to Her Majesty's in the Haymarket, the traditional home of Italian Opera, eventually winning the day. This T. was burned 1856, present building opened 15 May 1858. Renamed the Royal Opera in 1892 it became under the management of HARRIS one of Europe's leading opera theatres. In 1946 it was nationalized; it now runs a yearly international season from mid-September to the end of July. JB

Drury Lane, Theatre Royal. A theatre was built there in 1663; present building dates from 1812. Operatically its importance began in 19th *c.* under BUNN, with Eng. premieres of ROBERT LE DIABLE and FRA DIAVOLO. MAPLESON dir. opera there, 1867–77, after the burning of Her Majesty's T.; the first Eng. perfs of WAGNER operas were given there, FLIEGENDE HOLLÄNDER in 1870, TRISTAN UND ISOLDE and MEISTERSINGER in 1882. Carl Rosa made it his London theatre for some years from 1883. In the 20th c. BEECHAM gave his remarkable 1913–14 seasons there, introducing BORIS GODUNOV, MAID OF PSKOV, and PRINCE IGOR. After World War II it was the scene of a number of US musicals, beginning with OKLAHOMA!, 1947. The musical still dominates. LO

Her Majesty's Theatre (Haymarket). Continued the It. opera tradition of the King's T. Burned down 1867, rebuilt 1869; opera perfs resumed 1877. First perfs in English of VÊPRES SICILIENNES, GOUNOD's FAUST, and CARMEN were given there; in 1882 SEIDL gave the first perf. in Eng. of the RING. Pulled down 1891; replaced by present T., 1897. The Eng. premiere of ARIADNE AUF NAXOS was given there, 1913. The BNOC gave London seasons there 1924–8, since then it has faded out of the operatic scene. LO

King's Theatre (Haymarket). Built 1705; the scene of the first It. opera heard in London, Jakob Greber's *Gli Amori d'Ergasto*. For more than 100 years the centre of It. opera in London; most of HANDEL's operas were first given there. Burned down in 1789, a new and larger King's T. was built in 1793, renamed Her Majesty's on Queen Victoria's accession, 1837. LO

Lyceum Theatre. The orig. 1765 building was remodelled by ARNOLD, 1794, but the 'Patent Theatres', i.e. CG and DL, prevented him from using it as a theatre. When DL was burned in 1809 the Lyceum housed the opera. In 1810 its name was changed to The English O. House; rebuilt in 1815, and again in 1834 as The New T. Royal and English O. House. Opera was given there off and on during the 19th c. and esp. 1856–7, while CG was being rebuilt after the fire, and occasionally in the 20th c. It is now a dance hall. LO

Royal English Opera House. Built by Richard D'Oyly Carte in Cambridge Circus, London, as a home for Eng. opera; opened 31 Jan 1891 with IVANHOE, which ran successfully for 160 perfs. Though other operas, by Hamish McCunn, COWEN and A. G. THOMAS had been intended, none were wr., and *Ivanhoe* was followed, hurriedly, by BASOCHE, after which the opera house closed. The building is now the Palace T. LO

Sadler's Wells Opera. This evolved from the time of BAYLIS's management of the Old Victoria Music Hall (the Old Vic). By 1920 five opera perfs a fortnight were being given there. When the SW T. was opened in N. London in 1931 opera was given alternately here and at the Old Vic until 1934, which date can be regarded as the birthday of SW Opera Co. Since then there have been landmarks in profusion: BORIS GODUNOV, 1935; FALSTAFF, 1936; MEISTERSINGER, 1936; ROSENKAVALIER, 1939; after World War II PETER GRIMES, 1945; the first British prod. of KÁT'A KABANOVÁ, 1951. It became the ENO in 1974. LO

Sadler's Wells Theatre. Originally a music hall, built in 1683 by Dick Sadler. A new theatre was built in 1746, and refurbished in 1802; opera was occasionally perf. there in 19th c. Rebuilt in the 1930s under BAYLIS it became a N. London home for the Old Vic Co., from 1934 giving only opera and ballet. Forced to close during World War II it reopened in 1945 with premiere of PETER GRIMES. Remained the home of SW O. Co. until 1968; now used by visiting companies such as the D'Oyly Carte and the New O. Co. LO

See Rosenthal, *Two Centuries of Opera at Covent Garden* (London 1958); Arundell, *The Story of Sadler's Wells* (London 1965)

London [Burnstein], George, b. Montreal, 30 May 1920. Canadian bass-baritone whose parents settled in Los Angeles from 1935. Debut, 1941, as George Burnson (*sic*) at Hollywood Bowl in *Gainsborough* by A. COATES. Appeared in musical comedy; toured USA 1947 with Frances Yeend and Mario Lanza as Bel Canto Trio. Engaged by BÖHM for Vienna Staats O. from 1949: debut as AMONASRO. Bayreuth Fest. frequently from 1951 as AMFORTAS and FLIEGENDE HOLLÄNDER (title role). NY Met debut same year as Amonasro. Notable NY successes as BORIS GODUNOV and DON GIOVANNI (title roles) and SCARPIA, in addition to WAGNER. Sc. from 1952. London debut 1954 with Vienna Staats O. at Royal Fest. Hall (Don Giovanni). Sang title role in US premiere of LAST SAVAGE (NY Met 1964). Perfs distinguished by strong vocal char. and intense musical feeling as well as commanding stage presence. From 1968 mus. administrator John F. Kennedy Center for Performing Arts, Washington, DC; from 1971 gen. dir. Los Angeles Mus. Center O. Assn. NG

Loose, Emmy, b. Karbitz (now Chabařovice), 1914. Austrian soprano. Studied Prague. Debut as BLONDCHEN at Hanover (1939). Guest appearance at Vienna Staats O. 1941 as Ännchen (FREISCHÜTZ) led to a permanent engagement with that house, specializing in light sop. roles. Glyndebourne as BLONDCHEN (1953), CG with Vienna co. (1947) and with resident co. as SOPHIE and SUSANNA (1950). AB

Lorca, Federico García, b. Fuente Vaqueros, Granada, 15 Apr 1899; executed by fascist firing squad outside Granada, 19 Aug 1936. Spanish poet and dramatist. Two of his plays were adapted for operas by FORTNER, *Bodas de Sangre* (*Blood Wedding*) as BLUTHOCHZEIT (1957) and *Amor de Don Perlimplín con Belisa en su Jardín* as *In seinem Garten liebt Don Perlimplin Belisa* (1962) *Bodas de Sangre* and *La Zapatera Prodigiosa* were used as libs by CASTRO (1952 and 1943). FGB

Loreley, opera, 3 acts, Alfredo CATALANI, lib. Carlo d'Ormeville and Angelo Zanardini. Turin, T. Regio, 16 Feb 1890. This was a revision of Catalani's first opera, *Elda*, 4 acts, lib. d'Ormeville; altered to 3 acts by Zanardini. LO

Lorengar, Pilar, b. Saragossa, 1928. Spanish soprano. After appearing in Sp. houses made CG debut, 1955, as VIOLETTA. Glyndebourne as enchanting PAMINA 1956–7, 1960 and Countess ALMAVIVA 1958–9. NY Met debut 1966 as Donna ELVIRA (DON GIOVANNI). Other important roles incl. FIORDILIGI, Donna ANNA and Elisabeth (DON CARLOS). Clear, attractive sop. with typically Sp., quick vibrato. Appealing actress. AB

Lorenz, Max, b. Düsseldorf, 10 May 1901; d. Vienna, 12 Jan 1975. German tenor. Studied Berlin; debut Dresden Staats O. as Walther von der Vogelweide (TANNHÄUSER). Berlin Staats O. from 1931 and Vienna Staats O. from 1937. NY Met debut 1931 and CG debut 1934 as Walther (MEISTERSINGER). Bayreuth 1933–9 and 1952. One of the leading *Heldentenor* singers of his day, also a notable OTELLO (VERDI). He had a ringing voice, used with great histrionic force, and a fine presence. AB

Lortzing, Gustav Albert, b. Berlin, 23 Oct 1801; d. Berlin, 21 Jan 1851. German composer. Of his 12 operas the best are ZAR UND ZIMMERMANN, HANS SACHS, and *Der Wildschütz* (*The Poacher*), 1842, which developed the *opéra comique* and *Singspiel*, and remained popular during the 19th c. Others such as UNDINE and *Der Waffenschmied* (*The Armourer*), 1846, met with some success, but have not stayed the course. LO

Lothar, Mark, b. Berlin, 23 May 1902. German conductor and composer. Studied at Berlin Musikhochschule with SCHREKER, and later with WOLF-FERRARI. At Berlin Staats O. 1933–44, moved to Munich 1945. Has wr. several operas incl. SCHNEIDER WIBBEL (1938); *Tyll*, on the Till Eulenspiegel story (Weimar 1928); *Lord Spleen* (Dresden 1930), based on JONSON's *Epicoene*; *Rappelkopf* (Munich 1958), a magic opera. LO

Loughran, James, b. Glasgow, 30 June 1931. Scottish conductor. Assistant cond. in Bonn, Amsterdam, and Milan, then won the Philharmonia Young Conds' Competition. Cond. FIDELIO for the Chelsea O. Group 1963; CG debut 1964 (AIDA). Conducted at SW, Aldeburgh (ACIS AND GALATEA), and for SO (GONDOLIERS and TRAVIATA). In 1969 he cond. two operas for the BBC, Thomas Wilson's *Charcoal Burner* and MUSGRAVE's *Abbot of Drimock*. He is now principal cond. of the Hallé Orchestra, Manchester. EF

Louise, *roman musical*, 4 acts, CHARPENTIER, lib. comp. with assistance from others. Paris, OC, 2 Feb 1900; NY, Manhattan OH, 3 Jan 1908; London, CG, 18 June 1909. Charpentier's great success, an example of *verismo*, inspired by his socialist sympathies. Filmed in Fr. with THILL and G. MOORE. LO ★
See Kobbé

Louisville, Ky. Louisville Orchestral Commissions has commissioned several operas since *c.* 1950, by US and other comps. Among them are Peggy Glanville-Hicks's *The Transposed Heads* (1954); LIEBERMANN's *Die Schule der Frauen* (1955), and NABOKOV's *The Holy Devil* (1958, later revised as *The Death of Gregory Rasputin*). LO

Love for Three Oranges, The (*Lyubov k tryom apelsinam*), opera, 4 acts, PROKOFIEV, lib. composer after GOZZI. Chicago, Auditorium, 30 Dec 1921; Leningrad, State Acad. O. and Ballet T. (now the Kirov), 18 Feb 1926; Edinburgh, 21 Aug 1962; London, SW, 24 Apr 1963. By contrast to Prokofiev's other, realistic, operas of the period (GAMBLER, FIERY ANGEL), *The Love for Three Oranges* is a witty, satirical comedy. The protagonists are caricatures rather than characters, and the whole score is brilliantly imbued with a sense of the ludicrous and the grotesque. GN ○
See Kobbé

Love in a Village, *pasticcio*, lib. BICKERSTAFFE, adapted from the ballad opera, *The Village Opera* (1729), music (anon.) arr. ARNE. London, CG, 8 Dec 1762; Charleston, La, 10 Feb 1766. Popular throughout the 18th c.; chosen by BEARD for his farewell perf. 1767. Has been revived in modern times. LO

Lualdi, Adriano, b. Larino, 22 Mar 1885; d. Milan, 8 Jan 1971. Italian composer. Studied with Stanislao Falchi, Rome and WOLF-FERRARI, Venice. Operas, to his own libs, incl. two marionette operas, *Il Diavolo nel Campanile*, after POE, 1925, and *La Luna dei Caraibi* after Eugene O'Neill, 1953. LO

Lubin, Germaine, b. Paris, 1 Feb 1890. French soprano. Studied with Jacques Isnardon and LITVINNE; debut 1912, Paris, OC (CONTES D'HOFFMANN). Was a principal sop. at Paris O. for *c.* 30 years, 1914–44; also sang at CG, Berlin, Prague, Salzburg, and Vienna; was first Fr. singer of KUNDRY and ISOLDE at Bayreuth. Roles also incl. ALCESTE (GLUCK), ELEKTRA, LEONORE, and OCTAVIAN, later the MARSCHALLIN. Had a rich, well-trained voice and excelled in dramatic roles. LO

Lucca, Pauline, b. Vienna, 25 Apr 1841; d. Vienna, 28 Feb 1908. Austrian soprano. Studied Vienna; joined Vienna O. chorus. She triumphed at her debut in Olmütz [Olomouc], 4 Sept 1859 in ERNANI and was made principal sop. Sang NORMA and Valentine (HUGUENOTS) in Prague 1860, and subsequently sang in Berlin where she was made a permanent *Kammersängerin*. She appeared in London every season 1863–72 (except 1869) where she was a great favourite with the public; USA 1872–4. Associated with the Vienna O. until 1889, after which she retired. PS

Lucia di Lammermoor, opera, 3 acts, DONIZETTI, lib. CAMMARANO after SCOTT's *The Bride of Lammermoor*. Naples, T. S. Carlo, 26 Sept 1835; London, HM, 5 Apr 1838; New Orleans, 28 Dec 1841. Main chars: Lucia (sop.) Edgardo (ten.) Enrico (bar.) Raimondo (bass) Arturo (ten.). Lucia (Lucy Ashton), in love with her family's enemy Edgardo (Edgar Ravenswood) is persuaded during his absence by her brother Enrico (Henry) to marry Arturo

(Arthur Bucklaw). During the ceremony Edgardo returns unexpectedly and curses her for betraying him. Lucia goes mad and stabs her bridegroom. Edgardo kills himself. JB ○
See Kobbé

Lucio Silla (*Lucius Sulla*), *opera seria*, 3 acts, MOZART, lib. Giovanni da Gamerra, modified METASTASIO. Milan, T. Regio Ducale, 26 Dec 1772. Main chars: Cecilio (sop.) Cinna (sop.) Silla (ten.) Celia (sop.) Giulia (sop.). The plot concerns the rivalry of Silla (Sulla, the Roman dictator) and Cecilio (Caecilius, a proscribed senator) for the hand of Giulia. Cecilio plots to kill Silla but is discovered and imprisoned. Silla plays the magnanimous ruler, freeing Cecilio and uniting him with Giulia. Mozart's last opera wr. in Italy. JB ○

Lucky Peter's Journey, comedy, WILLIAMSON, lib. Edmund Tracey, derived from Strindberg's *Lycko-Pers Resa*. London, Coliseum, 18 Dec 1969. Main chars: Peter (bar.) Lisa (mezzo-sop.). After putting aside the false allurements of worldly success, Peter, a questing hero finds himself and true love. AB

Lucrezia Borgia, opera, prologue and 2 acts, DONIZETTI, lib. ROMANI after HUGO's *Lucrèce Borgia*, 1833. Milan, Sc., 26 Dec 1833; revived Sc. 11 Jan 1840 with ending altered to give more prominence to the tenor; London, HM, 6 June 1839; New Orleans, 27 Apr 1844. Main chars: Lucrezia (sop.) Gennaro (ten.) Alfonso (bass) Maffio Orsini (mezzo-sop.). Lucrezia Borgia is taken to meet Gennaro, the son whom she bore long ago, and who is unaware of her identity. She is discovered and taunted by his friends. Gennaro is arrested (for having insulted the Borgias) by Lucrezia's husband Alfonso, who poisons him; Lucrezia saves his life with an antidote. Lucrezia poisons all Gennaro's friends at a party, not realizing until too late that Gennaro himself was among them. He insists on sharing their fate. One of Donizetti's most dramatic and influential operas. Revived 1965 by American Opera Society with CABALLÉ. JB ○
See Kobbé

Ludwig II of Bavaria, b. Nymphenburg, 25 Aug 1845; d. Lake Starnberg, 13 June 1886. Succeeding to the throne in 1864, he dedicated his life to the promotion of WAGNER, providing him with lavish residences, arranging for premieres of TRISTAN UND ISOLDE, MEISTERSINGER, RHEINGOLD and WALKÜRE in Munich, and donating a huge sum toward the building of the Festspielhaus at Bayreuth. Ludwig, whose mental balance was highly unstable, and whose extravagance was in every way remarkable, lived and died (probably suicide) like a character in a romantic opera. FGB
See Blunt, *The Dream King* (London 1970)

Ludwig, Christa, b. Berlin, 16 Mar 1924. German mezzo-soprano. Debut 1946, Frankfurt, as Orlofsky (FLEDERMAUS); then sang at Darmstadt, Hanover, Hamburg, Salzburg, Vienna, and NY Met (since 1959). Though her repertory incl. MOZART (CHERUBINO, DORABELLA), ROSSINI (ROSINA, CENERENTOLA), VERDI (LADY MACBETH, EBOLI, AMNERIS), and WAGNER (VENUS, ORTRUD, KUNDRY), the richness, power and range of her voice are particularly suited to R. STRAUSS, and she sings KLYTEMNESTRA, OCTAVIAN, the MARSCHALLIN, the Composer (ARIADNE AUF NAXOS), the Dyer's Wife (FRAU OHNE SCHATTEN), and Clairon (CAPRICCIO). She is also a fine FIDELIO and Didon (TROYENS). EF

Luisa Miller, opera, 3 acts, VERDI, lib. CAMMARANO after SCHILLER's *Kabale und Liebe*. Naples, T. S. Carlo, 8 Dec 1849; Philadelphia, 27 Oct 1852; London, SW, 3 June 1858. Main chars: Luisa (sop.) Rodolfo (ten.) Miller (bar.) Federica (mezzo-sop.) Count Walter (bass) Wurm (bass). Luisa, daughter of a retired soldier on Count Walter's estate, is loved by the Count's son Rodolfo, though his father wishes him to marry his cousin, Federica. Wurm, Walter's steward, compels Luisa to write a love letter to himself which Rodolfo intercepts. Rodolfo poisons himself and Luisa; he discovers the truth too late. JB ○
See Kobbé

Lully, Jean-Baptiste, b. Florence, 28 Nov 1632; d. Paris, 22 Mar 1687. Italian composer. Went to Paris as a boy and remained there. With MOLIÈRE and QUINAULT he estab. a pattern of Fr. opera which endured for almost 100 years, with repercussions felt even today. His entertainments devised for the Sun King, perf. at Versailles or in the Acad. Royale de Musique founded by Pierre Perrin and CAMBERT in 1671, and taken over by Lully in 1672, consisted of ballets, *comédies-ballets* and 18 dramatic works, mostly to Quinault's words. The most important are *Cadmus et Hermione* (his first *tragédie* by Quinault), ALCESTE, PHAÉTON, AMADIS (1684), *Roland* (1685), and ARMIDE ET RENAUD. To Lully we also owe the orch. with its solid foundation of strings, which under his direction set an unsurpassed standard; and although not a native Frenchman, by modelling his vocal line on a diligent study of the delivery of the best Fr. actors of the time he

Lulu. WNO's production, Sept 1971, New Theatre, Cardiff; produced GELIOT; designed KOLTAI; costumes Freeda Blackwood; Carole Farley as Lulu; John Modenos as Dr Schön

was able to give to Fr. singing a characteristic style and authority that remained unchallenged until ROUSSEAU and the *guerre des bouffons* in the 18th c. *Cadmus and Hermoine* and *Alceste* are the only two so far prod. in Britain. LO

Lulu, 3 acts (third unfinished), BERG, lib. comp. derived from Frank Wedekind's *Erdgeist* and *Die Büchse der Pandora*. Zürich, 2 June 1937; London, SW by Hamburg O., 3 Oct 1962; Santa Fe, 7 Aug 1963. Main chars: Lulu (sop.) Geschwitz (mezzo-sop.) Alwa (ten.) Dr Schön (bar.). Lulu, a *femme fatale*, succeeds in destroying all her lovers. The only true feelings towards her are felt by the lesbian, Countess Geschwitz. Eventually she comes to London and is killed by Jack the Ripper. The work was left unfinished at Berg's death, but sufficient material in fact exists for the completion of the third act. Even as it is, *Lulu* is a powerful mus. drama, realistic and compelling. AB O
See Kobbé

Lumley [Levy], Benjamin, b. London, 1811; d. London, 17 Mar 1875. English theatre manager. Succeeded Pierre Laporte (1799–1841) as manager of HM until 1852. After CG was burned in 1856 re-opened at HM until 1859, when he retired and resumed his earlier legal profession. Introduced many It. operas to England incl. FILLE DU RÉGIMENT, DON PASQUALE, LINDA DI CHAMOUNIX, FAVORITE, ERNANI, ATTILA, NABUCCO, TRAVIATA, and TROVATORE. His co. also incl. some of the foremost singers of the time: LIND, Giovanni Tadolini, FREZZOLINI, PICCOLOMINI, and TIETJENS. LO
See his *Reminiscences of the Opera* (London 1864)

Luna, Pablo, b. Alhama de Aragón, 21 May 1880; d. Madrid, 28 Jan 1942. Spanish composer. Wrote operettas, revues and many *zarzuelas* including *Molinos de Viento*, *La Pícara Molinera*, *Miguelón*, and *El Niño Judio*. FGB

Lustigen Weiber von Windsor, Die (*The Merry Wives of Windsor*), opera, 3 acts, NICOLAI, lib. Salomon Hermann Mosenthal after SHAKESPEARE's *Merry Wives of Windsor*. Berlin, Hof O., 9 Mar 1849; Philadelphia, 16 Mar 1863; London, HM (in It.), 3 May 1864; CG (in Ger.), 16 Feb 1907. Nicolai's last and best opera, it remained very popular throughout the 19th c. LO

Lustige Witwe, Die (*The Merry Widow*), operetta, 3 acts, LEHÁR, lib. Victor Léon and Leo Stein, originally wr. for HEUBERGER, based on MEILHAC's *L'Attaché*. Vienna, T. a. d. Wien, 28 Dec 1905; London, Daly's T., 8 June 1907; NY, New Amsterdam T., 21 Oct 1907. The work on which Lehár's reputation is

Colour plates. Facing page: Design by Isak Rabinovich for the Horror in LOVE FOR THREE ORANGES, Moscow, Bolshoy T., 1927

Overleaf: David Hockney (b. 1937) designed sets and costumes for the 1975 revival of RAKE'S PROGRESS at Glyndebourne in a decor suggestive of the hatching of 18th-c. engravings, which harmonizes with the deliberate archaisms of STRAVINSKY's score.

Dal vero Angelo In

mainly based. Continually in the repertory at Vienna; revived SW 4 Mar 1958. LO O★
See Lubbock

Luxon, Benjamin, b. Redruth, 24 Mar 1937. British baritone. Local success as a boy singer; studied Guildhall School of Music, London; prizewinner at Munich International *Lieder* competition 1961. Joined EOG 1963: debut as Sid (ALBERT HERRING) and Tarquinius (RAPE OF LUCRETIA) on EOG tour of Russia. Later toured with EOG to Canada and Australia in addition to European fests. Created title role in OWEN WINGRAVE (BBC TV 1971; CG 1973), and Jester/Death in Maxwell DAVIES's *Taverner* (CG 1972). Other debuts 1972 at Glyndebourne Fest. in RITORNO D'ULISSE IN PATRIA (title role) and with Geneva O. in HANDEL's *Belshazzar* (Cyrus). His singing distinguished by its warmth, range and musical sensibility as well as strength of char. NG

Luzzati, Emanuele, b. Geneva, 3 June 1921. Italian painter, designer and costumist. Studied Lausanne. Has designed for many It. theatres incl. prods of ROSENKAVALIER, Sc. 1948; NABUCCO, Florence 1955; MALIPIERO's *Il Figliuolo Prodigo,* Florence 1957; LEHÁR's *Frasquita*, Trieste, 1958; PETRASSI's *Cordovano*, Sc. 1959; also ZAUBERFLÖTE, Glyndebourne, 1963 and ELISIR D'AMORE, Geneva 1974. LO

Lyceum Theatre *see* LONDON

Lyon, France. PHAÉTON was heard there in 1688; from 1756 perfs were frequent, in the Grand T. This was pulled down and rebuilt 1831. The present co. under Louis Erlo gives five or six operas each season, with an interesting repertory which incl. revivals of works like RAMEAU's *Zorastre* and novelties like GOOD SOLDIER SCHWEIK in addition to the standard repertory. LO

M

Maag, Peter Ernst, b. St Gallen, 10 May 1919. Swiss conductor. Has worked in most of the world's major opera houses, incl. the Vienna Staats O. and the NY Met. MOZART specialist. AB

Maazel, Lorin, b. Neuilly-sur-Seine, nr Paris, 6 Mar 1930. American conductor. Studied at Univ. of Pittsburgh and privately with Vladimir Bakaleinikoff. NY Met debut 1962 (DON GIOVANNI). Mus. dir. Deutsche O., Berlin, 1965–71, after which he continued to take charge of one prod. every season. Bayreuth, 1960 (LOHENGRIN), 1969–70 (RING DES NIBELUNGEN). AB

Macbeth, opera, 4 acts, VERDI, lib. PIAVE with additions by Andrea Maffei after SHAKESPEARE. Florence, T. alla Pergola, 14 Mar 1847; NY, Niblo's Garden, 24 Apr 1850. Second, definitive version Paris, TL, 21 Apr 1865; Glyndebourne, 21 May 1938. Main chars: Macbeth (bar.) Lady Macbeth (sop.) Macduff (ten.) Banco (bass). A straightforward, compressed setting of Shakespeare's tragedy. JB O
See Kobbé

McCormack, (Count) John, b. Athlone, 13 June 1884; d. Dublin, 16 Sept 1945. Irish tenor. During his short operatic career (he had virtually retired from the stage by 1914) he sang at CG, Manhattan OH, NY Met, Boston, and Philadelphia, where he created Paul Merrill in HERBERT's *Natoma* (1911). Much admired for his effortless singing, diction and phrasing, he lacked the dramatic drive needed for *Heldentenor* roles, confining himself to the It. repertory and some MOZART. LO

McCracken, John Eugene, b. Gary, Ind., 16 Dec 1926. American tenor. Studied NY; debut 1952, NY CC (BOHÈME). Joined NY Met in 1953, but left in 1957. Sang in many European opera houses, esp. successful at Zürich. After further study in Milan returned to Met in 1960 in title role of VERDI's OTELLO. Has since sung major roles at Vienna, Zürich, San Francisco, and many of the major European fests. A heroic ten. especially commended for his Otello. LO

MacFarren [Andrae], Natalia, b. Lübeck, 1827 (or 1828); d. Bakewell, Derbyshire, 9 Apr 1916. German, later British, contralto and translator. Wife of George Alexander MacFarren (1813–87), who wrote seven operas. She tr. operas for the pub. Novello: FRA DIAVOLO, PURITANI, FILLE DU RÉGIMENT, GUILLAUME TELL, TROVATORE, TANNHÄUSER, FREISCHÜTZ; also ed. OBERON. LO

McIntyre, Donald, b. 22 Oct 1934. New Zealand bass-baritone. British debut, 1959, with WNO (NABUCCO). Joined SW 1960; sang many roles incl. FIGARO (NOZZE DI FIGARO), Caspar (FREISCHÜTZ), PIZARRO, ATTILA, FLIEGENDE HOLLÄNDER and MÉPHISTOPHÉLÈS. Debut CG 1967; Bayreuth 1968. His repertory incl. ESCAMILLO, GOLAUD, Jokanaan (SALOME), Barak (FRAU OHNE SCHATTEN), TELRAMUND, AMFORTAS, KLINGSOR, and WOTAN, which he has sung in complete

Colour plate: Detail of painting, 1852, by Inganni Angelo, of the Teatro alla Scala, Milan, built by Giuseppe Piermarini in 1776–8

Madama Butterfly, London, CG, 1970–1; produced Robert Helpmann; designed FEDOROVICH; PILOU as Cio-Cio-San

RING DES NIBELUNGEN cycles at Bayreuth and CG. He created Heyst in VICTORY. EF

Mackerras, (Alan) Charles, b. Schenectady, NY, 17 Nov 1925. Australian conductor. Studied Sydney and Prague; debut 1948, SW (FLEDERMAUS). Has worked with EOG, and cond. premieres of BERKELEY's *Ruth* (1956) and BRITTEN's *Noyes Fludde* (1958), at Wexford (1958–9) and with WNO. CG debut 1964 (KATERINA IZMAYLOVA); first cond. of the Hamburg Staats O. (1966–9). Mus. dir. of SW 1970– . A JANÁČEK specialist, he cond. the first London stage perfs of KÁT'A KABANOVÁ (1951), MAKROPULOS CASE (1964), and FROM THE HOUSE OF THE DEAD (1965). A regular visitor at the Paris O. Cond. the opening concert at the new Sydney OH (1973). EF

Maconchy, Elizabeth, b. Broxbourne, Hertfordshire, 19 Mar 1907. English composer of Irish parentage. Studied in London, Prague, Vienna, and Paris. *The Sofa* (1959), based on the novel by Claude-Prosper Jolyot de Crébillon, and *The Departure* (1963) were both prod. by the New Opera Workshop at SW. *The Three Strangers*, adapted from the play made by Thomas Hardy from his own short story, was first perf. at Bishop's Stortford College in 1968, and broadcast on BBC Radio 3 in 1970. *The Jesse Tree* was prod. Dorchester Abbey, 1970. EF

Madama Butterfly, opera, 2 acts, PUCCINI, lib. ILLICA and GIACOSA after David Belasco's version of a story by John Luther Long, 1900. Milan, Sc., 17 Feb 1904; revived Brescia, 28 May 1904, in definitive form with last act split into two parts; London, CG, 10 July 1905; Washington DC, 15 Oct 1906. Main chars: Cio-Cio-San (sop.) Pinkerton (ten.) Sharpless (bar.) Goro (ten.) Suzuki (mezzo-sop.) the Bonze (bass) Kate Pinkerton (mezzo-sop.). Pinkerton, an American Navy lieutenant, marries and deserts a Japanese geisha girl who has renounced her religion for his sake. He returns with his newly married American wife to reclaim his child by the geisha, who in despair commits suicide. JB O
See Kobbé

Maderna, Bruno, b. Venice, 21 Apr 1920; d. Darmstadt, 13 Nov 1973. Italian, naturalized German, composer and conductor. Studied with MALIPIERO, in 1955 becoming interested in electronic music. Cond. first perf. of INTOLLERANZA 1960 (Venice 1961); his opera *Don Perlimplin* was broadcast on It. radio (1962). *Hyperion*, written in collaboration with Virginia Puechner, perf. at Venice, 1964, and *Von A bis Z* at Darmstadt, 1970. *Satyricon*, based on an episode from Petronius, prod. at Scheveningen, Holland, and at the Berkshire Fest., Tanglewood, Mass., 1973. EF

Madrid. First opera house inaugurated there was the T. de los Caños de Peral (1738). The T. del Zarzuela (1856) is used today for seasons of international opera, the T. Real (1850) now being unfit for stage perfs and employed instead for concerts. There are also *zarzuela* theatres. FGB

maestro di cappella (MdC). It. term without an exact Eng. equivalent: 'musical director' is the nearest; sometimes simply means 'conductor'. At 18th-c. courts the MdC was in charge of the complete mus. establishment. Ger.: *Kapellmeister*; Fr.: *maître de chapelle*. LO

Maeterlinck, Maurice, b. Ghent, 29 Aug 1862; d. Nice, 6 May 1949. Belgian author whose plays with their symbolism and poetry challenged the prevailing Realism of the theatre of the time. Sixteen operas have been based on his plays, the best known being ARIANE ET BARBE-BLEUE, PELLÉAS ET MÉLISANDE, and MONNA VANNA. Other works on which operas are based are *Le Mort de Tintagiles*, 1894 (Jean Nouguès, 1905); *Alladine et Palomides*, 1894 (E. F. BURIAN, 1923, CHLUBNA, 1925, BURGHAUSER, 1944); *Monna Vanna*, 1902 (Emil Ábrányi, 1907); *L'Oiseau Bleu*, 1909 (WOLFF, 1919); *Sœur Béatrice*, 1901 (François Rasse, 1938; Aleksandr Grechaninov, 1910; Guido Pannain, 1940; MITROPOULOS, 1919). LO

Magdalena, sop., Eva's nurse in MEISTERSINGER

Maggio Musicale Fiorentino. The Florentine May Fest. of Music was started by GUI in 1933. Operas are perf. in the T. Comunale and della Pergola, or the Boboli Gardens. FRAZZI's *Re Lear* (1939) and *Don Chisciotte* (1942), VOLO DI NOTTE (1940), and PRIGIONIERO (1950) received their premieres during the Fest. Notable revivals have incl. Busoni's *Turandot* (1940), DOKTOR FAUST (1942), DON CARLOS (1950), ROSSINI's *Armida*, COMTE ORY, PIETRA DEL PARAGONE, SCALA DI SETA, and TANCREDI (1952), SPONTINI's *Agnes von Hohenstaufen* (1954), ROBERT LE DIABLE (1968), AFRICAINE (1971), and a complete version of GUILLAUME TELL (1972). EF

Magic Flute, The *see* ZAUBERFLÖTE

magic opera *see* ZAUBEROPER

Mahagonny *see* AUFSTIEG UND FALL DER STADT MAHAGONNY

Mahler, Gustav, b. Kališt, Bohemia, 7 July 1860; d. Vienna, 18 May 1911. Austrian conductor and composer. After study in Vienna several conducting posts followed, leading to the important post at Hamburg, 1891–7 and the climax of his career, the 10 years at Vienna O. 1897–1907. Here his perfs of the great classics of opera were legendary, but his drive and unflinching idealism impaired his health and made him enemies. In 1892 he cond. the first RING DES NIBELUNGEN at CG, and after leaving Vienna he appeared at NY Met (TRISTAN UND ISOLDE, 1 Jan 1908) and cond. first US perfs of BARTERED BRIDE and QUEEN OF SPADES. LO
See Mitchell, *Gustav Mahler* (London 1958; Volume 2, London 1975)

Maid as Mistress, The *see* SERVA PADRONA

Maid of Orleans, The (*Orleanskaya deva*), opera, 4 acts, TCHAIKOVSKY, lib. composer after SCHILLER, tr. Vasily Zhukovsky. St Petersburg, Mariinsky, 25 Feb 1881. Main chars: Lionel (bar.) Thibaut (bass) Raimund (ten.) Joan of Arc (sop.). Tchaikovsky found it difficult to come to terms with the remote figure of Joan of Arc, and it is only in Act 2 and in the Farewell Scene in Act 1 that he manages to portray anything but the most superficial elements of the heroine. In the opera's dramatic conventions, he was much influenced by MEYERBEER. The first of Tchaikovsky's operas heard outside Russia (Prague, July 1882). GN O

Maid of Pskov, The (*Pskovityanka*), opera, 3 acts, RIMSKY-KORSAKOV, lib. composer after Lev Mey. 1st version: St Petersburg, Mariinsky, 13 Jan 1873; 3rd version: St Petersburg, Panayevsky, 18 Apr 1895; London, DL (in Russian), 8 July 1913. Main chars: Ivan the Terrible (bass) Prince Yury Tokmakov (bass) Nikita Matuta (ten.) Mikhail Tucha (ten.) Princess Olga (sop.). Ivan the Terrible, having destroyed Novgorod, is approaching Pskov. Olga is in love with Tucha, but is offered by Prince Tokmakov (apparently her father, but really her uncle) to Matuta. The Tsar enters Pskov, meets Olga, and learns of the doubt about her origins (it is rumoured that she is of very noble birth). He promises clemency to Pskov, and takes Olga with him. Later the Tsar reveals that Olga is his own daughter. Tucha tries to rescue her; a shot aimed at him kills Olga. Rimsky-Korsakov's first opera contains one of his finest mus. characterizations, Ivan the Terrible. A prologue that Rimsky-Korsakov comp. for the unperformed second version (1876–7) was later revised as a 1-act opera *Boyarynya Vera Sheloga* (Solodovnikov T., 27 Dec 1898). GN

Maillart, Aimé (Louis), b. Montpellier, 24 Mar 1817; d. Moulins, 26 May 1871. French composer. Pupil of J. F. HALÉVY at the Cons.; won *Prix de Rome* 1841. Wrote six operas, of which *Les Dragons de Villars* (Paris, TL, 19 Sept 1856) was the only one to be successful. LO

The Makropulos Case, Prague, National T., 15 Oct 1965; produced KAŠLÍK; designed SVOBODA; Libuše Prylová as Emilia Marty

Makropulos Case, The (*Věc Makropulos*), opera, 3 acts, JANÁČEK, lib. composer after ČAPEK's play (1922). Brno, NT, 18 Dec 1926; London, SW, 12 Feb 1964; NY, Philharmonic Hall, 12 Dec 1968. Main chars: Emilia Marty (sop.) Albert Gregor (ten.) Jaroslav Prus (bar.) Dr Kolenatý (bass-bar.). When Gregor is about to lose his family's long legal battle with Prus, Emilia Marty, a mysterious opera singer, appears at the offices of Gregor's solicitor, Dr Kolenatý, offering evidence that will reverse the case. Gregor falls in love with her, as does Prus, who, from his files, provides Emilia with what she has been seeking: the long-lost recipe for an elixir that prolonged her life 300 years ago. But it is too late now; she tells her strange story and dies as the recipe is burned. This work, one of Janáček's most gripping theatre pieces, has only recently found general acceptance. JT O
See Ewans, *Janáček's Tragic Operas* (London 1976)

Malatesta, bar., Pasquale's friend in DON PASQUALE

Malheurs d'Orphée, Les (*The Sorrows of Orpheus*), opera, 3 acts, MILHAUD, lib. Armand Lunel. Brussels, T. de la Monnaie, 7 May 1926; NY, 22 May 1958; London, St Pancras Town Hall, 8 Mar 1960. A re-creation of the ancient myth in terms of our own day. Neither Orpheus's manmade magic (he is a chemist) nor the sympathy of the animals he treats can save the life of his gypsy sweetheart, Eurydice. LO

Malibran [García], Maria Felicità, b. Paris, 24 Mar 1808; d. Manchester, 23 Sept 1836. Spanish mezzo-soprano. Daughter of GARCÍA I; sister of VIARDOT. First stage appearance in PAER's *Agnese* at T. S. Carlo, Naples, in a child's part. Studied with her father. Official debut 7 June 1825, King's T., London (ROSINA). Appeared in NY for two years with her father's co., and there, to escape her father's clutches, married a banker, François Eugène Malibran, from whom she was soon separated. Paris debut 1828, TI; her success led to engagements throughout Italy and in London. In 1835 she created the role of MARIA STUARDA for DONIZETTI at Sc., and in Mar 1836 m. the violinist Charles de Bériot. A fall from a horse left her with injuries from which she never recovered, and she died shortly after finishing a concert in Manchester, five months later. PS

Malipiero, Gian Francesco, b. Venice, 18 Mar 1882; d. Treviso, 1 Aug 1973. Italian composer. Wrote over 30 operas, none so far stabilized in the repertory. They incl. *La Bottega del Caffè* (1923, based on GOLDONI); two sets of trilogies, *L'Orfeide* (1925) and *Il Mistero di Venezia* (1932); *Giulio Cesare* (1936); *Antonio e Cleopatra* (1938); *Il Figliuolo Prodigo* (1953). Responsible for a complete edition of MONTEVERDI. His nephew Riccardo (b. 1914) comp. an opera, *La Donna è Mobile* (1957). LO

Mamelles de Tirésias, Les (*The Breasts of Tiresias*), *opéra bouffe*, 2 acts, POULENC, lib. Guillaume Apollinaire. Paris, OC, 3 June 1947; Waltham, Mass., 13 June 1953; Aldeburgh, 16 June 1958. Surrealist story of Husband (ten.) and Wife (sop.) changing sexes when the latter protests against the exploitation of women. The husband retaliates by finding a way of producing 40,000 babies before the couple agree to revert to their earlier roles. The music abounds in typical Gallic wit. FGB

Mamontov, Savva Ivanovich, b. Yalutorovsk, 15 Oct 1841; d. Moscow, 6 Apr 1918. Russian industrialist and patron of the arts. In 1885 he founded the Moscow Private Russian O., which functioned until 1904 (*see* ZIMIN). This staged a number of important premieres (incl. some of RIMSKY-KORSAKOV's operas) and attracted renowned artists, among them SHALYAPIN and RAKHMANINOV. GN

Mam'zelle Nitouche, operetta, 3 acts, HERVÉ, lib. MEILHAC, Albert Millaud, and Ernest Blum. Paris, T. des Variétés, 26 Jan 1883. One of Hervé's most popular operettas, frequently revived; perf. Marseille during 1974–5 season. LO

Maria Malibran in the premiere of VACCAI's *Giovanna Gray*, Milan, Scala, 1836 (the libretto was written by Carlo Pepoli, who wrote the libretto for PURITANI)

Manchester. Sir Charles Hallé in 1855 cond. operas in the T. Royal (the third of that name, built 1845). The same theatre saw the birth of the Carl Rosa Co. (MARITANA, 1 Sept 1873) and the first perf. in Britain of BOHÈME in 1897 (the comp. was present). The Opera House, opened as the New T. in 1912, was the scene of BEECHAM's opera seasons 1916–19. Now served by visits from CG and SW cos. LO

Mancinelli, Luigi, b. Orvieto, 5 Feb 1848; d. Rome, 2 Feb 1921. Italian conductor and composer. A cellist, like TOSCANINI suddenly called upon to cond. an opera, in this case AIDA (Rome 1874). Remained in Rome until 1881, then transferred to T. Comunale, Bologna. Engaged by HARRIS as chief cond. DL 1887, and CG 1888–1905. Was also mus. dir. at T. Real, Madrid, 1888–95. His three operas are *Isora di Provenza* (Bologna 1884); *Ero e Leandro* (first given in concert form at Norwich 1896, and staged at CG 1898), and *Paolo e Francesca* (Bologna 1907). Cond. several first perfs in England incl. FALSTAFF, WERTHER, TOSCA, and STANFORD's *Much Ado about Nothing*. LO

Manelli, Francesco, b. Tivoli, *c.* 1595; d. Parma, Sept 1667. Italian composer, singer, and impresario. Wrote 11 operas 1637–64. He and his wife Maddelena, also a singer, put on the first 'commercial' opera, *L'Andromeda* (Venice 1637). Active in Venice, Padua, Bologna, Parma. LO

Manhattan Opera Company *see* NEW YORK

Manners, Charles [Southcote Mansergh], b. London, 27 Dec 1857, d. Dundrum, Co. Dublin, 3 May 1935. Irish bass and manager. Began in D'Oyly Carte Co. (1881) and later sang with Carl Rosa. After an operatic tour in S. Africa (1896–7), founded with MOODY, whom he m. in 1890, the Moody-Manners O. Co. LO

Mannheim, W. Germany. The NT., built 1789, was destroyed 1943, rebuilt 1957. Vincenz Lachner (1811–93) was MdC there 1836–73; other mus. dirs have been WEINGARTNER (1889–91); BODANZKY (1909–15); FURTWÄNGLER (1915–20); E. KLEIBER (1922–3); ELMENDORFF (1937–43). H. STEIN apptd gen. mus. dir. 1963, Hans Wallet 1973. World premieres at Mannheim incl. ALKESTIS and ABSTRAKTE OPER NO. 1. LO

Manon, opera, 5 acts, MASSENET, lib. MEILHAC and Philippe Gille, based on PRÉVOST's *L'Histoire du Chevalier des Grieux et de Manon Lescaut*, 1731. Paris, OC, 19 Jan 1884; Liverpool, Carl Rosa (in Eng.), 17 Jan 1885; NY, Acad. of Music, 23 Dec 1885; London, CG (in Fr.), 19 May 1891. Main chars: Chevalier des Grieux (ten.) Count des Grieux (bass) Manon

Right: Manon. FARRAR in the title role, a role in which she excelled at the NY Met

Lescaut (sop.). The story deals with Chevalier des Grieux's passionate and ill-starred love affair with Manon, to the sorrow of his father, the Count; his attempt to rescue her from her dissipated Parisian life; her back-sliding and final downfall, condemned to transportation as a prostitute. She dies in des Grieux's arms on the road to Le Havre. LO ○
See Newman, *Opera Nights* (London 1943)

Manon Lescaut, opera, 4 acts, PUCCINI, lib. Marco Praga, Domenico Oliva, Giulio RICORDI, ILLICA and others, after PRÉVOST. Turin, T. Regio, 1 Feb 1893; London, CG, 14 May 1894; Philadelphia, Grand OH, 29 Aug 1894; revived Milan, Sc., 1 Feb 1923 under TOSCANINI in definitive form. Main chars: Manon (sop.) des Grieux (ten.) Lescaut (bar.) Geronte (bass) Edmondo (ten.). The young Chevalier des Grieux meets, falls in love and elopes with Manon. She is later living with the elderly Geronte; at the reappearance of des Grieux she escapes with him, but is arrested on Geronte's orders. An attempt to save her from deportation fails; des Grieux joins her on board ship. She dies in her lover's arms in a desert near New Orleans. His third opera and first real success; he modified it for 30 years. JB ○★
See Kobbé

Manrico, ten., the hero of TROVATORE

Manru, opera, 3 acts, Ignacy Jan Paderewski (1860–1941), lib. Alfred Nossig based on Józef Ignacy Kraszewski's novel *The Cabin Behind the Wood*, 1843. Dresden, 29 May 1901; NY Met, 14 Feb 1902. Paderewski's only opera. LO

Manzoni, Giacomo, b. Milan, 26 Sept 1932. Italian composer. Studied Messina and Milan. His first opera, *La Sentenza* (Bergamo 1960), lasting 40 minutes, was revived, Florence Maggio Musicale, 25 May 1973. *Atomtod* (Milan 1965) depicts horrors of post-nuclear war. *Per Massimiliano Robespierre* was prod. Bologna, 12 Apr 1975. LO

Mapleson, James Henry, b. London, 4 May 1830; d. London, 14 Nov 1901. English impresario. Studied London RAM; was a singer and viola player. Career as manager began in 1861, at the Lyceum, where BALLO IN MASCHERA was first prod. in Eng. Managed HM 1862 until it was burned down (1867); then took over DL for a season. After a short period at CG took over HM again (1877–81). Also managed NY Acad. of Music 1878–86 and again in 1896. His enterprise did much for opera in London and NY, introducing many new works and a variety of singers. LO
See Mapleson, *The Mapleson Memoirs* (London 1888; reprinted, ed. Rosenthal, London and New York 1966)

Marcellina, sop., Rocco's daughter in FIDELIO

Marcello, bar., one of the four Bohemians in BOHÈME

Marchesi, Blanche, b. Paris, 4 Apr 1863; d. London, 15 Dec 1940. French soprano, daughter of MARCHESI DE CASTRONE. Debut Prague 1900, as BRÜNNHILDE. After singing in Moody-Manners Co. (she appeared at CG in 1902 in CAVALLERIA RUSTICANA, TROVATORE, LOHENGRIN, and as ISOLDE) she settled in England as a teacher. LO
See autobiography, *Singer's Pilgrimage* (London 1923)

Marchesi, Salvatore, Cavaliere de Castrone, Marchese della Rajata, b. Palermo, 15 Jan 1822; d. Paris, 20 Feb 1908. Italian baritone, and husband of MARCHESI DE CASTRONE. Studied philosophy, law and singing, Palermo. Exiled in 1848 for political activities; debut NY in ERNANI. Returned to Paris, and studied with GARCÍA II; lived for some years in London where, like his wife, was successful teacher. Tr. several Fr. and Ger. operas into It. (VESTALE, MÉDÉE, IPHIGÉNIE EN AULIDE, LOHENGRIN, TANNHÄUSER). LO

Marchesi de Castrone [Graumann], Mathilde, b. Frankfurt, 23 Mar 1821; d. London, 17 Nov 1913. German mezzo-soprano. Studied with NICOLAI in Vienna and GARCÍA II in Paris, under whose guidance and encouragement she became one of the most eminent singing teachers in Europe. Highly praised by ROSSINI, her pupils incl. CALVÉ, DE MURSKA, EAMES, GARDEN and MELBA. She published a Method of Singing; her reminiscences, *Marchesi and Music*, appeared in 1897. She m. S. MARCHESI in 1852. LO

Marchisio, Barbara, b. Turin, 6 Dec 1833; d. Mira, 19 Apr 1919. Italian contralto. One of the most celebrated contraltos of the mid-19th c., she was solely responsible for many of the revivals of *bel canto* operas such as SEMIRAMIDE and CROCIATO IN EGITTO in the 1860s. With her sister, C. MARCHISIO, she studied under Luigi Fabbrica in Turin. Debut 1856, Madrid (ROSINA). Her career was spent mainly in Italy, although she appeared with spectacular success in the Paris revival of *Semiramide* (in Fr.) 1860, repeating the role of Arsace at HM, London, 1862. After touring Spain and Portugal, last appearance 1876 at T. Malibran,

Venice (BARBIERE DI SIVIGLIA). She came out of retirement in 1887 to sing in ROSSINI's *Stabat Mater* in Florence when the comp.'s ashes were brought back to Italy. PS

Marchisio, Carlotta, b. Turin, 6 Dec 1833; d. Turin, 28 June 1872. Italian soprano, twin sister of the above. Debut 1857, Madrid (ADALGISA). After successes in Italy and Paris she appeared at HM, London, in 1862 as Donna ANNA and Isabella in ROBERT LE DIABLE. In London she m. the bass, Eugenio Cosselli (Eugen Kuhn, 1835–75). She died in childbirth. PS

Marcoux, Vanni [Jean Émile Diogène], b. Turin, 12 June 1877; d. Paris, 22 Oct 1962. French bass-baritone. Studied Paris; debut Bayonne 1889; sang in first Nice perf. of BOHÈME same year. Sang at CG, Monte Carlo and elsewhere before appearing in USA (Boston 1912; Chicago 1913–14 and 1926–32). His wide repertory was confined mainly to It. and Fr. operas, with SCARPIA and MARCELLO among his best roles. Dir. of Grand T., Bordeaux 1948–51. LO

Maréchal, Charles Henri, b. Paris, 22 Jan 1844; d. Paris, 10 May 1924. French composer. Studied with MASSÉ, won *Prix de Rome* 1870. His seven operas incl. *Déidamie* (1893) and *Daphnis et Chloé* (1899). LO

Mařenka, sop., the heroine of BARTERED BRIDE

Maretzek, Max, b. Brno [Brünn], 28 June 1821; d. NY, 14 May 1897. Czech, later American, conductor and impresario. Cond. his own opera, *Hamlet* (Brno 1843). To USA, 1848, as cond. Astor Place OH, NY; later formed his own co., was manager of Niblo's Garden, NY, and Crosby OH, Chicago; took touring co. to Mexico and Havana. LO

Marguerite, sop., the heroine of GOUNOD's FAUST

Maria di Rohan, opera, 3 acts, DONIZETTI, lib. CAMMARANO after Édouard Lockroy's *Un Duel sous le Cardinal de Richelieu*. Vienna, KT, 5 June 1843; London, CG, 8 May 1847; NY, 10 Dec 1849. Main chars: Maria (sop.) Riccardo (ten.) Gondi (contr.) Chevreuse (bar.). JB
See Ashbrook, *Donizetti* (London 1965)

Maria Golovin, opera, 3 acts, MENOTTI, lib. composer. Brussels, Pavilion T. in World Fair, 20 Aug 1958 (commissioned by NBC); NY, Martin Becket T., 5 Nov 1958. Revised version Washington DC, 22 Jan 1965. LO

Mariani, Angelo, b. Ravenna, 11 Oct 1821; d. Genoa, 13 June 1873. Italian conductor. Dir. T. Carlo Felice, Genoa, 1852–73. Cond. It. premieres of LOHENGRIN (Bologna 1871) and TANNHÄUSER (Bologna 1872), and was a staunch friend and supporter of VERDI until the breach between the two in the 1870s. One of the most enlightened and forward looking conds in Italy at that time. LO

Maria Stuarda, opera, 3 acts, DONIZETTI, lib. Giuseppe Bardari after SCHILLER. Naples, T. S. Carlo, 18 Oct 1834 as *Buondelmonte*; revived under proper title Milan, Sc., 30 Dec 1835 with MALIBRAN in title role. London, Camden Fest., 1 Mar 1966; NY CC, Mar 1972; London, Col., by ENO (in Eng.), 13 Dec 1973. Main chars: Maria (sop.) Elisabetta (sop.) Leicester (ten.) Talbot (bar.) Cecil (bass). Elisabetta (Elizabeth I of England), in love with the Earl of Leicester, is persuaded by him to visit Maria (Mary Queen of Scots), held prisoner in Fotheringhay. During their interview Maria is provoked into insulting her cousin, for which she is put under close arrest and finally executed. Leicester, who himself loves Maria, is ordered to witness her fate. JB O

Marie, sop., Wozzeck's mistress in WOZZECK

Marinuzzi, Gino [Giuseppe], b. Palermo, 24 Mar 1882; d. Milan, 17 Aug 1945. Italian conductor and composer. Studied Palermo; debut Catania, with touring co.; then at Mantua, Milan (T. dal Verme) and Palermo, where his first opera, *Barbarina*, was perf. 1903, and where he cond. first Palermo perfs of TRISTAN UND ISOLDE (1909) and PARSIFAL (1914). Other engagements: Rome 1905, Madrid 1909–11, cond. first Madrid *Tristan und Isolde* 1911. Toured S. America several times, introducing operas by ZANDONAI, ALFANO, RESPIGHI, and PIZZETTI. Also cond. Chicago 1919–21 and Sc. 1934–44. One of the best It. conds of his generation, active in promoting not only new It. operas but those of R. STRAUSS and WOLF-FERRARI in Italy. LO

Mario [Giovanni Matteo de Candia], b. Cagliari, 17 Oct 1810; d. Rome, 11 Dec 1883. Italian tenor. Son of a general in the Piedmontese army, he was trained for a military career. A liaison with a ballet dancer forced him to flee to Paris in 1836; debut 1838, Paris O. (ROBERT LE DIABLE). Outstandingly handsome, he is considered the prototype of the romantic tenor. London debut 1839 (LUCREZIA BORGIA). In 1844 m. Giulia GRISI. Last appearance CG 1871 in FAVORITE, after which he retired to Rome. PS

Marionette operas. Operas for puppets have a history going back to Francesco Pistocchi's *Leandro* (Venice 1679). HAYDN wrote PHILÉMON ET BAUCIS for Prince Esterházy's puppet theatre. The 20th c. has seen several puppet operas incl. HINDEMITH's *Nusch-Nuschi* (1921), LUALDI's *Le Furie di Arlecchino* (1915), and *Guerin Meschino* (1920), both written for the T. dei Piccoli, founded in Rome by Vittorio Podrecca (1883–1959), and esp. RETABLO DE MAESE PEDRO. LO

Maritana, opera, 3 acts, V. WALLACE, lib. Edward Fitzball, after the melodrama by Adolphe-Philippe d'Ennery and Philippe François Dumanoir, *Don César de Bazan* (a character in HUGO's *Ruy Blas*). London, DL, 15 Nov 1845; Philadelphia, 9 Nov 1846. A popular stand-by in Britain throughout the 19th c. LO

Marmontel, Jean François, b. Bort, Limousin, 11 July 1723; d. Abloville, Eure, 31 Dec 1799. French librettist. His numerous libs incl. ZÉMIRE ET AZOR and HURON; *Acante et Céphise* (1751) for RAMEAU; *Atys* and *Roland* (1778) for PICCINNI; and *Démophon* (1788) for CHERUBINI. He wrote the article *Opéra* for the *Grande Encyclopédie*, and sided with Piccinni in the Piccinni/GLUCK controversy. LO

Mârouf, Savetier du Caire (*Mârouf, the Cobbler of Cairo*), opera, 4 acts, RABAUD, lib. Lucien Népoty based on ARABIAN NIGHTS' ENTERTAINMENTS. Paris, OC, 15 May 1914; NY Met, 19 Dec 1917. Rabaud's most popular opera, still seen in Fr. and Belg. opera houses. Mârouf goes to sea to escape his termagant wife; shipwrecked, he meets a friend, now become wealthy, who passes him off as a rich merchant to the Sultan. He marries the Sultan's daughter, living luxuriously at her father's expense. When the Sultan becomes suspicious the pair escape, pursued by the Sultan. Nemesis is avoided at the last minute by a magic ring that turns their desert abode into a palace, and all is forgiven. LO

Marriage, The (*Zhenitba*), opera, 1 act, MUSORGSKY, lib. GOGOL's prose comedy. St Petersburg, 1 Apr 1909. Main chars: Podkolesin (bar.) Stepan (bass) Fyokla (contr.) Kochkaryov (ten.). Podkolesin, a clerk, is undecided whether or not to marry Arafya, a merchant's daughter. Fyokla, the marriage broker, urges him not to delay, and Kochkaryov (whose own marriage, arranged by Fyokla, has collapsed) describes the happiness of married life. He persuades Podkolesin to visit his intended bride. Although Musorgsky finished only the first act of this comedy of manners (1868; the other three acts were completed by Mikhail Mikhaylovich Ippolitov-Ivanov for a version perf. 1931), it is a significant work, applying to prose DARGOMYZHSKY's principles of realism and melodic recitative, and employing *Leitmotiv* (for the first time in Russian opera) as a means to musical characterization. GN

Marriage of Figaro, The *see* NOZZE DI FIGARO

Marschallin, sop., Princess von Wedenberg in ROSENKAVALIER

Marschner, Heinrich August, b. Zittau, 16 Aug 1795; d. Hanover, 14 Dec 1861. German composer. Joint MdC with C. WEBER and MORLACCHI Dresden 1820–4, mus. dir. there 1824–6; MdC Leipzig 1827–31, then similar post at Hanover. Of his 14 operas he is remembered for VAMPYR, *Der Templer und die Jüdin* (1829, based on SCOTT's *Ivanhoe*), and HANS HEILING. Important in the history of Ger. romantic opera. LO

Marseille, France. In 1682 Pierre Gaultier was granted permission to establish opera at Marseille and at other towns in the Midi. Grand T. opened 1787; opera given there until it was burned out 1919. Present theatre dates from 1924. About a dozen operas are presented each season, some in conjunction with Aix or Bordeaux. First Fr. prod. of DEVILS OF LOUDUN (Feb 1972), and of Pascal Bentoiu's *Hamlet* (1973). Present gen. manager and mus. dir. Reynald Giovaninetti. LO

Martha, oder Der Markt von Richmond (*Martha, or Richmond Market*), opera, 4 acts, FLOTOW, lib. W. Friedrich [Friedrich Wilhelm Riese] after SAINT-GEORGES's ballet-pantomime *Lady Henriette ou La Servante de Greenwich*. Vienna, KT, 25 Nov 1847; London, DL, 4 July 1849; NY, Niblo's Garden, 1 Nov 1852. LO O
See Kobbé

Martin, Frank, b. Geneva, 15 Sept 1890; d. Naarden, Holland, 21 Nov 1974. Swiss composer. Best known for orch. and instrumental works. Dramatic works incl. the oratorio *Le Vin Herbé* (staged Salzburg 1948), the opera STURM, the scenic-oratorio *Le Mystère de la Nativité* (staged Salzburg 1960), and the comic opera MONSIEUR DE POURCEAUGNAC. FGB

Martinelli, Giovanni, b. Montagno, 22 Oct 1885; d. NY, 2 Feb 1969. One of the most notable Italian tenors of the 20th c. Voice discovered while serving in army by It. bandmaster. Studied Milan; debut there 1910, T. dal Verme (ERNANI). CG debut 1912 (CAVARADOSSI), returned there until World War I, and in 1919 and 1937. NY Met debut 1912 (RODOLFO), remaining there until 1946, singing almost 700 times in *c.* 40 roles. Among his most famous were RADAMES, CANIO, Don JOSÉ, MANRICO, ELÉAZAR, ALVARO and, in later years, VERDI's OTELLO. Sang Tristan (TRISTAN UND ISOLDE) at Chicago opposite FLAGSTAD. Final stage appearance as the Emperor in TURANDOT (Seattle 1967) – had sung his first CALAF at Coronation season, CG, 1937. His Verdian style was impeccable and an object lesson to all other tenors. His tone, perfectly focused, was silvery and bright, and used expressively in everything he did. AB

Martinů, Bohuslav, b. Polička, 8 Dec 1890; d. Liestal, Switzerland, 28 Aug 1959. Czech composer. Studied Prague Cons.; played second violin in the Czech Philharmonic. Settled in Paris 1923, where he had lessons with ROUSSEL. Spent World War II in the USA, returning to Europe in 1953, though he never went back to Czechoslovakia. His earliest opera was *The Soldier and the Ballerina* (*Voják a tanečnice*, 1928, after Plautus). He was influenced by jazz and Parisian trends in the 1920s as in his witty Dadaist operas *Les Larmes du Couteau* (1928, prod. 1969) and *Trois Souhaits* (1929, prod. 1971). Gradually, however, he achieved a synthesis in which Czech elements are more evident – e.g. *The Plays of Our Lady* (*Hry o Marii*), 1935 and *The Suburban Theatre* (*Divadlo za branou*, 1936). *Alexandre Bis*, wr. 1937, was prod. 1964. His best-known opera is JULIETTA, a surrealist work which captures the nostalgia of a permanent exile. Martinů wrote two one-act radio operas, *The Voice of the Forest* (*Hlas lesa*, 1935) and COMEDY ON A BRIDGE, and two TV operas, *What Men Live By* (1953, after TOLSTOY) and *The Marriage* (1953, after GOGOL). His last works incl. *La Plaint Contre Inconnu* (wr. 1953, unfinished), *Mirandolina* (1959, in It., after GOLDONI), GREEK PASSION and the 1-act opera inspired by CALLAS, *Ariadna* (1961). JT
See Large, *Martinů* (London 1975)

Martín y Soler, Vicente, b. Valencia, 18 June 1754; d. St Petersburg, 30 Jan 1806. Spanish composer. His tuneful but slender operas won considerable popularity, esp. in Vienna, where he lived 1785–8. A melody from COSA RARA is quoted by MOZART in the Supper Scene of DON GIOVANNI. LO

Martyrs, Les *see* POLIUTO

Masaniello *see* MUETTE DE PORTICI

Mascagni, Pietro, b. Livorno, 7 Dec 1863; d. Rome, 2 Aug 1945. Italian composer and conductor. Studied music at Livorno and Milan Cons. which he left prematurely to join a touring co. The international success of CAVALLERIA RUSTICANA estab. him for a while as the foremost It. comp. of his generation, but his career declined steadily. AMICO FRITZ still survives precariously. *I Rantzau* (Florence 1892) and *Guglielmo Ratcliff* (Milan 1895) return to heavy melodrama. *Silvano* (Milan 1895) combines the idyllic and veristic in a picturesque Adriatic setting. *Zanetto* (Pesaro 1896), perf. in the same year in which Mascagni was apptd dir. Pesaro Cons., is a miniature, a musical short story. IRIS was successful; *Le Maschere* (1901), given its premiere in seven different cities concurrently, failed in six. Later operas were *Amica* (Monte Carlo 1905), ISABEAU, *Parisina* (lib. D'ANNUNZIO, Milan 1913), LODOLETTA, the operetta *Si* (Rome 1919), PICCOLO MARAT, *Pinotta* (Rome 1932), and *Nerone* (Milan 1935). He died in poverty and isolation as a result of his former political affiliations. Despite a genuine melodic gift and a growing refinement of technique he lacked the ability in most of his works to sustain interest throughout an act. As a cond. he made successful tours abroad with It. orchestras. JB

Mascotte, La, operetta, 3 acts, AUDRAN, lib. Alfred Duru and Henri Charles Chivot. Paris, Bouffes-Parisiens, 28 Dec 1880; NY, Park T., 5 May 1881; Brighton, Sussex, 19 Sept 1881; London, Comedy T., 15 Oct 1881. Audran's most popular operetta, played 1,700 times in Paris alone to 1897. LO
See Lubbock

Maskarade, opera, 3 acts, NIELSEN, lib. Vilhelm Andersen based on a play by Ludvig Holberg. Copenhagen, 11 Nov 1906; London, BBC, 1965; St. Paul, Minn., 23 June 1972. Main chars: Henrik (bar.) Leander (ten.) Pernille (sop.) Arv (ten.) Magdalene (sop.) Jeronimo (bass). A young man refuses to marry the young lady of his parents' choice, preferring a girl he met at a masquerade – who turns out to be his official fiancée. EF

Masked Ball, A *see* BALLO IN MASCHERA

Masnadieri, I (*The Brigands*), opera, 4 acts, VERDI, lib. Andrea Maffei after SCHILLER's *Die Räuber*. London, HM, 22 July 1847 with LIND as prima donna. Main chars: Amalia (sop.) Carlo (ten.) Francesco (bar.) Massimiliano (bass) Moser (bass). Carlo, a wild student, banished from his home through the intrigues of his younger brother Francesco, forms his companions into a company of Robin Hood-like bandits. Francesco suborns a dependant to bring his father false evidence of Carlo's death. Amalia, Carlo's beloved, repulses Francesco's advances; Carlo burns down a city to rescue a comrade. Carlo is reunited with Amalia and rescues his father from starving to death in a tower. Still unrecognized by the old Count, he brings about Francesco's death, but when his men refuse to release him from his oath of loyalty to them he kills Amalia in their presence. Verdi's only opera wr. for England; only moderately successful and rarely revived. JB O

masque. A theatrical entertainment popular in It., Fr., and Eng. courts and palaces in 16th and 17th c. It featured music, dancing, elaborate costumes and scenery with machines; the subject matter was drawn from classical mythology or the It. pastoral, but there was little if any dramatic tension. Important in the early history of opera. LO

Massard, Robert, b. Pau. French baritone. Debut 1952, Paris O., as High Priest (SAMSON ET DALILA). Since sung most major bar. roles there. CG debut 1961 as Oreste (IPHIGÉNIE EN TAURIDE) and subsequently sung Fieramosca (BENVENUTO CELLINI) and the Toreador (CARMEN). Also appeared at Sc. Foremost Fr. bar. of his generation who maintains something of Fr. style in an era notably weak in that field. AB

Massé, Félix Marie [known as Victor], b. Lorient, 7 Mar 1822; d. Paris, 5 July 1884. French composer. Studied with J. F. HALÉVY, won *Prix de Rome* 1844. Chorus master Paris O. 1860–76. Wrote more than 20 operettas, incl. two charming *opérettes de famille*, pub. 1879, intended for private perf. *La Reine Topaze* (Paris, TL, 1856) was given, in Eng., at HM 1858; other works heard in London were *Les Noces de Jeanette*, lib. BARBIER and CARRÉ (Paris, OC, 1853; CG, in Eng., 1860 – his best work), and *Paul et Virginie*, same libs (Opéra-National-Lyrique 1876; CG, in It., 1878). LO
See Hughes, *Composers of Operetta* (London and New York 1962)

Massenet, Jules Émile Frédéric, b. Montaud, Loire, 12 May 1842; d. Paris, 13 Aug 1912. French composer. Studied with Ambroise THOMAS at the Cons., winning the *Prix de Rome* in 1863. His career was an almost unbroken success, his 25 operas bringing him a considerable fortune. *La Grand' Tante* (1867) and *Don César de Bazan* (1872) met with only moderate response, but ROI DE LAHORE and HÉRODIADE were well received; the next, MANON, was acclaimed with enthusiasm, and its popularity at the OC is rivalled only by CARMEN. CID, *Esclarmonde* (1889), and *Le Mage* (1891) made little impact, but with WERTHER he scored another hit, the next, THAÏS, being only slightly less successful. Operas followed steadily, every year or so – *Le Portrait de Manon* (a sequel to *Manon*, 1894); NAVARRAISE (wr. for CG); *Sapho* (1897); *Cendrillon* (based on PERRAULT's Cinderella story, 1899); GRISÉLIDIS; JONGLEUR DE NOTRE-DAME; *Chérubin* (1905); *Ariane* (1906); *Thérèse* (1907); *Bacchus* (1909); *Don Quichotte* (1910); *Roma* (1912); *Panurge* (1913); *Cléopâtre* (1914); *Amadis* (1922) (the last four wr. in 1910). His stylish and elegant music is returning to favour. LO
See Harding, *Massenet* (London 1970; New York 1971)

Jules Massenet. Poster for the first production of *Esclarmonde* (1889). The opera was revived, San Francisco, 1974.

Master Peter's Puppet Show *see* RETABLO DE MAESE PEDRO

Mastersingers of Nuremberg *see* MEISTERSINGER VON NÜRNBERG

Mastilović, Danica. Yugoslavian soprano. Studied Belgrade Acad. of Mus.; joined Frankfurt O. 1959. Has sung all over Germany, at Buenos Aires, Florence, Verona (1971), Sc. (1972), and CG (1973). Her powerful, bright-toned voice and dramatic style make her a fine ELEKTRA and TURANDOT; also sings Abigaille (NABUCCO), LEONORE, SENTA, BRÜNNHILDE, and Dyer's Wife (FRAU OHNE SCHATTEN). EF

Matačić, Lovro von, b. Sušak, 14 Feb 1899. Yugoslav conductor. Studied Vienna; debut Cologne 1919. Cond. BORIS GODUNOV (Paris 1930); after posts in Ljubljana and Zagreb apptd dir. of Belgrade O. 1938; similar post, Dresden 1956–8. Succeeded SOLTI at Frankfurt 1961. Has appeared as guest cond. in Sc., Vienna, Chicago and in 1971 cond. WALKÜRE – the first opera to be performed in the remodelled Paris O. LO

Materna, Amalia, b. Sankt Georgen, Styria, 10 July 1844; d. Vienna, 18 Jan 1918. Austrian soprano. Debut 1864, Graz, in light roles, continuing to sing such parts in Carl T., Vienna. Debut 1869 Vienna Staats O. (AFRICAINE); remained there until she retired in 1897. The first Bayreuth BRÜNNHILDE and KUNDRY. With her ample voice and fine stage presence was one of the best WAGNER singers of her generation. LO

Mathis, Edith, b. Lucerne, 11 Feb 1938. Swiss soprano. Studied Lucerne Cons. Stage debut Lucerne as second boy in ZAUBERFLÖTE. Cologne, 1959–63, then Deutsche O., W. Berlin. UK debut 1962, Glyndebourne (CHERUBINO), returning there 1963 in same role and in 1965 as SOPHIE. CG debut 1970 (SUSANNA). Has appeared regularly at Salzburg and Munich fests, notably as Susanna, PAMINA, and MÉLISANDE. AB

Mathis der Maler (*Matthias the Painter*), opera, 7 scenes, HINDEMITH, lib. composer. Zürich, 28 May 1938; London, Queen's Hall (concert), 15 Mar 1939; Edinburgh, King's T., 29 Aug 1952; Boston, 17 Feb 1956. Main chars: Mathis (bar.) the Cardinal (ten.) Riedinger (bass) Ursula (sop.) Schwalb (ten.) Regina (sop.). The opera recounts the life of the 16th-c. painter, Matthias Grünewald, master of the Isenheim altarpiece, his sympathy with the Peasants' Rebellion, his vision of the Temptation of St Anthony, his rejection of politics for art and, finally, his death. EF

Il Matrimonio Segreto, production at Milan, Piccola Scala, 1955–7; produced STREHLER; scenery DAMIANI; costumes Ezio Frigerio

Matrimonio Segreto, Il (*The Secret Marriage*), *opera buffa*, 2 acts, CIMAROSA, lib. BERTATI after George Colman and GARRICK. Vienna, BT, 7 Feb 1792; London, 11 Jan 1794; NY, 4 Jan 1834. Main chars: Paolino (ten.) Carolina (sop.) Geronimo (bass) Elisetta (sop.) Fidalma (mezzo-sop.) Count Robinson (bass). Paolino and Carolina are secretly married. Their plight is further embarrassed by Count Robinson, who, betrothed to Carolina's elder sister Elisetta, falls in love with Carolina herself, and by Carolina's aunt Fidalma who has designs on Paolino. All ends happily when the truth is revealed. Cimarosa's most famous opera, repeated in its entirety on the night of its first perf. JB
See Kobbé

Matzenauer, Margarete, b. Temesvár (now Timişoara), 1 June 1881; d. Van Nuy, Cal., 19 May 1963. Hungarian contralto, later soprano. Studied Berlin; debut 1901, Strasbourg, as Puck (OBERON). Moved to Munich 1904–11. NY Met debut 1911 (AMNERIS). After various mezzo-sop. roles she graduated to dramatic sop. parts such as BRÜNNHILDE and LEONORA (TROVATORE); remained at the Met until 1930, appearing more than 300 times in both Ger. and It. repertory. First Met EBOLI and Kostelnička (JENŮFA). AB

Maurel, Victor, b. Marseille, 17 June 1848; d. NY, 22 Oct 1923. French baritone. Trained Paris Cons.; debut 1868, O., as Nevers (HUGUENOTS) and appeared with increasing success in France and abroad in a wide variety of roles. His most important creations were in operas by VERDI: the Doge (in the revised SIMONE BOCCANEGRA), IAGO, and the title role in FAL-

STAFF. Rejoined Paris O. 1889–94; at OC 1896–1900. After a brief period as a straight actor in France, he returned to the opera stage in 1904, finally retiring to teach in NY. He was the best singing actor of his generation. JB

Mauro, Ermanno, b. nr Trieste, 29 Jan 1939; moved to Canada 1958. Canadian tenor. First operatic appearances 1962, Edmonton, as TAMINO and MANRICO; then entered Royal Cons. O. School in Toronto. Since 1965 has sung regularly with COC in Toronto and with other cos in Canada. Joined CG 1967; appeared as guest in continental Europe and with WNO. NY CC debut 1975 (CALAF). Has a rich lyric voice equally effective as EDGARDO, the Male Chorus in RAPE OF LUCRETIA, or Naisi in Healey Willan's *Deirdre*. CM

Mauro family. A dynasty – at least 15 – of Italian architects and designers, active *c.* 1660–1820, mainly in Austria and S. Germany. Alessandro, *fl.* 1709–49, worked in Venice, Vienna and Dresden, where he built the opera house, 1719. LO

Mavra, opera, 1 act, STRAVINSKY, lib. Boris Kokhno after PUSHKIN's *The Little House at Kolomna*. Paris, O., 2 June 1922 (earlier private perf. at the Hôtel Continental); Moscow, 2 Feb 1929; London, 27 Apr 1934 (radio); Philadelphia, Acad. of Music, 28 Dec 1934; Edinburgh 21 Aug 1956. Main chars: Parasha (sop.) Sosedka (mezzo-sop.) Mother (contr.) Hussar (ten.). Parasha's mother sends her to look for a replacement for the cook who has died. She disguises her lover, the Hussar, as a woman, and establishes him in the house. But he is caught shaving, and is ejected. *Mavra*, an *opera buffa* in the Russo-It. tradition, is dedicated to Pushkin, GLINKA, and TCHAIKOVSKY. The orchestration reflects the interest in wind instruments Stravinsky reveals in several other works of the period. GN O

Maw, Nicholas, b. Grantham, Lincolnshire, 5 Nov 1935. British composer. Studied Paris with Nadia Boulanger. Came to notice with his R. STRAUSS-like *Scenes and Arias*, a concert work, in 1962 (revised 1966). His comic opera in 2 acts, *One Man Show* (1964), showed distinct promise in writing for the stage confirmed by his full-length *The Rising of the Moon* (1970), wr. for Glyndebourne. His style is lyrical and lively. AB

Max, ten., the hero of FREISCHÜTZ

Maximilien, opera, 3 acts, MILHAUD, lib. Armand Lunel, tr. from play by Rudolf Stephen Hoffmann based on Franz Werfel's historical play, *Juarez und Maximilian*, 1924. Paris, O., 4 Jan 1932. Based on Archduke Maximilian's ill-fated Mexican adventure of 1864 – with CHRISTOPHE COLOMB and BOLIVAR making a 'New World' trilogy. Despite a lavish production and good cast the work failed to make an impression. LO

Maximowna, Ita, b. Pskov, 31 Oct 1914. Russian designer. Studied painting in Paris. Work began in Berlin 1945–52; active in Hamburg, Vienna, Milan, Edinburgh, Salzburg, Vancouver, Glyndebourne, etc. Operas she has designed for incl. LEONORE 40/45 (Sc. 1953); CARMEN and VIE PARISIENNE (both Hamburg 1955); PROZESS (Frankfurt 1958). LO

May Night (*Mayskaya Noch*), opera, 3 acts, RIMSKY-KORSAKOV, lib. composer after GOGOL. St Petersburg, Mariinsky, 21 Jan 1880; London, DL (in Russian), 26 June 1914. Main chars: the Headman (bass), Levko (ten.) Ganna (mezzo-sop.) Pannochka (sop.). Levko and Ganna are lovers. With the help of Pannochka, a water-nymph (formerly daughter of a landowner), Levko teaches his father (the Headman) a lesson for trying to seduce Ganna, and also manages to win permission to marry her. The first of Rimsky-Korsakov's fantasy operas, *May Night* has never been among his most popular works, despite its lyricism and gentle humour, and is now heard only occasionally in Russian opera houses. GN

Right: Giovanni Simone Mayr's MEDEA IN CORINTO. PASTA in the title role, a particular favourite of hers

Mayr, Giovanni Simone [Johann Simon], b. Mendorf, Bavaria, 14 June 1763; d. Bergamo, 2 Dec 1845. German–Italian composer. Studied Ingolstadt and Venice. His first opera, *Saffo* (T. La Fenice, 1794), was an immediate success. In the next 30 years he wrote nearly 70 operas. The most important are *Che Originali* (1798), which brought him international fame; *Ginevra di Scozia* (1801); *Elisa* (1804); *L'Amore Coniugale* (1805), based on the BOUILLY drama set the same year by BEETHOVEN as LEONORE; and *La Rosa Bianca e la Rosa Rossa* (1813), which began the vogue for operas on romantic Eng. historical themes. His masterpiece was MEDEA IN CORINTO. In 1802, he became MdC of Santa Maria Maggiore, Bergamo, and in 1805 founded the charity mus. school where, 1806–15, he taught DONIZETTI. Mayr introduced the technique of the pliable symphony orchestra from Germany to Italy, and particularly to It. opera, where he developed it to a degree that fascinated every comp. in Europe. PS

Mayr, Richard, b. Henndorf, 18 Nov 1877; d. Vienna, 1 Dec 1935. Austrian bass. Persuaded by MAHLER to take up a musical career, he studied at the Vienna Cons.; debut 1902, Bayreuth (HAGEN). Became principal bass with Vienna Staats O., 1902, and retained the position until retiring a few months before his death. Famous in WAGNER, he was celebrated above all for his OCHS, and at Salzburg he enjoyed great success as FIGARO (BARBIERE DI SIVIGLIA), LEPORELLO, and SARASTRO. Sang at CG 1924–31, and NY Met 1927–30. Created Barak (FRAU OHNE SCHATTEN). FGB

Mazepa, opera, 3 acts, TCHAIKOVSKY, lib. composer and Viktor Burenin, after PUSHKIN. Moscow, Bolshoy T., 15 Feb 1884; Liverpool, 6 Aug 1888; Boston, Boston OH, 14 Dec 1922. Main chars: Mazepa (bar.) Kochubey (bass) Mariya (sop.) Andrey (ten.). Mazepa asks to marry Kochubey's daughter Mariya, but is rejected. He carries her off. Andrey (in love with Mariya) takes his revenge by telling the Tsar that Mazepa is in league with the Swedes. But the Tsar (believing Mazepa rather than Andrey) arrests Kochubey and executes him. Andrey is shot by Mazepa; Mariya goes insane and sings a lullaby to the dead Andrey. Tchaikovsky failed to sympathize fully with either Mazepa or Mariya, and the characterization is consequently pale. But there are attractive and powerful moments in the score, and the orchestral interlude 'The Battle of Poltava' is a fine piece of programme music. GN

Mazurok, Yury Antonovich, b. Krasnik, 8 July 1931. Soviet baritone of Polish birth. Studied Moscow Cons., joined the Bolshoy in 1963 and later became a soloist there. Particularly noted for his interpretations of EUGENE ONEGIN, Eletsky (QUEEN OF SPADES), Andrey Bolkonsky (WAR AND PEACE), and FIGARO (BARBIERE DI SIVIGLIA). GN

Medea in Corinto, opera, 2 acts, G. S. MAYR, lib. ROMANI. Naples, T. S. Carlo, 28 Nov 1813; London, King's T., 1 June 1826. Mayr's finest work, written for COLBRAN and GARCÍA I, and a favourite role of PASTA. Main chars: Medea (sop.) Creusa (sop.) Ismene (mezzo-sop.) Giasone (ten.) Egeo (ten.) Creonte (bass). A retelling of the Medea story, to which Romani has added the character of Egeo, king of Athens, as the slighted lover of Creusa. The work was revised for Milan (1822), and this edition has been revived by Bavarian Radio (1963), in NY, and on record. The original Naples edition was perf. in London by Opera Rara, 18 June 1972, and at the Wexford Fest., 1974. PS O

Médecin Malgré Lui, Le (*The Doctor in Spite of Himself*), opera, 3 acts, GOUNOD, lib. BARBIER and CARRÉ based on MOLIÈRE's 1666 comedy. Paris, TL, 15 Jan 1858; London, CG (in Eng. as *The Mock Doctor*), 27 Feb 1865; Cincinnati, 20 Mar 1900. Gounod's only comedy, and his first success. LO

Médée (*Medea*), *tragédie lyrique*, 3 acts, CHERUBINI, lib. HOFFMAN, based T. CORNEILLE's *Médée*. Paris, T. Feydeau, 13 Mar 1797; London, HM, 6 June 1865; San Francisco, 12 Sept 1958. First revived in 20th c. by CALLAS (Florence 1953), and since then by other artists (FARRELL, G. JONES); also at Frankfurt (Mar 1971) with LACHNER's 1855 recitatives. Other operas on the Medea legend incl. those by CAVALLI (*Giasone*, 1649), Marc Antoine Charpentier (1634–1704), based on Thomas Corneille's play, *Médée* (1693), G. S. MAYR (MEDEA IN CORINTO – a great vehicle for PASTA), and MILHAUD (1939). LO O

Medium, The, opera, 2 acts, MENOTTI, lib. composer. NY, Columbia Univ., 8 May 1946; revised Barrymore T., 1 May 1947; London, Aldwych T., 29 Apr 1948. Main chars: Mme Flora (contr.) Monica (sop.) Toby (mute) Mrs Gobineau (contr.) Mr Gobineau (bar.). A medium cheats her clients, then becomes frightened when things happen in the occult that she cannot explain. EJ O
See Kobbé

Mefistofele (*Mephistopheles*), opera, prologue, 4 acts and epilogue, BOITO, lib. composer, after

Goethe. Milan, Sc., 5 Mar 1868: revised version Bologna, 4 Oct 1875; revived Venice, 13 May 1876 in definitive form; London, HM, 6 July 1880; Boston, 16 Nov 1880 (in Eng.). Main chars: Mefistofele (bass) Faust (ten.) Margherita (sop.) Elena (sop.). Mefistofele wagers Heaven that he will win the soul of Faust, a learned doctor, concerned to experience life to the full. Faust strikes the bargain for his soul, seduces the village girl Margherita, and is responsible for her madness and death; has a love affair with Helen of Troy, who symbolizes the spirit of classical Greece: and on his deathbed is saved by faith from falling into Mefistofele's power. JB ○
See Kobbé

Mehta, Zubin, b. Bombay, 29 Apr 1936. Indian conductor. Studied Vienna; debut there, 1959. Cond. at Florence 1964 (Traviata); Salzburg 1965 (Entführung aus dem Serail). NY Met debut 1965 (Aida); cond. the premiere of Mourning Becomes Electra there. His repertory incl. Trovatore, Verdi's Otello, Turandot, Carmen, Tristan und Isolde (which he cond. for It. Radio), Samson et Dalila (Israel Fest., 1972 at Caesarea), and Salome. As principal cond. of the Montreal Symphony Orch., he has cond. much opera in Canada. EF

Méhul, Étienne-Nicolas, b. Givet, Ardennes, 22 June 1763; d. Paris, 18 Oct 1817. French composer. Began as an organist, found his way to Paris *c.* 1778; was present at premiere of Iphigénie en Tauride, which inspired him to compose. Became friendly with Hoffman, whose *Euphrosine* he set (perf. TI, 4 Sept 1790). Twenty-four other operas followed rapidly; the most important are Caverne, Ariodant, *Uthal*, 1806, and his masterpiece Joseph – the last two written in the serious and lofty style he had learned from Gluck. LO

Meilhac, Henri, b. Paris, 21 Feb 1831; d. Paris, 6 July 1897. French dramatist and librettist. Wrote libs for Manon, in collaboration with Philippe Gille; for Mam'zelle Nitouche, with Albert Millaud and Ernest Blum; for Offenbach's *Vert-Vert* (1869) with Nuitter. His comedy, *L'Attaché*, was the basis for Lustige Witwe and his *Réveillon* (with L. Halévy) was the basis for Fledermaus. LO

Meiningen Players. A theatrical troupe founded and run, 1874–90, by George Duke of Saxe-Meiningen (1826–1914), whose ideas on stage costume, the handling of crowds and the total integration of stage perf. had far-reaching consequences on the mounting of plays and operas. It could be said that the Duke was the first modern producer. Stanislavsky was strongly influenced by him LO

Meistersinger von Nürnberg, Die (*The Mastersingers of Nuremberg*), music drama, 3 acts, Wagner, lib. composer. Munich, 21 June 1868; London, DL, 30 May 1882; NY, 4 Jan 1886. Main chars: Walther (ten.) Eva (sop.) Hans Sachs (bar.) Beckmesser (bar.) David (ten.) Magdalene (mezzo-sop.) Pogner (bass). Walther von Stolzing, a young nobleman, wishes to qualify for the singing contest of the Mastersingers, so as to win the hand of Eva; but he is ignorant of the poetic rules. With the help of the cobbler Hans Sachs, and in the teeth of opposition from the pedantic Beckmesser, he wins the contest with his Prize Song. JB ○★
See Kobbé

Melba, Nellie [Helen Porter Mitchell], b. Richmond, nr Melbourne (from which city she took her name), 19 May 1859; d. Sydney, 23 Feb 1931. Australian soprano. After studying piano, organ, theory, and voice, she m. Captain Charles Armstrong 1882. Travelled to Paris 1886 where she studied with Marchesi de Castrone. Debut 12 Oct 1887, Brussels (Gilda); 24 May 1888 sang Lucia di Lammermoor at CG where she was rapturously received. Paris debut 1889, first of many European triumphs. NY Met debut 4 Dec 1893, again as Lucia, and was praised for her 'most admirable musical instincts'. An attempt at Brünnhilde (1896) led to a temporary retire-

Nellie Melba as Nedda and Fernando de Lucia (1860–1925) as Canio in Pagliacci, London, CG, 19 May 1893. They also sang these roles at the NY Met.

Die Meistersinger von Nürnberg. Design by Barry Kay for Act II, London, CG, 24 Jan 1969; produced R. HARTMANN

ment. She appeared with the Damrosch O. Co., 1897, and until 1899 with the Manhattan O. Co. Perhaps the most famous sop. of all time, she enjoyed a dazzling career. Last US appearance 1920; last CG perf. 8 June 1926. Retired to Australia as dir. of Melbourne Cons. Awarded DBE 1918. PS
See autobiography, *Melodies and Memories* (London 1925); Colson, *Melba: An Unconventional Biography* (London 1932)

Melbourne, Victoria, Australia. The Melba Memorial Centre, opened 1973, houses the Melba Cons. of Music and has a theatre where the Victorian O. Co. and Australian O. Co. can perform. LO

Melchior, Lauritz, b. Copenhagen, 20 Mar 1890; d. Santa Monica, Cal., 18 Mar 1973. Danish-American baritone, later tenor. Debut 1913, Copenhagen (SILVIO). Was then persuaded to study ten. roles; debut as ten. 1918, also Copenhagen (TANNHÄUSER). CG debut 1924 (SIEGMUND), and from then specialized in the WAGNER repertory. Was frequent visitor to CG 1926–9, and to Bayreuth (he was Siegmund in the first post-World War I Fest. 1924). NY Met debut 1926; from then to 1950 he was its main Wagner ten. He perhaps made more Wagner appearances than any other ten., singing Tristan (TRISTAN UND ISOLDE) over 200 times, Siegfried over 100. His voice was a superb instrument, and at his best his Wagner interpretations could rank with the finest. LO

Mélesville [Anne Honoré Duveyrier], b. Paris, 13 Nov 1787; d. Paris, 8 Nov 1865. French librettist and dramatist. Wrote lib. for ZAMPA and, with SCRIBE and others, for A. ADAM's *Le Chalet* (1834) and DONIZETTI's *Betly* (1836) derived from it; for Donizetti's *Il Borgomastro di Saardam* (1827), and for CHERUBINI's *Ali Baba* (1834). LO

Mélisande, sop., the heroine of PELLÉAS ET MÉLISANDE

Melnikov, Ivan Aleksandrovich, b. St Petersburg, 4 Mar 1832; d. St Petersburg, 8 July 1906. Russian baritone. Studied in Italy; St Petersburg debut 6 Oct 1867 as Riccardo (PURITANI). Until 1890 he sang with the Mariinsky T., and was then a dir. there (1890–2). Created a number of Russian roles, incl. BORIS GODUNOV, PRINCE IGOR, William Ratcliff (CUI's opera of the same name), Prince Tokmakov (MAID OF PSKOV), Kalenik (MAY NIGHT), and Don Carlos (STONE GUEST); also noted for his interpretations of RUSLAN, and the Miller in DARGOMYZHSKY's *Rusalka*. He was much admired by TCHAIKOVSKY, and perf. in all his operas except IOLANTA. GN

melodrama 1. The popular usage, 'sensational dramatic piece with violent appeals to emotions and happy ending' (Concise Oxford Dictionary), has its obvious counterpart in opera. 2. A spoken text accompanied by instrumental mus. as in Wolf's Glen scene in FREISCHÜTZ. Extended dramatic pieces were wr. in this style in the 18th c. by e.g. BENDA. LO

melodramma (It.) sung drama, or opera

Mendelssohn (–Bartholdy), Felix, b. Hamburg, 3 Feb 1809; d. Leipzig, 4 Nov 1847. German composer. Though *Die Hochzeit des*

Camachos (1825, lib. Karl Klingemann, based on Cervantes) was the only opera publicly staged during Mendelssohn's lifetime (Berlin, 29 Apr 1827), it was not the only one completed. *Die Beiden Neffen, oder Der Onkel aus Boston*, 3 acts, was his fourth opera, and was rehearsed in the Mendelssohn house 3 Feb 1824. *Die Beiden Pädagogen*, one-act *Singspiel*, perf. at his grandmother's house, Berlin, 1825, has been successfully revived (E. Berlin, Staats O., Nov 1972). Another *Singspiel*, *Soldatenliebschaft*, and *Heimkehr aus der Fremde* (known in England as *Son and Stranger*), were perf. privately, 1829. Late in his life (1847) he tackled Emmanuel Geibel's *Loreley*, but this was left unfinished. His actor friend Eduard Devrient wrote Hans Heiling for him, and also offered a lib. on Gerusalemme Liberata, but Mendelssohn turned these down, as he did Planché's *Siege of Calais* and *Die Nibelungen*, which Dorn set in 1854. LO

Mendès, Catulle, b. Bordeaux, 22 May 1841; d. in a railway accident, St-Germain-en-Laye, 8 Feb 1909. French poet and librettist, a member of the *Parnassiens*, a Wagner disciple. Made pilgrimages to Bayreuth for Ring des Nibelungen 1876, and Parsifal 1882, and wrote a book on Wagner (1886). Wrote libs for Gwendoline, Hahn's *La Carmélite* (1902), Massenet's *Ariane* (1906) and *Bacchus* (1906), Messager's *Isoline* (1888), Leroux's *La Reine Fiammette* (1889), and Camille d'Erlanger's *Le Fils de l'Étoile* (1904); also for Chabrier's unfinished *Briseïs*. His *Rodrigue et Chimène*, based on Guilhen de Castro's *Las Mocedades del Cid*, was wr. for Debussy but never set. LO

Menotti, Gian Carlo, b. Cadegliano, Italy, 7 July 1911. Italian composer, librettist, and producer. Moved to USA 1927; studied at Curtis Institute, Philadelphia, graduating 1933. In contrast to many US opera comps he shows an inimitable theatrical skill and, as an Italian, a heritage of 19th-c. *verismo*. He writes his own libs which range from *buffa* trifles (Amelia Goes to the Ball), Christmas fantasy (Amahl and the Night Visitors), psychological thrillers (Medium) and political drama (Consul) to traditional operatic fare (Maria Golovin, Saint of Bleecker Street). His other operas are: *The Island God* (1942); Telephone; *The Unicorn, the Gorgon and the Manticore* (1956); Old Maid and the Thief; Last Savage; *Labyrinth* (TV 1963); Help, Help, The Globolinks!; *The Most Important Man* (1971), and *Tamu-Tamu* (1973). He also wrote the lib. of Vanessa and the revised Antony and Cleopatra, and is the founder of the Spoleto Fest. EJ

Méphistophélès, bass, the Evil One in Gounod's Faust

Mercadante, Saverio, b. Altamura, nr Bari, 17 Sept 1795; d. Naples, 17 Dec 1870. Italian composer. Studied Naples. His nearly 60 operas incl. *Amleto* (1822); *Elisa e Claudio* (1821; revived Naples 1971); an *opera buffa*, *I Due Illustri Rivali* (1838; revived Venice 1970); and probably his best work, *Il Giuramento* (1837; revived Spoleto 1971). *Orazi e Curiazi* (1846) was revived at Colston Hall, Bristol, 23 Apr 1975 and London, Queen Elizabeth Hall, 27 Apr 1975 (concert perfs by Opera Rara). LO

Merighi, Giorgio, b. Ferrara, 20 Feb 1939. Italian tenor. Studied at Pesaro. Debut 1962, Spoleto (GUSTAVE III). Has sung since throughout Italy incl. Sc. Wexford Fest. 1969 as Rodolfo (LUISA MILLER). CG debut 1971 (Gustave); returned 1974 for CAVARADOSSI. Bright, forward, typically Italianate ten. and good stage presence. AB

Mérimée, Prosper, b. Paris, 28 Sept 1803; d. Cannes, 23 Sept 1870. French author and archaeologist. Works on which operas are based incl. *Le Carrosse du Saint-Sacrement*, 1830 (PÉRICHOLE and operas by Lord Berners, 1923, and BUSSER); *Les Âmes du Purgatoire*, 1837 (*Don Juan de Mañara* by ALFANO, ENNA, TOMASI and GOOSSENS III); *Mosaïque*, 1833 (CUI, *Matteo Falcone*, 1907); *Colomba*, 1841 (PACINI, *La Fidanzata Corta*, 1842; Alexander Mackenzie, 1883; Busser; Tomasi); *Carmen*, 1845 (BIZET); *La Vénus d'Ille*, 1852 (SCHOECK; Hermann Wetzler, *Die Baskische Venus*, 1928); *La Dame de Pique*, tr. from PUSHKIN (J. F. HALÉVY, 1850). LO

Left: Méphistophélès. GHIAUROV in one of his most famous roles

Merrill, Robert, b. Brooklyn, NY, 4 June 1917. American baritone. Began singing professionally in light mus., incl. Radio City Music Hall, NY 1943. Debut 1944, Trenton, NJ (AMONASRO). Won Met O. Auditions of the Air 1945; NY Met debut 1945 (TRAVIATA). Since then a regular and much admired principal of Met in It. and Fr. repertory. Engaged by TOSCANINI for leading roles in studio broadcasts of *La Traviata* and BALLO IN MASCHERA (the cond.'s last broadcast). Dismissed from Met by BING 1951, for accepting Hollywood film engagement, but reinstated later that year. CG debut not until 1967 (GERMONT). NG
See Merrill, *Once More from the Beginning* (New York 1965)

Left: Gian Carlo Menotti's LAST SAVAGE, US premiere, 23 Jan 1964, NY Met; produced by the composer; sets and costumes Beni Montresor; conducted SCHIPPERS; G. LONDON as Abdul

Merriman, Nan, b. Pittsburgh, Pa., 28 Apr 1920. American mezzo-soprano. Studied Los Angeles. Stage debut 1942, Cincinnati, as La Cieca (GIOCONDA) but made reputation as Orphée (ORPHÉE ET EURYDICE), MAGDALENA and Emilia (VERDI's OTELLO) with TOSCANINI in broadcasts and records. Sang Baba the Turk in first British perf. of RAKE'S PROGRESS (Glyndebourne 1953), returning as DORABELLA (1956). A warm singer with char., and an amusing actress. AB

Merry Mount, opera, 3 acts, HANSON, lib. Richard Stokes derived from Nathaniel Hawthorne's *The May-Pole Lovers of Merry Mount*. NY Met, 10 Feb 1934. Main chars: Pastor Wrestling Bradford (bar.) Lady Marigold Sandys (sop.) Plentiful Tewke (contr.) Sir Gower Lackland (ten.) Thomas Morton (bass). A Puritan pastor's endeavour to save the soul of a beautiful sinner leads both of them to ultimate destruction by fiery immolation. The fourth full-length opera by an American comp. prod. by the Met since 1912. EJ

Merry Widow, The *see* LUSTIGE WITWE, DIE

Merry Wives of Windsor, The *see* LUSTIGEN WEIBER VON WINDSOR, DIE

Mess, Suzanne, b. Toronto, 2 Aug 1928. Canadian costume designer who works almost exclusively in opera. Beginning with MADAMA BUTTERFLY (1951), she has designed more than 35 prods for the COC. Her designs are also used by most other cos in Canada, and by many US cos, incl. those in Santa Fe, Boston, Houston, New Orleans, and Washington. As a staff designer for CBC she has designed for TV operas seen throughout Canada as well as in Britain and the USA. CM

Messager, André Charles Prosper, b. Montluçon, 30 Dec 1853; d. Paris, 24 Feb 1929. French composer and conductor. Studied Paris, École Niedermeyer, and also with SAINT-SAËNS and FAURÉ. Cond. Paris OC 1898–1908 (cond. first perf. of PELLÉAS ET MÉLISANDE); 1907–15 dir. and principal cond. at O.; art. dir. CG 1901–6. Wrote some 17 operas and operettas, many very popular in Paris and London, the chief of which are: BASOCHE; *Madame Chrysanthème* (1893); *Fortunio* (1907); VÉRONIQUE; MONSIEUR BEAUCAIRE. LO

Messel, Oliver Hilary Sambourne, b. Cuckfield, Sussex, 13 Jan 1904. British designer. His work for opera began with ZAUBERFLÖTE (1947) and continued with the following for Glyndebourne: ARIADNE AUF NAXOS (1950, at Edinburgh Fest.), IDOMENEO (1951); CENERENTOLA (1952), COMTE ORY (1954), BARBIERE DI SIVIGLIA (1954), NOZZE DI FIGARO (1955), ENTFÜHRUNG AUS DEM SERAIL and *Zauberflöte* (1956), ROSENKAVALIER (1959). Returned to CG to design QUEEN OF SPADES (1950) and HANDEL'S *Samson* (1958). *Nozze di Figaro* at NY Met 1961. One of the most fanciful of stage designers. AB

Messidor, opera, 5 acts, BRUNEAU, lib. ZOLA. Paris, O., 19 Feb 1897. 'Messidor' is the harvest month of the revolutionary calendar, 20 June–19 July. The story is symbolic, a struggle between capitalist Gold and life-giving Water: the characters themselves are symbolic,

Oliver Messel's design for Act I, sc. 2, of ROSSINI'S BARBIERE DI SIVIGLIA, Glyndebourne, 1954; produced C. EBERT

Guillaume typifying labour and Véronique representing religion. LO

Metastasio [Trapassi], Pietro, b. Rome, 3 Jan 1698; d. Vienna, 12 Apr 1782. Italian librettist, the foremost *opera seria* librettist of his time. A wealthy patron, Vincenzo Gravina, adopted him, educated him, and on his death when Metastasio was only 20, left him his fortune. His first libs were wr. for Naples (*Didone Abbandonata*, 1724) and Rome (*Catone in Utica*, 1727); in 1729 was invited to Vienna as Court Poet, succeeding ZENO. Most of his libs (*c.* 50 in all, incl. a few sacred dramas) were written for Vienna 1730–71 and first set by CALDARA, Georg Reutter, Luigi Predieri, Giuseppe Bonno, and HASSE. Many were set again and again; among the better known of these are: *Ezio*, 1728 (GLUCK and HANDEL); *Artaserse*, 1730 (set *c.* 50 times, incl. ARNE, JOMMELLI, PICCINNI); *Alessandro nell'Indie* (1729 – appearing sometimes as *Poro*) (PORPORA, VINCI, Hasse, Handel); *La Clemenza di Tito* (1734) (MOZART); *Il Re Pastore* (1751) (Mozart). An *Ipermestra* (1744) was still being set in the 19th c. – by MERCADANTE (1825). Whether labelled *festa teatrale*, *azione teatrale*, or *dramma*, the themes were drawn from eras in Roman history or (more rarely) mythology; plots were complex, of the A loves B, B loves C, who loves A (or D) variety, and the nub of the drama was usually a moral dilemma, the conflict between love and duty – patterns which, like Zeno, he took over from Fr. drama. LO

Metropolitan Opera House *see* NEW YORK

Mexico *see* LATIN AMERICA

Meyer, Kerstin, b. Stockholm, 3 Apr 1928. Swedish mezzo-soprano. Joined Stockholm Royal O. 1952: debut as AZUCENA. Further debuts: Berlin 1959 in W. WAGNER prod. of CARMEN (title role); NY Met 1960 as Carmen; CG 1960 as Didon (TROYENS); Glyndebourne Fest. 1961 as Caroline (ELEGY FOR YOUNG LOVERS); Bayreuth Fest. 1962 as BRANGÄNE. An actress of vivid dramatic insight as well as a singer of rare style and expression, she has created several memorable roles in modern operas, incl.: Agave in BASSARIDS (Salzburg 1966); Mrs Claiborne in VISITATION (Hamburg 1966); Mrs Arden in ARDEN MUSS STERBEN (Hamburg 1967); Gertrude in SEARLE's HAMLET (Hamburg 1968); Elisabeth in MAW's *The Rising of the Moon* (Glyndebourne 1970). Outstanding as Countess Geschwitz (LULU), Baba the Turk (RAKE'S PROGRESS), Kostelnička (JENŮFA), and Claire Zachanassian (BESUCH DER ALTEN DAME), she also sings mezzo-sop. roles in MOZART and R. STRAUSS (esp. KLYTEMNESTRA) with success. NG

Meyerbeer, Giacomo [Jacob Liebmann Beer], b. Berlin, 5 Sept 1791; d. Paris, 2 May 1864. German composer. Son of a wealthy Jewish industrialist. Studied with Muzio Clementi, Carl Friedrich Zelter, Anselm Weber, and Abbé Vogler. His first operas, *Jephtha's Gelübde*

(Munich 1812) and *Wirth und Gast* (Stuttgart 1813; Vienna 1814, as *Die Beiden Kalifen*; and Dresden 1820, as *Alimelek*) failed. In Vienna *Alimelek* was more happily received. Then he moved to Venice and in 1817 his first It. opera, *Costanza e Romilda*, was prod., at Padua, followed by *Semiramide Riconosciuta* (1819), *Emma di Resburgo* (1819), *Margherita d'Anjou* (1820), *L'Esule di Granata* (1822), and CROCIATO IN EGITTO. In 1825 he moved to Paris at ROSSINI's invitation, where he prod. the first of the Fr. grand operas that made him the most famous comp. in Europe, ROBERT LE DIABLE, followed by HUGUENOTS and PROPHÈTE. Meyerbeer's ability to combine heroic drama and action with ballet, pomp and spectacular visual effects, added to immense dramatic power, lyricism, and tremendous orchestral virtuosity, were to influence the later DONIZETTI, VERDI, and WAGNER. Appointed MdC Berlin, 1842, where he wrote *Ein Feldlager in Schlesien* (1844) to open the new Berlin opera house. He revised the work for Vienna as *Vielka* (1846) and again for the OC, Paris, as ÉTOILE DU NORD. He followed this with DINORAH. He worked for 25 years on his last opera, AFRICAINE, constantly revising even at rehearsal stage, but did not live to see it perf. PS

Meyerhold, Vsevolod Emilyevich, b. Penza, 9 Feb 1874; d. Moscow, 2 Feb 1940. Russian theatre director. He prod. at the Mariinsky (now Kirov) T., TRISTAN UND ISOLDE (1909), GLUCK's ORFEO ED EURIDICE (1911), ELEKTRA (1913), STONE GUEST (1917), and NIGHTINGALE (1918); and, at the Leningrad Maly T., QUEEN OF SPADES (1935). From 1938 he was a dir., and from 1939 principal dir., Stanislavsky O. T. GN

mezza voce (It. 'half voice') – i.e., quiet, unemotional singing, as in situations of peace and tranquillity. LO

mezzo-soprano (It. 'half soprano') – voice with TESSITURA lying between that of true SOPRANO and CONTRALTO. Quality usually darker, less brilliant, than a sop. even if singing at same pitch. LO

Micaëla, sop., a peasant girl in CARMEN

Micheau, Janine, b. Toulouse, 17 Apr 1914. French soprano. Studied Toulouse and Paris Cons.; debut 1933, Paris OC. Created Médée in first Paris perf. of MILHAUD's opera, Paris O., 1940, and Manuela in BOLIVAR 1950. Has also sung in Italy, Belgium, the Netherlands, S. America, and CG; she sang MICAËLA at the last in 1937. LO

Micheletti, Gaston, b. Tavaco, Corsica, 5 Jan 1892; d. Ajaccio, 21 May 1959. French tenor. Studied at the Paris Cons. After singing in the French provinces, made his debut at the Paris OC as DES GRIEUX (MANON), 1925. He remained there for 20 years as a leading lyric ten. Among his notable roles were DON JOSÉ (he recorded excerpts from CARMEN with SUPERVIA), Pylade (IPHIGÉNIE EN TAURIDE), Gérald (LAKMÉ), and the title role of CONTES D' HOFFMANN. His records show him to have been one of the foremost French tenors of his day with a forward, vibrant tone and great involvement. AB

Midsummer Marriage, The, opera, 3 acts, TIPPETT, lib. composer. London, CG, 27 Jan 1955. Main chars: Jenifer (sop.) Bella (sop.) Sosostris (contr.) Mark (ten.) Jack (ten.) King Fisher (bar.). A quest for sexual and spiritual fulfilment between one couple whose hindrances are philosophical and supernatural, and between another couple on a more material and social level; King Fisher symbolizes parental authority and the power of commercial self-interest. Literary concepts in the text were initially held to be an impediment to success in the theatre, but a different prod. (CG 1968) won wider acclaim for its wealth of romantic musical imagination. NG O

The Midsummer Marriage, London, CG, 10 Apr 1968; produced Ande Anderson; designed Tony Walton; BURROWS as Jack and HARWOOD as Bella

Midsummer Night's Dream, A, opera, 3 acts, BRITTEN, lib. composer and PEARS derived from SHAKESPEARE. Aldeburgh, 11 June 1960; London, CG, 2 Feb 1961; San Francisco, 10 Oct 1961. Main chars: Helena (sop.) Tytania (sop.) Hermia (mezzo-sop.) Oberon (counterten.) Lysander (ten.) Demetrius (bar.) Bottom (bar.). Ingenious and subtle evocation of

Shakespeare's play with some of Britten's most translucent and magical music. Clever parody of operatic conventions in the Pyramus and Thisbe 'play' in the third act. AB ○

Mignon, opera, 3 acts, Ambroise THOMAS, lib. BARBIER and CARRÉ from GOETHE's *Wilhelm Meisters Lehrjahre*, 1795–6. Paris, OC, 17 Nov 1866; London, DL, 5 July 1870; New Orleans, 9 May 1871. After WERTHER Thomas's most successful opera. LO
See Kobbé

Below: The Mikado, London, SW, 6 July 1962, a production for BBC TV. HAMMOND-STROUD (centre) as Ko-Ko; produced Douglas Craig; designed Peter Rice

Mikado, The, or The Town of Titipu, operetta, 2 acts, SULLIVAN, lib. GILBERT. London, Savoy T., 14 Mar 1885; Chicago, 6 July 1885. Main chars: Ko-Ko (buffo) Yum-Yum (sop.) Nanki-Poo (ten.) Mikado (bass) Pooh-Bah (bass-bar.) Katisha (contr.). Nanki-Poo, son of the Mikado, roaming Japan in disguise to escape the attentions of an elderly admirer, Katisha, falls in love with Yum-Yum, ward and fiancée of Ko-Ko, Lord High Executioner of Titipu. A complicated and dangerous situation is resolved by the marriage of Ko-Ko to Katisha. Sullivan's most famous operetta. JB ○★

Milan [Milano]. Capital of Lombardy before the unification of Italy, 1870. The name of its chief opera house, La Scala, is a byword throughout the world. Dating from 1778, replacing the T. di Corte burned down in 1776, it is still in use today, World War II damage having been repaired. In the 19th c. ROSSINI, BELLINI, DONIZETTI, VERDI, and BOITO all had premieres there. Among its mus. dirs the outstanding name is that of TOSCANINI, who uncompromisingly did battle with audiences and performers in the interest of artistic integrity. He introduced works by WAGNER, R. STRAUSS, DEBUSSY, and others to Milanese audiences; he was followed by SABATA, GAVAZZENI, and CHAILLY. Other Milan opera houses incl. the T. Cannobiana, opened 1779, demolished 1894; the T. Lirico, which replaced it (now a cinema); the T. Carcano, opened 1803, scene of the premiere of SONNAMBULA; and the T. dal Verme, opened 1872. LO

La Piccola Scala opened 1955 (with MATRIMONIO SEGRETO, cond. SANZOGNO, decor DAMIANI) in the main Sc. building. Used for chamber operas and for intimate perfs of earlier classics both major (COSÌ FAN TUTTE) and minor (BUONA FIGLIUOLA) as well as for works of modern comps. LO
See Hughes, *Great Opera Houses* (London 1956; New York 1969)

Milanov [Kunc], Zinka, b. Zagreb, 17 May 1906. Yugoslav soprano. Studied Zagreb; debut 1927, Ljubljana, as LEONORA (TROVATORE). Zagreb O. 1928–35, singing more than 350 perfs. Sang in VERDI's *Requiem* under TOSCANINI at Salzburg Fest. 1937, which led to her engagement at the NY Met; debut there 1937 as Leonora (*Trovatore*); remained until

Left: *A Midsummer Night's Dream*, London, CG, 2 Feb 1961; produced Sir John Gielgud; designed PIPER

1966, appearing more than 400 times, always in the lyric-dramatic roles, notably as LEONORA (FORZA DEL DESTINO), AIDA, Santuzza (CAVALLERIA RUSTICANA), and NORMA. CG as Leonora (*Trovatore*) and TOSCA (1956–7). One of the most authoritative and sensitive sopranos of her day. AB

Mildenburg, Anna von *see* BAHR-MILDENBURG, Anna

Milder-Hauptmann [Milder], Pauline Anna, b. Constantinople [Istanbul], 13 Dec 1785; d. Berlin, 29 May 1838. Austrian soprano. Debut 1803, Vienna, in revival of Franz Süssmayr's *Der Spiegel von Arkadien*; sang LEONORE in both 1805 and 1814 versions of FIDELIO. Sang in Berlin 1816–29, where she was most successful in classical roles of GLUCK and SPONTINI. See also ALFONSO UND ESTRELLA. LO

Mildmay, Audrey, b. Hurstmonceux, 19 Dec 1900; d. London, 31 May 1953. English soprano. Began career with Carl Rosa co. In 1931 m. CHRISTIE and inspired him in his founding of Glyndebourne Fest. (1934). From then until 1939 sang SUSANNA, ZERLINA, and NORINA at that house; in BEGGAR'S OPERA with Carl Rosa co. in London 1939–40. AB

Milhaud, Darius, b. Aix-en-Provence, 4 Sept 1892; d. Geneva, 22 June 1974. French composer. A member of 'Les Six' and immensely prolific in all forms of music, he wrote many operas, incl.: MALHEURS D'ORPHÉE, PAUVRE MATELOT, MAXIMILIEN, three 'Opéras-Minutes' (Wiesbaden 1928), *Médée* (Antwerp 1939), BOLIVAR, DAVID. His long association with CLAUDEL resulted in music for Claudel's translation of the Aeschylus *Oresteia*, the middle section of which, *Les Choéphores*, was staged at Brussels (1935), CHRISTOPHE COLOMB and his last opera, *Saint Louis* (wr. 1970–1), broadcast by It. Radio and later staged in Rio de Janeiro. EF

Right: *The Mines of Sulphur*. Ann Howard as Leda with Dennis Wicks as Sherrin; London, SW, 27 Sept 1973; produced GRAHAM; designed Alix Stone

Miller, Jonathan, b. London, 21 July 1934. British producer. Began to dir. opera 1974, the first Eng. perf. of ARDEN MUSS STERBEN for the New O. co. at SW, and COSÌ FAN TUTTE for Kent O. Prod. CUNNING LITTLE VIXEN (Glyndebourne 1975), and RIGOLETTO (Kent O., 1975). EF

Millöcker, Karl, b. Vienna, 29 May 1842; d. Baden, nr Vienna, 31 Dec 1899. Austrian composer and conductor. MdC Vienna, T. a. d. Wien 1869–83. Of his numerous operettas the best is BETTELSTUDENT; others such as *Gräfin Dubarry* (1879), *Gasparone* (1884), and *Der Arme Jonathan* (1890), have been revived at Bregenz and also at Berlin. LO
See Lubbock

Milnes, Sherrill Eustace, b. Dourren Grove, Ill., 10 Jan 1935. American baritone. Trained as a music teacher, sang in a Chicago choir, joined Boris Goldovsky's Grand O. Theater Co. 1960, making debut as Masetto (DON GIOVANNI). Ford Foundation award (1962) brought regional engagements throughout USA. In five years acquired repertory of more than 40 roles. NY debut 1964 with City O. (VALENTIN); Met 1965 in same role. Since then the leading Met baritone. Created Adam Brant (MOURNING BECOMES ELECTRA). European debuts: London, DL, 1969, as Barnaba in concert perf. of GIOCONDA; Milan, T. Nuovo, 1969, as FIGARO (BARBIERE DI SIVIGLIA); Vienna, Staats O., 1970 as MACBETH; London, CG, 1971 as RENATO. An outstanding VERDI and DONIZETTI baritone in richness of vocal char. and firmness of line, with an imposing stage presence. Has made a record with DOMINGO in which each conducts the orch. for the other's arias. NG

Mime, ten., brother of Alberich in RING DES NIBELUNGEN

Mimi, sop., the heroine of BOHÈME

Mines of Sulphur, The, opera, 3 acts, BENNETT, lib. Beverley Cross. London, SW, 24 Feb 1965; Milan, Sc., 25 Feb 1966; NY, Juilliard, 17 Jan 1969. Main chars: Jenny (sop.) Rosalind (mezzo-sop.) Boconnion (ten.) Tovey (bar.) Braxton (bar.). The owner of an 18th-c. manor house is murdered by Boconnion, a deserter, aided by the gypsy Rosalind. A group of stroll-

ing players who come to the house for refuge act as a catalyst. Bennett's music aptly matches the melodramatic story. Although it is serial in composition, much of the vocal writing is lyrical. AB

Ming, Cho Lee *see* LEE, Ming Cho

Mingotti Opera Company. One of the several touring companies operating in 18th-c. Germany. Run by two brothers, Piero (*c.* 1702–59), and Angelo (born *c.* 1700, date and place of death unknown). Besides touring in N. and S. Germany they also appeared in Scandinavia. GLUCK was associated with them for a time in the 1740s. LO

Minneapolis, Center Opera Company of (Minn.). Estab. 1963. About 20 perfs each season mainly of contemporary works, followed by tours. Novelties incl.: KLUGE (6 June 1965); E. Stokes, *Horspfal* (15 Dec 1969); EGK, *17 Days and 4 Minutes* (17 Jan 1970); Harrison Birtwistle, *Punch and Judy* (30 Jan 1970); John Gessner and W. Wesley Balk, *Faust Counter Faust*, musical collage (1971). Several of these experimental works were brought to NY (Hunter College) in Feb 1971. Gen. Mgr John Ludwig; dir. Philip Brunelle. EJ

Minton, Yvonne, b. Sydney, 4 Dec 1938. Australian mezzo-soprano. Studied Sydney Cons.; stage debut 1964 as Maggie Dempster, a role she created in MAW's *One Man Show*. CG debut 1965 in small roles before singing Marina (BORIS GODUNOV, 1965). Other CG opera roles incl. OCTAVIAN, DORABELLA, Sesto (CLEMENZA DI TITO) and BRANGÄNE; created Thea (KNOT GARDEN) there (1970). Debut Cologne O. 1969. US debut: Chicago 1970 (Octavian). Other debuts: Israel Fest. 1972 (DALILA); NY Met 1973 (Octavian); Bayreuth 1974 (Brangäne). Among the foremost mezzos of the 1970s, with feeling and artistry. AB

Miolan-Carvalho, Marie [Caroline Marie Félix], b. Marseille, 31 Dec 1827; d. Puys, 10 July 1895. French soprano. Studied with her father, an oboist, and DUPREZ 1843–7 at the Paris Cons. Debut 1849 in Duprez's benefit at the O., singing Act 1 of LUCIA DI LAMMERMOOR and a trio from JUIVE. Sang at OC 1850–5; London debut 1859 (DINORAH); appeared every season until 1864. Sang at O. and OC, 1868–83. Created the roles of MARGUERITE, MIREILLE, and JULIETTE. She m. CARVALHO 1853; retired 1885. PS

Mireille, opera, 5 acts, GOUNOD, lib. CARRÉ based on poem *Mireio* by Frédéric Mistral, 1859. Paris, TL, 19 Mar 1864; London, HM (in It. as *Mirella*), 5 July 1864; Chicago (in Eng.), 13 Sept 1880. Revised version, 3 acts, TL, 15 Dec 1864. A revival in 1954, Aix-en-Provence, used the original 5-act version. LO
See Kobbé

Yvonne Minton as Helen in KING PRIAM, London, CG, 19 May 1975

Misón, Luís, b. Barcelona; d. Madrid, 13 Feb 1766. Spanish composer. In addition to operas, gave the greatest impetus to the new form of the *tonadilla escénica*. His *tonadillas*, which number about 100, are full of national colour. FGB

Miss Julie, opera, 2 acts, Ned Rorem (b. 1923), lib. Kenward Elmslie, based on August Strindberg's play. NY CC, 4 Nov 1965. LO

Mr Brouček's Excursions (*Výlety páně Broučkovy*), operatic 'bilogy', JANÁČEK, lib. part 1 mainly by the composer, part 2 by František Procházka, both based on satirical novels by Svatopluk Čech (1889). Prague, NT, 23 Apr 1920; Edinburgh, King's T., 9 Sept 1970. Main chars: Mr Brouček (buffo ten.) Málinka/Etherea/Kunka (sop.) Mazal/Blankytný/Petřík (ten.) the Sacristan/Lunobor/Domšík (bass-bar.) Würfl/Čaroskvoucí/the Constable (bass). After drinking at his pub in the Prague Castle precincts, Mr Brouček, a Prague landlord, dreams that he is on the moon and, next evening, in the Hussite Wars of the 15th c. In the first dream Mr Brouček, representing the no-nonsense 19th-c. Czech towndweller, appears saner than the moon's (satirizing Prague's) over-refined 'artistic' society; in the second part Mr Brouček shows the cowardice of the modern Czech in contrast to his single-minded but heroic forebears. Janáček's only comic opera allows him few opportunities for his stronger dramatic attributes and its limited national application has prevented its spreading much abroad. JT O

Mitridate, Re di Ponto (*Mithridates, King of Pontus*), *opera seria*, 3 acts, MOZART, lib. Vittorio Amadeo Cigna-Santi after RACINE. Milan, T. Regio Ducale, 26 Dec 1770; revived Salzburg, 1971. Main chars: Mitridate (ten.) Aspasia (sop.) Sifare (sop.) Farnace (contr.) Ismene (sop.). The plot concerns the rivalry of Mitridate (Mithridates) and his two sons, Farnace (Pharnaces) and Sifare (Xiphares) for the affections of Aspasia. Farnace, betrothed to the princess Ismene, is also in league with his father's enemies, the Romans; but he redeems his honour by avenging Mitridate's defeat at their hands. His father, having taken poison, gives him his dying blessing. Mozart's first full-length *opera seria*, written at 14. JB

Mitropoulos, Dmitri, b. Athens, 1 Mar 1896; d. Milan, 2 Nov 1960. Greek conductor and composer. Studied Athens, Brussels, Berlin. Cond. a few operas at Athens, then was *répétiteur* at Berlin 1921–5. Debut NY Met 1954 (SALOME); stayed there until 1960, cond. TOSCA, BALLO IN MASCHERA, MADAMA BUTTERFLY and premiere of VANESSA. At his best in complex scores such as WOZZECK (Sc.) and ELEKTRA (Florence Maggio). LO

Mlada. In 1872 Stepan Aleksandrovich Gedeonov, dir. of the Imperial Theatres, commissioned a 4-act opera-ballet from BORODIN (Act 4), CUI (Act 1), MUSORGSKY and RIMSKY-KORSAKOV (Acts 2 and 3) and Ludwig Minkus (incidental ballet music), with a lib., set in 9th- and 10th-c. Pomerania, by Viktor Krylov. The project fell through because of expense, but Rimsky-Korsakov later returned to the subject for his own *Mlada*, revising Krylov's lib. himself. It was given at St Petersburg, Mariinsky, 1 Nov 1892. GN

Mödl, Martha, b. Nuremberg, 22 Mar 1912. German soprano. Originally a mezzo-sop.; debut 1944, Remschied (AZUCENA); then engaged at Düsseldorf, where she sang DORABELLA, KLYTEMNESTRA, OCTAVIAN, and MARIE. Debuts: CG 1949 (CARMEN), Berlin 1950 (LADY MACBETH), Bayreuth 1951 (KUNDRY). She sang FIDELIO at the reopening of the Vienna Staats O. (1955). An intelligent, highly dramatic singer, she was for many years a magnificent interpreter of SIEGLINDE, BRÜNNHILDE, GUTRUNE and, especially, ISOLDE. EF

Moffo, Anna, b. Wayne, Pa, 27 June 1932. American soprano. Studied Curtis Institute, Philadelphia, NY, and Rome. First appeared 1956 on It. TV before stage debut, 1956 Palermo (MICAËLA). US debut, 1957 Chicago (MIMI). NY Met debut, 1959 (VIOLETTA); and roles there until 1969 incl. MARGUERITE, GILDA, LIÙ, four heroines in CONTES D'HOFFMANN, LUCIA DI LAMMERMOOR, and MANON. CG debut, 1964 (GILDA). Agile, attractive sop. and appealing actress. AB

Moïse *see* MOSÈ IN EGITTO

Molière [Jean Baptiste Poquelin], b. Paris, 15 Jan 1622; d. Paris, 17 Feb 1673. French actor and playwright. His works have inspired more than 30 operas. LULLY cooperated with him in several *comédies-ballets*. Works on which operas are based incl.: *L'École des Femmes*, 1662 (LIEBERMANN, MORTARI, 1959); *L'Amour Médecin*, 1665 (WOLF-FERRARI, 1913); *Le Médecin Malgré Lui*, 1666 (GOUNOD); *Tartuffe*, 1667 (HAUG, 1937, and BENJAMIN); *L'Avare*, 1667 (BURGHAUSER, 1950); *Monsieur de Pourceaugnac*, 1669 (FRANCHETTI, 1897 and MARTIN); *Le Bourgeois Gentilhomme*, 1670 (R. STRAUSS, ARIADNE AUF NAXOS); *Le Malade Imaginaire*, 1673 (NAPOLI, 1939; Andrés Sas, *El Enfermo Imaginaire*, 1943; Haug, 1946). LO

Molinari-Pradelli, Francesco, b. Bologna, 4 July 1911. Italian conductor. Studied at Rome with Bernardino Molinari. Debut in opera 1946, Sc.; then cond. in all It. houses. CG debut 1955 (TOSCA, AIDA). San Francisco since 1957, Vienna since 1959. NY Met debut 1966 (BALLO IN MASCHERA). AB

Mombelli, (Maria) Ester, b. Bologna, 1794; d. ? Italian soprano. Daughter of the singer Domenico Mombelli (1751–1835) and Vincenza Viganò, sister of Salvatore Viganò, the celebrated choreographer. Debut 1809, T. Nuovo, Padua, with her father and sister, Annetta. The sisters were acclaimed in Milan 1811, and 18 May 1812 appeared in the first perf. of ROSSINI's *Demetrio e Polibio*, commissioned by their father, and set to a lib. by their mother, at the T. Valle, Rome. DONIZETTI wrote *Zoraide di Granata* and *L'Ajo nell'Imbarazzo* for Ester, and she created the title roles in MERCADANTE's *Donna Caritea, Regina d'España* and *Erode* (his version of Salome). She continued her career after her m. to Count Gritti, notably in the Paris premiere of CROCIATO IN EGITTO and the first perf. of Rossini's ill-fated *Il Viaggio a Reims* (1825). Annetta Mombelli m. the journalist Angelo Lambertini and retired to Bologna. PS

Mona, opera, 3 acts, PARKER, lib. Brian Hooker. NY Met, 14 Mar 1912. Main chars: Mona (mezzo-sop.) Enya (sop.) Arth (bass) Gloom (bar.) Caradoc (ten.). Mona, a princess of the Britons, leads her people in rebellion against the occupying Romans. Four perfs. EJ

Monaco *see* MONTE CARLO

Mond, Der: Ein kleines Welttheater (*The Moon: A Little World Theatre*), opera, 3 acts, ORFF, lib. composer from *Der Mond* by GRIMM. Munich, Staats O., 5 Feb 1939; NY CC, 16 Oct 1956. LO O

Mondo della Luna, Il (*The World on the Moon*), opera, 3 acts, HAYDN, lib. GOLDONI (orig. wr. for GALUPPI, 1750). Esterháza, 3 Aug 1777. First revival modern times, Schwering (in Ger.), 20 Mar 1932; NY, Greenwich Mews Playhouse (in Eng.), 7 June 1949; London, Scala T., by London O. Club, 8 Nov 1951 (incomplete); in H. C. Robbins Landon's edition, Holland Fest., 24 June 1959. Goldoni's text was set frequently in the 18th c., by GASSMANN, PAISIELLO, PICCINNI and others. LO

Moniuszko, Stanisław, b. Ubiel, 5 May 1819; d. Warsaw, 4 June 1872. Polish composer. Dir. for some years of the Warsaw O., he was a prolific comp., whose best-known operatic work, HALKA, was originally prod. in 2 acts in 1848 at Vilna (Wilno) and then in a 4-act version at Warsaw (1858). His other operas incl. *Loterya* (*The Lottery*, 1846); *Flis* (*The Raftsman*, 1858); *Hrabina* (*The Countess*, 1860); *Straszny Dwór* (*The Haunted Manor*, 1865, as popular in Poland as *Halka*); *Paria* (1869), and *Beata* (1872), all prod. at Warsaw. EF

Monk, Alan, b. Mission, BC, 19 Aug 1942. Canadian baritone. After training and early experience in Calgary, he joined the touring co. of the San Francisco O. and later the main co., singing some 50 roles. Resumed activity in Canada in 1971 at Ottawa as the Count in NOZZE DI FIGARO; in 1973 created Abelard in Charles Wilson's *Heloise and Abelard* with the COC. CM

Monnaie, Théâtre de la *see* BRUSSELS

Monna Vanna, *drame lyrique*, 4 acts, FÉVRIER, lib. MAETERLINCK's play of same name (1902). Paris, O., 13 Jan 1909; Boston, Mass., 5 Dec 1913. Another opera on same subject is by the Hungarian Emil Abrányi (1907). LO

Monostatos, ten., Sarastro's black slave in ZAUBERFLÖTE

Monsieur Beaucaire, operetta, prologue and 3 acts, MESSAGER, lib. Frederick Lonsdale (1881–1954), lyrics Adrian Ross, adapted from Booth Tarkington's novel (1901). Birmingham, Prince of Wales' T., 7 Apr 1919; London, Prince's T., 19 Apr 1919, where it had a long run; NY, 11 Dec 1919; Paris, in the new Marigny T., 20 Nov 1925. Set in Bath in the time of Beau Nash. In a classic case of mistaken identity 'M. Beaucaire' is revealed as the Duc d'Orléans in disguise. LO
See Lubbock

Monsieur de Pourceaugnac, comic opera, 3 acts, MARTIN, lib. composer based on MOLIÈRE's *comédie-ballet* of that name, music LULLY, 1669. Geneva, 23 Apr 1963; repeated Holland Fest. June 1963. LO

Monsigny, Pierre Alexandre, b. Fauquembergues, Pas de Calais, 17 Oct 1729; d. Paris, 14 Jan 1817. French composer. One of principal writers of *opéra comique*, whose best works found appreciation outside France. The most important are CADI DUPÉ, ROI ET LE FERMIER, *Rose et Colas* (1764), *Aline, Reine de Golconde* (1766), and his masterpiece, DÉSERTEUR. LO

Monte Carlo, Monaco. Opera house built by GARNIER, opened 25 Jan 1879 with recitations by Sarah Bernhardt; capacity 600, orch. stalls only, free admission (subsidized by the Casino). Its most glorious period was under Raoul Gunsbourg (1859–1955), dir. 1892–1954, with premieres of works by PUCCINI, FAURÉ, RAVEL, and esp. MASSENET. He also staged premiere of DAMNATION DE FAUST, 18 Feb 1893. Present art. dir. Renzo ROSSELLINI. LO
See Walsh, *Monte Carlo Opera, 1879–1909* (Dublin 1975)

Montemezzi, Italo, b. Vigasio, ?31 May 1875; d. Vigasio, 15 May 1952. Italian composer. *Bianca,* his first, unperformed opera, won a competition at the Milan Cons. *Giovanni Gallurese* (1905) and *Hellera* (1909) had their premieres at Turin; his most successful opera, AMORE DEI TRE RE, was first prod. at Sc. as were NAVE (1918) and *La Notte di Zoraima* (1931). *L'Incantesino* (1943), a radio opera, was staged at Verona in 1952. EF

Monteux, Pierre, b. Paris, 4 Apr 1875; d. Hancock, Maine, 1 July 1964. French conductor. Best known in the concert hall, esp. with San Francisco Symphony Orch. In the theatre cond. the notorious premiere of STRAVINSKY's *Rite of Spring*; at Paris O. 1913–14, NY Met 1917–19 and 1953–6, cond. Fr. repertory. Cond. US premieres of GOLDEN COCKEREL,

MÂROUF, and Xavier Leroux's *La Reine Fiammette*. His undemonstrative manner hid a consummate artistry, and his perfs were always convincing and authoritative. LO

Monteverdi, Claudio, b. Cremona, ? May 1567 (baptized 15th); d. Venice, 29 Nov 1643. Italian composer, the earliest opera comp. whose mus., after being consigned for centuries to a few lines in mus. histories, is played today. FAVOLA D'ORFEO was the first work of genius to spring from the Florentine Camerata. Of his second opera, *Arianna*, one item only survives; other operas have vanished completely, the most serious loss being a comedy, *La Finta Pazza* (*Feigned Madness*), lib. Giulio Strozzi, 1627. When public opera began in Venice 1637, his interest was reawakened. *Arianna* was revived there 1639; in 1641 he prod. *Le Nozze d'Enea con Lavinia* (also lost). In 1642 came his RITORNO D'ULISSE IN PATRIA and his masterpiece, INCORONAZIONE DI POPPEA. His operas are heard with increasing frequency, and his place among the great masters of mus. drama is now assured. LO
See Arnold, *Monteverdi* (London and New York 1963)

Montezuma, *opera seria*, 3 acts, GRAUN, lib. (in Fr.) Frederick the Great of Prussia, tr. into It. by the Court Poet. Berlin, 6 Jan 1755; Boston Center for the Arts, 14 Feb 1973. Recorded under BONYNGE. The first important treatment of ROUSSEAU's 'noble savage' theme (HURON was 1768; INDES GALANTES was more a *divertissement* than an opera; PURCELL's *Indian Queen* (1695), based on Dryden and Howard's *Indian Queen* (1664) was at best a semi-opera).

Other Montezuma operas incl. those by Antonio Vivaldi (1773); Francesco di Majo (1765); PAISIELLO (*c.* 1773); SACCHINI (1775); ZINGARELLI (1781); Ignaz Xaver von Seyfried (*c.* 1825); Roger Sessions (1964) (*see* following entry). FERNAND CORTEZ also treats the same subject, as does AZORA, DAUGHTER OF MONTEZUMA. LO

Montezuma, opera, 3 acts, Roger Sessions (b. 1896), lib. Giuseppe Antonio Borgese. Berlin, Staats O., 19 Apr 1964; Boston, Mar 1976. LO

Montezuma's Daughter *see* AZORA, DAUGHTER OF MONTEZUMA.

Montreal. Several different organizations have been responsible for the recent prod. of opera in Montreal. For about 30 years, from 1936, the Montreal Fests. gave a major opera prod. each summer. From 1941 until her death in 1969, the singer Pauline Donalda headed the Opera Guild of Montreal which annually presented one opera. The opening of the splendid Salle Wilfred Pelletier at the Place des Arts (1963) provided incentive for the Montreal Symphony Orch., first under MEHTA and later under Franz-Paul Decker, to stage two or three operas as part of its activities each season. Since 1971 opera has been prod by L'Opéra du Québec, not a regular performing co. but an administrative unit with provincial government support to organize operatic prod. in Montreal and in Quebec City.

As the site of Expo 67, Montreal saw prods by the Montreal Symphony, COC of Toronto, the Bolshoy, the EOG, the Hamburg O., Sc., Royal Swedish O., and the Vienna Staats O. Montreal is the centre for Fr.-language broadcasting in Canada and the source of many TV opera prods. CM

Moody, Fanny, b. Redruth, Cornwall, 23 Nov 1866; d. Dundrum, Co. Dublin, 21 July 1945. English soprano. Studied with Charlotte Sainton-Dolby; debut 1887 with Carl Rosa (BOHEMIAN GIRL). Was first Eng. TATYANA, 1892. Sang WAGNER roles with some success with Carl Rosa and with Moody-Manners Co. (she m. MANNERS in 1890), but her light sop. voice was more suited to such roles as CIO-CIO-SAN. LO

Moody-Manners Opera Company. A British touring co. founded by MANNERS and MOODY in 1898. There were three separate troupes, the first co. with 115 members and a repertory of *c.* 30 operas. The co. did useful, indeed remarkable, work for opera in Eng., and attempted, by offering prizes, to stimulate the writing of Eng. operas. It lasted until 1916. LO

Moore, Douglas Stuart, b. Cutchogue, L.I., NY, 10 Aug 1893; d. Greenpoint, LI, 25 July 1969. American composer. Studied at Yale with PARKER and abroad with d'INDY and Nadia Boulanger. Returned home to study with BLOCH. Joined faculty of Columbia Univ. (1926) and headed Dept of Music 1940–62. His operas incl. *White Wings* (Hartford, 9 Feb 1949; NY CC, 12 Dec 1961); DEVIL AND DANIEL WEBSTER; *Giants in the Earth* (NY, Columbia Univ., 28 Mar 1951), a story of the settling of Dakota by Norwegians; BALLAD OF BABY DOE; *Carry Nation*, lib. William North Jayme (Univ. of Kansas, 28 Apr 1966; NY CC, 28 Mar 1968), on life of the proponent of women's rights. EJ

Moore, Grace, b. Slabtown, Tenn., 5 Dec 1901; d. Copenhagen, 26 Jan 1947. American

Left: Douglas Moore's BALLAD OF BABY DOE, Santa Fe, 1961; produced Bill Butler; designed Eldon Elder. Mary McMurray (centre) as Augusta Tabor; surrounded by her four friends, apprentice artists Sharon Tebbenkamp, Marlene Kleinman, Mary Burgess and Iris Bala

soprano. Began career in NY singing in musical comedies. After further study in Europe, debut 1928, NY Met, where she sang frequently until 1946. Her best parts were MIMI (her only appearance at CG 1935) and LOUISE, which she sang at Paris OC and made a film of. Though critics found fault with her she was a great success with the public, who had enjoyed her perfs in *One Night of Love* (1934) and other films. She died in an air crash. LO
See autobiography, *You're Only Human Once* (New York 1944; London 1947)

Moore, Thomas, b. Dublin, 28 May 1770; d. Sloperton Cottage, nr Devizes, Wiltshire, 28 Feb 1862. Irish poet. His *Lalla Rookh*, 1817, consists of four stories: 1. *The Veiled Prophet of Khorassan*; 2. *Paradise and the Peri*; 3. *The Fire Worshippers*; 4. *The Light of the Harem*. Operas on these as follows: 1. STANFORD, 1893; 4. SPONTINI, *Nurmahal*, 1822; A. G. THOMAS, 1879. DAVID's *Lalla Rookh*, 1862 and RUBINSTEIN's *Feramors*, 1863, are based on the poem as a whole; FRANCHETTI's *Asrael*, 1888, is based on *Loves of the Angels*, 1823. LO

Moreau, Jean Michel (le Jeune), b. Paris, 26 Mar 1741; d. Paris, 30 Nov 1814). French painter, engraver, and designer, influential in reform of stage costume and the move toward historical correctness. The actress Mlle Saint-Huberty worked with him and he had the approval of GLUCK, who used his designs for the Vienna prod. of IPHIGÉNIE EN TAURIDE (1781). LO

Moreno Torroba, Federico, b. Madrid, 3 Mar 1891. Spanish composer and conductor. Works incl. *zarzuelas*, among which *Luisa Fernanda* is one of the most melodically rich and appealing in the entire repertoire. FGB

Moriani, Napoleone, b. Florence, 10 Mar 1808; d. Florence, 4 Mar 1878. Italian tenor, known as *il tenore della bella morte* since he excelled in death scenes. His career though short was glorious, earning him court honours in Vienna and Lisbon. Created leading roles in VACCAI's *Sposa di Messina* (Venice 1839), MERCADANTE's *Le Due Illustri Rivali* (Venice 1838), DONIZETTI's *Maria di Rudenz* (Venice 1838) and LINDA DI CHAMOUNIX; also Federico Ricci's *Luigi Rolla* (Florence 1841). For a revival of ATTILA (Milan 1847) VERDI wrote for him a romanza to be inserted into the last act. JB

Morlacchi, Francesco, b. Perugia, 14 June 1784; d. Innsbruck, 28 Oct 1841. Italian composer. Studied first with his father, and then with Luigi Caruso. His boyhood compositions excited enthusiasm and he was sent to study with ZINGARELLI, then later to Stanislao Mattei in Bologna. His first opera was *Il Simoncini* (1803); first big success was *Corradino* (Parma 1808). It was his 10th opera, *Le Danaide* (Rome 1810), that made him famous, and he was offered the position of mus. dir. of the It. O. in Dresden, for life. In 1817 a period of bitter rivalry began when C. WEBER was apptd MdC of the German O. in Dresden. Of Morlacchi's later operas, the most important is *Tebaldo ed Isolina* (1822), selected for VELLUTI's London debut (1825). Morlacchi's last work was *Il Rinegato* (1832). His music is abundantly tuneful. Weber described it as 'pretty and praiseworthy'. None of his operas has been heard this c. PS

Mortari, Virgilio, b. Passirana di Lainate, Milan, 6 July 1902. Italian composer. Best known as an editor of 17th- and 18th-c. works by CIMAROSA, GALUPPI, MONTEVERDI, PERGOLESI, PURCELL, A. SCARLATTI, and Antonio Vivaldi, he has also wr. several operas, which incl. *La Scuola delle Mogli* (1930, revised version, Piccola Sc., Milan, 1959); *La Figlia del Diavolo* (Sc. 1954) about Salome; and *Il Contratto*, broadcast by It. Radio (1962) and staged at Rome (1964). EF

Moscow [Moskva], USSR. An important centre for Russian opera only since the late 1770s, though various touring cos had perf. It. and Fr. opera in the city from the early 1730s. The first permanent theatre in Moscow was the Petrovsky (*see* BOLSHOY). Also important is the Stanislavsky-Nemirovich-Danchenko Music T., est. 1941. The Moscow Operetta T. was opened in 1927, and has given the premieres of many Soviet works, incl. KABALEVSKY's *Spring Sings* (1957), SHOStakovich's *Moscow–Cheremushki* (1959), and the Moscow premiere of Muradeli's *Moscow–Paris–Moscow* (1970). The city also has a Children's Music T., founded 1965, and a Chamber O. T. (1970).

Bolshoy Theatre. The leading Soviet music theatre. It developed from the Petrovsky T. (founded 1780), destroyed by fire in 1805; the co. then perf. in different theatres, and in 1806 came under the control of the Directorate of the Moscow Imperial Theatres. A new building was erected on the old site (1824) and opened on 18 Jan 1825 as the Bolshoy (i.e. Grand) Petrovsky. In 1853 it was again burned down, and was reconstructed to its present design by Alberto Cavos (1856). In 1924 the co. opened a smaller branch theatre (on the basis of Zimin's Free Opera), and since 1961 has had an additional stage at the Kremlin Palace of Congress (capacity 6,000). The Bolshoy has staged premieres of operas by Verstovsky (*Askold's Tomb*, 1835), Tchaikovsky (*The Voyevoda*, 1869; Mazepa, 1884; *Cherevichki*, 1887), and Rakhmaninov (*Aleko*, 1893; *The Miserly Knight* and *Francesca da Rimini*, 1906); and it has been particularly active in staging operas by Soviet comps, among them Dzerzhinsky (*Virgin Soil Upturned*, 1937), Shaporin (Decembrists, 1953), Khrennikov (*Mother*, 1957), Prokofiev (Story of a Real Man, 1960), and Muradeli (*October*, 1964). The opera co.'s first perf. abroad was in Italy (1964), and in 1975 it toured the United States. Among today's leading artists are Arkhipova, Mazurok, Evgeny Nesterenko, Elena Obraztsova, Aleksandr Ognivtsev, and I. Petrov. GN

Mosè in Egitto (*Moses in Egypt*), *azione sacra*, 3 acts, Rossini, lib. Andrea Tottola. Naples, T. S. Carlo, 5 Mar 1818; London, HM, as *Pietro l'Eremita*, 22 Apr 1822; NY, 2 Mar 1835. Refashioned with a ballet and new mus. added and substituted, *Moïse*, grand opera, 4 acts, lib. Giuseppe Luigi Balocchi and Jouy. Paris, O., 26 Mar 1827; London, CG, as *Zora*, 20 Apr 1850; NY, Acad. of Mus., 7 May 1860. Main chars in later version: Moïse (bass) Aménophis (ten.) Anaide (sop.) Pharaon (bar.) Sinaide (sop.). The Old Testament story of the Exodus, on which is grafted the theme of the love between Aménophis, Pharaon's son, and Anaide, niece of Moïse (Moses). Better known in the later It. version, tr. Calisto Bassi. JB

Moses und Aron, opera, 3 acts (only 1 and 2 completed), Schönberg, lib. composer. Hamburg Radio, 12 Mar 1954; Zürich, 6 June 1957; London, CG, 28 June 1965; Boston, 2 Nov 1966. Chief chars: Moses (bass-bar.) Aron (ten.) young girl (sop.) young man (ten.) priest (bass). Moses, unable to communicate his revelation of the word of God, allows his brother Aron (Aaron) to explain it to the people, by means of miracles and familiar images. When Moses, on his return from Sinai, finds the people worshipping the Golden Calf, he shatters the idol, but despairs of explaining his message without the aid of a distorting mouthpiece such as Aron. EF O★

Mother of Us All, The, opera, 3 acts, V. Thomson, lib. G. Stein, on the life of Susan B. Anthony, American feminist leader of the 19th c. NY, Columbia Univ., Brander Matthews T., 7 May 1947. LO

Mottl, Felix, b. Unter-Sankt-Veit, Austria, 24 Aug 1856; d. Munich, 2 July 1911. Austrian conductor. Studied Vienna; *répétiteur* at Vienna O. Assistant to Wagner at Bayreuth 1876, cond. there regularly 1888–1902. At Karlsruhe 1881–1903, notably raising the standard there; Munich 1903–11. Also cond. CG 1898–1900 and NY Met 1903–4, debut Walküre. A devoted and brilliant Wagnerian, he edited vocal scores of all the mus. dramas. LO

Mount-Edgcumbe, 2nd Earl of [Richard Edgcumbe], b. Plymouth, 13 Sept 1764; d. Richmond, Surrey, 26 Sept 1839. English writer and amateur composer. His *Musical Reminiscences of an Amateur, chiefly respecting the Italian Opera in England, for fifty years, 1773 to 1823* (London 1823, and later edns) offers valuable sidelights on operatic life in London. LO

Mourning Becomes Electra. Lear (left) as Lavinia Mannon and Collier as Christine Mannon; NY Met, 17 Mar 1967; produced Boris Aronson; sets Michael Cacoyannis

Mourning Becomes Electra, opera, 3 acts, Marvin David Levy, lib. Henry Butler based on Eugene O'Neill's play of same name, 1931. NY Met, 16 Mar 1967; Dortmund, Nov 1969. LO

Mozart, Wolfgang Amadeus, b. Salzburg, 27 Jan 1756; d. Vienna, 5 Dec 1791. Austrian composer. Son of the renowned violin teacher Leopold Mozart, he toured widely as an infant prodigy on keyboard and violin. As there was no regular opera at Salzburg, his first operatic essay, BASTIEN UND BASTIENNE (1768) was perf. privately in Vienna. FINTA SEMPLICE, a full-length *opera buffa,* refused perf. at the BT, was specially mounted in Salzburg 1769. In the early 1770s, Mozart made several journeys to Italy, where he prod. MITRIDATE, RE DI PONTO, ASCANIO IN ALBA, LUCIO SILLA, all of them competent examples of *opera seria*; and for the installation of Salzburg's new Archbishop he wrote *Il Sogno di Scipione* (*The Dream of Scipio*) (1771). More characteristic were FINTA GIARDINIERA and RE PASTORE, both belonging to the musical world of his violin concertos. After a fruitless tour of Germany and France 1777–8 he had to wait two years for his next operatic commission – IDOMENEO, an *opera seria* in a Franco-It. genre with much chorus and dramatic spectacle.

He left Salzburg in 1781 to settle in Vienna; meantime he had wr. part of a *Singspiel,* later published as ZAÏDE; this he hoped to complete and have perf. in Vienna; but the *Intendant* of the Ger. theatre proposed instead ENTFÜHRUNG AUS DEM SERAIL, which took Vienna and the Ger.-speaking countries by storm. In 1783 he began two comic subjects OCA DEL CAIRO and SPOSO DELUSO; then after the short SCHAUSPIELDIREKTOR, one of the many theatrical satires of the time, came NOZZE DI FIGARO, DON GIOVANNI and COSÌ FAN TUTTE; comedies written to libs by da PONTE, and all representing the high-water mark of Mozart's operatic career, though the last was written in increasing poverty. To the final year of his life belong CLEMENZA DI TITO (Prague), an old-fashioned *opera seria* modified to suit contemporary taste, and ZAUBERFLÖTE (Vienna), a fantastic *Singspiel* with the character of a religious testament. Together with VERDI and WAGNER, Mozart is one of the three supreme masters of opera; he extended the scope of every genre which he touched and played a key role in the evolution of Ger. opera. JB

Muck, Karl, b. Darmstadt, 22 Oct 1859; d. Stuttgart, 3 Mar 1940. German conductor. Studied Leipzig. Cond., A. NEUMANN's Co., Prague, 1886; was subsequently with Neumann's travelling Wagner Co. With Berlin Staats O. 1892–1912; also appeared at CG and regularly at Bayreuth 1901–30, where he proved one of the best WAGNER interpreters of the period. LO

Muette de Portici, La (*The Dumb Girl of Portici*), also known as *Masaniello,* opera, 5 acts, AUBER, lib. SCRIBE and Germaine Delavigne. Paris, O., 29 Feb 1828; London, DL (as *Masaniello*), 4 May 1829; NY, 15 Mar 1831. Based on a historical incident of 1647. Main chars: Masaniello (ten.) Alfonso (ten.) Fenella (mute). Masaniello, moved by the oppression of the people and the betrayal of his sister Fenella by Alfonso, Viceroy of Naples, leads a revolt against the Spaniards, which, initially successful, is crushed. Masaniello is killed, Fenella commits suicide. A perf. in Brussels (22 Aug 1830) sparked off the Belg. rising against the Dutch. LO
See Kobbé

Mugnone, Leopoldo, b. Naples, 29 Sept 1858; d. Naples, 22 Dec 1941. Italian composer and conductor. Only 12 when he wrote his first opera, and began cond. at 16 at T. La Fenice, Venice. Engagements incl. T. Costanzi, Rome, where he cond. first perfs of CAVALLERIA RUSTICANA and TOSCA, and Sc., where he cond. first perf. of FALSTAFF. At CG cond. Eng. premieres of ADRIANA LECOUVREUR, FEDORA, and IRIS. One of the best It. conds of his time. LO

Mulhouse, France. Since World War II has become increasingly important operatically, and has given notable premieres such as the first Fr. prod. of RAPE OF LUCRETIA and ATLANTIDE. Since 1972 has been part of Opéra du Rhin. LO

Müller, Wenzel [Václav], b. Trnávka, Moravia, 26 Sept 1759; d. Baden, nr Vienna, 3 Aug 1835. Austrian composer and conductor. Second cond., Brno T., 1783–5; after touring Germany and Italy, settled in Vienna 1786 as cond. at Marinelli's Leopoldstadt T., a rival of SCHIKANEDER's Freihaus T. Apart from 1808–13, when he was cond. of the Prague Estates T., he remained in Vienna all his life. He was one of the most productive and popular *Singspiel* comps of his time, writing over 200 works: the best known were *Das Neue Sonntagskind* (1793) and *Die Schwestern von Prag* (1794), which gave BEETHOVEN the theme for his 'Kakadu' Variations, op. 121a. His *Kaspar der Fagottist* (1791) has a lib. similar to that of ZAUBERFLÖTE (which it preceded by a few months); in 1818 Müller parodied the MOZART opera in *Die Travestierte Zauberflöte.* JT

Mullings, Frank, b. Walsall, 10 May 1881; d. Manchester, 19 May 1953. English tenor. Debut 1907, Coventry (GOUNOD'S FAUST). Sang in Denhof Co. 1913, and later in Beecham's Co.; the first to sing PARSIFAL in English (CG 1919). With BNOC 1922–6, singing WAGNER roles and VERDI'S OTELLO, parts for which his robust ten. was well suited. LO

Munich [München], W. Germany. Capital of Bavaria, with an operatic history going back to 1653. Comps connected with Munich incl. MOZART, WAGNER (premieres of TRISTAN UND ISOLDE, MEISTERSINGER VON NÜRNBERG, RHEINGOLD and WALKÜRE), and R. STRAUSS (b. there). The Residenz T., designed by Jean François de Cuvilliès, was built in 1753, damaged during World War II and restored 1958; IDOMENEO, perf. there 1781. The main T. is the Hof- und NT (the Bavarian State Opera). Built in 1818, burned down 1823, rebuilt 1825, destroyed in 1943 and re-opened 1963, its long line of distinguished mus. dirs runs from Franz Lachner through LEVI, MOTTL, WALTER, KNAPPERTSBUSCH, C. KRAUSS, LEITNER, SOLTI, KEMPE, FRICSAY, and KEILBERTH. The Prinzregenten T. was opened in 1901, modelled on Bayreuth. The Staats T. am Gärtnerplatz maintains a tradition of operetta and *Singspiele* dating from the 1870s. The Munich O. Fest. dates from 1901, and began by concentrating on Mozart and Wagner. Strauss soon became an important addition, balanced by a selection of 20th-c. works. LO

Muradeli, Vano Ilyich, b. Gori, 6 Apr 1908; d. Tomsk, 14 Aug 1970. Georgian composer. Educated at Tiflis (now Tbilisi) and Moscow Cons., he is known particularly for his first opera *The Great Friendship* (1947). Intended as a glorification of Stalin's native Georgia, it was, however, denounced as anti-Stalinist shortly after the premiere, because, it is thought, of the antagonism between Stalin and the opera's central char., Komissar Ordzhonikidze. *October* (1964) had a more lasting success and is still perf.; it was also an important landmark in the history of Soviet mus. as the first opera in which the char. of Lenin has a singing role. Muradeli composed two operettas, *The Girl with Blue Eyes* (1966) and *Moscow–Paris–Moscow* (1968, revised 1974). GN

Muratore, Lucien, b. Marseille, 29 Aug 1876; d. Paris, 16 July 1954. French tenor. Studied Marseille, as horn player, then voice at Paris Cons. Began as straight actor; debut as singer in HAHN'S *La Carmélite* (OC 1902). Engaged Paris O. 1905–11, then moved to USA, Boston 1913 and Chicago 1913–22. In 1913 m. L. CAVALIERI, and with her made US film of MANON LESCAUT 1914. Returned to France 1923. Created more than 30 roles incl. Bacchus (title role), Thésée (*Ariane*), and Lentulus (*Roma*), all by MASSENET; and Prinzivalle in MONNA VANNA. A perfectionist, one of the foremost singers of the period. Manager, Paris OC, 1943–5. LO

Musgrave, Thea, b. Edinburgh, 27 May 1928. Scottish composer. Studied composition at Edinburgh Univ. and in Paris with Nadia Boulanger. Operas are: *The Abbot of Drimock*, a 1-act chamber opera (lib. Maurice Lindsay) portraying the cupidity of a cleric routed by the honesty of young love, wr. 1955, first staged Morley Coll., London, 19 Dec 1962; *The Decision*, 3 acts (lib. also by Lindsay), the tragedy of a mine disaster, New O. Co., SW, 30 Nov 1967; and her major operatic work to date, VOICE OF ARIADNE. Musgrave's mature mus. is in a fluent lyrical serial idiom. SO commissioned her to write an opera on Mary, Queen of Scots, for prod. 1977. NG

Musical, The. Although *The Black Crook* (1866) is sometimes cited as the first US musical comedy, it was actually a spectacle and a revue put together by many hands, but its amalgam of music, dance, comedy, and scenic display pointed in new directions. In the USA, as elsewhere, the Viennese operetta was popular for *c.* 50 years until the pasteboard royalty and stratified society of Ruritania became tiresome and repetitious. Reginald De Koven's *Robin Hood*, 1890, set in medieval England, John Philip Sousa's *El Capitan*, 1897, in Peru, and HERBERT'S *Fortune Teller*, 1898, Budapest, were the first successes in a swashbuckling and romantic style, followed in 1887–1917 by a further 65 works of these composers.

The American musical comedy, arriving *c.* 1900, was a simpler form looking back to the SINGSPIEL. Boy meeting girl was no longer a prince but a youth from the hinterland, the suburbs or the inner city. George M. Cohan set the course with *Little Johnny Jones*, 1904, concerning an American jockey. Musically Cohan's works were inexpert, tuneful rather than melodious, with rudimentary orchestration and sung by inferior voices. Comps of this new style were frequently without musical training, needing professional assistance with their craft. The two types, represented by Cohan and the operetta, prospered until *c.* 1920, with a late flowering of the latter in ROMBERG'S *Blossom Time*, 1921, STUDENT PRINCE, 1924, and a few others sponsored by the brothers Shubert.

New strength and variety were infused into

the musical comedy by the acceptance of ragtime and jazz, and the emergence of newer men. GERSHWIN began as a tunesmith like Cohan and BERLIN, but acquired a substantial technique, and LADY, BE GOOD, like Vincent Youmans's NO, NO, NANETTE!, differed from Cohan's style chiefly in that it was more musicianly. It is worth noting that changes in the popular musical were resisted by producers. From now on the American subject was standard, drawn from an OKLAHOMA farm, a SHOW BOAT on the Mississippi, or the life styles of GUYS AND DOLLS in urban centres. With the works of the later Gershwin, with PORTER, RODGERS, LOEWE, LOESSER, BERNSTEIN, and their associates, the musical has to be considered as an integrated whole, the product of librettist, lyricist, composer, and choreographer, of whom HART, HAMMERSTEIN II, Otto Harbach, Jerome Robbins, Agnes de Mille, and Hanya Holm were among the most able. They adapted plays and novels by SHAKESPEARE, VOLTAIRE, Ferenc Molnar, Marcel Pagnol, George Bernard Shaw, Thornton Wilder or Edna Ferber to create works of greater depth and power than the simple situation comedies. Musicals of this type promise to endure as artistic entities, not merely as frameworks for popular songs. EJ
See Engel, *The American Musical Theater; A Consideration* (New York 1967)

Musical comedy. Victorian and Edwardian musical comedy in Eng. derives mainly from 1. 18th-c. plays with mus. and so-called operas of DIBDIN, SHIELD, and ARNE; 2. Fr. *opérette* esp. OFFENBACH and HERVÉ and the lighter operas of AUBER, A. ADAM and BOÏELDIEU. Impresarios like George Edwardes (1852–1913) and the American John Augustin Daly (1839–99) staged the works excellently. The steady stream of comps incl. CELLIER, S. JONES, Edward German (1862–1936), Lionel Monckton (1861–1924), Paul Rubens (1876–1917), Harold Fraser-Simpson (1873–1944), with SULLIVAN in a niche of his own. LO
See Hughes, *Composers of Operetta* (London and New York 1962)

Musorgsky, Modest Petrovich, b. Karevo, Pskov Government, 21 Mar 1839; d. St Petersburg, 28 Mar 1881. Russian composer. Before embarking on his only completed opera, BORIS GODUNOV, he contemplated and worked on several abortive projects: *Han d'Islande* (based on HUGO, 1856); *Oedipus in Athens* (Ozerov, 1858–60); *St John's Eve* (GOGOL, 1858); and *Salammbô* (FLAUBERT, 1863–6), in which he used some of the *Oedipus* mus., and from which he borrowed mus. for *Boris Godunov* and other works. Whereas *Salammbô* is notable above all for its lyricism, his next incomplete opera, MARRIAGE, goes to the opposite extreme of musical realism; these lyrical and realistic elements are perfectly balanced in *Boris Godunov*, his finest work. Between the two versions of *Boris Godunov*, Musorgsky began, in 1870, another opera, *The Landless Peasant* (after Spielhagen's *Hans und Grete*), and used one completed scene from it in KHOVANSHCHINA; mus. for the collective MLADA (for which he again drew on *Oedipus*) was also used in later works. His final project was *Pugachovshchina* (1877). *Khovanshchina*, based on late 17th-c. Russian history, lacks the cohesion of *Boris*, and the opera remained unfinished, partly because of other work (incl. another opera, SOROCHINTSY FAIR), partly because of the heavy drinking that was to be the cause of his death. GN
See Calvocoressi, *Mussorgsky* (completed by G. Abraham, London 1946; revised 1974)

Muti, Riccardo, b. Naples, 28 July 1941. Italian conductor. Won the CANTELLI prize for conds in 1967; principal cond. of the Maggio Musicale Fiorentino Orch. in 1969. Cond. in Vienna and Salzburg, and is admired for his interpretations of VERDI operas – MASNADIERI, FORZA DEL DESTINO, and AIDA. In Florence he has also cond. AFRICAINE, (1971), an uncut version of GUILLAUME TELL (1972), and SPONTINI's *Agnes von Hohenstaufen* (1974). He is now principal cond. of the New Philharmonia Orch., London. EF

Muzio, Claudia, b. Pavia, 7 Feb 1889; d. Rome, 24 May 1936. Italian soprano. Debut 1912, Arezzo (MANON); sang at CG and European opera houses before moving to USA (1916), where she spent most of her career: Met 1916–22; Chicago 1922–31. At her best in the great It. roles. LO

My Fair Lady, musical, LOEWE, book LERNER based on George Bernard Shaw's *Pygmalion*. NY, Mark Hellinger T., 15 Mar 1956; London, DL, 30 Apr 1958. EJ ○ ★
See Lubbock

N

Nabokov, Nicolas, b. Lyubcha, Minsk, 17 Apr 1903. Russian, naturalized American, composer. Studied Berlin and Paris, emigrating to USA 1933, later living in Paris. His opera about Rasputin, *The Holy Devil*, was prod. at Louisville 1958; a revised version, *Der Tod des Grigori Rasputin*, was perf. at Cologne 1959. In 1973

Love's Labour's Lost, a setting of SHAKESPEARE's play, lib. AUDEN and KALLMAN, was prod., in Eng., by the Deutsche O. of Berlin at the T. de la Monnaie, Brussels. EF

Nabucco [*Nabucodonosor*], opera, 4 acts, VERDI, lib. Temistocle Solera after Eugène Bourgeois and Cornu. Milan, Sc., 9 Mar 1842. London, HM, as *Nino*, 3 Mar 1846; NY, Astor Opera House, 4 Apr 1848. Main chars: Nabucco (bar.) Abigaille (sop.) Zaccaria (bass) Fenena (sop.) Ismaele (ten.). The story of Nabucco (Nebuchadnezzar), his capture of Jerusalem, the intrigues of his adopted daughter Abigaille against the legitimate Princess Fenena, his own blasphemy, madness and recovery after turning to the worship of Jehovah. Verdi's third opera and first unqualified success. JB O

Nacht in Venedig, Eine (*A Night in Venice*). *operetta*, 3 acts, J. STRAUSS, lib. F. Zell (Camillo Walzel) and GENÉE. Berlin, Friedrich-Wilhelm Städtisches T., 3 Oct 1883; NY, 8 Dec 1889; London, Cambridge T., 25 May 1944. New version by Hubert Marischka and KORNGOLD (Vienna, Staats O., 21 June 1923). An 18th-c. comedy of intrigue involving disguises and misunderstandings in a Venetian Carnival. Still frequently played in Germany and Austria. LO

Nachtlager von Granada, Das (*The Night Camp in Granada*), opera, 2 acts, KREUTZER, lib. Karl Johann Braun based on play of same name by Friedrich Kind. Vienna, Josefstadt T., 13 Jan 1834; London, Princes T. (in Ger.), 13 May 1840; NY, 15 Dec 1862. Kreutzer's most popular opera, in the style of the 18th-c. *Singspiel*. The story is similar to that of JAGD. LO

Nancy, France. Opera is given in the T. Municipal, *c.* eight or ten operas each season. Louis Ducreux succeeded Jean-Claude Riber as dir. in 1973. LO

Naples [Napoli], Italy. Once the capital of the independent Kingdom of Naples, and after Venice the most important centre in the history of opera. Its finest period was probably the 18th c.: PERGOLESI, LEO, and Francesco Provenzale founded *opera buffa*; PICCINNI and JOMMELLI continued the *opera seria* tradition begun by A. SCARLATTI and PORPORA. It continued to flourish in the 19th c.: ROSSINI, BELLINI, DONIZETTI, and VERDI all had premieres there. Its contribution to 20th-c. opera has been less notable.

Teatro San Carlo. One of the show theatres of the world. First built in 1737, completed in nine months. After alterations and improvements in 1777 and 1812 it was burned out in 1816 and rebuilt, in six months, by Antonio Niccolini. Damaged in World War II, it was restored by aid of the British Army. One of the biggest theatres (capacity 3,500), its audiences have the reputation of being vocally critical, chauvinistic, and conservative. Nevertheless 20th-c. operas such as NEUES VOM TAGE, WOZZECK, BOULEVARD SOLITUDE have been staged, often in enterprising prods. Like many large theatres elsewhere, and despite a generous subsidy, it faces ever-increasing financial difficulties. LO

See Robinson, *Naples and Neapolitan Opera* (Oxford 1972); Gishford, *Grand Opera: Story of the World's Leading Opera Houses and Personalities* (London 1973)

Napoli, Jacopo, b. Naples, 26 Aug 1911. Italian composer. Several of his comic operas, which incorporate Neapolitan songs, have received their first perfs at the T. S. Carlo, Naples: *Il Malato Immaginario* (1939), *Miseria e Nobiltà* (1946), *I Pescatori* (1954), and *Il Barone Avaro* (1970). *Un Curioso Accidente* was prod. Bergamo (1950); *Mas'Aniello*, Milan, Sc. (1953); *Il Tesoro*, Rome (1958); *Il Povero Diavolo*, Trieste (1963); *Il Rosario*, Brescia (1962). *Dubrovski II* was first perf. Naples (1973). EF

Nápravník, Eduard, b. Býšt, 24 Aug 1839; d. Petrograd, 23 Nov 1916. Czech conductor, working in Russia. Joined the Mariinsky T. in 1863, then succeeded Konstantin Lyadov as principal cond. in 1869. Cond. important premieres of Russian operas incl. STONE GUEST, second version of BORIS GODUNOV, MAID OF PSKOV, and TCHAIKOVSKY's *The Oprichnik* (1874), *Vakula the Smith* (1876), MAID OF ORLEANS, QUEEN OF SPADES and IOLANTA. Also comp. four operas: *Nizhegorodtsy* (1868), *Garold* (1886), *Dubrovsky* (1895), and *Francesca da Rimini* (1902). GN

National Broadcasting Co. (NBC Opera Co.), New York. Grew out of a broad musical programme begun in 1926, dir. Samuel Chotzinoff; incl. Walter DAMROSCH's Music Appreciation Hour, NY Philharmonic Orch., formation of the NBC Orch. under TOSCANINI, and broadcasts of Saturday matinees of the Met, sponsored by Texaco. The NBC O. Co. commissioned AMAHL AND THE NIGHT VISITORS (the first opera designed for TV) and sponsored Norman Dello Joio's *The Triumph of St Joan* (8 Apr 1956), also prods of WAR AND PEACE (13 Jan 1957), and DIALOGUES DES CARMÉLITES (1958). Only the sponsored broadcasts of the Met now survive. EJ

Naudin, Emilio, b. Parma, 23 Oct 1823; d. Bologna, 5 May 1890. Italian tenor. Studied with Giacomo Panizza in Milan; debut 1845 Cremona, in PACINI's *Saffo*. Sang in Italy, Vienna, and St Petersburg; London debut 2 June 1858, DL (DUCA DI MANTUA) returning 1862 in TROVATORE. After singing COSÌ FAN TUTTE and ALESSANDRO STRADELLA in Paris, CG debut 7 Apr 1863 as Masaniello (MUETTE DE PORTICI), singing there 1863–72 except 1865 when he was engaged to create the role of Vasco da Gama in AFRICAINE (he was named for the role in MEYERBEER's will). Last appeared in Spain and Italy in 1879, after which he became paralysed. PS

Naumann, Johann Gottlieb, b. Blazewitz, Dresden, 17 Apr 1741; d. Dresden, 23 Oct 1801. German composer. Studied in Italy; his first operas were perf. at Venice. His setting of *Clemenza di Tito* was prod. at Dresden (1769). Travelled to Stockholm 1777, where several of his operas were given: *Amphion* (1778), *Cora och Alonzo* (1782) and *Gustaf Wasa* (1786). His later works incl. *Medea* (Berlin 1788), *La Dama Soldato* (Dresden 1791), and *Aci e Galatea* (Dresden 1801). EF

Navarraise, La (*The Girl from Navarre*), *épisode lyrique*, 2 acts, MASSENET, lib. Jules Claretie and Henri Cain based on Claretie's story *La Cigarette*. London, CG, 20 June 1894; Paris, OC, 8 Oct 1895; NY Met, 11 Dec 1895. LO O
See Harding, *Massenet* (London 1970; New York 1971)

Navarrini, Francesco, b. Citadella, 1855; d. Milan, 23 Feb 1923. Italian bass. Debut 1878, Treviso, as Alfonso (LUCREZIA BORGIA). Sc. from 1883. Created Lodovico in VERDI's OTELLO (Sc., 1887). CG debut, as Alfonso, 1888. One of the most imposing voices and figures of his day. AB

Nave, La (*The Ship*), opera, prologue and 3 acts, MONTEMEZZI, lib. Tito RICORDI, from D'ANNUNZIO's *La Nave*, 1908. Milan, Sc., 3 Nov 1918; Chicago (in It.), 18 Nov 1919; revived Rome, 14 Dec 1938. LO

Nedbal, Oskar, b. Tábor, 26 Mar 1874; d. Zagreb, 24 Dec 1930. Czech conductor and composer. Studied comp. with DVOŘÁK, Prague Cons.; violist in the Bohemian Quartet 1891–1906; cond., Czech Philharmonic 1896–1906. Cond., Vienna Tonkünstlerverein 1906–18 and estab. his reputation as an operetta comp. (*Die Keusche Barbora*, 1910; *Polenblut*, 1913; *Die Winzerbraut*, 1916; *Die Schöne Saskia*, 1917; *Mamzel Napoleon*, 1918; *Donna Gloria*, 1925). With Czech independence in 1918, settled in Bratislava, becoming chief cond. of the opera (1923) and a vital instigator of Slovak musical life. Wrote one opera, *Sedlák Jakub* (*Jacob the Farmer*, 1922). JT

Nedda, sop., Canio's wife in PAGLIACCI

Neher, Caspar, b. Augsburg, 11 Apr 1897; d. Vienna, 30 June 1962. German designer and librettist. After working at Munich and Vienna (with ROLLER) went to Kroll O., Berlin, 1924–8 and Berlin Städtische O. 1931–3. Subsequently at Frankfurt (1934–41) and Hamburg (1945–7). Designed more than 50 operas for houses mentioned, and Glyndebourne, CG (WOZZECK), and Salzburg. Wrote libs for EINEM and WAGNER-RÉGENY. LO

Nemeth, Maria, b. Körmend, 13 Mar 1899; d. Vienna, 28 Dec 1967. Hungarian soprano. Studied Budapest; debut there, 1923. Vienna, Staats O., 1925–46; also sang at CG (1931, TURANDOT). Sang mainly It. roles; outstanding as Turandot and TOSCA. Had the brilliance and agility for the MOZART roles of CONSTANZE and Donna ANNA; was a remarkably fine QUEEN OF THE NIGHT. LO

Nemirovich-Danchenko, Vladimir Ivanovich, b. Ozurgety (now Makharadze), Georgia, 23 Dec 1858; d. Moscow, 25 Apr 1943. Russian theatre director. At the Moscow Arts T. (which he founded in collaboration with STANISLAVSKY in 1898), he estab. his Music Studio (1919); in 1926 it was named the Nemirovich-Danchenko Music T.; in 1941 combined with the Stanislavsky Opera T. and renamed the Stanislavsky-Nemirovich-Danchenko Music T. In the field of opera, Nemirovich-Danchenko is known particularly for his close association with KHRENNIKOV in the staging of *Into the Storm* (1939); but after his death the theatre continued to give important premieres, notably of the revised version of KATERINA IZMAYLOVA. Also wrote the lib. for RAKHMANINOV's *Aleko* (1893). GN

Nemorino, ten., the hero of ELISIR D'AMORE

Nerone (*Nero*), opera, 4 acts, BOITO, lib. composer. Milan, Sc., 1 May 1924 (posth.). Main chars: Nerone (ten.) Simon Mago (bass-bar.) Fanuel (bar.) Asteria (sop.) Rubria (mezzo-sop.) Tigellino (bass). Simon Mago (Magus), unmasked by Nerone as a fake magician, betrays the Christians to the Emperor, who condemns them to martyrdom in the circus. Simon and his followers set fire to the city; many of the victims escape, but Rubria is fatally wounded

Nerone. Act IV, sc. 1, Milan, Scala, 1939; produced Mario Frigerio; designed Pogliaghi

and dies in the arms of Fanuel. A fifth act was written but never set to mus.: the scoring of the previous acts was completed by Vincenzo Tommasini and TOSCANINI, who cond. the first perf. JB
See Kobbé

Nessler, Victor, b. Baldenheim, 28 Jan 1841; d. Strasbourg, 28 May 1890. German conductor and composer. Comp. 10 operas, of which *Der Rattenfänger von Hameln* (*The Ratcatcher of Hamelin*), 1879, and esp. *Der Trompeter von Säckingen* (*The Trumpeter of Säckingen*), 1884 (NY 1888), were the most successful. LO

Netherlands. Chief operatic centres are Amsterdam and The Hague. Nineteenth-c. Dutch comps who wrote operas incl. S. van Milligen (1849–1929), whose *Brunio* (1889) and *Dartula* (1898) were prod. in Holland. Cornelis Dopper (1870–1939) wrote *De Blinde van het Kasteel Cuillé* (1894), *Het Eere Kruis* (1903) and *William Ratcliff* (1909); Willem Landré (1874–1948) composed *De Roos van Dekama* (1897) and *Beatrijs* (1925). In the next generation, Willem Pijper (1894–1947) wrote a popular opera, *Halewijn* (1933), and Guillaume Landré (1905–68), son of Willem Landré, composed *De Snoek* (1938) and *Jean Lévecq* (1965). The Holland Fest., which grew out of the Scheveningen Summer fest., 1947, was started in 1948 and has staged several new works by Dutch comps, incl. ANDRIESSEN's *Philomela* (1950), Sem Dresden's *François Villon* (1958), BADINGS's *Martin Korda DP* (1960), LEEUW's *De Droom* (1965) and *Reconstructie* (1969), an opera by five joint comps, Louis Andriessen, Reinbert de Leeuw, Misha Mengelberg, SCHAT, and Jan van Vlijmen. Perfs, given by Nederlandse O., Holland Fest. O. or visiting foreign companies, of works by JANÁČEK, PROKOFIEV, STRAVINSKY, MARTIN, DALLAPICCOLA, MILHAUD, SHOSTAKOVICH, BRITTEN, and TOMASI, have also been staged. EF

Neues vom Tage. A scene at the Universal Service Bureau, where Mr Hermann (Loren Driscoll) fends off the attention of the secretarial staff; US premiere, Santa Fe, 12 Aug 1961; produced Don Moreland; designed Henry Heymann; conducted by the composer

Neues vom Tage (*News of the Day*), comic opera, 3 parts, HINDEMITH. lib. Marcellus Schiffer. Berlin, Kroll T., 8 June 1929; revised Naples, 7 Apr 1954; Santa Fe, 12 Aug 1961. Main chars: the Press Chief (bass) the Married Couple (sop. and bar.) the Agency employees (mezzo-sop. and ten.). A world press agency exploits a young married couple in order to provide sensational copy. The opera incl. a notorious scene, objected to by Dr Goebbels, in which the heroine, lying in her bath, hymns the joys of constant hot water. EF

Neumann, Angelo, b. Vienna, 18 Aug 1838; d. Prague, 20 Dec 1910. Austrian-Czech theatre director. After singing for 17 years as a bar., he became dir. Städtische O., Leipzig (1876–82), where he initiated the first RING DES NIBELUNGEN cycle and, 1882–3, toured Europe with a WAGNER co. From 1885 to his death he was director of the German T., Prague, which he made one of the leading cos in Europe, performing C. WEBER, WAGNER, and MOZART cycles, and touring St Petersburg (1889) and Berlin (1891) with the *Ring*. He also perf. many novelties incl. TIEFLAND (1903) and the first Prague prod. of PELLÉAS ET MÉLISANDE. He pub. *Erinnerungen an Richard Wagner* (Leipzig 1907). *See also* PRAGUE. JT

Neumann, František, b. Přerov, 16 June 1874; d. Brno, 25 Feb 1929. Czech conductor. Studied Leipzig Cons. (1896–7) before serving as a *répétiteur* in German, Austrian, and Czech theatres. In 1919, on JANÁČEK's recommendation, he became chief cond. of the newly reorganized Brno NT, where he did much to raise the standards of the co. and greatly enlarge its repertory. His great service was as cond. of the premieres of KÁT'A KABANOVÁ, CUNNING LITTLE VIXEN, *Šárka* (1925) and MAKROPULOS CASE, in which he worked closely with Janáček. Also cond. premieres of works by NOVÁK and OSTRČIL, and wrote several operas. JT

Neumann, Václav, b. Prague, 29 Oct 1920. Czech conductor. Studied Prague Cons; played violin and viola in the Smetana Quartet. After cond. posts in Bohemia he became cond. at the Berlin KO (1956–64) and worked with FELSENSTEIN in the celebrated prod. of CUNNING LITTLE VIXEN (1956). Since 1964 he has been cond. Czech Philharmonic (chief cond., 1968) and general mus. dir., Stuttgart Staats O. (1970–3). A versatile cond., he has achieved special success with his perfs and recordings of JANÁČEK operas. JT

Neway, Patricia, b. Brooklyn, NY, 30 Sept 1919. American soprano. Debut 1949, Chautauqua Summer O. (FIORDILIGI). Has sung at NY CC, Aix-en-Provence (IPHIGÉNIE EN TAURIDE), Paris OC (TOSCA and RISURREZIONE), and San Francisco. Created Magda Sorel in CONSUL (Philadelphia 1950), an opera she has sung over 500 times in USA and Europe. Also sang in the first perfs of David Tamkin's *The Dybbuk* (NY 1951) and MARIA GOLOVIN (Brussels 1958). Her repertory incl. MARIE, Female Chorus (RAPE OF LUCRETIA), and the Governess (TURN OF THE SCREW). EF

New London Opera Company. Gave It. opera for a few seasons beginning 1946 at Cambridge T. and Stoll T. with EREDE as cond. and BORGIOLI as prod. and vocal dir., with STABILE, GRANDI, DICKIE, FRANKLIN and I. WALLACE among the singers. Though perfs were perhaps not up to the finest international standards, the co. did valuable service, their operas sung stylishly in It., during the post-World War II period when CG was becoming estab. as the UK's national opera. LO

Newman, Ernest [William Roberts], b. Liverpool, 30 Nov 1868; d. Tadworth, Surrey, 6 July 1959. English critic and writer. Music critic, *Manchester Guardian* 1905–19; *Observer* 1919–20; *Sunday Times* 1920–58. Books incl. *Gluck and the Opera* (1895, reprinted 1964); *The Life of Richard Wagner,* 4 vols (1933–47). *Opera Nights* (1943), *Wagner Nights* (1949), and *More Opera Nights* (1954) contain long and scholarly essays on 56 operas. A forward-looking critic, he championed not only WAGNER but R. STRAUSS and other contemporaries. LO

Newmarch, Rosa, b. Leamington Spa, 18 Dec 1857; d. London, 9 Apr 1940. English critic. After studying painting (1880–3), became London journalist. Visited Russia several times, meeting leading comps (RIMSKY-KORSAKOV, Aleksandr Glazunov) and the critic Vladimir Stassov. Did much to further the cause of Russian and Czech opera in England. LO
See her *Russian Opera* (London 1914) and esp. her *Music of Czechoslovakia* (London 1942)

New Orleans. Important centre in 19th c. US premieres at the Fr. Opera House, built 1859, destroyed 1919, incl. DINORAH, MIGNON, GIORDANO's *Siberia* (1906), and SAMSON ET DALILA. Before 1859 US premieres had been more numerous, incl. VESTALE, HUGUENOTS, LUCIA DI LAMMERMOOR, and FAVORITE. The New Orleans T. of the Performing Arts, seating 2,300, was opened 1973 with MADAMA BUTTERFLY. Gen dir. of New Orleans Opera House Association, Arthur Cosenza; mus. dir. Knud Andersson. LO

New York. The most important centre for opera in the USA and the home of several eminent companies. Ballad operas were performed in the 18th c., culminating in one of the earliest indigenous US examples, James Hewitt's *Tammany, or The Indian Chief*, given at John Street T., 1794. It. opera first came to NY on 29 Nov 1825 with ROSSINI's BARBIERE DI SIVIGLIA at the **Park Theatre**, built 1825, the second theatre of this name (first built 1798). Enthusiasm and progress were reflected in opera houses built and companies founded, particularly in the latter half of the 19th c. and the early decades of the 20th.

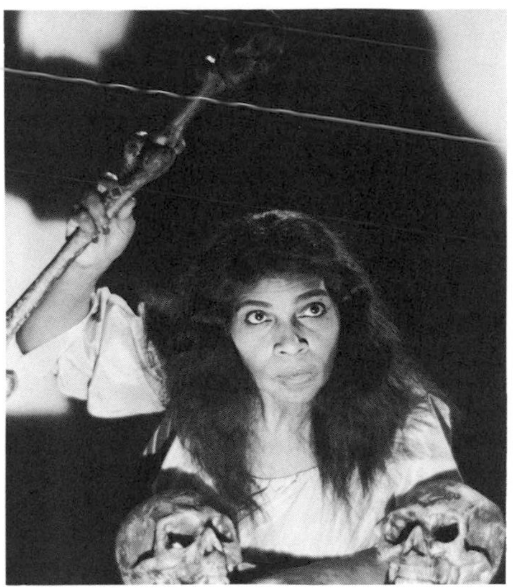

New York. ANDERSON as ULRICA, her first role at the NY Met, 1955

The **Academy of Music,** which succeeded the Astor Place OH, opened with NORMA on 2 Oct 1854. For over 30 years the city's leading house, it was the setting for the US debuts of numerous singers incl. Giulia GRISI, HAUK, MARIO, C. NILSSON, NORDICA, PATTI, and TIETJENS; among its US premieres were those of AIDA, COLA RIENZI, TRAVIATA, and TROVATORE. The first manager was MARETZEK; his successors included the influential MAPLESON. Opera perfs ceased in *c.* 1900, some years after the establishment of the NY Met, and the building was finally demolished in 1925.

New York City Center Opera, Lincoln Center (CC). Estab. 1944. Spring and fall seasons totalling 21 weeks in NY with intervening engagements in Los Angeles and Washington (Kennedy Center). Principal conds: HALASZ (1944–51), Joseph Rosenstock (1951–5), RUDEL (1957–). Housed in Mecca Temple 1944–64; NY State T. since 1964. Repertory of standard works with novelties, from MONTEVERDI and HANDEL to the present, and with constant encouragement of US comps and singers.

World premieres of operas by US comps incl.: STILL's *The Troubled Island* (31 Mar 1949); David Tamkin's *The Dybbuk* (4 Oct 1951); TENDER LAND; GOOD SOLDIER SCHWEIK; Lee Hoiby's *The Scarf* (5 Apr 1959); Hugo Weisgall's *Six Characters in Search of an Author* (26 Apr 1959); D. MOORE's *Wings of the Dove* (12 Oct 1961); CRUCIBLE; Jack Beeson's *Lizzie Borden* (25 Mar 1965); MISS JULIE; GIANNINI's *The Servant of Two Masters* (9 Mar 1967); Hugo Weisgall's *Nine Rivers Over Jordan* (9 Oct 1969); also US premieres of DUKE BLUEBEARD'S CASTLE; MOND; FIERY ANGEL; DANTONS TOD.

Columbia University, Brander Matthews Theater. Noteworthy for a brief period in which new works by US comps were given, aided by the Alice Ditson Memorial Fund. These incl.: Normand Lockwood, *The Scarecrow* (May 1945); MEDIUM (8 May 1946); MOTHER OF US ALL (7 May 1947); Otto Luening, *Evangeline* (comp. 1932, perf. 10 May 1948); Jan Meyerowitz, *The Barrier* (18 June 1950); D. MOORE, *Giants in the Earth* (28 Mar 1951).

Juilliard School of Music, the most highly endowed music school in the United States, now a part of LC, with an enterprising opera department. Several US premieres have been given there, among them CAPRICCIO, 1954, and MINES OF SULFUR, 1969. Musicians who have studied at Juilliard have found places in many major opera houses in America and Europe.

Manhattan Opera Company. Founded by HAMMERSTEIN I, opened 1906 in the Manhattan OH, which he built, and ran for four years as a serious rival to the Met, which eventually paid Hammerstein over $1,000,000 to discontinue prods. of opera in NY. Notable US premieres there were those of THAÏS, LOUISE, PELLÉAS ET MÉLISANDE and ELEKTRA; singers incl. GARDEN, NORDICA, TETRAZZINI, MCCORMACK, and ZENATELLO.

Metropolitan Opera House (Metropolitan Opera Association). Founded 1883 as a rival to the NY Academy of Music, with a roster of eminent singers, but after a year of resplendent sound and resounding deficit it went over to WAGNER under SEIDL and W. DAMROSCH. After 1886 an international repertory with prods unequalled anywhere gave the Met its worldwide renown. CARUSO appeared in 1903, SHALYAPIN in 1907; in 1908 TOSCANINI was apptd cond. and GATTI-CASAZZA manager. The latter reigned until 1935, followed by JOHNSON, 1935–50, succeeded by BING, 1950–72. When Bing retired GENTELE was appointed, but died (1972) before he could make his presence felt. The New Met in Lincoln Center was opened in 1966 with ANTONY AND CLEOPATRA. Schuyler Chapin followed Gentele; replaced in Jan 1975 by Anthony Bliss, Executive Dir., DEXTER, as Stage Dir., and LEVINE as chief cond. Current seasons of about 40 weeks, over 250 perfs of more than 20 operas, followed by a tour of six weeks and a June Fest. of 14 perfs in New York. Standard repertory with 19th-c. revivals and a limited number of new works, incl. RAKE'S PROGRESS, 1953; MOURNING BECOMES ELEKTRA, 1967; LAST SAVAGE, 1964; *Antony and Cleopatra,* 1966; DEATH IN VENICE, 1974; WOZZECK, 1974; JENŮFA, 1974.

Niblo's Garden. Orig. Sans Souçi T., opened at corner of Broadway and Prince Street in 1828 by William Niblo for summer variety shows. Opera seasons were given by visiting cos in the 1830s and 1840s. Burned down in 1846; rebuilt 1849. Here in 1866 was perf. *The Black Crook*, a spectacular song-and-dance show often cited as the forerunner of the Amer. MUSICAL. Seasons of ballet and opera given there occasionally until its closure in 1895. EJ/LO
See Kolodin, *The Metropolitan Opera 1883–1965* (New York 1966); Rubin, *The New Metropolitan in Profile* (New York 1974)

Nezhdanova, Antonina Vasilyevna, b. Krivaya Balka, nr Odessa, 29 July 1873; d. Moscow, 26 June 1950. Russian soprano. Studied with Umberto Mazetti at the Moscow Cons.; sang at the Bolshoy from 1902. In 1912 she appeared at the Paris O. One of the finest singers of the day, possessing a clear, coloratura voice and subtle acting ability. Known esp. for her Russian roles: the heroine in RUSLAN AND LYUDMILA, TATYANA, SNOW MAIDEN, Volkhova (SADKO), the Queen of Shemakhan (GOLDEN COCKEREL), Antonida (IVAN SUSANIN), Marfa (TSAR'S BRIDE); and also for many Western characters, including GILDA and ELSA. GN

Nibelungenlied, a combination of two German 13th-c. poems, the Burgundian cycle and the Brünnhilde cycle, telling the story of Siegfried and incl. elements found also in earlier Norse sagas and poems; the basis of several 19th-c. Ger. plays and in particular of WAGNER's tetralogy, RING DES NIBELUNGEN. LO
See Robertson, *A History of German Literature* (London 1953, 1970)

Niblo's Garden *see* NEW YORK

Nicaragua *see* LATIN AMERICA

Nice, France. Opera is given in the T. de l'Opéra, about six operas a season. Dir., Ferdinand Aymé. LO

Nicolai, Carl Otto Ehrenfried, b. Königsberg (now Kaliningrad), 9 June 1810; d. Berlin, 11 May 1849. German composer and conductor. Studied in Berlin; after a period in Rome moved to Vienna as principal cond. at KT (1837), returning to Italy 1838. His first opera *Enrico II* (Trieste 1839) failed, but his second, *Il Templario*, based on SCOTT's *Ivanhoe* (Turin 1840) became an international success. Appointed MdC of Vienna Hof O. 1841, and in 1847 MdC of Berlin Hof O., where on 9 Mar 1849 though seriously ill he cond. premiere of LUSTIGEN WEIBER VON WINDSOR. Two months later, the day he was elected a member of the Berlin Acad., he died of apoplexy. Other operas: *Odoardo e Gildippe* (Genoa 1841); *Il Proscritto* (Sc. 1841), reworked as *Die Heimkehr des Verbannten* (Vienna 1844). PS

Nicolini, also **Nicolino** [Niccolò or Nicola Grimaldi], b. Naples, Apr 1673; d. Naples, 1 Jan 1732. Italian male contralto, formerly soprano. One of the greatest singers of the 18th c. After being principal singer at Naples and singing elsewhere in Italy moved to London 1708. Created title part in RINALDO and perf. in other HANDEL operas. Was renowned for his acting as well as his singing. LO

Nielsen, Carl August, b. Nørre Lyndelse, Odense, 9 June 1865; d. Copenhagen, 3 Oct 1931. Danish composer. Studied Copenhagen; cond. of the Royal Danish O. there 1908–14. His two operas, *Saul og David* (1902) and MASKARADE, are still performed and are popular in Denmark. EF

Niemann, Albert, b. Erxleben, Magdeburg, 15 Jan 1831; d. Berlin, 13 Jan 1917. German tenor. Debut 1849, Dessau. After various engagements in Germany was at Berlin 1866–88. Sang in several WAGNER premieres: TANNHÄUSER, new version, Paris 1861; SIEGMUND, Bayreuth 1876 and London, 1882. At NY Met 1886–8 where he was first US TRISTAN and SIEGFRIED. LO

Nightingale, The (*Solovey*; *Le Rossignol*), opera, 3 acts, STRAVINSKY, lib. composer and Stepan Nikolayevich Mitusov after ANDERSEN. Paris, O., 26 May 1914; London, DL, 18 June 1914; NY Met, 6 Mar 1926. Between the composition of act 1 in Russia (1909) and acts 2 and 3 (1913–14), Stravinsky's style underwent considerable development with the ballets *The Firebird*, *Petrushka*, and *The Rite of Spring*, and the music to *The Nightingale* consequently displays a lack of unity; this Stravinsky managed to justify, at least to himself: 'the forest, with its nightingale, the pure soul of the child who falls in love with its song . . . all this gentle poetry . . . could not be expressed in the same way as the baroque luxury of the Chinese court; . . . all this exotic fantasy obviously demanded a different musical idiom'. Stravinsky also wrote a symphonic poem *Le Chant du Rossignol* (1917), based largely on mus. from Acts 2 and 3 of the opera, with the Fisherman's Song from Act 1. GN
See Kobbé

Nikisch, Artur, b. Lébényi Szant-Miklós, 12 Oct 1855; d. Leipzig, 23 Jan 1922. Hungarian conductor. Studied Vienna. Chorus master Leipzig 1877; chief cond. there 1879–89; dir. Budapest O. 1893–5. After that guest appearances incl. CG 1907 and 1913–14. Cond. of Leipzig Gewandhaus Orch. 1895–1922. LO

Nilsson, Birgit, b. Karup, 17 May 1918. Swedish soprano acclaimed as the outstanding WAGNER sop. of her time, the successor to FLAGSTAD. Studied Stockholm with HISLOP, joined Royal O. there; debut 1946 (AGATHE). Acquired wide repertory in Wagner and VERDI; won international fame from mid-1950s. Debuts: Glyndebourne Fest. 1951 as Elettra (IDOMENEO); Bayreuth Fest. 1954 (ELSA); Bavarian Staats O., Munich 1954–5 as Brünnhilde (WALKÜRE) and SALOME; Hollywood Bowl and San Francisco O. 1956 (Brünnhilde); London, CG, 1957 (Brünnhilde); Sc. 1958 (TURANDOT); NY Met 1959 (ISOLDE). Other roles closely associated with her incl. ELEKTRA, LADY MACBETH, LEONORE, Reiza in OBERON, and has sung both ELISABETH and VENUS at the same perf. She has the thrilling timbre, steely line, and powerful character of female singing at its most heroic. NG

Nilsson, Christine [Kristina], b. nr Växjö, 20 Aug 1843; d. Stockholm, 22 Nov 1921. Swedish soprano. Sang in Stockholm from an early age. Paris debut TL 1864, London debut HM 1867, both times as VIOLETTA. She created Ophelia in Ambroise THOMAS's HAMLET (Paris, O., 1868) and Edith in BALFE's *Talisman* (DL 1874). US debut Acad. of Music 1870, and sang MARGUERITE at the opening of the Met (1883). Her voice, immensely flexible and brilliant in timbre, easily encompassed roles as disparate as QUEEN OF THE NIGHT, ELSA and GIOCONDA. Her repertory incl. Donna ELVIRA (DON GIOVANNI), DESDEMONA (ROSSINI's), Lucia di Lammermoor, Mignon, and Margherita and Elena (MEFISTOFELE). EF

Nina, ou La Folle par Amour (*Nina, or Madness Through Love*), *comédie*, 1 act, *en prose mêlée d'ariettes*, DALAYRAC, lib. Benoît Joseph Marsollier. Paris, TI, 15 May 1786. A *comédie larmoyante*: Nina awaits her lover, who never arrives (he has been killed *en route*); her reason goes. Each day she walks to the trysting place; he is not there; but she will come again tomorrow. An early example of the mental disarray to become so popular a few years later. Marsollier's text formed the basis of It. operas by PAISIELLO (1789) and Pier Antonio Coppola (1835). Paisiello's was revived, Mantua 1974. LO

Birgit Nilsson as TURANDOT, London CG, 1970–1; produced Sandro Sequi; designed Cecil Beaton

Ninette à la Cour, ou Le Caprice Amoureux, (*Ninette at Court, or The Amorous Caprice*), *opéra comique*, 2 acts, DUNI, lib. FAVART. Parma 1755. Based on GOLDONI's *Bertoldo, Bertoldino e Cacasenno*, 1747. The simple Ninette succumbs to the glamour of courtly life, but is finally restored to her village lover. HILLER's *Singspiel, Lottchen am Hofe* (Leipzig 1767) is a Ger. version; the theme recurs frequently, e.g. ZERLINA. LO

Nissen, Hans Hermann, b. Danzig (now Gdańsk), 20 May 1893. German bass-baritone. Studied Berlin. Debut 1924, Berlin Volks O. Bavarian Staats O. at Munich 1925–67. Only CG appearances 1928, as WOTAN and HANS SACHS, his two most famous roles. NY Met 1938–9 as Wotan, WOLFRAM, TELRAMUND, and KURWENAL. Also sang at Sc., Vienna, and Berlin. One of the firmest, most sonorous heroic bass-bars of the interwar years. AB

Noble, Dennis, b. Bristol, 25 Sept 1899; d. Spain, 14 Mar 1966. English baritone. Studied Bristol. CG debut 1923 as SILVIO with the BNOC; sang there frequently until 1937, appreciably as GERMONT and in the roles of ESCAMILLO and Lescaut (MANON LESCAUT). Also sang with Carl Rosa, notably FIGARO (BARBIERE DI SIVIGLIA). One of the most sensitive and mellifluous British singers. AB

Nono, Luigi, b. Venice, 29 Jan 1924. Italian composer. Studied Venice with MALIPIERO, MADERNA, and SCHERCHEN. His opera INTOLLERANZA 1960 provoked a riot at its premiere in 1961, less for its advanced musical technique than for the political views of its lib. An updated version, *Intolleranza 1970*, was perf. in Germany. *Non Consumiamo Marx* received its first perf. in Paris (1969); *Al Gran Sale Carico d'Amore*, T. Lirico (staged Sc.), Milan, 4 Apr 1975. EF

No, No, Nanette!, operetta, Vincent Youmans, book Otto Harbach and Frank Mandel, lyrics Irving Caesar and Otto Harbach. London, Palace T., 11 May 1925; NY, Globe T., 16 Sept 1925; dances Busby Berkeley. Revived NY, 46th Street T., 19 Jan 1971. EJ ○★
See Lubbock; also Dunn, *The Making of 'No, No, Nanette!'* (New York and London 1972)

Nordica [Norton], Lillian, b. Farmington, Maine, 12 May 1857; d. Batavia, Java, 10 May 1914. American soprano. Studied New England Cons. of Music, Boston; began as a concert singer in USA and London. Operatic debut 1879, Milan (TRAVIATA). Engagements in Berlin, Danzig, and St Petersburg led to appearances at Paris O. 1882 (GOUNOD's FAUST, Ambroise THOMAS's HAMLET), and NY debut 1883, at the Acad. of Music with Mapleson's Co. After a brief first marriage (her husband was killed in a balloon accident) she sang at CG 1887 (VIOLETTA) and during the next ten seasons. So far she had confined her singing to the Fr. and It. repertory, but her rich voice was ideally suited to WAGNER, and in 1889 she sang ELSA at CG, repeating this at Bayreuth in 1894 – the first US singer there. Subsequently she made BRÜNNHILDE and ISOLDE her great roles, and was acclaimed as one of the finest Wagner singers of her day. In 1913 she began a farewell tour round the world; her ship was wrecked near Java, where she died. LO

Lillian Nordica as BRÜNNHILDE, one of her most famous roles

Norena, Eide [Kaia Hansen Eide], b. Horten, Norway, 26 Apr 1884; d. Monthei, VS, Switzerland, 13 Nov 1968. Norwegian soprano. Studied Oslo, Weimar, London, Paris. Debut Oslo, in ORPHÉE ET EURYDICE; first really made her name at Sc. under TOSCANINI (GILDA, 1924). Sang at CG for several seasons, also at Chicago 1926–8, and NY Met 1933–8. A fine actress and musicianly singer, she specialized in It. roles; she excelled as Gilda and was 'an extraordinarily beautiful and moving DESDEMONA'. LO

Norina, sop., the young widow in DON PASQUALE

Norma, opera, 2 acts, BELLINI, lib. ROMANI after Louis Alexandre Soumet. Milan, Sc., 26 Dec 1831; London, King's T., 26 June 1833; New Orleans, 1 Apr 1836. Main chars: Norma (sop.) Adalgisa (sop. or mezzo-sop.) Pollione (ten.) Oroveso (bass). Norma, a Druid priestess, discovers an intrigue between the young novice, Adalgisa, and Pollione, a Roman proconsul, the father of her own two children. Having vainly tried to induce him to renounce Adalgisa, Norma accuses herself publicly of having betrayed her country and religion. She is condemned to be burned alive: Pollione, moved by her courage, decides to share her fate. Bellini's most famous opera. JB ○
See Kobbé

Norman, Jessye, b. Augusta, Ga., 1935. American soprano. Won singing awards as univ. student (Washington DC) and teacher (Univ of Michigan); began European career after winning first prize in Bavarian Radio international competition, Munich 1968. Joined Deutsche O., Berlin, 1969; debut there (ELISABETH). Other debuts: Florence Maggio Musicale 1971 (AFRICAINE; title role); Sc. 1972 (AIDA); CG 1972 as Cassandre (TROYENS). Has continued

Above: Norma. PASTA in the title role; DONZELLI as Pollione, and Giulia GRISI as Adalgesa, in the premiere, Milan, Scala, 26 Dec 1831

to parallel operatic career as concert and *Lieder* singer, esp. in Fr. repertory (initially studied with Pierre Bernac). Admired for musical sensitivity supported by generous personality and physical presence. NG

Norway. Apart from ballad operas such as *Fjeldeventyret* (*The Mountain Adventure*) by Waldemar Thrane, which was given a concert perf. 1824 and first staged at Christiania (now Oslo) 1850, Norwegian opera did not really come into existence until the beginning of the 20th c. Ole Olsen (1850–1927) wrote four operas, but only one, *Lajla*, was prod. (Oslo 1908), when it shared the bill with the first stage prod. of Edvard Grieg's unfinished opera, *Olaf Trygvason* (begun as early as 1873). Christian Sinding (1856–1941) wrote an opera, *Der Heilige Berg*, to a German text (Dessau 1914; concert perf. Oslo 1931, with FLAGSTAD). Sigwardt Aspestrand (1856–1941) and Gerhard Schjelderup (1859–1933) both comp. operas which were perf. in Germany. Arne Eggen's (1881–1955) very popular *Olav Liljekrans* was first prod. at the Oslo NT 1940, and Ludvig Paul Irgens Jensen (b. Oslo, 1894) also had several operas staged there: *Kong Baldvines Armring* (1935), *Driftekaren*, *Mennesket*, and *Robin Hood* (1945); *Heimferd*, an oratorio first perf. Trondheim 1930, was adapted as an opera at Oslo 1947. EF

Nose, The (*Nos*), opera, 3 acts, SHOSTAKOVICH, lib. composer and others after GOGOL. Leningrad, Maly, 18 Jan 1930; Sante Fe Opera, 11 Aug 1965; London, SW, 4 Apr 1973. Main chars: Kovalyov (bar.) Yakovlevich (bass-bar.) Police Inspector (high ten.) the Nose (ten.) Madame Podtochina (mezzo-

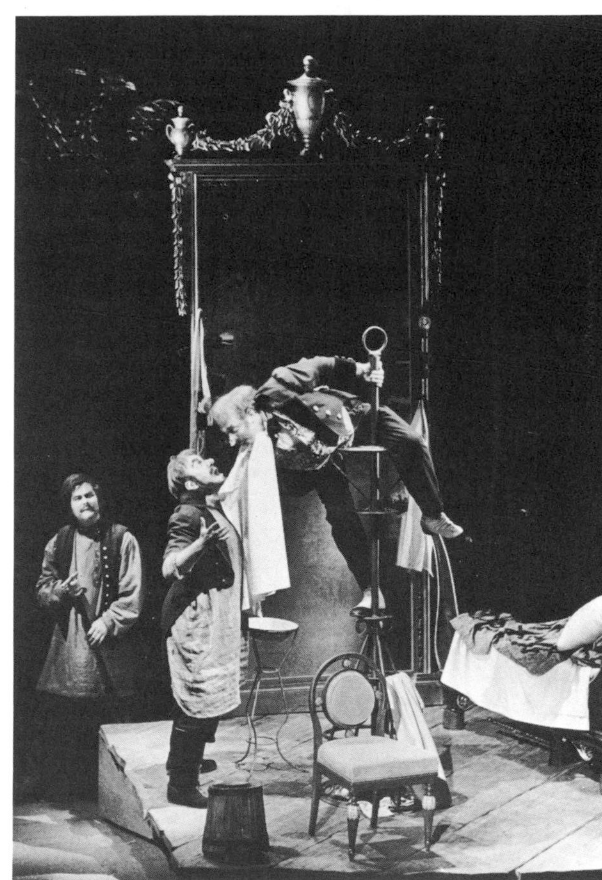

Right: The Nose, Berlin Staats O., 23 Feb 1969: Reiner Sülz as Kovalyov; Peter Olesch as Yakovlevich; Peter Bindseus as Ivan, Koyalyov's servant; produced Erhard Fischer; designed Wilfried Werz

sop.). Yakovlevich finds a nose in his breakfast roll; he tries to dispose of it, but is arrested by the Police Inspector. Kovalyov, a civil servant, finds that his nose is missing; on his way to inform the police he sees the Nose in the cathedral, but it escapes. He tries to advertise for the Nose, but the newspaper refuses to accept the advertisement. Then the Nose is returned by the police, but Kovalyov cannot make it stay on his face; he suspects that Madame Podtochina has cast a spell because he shows no interest in her daughter, but she denies it. Finally the Nose is restored to its proper place, and Kovalyov strolls happily along the Nevsky Prospekt. The sharp, satirical comedy and the extreme complexity of the score proved unacceptable in the anti-formalist atmosphere generated during the 1930s, and the opera quickly disappeared from the Soviet repertory. It was revived by the Moscow Chamber Music T. in 1974. GN

Nourrit, Adolphe, b. Paris, 3 Mar 1802; d. Naples, 8 Mar 1839. French tenor, son of Louis Nourrit (1780–1831), also a ten. at the Paris O. and a diamond merchant, who intended his son for the business. Studied with GARCÍA I, debut 1821 Paris O. as Pylade (IPHIGÉNIE EN TAURIDE). Succeeded his father there as principal ten. 1826, but DUPREZ's appointment (1837) caused him to leave Paris. Sang for a time in Italy, but became a prey to melancholia and committed suicide by jumping from his hotel window. Created the roles of ARNOLD, ROBERT LE DIABLE, ELÉAZAR and Raoul (HUGUENOTS). Also wrote book for the ballet *La Sylphide*. LO

Novák, Vítězslav, b. Kamenice nad Lipou, 5 Dec 1870; d. Skuteč, 18 July 1949. Czech composer. While studying law he attended Prague Cons. (1889–92) under DVOŘÁK and BENDL, and from 1908 taught at the Cons., taking master classes in composition from 1918. In his day he was a leading Czech comp. and one of the most accomplished and respected, but after World War I he was eclipsed by the older JANÁČEK. Though a full-blown Romantic in his youth and later influenced by French Impressionism, all his four operas have libs by Czech authors and deal with Czech subjects. The most popular, *Karlštejn* (1916) and *The Lantern* (*Lucerna*, 1923), have strong patriotic elements. His other operas are the 1-act *Imp of Zvíkov* (*Zvíkovský rarášek*, 1915) and *The Grandfather's Heritage* (*Dědův odkaz*, 1926). JT

Colour plate: Alexandra Hunt as Curley's wife and William Neill as Lennie, in OF MICE AND MEN, St Paul Opera Assn, 1970

Novello, Clara (Anastasia), b. London, 10 June 1818; d. Rome, 12 Mar 1908. English soprano. Daughter of Vincent Novello, at the age of three sang MOZART and HANDEL arias. Studied with Alexandre Étienne Choron in Paris 1829; first public appearance at Worcester Fest. 1833, in oratorio. Operatic debut 1841, Padua (SEMIRAMIDE). Sang PACINI's *Saffo* and ACIS AND GALATEA (London 1843), after which she m. Count Gigliucci and retired. Circumstances forced her to return in 1850 at principal oratorio fests. Her last stage appearance in Britain was in PURITANI (DL 1853). She had a voice of 'silvery sweetness' ranging from C below the stave to high D. PS

Novels as bases for operas. The first important opera founded on the 'novel' was BUONA FIGLIUOLA, 1760, derived from Samuel Richardson's *Pamela*, 1740 (previously used by DUNI, 1757). This was followed in 1765 by TOM JONES, based on Henry Fielding's novel, 1749. The earliest work to be so used is PRÉVOST's *Manon*, 1731. Some of the more important novelists are SCOTT; Stendhal, 1783–1842 (*La Chartreuse de Parme*, SAUGUET); Alessandro Manzoni, 1785–1873 (*I Promessi Sposi*, PONCHIELLI, Enrico Petrella, 1869); GOETHE; DICKENS; Herman Melville, 1819–91 (BILLY BUDD); DOSTOYEVSKY; DUMAS; TOLSTOY; FLAUBERT; GOGOL; HUGO; MÉRIMÉE; George du Maurier, 1834–96 (PETER IBBETSON); ZOLA; Anatole France, 1844–1924 (THAÏS; Charles Levadé's *La Rôtisserie de la Reine Pédauque*, 1920) Thomas Hardy, 1840–1928 (*Tess of the D'Urbervilles*, d'Erlanger, 1906); Joseph Conrad, 1857–1924 (VICTORY); LORCA; KAFKA. LO

Novotná, Jarmila, b. Prague, 27 Sept 1907. Czech soprano. Studied Prague with DESTINN; debut there 1926 (VIOLETTA). Berlin Staats O. 1928, Vienna Staats O. 1933–8, Salzburg Fest. 1935–7, NY Met 1939–53; debut there in BOHÈME and much admired as Violetta, CHERUBINO, and OCTAVIAN. Created title role in GIUDITTA. One of the most intelligent and characterful acting singers of her day. AB

Nozze di Figaro, Le (*The Marriage of Figaro*), *dramma giocoso*, 4 acts, MOZART, lib. da PONTE after BEAUMARCHAIS's *La Folle Journée, ou le Mariage de Figaro*, 1778. Vienna, BT, 1 May 1786: revived there 29 Aug 1789 with two sop. arias substituted; London, HM, 18 June 1812; NY, Park T., 10 May 1824. Main chars: Figaro (bass or bar.) Susanna (sop.) Countess (sop.) Count (bar.) Bartolo (bass) Marcellina (sop. or mezzo-sop.) Cherubino (sop. or mezzo-sop.) Basilio (ten.). Count Almaviva, pursuing the maid Susanna, tries to prevent her marriage to Figaro, but is continually thwarted. The most 'human' of Mozart's three comic operas writ-

Le Nozze di Figaro, London, CG, 7 Jan 1976, produced COPLEY; scenery Stefano Lazaridis; costumes Michael Stennett; Julia Hamaii as Cherubino; LORENGAR as the Countess; STRATAS as Susanna

ten with da Ponte (*see* DON GIOVANNI, COSÌ FAN TUTTE) and the least dependent on star singers. JB O★
See Kobbé

Nuitter [Truinet], Charles Louis Étienne, b. Paris, 24 Apr 1828; d. Paris, 24 Feb 1899. French librettist and historian of opera, archivist at the O. from 1865. Wrote libs for operas and operettas incl. some for LECOCQ and OFFENBACH, and tr. numerous It. and Ger. libs into Fr. for the TL (OBERON, ZAUBERFLÖTE, COLA RIENZI, etc.). His most important book is *Les Origins de l'Opéra Français* (with Ernest Thoinan, Paris 1886). LO

Oberon, or the Elf-King's Oath, opera, 3 acts, C. WEBER, lib. in Eng. PLANCHÉ, from WIELAND's poem based on the story *Huon de Bordeaux* in *La Bibliothèque Bleue*. London, CG, 12 Apr 1826 with PATON, VESTRIS, BRAHAM, Weber cond.; NY, Park T., 9 Oct 1828. The music has been revised Franz Gläser, BENEDICT, MAHLER among others. Main chars: Huon (ten.) Reiza (sop.) Sherasmin (bar.) Fatima (mezzo-sop.) Oberon (ten.). Oberon and Titania quarrel. She swears never to return until he finds two lovers who will remain faithful despite all obstacles. Oberon chooses Sir Huon and Reiza who undergo, with Oberon's help, shipwreck, capture by pirates, slavery and sentence of death before Oberon and Titania, reconciled, save them and transport them to Charlemagne's court. The culmination of Weber's career; considered a cornerstone of Ger. Romantic opera. The cumbersome lib. has been subject to many revisions, most recently Wexford Fest. 1972, without success. PS O
See Kobbé

Colour plate: Members of the chorus in Cecil Beaton's classic Ascot scene from the film directed by George Cukor of MY FAIR LADY (1964)

Oberto, Conte di San Bonifacio, opera, 2 acts, VERDI, lib. Temistocle Solera, probably based on Antonio Piazza's lib., *Rocester*. Milan, Sc., 17 Nov 1839. Main chars: Leonora (sop. or mezzo-sop.) Cuniza (contr.) Riccardo (ten.) Oberto (bass). Oberto returns from exile to fight a duel with Riccardo, his daughter's seducer, who is about to marry another woman. Oberto is killed and Riccardo flees the country. Verdi's first opera. JB

Obukhova, Nadezhda Andreyevna, b. Moscow, 6 Mar 1886; d. Feodosiya, 15 Aug 1961. Russian mezzo-soprano Studied Moscow Cons. under Umberto Mazetti, then sang at the Bolshoy T. (1916–48). Among her most famous roles were Marfa (KHOVANSHCHINA), DALILA, and FRICKA. A radio recital of hers is the subject of a conversation in Aleksandr Isayevich Solzhenitsyn's *The First Circle*. GN

Oca del Cairo, L' (*The Goose of Cairo*), unfinished *opera buffa*, MOZART, lib. Giovanni Battista Varesco. Main chars: Don Pippo (bar.) Celidora (sop.) Lavina (sop.) Brondello (ten.) Calandrino (ten.) Auretta (sop.) Chichibio (ten.). A typical roundabout of amorous intrigue. Begun in 1783; seven numbers in various stages of completion. JB

Ochs, Baron, bass, the Marschallin's cousin in ROSENKAVALIER

Octavian, sop., the hero of ROSENKAVALIER

Odessa *see* UKRAINE

Oedipus der Tyrann (*Oedipus the Tyrant*), opera, 3 acts, ORFF, lib. Friedrich Hölderlin's tr. of SOPHOCLES. Württemberg Staats O., Stuttgart, 11 Dec 1959. The second of Orff's trilogy of Gr. drama. LO O

Oedipus Rex, opera-oratorio, 2 acts, STRAVINSKY, lib. COCTEAU after SOPHOCLES, tr. into Latin Jean Daniélou. Paris, T. Sarah Bernhardt, 30 May 1927 (concert perf.); Vienna, 23 Feb 1928; Philadelphia, Metropolitan OH, 10 Apr 1931; Edinburgh, 21 Aug 1956. Stravinsky dispenses with all but the bare minimum of stage action (the masked characters move only their head and arms, giving 'the impression of living statues'); and this enhances the effectiveness of the lib., which is deliberately

written in a dead language to lend the tragedy a timeless quality. GN O
See Kobbé

Oenslager, Donald, b. Harrisburg, Pa., 7 Mar 1902; d. Bedford, NY, 20 June 1975. American designer and historian of stage design. His more than 150 sets include a number of Broadway prods and a wide variety of designs for the NY Met and CC operas beginning with SALOME and TRISTAN UND ISOLDE at the Met, 1934, then VERDI's OTELLO, 1935. For CC his designs have included TRAVIATA, 1942, FIDELIO, 1947, SCHÖNE GALATHEE, 1951, BOHÈME and CARMEN, 1952, BALLAD OF BABY DOE, 1956 and MIKADO, 1959. For Yale Univ., where for some time he was Professor of T., he designed DIDO AND AENEAS and MARTINŮ's *Comedy on a Bridge*, 1952. LO
See his *Stage Design* (London and NY, 1975)

Offenbach, Jacques [Jakob Eberst], b. Cologne, 20 June 1819; d. Paris, 4 Oct 1880. German composer, lived in France from 1833. After studying at the Cons. and with J. F. HALÉVY his first post was as cond. at the Comédie Française, 1850–5. In 1855 he opened his own theatre, the Bouffes-Parisiens, where his first *opérette*, *Les Deux Aveugles* (1855) was prod. It was followed by nearly 100 more, some of the best known being BELLE HÉLÈNE, *Les Brigands*, 1869, GRANDE DUCHESSE DE GÉROLSTEIN, ORPHÉE AUX ENFERS, VIE PARISIENNE, *Robinson Crusoé*, 1867, and PÉRICHOLE. CONTES D'HOFFMANN, his last work, left unfinished at his death, stands apart from the rest, being his one attempt to move outside the operetta. His works had a significant influence on the Viennese J. STRAUSS and SUPPÉ as well as on the London musical comedy of CELLIER and SULLIVAN; the best of them have never lost their appeal. LO
See Kracauer, *Offenbach and the Paris of his Time* (London 1937)

Of Mice and Men, opera, 3 acts, FLOYD, lib. composer, based on novel by John Steinbeck. Seattle O., 20 Jan 1970. Two ranch workers, George and Lennie, look forward to buying a ranch of their own, but the half-witted Lennie commits murder and George, rather than have him face trial, shoots him. LO

Of Thee I Sing, musical, GERSHWIN, book Morrie Riskin and George Kaufman. NY, Music Box T., 26 Dec 1931. Wintergreen and Throttlebottom run for President on a platform of Love. The first musical to win a Pulitzer Prize. EJ O
See Lubbock

Jacques Offenbach. Music sheet for *Les Deux Aveugles*, which opened Offenbach's theatre, the Bouffes-Parisiens, in 1855

Ohana, Maurice, b. Gibraltar, 12 June 1914. French composer of Spanish origin. Studied in Barcelona, Paris, and Rome. His dramatic works include *Chanson de Toile*, a marionette opera (Paris 1960), *Syllabaire pour Phèdre* (Paris 1969), a radio opera, *Grida*, which won the Italia prize in 1969, and *Auto-da-Fe* (Lyon 1972). EF

Oklahoma!, musical, RODGERS, book and lyrics HAMMERSTEIN II based on a novel, *Green Grow the Lilacs*, by Lynn Riggs, dances Agnes de Mille. NY, St James T., 31 Mar 1943; London, DL, 30 Apr 1947. Revived 1969 NY CC. EJ O★
See Lubbock

Olczewska [Berchtenbreitner], Maria, b. Augsburg, 12 Aug 1892; d. Klagenfurt, 17 May 1969. German mezzo-soprano. Began career in operetta; heard by NIKISCH who engaged her for Leipzig; debut there 1920. Debut Vienna Staats O. 1923; first CG appearance as Herodias (SALOME); sang there regularly until 1932 in

Wagnerian roles, also OCTAVIAN and CARMEN. NY Met debut as BRANGÄNE (1932), having sung at Chicago since 1928. Her voice was a warm, rich mezzo and she was a good actress. She m. the heroic baritone Emil Schipper. AB

Old Maid and the Thief, The, opera, 1 act, MENOTTI, lib. composer. NY, commissioned NBC, radio, 22 Apr 1939. Staged Philadelphia, 11 Feb 1941. Main chars: Miss Todd (contr.) Laetitia (sop.) Miss Pinkerton (sop.) Bob (bar.). A young man, befriended by three adoring ladies, departs in his own good time and in the process takes everything of value he can lay his hands on. EJ

Old Vic Theatre *see* LONDON

Olimpiade, L', one of the most popular of METASTASIO's libs, first set by CALDARA, 1733, followed by PERGOLESI, HASSE, PAISIELLO, CIMAROSA, and *c.* 30 other comps in the 18th c. LO

Olivero, Magda, b. Saluzzo, 1914. Italian soprano. Debut Turin as LAURETTA (1933); sang regularly in It. opera houses, where her ADRIANA LECOUVREUR, VIOLETTA, and LIÙ were much admired, until an early retirement in 1941 when she married. Returned to the stage as Adriana in 1950–1 season. London debut at Stoll T. as MIMI (1952). US debut as Medea (MEDEA IN CORINTO) at Dallas (1967). In reputedly her final stage appearances, she made her Met debut as TOSCA (1975). A fine singing actress. AB

Olympia, sop., Hoffmann's first love in CONTES D'HOFFMANN

Olympians, The, opera, 3 acts, BLISS, lib. J. B. Priestley. London, CG, 29 Sept 1949; RFH, 21 Feb 1972. Main chars: Diana (sop.) Madeleine (sop.) Mme Bardeau (mezzo-sop.) Hector (ten.) Curé (ten.) Bacchus (ten.) Jupiter (bar.) Mars (bass) Lavette (bass). The Olympian gods and goddesses, now a company of strolling players, regain for one night their ancient power and glory. EF

Olympie, grand opera, 3 acts, SPONTINI, lib. Michael Dieulafoy and Charles Brifaut after VOLTAIRE. Paris, O., 22 Dec 1819; revised version Berlin, 14 May 1821; final version Paris, O., 28 Feb 1826. Main chars: Olympie (sop.) Statire (mezzo-sop.) Cassandre (ten.) Antigone (bass). The plot concerns the rivalry of Alexander the Great's successors for the hand of his daughter Olympie. Cassandre, her own choice, is opposed by Alexander's widow Statire, disguised as a priestess, who is convinced that he poisoned her husband. In a battle with Cassandre's troops Antigone is mortally wounded and dies confessing to Alexander's murder. The lovers are united and Statire enthroned as supreme ruler. JB

O'Mara, Joseph, b. Limerick, 16 July 1866; d. ?5 Aug 1927. Irish tenor. Debut 1891, in IVANHOE; later sang at CG and DL, then with Moody-Manners, then founded his own opera co. Retired 1926. LO

Oncina, Juan, b. Barcelona, 15 Apr 1925. Spanish tenor. Studied Barcelona with Mercedes Capsir; debut there as DES GRIEUX (MANON), 1946. Sang throughout It. in ROSSINI and DONIZETTI repertory 1946–52 and at Glyndebourne 1952–61. Later sang heavier parts with less distinction. An outstanding interpreter of COMTE ORY, Ramiro (HEURE ESPAGNOLE), and Lindoro (ITALIANA IN ALGERI). AB

Onegin [Hoffmann], Sigrid, b. Stockholm, 1 July 1891; d. Magliaso, Switzerland, 16 June 1943. Swedish contralto. Debut Stuttgart, 1922, as CARMEN. Appeared Munich, Berlin, NY Met (debut there 1922, AMNERIS) and CG, singing all the great contr. roles. Sang in premiere of ARIADNE AUF NAXOS. LO

Open-air performances. Some of LULLY's operas were perf. in the garden at Versailles, and in Vienna and Prague some of FUX's operas were mounted with great splendour out of doors. PROMÉTHÉE was one of several perf. at Béziers Arena, 1900. Today places offering open-air perfs incl. Aix-en-Provence, Bregenz, Chicago (Ravinia Park), Cincinnati (Zoo Opera), Dubrovnik, Florence (Boboli Gardens), Orange, Rome (Caracalla Baths), and Verona. LO

opéra-ballet, term used by 18th-c. Fr. composers, esp. RAMEAU, to describe stage works combining ballet with some (perhaps rudimentary) drama. Examples: INDES GALANTES; *Les Fêtes d'Hébé*, 1739; CAMPRA's *Europe Galante*, 1697. The genre is similar to the COMÉDIE-BALLET of LULLY. LO

opéra bouffe (Fr.), *opera buffa* (It.), comic opera (It. *buffo*, 'comedian'). Terms applied esp. in 18th c. *Opéra bouffe* usually has spoken dialogue, *opera buffa* has *recitativo secco* (*see* RECITATIVE). LO

Opéra-Comique *see* PARIS

opéra comique (Fr. 'comic opera'), *c.* 1790–*c.* 1900 used to denote a genre that involves set numbers linked by spoken dialogue, a wide variety of musical forms and sometimes a tragic plot (e.g. CARMEN in its original form). JB

Opéra du Rhin, an association of opera houses of Colmar, Mulhouse, and Strasbourg, formed 1972 to coordinate and combine prods. Admin. dir., Jean-Pierre Wurtz; Art. dir., LOMBARD. Nathaniel Merrill is resident designer. LO

Opera handbooks. Hugo Riemann's *Opernhandbuch* (Leipzig 1887) was followed in Germany by several other 'guides', giving résumés of the action and sometimes notes on the music of standard operas, a practice soon copied in Britain and the USA. The best known is KOBBÉ's *Complete Opera Book* (New York and London 1919 and later editions). NEWMAN's three volumes contain more detailed essays. Others are George W. Martin's *The Opera Companion* (London 1964, New York 1970), *The Pan Book of Opera*, ed. Arthur Jacobs and Stanley Sadie (London 1969, published New York 1972 as *Opera: A Modern Guide*), and the *Harrap Opera Guide*, ed. Sir Alexander Morley (London 1970, New York 1971). For light opera, Mark Lubbock's *Complete Book of Light Opera* (New York and London 1962) is indispensable. LO

opera seria (It. 'serious opera'), in the 18th c. a technical term for an operatic genre with certain fixed conventions: e.g. plots that involve noble or mythological characters, long formal arias, *castrato* singers, and a conception of music drama as a succession of contrasting emotional states. JB

Operetta. Francis (Francisco) Lopez's (b. 1916) *Gipsy*, performed Paris, 17 Feb 1972; José Todaro, surrounded by Bohemians

Right: opéra comique. DIAMANTS DE LA COURONNE, premiere at Paris OC, 6 Mar 1841

operetta, opérette (It., Fr. 'little opera'), virtually synonymous with light opera and musical comedy. The 'little' applies to dramatic and musical pretensions rather than length; the plots are romantic or improbable, even farcical, the music tuneful and undemanding, usually with spoken dialogue, the whole often of considerable artistry. Typical comps are FALL, LEHÁR, OFFENBACH, STRAUS, J. STRAUSS, SULLIVAN, and SUPPÉ. LO
See Hughes, *Composers of Operetta* (London and New York 1962)

Orchestra. Its basic shape for opera is due to LULLY, namely a core of strings, oboes and/or flutes added for pastoral scenes, trumpets and timpani for warlike effects. From the first it was used not simply as an accompaniment but to colour the dramatic situation. Since then there has been a consistent expansion of the orchestra, and by RAMEAU's time there were complaints that it was too noisy. New instruments were added: the horn, for hunting scenes, from *c.* 1720; trombones, for solemnity (GLUCK used them in ORFEO ED EURIDICE, 1762). The clarinet appeared sporadically from *c.* 1750, but its full value was not realized until MOZART. By now the wind instruments had become a family, so that it was possible, as in ZAUBERFLÖTE, to accompany soloists or chorus with a wind 'choir'. The 19th c. saw yet larger orchestras, until with WAGNER and esp. R. STRAUSS they had swollen to *c.* 100 players, requiring a vast orchestra pit and threatening singers' audibility – a problem solved at Bayreuth by covering the orchestra completely. Besides its function as accompanist and its illustrative function (in evidence as early as Lully), it is a distinct auxiliary to the drama, reinforcing or contradicting what happens on stage, throwing in comments and interjections; and in Wagner's music-dramas its tissue of *Leitmotive* almost usurps the singers' prerogatives. In 19th-c. Italian opera the orchestra remains more subservient to the singer; nevertheless its three roles – accompaniment, illustration, dramatic significance – are still noticeable, if held in check by fairly strict conventions, no sop. for example being allowed to take leave of her senses unless accompanied by her faithful flute. LO

Orfeo (MONTEVERDI) *see* FAVOLA D'ORFEO; for other operas on the Orpheus legend *see* ORFEO ED EURIDICE and under titles with ORPHÉE

Orfeo ed Euridice, *azione teatrale*, 3 acts, GLUCK, lib. CALZABIGI. Vienna, BT., 5 Oct 1762; London, King's T., with additional music by J. C. BACH and Pietro Guglielmi, 7 Apr 1770. Though GUADAGNI, the original *castrato* Orfeo, sang again here, the addition of fresh music and several new characters must have made this something of a travesty. For other revivals *see* ORPHÉE ET EURYDICE. This was Gluck's first 'reform' opera, published, with an important preface, in Paris in 1764. LO O

Orff, Carl, b. Munich, 10 July 1895. German composer. His stage works, plays with music rather than true operas, have aroused controversy. The most important of them are CARMINA BURANA, MOND, KLUGE, *Antigonae*, 1949, BERNAUERIN, and OEDIPUS DER TYRANN. His interest in folk material and his search for the elemental in drama led to a simplicity of utterance opposed alike to Wagnerian complexity and the involved language of *avant-garde* comps, but his works have yet to become absorbed in the general operatic repertory. LO
See Liess, *Carl Orff* (London and New York 1966)

Orgeni [Görger St Jorgen], Anna Maria Aglaia, b. Rimaszombat (now Rimavská Sobota), 17 Dec 1841; d. Vienna, 15 Mar 1926. Hungarian soprano, pupil of VIARDOT. Debut Berlin, 1865, in SONNAMBULA. Sang only one season at CG (1866); subsequently went to Vienna; was also heard at Leipzig, Hanover, Dresden, and elsewhere. A singer and actress of distinction, she ended her career as a notable singing teacher in Vienna. LO

Oriental and exotic subjects. The New World made an appeal in the 18th c. (MONTEZUMA, HURON, and a little later FERNAND CORTEZ) as did the Orient (GLUCK's *Le Cinesi*, 1754), influencing decor and costumes but with little impact on the music. In the late 19th c. Japan inspired a number of operas and operettas, e.g. MADAMA BUTTERFLY and MIKADO. India furnished themes for ROI DE LAHORE, LAKMÉ, PADMÂVATÎ, and SĀVITRI; Egypt and Arabia, popular since RENCONTRE IMPRÉVUE, have suggested comedies such as BARBIER VON BAGDAD and MÂROUF, the dramatic AIDA as well as colouring ZAUBERFLÖTE. Orientalism and exoticism were exploited by the Russians instinctively, demonstrated brilliantly in the operatic works of both BORODIN and RIMSKY-KORSAKOV. LO

Ormindo, L', opera, 3 acts, CAVALLI, lib. Giovanni Battista Faustini. Venice, T. S. Cassiano, Carnival 1644; New York, 24 Apr 1968. Other revivals at Glyndebourne (LEPPARD's realization), prod. RENNERT, 1967, and Scheveningen, 1970. LO O

ornamentation, the art of embellishing a melody. Ornaments may be written out by the comp., indicated by him with a symbol or added by the performer. In the 18th and early 19th c. singers and continuo players were expected to embellish far more freely than the printed notes suggest (*see also* APPOGGIATURA). JB

Oroveso, bass, the High Priest in NORMA

Orphée aux Enfers (*Orpheus in the Underworld*), *opéra féerie*, 2 acts, OFFENBACH, lib. Hector Crémieux and L. HALÉVY. Paris, T. Bouffes-Parisiens, 21 Oct 1858; NY, Stadttheater, Mar 1861; London, HM, tr. and adapted by PLANCHÉ as *Orpheus in the Haymarket*, 26 Dec 1863; SW, in Eng., tr. DUNN, 17 May 1960. An amusing skit on the Orpheus story, with a good lib. that launched shafts against the complacency of Second Empire Paris. One of Offenbach's best scores, it played for 228 perfs and set the seal on his reputation. LO

Orphée et Eurydice, *tragédie opéra*, 3 acts, GLUCK (his 1762 ORFEO, with alterations and additions), lib. Pierre-Louis Moline, tr. from CALZABIGI, with additions. Paris, O., 2 Aug 1774. A significant change was the casting of Orpheus as ten. in place of the original contr.; the opera was also lengthened, with additional ballets and arias. In 1859 BERLIOZ prepared a version restoring Orpheus as a contr. (for VIARDOT); this has been the basis of most sub-

sequent perfs: London, CG, 27 June 1860 (in It.); NY, Winter Garden, 25 May 1863. LO ○
See Kobbé

Orpheus. For operas based on this legend *see* FAVOLA D'ORFEO, ORFEO ED EURIDICE and under titles with ORPHÉE

Orpheus in the Underworld *see* ORPHÉE AUX ENFERS

Orr, Robin [Robert Kemsley], b. Brechin, 2 June 1909. Scottish composer. Chairman of SO, he has written a short opera, *Full Circle* (SO, Perth, 1968, also shown on TV). *Hermiston*, a full-length work adapted from the novel by R. L. Stevenson, was staged at the 1975 Edinburgh Fest. EF

Ortrud, mezzo-sop., Telramund's wife in LOHENGRIN

Oslo (formerly Christiania). Foreign touring companies have visited Oslo since the early 18th c. The Norwegian State Opera House opened in 1900 and Den Norske Oper (The Norwegian O.), with FLAGSTAD as its first dir., was established in 1959 (*see* NORWAY). EF

Osmin, bass, the keeper of the seraglio in ENTFÜHRUNG AUS DEM SERAIL

Ossian, ou les Bardes, opera, 5 acts, LESUEUR, lib. P. Dercy and Jacques Marie Deschamps. Paris, O., 10 July 1804. This, the first Ossian opera, was suggested by Napoleon, an enthusiastic admirer of 'Ossian' (really James MacPherson, 1736–96, whose alleged Ossianic poems had been published in the 1760s). The work included an effective 'dream scene' (Ossian seeing in a vision the heroes of his race) and a lavish palace scene '*d'un effet magique*'. Other Ossian operas include MÉHUL's *Uthal* (1806), WINTER's *Colmal* (1809) and Edgar Bainton's *Oithona* (Glastonbury Fest., 1915). LO

Osten, Eva von der, b. Heligoland, 19 Aug 1881; d. Dresden, 5 May 1936. German soprano. Studied Dresden; debut there and was principal sop. 1902–30. Created OCTAVIAN; stage-directed premiere of ARABELLA. In London, CG, in 1913–14, sang Octavian, ARIADNE AUF NAXOS, ISOLDE, SIEGLINDE, and KUNDRY. Also famous as TOSCA. She m. Friedrich Plaschke, leading bass at Dresden. FGB

Ostrava [Ostrau], Czechoslovakia. Regular operatic perfs took place from 1908 in the National House (built 1894) and, after the establishment of the Czechoslovak Republic in 1918, also in the German theatre (built 1908). This bigger theatre, bombed in World War II, was renovated and in 1948 renamed the Zdeněk Nejedlý T.; it has since been used only for opera, the smaller theatre for operetta and plays. The company was transformed under VOGEL (1927–43); notable successors include B. GREGOR and KOŠLER. JT

Ostrčil, Otakar, b. Prague, 25 Feb 1879; d. Prague, 20 Aug 1935. Czech composer and conductor. Studied modern languages at Prague Univ. and composition with FIBICH (1895–1900). After conducting an amateur orch., he became cond. at the Vinohrady T. in Prague (1914–19) and then head of opera at the Prague NT (1920–35). As KOVAŘOVIC's successor he renewed the repertory with modern international works (STRAVINSKY, SZYMANOWSKI, ROUSSEL, and early performances of WOZZECK, 1926) and consolidated it with cycles of MOZART, DVOŘÁK, SMETANA, Fibich, FOERSTER, and NOVÁK operas. He had a close friendship with JANÁČEK, introducing several of his operas to Prague and conducting the premiere of MR BROUČEK'S EXCURSIONS. As well as the very successful *Johnny's Kingdom* (*Honzovo království*, 1934), his own operas include *The Death of Vlasta* (*Vlasty skon*, 1904), *Kunala's Eyes* (*Kunálovy oči*, 1908), *The Bud* (*Poupě*, 1912), and *The Legend of Erin* (*Legenda z Erinu*, 1921). JT

Otello, opera, 4 acts, VERDI, lib. BOITO after SHAKESPEARE. Milan, Sc., 5 Feb 1887; NY, 16 Apr 1888; London, Lyceum T., 5 July 1889; Paris, O., 12 Oct 1894 with added ballet and modified finale to Act III. Main chars: Otello (tenor) Iago (bar.) Desdemona (sop.) Cassio (ten.). The plot follows Shakespeare's play apart from omitting the first, Venetian, act. The greatest tragic opera in the Italian repertoire. JB ○★
See Kobbé

Otello, ossia il Moro di Venezia (*Othello, or The Moor of Venice*), opera, 3 acts, ROSSINI, lib. Berio di Salsa after SHAKESPEARE. Naples, T. Fondo, 4 Dec 1816; London, King's T., 16 May 1822; NY, Park T., 7 Feb 1826. Main chars: Desdemona (sop.) Emilia (mezzo-sop.) Otello (ten.) Rodrigo (ten.) Iago (ten.) Elmiro (bass). Although requiring three virtuoso tenors, the opera remained popular until supplanted by VERDI'S OTELLO, for whose last act it had provided the pattern. JB

Ottavio, Don., ten., Donna Anna's lover in DON GIOVANNI

Ottawa *see* CANADA

Ouragan, L' (*The Hurricane*), opera, 4 acts, BRUNEAU, lib. (in prose) ZOLA. Paris, OC, 29 Apr 1901. Symbolic, the physical hurricane mirroring 'the inward tempest raging in the hearts of the main characters', themselves symbolic, representing three different aspects of love in the three heroines, quite different from the realism of ATTAQUE DU MOULIN. LO

Our Man in Havana, opera, 3 acts, WILLIAMSON, lib. Sidney Gilliat, based on novel by Graham Greene. London, SW, 2 July 1963. Main chars: Bramble (ten.) Milly (sop.) Beatrice (sop.) Segura (bar.) Hasselbacher (bass). A British vacuum-cleaner salesman, living in Cuba, becomes a secret agent to provide luxuries for his teenage daughter. Having no genuine information, he sends his superiors plans of 'secret installations' – in reality blown-up drawings of vacuum-cleaner components. EF

overture (Fr. *ouverture*, It. *apertura* 'opening'), instrumental music played before the opera begins. Originally just a short prelude as in FAVOLA D'ORFEO. LULLY developed the Fr. overture, a slow movement with a characteristic dotted rhythm followed by a quicker, usually contrapuntal, movement, often ending with a dance. The It. overture developed by A. SCARLATTI used the scheme quick, slow, quick. In the 19th c. the overture became more elaborate; it was sometimes built on material drawn from the following opera (e.g. in MEISTERSINGER, BARTERED BRIDE). A later development was to dispense with the overture and revert to the short prelude, as in TOSCA. Artistically the overture's function is to set the mood of the coming opera. LO

Owen Wingrave, opera, 2 acts, BRITTEN, lib. Myfanwy Piper, derived from a short story by JAMES. BBC TV, 24 May 1971; London, CG, 10 May 1973; Santa Fe, 9 Aug 1973. Main chars: Owen Wingrave (bar.) Kate Julian (mezzo-sop.) Lechmere (ten.) Coyle (bass-bar.). Britten originally conceived his setting of Henry James's mysterious story in televisual terms, but it transferred successfully to the stage. As in Britten's earlier operas, one figure, in this case the pacific Wingrave, is set against an uncomprehending society, his own militaristic family. The conflict is presented in bleakly black-and-white terms; the musical characterization of each side is strong. AB O

Oxford University Opera Club. Inaugurated in 1925 with a prod. of FAVOLA D'ORFEO, ed. and cond. J. A. Westrup, the Club has staged INCORONAZIONE DI POPPEA, CASTOR ET POLLUX, DEVIL AND KATE, IDOMENEO, CLEMENZA DI TITO, TROYENS, HANS HEILING, JOLIE FILLE DE PERTH, *Men of Blackmoor* (BUSH), *Testament de la Tante Caroline* (ROUSSEL), *Rosinda* (CAVALLI), and the first performance of *Incognita* (Egon Wellesz, 1951). In 1975 *Favola d'Orfeo*, edited and conducted by Jane Glover, was presented again to celebrate the Club's 50th anniversary. EF

P

Pacchierotti, Gasparo, b. Fabriano, nr Ancona, *c.* 21 May 1740; d. Padua, 28 Oct 1821. Italian male soprano. Appeared at the principal opera houses in Italy and in London from 1769 to 1792; he was among the greatest *castrati* of his time, highly praised by BURNEY for the range of his voice and the perfection of his technique. LO

Pacini, Giovanni, b. Catania, Sicily, 17 Feb 1796; d. Pescia, 6 Dec 1867. Italian composer. Very popular in Italy, he wrote over 70 operas, the best known of which include *L'Ultimo Giorno di Pompei* (1825), *Saffo* (1840), and *Medea* (1843). LO

Padmâvatî, opera-ballet, 2 acts, ROUSSEL, lib. Louis Laloy, based on the Indian story of Padmâvatî, legendary Queen of Tchitor. Paris, O., 1 June 1923. Begun in 1914, it utilizes the Fr. mixture of opera and ballet popular ever since LULLY. Roussel's first and most successful stage work. LO
See Deane, *Albert Roussel* (London 1961)

Paer, Ferdinando, b. Parma, 1 June 1771; d. Paris, 3 May 1839. Italian composer. Trained in Parma; MdC in Venice (1790–8), Vienna (1798–1803), Dresden (1803–6), and Paris (1807–14), which became his home. Dir. TI, 1812–27, latterly in partnership with ROSSINI. With G. S. MAYR, Paer was one of the two foremost practitioners of It. opera in the generation between PAISIELLO and Rossini, excelling particularly in *semi-seria.* Of his more than 40 operas the outstanding are: *Griselda* (Parma 1798), *Camilla* (Vienna 1799), *Achille* (Vienna 1801), *I Fuorusciti di Firenze* (Dresden 1803), *Sargino* (Dresden 1803), *Leonora* (Dresden 1804), *Sofonisba* (Bologna 1805), *Agnese di Fitzhenry* (Parma 1809). The satirical comedy, *Le Maître de Chapelle* (Paris 1821) is occasionally revived today. JB

Pagliacci (*The Strolling Players*), opera, prologue and 2 acts, LEONCAVALLO, lib. composer. Milan, T. dal Verme, 21 May 1892; London, CG, 19 May 1893; NY, Grand O. House, 15 June 1893. Main chars: Nedda (sop.) Canio (ten.) Tonio (bar.) Silvio (bar.) Beppo (ten.). Canio, leader of a troupe of strolling players, finds that his wife has a lover and murders her in the course of the play that they enact before the audience. Leoncavallo's most popular opera, usually coupled with CAVALLERIA RUSTICANA in a double bill of *verismo*. JB ○★
See Kobbé

Paisiello, Giovanni, b. Taranto, 8 May 1740; d. Naples, 5 June 1816. Italian composer. Trained at Naples Cons, he first made his name in the northern It. cities, settling in Naples in 1766 where he established himself as chief rival to PICCINNI with his *L'Idolo Cinese* (1767). At the court of Catherine the Great of Russia, 1776–84; his works there incl. BARBIERE DI SIVIGLIA. On his return he wrote *Il Re Teodoro di Venezia* (1784) for Vienna; that same year Ferdinand IV of Naples created him court MdC; during the next 15 years he prod. his finest works, *Pirro* (1787), *La Molinara* (1788), *Fedra* (1788), *Nina* (1789). Summoned to Paris by Napoleon (1801), a great admirer of his music. But *Proserpine* (T. de l'Opéra, 1803) was a failure. Returned finally to Naples 1804; died in comparative poverty.

The leading It. opera comp. of his generation, having written at least 83 works in a wide range of styles. Best known for his *opere buffe*, he shows in *Fedra* a mastery of the Fr.-It. genre of serious opera exploited by TRAETTA and, in IDOMENEO, by MOZART; *Nina* pioneers the sentimental *comédie larmoyante* that became so popular in the 19th c. JB

Palermo, Sicily. Its operatic history goes back to the 17th c. The T. Santa Lucia, built 1726, became in 1809 the Reale T. Carolina, and in 1860 the T. Bellini. The first opera house built and run by the municipality was the Politeama Garibaldi, opened 1874. Opera is now given in the big T. Massimo, opened in 1897 with FALSTAFF. LO

Palestrina, opera, 3 acts, PFITZNER, lib. composer. Munich, NT, 21 June 1917. Main chars: Palestrina (ten.) Cardinal Borromeo (bass-bar.). Tells how Palestrina saved the art of contrapuntal music in the 16th c. through the composition of his *Missa Papae Marcelli*, overcoming the conservatism represented by the not entirely unsympathetic figure of Borromeo. Palestrina's emotional and vocational struggle is depicted in acts 1 and 3, while act 2 is a lively and detailed portrait of the Council of Trent. This late Romantic score owes something to the inspiration of MEISTERSINGER, but Pfitzner had something peculiarly his own, conservative but never dull, to offer, and the score does not deserve its comparative neglect. Karl Erb and PATZAK have been famous interpreters of the title role. AB ○
See Kobbé

Paliashvili, Zakhary Petrovich, b. Kutaisi, 16 Aug 1871; d. Tbilisi, 6 Oct 1933. Georgian composer. After working in various Georgian churches he studied at Tbilisi Music College (1891–9), then with Sergey Taneyev at Moscow Cons. (1900–3). His interest in Georgian folklore is reflected in his monumental opera *Abesalom and Eteri* (1919), based on a Georgian legend and using idioms of Georgian folksong. He also composed TWILIGHT and *Latavra* (1928). GN

Pamina, sop., the heroine of ZAUBERFLÖTE, loved by Tamino

Pampanini, Rosetta, b. Milan, 2 Sept 1900; d. Corbola, 2 Aug 1973. Italian soprano. Debut Rome as MICAËLA (1920). Further study led to engagements at Naples and Bergamo. TOSCANINI heard her and she was engaged for Sc.; debut there (1925) as CIO-CIO-SAN, to become her most significant role. CG debut in same role (1928); also sang LIÙ and NEDDA, reappearing as MIMI and MANON LESCAUT (1929), and (1933) as Mimi and DESDEMONA (OTELLO), another of her best parts. Only US appearances at Chicago (1932–3). Took on heavier roles towards end of career. Retired in 1944 to teach. Her pupils incl. SHUARD. She had a well-formed and intelligently used lyric sop. and was an appreciable actress. AB

Panizza, Ettore [Héctor], b. Buenos Aires, 12 Aug 1875; d. Milan, 29 Nov 1967. Argentine conductor and composer of Italian descent. Studied Milan. After engagements in Italy, appointed CG 1907–14. Debut Sc. 1916; TOSCANINI's assistant there, 1921–9. SERAFIN's successor at NY Met, 1934–42. Has also been one of the principal conds at T. Colón, esp. since World War II until his retirement, 1954. His four operas are *Il Fidanzato del Mare* (1897), *Medio Evo Latino* (1900), *Aurora* (1908), and *Bisanzio* (1939). MK

Papagena, sop., Papageno's lover in ZAUBERFLÖTE

Papageno, bar., Tamino's attendant in ZAUBERFLÖTE

Papp, Gustáv, b. Čierny Blh, 28 Sept 1919. Slovak tenor. A qualified doctor, he studied singing at Bratislava Cons. and since 1955 has been a permanent member of the Bratislava NT. Has sung most of the dramatic and lyric Czech repertory as well as Wagnerian roles in Leipzig, Dresden, and the USSR. Has also taken part in the premieres of several CIKKER operas. JT

Pardon de Ploërmel, Le *see* DINORAH

Pareto, Graziella, b. Barcelona, 6 Mar 1888. Spanish soprano. Studied Milan; debut Madrid, 1908. Sang in S. America and St Petersburg before CG debut in 1920. She sang at CG for only one season, as Leïla (PÊCHEURS DE PERLES), NORINA, and VIOLETTA. Appeared in Chicago, 1923–5, and at the Salzburg Fest., as Carolina (MATRIMONIO SEGRETO, 1931). Possessed one of the purest, most limpid coloratura voices of her day. AB

Paride ed Elena (*Paris and Helen*), *dramma per musica*, GLUCK, lib. CALZABIGI, based on Ovid. Vienna, BT, 30 Nov 1770; never staged since, though a concert perf. was given NY, 15 Jan 1954 by American O. Soc. Some of the music is familiar as it was included in later operas such as ORPHÉE ET EURYDICE, IPHIGÉNIE EN AULIDE, and the Fr. ALCESTE. Lacking the dramatic force of these later works, this opera, concerned entirely with the love between Paris and Helen, reveals the composer in a softer and tenderer light than he usually shows. LO

Paris. An important centre of opera since LULLY. In 18th-c. Paris the *guerre des bouffons* (war of the comedians), a lively pamphleteering quarrel between the champions of Fr. opera *à la* RAMEAU and those, headed by ROUSSEAU, advocating It. operatic methods, had repercussions all over Europe. In the 19th and 20th c. grand opera and the ideals of DEBUSSY have materially influenced musical thought. The theatres where opera or operetta have been given incl. the O., OC, TL, T. Bouffes-Parisiens, the Gaieté, T. Châtelet, T. Éden, T. Champs-Élysées.

Théâtre Bouffes-Parisiens. A small theatre, originally *Salle des Folies Marigny*, in Champs-Élysées, opened 5 July 1855 with OFFENBACH's *Deux Aveugles*. Later, Dec 1855, Offenbach moved to the rather larger T. Salle Choiseul, also in Champs-Élysées, until 1868. The T. Bouffes-Parisiens reopened 1871, after the Franco–Prussian war, giving operettas by Offenbach, HERVÉ, LECOCQ, AUDRAN, and MESSAGER.

Opéra (Académie de Musique). The principal opera house of France. Beginning as L'Académie d'Opéra, under Pierre Perrin in 1669, it became L'Académie Royale de Musique when LULLY took over, 1672. From 1674 to 1763 this was in the Palais Royal. Following a fire in 1763 the Opéra moved to the Salle des Machines, and back to a rebuilt theatre in Palais Royal, 1770. This was the period of GLUCK's Paris triumphs. After another fire in 1781 the Opéra moved to a 'temporary' building in Boulevard St Martin, until 1792. The Revolution occasioned some changes of name (Académie de Musique; Opéra et Opéra National; T. des Arts). In 1822 the Opéra moved to a new theatre in Rue Peletier; here grand opera under MEYERBEER was at its most resplendent. Burned down in 1873 it was replaced in 1875 by GARNIER's present building. Since World War II the Opéra, first under M. LEHMANN and then under LIEBERMANN, and with an enormous subsidy, has again assumed an important role in international opera.

Opéra-Comique (OC). Paris's second opera house. The name dates from 1714, when a compromise agreement was reached between the Opéra and the Comédie Française, which enjoyed monopolies over singing and speaking perfs, and the actors playing vaudevilles in the Paris Fairs. The real birth of the OC, however, dates from 1762, with the amalgamation of the OC with the Comédie Italienne. With its own premises (the most recent erected 1898), the OC has been the home of France's most distinctive operatic genre, the *opéra comique*, and has also sheltered others works such as PELLÉAS ET MÉLISANDE and HEURE ESPAGNOLE which the Opéra found not suitable. A recent reorganization has deprived the OC of its independent existence. *See* Genest, *L'Opéra-Comique Connu et Inconnu* (Paris 1925)

Théâtre-Lyrique (TL). Under CARVALHO the scene of many important premieres including GOUNOD's FAUST, ROMÉO ET JULIETTE, and the second part of TROYENS, 1863. Rebuilt 1874, renamed T. des Nations. The OC was there, 1887–98, while its own theatre was being rebuilt. Since then has been used for opera only occasionally. LO

Parker, Horatio William, b. Auburndale, Mass., 15 Sept 1863; d. Cedarhurst, NY, 18 Dec 1919. American composer. Studied in Boston and Munich, returning to Boston as a church musician, an association earnestly followed throughout his career. Professor of Music at Yale Univ., head of its music school (1894) and among the foremost US comps of his time. His opera MONA won a prize of $10,000 offered by the NY Met, where it was perf., 1912. The music, however, was not sufficiently vital to compensate for lack of theatrical experience, and *Mona* enjoyed only a *succès d'estime*. A later work, *Fairyland*, was prod. at Los Angeles 1915. EJ

Park Theater *see* NEW YORK

parlando (It. 'speaking'). Singers are often directed to sing thus, in a 'speaking' fashion, when the need for clarity is imperative (e.g. in a conspiratorial whisper). LO

Parma, Italy, one-time capital of the Duchy of Parma. The T. Farnese was built inside the palace in 1618 (partly destroyed during World War II, now being meticulously rebuilt). The T. Regio opened in 1829 with BELLINI's *Zaira*. Present art. dir. MAAG. LO

Parody. Serious opera has always invited parody. Either the style is parodied, exaggerating the conventions to the point of absurdity (e.g. SCHAUSPIELDIREKTOR and the GILBERT and SULLIVAN comic operas); or specific operas are parodied, as in ORPHÉE AUX ENFERS or the several parodies of ZAUBERFLÖTE, or SUPPÉ's WAGNER parody, *Tannenhäuser*, 1848. The practice was common in the 18th c. and early 19th c. LO

Parsifal, sacred fest. drama, 3 acts, WAGNER, lib. comp. Bayreuth, 26 July 1882. London, RAH, 10 Nov 1884; NY, 3 Mar 1886 (concert perfs); NY Met, 24 Dec 1903 (before the Bayreuth copyright had expired); London, CG, 2 Feb 1914. Main chars: Parsifal (ten.) Kundry (sop.) Gurnemanz (bass) Amfortas (bar.) Titurel (bass) Klingsor (bar.). Amfortas, king of the Knights of the Grail, has long suffered from a wound inflicted by the spear of Klingsor, the Grail's enemy, and can only be healed by a 'holy fool'. The feat is accomplished against all expectations by Parsifal who withstands the temptations of Kundry and the flower maidens in Klingsor's magic garden and captures the spear. Wagner's last music drama. JB O
See Kobbé

Pasatieri, Thomas, b. 1946. American composer. Operas incl. *Black Widow* (Seattle 1972), *The Trial of May Lincoln* (New York 1972), *Calvary* (New York 1972), *The Seagull*, based on CHEKHOV (Houston 1974), and *Ines de Castro* (Baltimore 1975). LO

Pashchenko, Andrey Filippovich, b. Rostov-on-Don, 15 Aug 1885. Soviet composer. Of his 10 operas, the most significant is *The Eagle's Revolt* (1925), based on the Pugachov uprising, though he has become more widely known for his satirical comedies, particularly *Tsar Maximilian* (1930). GN

Pashley, Anne, b. Sheffield, 4 Feb 1938. English sop. Studied Guildhall School of Music, London. Has sung intermittently with most British cos, mainly in MOZART roles at which she is adept, being a fine Idamante (IDOMENEO), Donna ELVIRA (DON GIOVANNI), ZERLINA, and Amyntas (RE PASTORE), a role she has sung at Wexford and Camden Fests. An outstanding singer-actress. AB

Pasta [Negri], Giuditta, b. Saronno, nr Milan, 9 Apr 1798; d. Blevio, Lake Como, 1 Apr 1865. Italian soprano. Studied Milan. Early career was not remarkable, but she made her name in the 1820s in ROSSINI operas. At her best in tragic roles such as Medea (MEDEA IN CORINTO) or NORMA and ANNA BOLENA, written expressly for her. Her voice had an enormous range, with powerful low notes which BELLINI exploited; her coloratura as in ADINA, also written for her, was never as secure as that of some of her rivals. Nevertheless she was an outstanding singer, renowned for her dramatic ability as much as for her singing, a superb interpreter in an era of superlative performers. After about 1840 her voice had deteriorated markedly, and she retired in 1850. LO

Right: Mary Ann Paton as SUSANNA, the role in which she made her stage debut. She was an accomplished pianist and violinist as well as a singer, and well known as a performer before her operatic debut.

Parsifal, Act I, sc. 2, produced at Bayreuth in 1951 by Wieland WAGNER, with WINDGASSEN as Parsifal and LONDON as AMFORTAS

pasticcio (It. 'pie'; the Fr. term is *pastiche*). An opera pieced together from previously comp. operas by one or more comps; common practice in early 18th c. esp. in London. The typical METASTASIO aria was loosely applicable to a variety of situations, there was stylistic similarity between comps, so that though the practice cannot be condoned there was less objection than would have been felt later. A somewhat different type of *pasticcio* arises when as in SUPPÉ's *Franz Schubert* (1864) an opera is constructed from a single comp's non-operatic music (here, SCHUBERT's songs). LO

pastoral(e). From It. *pastore*, a shepherd; hence plays or operas involving shepherds and shepherdesses, often of a rather artificial nature. The first pastoral play was TASSO's *Aminta* (1573) followed by GUARINI's *Il Pastor Fido* (*c.* 1590). The pastoral appears in LULLY, e.g. ACIS ET GALATÉE; other examples: ACIS AND GALATEA, PASTOR FIDO, and RE PASTORE. LO

Pastor Fido, Il, opera, 3 acts, HANDEL, lib. Giacomo Rossi after Giovanni Battista Guarini. London, HM, 3 Dec 1712; new version there 29 May 1734. Main chars: Mirtillo (sop.) Amarilli (sop.) Eurilla (sop.) Silvio (contr.) Dorinda (mezzo-sop.). Amarilli and Mirtillo are in love; but she is unwillingly betrothed to Silvio, who, though loved by Dorinda, cares only for hunting. Eurilla, who also loves Mirtillo, traps her rival into a compromising situation, the penalty for which is death. Silvio shoots Dorinda in mistake for an animal and falls in love with her; the high priest of Diana spares Amarilli on divine instructions, and unites her with Mirtillo and Dorinda with Silvio. JB

Patané, Giuseppe, b. Naples, 1 Jan 1932. Italian conductor. Son of cond. Franco Patané; debut Naples 1951 with TRAVIATA. Engaged at the Landes T., Linz, 1961–2, he then worked for six years at the Deutsche O., Berlin. Debut San Francisco in 1967 (GIOCONDA); at Sc. in 1969 (RIGOLETTO) and at CG in 1973 (FORZA DEL DESTINO). Other operas he has cond. incl. ELISIR D'AMORE, LUCIA DI LAMMERMOOR, TROVATORE, ERNANI, MACBETH, and TURANDOT. EF

Patience, or Bunthorne's Bride, operetta, 2 acts, SULLIVAN, lib. GILBERT. London, Opéra Comique, 25 Apr 1881; St Louis, 28 July 1881. Main chars: Bunthorne (buffo) Patience (sop.) Grosvenor (bar.) Lady Jane (contr.) Colonel (bass). A satire on the aesthetic movement with two fashionable poets as rivals for the hand of the milkmaid, Patience. JB O

Paton, Mary Ann, b. Edinburgh, Oct 1802; d. Chapelthorpe, 21 July 1864. Scottish soprano. Stage debuts as SUSANNA (London, HM, 3 Aug 1822) and CG same year as Polly (BEGGAR'S OPERA), and Mandane (ARTAXERXES). She sang AGATHE in 1824; created Reiza (OBERON) 1826. C. WEBER called her 'a singer of the very first rank'. Renowned for her beauty and her command of the florid style. Her sisters Eliza and Isabella were also singers. PS

Patti, Adelina [Adela Juana Maria], b. Madrid, 10 Feb 1843; d. Craig-y-Nos, Wales, 27 Sept 1919. Italian soprano. Taken by her parents, who were both singers, to the USA as a child, she studied with Ettore Barili and Maurice Stakosch (later her brother-in-law); debut NY in LUCIA DI LAMMERMOOR, 1859. London debut in SONNAMBULA, 1861. Thereafter she reigned as the supreme coloratura singer until her last CG appearances in 1895. She limited her roles to the It. and Fr. repertory and was unsurpassed in lyric parts, for which she was acclaimed wherever she sang in Britain, USA, France or Italy. She bought a castle in Wales and in 1891 built a private theatre there. LO
See Klein, *The Reign of Patti* (New York and London 1920)

Patzak, Julius, b. Vienna, 9 Apr 1898; d. Rottach, 26 Jan 1974. Austrian tenor. After studying to be a cond. his voice was discovered; debut as RADAMES at Reichenberg (1926). Appearances at Brno before joining the Bavarian Staats O. in 1928, where he took all the major and minor lyric ten. roles until 1945, appearing

Left: Adelina Patti as Juliette, 1879

more than 1,000 times. Vienna Staats O. 1945–60. In later years his Florestan and Palestrina were memorable portrayals. CG debut 1938 as Tamino; returned with Vienna Staats O. 1947, singing Florestan and Hoffmann (Contes d'Hoffmann), 1954. Created roles in Dantons Tod and Martin's *Le Vin Herbé* at Salzburg, 1947–8; sang an unforgettable Florestan there under Furtwängler, 1949–50. A ten. of the utmost refinement and musicianship, who showed complete identification with all his characters. AB

Pauer, Jiří, b. Libušin, Bohemia, 22 Feb 1919. Czech composer. A pupil of Hába. One of the most prolific and successful of contemporary Czech opera comps. His works range from the fairy-tale operas *The Garrulous Slug* (*Žvanivý Slimejš*, 1958) and *Little Red Riding Hood* (*Červená Karkulka*, 1960) to the romantic opera *Zuzana Vojířova* (1958) and the comic operas *Matrimonial Counterpoints* (*Manželské kontrapunkty*, 1968) and *Le Malade Imaginaire* (*Zdravý nemocný*, 1970). JT

Pauly, Rosa [Rose Pollak], b. Eperjes, 15 Mar 1894; d. Tel Aviv, 14 Dec 1975. Hungarian soprano. Studied Vienna; debut in Aida, Hamburg 1918. Cologne, 1922–7; Berlin, 1927–31; Vienna, 1931–8. Has also sung widely in the New World, at NY Met, 1938–40, and at Chicago, San Francisco, and Buenos Aires. A fine actress and an outstanding Elektra. LO

Pauvre Matelot, Le (*The Poor Sailor*), opera, 3 acts, Milhaud, lib. Cocteau. Paris, OC, 16 Dec 1927; Philadelphia, 1 Apr 1937; London Opera Club, 1950. Main chars: Wife (sop.) her Father (bass) his Friend (bar.) Sailor (ten.). The Wife has faithfully waited 15 years for her sailor husband's return, rejecting the Friend and refusing her Father's advice to find another man. The Sailor returns, but tells his Wife, who does not recognize him, he is the rich friend of her husband, who has remained poor. The Wife kills him for the money, then sings lyrically of her husband's eventual return. Lasting less than 40 minutes, the opera heightens the complete unreality of the story with music of playful banality. FGB
See Kobbé

Pavarotti, Luciano, b. Carpi, nr Modena, 12 Oct 1935. Italian tenor. Debut 1961, Carpi, as Duca di Mantua, then sang at CG (1963), Sc. (1964), Glyndebourne (1964), with the Sutherland company in Australia (1965), San Francisco (1967) and the NY Met (1968). He has a robust, but lyrical voice, with a strong upper register, and his repertory includes Idamante (Idomeneo), Elvino (Sonnambula), Nemorino, Edgardo, Tonio (Fille du Régiment), Alfredo, Riccardo (Ballo in Maschera), and Rodolfo, his favourite role. EF

Right: Peter Pears as von Aschenbach in EOG's production, 1973, of Death in Venice

Pearl Fishers, The *see* Pêcheurs de Perles

Pears, Peter, b. Farnham, Surrey, 22 June 1910. English tenor; close associate of Britten. Solo stage debut, Strand T., London, 1942, as Hoffmann (Contes d'Hoffmann). With SW, 1943–6 and created title role in Peter Grimes. Founder member with Britten of English Opera Group, 1946. He created following roles in later Britten operas: Male Chorus (Rape of Lucretia); title role, Albert Herring; Captain Vere (Billy Budd); Essex (Gloriana); Quint (Turn of the Screw); Flute (Midsummer Night's Dream); Madwoman (Curlew River); Nebuchadnezzar (Burning Fiery Furnace); Tempter/Abbot (Prodigal Son); General Wingrave (Owen Wingrave); von Aschenbach (Death in Venice). Also created Pandarus in Troilus and Cressida. Special success as Tamino and Vašek for both SW and CG, also David (Meistersinger) for CG. Has toured USA, USSR, and Far East with EOG in Britten operas; NY Met debut, 1974, in *Death in Venice*. Combines exceptional musical intelligence with subtlety of character and expression, and is renowned in song as well as opera. Awarded CBE 1957. NG

Pease, James, b. Indianapolis, 9 Jan 1916; d. NY, 26 Apr 1967. American baritone. Studied Philadelphia; debut there 1941. Engaged with NY CC 1946–53; Hamburg Staats O. 1953–8; Zürich 1960–2. Has also appeared at Bayreuth. Sang in US premieres of PETER GRIMES and ALBERT HERRING. LO

Pêcheurs de Perles, Les (*The Pearl Fishers*), opera, 3 acts, BIZET, lib. CARRÉ and Eugène Cormon. Paris, TL, 30 Sept 1863; London, CG, in It. as *Leila* (the intended original title), 22 Apr 1887; Philadelphia, 23 Aug 1893. The plot, set in Ceylon (it was originally to have been Mexico), is a bowdlerized 'vestal virgin' theme; Leila, a priestess of Brahma, breaks her sacred vows for love. LO O
See Curtiss, *Bizet and his World* (London 1959; 1964)

Pécs, Hungary. The opera company (housed in the NT building of 1895) has been in existence since 1959. GN

Pedrell, Felipe, b. Tortosa, 19 Feb 1841; d. Barcelona, 19 Aug 1922. Spanish composer, musicologist, and champion of his country's national music. After composing a few youthful *zarzuelas*, turned to operas on an ambitious scale which earned him the title of 'the Spanish Wagner', though the quality of his music in no way warrants this. His operas include *Los Pirineos* (1894), *La Celestina* (1903), and *El Conde Arnau* (1921). Important as a teacher, his pupils included FALLA. FGB

Peerce, Jan [Jacob Pincus Perelmuth], b. NY, 3 June 1904. American tenor. Played as violinist in dance bands and sang at Radio City Music Hall, NY, 1933–9 before operatic debut Philadelphia, 1938, in RIGOLETTO. NY Met debut 1941 in TRAVIATA; leading ten. there since then. Has also appeared in USSR (first American singer to appear at the Bolshoy), Germany, and the Netherlands. Esp. successful in Fr. and It. repertory. LO

Pelléas et Mélisande, opera, 5 acts, DEBUSSY, lib. from MAETERLINCK's play of the same name. Paris, OC, 30 Apr 1902; NY, Manhattan OH, 19 Feb 1908; London, CG, 21 May 1909. Main chars: Pelléas (ten.) Mélisande (sop.) Golaud (bar.) Geneviève (alto) Yniold (sop.) Arkel (bass). Debussy set Maeterlinck's play almost as it stood, cutting four unimportant scenes but otherwise without rewriting; Maeterlinck initially opposed the opera. It uses a Wagnerian-style orchestra to achieve an almost anti-Wagnerian character in a succession of short, concentrated scenes, creating a haunting drama of the spirit with figures in a landscape of illusion. They are nevertheless creatures of flesh and blood, who illustrate ROUSSEAU's definition of existence as 'Nothing but a succession of moments perceived through the senses'. The opera remains unique of its kind, frequently and widely perf. NG O
See Kobbé; Newman, *Opera Nights* (London 1943); Lockspeiser, *Debussy: His Life and Mind*, Vol. 1 (London and New York 1962)

Pellegrini, Maria, b. Pescara, Italy, ?1939. Italian-Canadian soprano. Her family moved to Canada when she was a child but five years later went back to Italy. Pellegrini returned to Canada to study at the Opera School of the Royal Cons. in Toronto. Debut with COC as the priestess in AIDA 1963. In 1965 sang GILDA with the co., a role that, with VIOLETTA and CIO-CIO-SAN, is one of her most successful. She sang at London, SW (1967), and CG (1968). Since then she has appeared in Genoa, Bologna, Parma, and with the WNO as well as in Canada; US debut Pittsburgh 1974. CM

Pelletier, Wilfred, b. Montreal, 20 June 1896. Canadian conductor. Studied Paris. Cond. Montreal Opera Guild 1913–14; apptd asst cond. NY Met 1922–32; a principal cond. there from 1932, cond. Fr. and It. repertory. Cond. of summer opera, Ravinia Park, Chicago, 1921–31. LO

Penderecki, Krzysztof, b. Dębica, 23 Nov 1933. Polish composer. His first opera, DEVILS

OF LOUDUN, created a sensation at its premiere in 1969, and has since been prod. all over Europe and in the USA. The Lyric O., Chicago, has commissioned a work from him for 1976, lib. Christopher Fry, based on Milton's *Paradise Lost*. The *St Luke Passion*, comp. 1963–5, has also been staged. EF

Pénélope, *drame lyrique*, 3 acts, FAURÉ, lib. René Fauchois, based on HOMER. Monte Carlo, 4 Mar 1913; Paris, T. Champs-Élysées, 10 May 1913; Cambridge, Mass., 29 Nov 1945; London, RAM, 20 Nov 1970. The title role was created by BRÉVAL, who in 1907 had suggested the subject, the familiar story of the return of Ulysses and the routing of Penelope's suitors. LO

Penny for a Song, A, opera, 2 acts, BENNETT, lib. GRAHAM, based on the play of the same name by John Whiting, commissioned by SW and the Calouste Gulbenkian Foundation. London, SW, 31 Oct 1967. Main chars: Dorcas Bellboys (sop.) Hester Bellboys (mezzo-sop.) Hallam Matthews (ten.) Edward Sterne (bar.) Sir Timothy Bellboys (ten.) Lamprett Bellboys (bar.) Humpage (bass). In an Eng. coastal house in 1804, the Bellboys brothers, middle-aged eccentrics, prepare to deal with the threatened Napoleonic invasion, keeping their butler, Humpage, permanently up a tree as a lookout. Dorcas, daughter of Lamprett, meanwhile falls in love with Edward, a returning mercenary sickened by the futility of war, whose views clash with those of Hallam, a sophisticated cynic also half in love with Dorcas, wanting only to preserve the status quo. Bennett's music delineates each main character with distinctive motifs and instrumentation in a mainly harmonic idiom, seldom extending conversational word setting beyond modest *arioso*, but expressing qualities of wry humour, subdued poetry and skilful musical colour. NG

Pepusch, John Christopher [Johann Christoph], b. Berlin, 1667; d. London, 20 July 1752. English composer of Ger. birth. A musician at the Prussian court 1681–97; moved to London 1700 where he played in the DL orch. HANDEL's predecessor as organist and comp. to Duke of Chandos, 1712–18; mus. dir., Lincoln's Inn Fields T., for which he comp. several masques. In 1718 m. the wealthy singer Margherita de l'Épine. Arranged music for BEGGAR'S OPERA and POLLY. A respected teacher, his pupils incl. William Boyce and Benjamin Cooke. PS

Peragallo, Mario, b. Rome, 25 Mar 1910. Italian composer. His operas include *Ginevra degli Almieri* (Rome 1937), *Lo Stendardo di S. Giorgio* (Genoa 1941), *La Gita in Campagna*, a 1-act opera, lib. Alberto Moravia (Sc. 1954), and *La Parrucca dell'Imperatore* (Spoleto 1959). EF

Perfect Fool, The, opera, 1 act, HOLST, lib. composer. London, CG, 14 May 1923; Wichita, 20 Mar 1962. Main chars: Princess (sop.) Troubadour (ten.). An allegory in Elizabethan style parodying WAGNER, VERDI, and earlier opera comps. AB

Pergola, Teatro della *see* FLORENCE

Pergolesi, Giovanni Battista, b. Jesi, 4 Jan 1710; d. Pozzuoli, 16 Mar 1736. Italian composer. Studied Naples Cons.; operatic debut in that city with *Salustia*, of which the music is now lost. Of his other stage works the most important are the full-length comedy *Lo Frate 'Nnamorato* (Naples 1732), the two *opere serie* *Adriano in Siria* (Naples 1734) and *L'Olimpiade* (Rome 1735), and above all SERVA PADRONA whose perf. by an It. co. in Paris in 1753 sparked off the *guerre des bouffons*, in which Pergolesi's score, with its sharp rhythms and vivid verbal accentuation, was upheld by ROUSSEAU and others as a model of what comic opera should be. In this respect Pergolesi is the father of *opéra comique* as well as classical *opera buffa*. So great was his posthumous reputation that various works were falsely pub. under his name (including, e.g. *Il Maestro di Musica* and *Il Geloso Schernito*). JB

Peri, Jacopo, b. Rome, 20 Aug 1561; d. Florence, 12 Aug 1633. Italian singer and composer. A member of the Florentine Camerata, and important in the early history of opera. His DAFNE was probably the first opera; his EURIDICE is the first of which the music is preserved. Other operas incl. *Tetide*, comp. 1608, and *Adone*, comp. 1620, but it is not certain that they were ever perf. LO

Périchole, La, *opéra bouffe*, 3 acts, OFFENBACH, lib. MEILHAC and L. HALÉVY based on MÉRIMÉE's 1-act play *Le Carrosse du Saint Sacrement*. Paris, T. des Variétés, 6 Oct 1868; NY, Grand OH, 4 Jan 1869; London, Princess's T., 27 June 1870. Sung frequently in Eng. in the 1880s; often revived. LO

Périer, Jean Alexis, b. Paris, 2 Feb 1869; d. Paris, 6 Nov 1954. French baritone of Belgian origin. Studied Paris Cons. Debut OC 1892 (MONOSTATOS), where he sang until 1895 and again after 1900. Esp. distinguished in Fr. opera both serious and comic (sang in operettas by MESSAGER, LECOCQ and others), he created

La Périchole, Act I, as performed at the T. des Variétés, Paris, 6 Oct 1868

many roles, notably Ramiro in HEURE ESPAGNOLE, MÂROUF and, above all, PELLÉAS. His acting was as remarkable as his singing; he frequently appeared in the straight theatre as well as on the opera stage. LO

Perrault, Charles, b. Paris, 12 Jan 1628; d. Paris, 16 May 1703. French writer whose fairy tales *Les Contes de Ma Mère l'Oye* (1697) have provided material for operas, the main ones being: *Cendrillon*, his Cinderella story (Jean Louis Laruette, 1759; ISOUARD; ROSSINI, CENERENTOLA; MASSENET; WOLF-FERRARI, 1900); *Le Petit Chaperon Rouge* (BOÏELDIEU, 1818; PAUER, 1960); *La Belle au Bois Dormant* (CARAFA, 1825; LECOCQ, 1898; RESPIGHI, *La Bella Addormentata*, 1909; HUMPERDINCK, *Dornröschen*, 1902); *La Belle et la Bête* (MALIPIERO, *La Bella e il Mostro*, 1930); *Le Chat Botté* (CUI, 1911); *Riquet à la Houppe* (Georges Huë, 1928); *La Forêt Bleue* (AUBERT). LO

Persiani [Tacchinardi], Fanny, b. Rome, 4 Oct 1812; d. Neuilly, Paris, 3 May 1867. Italian soprano. Daughter of the celebrated ten. TACCHINARDI (1776–1859), she m. the comp. Giuseppe Persiani (1799–1869) in 1830; debut Livorno 1832. Engaged by the major It. opera houses; DONIZETTI wrote *Rosmonda d'Inghilterra* (Florence 1834), LUCIA DI LAMMERMOOR and *Pia de' Tolomei* (Venice 1837) for her. Paris debut 12 Dec 1837 as Lucia; sang SONNAMBULA in London 1838. Her voice was described as clear and penetrating, but thin, with a tendency to be off pitch, but much admired by connoisseurs. She sang in London 1847–9, the Netherlands 1850, then in Russia; reappeared at DL 1858 in several of her most famous roles. PS

Pertile, Aureliano, b. Montagnana, 9 Nov 1885; d. Milan, 11 Jan 1952. Italian tenor. Debut Lionel (MARTHA), Vicenza, 1911. Sang NY Met 1921–2, and Milan, Sc., 1921–37 as TOSCANINI's favourite ten. Created title role in NERONE, 1924. His dazzlingly bright voice encompassed lyrical roles in DONIZETTI and the heroics of LOHENGRIN and VERDI's OTELLO. The first ten. to combine suave *bel canto* technique with the highly emotional style of *verismo*. Retired in 1946 but continued to teach until his death. FGB

Peru *see* LATIN AMERICA

Peter Grimes, opera, 3 acts, BRITTEN, lib. Montagu Slater, derived from George Crabbe's poem *The Borough*. London, SW, 7 June 1945; Tanglewood, 6 Aug 1946. Main chars: Peter Grimes (ten.) Ellen Orford (sop.) Balstrode (bar.). First and most frequently heard (until rivalled by DEATH IN VENICE) of Britten's operas. Established his sympathy with the 'outsider' and his ability to express character in deeply felt music. Also showed his talent in dramatic timing. The premiere immediately after World War II was an exciting event and immediately brought Britten to international prominence. AB O
See Kobbé

Peter Ibbetson, opera, 3 acts, TAYLOR, lib. Constance Collier and composer from the George du Maurier novel. NY Met, 7 Feb 1931. Main chars: Peter Ibbetson (ten.) Colonel Ibbetson (bar.) Mary, Duchess of Towers (sop.) Mrs Deane (contr.). Peter Ibbetson, abused by a cruel uncle, finds escape in dreams about his childhood. Returning to his birthplace, he meets a playmate, Mary. For killing his uncle, Peter is sentenced to life imprisonment where, over 40 years, he finds solace in dreams as Mary visits him. Learning of her death, he joins her. The work is traditional in form. EJ

Peters, Roberta, b. NY, 4 May 1930. American soprano. Studied NY with William Hermann. Debut NY Met as ZERLINA (1950); has since sung there regularly, roles incl. QUEEN OF THE NIGHT, ROSINA, DESPINA, GILDA, Oscar (BALLO IN MASCHERA) LUCIA DI LAMMERMOOR, and ADINA. CG debut as Arline in BOHEMIAN GIRL under BEECHAM (1951); returned for Gilda (1961). AB

Petrassi, Goffredo, b. Zagarolo, Rome, 16 July 1904. Italian composer. Studied Rome; 1937–9 was Superintendent, T. La Fenice, Venice. His comic opera *Il Cordovano*, based on CERVANTES, was prod. Sc. (1949); *Morte dell' Aria* was perf. Rome (1950). EF

Petrov, Ivan Ivanovich, b. Irkutsk, 29 Feb 1920. Soviet bass. Has sung at the Bolshoy since 1943. Particularly successful as Ruslan (RUSLAN AND LYUDMILA), BORIS GODUNOV, Dosifey (KHOVANSHCHINA), Don BASILIO (BARBIERE DI SIVIGLIA), and MÉPHISTOPHÉLÈS. Has toured extensively in W. Europe; made an honorary member of the Paris O., 1954. GN

Petrov, Osip Afanasyevich, b. Elizavetgrad, 15 Nov 1806; d. St Petersburg, 12 Mar 1878. Russian bass. Debut 1826; first appeared in St Petersburg in 1830. He had a wide-ranging voice and colourful acting ability, and created many important Russian roles: IVAN SUSANIN and Ruslan (RUSLAN AND LYUDMILA), the Miller in DARGOMYZHSKY's *Rusalka*, and Leporello (STONE GUEST), Varlaam (BORIS GODUNOV), SEROV's Oziya (*Judith*), and Vladimir (*Rogneda*), Ivan the Terrible (MAID OF PSKOV), Prince Gudal (DEMON), and the Mayor in TCHAIKOVSKY's *Vakula the Smith*. His wife was the contr. Anna Yakovlevna Vorobyova (1816–1901), for whom GLINKA wrote the part of Vanya in *Ivan Susanin*. GN

Petrovics, Emil, b. Nagybecskerek, Yugoslavia, 9 Feb 1930. Hungarian composer. The 1-act *C'est la Guerre* (1962), which shows the influence of BERG, was staged with such success that he was encouraged to write a second opera, *Lysistrate* (concert perf. Budapest 1962; staged Budapest 1971). His other opera is the 3-act *Crime and Punishment* (1970), based on DOSTOYEVSKY's novel. GN

Pfitzner, Hans Erich, b. Moscow, 5 May 1869; d. Salzburg, 22 May 1949. German conductor and composer. Studied with his father, a dir. of the Frankfurt O. Taught piano and cond. while beginning to comp. Dir., Strasbourg O., 1910–16. His major work was PALESTRINA, but his other operas enjoyed a success in their own day: ARME HEINRICH (1895), *Die Rose vom Liebesgarten* (1901), *Christelflein* (1906, revised 1917), and *Das Herz* (1931). His operas are traditional in style and outlook, well made; he had a keen ear for characterization. AB

Phaéton, *tragédie lyrique*, prologue and 5 acts, LULLY, lib. QUINAULT. Versailles, at Fr. court, 6 Jan 1683; Paris, O., 23 Apr 1683. A spectacle opera, with emphasis on The Temple of Isis, The Sun Palace, Phaéton's Chariot, etc. Parodied at the Foire Ts. as *Le Cocher Maladroit*. LO

Philadelphia. The most opera-conscious city in the USA from earliest days. Its early history is well documented through the 19th c. Various companies have staged unusual works, incl. ARIADNE AUF NAXOS (1 Nov 1928). Leopold Stokowski cond. the first US perf. of WOZZECK in 1931 (Nelson Eddy as the Soldier). The newly founded Curtis Institute staged OEDIPUS REX (21 Apr 1931) and MAVRA (28 Dec 1934). PAUVRE MATELOT was combined with AMELIA GOES TO THE BALL (1 Apr 1937).

For many years the NY Met journeyed to Philadelphia on Tuesday evenings during the season (alternating with Brooklyn) to offer novelties and standard works. Rising costs brought this to an end. Philadelphia was also served by two locally sponsored units, the Philadelphia Grand and Philadelphia Lyric O. cos each offering a series of about six works from the standard repertory.

In 1975 these two merged to form the Opera Co. of Philadelphia; Gen. Mgr Max M. Leon; Art Dir. Carl Suppa. *See also* CHICAGO. EJ

Philémon et Baucis, opera, 3 acts, GOUNOD, lib. BARBIER and CARRÉ based on Ovid. Paris, TL, 18 Feb 1860; London, CG (in Fr.), 24 Oct 1891; DL (in Eng., tr. Joseph Bennett), 26 Apr 1894; NY Met (in Eng.) 16 Nov 1893, (in Fr.) 29 Nov 1893. Originally 1 act, intended for Baden-Baden; expanded into 3 acts at request of CARVALHO; reduced to 2 acts in a further revision. Also set by GLUCK (1769, 1 act), and (for marionettes) HAYDN, 1973. LO

Philidor, François André Danican, b. Dreux, 7 Sept 1726; d. London, 24 Aug 1795. French composer and chess player. His more than 30 *opéras comiques*, of which TOM JONES is the best known, were very popular in his lifetime and are important in the history of the genre. LO

Philippe [Philip II], bass, the King of Spain in DON CARLOS

Piave, Francesco Maria, b. Murano, 18 May 1810; d. Milan, 5 Mar 1876. Italian librettist. Resident poet and stage mgr of T. La Fenice, Venice, 1843–67. Wrote over 70 libs, incl. 9 for VERDI: FORZA DEL DESTINO, MACBETH, SIMONE BOCCANEGRA (first version; revised BOITO), RIGOLETTO, TRAVIATA, *Il Corsaro* (1948), STIFFELIO and its revision, *Aroldo*, and DUE FOSCARI. LO

Piccaver, Alfred, b. Long Sutton, Lincolnshire, 15 Feb 1884; d. Vienna, 23 Sept 1958. English

Colour plate: JURINAC as the Marschallin in ROSENKAVALIER, London CG, 1966; produced and designed VISCONTI

tenor. Debut 1907, Prague, title role ROMÉO ET JULIETTE. Completed studies at Milan. First appeared at Vienna Hof O. in 1910 as substitute for another ten. during the It. season, immediately successful and remained with the Hof O. (later the Vienna Staats O.) until 1937, singing mainly It. roles, and appearing in the first Austrian perf. of FANCIULLA DEL WEST. At Chicago, 1923–5. Only CG appearances as CAVARADOSSI and DUCA DI MANTUA (1924). Taught in London, 1937–55. Possessed a lyric ten. of beautiful timbre and easy production. AB

Piccinni, Niccolò, b. Bari, 16 Jan 1728; d. Passy, France, 7 May 1800. Italian composer. A pupil of LEO and Francesco Durante at Naples, he first made his mark with a number of comedies beginning with *Le Donne Dispettose* (Naples 1754). His greatest triumph was with BUONA FIGLIUOLA which established him as the leading comp. of *opera buffa* after LOGROSCINO. Invited to Paris 1776 where his *Roland* (1778), a *tragédie lyrique*, was favourably received. His admirers set him up against his will as GLUCK's rival; however, his *Iphigénie en Tauride* (1781) was unable to hold its own against Gluck's masterpiece. *Didon* (1783) survived into the 19th c. to influence BERLIOZ's grand opera TROYENS. In his last years Piccinni, like CIMAROSA, was a victim of political events in Paris and Naples. JB

Piccola Scala, La *see* MILAN

Piccolo Marat, Il, opera, 3 acts, MASCAGNI, lib. FORZANO. Rome, T. Costanzi, 2 May 1921. Main chars: Il Piccolo Marat (ten.) Mariella (sop.) l'Orco (bass) il Soldato (bar.) il Carpentiere (bar.). In order to free his mother, imprisoned and condemned to death by the Jacobins, the young prince Jean-Charles de Fleury insinuates himself into the good graces of the President of the Council and becomes known as il Piccolo ('Little') Marat through his revolutionary zeal. With the help of Mariella and the carpenter he binds the President as he lies in drunken sleep, forces him to sign a release order for the Princess, and though wounded, escapes to freedom. JB

Piccolomini, Marietta, b. Siena, 15 Mar 1834; d. Poggio Imperiale, nr Florence, 23 Dec 1899. Italian soprano. Daughter of a Tuscan family, studied Florence; debut there 1852 as LUCREZIA BORGIA. She was noted for her VIOLETTA in Rome, Siena and Turin, and in London in 1856 where she became all the rage. A clever actress, she introduced the now obligatory consumptive cough into the role. She sang in Paris, and at HM, London, 1857–8 as ADINA, ZERLINA, SUSANNA, and LUISA MILLER. After a successful debut in America (1858) she returned to London in 1860, and the same year m. the Marchese Gaetani della Fargia and retired. She reappeared at DL for four nights in 1863 for LUMLEY's benefit. PS

Pierné, (Henri Constant) Gabriel, b. Metz, 16 Aug 1863; d. Ploujean, 17 July 1937. French organist, conductor, and composer. His eight operas include a comedy, *On ne Badine pas avec l'Amour*, 1910, based on Alfred de Musset's work of the same name, 1834, and *Sophie Arnould*, 1927, based on the life of the 18th-c. singer. LO

Colour plate: SALOME dancing before Herod, painting by Gustave Moreau (1826–98). Moreau was one of the French Symbolist painters. His evocative picture illustrated here epitomizes the *fin de siècle* preoccupation with the evil aura surrounding Salome which WILDE, R. STRAUSS and MASSENET were to express in the theatre.

La Pietra del Paragone, Glyndebourne, 17 June 1964. Left to right: Heinz Blankenburg as Pacuvio; Alberta Valentini as Fulvia; Anna Reynolds as Ortensia; ROUX as Macrobio; produced RENNERT; designed LANCASTER

Pietra del Paragone, La (*The Touchstone*), *opera buffa*, 2 acts, ROSSINI, lib. ROMANELLI. Milan, Sc., 28 Sept 1812; London, St Pancras Town Hall, 19 Mar 1963. Main chars: Asdrubale (bar.) Clarice (mezzo-sop.) Pacuvio (bar.) Macrobio (bar.) Giocondo (ten.) Fulvia (sop.). In order to test the genuineness of his friends, Count Asdrubale pretends to have been dispossessed of his wealth by an African prince whom he then impersonates. All fail the test disastrously except for Giocondo, and Clarice, with whom Asdrubale is in love. JB O

Pilarczyk, Helga, b. Schöningen, Brunswick [Braunschweig], 12 Mar 1925. German soprano. Debut 1951 at Brunswick as a mezzo-sop. in LORTZING's *Waffenschmied*, and sang CARMEN, LADY MACBETH, and AMNERIS. Engaged at Hamburg (1954); has sung at Glyndebourne (1958), CG (1959), Sc. (1963), the NY Met and Chicago (1965). Particularly noted for her perfs in modern operas, she sang at the premieres of KŘENEK's *Pallas Athene Weint* (1955) and *Der Goldene Bock* (1964). Her repertory incl. SALOME, MARIE, LULU, and roles in ERWARTUNG, FIERY ANGEL, FERNE KLANG, and ANIARA. EF

Pilger von Mekka, Die *see* RENCONTRE IMPRÉVUE

Pilgrim's Progress, The, morality, 4 acts, VAUGHAN WILLIAMS, lib. composer derived from John Bunyan's allegory. London, CG, 26 Apr 1951. Main char: Pilgrim (bar.). A series of tableaux showing the temptations and vicissitudes affecting the Pilgrim on his journey to the Celestial City. The most famous episode, the Shepherd of the Delectable Mountains, was set separately as a 1-act piece in 1922. Although the work is not wholly effective dramatically, the sincerity and conviction of the comp. are admirably conveyed in the music. AB O
See Kobbé

Pilou, Jeannette, b. Alexandria, Egypt, of Greek parents. Soprano. Studied Milan; debut T. Smeraldo as VIOLETTA (1959). First appearance at Vienna Staats O. was as MIMI (1965) and at NY Met as JULIETTE (1967). First CG appearance as CIO-CIO-SAN (1971). Roles also incl. MANON, MARGUERITE, and MICAËLA. An affecting singer and actress. AB

Pimen, bass, a monk in BORIS GODUNOV

Pimpinone, oder Die Ungleiche Heirat (*Pimpinone, or The Unequal Marriage*), intermezzo, 2 parts, TELEMANN, lib. Johann Peter Praetorius, after Pietro Pariati. Hamburg, T. am Gänsemarkt, 27 Sept 1725. Main chars: Pimpinone (bar.) Vespetta (sop.). For plot, *see* SERVA PADRONA. Telemann's best-known stage work. JB O

Pini-Corsi, Antonio, b. Zara, June 1858; d. Milan, 22 Apr 1918. Italian baritone. Debut Cremona 1878 as Dandini (CENERENTOLA). After singing *buffo* parts in secondary theatres in Italy international career began in LAKMÉ, Kroll O., 1889. Created FORD (1893) and SCHAUNARD (1896). Sang frequently at CG and NY Met. At his best in the comic parts of ROSSINI and MOZART. LO

Pinkerton, ten., CIO-CIO-SAN's lover in MADAMA BUTTERFLY

Pinza, Ezio [Fortunio], b. Rome, 18 May 1892; d. Stamford, Conn., 9 May 1957. Italian bass, one of the finest of the interwar years. After military service, debut Rome, 1921; then engaged at Sc., 1921–4. Most of his career was centred on the NY Met, 1926–48, singing an enormous variety of roles from MOZART (esp. DON GIOVANNI and FIGARO) to VERDI, RIMSKY-KORSAKOV, and MUSORGSKY. A fine actor, he also made a career in musicals and films, his appearance in SOUTH PACIFIC (1949), being particularly noteworthy. LO

Pipe of Desire, The, opera, 1 act, CONVERSE, lib. George Edward Burton. Boston, 31 Jan 1906; the first US opera prod. at NY Met, 18 Mar 1910. LO

Piper, John, b. 13 Dec 1903. English painter and stage designer. A founder member of the EOG in 1947. Has designed the sets for many of the premieres of BRITTEN's operas: RAPE OF LUCRETIA, ALBERT HERRING, BILLY BUDD, TURN OF THE SCREW; perhaps most notably MIDSUMMER NIGHT'S DREAM and DEATH IN VENICE. Also designed prods for Glyndebourne, CG, and SW. His sets follow the atmospheric, rather shaded, style of his paintings. AB

Pipkov, Lyubomir, b. Lovech, 6 Sept 1904. Bulgarian composer. After studying in Sofia and Paris, he worked at the Sofia National Opera as *répétiteur*, then as chorus master; later he was dir. (1944–7). He comp. three operas, which show a use of folksong: *Jana's Nine Brothers* (1937), *Momchil* (1948), and *Antigona 43* (1963). GN

Pique Dame, La *see* QUEEN OF SPADES

Pirata, Il (*The Pirate*), opera, 2 acts, BELLINI, lib. ROMANI after *Bertram or The Castle of St Aldobrand* by Charles Maturin. Milan, Sc., 27 Oct 1827; London, HM, 17 Apr 1830; NY, 5 Dec 1832. Main chars: Imogene (sop.) Gualtiero (ten.) Ernesto (bar.). Gualtiero, dispossessed of his estates and turned pirate after the battle of Benevento, returns to find his beloved Imogene married to his enemy Ernesto. Ernesto surprises his wife in a secret rendezvous with her former lover and challenges him to a duel. Ernesto is killed, Gualtiero arrested, and Imogene loses her reason. Bellini's third opera; the first to bring him international fame. Revived Palermo 1958 with CALLAS. JB ○

Pirates of Penzance, The, or **The Slave of Duty,** operetta, 2 acts, SULLIVAN, lib. GILBERT. Paignton, Bijou T., 30 Dec 1879; NY, New Fifth Avenue T., 31 Dec 1879. Main chars: Frederick (ten.) Mabel (sop.) Major General Stanley (buffo) Pirate King (bass) Ruth (contr.) Police Sergeant (bass bar.). Frederick, apprenticed to a gang of pirates until his 21st birthday, is thwarted in his desire to leave them by the discovery that he was born on 29 February. Led by Frederick and the Pirate King the pirates overcome the forces of law but yield when an appeal is made to their patriotism. JB ○

Right: Ildebrando Pizzetti's ASSASSINIO NELLA CATTEDRALE, London, SW, 3 July 1962; produced Basil Coleman. GARRARD as Becket; MCINTYRE as the fourth Knight

Pirogov, Aleksandr Stepanovich, b. Novoselki, Ryazan Government, 4 July 1899; d. Moscow, 26 June 1964. Russian bass. Sang in ZIMIN's Free O. (1922–4), then at the Bolshoy from 1924. He was particularly known for his interpretations of IVAN SUSANIN, Ruslan (RUSLAN AND LYUDMILA), and Boris and Varlaam (BORIS GODUNOV). GN

Pisaroni, Benedetta Rosamunda, b. Piacenza, 6 Feb 1793; d. Piacenza, 6 Aug 1872. Italian soprano, later contralto. Debut as sop., Bergamo, 1911; lost her high notes through illness. Though disfigured by smallpox (she always sent her picture to impresarios so that they should have no illusions as to her appearance), she was a good actress as well as a singer, excelling in ROSSINI. LO

Pitt, Percy, b. London, 4 Jan 1870; d. London, 23 Nov 1932. English conductor. Mus. dir. CG Grand Opera Syndicate, 1907–28. Also cond. with BEECHAM's Co., 1915–18, and art. dir., BNOC 1920–4. Cond. many CG premieres including IVANHOE, HEURE ESPAGNOLE, and KHOVANSHCHINA. LO

Pizarro, bar., the prison governor in FIDELIO

Pizzetti, Ildebrando, b. Parma, 20 Sept 1880; d. Rome, 13 Feb 1968. Italian composer. Like WAGNER began by writing plays, when he was *c.* 14. After three early 1-act operas, in 1909 began work on FEDRA. DEBORA E JAELE, *Lo Straniero*, 1930, and *Fra Gherardo*, 1928, were conceived as a sort of 'moral trilogy'. FIGLIA DI JORIO and ASSASSINIO NELLA CATTEDRALE have been the most successful of his post-World War II operas, and indeed have been the only ones of his 13 operas to find much favour with the international public. LO

Pizzi, Pier Luigi, b. Milan, 15 June 1930. Italian scenographer. Has designed sets for most of the major opera houses incl. Florence (MARIA STUARDA, 1967); Sc. (VÊPRES SICILIENNES, 1970–1), Glyndebourne (QUEEN OF SPADES, 1971); Verona (NABUCCO, 1971); Venice Fest. (a fine BORIS GODUNOV), 1973, and Vienna (FORZA DEL DESTINO, 1974). LO

Planché, James Robinson, b. London, 27 Feb 1796; d. London, 30 May 1880. English writer of Huguenot descent. His numerous libs incl. *Maid Marian* (1822) and *Cortez* (1823), both set by BISHOP; OBERON; *The Siege of Calais by Edward III*, intended for MENDELSSOHN; *Lover's Triumph*, V. WALLACE. Also tr. operas by AUBER (GUSTAVE III), BELLINI (NORMA), HÉROLD, MARSCHNER, MOZART (ZAUBERFLÖTE, NOZZE DI FIGARO), and ROSSINI (GUILLAUME TELL). Wrote a *History of British Costume* (London 1834) and published *Recollections and Reflections* (London 1872). LO

Plançon, Pol Henri, b. Fumay, Ardennes, ?12 July 1854; d. Paris, 11 Aug 1914. French bass. Pupil of DUPREZ and Giovanni Sbriglia; debut Lyon 1877; Paris debut, T. de la Gaieté, 1880. Career at the O. began 1883 with MÉPHISTOPHÉLÈS at which he excelled; CG debut in same part, 1891; regular visitor there until 1904. NY Met debut 1893 in PHILÉMON ET BAUCIS; sang frequently there until 1908. Parts he created incl. Francis I in SAINT-SAËNS's *Ascanio*, General Garrido in NAVARRAISE,

Francis in STANFORD's *Much Ado About Nothing*. A *basso profundo* of great range, evenness, ease of delivery and superb quality, more at home in the Fr. and It. repertory than the Ger. LO

Planquette, Jean-Robert, b. Paris, 31 July 1848; d. Paris, 28 Jan 1903. French composer of *c.* 20 operettas of which *Les Cloches de Corneville*, Paris, T. des Folies-Dramatiques, 19 Apr 1877; NY, 22 Oct 1877; London, Folly T., (in Eng.), 23 Feb 1878, was the most outstandingly successful. LO
See Lubbock

Platée, *comédie-ballet*, prologue, 3 acts, RAMEAU, lib. Jacques Autreau and Adrien-Joseph le Valois d'Orville. Versailles, 31 Mar 1745; Paris, O., 4 Feb 1749. The story, an unpleasant treatment of ugliness as a theme for comedy, is of a mock marriage between an ill-favoured woman and a god. One of the very earliest comic operas, as distinct from operas which include comic scenes. Revived Munich 1901 (in Ger., with some drastic changes); Aix Fest., July 1956. LO
See Girdlestone, *Jean-Philippe Rameau* (London 1957)

Plzeň [Pilsen]. A theatre was built in 1830–2 but was used mostly for plays by the German population until 1868, when a permanent Czech opera co. (the first outside Prague) was established. A new building was erected in 1902; this is now used for opera, the earlier theatre for plays and operetta. Czech premieres at Plzeň include operas by HANUŠ, HURNÍK, and JIRÁSEK. JT

Poe, Edgar Allan, b. Boston, 19 Jan 1809; d. Baltimore, 7 Oct 1849. American writer. Exerted strong influence on European, esp. Fr., literature. Works on which operas are based incl.: *The Pit and the Pendulum*, 1843 (BETTINELLI, *Il Pozzo e il Pendolo*, 1967); *The Devil in the Belfry*, 1839 (LUALDI, *Il Diavolo nel Campanile*, 1925); *Some Words with a Mummy* (VIOZZI, *Allamistakeo*, 1954); *The System of Doctor Tarr and Professor Fether* (TOSATTI, *Il Sistema della Dolcezza*, 1950). DEBUSSY began operas on *The Fall of the House of Usher*, 1839 (*Chute de la Maison Usher*) and *The Devil in the Belfry* (*Diable dans le Beffroi*); in 1908 he contracted with GATTI-CASAZZA, giving the NY Met priority for them. LO

Pogner, bass, Eva's father in MEISTERSINGER

Poisoned Kiss, The, romantic extravaganza, 3 acts, VAUGHAN WILLIAMS, lib. Evelyn Sharp, considerably revised on various occasions by Ursula Vaughan Williams, derived from Richard Garnett's *The Poison Maid*. Cambridge, 12 May 1936; NY, Juilliard School, 21 Apr 1937. Main chars: Tormentilla (sop.) Amaryllus (ten.) Dispascus (bass). A facetious fantasy about rival necromancers, poisons, antidotes, and goblins, often redeemed by music of charm and some passion. Love finally triumphs over evil. AB
See Kobbé

polacca *see* POLONAISE

Polacco, Giorgio, b. Venice, 12 Apr 1875; d. New York, 30 Apr 1960. Italian conductor. Studied Venice and Milan; debut London, Shaftesbury T., 1893. During next few years gained wide experience in Europe and S. America (Buenos Aires and Rio de Janeiro). Cond. first It. perf. of PELLÉAS ET MÉLISANDE, Sc. First US appearance San Francisco, 1906; NY Met, 1912–17, debut MANON LESCAUT. Chicago 1918–30. Cond., CG 1913–14 and 1930 (*Pelléas et Mélisande*). A versatile cond., he was especially at home in the It. repertory. LO

Poland. The first Polish operatic composer was Maciej Kamieński (1734–1821), whose *Nędza Uszczęśliwiona* (*Misery Contented*) was prod. at Warsaw in 1778. Kamieński had five other operas perf. in Poland, incl. *Zośka* and *Prostota Cnotliwa* (1779). Ksawery Józef Elsner (1769–1854) wr. 32 operas, of which *Andromeda* and *Trybunal Niewidzialny* (*The Invisible Tribunal*) were prod. at Warsaw in 1807. The most successful of Karol Kurpiński's (1785–1857) 24 operas was *Pałac Lucypera* (*The Palace of Lucifer*); he also wr. *Dwie Chatki* (1811), *Jadwiga, Królowa Polski* (1814), *Aleksander i Apelles* and *Nadgroda* (1815), as well as *Wanda*, first given at Poznań [Posen] in 1826. I. F. Dobrzynski (1807–67) comp. an opera, *Monbar* (*The Filibuster*) but the best-known and most prolific mid-19th-c. operatic comp. in Poland was MONIUSZKO, whose HALKA became the Polish national opera. Ignacy Jan Paderewski (1860–1941) wr. one opera, MANRU, performed in 1901. Two works by Adam Wieniawski (1876–1950), *Megaë* (1922) and *Wyzwolony* (1928) were perf. at Warsaw. SZYMANOWSKI wr. two operas of which the second, KING ROGER, has achieved both national and international fame. DEVILS OF LOUDUN has been perf. all over W. Europe. EF

politeama. It. term for theatrical building, usually of large size, catering for variety of uses, even for a circus. Examples: Bari, Politeama di

Giosa; Genoa, Politeama Regina Margherita; Palermo, Politeama Garibaldi. LO

Poliuto, opera, 3 acts, DONIZETTI, lib. CAMMARANO after CORNEILLE's *Polyeucte*. Naples, T. S. Carlo, 30 Nov 1848 (posth.); revised version *Les Martyrs*, grand opera, 4 acts, lib. SCRIBE, Paris, O., 10 Apr 1840. Main chars: Poliuto (Polyeucte – ten.) Paolina (Pauline – sop.) Severo (Sévère – bar.) Nearco (Néarche – bass). Poliuto (Polyeuctes), a secret Christian convert, is arrested and condemned to martyrdom. His wife, Paolina (Pauline), though still half in love with her former fiancé, the proconsul Severo (Severus), decides to share her husband's fate. Orig. version comp. 1838 but forbidden a stage perf. by the Neapolitan censors. JB

polka. Dance, in quick 2/4 time, which apparently originated in Bohemia *c.* 1830 and rapidly became popular. SMETANA made effective use of it in his operas, esp. BARTERED BRIDE. Also used by the Viennese operetta comps. LO

Pollione, ten., the Roman proconsul in NORMA

Polly, ballad opera, 3 acts, music arr. PEPUSCH from popular songs and ballads, lib. GAY. London, HM, 19 June 1777. Revived 1922, Kingsway T., London, revised text by Clifford Bax, music arr. Frederic Austin; NY, Cherry Lane Playhouse, 10 Oct 1925. Written in 1729 as a sequel to BEGGAR'S OPERA, it was in rehearsal when the Lord Chamberlain banned it, probably at the instigation of Sir Robert Walpole, who had been satirized in *The Beggar's Opera*. The score, nevertheless, was pub., and earned Gay £1,000. When *Polly* finally reached the stage, 45 years after Gay's death, six songs by S. ARNOLD were added. PS

polonaise (Fr.) **polacca** (It.). Term for a ceremonious Polish dance in 3/4 time with a cadence on the second beat and, in the 19th and 20th c., a characteristic accompaniment. Famous operatic examples incl. those in PURITANI, BORIS GODUNOV and EUGENE ONEGIN. The vaudeville finale of BARBIERE DI SIVIGLIA is a polonaise in all but name. JB

Pomo d'Oro, Il (*The Golden Apple*), *festa teatrale*, prologue and 5 acts, CESTI, lib. Francesco Sbarra. Vienna, Carnival, 1667. One of the most splendid spectacle operas, written for wedding of Leopold I, Emperor of Austria and Infanta Margherita of Spain, 12 Dec 1666. Based on the myth of Paris and the Golden Apple, it was perf. in a theatre built specially by BURNACINI, who also designed the 21 separate stage sets. LO

Pomone, *pastorale*, prologue and 5 acts, CAMBERT, lib. Pierre Perrin. Paris, O., 19 Mar 1671. The first Fr. opera; the first to be prod. at the new Académie Royale de Musique. LO

Ponchielli, Amilcare, b. Paderno Fasolaro, Cremona, 1 Sept 1834; d. Milan, 17 Jan 1886. Italian composer. Studied Milan Cons.; later became a professor there, incl. among his pupils PUCCINI and MASCAGNI. Of his nine operas only GIOCONDA (Milan 1876) has survived in the repertory. The remainder are: *I Promessi Sposi* (Cremona 1856, revised version Milan 1872), *La Savojarda* (Cremona 1861, revised version, *Lina,* Milan 1877), *Roderico* (Piacenza 1863), *Bertrand de Born* (1867, not performed), *I Lituani* (Milan 1874, revised version there 1875; 2nd version as *Aldona*, St Petersburg 1884), *I Mori di Valenza* (Monte Carlo 1914, posth.), *Il Figliuol Prodigo* (Milan 1880), *Marion Delorme* (Milan 1885). The last comp. of stature in the tradition of VERDI and DONIZETTI. His penchant for ballet, of which he wr. several examples, is shown in the famous 'Dance of the Hours' from *La Gioconda*. JB

Ponnelle, Jean-Pierre, b. Paris, 19 Feb 1932. French designer and producer. As designer, his first operatic assignment was BOULEVARD SOLITUDE (Hanover 1952). During the next decade his designs incl. KÖNIG HIRSCH (Berlin, Städtische O.), ROSENKAVALIER (Hamburg, CARMINA BURANA and KLUGE (San Francisco), MESSAGER'S *Isoline* (Paris OC), KLEBE'S *Die Tödlichen Wünsche* (Düsseldorf) and ALKMENE (Essen), INTERMEZZO (Munich) and OBERON (Stuttgart). In 1962 he prod. his first WAGNER opera, TRISTAN UND ISOLDE (Düsseldorf). Since then he has both dir. and designed MIDSUMMER NIGHT'S DREAM, JUNGE LORD, ZAUBERFLÖTE (Strasbourg); BARBIERE DI SIVIGLIA, COSÌ FAN TUTTE, NOZZE DI FIGARO (Salzburg); DON CARLOS, CENERENTOLA, ITALIANA IN ALGERI (Sc.); CLEMENZA DI TITO, BORIS GODUNOV, DON GIOVANNI (Cologne); VERDI'S OTELLO, TOSCA, RIGOLETTO (San Francisco); DON PASQUALE (CG), CARMEN (Stockholm), and PELLÉAS ET MÉLISANDE (Munich). EF

Pons, Lily [Alice Joséphine], b. Cannes, 16 Apr 1904; d. Dallas, Tex., 13 Feb 1976. French coloratura soprano. Studied Paris, debut Mulhouse in LAKMÉ. After singing in smaller opera houses in France her opportunity came when GATTI-CASAZZA engaged her for the NY Met;

debut in LUCIA DI LAMMERMOOR (1931). Made her home in USA; sang at the Met for over 25 years. Appeared in London only once, at CG, 1935, in BARBIERE DI SIVIGLIA. With her brilliant, flexible but light voice, attractive appearance and elegant stage presence, she was at her best in the operas of BELLINI, DONIZETTI, and the Fr. school. LO

Ponselle [Ponzillo], Rosa, b. Meriden, Conn., 22 Jan 1897. American soprano, of immigrant Neapolitan parents. Was singing with her sister, Carmella, in cinemas and church choirs before real vocal study in NY. CARUSO, who heard her, recommended her to GATTI-CASAZZA; debut, Met, 15 Nov 1918 in FORZA DEL DESTINO. The Met was to be her home base until she retired in 1937. NORMA was revived there for her, and her CG debut, 1929, was in this opera. In 1930 her VIOLETTA was hailed as 'an alliance between first-class singing and first-class intelligence'; and indeed her dramatic management of a glorious voice combined with an arresting stage presence and acting ability made her one of the great all-time operatic stars. Since 1954 art. dir., Baltimore Civic O. LO

Ponte, Lorenzo da [Emanuele Conegliano], b. Ceneda, 10 Mar 1749; d. NY, 17 Aug 1838. Italian poet and librettist. Libs incl. NOZZE DI FIGARO, DON GIOVANNI and COSÌ FAN TUTTE. Others are EQUIVOCI, based on SHAKESPEARE's *Comedy of Errors*, and COSA RARA. Also tr. TARARE into It. as *Axur, Re d'Ormus*. His last years were spent at Columbia Univ., NY, teaching It. Helped to estab. It. opera there. LO

Popp, Lucia, b. Bratislava, 12 Nov 1939. Czech-born Austrian soprano. Studied Bratislava; debut there as QUEEN OF THE NIGHT. Debut Vienna Staats O. in same role (1963). CG debut as Oscar (BALLO IN MASCHERA, 1966), later appearing as DESPINA, SOPHIE and GILDA. NY Met debut as Queen of the Night (1967). Other roles incl. CONSTANZE (formerly BLONDE), SUSANNA, ZERLINA and Marzelline (FIDELIO), all of which she has sung at Vienna and throughout Germany, esp. at Cologne, her resident co. Attractive and intense sop. AB

Poppea, sop., heroine of INCORONAZIONE DI POPPEA

Porgy and Bess, folk opera, 3 acts, GERSHWIN, lib. Du Bose Hayward and Ira Gershwin, derived from Du Bose Hayward's novel *Porgy* (1925) and the play by Dorothy and Du Bose Hayward (1927). Boston, 30 Sept 1935; NY, 10 Oct 1935; revived 1941; Zürich 1945; Copenhagen 1946; toured western Europe (Berlin, Vienna, London), South America and the USSR from 1952, sponsored by the US Dept of State; London, Stoll T., 9 Oct 1953. Main chars: Porgy (bar.) Crown (bass) Bess (sop.) Sportin' Life (ten.). The plot centres on the contest between Porgy, a cripple confined to a goat cart and Crown, a gambling stevedore, for the affections of Bess. In the end Crown is killed by Porgy; Bess, lured by Sportin' Life, leaves for New York and Porgy decides to follow. Large in style, employing major operatic orch. and vocal resources, *Porgy* is also noteworthy as a new US genre, reflecting the Broadway 'musical' idiom, noting trends then current in Paris and capturing the Negro inflection of the South. EJ O★
See Kobbé; Capote, *The Muses are Heard* (Toronto 1956; London 1959); Chase, *America's Music* (New York 1955, 1966, 1967)

Porpora, Nicola, b. Naples, 17 Aug 1686; d. Naples, 3 Mar 1768. Italian composer, singer and teacher. His *c.* 50 operas were admired in their day but he is now remembered almost solely as a great singing teacher; his pupils incl. FARINELLI and CAFFARELLI. LO

portamento (It. 'carrying'). The vocal art of bridging an interval between two notes without any break in the sound and with a slight anticipation of the second note. JB

Porter, Cole, b. Peru, Ind., 9 June 1892; d. Santa Monica, 15 Oct 1964. American composer. Showed early promise, his first song published at age 11. Attended Worcester Acad., graduated from Yale (1912) and entered Harvard Law School; soon transferred to Music Dept at Harvard where he studied three years. Served in World War I, stationed in Paris. Remained to study with d'INDY at the Schola Cantorum. His extraordinary lifestyle, owing to great wealth, and his entertainments became famous. His first success in the theatre was *Paris* (1928), followed by *Fifty Million Frenchmen* (1929), *The Gay Divorcée* (1932), *Jubilee* (1935), and esp. KISS ME KATE with other works for stage and screen. EJ
See Kimball (ed.), *Cole* (London and New York 1972)

Portugal. Music had vital patrons in the kings of the Braganza dynasty, and under John V the first known opera by a Port. comp., Francisco António de Almeida's *La Pazienza di Socrate*, was perf. in Lisbon in 1733. PORTUGAL comp. 22 Port. operas and almost 40 in It. COELHO is regarded as the founder of modern Port. opera, though no works by him or his compatriots have made international headway. Regular opera seasons are given in Lisbon. FGB

Portugal [Portogallo], Marcus Antonio da Fonseca, b. Lisbon, 24 Mar 1762; d. Rio de Janeiro, 7 Feb 1830. Portuguese composer. Wr. several operas for Lisbon, then went to Italy in 1792. His 35 It. operas include *Alceste*, 1798 and a *Nozze di Figaro*, 1799, both Venice; an *Orazi e Curiazi*, Ferrara, 1798, and what is probably his masterpiece, *Fernando nel Messico*, Venice 1798. In 1800 he returned to Lisbon as dir. of the San Carlo T., in 1810 following the Port. Court, which had fled to Brazil in 1807. LO

Postillon de Longjumeau, Le, *opéra comique,* 3 acts, A. ADAM, lib. Adolphe de Leuven and Léon Brunswick. Paris, OC, 13 Oct 1836; London, St James's T., 13 Mar 1837; NY, Park T., 30 Mar 1840. Adam's best and most successful *opéra comique*, an important precursor of OFFENBACH. Recent revivals: Stockholm, 1952; Deutsche O. am Rhein, 1968; Rouen, Jan 1975. LO
See Lubbock

Poulenc, Francis, b. Paris, 7 Jan 1899; d. Paris, 30 Jan 1963. French composer. Studied piano with Ricardo Viñes, then joined group of 'Les Six'. Comp. with individual delicate style in all music forms. Operas are *Le Gendarme Incompris* (1920), a *comédie bouffe*, MAMELLES DE TIRÉSIAS, DIALOGUES DES CARMÉLITES, and VOIX HUMAINE. FGB

Pousseur, Henri, b. Malmédy, 23 June 1929. Belgian composer. His *fantaisie variable du genre opéra, Votre Faust*, lib. Michel Butor, was prod. Piccola Sc., Milan, 15 Jan 1969, cond. by the comp. Theoretically the audience can interrupt the action of the work and so alter its course, but in practice actors are planted in the theatre to make the interruptions. EF

Powers, Marie, b. Mount Carmel, Pa., *c.* 1910; d. New York, 28 Dec 1973. American contralto. After appearing in Europe during the 1930s, she toured the USA with the San Carlo co., singing AZUCENA, AMNERIS, LAURA, and La Cieca (GIOCONDA). In 1947 she scored a huge success as Mme Flora in MEDIUM (New York) and created the Mother at the premiere of CONSUL (Philadelphia). Also sang Mme Flora at the Aldwych T., London (1948); FRICKA at the Paris O. (1951), and Mistress Quickly (FALSTAFF) at the OC (1952). EF

Poznań [Posen], Poland. The State O., dedicated to MONIUSZKO in 1919, is a flourishing

Right: Marie Powers as Mme Flora in MEDIUM, New York, 1947

centre of activity. Administrators since World War II have incl. Zygmunt Latoszewski and Zdzisław Gorzynski; Robert Satanowski became mus. dir. in 1963. Repertory incl. Polish national classics as well as JONNY SPIELT AUF, KATERINA IZMAYLOVA and SZOKOLAY's *Blood Wedding* (comp. 1964). EF

Prague [Praha, Prag]. Though Italian opera was presented by travelling cos in the 17th c. and regularly at Prague Castle and other venues by local cos in the 18th c., the first permanent home of opera was the Nostitz T., built by Count Nostitz-Rieneck (1781–3), and known from 1798 as the Estates T. and from 1948 as the Tyl T. Brought by the opera's dir. Bondini, MOZART saw NOZZE DI FIGARO here and cond. the two operas he wr. for Prague, DON GIOVANNI (1787) and CLEMENZA DI TITO (1791). Early conds incl. MÜLLER (1808–13) and C. M. WEBER (1813–16). Though the theatre was built to serve Prague's large Ger. community, regular perfs in Czech took place from 1823, the first opera written in Czech was ŠKROUP's *The Tinker*, 1826, and Škroup himself was cond. 1827–57.

The importance of the Estates T. diminished with the opening (1862) of the Czech Provisional T., where, despite the modest resources Czech opera achieved real impetus under J. N. Maýr (1862–6, 1874–81) and SMETANA (1866–74). Most of Smetana's operas received their premieres here, as did five of BENDL's operas, BLODEK's IN THE WELL, the early operas of FIBICH and DVOŘÁK, and works by many other Czech comps, while the international repertory was much expanded. In 1881 the NT, a project which had stirred emerging Czech national consciousness since the 1848 Revolution, was opened on a commanding site on the banks of the Vltava with the premiere of LIBUŠE; it was burned down less than two months later but reopened in 1883. The greatest period of the NT was under KOVAŘOVIC (1900–20) and OSTRČIL (1920–35), both comp.-conds of genius who introduced works by JANÁČEK, NOVÁK and FOERSTER and cultivated an international repertory. TALICH continued this tradition to 1945.

The New German T. served the Prague Ger. population from 1888 to 1945. Under A. NEUMANN, its first dir., it soon became the finest Ger. opera house outside Germany, employing conds of the calibre of SEIDL, MAHLER, MUCK, BLECH and KLEMPERER; the high standards continued under A. Von Zemlinsky (1911–27) and SZELL (1929–37). After the war it was known as the T. of the 5 May and from 1949 as the Smetana T., becoming with the Tyl T. part of the NT complex. Plays, ballet and opera are presented in the two larger theatres; the Tyl T. is limited to smaller-scale works, Mozart operas in particular. There are also two theatres for operetta. Since World War II conds, *Dramaturgen* and dirs have included JEREMIÁŠ, CHALABALA, VOGEL, PAUER, B. GREGOR, KREJČÍ, PUJMAN, KAŠLÍK and KROMBHOLC. A comprehensive renovation of the Smetana T. was completed in 1973, and a similar project for the NT began in 1976. JT

Pratella, Francesco Balilla, b. Lugo di Romagna, 1 Feb 1880; d. Ravenna, 18 May 1955. Italian composer. Associated with the Futurist Movement in Italy, 1910–17. His operas incl. one on flying, *L'Aviatore Dro*, 1920. LO

Pré aux Clercs, Le, *opéra comique,* 3 acts, HÉROLD, lib. François de Planard based on MÉRIMÉE's *Chronique du Règne de Charles IX,* 1829. Paris, OC, 15 Dec 1832; London, Adelphi T. (in Eng., arr. PLANCHÉ, as *The Court Masque, or Richmond in the Olden Times*), 9 Sept 1833; NY (in Fr.), 3 July 1843. Hérold's last opera, very successful, with 1,000 perfs in first 40 years in Paris. Set in Paris at the time of the St Bartholomew Massacre; the Baron de Mergy and the Comte de Comminges are rivals for the hand of Isabella, ward of Marguerite de Valois. They meet on the field called Pré aux Clercs, and Comminges is killed. LO

Prêtre, Georges, b. Waziers, 14 Aug 1924. French conductor. Studied in Paris with CLUYTENS; debut in 1947 at Marseille (ROI D'YS). First cond. at the Paris OC in 1955 (CAPRICCIO) and the Paris O. in 1959 (GOUNOD's FAUST). Chicago debut 1959 (THAÏS), San Francisco 1963, NY Met 1964 (SAMSON ET DALILA). Cond. TOSCA at CG (1965), *Faust* at Sc., Milan (1966) and ENFANT ET LES SORTILÈGES at Florence (1970), where he also cond. TURANDOT and PADMÂVATÎ (1971). EF

Preussisches Märchen (*Prussian Fable*), opera-ballet, 5 scenes, BLACHER, lib. Heinz von Cramer based on Carl Zuckmayer's *Der Hauptmann von Köpenick.* Berlin, Städtische O., 22 Sept 1952. LO

Previtali, Fernando, b. Adria, 16 Feb 1907. Italian conductor. Assistant to GUI at Florence, 1928–36; cond. the first perf. of DALLAPICCOLA's *Volo di Notte* there (1940), and the premieres of GHEDINI's *Re Hassan* at Venice (1939) and *Le Baccanti* at Sc. (1948). Other 20th-c. works he has cond. incl. Alfredo Casella's *Donna Serpente*, BUSONI's *Turandot*, DOKTOR FAUST, HONEGGER's JUDITH, and PETER GRIMES. As dir. of It. Radio Orch. he cond. DONIZETTI's works including *Duca d'Alba,* LOUISE, PELLÉAS ET MÉLISANDE, and DAPHNE. EF

Prévost, Antoine François, Abbé, b. Hesdin, Artois, 1 Apr 1697; d. Chantilly, 23 Nov 1763. French writer. His *L'Histoire du Chevalier des Grieux et de Manon Lescaut* (1731) was the first modern 'novel' to be used as basis for opera, first by AUBER, lib. SCRIBE (Paris, OC, 23 Feb 1856), then by Richard Kleinmichel (*Das Schloss de l'Orme*, 1883), MASSENET, PUCCINI, and HENZE (BOULEVARD SOLITUDE). In 1894 Massenet wrote a 1-act sequel, *Le Portrait de Manon.* Prévost also tr. into Fr. Samuel Richardson's *Pamela, Clarissa Harlowe* and *Sir Charles Grandison* – works which influenced Fr. and It. libs of *opéras comiques* and *opere buffe.* LO

Prey, Hermann, b. Berlin, 11 July 1929. German baritone. Studied Berlin; debut in 1952 at Wiesbaden. Engaged at Hamburg 1953–60, sings at Vienna, Munich, Salzburg, the NY Met, Aix-en-Provence, San Francisco, Sc., Milan and CG, where he made his debut in 1973 as FIGARO (BARBIERE DI SIVIGLIA). Particularly admired for his MOZART interpretations – DON GIOVANNI, GUGLIELMO and PAPAGENO – he also sings several R. STRAUSS roles – Harlekin (ARIADNE AUF NAXOS), Storch (INTERMEZZO), the Barber (SCHWEIGSAME FRAU), and Olivier (CAPRICCIO). He took part in the premiere of KŘENEK's *Pallas Athene Weint* (1955). EF

Right: Leontyne Price as AIDA, Paris O., 1 Feb 1968

Přibyl, Vilém, b. Náchod, 10 Apr 1925. Czech tenor. Worked as an engineer, taking private singing lessons and perf. in amateur cos, before joining the opera co. in Ústí nad Labem in 1960 and, a year later, the Brno NT. His appearance as DALIBOR with the Prague NT in Edinburgh (1964) resulted in foreign engagements, notably at London, CG and in America. The outstanding Czech ten. of his generation, he has sung several *Heldentenor* roles with great distinction (FLORESTAN, VERDI'S OTELLO, DALIBOR); though he has surprising reserves of power for such parts, his clear, exceptionally well-placed tone and intelligence are even better suited to more intimate roles such as Laca in JENŮFA. JT

Price, Leontyne, b. Laurel, Miss., 10 Feb 1927. American soprano. Studied NY Juilliard School 1949–52, singing Mistress Ford in FALSTAFF, and taking roles in FOUR SAINTS IN THREE ACTS in NY and Paris. Major debut as Bess in PORGY AND BESS, 1952, when she m. bar. William Warfield (who sang Porgy). Remained with this co. in NY, on US tour and in Europe until 1954, incl. London debut, Stoll T., 1953. Other debuts incl. NBC TV 1955 as TOSCA; San Francisco O. 1957, Madame Lidoine (DIALOGUES DES CARMÉLITES); CG 1958, Vienna Staats O. 1958, Sc. 1960, all in title role of AIDA, and became protégée of KARAJAN; Salzburg Fest. 1960, Donna ANNA; NY Met. 1961, LEONORA (TROVATORE). Created Cleopatra in ANTONY AND CLEOPATRA. Acclaimed in 1960s as the finest Aida in Europe and the USA, for warmth of feeling and lusciousness of tone, and instinctive response to femininity of dramatic character. NG

Price, Margaret Berenice, b. Blackwood, 13 Apr 1941. Welsh soprano. Studied Trinity College of Music, London. Debut as CHERUBINO with WNO (1962) and in same role at CG in 1963 when BERGANZA fell ill. EOG (1967) as Tytania (MIDSUMMER NIGHT'S DREAM) and Galatea (ACIS AND GALATEA). First Glyndebourne appearance 1968 as CONSTANZE. CG roles incl. FIORDILIGI, PAMINA, Countess ALMAVIVA, and Donna ANNA, in which she conclusively proved herself one of the most accomplished MOZART singers of the day. Debut Salzburg Fest. as Constanze (1975). Has also sung regularly at Paris O., Munich and Cologne, mostly in her Mozart repertory but also as Amelia (SIMONE BOCCANEGRA). DESDEMONA (VERDI) at Paris O. (1976). One of the smoothest, most sure sops of the day. AB

Prigioniero, Il (*The Prisoner*), opera, 1 act, DALLAPICCOLA, lib. composer, based on *La Torture par l'Espérance* by Villiers de l'Isle Adam. Turin Radio, 30 Nov 1949; Florence, T. Comunale, 20 May 1950; NY, Juilliard School, 15 Mar 1951; London, New Opera Co. at SW, 27 July 1959. Main chars: the Prisoner (bar.) the Mother (mezzo-sop.) the Gaoler/Grand Inquisitor (ten.). A prisoner of the Spanish Inquisition, his spirit unbroken by physical torture, is defeated by the worst torture of all – the illusion of liberty. EF ○

prima donna, primo uomo. (It. 'first lady', 'first man'); the lead female or male singer in a cast or company. LO

Prima Donna, opera, 1 act, BENJAMIN, lib. Cedric Cliffe. London, Fortune T., 23 Feb

Prince Igor, Bolshoy T., Moscow; Vladislav Romanovsky in the title role

1949; Philadelphia, 5 Dec 1955. Comp. 1933, it is a satire on the vanities and jealousies of two rival singers; cf. SCHAUSPIELDIREKTOR. LO

Prince Igor (*Knyaz Igor*), opera, prologue and 4 acts, BORODIN, lib. composer after Vladimir Vasilyevich Stasov's scenario. St Petersburg, Mariinsky, 4 Nov 1890; London, DL, 8 June 1914; NY Met, 30 Dec 1915. Main chars: Igor (bar.) Yaroslavna (sop.) Vladimir Igorevich (ten.) Vladimir Yaroslavich (bass) Konchak (bass) Konchakovna (mezzo-sop.). Unfinished at Borodin's death; completed and partly orch. by RIMSKY-KORSAKOV and Aleksandr Glazunov. One of the finest 19th-c. Russian operas – an epic in the tradition of IVAN SUSANIN. GN ○
See Kobbé

Pring, Katherine, b. Brighton, 4 June 1940. English mezzo-soprano. Joined SW 1968; CG debut 1971 as Thea (KNOT GARDEN). Debut Bayreuth in 1972. Her repertory incl. DORABELLA, CARMEN, AZUCENA, EBOLI, Preziosilla (FORZA DEL DESTINO), FRICKA, and Waltraute (RING DES NIBELUNGEN), Santuzza (CAVALLERIA RUSTICANA), Jocasta (OEDIPUS REX), and Kate (OWEN WINGRAVE). A highly intelligent, dramatic singer, she scored a great success as Agave in the first London perf. of BASSARIDS (ENO at Coliseum 1974). EF

Prinz von Homburg, Der, opera, 3 acts, HENZE, lib. Ingeborg Bachmann based on drama by KLEIST. Hamburg, 22 May 1960; Spoleto, 1960; London SW (Hamburg Staats O.), 26 Sept 1962. Main chars: Prince Friedrich (bar.) Elector of Brandenburg (ten.) Natalie (sop.). Prince Friedrich, condemned to death by the Elector for military disobedience, though his exploits have won the battle, accepts his sentence only to be pardoned and united with his beloved Natalie. EF

Pritchard, John, b. London, 5 Feb 1921. English conductor. *Répétiteur* at Glyndebourne in 1947, then chorus master and, in 1951, cond. Guest cond., Vienna Staats O. 1951; has since returned many times. CG debut 1952, where he has since conducted premieres of GLORIANA, MIDSUMMER MARRIAGE, and KING PRIAM. Became Principal Cond. Glyndebourne, 1963; now mus. dir. Has cond. opera and concerts all over the world. Commands a wide repertoire, specializing in MOZART. FGB

Private opera houses. The opera houses of the princely families of Europe such as those at Esterháza, Schönbrunn, and Versailles were es-

sentially private houses, not open to the general public. In 1632 Cardinal Barberini built one in his Rome palace, reputedly seating 3,000. In the 19th c. several rich landowners in Russia had opera houses on their country estates, often with serfs performing; MAMONTOV and ZIMIN in Moscow and Lapitsky in Leningrad built private opera houses, important in the history of Russian opera. The most notable 20th-c. example is probably Glyndebourne, established 1934. PATTI was one of several singers who provided themselves with small private theatres after their retirement, hers being at Craig-y-Nos, S. Wales. LO

Prodigal Son, The, church parable, 1 act, BRITTEN, lib. William Plomer, derived from the New Testament parable. Orford Church, 10 June 1968; Caramoor Fest., Katonah, NY, 29 June 1969. Main chars: Tempter (Abbot) (ten.) Younger Son (ten.) Elder Son (bar.) Father (bass). See CURLEW RIVER for description of genre. A tempter persuades the younger son to leave the security of home for the adventures of the city; he eventually returns to his forgiving father. The writing is taut and effective, as is the dramatic impact, esp. the arrival of the Tempter. AB

producer (US director; Ger. *Spielleiter*, Fr. *Régisseur*; It. *regista*). A comparatively modern term for the person who coordinates a play or opera – a duty previously perf. by the stage manager or cond. Comps supervised their own operas – GLUCK, C. WEBER, SPONTINI, MEYERBEER, VERDI and WAGNER did so meticulously. The emergence of the prod. is due principally to the Meiningen Players. The prod. must work closely with designer and cond.; the functions are often combined, e.g. KARAJAN conds and prods, and VISCONTI and ZEFFIRELLI both prod. and design. LO

Private opera houses. The little theatre, added 1891 to Craig-y-Nos by PATTI and her second husband, the tenor Ernest Nicolas (Nicolini). They built a small stage; the orchestral pit could seat about 20 players. The floor of the room could be tilted so that the audience could see the stage more easily.

Prokofiev, Sergey Sergeyevich, b. Sontsovka, Ekaterinoslav Government (now Krasnoye, Donetsk District), 23 Apr 1891; d. Moscow, 5 Mar 1953. Soviet composer. After several youthful attempts, he comp. his first important opera, the one-act *Maddalena*, in 1911 (revised 1913). Although it reveals many of the dramatic skills which were to blossom in his more mature works, for a variety of reasons (notably copyright complications) it has remained unperf. and unpub. He comp. GAMBLER in 1915–16 (revised 1927) and, though accepted by the Mariinsky T., the premiere was cancelled because of the Revolution and did not take place until 1929. By then he had comp. his comic opera LOVE FOR THREE ORANGES and also the brutally dramatic FIERY ANGEL. In contrast to both of these is *Semyon Kotko* (1940), based on a Soviet story (Valentin Katayev's *I, Son of the Working People*) and set in 1918 against the background of World War I and the revolution in the Ukraine. Prokofiev was concerned with expressing similar patriotic sentiments in WAR AND PEACE, perf. in 1946, the same year as his comedy DUENNA (comp. 1940). His last opera, STORY OF A REAL MAN (1947–8, perf. 1960), was a comparatively unsuccessful essay in socialist realism. GN
See Seroff, *Sergei Prokofiev: A Soviet Tragedy* (New York 1968; London 1969)

Sergey Prokofiev. Sketch of hussars' costumes by Isak Rabinovich for LOVE FOR THREE ORANGES, Moscow, 1927

Prométhée, *tragédie lyrique*, 3 acts, FAURÉ, lib. Jean Lorrain and Ferdinand Hérold. Béziers Arena, 27 Aug 1900; Paris, O. (revised scoring), 17 May 1917. Designed for open-air perf., large orch. forces were used – the local orch. society, 12 harps, military band (the scoring by the bandmaster of a regiment of engineers). The theme is Prometheus's seizing of fire, his punishment, and the opening of Pandora's box. LO

Prophète, Le (*The Prophet*), opera, 5 acts, MEYERBEER, lib. SCRIBE. Paris, O., 19 Apr 1849; London, CG, 24 July 1849 (in It.) with VIARDOT and MARIO. New Orleans, 2 Apr 1850. Main chars: John of Leyden (ten.) Fidès (contr.) Bertha (sop.) Count Oberthal (bar.) Zacharias (bass). Count Oberthal threatens to put Fidès, John's mother, to death unless John surrenders his sweetheart, Bertha. John, hailed by the Anabaptists as a prophet, becomes their leader and leads them to victory in Münster where he is crowned king. Distressed at being forced to renounce his mother, John promises to leave the Anabaptists and return to Leyden. Bertha appears and on learning John is the prophet, kills herself. The Emperor's troops, led by Oberthal, set fire to the palace, Fidès braves the flames to join her son in death. Perhaps the most stirring and spectacular of Meyerbeer's operas, it is unusual in the prominence given to the role of the mother, a role written specially for Viardot. It was revived by It. Radio, Turin, in 1970 as a vehicle for HORNE. PS

Prozess, Der (*The Trial*), opera, 2 acts, EINEM, lib. BLACHER and Heinz von Cramer, based on KAFKA's novel of same name, 1925. Salzburg, 17 Aug 1953; NY CC, 22 Oct 1953; London, Collegiate T. (in Eng.), 24 May 1973 – the first of Einem's operas to be prod. in Britain. A disturbing story of arrest, imprisonment, and condemnation for unspecified crimes. Also set by SCHULLER. LO

Puccini, Giacomo, b. Lucca, 22 Dec 1858; d. Brussels, 29 Nov 1924. Italian composer. Studied Milan Cons. where his teachers included PONCHIELLI. His VILLI failed to win the Sanzogno prize for which it was submitted, but had a modest success at the T. dal Verme, Milan. EDGAR (1888) was judged a failure; but his publisher Giulio RICORDI's faith in Puccini as VERDI's successor was rewarded by the triumph of MANON LESCAUT (1893). The upward trend continued with BOHÈME, TOSCA, and MADAMA BUTTERFLY, though the last was initially a fiasco. All are marked by strong emotional situations and abundant melody. With FANCIULLA DEL WEST Puccini

began to widen his stylistic range and economize on facile lyricism. RONDINE, an essay in light sentimentality in the manner of LEHÁR, has never quite survived its weak finish, but with the TRITTICO and the unfinished TURANDOT he broadened his scope still further with influences from DEBUSSY and, in the last, STRAVINSKY. Puccini is the greatest of the *veristi*, whose style was largely defined by CAVALLERIA RUSTICANA. As an operatic craftsman he is unrivalled. Though they include self-contained numbers his operas are organized motivically in a personal and more vocally orientated variant of WAGNER's manner. Personal emotion and local atmosphere form their two main points of reference. JB
See Carner, *Giacomo Puccini* (London 1958; New York 1959)

Puerto Rico *see* LATIN AMERICA

Pujman, Ferdinand, b. Nižkov, Bohemia, 23 May 1889; d. Prague, 17 Dec 1961. Czech producer. Trained as an engineer and a singer, he also worked as a music critic and developed theories of opera prod. He was able to put these into practice when he became prod. at the Brno NT (1920–1) and at the Prague NT (1921–57), where he collaborated fruitfully with OSTRČIL on a great variety of new prods. He aimed at a style pared down to essentials and which made greater use of stage space and lighting. JT

Puppet operas *see* MARIONETTE OPERAS

Purcell, Henry, b. London, ?1659; d. London, 21 Nov 1695. English composer. In 1669 became a chorister of the Chapel Royal. After his voice broke studied comp. with John Blow, 1674; 1677 appointed comp. to the King's Band, in 1679 organist Westminster Abbey and 1682 one of the three organists of the Chapel Royal. Besides his one true opera DIDO AND AENEAS he comp. a large amount of incidental music to plays incl. Thomas Betterton's adaptation of Sir Francis Beaumont and John Fletcher's *The Prophetess, Dioclesian*, 1690, John Dryden's *King Arthur*, 1690, and *The Indian Queen*, 1691 and FAIRY QUEEN. PS
See Westrup, *Purcell* (London and New York 1937)

I Puritani di Scozia, London, CG, 20 Mar 1964; produced ZEFFIRELLI; designs Zeffirelli and Peter Hall; sets and costumes from a production at T. Massimo, Palermo

Puritani di Scozia, I (*The Puritans of Scotland*), opera, 3 acts, BELLINI, lib. Carlo Pepoli after *Têtes Rondes et Cavaliers* by Jacques Ancelot and Xavier Boniface Saintine. Paris, TI, 25 Jan 1835; London, King's T., 21 May 1835; Philadelphia, 22 July 1843. Main chars: Elvira (sop.) Arturo (ten.) Riccardo (bar.) Giorgio (bass) Enrichetta (mezzo-sop.). Arturo (Lord Arthur Talbot), a royalist, is about to marry Elvira, niece of the Puritan Giorgio (George Walton); but in aiding the escape to France of Enrichetta (Henrietta Maria), widow of King Charles I, is thought to have deserted his bride, who goes mad in consequence, recovering her sanity when he returns. Bellini's last opera,

Henry Purcell's *King Arthur*, EOG, 1969, produced GRAHAM; designed Tim Goodchild; LUXON as Arthur; Denis Dowling as Merlin

written for the famous quartet of soloists, Giulia GRISI, RUBINI, TAMBURINI and LABLACHE. JB O
See Kobbé

Pushkin, Aleksandr Sergeyevich, b. Moscow, 26 May 1799; d. St Petersburg, 29 Jan 1837. Russian poet and writer. He occupied a similar position in Russian literature to that of GLINKA in music, and his works have been set to music more than those of any other Russian poet, both because of their diversity of subject and because of their sheer musicality of language. Prose works on which operas are based incl. *Peter the Great's Moor*, 1827–8 (Boris Aleksandrovich Arapov, *The Frigate 'Victory'*, comp. 1948–58; Arthur Lourié, 1958); *The Lady Peasant*, 1830 (five operas, incl. Yury Sergeyevich Biryukov, 1947; Iosif Naumovich Kovner, *Akulina*, operetta, 1948); *The Post-Station Master*, 1830 (Vladimir Nikolayevich Kryukov, 1940; F. von Reuter, *Postmeister Wyrin*, 1946); *The Snowstorm*, 1830 (DZERZHINSKY, *On a Winter's Night*, 1946); *The Undertaker*, 1830 (Boris Karlovich Yanovsky, comp. 1923; Johann Admoni, comp. 1934–5); *Dubrovsky*, 1832–3 (NÁPRAVNÍK, 1895); *The Queen of Spades*, 1833 (J. F. HALÉVY, 1850; TCHAIKOVSKY, 1890); *The History of the Pugachov Rising*, 1831–4 (MUSORGSKY, projected opera, *Pugachovshchina*, 1877); *The Captain's Daughter*, 1833–6 (CUI, 1911; Sigismund Kats, radio, 1941, revised, comp. 1946).

Poems on which operas are based incl.: *Ruslan and Lyudmila*, 1817–20 (Glinka, 1842); *A Prisoner in the Caucasus*, 1820–1 (Aleksandr Alyabyev, melodrama, 1828; two operas, incl. Cui, 1883); *The Fountain of Bakhchisaray*, 1821–3 (eight operas, incl. L. E. Mečura, *Marie Potocká*, 1871; A. F. Fyodorov, 1895; M. Zubov, comp. 1898; Aleksandr Aleksandrovich Ilyinsky, 1911; P. Krylov, comp. 1912; A. V. Parusinov, comp. 1912; I. K. Shaposhnikov, radio, 1937, staged 1950); *The Gypsies*, 1824 (17 operas, incl. Vladimir Kashperov, unfinished, comp. 1850; Grigory Andreyevich Lishin, unfinished, comp. 1876; RAKHMANINOV, *Aleko*, 1893; M. Zubov, comp. 1894; A. Ferretto, 1900; A. Schäfer, 1901; A. Ziks, comp. 1906; Konstantin Galkauskas, 1908; LEONCAVALLO, 1912; Vasily Pavlovich Kalafati, comp. 1941; Nikolay Shakhmatov, 1949); *Boris Godunov*, 1824–5 (Musorgsky, 1874); *Count Nulin*, 1825 (Grigory Lishin, comp. 1876; M. Zubov, comp. 1894; Nikolay Mikhaylovich Strelnikov, comp. 1938; Marian Viktorovich Koval, *The Country Estate*, comp. 1929–49); *Poltava*, 1828 (three operas, incl. Tchaikovsky, MAZEPA, 1884); *Eugene Onegin*, 1823–30 (Tchaikovsky, 1879); *Mozart and Salieri*, 1826–30 (RIMSKY-KORSAKOV, 1898); *A Feast in Time of Plague*, 1830 (seven operas, incl. Cui, 1901; Arthur Lourié, opera-ballet, comp. ?1939–40; Aleksandr Goldenveyzer, 1945); *The Miserly Knight*, 1826–30 (two operas, incl. Rakhmaninov, 1906); *The Stone Guest*, 1826–30 (two operas, incl. DARGOMYZHSKY, 1872); *The Little House at Kolomna*, 1830 (two operas, incl. STRAVINSKY, MAVRA, 1922); *The Tale of the Priest and his Workman Balda*, 1830 (two operas, incl. Leonid Ovanesovich Bakalov, radio, 1938); *The Tale of Tsar Saltan*, 1831 (three operas, incl. Rimsky-Korsakov, 1900); *Rusalka*, 1826–32 (Dargomyzhsky, 1856); *The Bronze Horseman*, 1833 (Gavril Nikolayevich Popov, unfinished, comp. 1937; Boris Vladimirovich Asafyev, comp. 1942); *The Tale of the Dead Princess*, 1833 (eight operas, incl. Mikhail Ivanovich Krasev, comp. 1924; Yuliya Lazarevna Veysberg, radio 1937, staged 1941; M. K. Chernyak, 1947, revised 1951; Arkady Kotilko, 1947); *The Tale of the Fisherman and the Fish*, 1833 (five operas, incl. Leonid Alekseyevich Polovinkin, 1935; Boris Dmitriyevich Gibalin, comp. 1936; Nikolay Parkhomenko, comp. 1936); *The Tale of the Golden Cockerel*, 1834 (two operas, incl. Rimsky-Korsakov, 1909). GN
See Stöckl, *Puškin und die Musik* (Leipzig 1974)

Pygmalion. The legend of the Cyprus sculptor and his beautiful statue, Galatea, brought to life by Venus, has been the source of operas by Antoine Houdar de Lamotte, 1748 (lib. ROUSSEAU), Franz Aspelmayr, 1770; SCHWEITZER, BENDA, CHERUBINI (*Pimmalione*, 1809), DONIZETTI (*Il Pigmalione*, 1816), and several others. The musical MY FAIR LADY is based on George Bernard Shaw's *Pygmalion*. LO

Q

Quaglio family, dynasty of designers of Italian origin, beginning with **Giulio I** (1601–58); ending with **Eugen** (1857–1942). **Simon** Quaglio, b. Munich, 23 Oct 1795; d. Munich, 8 Mar 1878. Chief designer, Munich, for 32 years, responsible for over 100 prods incl. a remarkable ZAUBERFLÖTE (1818). Followed by his son, **Angelo**, b. Munich, 13 Dec 1829; d. Munich, 5 Jan 1890. Designed TANNHÄUSER (1855) and LOHENGRIN (1858); also assisted WAGNER in premieres at Munich of TRISTAN UND ISOLDE, MEISTERSINGER, RHEINGOLD, and WALKÜRE. LO

Quattro Rusteghi, I (*The Four Boors*), opera, 4 acts, WOLF-FERRARI, lib. Giuseppe Pizzolato

after GOLDONI. Munich, 19 Mar 1906 (in Ger. as *Die Vier Grobiani*); Milan, Sc. (in It.), 2 June 1914; London, SW (in Eng. as *The School for Fathers*), 7 June 1946; NY CC (in Eng. as *The Four Ruffians*), 18 Oct 1951. Main chars: Lunardo (bass) Margarita (mezzo-sop.) Lucieta (sop.) Maurizio (bass or bass-bar.) Filipeto (ten.) Marina (sop.) Simon (bass-bar.) Canciano (bass) Felice (sop.). Four wives teach their elderly, churlish husbands a lesson by interfering with plans for a marriage of convenience between two of their offspring – who do in fact fall in love with each other. The It. text is in Venetian dialect. JB
See Kobbé

Queen of Spades, The (*Pikovaya dama*), opera, 3 acts, TCHAIKOVSKY, lib. comp. and Modest Tchaikovsky, after PUSHKIN. St Petersburg, Mariinsky T., 19 Dec 1890; NY Met, 5 Mar 1910; London, London O. House, 29 May 1915. Main chars: Hermann (ten.) Countess (mezzo-sop.) Lisa (sop.). In this, his penultimate opera, Tchaikovsky successfully combines elements of melodrama and the supernatural with delicate 18th-c. pastiche, at the same time borrowing certain numbers from 18th-c. Russ. and Fr. music. The sense of Fate underlying the death of Hermann emphasizes the fact that the opera was comp. between his last two Fate symphonies, the Fifth and Sixth. GN O
See Kobbé

Queen of the Night, The, sop., Pamina's mother in ZAUBERFLÖTE

Quiet Flows the Don (*Tikhiy Don*), opera, 4 acts, DZERZHINSKY, lib. Leonid Dzerzhinsky after books 1 and 2 of Mikhail Sholokhov's novel. Leningrad, Maly T., 22 Oct 1935; Detroit, Masonic Temple Auditorium, 25 Mar 1945. Main chars: Grigory Melekhov (ten.) Natalya (sop.) Aksinya (mezzo-sop.) Evgeny Listinsky (bar.). Time, 1914–17. Grigory is forced by his parents to marry Natalya; but Aksinya, his real love, arrives at the wedding celebrations, and they elope. Grigory then goes off to fight in the war. Aksinya, working as a cook in General Listinsky's house, learns that her daughter is dying and that Grigory has been killed; she is seduced by her employer's son, Evgeny. But Grigory is alive. At the Austrian front he tells his fellow soldiers that the Tsar will be overthrown and the war concluded. He returns home and, learning of Aksinya's adultery and of his daughter's death, kills Evgeny, before marching off with the revolutionary forces. Dzerzhinsky's tuneful, uncomplicated score (with its patriotic and revolutionary elements) was a landmark in Soviet music and a precedent to many more such 'song operas'. GN

Quilico, Louis, b. Montreal, 14 Jan 1929. Canadian baritone. Besides singing with the COC from 1966, has perf. at NY CC 1955, San Francisco 1956, Spoleto 1960, CG 1960–3, and Paris O. 1963–4, 1968–9. Roles incl. AMONASRO, GERMONT, RIGOLETTO, IAGO, SCARPIA, and SHARPLESS. NY Met debut 1972 as GOLAUD; has also sung Germont at Vienna 1974. LO

Quinault, Philippe, b. Paris, 3 June 1635; d. Paris, 26 Nov 1688. French dramatist, who collaborated willingly with LULLY in laying the foundations of Fr. opera in *Cadmus et Hermione* (1673); ALCESTE; *Thésée* (1675); *Atys* (1676); *Isis* (1677); *Proserpine* (1680); *Persée* (1682); PHAÉTON; AMADIS; *Roland* (1685); ARMIDE ET RENAUD. The last two also used by PICCINNI; GLUCK also set ARMIDE unchanged. Quinault's tragedies, with those of RACINE, were the models for ZENO and METASTASIO; but while the Italians sought inspiration in the heroes of history Quinault was more drawn to the fabulous and mythical. LO

R

Rabaud, Henri, b. Paris, 10 Nov 1873; d. Paris, 11 Sept 1949. French composer and conductor. Studied with MASSENET at Paris Cons., of which he became head in 1919. Wr. eight operas, the most successful being MÂROUF. *L'Appel de la Mer* (1924), lib. comp., was based on John Millington Synge's *Riders to the Sea*, 1904. Cond. at Paris O. 1908–14; dir. 1914–18. LO

Racine, Jean Baptiste, b. Le Ferté-Milon, nr Soissons, 21 Dec 1639; d. Paris, 21(?) Apr 1699. French dramatist. His tragedies with those of CORNEILLE and QUINAULT were the models for the libs of ZENO and METASTASIO esp. in their involved love tangles and the notion of the benevolent despot. The outstanding opera based fairly closely on one of his plays (*Iphigénie*, 1675) is IPHIGÉNIE EN AULIDE. LO

Radames, ten., the hero of AIDA

Radford, Robert, b. Nottingham, 13 May 1874; d. London, 3 Mar 1933. English bass. Studied London, RAM, with Albert Randegger. Debut 1904, CG, as Commendatore (DON GIOVANNI); his roles have ranged from OSMIN to BORIS GODUNOV (the first Boris in Eng.)

and WAGNER. With BEECHAM was active in promoting Eng. opera and opera in Eng.; a founder member and director, BNOC. LO

Radio opera. Sound broadcasts go back to the early days of radio, e.g., HÄNSEL UND GRETEL, broadcast from CG, 1923. Studio broadcasts, often of unusual operas, are frequent; operas are also transmitted, live or recorded, from the stage. In the 1970s BBC radio alone averaged 130 operas a year.

Among comps who have wr. operas specially for sound broadcast are BLACHER, Niccolò Castiglione, b. 1932 (*Attraverso lo Specchio*, 1961), EGK, Orazio Fiume, b. 1908 (*Il Tamburo di Panno*, 1962), GIANNINI, PIZZETTI (*Ifigenia*, 1950), and SUTERMEISTER, many of them commissioned by It. radio. *See also* NATIONAL BROADCASTING CO. LO

Raimondi, Ruggero, b. Bologna, 3 Oct 1941. Italian bass. Studied Rome; won first prize in Spoleto Fest. competition 1962; debut there 1962 (BOHÈME). Sang with increasing success throughout Italy, incl. Sc. 1970 as Procida (VÊPRES SICILIENNES). Other debuts: Wiesbaden Fest. 1965, with Venice O. Co. as Roger in *Jérusalem* (*see* LOMBARDI ALLA PRIMA CROCIATA); London, RFH, 1968, concert perf. of LUCREZIA BORGIA (Alfonso); Glyndebourne Fest. 1969, DON GIOVANNI (title role); NY Met 1970, ERNANI (Don Ruy de Silva); CG 1972, SIMONE BOCCANEGRA (Fiesco). An outstanding *basso cantante* in the 19th-c. It. repertory; a notable BORIS GODUNOV, with a voice of warm resonance and majestic dramatic power. NG

Rake's Progress, The, opera, 3 acts and epilogue, STRAVINSKY, lib. AUDEN and KALLMAN. Venice, T. La Fenice, 11 Sept 1951; NY Met, 14 Feb 1953; Edinburgh, 25 Aug 1953. Based on Hogarth's series of engravings, it represents the culmination of the neoclassical period of Stravinsky's career. Influences in the lib. and the music are drawn from a wide variety of sources but the score still displays striking individuality in the treatment of the subject. GN O

Rakhmaninov, Sergey Vasilyevich, b. Semyonovo, 1 Apr 1873; d. Beverly Hills, 28 Mar 1943. Russian pianist and composer. Graduated from Moscow Cons. (1892), comp. his first opera *Aleko* (1893) as an examination exercise. This was followed by *The Miserly Knight* and *Francesca da Rimini* (both 1906). Though the music to all three displays a fine sense of drama, the libs make poor theatre and none is ever staged with much success. Another opera, *Monna Vanna*, was not completed, and a detailed scenario that Rakhmaninov devised for *Salammbô* was never used. As a cond. he appeared with MAMONTOV's co. (1897–8) and at the Bolshoy (1904–6). GN

Ralf, Torsten, b. Malmö, 2 Jan 1901; d. Stockholm, 27 Apr 1954. Swedish tenor. Debut 1930, Stettin (CAVARADOSSI); then sang at Frankfurt and Dresden, where he created the role of Apollo (DAPHNE). Appeared at CG 1935; NY Met 1945–8. His repertory was mainly Ger., incl. Erik (FLIEGENDE HOLLÄNDER), TANNHÄUSER, LOHENGRIN, WALTHER VON STOLZING, PARSIFAL, and Bacchus (ARIADNE AUF NAXOS), but he also sang RADAMES and VERDI's OTELLO with some success. EF

Rameau, Jean-Philippe, b. Dijon, 25 Sept 1683; d. Paris, 12 Sept 1764. French organist, theorist and composer. His introduction to the theatre came soon after he settled in Paris in 1723, writing music for sketches written by his fellow townsman Alexandre Piron. Famed as organist (at cathedral of Clermont-Ferrand) and as writer of harmony textbooks (1722 and later) before writing his first opera, aged 50. His *c.* 30 works for the stage incl. *ballets*, *opéras-ballets*, *comédies-ballets*, *tragédies lyriques*, and *pastorales* – to use his own terminology. The most important are: HIPPOLYTE ET ARICIE (his first), CASTOR ET POLLUX, DARDANUS, INDES GALANTES, and PLATÉE, all written for Paris, some perf. elsewhere in France (e.g. Bordeaux). His last, *Les Boréades*, was perf. for the first time, London, Queen Elizabeth Hall, in concert version, 19 Apr 1975. A follower of the Fr. style rather than the more international It. style, and the most substantial Fr. composer between LULLY and BERLIOZ, his operas have made little headway outside France; not one has appeared for example at CG, though there have been revivals elsewhere. LO
See Girdlestone, *Jean-Philippe Rameau* (London 1957)

Ranalow, Frederick Baring, b. Kingstown, 7 Nov 1873; d. London, 8 Dec 1953. Irish baritone. Studied London, RAM. A leading bar. in BEECHAM's O. Co.; also Macheath in Nigel Playfair's revival of BEGGAR'S OPERA at the Lyric T., Hammersmith, 5 June 1920–17 Dec 1923. A versatile artist at his best in comedy roles. LO

Rankl, Karl, b. Gaden, nr Vienna, 1 Oct 1898; d. St Gilgen, 6 Sept 1968. Austrian, later British, conductor. KLEMPERER's assistant at Kroll T. 1928–31; Graz 1932–7; Prague 1937–9, where he cond. première of KŘENEK's *Karl V*.

After World War II became mus. dir., CG, 1946–51, where he built up a completely new co. LO

Rape of Lucretia, The, opera, 2 acts, BRITTEN, lib. Ronald Duncan, derived from a play by André Obey, *Le Viol de Lucrèce* (1931), in turn based on SHAKESPEARE's poem *The Rape of Lucrece* and on Livy. Glyndebourne, 12 July 1946; Chicago, 1 June 1947. Main chars: Lucretia (contr.) Female Chorus (sop.) Male Chorus (ten.) Tarquinius (bar.) Collatinus (bass). First of Britten's chamber operas, with an orch. of 12 instruments. The music is concise and concentrated, often of great eloquence in retelling from a Christian standpoint of the testing of Lucretia's fidelity and her eventual rape. The Male and Female Chorus draw the Christian moral. AB O
See Kobbé

Raskin, Judith, b. NY, 21 June 1932. American soprano. Made her name first in TV, then appeared at Santa Fe 1958; began to sing for NY CC 1959. Since 1962 has sung at NY Met; has also appeared at Glyndebourne. Has made a fine reputation as a MOZART singer and as SOPHIE. LO

Raskolnikoff, opera, 2 acts, SUTERMEISTER, lib. Peter Sutermeister based on DOSTOYEVSKY's *Crime and Punishment*. Stockholm, 14 Oct 1948. LO

Ravel, Maurice, b. Ciboure, 7 Mar 1875; d. Paris, 28 Dec 1937. French composer. Studied Paris Cons. and first became famous for his piano pieces, then as a comp. of music in exquisite style and a master of imaginative orchestration. His operas are HEURE ESPAGNOLE and ENFANT ET LES SORTILÈGES, both miniature masterpieces of subtle originality. FGB

recitative, free musical declamation following the rhythms of ordinary speech; in 18th-c. opera divided into *recitativo secco*, accompanied by keyboard and occasionally a string bass, and *recitativo stromentato* accompanied by the orchestra. The first category is used for the dialogue that carries the plot forward between set numbers; the second, more emphatic, prepares the way for an especially powerful aria or duet. In the 19th c. *recitativo secco* gradually disappears while the bounds between recitative in general and formal number become increasingly faint. JB

Recorded operas. The gramophone (phonograph), reproducing sound from a disc, dates from 1888, when Emile Berliner replaced

Maurice Ravel's ENFANT ET LES SORTILÈGES, Santa Fe, 1973; produced Bliss Hebert; designed Allen Charles Klein. Rita Shane as The Fire

Thomas Edison's cylinder with the familiar shellac plate. By the end of the 19th c. CARUSO and SHALYAPIN were already recording, and by early in the 20th c. complete operas had been recorded. Electrical recording dates from the 1920s, the improvement in sound quality leading to a vast increase in operatic recording. The introduction of the long-play micro-groove record in the 1950s encouraged still further the production of complete operas. With the coming of stereophonic, and the still more recent quadrophonic sound, the reproduction of music has become, it might be said, pluperfect, with a standard of reproduction impossible to match in real life in the concert hall or opera house. The tape recorder and the cassette have opened up still more opportunities for the armchair listener, who can now record perfs for himself at home. The voices of most of the singers mentioned in this book, esp. those active since 1930, are available on disc, and those operas, recorded in full, that are currently obtainable are indicated by the symbol O. LO

Reeves, Sims [John], b. Woolwich, 26 Sept 1818; d. Worthing, 25 Oct 1900. English tenor. First studied with his father, a bassoonist in a military band; debut as bar. 1838, Newcastle (BISHOP's *Guy Mannering*). Debut as ten. 1841, DL. After further study in Paris and Milan, Sc. debut 1836 (EDGARDO); same role, in Eng. DL 1847. Sang in BALFE's *Maid of Honour* 1847 and in DAMNATION DE FAUST 1848, both under

BERLIOZ. From 1848 engaged at HM, where he sang in first perf. in England of GOUNOD's FAUST (1864). Equally at home in opera and oratorio, he devoted his last years to the concert platform; his farewell concert was at the RAH, London, 11 May 1891. PS

Reformed Drunkard, The see IVROGNE CORRIGÉ

Reggio Emilia, Italy. The handsome T. Municipale was built in 1857 and is still used as the opera house. LO

Regina, opera, 3 acts, BLITZSTEIN, book and lyrics composer, based on Lillian Hellman's play *The Little Foxes*. NY, 46th Street T., 31 Oct 1949; revived NY CC 2 Apr 1953. Main chars: Horace Giddens, Regina, Alexandra. A vitriolic play of revenge in which a Southern family is dominated by Regina Giddens, who destroys all around her, incl. her husband. Her final control of a lucrative family business is a hollow victory, for she is tortured by fear and is hated by her own daughter. A work midway between mus. play and opera but with recitatives and orch. score of operatic proportions. EJ

régisseur, regista see PRODUCER

Reine de Saba, La (*The Queen of Sheba*), opera, 4 acts, GOUNOD, lib. BARBIER and CARRÉ based on a poem by Gérard de Nerval. Paris, O., 28 Feb 1862; Manchester, by Frederick Archer's O. Co., 10 Mar 1880; New Orleans, French OH, 12 Jan 1889. LO

Reiner, Fritz, b. Budapest, 19 Dec 1888; d. NY, 15 Nov 1963. Hungarian conductor. Worked mainly in the concert hall, but began career in opera, at Ljubljana 1910; Budapest 1911–14; Dresden 1914–21. Also cond. CG 1936–7, San Francisco 1936, and NY Met 1949–53. A noted interpreter of R. STRAUSS and WAGNER. LO

Reinhardt [Goldmann], Max, b. Baden, nr Vienna, 9 Sept 1873; d. NY, 30 Oct 1943. Austrian actor, manager, and producer. Prod. mainly plays; influence on opera mainly through his genius for handling crowds, as in HOFMANNSTHAL's *Jedermann* (Salzburg 1920). Collaborated with ROLLER in premiere of ROSENKAVALIER. Other operas prod. incl. FLEDERMAUS (1929); BELLE HÉLÈNE (1931); CONTES D'HOFFMANN (1932). LO

Reiss, Albert, b. Berlin, 23 Feb 1870; d. Nice, 19 June 1940. German tenor. Debut 1897, Königsberg (ZAR UND ZIMMERMANN). Engaged NY Met 1901–20; also sang frequently at CG. Much admired as MIME and DAVID. Retired 1938, to live in Nice. LO

Remedios, Alberto, b. Liverpool, 27 Feb 1935. English tenor of Spanish descent. Debut 1957, SW, as Tinca (TABARRO); at first sang lyric roles such as Don OTTAVIO, TAMINO, ALFREDO and GOUNOD's FAUST. In 1965 toured Australia with the SUTHERLAND co.; CG debut as Dimitry (BORIS GODUNOV). His repertory widened to incl. MAX, FLORESTAN, Erik (FLIEGENDE HOLLÄNDER), Bacchus (ARIADNE AUF NAXOS) and WALTHER VON STOLZING. Though he still sings DON CARLOS, DAMNATION DE FAUST and MANON, he now undertakes LOHENGRIN, SIEGMUND and SIEGFRIED, which he sang in the Eng. RING cycle (Col., 1973). EF

Renard, *histoire burlesque chantée et jouée* (*The Fox: A Burlesque*), 2 acts, STRAVINSKY, lib. comp. and Charles Ferdinand Ramuz. Paris, O., 2 June 1922; NY, Vanderbilt T., 2 Dec 1923 (concert perf.); NY, Hunter College Playhouse, 13 Jan 1947 (staged). Twice the cock is rescued from the fox by the cat and the goat; finally the fox is killed. There are a number of innovations, particularly the placing of the singers (two tenors and two basses) in the orch. The actors, 'preferably on a trestle stage placed in front of the orchestra', do not speak. GN O

Renato, bar., Amelia's husband in BALLO IN MASCHERA

Renaud, Maurice, b. Bordeaux, 24 July 1861; d. Paris, 16 Oct 1933. French baritone. Studied Paris and Brussels; debut 1883, T. de la Monnaie. Stayed there until 1890, creating Gunther in SIGURD and Hamilcar in SALAMMBÔ. Paris O. 1891–1902. Appeared frequently at CG 1897–1904. Debut New Orleans 1893 (SAMSON ET DALILA); sang in NY, Manhattan OH 1906–10, Met 1911–12. Sang a wide variety of roles in MOZART, VERDI, and WAGNER, several of the latter for the first time at the Paris O. (BECKMESSER was particularly prized) as well as the Fr. repertory. Admired for his voice and for his acting and general artistry. LO

Rencontre Imprévue, La (*The Unexpected Meeting*), *comédie mêlée d'ariettes*, 3 acts, GLUCK, lib. L. H. Dancourt. Vienna, BT (in Fr.), 7 Jan 1764; Frankfurt (in Ger. as *Die Pilger von Mekka*), 1770; Loughton, Essex (in Eng. tr. by DUNN), 21 July 1939; Cleveland, Ohio,

Maurice Renaud as BECKMESSER, one of his well-known roles

8 June 1951. Gluck's last, most complete and best *opéra comique*, based on play by Alain-René Le Sage and d'Orneval, *Les Pèlerins de la Mecque* (1731). It had a successor in ENTFÜHRUNG AUS DEM SERAIL; cf. HAYDN's *L'Incontro Improviso* (1775). Frequently revived in Germany. LO

Rennert, Günther, b. Essen, 1 Apr 1911. German producer and *Intendant*. An important figure in post-World War II Germany. *Intendant* Hamburg 1946–56, raising Hamburg to a pre-eminent position among opera houses during this period. Prod. NY Met, 1960–7; since then *Intendant* Munich Staats O. Has dir. at Stuttgart, Milan, Glyndebourne, Schwetzingen (Günter Bialas's *Der Gestiefelte Kater*, June 1975), Vienna, and CG. LO

Re Pastore, Il (*The Shepherd King*), opera, 2 acts, MOZART, lib. METASTASIO. Salzburg, 23 Apr 1775; London, St Pancras Town Hall, 8 Nov 1954; Norfolk, Va., 7 July 1971. Main chars: Aminta (sop.) Elisa (sop.) Agenore (ten.) Alessandro (ten.) Tamiri (sop.). Aminta (Amyntas), a poor shepherd, is discovered by Alessandro (Alexander the Great) to be the rightful heir to the throne of Sidon. Having reinstated him, Alessandro intends him to marry Tamiri (Tamiris), daughter of the former usurper, unaware that she is in love with Agenore. But Aminta renounces his crown rather than be parted from his beloved shepherdess Elisa. Alessandro gives in and appoints Aminta 'shepherd king' of Sidon with Elisa as his queen. Famous for the aria with violin obbligato, *'L'amerò, sarò costante'*. JB O

répétiteur (Fr. 'rehearser'). A musician and pianist attached to an opera co. whose task is to teach the singers their notes.

rescue opera. Term signifying an opera featuring the more or less spectacular rescue of hero or heroine from death or catastrophe. Seen in embryo in RICHARD CŒUR DE LION, it appears in its full melodramatic form in DEUX JOURNÉES and intensified in LODOÏSKA. The best-known, and best, example is FIDELIO. LO

Resnik, Regina, b. NY, 30 Aug 1922. American mezzo-soprano, formerly soprano. Debut 1942, Brooklyn Acad. of Mus., and with New O. Co. as LADY MACBETH. NY Met debut 1944 as LEONORA (TROVATORE). Leading sop. roles in next 10 years; created Delilah in Bernard Rogers's *The Warrior* (1945). Sang in US premieres of PETER GRIMES as Ellen Orford and RAPE OF LUCRETIA as Female Chorus; sang title role, 1957, Stratford, Ont. European debut Bayreuth Fest. 1953 (SIEGLINDE). Changed to mezzo-sop. 1955; debut in this register at Cincinnati (AMNERIS). Created Baroness in VANESSA. CG 1957 as notably successful CARMEN, followed in later seasons by KLYTEMNESTRA, ULRICA, Nurse (FRAU OHNE SCHATTEN). Other European debuts incl. Salzburg Fest. as EBOLI, Berlin as Carmen, both 1960. Returned to Bayreuth 1961 as FRICKA, the first singer to appear there in two voice ranges. Her 25th anniversary at NY Met celebrated (1970) with *Carmen*, having sung 37 different roles with the co. In 1971 she turned prod., staging *Carmen* at Hamburg, ELEKTRA at Venice. Her singing expressed vivid stage char. through voice of rich quality and flexibility. NG

Respighi, Ottorino, b. Bologna, 9 July 1879; d. Rome, 18 Apr 1936. Studied Liceo Musicale, Bologna, and with RIMSKY-KORSAKOV in St Petersburg and BRUCH in Berlin. A violinist and quartet leader, he devoted himself exclusively to teaching and comp. after 1908; professor, Rome Cons., 1912. Best known for his orchestral tone poems, he wrote nine operas in a late romantic manner influenced partly by R. STRAUSS, partly by the Russians, but unmistakably Italian. Of these the most notable are the fable *La Bella Addormentata nel Bosco* (Rome

1922), the comedy *Belfagor* (Milan 1923), *La Campana Sommersa* (Hamburg 1927), and *La Fiamma* (Rome 1934). Keenly interested in pre-classical mus., he made a free transcription of FAVOLA D'ORFEO (Milan 1935). JB

Retablo de Maese Pedro, El (*Master Peter's Puppet Show*), puppet opera, 1 act, FALLA, lib. composer, based on incident in CERVANTES' *Don Quixote*. Seville, 23 Mar 1923 (concert perf.); Paris, 25 June 1923 (staged); Clifton, England, 14 Oct 1924; NY, 29 Dec 1925. In the stable of an inn, Master Peter's puppets perf. the story of Melisendra's rescue from the Moors, watched by an audience incl. Don Quixote and Sancho Panza. The Don sees the puppets as human figures in need of support and leaves his place to do battle, thereby ruining the perf. Falla specified two sizes of puppets for performers and audience, with singers placed with the pit orch. At a Spoleto Fest. prod. (1969), children took the puppet roles. The mus., scored for chamber orch. of not more than 23 players, marked a change in Falla's style away from the Span. folk and regional idiom: it derived more from medieval Span. music, both courtly and popular, impregnated with Castilian restraint and *dignidad*. NG O
See Pahissa, *Manuel de Falla, His Life and Works* (London 1954)

Rethberg [Sättler], Elisabeth, b. Schwarzenburg, 22 Sept 1894. German-American soprano. Studied Dresden; sang there 1915–22 (debut as Arsena in ZIGEUNERBARON, 1915). NY Met (debut as AIDA), 1922–42. CG 1926 (debut as CIO-CIO-SAN and Aida, much praised) and 1934–9. Returned to Dresden to create title role in ÄGYPTISCHE HELENA. Had a lyric *spinto* voice of surpassing beauty, and was as at home in the Ger. as the It. repertory. Her leading roles also incl. VERDI'S DESDEMONA, AMELIA, ELSA, and ELISABETH. AB

Rêve, Le (*The Dream*), opera, 4 acts, BRUNEAU, lib. GALLET, based on novel, *Le Rêve*, ZOLA, 1888. Paris, OC, 18 June 1891; London, CG, 29 Oct 1891. Widely perf. in France and Belgium, also in Hamburg (cond. MAHLER). Angélique, dreamy, romantic, falls in love with Félicien, son of Bishop Jean d'Hautecoeur, who forbids the marriage. Angélique goes into a decline; Félicien implores the Bishop to perf. a miracle and restore her to health. The miracle takes place, apparently; the couple are wed, but Angélique dies. LO

Revisor, Der (*The Government Inspector*), opera, 5 acts, EGK, lib. composer adapted from GOGOL. Schwetzingen, 9 May 1957; London, New O. Co. at SW, 25 July 1958; NY CC, 19 Oct 1960. Main chars: Chlestakov (ten.) Mayor (bass) Mayor's wife (mezzo-sop.) Mayor's daughter (sop.). A penniless civil servant is mistaken for the Government Inspector, and entertained by the Mayor's household. EF

Reyer, Ernest [Louis Étienne Rey], b. Marseille, 1 Dec 1823; d. Le Lavandou, Hyères, 15 Jan 1909. French composer. Wrote five operas: *Maître Wolfram* (1854), 1-act *opéra comique*; *La Statue* (1861), based on an ARABIAN NIGHTS story, 3 acts; rewritten, 5 acts, for the O. 1903; *Erostate* (Baden 1862), 2 acts; SIGURD; and SALAMMBÔ. Also worked as mus. critic; reported the premiere of AIDA. LO

Rezniček, Emil Nikolaus von, b. Vienna, 4 May 1860; d. Berlin, 2 Aug 1945. Austrian composer and conductor. Best known for comic opera, particularly DONNA DIANA and *Till Eulenspiegel* (1902). Court cond. Weimar 1896 and Mannheim 1896–9; cond. Warsaw O. 1906–9, KO, Berlin 1909–11. GN

Rheingold, Das *see* RING DES NIBELUNGEN

Ricciarelli, Katia, b. Rovigo, 18 Jan 1946. Italian soprano. Debut 1969, Mantua (MIMI), then won the Verdi Award for young opera singers at Parma (1970) and the It. Radio New Verdi Voices Contest at Milan (1971). VERDI operas she has sung incl. DUE FOSCARI, GIOVANNA D'ARCO, CORSARO, TROVATORE, SIMONE BOCCANEGRA, BALLO IN MASCHERA, DON CARLOS, and OTELLO. Sc. debut 1973 (SUOR ANGELICA); CG debut 1974 (Mimi). She has sung all over Italy and at Chicago, while her roles range from Corinna (ANACRÉON) and Julietta (CAPULETI ED I MONTECCHI) to ELSA. EF

Richard Cœur de Lion, *comédie en prose mêlée d'ariettes* (*Richard Lionheart*, prose comedy with ariettas), 3 acts, GRÉTRY, lib. SEDAINE. Paris, CI, 21 Oct 1784; London, CG, 16 Oct 1786; Boston, Mass., 23 Jan 1797; T. Royal, Halifax, Canada, 14 Feb 1798. Revived Ghent 1974–5. Grétry's masterpiece tells the story of Richard's rescue by his minstrel, Blondel, thus presaging the later RESCUE OPERA. LO

Richter, Hans, b. Györ [Raab], 4 Apr 1843; d. Bayreuth, 5 Dec 1916. Hungarian conductor. Worked closely with WAGNER; cond. first perf. of RING DES NIBELUNGEN. Principal cond., Vienna, 1875–1900; mus. dir. there, 1893. Cond. first perfs in England of TRISTAN UND ISOLDE and MEISTERSINGER (DL 1882), and first *Ring* in English (CG 1909). LO

Ricordi. Publishing house in Milan, founded by **Giovanni** Ricordi (1785–1853) in 1808; carried on by his son **Tito** (1811–88), grandson **Giulio** (1840–1912), and great-grandson **Tito** (1865–1933). Pub. operas by most 19th-c. It. comps incl. BELLINI, DONIZETTI, VERDI, and PUCCINI. The firm's archives contain a valuable collection of autograph scores. Present head of firm, Dr Carlo Clausetti. LO

Ridderbusch, Karl, b. Recklinghausen, 1932. German bass. Encouraged to take up singing by Rudolf Schock with whom he appeared in a film. Studied Folkwang School, Essen. After appearing with the Münster and Essen cos, joined the Deutsche O. am Rhein, Düsseldorf, 1965. Bayreuth debut 1967, King Henry (LOHENGRIN) and FASOLT; has since sung there regularly as POGNER, HAGEN, and HANS SACHS. CG debut 1971 (Fasolt, HUNDING, and Hagen); returned for the Landgrave (TANNHÄUSER) 1973. NY Met debut 1967 (Hunding). Other roles incl. OCHS, PHILIPPE, and the Commendatore (DON GIOVANNI). One of the foremost Ger. basses of today. AB

Riders to the Sea, opera, 1 act, VAUGHAN WILLIAMS, lib. from John Millington Synge's tragedy of the same name. London, RCM, 30 Nov 1937; Cleveland, Ohio, 26 Feb 1950. Main chars: Cathleen (sop.) Nora (sop.) Maurya (contr.) Bartley (bar.). Set on the West coast of Ireland, Maurya loses her husband and sons to the sea. The comp. develops her char. in finely expressive music. Often called the Eng. PELLÉAS ET MÉLISANDE, this short, intense piece is undoubtedly the comp.'s stage masterpiece. AB ○

Rienzi *see* COLA RIENZI

Rieti, Vittorio, b. Alexandria, Egypt, 28 Jan 1898. Italian, naturalized American, composer. Studied Milan and Rome; his earlier works incl. an unperf. opera, *Orfeo Tragedia* (wr. 1928), and *Teresa nel Bosco* (Venice 1934). Moved to the USA 1940; his later operas, *Don Perlimplin* (1952), *The Pet Shop* (1958), and *The Clock* (1960), have all been perf. there. Has also wr. a radio opera, *Viaggio d'Europa* (1954). EF

Riga *see* LATVIA

Rigoletto, opera, 3 acts, VERDI, lib. PIAVE after HUGO's *Le Roi s'amuse*. Venice, T. La Fenice, 11 Mar 1851; London, CG, 14 May 1853; NY, Acad. of Music, 19 Feb 1855. Main chars: Rigoletto (bar.) Gilda (sop.) Il Duca (ten.) Sparafucile (bass) Maddalena (contr.). Rigoletto, court jester, intending to have the Duke murdered for having seduced his daughter, Gilda, brings about the murder of the girl herself. The first of the 'romantic trilogy' (see TROVATORE, TRAVIATA). JB ○
See Kobbé

Rimsky-Korsakov, Nikolay Andreyevich, b. Tikhvin, Novgorod Government, 18 Mar 1844; d. Lyubensk, St Petersburg Government, 21 June 1908. Russian composer. His finest mus. is contained in his operas, particularly those fantasy works in which he could exploit his talent for vivid, exotic harmony and orchestration. This largely compensates for a lack of characterization which is felt in most of his works. MAID OF PSKOV, his first opera, is an exception, containing a powerfully drawn Ivan the Terrible; it also differs from much of his later mus. in that (much like BORIS GODUNOV) lyricism is combined with the mus. realism first mooted in STONE GUEST. His next two operas, MAY NIGHT and SNOW MAIDEN, are unprofound but delicate, appealing stories embracing the real and imaginary worlds, whereas the opera-ballet MLADA and *Christmas Eve* (1895) contain much dry mus. and ineffective drama; the latter also came in for criticism from the censor for its depiction of a tsarina (clearly Catherine II). Both operas, however, were useful preparatory exercises for the far finer SADKO, a *bylina* (epic) opera in the tradition of PRINCE IGOR. For his next ideas Rimsky turned away from Russian folklore: sketches for *The Barber of Bagdad* (1895) came to nothing, but he did complete *Mozart and Salieri* (1898), a setting of one of PUSHKIN's 'little tragedies'. After making a separate opera, *Boyarinya Vera Sheloga* (1898), out of the prologue for the unperf. second version of *The Maid of Pskov*, he comp. TSAR'S BRIDE which, like *The Maid*, is concerned not with fantasy but wholly with human emotions. TALE OF TSAR SALTAN in many respects recalls *May Night*, *Mlada*, and *Christmas Eve*, but the writing is altogether more skilfully imaginative. *Serviliya* (1902) and *Pan Voyevoda* (1904) are both dull pieces (the former is a 5-act opera set in ancient Rome; the latter is in 4 acts, set in 16th- and 17th-c. Poland) but between these came the 1-act *Kashchey the Immortal* (1902), another piece of folklore in which the mood is (by contrast to other works) 'sombre and cheerless, with rare shafts of light and sometimes sinister gleams'. His last two operas are his finest: LEGEND OF THE INVISIBLE CITY OF KITEZH for its warmth, lyricism, and unusually clear characterization, GOLDEN COCKEREL for its scintillating orchestration and sharp wit. GN
See Calvocoressi and Abraham, *Masters of Russian Music* (London and New York 1936)

Der Ring des Nibelungen. A scene from the ENO's production of RHEINGOLD, revived at the Coliseum, 13 Mar 1975 with (left to right) PRING as Fricka; Emile Belcourt as Loge; HERINCX as Wotan; Norman Welsby as Donner; GRANT as Fafner; Robert Ferguson as Froh; Robert Lloyd as Fasolt; and Lois McDonald as Freia

Rinaldo, opera, 3 acts, HANDEL, lib. Giacomo Rossi based on GERUSALEMME LIBERATA. London, HM, 24 Feb 1711. Handel's first London opera, very successful, and perf. Hamburg (1715), Naples, Milan, and Venice (all 1718). The story is basically the same as that of ARMIDE. LO

Ring des Nibelungen, Der (*The Ring of the Nibelungs*), operatic tetralogy comprising *Das Rheingold, Die Walküre, Siegfried, Götterdämmerung*, WAGNER, lib. comp. First perf. as a cycle, Bayreuth 13, 14, 16, 17 Aug 1876. London, HM, 5–9 May 1882; NY, 4–11 Mar 1889. Main chars: *Rheingold*: Alberich (bar.) Wotan (bar. or bass-bar.) Fricka (mezzo-sop.) Loge (ten.) Fasolt (bass) Fafner (bass) Mime (ten.) Erda (contr.) Freia (sop.) Froh (ten.) Donner (bar.). *Die Walküre*: Siegmund (ten.) Sieglinde (sop.) Hunding (bass) Wotan (bar. or bass-bar.) Fricka (mezzo-sop.) Brünnhilde (sop.). *Siegfried*: Siegfried (ten.) Mime (ten.) Wotan (bar. or bass-bar.) Alberich (bar.) Fafner (bass) Woodbird (sop.) Erda (contr.) Brünnhilde (sop.). *Götterdämmerung*: Siegfried (ten.) Brünnhilde (sop.) Gunther (bar.) Gutrune (sop.) Hagen (bass) Alberich (bar.) Waltraute (mezzo-sop.). A personal version of the Teutonic epic, the *Nibelungenlied*, developed as a parable of humanity and its search for power, it tells of the theft of the Rhinegold and the misfortune it brings to all who possess it. Wagner's most monumental mus. drama, it is the one which conforms most closely to the theories propounded in his pub. writings. JB O
See Kobbé

Rinuccini, Ottavio, b. Florence, 20 Jan 1562; d. Florence, 28 Mar 1621. Italian poet, member of Florentine Camerata and the first operatic librettist. His *Dafne* was set by PERI (1597) and Marco Gagliano (1608) and, in Ger. tr., by Heinrich Schütz (1627); *Euridice* was set by Peri (1600) and CACCINI (1602); his *Arianna* and *Il Ballo delle Ingrate* were both set by MONTEVERDI (1608). LO

Rio de Janeiro. The **Teatro Municipal**, inaugurated 14 July 1909, a year after the T. Colón, Buenos Aires, was the main opera house in Rio de Janeiro, capital of Brazil, until 21 Apr 1960. It has had its own national opera co., ballet school, chorus, and orchestra since 1931. Besides engaging international performers and producing classic 20th-c. works e.g. PETER GRIMES and WOZZECK, it has given premieres of Brazilian operas, incl. Francisco Mignone's *O Contratador de Diamantes* (1924, 1956), Oscar Lorenzo Fernândez's *Malazarte* (1941), Camargo Guarnieri's *Pedro Malazarte* (1952, 1959), and VILLA-LOBOS's *Izath* (wr. 1918, 1958). MK

Rip Van Winkle, opera, 3 acts, BRISTOW, lib. Jonathan Howard Wainwright. Based on story of the same title by Washington Irving (1820). NY, Niblo's Garden, 27 Sept 1855. Semi-professional revival by American Music Group, Univ. of Illinois, 2–3 Feb 1974. The first US grand opera on an American subject, with spoken dialogue. Rip, a good-natured ne'er-do-well with a termagant wife, wanders off to the mountains where, after an encounter with a colony of dwarfs, he falls asleep for 20 years. Unaware of the passage of time, he returns to find his wife gone, his child grown, and himself a figure of ridicule. Professing loyalty to the King, he learns that America is now a republic. Because Rip's daughter follows her lover to the Revolutionary War, the plot (and some of the music) resembles that of FILLE DU RÉGIMENT. The librettist, who was a military man, added many drills, marches and soldiers' choruses, and introduced a love interest not in the original story. EJ

Rise and Fall of the City of Mahagonny *see* AUFSTIEG UND FALL DER STADT MAHAGONNY

Risurrezione (*Resurrection*), opera, 4 acts, ALFANO, lib. Cesare Hanau after TOLSTOY's novel, *Resurrection*, 1900. Turin, T. Vittorio Emanuele, 30 Nov 1904. Chicago, 31 Dec 1925. Main chars: Katiusha (sop.) Dimitri (ten.) Simonson (bar.). Katiusha is seduced and abandoned by her childhood friend Prince Dimitri. She tries and fails to meet him at a railway station. He comes, remorseful, to rescue her from being sentenced to Siberia on a false charge, but she spurns him proudly. He seeks her out in Siberia again offering marriage; but although she still loves Dimitri she decides to marry her fellow convict, Simonson, instead. JB

Rita ou Le Mari Battu (*Rita, or The Beaten Husband*), *opéra comique*, 1 act, DONIZETTI, lib. by Gustave Vaëz. Paris, OC, 7 May 1860 (posth.); NY, Hunter College, 14 May 1957; London, National School of Opera, 12 Dec 1962. Chars: Rita (sop.) Beppe (ten.) Gasparo (bar.). A hen-pecked husband meets his wife's former spouse, believed dead. Both play a game of chance for the privilege of losing her. Beppe, the present incumbent, loses; but Rita promises to reform.

The opera was wr. 1841, but never given in Donizetti's lifetime. JB
See Ashbrook, *Donizetti* (London 1965)

Ritorno d'Ulisse in Patria, Il (*Ulysses' Return to his Country*), opera, prologue and 5 acts, MONTEVERDI, lib. Giacomo Badoaro. Venice, T. S. Cassiano, Feb 1641; Florence Maggio Musicale, in version by DALLAPICCOLA, 1942; London, St Pancras Arts Fest., 16 Mar 1965. Washington DC, in LEPPARD's realization, 18 Jan 1974. Ulysses returns to the waiting Penelope disguised as an old beggar. The suitors surrounding her are unable to bend Ulysses' bow, which he does with ease, then kills them. LO ○

Roar, Leif. Danish baritone. Debut Copenhagen; then sang at Kiel 1967, Düsseldorf 1967, Munich 1971, Stuttgart, Salzburg 1973, the T. Colón, Buenos Aires, Sc., and Schwetzingen, where he took part in the premiere of KLEBE's *Märchen von der Schönen Lilie* (1969). His repertory incl. PIZARRO, DI LUNA, Posa (DON CARLOS), Jokanaan (SALOME), Mandryka (ARABELLA), MATHIS DER MALER, Nick Shadow (RAKE'S PROGRESS), ULISSE and several WAGNER roles: FLIEGENDE HOLLÄNDER, WOLFRAM, TELRAMUND, KURWENAL, AMFORTAS, Donner (RHEINGOLD), and WOTAN. EF

Robert le Diable (*Robert the Devil*), opera, 5 acts, MEYERBEER, lib. SCRIBE and Germain Delavigne. Paris, O., 21 Nov 1831; London, DL, 20 Feb 1832 (in Eng. as *The Daemon*); CG, 21 Feb 1832 (in Eng. as *The Fiend Father*). New Orleans, 24 Dec 1836. Main chars: Robert (ten.) Bertram (bass) Isabella (sop.) Alice (sop.). Robert, Duke of Normandy, is the son of the devil (masquerading as Bertram) and a mortal woman. Bertram offers Robert the love of Isabella in exchange for his soul. Alice, his foster-sister, dissuades him, and Robert, now redeemed, and Isabella are married, and Bertram returns to hell. One of the greatest operatic successes of all time but modern perfs are rare. It received a major revival at the Maggio Musicale, Florence, in 1968 (in It.) with SCOTTO as Isabella and CHRISTOFF as Bertram. PS

Roberto Devereux, Conte d'Essex, opera, 3 acts, DONIZETTI, lib. CAMMARANO after François Ancelot's *Élisabeth d'Angleterre*. Naples, T. S. Carlo, 2 Oct 1837: London, 24 June 1841: NY, 15 Jan 1849. Main chars: Roberto (ten.) Sara (sop. or mezzo-sop.) Elisabetta (sop.) Nottingham (bar.). Roberto (Robert, Earl of Essex), loved by Elisabetta (Queen Elizabeth I of England), is secretly in love with Sara, Countess of Nottingham. Already in disgrace and suspected of rebellion, he is condemned to death by the jealous Queen. JB ○
See Ashbrook, *Donizetti* (London 1965)

Robinson, Anastasia, b. Italy, *c.* 1695; d. Southampton, Apr 1755. English contralto. Daughter of a portrait painter; studied singing with William Croft and Pier Giuseppe Sandori. Debut 1714, London, in a *pasticcio*, *Creso*; in premiere of HANDEL's *Amadigi* (1715). Triumphed at King's T. 1720–4 in D. SCARLATTI's *Narciso*, BONONCINI's *Griselda*, and esp. in Handel's *Floridante* (1721), *Flavio* (1723), *Ottone* (1723) and GIULIO CESARE. In 1722 she had secretly m. the Earl of Peterborough who, in

Robert le Diable. CICERI's design for Act III of the premiere, Paris O., 21 Nov 1831

defence of her honour, once whipped the castrato Senesino [Francesco Bernardi]. She is buried in Bath Abbey. Her sister Elizabeth was also a singer of note. PS

Robinson, Forbes, b. Macclesfield, 21 May 1926. English bass. Began as a repertory actor and choral singer, turned to opera after winning the 1952 Mario Lanza competition in London, which brought him a year's study at Sc. Joined CG 1954; debut as Schlemil (CONTES D'HOFFMANN). Acquired repertory of over 70 large and small roles as one of the co.'s most consistent singers. Created title role in KING PRIAM; won major success as the bullying Claggart in BILLY BUDD (revised version, CG 1964, and NY same year); played Moses (speaking role) in MOSES UND ARON in UK stage premiere. He was the first Eng. DON GIOVANNI at CG (1970) since SANTLEY in 1868. Frequent appearances with EOG, SO, WNO. His vocal char. ranges from dark menace to buffo comedy, informed by deep musical understanding. NG

Rocca, Lodovico, b. Turin, 29 Nov 1895. Italian composer. Educated Turin and Milan; 1940–6 dir. Cons. G. Verdi at Turin. His operas incl. *La Morte di Frine* (comp. 1920; prod. Sc. 1937); *In Terra di Leggenda* (comp. 1922–3 as *La Corona del Re Gaulo*; prod. Bergamo 1936); *Il Dibuk* (Sc. 1934); *Monte Ivnor* (Rome 1939); and *L'Uragano*, based on Aleksandr Nikolayevich Ostrovsky's play, *The Storm* (Sc. 1952). EF

Rocco, bass, the jailer in FIDELIO

Rodelinda, *opera seria*, 3 acts, HANDEL, lib. Antonio Salvi, altered by Nicola Haym. London, Haymarket T., 24 Feb 1725. Northampton, Mass., Smith College, 9 May 1931. Main chars: Rodelinda (sop.) Bertarido (mezzo-sop.) Edwige (contr.) Grimaldo (ten.) Garibaldo (bass). Bertarido, rightful king of Lombardy, believed dead, returns home secretly to find the usurper Grimaldo trying to force his wife Rodelinda into marriage with him. Bertarido is arrested and imprisoned; escaping, he prevents Grimaldo from being killed by his own villainous henchman Garibaldo. In return Grimaldo gives up the throne, and kneels in homage to the true sovereign. JB ○

Rodgers, Richard, b. Long Island, NY, 28 June 1902. American composer of musicals. Learned his craft by attending theatre and admiring great works of his day. Seeing *Very Good, Eddie* (1916), he rejected European operetta for US subjects. His meeting with HART (1918) established immediate rapport that lasted until early 1940s when Rodgers turned to HAMMERSTEIN II for OKLAHOMA!. Their collaboration prod. 27 musical shows in 25 years incl. CAROUSEL, SOUTH PACIFIC, KING AND I. EJ
See Ewen, *Richard Rodgers* (New York 1957); Rodgers, *Musical Stages* (New York 1975)

Rodolfo, ten., one of the four Bohemians in BOHÈME

Rodrigo, bar., the Marquis of Posa in DON CARLOS

Rodríguez de Hita, Antonio, b. 1724; d. Madrid, 21 Feb 1787. Spanish composer. His meeting with the dramatist CRUZ resulted in the heroic *zarzuela Briseida* (1768), the *zarzuela* of peasant life *Las Segadoras de Vallecas* (1768) and LABRADORAS DE MURCIA, which were of the utmost importance to the subsequent development of the *zarzuela*. FGB

Rodzinsky [Rodziński], Artur, b. Split [Spalato], 2 Jan 1894; d. Boston, 27 Nov 1958. Polish conductor. Cond. opera in Warsaw in the 1920s; moved to USA, chiefly as orch. cond., but from 1933 gave interesting concert perfs of opera, Cleveland, and cond. first US perf. of *Lady Macbeth of the Mtsensk District* (*see* KATERINA IZMAYLOVA (1935). Has also cond. at Sc., Salzburg and Florence Maggio Musicale, where he gave first perf. outside USSR of WAR AND PEACE. LO

Roi David, Le (*King David*), lyric drama, in 2 parts and 31 scenes, HONEGGER, lib. René Morax. Mézières, 11 June 1921; NY, 26 Oct 1925; London, RAH, 17 Mar 1927. Main chars:

King David (ten.) young David (mezzo-sop.) Michal (sop.) Angel (sop.). Taken from the Old Testament Books of Samuel I and II. EF O

Roi de Lahore, Le (*The King of Lahore*), opera, 5 acts, MASSENET, lib. GALLET, based on story from the Hindu poem *Mahabharata*. Paris, O., 27 Apr 1877; London, CG (in It.), 28 June 1879; New Orleans (in Fr.) Dec 1883; NY (in Fr.) 29 Feb 1924. Massenet's first work at the O., and his first real success in France and Italy. Sita is loved by King Alim and his minister, Schindia. The latter kills Alim, who is allowed by the god Indra to return, as a beggar. Sita kills herself, to be with Alim in paradise. LO

Roi d'Ys, Le (*The King of Ys*), opera, 3 acts, LALO, lib. Édouard Blau. Paris, OC, 7 May 1888; New Orleans, 23 Jan 1890; London, CG, 17 July 1901. The Breton legend on which this is loosely founded is that drawn on by DEBUSSY for his piano prelude *La Cathédrale Engloutie*. LO

Roi d'Yvetot, Le (*The King of Yvetot*), *opéra comique*, 4 acts, IBERT, lib. Jean Limzon and André de la Tourasse, based on a ballad of the same name. 1813, by Pierre-Jean Béranger. Paris, OC, 15 Jan 1930; Tanglewood, 7 Aug 1950. A. ADAM wrote an opera, 1842, on the same subject. LO

Roi et le Fermier, Le (*The King and the Farmer*), *comédie mêlée d'ariettes*, 3 acts, MONSIGNY, lib. SEDAINE. Paris, TI, 22 Nov 1762. The basis of JAGD; in turn founded on *The King and the Miller of Mansfield* (1737) by Robert Dodsley (1703–64). The king, out hunting, shelters in a farmer's cottage. As a reward he enables the farmer to win Jenny. LO

Roi Malgré Lui, Le (*The King against his Will*), *opéra comique*, 3 acts, CHABRIER, lib. Émile de Najac and Paul Burani, with emendations by Jean Richepin and the comp. Paris, OC, 18 May 1887. LO
See Myers, *Emmanuel Chabrier and His Circle* (London 1969; Rutherford, N.J. 1970)

Roller, Alfred, b. Vienna, 10 Feb 1864; d. Vienna, 21 June 1935. Austrian artist and stage designer. With Gustav Klimt a member of Vienna Secession, and a disciple of APPIA and Gordon Craig. Closely associated with MAHLER at Vienna from the designing of TRISTAN UND ISOLDE, 1903. Designed for first perfs of ROSENKAVALIER and FRAU OHNE SCHATTEN. Taught for 25 years at the Vienna School of Arts and Crafts. One of the most influential designers of his time. LO

romance (It. *romanza*, Ger. *Romanze*). A solo song of lyrical and intimate char.; in 19th-c. It. opera a technical term describing an aria in a single, slow movement (*see also* CANTABILE). JB

Romanelli, Luigi, b. Rome, 21 July 1751; d. Milan, 1 Mar 1839. Italian librettist. Professor of declamation and belles lettres at Milan Cons., 1816–31, he wr. over 60 libs, the most notable being PIETRA DEL PARAGONE, *Elisa e Claudio* (MERCADANTE), *La Vestale* (PACINI), and *Le Finte Rivali* (G. S. MAYR). PS

Romani, Felice Giuseppe, b. Genoa, 31 Jan 1788; d. Moneglia, 18 Jan 1865. Italian librettist, the most important of his day. Trained as a lawyer. Wr. libs for most of the major, esp. It., comps of the 19th c. beginning with G. S. MAYR's *Rosa Bianca e Rosa Rossa* (1813). He wr. PIRATA, STRANIERA, *Zaira* (1829), CAPULETI ED I MONTECCHI, SONNAMBULA, and NORMA for BELLINI; ten for DONIZETTI incl. ANNA BOLENA and LUCREZIA BORGIA, 16 for MERCADANTE, and others for ROSSINI (TURCO IN ITALIA, *Aureliano in Palmira,* 1813 and *Bianca e Falliero*, 1819), Mayr incl. MEDEA IN CORINTO, and MEYERBEER (*L'Esule di Granata*, 1822, and *Margherita d'Anjou*, 1820). GIORNO DI REGNO was a re-setting of *Il Finto Stanislao* wr. for Adalbert Gyrowetz, 1818. After 1834 he became editor of the *Gazetta Piemontese*; later he went blind and was granted a government pension. His libs are able to reveal a char.'s innermost feelings. PS

Romania. Opera was provided by visiting cos until the mid-19th c. Of the numerous Romanian opera composers few are known outside Romania. They incl. Eduard Caudella, 1841–1923 (*Petru Rareț*, Bucharest, 1900); Gheorghe Dima, 1847–1925; Tiberiu Brediceano, 1877–1968 (he was dir. of the National O. at Cluj); Sabin Dragoiu, 1894–1968; Georges Enesco, 1881–1955 (*Oedipe*, 1936); and Paul Constantinescu, 1908–63 (*The Stormy Night*, 1935, *Pana Lesnea*, 1956, both Bucharest). *See* BUCHAREST, CLUJ. LO

Romberg, Sigmund, b. Nazy Kaniza, 29 July 1887; d. NY, 9 Nov 1951. Hungarian, later American, composer of operettas. Wrote *c.* 50, mainly for NY (Broadway), where he went in 1909 – among them *Blossom Time* (1921), STUDENT PRINCE; *The Desert Song* (1926), and *The New Moon* (1928). LO
See Lubbock

Rome [Roma]. The first opera perf. there was Filippo Vitali's *L'Aretusa* (1620); in 1632 Stefano Landi's *Sant'Alessio* was given in Cardinal Barberini's private opera house. Comic opera was developed there a little later, with Giulio Rospigliosi's *Chi Soffre, Speri*, 1639, and *Dal Male il Bene*, 1654. Its main opera house was the Argentina, superseded by the T. Costanzi. Opera is perf. in the open at the Caracalla Baths.

Teatro Costanzi. Built by Domenico Costanzi in 1880; rebuilt and modernized, 1926–7, renamed **Teatro Reale dell'Opera** in 1928; now known as **Teatro dell'Opera**. Premieres there have incl. TOSCA and ZANDONAI's *Giulietta e Romeo* (1922). Like many It. opera houses it is now undergoing a period of financial strain. Dir. since 1968, ZAFRED. LO

Roméo et Juliette, opera, 5 acts, GOUNOD, lib. BARBIER and CARRÉ, based on SHAKESPEARE. Paris, TL, 27 Apr 1867; London, CG (in It.), 11 July 1867; NY, Acad. of Music (in It.), 15 Nov 1867; also in Eng. 14 Jan 1881 and in Fr. 8 Dec 1893. Given with some revisions by Gounod, Paris O., 28 Nov 1888; this version, in Fr., was heard at CG, 15 June 1889, cond. MANCINELLI, with a cast incl. both DE RESZKES and MELBA. For other Romeo and Juliet operas *see* following entry and SHAKESPEARE. LO ○

Romeo und Julia, opera, 2 acts, SUTERMEISTER, lib. composer after Schlegel's Ger. tr. of SHAKESPEARE's play. Dresden, 13 Apr 1940; London, SW (in Eng.), 12 Mar 1953. Main chars: Romeo (ten.) Julia (sop.) Friar Lawrence (bass) Nurse (mezzo-sop.) Capulet (bar.) Lady Capulet (mezzo-sop.). Sutermeister's concise treatment of the drama concentrates on the lovers themselves, leaving other characters as shadowy figures. His mus. is simple and direct, with an easy lyrical flow. FGB

Ronconi, Giorgio, b. Milan, 6 Aug 1810; d. Madrid, 8 Jan 1890. Italian baritone. Studied with his father, the singer Domenico Ronconi (1772–1839); debut 1831, Pavia. DONIZETTI's favourite baritone, he created leading roles in *Il Furioso nell'Isola di San Domingo*, *Torquato Tasso*, *Pia de' Tolomei*, *Il Campanello*, *Maria de Rudenz*, *Maria Padilla* and MARIA DI ROHAN. M. mezzo-sop. Elguerra Giannoni (1837), who frequently sang with him. VERDI's first NABUCCO at Sc. 1842; London debut the same year. He sang in London regularly 1847–66, and 1866–74 in USA. A famous RIGOLETTO, he excelled in the *bel canto* repertoire. After retirement he taught singing in Madrid and Granada. His brother Felice (1811–75) was a noted professor of singing in Würzburg, Frankfurt, Milan, London, and St Petersburg. Another brother, Sebastiano (1814–1900) was also a celebrated bar. Debut 1836, Lucca, as Donizetti's Torquato Tasso; sang in London 1836, 1837, 1860; retired in 1871 and became a singing teacher. PS

Rondine, La (*The Swallow*), opera, 3 acts, PUCCINI, lib. ADAMI after WILLNER and Heinrich Reichert. Monte Carlo, 27 Mar 1917. NY Met, 10 Mar 1928; London, Fulham Town Hall by Opera Viva, 9 Dec 1966. Main chars: Magda (sop.) Ruggiero (ten.) Lisette (sop.) Prunier (ten.) Raimbaud (bar.). Magda, mistress of a rich Parisian business man, falls in love with Ruggiero, a guest at one of his parties. In disguise, she meets him in a Bohemian café and they decide to elope. They live together in the South of France and Ruggiero proposes marriage, but rather than face his family's disapproval, Magda returns to Paris and her former protector. Originally planned as an operetta for Vienna. JB ○
See Kobbé

Rosamunde, Fürstin von Cypern (*Rosamund, Princess of Cyprus*), romantic play with music, 4 acts, SCHUBERT, lib. Helmiña von Chézy. Vienna, T. a. d. Wien, 20 Dec 1823. The play is lost, only the lyrics are preserved; of the music the *entr'acte* between Acts III and IV and the ballet music are familiar. Not an opera, but deserves recording as one of the few Schubert stage works to reach perf. LO ○

Rosbaud, Hans, b. Graz, 22 July 1895; d. Lugano, 29 Dec 1962. Austrian conductor. Well known for his sympathy with and interpretation of modern scores; cond. premiere of MOSES UND ARON. Chief cond. Aix-en-Provence Fest. 1947–59. LO

Rose Marie, operetta, FRIML and Herbert Stothart, book and lyrics Otto Harbach and HAMMERSTEIN II. NY, Imperial T., 2 Sept 1924; London, DL, 20 Mar 1925. EJ ○★
See Lubbock

Rosenkavalier, Der (*The Knight of the Rose*), opera, 3 acts, R. STRAUSS, lib. HOFMANNSTHAL. Dresden, 26 Jan 1911; London, CG, 29 Jan 1913; NY Met, 9 Dec 1913. Main chars: the Marschallin (sop.) Octavian (mezzo-sop.) Sophie (sop.) Baron Ochs (bass) Faninal (bar.) Valzacchi (ten.) Annina (sop.). The Marschallin, Princess von Werdenberg, the most sympathetic of all the characters, is faced with the perennial problem of the older woman who must lose her youthful lover, Octavian, but she at least enjoys the satisfaction of seeing that he, rather than her boorish cousin, Ochs, finally marries the attractive young Sophie. This ro-

Der Rosenkavalier, Berlin Staats O., 8 July 1973; produced Erhard Fischer; sets and costumes Wilfried Werz. Isabella Nawe as Sophie; Ingeborg Springer as Octavian

mantic opera finds Strauss at his mellowest and most melodically inventive, his music dealing most subtly with intimate personal relationships in the aristocratic setting of Maria Theresa's Vienna. Except for some crudity in the characterization of Ochs this is comic opera of Mozartian graciousness. FGB O★
See Mann, *Richard Strauss* (London 1964; New York 1966); Kobbé

Rosina, mezzo-sop., the heroine of BARBIERE DI SIVIGLIA

Rossellini, Renzo, b. Rome, 2 Feb 1908. Italian composer. His earlier operas, *La Guerra* (1956), *Il Vortice* (1958) and *La Piovra* (1958), comp. to his own libs, were prod. at Naples. *Uno Sguardo dal Ponte*, a setting of Arthur Miller's play, *A View from the Bridge*, had its premiere Rome 1961, dir. by the comp.'s brother Roberto. *Il Linguaggio dei Fiori* (1963) and *La Leggenda del Ritorno* (1966), based on an episode from DOSTOYEVSKY's novel *The Brothers Karamazov*, were perf. at Sc. He has also wr. *L'Avventuriero* (Monte Carlo 1968), *L'Annonce Faite à Marie*, adapted from the play by CLAUDEL (Paris 1970) and a TV opera, to his own text, *Le Campane* (1959). Art. dir., Monte Carlo, since 1973. EF

Rossellini, Roberto, b. Rome, 8 May 1906. Italian film director and producer. The first opera he dir. was VERDI'S OTELLO (T. S. Carlo, Naples, 1953), where the same year he staged JEANNE D'ARC AU BÛCHER in a prod. later seen at Milan, Paris, London and elsewhere. He also prod. FIGLIA DI JORIO (Sc. 1954) and his brother Renzo's opera, *Uno Sguardo dal Ponte*. EF

Rossi, Gaetano, b. Verona, 18 May 1774; d. Verona, 25 Jan 1855. Italian librettist, a prolific one, writing over 100. Official playwright of T. La Fenice, Venice, he provided texts for ROSSINI, DONIZETTI, MEYERBEER and NICOLAI, the most famous being SEMIRAMIDE, TANCREDI, CROCIATO IN EGITTO, LINDA DI CHAMOUNIX and *Maria Padilla* (Donizetti). PS

Rossi, Mario, b. Rome, 29 Mar 1902. Italian conductor. Debut Rome, then worked at the Florence Maggio Musicale (1936–44). Also regularly on Italian Radio. CG, MACBETH (1964). AB

Rossi-Lemeni, Nicola, b. Constantinople (now Istanbul), 6 Nov 1920. Italian bass, whose Russian mother taught singing at Odessa. Forsook plans for a diplomatic career in favour of singing; stage debut 1946, Venice, as Varlaam (BORIS GODUNOV). Other debuts: Sc. 1947; San Francisco O. 1951 (Boris Godunov); CG 1952 (Boris Godunov); NY Met 1953 (MÉPHISTOPHÉLÈS). Created Thomas à Becket (ASSASSINIO NELLA CATTEDRALE). Has also sung in other contemporary operas by BLOCH

(*Macbeth*), GRUENBERG (EMPEROR JONES), and Renzo ROSSELLINI (*Uno Sguardo dal Ponte*), but is chiefly distinguished for his vigour of stage and vocal char. as Boris Godunov and Méphistophélès. Married the sop. Virginia ZEANI. NG

Rossini, Gioacchino Antonio, b. Pesaro, 29 Feb 1792; d. Passy, nr Paris, 13 Nov 1868. Italian composer. The son of a horn player and a singer; studied Bologna Liceo Musicale with Stanislao Mattei. His first public commission came for a one-act *farsa* CAMBIALE DI MATRIMONIO (1810) for the Venetian T. S. Moïse. Over the next three years four more *farse* for the same theatre followed, incl. SCALA DI SETA (1811) and *Il Signor Bruschino* (1813); his first full-length comedy was *L'Equivoco Stravagante* (Bologna 1811). The success of PIETRA DEL PARAGONE (Milan 1812) procured him exemption from military service: while TANCREDI and ITALIANA IN ALGERI (Venice 1813) est. his pre-eminence in both serious and comic fields. Engaged by BARBAIA as *maestro al cembalo* at the T. S. Carlo, Naples, 1815–23, with a contract for two operas a year. To this period belong most of his famous works, ELISABETTA, REGINA D'INGHILTERRA, BARBIERE DI SIVIGLIA, CENERENTOLA, GAZZA LADRA, OTELLO, *Armide* (Naples 1817), MOSÈ IN EGITTO, *Ermione* (Naples 1819) and DONNA DEL LAGO. His It. career closed with SEMIRAMIDE (1823); went to Paris 1824 as mus. dir., T. des Italiens. He adapted his *Maometto II* and *Mosè in Egitto* for the Paris O. as respectively *Le Siège de Corinthe* (1826) and *Moïse* (1827) adding and substituting new music. His first wholly original Fr. opera was the comedy COMTE ORY (1828), followed by GUILLAUME TELL, his last stage work. During the 1830s, he acted as unofficial adviser to the TI and was responsible for engaging DONIZETTI and BELLINI in 1835. Separated from his first wife, COLBRAN, who had created sop. roles in many of his operas, he eventually m. Olimpe Pélissier, mistress of the painter Horace Vernet. After a period in Bologna and Florence, Rossini returned to Paris 1855 where he held court until his death. Apart from his unique comic gift, Rossini remains the founder of It. romantic opera, having est. the forms and procedures through which it developed. JB
See Weinstock, *Rossini: A Bibliography* (London and New York 1968)

Rostand, Edmond, b. Marseille, 1 Apr 1868; d. Paris, 2 Dec 1918. French poetic dramatist. Works on which operas are based incl. *Cyrano de Bergerac*, 1897 (W. DAMROSCH, 1913; ALFANO, 1936); *La Princesse Lointaine*, 1895 (Georges-Martin Witkowsky, 1934; MONTEMEZZI, unfinished); *La Samaritaine*, 1897 (Max d'Ollone, 1937); *L'Aiglon*, 1900 (HONEGGER and IBERT, 1937); *Les Romanesques*, 1894 (Fritz Hart, 1918). LO

Rosvænge [Rosenving-Hansen], Helge, b. Copenhagen, 29 Aug 1897; d. Munich, 19 June 1972. Danish tenor. Debut 1921, Neustrelitz (Don JOSÉ). Berlin, Staats O., 1924–45; Vienna Staats O. from 1936 and Salzburg 1933–9, where he was a notable Huon (OBERON), FLORESTAN, and TAMINO. Bayreuth 1934 and 1936 (PARSIFAL). Only CG appearance as Florestan. In later years was renowned for more heroic roles such as CALAF and RADAMES, also for operetta. His career continued almost to the end of his life. His voice was exciting, with a brilliant ring to the tone. AB

Rota, Nino, b. Milan, 3 Dec 1911. Italian composer. After a student work, *Il Principe Porcaro*, based on ANDERSEN's tale *The Prince and the Swineherd*, his operas *Ariodante* (1942) and *Torquemada* (1943) were perf. at Parma. *Il Cappello di Paglia di Firenze*, adapted from the farce by Labiche (Palermo 1955), *Lo Scoiattolo in Gamba* (Venice 1959) and *La Scuola di Guida* (Spoleto 1959), were followed by *Aladino e la Lampada Magica* (Naples 1968) and *La Visita Meravigliosa*, taken from H. G. Wells (Palermo 1970). Has also wr. two radio operas, *I Due Timidi* (1950), and *La Notte di un Nevrastenico*, which won the Italia prize (1959) and was staged in Milan (1960). EF

Rothenberger, Anneliese, b. Mannheim, 19 June 1924. German soprano. Studied Mannheim mus. acad.; debut 1948, Coblenz; Hamburg O. 1949–56; then Vienna Staats O. Appeared regularly at Salzburg Fest. until 1969 when she sang FIORDILIGI. NY Met debut 1960 as Zdenka (ARABELLA). Glyndebourne 1959–60 as SOPHIE. Much admired in roles such as Sophie and Zdenka, and in operetta for her light and charming voice. AB

Rothmüller, Marko, b. Trnjani, 31 Dec 1908. Yugoslav baritone. Studied Vienna; debut 1932, Hamburg. Sang Zagreb (1933), Zürich (1935), CG (1939 and 1948–55), Vienna (1946–9), Edinburgh and Glyndebourne (1949–52), NY CC (1948–52) and Met (1949–60). His repertory ranged from MOZART, ROSSINI, GIORDANO, and PUCCINI to GOUNOD, BIZET, WAGNER, and R. STRAUSS. He also sang the bar. roles in VERDI'S MACBETH, LUISA MILLER, RIGOLETTO, TROVATORE, TRAVIATA, BALLO IN MASCHERA, SIMONE BOCCANEGRA, FORZA DEL

DESTINO, DON CARLOS, AIDA, OTELLO, and FALSTAFF. He was much admired as WOZZECK, which he sang at CG under E. KLEIBER. EF

Rouen, France. In 1688 Bernard Vaultier opened an Académie de Musique with PHAÉTON. The Grand T. was opened 29 June 1776; after the Revolution known as T. des Arts. Burned out 1876, rebuilt 1882, destroyed again in World War II; since rebuilt as the present T. des Arts. About 12 operas are given each season, Oct–Apr. Dir. André Cabourg. LO

Rouleau, Joseph, b. Matane, Quebec, 28 Feb 1929. Canadian bass. Debut 1954 Canada; USA debut 1955 New Orleans; CG 1957 (COLLINE); Paris O. 1960 as Raimondo (LUCIA DI LAMMERMOOR). His extensive repertory incl. Giorgio (PURITANI), OROVESO, Count Rodolfo (SONNAMBULA), SPARAFUCILE, Fiesco (SIMONE BOCCANEGRA), Ramfis (AIDA), PHILIPPE and Grand Inquisitor (DON CARLOS), Dosifey (KHOVANSHCHINA), BORIS GODUNOV and PIMEN, MÉPHISTOPHÉLÈS and MASSENET's Don Quichotte. EF

Rousseau, Jean-Jacques, b. Geneva, 28 June 1712; d. Ermenonville, 2 July 1778. Swiss philosopher. At the centre of the *guerre des bouffons* in Paris in the 1750s. Prod. a *Dictionary of Music* (1768), and contributed articles on mus. to Diderot's *Grande Encyclopédie*. Of his three attempts at opera, the second, DEVIN DU VILLAGE, met with considerable success; the third, *Pygmalion* (1770), wr. in collaboration with the comp. Horace Coignet, was an experiment in melodrama similar to those of BENDA. LO

Roussel, Albert, b. Tourcoing, 5 Apr 1869; d. Royan, 23 Aug 1937. French composer. A pupil of d'INDY, he later turned to Oriental mus. for his inspiration and prod. a work of highly individual genius in the opera-ballet PADMÂVATÎ. His other operas are *Le Naissance de la Lyre* (1924), after SOPHOCLES, and the comedy *Le Testament de la Tante Caroline* (1933). FGB
See Deane, *Albert Roussel* (London 1961)

Roux, Michel, b. Angoulème, 1924. French baritone of vivid stage character. Studied Paris Cons. Appearances Paris O. since 1949 (debut OC in LAKMÉ), and throughout Europe, incl. Sc. 1953 (GOLAUD); Glyndebourne Fest. 1956 as Count ALMAVIVA (NOZZE DI FIGARO). Returned to Glyndebourne frequently to 1969, as Count (SEGRETO DI SUSANNA), Golaud, Macrobio (PIETRA DEL PARAGONE), and Don ALFONSO. Teaches char. and interpretation in Paris. NG

Rusalka, Prague, National T., 29 Jan 1960; produced KAŠLÍK; designed SVOBODA; dancer Z. Šemberová

Rovescalli, Odourdo Antonio, b. Crema, 21 Dec 1864; d. Milan, 12 Dec 1936. Italian designer, one of the most active in 19th-c. Italy. Worked for Milan, Sc. and T. Lirico, and for Rome, T. Costanzi, where he designed MASCAGNI's *Amica*, IRIS, PICCOLO MARAT. Milan designs incl., besides several PUCCINI operas, NIGHTINGALE, PELLÉAS UND MÉLISANDE, TRISTAN UND ISOLDE (T. Lirico), FEUERSNOT (Sc., 1913). LO

Royal Opera House, Covent Garden *see* LONDON

Rozhdestvensky, Gennady Nikolayevich, b. Moscow, 4 May 1931. Soviet conductor. Studied cond. Moscow Cons. with his father, Nikolay Anosov; debut aged 20 in a Bolshoy T. prod. of TCHAIKOVSKY's *Nutcracker*. At the same theatre he was cond. (1951–61), then principal cond. (1964–70), and was involved in a number of important Bolshoy premieres, incl. WAR AND PEACE and MIDSUMMER NIGHT'S DREAM. London debut with the Bolshoy Ballet (1956); he first appeared with the Royal O. in BORIS GODUNOV (20 Feb 1970). One of the most gifted of the younger Russ. conductors. GN

Rubini, Giovanni-Battista, b. Romano, 7 Apr 1795; d. Romano, 2 Mar 1854. Italian tenor. Studied Bergamo, sang with touring cos. After further study Naples, engaged by BARBAIA 1816. He m. Fr. mezzo-sop. Adelaide Comelli [Chaumel] 1819, with whom he frequently appeared. After leaving Barbaia, alternated between Paris and London 1831–43. A poor actor, but a singer of genius, he created eight roles for DONIZETTI incl. Riccardo Percy in ANNA BOLENA and four for BELLINI, in *Bianca e Gernando* (*see* BIANCA E FERNANDO), PIRATA, SONNAMBULA and PURITANI. His brothers Geremia and Giacomo were also tenors. PS

Rubinstein, Anton Grigoryevich, b. Vikhvatinets, Podolsk Government, 28 Nov 1829; d. Peterhof, 20 Nov 1894. Russian pianist and composer. Of his 18 operas, only DEMON, set in the manner of Fr. lyric opera, has achieved much popularity. Some of his works – *Dmitry Donskoy* (1852), *Tom the Fool* (1853) and *Kalashnikov the Merchant* (1880) – contain nationalist touches, but much more of his mus. reveals the influence of MEYERBEER and MENDELSSOHN, the former particularly in heroic operas like *Die Makkabäer* (1875) and *Nero* (1879), the latter in his several sacred operas: *Das Verlorene Paradies* (1856), *Der Thurm zu Babel* (1870), *Moses* (1892), and *Christus* (1895), as well as the opera-oratorio *Sulamith* (1883). GN

Ruddigore or The Witch's Curse, operetta, 2 acts, SULLIVAN, lib. GILBERT. London, Savoy T., 22 Jan 1887; NY 21 Feb 1887. Main chars: Robin Oakapple (Sir Ruthven Murgatroyd) (buffo) Richard Dauntless (ten.) Mad Margaret (mezzo-sop.) Sir Despard Murgatroyd (bass bar.) Dame Hannah (contr.) Sir Roderic Murgatroyd (bass) Rose Maybud (sop.). A satire on the Gothic novel. JB ○

Rudel, Julius, b. Vienna, 6 Mar 1921. Austrian conductor, since 1941 a naturalized US citizen. Joined NY CC as coach; debut there as cond. 1944 (ZIGEUNERBARON). Since 1957 mus. dir. there, presenting many premieres esp. of US operas. Has also cond. in Europe, e.g. BOHÈME, Paris O., 1973–4 season. LO

Ruffo, Titta [Ruffo Cafiero Titta], b. Pisa, 9 June 1877; d. Florence, 6 July 1953. Italian baritone. Studied Rome and Milan. Debut 1898, Rome, as the Herald (LOHENGRIN). Only CG appearance 1903 as Lord Henry Ashton (LUCIA DI LAMMERMOOR). US debut 1912, Chicago (RIGOLETTO). NY Met (debut as FIGARO in BARBIERE DI SIVIGLIA) 1922–9. Had one of the most powerful and rich bar. voices of his day. Famous for his SCARPIA, TONIO, and RIGOLETTO. AB

Rusalka, opera, 3 acts, DVOŘÁK, lib. by Marie Červinková-Riegrová. Prague, NT, 31 Mar 1901; London, Peter Jones T., 9 May 1950; London, SW, 18 Feb 1959; Chicago, 10 Nov 1935. Main chars: Rusalka (sop.) Prince (ten.) Foreign Princess (sop.) Water Goblin (bass) Ježibaba (mezzo-sop.). The waternymph Rusalka wishes to become human in order to gain the love of the Prince. Ježibaba the witch makes two conditions for this: that Rusalka be dumb and that her lover be true – otherwise both will be damned. But the Prince abandons Rusalka for the Foreign Princess; repenting, he frees Rusalka from the curse but dies himself. This fairy-tale opera is Dvořák's most successful and is a popular favourite in Czechoslovakia. JT ○
See Clapham, *Antonín Dvořák, Musician and Craftsman* (London 1966)

Ruslan and Lyudmila, opera, 5 acts, GLINKA, lib. Valeryan Fyodorovich Shirkov and others, after PUSHKIN. St Petersburg, Bolshoy T., 9 Dec 1842; London, Lyceum T., 4 June 1931; NY, Town Hall, 26 Dec 1942 (concert perf.). Main chars: Svetozar (bass) Lyudmila (sop.) Ruslan (bar.) Ratmir (contr.) Farlaf (bass) Gorislava (sop.) Finn (ten.) Naina (mezzo-sop.) Chernomor. A dramatic hotchpotch, *Ruslan* nevertheless contains some of Glinka's finest mus. and, more so than IVAN SUSANIN, presages later 19th-c. Russian opera in many aspects of harmony, melody and orchestration. Also, its elements of fantasy and heroism were taken up by, particularly, RIMSKY-KORSAKOV and in the epics of BORODIN and MUSORGSKY. GN
See Kobbé

Russia and the Soviet Union. Until the 18th c., Russ. mus. remained isolated from the evolutionary processes of the West, and it was not until 1731 that the first opera was perf. in Moscow, by an It. touring co.: Giovanni Alberto Ristori's *commedia per musica, Calandro.* ARAIA's *La Forza dell'Amore e dell'Odio* was given at St Petersburg in 1736, the year after he had been appointed MdC to the Empress Anna, thus paving the way for a great many other foreign musicians who were employed by the Russ. court: Hermann Friedrich Raupach (who comp. one of the earliest operas to a Russ. text, *Alcestis* (1758), Araia having comp. the first in 1755), Vincenzo Manfredini, GALUPPI, TRAETTA, PAISIELLO, SARTI, CIMAROSA, MARTÍN Y SOLER. Araia remained in St Petersburg for many years, and thrived on the court's taste for It. opera which lasted until *c.*

Russia and the Soviet Union. The Opera and Ballet Theatre at Novosibirsk, Siberia

1764, when a Fr. troupe began to perf. *opéra comique* in the city. The earliest Russ. opera to have survived is Zorin's *Rebirth*, perf. 1779, the same year as another, more substantial, Russ. comic opera, Sokolovsky's *The Miller-Magician, Cheat and Matchmaker*, later revised by Evstigney Fomin (1761–1800) and the Bohemian Arnošt Vančura (*c.* 1750–1801), who in 1787 set one of Catherine II's own libs, *The Brave and Bold Knight Akhrideich.* Fomin, Maxim Berezovsky (1745–77), and Dmitry Bortnyansky (1751–1825), all of whom were trained in Italy, were, with Mikhail Matinsky (1750–*c.* 1825) and Vasily Pashkevich (*c.* 1742–*c.* 1797), the earliest significant native Russ. comps of opera, often incorporating folk tunes into their music and imbuing their scores with local colouring. Fomin is known particularly for *The Postdrivers* (1787), *The Americans* (comp. 1788, perf. 1800) and his fine 2-act melodrama *Orpheus and Eurydice* (1792); Berezovsky for the *opera seria Demofoonte* (1773); Bortnyansky for *Le Faucon* (1786) and *Le Fils-rival* (1787), as well as a number of It. operas; Matinsky for *The St Petersburg Bazaar* (1782); and Pashkevich for *Fevey* (1786) and the 'historical spectacle' *The Early Reign of Oleg* (1790) which he wr. in collaboration with Canobbio and Sarti. Caterino Cavos (1776–1840), a Venetian comp. and cond. (*see* KIROV T. under LENINGRAD) adopted a Russ. idiom for his *Ilya the Hero* (1807) and *Ivan Susanin* (comp. 1815, perf. 1822), based on the same subject as GLINKA's opera, the premiere of which he cond.

Against the background est. by these comps and by others such as Stepan Davydov (1777–1825) and VERSTOVSKY, Glinka emerged: he possessed great natural musical abilities, and his operas, which have that degree of professionalism lacking in earlier Russ. opera, had a decisive influence on the mus. of BORODIN, MUSORGSKY (who was also influenced by DARGOMYZHSKY), RIMSKY-KORSAKOV, TCHAIKOVSKY, PROKOFIEV, and STRAVINSKY.

After the 1917 Revolution there followed a substantial period of ideological discussion in artistic circles. But, by the 1930s, policies had been formulated, and the modernist traits in operas like NOSE and KNIPPER's *The North Wind* (1930) were criticized, and the works withdrawn shortly after their premieres. The denunciation of SHOSTAKOVICH's *Lady Macbeth of the Mtsensk District* (*see* KATERINA IZMAYLOVA) in 1936, and the simultaneous praise of QUIET FLOWS THE DON clearly showed the path of development that opera was expected to follow, and as a result a large number of lyrical 'song operas' were prod. by KABALEVSKY, KHRENNIKOV, MURADELI, and many others. The rigours of the Stalinist era culminated in the notorious Zhdanov censures (1948), in which the mus. of Prokofiev, Shostakovich and other leading comps was condemned for 'formalism' – the separation of form from content. But in the cultural thaw that has largely continued since Stalin's death (1953), notable operas have been successfully prod. by such comps as SHAPORIN, Rodion Shchedrin (b. 1932: *Not Love Alone*, 1961), SHEBALIN, Sergey Slonimsky (b. 1932: *Virineya*, 1967), and SPADAVECCHIA.

The chief musical centres of Russia are Moscow and Leningrad. Important national schools of composition have also developed in the individual republics, particularly Armenia (*Almast*, 1930, by Aleksandr Spendiarov, 1871–1928; *Arshak II*, comp. 1868, perf. 1945, by Tigran Chukhadjian, 1837–98), Azerbaijan (*see* BAKU), Georgia (*see* TBILISI), LATVIA, LITHUANIA, and the UKRAINE. GN

Rysanek, Leonie, b. Vienna, 14 Nov 1926. Austrian soprano. Studied Vienna Mus. Acad. with JERGER and Rudolf Grossmann. Debut 1949, Innsbruck (AGATHE), moving to Saarbrücken (1950–2), then to Munich. Bayreuth debut 1951 (SIEGLINDE); sang there regularly for 20 years. Vienna Staats O. since 1954. Visited CG with the Bavarian Staats O. 1953, when she sang Danae (LIEBE DER DANAE), returning for Sieglinde with the regular co. 1955. In subsequent seasons was heard as the MARSCHALLIN and TOSCA. NY Met debut 1955 (MACBETH), returning in subsequent seasons in all her leading roles incl. LEONORE, SENTA, Marschallin, CHRYSOTHEMIS, AMELIA, and the Empress (FRAU OHNE SCHATTEN). Returned to Salzburg in *Frau ohne Schatten* for a significant revival there 1974–5. Her rich, expansive voice (especially in the top register) has made her an ideal exponent of R. STRAUSS roles post World War II. Her eloquent singing and acting are also much admired in her Senta, Sieglinde, and VERDI roles. AB

S

Sabata, Victor de, b. Trieste, 10 Apr 1892; d. Santa Margherita, 11 Dec 1967. Italian conductor. First important operatic post Monte Carlo, 1919–29, where he cond. premiere of ENFANT ET LES SORTILÈGES; Sc. 1929–53 as cond. and later as art. and mus. dir. Has also cond. at Bayreuth, CG, Salzburg, and Florence Maggio Musicale. One of the outstanding conds of his day, whose VERDI was especially admired. LO

Sabina, Karel, b. Prague, 29 Dec 1813; d. Prague, 9 Nov 1877. Czech writer. Wrote the libs for SMETANA's first two operas *The Brandenburgers in Bohemia* (1866) and BARTERED BRIDE and his humorous verses about an elderly bridegroom formed the basis for three more libs: IN THE WELL, Josef Richard Rozkošný's *Mikuláš* (1870) and BENDL's *The Old Bridegroom* (1882). His finest work of all these was probably the lib. for FIBICH's *Bukovín* (1874). JT

Sacchini, Antonio (Maria Gasparo Gioacchino), b. Florence, 14 June 1730; d. Paris, 6 Oct 1786. Italian composer. Studied Naples Cons. di Loreto with which he was associated until 1762; his first stage work, the intermezzo *Fra Donato* was prod. with success there 1758. Travelled widely in Italy and Germany; lived in London 1772–84, where he prod. 17 operas with varying success. His last years were spent in Paris, where he d. soon after completing his masterpiece *Oedipe à Colone* (1786), a pillar of the 'grand' repertoire until the mid-19th c., sharing many of the qualities of GLUCK. JB

Sachs, Milan, b. Lišov, Bohemia, 28 Nov 1884; d. Zagreb, 4 Aug 1968. Yugoslav conductor of Czech origin. Studied Prague Cons. (1899–1905); settled in Zagreb 1911–32, first as leader, then as cond., dir. (1920–9) and finally chief cond. (1929–32) of the Zagreb O. Cond. Brno NT 1932–8, conducting all SMETANA's operas and contributing greatly to the Brno JANÁČEK tradition. As a Jew, he fled Czechoslovakia 1938 and was forced into retirement in Yugoslavia. Returned as head of Zagreb O. 1945, and before his retirement (1955) brought the co. on a very successful tour of London, with 10 perfs of PRINCE IGOR. JT

Sadko, opera, 7 scenes, RIMSKY-KORSAKOV, lib. comp. and Vladimir Ivanovich Belsky. Moscow, Solodovnikov T., 7 Jan 1898; NY Met, 25 Jan 1930; London, Lyceum T., 9 June 1931. Main chars: Sadko (ten.) Lyubava (mezzo-sop.) Sea King (bass) Volkhova (sop.). The Novgorod merchants ask Sadko to seek wealth for the city. He meets Volkhova, the Sea Princess, who falls in love with him and tells him he will catch three golden fish in the lake. Sadko wins a bet with the crowd that he will catch the fish, then sets sail. On his way back from accumulating treasure, his fleet is becalmed because he has not offered a sacrifice to the Sea King; treasure is poured overboard, and Sadko is set adrift on a plank. He sinks to the seabed, and is offered the hand of Volkhova. At the wedding celebrations the vigorous dancing causes ships to sink. The end of the Sea King's reign is proclaimed and Sadko and Volkhova are carried off in a shell drawn by birds. Next morning, Volkhova is transformed into the river which now bears her name, and Sadko is discovered by his wife Lyubava. One of the comp.'s most appealing fairy-tale operas (with its vivid Harbour Scene), *Sadko* was nevertheless rejected by the Imperial Theatres, and was first perf. by MAMONTOV's co. GN O

Saint-Georges, Jules-Henri Vernoy de, b. Paris, 7 Nov 1799; d. Paris, 23 Dec 1875. French librettist. Provided, alone or in collaboration, more than 80 opera books for many of the 19th-c. Fr. comps incl. AUBER (DIAMANTS DE LA COURONNE), BIZET (JOLIE FILLE DE PERTH), J. F. HALÉVY, and HÉROLD. LO

Saint of Bleecker Street, The, opera, 3 acts, MENOTTI, lib. comp. NY, Broadway T., 27 Dec 1954; Milan, Sc., 8 May 1955; London, BBC TV, 4 Oct 1956. Main chars: Maria (sop.) Anninia (sop.) Michele (ten.) Desideria (mezzo-sop.). Anninia, a religious mystic, receives stigmata on her palms, inspiring religious awe among her Catholic neighbours. Her brother Michele, although an agnostic, is devoted to her while Desideria, his sweetheart, shows extreme jealousy. Desideria is killed in a quarrel whereupon Michele flees. He returns later and is taken. EJ

St Paul Opera Association, Minnesota. About 40 perfs annually. Many standard works with novelties by James Neilsen, Lee Hoiby (*Summer and Smoke*, 1971), FLOYD (OF MICE AND MEN, 22 Jan 1970), ANTHEIL (*Venus in Africa*, 1970). Staging is highly experimental. Dir. Igor Buketoff. EJ

Saint-Saëns, (Charles) Camille, b. Paris, 9 Oct 1835; d. Algiers, 16 Dec 1921. French composer. Studied Paris Cons. and privately under GOUNOD before taking up a long career as organist at the Madeleine. Comp. prolifically in almost every form and wr. many books on music. Operas are *La Princesse Jaune* (1872), *Le Timbre d'Argent* (1877), SAMSON ET DALILA, *Étienne Marcel* (1879), HENRY VIII, *Proserpine* (1887), *Ascanio* (1890), *Phryné* (1893), *Déjanire* (1898), *Les Barbares* (1901), *Hélène* (1904), *L'Ancêtre* (1906). A frequent visitor to Britain as pianist, organist and cond., he was made Hon. D. Mus. at Cambridge 1893. His music is remarkable for its fluent craftsmanship and refinement rather than for any robust originality. FGB
See Harding, *Saint-Saëns and His Circle* (London 1965)

Sakuntala, Hindu play by Kalidasa (*fl.* 5th c. AD), tr. Sir William Jones 1789. Operas based on it are by ALFANO, 1921; Louis Coerne (1870–1922), 1904; WEINGARTNER, 1884. F. SCHUBERT began one in 1820. LO

Salammbô, opera, 5 acts, REYER, lib. LOCLE based on FLAUBERT's novel, 1862. Brussels, T. de la Monnaie, 10 Feb 1890; Paris, O., 16 May 1892; New Orleans, Fr. Opera House, 25 Jan 1900; NY Met 20 Mar 1901. Matho, leader of the besiegers of Carthage, loves Salammbô, priestess and daughter of Hamilcar. He steals a sacred veil from the Temple of Tanit, and is condemned to die by Salammbô's hand. She kills herself in his place, and Matho stabs himself. MUSORGSKY began an opera on the same subject, 1863–5; other operas by Nicolò Massa, 1886; Vincenzo Fornari (*Salammbô e Zuma*, 1881), and Josef Mathias Hauer, 1930. LO

Saléza, Albert, b. Bruges, Basses-Pyrénées, 28 Oct 1867; d. Paris, 26 Nov 1916. French tenor. Studied Paris Cons.; debut 1892, Paris, OC (ROI D'YS). Later sang in Brussels (premiere of SALAMMBÔ), Monte Carlo, Nice in *La Prise de Troie* (see TROYENS) and London (CG debut, 1898, in ROMÉO ET JULIETTE). Excellent singer especially in Fr. roles, who impressed by the quality of his voice and the intelligence of his interpretations. LO

Salieri, Antonio, b. Legnano, 18 Aug 1750; d. Vienna, 7 May 1825. Italian composer. Studied Venice with GASSMANN who took him to Vienna, his future home, in 1766. Here he became Court Comp. 1744, court MdC 1788. A teacher, he incl. F. SCHUBERT and BEETHOVEN among his pupils. A rumour that he had poisoned MOZART appealed to the romantic imagination but, though believed by Mozart himself, is almost certainly false. Of his 35 operas, which begin with *Le Donne Letterate* (1770) most were wr. for the Ger. or It. theatres in Vienna. GLUCK's influence secured him several commissions for the Paris O. of which DANAÏDES is the most notable. Salieri's music is typically Viennese-Italian: fluent, melodious and with well-nourished instrumental textures. His most admired works incl. *La Grotta di Trofonio* (Vienna 1785) and *Falstaff* (Vienna 1799). JB

Salle des Machines. A small theatre built in Paris by order of Cardinal Mazarin by Gaspare Vigarani (1586–1663) intended to house the spectacular shows for Louis XIV's wedding in 1660. In fact it was not ready in time, and the gala opera, CAVALLI's *Xerxes*, was perf. in the Grand Gallery of the Louvre. The first opera given in the new theatre was Cavalli's *Ercole Amante* (1662). Well equipped as its name suggests, it was later successively under the direction of BÉRAIN and SERVANDONY, and is important in the history of stage scenery. The Paris O. was there 1763–9. LO

Salome, opera, 1 act, R. STRAUSS, after the drama by WILDE, tr. Hedwig Lachmann. Dresden, 9 Dec 1905; NY Met, 22 Jan 1907; London, CG, 8 Dec 1910. Main chars: Salome (sop.) Herod (ten.) Herodias (mezzo-sop.) Jokanaan (bar.) Narraboth (ten.) Page of Herodias (contr.). Having perf. the Dance of the Seven Veils for Herod, Tetrarch of Judea, Salome demands as her reward the head of Jokanaan (John the Baptist), who has repulsed her sexual advances. Strauss provided such appropriately

erotic music for the text, fusing the two elements to perfection, that the Kaiser in Berlin, the Lord Chamberlain in London and the churches in NY condemned the opera as obscene and several projected perfs were even cancelled. Strauss and the critics stood firm, good sense finally prevailed, and *Salome* is now universally regarded as a classic. FGB ○ ★
See Mann, *Richard Strauss* (London 1964; New York 1966); Kobbé

Salzburg, Austria, MOZART's birthplace. The summer fest. began there 1921, in the Landes T., with artists from Vienna. The Festspielhaus, converted from the old Riding School, was opened 1927; the new Festspielhaus was built 1960 at a cost of nearly £3,500,000, offering first-class acoustics and every stage convenience. Its repertory naturally gives pride of place to Mozart, with R. STRAUSS a close second, but several premieres by BLACHER, EGK, LIEBERMANN and ORFF have been given. Besides the summer fest. there is also an Easter fest., begun 1967, presided over by KARAJAN. LO

Sammarco, Mario, b. Palermo, 13 Dec 1868; d. Milan, 24 Jan 1930. Italian baritone. Studied Palermo; debut there 1888. Soon established himself as one of Italy's leading bars, singing at Sc. from 1896. Appeared regularly CG 1904–14, where his accomplished singing made a profound impression. Also sang NY Manhattan OH, 1908–12, and with Chicago O. 1911–12. Heard to best effect in the It. repertory, especially as SCARPIA and in RIGOLETTO. Created roles in ZAZA and HERBERT's *Natoma* (Philadelphia 1911). LO

Samson et Dalila, opera, 3 acts, SAINT-SAËNS, lib. Ferdinand Lemaire after the biblical story. Weimar, Grand Ducal T. (in Ger.), 2 Dec 1877; Rouen, 3 Mar 1890; NY (concert version) 25 Mar 1892; New Orleans (staged) 4 Jan 1893; London, CG (concert version), 25 Sept 1893; London CG, (staged), 26 Apr 1909. Main chars: Dalila (mezzo-sop.) Samson (ten.) High Priest of Dagon (bar.). Samson leads a successful revolt by the Hebrews against their Philistine conquerors but is afraid of the lure of Dalila's beauty. Prompted by the High Priest, Dalila renders Samson powerless by cutting off his hair. Samson recovers his strength through prayer and destroys the Temple of Dagon. Saint-Saëns's only lasting stage success, the opera provides a lavish spectacle and incl. two superb arias for Dalila, *'Amour! viens aider ma faiblesse'* and *'Mon coeur s'ouvre à ta voix'* as well as impressive choruses. FGB ○
See Kobbé

San Carlo Opera House *see* NAPLES

Sanderson, Sybil, b. Sacramento, Cal., 7 Dec 1865; d. Paris, 15 May 1903. American soprano. Studied Paris with MARCHESI DE CASTRONE and Giovanni Sbriglia. Debut 1888, The Hague, in the Dutch premiere of MANON (under pseudonym Ada Palmer). Her engagement there was due to MASSENET, who had heard her sing, and been overcome by her beauty and her voice. He regarded her as the ideal interpreter of his female roles, and his *Esclarmonde* (1889) and THAÏS were wr. expressly for her, as was SAINT-SAËNS's *Phryné* (1893), but the success she achieved in Paris in these operas was not matched either in London or her native country. LO

San Francisco Opera Company. Founded 1923 by Gaetano Merola, dir. 1923–53, who kept largely to standard It. and Ger. works. Succeeded by present dir., K. H. ADLER. About 56 perfs a season are given in War Memorial OH (opened 1932). Adler has blended standard works with novelties, often for the first time in the USA, such as DIALOGUES DES CARMÉLITES, FRAU OHNE SCHATTEN, Norman Dello Joio's *Blood Moon* (1961), KATERINA IZMAYLOVA, DVOŘÁK's *Turdé Palice* (1974) and MASSENET's *Esclarmonde* (1974). EJ
See Bloomfield, *Fifty Years of the San Francisco Opera* (San Francisco 1972)

Sanjust, Filippo, b. Rome, 9 Sept 1925. Italian producer and designer. Prods incl. RIGOLETTO (Rome 1966); W. BURKHARD's *Ein Stern geht auf aus Jaakob* (Hamburg 1970); INCORONAZIONE DI POPPEA (Holland Fest. 1971); PELLÉAS ET MÉLISANDE (Scheveningen 1973); LULU (Berlin 1973); and ERISMENA (Holland Fest. 1974). LO

Sanquirico, Alessandro, b. Milan, 27 July 1777; d. Milan, 12 Mar 1849. Italian stage designer. The foremost scenographer in Italy in his day, he worked entirely in Milan, designing for the ballets of Salvatore Viganò and Filippo Taglioni and the operas of BELLINI, ROSSINI, MERCADANTE, DONIZETTI, and PACINI. His style was basically neoclassical, but he could react to the mounting pressures of romanticism inherent in the new It. school of composition. In 1829 he redecorated the interior of Sc. (*see* MILAN). Some hundreds of his drawings are extant; a number are available in fine quality prints. LO

Santa Fe Opera (The Opera Association of New Mexico). Founded 1957 by present gen. manager John Crosby; 26 perfs each summer season, with strong emphasis on novelties, always with high standard of dir. and prod. World premieres there have incl.: Marvin David Levy, *The Tower*, 2 Aug 1957; FLOYD, *Wuthering Heights*, 16 July 1958; Luciano Berio, *Opera*, 12 Aug 1970; VILLA-LOBOS, *Yerma* (comp. 1955), 12 Aug 1971; Aribert Reimann, *Melusine*, 21 Aug 1972. US premieres incl.: NEUES VOM TAGE; LULU; DAPHNE (first US stage perf.); SCHÖNBERG's *Jakobsleiter*, 14 Aug 1968; KÖNIG HIRSCH; NOSE; CARDILLAC; BOULEVARD SOLITUDE; BASSARIDS; DEVILS OF LOUDUN; HELP, HELP, THE GLOBOLINKS!; OWEN WINGRAVE; CAVALLI's *L'Egisto*, 1 Aug 1974. EJ

Santley, (Sir) Charles, b. Liverpool, 28 Feb 1834; d. London, 22 Sept 1922. English baritone. After studying with his father, a music teacher, and a period as a chorister, he went to Milan. Debut 1855, Pavia, as the Doctor (TRAVIATA); returned to London 1857 to study with GARCÍA II. British stage debut 1859 CG, as Hoël (DINORAH). It was for Santley that GOUNOD wr. 'Even bravest heart' for the perf. of FAUST in Eng. 1864. He toured the USA 1871; joined the Carl Rosa co. 1875. Knighted 1907. He last sang in 1915, in concert. In 1859 he m. Gertrude Kemble, a former sop. Their daughter Edith was also a singer. PS

Santoliquido, Francesco, b. S. Giorgio a Cremano, Naples, 6 Aug 1883; d. Naples, 24 Aug 1971. Italian composer. Studied Rome; then lived in Tunisia 1912–33. His operas incl. *La Favola di Helga* (Milan 1910), *L'Ignota* (unperf.), *Ferhuda* (Tunis 1919) and *La Porta Verde* (Bergamo 1953). EF

Sanzogno, Nino, b. Venice, 13 April 1911. Italian conductor. First cond. Sc. 1941 (SALOME); and at the Piccola Sc. on its opening in 1955 (MATRIMONIO SEGRETO). Has cond. many 18th-c. works and some standard repertory operas, but best known as an interpreter of 20th-c. comps. Cond. the premieres of DAVID, DIALOGUES DES CARMÉLITES, Guido Turchi's *Buon Soldato Svejk* (1962) and has given perfs of operas by BERG, PROKOFIEV, STRAVINSKY, WALTON, BRITTEN, DALLAPICCOLA, MALIPIERO, PETRASSI, PERAGALLO, Bruno Bartolozzi and others. Cond. TABARRO and CARMINA BURANA at San Francisco 1971. EF

Sarastro, bass, the priest of Isis in ZAUBERFLÖTE

Sardou, Victorien, b. Paris, 7 Sept 1831; d. Paris, 8 Nov 1908. French playwright whose fashionable dramas provided material for several operas: *Patrie*, 1869 (Émile Paladilhe, O., 1886); *Fédora*, 1880 (GIORDANO, FEDORA); *Les Barbares*, 1901 (SAINT-SAËNS, *Les Barbares*, O., 1901); *Tosca*, 1887 (PUCCINI); *Madame sans Gêne*, 1893 (Giordano, *Madame sans Gêne*, NY 1915). Collaborated with OFFENBACH in *Le Roi Carotte* (1872) and *Fantasio* (1872) and, with Philippe Gille, wrote lib. for LECOCQ's *Les Prés St Gervais* (1874). J. STRAUSS's *Karneval in Rom* (Vienna 1873) is based on Sardou's comedy *Piccolino*; he also wrote a lib. *Grisélidis*, for BIZET, who worked on it 1870–1. LO

Šárka, opera, 3 acts, FIBICH, lib. Anežka Schulzová. Prague, NT, 28 Dec 1897. Main chars: Přemysl (bar.) Ctirad (ten.) Vlasta (mezzo-sop.) Šárka (sop.). After Libuše's death, the women lose their influence at Přemysl's court, and when their appeal to Přemysl is rebuffed, the hot-blooded Šárka challenges Ctirad, the women's greatest opponent, to a duel. He scornfully refuses. In the war that follows, Šárka tricks Ctirad into 'rescuing' her when he finds her tied to a tree. Instead of calling her women warriors, Šárka falls in love with Ctirad, and warns him of the ambush. He, equally in love with Šárka, refuses to run away and summons the women himself. He is taken away, wounded. Šárka tells Přemysl where Ctirad is being held; the men rescue him and kill the women, and in remorse Šárka leaps to her death. Fibich's most popular opera shares its subject with JANÁČEK's first opera and SMETANA's tone poem, *Šárka*; this incident from Czech mythology is itself a sequel to LIBUŠE. JT O

Sarti, Giuseppe, b. Faenza, ? Nov (baptized 1 Dec) 1729; d. Berlin, 28 July 1802. Italian composer. Had posts in Denmark 1753–75, and Russia 1784–1802. His *c.* 70 operas, full of graceful music, are forgotten; *Fra Due Litiganti* (Milan 1782) is remembered by one aria quoted in the last act of DON GIOVANNI. LO

Sauguet, Henri [Henri-Pierre Poupard], b. Bordeaux, 18 May 1901. French composer. A friend of POULENC, MILHAUD and other members of 'Les Six', he has wr. several operas, incl. *Le Plumet du Colonel* (1924), *La Contrebasse* (1930) and *La Voyante* (1932), a one-act monologue for sop. *La Chartreuse de Parme*, based on the novel by Stendhal, was prod. at the Paris O. (1939), *La Cageure Imprévue* at the Paris OC (1944) and *Les Caprices de Marianne*, an adaptation of the play by Alfred de Musset, at Aix-en-Provence (1954). EF

Savage Opera Company. When Henry W. Savage (1859–1927), a Boston realtor, took over the bankrupt Castle Square T. (1895), he experimented with light opera in Eng. at popular prices. Immediate success led him to alternate seasons in Baltimore, then to brief engagements at the NY Met as the Eng. O. Co., and to national tours. He sponsored a tour of PARSIFAL 1904–5, gave first US prod. of MADAMA BUTTERFLY, and toured with FANCIULLA DEL WEST 1911–12. Savage managed several companies, the Castle Square for sure-fire novelties, as LUSTIGE WITWE (1906) and the Eng. O. Co. for more serious works. Prods were well staged, youthfully sung and supported by adequate orchs. EJ

Sāvitri, 1 act, HOLST, lib. comp., derived from an episode in the *Mahabhrata*. London, Wellington Hall, 5 Dec 1916; Chicago, 23 Jan 1934. Main chars: Sāvitri (sop.) Satyavan (ten.) Death (bass). In this highly stylized story, telling how Sāvitri cheats Death, come to claim her husband, Holst's refined and beautiful score creates a world very much of its own by extraordinarily economical means. BAKER took the title role in a moving revival of the work at the 1974 Aldeburgh Fest. AB O
See Kobbé

Sawallisch, Wolfgang, b. Munich, 26 Aug 1923. German conductor. Studied Munich. Has held posts at Augsburg (1947–53); Aachen (1953–5); Wiesbaden (1957–9); Cologne (1959–63). Principal cond. Munich since 1969. Has cond. Bayreuth (TRISTAN UND ISOLDE, 1957; FLIEGENDE HOLLÄNDER, 1959; TANNHÄUSER, 1961), Edinburgh and at other fests. LO

Sayão [Baldwin de Oliveira], Bidù, b. Rio de Janeiro, 11 May 1902. Brazilian soprano. Studied with Jean DE RESZKE at Nice. Debut 1926 Rome as ROSINA. US debut 1937, NY Met (MANON); her roles there until 1951 incl. VIOLETTA, MIMI, SUSANNA, ZERLINA, and MÉLISANDE. Her voice was light and flexible, her acting appealing. AB

Scala, Teatro alla *see* MILAN

Scala di Seta, La (*The Silken Ladder*), *farsa*, 1 act, ROSSINI, lib. Giuseppe Foppa after François Planard. Venice, T. S. Moïse, 9 May 1812; London, SW, 26 Apr 1954. Main chars: Giulia (sop.) Dorvil (ten.) Blansac (bar.) Lucilla (mezzo-sop.) Dormont (basso-buffo) Germano (basso-buffo). Giulia, secretly married to Dorvil, devises various plans to ward off the attentions of the servant, Germano, and Dorvil's friend Blansac, and to keep her marriage a secret from her guardian, Dormont. The dénouement and general reconciliation takes place by the 'silken ladder' whereby Dorvil enters his wife's apartment. JB
See Weinstock, *Rossini, A Biography* (London and New York 1968)

Scaria, Emil, b. Graz, 18 Sept 1838; d. Blasewitz, nr Dresden, 22 July 1886. Austrian bass. Studied Vienna; debut 1860, Pest (HUGUENOTS). After further study with GARCÍA II in London engaged Dessau, Leipzig, 1863–5 and Dresden, 1865–72. His great reputation was established in Vienna, 1872–86. Outstanding in WAGNER roles, he created Gurnemanz in PARSIFAL (Bayreuth 1882), and was the first Bayreuth WOTAN. He died insane. LO

Scarlatti, Alessandro, b. Palermo, 2 May 1660; d. Naples, 24 Oct 1725. Italian composer, the first great master of the Neapolitan School of comp. Of his *c.* 115 operas *c.* 70 survive, but few have been revived. The perfecting of the tripartite ARIA form and the It. overture (quick, slow, quick – the basis for subsequent symphonic developments) are generally credited to him; his music, grateful to sing, is an essential foundation for the BEL CANTO style. In such operas as have been revived, however, it is the dramatic quality which, though sensed by his contemporaries, eludes us. LO
See Dent, *Alessandro Scarlatti: His Life and Works* (London 1905; 2nd ed., with Preface and Notes by Frank Walker, London 1960)

Scarlatti, Domenico, b. Naples, 26 Oct 1685; d. Madrid, 23 July 1757. Italian composer, son of the above. Though best known for his harpsichord comps, he wrote several operas for Rome and London incl. two on Iphigenia and an *Amleto*, lib. ZENO and Pietro Pariati (Rome 1715), one of the earliest Hamlet operas. LO

Scarpia, bar., the chief of police in TOSCA

scena (It. 'scene') 1. A segment of an act during which the scenery and/or the number of chars on stage remains constant. 2. The non-formal, declamatory part of any large-scale solo on ensemble (e.g. *scena ed aria, scena e duetto* etc.). JB

Schalk, Franz, b. Vienna, 27 May 1863; d. Edlach, 2 Sept 1931. Austrian conductor. Studied Vienna. After appointments in Graz (1889–95), Prague (1895–8) and Berlin (1899–1900) returned to Vienna as chief cond. at Hof O., becoming dir. 1918, succeeding Hans Gregor. R. STRAUSS was his associate there 1919–24 until differences led to Strauss's resignation. Cond. three RING DES NIBEL-

UNGEN cycles at CG; also at NY Met 1898–9. One of founders of Salzburg Fest. LO

Schat, Peter, b. Utrecht, 5 June 1935. Dutch composer. His opera, *Het Labyrinth*, was prod. Amsterdam 1966. EF

Schaunard, bar., one of the four Bohemians in BOHÈME

Schauspieldirektor, Der (*The Impresario*), *Singspiel*, 1 act, MOZART, lib. Gottlieb Stephanie jr. Vienna, Schönbrunn T., 7 Feb 1786; London, St James's T., 30 May 1857; NY, 9 Nov 1870. Main chars: Mme Herz (sop.) Mme Silberklang (sop.) Herr Vogelsang (ten.). A theatrical satire with two quarrelling prima donnas and a tenor who tries to keep the peace. Five numbers only incl. an overture. Usually given with altered lib. JB O

Schenk, Otto, b. Vienna, 12 June 1930. Studied at Vienna to become an actor, and began his career in that capacity at the Josefstadt T. First opera prod. ZAUBERFLÖTE (Salzburg 1963), followed by JENŮFA (Vienna Staats O. 1964). Has since prod. regularly there and at Munich. Prod. FIDELIO, cond. BERNSTEIN, for the BEETHOVEN bicentenary (T. a. d. Wien, 1970). CG with BALLO IN MASCHERA (1975). One of the most sensitive and perceptive of modern producers. AB

Scherchen, Hermann, b. Berlin, 21 June 1891; d. Florence, 12 June 1966. German conductor. Best known in the concert hall, but has cond. premieres of several modern operas incl. PRIGIONIERO, *Das Verhör des Lukullus* (*see* VERURTEILUNG DES L.), and KÖNIG HIRSCH. Other present-day works he has cond. incl. ABSTRAKT OPER NO. 1, HINDEMITH's *Hin und Zurück* and VON HEUTE AUF MORGEN and SALOME. LO

Scheveningen, the Netherlands. Opera is perf. at the Kurhaus during the summer. In 1947 a Summer Fest. was held there which evolved, the following year, into the Holland Fest., based mainly in Amsterdam and The Hague. *See* Netherlands. EF

Schikaneder, Emanuel (Johann Joseph), b. Straubing, 1 Sept 1751; d. Vienna, 21 Sept 1812. Austrian actor, playwright and impresario. As manager of the T. a. d. Wieden, built by him 1787, he commissioned ZAUBERFLÖTE, in which he played PAPAGENO. Built T. a. d. Wien 1801, managing this until 1806. Wr. at least 35 libs, for PAISIELLO, Franz Süss-Mayr, WINTER and others. *Vestas Feuer* (1805) was wr. for BEETHOVEN, who set a portion of it to music but did not finish it. LO

Schiller, Johann Christoph Friedrich von, b. Marbach, 10 Nov 1759; d. Weimar, 9 May 1805. German poet and dramatist. His works have been the basis for over 20 operas, incl. *Die Räuber*, 1782 (MASNADIERI; Ivan Zacj, *Amelia*, 1860; KLEBE, 1957); *Kabale und Liebe*, 1783 (LUISA MILLER); *Don Carlos*, 1784–7 (DON CARLOS); *Wallenstein*, 1789–9 (WEINBERGER, 1937; ZAFRED, 1965); *Das Lied von der Glocke*, 1799 (d'INDY, *Le Chant de la Cloche*, 1912); *Die Jungfrau von Orleans*, 1801 (VACCAI, *Giovanni d'Arco*, 1827; GIOVANNI D'ARCO; MAID OF ORLEANS; REZNIČEK, 1886); *Wilhelm Tell*, 1804 (GUILLAUME TELL). GRÉTRY's *Guillaume Tell*, 1791, and ARCHERS, 1796, given in some reference books as founded on Schiller, obviously cannot be. LO

Schillings, Max von, b. Düren, 19 Apr 1868; d. Berlin, 23 July 1933. German composer, conductor, and director. Chorus master, Bayreuth, 1902; gen. mus. dir. Stuttgart, 1911–18; and *Generalintendant*, Berlin Staats O., 1919–25. *Mona Lisa* (1915) was his only opera to achieve any success. LO

Schinkel, Karl Friedrich, b. Neuruppin, 13 Mar 1781; d. Berlin, 9 Oct 1841. German architect and stage designer. Appointed Prussian State Architect in 1815 aged 34, he was responsible for much of the architecture in the city and remodelled the Hof O. Designed for over 30 plays and operas 1815–32, incl. UNDINE, ARMIDE and (1815) ZAUBERFLÖTE, the sets of which were used in BEECHAM's Grand O. Season, CG, 1938. Schinkel was one of the most imaginative designers working in Germany. Like DAGUERRE in Paris he was experimenting with dioramas and cycloramas: by painting scenery with semi-transparent watercolours and contrasted opaque colour and applying varied lighting he could effect a transition from sunlight to overcast conditions, or create the illusion of moonlight. His ideas on opera prod. anticipated those of WAGNER, and later continental European designers owed much to his work. LO

Schipa, Tito [Raffaele Attilio Amadeo], b. Lecce, 2 Jan 1889; d. NY, 16 Dec 1965. Italian tenor. Studied Lecce and Milan. Debut 1911, Vercelli (ALFREDO); appeared at Rome and Sc. Created Ruggero (RONDINE). Chicago (US debut) 1919–32; NY Met (debut as NEMORINO) 1932–5 and 1940–1. Continued to appear at Sc. until 1949. One of the most musicianly and stylish tenors of his age, particularly noted in the ROSSINI, BELLINI and DONIZETTI repertory, but also a fine DES GRIEUX, Alfredo, FENTON (FALSTAFF) and Wilhelm Meister (MIGNON). AB

Schippers, Thomas, b. Kalamazoo, Mich., 9 Mar 1930. American conductor. Debut 1948, NY; cond. London premiere of CONSUL. First engaged at the NY Met 1955, the same year he cond. SAINT OF BLEECKER STREET at Sc. Associated since its inception (1958) with the Fest. of Two Worlds, Spoleto, he has cond. many operas there, incl. DONIZETTI's *Duc d'Albe* (1959), COMTE ORY (1962), ITALIANA IN ALGERI (1969) and MERCADANTE's *Giuramento* (1970). Cond. premieres of FALLA's *Atlàntida* (Sc. 1968) and ANTONY AND CLEOPATRA (Met 1966). Bayreuth debut 1963 (MEISTERSINGER); CG debut 1968 (ELEKTRA). EF

Schlusnus, Heinrich, b. Braubach, 6 Aug 1888; d. Frankfurt, 19 June 1852. German baritone. Debut 1915, Hamburg (LOHENGRIN); engaged Nuremberg 1915–17; Berlin till 1945. Guest appearances CG, Vienna, Chicago O. and Bayreuth. A fine interpreter of WAGNER and VERDI; famous as *Lieder* singer. LO

Schmedes, Erik, b. Gentofte, nr Copenhagen, 27 Aug 1868; d. Vienna, 23 Mar 1931. Danish tenor, who began career as baritone. Studied with ARTÔT at Paris. Debut 1891, as bar., Wiesbaden, as the Herald (LOHENGRIN). After singing as bar. at Nuremberg and Dresden, debut 1898, as ten. Vienna (SIEGFRIED). Remained there as leading *Heldentenor* until 1924. Bayreuth 1899–1902 as Siegfried and PARSIFAL; NY Met 1908–9. One of the leading heroic tenors of his day. AB

Schneider, Hortense, b. Bordeaux, 30 Apr 1833; d. Paris, 6 May 1920. French soprano, daughter of a Ger. master tailor who settled in Bordeaux and m. a Frenchwoman. Went to Paris 1855, and at once engaged by OFFENBACH, in whose works, especially BELLE HÉLÈNE and GRANDE DUCHESSE DE GÉROLSTEIN, she scored her greatest successes. Combining a fine voice, commanding stage presence and an inimitable sense of comedy, she was one of the great stars of 19th-c. light opera. She last appeared in 1881 in a revue, *Les Parfums de Paris*. LO

Schneider-Siemssen, Günther, b. Augsburg, 7 June 1926. Austro-German designer. Studied with C. KRAUSS and at Munich Staats O. with Emil Praetorius and Ludwig Sievert. At Munich 1948–52. In 1952 designed scenes for Salzburg Marionettes (ZAUBERFLÖTE, DON GIOVANNI etc.); from 1962 at Vienna Staats O. Has also worked at Stuttgart, Cologne, Frankfurt, Hamburg, and London. LO

Schneider Wibbel (*Tailor Wibbel*), comic opera, 4 acts, LOTHAR, lib. Hans Müller-Schlösser. Berlin, Staats O., 12 May 1938. Lothar's most successful opera, with perfs all over Germany. Revived Munich, Gärtnerplatz T., 1962. LO

Schnorr von Carolsfeld, Ludwig, b. Munich, 2 July 1836; d. Dresden, 21 July 1865. German tenor. Debut 1858, Karlsruhe (JOSEPH). Leading ten. Dresden 1860–5. WAGNER, who heard him sing LOHENGRIN (Karlsruhe 1862), was so impressed that he entrusted the creation of the part of TRISTAN to him. He died shortly after the premiere. LO

Schock, Rudolf Johann, b. Duisburg, 4 Sept 1915. German tenor. Sang in the chorus at Duisburg; debut as soloist 1937, Brunswick. Sang in Berlin 1943, Hanover 1945, Hamburg 1946, Salzburg 1948, CG 1949, Edinburgh 1952, and Vienna 1953. A lyric ten. with a smoothly prod. and warm-toned voice, he has a large repertory incl. RODOLFO, PINKERTON, ALFREDO, TAMINO, MAX, Bacchus (ARIADNE AUF NAXOS), and WALTHER VON STOLZING, which he sang at Bayreuth (1959). EF

Schoeck, Othmar, b. Brunnen, 1 Sept 1886; d. Zürich, 8 Mar 1957. Swiss composer. His six operas include a comedy, *Don Ranudo de Colibrados* (1919), based on Ludvig af Holberg's play; *Venus* (1922), based on MÉRIMÉE's *Vénus d'Ille*; and *Penthesilea* (1927), based on KLEIST. They have made little headway outside Switzerland. LO

Schöffler, Paul, b. Dresden, 15 Sept 1897. German, later Austrian, baritone. Studied Dresden, Berlin and Milan; debut Dresden 1925, where he remained until 1937 when he went to Vienna. Has sung at CG, 1934–9, 1948–53, and at NY Met; also at Bayreuth, Salzburg and elsewhere. A fine WAGNER bar., esp. admired as HANS SACHS. Created Jupiter in LIEBE DER DANAE. LO

Schönberg, Arnold, b. Vienna, 13 Sept 1874; d. Brentwood, Cal., 13 July 1951. Austrian composer. His first two operas, ERWARTUNG and GLÜCKLICHE HAND, are wr. in post-romantic, atonal style; VON HEUTE AUF MORGEN is the first wholly dodecaphonic opera. In 1932 he completed the first two acts of MOSES UND ARON, but in 1933 was driven by the Nazis from Berlin, where he taught at the

Acad. of Arts, and settled in the USA. Though he recommenced work on *Moses und Aron* in 1951, the opera was left unfinished at his death. EF

Schöne, Lotte [Charlotte Bodenstein], b. Vienna, 15 Dec 1891. Austrian soprano. Studied Vienna; debut 1912, Vienna O., as a bridesmaid in FREISCHÜTZ. Vienna Staats O. 1917–25, singing all the major light, lyrical roles; Salzburg 1922–34 (ZERLINA, DESPINA, and BLONDE). Also a regular visitor to Berlin Staats O. 1925–33, graduating to heavier parts such as MANON, MIMI and CIO-CIO-SAN. Was the first London LIÙ in her only CG season (1927). After the Nazis came to power, moved to Paris and joined OC, where her MÉLISANDE (1933) was much admired. Sang MARCELLINA and Zerlina under WALTER (Paris O. 1937), after which she virtually retired from the stage. One of the most enchanting sopranos of her day, esp. famed for MOZART and R. STRAUSS parts. AB

Schöne Galathee, Die (*The Beautiful Galatea*), operetta, 1 act, SUPPÉ, lib. Poly Henrion [Leopold K. Dittmar Kohl von Kohlenegg]. Berlin, Meysel's T., 30 June 1865; London, Gaiety T. (as *Ganymede and Galatea*), 20 Jan 1872; NY, 14 Sept 1882. LO
See Lubbock

Schorr, Friedrich, b. Nagyvárad, 2 Sept 1888; d. Farmington, Conn., 14 Aug 1953. Hungarian, later American, bass-baritone. Studied Vienna; first appearances in minor roles at Chicago 1912. Debut 1912, Graz (WOTAN). After engagements there, at Prague and Cologne, joined Berlin Staats O. 1923. NY Met debut 1924 as WOLFRAM; principal Wagnerian bar. there until 1943. CG debut 1924 as RHEINGOLD Wotan; sang there regularly until 1933. Bayreuth 1925–33. Leading Wotan, HANS SACHS and FLIEGENDE HOLLÄNDER of the 1920s and 1930s, a noble, warm singer of great dramatic truth. AB

Schreier, Peter, b. Meissen, 25 July 1935. German tenor. Debut 1961, Dresden; sang at the Berlin Staats O. since 1962. London debut 1966 with the Hamburg O. at SW; has appeared at Rome, Vienna, Salzburg, Sc., Buenos Aires and the NY Met (1968). A very stylish MOZART singer, he incl. Idamante (IDOMENEO), BELMONTE, Don OTTAVIO, FERRANDO, TAMINO, and the early MITRIDATE, RE DI PONTO in his repertory. He also sings lyric ten. roles such as Jacquino (FIDELIO), ALMAVIVA (BARBIERE DI SIVIGLIA), DAVID, Da-Ud (ÄGYPTISCHE HELENA), and Flamand (CAPRICCIO). EF

Schreker, Franz, b. Monaco, 23 Mar 1878; d. Berlin, 21 Mar 1934. Austrian composer. A contemporary of SCHÖNBERG, his music, which seemed advanced at the time, has suffered neglect since his death. His first opera, FERNE KLANG, made some stir; of his six others *Das Spielwerk und die Prinzessin* (1913) and *Der Schatzgräber* (1920) were the most successful in Germany but made no headway elsewhere. LO

Schröder-Devrient, Wilhelmine, b. Hamburg, 6 Dec 1804; d. Coburg, 21 Jan 1860. German soprano, perhaps the finest dramatic singer of her day. Her father, Friedrich Schröder, was a singer, her mother, Antoinette Sophie Bürger, an actress; both parents taught her. Debut 1821, Vienna (PAMINA). Dresden 1823–47, where she created Adriano (COLA RIENZI), SENTA, and VENUS. Other roles incl. Donna ANNA, EURYANTHE, and LEONORE (CG 1832). She m. the actor Karl Devrient 1823, divorced 1828. LO

Schubert, Franz Peter, b. Vienna, 31 Jan 1797; d. Vienna, 19 Nov 1828. Austrian composer, whose astonishing output incl. some 17 attempts at opera: *Des Teufels Lustschloss*, 3 acts, lib. August von Kotzebue, 1813–14; *Der Vierjährige Posten*, 1-act *Singspiel*, lib. Theodor Körner, May 1815 (Dresden 23 Sept 1896); *Fernando*, 1-act *Singspiel*, lib. Albert Stadler, 1815 (Magdeburg 18 Aug 1918); *Claudine von Villa Bella*, lib. GOETHE, 1815 (incomplete); *Die Freunde von Salamanka*, 2-act *Singspiel*, lib. Johann Mayrhofer, 1815 (Halle 6 May 1928); *Die Bürgschaft*, lib. unknown, 1816 (incomplete); *Die Zwillingsbrüder*, 1-act *Singspiel*, lib. Georg von Hofmann, 1819 (commissioned by KT, perf. 14 June 1820, seven perfs); *Die Zauberharfe*, magic play with music, lib. Hofmann, 1819–20 (T. a. d. Wien 19 Aug 1820, eight perfs); *Sakuntala*, opera, 3 acts, lib. Johann Philipp Neumann after Kalidasa's Indian play, 1820 (incomplete); ALFONSO UND ESTRELLA; *Fierabras*, opera, lib. Josef Kupelweiser, 1823 (Karlsruhe 9 Feb 1897); *Der Häusliche Krieg*, 1-act *Singspiel*, lib. Ignaz Castelli after Aristophanes, 1823 (Frankfurt 29 Aug 1861; occasionally revived). LO

Schubert, Richard, b. Dessau, 14 Dec 1885; d. Oberstaufen, 12 Oct 1959. German tenor. Debut (as bar.) 1909, Strasbourg. Became ten. and studied Dresden; ten. debut 1911, Nuremberg. Engagements there, at Wiesbaden and Hamburg (1917–35); Vienna Staats O. debut 1920; guest there until 1929 in many of the *Heldentenor* roles and lyric-dramatic parts in the It. repertory. NY Met 1922 (TANNHÄUSER); Chicago 1922–3. Created Paul in TOTE STADT.

Possessed one of the most beautiful heroic voices of his day and cut a fine figure on stage. AB

Schuch, Ernst von, b. Graz, 23 Nov 1846; d. Dresden, 10 May 1914. Austrian conductor. Studied Graz and Vienna. His principal post was at Dresden, where he was cond. from 1873 and gen. mus. dir. 1882–1914, a period of splendour for the Dresden O. Cond. premieres of FEUERSNOT, SALOME, ELEKTRA, and ROSENKAVALIER. LO

Schuh, Oscar Fritz, b. Munich, 15 Jan 1904. German producer. Studied philosophy and art history. After staging works in Oldenburg, Osnabrück, Darmstadt, and elsewhere went to Hamburg as resident prod. 1932–40; similar post at Vienna 1940–5. Active in other centres too: at Venice Fest. (CARDILLAC, 1948); Naples (TANNHÄUSER, 1948; WOZZECK, 1950); Salzburg, with notable prods of MOZART and of modern works: DANTONS TOD (1947); PROZESS (1953); ORFF's *Antigonae* (1949); LIEBERMANN's *Penelope* (1954); IRISCHE LEGENDE (1955). *Generalintendant* Cologne 1959, where he prod. first Ger. perf. of FIERY ANGEL. LO

Schuller, Gunther, b. NY, 22 Nov 1925. American composer, conductor, and teacher. President of New England Cons. Was a horn player in Cincinnati and Met orchestras. Operas are VISITATION and a children's opera, *The Fisherman and his Wife*; the latter was based on a GRIMM fairy tale (Boston, 8 May 1970). LO

Schumann, Elisabeth, b. Merseburg, 13 June 1885; d. NY, 23 Apr 1952. German soprano. Studied Hamburg, debut there 1909 (Shepherd in TANNHÄUSER). Sang Vienna Staats O. 1919–37, when she left Austria for the USA. A frequent visitor to CG, 1924–31, and at Salzburg and Munich Fests. Her reputation was based on Ger. opera and *Lieder*; her MOZART and R. STRAUSS were unsurpassed. LO

Schumann, Robert Alexander, b. Zwickau, 8 June 1810; d. Endenich, 29 July 1856. German composer and critic. He toyed with several operatic projects, among them BYRON's *Corsair*, fragments of which exist, and HOFFMANN's *Doge und Dogaressa*, but completed only GENOVEVA. As a critic he was out of sympathy with much of the opera of his time though he praised EURYANTHE. His judgment on reading the score of TANNHÄUSER was unfavourable but he gave it a guarded welcome after hearing it. LO

Schumann-Heink, Ernestine Rössler, b. Lieben, 15 June 1861; d. Hollywood, Cal., 17 Nov 1936. Czech, later American, contralto. Studied Graz and Dresden; debut 1878, Dresden (AZUCENA). Hamburg 1882–98; then Berlin, Chicago and (1899) the NY Met (debut as ORTRUD), remaining there for many seasons until 1932. CG debut 1892, singing ERDA, FRICKA and Waltraute in the house's first RING DES NIBELUNGEN and returning 1897–1900. Bayreuth 1896–1906. Created KLYTEMNESTRA. Her full, opulent voice, amazing flexibility, and dramatic ability made her one of the great singers of her age. AB

Schwanda the Bagpiper (*Švanda dudák*), opera, 2 acts, WEINBERGER, lib. Miloš Kareš after J. K. Tyl. Prague, NT, 27 Apr 1927; NY Met, 7 Nov 1931; London, CG, 11 May 1934. Main chars: Švanda (bar.) Dorotka (sop.) the Queen (mezzo-sop.) the Devil (bass). The work, with its obvious folk-music elements, was extremely popular in Europe and America for 20 years; today it is rather better known for the concert performances of its polka and fugue. JT
See Kobbé

Schwarzkopf, Elisabeth, b. Jarocin, nr Posen (now Poznań), 9 Dec 1915. German soprano much admired in MOZART and R. STRAUSS, and an outstanding *Lieder* singer. Studied Berlin Hochschule für Musik, and with IVOGÜN. Debut Berlin Deutsche O. 1938 as First Flowermaiden (PARSIFAL); Vienna Staats O. 1942 (ZERBINETTA). Remained with Vienna co. to 1948, mainly as coloratura sop., changing to lyric sop. about 1947, when she first sang at CG as Donna ELVIRA (DON GIOVANNI) with Vienna co. in guest season. Resident member of CG 1948–52, singing in Eng., incl MANON, MARCELLINA, VIOLETTA, CIO-CIO-SAN and MIMI, in addition to Mozart and Strauss; EVA (in Ger.); and GILDA (in It.). Sang Countess ALMAVIVA 1948 under KARAJAN at both Sc. and Salzburg Fest. Created Anne Trulove (RAKE'S PROGRESS). US debuts: San Francisco O. 1955, NY Met 1964, both as MARSCHALLIN, a role for which she was widely praised, and which was filmed in a 1960 Salzburg Fest. prod. as well as being among many roles she sang on records prod. by her husband, Walter Legge (m. 1950). Dramatic char. sometimes acquired tinge of artificiality through exceptional refinement of vocal technique, but beauty of tone and phrasing allied to glamour of appearance gained her musical respect as well as deserved popularity. NG
See Rosenthal, *Sopranos of Today* (London 1956)

Schweigsame Frau, Die (*The Silent Woman*), opera, 3 acts, R. STRAUSS, lib. ZWEIG after JONSON's *Epicoene, or The Silent Woman*. Dresden, 24 June 1935 (banned by the Nazis after four perfs); NY, City O., 7 Oct 1958 (in Eng.); London, CG, 20 Nov 1961 (in Eng.). Main chars: Sir Morosus (bass) Henry Morosus (ten.) Aminta (sop.) Housekeeper (contr.) Barber (bar.). The bad-tempered Sir Morosus, who has an obsessive hatred of noise, is made to see the brighter side of life by his nephew through a fake marriage to a timid 'wife' who turns outrageously noisy after the ceremony. FGB
See Mann, *Richard Strauss* (London 1964; New York 1966); Kobbé

Schweitzer, Anton Theodor Heinrich, b. Coburg 1735 (baptized 16 June); d. Gotha, 23 Nov 1787. German composer and conductor. MdC, Hildburghausen, *c.* 1766–9; after being mus. dir. at Weimar in GOETHE's time succeeded BENDA at Gotha. His *c.* 12 operas incl. an *Alceste* (1773) lib. Christoph Martin Wieland) and several *Singspiele*. LO

Schwetzingen, W. Germany. Fests began there 1956, in the theatre in the castle. Revivals of 18th-c. works are given, also contemporary operas incl. premieres of REVISOR, ELEGY FOR YOUNG LOVERS, FORTNER's *In seinem Garten liebt Don Perlimplin Belisa* (1962). LO

Schwind, Moritz von, b. Vienna, 21 Jan 1804; d. Vienna, 8 Feb 1871. Austrian painter, friend of F. SCHUBERT, Franz Lachner, and other musicians. The charming panels he painted in the foyer of the Vienna O. on the theme of MOZART and especially of ZAUBERFLÖTE escaped destruction when the house was bombed in 1945. LO

Sciammarella, Valdo, b. Buenos Aires, 20 Jan 1924. Argentine composer. His only opera, *Marianita Limeña* (1957) was chosen for perf. at the Brussels World's Fair (1958) and revised for its premiere at the T. Colón (1962). Francisco Javier's lib. is based on *El Divorcio de la Condesita*, from Ricardo Palma's *Tradiciones Peruanas*, which records the first marital annulment case in the Spanish colonies (Lima 1755). MK

Sciutti, Graziella, b. Turin, 17 Apr 1932. Italian soprano. Studied Rome. Debut 1951, Aix, as Lucy (TELEPHONE). British debut 1954, Glyndebourne (ROSINA), returned as Nannetta (FALSTAFF) and SUSANNA (1958), DESPINA (1959). CG debut 1957 as Oscar (BALLO IN MASCHERA). A notable soubrette of the day, with a lively stage presence. Outstanding roles: Susanna, NORINA, and Oscar. AB

Scott, Sir Walter, b. Edinburgh, 15 Aug 1771; d. Abbotsford, 21 Sept 1832. Scottish poet and novelist. Some 27 operas are based on his works, the chief ones being: *The Lady of the Lake*, 1810 (DONNA DEL LAGO); *Guy Mannering*, 1815 (DAME BLANCHE); *The Bride of Lammermoor*, 1819 (LUCIA DI LAMMERMOOR); *Ivanhoe*, 1819 (MARSCHNER, *Der Templer und die Jüdin*, 1829; SULLIVAN); *Kenilworth*, 1821 (DONIZETTI, 1829); *The Fair Maid of Perth*, 1828 (JOLIE FILLE DE PERTH). LO

Scotti, Antonio, b. Naples, 25 Jan 1866; d. Naples, 26 Feb 1936. Italian baritone. Debut 1889, Malta (AMONASRO); Sc. debut 1898 (HANS SACHS); CG and NY Met debuts 1899 (DON GIOVANNI). SCARPIA at the first CG (1900) and Met (1901) perfs of TOSCA, he also sang ALMAVIVA (NOZZE DI FIGARO), Alfonso (LUCREZIA BORGIA), VALENTIN, ESCAMILLO, many VERDI roles – GERMONT, RIGOLETTO, IAGO and FALSTAFF; also MARCELLO, De Siriex (FEDORA) and Chim-Fen in Franco Leoni's *Oracolo*, with which he took his farewell at the Met in 1933. EF

Scottish Opera (SO). Founded 1962 by GIBSON, now art. dir. Its achievement to date has been remarkable, with some notable perfs, e.g. TROYENS (1969), and the RING DES NIBELUNGEN (1971). Gave first perf. in Britain of VOLO DI NOTTE, and commissioned ORR's *Full Circle* (1968), and *Weir of Hermiston* (1975). Dir. of prods, P. EBERT. The T. Royal, Glasgow, became its permanent home in Oct 1975; it also tours in Scotland and England. LO

Scotto, Renata, b. Savona, 24 Feb 1934. Italian soprano. Studied Milan with Mercedes Llopart. Debut 1953, T. Nazionale, Milan (VIOLETTA). Sc. debut 1954 as Walter (WALLY); has appeared there regularly since. London debut as MIMI (Stoll T. 1957) where she also sang ADINA, Violetta, and Donna ELVIRA (DON GIOVANNI). In 1957 replaced CALLAS in final perf. of SONNAMBULA at the Edinburgh Fest. to much acclaim. CG debut 1962 (Mimi); has since sung there as CIO-CIO-SAN, MANON, GILDA, Violetta and Amina (*Sonnambula*). NY Met debut 1965 (Cio-Cio-San). More recently has taken heavier roles, e.g. Elena (VÊPRES SICILIENNES) and Amelia (SIMONE BOCCANEGRA). One of the most intelligent and successful It. sopranos since CALLAS. AB

Scribe, Augustin Eugène, b. Paris, 25 Dec 1791; d. Paris, 21 Feb 1861. French dramatist and librettist. A prominent figure in the Fr. theatre for more than 40 years, he wr. *c.* 300 plays, and libs for nearly all the leading Fr.

Colour plates.
Facing page: Henriette SONTAG as ROSINA in BARBIERE DI SIVIGLIA, 1849
Overleaf: Set by Karl Friedrich SCHINKEL (1781–1841) for ZAUBERFLÖTE, Act I, sc. 6 (1815)

J. Brandard del et lithog.   M & N Hanhart lith. Printers

MADAME SONTAG,

AS ROSINA "BARBER OF SEVILLE".

comps and some It. ones (ELISIR D'AMORE and FAVORITE; VÊPRES SICILIENNES). Was equally at home in *opéra comique* and the grand opera of SPONTINI/MEYERBEER – a category he largely helped to create. His output incl. libs for JUIVE, MUETTE DE PORTICI (with Casimir Delavigne), PROPHÈTE, ROBERT LE DIABLE (with Delavigne), HUGUENOTS, AFRICAINE, DAME BLANCHE, GUSTAVE III (for AUBER, later adapted for BALLO IN MASCHERA) and ADRIANA LECOUVREUR. LO
See Smith, *The Tenth Muse* (New York 1970; London 1971)

Searle, Humphrey, b. Oxford, 26 Aug 1915. English composer. Studied with Anton Webern in Vienna. His operas are the 1-act *Diary of a Madman*, derived from GOGOL (Städtische O., Berlin, 1958; New O. Co., SW, 1960); *The Photo of the Colonel* (based on Eugène Ionesco's play, Frankfurt 1964); and HAMLET. EF

Seattle, Washington, USA. Opera began in a modest way in 1964, gradually enlarging its scope. Pacific Northwest Fest. held there, with a RING DES NIBELUNGEN cycle in Ger. and Eng. OF MICE AND MEN first prod. there. Present prod. G. LONDON. LO

Sebastian, George, b. Budapest, 17 Aug 1903. Hungarian conductor. Studied with KODÁLY and with WALTER in Munich. Held posts at Leipzig 1924–7; Berlin, Städtische O., 1927–31; San Francisco 1944–7. Since then has been chief cond. Paris O. LO

Secret, The (*Tajemství*), opera, 3 acts, SMETANA, lib. KRÁSNOHORSKÁ. Prague, New Czech T., 18 Sept 1878; Oxford, 7 Dec 1956. Main chars: Malina (bass) Roza (contr.) Kalina (bar.) Bonifác (bass) Blaženka (sop.) Vítek (ten.). The rivalry of Kalina and Malina in a small 18th-c. Bohemian town prevents their children from marrying and has prevented Malina's sister Roza from marrying the once poor Kalina. Directions to the 'secret' (which the deceased Friar Barnabáš had promised would enable Kalina to marry Roza) turn out to be directions to a tunnel to her house, where the two pairs of lovers are united. Smetana's opera is remarkable for its skilled ensemble writing and delicate characterization. JT O
See Large, *Smetana* (London 1970)

Sedaine, Michel Jean, b. Paris, 4 July 1719; d. Paris, 17 May 1797. French playwright and librettist, important in 18th-c. *opéra comique*. Among his many libs are those for GRÉTRY'S RICHARD CŒUR DE LION and *Guillaume Tell* (1791); MONSIGNY'S ROI ET LE FERMIER, *Aline, Reine de Golconde* (1766), DÉSERTEUR, *Rose et Colas* (1764); PHILIDOR'S *Le Diable à Quatre* (1759) and *Blaise le Savetier* (1759). SAUGUET'S *La Gageure Imprévue* (1944) also uses a Sedaine lib. LO

Seefried, Irmgard, b. Köngetried, Bavaria, 9 Oct 1919. German soprano. Debut 1939, Aachen, as the Priestess (AIDA). Engaged at the Vienna Staats O. since 1943, first sang at Salzburg 1946, CG 1947, Sc. 1948 and NY Met 1955. A sensitive interpreter of SUSANNA, ZERLINA, FIORDILIGI and PAMINA, she has also sung Cleopatra (GIULIO CESARE), MARCELLINA, EVA, MAŘENKA, OCTAVIAN, the Composer (ARIADNE AUF NAXOS), MARIE, and Blanche (DIALOGUES DES CARMÉLITES). Though now virtually retired from the stage, she still occasionally sings char. parts, such as the Marquise (FILLE DU RÉGIMENT). EF

Segreto di Susanna, Il (*Susanna's Secret*), opera, 1 act, WOLF-FERRARI, lib. Enrico Golisciani. Munich, 4 Dec 1909 (in Ger.); NY, 14 Mar 1911 (in It.); London, CG, 11 July 1911. Main chars: Gil (bar.) Susanna (sop.). Count Gil, smelling tobacco smoke about the house, suspects that his wife has a lover: in fact she is a secret smoker herself. Wolf-Ferrari's best-known opera. JB
See Kobbé

Seidl, Anton, b. Pest, 7 May 1850; d. NY, 28 Mar 1898. Hungarian conductor. Studied Leipzig. Assisted WAGNER at first Bayreuth Fest. 1876. Cond. Leipzig 1879–82, then toured with A. NEUMANN'S Wagner Co. After Bremen, 1883–5, moved to NY Met as cond. of Ger. opera, cond. US premieres of MEISTERSINGER VON NÜRNBERG, RHEINGOLD, SIEGFRIED, GÖTTERDÄMMERUNG and TRISTAN UND ISOLDE. Also cond. first Eng. RING DES NIBELUNGEN, and premiere of PARSIFAL at Bayreuth. LO

Sellner, Gustav Rudolf, b. Traunstein, Bavaria, 25 May 1905. German producer. Studied Munich. After appointments at Oldenburg and Göttingen was *Intendant*, Hanover, 1943–4, Darmstadt 1951–61 and since 1961 at Berlin Deutsche O. Began as prod. of straight plays; his operas prod. since 1959 incl. MOSES UND ARON, 1959; ALKMENE, 1961; FRAU OHNE SCHATTEN, 1964; BESUCH DER ALTEN DAME, 1971. LO

Sembrich, Marcella [Marcelline Kochanska], b. Wisniewczyk, 18 Feb 1858; d. NY, 11 Jan 1935. Polish soprano. Taught by her father, a

Colour plate:
Amy SHUARD in the title role of TURANDOT, London, CG, 1973; produced Charles Hamilton; scenery and costumes Cecil Beaton

noted concert violinist; then studied Lemberg Cons. On LISZT's advice she studied singing in Vienna and Milan. She m. her teacher, Wilhelm Stengel, from Lemberg Cons. Debut 3 June 1877, Athens (PURITANI); German debut 1878, Dresden (LUCIA DI LAMMERMOOR); CG debut 1880 in same role, returning for four successful seasons; NY debut 24 Oct 1883 again as Lucia. She sang throughout Europe until 1898; was a great favourite at the Met 1898–1909, after which she retired to teach at the Curtis Institute, Philadelphia, and the Juilliard School of Music, NY. She was also a notable *Lieder* singer. PS

Semele, secular oratorio, 3 acts, HANDEL, lib. William Congreve with one air by Alexander Pope. London, CG (concert form), 10 Feb 1744; Cambridge (staged), 1925; Evanston, Ill., 30 Jan 1959. Main chars: Semele (sop.) Ino/Juno (contr.) Jupiter (ten.) Athamas (counter-ten. or contr.) Cadmus (bass) Somnus (bass). Semele, one of Jupiter's earthly mistresses, is provoked by the disguised Juno into making her lover promise to reveal himself to her in all his glory. He does so, burning her to a cinder. JB O

Semiramide (*Semiramis*), opera, 2 acts, ROSSINI, lib. G. ROSSI after VOLTAIRE. Venice, T. La Fenice, 3 Feb 1823; London, HM, 15 July 1824; New Orleans, 1 May 1837. Main chars: Semiramide (sop.) Arsace (contr.) Oroe (bass) Assur (bar.) Idreno (ten.). Semiramide, Queen of Babylon, who has murdered her husband Nino with the aid of Assur, hopes to marry the young general Arsace. As she announces her choice in the temple, the ghost of Nino appears and forbids the ceremony. Then Semiramide and Arsace are revealed to each other as mother and son. In her attempt to protect Arsace from the vengeance of Assur, Semiramide is killed accidentally by her son. Rossini's last opera for Italy. JB O
See Kobbé

Semper, Gottfried, b. Hamburg, 29 Nov 1803; d. Rome, 15 May 1879. German architect. Designer of Dresden O. House (1841) which was destroyed by fire (1869) and rebuilt by his son, Manfred. Worked with WAGNER on designs for a Munich Festspielhaus, some features of which were incorporated into the Bayreuth Festspielhaus. LO

Senta, sop., the heroine of FLIEGENDE HOLLÄNDER

Serafin, Tullio, b. Rottanova di Cavarzere, 8 Dec 1878; d. Rome, 2 Feb 1968. Italian conductor. Studied Milan; debut 1900 Ferrara. His numerous posts have incl. NY Met 1924–34; Rome, cond. and art. dir., 1934–43 as well as appearing frequently at Sc., CG, Chicago. Returned to Rome O. 1962. Premieres he has cond. incl. EMPEROR JONES, KING'S HENCHMAN and others at the Met, and the first It. prod. of PETER GRIMES. LO

Seraglio, Il *see* ENTFÜHRUNG AUS DEM SERAIL

Serbia *see* YUGOSLAVIA

serenata (It. 'serenade') 1. Evening song addressed by a lover, outside, to his lady, inside, at her balcony window – a frequent custom in Italy and Austria, immortalized in DON GIOVANNI by 'Deh, vieni'. 2. Name applied occasionally in the 18th c. to a dramatic cantata, or a work smaller in scale than the usual opera. ACIS AND GALATEA was thus described. LO

Serov, Aleksandr Nikolayevich, b. St Petersburg, 23 Jan 1820; d. St Petersburg, 1 Feb 1871. Russian critic and composer. An opponent of the Russian nationalist school, a fact clearly revealed in his first and finest opera, the Meyerbeerian *Judith* (1863), which enjoyed considerable success in Russia. It was followed by *Rogneda* (1865). *The Power of Evil* (1871), left unfinished, under the terms of his will was completed by his widow and Nikolay Solovyov. None of Serov's operas has been staged complete in the West, though Act 4 of *Judith* was given in Paris during DYAGILEV'S 1909 season. GN

Serrano, José, b. Sueca, 14 Oct 1873; d. Madrid, 8 Nov 1941. Spanish composer. His more than 50 *zarzuelas* incl. *El Motete*, *La Canción del Olvido*, *El Carro del Sol*, *Los de Aragon*, *La Dolorosa*, and *El Trust de los Tenorios*. FGB

Serse (*Xerxes*), opera, 3 acts, HANDEL, lib. Niccolò Minato with alterations. London, Haymarket T., 26 Apr 1738; Northampton, Mass., 12 May 1928. Main chars: Serse (contr.) Arsamene (mezzo-sop.) Elviro (bass) Atalanta (sop.) Romilda (sop.) Amastre (mezzo-sop.). Serse (Xerxes, king of Persia), engaged to Amastre, falls in love with his brother's fiancée Romilda, so setting off the usual chain reactions of jealousy, misunderstanding and despair. Further complications result from the incompetence of Elviro, Arsamene's comic servant. Amastre observes the proceedings in male disguise, finally revealing herself so as to bring her royal lover to heel. Famous for Serse's aria 'Ombra mai fu', sometimes known as 'Handel's Largo'. JB O

Servandony, Jean Nicolas, b. Florence, 2 May 1695; d. Paris, 19 Jan 1766. Italian architect and stage designer. Trained in Italy, then went to Paris O., 1724, and later at the Salle des Machines, 1738–42. Designed decor for INDES GALANTES. Was also active in Lisbon, Bordeaux, Dresden, Vienna, Stuttgart, and London, where in 1749 he was in charge of fireworks in St James's Park. LO

Serva Padrona, La (*The Maid as Mistress*), *intermezzo*, 2 parts, PERGOLESI, lib. Gennaro Antonio Federico. Naples, T. S. Bartolomeo, 28 Aug 1733 between the acts of his *opera seria*, *Il Prigioniero Superbo*; London, HM, 27 Mar 1750; Baltimore, 13 June 1790. Main chars: Uberto (bar.) Serpina (sop.). Serpina, a chambermaid, tricks her master into marrying her. Pergolesi's most famous dramatic work. JB O

Shakespeare, William, b. Stratford-on-Avon, 22/23 Apr 1564; d. Stratford-on-Avon, 23 Apr 1616. English poet and dramatist. The most complete list at time of publication of operas based on his works is in Hartnoll (ed.), *Shakespeare and Music* (London 1964), which catalogues 188 operas drawn from 27 plays. *The Tempest*, 1611–12, tops the list with 31, incl. those by WINTER, 1793, FIBICH, 1895, SUTERMEISTER, and MARTIN. Next comes *Romeo and Juliet*, 1594–5, 24 (ZINGARELLI, 1796, VACCAI, 1825, BELLINI, GOUNOD); then *Hamlet*, 1600–1, 14 (MERCADANTE, 1822; Ambroise THOMAS, ZAFRED, SEARLE); *A Midsummer Night's Dream*, 1595–6 (PURCELL, FAIRY QUEEN, Thomas, 1850, ORFF, 1952, BRITTEN); *The Merchant of Venice*, 1596, 11 (HAHN, 1935, CASTELNUOVO-TEDESCO); *The Merry Wives of Windsor*, 1600–1, 10 (BALFE, 1838, NICOLAI, VERDI, VAUGHAN WILLIAMS). Others are *Antony and Cleopatra*, 1606–7 (BARBER); *The Comedy of Errors* (S. STORACE, KREJČÍ, 1946); *Coriolanus*, 1607–8 (CIKKER, 1973); *King Lear*, 1605–6 (FRAZZI, 1939); *Macbeth*, 1605–6 (Hippolyte Chélard, 1827, Verdi, BLOCH); *Measure for Measure*, 1604–5 (WAGNER, LIEBESVERBOT); *Much Ado about Nothing*, 1608–9 (BERLIOZ, STANFORD); *Othello*, 1604–5 (ROSSINI, Verdi); *The Taming of the Shrew*, 1593–4 (GÖTZ, GIANNINI, 1953); *The Winter's Tale*, 1610–11 (BRUCH, *Hermione*, 1872, GOLDMARK). Operas with Shakespearean titles not based on his plays incl. GIULIO CESARE, HENRY VIII, and TROILUS AND CRESSIDA. LO

Below: Feodor Shalyapin as Prince Galitsky in PRINCE IGOR, one of his most famous roles

Right: Yury Shaporin's DECEMBRISTS, Act III, sc. 1, Bolshoy T., Moscow, 1953. Aleksandr Ognivtsyov (centre) as Nikolay

Shalyapin, Fyodor, b. Kazan, 11 Feb 1873; d. Paris, 12 Apr 1938. Russian bass. Debut in 1890 at Ufa as Stolnik in HALKA; then sang at Tiflis, St Petersburg, Nizhni-Novgorod [Gorki], and Moscow. He first appeared at Sc. 1901; NY Met 1907; Paris O. 1908; DL 1913 and CG 1926. Apart from the Russian repertory – BORIS GODUNOV, Dosifey (KHOVANSHCHINA), IVAN SUSANIN, IVAN THE TERRIBLE, Galitsky (PRINCE IGOR) and Prince Gremin (EUGENE ONEGIN), in which he was unrivalled – he also sang MÉPHISTOPHÉLÈS, MEFISTOFELE, LEPORELLO, Don BASILIO (BARBIERE DI SIVIGLIA), PHILIPPE, and MASSENET's *Don Quichotte*, which he created at Monte Carlo in 1910. EF

Shanewis, or The Robin Woman, opera, 2 acts, CADMAN, lib. Nelle Richmond Eberhart. NY Met, 23 Mar 1918. Main chars: Shanewis (contr.) Mrs Everton (sop.) Amy (sop.) Linnel (ten.) Philip (bar.). An Indian girl with a promising vocal talent falls in love with the son of her benefactress who is engaged to a white girl. The ending is tragic. EJ
See Kobbé

Shaporin, Yury Aleksandrovich, b. Glukhov, 8 Nov 1887; d. Moscow, 9 Dec 1966. Russian composer. Graduated in law from St Petersburg Univ. (1912), then (1913–18) studied at the Cons. Known particularly for his monumental opera DECEMBRISTS with which he was occupied for much of his life. GN

Sharpless, bar., the US Consul in MADAMA BUTTERFLY

Shaw, Glen Byam, b. London, 13 Dec 1904. English producer. Began career as an actor,

then dir. for the straight stage before becoming Dir. of Prods for SW (now ENO) in 1962. For that co. his prods incl.: RAKE'S PROGRESS and IDOMENEO (1962), COSÌ FAN TUTTE and FREISCHÜTZ (1963), FAUST (1964), FLEDERMAUS (1966), the RING, with John Blatchley (1970–2). His strength as a prod. lies in the bringing out of char. through the music, with simple but significant movement. AB

Shebalin, Vissarion Yakovlevich, b. Omsk, 11 June 1902; d. Moscow, 28 May 1963. Soviet composer. Best known for his skilful, lyrical and witty opera *The Taming of the Shrew* (1957), based on SHAKESPEARE. His other opera is *The Sun over the Steppe* (concert perf. 1958). GN

Sheridan, Margaret, b. Castlebar, 15 Oct 1889; d. Dublin, 16 Apr 1958. Irish soprano. Educated at convent in Ireland, then studied London, RAM, and Italy. Debut 1918, Rome. The first CG IRIS, 1919. Sang at Sc. 1921–4, and CG 1925–30. With her lyric sop. and beauty she made an appealing MIMI and CIO-CIO-SAN. LO

Shield, William, b. Whickham, Co. Durham, 5 Mar 1748; d. Brightling, Sussex, 25 Jan 1829. English composer, engaged at CG 1778–91 and 1792–7. The most successful of his many operas was *Rosina* (1783) which has been revived and recorded. LO

Shirley, George, b. Indianapolis, 18 Apr 1934. American tenor. Trained as choral cond., Wayne Univ. Detroit. Opera debut 1959, Woodstock, NY (FLEDERMAUS). Prizewinner in Concorso di Vercelli, Italy, brought European debuts 1960 as RODOLFO (T. Nuovo, Milan, and Florence). Won NY Met 'Auditions of the Air' 1961; Met debut 1961 (FERRANDO). Also appeared NY City O., San Francisco O., Santa Fe O., and Spoleto Fest. UK debut, 1966, Glyndebourne Fest. (TAMINO); Glasgow, May 1967, with SO as Rodolfo; CG, July 1967, as Don OTTAVIO (DON GIOVANNI). His light, lyrical quality of voice and sense of classical line has been heard to good effect in roles mentioned, plus PELLÉAS, Erik (FLIEGENDE HOLLÄNDER) and DAVID. NG

Shirley-Quirk, John, b. Liverpool, 28 Aug 1931. English bass-baritone. Originally a science teacher, then studied with Roy Henderson, and began his career with choral work. Stage debut 1962, Glyndebourne, as the Doctor (PELLÉAS ET MÉLISANDE). Joined EOG 1964; created various parts in BRITTEN's church operas and, 1973, the *alter ego* roles in DEATH IN VENICE with which he made his NY Met debut 1974. CG debut 1973 as Mr Coyle (OWEN WINGRAVE), a role he created on TV (1971). With SO he has sung Count ALMAVIVA (NOZZE DI FIGARO), Don ALFONSO, DON GIOVANNI, GOLAUD, and Mittenhofer in ELEGY FOR YOUNG LOVERS (Edinburgh Fest. 1970). Intensity and complete commitment are the hallmarks of his interpretations. AB

Shostakovich, Dmitry Dmitriyevich, b. St Petersburg, 25 Sept 1906; d. Moscow, 9 Aug 1975. Russian composer. During the years of musical experimentation in Russia following the 1917 revolution, he comp. his first opera NOSE, based on GOGOL's satirical story. His only other opera, *Lady Macbeth of the Mtsensk District*, was enthusiastically received at its premiere (1934). But in 1936, when QUIET FLOWS THE DON was being acclaimed, a *Pravda* article (entitled 'Chaos instead of Music') attacked *Lady Macbeth* for its modernism and vulgarity. The opera was withdrawn. In 1956 Shostakovich revised the lib. and certain details of orchestration, and comp. two new orchestral *entr'actes*; a second premiere was given under the title KATERINA IZMAYLOVA in 1962. Shostakovich also comp. the musical comedy *Moscow–Cheremushki* (1959). GN

Show Boat, musical, KERN, book and lyrics HAMMERSTEIN II based on the novel by Edna Ferber. NY, Ziegfeld T., 27 Dec 1927; London, DL, 3 May 1928; revived 1932; 1946; NY CC, Apr 1954. Life on the Mississippi in the 1880s. EJ O★
See Lubbock

Shuard, Amy, b. London, 19 July 1924; d. 18 Apr 1975. English soprano. Debut 1949, Johannesburg (AIDA). At SW 1949–55, her roles there incl. MARGUERITE, Amelia (SIMONE BOCCANEGRA), EBOLI, TATYANA, Musetta (BOHÈME), CIO-CIO-SAN and NEDDA. Debuts: CG 1954; Sc. 1962; San Francisco 1963; Bayreuth 1968. As her voice developed from lyric to dramatic sop. she undertook a heavier repertory, singing FIDELIO, LADY MACBETH, Amelia, Cassandre (TROYENS), Santuzza (CAVALLERIA RUSTICANA), TURANDOT, BRÜNNHILDE, KUNDRY, and ELEKTRA. Earlier a fine exponent of KÁT'A KABANOVÁ and JENŮFA, she then sang Kostelnička (*Jenůfa*). EF

Sicilian Vespers *see* VÊPRES SICILIENNES

Siegfried *see* RING DES NIBELUNGEN

Sieglinde, sop., Hunding's wife in WALKÜRE

Siegmund, ten., Sieglinde's brother in WALKÜRE

Siems, Margarethe, b. Breslau (now Wrocław), 30 Dec 1879; d. Dresden, 13 Apr 1952. German soprano. Studied with ORGENI; debut 1902, Prague. Dresden 1908–22, where she was associated with R. STRAUSS, creating CHRYSOTHEMIS, the MARSCHALLIN, and ZERBINETTA. LO

Siepi, Cesare, b. Milan, 10 Feb 1923. Italian bass. Mainly self-taught; in his teens, a competition prizewinner at Florence; awarded scholarship to Milan Cons.; debut 1941, Schio, nr Venice (SPARAFUCILE). After wartime flight to Switzerland and internment, resumed operatic career at Venice, 1946, as Zaccaria (NABUCCO); sang same role at reopening perf. of Sc. later that year. Principal bass at Milan and elsewhere in Italy to 1950. Debuts that year: CG with Sc. co. as Pistol (FALSTAFF); NY Met (PHILIPPE). Regular member of NY Met co. into 1960s, with particular success as DON GIOVANNI and BORIS GODUNOV and VERDI roles. Debut Salzburg Fest. 1953 as Don Giovanni, in a prod. which was filmed. His perfs combine expressive subtlety with richness of tone, as well as elegance of stage character. NG

Siface [Giovanni Francesco Grossi], b. Uzzanese Chiesina, 12 Feb 1653; d. nr Ferrara, 29 May 1697. Italian male soprano, the first to be heard in England (1687) – not in opera, but in King James II's private chapel. He got his name from the part of Syphax in CAVALLI's *Scipione Africano*, which he sang in Venice 1678. He was murdered on the way from Bologna to Ferrara. LO

Signor Bruschino, Il, o Il Figlio per Azzardo (*Mr B., or The Son by Accident*), *farsa*, 1 act, ROSSINI, lib. Giuseppe Foppa after Alisan de Chazet and Maurice Ourry. Venice, T. S. Moïse, Jan 1813; NY Met, 6 Dec 1932; Orpington, Kentish O. Group, 14 July 1960. Main chars: Sofia (sop.) Florville (ten.) Gaudenzio (buffo-bass) Bruschino (buffo-bass). In order to win Sofia, Florville impersonates the young man to whom she has been betrothed sight unseen. The father of the real fiancé arrives: at first indignant, he later aids the deception for his own reasons. The last of Rossini's one-act *farse*, frequently revived; famous for an overture in which the violinists strike the strings with the wood of the bow. JB O

Sigurd, opera, 5 acts, REYER, lib. LOCLE and Alfred Blau. Brussels, T. de la Monnaie, 7 Jan 1884; London, CG (in It.), 15 July 1884; Paris, O. (in a version so mutilated that Reyer refused to stay in the house), 12 June 1885; New Orleans, Fr. O. House, 24 Dec 1891. Based on the Nibelung story; begun in 1870, but Reyer's work as a music critic interfered with its progress. LO

Silent Woman, The *see* SCHWEIGSAME FRAU

Silja, Anja, b. Berlin, 17 Apr 1940. German soprano. Debut 1956, aged 15, Brunswick (ROSINA). Sang ZERBINETTA just before her 17th birthday (1957) at same theatre. Joined Stuttgart co. for a year (1958); returned on regular engagement 1965. First sang CONSTANZE, FIORDILIGI, Santuzza (CAVALLERIA RUSTICANA), and TURANDOT, an extraordinary range for a young singer, at Frankfurt from 1959; widened her repertory in 1970s to incl. roles such as Renata (FIERY ANGEL), KÁT'A KABANOVÁ and Hanna (LUSTIGE WITWE). Bayreuth debut 1960 (SENTA); remained there in many leading roles until W. WAGNER's death in 1966. Also sang WAGNER and other roles, notably SALOME, MARIE, LULU and LEONORE, in his prods at other centres. Has appeared regularly at Vienna Staats O. CG debut 1967 (Leonore); returned to sing the part under KLEMPERER 1969; also heard there as Senta and Marie. One of the most eloquent singing actresses of the day, with an uncanny ability to move an audience. AB

Sills, Beverly [Belle Silverman], b. Brooklyn, 25 May 1929. American soprano. Debut 1947, aged 18, Philadelphia, as Frasquita (CARMEN); San Francisco debut 1953; at NY City O. since 1957. Sang at Sc. 1969, CG 1970; NY Met debut 1975 as Pamira in ROSSINI's *Assedio di Corinto*. Though her voice is not large, her extreme facility in coloratura allows her to sing a wide repertory, which incl. Cleopatra (GIULIO CESARE), MARGUERITE, Philine (MIGNON), MANON, NORMA, VIOLETTA, Queen of Shemakhan (GOLDEN COCKEREL) and ZERBINETTA. But it is in the operas of DONIZETTI, ROBERTO DEVEREUX, MARIA STUARDA, ANNA BOLENA, LUCIA DI LAMMERMOOR and FILLE DU RÉGIMENT, that she has scored her greatest successes. EF

Silva, bass, Ernani's rival in ERNANI

Silveri, Paolo, b. Ofena, nr Aquila, 28 Dec 1913. Italian singer, in succession bass, baritone and tenor. First sang bass (Rome 1939). Bar. debut Rome O. 1944 as Giorgio Germont (TRAVIATA). At CG, 1946, with co. from S. Carlo T., Naples (MARCELLO and FIGARO in NOZZE DI FIGARO). Joined CG 1947–9, singing in Eng. (incl. RIGOLETTO, BORIS GODUNOV, DI LUNA, and ESCAMILLO). Also remained active in Italy at this time; returned to CG 1950 with co. from Sc. (FORD and IAGO). NY Met debut 1950. Later ventured into ten. repertory: debut 1959, Dublin (VERDI's OTELLO). Reverted to bar. (his most successful vocal range); last heard at Camden Fest., London, 1967, as Israele in DONIZETTI's *Marino Faliero*. NG

Silvio, bar., Nedda's lover in PAGLIACCI

Simionato, Giulietta, b. Forlì, 15 Dec 1910. Italian mezzo-soprano. Studied Rovigo. Won first prize Florence Bel Canto competition (1933); sang small roles in It. houses; major debut 1938, T. Comunale, Florence, as Young Mother in PIZZETTI's *L'Orseleo*. Sc. as CHERUBINO and ROSINA (1943–4), and Asteria in NERONE under TOSCANINI (1948). British debut 1947, Edinburgh Fest. with Glyndebourne co. (Cherubino); CG debut 1953 Coronation season (ADALGISA, AMNERIS, and AZUCENA, all with CALLAS). US debut as CHARLOTTE at San Francisco (1953); Chicago from 1954; CAPULETI ED I MONTECCHI revived for her at Palermo (1954); Valentine in HUGUENOTS (Sc. 1962). NY Met debut 1959 (Azucena); also sang three of her other famous roles there: Rosina, Santuzza (CAVALLERIA RUSTICANA) and DALILA. Her agile coloratura mezzo-sop. was much admired in the ROSSINI roles for that voice; equally effective in the dramatic mezzo-sop. parts, for which her strong, even voice was ideal. Acted with great authority. AB

Simoneau, Léopold, b. Quebec City, 3 May 1918. Canadian tenor. Debut 1943 Montreal as Wilhelm Meister (MIGNON). Other debuts: NY CC 1946, Paris O. and OC 1949, Aix-en-Provence 1950, Glyndebourne 1951, London, RFH, and Chicago 1954, and NY Met 1963. A very stylish singer, particularly admired as Idamante (IDOMENEO), BELMONTE, Don OTTAVIO (DON GIOVANNI), FERRANDO, TAMINO and Tito (CLEMENZA DI TITO), he has appeared in many Fr. operas: INDES GALANTES, MIREILLE, LAKMÉ, PÊCHEURS DE PERLES; has also sung ALMAVIVA (BARBIERE DI SIVIGLIA), Lionel (MARTHA), EDGARDO, NEMORINO, Ernesto (DON PASQUALE), ALFREDO, and Tom Rakewell (RAKE'S PROGRESS). EF

Simone Boccanegra, opera, prologue and 3 acts, VERDI, lib. PIAVE with additions by Giuseppe Montanelli after García Gutiérrez. Venice, T. La Fenice, 1 Mar 1857; revived Milan, Sc., 24 Mar 1881 in definitive version with additions to text by BOITO; NY Met, 28 Jan 1932; London, SW, 27 Oct 1948. Main chars: Simone (bar.) Amelia (sop.) Gabriele (ten.) Fiesco (bass) Paolo (bar.). Simone Boccanegra, a corsair, is elected Doge of Genoa, finds his long lost daughter, foils more than one plot against his life and pardons the instigators, is finally reconciled with his enemy, Fiesco, but dies of a slow poison through the villainy of his former friend, Paolo. JB O
See Kobbé

Singspiel (Ger. 'song-play'). The Ger. equivalent of *opéra comique*, with sung airs and spoken dialogue; 18th-c. examples by GLUCK and HILLER were often translations of Fr. *opéras comiques*. The genre strictly incl. such works as ZAUBERFLÖTE, FIDELIO, and FREISCHÜTZ. LO

Sir John in Love, opera, 4 acts, VAUGHAN WILLIAMS, lib. comp. on texts selected from SHAKESPEARE's *The Merry Wives of Windsor*. London, RCM, 21 Mar 1929; NY, Columbia Univ., 20 Jan 1949. Main char.: Falstaff (bar.). In this work closely following Shakespeare's play, the comp. uses his beloved folksong idiom to create a work of high spirits, also shot through with ardent love music. AB O

Škroup, František Jan, b. Osice u Pardubice, 3 June 1801; d. Rotterdam, 7 Feb 1862. Czech composer and conductor. Active as singer and cond. in attempts to organize a permanent opera at the Estates T., Prague, and sang the title role in his *Singspiel The Tinker* (*Dráteník*, 1826), the first opera wr. in Czech. Became second cond. (1827–37) and chief cond. (1837–57), Estates T., where he introduced works by SPOHR, J. F. HALÉVY, MARSCHNER, MEYERBEER, and WAGNER. Later he emigrated to Rotterdam. He wr. two other Czech operas, *Oldřich and Božena* (1828) and *Libuše's Marriage* (*Libušin sňatek*, 1835, the subject of SMETANA's later opera), as well as seven Ger. operas and other theatre works. These incl. the incidental music to J. K. Tyl's *Fidlovačka* (1834), from which the song '*Kde domov můj*' became the Czech national anthem in 1918. JT

Slezak, Leo, b. Krásna Hora, Bohemia, 18 Aug 1873; d. Egern-am-Tegernsee, 1 June 1946. Austrian tenor. Debut 1896, Brno (LOHENGRIN). Appeared Berlin 1898–9 and CG 1900 (Lohengrin); joined Vienna Staats O. 1901, and remained its leading dramatic ten. until 1926. CG 1909, as VERDI's OTELLO, one of his most famous roles with which he also made his NY Met debut 1909, singing there until 1913. His frame and voice were of an equally imposing size, and much admired in Verdi and WAGNER roles. AB

Slovenia *see* YUGOSLAVIA

Smareglia, Antonio, b. Pola, 5 May 1854; d. Grado, 15 Apr 1929. Italian composer. A pupil of FACCIO at the Milan Cons., his first operatic work was *Preziosa* (Milan 1879). Already blind in 1900 he continued to comp. His style, like Alfredo CATALANI's, was formed before the advent of *verismo*, and his music was much praised in Germany for combining Ger. science with It. lyricism. Outstanding among his nine operas are *Le Nozze Istriane* (Trieste 1895) and his masterpiece, *Oceana* (Milan 1903). JB

Smetana, Bedřich, b. Litomyšl, 2 Mar 1824; d. Prague, 12 May 1884. Czech composer. While piano tutor to Count Thun's family, he received a systematic musical training from Josef Proksch in Prague (1844–7) and opened a music institute (1848). Moved to Göteborg, Sweden, 1856. Successful as cond. and pianist; wr. his first important works – three Lisztian tone poems. Returned permanently to Prague 1862, hoping to become chief cond. at the newly opened Prague PT, but it was not until after perfs of his first opera *The Brandenburgers in Bohemia* (*Braniboři v Čechách*, 1866) and, a few months later, BARTERED BRIDE, that he was appointed. Despite vicious conservative opposition he worked hard at enlarging the repertory but total deafness in 1874 brought his effective work as a cond. to an end. He continued courageously to comp., slowed down by increasingly physical and mental deterioration: the cycle of six tone poems *Má Vlast* (*My Fatherland*) dates from this period as do three more operas, KISS, SECRET, and DEVIL'S WALL, all to libs by KRÁSNOHORSKÁ. A final opera, *Viola* (after SHAKESPEARE) was left incomplete.

Smetana's eight operas provided, at a time of growing national awareness, a definitive body of Czech national opera and it is for this that Smetana, rather than DVOŘÁK, is considered by the Czechs to be 'the father of modern Czech music'. Smetana's operas are also a considerable artistic achievement; they range from tuneful *Singspiel*-based works (*Bartered Bride*, TWO WIDOWS) to fest. opera (LIBUŠE) and dramatic opera (DALIBOR) in which musical integration is achieved through a system of thematic transformation. The late operas, with their wise, resigned humour, remarkable ensembles and depth of psychological penetration represent a unique genre, and are unjustly neglected. JT
See Large, *Smetana* (London and New York 1970)

Bedřich Smetana's BARTERED BRIDE, Prague, Smetana T., 21 May 1971; produced Přemysl Kočí; designed Jaroslav Gruss. Gabriela Beňačková as Mařenka; ŽÍDEK as Jeník

Smyth, Ethel (Mary), b. London, 23 Apr 1858; d. Woking, 8 May 1944. English composer. Studied Leipzig Cons. Comp. six operas, the first *Fantasio* (1898) for Weimar to her own lib. based on Alfred de Musset's play. Most important works: WRECKERS and BOATSWAIN'S MATE; other operas: *Der Wald* (Dresden 1901), *Fête Galante* (1923) and *Entente Cordiale* (1925). Her works show a remarkable understanding of the stage. Played a major role in the fight for women's suffrage; DBE 1920; suffered from deafness in later life. Last important work, *The Prison*, for sop., bass-bar., choir and orch., Queen's Hall, 24 Feb 1931. Wrote nine books incl. *Impressions That Remained* (London 1919) and *Streaks of Life* (London 1921). PS

Snow Maiden, The (*Snegurochka*), opera, 4 acts, RIMSKY-KORSAKOV, lib. comp. after Aleksandr Nikolayevich Ostrovsky. St Petersburg, Mariinsky T., 10 Feb 1882; NY, 23 Jan 1922; London, SW, 12 Apr 1933. Main chars: Tsar Berendey (ten.) Spring (mezzo-sop.) Snow Maiden (sop.) Kupava (sop.) Mizgir (bar.). Winter is ending, but the Snow Maiden pleads with Spring to allow her to stay. Mizgir falls in love with her; his former love, Kupava, complains to Tsar Berendey, but he is captivated by the Snow Maiden's beauty. The Snow Maiden is frightened by Mizgir's passionate entreaties, and she asks Spring to give her some warmth of heart. Spring does so, but warns her to keep her love secret from the Sun. But the Sun finds out, and his rays melt the Snow Maiden. Mizgir drowns himself. Like MAY NIGHT, *The Snow Maiden* combines elements of the human and fantasy worlds in a score of great delicacy and charm. GN O

Sobinov, Leonid Vitalyevich, b. Yaroslavl, 7 June 1872; d. Riga, 14 Oct 1934. Russian tenor. Sang at the Bolshoy (from 1897) and at St Petersburg (particularly the Mariinsky, now the Kirov), also appearing at Sc. and other west European opera houses. Had a wide operatic repertory which incl. ALFREDO, DES GRIEUX, DUCA DI MANTUA, GOUNOD'S FAUST, LOHENGRIN, ROMÉO, and Vladimir (PRINCE IGOR); he was also renowned in the role of LENSKY. GN

Söderström, Elisabeth, b. Stockholm, 7 May 1927. Swedish soprano of wide musical sensibility and versatile repertory. Studied Swedish Royal Acad. of Mus. Debut 1947, Drottningholm Court T. as Bastienne (BASTIEN UND BASTIENNE). Joined Swedish Royal O. 1950; sang increasing variety of classical and modern roles. Foreign debuts: Salzburg Fest. 1955 as Ighino (PALESTRINA); Glyndebourne Fest. 1957 as the Composer (ARIADNE AUF NAXOS), and returned there many times; NY Met 1959 (SOPHIE); CG 1960, with Swedish Royal O. as Daisy-Doody (ANIARA); CG 1967, with Royal O., as Countess ALMAVIVA, changing to SUSANNA at one perf. Has unique record of singing all three sop. roles in ROSENKAVALIER in course of one year (1959): Sophie (NY Met); OCTAVIAN (Glyndebourne); MARSCHALLIN (Stockholm). Much admired for other roles incl. TATYANA, Countess (CAPRICCIO), MARIE, Elisabeth (ELEGY FOR YOUNG LOVERS), Governess (TURN OF THE SCREW), Emilia Marty (MAKROPULOS CASE). As successful in tragic roles as in comic opera and operetta, especially by close identification with stage characters (she claims that it took 15 years for her to sing Tatyana without weeping), and by her instinctive charm of personality. NG

Sofia. Opera has been perf. in the Bulgarian capital since 1890; the Dramatic O. Co. was formed 1891. The O. Society opened at the NT 1908; given state support 1921 and became the Sofia National O. This has developed into an internationally known co., whose artists frequently appear abroad. Operetta also occupies an important place in Bulgarian musical life, and has been perf. by several professional groups: the Cooperative T. (1922–39), the Free T. (1918–27), the Renaissance (1920–22), the Odeon (1935–44), and the Operetta Arts T. (1942–6). The State Stefan Makedonski Music T., specializing in operetta, was founded 1948. GN

Die Soldaten, Edinburgh, Deutsche O. am Rhein, 21 Aug 1972. Catherine Gayer as Marie and Marius Rintzler as Wesener; produced Georg Reinhardt; designed Heinrich Hendel

Soldaten, Die (*The Soldiers*), opera, 4 acts, ZIMMERMANN, lib. a rearrangement by comp. of play by Jakob Michael Lenz. Cologne, 15 Feb 1965; Edinburgh, Deutsche O. am Rhein, King's T., 21 Aug 1972. Chief chars: Marie (sop.) Charlotte (mezzo-sop.) Countess de la Roche (mezzo-sop.) Desportes (ten.) Stolzius (bar.) Wesener (bass). Marie, a respectable, bourgeois girl, engaged to Stolzius, is seduced by the aristocratic officer, Baron Desportes, and eventually becomes a soldiers' whore. Zimmermann has used every ingredient of total music theatre in his score: a huge orch., divided into several groups; song, speech, taped and electronic music; non-musical sound effects, as well as film, dance and mime. Some of the scenes take place simultaneously. EF

Soldier's Tale, The *see* HISTOIRE DU SOLDAT

Solti, Georg, b. Budapest, 21 Oct 1912. Hungarian conductor. Studied Budapest. Most important posts have been mus. dir. Munich Staats O. 1947–51, Frankfurt 1951–61, and CG 1961–71; has also cond. at Salzburg, San Francisco, Glyndebourne, and Chicago. His readings are characterized by intensity; his regimes at Frankfurt and CG were noteworthy for vital and exciting perfs of operas by VERDI, R. STRAUSS, and A. BERG. LO

Somers, Harry, b. Toronto, 11 Sept 1925. Canadian composer. Works incl. two 1-act operas, *The Fool* (1953) and *The Homeless Ones* (1955), texts Michael Fram; major opera is *Louis Riel* (1967), commissioned by COC in Toronto, about a controversial figure in 19th-c. Canada. The text by Mavor Moore and Jacques Languirand is in Fr. or Eng. as the dramatic situation requires. Somers's eclectic score incl. some electronic sounds, some dramatically effective tonal writing, and a personal contemporary harmonic idiom. Vocal material ranges from the spoken to the rhapsodically lyrical. The COC has given *Louis Riel* in 1967, 1969, and 1975, and has perf. it in Toronto, Montreal, Ottawa, and in Washington, DC. It has also been broadcast on radio and TV in Canada. CM

Sondheim, Stephen Joshua, b. New York, 22 Mar 1930. American composer and lyricist. Wr. lyrics for WEST SIDE STORY; other musicals incl. *Company* (1970) and *Pacific Overtures* (1976). EJ

Sonnambula, La (*The Sleepwalker*), opera, 2 acts, BELLINI, lib. ROMANI. Milan, T. Carcano, 6 Mar 1831; London, King's T., 28 July 1831; NY, Park T., 13 Nov 1935. Main chars: Amina (sop.) Elvino (ten.) The Count (bass) Lisa (sop.). Amina, a sleepwalker, is discovered in the bedroom of the newly returned Lord of the Manor, suspected of immorality and renounced by her fiancé, Elvino. All is forgiven when she is seen to sleepwalk over a dangerous bridge. JB O
See Kobbé

Sontag, Henriette [Gertrud Walburga], b. Koblenz, 3 Jan 1806; d. Mexico City, 17 June 1854. German soprano, one of the most remarkable artists of her day. First public appearance aged six, in a *Singspiel*, *Donauweibchen*, by Ferdinand Kauer. Taken in 1815 by her mother to Prague; studied at Cons. there; debut, 1821, aged 15, as substitute in BOÏELDIEU's *Jean de Paris*. Then went to Vienna where C. WEBER, hearing her in DONNA DEL LAGO, offered her the title role in EURYANTHE. An unbroken series of triumphs followed, in Berlin, Paris, London (1828, at King's T., as ROSINA). In 1830 m. Count Rossi and retired from the stage, taking up the duties of an ambassador's wife; returned after the political upheavals of 1848, with her voice as fresh as ever. Moved to USA 1852, acclaimed there as enthusiastically as in Europe. Last appearance in LUCREZIA BORGIA, in Mexico City, where she died of cholera. As a singer she had no superior; her beauty and charm endeared her wherever she went. BEETHOVEN, by then completely deaf, met her and was fascinated by her; she sang in the first perfs of his 9th Symphony and the Mass in D. LO

Sophie, sop., the young heroine of ROSENKAVALIER

Sophocles, b. Colonus, nr Athens, 495 BC; d. 406 BC. Greek dramatist. Of his *c.* 100 plays only seven are extant; ones on which operas are based are: *Antigone* (*c.* 30, incl. those by HONEGGER and ORFF); *Electra* (Jean Baptiste Lemoyne, lib. GUIRAUD, 1782; Johann Haeffner, 1787; ELEKTRA); *Oedipus Rex* (LEONCAVALLO, 1920; STRAVINSKY; OEDIPUS DER TYRANN); *Oedipus at Colonus* (SACCHINI, 1786; ZINGARELLI, 1802). LO

sopranist, male SOPRANO, *see* CASTRATO

soprano (It., from *sopra*, 'above'). The highest range of female voice; also the highest range of CASTRATO voice. Since this can most easily ride over the orch. it is the most frequently used female voice for all kinds of roles, both dramatic and lyric. Like other high instruments a sop. voice 'speaks' readily, so it lends itself to the brilliant coloratura writing of the 18th c. and the florid It. school of the 19th c. LO

Sorcerer, The, operetta, 2 acts, SULLIVAN, lib. GILBERT. London, O. Comique, 17 Nov 1877; NY, Broadway T., 21 Feb 1879. Main chars: Sir Marmaduke Pointdextre (bass) Alexis (ten.) Dr Daly (bass bar.) John Wellington Wells (buffo) Lady Sangazure (contr.) Aline (sop.) Constance (mezzo-sop.) Mrs Partlet (contr.). A variation on Gilbert's long-cherished theme of an elixir that causes the most unsuitable couples to fall in love. JB O

Sorochintsy Fair (*Sorochinskaya yarmarka*), opera, 3 acts, MUSORGSKY, lib. comp. after GOGOL. Main chars: Cherevik (bass) Khivrya (mezzo-sop.) Parasya (sop.) Gritsko (ten.). The opera, which makes considerable use of Ukrainian folk tunes, was unfinished at Musorgsky's death. Several later editions were prepared, the earliest being Anatoly Lyadov's and Vyacheslav Karatygin's. A version based on these two editions (together with RIMSKY-KORSAKOV's version of *Night on the Bare Mountain*) was given at the Moscow Free T., 21 Oct 1913; a version by CUI at the Petrograd Music Drama T., 26 Oct 1917. But the version known in the West is by CHEREPNIN (Monte Carlo, 17 Mar 1923; NY Met, 29 Nov 1930; London, Fortune T., 17 Feb 1934). Another version, by SHEBALIN, was given at the Maly T., Leningrad, 21 Dec 1931. GN
See Kobbé

Sorozábal, Pablo, b. San Sebastián, 18 Sept 1897. Spanish composer and conductor. His works incl. many *zarzuelas* of which the following have been recorded: *La Tabernera del Puerto*, *Don Manolito*, *Katiuska*, *La Del Manojo de Rosas*, *Adiós a la Bohemia*, *Black el Payaso*, *Las de Cain*, and *La Eterna Canción*. FGB

Sosarme, Re di Media (*Sosarmes, King of the Medes*), *opera seria*, HANDEL, lib. altered from

Matteo Noris's *Alfonso Primo* first set by Carlo Francesco Pollarolo, 1694. London, HM, 15 Feb 1732. Revived Göttingen, 1973. LO

Souez [Rains], Ina, b. Windsor, Col., 1908. American soprano. Studied Denver and Milan; debut 1928 Ivrea (MIMI), then sang at Palermo. CG debut 1929 (LIÙ); returned for MICAËLA 1935. Glyndebourne (1934–9) as FIORDILIGI and Donna ANNA. AB

Souliotis, Elena, b. Athens, 28 May 1943. Greek soprano. Studied with Mercedes Llopart. Debut 1964, T. S. Carlo, Naples, as Santuzza (CAVALLERIA RUSTICANA). Sc. debut 1966 as Abigaille (NABUCCO). Sang same role at a concert perf. in London (1968) before undertaking it at CG (1972). CG and NY Met debuts 1969 (LADY MACBETH). Has a bold, uneven voice of considerable dramatic power, but her career seems to have been attenuated by faulty vocal production. AB

South Africa. Main centres for opera are Cape Town, Durban, and Johannesburg. CHISHOLM staged a number of unusual operas incl. DUKE BLUEBEARD'S CASTLE. On the whole the Union has had to rely on visiting cos such as Carl Rosa and Moody-Manners. LO

South Pacific, musical, RODGERS, book and lyrics HAMMERSTEIN II, based on *Tales of the South Pacific* by James Michener. NY, Majestic T., 7 Apr 1949; London, DL, 1 Nov 1951; NY CC 1967. EJ O★
See Lubbock

Spadavecchia [Spadavekkia], Antonio (Emmanuilovich), b. Odessa, 3 June 1907. Soviet composer of Italian descent. Graduated from SHEBALIN'S comp. class at the Moscow Cons. 1937. First opera, *The Magic Horse* (1942, revised version 1952), based on a Bashkir legend, was wr. in collaboration with the Bashkir comp. Zaimov. Other operas: *The Hotel Landlady* (1949), *Way Through Hell* (1953, revised as *The Fiery Years*, 1967) based on A. N. Tolstoy's novel, *The Gadfly* (1957), the satirical *Gallant Soldier Shveyk* (1963), and *Yucci* (1969). GN

Spain. The first known comp. of Sp. opera was Juan Hidalgo with his setting of CALDERÓN'S *Celos Aun del Aire Matan* (1660). Native opera did not establish itself, however, and with the arrival of the male sop. FARINELLI at the Sp. court in 1737 It. domination became complete. In the 19th c. PEDRELL, the 'father of modern Spanish music', and BRETÓN tried to give new impetus to native opera, but only FALLA has enjoyed lasting international success. Sp. comps have expressed themselves more fruitfully in the lighter, more popular vein of the *zarzuela* and the *tonadilla.* There is a strong tradition of opera singers from MALIBRAN through SUPERVIA to de los ANGELES and CABALLÉ. Leading opera houses are found in Madrid, Barcelona, Bilbao, and Valencia. FGB
See Gilbert Chase, *The Music of Spain* (New York 1941, 2nd rev. ed. 1959)

Sparafucile, bass, the hired assassin in RIGOLETTO

Spectacle opera. Theatrical perfs where the visual tends to overbalance the musical and dramatic sides. A famous and extreme example was POMO D'ORO, but many *opere serie* and most *feste teatrali* were of this type. GLUCK'S *I Cinesi* (1754) was an elaborately decorated 'show' full of fanciful coloured prisms, rich costumes and *chinoiserie* scenery; FUX'S *Costanza e Fortezza* (1723) was a vast outdoor spectacle; the five acts of DESTOUCHE'S *Issé* (Paris O. 1697) were: The Garden of Hesperides; Issé's Palace; A Forest; A Grotto (inhabited by Echo, Slumber, Dreams, Zephyrs, Nymphs); A Solitary Place, changing to a magnificent Palace, the Hours descending in a cloud machine, followed by a cortège of the God of Light. The modern equivalent is to be seen in the arena prods at Verona and elsewhere, but more so perhaps in MGM's 'glorious technicolor' filmed musical shows of the 1930s and 1940s. LO

Speziale, Lo, opera, 3 acts, HAYDN, lib. GOLDONI (orig. wr. for Vincenzo Pallavicino and Domenico Fischietti, 1755). Esterháza, autumn 1768; London, King's T., Hammersmith, 3 Nov 1925 (in Eng. version by André Skalski and Kingsley Lark); NY, Neighborhood Playhouse, 16 Mar 1926 (in Eng. version by Ann Macdonald). Set in Ger. (tr. Johann Jacob Engel) as *Die Apotheke* by Christian Gottlob Neefe, Berlin 13 Dec 1771. LO

Spohr, Louis, b. Brunswick [Braunschweig], 5 Apr 1784; d. Kassel, 22 Oct 1859. German violinist, conductor and composer; embarked on his first concert tour at 14. Accepted post under the Duke of Gotha, 1805, and had his first opera, *Die Prüfung*, perf. in concert version. After short period in Vienna at the new T. a. d. Wien, 1812, went to Kassel which remained his headquarters for the rest of his life. First important opera, FAUST (not based on GOETHE) was followed by his fairy opera ZEMIRE UND AZOR and, his most successful, JESSONDA. *Der Berggeist* (1823), *Pietro von Albano* (1827), and *Der Alchymist* (1830) made less impact. At Kassel his

work as cond. was important. Staged FLIEGENDE HOLLÄNDER 1843 (same year as its premiere in Dresden); a prod. of TANNHÄUSER was vetoed by the Elector. Spohr was a bridge between the older classical ideals and the new romanticism; but his music, facile but lacking in depth, could not compete with the richness in the music of his contemporaries and successors, BEETHOVEN, C. WEBER, BERLIOZ, and WAGNER. LO
See his *Autobiography* (Ger. ed. 1860, 1861; tr. Eng. London 1865)

Spoleto Festival, Italy. The Fest. of Two Worlds was founded here by MENOTTI 1958. It has successfully revived some 19th-c. works such as DONIZETTI's *Il Furioso all'Isola di San Domingo* and MERCADANTE's *Il Giuramento*, and staged several modern operas, incl. BERIO's *Laborintus II* and SAINT OF BLEECKER STREET. At the 1973 Fest. VISCONTI staged an outstanding revival of MANON LESCAUT. AB

Spontini, Gasparo (Luigi Pacifico), b. Maiolati, nr Jesi, 14 Nov 1774; d. Maiolati, 24 Jan 1851. Italian composer and conductor. Studied Naples 1793–5; his first opera *I Puntigli delle Donne* (Rome 1795) was followed by at least eight others all written in the prevailing It. style. Left Italy 1803 for Paris where he first made his mark with the *opéra comique*, *Milton* (1804). Through the Empress Joséphine's influence and despite opposition from the Fr. musical establishment he prod. the grandiose VESTALE at the O. with immense success, so becoming in effect the official comp. of the First Empire. It was followed by FERNAND CORTEZ and OLYMPIE. Mus. dir., Royal T., Berlin, 1820–40, where he prod. his last important stage work, *Agnes von Hohenstaufen* (1829). A project to develop his earlier *Milton* into a grand opera, *Der Verlorene Paradies*, remained unfinished at his death. During his last years he made various appearances in France and Germany as a cond. Known as 'the father of grand opera', he forms a musical link between GLUCK and WAGNER. JB

Gasparo Spontini's OLYMPIE, in Italian as *Olimpia*, Milan, Scala, Jan 1966, produced MOLINARI-PRADELLI; set by Piero Zuffi; left to right: SOULIOTIS as Olimpia; Nicola Zaccaria as Staria; Giangiacomo Guelfi as Antigono

Sposo Deluso, Lo (*The Deluded Husband*), unfinished *opera buffa*, MOZART, lib. attributed da PONTE. Main chars: Bettina (sop.) Pulcherio (ten.) Bocconio (bass) Eugenia (sop.) Don Asdrubale (ten.). Begun in 1783. Five numbers only, three complete and two sketched. JB

Sprechstimme, Sprechgesang (Ger. 'speech-song'), a term associated esp. with the Ger. 12-note school of comp. (SCHÖNBERG, A. BERG, KŘENEK), indicating a kind of RECITATIVE midway between speech and song. The pitch is notated in a special way. The device was first used by HUMPERDINCK in the first version of his KÖNIGSKINDER, 1897, but omitted in the 1910 version. LO

Stabile, Mariano, b. Palermo, 1888; d. Milan, 11 Jan 1968. Italian baritone. Studied Santa Cecilia Acad., Rome. Debut 1909, Palermo (MARCELLO). Sc., Milan, from 1922, when he opened the season as FALSTAFF under TOSCANINI. CG debut 1926 (DON GIOVANNI, IAGO, and Falstaff); sang there regularly until 1931. Glyndebourne 1936–9, 1948 (Edinburgh) (FIGARO, MALATESTA and Don ALFONSO); Cambridge T. as Malatesta and Falstaff (1946–8); Salzburg 1935–9. Although his voice was never beautiful, he always used it with intelligence and style. AB

Stade, Frederica von, b. Somerville, NJ, 1 June 1946. American mezzo-soprano. A semifinalist of the Met Auditions (1969), she sang Hänsel (HÄNSEL UND GRETEL) while still a student at Mannes College of Music, NY. Debuts: NY Met 1970, San Francisco 1971, Santa Fe 1972, Glyndebourne and Paris O. 1973. A young singer with great vocal and dramatic gifts, she has a repertory that incl. ZERLINA, CHERUBINO, DORABELLA, Sesto (CLEMENZA DI TITO), CENERENTOLA, Siebel (FAUST), Nicklausse (CONTES D'HOFFMANN), Stephano (ROMÉO ET JULIETTE) and MÉLISANDE. She sang Nina at the premiere of PASATIERI's *Seagull* (Houston 1974); CG debut 1975 (ROSINA). EF

stagione (It. 'season'). The most important *stagione* in 18th and 19th c. was the Carnival season, beginning on 26 Dec and running through to Lent. Other, less important, ones were the spring season, beginning after Lent, and the autumn season, before Advent. LO

Stanford, (Sir) Charles Villiers, b. Dublin, 30 Sept 1852; d. London, 29 Mar 1924. Irish composer. Wr. 10 operas incl.: *The Veiled Prophet of Khorassan* (Hanover 1881); *Shamus O'Brien* (London, O. Comique, 1896); *Savonarola* (Hamburg 1884); *The Canterbury Pilgrims* (DL 1884); *Much Ado about Nothing* (CG 1901); *The Critic* (London, Shaftesbury T., 1916). His last, *The Travelling Companion* (Bristol, T. Royal, 1926), was in SW repertory for some time just before World War II. Stanford also did much good work at the RCM, training young singers in the opera class there. LO

Stanislavsky, (Alekseyev) Konstantin Sergeyevich, b. Moscow, 17 Jan 1863; d. Moscow, 7 Aug 1938. Russian theatre director. With NEMIROVICH-DANCHENKO founded the Moscow Arts T. (1898), where he first tried out his ideas of realistic prod., encouraging his actors to identify completely with the characters by studying their psychological and social backgrounds. Established his O. Studio at the Bolshoy 1918. It was named the Stanislavsky O. Studio 1924, the Stanislavsky O. Studio T. 1926, and the Stanislavsky O. T. 1928. Stanislavsky himself dir. many operas, incl. EUGENE ONEGIN (1922), TSAR'S BRIDE (1926), MAY NIGHT (1928), BORIS GODUNOV (1929), QUEEN OF SPADES (1930), GOLDEN COCKEREL (1932), as well as Western operas; after his death the theatre gave the premiere of PROKOFIEV'S *Semyon Kotko* (1940). In 1941 the theatre was amalgamated with the Nemirovich-Danchenko Music T. and renamed the Stanislavsky-Nemirovich-Danchenko Music T. GN

Staudigl, Joseph, b. Wöllersdorf, 14 Apr 1807; d. Döbling, nr Vienna, 28 Mar 1861. Austrian bass. Son of an imperial huntsman; entered the philosophical college, Krems, 1823; became a novitiate at the Benedictine monastery of Melk 1825. Went to Vienna to study surgery 1827, but running short of funds, joined the chorus of KT. Debut in a major role as Pietro (MUETTE DE PORTICI). Joined the T. a. d. Wien 1845, returning to the Court T. 1845–54. Associated more with oratorio than opera, particularly *Elijah*, which he created in 1846. He was also a famous F. SCHUBERT singer. His son, Joseph (1850–1916) was also a bar. of note. PS

Steber, Eleanor, b. Wheeling, Va., 17 July 1916. American soprano. Studied Boston. Won NY Met 'Auditions of the Air' 1940; debut there 1940 as SOPHIE (later sang successful MARSCHALLIN). Remained with co. for almost 20 years, a popular principal in wide range of Fr., Ger., and It. roles. Created title role in VANESSA. UK debut, first Edinburgh Fest. 1947, with Glyndebourne co., (Countess ALMAVIVA), Bayreuth Fest. 1953 (ELSA). Teaches at Cleveland Inst. of Music. Has rich, firm tone and eloquence of feeling. NG

Stein, Gertrude, b. Allegheny, Pa., 3 Feb 1874; d. Neuilly, nr Paris, 27 July 1946. American writer; lived in Paris from 1902 until her death. Wrote libs for FOUR SAINTS IN THREE ACTS and MOTHER OF US ALL. LO

Stein, Horst, b. Elberfeld, 2 May 1928. German conductor. After engagements at Mannheim and Wuppertal, he was cond. at Hamburg 1951–5, Berlin Staats O. 1955–61, and again at Hamburg 1961–3. San Francisco debut 1965 (LOHENGRIN); appointed principal cond. Vienna Staats O., 1968. He first cond. Bayreuth 1969 (PARSIFAL) and has since returned for the RING and TANNHÄUSER. Cond. *Parsifal* at the Paris O. 1973. EF

Steinberg, William [Hans Wilhelm], b. Cologne, 1 Aug 1899. German, later American, conductor. Studied Cologne; was KLEMPERER'S assistant there. Prague 1925–9; Frankfurt 1929–33. Mainly known as an orch. cond., but has dir. operas at San Francisco and NY Met, incl. AIDA (1965). LO

Stevens, Risë, b. NY, 11 June 1913. American mezzo-soprano. Studied at Juilliard School and in Vienna with Marie Gutheil-Schoder. Debut 1936, Prague (MIGNON). NY Met debut 1938 (OCTAVIAN); remained there until 1955 singing Mignon, FRICKA, ERDA, CHERUBINO, DALILA, LAURA, CARMEN, Marina (BORIS GODUNOV) and Orphée (ORPHÉE ET EURYDICE) among others. Glyndebourne 1939 and 1955 (Cherubino). Also appeared in films. AB

Stewart, Thomas, b. San Saba, Texas, 29 Aug 1928. American baritone. Debut 1954, Chicago (LUCIA DI LAMMERMOOR) and was engaged for a season at NY CC. Went to Berlin 1957; CG debut 1960 (ESCAMILLO). Debuts: Bayreuth 1960, San Francisco and NY Met 1965; Salzburg Easter Fest. 1967. His repertory incl. all the WAGNER bar. roles from FLIEGENDE HOLLÄNDER to AMFORTAS; DON GIOVANNI, ALMAVIVA (NOZZE DI FIGARO); VERDI'S AMONASRO, IAGO and FORD; EUGENE ONEGIN, GOLAUD, SCARPIA, Orest (ELEKTRA) and the Count (CAPRICCIO). He m. the sop. LEAR. EF

Stich-Randall, Teresa, b. W. Hartford, Conn., 24 Dec 1927. American soprano. Studied Hartford School of Music. Sang in premiere of MOTHER OF US ALL, also in NBC broadcasts under TOSCANINI as Nannetta (FALSTAFF) and Priestess (AIDA). To Europe 1951, winning 1st prize in Lausanne competition. Joined Basel O., then Vienna Staats O. from 1952; debut there as VIOLETTA. Other debuts: Aix-en-Provence 1953; Chicago Lyric O. 1955; NY Met 1961 (FIORDILIGI). Much admired in MOZART for elegance of line and creaminess of tone. NG

Stiedry, Fritz, b. Vienna, 11 Oct 1883; d. Zürich, 9 Aug 1968. Austrian conductor. Studied Vienna. Principal cond., Berlin 1914–23; Vienna, Volks O., 1924–5; Berlin, Städtische O., 1929–33. To USA 1938; at NY Met 1946–58, specializing in Ger. repertory. Has also cond. Glyndebourne and CG. LO

Stiffelio, opera, 3 acts, VERDI, lib. by PIAVE after *Le Pasteur* by Émile Souvestre and Eugène Bourgeois. Trieste, T. Grande, 16 Nov 1850. Main chars: Stiffelio (ten.) Lina (sop.) Stankar (bar.) Jorg (bass) Raffaele (ten.). Stiffelio, a Protestant minister, returns home to find that his wife has been unfaithful to him. His father-in-law Stankar is determined to prevent him from finding out the identity of the seducer, Raffaele, but Stiffelio, preventing a duel between Stankar and Raffaele, finds out the truth and offers his wife a divorce. Stankar kills Raffaele; Stiffelio forgives Lina from the pulpit. As the last scene never escaped intact from religious censorship, Verdi remade the opera in four acts as *Aroldo*, altering and adding to the music. Rimini, T. Nuovo, 16 Aug 1857; London, Camden Fest., 25 Feb 1964. Main chars: Aroldo (ten.) Mina (sop.) Egberto (bar.) Briano (bass) Godvino (ten.). Aroldo, now a returned English Crusader, divorces his wife, then flees with the hermit Briano to Loch Lomond where his penitent wife joins him and is forgiven. JB

Stignani, Ebe, b. Naples, 10 July 1904; d. Imola, 5 Oct 1974. Italian contralto. Debut 1925, T. S. Carlo, Naples (AMNERIS, destined to be one of her most famous roles). Sc., Milan, 1925–56, where her notable roles were AZUCENA, Amneris, ADALGISA, and EBOLI. CG debut 1937 (Amneris); returned there intermittently until 1957. US debut 1938 San Francisco as Santuzza (CAVALLERIA RUSTICANA); returned 1948 in same role and as Dame Quickly (FALSTAFF). Her voice was regal and dramatic, capable of noble expression. It is heard at its most opulent on 78 rpm discs which were made before World War II. AB

Still, William Grant, b. Woodville, Miss., 11 May 1895. American composer of part Negro, part Indian descent. His nine operas incl. *The Troubled Island* (comp. 1938, NY CC 1949) and *A Bayou Legend* (comp. 1940, Jackson, Miss., 1974). LO

Stockholm, Sweden. Fr. and It. opera was given in the Court theatres from the mid-17th c. A public opera house in the Bollhus was opened 1773 with Francesco Uttini's *Thetis och Pelée*. The Royal O. House was inaugurated 1782 with NAUMANN's *Cora och Alonso*, and entirely rebuilt 1898; Armas Järnefelt was chief cond. 1907–32, and dirs have incl. FORSELL, Harald André, BERGLUND, SVANHOLM, and GENTELE. EF
See Hillström, *The Royal Opera, Stockholm* (Stockholm 1960, in Eng.)

Stoltz, Rosine [Victoire Noël], b. Paris, 13 Feb 1815; d. Paris, 28 July 1903. French mezzo-soprano. Studied Paris, sang minor roles (as Mlle Victoire Ternaux, then as Heloïse Stoltz, a modification of her mother's maiden name); then roused attention by her perf. of Rachel (JUIVE), Brussels 1836. Sang at Paris O. 1837–47, creating numerous roles incl. Léonore (FAVORITE) and Catarina (J. F. HALÉVY's *Reine de Chypre*, 1841). During this time was the mistress of Léon Pillet, manager of the O.; she was a favourite with the public, and exploited the prima donna's 'temperament' to the full. M. to A. Lescuyer, manager of T. de la Monnaie, 1837, and to Duke Carlo Lesignano, 1872 (taking title of Baroness von Ketschendorf). Made a tour of Brazil 1850–9 under protection of Emperor Don Pedro. Last stage appearance 1860 at Lyon. LO

Stolz, Teresa [Terisina Stolzová], b. Kostelec nad Labem, 2 June 1834; d. Milan, 23 Aug 1902. Bohemian soprano. Studied Prague from 1849 and with her brother-in-law Luigi Ricci in Trieste from 1852. Debut 1865, Sc. (GIOVANNA D'ARCO); VERDI later recognized in her an ideal interpreter of his music. She was Elisabeth in the It. premiere of DON CARLOS (Bologna 1867), Leonora in the revised FORZA DEL DESTINO (Milan 1869) and the first AIDA in Italy (Milan 1872); also created the sop. role in the *Requiem* (Milan 1874) the autograph of which Verdi inscribed to her. JB

Stone Guest, The (*Kamenny gost*), opera, 3 acts, DARGOMYZHSKY, lib. PUSHKIN's poem set unaltered. St Petersburg, Mariinsky T., 28 Feb 1872. Main chars: Don Juan (ten.) Leporello (bass) Donna Anna (sop.) Don Carlos (bar.). The lib., one of Pushkin's 'little tragedies', is based on the Don Juan legend. The opera, unfinished at Dargomyzhsky's death, was completed by CUI and orchestrated by RIMSKY-KORSAKOV. GN

Storace, Ann Selina [Nancy], b. London, 27 Oct 1766; d. London, 24 Aug 1817. English soprano, daughter of an It. immigrant. Studied with Venanzio Rauzzini, and later in Venice. Engaged by Vienna BT 1784; was the original SUSANNA there 1786. Returned to England 1787, where she continued her career until 1808. Excelled as a comedienne. LO

Storace, Stephen, b. London, 4 Jan 1763; d. London, 19 Mar 1796. English composer, brother of the above. Among his many stage works are *The Haunted Tower* (DL 1789), which ran for 50 nights; *No Song, No Supper* (DL 1790); and EQUIVOCI. LO

Storchio, Rosina, b. Mantua, 19 May 1876; d. Milan, 25 July 1945. Italian soprano. Debut 1892, T. dal Verme, Milan (MICAËLA). Sc. debut 1895 as Sophie (WERTHER) and sang there until 1918. She created Musetta in LEONCAVALLO's *La Bohème* (Venice 1897), ZAZA, CIO-CIO-SAN, Stefana in GIORDANO's *Siberia* (Sc. 1903) and LODOLETTA. A lyric sop. with a beautiful, flexible voice, she also sang SUSANNA, Zerlina (FRA DIAVOLO), Amina (SONNAMBULA), NORINA, VIOLETTA, MIGNON, MARGUERITE, MANON, and MIMI. EF

The Story of a Real Man. Evgeny Kibkalo as Aleksey, Moscow, Bolshoy T., 7 Oct 1960

Story of a Real Man, The (*Povest o nastoyashchem cheloveke*), opera, 3 acts, PROKOFIEV, lib. comp. and Mira Mendelson-Prokofieva after Boris Polevoy. Moscow, Bolshoy T., 7 Oct 1960. Main chars: Aleksey (bar.) Olga (sop.) Andrey (bass) Commissar (bass). Time, 1942. Aleksey's plane is shot down, and he crashes into a dense forest. The thought of Olga, his fiancée, gives him strength, and, seriously wounded, he wanders for 18 days before being spotted by two children. Eventually he is transferred to hospital, where both his feet are amputated; he lies in bed delirious and obsessed with the thought that he will not fly again. But the Commissar tells him of a pilot named Karpovich, who continued to fly after losing a foot; and Aleksey resolves to do the same. At first, doctors forbid him to return to the front, but, impressed by his determination, they agree to let him fly again. Finally he is reunited with Olga. While writing this, his last opera (1947–8), Prokofiev, like many Soviet comps, was severely attacked in the Zhdanov censures. Despite his own confidence that the score would conform to the authorities' stringent requirements, it was rejected after a private perf. at the Kirov T. (3 Dec 1948), and was not given its public premiere (with the orig. four acts condensed to three) until seven years after the comp.'s death. GN O

Straniera, La (*The Stranger*), opera, 2 acts, BELLINI, lib. ROMANI after novel by Victor-Prévost, Vicomte d'Arlincourt. Milan, Sc., 14 Feb 1829; London, King's T., 23 June 1832; NY, 10 Dec 1834. Main chars; Alaide (sop.) Isoletta (sop. or mezzo-sop.) Arturo (ten.) Valdeburgo (bar.). Arturo, about to marry Isoletta, meets and falls in love with the unknown Alaide, considered a witch. Seeing her in secret colloquy with Valdeburgo (in fact her brother), he challenges his supposed rival to a duel, causing him to fall and apparently drown. Alaide is accused of the murder, despite Arturo's attempts to take the blame. Valdeburgo, however, is discovered to be alive; at his insistence Arturo agrees to marry Isoletta; but at the end, discovering Alaide to be the French king's unlawfully married wife, kills himself. JB

Strasbourg, France. Important provincial centre for opera; several first perfs in Fr. have been given there, incl. BÉATRICE ET BÉNÉDICT, PRIGIONIERO, and WOZZECK. T. Municipal, built 1821, was destroyed 1870, rebuilt 1870–72 to same plans. Now a member of l'Opéra du Rhin. Mus. dir. LOMBARD; resident producer, Nathaniel Merrill; principal cond. Ignaz Strasfogel. LO

Stratas, Terese [Anastasia Strataki], b. Toronto, 26 May 1938. Canadian soprano of Greek extraction. Studied Cons. of Toronto; debut 1958, Toronto O. (MIMI). Besides her many perfs with COC has also sung at NY Met (debut Mimi, 1962), at Paris O. (DESPINA), and elsewhere in Europe. Her roles incl. ZERLINA, LIÙ, MICAËLA, NEDDA, the Composer (ARIADNE AUF NAXOS), and Lisa (QUEEN OF SPADES). Has also sung SALOME in a filmed version, cond. BÖHM. LO

Stratford, Ontario *see* CANADA

Straus, Oscar, b. Vienna, 6 Mar 1870; d. Bad Ischl, 11 Jan 1954. Austrian composer of operettas. Studied with Hermann Gradener, Vienna, and BRUCH, Berlin. Like SCHÖNBERG was for a time cond. at Ernst von Wolzogen's Berlin cabaret Überbrettl. The best known of his operettas are *Ein Walzertraum* (Vienna 1907) and *Der Tapfere Soldat* (based on George Bernard Shaw's *Arms and the Man*, Vienna 1908), popular in Britain as *The Chocolate Soldier*. LO
See Lubbock

Strauss, Johann, b. Vienna, 25 Oct 1825; d. Vienna, 3 June 1899. Austrian composer, son of Johann Strauss (1804–49) of Viennese waltz fame. Wrote 16 operettas beginning with *Indigo oder der Vierzig Räuber* (1871) and ending with *Die Göttin der Vernunft* (1897). His first great success, FLEDERMAUS, carried his name all over the world. Among the others are *Der Karneval in Rom* (1873); *Cagliostro in Wien* (1875); NACHT IN VENEDIG, and ZIGEUNERBARON – the second peak in his work. With their lilting melodies, captivating dance rhythms (polkas and galops as well as waltzes) and brilliant orchestration they voiced a nostalgia for an idealized Vienna and stamped the Viennese operetta with an individuality that was carried over into the work of his successors STRAUS and LEHÁR. LO
See Jacob, *Johann Strauss: A Century of Light Music*, tr. Wolff (London and Melbourne 1940)

Strauss, Richard, b. Munich, 11 June 1864; d. Garmisch-Partenkirchen, 8 Sept 1949. German composer and conductor. Son of a famous horn player, he was a musical prodigy, his early tone poems establishing him as a comp. of vivid originality. His first opera, GUNTRAM, inspired by admiration for WAGNER, was a failure, his second, FEUERSNOT, only a qualified success. The sensational SALOME, followed by the savage ELEKTRA, made him internationally famous, even if as an *enfant terrible* in some quarters. ROSENKAVALIER, with its rich humanity, won him universal admiration, as did ARIADNE AUF NAXOS. After this point, his inspiration seemed to flag, though the somewhat pretentious FRAU OHNE SCHATTEN, the highly romantic ARABELLA, and the conversational CAPRICCIO have all held their places in the international repertoire. The remaining operas, revived less frequently, are INTERMEZZO, ÄGYPTISCHE HELENA, SCHWEIGSAME FRAU, FRIEDENSTAG, DAPHNE, and LIEBE DER DANAE. With PUCCINI, one of the last of the great popular opera comps. FGB
See Mann, *Richard Strauss* (London 1964; New York 1966)

Stravinsky, Igor Fyodorovich, b. Oranienbaum (now Lomonosov), 17 June 1882; d. NY, 6 Apr 1971. American composer, of Russian birth. His first opera was NIGHTINGALE. With *The Wedding* (comp. 1914–17, orch. and perf. 1923) he began to explore new ideas of stage perf. (the work is described as 'Russian dance scenes with song and music'), and these tendencies were continued in HISTOIRE DU SOLDAT and in RENARD. MAVRA is a conventional comic opera, but OEDIPUS REX a less orthodox opera-oratorio; his fascination for classical subjects is revealed again in the melodrama *Persephone* (1934). His finest opera is RAKE'S PROGRESS; his television opera *The Flood* (1962) was a comparatively unsuccessful essay in serial technique. GN

Strehler, Giorgio, b. Barcola, Trieste, 14 Aug 1921. Italian producer. Studied Milan; served in It. army until 1943, then after sheltering in Switzerland returned to Milan, 1945, prod. plays (*L'Assassinio nella Cattedrale*, 1945, Geneva and Milan) and operas, TRAVIATA (1947); PETRASSI's *Il Cordovano* (1949), and, at Venice Fest., LULU (1949) and FIERY ANGEL (1955). More recently has prod. ENTFÜHRUNG AUS DEM SERAIL (Salzburg 1971), the first It. perf. of AUFSTIEG UND FALL DER STADT MAHAGONNY (1971) and VERURTEILUNG DES LUKULLUS (T. Lirico, Milan, 1973). Since 1955 has been co-dir. of La Piccola Sc., Milan. LO

Streich, Rita, b. Barnaul, Siberia, 18 Dec 1920. German soprano. Studied with IVOGÜN and BERGER. Stage debut Aussig; went to the Berlin Staats O. immediately after World War II; debut there as Amor (ORFEO ED EURIDICE); then sang OLYMPIA and BLONDE. Berlin Städtische O. from 1950; Bayreuth as the Woodbird (SIEGFRIED) 1952–3. Vienna debut 1953; sang there regularly for the rest of her career in roles such as SOPHIE, SUSANNA, ZERBINETTA, ZERLINA, and QUEEN OF THE NIGHT. London debut 1954 with Vienna co. at RFH. US debut 1957, San Francisco, as Zerbinetta, a role she sang at Glyndebourne (1958). One of the most successful lighter sopranos in the Ger. repertory since World War II. AB

Strepponi, Giuseppina, b. Lodi, 8 Sept 1815; d. Busseto, 14 Nov 1897. Italian soprano, especially famous during the late 1830s. Created leading roles in several operas incl. DONIZETTI's *Adelia* (Rome 1841), Federico Ricci's *Luigi Rolla* (Florence 1841), and NABUCCO. Overwork and a liaison with MORIANI involving three pregnancies brought her singing career to a premature end. After a brief period as a singing teacher in Paris, in 1847 she became the life partner of VERDI, already a widower; they were m. in 1859. JB

stretta, a technical term in 19th-c. It. opera denoting the fast complement to the *largo concertato* of a central finale, bringing down the curtain in a blaze of sound and on an unresolved situation. JB

Student Prince, The, operetta, ROMBERG, book and lyrics Dorothy Donnelly. NY,

Jolson T., 2 Dec 1924; London, HM, 3 Feb 1926. EJ ○ ★
See Lubbock

Sturm, Der (*The Tempest*), opera, MARTIN, lib. August von Schlegel's Ger. tr. of SHAKESPEARE's play (almost word-for-word and therefore of inordinate length). Vienna, Staats O., 1956. Its vocal style is declamatory, with the use of jazz elements to portray court society and an offstage chorus for the songs of Ariel, a role taken by a dancer. FGB

Stuttgart, Germany. One of the oldest of Germany's operatic centres, Stuttgart has had perfs since the 17th c., with an exceptionally brilliant period in the 18th c. under JOMMELLI. The modern history of its co. dates from the opening of the present house in 1912 with ARIADNE AUF NAXOS. Both before and after World War II, the house was notable for its excellent ensemble of singers. After the war, WINDGASSEN and RENNERT did some of their best work as prods at Stuttgart, often with LEITNER, the co.'s mus. dir., as cond. A certain emphasis on WAGNER and R. STRAUSS, also considerable interest in 20th-c. repertory, especially operas of JANÁČEK. AB

Suchoň, Eugen, b. Pezinok, Slovakia, 25 Sept 1908. Slovak composer. Studied Bratislava Cons. 1927–31, and with NOVÁK at Prague 1931–3. Since 1941 has held teaching posts at Bratislava Cons., Acad. and Univ. The first Slovak comp. to gain international recognition, notably with his opera *The Whirlpool* (*Krútňova*, 1949), which owes something in its use of folk ceremony and strong, emotionally explored emotions to JENŮFA. *Svätopluk* (1960) deals with events in the 9th-c. Great Moravian Empire and like LIBUŠE is an attempt at national heroic opera. JT

Sukis, Lillian, b. Lithuania, 1943 (?), moved to Canada in 1950. Canadian soprano. Took BA at McMaster Univ., and studied piano. Vocal studies at the Royal Cons., Toronto, 1960; professional debut 1965, Stratford Fest. (Countess ALMAVIVA). NY Met debut 1967 (MOURNING BECOMES ELECTRA). Has since sung mostly in Germany, principally at the Bavarian Staats O., with which co. she created the title role of Isang Yun's *Sim Tjong* (1972). CM

Sullivan, (Sir) Arthur (Seymour), b. London, 13 May 1842; d. London, 22 Nov 1900. English composer. A boy chorister of the Chapel Royal, he studied at the RAM, London, and the Leipzig Cons., returning to England 1861; thereafter active as organist, cond. and fashionable comp. His first operetta, *Cox and Box* (London 1867) disclosed a talent for comedy which came to fruition in the so-called Savoy Operas written with GILBERT; these form a unique contribution to the English musical stage. During an estrangement between the partners Sullivan prod. his only grand opera, IVANHOE. He also collaborated with other writers on operettas but with only modest success. Well versed in It. opera, he edited several operas by BELLINI and DONIZETTI for English publication. His qualities incl. a limited but distinct originality, melodic fluency, a gift for parody and for setting Eng. words.

Operettas written to Gilbert's words are: *Cox and Box*; *Trial by Jury* (1875); SORCERER; H.M.S. PINAFORE; PIRATES OF PENZANCE; PATIENCE; IOLANTHE; *Princess Ida* (1884); MIKADO; RUDDIGORE; YEOMEN OF THE GUARD; GONDOLIERS; *Utopia Limited* (1893); *The Grand Duke* (1896). JB
See Young, *Sir Arthur Sullivan* (London and New York 1971

Suor Angelica (*Sister Angelica*), opera, one act, PUCCINI, lib. FORZANO. NY Met, 14 Dec 1919; London, RAM, 29 July 1931. Main chars: Angelica (sop.) The Princess (mezzo-sop.) Genoveva (sop.). Sister Angelica has become a nun in order to expiate the sin of having borne an illegitimate child. Her aunt, the Princess, arrives at the convent to get her to sign away all her worldly inheritance as dowry for her younger sister. She adds that Angelica's child is dead. Angelica commits suicide but receives a sign from heaven that her mortal sin is forgiven. For women's voices only; the second of the TRITTICO. JB ○
See Kobbé

Supervia, Conchita [Concepción Supervia Pascual], b. Barcelona, 8 Dec (?) 1899; d. London, 30 Mar 1936. Spanish coloratura mezzo-soprano. Studied Barcelona; debut 1910, T. Colón, Buenos Aires (BRETÓN's *Los Amantes de Teruel*). Sang OCTAVIAN in first It. perf of ROSENKAVALIER (Rome 1911). Sang in Chicago 1915–16 and at Sc. 1924–9. London debut 1930, Queen's Hall; m. an Englishman and settled in London; CG debut 1934 only two years before dying in childbirth. Most famous for her singing of ROSSINI roles in their original keys and for her controversial CARMEN. Her recordings of arias from *Carmen* and various Rossini operas reveal the seductive brilliance of her voice and hint at the magic of her impishly charming stage personality. FGB

Conchita Supervia as CARMEN, a role she sang in New York and at London, CG, in her second and last season there in 1935

Suppé, Franz von [Francesco Ezechiele Ermenegildo Suppe Demelli], b. Split, 18 Apr 1819;

d. Vienna, 21 May 1895. Austrian composer, father of Belgian origin, mother Austrian. The founder of the Viennese Light Opera school. Went to Vienna 1835, on death of his father; held posts successively at Josefstadt T. (1840); T. a. d. Wien (1862); Leopoldstadt T. (Carltheater) (1865 until his death). *Das Mädchen vom Lande* (1847) was his first success; the one-act operettas he wr. from 1860 incl. *Leichte Kavallerie* (1866), *Banditenstreiche* (1867), and SCHÖNE GALATHEE. First full-length operetta was the successful FATINITZA, followed by BOCCACCIO, *Donna Juanita* (1880), *Gascogner* (1881), and others. One of his operettas, *Franz Schubert* (1864) is based on SCHUBERT's life. The overtures to *Leichte Kavallerie* and *Dichter und Bauer* (1846) have in their time been very popular. LO

Susanna, sop., Countess Almaviva's maid in NOZZE DI FIGARO

Susannah, opera, 3 acts, FLOYD, lib. comp. Tallahassee, Fla., 24 Feb 1955. Main chars: Susannah (sop.) Olin Blitch (bass) Sam (ten.). Susannah, bathing in a public place in rural Tennessee, is spied upon by elders of the parish and considered wanton. A travelling revivalist, Blitch, preaching in the town, fails to convert Susannah while himself becoming enamoured of her. Tormented, he visits her to plead his love and is killed by her brother. At the end, Susannah is left alone, embittered and withdrawn. The story draws on folk materials: fiddler of square dances, rural superstitions, religious mysticism, and primitive hellfire. EJ

Susanna's Secret *see* SEGRETO DI SUSANNA

Sutermeister, Heinrich, b. Feuerthalen, 12 Aug 1910. Swiss composer. Among works in a variety of forms he has wr. *c.* 10 operas incl. *Die Schwarze Spinne* (1936 for radio, 1949 revised for perf. at Berlin Staats O.); ROMEO UND JULIA; *Die Zauberinsel* (based on SHAKESPEARE's *The Tempest*; Dresden, Oct 1942); RASKOLNIKOFF; *Titus Feuerfuchs* (Basel 1958); *Madame Bovary* (1967). FGB

Sutherland, Joan, b. Sydney, 7 Nov 1926. Australian soprano. Won Sydney Sun Aria competition and Mobil Quest; London debut 1952, CG, as First Lady (ZAUBERFLÖTE). Sang many lyric roles: AGATHE, MICAËLA, GILDA, VERDI's DESDEMONA, EVA, and created Jennifer (MIDSUMMER MARRIAGE), before her perf. of LUCIA DI LAMMERMOOR turned her overnight into a coloratura sop. celebrity. Since then she has sung all over Europe, USA, and Australia in a repertory that incl. ALCINA, RODELINDA, GIULIO CESARE, SEMIRAMIDE, SONNAMBULA, PURITANI, BEATRICE DI TENDA, NORMA, MARIA STUARDA, FILLE DU RÉGIMENT, HUGUENOTS, and MASSENET's *Esclarmonde*. She m. BONYNGE, who has contributed greatly to her success. EF
See Braddon, *Joan Sutherland* (London and New York 1962)

Suzuki, mezzo-sop., Cio-Cio-San's servant in MADAMA BUTTERFLY

Svanholm, Set, b. Västerås, 2 Sept 1904; d. Saltsjö-Duvnäs, 4 Oct 1964. Swedish tenor. Debut 1930 as a bar. (SILVIO); in 1936 emerged as a ten. (RADAMES). Sang at Vienna, Salzburg (1938), Sc., Bayreuth (1942), Rio de Janeiro, San Francisco, NY Met (1946–56), CG (1948–57). A most musicianly singer, outside Sweden he was best known as a WAGNER ten., and had Erik (FLIEGENDE HOLLÄNDER), TANNHÄUSER, LOHENGRIN, Tristan (TRISTAN UND ISOLDE), WALTHER VON STOLZING, LOGE, SIEGMUND, SIEGFRIED and PARSIFAL in his repertory. At the Stockholm Royal O., of which he was dir. 1956–63, he also sang FLORESTAN, MAX, MANRICO, Don JOSÉ, CANIO, VERDI's OTELLO, Bacchus (ARIADNE AUF NAXOS), and PETER GRIMES. EF

Svoboda, Josef, b. Čáslav, 10 May 1920. Czech designer. Qualified as an architect; in 1948 became chief designer Prague NT, where he has exerted a strong influence on Czech stage

Joan Sutherland as Elvira, in PURITANI, London, CG, 20 Mar 1964

design. A feature of his style is a type of set that can change fluidly and magically during the course of the work, as in DALIBOR (his British debut with the Prague NT, Edinburgh, 1964), with oppressive, monolithic blocks which shift smoothly into new shapes, or in the RING DES NIBELUNGEN (London, CG, 1974–6), where the tilting stage reveals the Rhine and Nibelheim beneath it or itself forms the steep steps to Valhalla. He has worked in every major centre and has designed over 300 sets for plays and ballets as well as operas. JT

Swarthout, Gladys, b. Deepwater, Miss., 24 Dec 1904; d. La Bagnaia, Italy, 6 July 1969. American mezzo-soprano. Studied Chicago and with MUGNONE. Debut 1904, Chicago, as Shepherd Boy (TOSCA); NY Met 1929–38 and several seasons later. Sang in US premiere of SADKO and MERRY MOUNT. Other roles incl. CARMEN and MIGNON. LO

Sweden. The first opera with a Swedish text was *Syrinx, eller Den uti vass förvandlade Vattennymphen* (*Syrinx, or The Waternymph changed into a Reed*) (Stockholm 1747), a pastiche with music by HANDEL and others. NAUMANN's *Cora och Alonso* (1782) and *Gustaf Vasa* (1786) were also wr. and perf. in Swedish. Other operas on national historical subjects incl. Carl Stenborg's *Konung Gustav Adolfs Jakt* (1777), *Skeppar Rolf och Gunhild* (1778), *Gustav Vasa i Dalarna* (1787) and Georg Joseph (Abbé) Vogler's *Gustav Adolf och Ebbe Brahe* (1788). Franz Berwald (1796–1868) comp. two operas: *Estrella de Soria* (Stockholm 1862) and *Drottningen av Golconda*, originally wr. for C. NILSSON, but not perf. until 1968, with SÖDERSTRÖM in the title role. HALLSTRÖM wr. many light operas; Johan Andreas Hallén (1842–1925), who was strongly influenced by WAGNER, comp. *Harald der Wiking* to a German text (1881), originally prod. Leipzig, and *Häxfällan* (1896). Hallén's *Waldemarsskatten* (1899) was one of the operas commissioned for the opening of the new Royal O.; another was *Tirfing* (1898) by Wilhelm Stenhammar (1871–1927), who also wr. *Gildet på Solhaug* (Stuttgart 1899 and Stockholm 1902). Wilhelm Peterson-Berger (1867–1942) comp. several successful operas, incl. *Arnljot* (1910), *Domedagsprofeterna* (1919), and *Adils och Elisiv* (1927). N. BERG wr. both texts and music for his operas. ATTERBERG comp. *Härvard Harpolekare* (1919), *Bäckahästen* (1925), *Fanal* (1934), *Aladdin* (1941), and *Stormen* (1948), based on SHAKESPEARE's *Tempest*. Hilding Rosenberg's (b. 1892) operas, all prod. Stockholm, incl. *Resan till Amerika* (1932), *Marionetter* (1939), *De Två Kungsdöttrarna* (1940), *Lycksalighetens Ö* (1945), *Kaspers Fettigsdag* (1954), *Porträttet* (1956), and *Salome* (1963). In the second half of the 20th c., the two most admired operas by Swedish comps have been ANIARA and DRÖMMEN OM THÉRÈSE. EF

Switzerland. Comps incl. HAUG, HUBER, HONEGGER, Rudolf Kelterborn (b. 1890; *Die Erettung Thebens*, 1962), P. BURKHARD, MARTIN, SCHOECK, SUTERMEISTER, Roger Vuataz (b. 1898; *Monsieur Jabot*, Geneva, 1958). The most important centres are BASEL, BERN, GENEVA, and ZÜRICH. LO

Sydney, New South Wales, Australia. The headquarters of the Australian O. Co. The 1955 international competition for a new opera house was won by a Dane, Jørn Utzon; the building after many delays and especially financial difficulties opened 1973 (*see* AUSTRALIA). The building contains two main halls; the larger one, originally intended for opera, was changed into a concert hall, the smaller house becoming the Sydney Opera House. LO

Sydney. The opera house designed by Jørn Utzon and opened in 1973

Szell, Georg, b. Budapest, 7 June 1897; d. Cleveland, Ohio, 29 July 1970. Hungarian, later American, conductor. Studied Vienna and Leipzig. Persuaded by R. STRAUSS to take up cond. Became cond. Strasbourg 1917; appearances in Prague and Düsseldorf; principal cond., Berlin Staats O., 1924–9. Mus. dir., Prague, German O., 1929–37. NY Met debut 1942 (SALOME); remained there until 1946, specializing in the Ger. repertory but also cond. VERDI's OTELLO and BORIS GODUNOV with success. Debut Salzburg Fest. 1949; appeared there several succeeding seasons incl. LIEBERMANN and EGK premieres. A consistent seeker after accuracy of detail, he was often difficult to please and to work with, but his perfs were worth the trouble he took over them, both in concert hall and opera house. AB

Karol Szymanowski. Hanna Runowska as Roxana in KING ROGER, Warsaw Grand T., Nov 1965

Szokolay, Sándor, b. Kunagota, 30 Mar 1931. Hungarian composer. Known particularly for his powerful three-act opera *The Blood Wedding* (comp. 1964), based on LORCA's drama, *Bodas de Sangre*. Also comp. *Hamlet* (1968) and *Samson* (1973). GN

Szymanowski, Karol, b. Timoshovka, 6 Oct 1882; d. Lausanne, 29 Mar 1937. Polish composer. His first opera, *Hagith*, wr. 1913, was prod. Warsaw 1922; his second, KING ROGER, is still perf. quite frequently in Poland. EF

T

Tabarro, Il (*The Cloak*), opera, one act, PUCCINI, lib. ADAMI after Didier Gold's *La Houppelande*. NY Met, 14 Dec 1919; London, SW, 23 Oct 1935. Main chars: Georgetta (sop.) Michele (bar.) Luigi (ten.). Michele, a Parisian bargee, discovers his wife's infidelity with Luigi, a young stevedore; murders him as he is about to keep an assignation, and presents the body to his wife, having wrapped it in the cloak of the title. An exercise in operatic Grand Guignol: the first of the TRITTICO. JB O

Tacchinardi, Niccolò, b. Livorno, 3 Sept 1772; d. Florence, 14 Mar 1859. Italian tenor. Despite his appearance (he was almost a hunchback) the beauty of his voice overcame this, and he triumphed even as DON GIOVANNI (transposed for him). Between 1804 and 1831 he sang in most continental European centres including Paris, Venice, Florence, Milan, and Vienna, but never in England. After retirement, 1831, he built himself a small theatre where his pupils could train; they incl. his daughter, PERSIANI, and FREZZOLINI. LO

Taddei, Giuseppe, b. Genoa, 26 June 1916. Italian baritone. Debut 1936, Rome. Vienna Staats O. since 1946. English debut 1947 with New London Co. at Cambridge T. US debut 1957, San Francisco (MACBETH and SCARPIA, two of his best parts). CG debut 1959–60 (IAGO and Macbeth). Other roles incl. RIGOLETTO, FALSTAFF, FIGARO (MOZART and ROSSINI) and DON GIOVANNI. One of the leading singing actors of the postwar era. Was still singing *buffo* parts in 1975. AB

Tagliavini, Ferruccio, b. Reggio Emilia, 14 Aug 1913. Italian tenor. Studied Parma and Florence (with Amedio Bassi). Debut 1939, Florence (RODOLFO). Sc. debut 1940; during World War II the leading It. lyric ten. NY Met debut 1947 (Rodolfo); sang there until 1954, notably as Alfredo (ELISIR D'AMORE), NEMORINO, EDGARDO, and CAVARADOSSI, three of his leading roles. CG debut 1950 with Sc. as Nemorino, returned 1956 as Cavaradossi. In his early years had one of the sweetest tenors of the day. Suffered later from taking on too heavy roles. AB

Tajo, Italo, b. Pinerolo, 25 Apr 1915. Italian bass. Studied Turin; debut there 1935 (FAFNER). Also 1935 sang with Glyndebourne Fest. chorus in Britain (at suggestion of BUSCH). After wartime interruption, his career flourished with debuts at Chicago Lyric O., 1946, as Ramfis (AIDA); 1st Edinburgh Fest. 1947, with Glyndebourne co. as FIGARO (NOZZE DI FIGARO); London, Cambridge T., 1947, title role in DON PASQUALE; NY Met 1948, Don BASILIO (BARBIERE DI SIVIGLIA); CG 1950, with Sc. co. as Dulcamara (ELISIR D'AMORE). In late 1940s appeared in Italian opera films of *Barbiere di Siviglia* and *Elisir d'Amore*. Vivid sense of comedy and generous personality in *buffo* roles; also successful in title role of BORIS GODUNOV, PHILIPPE, MÉPHISTOPHÉLÈS. NG
See: Rosenthal (ed.), *Opera Annual 7:* 'Italo Tajo', Ronald Hastings (London 1960)

Tal [Grünthal], Josef, b. Pinne, Posen (now Poznań), 18 Sept 1910. Israeli composer. Studied Berlin; emigrated to Palestine 1934. Dir., Acad. of Mus., Jerusalem, 1948–52. His operas incl. *Saul at Endor* (Ramat Gan 1957), *Amnon and Tamar* (Wiesbaden 1961), *Ashmodai* (Hamburg 1971), and *Masada 967* (Jerusalem 1973). EF

Tale of Tsar Saltan, The (*Skazka o Tsare Saltane*), opera, prologue and 4 acts, RIMSKY-KORSAKOV, lib. Vasily Ivanovich Belsky after PUSHKIN. Moscow, Solodovnikov T., 2 Nov

1900; London, SW, 11 Oct 1933; NY, St James T., 27 Dec 1937. Main chars: Tsar Saltan (bass) Milistrisa (sop.) Prince Gvidon (ten.) Swan Princess (sop.). As a result of a plan devised by her jealous sisters, the Tsarina Milistrisa and her son Gvidon are put in a cask and thrown into the sea. They are washed up on Buyan Island, where Gvidon rescues a princess disguised as a swan; she turns him into a bee. The sisters try to prevent the Tsar visiting the island, and Gvidon stings them. He then turns the swan back into a princess, and she restores Milistrisa to the Tsar. One of Rimsky-Korsakov's most sparkling, subtly satirical scores, *Tsar Saltan* is still perf. frequently in Russia. GN

Tales of Hoffmann, The *see* CONTES D'HOFFMANN

Talich, Václav, b. Kroměříž, Moravia, 28 May 1883; d. Beroun, Bohemia, 16 Mar 1961. Czech conductor. Trained as a violinist with Otakar Ševčík and was leader under NIKISCH in Berlin (1903). In 1919 became cond., Czech Philharmonic, where he established a worldwide reputation with foreign tours. Though less at ease in the theatre, he was an authoritative opera cond. and 1935–47 headed the Prague NT. Gave the premiere of JULIETTA and cond. several JANÁČEK works, incl. his own reorchestration of CUNNING LITTLE VIXEN (1925). JT

Talvela, Martti, b. Hiitola, 4 Feb 1935. Finnish bass. Studied Stockholm with Carl Martin Öhmann; debut 1961, Royal Stockholm O. After two seasons moved to Berlin Deutsche O. where he remains resident. Bayreuth debut 1962 as Titurel (PARSIFAL); in following seasons sang most of leading WAGNER bass roles there. HUNDING under KARAJAN, Salzburg 1968; appeared at NY Met in same prod. 1968 after debut as Grand Inquisitor (DON CARLOS). CG debut 1970 as FASOLT, Hunding, and HAGEN. Has dir. fest. at Savonlinna, Finland, since 1973, when he first sang there as SARASTRO. Other roles incl. PHILIPPE, the Commendatore (DON GIOVANNI) and KING MARK, which he sang unforgettably in the W. WAGNER prod. at Bayreuth in the late 1960s. Imposing actor, with firm, warm, eloquent singing, helped by his great height. AB

Left: Martti Talvela as BORIS GODUNOV in the original MUSORGSKY version at the Olavinlinna fortress, at the 1975 Savonlinna Fest. He had an inflamed foot, was carried to the castle on a stretcher and sang with his leg in plaster, giving a magnificent performance.

Tamagno, Francesco, b. Turin, 28 Dec 1850; d. Varese, 31 Aug 1905. Italian tenor. Trained Turin Cons.; debut in a revival of BALLO IN MASCHERA (Palermo 1873). Created Gabriele in revised SIMONE BOCCANEGRA (Milan 1881) and the name part of VERDI's OTELLO, the death scene from which he twice recorded. With his powerful, trumpetlike tone he set the pattern for singers of this exacting role. JB

Tamberlik, Enrico, b. Rome, 6 Mar 1820; d. Paris, 13 Mar 1889. Italian tenor. Studied Rome and Naples; debut 1840 Naples; sang in Spain and Portugal before London appearances 1850–64. A dramatic ten., he excelled not only in VERDI, but in the French repertoire and more robust *bel canto* roles such as ROSSINI's OTELLO and POLLIONE. Sang in N. and S. America and in St Petersburg where he created the role of ALVARO. Despite a persistent vibrato and a poor sense of time, he won the public with the great power of his high notes and at the age of 57 was still able to thrill audiences with the ringing high C that he had been the first to introduce in 'Di quella pira' in TROVATORE. He reappeared in London 1870 and 1877, after which he settled in Madrid where he became first a singing teacher and then an arms manufacturer. PS

Tamburini, Antonio, b. Faenza, 28 Mar 1800; d. Nice, 9 Nov 1876. Italian baritone. Son of a bandmaster, and himself a horn player, Tamburini studied with Aldobrando Rossi, and sang in the Faenza opera chorus. Debut 1818, Cento, in GENERALI's *La Contessa di Colle Erboso*. Appeared in Rome, then member of BARBAIA's co. for four years, singing in Naples, Milan, and Vienna. From 1832 idol of Paris and London; returned to Italy 1841; 1842–52 sang in St Petersburg, after which he appeared in London, the Netherlands, and Paris. His voice gradually deteriorated, and he sang in London for the last time 1859, then retired to Nice. He created many important roles incl. those in PIRATA, STRANIERA, and PURITANI, and 11 for DONIZETTI, most importantly MALATESTA. PS

Taming of the Shrew, The *see* WIDERSPENSTIGEN ZÄHMUNG

Tamino, ten., the hero of ZAUBERFLÖTE

Tancredi (*Tancred*), opera, 2 acts, ROSSINI, lib. G. ROSSI after VOLTAIRE'S *Tancrède*, 1760. Venice, T. La Fenice, 6 Feb 1813; London, 4 May 1820, NY, 31 Dec 1825. Main chars: Amenaide (sop.) Argirio (ten.) Tancredi (contr.) Orbazzano (bar.). Tancredi returns from exile to Sicily in time to prevent the marriage of his beloved Amenaide to his rival Orbazzano. But Orbazzano intercepts a letter from her to Tancredi, and declares that it is addressed to the chief of the Saracens, the Sicilians' enemies. Amenaide is imprisoned and condemned to death for treason, unless a champion can be found to fight for her. Tancredi though believing her guilty offers himself and wins, then leads a triumphant expedition against the Saracens. The truth is revealed and the lovers are reconciled. Rossini's first international success, heralding a renaissance of It. serious opera. An alternative tragic end, written for a prod. in Ferrara (1813), has recently come to light. JB

Tanglewood *see* BERKSHIRE MUSIC FESTIVAL

Tannhäuser und der Sängerkrieg auf der Wartburg (*Tannhäuser and the Singing Contest at the Wartburg*), opera, 3 acts, WAGNER, lib. composer. Dresden, 19 Oct 1845; NY, 4 Apr 1859; London, CG, 6 May 1876; revived in definitive form with ballet, Paris, O., 13 Mar 1860. Main chars: Tannhäuser (ten.) Elisabeth (sop.) Wolfram (bar.) Landgraf (bass) Venus (sop. or mezzo-sop.). Tannhäuser, a Christian minstrel, has been seduced by the pagan goddess Venus; surfeited by pleasure he returns to his comrades and takes part in the minstrels' contest for the hand of Elisabeth. But the words of his song betray carnal experience, and he is ordered to make the pilgrimage to Rome, from which he returns unshriven. He is finally saved by the self-sacrifice of Elisabeth. JB ○ *See* Kobbé

Tarare, opera, prologue and 5 acts, SALIERI, lib. BEAUMARCHAIS. Paris, O., 8 June 1787; London, Lyceum T. (in Eng.), 15 Aug 1825; revised, in free tr. by da PONTE, Vienna, 8 Jan 1788 as *Azur, Re d'Ormus*. One of Salieri's best operas; very successful in Paris. LO

Tasso, Torquato, b. Sorrento, 11 May 1544; d. Rome, 23 Apr 1595. Italian poet and dramatist. His *Aminta* (1573) was the prototype of the PASTORAL which led to a number of operas. GERUSALEMME LIBERATA which incl. the story of Rinaldo and Armida furnished themes for over 30. DONIZETTI'S *Torquato Tasso* (1833) is based on his life. LO

Tatyana, sop., the heroine of EUGENE ONEGIN

Tauber, Richard [Ernst Seifert], b. Linz, 16 May 1892; d. London, 8 Jan 1948. Austrian tenor. Debut 1913, Chemnitz (TAMINO). Dresden 1913–25; Vienna Staats O. 1925–38, while also singing, mainly in operetta, in Germany and England. CG debut 1938 (BELMONTE); returned 1939; final stage appearance 1947, as Don OTTAVIO, when the Vienna Staats O. visited London. He was a noted Mozartian, but also excelled in many of the It. and Fr. lyric roles, and especially in LEHÁR. He brought a highly individual voice and manner to all he did. AB

Tauberová, Marie, b. Vysoké Mýto, 28 Apr 1911. Czech coloratura soprano. Studied Vienna and Milan; debut 1936 Prague NT, where she has been a permanent member of the co. Her bright, light voice and technical agility were particularly suitable for DONIZETTI, ROSSINI, and VERDI parts, though she was also well known for her MOZART and her enthusiastic espousal of modern works. JT

Taylor, Deems, b. NY, 22 Dec 1885; d. NY, 3 July 1966. American composer and critic. Graduated NY Univ. 1906; largely self-taught in music with occasional successes in the entertainment world; wrote perceptive and witty music criticism for the *New York World* 1921–5. His best operas are KING'S HENCHMAN, commissioned by the NY Met,

Tannhäuser. NORMAN as Elisabeth; RIDDERBUSCH as the Landgraf, London, CG, 11 Oct 1973; produced KAŠLIK; scenery SVOBODA; costumes Jan Skalicky

and PETER IBBETSON. Other operas are *Ramuntcho* (Philadelphia, 10 Feb 1942) and *The Dragon*, wr. for amateurs (NY, 6 Feb 1958). EJ

Tbilisi (formerly Tiflis). Capital of the Georgian SSR. The opera house opened 1851, staging first It., then Russ. opera. Native Georgian opera began to emerge only in the 20th c., with ARAKISHVILI's *The Legend of Shota Rustaveli* (1919), and PALIASHVILI's *Abesalom and Eteri* (1919) and TWILIGHT. The city has continued to give premieres of national operas, incl. Mshvelidze's *The Tale of Tariel* (1946) and *The Great Master's Right Hand* (1961), and Taktakishvili's *Mindiya* (1961) and *Three Novels* (1967). GN

Tchaikovsky, Pyotr Ilyich, b. Kamsko-Votkinsk, 7 May 1840; d. St Petersburg, 6 Nov 1893. Russian composer. He was constantly attracted to opera, even though he only rarely managed to fully realize his characters in musical terms. His first opera *The Voyevode* (1869), though initially successful, did not maintain a place in the repertory. He burned the score of his next opera *Undine* (comp. 1869), salvaging some of it for the Second Symphony and *Swan Lake*, and he completed only the Chorus of Flowers and Insects for *Mandragora* (1869). He then reworked some of the material from *The Voyevode* for *The Oprichnik* (1874), a melodramatic 'number' opera which in some characteristic touches offers a foretaste of more strikingly individual works. *Vakula the Smith* (1876; revised as *Cherevichki*, or *The Little Shoes*, 1887) is a more assured piece, presaging in some respects EUGENE ONEGIN, in which he found himself entirely in sympathy with the character of Tatyana (far more so than with the remote figure of Onegin). He chose a SCHILLER subject for his next opera, MAID OF ORLEANS, but returned to Russ. literature for MAZEPA and for the dramatically disorganized *The Sorceress* (1887). QUEEN OF SPADES is his most powerful and, with *Eugene Onegin*, most popular opera; and Hermann is one of his most sharply defined characters. By comparison IOLANTA is pale. GN

See Warrack, *Tchaikovsky* (London and New York 1973)

Tcherepnin *see* CHEREPNIN

Tear, Robert, b. Barry, S. Wales, 8 Mar 1939. Welsh tenor. At first a professional chorister at St Paul's Cathedral; operatic debut 1964 with EOG as Quint (TURN OF THE SCREW), and has also sung in RAPE OF LUCRETIA, BILLY BUDD, CURLEW RIVER, BURNING FIERY FURNACE and PRODIGAL SON. He has appeared with WNO and SO; CG debut 1970 as Dov at the premiere of KNOT GARDEN. A versatile and very musical singer, he has a repertory incl. Nerone (INCORONAZIONE DI POPPEA), Admète (GLUCK's ALCESTE), LENSKY, Galitsin (KHOVANSHCHINA), Matteo (ARABELLA), and Paris (KING PRIAM). EF

Tebaldi, Renata, b. Pesaro, 1 Feb 1922. Italian soprano. Studied Parma; debut 1944, Rovigo, as Elena (MEFISTOFELE). Her career flourished after TOSCANINI chose her for the concerts that reopened Sc., Milan, 1946. Principal sop. there 1949–54, much admired in VERDI, PUCCINI, and other *verismo* roles for consistent beauty of voice and expressive character. Other debuts: CG 1950, with Milan Sc. co. (Verdi's DESDEMONA); San Francisco O. 1950 (AIDA); NY Met 1955 (Desdemona); returned London, 1955, as TOSCA with CG O. Since 1955 based mainly at NY Met, where the rare elegance and style of her singing, and a personality reflecting these qualities won many devoted admirers. NG

Telemann, Georg Philipp, b. Magdeburg, 14 Mar 1681; d. Hamburg, 25 June 1767. German composer. Self-taught; held successive appointments at Sorau (1704), Eisenach (1709), Frankfurt-am-Main (1712), Bayreuth (1716), and Hamburg (1721) where he remained until his death. His over 40 operas keep pace steadily with the stylistic developments of his age; among the few surviving are *Der Geduldige Sokrates* (Hamburg 1721) and PIMPINONE. JB

Telephone, The, *opera buffa*, 1 act, MENOTTI, lib. comp. NY, Hekscher T., 18 Feb 1947; transferred to Barrymore T.; London, Aldwych T., 29 Apr 1948. A young man comes to visit his fiancée with the intention of proposing marriage, but she is so enthralled with a newly installed telephone that she has no time for him. In frustration he rushes to the nearest telephone kiosk and finds her a willing listener. *The Telephone*, frequently perf. in continental Europe, is most often sung as curtain raiser to MEDIUM. EJ

Television opera. The first opera written for TV was AMAHL AND THE NIGHT VISITORS; the most important one to date is OWEN WINGRAVE. Other operas specially wr. for TV incl.: Jack Beeson, *My Heart's in the Highlands*, 1969; FLOYD, *The Sojourner and Mollie Sinclair*, 1963; FOSS, *Griffelkin*, 1955; HENZE, *Rachel la Cubana*, 1974; MARTINŮ, *The Marriage*, 1953; and Renzo ROSSELLINI, *Le Campane*, 1963. LO

Telramund, bar., a Count of Brabant in LOHENGRIN

Tender Land, The, opera, 3 acts, COPLAND, lib. Horace Everett. NY, City O., 1 Apr 1954; revised form, Berkshire Music Center, 2 Aug 1954. Set in the American Midwest in the 1930s it seeks to evoke a rustic atmosphere for an unsophisticated story by means of folklike and homely material. LO

tenor, high male voice with a compass of approx. two octaves from C below middle C to the C above.

Ternina, Milka, b. Vezisce, Croatia, 19 Dec 1863; d. Zagreb, 18 May 1941. Yugoslav soprano. Studied Zagreb and Vienna; debut 1882 (BALLO IN MASCHERA). Several engagements in Ger. before Munich, 1890–9. US debut 1896, Boston, with Damrosch OC. Sang several seasons in London 1898–1906, and was first London TOSCA. Sang at Bayreuth 1899, but never again as she created KUNDRY in USA, 1903, in breach of agreement with Bayreuth. One of the outstanding WAGNER singers of her era, with a magnificent voice and great dramatic power; also a great Tosca. Retired 1916 after an attack of paralysis. LO

tessitura (It. 'texture'), the mean compass of a voice or a vocal role.

Tetrazzini, Luisa, b. Florence, 29 June 1871; d. Milan, 28 Apr 1940. Italian soprano. Studied Liceo Musicale, Florence, and with her sister Eva (1862–1938). Debut 1890, Florence (AFRICAINE). After engagements at Rome and other It. towns went to Buenos Aires (1898), Mexico, and San Francisco. CG 1907–12, with a sensational debut as VIOLETTA; NY, Manhattan Co., 1908–10, Met 1911–12, Chicago 1913–14. Her repertory was confined to the light agility roles of It. and Fr. opera, in which her brilliance was unrivalled. LO

Teyte [Tate], Maggie, b. Wolverhampton, 17 Apr 1888. After study at RCM, London, and with J. DE RESZKE, debut 1907, Monte Carlo (DON GIOVANNI). Was then engaged by Paris OC, where she sang MÉLISANDE in 1908. Sang frequently at CG from 1910 (debut there in TIEFLAND), where her roles incl. CIO-CIO-SAN and Hänsel (HÄNSEL UND GRETEL). Created the Princess role in PERFECT FOOL. Also sang in Chicago 1911–14, and Boston 1915–17, and after World War II with NY CC. A singer of great artistry and refinement. Her Mélisande won high praise from all sides, though DEBUSSY voiced conflicting opinions on her performance. LO
See autobiography, *Star on the Door* (London 1958)

Thaïs, *comédie lyrique*, 3 acts, MASSENET, lib. GALLET based on Anatole France's novel, 1890, in turn an expansion of his poem *La Légende de Sainte Thaïs*, 1867. Paris, O., 16 Mar 1894; NY, Manhattan OH, 25 Nov 1907; London, CG, 18 July 1911. Written with SANDERSON in mind as the Egyptian courtesan Thaïs, converted by the ascetic monk Athanaël, who is in turn destroyed by her. The oasis scene and a new ballet were added after the first perf. LO **O**
See Newman, *Opera Nights* (London 1943)

Thebom, Blanche, b. Monessen, Pa., 19 Sept 1918. American mezzo-soprano. Studied with MATZENAUER and WALKER. Debut 1944, NY Met (FRICKA) and appeared there until 1965 in most of the leading mezzo roles. Appeared at CG as Didon (TROYENS, 1957–8). Recorded BRANGÄNE under FURTWÄNGLER with FLAGSTAD as ISOLDE. Created Bearded Lady in RAKE'S PROGRESS. AB

Thieving Magpie, The *see* GAZZA LADRA

Thill, Georges, b. Paris, 14 Dec 1897. French tenor. Studied Paris and Naples; debut 1918, Paris, OC (CARMEN); O. 1924 (THAÏS). For many years a leading ten. there, he also sang at CG, T. de la Monnaie, Sc., and for two seasons at NY Met. A sensitive artist with a robust and vibrant voice, though limited in compass. LO

Thomas, Arthur Goring, b. Ratton Park, Sussex, 20 Nov 1850; d. London, 20 Mar 1892. English composer. Studied Paris, London RAM and with BRUCH. His first opera, *Esmeralda*, lib. Theophilus Marzials and Albert Randegger after HUGO's *Notre-Dame de Paris*, was commissioned by Carl Rosa, prod. DL 26 Mar 1883, and subsequently in Germany (in Ger.) and, in Fr., at CG. A second, *Nadeshda*, prod. Carl Rosa 1885, had less success. LO

Thomas, (Charles Louis) Ambroise, b. Metz, 5 Aug 1811; d. Paris, 12 Feb 1896. French composer. Entered Paris Cons. 1828, won the *Prix de Rome* 1832. Wrote 13 operas for the OC, beginning with *La Double Échelle* (1837). His first successes were *Le Caïd* (1849) and *Le Songe d'une Nuit d'Été* (1850). Others incl. *Raymond* and his best work, MIGNON. He also wrote a five-act *Hamlet* (1868) for the O., his last important work. He succeeded AUBER as dir. of the Cons. 1871. His operas, elegant and refined rather than robust, have almost entirely dropped out of the international repertoire. LO

Thomas, Jess, b. Hot Springs, S. Dak., 4 Aug 1927. American tenor. Debut 1957, San Francisco, as Malcolm (MACBETH), and then sang

Left: Jess Thomas as Augustus Caesar in the premiere of ANTONY AND CLEOPATRA, which opened the new NY Met, 1966

in Karlsruhe, Munich, Salzburg and Bayreuth, (debut 1961 as PARSIFAL). Has sung at the NY Met since 1962 and at CG since 1969. A versatile singer, able to encompass both dramatic and heroic ten. roles, his repertory incl. TANNHÄUSER, LOHENGRIN, WALTHER VON STOLZING, SIEGMUND, SIEGFRIED, TRISTAN, Bacchus (ARIADNE AUF NAXOS), Emperor (FRAU OHNE SCHATTEN), LENSKY, RADAMES, and PETER GRIMES. Sang Augustus Caesar at the premiere of ANTONY AND CLEOPATRA which opened the new Met 1966. EF

Thomas and Sally; or, The Sailor's Return, opera, 3 acts, ARNE, lib. BICKERSTAFFE, London, CG, 28 Nov 1760; revived Lyric T., Hammersmith, London, 10 Apr 1926. A true opera, with recitative, not spoken dialogue. The sailor returns home in the nick of time to save Sally from the Squire's intentions. LO ○

Thomson, Heather, b. Vancouver, 7 Dec 1940. Canadian soprano. Studied Royal Cons. O. School, Toronto; debut 1962 with COC as the Dew Fairy (HÄNSEL UND GRETEL). The following season she sang MIMI; since then has sung many roles with the COC, incl. MARGUERITE, TATYANA, and Heloise (in WILSON'S *Heloise and Abelard*, 1973). SW debut 1966; NY CC 1969. CM

Thomson, Virgil, b. Kansas City, Mo. 25 Nov 1896. American composer and critic. Graduated from Harvard 1922; won a Paine Fellowship for study abroad, residing in Paris during the 1920s and 1930s. His works show the influences of study with Nadia Boulanger, and contact with the theories of 'Les Six' and of Erik Satie, as well as the vernacular tradition of his own folk, and the religious hymnody of Protestant revivalism. His collaboration with G. STEIN resulted in two operas, MOTHER OF US ALL and FOUR SAINTS IN THREE ACTS. EJ

Tibbett, Lawrence, b. Bakersfield, Calif., 16 Nov 1896; d. NY, 15 July 1960. American baritone. Began in light opera, then after study in NY, debut Met 1923 as monk (BORIS GODUNOV). In 1925 his singing at short notice of FORD was sensational; thereafter a leading bar. at the Met for 25 years. Created roles in several American operas, his perf. in EMPEROR JONES being outstanding; sang in Met premieres of SIMONE BOCCANEGRA, PETER GRIMES, and KHOVANSHCHINA, while at CG at E. GOOSSENS III's request he created title role in *Don Juan de Mañara* (1937). Was ideal in VERDI and PUCCINI. LO

Tichatschek [Tikáček], Joseph (Aloys), b. Ober-Wechseldorf, 11 July 1807; d. Blasewitz, nr Dresden, 18 Jan 1886. Czech tenor. Studied Vienna. At first a chorus ten.; solo debut 1837, Dresden (GUSTAVE III). Lived Dresden until retirement 1870. Coached by SCHRÖDER-DEVRIENT and admired by WAGNER, who chose him to create RIENZI and TANNHÄUSER. LO

Tieck, Johann Ludwig, b. Berlin, 30 May 1773; d. Berlin, 23 Apr 1853. German poet and dramatist. Prominent Romantic and friend of C. WEBER. His *Historie von der Melusina* (1799) formed basis of Conradin Kreutzer's *Melusina* (1833); *Der Leben und Tod der Heiligen Genoveva* (1799) that of GENOVEVA. LO

Tiefland (*The Lowlands*), opera, prologue and 2 (orig. 3) acts, d'ALBERT, lib. Rudolf Lothar based on a Catalan play *Terra Baixa* (1896) by Angel Guimerá. Prague, German T., 15 Nov 1903; NY Met, abridged version, 23 Nov 1908; London, CG (in Eng.), 5 Oct 1910. The mountain shepherd Pedro, living in the pure upper air of the Pyrenees, is offered a bride, Martha, by a landowner, Sebastiano. She, Sebastiano's mistress against her will, mistrusts Pedro who, goaded by the villagers, turns on her. She eventually realizes that Pedro loves her. In the last scene Pedro strangles Sebastiano and takes Martha back with him to the serenity of the mountains. D'Albert's most successful opera, still played in Germany. LO

Tietjen, Heinz, b. Tangier, 24 June 1881, d. Bayreuth, 30 Nov 1967. German conductor and producer. Studied cond. with NIKISCH.

Debut 1907 as cond., Trier; remained there as cond./prod., later *Intendant* until 1919. Engagements at Saarbrücken and Breslau; then *Intendant*, Berlin Städtische O., 1925–30. From 1930 worked as cond. and prod. at Berlin Staats O. and Kroll T. Art. dir., Bayreuth, 1931–44. Returned to Berlin Städtische O. 1948–54; worked in Hamburg 1954–9. CG, prod. FLIEGENDE HOLLÄNDER (1950), PARSIFAL, and MEISTERSINGER VON NÜRNBERG (1951); Bayreuth again, cond. LOHENGRIN (1959). One of the last of the traditional prods of WAGNER's works. AB

Tietjens, Therese (Cathline Johanna Alexandra), b. Hamburg, 17 July 1831; d. London, 3 Oct 1877. German soprano, purportedly of Dutch and Hungarian extraction. Debut 1849, Hamburg (LUCREZIA BORGIA). This led to engagements in Frankfurt, and in 1856, Vienna (debut as Valentine in HUGUENOTS). Engaged by LUMLEY; and appeared at HM, London, in 1858, in the same role, becoming an immediate favourite with audiences, and making London her home. Apart from engagements in Paris (1863) and USA (1876), she sang only in England. Her voice has been described as a mezzo-sop. with an extended register, permitting her to sing roles as diverse as Fidès (PROPHÈTE) and Countess ALMAVIVA. MÉDÉE was revived for her with great success. PS

Tinsley, Pauline, b. Wigan, 27 Mar 1928. English soprano. Studied Manchester and London (Guildhall School of Music, National O. School). Sang with EOG chorus and BBC Northern Singers. Solo opera debut 1961, St Pancras (now Camden) Fest. (ROSSINI's DESDEMONA), followed by Amalia (MASNADIERI) and Elvira (ERNANI) in successive years. Leading roles with WNO from 1962 in NABUCCO, MACBETH, AIDA, TURANDOT, LOHENGRIN, etc. SW O. from 1963, first as GILDA, then a variety of dramatic sop. roles incl. LEONORA (FORZA DEL DESTINO), LEONORE, Elisabetta (MARIA STUARDA). CG debut 1965 as the Overseer (ELEKTRA); Hamburg from 1968 (Abigaille in *Nabucco*); in USA at Santa Fe Fest. 1969 (ANNA BOLENA), and NY City O. 1971 as Elisabetta (*Maria Stuarda*). Her voice has a brightness of tone and steadiness of line ideal for It. roles, and her perfs convey a wealth of dramatic character. NG

Tippett, Michael (Kemp), b. London, 2 Jan 1905. English composer. Studied comp. at the RCM under Charles Wood and Reginald Owen Morris; cond. with Adrian Boult and Malcolm Sargent. Dir. of Music, Morley College, London, 1940–51. After building a major reputation in concert works, his first opera, MIDSUMMER MARRIAGE, confirmed his richness of musical and theatrical imagination in a style of romantically expressive polyphony. He has continued to wr. his own libs in subsequent operas, KING PRIAM and KNOT GARDEN. His fourth opera, provisionally entitled *The Ice Break*, is planned for prod. at CG 1976–7. Awarded CBE 1959; knighted 1966. NG
See Tippett, *Moving into Aquarius* (Essays) (London 1959); Schafer, *British Composers in Interview* (London 1963); Kemp (ed.), *Michael Tippett: A Symposium on his 60th Birthday* (London 1965)

Tofts, Catherine, b. ?; d. Venice, 1756. English soprano, the first Eng. singer in It. opera. Sang in Thomas Clayton's *Arsinoe* (1705), and *Rosamund* (1707); BONONCINI's *Camilla* (1706), and PEPUSCH's *pasticcio*, *Thomyris* (1707). M. to Joseph Smith, Eng. Consul at Venice, where she died insane. LO

Tolstoy, Lev Nikolayevich, b. Yasnaya Polyana, 9 Sept 1828; d. Astapovo, 20 Nov 1910. Russian writer. As a genre, opera was directly opposed to his ideas that one art should be fully capable of expression without combination with another. But several operas have been based on his works, particularly his two epic novels: *War and Peace*, 1863–9 (Aël, *Eingeäschertes Moskau*, 1914; WAR AND PEACE); *Anna Karenina*, 1873–7 (Salvatore Sassano, 1905; E. Granelli, 1912; E. Malherbe, 1914; HUBAY, 1923; Igino Robbiani, 1924; Stanislav Goldbach, 1930; JANÁČEK, unfinished, wr. 1907). Stories and novels upon which operas are based incl.: *What Men Live By*, 1881 (MARTINŮ, 1953); *The Tale of Ivan the Jester and his Two Brothers*, 1888 (Rudolf Reti, *Iwan und die Trommel*, 1933; OSTRČIL, *Johnny's Kingdom*, 1934); *Resurrection*, 1899 (ALFANO, 1904; CIKKER, 1962); *The Living Corpse*, 1902 (Janáček, *The Living Dead*, unfinished, wr. 1916); *What For?*, 1906 (Nikolay Mikhaylovich Strelnikov, *The Fugitive*, 1933). GN

Tomasi, Henri, b. Marseille, 17 Aug 1901; d. Avignon, 13 Jan 1971. French composer. Cond. of the Casino, Vichy and the O., Monte Carlo, 1946–50. His operas incl. ATLANTIDE, *Miguel Mañara* (Munich 1956), *Sampiero Corso* (Bordeaux 1956), *Le Triomphe de Jeanne* (Rouen 1956), *Princesse Pauline* (Paris 1962), *L'Élixir du Révérend Père Gaucher* (Toulouse 1964), and *Le Silence de la Mer*, taken from the book by Vercors (Toulouse 1964). EF

Tom Jones, *comédie en prose mêlée d'ariettes*, 3 acts, PHILIDOR, lib. Antoine Poinsinet. Paris,

TI, 27 Feb 1765. An early example of the novel-based opera, taken from Henry Fielding's *Tom Jones, a Foundling* (1749). Philidor's best opera. Another *Tom Jones* opera by Thomas Linley, 1785. LO

Tonadilla escénica, a form of popular musical theatre that grew up in Spain during the temporary eclipse of the ZARZUELA *c.* 1750–*c.* 1830. It developed when two or more characters sang *tonadillas* (songs) in dialogue, with stage action and orch. accompaniment. Comps quick to take up the form were MISÓN, Antonio Guerrero, Pablo Esteve, Ventura Galván, and José Palomino. Hundreds were comp., for they were short works enjoying equally short lives, and were mostly picaresque or satirical in style. Their use of the popular Sp. musical idiom was not without subsequent influence on BIZET and others who wanted to create Sp. atmosphere in their works. FGB

Tonio, bar., the clown in PAGLIACCI.

Tooley, John, b. Rochester, 1 June 1924. English administrator. Assistant to the General Administrator, Royal O. House, CG, 1955; Assistant General Administrator 1960; General Administrator 1970. EF

Torelli, Giacomo, b. Fano, ? 1 Sept 1608; d. Fano, 17 June 1678. Italian scenographer. After working with Giovanni Battista Aleotti at Parma went to Venice 1641, where he built the T. Novissimo, and mounted eight operas with unsurpassed brilliance; went to Paris 1645 to stage plays and operas for Cardinal Mazarin. He made improvements in the CLOUD MACHINE, and invented a system of quick-change scenery (flats running in grooves on the stage, controlled from below). LO

Giacomo Torelli's decor for Act II of a Paris production of *Venus Jalouse* (a French translation of *Venere Gelosa* by Francesco Sacrati, first performed Venice 1644)

Toronto. The main organization is the Canadian Opera Co. (COC), the first co. to present regular seasons of opera in the city despite many unsuccessful attempts dating back to the 1860s. The basis for the COC was an opera school set up 1946 at the Royal Cons., Toronto, with Arnold Walter as administrative dir., Nicholas Goldschmidt as mus. dir. and, in 1948, GEIGER-TOREL as stage dir. In 1953 Ernesto Barbini became mus. dir. Since 1969 the School has been a dept of the Faculty of Music, Univ. of Toronto, and has among its assets a fully equipped theatre and work rooms. A significant number of Canadian singers have been students there, incl. BONHOMME, BRAUN, GARRARD, LITTLE, MAURO, PELLEGRINI, STRATAS, SUKIS, H. THOMSON, VICKERS, and ZAROU. Each year the School mounts two fully staged operas with orch.

As an outgrowth of the O. School three perfs were mounted professionally in 1950 by the Royal Cons. O. Co. From this success evolved the O. Fest. Co. (1954) which in 1959 changed its name to the Canadian O. Co. with Geiger-Torel as Gen. Dir. The co. has a permanent administrative staff in Toronto where it presents six or seven operas each fall season. The full co. also gives four perfs in Ottawa and since 1958 a special touring co. has been sent with a fully staged opera (since 1968 with its own orch.) throughout Canada and to many places in the USA, travelling about 20,000 miles. In Toronto the orch. is the Toronto Symphony. The mus. and prod. staff are mainly drawn from Canada but with many guest singers, conds and dirs. Three works have been written for the co.: *The Luck of Ginger Coffey* (1967, Raymond Pannell), *Louis Riel* (1967, SOMERS), and *Heloise and Abelard* (1973, WILSON). By 1975 the COC had given 53 different operas.

As the centre for Eng. language broadcasting in Canada, Toronto is the source of many opera prods of the CBC. CM

Tosatti, Vieri, b. Rome, 2 Nov 1920. Italian composer. His five operas are: *Dionisio* (comp. 1946); *Il Sistema della Dolcezza*, based on *The System of Doctor Tarr and Professor Fether* by POE (Bergamo 1950); *Partita a Pugni* (*Fist Fight* – a boxing opera), 1 act (Venice Fest. 1953); *Il Giudizio Universale* (1955); *L'Isola del Tesoro*, based on Robert Louis Stevenson's *Treasure Island* (Bologna 1958). LO

Tosca, opera, 3 acts, PUCCINI, lib. ILLICA and GIACOSA after SARDOU. Rome, T. Costanzi, 14 Jan 1900; London, CG, 12 July 1900; NY Met, 4 Feb 1901. Main chars: Tosca (sop.) Cavaradossi (ten.) Scarpia (bar.). Floria Tosca, a prima donna, pursued by Scarpia, chief of the

Roman police, unwittingly helps to destroy her lover, the painter Cavaradossi, a liberal patriot, having attempted to save his life by apparently yielding to Scarpia's wishes, then killing him. JB O★
See Kobbé

Toscanini, Arturo, b. Parma, 25 Mar 1867; d. NY, 16 Jan 1957. Italian conductor. A cellist; sensational debut at Rio de Janeiro conducting AIDA, from memory, replacing the Co.'s regular cond. at their request, 25 Jan 1886. Engagements at Turin and Milan (T. dal Verme) followed; principal cond., Sc., 1898–1902 (left after demonstration against him for refusing an encore); returned 1906–8 and 1921–9, leaving only after increasing friction between him and the Fascists. At NY Met 1908–15 with GATTI-CASAZZA. Premieres he cond. incl. BOHÈME, DEBORA E JAELE, FANCIULLA DEL WEST, TURANDOT. At Sc. he introduced WAGNER, SALOME, LOUISE, PELLÉAS ET MÉLISANDE. Gifted with a prodigious memory, his repertory was enormous. A perfectionist, he demanded, and got, the utmost from his singers and players. He was a martinet, but his ruthlessness was directed entirely toward the highest realizations of the comp.'s intentions. LO

Tosi, Adelaide, b. Milan, *c.* 1800; d. Naples, 27 Mar 1859. Italian soprano. Daughter of a Milanese lawyer; studied with Girolamo Crescentini at Milan Cons., debut 1821, Sc. in G. MAYR's *Fedra*. In the 1820s many works were comp. expressly for her incl. DONIZETTI's *Il Paria*, *L'Esule di Roma*, and *Castello di Kenilworth*, Mayr's *Demetrio*, MEYERBEER's *L'Esule di Granata* and CROCIATO IN EGITTO, MERCADANTE's *Ipermestra*, *I Normanni a Parigi* and *Il Conte d'Essex*, and BIANCA E FERNANDO. PS

Tote Stadt, Die (*The Dead City*), opera, 3 acts, KORNGOLD, lib. Paul Schott after Georges Rodenbach's novel *Bruges-la-Morte*. Hamburg, 4 Dec 1920; NY Met, 19 Nov 1921. Main chars: Marietta (sop.) Marie (sop.) Paul (ten.). Paul mourns his dead wife Marie. He sees her image in Marietta, a dancer, and dreams that Marie is restored to him; but Marietta proves unfaithful, and in his dream, he strangles her with her long golden hair. EF O

Toulouse, France. The capital of old Languedoc. An Académie de Musique founded 1724, but opera had been given there 1696 by Jacques and Pierre Gautier's Marseille troupe. Opera is given in the T. du Capitole, first built 1736; prods are often shared with Bordeaux or Marseille; recently T. has joined with Bordeaux in a more formal agreement to share resources and mount joint prods. Art. dir. Michel Plaçon. LO

Tourel, Jennie, b. Montreal, 26 June 1910; d. NY, 23 Nov 1973. French-Canadian mezzo-soprano of Russian parentage. Debut 1930 singing small parts at Chicago; sang at Paris OC 1933–40. NY Met debut 1937; sang there again 1943–7. A famous CARMEN, MIGNON, and CHARLOTTE, she also sang ROSINA, ADALGISA, Lisa and the Countess (QUEEN OF SPADES). Created Baba the Turk in RAKE'S PROGRESS; her final appearance, Chicago, 26 Oct 1973, as the Duchess of Krackenthorp (FILLE DU RÉGIMENT). EF

Touring companies. These have existed since the early days of opera, and MANELLI's troupe was possibly the first. Such cos were certainly in being in the early 18th c. The MINGOTTI brothers ran two; GLUCK was their cond. in the 1740s. Another It. co. touring Austria and S. Germany was the Locatelli. Germany had several itinerant cos of travelling actors, such as the Seyler, Kock, and Ackermann cos, which sometimes incl. *Singspiele* in their repertories. With the coming of the railways in the 19th c. cos multiplied. In Germany the Merelli co., in Britain the Phillips, MOODY-MANNERS, CARL ROSA, DENHOF, and others took opera to the provinces; in the USA the EMMA ABBOTT, ABORN, San Carlo, KELLOGG and several others transported opera westwards from the eastern seaboard. In Britain in the 20th c. the Carl Rosa was in competition with BEECHAM's co. and the BNOC; today Glyndebourne, SO, WNO, and ENO all periodically make sorties from their headquarters. The D'OYLY CARTE co. exists solely for GILBERT and SULLIVAN, and in the 1890s the singer A. NEUMANN assembled a group to tour Europe with WAGNER operas. More recently compromises have begun to be worked out, with nearby towns joining forces to share prods and expenses, as in the OPÉRA DU RHIN and the DEUTSCHE OPER AM RHEIN – an attempt at trimming the vast expenses of opera while avoiding the inherent weaknesses of the older types of touring cos. LO

Traetta, Tommaso (Michele Francesco Saverio), b. Bitonto, 30 Mar 1727; d. Venice, 6 Apr 1779. Italian composer. A pupil of Francesco Durante at Naples; successful operatic debut with *Farnace* (Naples 1751), thereafter receiving commissions from most of the leading It. cities. Settled in Parma 1759–65 as MdC; here he instituted a reform of It. opera along the lines of Fr. *tragédie lyrique*, using translations of texts that had served RAMEAU and LULLY, e.g.

Ippolito ed Aricia (Parma 1759), *I Tintaridi* (Parma 1760), *Armide* (Vienna 1761). His *Ifigenia in Tauride* (Vienna 1763) anticipates certain features of GLUCK's more famous setting. Of his 40-odd operas the greatest by general consent is *Antigona* (St Petersburg 1772) which combines the dramatic truth of Gluck with a native It. sweetness of melody. JB

Traubel, Helen, b. St Louis, 20 June 1899; d. Santa Monica, Cal., 28 July 1972. American soprano. Studied St Louis, began as a concert singer. Invited by W. DAMROSCH to sing the lead in his *The Man without a Country* (NY Met 1937). Leading WAGNER singer at the Met 1939–53, and when FLAGSTAD left (1941) her supremacy was unchallenged. Left Met 1953 over a disagreement with BING about her appearances in night clubs. Appeared in opera in Chicago, Philadelphia, San Francisco, Latin America, and Japan, but not in Europe. Apart from the MARSCHALLIN her repertory was confined almost entirely to Wagner. LO
See autobiography, *St Louis Woman* (New York 1959)

Traubmann, Sophie, b. NY, 12 May 1867; d. NY, 16 Aug 1951. American soprano. Studied NY and Paris (with VIARDOT and MARCHESI DE CASTRONE), and was coached in WAGNER parts by Cosima Wagner. Debut, NY Acad. of Music (VENUS); the first US Woglinde (RING). LO

travesti roles (It., from *travestire* 'to disguise'). Name given to parts involving dress of opposite sex, especially man's part played by a woman, e.g. CHERUBINO, LEONORA dressed as a boy in FIDELIO, Romeo in CAPULETI ED I MONTECCHI, and OCTAVIAN. LO

Traviata, La (*The Lady Gone Astray*), opera, 3 acts, VERDI, lib. PIAVE after Alexandre DUMAS *fils*. Venice, T. La Fenice, 6 Mar 1853; revival in definitive form Venice, T. Gallo, 6 May 1854; London, HM, 24 May 1856; NY, Acad. of Music, 3 Dec 1858. Main chars: Violetta (sop.) Alfredo (ten.) Germont (bar.). Violetta, a *demimondaine*, renounces her life of pleasure for the sake of Alfredo; but is persuaded by his father to give him up for his own and his family's good. She returns to her former protector, with whom Alfredo fights a duel and is forced to flee the country. He returns to find her dying of consumption. JB O★
See Kobbé

Trebelli [Gillebert], Zélia, b. Paris, 1838; d. Étretat, 18 Aug 1892. French mezzo-soprano. Debut 1859, Madrid (ROSINA); soon acknowledged as one of the most accomplished mezzo-sops of her day. HAUK called her voice one of the finest real contr. voices she had ever heard. Sang in the USA with Henry Abbey's co. Roles incl. CARMEN, which she was the first to sing at the NY Met (1884), and she enjoyed *travesti* parts such as Siebel (FAUST) and Federico (MIGNON). LO

Trecate, Luigi Ferrari *see* FERRARI-TRECATE, Luigi

Treigle, Norman, b. New Orleans, 6 Mar 1927; d. New Orleans, 16 Feb 1975. American bass-baritone. Studied Loyola Univ. Debut 1947, New Orleans O., as Lodovico (VERDI's OTELLO). NY City O. debut (where most of his career was spent) 1953 (COLLINE). Rapidly established himself as a fine singer-actor in roles such as four villains in CONTES D'HOFFMANN, MÉPHISTOPHÉLÈS, BORIS GODUNOV, ESCAMILLO, DON GIOVANNI, GIANNI SCHICCHI. Created several roles in operas by FLOYD. First appeared in Britain in a semi-staged perf. of MEFISTOFELE (1972) and made his only CG appearance in GOUNOD's FAUST (1974). AB

Trial, The *see* PROZESS

Trieste, Italy. Main opera house is T. Verdi, opened 1801 as T. Nuovo; renamed T. Grande 1819; taken over by the city and renamed T. Comunale 1861. Closed during World War I, but opened 1917 with singers from Vienna Volks O. and in 1918 with a visit from Zagreb opera; reopened 1919 with its own co. Renamed T. Comunale Giuseppe Verdi 1931. Since World War II under *Sovrintendenti* Giuseppe Antonielli (1936–45, 1951–66), and ZAFRED (1966–8) its fortunes have prospered. LO

Tristan und Isolde. Act I of the 1962 production by Wieland WAGNER, Bayreuth, with WINDGASSEN as Tristan, Birgit NILSSON as ISOLDE, WÄCHTER as KURWENAL. Its stark simplicity is in the strongest contrast to the elaboration of the stage set of WAGNER's time illustrated in the colour plate on page 154.

Tristan und Isolde, music drama, 3 acts, WAGNER, lib. comp. Munich, 10 June 1865; London, DL, 20 June 1882; NY, 1 Dec 1886. Main chars: Tristan (ten.) Isolde (sop.) King Mark (bass) Kurwenal (bar.) Brangäne (mezzo-sop.) Melot (ten.). Tristan, bringing home the Irish queen Isolde to be the bride of King Mark of Cornwall, drinks with her what both believe to be poison, but is in fact a love potion. Later they are discovered in a midnight rendezvous by King Mark. Tristan flees wounded to France, where Isolde finds him dying, and herself dies by his side. Wagner's greatest love drama. JB O
See Kobbé

Trittico, Il *see* GIANNI SCHICCHI, SUOR ANGELICA, TABARRO

Troilus and Cressida, opera, 3 acts, WALTON, lib. Christopher Hassall, derived from a poem by Geoffrey Chaucer. London, CG, 3 Dec 1954; San Francisco, 7 Oct 1955. Main chars: Cressida (sop.) Troilus (ten.) Pandarus (ten.) Diomede (bar.). Walton's predominantly lyrical score tells the classical story in suitably impassioned terms, with much subtle char. music in support. The work has not perhaps had the success that is undoubtedly its due. AB

Trouble in Tahiti, opera, 1 act, BERNSTEIN, lib. comp. Waltham, Mass., 12 June 1952. A domestic comedy of two bickering Americans in suburbia. They make up their rather pointless quarrel in the evening by seeing the film, *Trouble in Tahiti*. LO O

Troutbeck, John, b. Blencowe, Cumberland, 12 Nov 1832; d. Westminster, 11 Oct 1899. English clergyman (precentor, Manchester, 1865–9, then minor canon at Westminster) and translator. Tr. GLUCK's two IPHIGÉNIES; ALCESTE; ORPHÉE ET EURYDICE; WIDERSPENSTIGEN ZÄHMUNG; ENTFÜHRUNG, AUS DEM SERAIL; FLIEGENDE HOLLÄNDER, and C. WEBER's *Preziosa* (1821). LO

Trovatore, Il (*The Troubadour*), opera, 4 acts, VERDI, lib. CAMMARANO after García Gutiérrez. Rome, T. Apollo, 19 Jan 1853; NY, Acad. of Music, 2 May 1855; London, CG, 10 May 1855. Main chars: Leonora (sop.) Azucena (mezzo-sop.) Manrico (ten.) Conte di Luna (bar.) Ferrando (bass). The story concerns the rivalry of two brothers for Leonora; and Azucena's conflict between the duty to avenge her mother and love for a son not her own. Verdi's most popular opera during his lifetime. JB O
See Kobbé

Troyanos, Tatiana, b. NY. American mezzo-soprano of Greek parentage. Studied NY Juilliard School, joined NY CC O. 1963–5. To Europe 1965, and resident principal with Hamburg Staats O. 1965–8; debut there as Preziosilla (FORZA DEL DESTINO). Major success at Aix Fest. 1966, as Composer (ARIADNE AUF NAXOS), thereafter debuts at Vienna Staats O. 1967; NY Met 1967 as Baba (RAKE'S PROGRESS); CG 1968 (OCTAVIAN). Created leading role of Sister Jeanne (DEVILS OF LOUDUN); a popular CARMEN since she first sang this with Bavarian Staats O., Munich, 1969. Her versatility of style ranges from E. di CAVALIERI and PURCELL to BARTÓK and BRITTEN, and her singing is rich in both quality and character. NG

Troyens, Les (*The Trojans*), opera, two parts (*La Prise de Troie* and *Les Troyens à Carthage*), prologue and five acts, BERLIOZ, lib. comp. after VIRGIL's *Aeneid*. Paris, TL, 4 Nov 1863 (part 2 only); Karlsruhe, 6 Dec 1890 (part 1 in Ger.); Paris, O., 10 June 1921 (both parts, reduced); Boston, 27 Mar 1955; London, CG, 8 June 1957 (complete perf. in Eng.). Main chars: Cassandre (sop.) Chorèbe (bar.) Hécube (mezzo-sop.) Priam (bass) Didon (mezzo-sop.) Enée (ten.) Narbal (bass) Ascagne (mezzo-sop.). Enée (Aeneas) escapes from the sack of Troy with his family, is welcomed at Carthage by Didon (Dido) who falls in love with him and kills herself when he leaves her to found a new empire in Italy. Berlioz's operatic masterpiece. JB O
See Kobbé

Tsar and Carpenter *see* ZAR UND ZIMMERMANN

Tsar Saltan *see* TALE OF TSAR SALTAN

Tsar's Bride, The (*Tsarskaya nevesta*), opera, 4 acts, RIMSKY-KORSAKOV, lib. composer and I. F. Tyumenev, after Lev Aleksandrovich Mey. Moscow, Solodovnikov T., 3 Nov 1899; San Francisco, Columbia T., 9 Jan 1922; London, Lyceum T., 19 May 1931. Main chars: Marfa (sop.) Grigory Gryaznoy (bar.) Ivan Lykov (ten.) Lyubasha (mezzo-sop.). Gryaznoy and Lykov are both in love with Marfa, and Gryaznoy decides to win her with a love potion. His mistress, Lyubasha, overhears and substitutes a poison. Marfa is chosen by Ivan the Terrible as his bride. She drinks the poison. The Tsar executes Lykov (who, under torture, has confessed to poisoning Marfa); Marfa goes mad, and Gryaznoy kills Lyubasha. Although *The Tsar's Bride* does not reach the heights of Rimsky-Korsakov's previous full-length opera

SADKO, Marfa's aria is one of his finest pieces of writing. GN ○★

Tucker, Richard [Reuben Ticker], b. Brooklyn, NY, 28 Aug 1913; d. Kalamazoo, Mich., 8 Jan 1975. American tenor. Father was a Romanian Jew; he studied singing, with ALTHOUSE, intending to be a Cantor in the Synagogue, but m. to PEERCE's sister (1936) prompted a desire to be an opera singer. Debut 1945, NY Met (GIOCONDA), stayed with the Met for 30 years, singing wide variety of roles especially in It. and Fr. repertoire. Made several visits to Europe, singing in Verona 1947 (in *La Gioconda* with CALLAS), Rome, Sc., and CG. Recorded RADAMES under TOSCANINI. LO

Turandot, opera (unfinished), 3 acts, PUCCINI, lib. Renato Simoni and ADAMI after GOZZI. Milan, Sc., 25 Apr 1926 under TOSCANINI. Later perfs with last act completed from the comp.'s sketches by ALFANO. NY Met, 16 Nov 1926; London, CG, 7 June 1927. Main chars: Turandot (sop.) Calaf (ten.) Liù (sop.) Timur (bass) Ping (bass) Pang (bar.) Pong (ten.). Prince Calaf wins the hand of the Princess Turandot by answering her three riddles; failure to solve them would have meant his death. In turn he challenges her to find out his name before next day. She tortures his father's slave girl Liù who kills herself rather than be forced to reveal Calaf's secret. Puccini's last opera. JB ○
See Kobbé

Turco in Italia, Il (*The Turk in Italy*), *opera buffa*, 2 acts, ROSSINI, lib. ROMANI. Milan, Sc., 14 Aug 1814; London, HM, 19 May 1821; NY, 14 Mar 1826. Main chars: Prosdocimo (bar.) Fiorilla (sop.) Zaida (mezzo-sop.) Don Narciso (ten.) Albazar (ten.) Don Geronio (buffo bass) Seoim (buffo bass). A Pirandellian plot in which the poet Prosdocimo manipulates his characters *in propria persona*. These incl. an elderly cuckold, his flighty wife, her young admirer and a Turk with whom she is flirting. Revived frequently since the 1950s. JB

Turgeon, Bernard, b. Edmonton, 20 Oct 1932. Canadian baritone. Appeared with COC, Toronto; joined SW 1959; sang at Glyndebourne 1960. US debut 1966, Central City, Col. Has made three tours of USSR; sang RIGOLETTO with the Bolshoy Co. 1972. Had spectacular success in creating the title role of SOMERS's *Louis Riel* with the COC, 1967, a role he has repeated on TV and in all subsequent stage prods. In charge of vocal and operatic training at the Univ. of Alberta, Edmonton, 1969–75. CM

Turiddu, ten., the hero of CAVALLERIA RUSTICANA

Turin [Torino]. Capital of Piedmont before the unification of Italy (1870). Opera was given in 17th c. in the T. of the Royal Palace. The T. Regio, designed by Benedetto Alfieri, was built 1741; burned down 1936. Premieres there incl. MANON LESCAUT, BOHÈME, FRANCESCA DA RIMINI, and RISURREZIONE. Its successor, the new T. Regio, was opened 10 Apr 1973 with VÊPRES SICILIENNES. The T. Carignano, the scene of TOSCANINI's first cond. in Italy, was opened 1853. LO

Turina, Joaquín, b. Seville, 9 Dec 1882; d. Madrid, 14 Jan 1949. Spanish composer. Though chiefly interesting for his orch. and piano music, his works incl. the operas *Margot* (1914), *La Adúltera Penitente* (1917), and *Jardín de Oriente* (1923). Also well known as a teacher and pianist. FGB

Turner, Dame Eva, b. Oldham, 10 Mar 1892. English soprano. Studied RAM; joined Carl Rosa as chorus member 1916, before graduating to minor roles. Remained with that co. until 1924, when TOSCANINI engaged her as Freia (RHEINGOLD) at Sc. CG debut 1920 with Carl Rosa; also sang there with BNOC before appearing in the international seasons, beginning in 1928 in three of her outstanding roles – TURANDOT, AIDA, and Santuzza (CAVALLERIA RUSTICANA). Appeared there in several seasons until 1948. Also sang at Chicago and Buenos Aires. Her voice was a true dramatic sop.; heard to advantage in VERDI, WAGNER and, above all, as Turandot of which she was the greatest exponent of her day. AB

Turn of the Screw, The, opera, prologue and 2 acts, BRITTEN, lib. Myfanwy Piper, derived from a novel by JAMES. Venice, 14 Sept 1954; London, SW (by EOG), 6 Oct 1954; NY College of Music, 19 Mar 1958. Main chars: The Governess (sop.) Miles (boy sop.) Flora (sop.) Quint (ten.) Miss Jessel (sop.) Mrs Grose (sop.). The Governess, sent to look after two children in an isolated manor, comes to realize that they are infected by two evil spirits. The score is dramatically gripping. The 16 scenes are all based on a theme that 'turns' through 15 variations during the course of the action and interludes. Although the opera has never become generally popular, its musical tautness has been appreciated at every revival. AB ○

Turp, André, b. Montreal, 21 Dec 1925. Canadian tenor. After singing in Canada and the USA, engaged at CG 1960 (debut as

EDGARDO); first heard at the Paris O. 1962, in same role. Has sung at Glyndebourne, Rio de Janeiro, Lisbon, Barcelona, and Marseille. A lyric ten. with a fine stage presence, he has a repertory incl. Macduff (MACBETH), ALFREDO, DON CARLOS, TURIDDU, RODOLFO, PINKERTON, CAVARADOSSI, and JENÍK, but is most at home in the Fr. repertory: Pylade (IPHIGÉNIE EN TAURIDE), DES GRIEUX (MANON), WERTHER, and Don JOSÉ. EF

Twilight (*Daisi*), opera, 3 acts, PALIASHVILI, lib. V. Guniya. Tbilisi, 19 Dec 1923. Main chars: Maro (sop.) Nano (mezzo-sop.) Malkhaz (ten.) Kiazo (bar.) Tsangala (bass). Maro is betrothed to a soldier, Kiazo. Her real love, Malkhaz, returns from abroad, and Tsangala tells Kiazo of their affection. Kiazo swears vengeance, but is called away to defend his country against the enemy. Jealousy gets the better of him: he returns to his village, is spurned by Maro, and kills Malkhaz. The troops march off to war. One of the earliest and most dramatic of Georgian lyric operas. GN

Two Hundred Thousand Talers *see* ZWEIHUNDERTTAUSEND TALER

Two Widows, The (*Dvě vdovy*), opera, 2 acts, SMETANA, lib. Emanuel Züngel after Félicien Mallefille's *Les Deux Veuves*, 1859. Prague, PT, 27 Mar 1874 (spoken dialogue); Prague, PT, 15 Mar 1878 (enlarged cast, through-comp.); NY, Sokol Hall, 23 Oct 1949; London, Guildhall School of Music and Drama, 17 June 1963. Main chars: Karolina (sop.) Anežka (sop.) Ladislav Podhajský (ten.) Mumlal (bass). Ladislav manages to meet his earlier love, Anežka, now a widow, by having himself arrested for poaching by Mumlal, the gamekeeper on the estate of Anežka's cousin Karolina. Though Anežka is at first unwilling to receive his attentions, Karolina spurs her on by flirting with him and the couple are finally united. This 'conversation piece' is Smetana's lightest opera with set numbers and a polka as a principal theme. JT O *See* Large, *Smetana* (London 1970)

U

Uhde, Hermann, b. Bremen, 20 July 1914; d. Copenhagen, 24 Oct 1965. German baritone. Studied Bremen; debut there as Titurel (PARSIFAL) 1936. After an engagement at Freiburg, he went to Munich, Hanover and Hamburg before returning to Munich, where he was principal bar. from 1951 until his death. Bayreuth 1951–7, 1960, where he was a notable Dutchman (FLIEGENDE HOLLÄNDER), TELRAMUND and KLINGSOR. CG debut with Munich co. as Mandryka (ARABELLA) 1953; sang there 1954–60, notably as the four villains in CONTES D' HOFFMANN and as GUNTHER. NY Met debut as Telramund 1955; appeared there until 1961, notably as WOZZECK, AMFORTAS and PIZARRO. AB

Ukraine. The Ukraine has always been noted for its fine singers. GLINKA went there in 1838 to recruit choir members for the Imperial Chapel in St Petersburg, choosing among others the bass-bar. Semyon Gulak-Artemovsky (1813–73), comp. of the first distinctively Ukrainian opera, *A Cossack Beyond the Danube* (1863); the most significant Ukrainian comp. was Nikolay Lysenko (1842–1912), known particularly for *Taras Bulba* (1924) and other GOGOL operas. During the Soviet period, notable operas have included *The Young Guard* (1947) by Yuly Meytus (b. 1903) and *'Arsenal'* (1960) by Georgy Mayboroda (b. 1913). The principal musical centres are Kharkov, Kiev (the capital) and Odessa. At Kharkov the Lysenko Opera and Ballet T. was founded in 1874, at Kiev the Shevchenko Academic Opera and Ballet T. in 1867. At Odessa the Opera and Ballet T. was opened as early as 1809; twice burned down (1873, 1925), it was finally rebuilt in 1926. The city also has the Ukrainian October Revolution Music and Drama T., and the Musical Comedy T. GN

Ulisse, opera, 2 acts, prologue and epilogue, DALLAPICCOLA, lib. composer after HOMER. Berlin, 29 Sept 1968; London, BBC, 20 Sept 1969; Sc., Milan, 13 Jan 1970. Main chars: Ulisse (bar.) Nausicaa (sop.) Circe/Melanto (contr.) Demodoco/Tiresio (ten.) Calypso/Penelope (sop.) Eumete (ten.) Telemaco (counter-ten./mezzo-sop.). The action follows Homer's account of Ulysses' return to Ithaca after the Trojan war. EF

Ulrica, mezzo-sop., the fortune teller in BALLO IN MASCHERA

Umlauf[f], Ignaz, b. Vienna, 1746; d. Vienna, 8 June 1796. Austrian composer. Worked at Vienna Hof T. first as violist, 1772, then, 1778, as MdC of *Singspiel* and, 1789, deputy MdC to SALIERI. His *Bergknappen* was chosen to inaugurate Franz Josef II's *Nationalsingspiel*, 17 Feb 1778 – the first Ger. *Singspiel* prod. at the Vienna BT. LO

Undine 1. Opera, 3 acts, HOFFMANN, lib. composer after Friedrich la Motte Fouqué's story, 1811. Berlin, 3 Aug 1816. This fairy tale of the union of a waternymph with a mortal, with beautiful and evocative decor by SCHINKEL, was one of the most important pre-C. WEBER romantic operas. 2. Opera, 4 acts, LORTZING, lib. comp. after la Motte Fouqué. Magdeburg, 21 Apr 1845; NY, Niblo's Garden, 9 Oct 1856. LO

Unger, Caroline, b. Vienna, 28 Oct 1803; d. nr Florence, 23 Mar 1877. Austro-Hungarian soprano. Studied with Aloysia Lange, MOZART's sister-in-law, Johann Michael Vogl and, in Italy, with Domenico Ronconi. Debut Vienna as DORABELLA 1821; 7 May 1824 sang the contr. part in the first perf. of BEETHOVEN's 9th Symphony, and it was she who turned the deaf composer around to acknowledge the applause. Many operas were written for her incl. DONIZETTI's *Parisina*, *Belisario*, and *Maria de Rudenz*; she was the first Isoletta in STRANIERA, 1829. Enjoyed a success at the TI, Paris, 1833. Retired after m. François Sabatier. ROSSINI described her as having 'the ardour of the south, the energy of the north, brazen lungs, a silver voice and a golden talent'. PS

United States of America. There are more than 100 opera cos of professional standing active at present in the USA, from Seattle to Miami, Sante Fe to Boston. The number of college and university groups is larger, their inventive ideas tempered by lean budgets and varying competencies. More than 20 communities sponsor annual seasons in which the success of standard works offsets the risk of the unusual. Thus DOKTOR FAUST, VILLAGE ROMEO AND JULIET, DEATH IN VENICE and DUKE BLUEBEARD'S CASTLE are heard alongside a fair quantity of American works by such composers as D. MOORE, FLOYD, Jack Beeson, BARBER and V. THOMSON. The former Fr. city of New Orleans was hearing opera by GRÉTRY, BOÏELDIEU, MÉHUL, and PAISIELLO at the time of the Louisiana Purchase, 1803. The Northeast, then heartland of America, heard its first grand opera when GARCÍA I, ROSSINI's original ALMAVIVA, brought BARBIERE DI SIVIGLIA to NY, with MALIBRAN as ROSINA. Rossini's OTELLO, TANCREDI and CENERENTOLA were sung, and then DON GIOVANNI, at the instigation of da PONTE, a US citizen since 1805 and teaching It. at Columbia College. A Fr. troupe under Montresor toured northern cities 1827–33. Perfs on a large scale came in 1849 with MARETZEK and his Havana Co. presenting works by BELLINI, DONIZETTI and the early VERDI. A co. managed by the Strakosch brothers followed in 1857 presenting the great voices of SONTAG, ALBONI, MARIO, and Giulia GRISI. Opera houses were built, scenery improved, and adequate orchs assembled for the major cities. Then came MAPLESON 1878–86 with the later Verdi, with CARMEN as a new type of heroine; his singers incl. Etelka Gerster, HAUK, and PATTI. The American Opera Co., 1886–9, cond. Theodore Thomas, presented opera in Eng. sung by US singers (GLUCK's ORFEO, MARTHA, ZAUBERFLÖTE, LOHENGRIN, LAKMÉ, etc.). By this time the NY Met, built 1883, had replaced the Acad. of Music and from 1886 presented an international repertory (*see under* NEW YORK). Subsequent managers incl. W. DAMROSCH, GATTI-CASAZZA, JOHNSON, and BING. In 1906–10 HAMMERSTEIN I at the Manhattan OH adjusted the balance toward the Fr., with a galaxy of stars incl. TETRAZZINI and GARDEN.

As to other cities, Boston had a brief era with its own Co., 1908–17; Chicago under CAMPANINI and POLACCO rivalled NY from 1910 until the fiscal debacle of 1933. For BLOOMINGTON, Ind., DALLAS, HOUSTON, PHILADELPHIA, SAN FRANCISCO, SEATTLE, SANTA FE *see* separate entries. There are, too, spring tours by NY Met and NY CC which uphold standards few resident forces can approach in inflationary times.

Operas on American subjects began with RIP VAN WINKLE, 1855, followed by a spate of works that proved ephemeral, such as W. Damrosch's patently Wagnerian *Scarlet Letter*, 1896. There was a period of dedication to Indian themes; of the 84 operas, mostly written between 1900 and 1918, Ethelbert Nevin's *Poia* (Berlin 1910), HERBERT's *Natoma* (1911) and esp. SHANEWIS attracted some attention. MERRY MOUNT, MOTHER OF US ALL and CRUCIBLE all dealt with the American past; CRADLE WILL ROCK, REGINA and VISITATION depicted current social and racial conflicts, as did PORGY AND BESS. Colloquial Americana is at the heart of JUMPING FROG OF CALAVERAS COUNTY, DEVIL AND DANIEL WEBSTER, EMPEROR JONES and TROUBLE IN TAHITI. None of these is the stuff of 'grand opera', but some such as SUSANNAH and BALLAD OF BABY DOE have sustained themselves in the repertory, while *The Crucible* and GOOD SOLDIER SCHWEIK have proved their worth in Europe. Many comps have turned from the American subject to other themes for their larger works, as for example KING'S HENCHMAN, PETER IBBETSON or VANESSA. Floyd, after the 'folksy' *Susannah*, turned to *Wuthering Heights* for his next opera, 1959. D. Moore turned from *Ballad of Baby Doe* to JAMES in *The Wings of the Dove*, 1961, but his last work, *Carry Nation*, 1966, again celebrated an American heroine.

On the whole, opera in the USA is

flourishing. A survey of the performing arts in the USA by the Ford Foundation, 1974, states: 'From its elitist heights, the grand opera has come into fairly broad popularity'. Capacity audiences are the rule; society continues to value opera, but with less snobbery than in the days of the Golden Horseshoe. Entire prods have been financed by individual and corporate donors; the National Foundation for the Arts, a government agency, now contributes, liberally by previous standards, not sufficiently generous by European standards. EJ
See Johnson, *Operas on American Subjects* (New York 1964); Chase, *America's Music* (New York 1955, 1966)

Urban, Joseph, b. Vienna, 26 May 1872; d. New York, 10(?) July 1933. Austrian, later American, scenographer, a member of the art group known as the Vienna Secession. After working with MAHLER and ROLLER at Vienna Opera and designing for other Continental houses, e.g. RING at Budapest, went to Boston Opera as art. dir. and designer in 1911. From there he moved to NY, designing the 1915 *Ziegfeld Follies*; shortly afterward, in 1917, GATTI-CASAZZA commissioned FAUST from him at the Met, followed by NORMA, PARSIFAL (sets which did duty for many years), VERDI'S OTELLO and others. Also designed for the Broadway musicals of J. KERN, ROMBERG, GERSHWIN, and RODGERS. LO

Urlus, Jacques, b. Hergenrath, nr Aachen, 6 Jan 1867; d. Noordwijk, 6 June 1935. Dutch tenor. Debut PAGLIACCI, 1894, in Amsterdam, where he stayed until 1900. Engagements in Germany followed, at Leipzig and Bayreuth. He was also heard in London, NY Met (1912–17) and Boston. A noted WAGNER singer. LO

Ursuleac, Viorica, b. Cernăuţi (now Chernovtsy), 26 Mar 1899. Romanian soprano. Studied with Lilli LEHMANN; debut Frankfurt (1924), where she met C. KRAUSS whom she later m. Principal sop. Staats O. at Vienna, Berlin, and the Bavarian, Munich, with highly successful guest appearances at Sc. and CG. Sang for many years at Salzburg Fest. Considered by R. STRAUSS the ideal sop. for his operas, she created the roles of ARABELLA, Maria in FRIEDENSTAG and the Countess in CAPRICCIO. Her lyric-dramatic voice was also much admired in MOZART and WAGNER. FGB

Uruguay *see* LATIN AMERICA

Usandizaga, José María, b. San Sebastián, 31 Mar 1887; d. Yanthi, 5 Oct 1915. Spanish composer. After studying in Paris he returned home to champion his native Basque music. More important than his orchestral, choral, chamber and piano works are the three operas *Mendy-Mendiyan* (Bilbao 1910), *Las Golondrinas* (*The Swallows*) with a story of love and jealousy among circus folk (Madrid 1914), and *La Llama* (*The Flame*), which was prod. Madrid 1915. FGD

USSR *see* RUSSIA AND THE SOVIET UNION

Ustinov, Peter, b. London, 16 Apr 1921. British author, actor, producer and designer. His operatic prods incl. a triple bill of HEURE ESPAGNOLE, ERWARTUNG and GIANNI SCHICCHI at CG (1962), ZAUBERFLÖTE at Hamburg (1968), DON GIOVANNI, for which he also designed the sets, at Edinburgh (1973), and MASSENET'S *Don Quichotte* at the Paris O. (1974). EF

V

Vaccai, Nicola, b. Tolentino, 15 Mar 1790; d. Pesaro, 5 Aug 1848. Italian composer and singing teacher. Originally intended for the law, he studied music in Rome and with PAISIELLO in Naples, where he prod. his first opera, *I Solitari di Scozia* (1815). His operas enjoyed a brief vogue in N. Italy in the mid-1820s, but he was soon eclipsed by BELLINI; he spent 1830–3 mostly in London as a highly successful singing teacher, returning to Italy on the death of his father. On the staff of the Milan Cons. 1836–43, becoming its dir. 1838. Of his 17 operas, the most famous is *Giulietta e Romeo* (Milan 1825), whose penultimate scene was often interpolated into CAPULETI ED I MONTECCHI. Here and in *Zadig ed Astartea* he anticipates Bellini in giving a subtly Romantic inflection to the prevailing Rossinian style. *Marco Visconti* (Turin 1838) shows an attempt to come to grips with the dramatic style of DONIZETTI; *Virginia* (Rome 1845) is a *Risorgimento* style opera recalling SPONTINI rather than VERDI. His *Metodo pratico del canto italiano* (pub. in 1833) sheds a valuable light on performance practice of the day. JB

Vagabond King, operetta, FRIML, book and lyrics Brian Hooker and W. H. Post, based on the novel *If I Were King* by Justin Huntly McCarthy. NY, Casino T., 21 Sept 1925; London, Winter Garden T., 19 Apr 1927. EJ O★
See Lubbock

Valentin, bar., Marguerite's brother in FAUST

Vallin, Ninon [Eugénie Vallin-Pardo], b. Montalieu-Vercien, Isère, 9 Sept 1886; d. Lyon, 22 Nov 1961. French soprano. Studied Lyon and Paris; debut, 1912, as MICAËLA. During World War I was at Buenos Aires, 1914–17, then returned to Paris, OC. One of best-known Fr. singers between the wars, she created several roles at the OC, and was heard at Sc., NY, Washington and Moscow. She was excellent in Fr. roles such as LOUISE, MANON, and CHARLOTTE. LO

Valverde, Joaquín, b. Badajoz, 27 Feb 1846; d. Madrid, 17 Mar 1910. Spanish composer. Of his more than 30 *zarzuelas* the most popular are *La Gran Vía* (with CHUECA), *Salón Eslava* and *La Boda de Serafin*. FGB

Valverde, Sanjuán, b. Madrid, 2 Jan 1875; d. Mexico, 4 Nov 1918. Spanish composer (son of the above). His output of some 250 *zarzuelas*, many in collaboration with other comps, is prodigious even in a field where it is customary to be prolific. He began comp. at 15 with *Con las de Caín*. FGB

Vampyr, Der (*The Vampire*), opera, 2 acts, MARSCHNER, lib. Wilhelm August Wohlbrück based on a Fr. melodrama by Charles Nodier, possibly based on BYRON. Leipzig, 29 Mar 1828; London, Lyceum T., 25 Aug 1829. The Scottish Lord Ruthven, a vampire, his soul sold to Satan, obtains respite by sacrificing pure maidens, and is finally destroyed by lightning. LO

Van Allan, Richard, b. Chipston, Nottinghamshire, 28 May 1935. Debut 1964 in Glyndebourne chorus; won John Christie Award for 1966–7. Has sung at Wexford, Nice, Paris O., Bordeaux and appears with WNO, the ENO at the Coliseum, and CG, where he was first heard in 1971 as the Mandarin (TURANDOT). A very versatile singer and a fine actor, he has a large repertory incl. OSMIN, FIGARO (NOZZE DI FIGARO), LEPORELLO, DON GIOVANNI, Don ALFONSO, Zaccaria (NABUCCO), Banco (MACBETH), PHILIPPE and Grand Inquisitor (DON CARLOS), Ramfis and the King (AIDA) and Pistol (FALSTAFF). Also sings PIZARRO, COLLINE, and created Colonel Jowler in MAW's *Rising of the Moon* (Glyndebourne 1970). EF

Vancouver. Opera was first seen in Vancouver in 1891 (LOHENGRIN, with JUCH), but regular prods date only from 1958 with the establishment of the Vancouver Fest. under Nicholas Goldschmidt. Over the next decade the Fest. presented a major work each summer; in 1958 the North American debuts of SUTHERLAND and RENNERT, and in 1961 the North American premiere of MIDSUMMER NIGHT'S DREAM.

In 1959 the new Queen Elizabeth T. was opened and the Vancouver O. Assn was set up with GUTTMAN as art. dir. Since 1960 it has prod. three or four operas each winter, mostly from standard repertoire and with some notable guest singers such as Sutherland, HORNE and RESNICK. In 1974 it formed the Canadian Artists' Co. of eight young singers, on salary, to form a permanent nucleus for major prods and to be the leading singers in chamber opera prods. The Assn also owns a large shop for scene construction which supplies sets for many other opera cos in North America.

In 1974 Guttman was succeeded as art. dir. by BONYNGE. CM

Vanessa, opera, 4 acts, BARBER, lib. MENOTTI. NY Met, 15 Jan 1958. Main chars: Vanessa (sop.) Anatol (ten.) Erika (mezzo-sop.) Baroness (mezzo-sop.) Doctor (bar.) Major-Domo (bass). In Scandinavia, 1905, Vanessa has been waiting 20 years for the return of her lover, who is dead. His son Anatol arrives and has an affair with Vanessa's niece Erika who at length rejects him. Finally Anatol goes off with Vanessa, leaving Erika as the woman waiting in vain. EJ

Varesi, Felice, b. Calais, 1813; d. Milan, 13 Mar 1889. Italian baritone. One of the leading It. bars of his day. Created title roles in MACBETH and RIGOLETTO, also GERMONT, when his singing was allegedly partly to blame for the fiasco of the first performance. He was the father of the sop. Elena Boccabadati. LO

Varnay, Astrid, b. Stockholm, 25 Apr 1918. American soprano. Debut 1941 at the NY Met as SIEGLINDE, substituting at short notice for Lotte LEHMANN. San Francisco debut 1946, CG 1948, she appeared at Bayreuth from 1951 to 1967, singing BRÜNNHILDE, ISOLDE, ORTRUD, GUTRUNE, SENTA and KUNDRY. Has also sung ELSA, ELISABETH, VENUS and EVA, LADY MACBETH, SALOME and ELEKTRA. An intensely dramatic singer, who immerses herself completely in her roles, she is particularly fine as Kostelnička (JENŮFA). EF

Varviso, Silvio, b. Zürich, 26 Feb 1924. Swiss conductor. Studied Zürich Cons.; cond. St Gallen, 1946–50; Basel Stadt T., 1950–9; San Francisco 1959–61, then at NY Met. Mus. dir. Stockholm 1965–72; in 1973 succeeded Vaclav Neumann at Stuttgart. Guest appearances at other opera houses incl. CG (conducting ARABELLA, 1973) and Berlin. LO

Vašek, ten., the son of Mícha in BARTERED BRIDE

Vasilenko, Sergey Nikiforovich, b. Moscow, 30 Mar 1872; d. Moscow, 11 Mar 1956. Russian composer. In collaboration with Mukhtar Ashrafi, he comp. the first important Uzbek opera, *Buran* (1939), which makes use of Uzbek folk music. He also comp. *Son of the Sun* (1929), *Christopher Columbus* (comp. 1933, unperf.), *The Great Canal* (1941) and *Suvorov* (1942). GN

vaudeville. French term used in opera to describe the kind of finale in which each char. in turn sings a verse followed by a general refrain. E.g. in ENTFÜHRUNG AUS DEM SERAIL and ROSSINI'S BARBIERE DI SIVIGLIA. JB

Vaughan, Elizabeth, b. Llanfyllin, Montgomeryshire, 12 Mar 1936. Welsh soprano. Debut 1960 with WNO at Cardiff as Abigaille (NABUCCO), repeating the role at SW. CG debut 1961 as Isotta (SCHWEIGSAME FRAU), and has appeared at Montreal, Vienna, Düsseldorf, Miami and in Australia. NY Met debut 1972 as Donna ELVIRA. Her repertory incl. NEDDA, Musetta (BOHÈME), CIO-CIO-SAN, LIÙ, Tytania (MIDSUMMER NIGHT'S DREAM), and Teresa (BENVENUTO CELLINI), as well as roles in RIGOLETTO, TRAVIATA, TROVATORE, BALLO IN MASCHERA, SIMONE BOCCANEGRA, and FALSTAFF (Alice). EF

Vaughan Williams, Ralph, b. Down Ampney, 12 Oct 1872; d. London, 26 Aug 1958. English composer. Studied with BRUCH and RAVEL. Much influenced by Eng. folksongs, as can be heard in his first opera, HUGH THE DROVER. SIR JOHN IN LOVE, about Falstaff, is a robust, lyrical evocation of the Fat Knight and his surroundings. RIDERS TO THE SEA, a direct setting of a John Millington Synge tragedy, is poignant and concise. POISONED KISS, described by the comp. as a 'Romantic extravaganza', has much delightful music but a questionable plot. PILGRIM'S PROGRESS is his best score in the genre. In spite of its episodic nature, it conveys his profound faith in music of a personal if none too dramatic a nature. It incl. *The Shepherds of the Delectable Mountains*, opera-oratorio in one episode, wr. 1922. AB

Josephine Veasey as Amneris and VAN ALLAN as the King of Egypt in AIDA, London, CG, Jan 1974; a revival of the 1968 production, produced Peter Potter; decor Nicholas Georgiadis

Veasey, Josephine, b. London, 10 July 1930. English mezzo-soprano. Studied with Audrey Langford, then joined CG chorus (1949), becoming a principal with resident co. 1955; debut as Shepherd Boy (TANNHÄUSER). Graduated to most of the major mezzo roles in the repertory, notably FRICKA, Waltraute (WALKÜRE), OCTAVIAN, BRANGÄNE, Marina (BORIS GODUNOV) and both Cassandre and Didon (TROYENS). Glyndebourne debut as Zulma (ITALIANA IN ALGERI, 1957), followed by CHERUBINO (1958–9), Clarice (PIETRA DEL PARAGONE, 1964) and CHARLOTTE (1969). Salzburg Easter Fest. as Fricka (1968) and NY Met debut in same prod. under KARAJAN (1968). Paris O. debut as KUNDRY (1973). One of the leading mezzos of the day, with a rich, pungent voice and dedication in her acting. Particularly admired as Fricka, Waltraute, Didon and Charlotte. AB

Velluti, Giovanni Battista, b. Montolmo [now Panusula], Ancona, 28 Jan 1780; d. San Brusone, Feb 1861. Italian male soprano, the last great *castrato*. Sang in several small It. theatres, then established his reputation in Rome, 1805. Engagements in Naples, Milan, Turin and Vienna confirmed him as one of the greatest singers of his day, but in London in 1825, in CROCIATO IN EGITTO, the unusual sound of his voice failed to please; audiences had no recollection of such a style and found it distasteful. LO

Venezuela *see* LATIN AMERICA

Venice, Italy. The birthplace of commercial opera. The T. San Cassiano was opened in 1637, followed in 1639 by the T. SS Giovanni e Paolo where INCORONAZIONE DI POPPEA was given. By 1700 16 theatres had been built. Comps associated with opera in its early days were MONTEVERDI, CAVALLI, Antonio Vivaldi and many others; names in the 18th c.

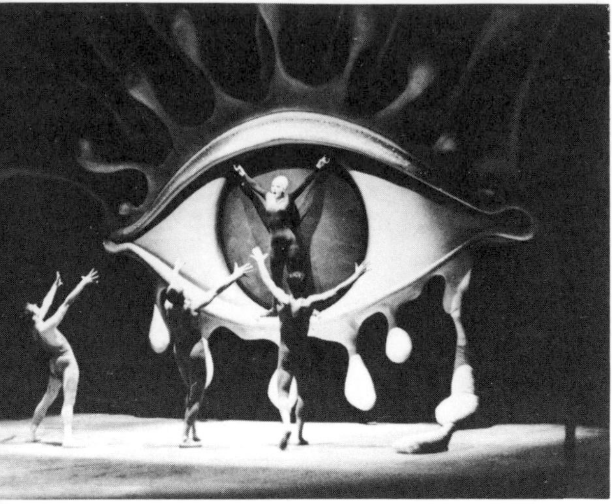

Left: Venice. Set by Salvador Dali (b. 1904) for GALUPPI's *Scipione nella Spania (Scipio in Spain)*, first performed Venice 1746), La Fenice, 25 Aug 1961

include GALUPPI and the librettists GOLDONI and GOZZI. The 19th c. saw premieres of operas by BELLINI, DONIZETTI, ROSSINI and VERDI, and others. They were given in the T. La Fenice, begun 1790, burned down in course of construction, rebuilt and opened 16 May 1792 with PAISIELLO's *I Giuochi d'Agrigento*. Destroyed again by fire, 1836, rebuilt 1837, the theatre stands today as one of the most elegant of all opera houses. Several of Verdi's operas were first heard there including RIGOLETTO and TRAVIATA. Operas first given at the Venice Biennial Fest. of Contemporary Music have incl. RAKE'S PROGRESS, TURN OF THE SCREW, and INTOLLERANZA 1960. LO

Venus, sop., the goddess of love in TANNHÄUSER

Vêpres Siciliennes, Les (*The Sicilian Vespers*), grand opera, 5 acts, VERDI, lib. SCRIBE and Charles Duveyrier. Paris, O., 13 June 1855; London, DL, 27 July 1859; NY, 7 Nov 1859; revived 20 July 1863 with new ten. romance. Main chars: Hélène (sop.) Henri (ten.) Montfort (bar.) Procida (bass). The story concerns the uprising of the Sicilians against their Fr. oppressors in 1282, and the conflicting loyalties of the Sicilian Henri towards his Fr. father Montfort, the conspirators under Procida and the patriotic Hélène with whom he is in love. Verdi's first essay in Meyerbeerian grand opera. JB ○

Verbena de la Paloma, La (*The Feast of Our Lady of the Dove*), *zarzuela*, 1 act, 3 scenes, BRETÓN, lib. Ricardo de la Vega. Madrid, T. Apolo, 19 Feb 1894. This most popular and typical of the thousands of *zarzuelas* wr. during the 19th c. presents a realistic slice of Madrid life. Don Hilarión (char. part), an old apothecary, takes a young blonde (Susana, sop.) and a young brunette (Casta, sop.) to the fiesta but loses the former to her lover Julián (bar.) and the latter to one of his friends. FGB

Verdi, Giuseppe (Fortunino Francesco), b. Le Roncole, nr Busseto, 10 Oct 1813; d. Milan, 27 Jan 1901. Italian composer. Studied music in Busseto, then privately with Lavigna in Milan 1832–5, having failed entrance examination to the Cons. After nearly three years as dir. of music school in Busseto (1836–8) returned to Milan where his first opera, OBERTO, CONTE DI SAN BONIFACIO was produced at Sc. (1839) with fair success. There followed the fiasco of GIORNO DI REGNO (1840), soon offset by the triumph of NABUCCO (1842). With this and the following two operas, LOMBARDI ALLA PRIMA CROCIATA (1843) and ERNANI (1844) his early style crystallized. For the next five years he prod. operas sometimes at the rate of two or three a year; among these MACBETH (1847 – first version) and LUISA MILLER (1849) stand out as landmarks. This first phase of his career reached its climax with the so-called 'romantic trilogy' of RIGOLETTO (1851), TROVATORE (1853) and TRAVIATA (1853). Thereafter his style became enriched with elements from Fr. grand opera, two examples of which he comp. for Paris – VÊPRES SICILIENNES (1885) and DON CARLOS (1867, revised 1884). Within this transitional period fell BALLO IN MASCHERA (1859), FORZA DEL DESTINO (1862, revised 1869) and SIMONE BOCCANEGRA (1857, revised 1881). Perfection in the 'grand' manner was reached in AIDA (1871). Verdi's crowning achievements were the Shakespearean operas OTELLO (1870) and FALSTAFF (1893) wr. to libs by BOITO, both revealing a depth and refinement of musical thought that has nowhere been surpassed. Verdi is not only Italy's greatest opera comp.: in his life, no less than his prodigious artistic development, he embodied the spiritual ideals of the It. nation that came into existence during his lifetime. Widowed in 1840, he later m. the singer STREPPONI. JB

See Budden, *The Operas of Verdi* (Vol. 1, London and New York 1973); Toye, *Giuseppe Verdi: His Life and Works* (London 1931); Walker, *The Man Verdi* (London and New York 1962)

Verhör des Lukullus *see* VERURTEILUNG DES LUKULLUS

verismo (It. 'realism'). Term used especially in Italian opera *c.* 1890 for naturalistic operas dealing with actual, often low-life, situations, e.g. TABARRO, CAVALLERIA RUSTICANA. The type in essence goes back to CARMEN. ATTAQUE DU MOULIN and LOUISE are Fr. examples of the genre. LO

Verkaufte Braut, Die *see* BARTERED BRIDE

Verlobung in San Domingo, Die (*The Betrothal in San Domingo*), opera, 2 acts, EGK, lib composer after KLEIST's novel of same name, 1810. Munich, 27 Nov 1963; St Paul, Minn., 12 July 1974. LO

Vernon, Lyn, b. Vancouver, 19 Aug 1944. Canadian mezzo-soprano. Made early appearances in Vancouver in small roles; member of the Zürich O, 1971–5. Returned to Canada in 1974 when she sang with great success the Female Chorus in RAPE OF LUCRETIA at the Guelph Fest., and Marina in BORIS GODUNOV and Judith in DUKE BLUEBEARD'S CASTLE in Toronto. London Col debut as OCTAVIAN 1975. Her voice is distinguished by great power and evenness over a very wide range. CM

Verona, Italy. The summer open air festival in the Roman arena began there in 1913 (AIDA, conducted by SERAFIN); has continued annually except for 1915–18 and 1940–5. Operas, staged on a magnificent scale, have incl. BOHÈME, CARMEN, NORMA, NABUCCO, and TOSCA. LO

Véronique, opera, 3 acts, MESSAGER, lib. Albert van Loo and Georges Duval. Paris, T. Bouffes-Parisiens, 10 Feb 1898; London (in Fr.), Coronet T., Notting Hill Gate, 5 May 1903; (in Eng.), Apollo T., 18 May 1904; NY, Broadway T., 30 Oct 1905. Based on a good lib., this is among Messager's better works. LO
See Lubbock

Verrett, Shirley, b. New Orleans, ?1933. American mezzo-soprano of major international reputation. Studied Los Angeles; debut in title role of RAPE OF LUCRETIA, 1957 (Antioch College Shakespeare Fest., Yellow Springs), then to Juilliard School, NY. First NY appearance in *Lost in the Stars* (WEILL) 1958, and in Europe at Cologne, 1959, in *The Death of Rasputin* (NABOKOV). After developing concert experience, returned to Europe, 1962, and won major success as CARMEN at Spoleto Fest., Italy, in prod. by MENOTTI. Further debuts as Carmen at Bolshoy T., Moscow, 1963; NY City O., 1964; Sc. 1966. Then CG, 1966, as ULRICA and notable distinction here in following years as AMNERIS, EBOLI, Carmen, AZUCENA; also at Edinburgh Fest. 1969 as Elisabetta (MARIA STUARDA) with Maggio Musicale Fiorentino Co. Debut NY Met 1973 as Cassandre (TROYENS). Her lustrous voice, vibrant intensity of expression and dramatic char., as well as beauty of appearance, brought her widespread admiration, and additionally renewed interest in such other roles as Leonore in FAVORITE (Dallas 1971) and Selika in AFRICAINE (San Francisco 1972). She commands an unusually brilliant top register, but has so far resisted offers of full sop. roles she considers unsuitable. NG

Versailles. The magnificent royal palace to the west of Paris began as a hunting lodge, built by Louis XIII, 1624. The gardens were laid out by André le Notre, under Louis XIV in 1661; here LULLY's *comédies-ballets* and operas were perf., in the open air. The beautiful Salle de l'Opéra in the north wing, designed by Ange-Jacques Gabriel, 1768, used for perf. at Marie Antoinette's m. to Louis XVI, was neglected during the 19th c. but re-opened 1952. LIEBERMANN's Paris regime began with NOZZE DI FIGARO here, 30 Mar 1973. Its use now is confined to special occasions. LO

Verstovsky, Aleksey Nikolayevich, b. Seliverstovo estate, Tambov Government, 1 Mar 1799; d. Moscow, 17 Nov 1862. Russian composer. Known esp. for his opera *Askold's Tomb* (1835), which combines distinctively Russian characteristics with elements clearly inspired by FREISCHÜTZ. It enjoyed enormous popularity in its day, and had a considerable influence on the development of 19th-c. Russian opera, esp. in that, though containing spoken dialogue, it makes greater use of recitative to advance the drama. He also comp. *Pan Tvardovsky* (1828), *Vadim* (1832), *Longing for the Homeland* (1839), *The Waking Dream* (1844), *Gromoboy* (1857), and about 30 vaudevilles. GN

Verurteilung (or **Verhör**) **des Lukullus** (*The Sentencing*, or *Trial*, *of Lucullus*), opera, 12 scenes, DESSAU, lib. BRECHT. Berlin Staats O., 17 Mar 1950; Cambridge (in Eng.), 30 Jan 1970. O

The same subject used by Roger Sessions, *The Trial of Lucullus*, Berkeley, Cal., 18 Apr 1947. LO

Vestale, La, grand opera, 3 acts, SPONTINI, lib. JOUY. Paris O., 16 Dec 1807; London, King's T., 2 Dec 1826; New Orleans, 17 Feb 1828. Main chars: Giulia (sop.) Licinio (ten.) Cinna (bar.) High Priestess (mezzo-sop.) Pontifex Maximus (bass). Giulia, a Vestal virgin, is in love with the general Licinio, who visits her during her vigil in the temple. The sacred flame is extinguished; Giulia is about to be buried alive, when the flame is re-kindled by divine intervention. She is released from her vows and united with her lover. Spontini's best-known opera, whose first production inaugurated a new tradition of grandeur at the O., recently re-opened as the Académie Imperiale de Musique. Other operas on same subject by Vincenzo Puccita, 1810; GENERALI, 1816; PACINI, 1823; MERCADANTE, 1840. GLUCK's *Innocenza Giustificata*, 1755, was renamed *La Vestale* when it was repeated, 1768. JB

Vestris [Bartolozzi], Lucia Elisabetta, b. London, 3 Jan or 2 Mar 1787; d. London, 8 Aug 1856. English contralto. In 1813 she m. Auguste Armand Vestris, *maître de ballet* of the King's T. Studied with Domenico Corri; debut King's T. 1815, at her husband's benefit in WINTER's *Il Ratto di Proserpina*. She appeared in opera and drama at DL; 1821–5 sang at the King's T. At the TI, she was first London Pippo (GAZZA LADRA) and Malcolm Graeme (DONNA DEL LAGO). CG 1826 created the role of Fatima in OBERON. She became manager of CG and other cos in London, and appeared in Eng. versions of many operas, as well as singing the title role in DON GIOVANNI and Macheath in BEGGAR'S OPERA. She was deserted by Vestris and in 1838 m. Charles Mathews. PS

Viardot, [García] Pauline [Michelle Ferdinande], b. Paris, 18 July 1821; d. Paris, 18 May 1910. French mezzo-soprano. Daughter of GARCÍA I and sister of MALIBRAN, she studied singing with her parents, composition with Reicha and piano with LISZT. Debut Brussels 1837; London debut 1839 (ROSSINI's OTELLO). She sang at the Paris TI and, 1841, m. its dir., Louis Viardot. She created the role of Fidès (PROPHÈTE) (1849) and GOUNOD's Sapho (1851) and also appeared in Paris in BERLIOZ's arrangement of ORPHÉE ET EURYDICE (1859) and the revival of ALCESTE (1861), by which time her voice was showing signs of wear. She retired in 1863, and wrote a number of plays, poems, songs and operettas to texts by Ivan Sergeyevich Turgenev, whose mistress she had become. She was the subject of George Sand's novel *Consuelo*, and SAINT-SAËNS wrote DALILA for her. In 1870 she sang the first performance of Johannes Brahms' *Alto Rhapsody* at Jena. From 1871 to 1875 she taught at the Paris Cons. Her daughter Louise (1841–1918) became a contr., and her son Paul was a noted violinist. Viardot's voice ranged from low G to high F and was described as unequal, harsh, thin but expressive. 'Don't do as I do,' she advised her pupils. 'I wanted to sing everything and I spoilt my voice.' PS
See Fitzlyon, *The Price of Genius: A Life of Pauline Viardot* (London 1964; New York 1965); Pleasants, *The Great Singers* (New York 1966)

Vickers, Jon, b. Prince Albert, 29 Oct 1926. Canadian tenor. Sang in Canada and the USA for some years; CG debut 1957 (BALLO IN MASCHERA). Bayreuth debut 1958 (SIEGMUND). Sings at Vienna, San Francisco, Sc., Salzburg, Chicago and the NY Met (debut 1960 as CANIO). His repertory, embracing both lyrical and dramatic roles, incl. Jason (MÉDÉE), Samson (both HANDEL's and SAINT-SAËNS's), DON CARLOS, VERDI's OTELLO, FLORESTAN, Don JOSÉ, Énée (TROYENS), PARSIFAL, Tristan (TRISTAN UND ISOLDE), PETER GRIMES and Laca (JENŮFA). One of the outstanding heroic tenors of his generation, in 1974 he sang both Herod (SALOME) and POLLIONE in the vast open-air arena at Orange. EF

Victory, opera, 3 acts, BENNETT, lib. Beverley Cross, derived from the novel by Joseph Conrad. London, CG, 13 Apr 1970. Main chars: Lena (mezzo-sop.) Heyst (bass-bar.) Schomberg (bass). Heyst, a philosophical Swede, is trying to hide away from the world on an island in the Java Sea. A kindly action of rescue involves him in the everyday world: he is moved by Lena, an ill-treated English girl of a travelling troupe, and becomes emotionally involved with her, a love that ends fatally when villains invade their idyllic peace. The work is a full-blooded realization of the novel written in a freely lyrical, serial idiom that sometimes lacks formal discipline and shape. AB

Vida Breve, La (*Life is Short*), opera, 2 acts, FALLA, lib. Carlos Fernández Shaw. Nice, 1 Apr 1913; NY Met, 6 Mar 1926; Edinburgh, King's T., 9 Sept 1958. Main chars: Salud (sop.) Paco (ten.) Carmela (mezzo-sop.). Salud, a gypsy girl in Granada, is in love with Paco, who vows his own love while secretly planning to marry Carmela. Salud discovers the truth at the wedding celebration, denounces Paco and dies heartbroken at his feet. Falla had never set foot in Granada at the time he comp. this opera, which won a national competition in 1905 for an opera on a Spanish subject, but his portrait of the betrayed Salud, his evocation of the Andalusian char. and scene in two dances and the opera's Intermezzo, are considered models of their kind. NG O
See Kobbé; Pahissa, *Manuel de Falla: His Life and Works* (London 1954)

Vienna. The most notable opera produced there in the 17th c. was POMO D'ORO, in the theatre built by BURNACINI. In the early 18th c. it was the main bastion of It. *opera seria*, with CALDARA, FUX, Giuseppe Bonni and others setting libs by ZENO, Pietro Pariati and METASTASIO. Later it was the scene of GLUCK's reform operas and MOZART's masterpieces and, in the 19th c., of BEETHOVEN's only opera FIDELIO. The building of the new Hof O. in 1869 inaugurated a brilliant period esp. under MAHLER. Since World War II Vienna has regained much of its former glory, first under BÖHM and KRIPS, later under KARAJAN. Another feature of Viennese operatic life has been the operetta, under SUPPÉ, J. STRAUSS, STRAUS and LEHÁR.

Burgtheater, Theater bei der Hofburg. The ancestor of the present Staats O., opened 1748 with GLUCK's *Semiramide Riconosciuta*. ORFEO ED EURIDICE, ALCESTE, PARIDE ED ELENA, ENTFÜHRUNG AUS DEM SERAIL and COSÌ FAN TUTTE were given there. It became mainly a home for drama in the 19th c.; destroyed 1945.

Theater am Kärntnerthor. Built 1708 as an opera house for the Viennese public (the Hofburg T. had been a court monopoly). Came into prominence in the early 19th c. when BARBAIA was at the helm.

Staatsoper. As part of the rebuilding of Vienna, 1857, a new opera house was planned. The new Hof O., renamed Staats O. in 1918, was opened 25 May 1869 with DON GIOVANNI. A fine ensemble was built up, first under Johann von Herbeck, 1870–5, then Franz Jauner, 1875–80, Wilhelm Jahn and RICHTER, 1880–96 and esp. Mahler, 1897–1907. The first dir. of the Staats O. was SCHALK, 1918–29, followed by C. KRAUSS, WEINGARTNER and WALTER. The Staats O. was destroyed by bombs, 1945; the rebuilt house opened 5 Nov 1955 with *Fidelio*.

Theater an der Wien. Built by SCHIKANEDER, a successor to T. auf der Wieden. *Fidelio* first prod. here. Managed by BARBAIA, 1820–2, who gave Viennese premieres of ROSSINI and other It. operettas by J. Strauss, incl. LUSTIGE WITWE, Lehár and others of the Viennese operetta school were perf. here from the 1870s. It housed the Staats O. 1945–55, and is now given over to drama and operettas.

Theater auf der Wieden. Built by Schikaneder, 1787. ZAUBERFLÖTE first perf. here. Closed 1801.

Volksoper. Built 1898, originally for drama. Opera began here 1904 with FREISCHÜTZ. Mus. dirs have incl. Weingartner, STIEDRY, BLECH. In 1945 its doors were opened to the bombed-out Staats O., resuming its own identity in 1955. Its repertory includes operas, operettas and musicals. LO

Vie Parisienne, La, operetta, OFFENBACH, 5 acts, lib. MEILHAC and L. HALÉVY. Paris, T. du Palais Royal, 31 Oct 1866; NY, 29 Mar 1869 (in Fr.); London, Holborn T. (in Eng. tr. Francis Cowley Burnand), 30 Mar 1872; revived SW, 24 May 1961. One of Offenbach's best, it surveys the Parisian scene on the eve of the 1867 *Exposition Universelle* with caustic wit and brilliant musical invention, the city's foreign visitors being willing and credulous victims of its gay but dubious attractions. LO
See Lubbock

Vieuille, Félix, b. Saugeon, Charente-Inférieure, 15 Oct 1872; d. Saugeon, 28 Feb 1953. French bass. Studied Paris Cons., winning first prize for *opéra comique* 1897. Debut 1897, Aix-les-Bains, in DON GIOVANNI; then engaged at OC 1898, where for 20 years he was chief bass. Created ARKEL, also roles in MÂROUF, ARIANE ET BARBE-BLEUE and PÉNÉLOPE. With a rich voice of wide range and sound technique and a gift for acting, he played a wide variety of roles at the OC but rarely sang outside Paris. LO

Village Romeo and Juliet, A, opera, prologue and 3 acts, DELIUS, lib. composer based on Gottfried Keller's story *Romeo und Julia auf dem Dorfe*, 1856. Berlin, 21 Feb 1907 (in Ger.); London, CG, 22 Feb 1910; Washington, DC, 26 Apr 1972. Main chars: Vreli (sop.) Sali (ten.) Manz (bar.) Marti (bar.) Dark Fiddler (bar.). The children of two rival farmers love each other, but are forced by their feuding elders to seek their only hope of union in suicide. FGB O
See Kobbé

Villa-Lobos, Heitor, b. Rio de Janeiro, 5 Mar 1887; d. Rio, 17 Nov 1959. Brazilian composer. His extensive list of compositions includes nine stage works, only three of which have been perf. They are *Izath*, comp. 1918, an amplified version of an earlier 1-act opera, *Eliza*, comp. *c.* 1915, perf. Rio, T. Municipal, 13 Dec 1958; *Magdalena*, Los Angeles, 26 July 1948 (which also had a run on Broadway, NY) and *Yerma*, comp. 1955, perf. Santa Fe, 12 Aug 1971. MK

Villi, Le (*The Witches*), opera, 1 act, PUCCINI, lib. FONTANA after HEINE. Milan, T. dal Verme, 31 May 1884; revived in 2 acts, Turin, T. Regio, 26 Dec 1884; Manchester, 24 Sept 1897; NY Met, 17 Dec 1908. Main chars: Anna (sop.) Roberto (ten.) Guglielmo Wulf (bar.). Roberto deserts his village sweetheart, Anna, who dies of grief, and becomes one of the nocturnal spirits who lure faithless lovers and cause them to dance until they die of exhaustion. Puccini's first opera. JB O

Vinay, Ramón, b. Chillán, 31 Aug 1912. Chilean tenor and baritone, famous for heroic tenor roles. Self-taught as singer, winning radio competition for amateurs in New Mexico while working in family saddlery business. Engaged Mexico City O.: debut 1938 bar. as DI LUNA. Changed to ten. from 1943, first as Don JOSÉ at Mexico City, where in 1944 he first sang VERDI's OTELLO – a role that later brought him fame in three continents. Other debuts: NY CC 1945, NY Met 1946, both as Don José; Sc. 1947, CG 1950 (with Sc. co.), both as Otello. Specially coached in this role by TOSCANINI, with whom he recorded it in a perf. generally considered one of the great gramophone classics of opera. In 1950 he first sang WAGNER: Tristan (TRISTAN UND ISOLDE) with San Francisco O. (and FLAGSTAD as ISOLDE). Debut Bayreuth Fest. 1952, in same role. Returned there regularly to 1958, and to London with CG O., 1953–60, in various Wagner roles.

Vinay's voice blended ringing timbre with darkly expressive character as an intelligent singing-actor of vivid intensity. In 1962 he reverted to bar., singing TELRAMUND at Bayreuth, and IAGO, FALSTAFF and SCARPIA elsewhere. NG

Vinci, Leonardo, b. Strongoli, 1690; d. Naples, 28 May 1730. Italian composer prominent in the 18th-c. Neapolitan school of composition. Educated Naples; succeeded A. SCARLATTI in 1725 as acting MdC there. Wrote *c.* 40 operas, mostly for Naples, Venice or Rome; *c.* 20 survive in manuscript. None has been revived. LO

Violetta, sop., the heroine of TRAVIATA

Violins of St Jacques, opera, 3 acts, WILLIAMSON, lib. William Chappell, derived from novel of the same name by Patrick Leigh Fermor. London, SW, 29 Nov 1966. Main chars: Berthe (sop.) Josephine (mezzo-sop.) Sosthène (ten.) Marcel (bar.). Set on the Caribbean island of St Jacques just before a volcano overwhelms the place, the story tells of a complicated tangle of human relationships inevitably resolved by the eruption and its resultant destruction, leaving one char. Berthe, to ponder as the sole survivor on the meaning of it all. The exotic setting is matched in the orchestral writing. The vocal music is predominantly lyrical, with ariosos and set numbers. AB

Viozzi [Weutz], Giulio, b. Trieste, 5 July 1912. Italian composer. His first opera, *Allamistakeo* (1954), based on POE, was prod. at Bergamo. *Un Intervento Notturno* (1957), *Il Sasso Pagano* (1962) and *La Giacca Dannata* (1967) were all perf. at Trieste. He has also wr. a radio opera, *La Parete Bianca* (1954). EF

Virgil [Publius Vergilius Maro], b. Andes, nr Mantua, 15 Oct 70 BC; d. Brundusium (Brindisi), 22 Sept 19 BC. His epic *Aeneid* has provided material for *c.* 70 operas. About half use METASTASIO's libretto *Didone Abbandonata*, and *c.* 20 have Aeneas in the title. PURCELL's DIDO AND AENEAS is one of the best known and one of the earliest; the most ambitious is BERLIOZ's masterpiece, TROYENS. LO

Visconti, Luchino [Conte L. V. di Modrone], b. Milan, 2 Nov 1906; d. Rome, 17 Mar 1976. Italian film director, stage producer and designer. His first operatic prod. was VESTALE in 1954 at Sc., where he also directed SONNAMBULA, TRAVIATA, ANNA BOLENA and IPHIGÉNIE EN TAURIDE, all with CALLAS. In 1958 he staged and designed DON CARLOS at CG, and later returned there to prod. TROVATORE, ROSENKAVALIER, and *La Traviata*. He staged MACBETH at the inaugural production of the Fest. of Two Worlds, Spoleto (1958), and also dir. DONIZETTI's *Duc d'Albe*, SALOME, *La Traviata*, and MANON LESCAUT at Spoleto. In 1966 he prod. FALSTAFF at Vienna. EF

Vishnevskaya, Galina Pavlovna, b. Leningrad, 25 Oct 1926. Soviet soprano. Studied Leningrad, and in 1952 joined the Bolshoy, where she has sung a wide variety of roles, incl. TATYANA, Marfa (KHOVANSHCHINA), VIOLETTA, TOSCA and LEONORE. Debuts: NY Met 1961 (AIDA and CIO-CIO-SAN), CG 1962 (Aida), Sc. 1964 (LIÙ). She is one of the finest Soviet sops, combining a flexible, even voice with an intense acting style. She m. Mstislav Rostropovich, the cellist, 1955. GN

Visitation, The, opera, 3 acts, SCHULLER, lib. composer based on KAFKA's novel *Der Prozess*, 1925 but transposed to racial conflict in southern USA. Hamburg O., 12 Oct 1966; NY (by Hamburg O.), 28 June 1967. Commissioned by Hamburg. For another treatment of the plot *see* PROZESS. LO

Visit of the Old Lady, The *see* BESUCH DER ALTEN DAME

Vives, Amadeo, b. Collbató, nr Barcelona, 18 Nov 1871; d. Madrid, 2 Dec 1932. Spanish composer. Began by writing ambitious operas, of which only *Maruxa* (1913) has any particular distinction, but later moved into the field of the *zarzuela*. Of his more than 100 *zarzuelas*, *Doña*

Francisquita (1923) has become a modern classic, while *Bohemios, La Villana* and *La Generala* have remained widely popular. One of the founders of the choral society Orfeó Català, dedicated to the fostering of Catalan music, and Professor of Composition at the Madrid Cons. FGB

Vogel, Jaroslav, b. Plzeň [Pilsen], 11 Jan 1894; d. Prague, 2 Feb 1970. Czech conductor and composer. Studied Munich and Paris before becoming *répétiteur* at Prague NT (1913–14) and cond. at Plzeň (1914–15), and completing his conducting studies under KOVAŘOVIC and TALICH. He held a number of posts in the republic, notably at the Prague NT (1948–58) and as head of Ostrava O. (1927–43), and cond. Fr. and Russian operas as well as WAGNER and JANÁČEK (he made the first complete recording of JENŮFA). As a friend of Janáček, a comp. (of three operas) and an exceptionally well-read and erudite scholar, he was well equipped to write the first large-scale monograph on Janáček, 1958. JT

Vogl, Heinrich, b. Munich, 15 Jan 1845; d. Munich, 21 Apr 1900. German tenor. Studied with Franz Lachner; debut Munich, 1865, in FREISCHÜTZ. Closely associated with the WAGNER music dramas, the leading Tristan (TRISTAN UND ISOLDE) of his day following SCHNORR VON CAROLSFELD, he sang at Bayreuth 1876–97 and in 1882 was first London LOGE and SIEGFRIED. His wife, **Therese** [Thoma], b. Tutzing, 12 Nov 1845; d. Munich, 29 Sept 1921, was also a leading Wagner singer, creating SIEGLINDE and was first London BRÜNNHILDE, 1882. LO

Voice of Ariadne, The, opera, 3 acts, MUSGRAVE, lib. Amalia Elguera after *The Last of the Valerii* by JAMES, commissioned by the Calouste Gulbenkian Foundation for EOG. Aldeburgh, Jubilee Hall, 11 June 1974; London, SW, 7 Oct 1974. Main chars: Countess (sop.) Bianca (sop.) Mrs Tracy (mezzo-sop.) Baldovino (ten.) Count Marco Valerio (bar.) Mr Lamb (bass). An Italian nobleman is obsessed by the legend of a statue buried in his garden. A dig discloses only a pedestal inscribed with the name of Ariadne. The Count imagines he hears Ariadne's voice calling to him, estranging him from the Countess. As he grows further from her, she seems to become the embodiment of Ariadne, so that he finally recognizes her as the source of a happiness he has pursued without realizing he already possessed it. The comp. extends her lyrical serial idiom to full-throated Straussian cantilena in an opera filled with melodic grace and beauty as well as sharp-featured character and comedy, incorporating a discreet use of electronic tape to supplement the resourceful writing for an orch. limited to 13 players. NG

Voix Humaine, La (*The Human Voice*), opera, 1 act, POULENC, lib. COCTEAU. Paris, OC, 6 Feb 1959; NY, Carnegie Hall, 23 Feb 1960; Edinburgh Fest., 30 Aug 1960; Palo Alto, Cal., 1 Mar 1962. This 45-minute monologue is for a young woman (sop.) who converses over the telephone with the lover who has betrayed her. The role is a speciality of its creator, DUVAL. FGB

Volo di Notte (*Night Flight*), opera, 1 act, DALLAPICCOLA, lib. composer based on Antoine St-Exupéry's novel *Vol de Nuit*, 1931. Florence, Pergola T., 18 May 1940; Glasgow, SO, 29 May 1963. LO

Voltaire, François-Marie Arouet de, b. Paris, 24 Nov 1694; d. Paris, 30 May 1778. French philosopher, dramatist and novelist. Works on which operas are based incl.: *Zaire*, 1732 (WINTER, 1805; Vincenzo Federici, 1806; Lavigna, 1809; MERCADANTE, 1831; BELLINI, 1833; Duke of Saxe-Coburg, 1846); *Alzire*, 1736 (ZINGARELLI, 1794; Giuseppe Niccolini, 1797; Francesco Bianchi, 1801; VERDI, 1845); *Mahomet*, 1742 (ROSSINI, 1820); *Mérope*, 1743 (GRAUN, 1756); *Zadig*, 1748 (Jean Dupérier, 1939); *Sémiramis*, 1748 (Graun, 1754; Bianchi, 1790; Charles Catel, 1802; Rossini, 1823); *L'Orphelin de la Chine*, 1755 (Giuseppe Bonno, 1756?; Winter, 1802); *Candide*, 1756 (KNIPPER, 1926–7; BERNSTEIN, 1958); *Tancrède*, 1760 (Johann Apell, *c.* 1789; Rossini, 1813); *Ce Qui Plaît aux Dames*, 1764 (DUNI, *La Fée Urgèle*, 1765); *Olympie*, 1764 (Christian Kalkbrenner, 1798; SPONTINI, 1819); *L'Ingénu*, 1767 (HURON); *La Bégueule*, 1772 (MONSIGNY, *La Belle Arsène*, 1773). Voltaire also collaborated with RAMEAU in a sacred opera, *Samson*, never publicly perf., though parts were given privately in 1734 and 1735; in *La Princesse de Navarre* (1748) and *Le Temple de la Gloire* (1745). LO

Von Heute auf Morgen (*From Day to Day*), comic opera, 1 act, SCHÖNBERG, lib. 'Max Blonda' (the composer's wife Gertrud). Frankfurt, 1 Feb 1930; BBC, Holland Fest. perf., 1958. Chars: the Wife (sop.) the Husband (bar.) the Singer (ten.) his Friend (sop.). A marriage is on the point of breaking up, but, through the wife's efforts, the couple are finally reconciled. EF O

Vostřák, Zbyněk, b. Prague, 10 June 1920. Czech composer and conductor. A pupil of

KAREL (he completed his *Three Hairs of an Old Wise Man*, 1948), he has wr. several operas. These include *Rohovín Čtverrohý* (1949), *The King's Mintmaster* (*Králův mincmistr*, 1955), *Prague Nocturne* (*Pražské nocturno*, 1960) and *The Broken Jug* (*Rozbitý džbán*, 1963). JT

Vyvyan, Jennifer, b. Broadstairs, 13 Mar 1925; d. London, 28 Mar 1974. English soprano. Studied with Roy Henderson and Fernando Carpi. Debut as Jenny Diver in BEGGAR'S OPERA with EOG (1947). Created four roles in BRITTEN'S operas: Lady Penelope Rich in GLORIANA, the Governess in TURN OF THE SCREW, Tytania in MIDSUMMER NIGHT'S DREAM and Mrs Julian in OWEN WINGRAVE (on TV). SW as CONSTANZE and Donna ANNA (1952). Created Countess of Serendin in VIOLINS OF ST JACQUES, various roles in LUCKY PETER'S JOURNEY. Elettra in IDOMENEO at Glyndebourne (1953). Also well known for her singing in various HANDEL operas. Her vivid portrayals were projected on firm, incisive tone. Her coloratura was astonishingly flexible. AB

Wächter, Eberhard, b. Vienna, 8 July 1929. Austrian baritone. Debut 1953, Vienna Volks O. (SILVIO); at Vienna Staats O. 1954. First sang at CG, 1956, at Bayreuth 1958, at Sc., 1960, at Chicago and NY Met, 1961. A fine DON GIOVANNI and Count ALMAVIVA (NOZZE DI FIGARO), he also sings GOLAUD, RENATO, Posa (DON CARLOS) and PRIGIONIERO, as well as AMFORTAS, WOLFRAM, and KURWENAL. EF

Wagner, Richard, b. Leipzig, 22 May 1813; d. Venice, 13 Feb 1883. German composer. After desultory musical study at Leipzig Univ., he was engaged as *répétiteur* and chorus-master at Würzburg (1833) where his first opera *Die Feen* was written though never perf. in his lifetime. Successive appointments followed at Magdeburg (1834) and Riga (1836). During this time he wr. LIEBESVERBOT and in 1838 began work on COLA RIENZI. He visited Paris 1839, hoping to have *Rienzi* staged at the O.; disappointed, he spent the next three years in journalism, making piano arrangements of L. HALÉVY and DONIZETTI, and comp. FLIEGENDE HOLLÄNDER. In 1842 a successful perf. of *Rienzi* at Dresden led eventually to Wagner's engagement as mus. dir. at the theatre. There followed *Der Fliegende Holländer* and TANNHÄUSER: Wagner's interest in medieval legend continued with LOHENGRIN, finished in 1848. Wagner meanwhile had been involved in the 1848 revolution and with its defeat was forced to leave Germany, eventually settling in Zürich. During the first three years of his exile he worked out new theories of music drama in a number of pamphlets – *Oper und Drama, Der Kunstwerk der Zukunft, Eine Mitteilung zu meiner Freunden* – and then began to put his theories into practice with the libretto *Siegfrieds Tod*. By 1852 the poem of the RING DES NIBELUNGEN had been completed. Thereafter Wagner divided his time between composition and occasional cond. (In 1855 he introduced excerpts of *Lohengrin* and *Tannhäuser* to England.) The music of RHEINGOLD was finished in 1854, that of WALKÜRE in 1856. He broke off work on *Siegfried* to write TRISTAN UND ISOLDE (1859–62) inspired partly by his admiration for Arthur Schopenhauer, partly by his own love affair with Mathilde Wesendonck. But his fortunes were running out. *Tannhäuser*, given with ballet at the Paris O., was a failure and his latest works remained unperf. Then in 1864 the newly crowned Bavarian King LUDWIG II summoned him to Munich, where *Tristan und Isolde* was perf. in 1865: but at the end of 1865 Wagner was again forced to leave Germany for political reasons. He settled in Triebschen in Switzerland; here MEISTERSINGER was finished in 1867 and given at Munich in 1868. Perfs followed of *Das Rheingold* (1869) and *Die Walküre* (1870); but Wagner was set on the construction of a special theatre for the perf. of his own works. A site in Bayreuth was chosen, and Ludwig of Bavaria headed the list of subscribers for the project, which was not realized until 1876. The theatre was inaugurated by three perfs of the *Ring* cycle, of which SIEGFRIED had been completed in 1869 and GÖTTERDÄMMERUNG in 1874. The next six years were spent in travel and in comp. PARSIFAL, a final expression of a personal Christianity, sketched as early as 1857: several pamphlets date from his last years including a diatribe against vivisection.

Wagner was the most influential comp. in the 19th c. after BEETHOVEN. Man of letters no less than musician, his ideal was a union of the arts which he first regarded as attainable in a Germanization of Fr. grand opera. After *Lohengrin* he evolved his own theory of music drama, based like those of the Florentine Camerata on Aristotle's *Poetics*, but more systematically worked out with special roles assigned to voices and orchestra and a musical organization based on the symphonic working of motifs, each of which has specific dramatic connotations. JB
See Newman, *The Life of Richard Wagner*, 4 vols (London and New York 1933–47)

Wagner, Siegfried, b. Triebschen, nr Lucerne, 6 June 1869; d. Bayreuth, 4 Aug 1930. German conductor and composer. Son of R. WAGNER and Cosima von Bülow. Art. dir., Bayreuth Fest., 1909–30. None of his 15 operas has held the stage. LO

Wagner, Wieland, b. Bayreuth, 5 Jan 1917; d. Munich, 16 Oct 1966. German designer and producer. Grandson of R. WAGNER. With his brother, Wolfgang (b. Bayreuth, 30 Aug 1919), art dirs of Bayreuth Fest. since 1951. Their non-realistic, simplified prods, based on APPIA's ideas, caused much controversy but eventually were accepted at Bayreuth and elsewhere. Since Wieland's death the pendulum has begun to swing back again. LO

Wagner-Régeny, Rudolf, b. Szász-Régen, 26 Aug 1903; d. Berlin, 18 Sept 1969. Hungarian-born German composer. Studied Leipzig and Berlin. His operas incl. *Der Günstling*, based on BÜCHNER's version of HUGO's *Marie Tudor*, 1935; *Der Nackte König*, based on ANDERSEN's *The Emperor's New Clothes*, 1928; *Die Bürger von Calais*, 1939; *Johanna Balk*, 1941; *Prometheus*, 1959, and *Das Bergwerk zu Falun*, 1961. They have made little impression outside Germany. LO

Wakhevitch, Georges (Georgij Vachevič), b. Odessa, Ukraine, 18 Aug 1907. Russian painter, scenographer, costume designer for theatre and film. Studied Paris. Has designed for most European opera houses incl. CG (BORIS GODUNOV, 1949), Sc. (CONSUL, 1950–1), Paris (DIALOGUES DES CARMÉLITES, 1957), Marseille (DEVILS OF LOUDUN, 1971), a superb FORZA DEL DESTINO for Rouen, 1972, Rome (BALLO IN MASCHERA, 1973) and for Vienna, Turin, Zürich, and Salzburg. His approach is that of a painter designing solidly constructed and spatial scenes. LO

Wales *see* WELSH NATIONAL OPERA

Walker, Edyth, b. Hopewell, NY, 27 Mar 1867; d. New York, 19 Feb 1950. American mezzo-soprano. Studied Dresden with ORGENI; debut Berlin 1894 in PROPHÈTE. Vienna, 1895–1902; NY Met 1903–6 (debut in AIDA), thereafter Hamburg, 1906–12, and Munich, 1912–17; also at CG, where she was the first London ELEKTRA, and Bayreuth. One of the earliest American singers to be established securely in the great European opera houses, and described by Harold Rosenthal in *Two Centuries of Opera at Covent Garden* (London 1958) as 'one of the greatest Wagnerian artists to have sung there'. LO

Walküre, Die *see* RING DES NIBELUNGEN

Wallace, Ian, b. London, 10 July 1919. English bass, acclaimed in *buffo* roles. Initially an actor, appearing in several London prods and singing in light entertainment. Engaged New London O. Co., Cambridge T., 1946: debut as SCHAUNARD. Joined Glyndebourne co. at Edinburgh Fest., 1948, Masetto (DON GIOVANNI); Glyndebourne Fest. from 1952, appearing regularly to 1960s in variety of comedy roles, notably BARTOLO (NOZZE DI FIGARO) and Don Magnifico (CENERENTOLA). Has sung these and similar roles with SW, EOG, SO, and abroad at Parma (1950), Berlin (1954), Rome (1955), Venice (1956), Bregenz (1965–6). His memorable char. portraits are a blend of stage experience in spoken drama with a voice of expressive verbal inflection and tone colour. NG
See Wallace, *Promise Me You'll Sing Mud* (London 1975)

Wallace, (William) Vincent, b. Waterford, 11 Mar 1812; d. Château de Bagen, nr Vieuzos, Hautes-Pyrénées, 12 Oct 1865. Irish composer. Remembered for two operas, MARITANA and *Lurline* (CG, 23 Feb 1860). LO

Wallerstein, Lothar, b. Prague, 6 Nov 1882; d. New Orleans, 18 Nov 1949. Czech, later American, producer. Main fields of activity Vienna, 1927–38; Salzburg Fest., 1926–37; NY Met 1941–6. Prod. PELLÉAS ET MÉLISANDE at first Holland Fest., 1948; also guest prod. at other theatres incl. Sc. and T. Colón. LO

Wallmann, Margherita [Margarethe], b. Vienna, 22 June 1904. Austrian choreographer and producer. Originally a dancer, she first staged opera 1936, Salzburg (ORFEO ED EURIDICE). Worked at T. Colón, Buenos Aires, 1937–48. Since 1952, when she dir. LIEBE DER DANAE at Sc. she has staged innumerable prods there, incl. the premieres of DAVID, DIALOGUES DES CARMÉLITES, ASSASSINIO NELLA CATTEDRALE and *Calzare d'Argento* (PIZZETTI), ATLANTIDE and Renzo ROSSELLINI's *Linguaggio dei Fiori*, as well as MÉDÉE, GLUCK's ALCESTE, FIAMMA, NORMA, IRIS, TOSCA, TURANDOT, VERDI's OTELLO, DON CARLOS, and MARIA STUARDA. At CG she has dir. AIDA and the *Dialogues des Carmélites*; at the Paris O., BALLO IN MASCHERA and TROYENS; at Chicago, CARMEN; and at the NY Met, LUCIA DI LAMMERMOOR. EF

Wally, La, opera, 4 acts, Alfredo CATALANI, lib. ILLICA after novel by Wilhelmine von Hillern. Milan, Sc., 20 Jan 1892. NY, 6 Jan

1909; Manchester, 27 Mar 1919. Main chars: Wally (sop.) Walter (sop.) Hagenbach (ten.) Gellner (bar.) Stromminger (bass) Afra (contr.). Wally, a strange, hoydenish girl, loves Hagenbach, but he humiliates her and she plots to have him killed. Gellner carries out her plan and pushes Hagenbach down a ravine, but Wally, now repentant, rescues him. Finally they are both killed in an avalanche. Catalani's last and most famous opera. JB O
See Kobbé

Walter [Schlesinger], Bruno, b. Berlin, 15 Sept 1876; d. Beverley Hills, Cal., 17 Feb 1962. German conductor. Studied Berlin; became asst to MAHLER at Vienna O., 1901, remaining there until 1912. Gen. mus. dir., Munich, 1913–22, where he cond. many contemporary operas. Closely identified with Salzburg Fest., 1922–37. Also cond. at CG, where he was first Ger. cond. after World War I, 1924. Back at Vienna as gen. mus. dir. 1936, but had to leave Austria in 1938. Moved to USA where from 1941 he was a welcome guest at the NY Met. His warm and sympathetic personality was reflected in his interpretations, his readings of the Ger. classics being notable for their relaxed flow and sensuous line. LO
See autobiography (tr. Galston), *Theme and Variations* (New York 1946; London 1947)

Walters, Jess, b. New York. American baritone. NY debut with small co. as MACBETH (1941). Joined CG in 1947 and remained until 1959 as leading bar. Sang with Nederlandse O. (1960–4). AB

Walther von Stolzing, ten., hero of MEISTERSINGER

Walton, (Sir) William (Turner), b. Oldham, 29 Mar 1902. English composer. Came to opera when well established in other kinds of composition. Wr. TROILUS AND CRESSIDA (1954) for CG, a large-scale, neo-Romantic work. His only other opera is the 1-act *The Bear* (1967), written for the Aldeburgh Fest. Based on a CHEKHOV short story, it is a light, comic work, containing witty parodies of several comps. AB

War and Peace (*Voyna i mir*), opera, 13 scenes, PROKOFIEV, lib. composer and Mira Mendelson-Prokofieva after TOLSTOY's novel. Leningrad, Maly, 12 June 1946; London, Col., 11 Oct 1972; NY, NBC, 13 Jan 1957 (TV perf.). Main chars: Prince Andrey Bolkonsky (bar.) Natasha Rostova (sop.) Sonya (mezzo-sop.) Mariya Akhrosimova (mezzo-sop.) Count Ilya Rostov (bass) Pierre Bezukhov (ten.) Hélène Bezukhova (contr.) Prince Anatol Kuragin (ten.) Kutuzov (bass) Napoleon (bar.). The Russian people declare their defiance of the French. Andrey sees Natasha and then meets her at a ball; Anatol, with the help of his scheming sister Hélène Bezukhova, plans to seduce Natasha. Andrey leaves for the war, and Anatol endears himself to Natasha. They plan to elope, but the attempt is foiled, and Mariya Akhrosimova persuades Pierre to reveal to Natasha that Anatol is already married. Napoleon invades Russia; war begins. Kutuzov retreats and the French take Moscow, but the city is set alight by the inhabitants. Natasha finds Andrey dying among the wounded soldiers; in the final scene the French retreat and Russia is victorious. The obvious analogy between the war of 1812 and World War II lent *War and Peace* particular pungency when it was first prod.; it remains one of Prokofiev's most powerful scores. GN O

Ward, David, b. Dumbarton, 3 July 1922. Scottish bass. Joined the SW chorus in 1952, the following year sang Count Walter (LUISA MILLER) and remained at SW until 1959. CG debut 1960 as POGNER, sang at Glyndebourne as Lord Walton (PURITANI) and at Bayreuth as Titurel (PARSIFAL). In 1963 he sang BORIS GODUNOV with SO and in 1964 made his NY Met debut as SARASTRO. He also sings at Buenos Aires, San Francisco and all over Europe. His large repertory includes Zaccaria (NABUCCO), Fiesco (SIMONE BOCCANEGRA), PHILIPPE and Grand Inquisitor (DON CARLOS), Padre Guardiano (FORZA DEL DESTINO), ARKEL, Prince Ivan Khovansky (KHOVANSHCHINA), and Morosus (SCHWEIGSAME FRAU); and he sings both bass and bass-bar. WAGNER roles: FASOLT, HUNDING, KING MARK, as well as the Dutchman (FLIEGENDE HOLLÄNDER), WOTAN, and Wanderer. EF

Ward, Robert, b. Cleveland, Ohio, 13 Aug 1917. American composer. Studied Eastman School, Rochester, NY, and Juilliard, New York City; bandmaster in World War II; taught at Juilliard School, Columbia Univ. and elsewhere. His operas are: *He Who Gets Slapped* (originally *Pantaloon*), 3 acts (1957); CRUCIBLE; *The Lady from Colorado*, based on a novel by Homer Croy, for Central City, Col., 1964. EJ

Warren [Vaarenov], Leonard, b. New York, 21 Apr 1911; d. New York, 4 Mar 1960. American baritone, admired in VERDI roles. Began commercial career; studied singing in NY from 1933, later in Milan, then joined chorus of Radio City Music Hall, NY. Won Met O. 'Auditions of the Air', 1938, and debut

NY Met, 1939, as Paolo (SIMONE BOCCANEGRA). Sang regularly there until his death, and with success throughout North and South America. Limited appearances in Europe incl. Sc. 1953, and tour of USSR, 1958. A popular radio and TV singer in addition to his operatic reputation for forthright dramatic char. and vocal style. He died at the Met, during a perf. of FORZA DEL DESTINO. NG

Warsaw [Warszawa]. Italian opera was introduced to Warsaw early in the 18th c., but a Polish national opera was not established until 1778, when Maciej Kamienski's *Nędza Uszczęśliwiona* (*Misery Contented*) was produced at the NT. During the 19th c. MONIUSZKO was for many years dir. of the O. The theatre was destroyed in World War II, and reopened in 1965. *See* POLAND. EF

Washington, Opera Society of. Established 1936. About 15 perfs annually at Kennedy Center, two novelties and two works, often unusual, by standard comps, complementing visits of NY CC with which there is close cooperation. The co. also perfs as part of the Philadelphia Lyric Opera's season. US Premieres incl. KOANGA, VILLAGE ROMEO AND JULIET, RITORNO D'ULISSE IN PATRIA; BOMARZO. Unusual works by comps of all periods are given; several recorded. Dir. Ian Strasfogel. EJ

Wasserbauer, Miloš, b. Svatoslav, 14 June 1907; d. Brno, 17 Aug 1970. Czech producer. After working in films, he held posts at Brno (1946–53, 1960 until his death) and Bratislava (1953–60) opera theatres. He aimed at a realistic style, influenced both by FELSENSTEIN and the Soviet operas he introduced in the early 1950s. He was best known for his JANÁČEK prods. JT

Water Carrier, The *see* DEUX JOURNÉES

Watson, Claire, b. New York, 3 Feb 1927. American soprano, whose major career was in Europe. Studied at Eastman School, Rochester, NY, and with E. SCHUMANN. Debut at Graz as DESDEMONA (1951). Frankfurt, 1956–8, singing major roles in It. and Ger. repertory. CG debut, as the MARSCHALLIN (1958), a role she sang at Glyndebourne in 1960. At opening of the rebuilt Cuvilliés T., Munich (1958), sang Countess ALMAVIVA. Has since appeared regularly with Bavarian Staats O. with particular success in MOZART, R. STRAUSS and WAGNER. Countess Almaviva at Salzburg (1966–8). Her portrayals are distinguished by her radiant, attractive stage personality and by her scrupulous musicianship. AB

Weber, Aloysia, b. Zell, Baden, 1761; d. Salzburg, 8 June 1839. German soprano. MOZART's first love; elder sister of Constanze Weber (1763–1842) whom Mozart married; cousin of C. WEBER. Engaged Vienna Hof O. 1780; the part of CONSTANZE was wr. for her. Her elder sister Josepha (d. 1820) was the first QUEEN OF THE NIGHT. LO

Weber, Carl Maria (Friedrich Ernst) von, b. Eutin, nr Lübeck, 18 Nov 1786; d. London, 5 June 1826. German composer. A childhood hip disease left him with a lifelong limp. He had some instruction in comp. first from Michael Haydn, later from Georg Joseph Vogler. His first two operas were wr. when he was still a boy; the second, *Das Waldmädchen*, 1800, was later remodelled as *Silvana* (1810). Two others, *Peter Schmoll* (1803) and *Der Beherrscher des Geisters* (1805), were wr. before *Abu Hassan* (1811) was prod. in Munich. Appointed MdC, Prague, 1813–16; Dresden 1816–26, FREISCHÜTZ being wr. for the latter. His last two operas were EURYANTHE and OBERON; *Die Drei Pintos*, left unfinished, was completed by MAHLER, perf. Leipzig 1888. Weber m. singer Caroline Brandt, the first AGATHE. He died two weeks after the premiere of *Oberon*. Buried in London, his body was moved to Dresden in 1844 at the instigation of WAGNER, who wrote the music for his reburial service and delivered the eulogy. Weber laid the cornerstone of Ger. national opera; his use of *Leitmotiv*, the dramatic employment of recitative, and the symphonic importance of the orch. led directly to Wagner. PS
See Warrack, *Carl Maria von Weber* (London and New York 1968)

Weber, Ludwig, b. Vienna, 29 July 1899; d. Vienna, 13 Oct 1974. Austrian bass. Studied Vienna; debut there, Volks O., 1920. Main engagements Munich, 1933–45; Vienna from 1945. Sang frequently at CG and regularly Bayreuth 1951–60. Repertory confined to the great Ger. bass roles, esp. WAGNER, in which he was unexcelled. LO

Webster, (Sir) David, b. Liverpool, 3 July 1903; d. London, 11 May 1971. English operatic manager. The first gen. administrator, CG, after World War II, appointed 1945, retired 1970. From virtually nothing he raised the CG Opera Co. to become one of the great European opera centres. Succeeded by TOOLEY. LO

Weill, Kurt, b. Dessau, 2 Mar 1900; d. New York, 3 Apr 1950. German composer. Working with BRECHT he wrote DREIGROSCHENOPER, AUFSTIEG UND FALL DER STADT

Kurt Weill and BRECHT's AUFSTIEG UND FALL DER STADT MAHAGONNY; revival at Frankfurt, 1 Dec 1966. Olive Moorefield as Jenny and Charles O'Neill as Jim Mahonney

MAHAGONNY, *Der Jasager* (Berlin 1930), and *Die Burgschaft* (Berlin 1932), all in a satirical vein and in popular, anti-highbrow style. Having to leave Nazi Germany, he moved to USA 1935 where his musicals met with some success. LO

Weimar, E. Germany. Its golden period was 1847–58 under LISZT, with premieres of LOHENGRIN and BARBIER VON BAGDAD, and interesting prods of BENVENUTO CELLINI and GENOVEVA. Opera is given in the Deutsches NT (formerly Hof T.). LO

Weinberger, Jaromír, b. Prague, 8 Jan 1896; d. St Petersburg, Fla., 8 Aug 1967. Czech composer. A highly talented pupil of KŘIČKA and NOVÁK (1910–13) in Prague and of Max Reger in Leipzig (1916), he won a worldwide reputation with his opera SCHWANDA THE BAGPIPER (1927). He did not repeat this success with his three following operas, nor with his subsequent operettas. He settled permanently in the USA in 1938. JT

Weingartner, (Paul) Felix (von), b. Zara (now Zadar), Croatia, 2 June 1863; d. Winterthur, Switzerland, 7 May 1942. Austrian conductor and composer. One of the greatest conds of his day, superb in concert hall and theatre. His career took him to many towns in Germany; the most important of his theatre posts were Berlin, 1891–8, Vienna Staats O. 1908–10 and Volks O. 1919–24. Also cond. Boston 1912–13, CG 1939 (debut PARSIFAL) – an association cut short by outbreak of World War II. LO

Weisse, Christian Felix, b. Annaberg, Saxony, 28 Jan 1726; d. Leipzig, 16 Dec 1804. German dramatist and librettist, important in history of the *Singspiel*. In 1752 did new tr. and adaptation of DEVIL TO PAY for Johann Christian Standfuss, and re-drafted it for HILLER, 1766. His other libs for Hiller include *Lottchen am Hofe* 1767, JAGD and *Der Dorfbarbier*, 1770. LO

Welitsch [Velichkova], Ljuba, b. Borisovo, 10 July 1913. Bulgarian soprano. Studied Sofia and Vienna; debut as NEDDA at Graz (1937), then graduated via Hamburg and Munich to Vienna. She enjoyed sensational London and New York debuts as SALOME, a role she had first sung under the comp.'s dir. She was also famous for highly dramatic portrayals of TOSCA, Donna ANNA, AIDA, and AMELIA. Since 1955 she has appeared only rarely. FGB

Welsh National Opera (WNO). Wales, traditionally the land of singers, has had an opera co. since 1946. Based on Cardiff, it tours the W. of England and Wales; has also visited London, SW, and made excursions to continental Europe (Lausanne and Zürich, 1973; Barcelona, 1975). The repertory is largely standard with occasionally a more adventurous work such as LULU, 1971. LO

Werle, Lars Johan, b. Gävle, 23 June 1926. Swedish composer. His experimental chamber opera-in-the-round, DRÖMMEN OM THÉRÈSE, was successfully prod. Stockholm 1964; his second, equally unconventional, opera, *Resan* (*The Journey*), was first perf. at Hamburg 1969. A third, *Tintomara*, Stockholm 1973. EF

Werther, *drame lyrique*, 4 acts, MASSENET, lib. Édouard Blau, Paul Milliet and Georges Hartmann, based on GOETHE's novel, 1774. Vienna O., 16 Feb 1892; Paris, OC, 16 Jan 1893; Chicago, 29 Mar 1894; London, CG, 11 June 1894. The premiere was in Vienna because the OC had burned down, 1887, while Massenet was wr. the opera. Though received with little enthusiasm in Britain it has had over 1,400 perfs at the OC. Other operas on the same subject are by Rodolphe Kreutzer, 1792; Vincenzo Puccita, 1804; Raffaele Gentili, 1864. LO O
See Harding, *Massenet* (London 1970; New York 1971)

West Germany *see* GERMANY

West Side Story, musical, BERNSTEIN, lyrics SONDHEIM, dir. and chor. Jerome Robbins, based on a play by Arthur Laurents. NY, Winter Garden T., 26 Sept 1957; London, HM, 12 Dec 1958; revived NY 1973. A reworking of the Romeo and Juliet theme in New York's Puerto Rican community. EJ O★
See Lubbock

Wexford, Irish Republic. Festival founded by Dr T. J. Walsh in 1951. Opera is performed in the tiny Theatre Royal, and the event has become notable for its revival of rarely heard works. Under Walsh's aegis the emphasis was on 19th-c. opera. When Brian Dickie took over in 1966, more Fr. works were added, and his successor, Thomson Smillie, who became dir. in 1974, has carried on both traditions. The fest. has often managed to persuade well-known singers to take part in the perfs, while encouraging promising newcomers too. AB

Whitehill, Clarence, b. Marengo, Iowa, 5 Nov 1871; d. New York, 19 Dec 1932. American baritone. Studied Chicago and Paris; debut Brussels, 1899, in ROMÉO ET JULIETTE. Toured in USA with Savage Opera Co., then returned to Europe for further study esp. of WAGNER,

West Side Story. George Chakiris (centre) and members of the chorus in the film (1961) directed by Robert Wise and Jerome Robbins

singing Bayreuth 1904 (WOLFRAM) and at Cologne, 1903–8. Debut NY Met as AMFORTAS 1909. Sang in several seasons at CG and was at the Met 1918–32. Noted for Wagner, also good in Fr. opera; sang in first Met perfs of LOUISE and PELLÉAS ET MÉLISANDE. LO

Widdop, Walter, b. Norland, nr Halifax, 19 Apr 1892; d. London, 6 Sept 1949. English tenor, one of the mainstays of BNOC, and of CG between the two world wars, equally at home in the It. repertory and WAGNER. LO

Widerspenstige Heilige, Der (*The Wayward Saint*), opera (*heitere Legende*), 3 acts, LOTHAR, lib. composer after Paul Vincent Carroll's comedy *The Wayward Saint*, 1955. Munich, 8 Feb 1968. LO

Widerspenstigen Zähmung, Der (*The Taming of the Shrew*), opera, 4 acts, GÖTZ, lib. Joseph Viktor Widmann based on SHAKESPEARE's play. Mannheim, 11 Oct 1874; London, DL, 12 Oct 1878; NY, Acad. of Music, 4 Jan 1886. LO

Wiesbaden, W. Germany. Under *Intendant* Alfred Erich Sistig, the summer fest., founded 1950, has brought visiting cos from Belgrade, Bratislava, Bucharest, Budapest, Dresden, Halle, Leipzig, Moscow, Prague, Sofia, Warsaw, and Zagreb. LO

Wilde, Oscar Fingal O'Flahertie Wills, b. Dublin, 16 Oct 1856; d. Paris, 30 Nov 1900. Irish playwright and novelist. Works on which operas are based incl.: *The Happy Prince*, 1888 (WILLIAMSON, 1965); *The Selfish Giant*, 1888 (WILSON, 1973); *The Nightingale and the Rose*, 1888 (Renzo Bossi, *Rosa Rossa*, 1940); *The Canterville Ghost*, 1891 (KŘIČKA, *Bily Pan*, 1929; Alexander Khaifel, 1974); *The Picture of Dorian Gray*, 1891 (Hans Kox, 1974); *A Florentine Tragedy*, 1891 (A. von Zemlinsky, *Eine Florentinische Tragödie*, 1917); *The Dwarf* (Zemlinsky, *Der Zwerg*, 1921); *The Duchess of Padua*, 1893 (WAGNER-RÉGENY, *La Sainte Courtesane*, 1930); *Salome*, 1893 (R. STRAUSS, 1905; Antoine Mariotte, 1908); *The Importance of Being Earnest*, 1895 (CASTELNUOVO-TEDESCO, 1962). LO

Williamson, Malcolm (Benjamin Graham Christopher), b. Sydney, 21 Nov 1931. Australian composer. Studied with GOOSSENS III, Elisabeth Lutyens and Erwin Stein; was pianist and organist before becoming comp. First major opera OUR MAN IN HAVANA, a melodrama with satirical overtones. *Julius Caesar Jones* (1966) is an accessible, tonal work for children with several roles for adults. VIOLINS OF ST JACQUES, a highly effective fantasy with a keen-edged, neo-romantic score, was followed by LUCKY PETER'S JOURNEY, based on a fairy tale by August Strindberg, an opera intended for audiences of all ages. Williamson has also wr. several pieces using smaller forces effectively and ingeniously, e.g. *English Eccentrics* (1965) and *The Growing Castle* (also based on Strindberg, 1968). His style is always lucid, and he employs it with considerable dramatic flair. Master of the Queen's Musick 1975. AB

William Tell *see* GUILLAUME TELL

Willner, Alfred Maria. Austrian librettist. Wrote lib. of HEIMCHEN AM HERD and, in collaboration with others, libs of FALL's *Dollarprinzessin*, LEHÁR's *Graf von Luxembourg*, *Zigeunerliebe*, *Eva*, *Wo die Lerche Singt*, and *Frasquita*; also *Dreimäderlhaus* (*Lilac Time*) to F. SCHUBERT's music. LO

Wilson, Charles, b. Toronto, 8 May 1931. Canadian composer. Works include 1-act opera *The Summoning of Everyman* (1973, lib. Eugene Benson) and 1-act opera for children, *The Selfish Giant* (1973, lib. WILDE). Large-scale opera *Heloise and Abelard* (1973, text Benson) commissioned by the COC in Toronto, successfully prod. there and in Ottawa. CM

Windgassen, Wolfgang, b. Annemasse, France, 26 June 1914; d. Stuttgart, 5 Sept 1974.

German tenor. Son of Fritz Windgassen (ten.) and Vally von der Osten (sop.); debut in 1939 at Pforzheim as ALVARO. Engaged at Stuttgart from 1945 until his death, he first sang at Vienna in 1953, CG in 1954, and the NY Met in 1956. Appeared every year 1951–70 at Bayreuth, singing all the major ten. Wagnerian roles from Erik (FLIEGENDE HOLLÄNDER) to PARSIFAL, from Froh (RHEINGOLD) to SIEGFRIED. He also sang FLORESTAN, MAX, COLA RIENZI, Don JOSÉ, OTELLO (VERDI), and the Emperor (FRAU OHNE SCHATTEN). His interpretative artistry was best demonstrated in TRISTAN UND ISOLDE. In 1970 he became Dir., Stuttgart O., where he made his final appearance (as Florestan) a week before he died. EF

Winter, Peter von, b. Mannheim, ? Aug 1754 (baptized 28 Aug); d. Munich, 17 Oct 1825. German composer. Studied violin with Johann Baptist Cramer and comp. with Georg Joseph Vogler; at 18 became dir., German O. at Mannheim. Moved to Munich where he stayed for the rest of his life. His most successful opera was *Das Unterbrochene Opferfest* (Vienna 1796). He comp. four operas for the King's T., London, incl. *Il Ratto di Proserpina* (1804) to da PONTE's lib. for BILLINGTON and GRASSINI, and *Zaira* (1805) for Grassini. Among the 37 operas he wr. for Germany, Italy, Vienna, Prague, and London, were *Das Labirint* (1798), the sequel to ZAUBERFLÖTE, lib. SCHIKANEDER, and *Maometto II* (1817), lib. ROMANI. PS

Wintermärchen, Ein, opera, 4 acts, GOLDMARK, lib. WILLNER, after SHAKESPEARE's *The Winter's Tale*, 1610–11. Vienna Staats O., 2 Jan 1908. LO

Winter's Tale, A *see* WINTERMÄRCHEN

Witherspoon, Herbert, b. Buffalo, NY, 21 July 1873; d. New York, 10 May 1935. American bass and administrator. Debut NY Met 1908, in PARSIFAL; at Met until 1914. Art. dir., Chicago Civic O., 1930; appointed to succeed GATTI-CASAZZA at the Met in 1935, but died of a heart attack at the time of taking office. LO

Wolf, Hugo, b. Windischgraz (now Slovenjgradec), 13 Mar 1860; d. Vienna, 22 Feb 1903. Austrian composer. Chiefly self-taught, he is most famous for his highly distinctive, intensely concentrated songs. Also remembered as a vitriolic critic. Only completed opera is CORREGIDOR, his *Manuel Venegas* remaining unfinished at his death. FGB

Wolff, Albert Louis, b. Paris, 19 Jan 1884; d. Paris, 20 Feb 1970. French conductor and composer. Studied Paris Cons. Cond. Paris OC from 1911; mus. dir. there 1921–4. At NY Met 1919–21, cond. Fr. repertory including premiere of his own *L'Oiseau Bleu*, 1919. Cond. Fr. repertory, T. Colón, in World War II. LO

Wolf-Ferrari, Ermanno, b. Venice, 12 Jan 1876; d. Venice, 21 Jan 1948. Italian composer. Son of a German painter; studied in Munich with Josef Rheinberger, returning to Venice in 1899, where his first opera, *Cenerentola* (1900), was unsuccessful, though liked in its Ger. version *Aschenbrödel* (Bremen 1902). His next two operas, DONNE CURIOSE and QUATTRO RUSTEGHI, were the first of several based on GOLDONI and set in Venice. The one-act curtain-raiser SEGRETO DI SUSANNA, his most popular work, was followed by GIOIELLI DELLA MADONNA, his one venture into veristic opera. With *L'Amore Medico* (Dresden 1913) based on MOLIÈRE, he returned to classical comedy, which was to remain his field until the end, and in which his style was to remain constant – delicate (despite the use of a large orch.), melodious, rhythmically vital, somewhat archaic and with splashes of local Venetian colour where appropriate. His remaining works are *Gli Amanti Sposi* (Venice 1925), *Das Himmelskleid* (Munich 1927), *Sly*, after SHAKESPEARE (Milan 1927), *La Vedova Scaltra* (Rome 1931), *Il Campiello* (Milan 1936), *La Dama Baba* (Milan 1939), *Gli Dei a Tebe* (Hanover 1943). All continue the tradition of VERDI's FALSTAFF in lighter vein. JB

Wolfram, bar., friend of TANNHÄUSER

Wotan, bass-bar., the ruler of the gods in RING DES NIBELUNGEN

Wozzeck, opera, 3 acts, A. BERG, lib. composer, derived from BÜCHNER's play of same name. Berlin, Staats O., 14 Dec 1925; Philadelphia, 19 Mar 1931; London, CG, 22 Jan 1952. Main chars: Marie (sop.) Wozzeck (bar.). The short scenes of the opera are each based on a specific musical form that keeps the structure and drama succinct and relevant. One of the seminal works of 20th-c. opera, it employs a freely declamatory kind of *Sprechstimme*, emphasizing the gruesome, almost fantastic nature of the tale, which for all its apparent alienation at first hearing becomes increasingly eloquent on repetition. The orchestration is rich and original, calling at different times for a military band, a restaurant orch. (on stage) and an out-of-tune piano (on stage). At others the texture is of a chamber-music-like delicacy. Marie's lullaby to her child, folk-like in its simplicity, her Bible-reading scene, the terror of Wozzeck just

before he drowns in searching for the fatal knife, and the child playing in the final scene unaware of the death of his parents are among the most compelling in all opera. AB ○★
See Kobbé

Wreckers, The, opera, 3 acts, SMYTH, lib. (in Fr., *Les Naufrageurs*) Henry Brewster from his Cornish drama. Leipzig, 11 Nov 1906 (*Strandrecht*, Ger. version by H. Decker and John Bernhoff); London, Queen's Hall, 30 May 1908 (concert perf.); HM, 22 June 1909 (in Eng., tr. comp. and Alma Strettell); CG 1910; SW 1939 in revised version. Main chars: Pascoe (bass) Thirza (mezzo-sop.) Mark (ten.). In 18th-c. Cornwall, the villagers pray to God to send ships to the coast for them to wreck and rob. Thirza, wife of the headman, Pascoe, is repelled by their savagery. She and her lover, Mark, are discovered lighting warning fires on the cliffs, and are locked in a cave where the rising tide will drown them. PS

Wunderlich, Fritz, b. Kusel, 26 Sept 1930; d. Heidelberg, 17 Sept 1966. German tenor. Studied Freiburg; debut there as TAMINO. Stuttgart O. from 1955. He sang there and at Munich regularly until the end of his career, cruelly cut short by a fatal accident. He first appeared at the Salzburg Fest. as Henry Morosus (SCHWEIGSAME FRAU) in 1959 and after that in many MOZART prods there and at the Munich Fest., where his Tamino was particularly admired. CG; as OTTAVIO, 1965. Created *Tiresias* in OEDIPUS REX and Christoph in VERLOBUNG IN SAN DOMINGO. One of the leading lyric tens of his day, also adept in operetta. AB

Y

Yeoman of the Guard, The, or The Merryman and His Maid, operetta, 2 acts, SULLIVAN, lib. GILBERT. London, Savoy T., 3 Oct 1888; NY, Casino T., 17 Oct 1888. Main chars: Colonel Fairfax (ten.) Sergeant Meryll (bass) Jack Point (buffo) Elsie Maynard (sop.) Phoebe Meryll (mezzo-sop.) Dame Carruthers (contr.) Wilfred Shadbolt (bass-bar.). Colonel Fairfax, a prisoner in the Tower of London, in order to disinherit a hated relative, undergoes a marriage blindfold to Elsie, the strolling player, loved by her partner, Jack Point. Having escaped, he woos and wins his unknown bride in earnest, causing Jack Point to die of a broken heart. Sullivan's most ambitious operetta. JB ○

Young Lord, The *see* JUNGE LORD

Yugoslavia. Country formed after World War I by fusion of several Balkan states notably Croatia, Serbia, and Slovenia. The Croatian capital was Zagreb; theatre built there 1834. Housed operetta (OFFENBACH, SUPPÉ), 1863–70, and in 1870 the Croatian National O. was founded, dir. by Ivan Zajc, 1832–1914, who wrote first Croatian national opera, *Nikola Subic Zrinsky*, 1876, revived for opening of present theatre, 1895. Other Croatian comps incl. Vatroslav Lisinsky, 1819–54, who wrote first opera in Croatian, *Ljubav i Zloba* (*Love and Malice*), 1846; Ivo Lhotka-Kalinsky, b. 1913; Boris Papandopulo, b. 1906; Ivan Brkanovic, b. 1906; Natko Devcic, b. 1914; Stjepan Sulek, b. 1914. The Dalmatian comp. Jakov Gotovac, b. 1895, was dir. of opera at Zagreb from 1923. His most important opera was *Ero s Onoga Svijeta*, Zagreb 1935.

Serbia, long subjected to Turkish rule, became important operatically only in the 19th c. Stanislav Binicki, 1872–1942, first dir. of Belgrade O., wrote first Serbian opera, *Na Uranka*, 1903. Other Serbian comps incl. Petar Konjovic, 1882–1970; Isador Bajic, 1878–1915; Dragomar Krancevic, 1847–1929, who founded a private opera co. in 1909; Petar Stojanovic, b. 1883; Mihovil Logar, b. 1902; Svetomir Nastasijevic, b. 1902. In Slovenia (cap. Ljubljana) an It. opera was perf. as early as 1652, but first Slovene comp. was Jakob Zupan, 1734–1810, whose *Belin* was perf. 1780. Other Slovene comps incl. Jurij Mihevuc, 1805–82; Gaspar Masek, 1794–1873; Slavsko Osterk, 1895–1941 and Matej Bravnicar, b. 1897. Apart from Belgrade, Ljubljana and Zagreb opera is perf. at other towns incl. Dubrovnik (open air), Sarajevo, and Split. LO

Wozzeck, Prague, National T., 28 May 1959; produced PUJMAN; designed František Tröster. Alena Miková as Marie; ŽÍDEK as a regimental musician.

Z

Zafred, Mario, b. Trieste, 2 Mar 1922. Italian composer. Art. dir., T. Verdi, Trieste (1966) and the Rome O. (1968), he has comp. a SHAKESPEARE opera, *Amleto* (1961), and one derived from SCHILLER, *Wallenstein* (1965), both prod. Rome O. EF

Zagreb *see* YUGOSLAVIA

Zaide, unfinished opera, MOZART, lib. Johann Andreas Schachtner after Joseph von Friebert. London, Toynbee Hall, 10 Jan 1955; Tanglewood, 8 Aug 1955. Main chars: Gometz (ten.) Zaide (sop.) Allazim (bass) the Sultan (ten.) Osmin (bar.). Allazim, Zaide and Gometz, members of a European family enslaved to a Turkish Sultan, discover each other's identity, attempt to escape, but are recaptured. Fifteen numbers only; spoken dialogue is lost, but there are two striking instances of 'melologue', or melodrama, i.e. speech over music. The final quartet uses a theme later transferred to ENTFÜHRUNG AUS DEM SERAIL. JB

Zampa, ou la Fiancée de Marbre (Z., or *The Marble Bride*), *opéra comique*, 3 acts, HÉROLD, lib. MÉLESVILLE. Paris, OC, 3 May 1831; London, Haymarket T., 19 Apr 1833; in Eng., adapted by John Oxenford as *The Bridal Promise*, T. Olympic, 10 June 1833; NY (in Fr.), 12 Aug 1833. Hérold's most popular opera, last seen in England in 1922 (Birmingham). Zampa, the bandit chief, as sacrilegious as DON GIOVANNI, meets a similarly sinister end at the hand of the marble bride of the title. LO

Zandonai, Riccardo, b. Sacco, 28 May 1883; d. Pesaro, 5 June 1944. Italian composer. A pupil of MASCAGNI at the Liceo Musicale of Pesaro, whose dir. he became in 1939. Operatic debut with *Il Grillo sul Focolare* (Turin 1908); was taken up by the publisher Tito RICORDI II who hoped to groom him as PUCCINI's successor. The effective *Conchita* (Milan 1911) was followed by his masterpiece, FRANCESCA DA RIMINI. Of his remaining seven operas the most outstanding are *Giulietta e Romeo* (Rome 1922) and *I Cavalieri di Ekebu* (Milan 1925). His music combines the melodic style of *verismo* with a more modern orchestral technique similar to that of RESPIGHI. JB

Zarou, Jeannette, b. Ramallah, Palestine, moved to Canada in 1947. Canadian lyric soprano. Studied Royal Cons. O. School, Toronto. Professional debut was as the Priestess in AIDA with the COC in Toronto in 1964. In 1966 she sang the title role of Healey Willan's *Deirdre* with the Co. Since 1967 she has been a regular member of the Deutsche O. am Rhein; with frequent appearances in Toronto. Her important roles include SOPHIE, ANTONIA and PAMINA. CM

Zar und Zimmermann (*Tsar and Carpenter*), opera, 3 acts, LORTZING, lib. composer based on play by MÉLESVILLE, Jean Toussaint Merle and Eugène Cantiran de Boirie, 1818. Leipzig, 22 Dec 1837; NY, Astor Place O. House, 9 Dec 1851; London, Gaiety T., 15 Apr 1871. LO O

Zarzuela. A form of musical theatre, generally comic, restricted entirely to Spain and, more recently, Latin America. Its name is derived from the palace of La Zarzuela (so called because of its nearby thickets of *zarza*, or bramble) near Madrid. CALDERÓN wrote the text of the first known *zarzuela*, *El Jardín de Falerina* (1648), and of *El Golfo de las Sirenas* (1657), the first actually given at the palace. Classical subject matter gave way to comedies of popular life and humbler characters with LABRADORAS DE MURCIA (1769). The rise of It. opera pushed the *zarzuela* into decline *c.* 1780, when for 50 years its place was taken by the TONADILLA ESCÉNICA. The *zarzuela* returned with *El Novio y el Concierto* (1839), oddly enough by an Italian, Basilio Basili. Spanish comps began to turn out *zarzuelas* in their hundreds; sometimes comp. in three acts, but most in the 1-act category of *género chico*. Because they are rooted in Spanish national life, with local and topical allusion and even improvisation in their dialogue, they have not proved exportable. The most prominent comps are BARBIERI, GAZTAMBIDE, and ARRIETA Y CORERA, also ALONSO, BRETÓN, CABALLERO, CAMPO, CHAPÍ Y LORENTE, CHUECA, GUERRERO, JIMÉNEZ, LUNA, MISÓN, MORENO TORROBA, SERRANO, SOROZÁBAL, J. and S. VALVERDE, and VIVES. FGB
See Chase, *The Music of Spain* (New York 1941; London 1941; 2nd rev. ed. New York 1959)

Zauberflöte, Die (*The Magic Flute*), opera (*Singspiel*), 2 acts, MOZART, lib. SCHIKANEDER. Vienna, T. auf der Wieden, 30 Sept 1791; London, HM, 6 June 1811; NY, Park T., 17 Apr 1833. Main chars: Tamino (ten.) Pamina (sop.) Papageno (bar.) Sarastro (bass) Queen of the Night (coloratura sop.) Monostatos (ten.) Papagena (sop.). The story, a 'Pilgrim's Progress' of the Enlightenment, tells of Prince Tamino's quest for Pamina and his initiation into the Brotherhood of Light. JB O★
See Kobbé

Die Zauberflöte. Singers dressing for a performance; watercolour (1794) by Georg-Melchior Kraus (1737–1806), court painter at Weimar

Zauberoper (Ger. 'magic opera'). Magical transformations have always appealed to the scenographer, from LULLY to the present day, but the term *Zauberoper* refers more specifically to Vienna in *c*. 1780–1820, where at the T. auf der Wieden and the later T. an der Wien plays of broad comedy which included both music and some sort of ritual magic were popular. The transcendental example, ZAUBERFLÖTE, is only one of several operas on magic fiddles, zithers, etc., culminating in F. SCHUBERT's *Zauberharfe* (*The Magic Harp*) of 1820. LO

Zaza, opera, 4 acts, LEONCAVALLO, lib. composer after play by Pierre Berton and Charles Simon. Milan, T. Lirico, 10 Nov 1900; San Francisco, 27 Nov 1903; London, Coronet T., 30 Apr 1909. Originally successful, occasionally revived in Italy. LO O

Zeffirelli [Corsi], Franco, b. Florence, 12 Feb 1923. Italian film director, theatre designer and producer. Since 1953, when he designed sets and costumes for ITALIANA IN ALGERI, and 1954, when he dir. and designed CENERENTOLA, both at Sc., he has been responsible for innumerable prods, usually to his own designs, throughout Europe and America. These include TURCO IN ITALIA, PUCCINI's BOHÈME, AIDA and BALLO IN MASCHERA at Sc.; DON PASQUALE, PICCINNI's *Cecchina* and CIMAROSA's *Astuzie feminili* at the Piccola Sc.; LINDA DI CHAMOUNIX, FILLE DU RÉGIMENT and PURITANI at Palermo; BARBIERE DI SIVIGLIA and TROVATORE at Genoa; ALCINA at Venice; LUCIA DI LAMMERMOOR, CAVALLERIA RUSTICANA, PAGLIACCI, FALSTAFF, DON GIOVANNI, RIGOLETTO, and TOSCA at CG; ELISIR D'AMORE at Glyndebourne; THAÏS and TRAVIATA at Dallas; ANTONY AND CLEOPATRA and VERDI's OTELLO at the NY Met. EF

Zeller, Carl (Johann Adam), b. St Peter-in-der-Au, 19 June 1842; d. Baden, nr Vienna, 17 Aug 1898. Austrian composer of operettas. The most successful were *Der Vogelhändler* (Vienna 1891) and *Der Obersteiger* (Vienna 1894). LO
See Lubbock

Zémire et Azor, *comédie-féerie*, 4 acts, GRÉTRY, lib. MARMONTEL based on comedy by Pierre-Claude Nivelle de la Chaussée, in turn based on PERRAULT's *Beauty and the Beast*. Fontainebleau, 9 Nov 1771; London, DL, 5 Dec 1776; NY, 1 June 1787; revived Bath Fest., 1955; Drottningholm, 1968. For other operas on the theme, see next entry. LO

Zemire und Azor, opera, SPOHR, lib. Johann Jakob Ihlee based on MARMONTEL. Frankfurt, 4 Apr 1819; London, CG (as *Azor and Zemira, or The Magic Rose*), 5 Apr 1831. Other operas on the same subject incl. ones by Karl Baumgarten (1775); Christian Gottlob Neefe (1778);Ignaz Seyfried (1818); and GARCÍA I, *c*. 1827. LO

Zenatello, Giovanni, b. Verona, 22 Feb 1876; d. New York, 11 Feb 1949. Italian tenor, orig. baritone. Debut (as bar.) at Naples as SILVIO (1898). Ten. debut as CANIO at Naples (1899);

Sc. 1903–7, where he created PINKERTON. CG debut as Riccardo (BALLO IN MASCHERA) in 1905, when he scored a great success as Pinkerton and ANDREA CHÉNIER. Returned 1906, 1908–9, and 1926, when his OTELLO (VERDI) was much admired. US debut with Manhattan O. (1907) as Enzo (GIOCONDA). Boston, 1909–14; Chicago, 1912–13. Helped to launch opera in the Verona Arena in 1913, with his wife, mezzo-sop. Maria Gay. One of the leading Italian lyric-dramatic tens of his day, famed particularly for his Otello; he sang the part more than 300 times. AB

Zeno, Apostolo, b. Venice, 11 Dec 1668; d. Venice, 11 Nov 1750. Italian scholar and librettist. Succeeded Silvio Stampiglia (1664–1725) as Caesarian Poet, Vienna, 1718. The large number of libs he wrote, often in collaboration with Pietro Pariati, were modelled on the Fr. classic theatre of CORNEILLE and RACINE and were set by all the important comps of the day, e.g. CALDARA, Francesco Gasparini, GRAUN, Pietro Guglielmi, HANDEL, TRAETTA, VINCI and Marco Antonio Ziani. LO

Zerbinetta, sop., the leader of the Harlequin troupe in ARIADNE AUF NAXOS

Zerlina, sop., the peasant girl in DON GIOVANNI

Zhelobinsky, Valery Viktorovich, b. Tambov, 27 Jan 1913; d. Leningrad, 13 Aug 1946. Russian pianist and composer. His operas contributed little to the development of Soviet music, largely because of unsatisfactory libs. But *Nameday* (1935) is similar to SHOSTAKOVICH's *Lady Macbeth of the Mtsensk District* (see KATERINA IZMAYLOVA) in its sumptuous harmonies and its sharp contrasts of the lyrical and the grotesque; when Shostakovich's opera was being denounced in 1936, Zhelobinsky's *Kamarinsk Peasant* (1933) was being praised by the Leningrad Soviet Composers' Union for its 'ideological and political content' and for its 'positive value to a general audience'. His other opera was *Mother* (1939). GN

Žídek, Ivo, b. Kravaře, nr Opava, 4 June 1926. Czech tenor. After singing for three years with Ostrava O. (debut there at 19 in title role of WERTHER), he joined the Prague NT in 1948. Also sang at the Berlin Staats O. (1963–8), from 1957 at the Vienna Staats O., and in many European and American centres. A strong lyric ten. with a fresh, clear voice, exemplary enunciation and a dependable technique, he is best known in Czech opera (an outstanding JENÍK, Gregor in MAKROPULOS CASE) but his repertory also incl. VERDI, BIZET, TCHAIKOVSKY, MOZART, and WAGNER. JT

Zigeunerbaron, Der (*The Gypsy Baron*), operetta, 3 acts, J. STRAUSS, lib. Ignaz Schnitzer based on a story, *Saffi*, by Maurus Jókai. Vienna, T. an der Wien, 24 Oct 1885; NY, Casino T., 15 Feb 1886; London (amateur prod. in Eng.), Rudolf Steiner Hall, 12 Feb 1935. Revived often in Ger. opera houses. Hungarian and Viennese styles are fused to make this a masterwork in the operetta genre. LO ○
See Lubbock

Zimin, Sergey Ivanovich, b. Orekhovo-Zuyevo, 3 July 1875; d. Moscow, 26 Aug 1942. Russian music patron. He formed an opera troupe in 1904, employing many members of MAMONTOV's company, recently disbanded. From 1908 it perf. regularly at the Solodovnikov T. When the company was nationalized in 1917, Zimin became a member of the directorate; 1922–4 it was known as Zimin's Free Opera. In 1924 the theatre was taken over as a branch of the Bolshoy, to which Zimin was an art. adviser (1924–42). Zimin's company followed Mamontov's example of promoting Russian opera, and in 1909 gave the premiere of GOLDEN COCKEREL. GN

Zimmermann, Bernd-Alois, b. Bliesheim, Cologne, 20 Mar 1918; d. Cologne, 10 Aug 1970. German composer. His opera SOLDATEN (comp. 1957–60, and first prod., in a reduced version, Cologne 1965), has since been perf. with success by several other Ger. opera cos, despite enormous technical difficulties of staging and musical perf. EF

Zingarelli, Nicola Antonio, b. Naples, 4 Apr 1752; d. Torre del Greco, 5 May 1837. Italian composer. Of his 34 operas the best known was *Giulietta e Romeo*, to a lib. by Giovanni Foppa, Milan, 1796. Head from 1813 of the Reale Collegio di Musica, Naples; BELLINI was one of his pupils. LO

Zítek, Vilém, b. Prague, 9 Sept 1890; d. Prague, 11 Aug 1956. Czech bass. Engaged as a soloist at the Prague NT in 1912; by 1916 was singing KECAL and PIZARRO and by 1918 Malina in SECRET. One of the leading singers in KOVAŘOVIC's co., his development as a singer continued under OSTRČIL. After studying in Milan (1925–6) accepted many short engagements in Turin, Milan, Paris, Berlin etc. His resonant and richly coloured voice was aided by a fine acting technique and served him well in the wide variety of parts he undertook; outside Czech opera these included PHILIPPE and BORIS GODUNOV. JT

Zola, Émile, b. Paris, 2 Feb 1840; d. Paris, 29 Sept 1902. French novelist. Wrote a cycle of 20 novels under the generic title of *Les Rougon-Macquart*, 1871–93; it incl. *La Faute de l'Abbé Mouret*, 1875, which MASSENET thought of setting, *Nana*, 1880 (set by GURLITT), and *Le Rêve*, 1888. His stories, considered at the time outspoken and scandalous, provided bases for operas by BRUNEAU. LO

Zürich, Switzerland. The small opera house by the lake, built 1891, has had a distinguished history, giving a number of interesting premieres – the first Swiss and the second European perf. of PARSIFAL outside Bayreuth in 1913; MATHIS DER MALER; first European perf. of PORGY AND BESS, LULU and MOSES UND ARON. Conds and prods there incl. ROSBAUD, 1955–8; P. BURKHARD, 1939–44; Hans Zimmermann, 1937–56 (as dir.); GRAF as art. dir. 1960–3. Present dir. Hermann Juch, with LEITNER as cond. LO

Zweig, Stefan, b. Vienna, 28 Nov 1881; d. Petropolis, nr Rio de Janeiro, 23 Feb 1942. Austrian writer, friend of R. STRAUSS. Wr. lib of SCHWEIGSAME FRAU (after JONSON). Also had a hand in the synopses of CAPRICCIO, FRIEDENSTAG and DAPHNE. LO

Zweihunderttausend Taler (*200,000 Talers*), opera, 3 acts and epilogue, BLACHER, lib. based on Sholom Aleichem's anti-capitalist comedy *The Two Hundred Thousand*, 1964. Berlin, Deutsche O., 25 Sept 1969. LO

Zwischenfälle bei einer Notlandung (*Incidents at a Forced Landing*), opera, 'two phases, fourteen situations', BLACHER, lib. Heinz von Cramer. Hamburg, 4 Feb 1966. LO

Zylis-Gara, Teresa, b. Vilnius [Vilna], 23 Jan 1937. Polish soprano. Studied Lodz; began career in Poland and North Germany. British debut Glyndebourne as OCTAVIAN (1966); CG debut as VIOLETTA (1968) and has returned there several times as Donna ELVIRA (DON GIOVANNI). NY Met debut as Donna Elvira in 1969, the year she sang same role at Salzburg Fest. Other roles incl. ANNA BOLENA, POPPEA and DESDEMONA (VERDI). Has a fresh, lyric sop. which she uses with great technical accomplishment. AB

Acknowledgments and Notes on Illustrations

The producers of this book wish to express their grateful thanks to all the contributors and others who suggested sources of information and illustrations, and also all those who are indicated by the following list of illustrations, especially the governing bodies and staffs of the Royal Opera House, Covent Garden, the libraries and museums and the individual owners of photographs. Every effort has been made to trace the primary sources of illustrations; in one or two cases where it has not been possible, the producers wish to apologize if the acknowledgment proves to be inadequate; in no case is such inadequacy intentional and if any owner of copyright who has remained untraced will communicate with the producers a reasonable fee will be paid and the required acknowledgment made in future editions of the book. The producers are particularly indebted to Colin Graham, Anke Kempter, Helen O'Neill, Vicki Robinson and Marilynn Zipes for assistance, and to Robert Stevenson for access to unpublished information on Puerto Rican opera.

COLOUR PHOTOGRAPHS

49 Opera Rara Ltd. Photo: Derrick Witty
50 Photo: Victor Glasstone
67 Photo: Houston Rogers
68 From *Costumes des Théâtres*, British Museum. Photo: R. B. Fleming
109 Photo: Dr Jaromír Svoboda, Prague
110–11 R. Dobujinsky
112 Photo: Reg Wilson
153 Photo: Syndication International
154 Photo: Werner Neumeister
171 Erté. Photo: Electrum Gallery
172 Society for Cultural Relations with the USSR. Photo: Derrick Witty
172 Bibliothèque Nationale, Paris
213 Society for Cultural Relations with the USSR. Photo: Derrick Witty
214–15 Photo: Guy Gravett
216 Photo: Scala, Florence
257 St Paul Opera Assn, Minn.
258 Cecil Beaton
275 Photo: Reg Wilson
276 Photo: Jacqueline Hyde
317 From *Queen's Boudoir*, 1849, courtesy Royal Opera House archives. Photo: Derrick Witty
318–19 British Museum. Photo: Bendall
320 Photo: Syndication International

MONOCHROME PHOTOGRAPHS

13 a. Royal Opera House, Covent Garden. Photo: Zoë Dominic
13 b. Deutsche Staatsoper, Berlin. Photo: Marion Schöne
15 English Music Theatre. Photo: Zoë Dominic
16 Teatro La Fenice, Venice. Photo: Giacomelli
17 Royal Opera House, Covent Garden. Photo: Donald Southern
19 Photo: NBC
21 Photo: E. Piccagliani, Milan
22 Royal Opera House, Covent Garden. Photo: Donald Southern
25 Deutsche Staatsoper, Berlin. Photo: Marion Schöne
29 Royal Opera House, Covent Garden. Photo: Donald Southern
30 Photo: Guy Gravett
31 Royal Opera House, Covent Garden. Photo: Donald Southern
32 Royal Opera House, Covent Garden. Photo: Reg Wilson
34 Opera for All
35 Festspielleitung, Bayreuth. Photo: Festspiele Bayreuth/Siegfried Lauterwasser
37 Victoria and Albert Museum, London
39 Photo: Guy Gravett
41 Photo: Victor Glasstone
42 Royal Opera House, Covent Garden. Photo: Houston Rogers
44 Victoria and Albert Museum, London
45 a. Society for Cultural Relations with the USSR, London. Photo: Derrick Witty
45 b. Royal Opera House, Covent Garden. Photo: Reg Wilson
48 Royal Opera House, Covent Garden. Photo: Clive Barda
52 Royal Opera House, Covent Garden. Photo: Donald Southern
53 Photo: Guy Gravett
54 Novosti Press Agency, London
55 Photo: Guy Gravett
58 English Music Theatre. Photo: Zoë Dominic
61 Teatro Colón, Buenos Aires
62 Pressebüro, Salzburger Festspiele
64 Royal Opera House, Covent Garden. Photo: Donald Southern
66 a. Royal Opera House, Covent Garden. Photo: Donald Southern
66 b. Royal Opera House, Covent Garden. Photo: Donald Southern
69 Roger-Viollet
72 a. Photo: E. Piccagliani, Milan
72 b. Royal Opera House, Covent Garden. Photo: Reg Wilson
74 Royal Opera House, Covent Garden. Photo: Houston Rogers
75 Victoria and Albert Museum, London, Enthoven Collection
76 Royal Opera House, Covent Garden. Photo: Houston Rogers
77 Maggio Musicale Fiorentino

79 Photo: E. Piccagliani, Milan
80 Royal Opera House, Covent Garden. Photo: Donald Southern
81 Royal Opera House, Covent Garden. Photo: Reg Wilson
84 Lipnitzki-Viollet
85 Photo: E. Piccagliani, Milan
87 a. Royal Opera House, Covent Garden. Photo: Houston Rogers
87 b. Royal Opera House, Covent Garden. Photo: Reg Wilson
89 Opera Rara Ltd
90 Dr Jaromír Svoboda, Prague
92 Dr Jaromír Svoboda, Prague
93 Photo: E. Piccagliani, Milan
95 Royal Opera House, Covent Garden. Photo: Stuart Robinson
96 Opera Rara Ltd. Photo: Derrick Witty
98 a. Royal Opera House Archives. Photo: Derrick Witty
98 b. Royal Opera House Archives. Photo: Derrick Witty
100 Deutsche Staatsoper, Berlin. Photo: Hella Köppel
101 Royal Opera House, Covent Garden. Photo: Houston Rogers
102 Photo: E. Piccagliani, Milan
104 Royal Opera House, Covent Garden. Photo: Donald Southern
105 Royal Opera House, Covent Garden. Photo: Stuart Robinson
106 Teatro Colón, Buenos Aires
107 Royal Opera House, Covent Garden. Photo: Stuart Robinson
114 a. Roger-Viollet
114 b. Dr Jaromír Svoboda, Prague
116 Royal Opera House, Covent Garden. Photo: Donald Southern
117 Royal Opera House, Covent Garden. Photo: Stuart Robinson
119 Novosti Press Agency, London
120 Royal Opera House, Covent Garden. Photo: Anthony Crickmay
121 Royal Opera House, Covent Garden. Photo: Donald Southern
123 a. Victoria and Albert Museum, London; Guy Little Bequest vol. 6. Photo: Caldesi & Co.
123 b. English National Opera, London Coliseum. Photo: Donald Southern
124 Photo: E. Piccagliani, Milan
126 Royal Opera House, Covent Garden. Photo: Donald Southern
127 Contemporary Films Ltd
128 Finnish Tourist Board. Photo: Posse
129 a. Roger-Viollet
129 b. Keystone
130 a. Reproduction: Margaret Smithers
130 b. Deutsche Staatsoper, Berlin. Photo: Marion Schöne
131 Royal Opera House, Covent Garden. Photo: Reg Wilson
133 Photo: Victor Glasstone
134 Royal Opera House, Covent Garden. Photo: Houston Rogers
135 a. Reproduction: Margaret Smithers
135 b. Royal Opera House, Covent Garden. Photo: Houston Rogers
136 Dr Jaromír Svoboda, Prague
138 a. Roger-Viollet
138 b. Novosti Press Agency
139 Reproduction: Margaret Smithers
140 Bibliothèque Nationale, Paris
141 English National Opera, London Coliseum. Photo: Reg Wilson
145 New York City Opera. Photo: Fred Fehl
147 a. Photo: Guy Gravett
147 b. Photo: Syndication International
148 Novosti Press Agency, London
151 Bibliothèque de l'Opéra, Paris. Photo: Françoise Foliot
161 English National Opera, London Coliseum. Photo: Dominic
162 Reproduction: Margaret Smithers
164 English National Opera, London Coliseum. Photo: Donald Southern
165 English National Opera, London Coliseum. Photo: Donald Southern
167 Bridget d'Oyly Carte Ltd. Photo: John Blomfield
169 Photo: Victor Glasstone
173 Photo: Guy Gravett
175 English National Opera, London Coliseum. Photo: John Garner
176 Novosti Press Agency, London
178 Teatro Colón, Buenos Aires
181 a. Radio Times Hulton Picture Library
181 b. Dr Jaromír Svoboda, Prague
184 a. and b. Dr Jaromír Svoboda, Prague
187 Society for Cultural Relations with the USSR, London. Photo: Derrick Witty
189 Dr Jaromír Svoboda, Prague
192 Royal Opera House, Covent Garden. Photo: Donald Southern
196 Bridget d'Oyly Carte Ltd. Photo: Donald Southern
201 Novosti Press Agency, London
203 Royal Opera House, Covent Garden. Photo: Donald Southern
205 Victoria and Albert Museum, London, Enthoven Collection. Photo: John R. Freeman Ltd
206 Roger-Viollet
207 Royal Opera House, Covent Garden. Photo: Donald Southern
212 Welsh National Opera

218 Royal Opera House, Covent Garden. Photo: Donald Southern
220 Photo: Dr Jaromír Svoboda, Prague
221 a. Opera Rara Ltd
221 b. Metropolitan Opera Archives, New York
226 Opera Rara Ltd
227 Photo: E. Piccagliani, Milan
228 Opera Rara Ltd
230 Victoria and Albert Museum; Enthoven Collection. Photo: Alfred Ellis
231 Royal Opera House, Covent Garden. Photo: Houston Rogers
232 a. Bibliothèque Nationale, Paris
232 b. Metropolitan Opera Archives, New York
234 Photo: Guy Gravett
235 Royal Opera House, Covent Garden. Photo: Reg Wilson
236 a. Royal Opera House, Covent Garden. Photo: Houston Rogers
236 b. English National Opera, London Coliseum. Photo: Dominic
237 English National Opera, London Coliseum. Photo: John Garner
238 Royal Opera House, Covent Garden. Photo: Donald Southern
242 Santa Fe Opera. Photo: Tony Perry
243 Metropolitan Opera Archives. Photo: Louis Mélançon, New York
249 a. Photo: E. Piccagliani, Milan
249 b. Santa Fe Opera. Photo: Tony Perry
251 Metropolitan Opera Archives, New York
253 Royal Opera House, Covent Garden. Photo: Donald Southern
254 Reproduction: Margaret Smithers
255 a. Opera Rara Ltd
255 b. Deutsche Staatsoper, Berlin. Photo: Marion Schöne
259 Royal Opera House, Covent Garden. Photo: Stuart Robinson
260 British Museum. Photo: John R. Freeman Ltd
262 a. Keystone; b. Bibliothèque Nationale, Paris
268 Festspielleitung Bayreuth. Photo: Festspiel Bayreuth/Wilhelm Rauh
269 Royal Opera House Archives. Photo: Derrick Witty
270 Royal Opera House Archives. Photo: Derrick Witty
271 English Music Theatre. Photo: John Garner
273 Bibliothèque de l'Opéra, Paris. Photo: Françoise Foliot
277 Photo: Guy Gravett
279 English National Opera, London Coliseum. Photo: Donald Southern
283 Reproduction: Margaret Smithers
285 a. Keystone
285 b. Novosti Press Agency, London
286 Photo: Victor Glasstone
287 Novosti Press Agency, London
288 a. Royal Opera House, Covent Garden. Photo: Houston Rogers
288 b. English Music Theatre. Photo: Zoë Dominic
292 Santa Fe Opera. Photo: Martin Weil
294 Bibliothèque Nationale, Paris
297 English National Opera, London Coliseum. Photo: John Garner
299 Bibliothèque Nationale, Paris
302 Deutsche Staatsoper, Berlin. Photo: Marion Schöne
304 Photo: Dr Jaromír Svoboda, Prague
306 Novosti Press Agency, London. Photo: E. Ettinger
323 a. Bakhrushin Theatre Museum, Moscow. Novosti Press Agency, London
323 b. Novosti Press Agency, London
327 Photo: Dr Jaromír Svoboda, Prague
328 Photo: Fred Kliché, Dusseldorf
331 Keystone.
334 Novosti Press Agency, London
336 Reproduction: Margaret Smithers
337 Royal Opera House, Covent Garden. Photo: Houston Rogers
338 Australian Information Service. Photo: Mike Brown
339 Photo: CAF Warsaw
340 Finnish Tourist Board. Photo: Leif Öster
341 Royal Opera House, Covent Garden. Photo: Donald Southern
344 Metropolitan Opera Association Inc. Photo: Louis Mélançon, New York
346 Bibliothèque de l'Opéra, Paris. Photo: Roger-Viollet
348 Festspielleitung Bayreuth. Photo: Festspiele Bayreuth/Wilhelm Rauh
355 Royal Opera House, Covent Garden. Photo: Donald Southern
356 Keystone
365 Keystone
367 United Artists Corp. Ltd
369 Photo: Dr Jaromír Svoboda, Prague
371 Nationale Forschungs- und Gedenkstätten der klassischen deutschen Literatur, Weimar

endpapers Design by Josef Svoboda for *Die Frau ohne Schatten*, London, Covent Garden, 12 June 1967. Royal Opera House, Covent Garden. Photo: Reg Wilson